Mercedes

Rainer W. Schlegelmilch

Text: Hartmut Lehbrink & Jochen von Osterroth

Mercedes

h.f.ullmann

Contents · Inhalt · Sommaire

Bruno Sacco: Fascination Mercedes

Highway 405, en route to Los Angeles Airport. It's 19 August 1997, around 9 am. The link is OK, and Mr. S... is on the other end of the line. The book is already in production, he explains, almost ready to go to press. It's planned as a photographic record of the most interesting and beautiful Mercedes vehicles. He's a photographic designer. Only at the second time of asking do I get his name: Rainer Schlegelmilch. I'm familiar with his pictures for the Car Museum in Untertürkheim. They're good.

Hartmut Lehbrink is responsible for the text. Would I like to write a foreword? I call back ten minutes later. I'll do it.

I've been a devotee of Mercedes cars since 1952, which seems a long time ago now. What happened in 1952? A one-two in the Le Mans 24 Hour race. And the Carrera Panamericana. And then, in 1954 in Reims, "veni, vidi, vici," the rest of the world had to give best to the new Mercedes phalanx of Nallinger, Uhlenhaut and Neubauer with worldclass drivers like Fangio, Herrmann and Kling at the wheel. The same year saw the launch of the 300 SL, one of the most beautiful cars of all time. So it was that I joined Mercedes in 1958. And I've remained faithful to Mercedes ever since. Why? The answer lies in the fascination that Mercedes cars exerted and still exert on me, naturally at different levels of perception. It was Leo Levine who said in 1988: "Why cars look the way they do, and why Mercedes-Benz automobiles look the way they do, are fascinating subjects."[1] How right he was!

The history of the invention of the motor car undoubtedly began long before Karl Benz and Gottlieb Daimler. However, Karl Benz and Gottlieb Daimler were the first to build "machines" that really ran and were therefore usable. One fact which is of great importance in historical terms too is that neither of them was a mere tinkerer who had managed to create some one-day wonder or other. They were experienced engineers who had arrived – separately at their goal as a result of methodical work and then continued to refine and improve their inventions and eventually bring them to industrial fruition. They produced the first saleable products of this type, even if the manufacturing process used for these cars was not comparable with that of what we would now term production cars: these earliest models were lovingly built by highly specialized craftsmen who overcame all kinds of difficulties in the process.

Your next question will be: What is fascinating? Let's take the example of Benz's three-wheeler (1885/86), Daimler's motor carriage (1886) and their direct derivatives such as the Daimler Stahlradwagen. With these models I would refer to the fascination of the spirit of invention. What's next? The Benz Victorias and Velos, and the Daimler Riemenwagen and Phoenix. Not the most visually attractive of cars, if we're honest. However, what is fascinating about them is that they represent the clear progression

Highway 405, auf dem Weg zum Flughafen Los Angeles. Es ist der 19. August 1997, so um 9 Uhr vormittags herum. Die Verbindung funktioniert, auf der anderen Seite der Leitung Herr S... Das Buch befindet sich bereits in der Herstellungsphase, ist sozusagen »im Druck«. Es soll ein Bildband über die interessantesten und schönsten Mercedes-Fahrzeuge werden. Er sei Fotodesigner. Erst beim zweiten Anlauf verstehe ich seinen Namen: Rainer Schlegelmilch. Ich kenne seine Aufnahmen für das Untertürkheimer Automobil-Museum. Gute Arbeiten.

Den Text soll Hartmut Lehbrink verfassen. Ob ich doch ein Vorwort schreiben möchte? Nach zehn Minuten rufe ich zurück. Ich werde es schreiben.

Mercedes-Fahrzeuge haben mich in ihren Bann gezogen seit dem inzwischen fernen 1952. Was war geschehen? 1. und 2. Platz bei den 24 Stunden in Le Mans. Und die Carrera Panamericana. Und dann, 1954 in Reims, »veni, vidi, vici«, der Rest der Welt musste sich der neuen Mercedes-Phalanx der Nallinger, Uhlenhaut und Neubauer beugen, gefahren von Weltklasse-Piloten wie Fangio, Herrmann und Kling. Dann erschien im selben Jahr der 300 SL. Eines der schönsten Sportwagen aller Zeiten. So kam ich zu Mercedes 1958. – Und blieb auch Mercedes treu. – Warum eigentlich? Die Antwort liegt in der Faszination die Mercedes-Automobile, natürlich auf unterschiedlichen Ebenen des Wahrnehmbaren, auf mich ausübten und noch ausüben. Sagte doch Leo Levine 1988: »Why cars look the way they do, and why Mercdes-Benz automobiles look the way they do, are fascinating subjects«[2] – wie recht er hatte!

Die Geschichte der Erfindung des Automobils beginnt sicher lange vor Karl Benz und Gottlieb Daimler. – Es waren aber Karl Benz und Gottlieb Daimler die ersten, die wirklich laufende und somit brauchbare »Maschinen« schafften. Was auch historisch betrachtet sehr wichtig ist: beide waren keine Tüftler, die irgendwelche Eintagsfliegen zusammenbastelten. Sie waren erfahrene Ingenieure, die methodisch arbeitend – getrennt – zum Ziel gekommen waren und Schritt für Schritt ihre Erfindungen weiterentwickelten, verbesserten und schließlich bis zur industriellen Reife führten. Sie erzeugten die ersten verkäuflichen Produkte dieser Gattung, auch wenn diese Automobile in ihrem Herstellungsprozess nicht vergleichbar waren mit sogenannten Serienautos: Handwerker mit hohem Spezialisierungsgrad bauten diese ersten Stücke liebevoll und unter Überwindung allerlei Schwierigkeiten zusammen.

Sie werden nun fragen: Was ist faszinierend? Nehmen wir doch das Dreirad von Benz (1885/86), die Motorkutsche von Daimler (1886) und ihre unmittelbaren Derivate, wie z.B. der Daimler-Stahlradwagen. Bei diesen Objekten würde ich von Faszination durch den Erfindergeist sprechen. Was kommt danach? Es sind die Benz Victorias und Velos, die Daimler Riemenwagen und Phoenix. Eigentlich keine optisch absolut

Autoroute 405, je suis en route vers l'aéroport de Los Angeles. Nous sommes le 19 août 1997, vers neuf heures du matin. Le téléphone sonne, c'est un certain monsieur S... qui m'appelle. Le livre est déjà en cours de réalisation, pour ainsi dire « en phase d'impression », dit-il. Il s'agira d'un ouvrage photographique sur les plus intéressantes et les plus belles des Mercedes. Il est photographe, ajoute-t-il. Ce n'est qu'à contrecœur que je comprends son nom : Rainer Schlegelmilch. Je connais les photos qu'il a faites pour le musée de l'Automobile d'Untertürkheim. Du bon travail.

Le texte sera signé Hartmut Lehbrink. Ne pourrais-je pas écrire une introduction ? Après dix minutes de réflexion, je le rappelle. Je l'écrirai.

Je suis tombé sous le charme des Mercedes un jour qui remonte déjà loin, c'était en 1952. Que s'est-il passé ?

Première et deuxième places aux 24 Heures du Mans. Et la Carrera Panamericana. Puis en 1954, à Reims, *veni, vidi, vici*, le reste du monde a dû plier l'échine sous les coups de butoir de la nouvelle phalange de Mercedes réunie par les Nallinger, Uhlenhaut et Neubauer, dont les voitures sont conduites par des pilotes d'exception comme Fangio, Herrmann et Kling. C'est alors qu'apparaît, la même année, la 300SL, l'une des plus belles voitures de sport de tous les temps. Et c'est ainsi que je me suis retrouvé chez Mercedes en 1958, et que j'y suis resté fidèle. Pourquoi ? En raison de la fascination que les voitures de chez Mercedes ont exercée sur moi, et exercent encore. N'était-ce pas Leo Levine qui disait, en 1988 : « Why cars look the way they do, and why Mercedes-Benz automobiles look the way they do, are fascinating subjects[1] » – comme il avait raison !

L'histoire de l'invention de l'automobile aura sans doute commencé longtemps avant Karl Benz et Gottlieb Daimler. Mais ce sont eux qui auront été les premiers à réaliser des « machines » qui roulaient réellement, donc viables. Autre considération très importante sur le plan historique : les deux hommes n'étaient pas du genre « bricoleur ». Ingénieurs expérimentés, ils travaillaient avec méthode – séparément – et ont atteint leur objectif puis, pas à pas, ont perfectionné leurs inventions, les ont améliorées, jusqu'à ce qu'elles parviennent enfin à la maturité industrielle. Constructeurs, ils sont aussi les premiers véritables vendeurs automobiles, même si ces engins n'étaient en rien comparables avec ce que l'on pourrait appeler des voitures de série, de par leur processus de fabrication : des artisans doués d'un haut niveau de spécialisation construisaient ces premiers exemplaires avec amour et ingéniosité pour surmonter toutes les difficultés.

Vous allez maintenant me demander : Qu'y a-t-il de passionnant ? L'invention et la nouveauté que représentent le tricycle de Benz, mû par un moteur à essence (1885-1886), la calèche à moteur de Daimler (1886) et ses dérivés directs, par exemple la voiture à roues d'acier de Daimler. Évoquant

from the original spirit-of-adventure prototypes to very saleable cars built in factories in small series. Just take a moment to consider the almost insurmountable variety of difficulties that these two inventors must have encountered. Everything was new, and even certain borrowings from coachbuilding techniques of the time cannot lessen these enormous achievements. The fascination, therefore, of skillful problem-solving and consolidation.

I don't wish to repeat the genesis of the first "Mercedes" here. One thing is clear, however: in addition to providing the name for the small series of cars which he had ordered, Emil Jellinek undoubtedly prompted the first modern car of the emerging century. A delicate masterpiece of engineering esthetics, which is sadly missing from the company's own museum. On the instructions of Prof. Werner Breitschwerdt, the then senior designer, I commissioned the museum's 1:4 scale model from the late modelmaker Carlo Brianza. The first Mercedes had a very clearly defined structure: the axles, the drive, the very low, horizontally configured floor, the seat bases, the front bulkhead, the steering gear, everything was in its "correct" place in the considered overall architectural plan.

The artistic freedom granted to the designer in putting together the SLK shows on the one hand the positive points of the sports car design of 1901 while, on the other, the photo provides the clearest evidence of just what a long route there was to the thoroughbred sports car of 1996. Wilhelm Maybach, the designer responsible at that time at Daimler, developed this car series. These "Mercedes" overshadowed everything else when they appeared and raced in Nice in 1901. It was the dawn of a new automotive era. The fascination of innovation!

From then on, it was a constant cavalcade. To name but a few models, take the Mercedes-Simplex, the Benz-Parsifal, the brilliant Blitzen-Benz, the Mercedes 38/100. Everything would probably have continued like this as Daimler unveiled a new racing car in 1914 which left all others in its wake on the track in Reims (where Mercedes took a 1-2-3), but then the First World War broke out. An obligatory break therefore ensued. After the war things picked up and proceeded again slowly, and the sedan body designs throughout the world came to resemble each other very closely. Daimler and Benz then merged. The newly formed company was an absolute world-beater in three fields:

1. The victorious racing car of 1914 was like the initial charge for a series of thoroughbred sports cars which were gradually developed over the years, i.e. up to about 1939, into imposing touring cars. I'm referring here to the "s," the "κ," the "ssκ," the "ssκL," and then the 500 κ and 540 κ series. The fascination of this group is based on power and restrained beauty. Some 500κ models fitted with "Sindelfingen bodies" are now amongst the most successful cars at the most prestigious concours d'élégance around the world.

2. Daimler-Benz became one of the few specialists in the development and production of prestige cars. The

begehrenswerten Automobile. Es ist aber der klare Schritt von den einstigen Erfindergeist-Prototypen zu den manufakturell in kleinen Serien zusammengebauten, durchaus verkäuflichen Automobilen, der für Faszination sorgen muss. Man denke an die fast unüberwindbare Vielfalt von Schwierigkeiten, die diesen beiden Erfindern begegnet sein müssen! Es war alles neu und selbst gewisse Anleihen an den damaligen Kutschenbau können diese gigantischen Leistungen nicht schmälern. Also: Faszination durch gekonnte Problemlösung und Konsolidierung.

Ich möchte hier die Geschichte der Entstehung des ersten »Mercedes« nicht wiederholen. Eines ist aber klar: Neben der Namensgebung für die von ihm bestellte kleine Serie von Fahrzeugen hat Emil Jellinek zweifellos den Anstoß zum ersten modernen Automobil des aufbrechenden Jahrhunderts gegeben. Ein delikates Meisterwerk der technischen Ästhetik, welches im werkseigenen Museum fehlt. Das Automobil im Maßstab 1:4 hatte ich im Auftrag von Prof. Werner Breitschwerdt, damals noch Entwicklungschef, beim

Mercedes 1901 & Mercedes-Benz SLK 1996

inzwischen verstorbenen Modellbauer Carlo Brianza bauen lassen. Der erste Mercedes war klar gegliedert, die Achsen, der Antrieb, der sehr tief liegende und horizontal verlaufende Wagenboden, die Sitzböcke, die vordere Trennwand, die Lenkung, alles lag in einer durchdachten architektonischen Gesamtkonzeption am »richtigen« Platz.

Die künstlerische Freiheit des Autors bei der Zusammenstellung mit dem SLK zeigt einerseits, was in diesem Sportwagenkonzept von 1901 »drin« steckte, andererseits liefert diese Aufnahme den besten Beweis dafür, wie weit der Weg bis zum reinrassigen Sportwagen von 1996 doch noch gewesen wäre. Wilhelm Maybach, der damalige verantwortliche Konstrukteur bei Daimler, entwickelte diese Fahrzeugserie. Bei ihrem Erscheinen und Renneinsatz in Nizza stellten diese »Mercedes« alles in den Schatten. Eine neue Automobilära war eingeleitet worden. – Faszination durch Innovation!

Von da an geht es weiter wie ein Feuerwerk, es seien lediglich einige Fahrzeugtypen genannt, wie z.B. der Mercedes-Simplex, der Benz-Parsifal, der fulminante Blitzen-Benz, der Mercedes 38/100. Alles wäre wahrscheinlich auch so weitergegangen, 1914 stellte Daimler einen neuen Rennwagen vor, der auf dem Rundkurs von Reims alle anderen hinter sich ließ (1., 2., 3. Platz: Mercedes!) – aber dann brach der Erste Weltkrieg aus. Es gab somit eine Zwangspause. Nach diesem Krieg ging es langsam wieder weiter, die Karosserie-

ces objets, je les qualifierais de fascinants eu égard au génie inventeur dont ils relèvent. Ensuite? Ce sont les Benz Victoria et Velo, les voitures à courroie et Phoenix de Daimler. Des voitures qui, à proprement parler, n'ont esthétiquement rien qui puisse les rendre si désirables. Mais c'est le passage sans équivoque des anciens prototypes issus d'un génie créateur aux automobiles tout à fait commercialisables et construites en petites séries dans des manufactures, c'est ce passage qui engendre la fascination. Imaginons seulement le nombre presque incalculable de difficultés auxquelles ces deux inventeurs ont dû être confrontés! Tout était nouveau, alors, et ce ne sont pas quelques emprunts à la construction de calèches de cette époque qui peuvent minimiser leur immense mérite. Autrement dit: fascination par la maîtrise à résoudre les problèmes techniques et par la consolidation.

Il n'est pas dans mes intentions de réécrire ici l'histoire de la première « Mercedes ». Mais une chose est sûre: outre le nom de baptême donné à la petite série de voitures qu'il avait commandées, Emil Jellinek (voir encadré p. 21) a sans aucun doute donné l'impulsion pour la première voiture moderne d'un siècle encore tout jeune. Un chef-d'œuvre raffiné d'esthétique technique dont on regrette l'absence dans notre propre musée. Sur ordre du professeur Werner Breitschwerdt, alors encore chef du développement, j'avais fait construire la voiture à l'échelle 1:4 chez le maquettiste Carlo Brianza, entre-temps décédé. La première Mercedes était clairement structurée, les essieux, la chaîne cinématique, le plancher de voiture très bas et horizontal, les banquettes, l'auvent antérieur, la direction, tout était au « bon » endroit dans une conception générale pensée dans les derniers détails sur le plan architectural.

La liberté artistique accordée à l'auteur pour le dessin de la SLK montre tout ce que renfermait déjà ce concept de voiture de sport de 1901. Mais aussi, rétrospectivement, combien le chemin allait encore être long jusqu'à la voiture de sport racée de 1996. Wilhelm Maybach, alors chef constructeur chez Daimler, a conçu cette série de voitures. Lors de leur sortie et de leur première participation à une course, à Nice en 1901, ces « Mercedes » ont ridiculisé le reste du plateau. Une nouvelle ère automobile venait d'être inaugurée. Fascination par l'innovation!

Dès lors, c'est un véritable feu d'artifice qui s'ensuit et nous nous contenterons de citer quelques types de voitures tels que la Mercedes-Simplex, la Benz-Parsifal, la météorique Blitzen-Benz, la Mercedes 38/100. Tout aurait probablement continué ainsi – en 1914, Daimler dévoila une nouvelle voiture de course qui, sur le circuit de Reims, domina toutes les autres voitures de la tête et des épaules (1re, 2e et 3e places à Mercedes!) –, mais c'est alors qu'éclata la Première Guerre mondiale. Toute compétition cessa séance tenante. Après la fin des hostilités, les choses ne redémarrèrent que lentement et les carrosseries des berlines se ressemblaient toutes dans le monde entier. C'est alors que Daimler et Benz fusionnèrent. La nouvelle firme baptisée Daimler-Benz devint ensuite championne absolue dans trois domaines:

rather conservative Stuttgart model was followed by the legendary Nürburg (Pope Pius XII's and Emperor Hirohito's Nürburgs can be admired in the Daimler-Benz Museum in Stuttgart). But the 770 K series was also highly suitable as an official car. I would claim the "fascination of authority" for this particular type of automotive monument.

3. If the victorious racing car of 1914 can be regarded as the precursor for the road-going sports car, straightforward refinement of its design would not have been quite enough to yield the spectacular W 25, W 25 and W 54 series. These required an almost unimaginable research and development effort. This must be termed the "fascination of the will to win, accompanied by technological superiority." From 1935 to 1940 these cars dominated the racetracks of Europe, but the outbreak of the Second World War in 1939 brought this era to an abrupt close.

After 1945 the company had to adapt to new market conditions. The age of the 540 K had been ended once and for all by the devastating events of the war. The chosen vehicle for Daimler-Benz's new start was a pre-war car, a four-door sedan designated the 170 V. Different bodies were added, and new series (220, 300) expanded the range. The 300 was the new high-status car for Germany. Attractive body variations, e.g. the cabriolet and coupé, were also built. Although these cars were still reminiscent of the style of pre-war designs, they had a fascination founded on solidity and reliability. From 1952 onwards Mercedes cars once again set new standards. Having dealt in some detail with this period which was of such significance for the starmarque cars (and for myself) above, I don't intend to say much more. I shall merely summarize as follows: 1952 the 300 SL road-going sports car, 1954 the racing cars, the 300 SL Gullwing Coupé, 1957 the 300 SL Roadster. In short: fascination upon fascination.

W 120 and W 180, the new, modern sedans with the monocoque body using the more contemporary unit-body construction are also products of this time. The fascination did not, understandably, reach the pinnacles of the sports cars. But the W 120 and W 180 enabled Daimler-Benz to further strengthen its reputation as a manufacturer of highclass, high-quality automobiles. The fascination of consolidation.

1959 saw the launch of the W 111, now better known as the "Fin" to lay admirers and specialists alike. This was actually the first modern top-of-the-range Mercedes sedan, the true "King of the Road." The coupé was unveiled two years later: "The 1961 220 SE Coupé is one of the most beautiful Mercedes ever designed, but not only that: it is one of the most beautiful cars ever designed anywhere," I stated in 1988 in Pebble Beach to an audience of 20 leading North American motoring journalists, and none ventured any contradiction. This was followed by the "Pagoda," the W 113. Then the 600 (W 100), again a car for prestigious official roles. After that there was the W 108, the stylistically more convincing replacement for the "Fin." W 115/114; C 111/1 and

formen der Limousinen ähnelten sich stark auf der ganzen Welt. Daimler und Benz fusionierten. Auf drei Gebieten entwickelte sich die neu entstandene Firma Daimler-Benz zur absoluten Spitze:

1. Der siegreiche Rennwagen von 1914 war wie eine Initialzündung bei einer Reihe von reinrassigen Sportwagen, die im Laufe der Zeit, d.h. bis etwa 1939, allmählich zu imposanten Tourenwagen hin entwickelt wurden. Ich meine damit die »S«, die »K«, die »SSK«, die »SSKL«, danach die 500 K und die 540 K Baureihen. Bei dieser Gruppe kann man von Faszination durch Kraft und kühle Schönheit sprechen. Einige 500 K mit der sogenannten »Sindelfinger Karosserie« gehören zu den meist ausgezeichneten Autos auf den prestigeträchtigsten Concours d'Elegance weltweit.

2. Daimler-Benz wurde einer der wenigen Spezialisten bei der Entwicklung und beim Bau von repräsentativen Fahrzeugen. Auf den etwas bieder anmutenden Typ Stuttgart folgte der legendäre Nürburg (Papst Pius XII und Kaiser Hirohitos Nürburgs können im Stuttgarter Daimler-Benz-Museum bewundert werden). Aber auch die Baureihe 770 K eignete sich bestens als Repräsentationsfahrzeug. Bei dieser Gattung von Automobil-Denkmälern würde ich für »Faszination durch Autorität« plädieren.

3. Wenn der siegreiche Rennwagen von 1914 als Vorläufer für die Straßensportwagen gelten kann, so wäre seine Konzeption nicht ganz geeignet gewesen, um durch einfache Weiterentwicklung zu den spektakulären W 25, W 125 und W 154 gelangen zu können. Dafür wurde eine fast unvorstellbare Entwicklungs- und Forschungsarbeit geleistet. Hier hat man von »Faszination durch Siegeswillen, flankiert von erreichter technologischer Führerschaft« zu sprechen. Von 1935 bis 1940 waren das die Protagonisten auf den Rennstrecken Europas. Diese Ära ging mit dem Ausbruch des Zweiten Weltkrieges 1939 abrupt zu Ende.

Nach 1945 musste man sich den neuen Gegebenheiten des Marktes anpassen. Die Zeit der 540 K war endgültig durch die verheerenden Kriegsereignisse weggewischt worden. Daimler-Benz begann wieder mit dem Bau eines Vorkriegs-Fahrzeugs, einer viertürigen Limousine mit der Typbezeichnung 170V. Es kamen Karosserievarianten dazu, neue Baureihen (220, 300) ergänzten das Programm. Der 300er war der neue »high status car« für Deutschland. Davon wurden auch schöne Karosserievarianten als Cabriolet bzw. als Coupé gebaut. Stilistisch noch an den Fahrzeugen der Vorkriegszeit orientiert, faszinieren diese Autos hauptsächlich ihrer Solidität und Zuverlässigkeit wegen. Ab 1952 setzen Mercedes-Autos wieder neue Zeichen. Ich werde mich an dieser Stelle nicht länger fassen; ich habe zu Beginn meiner Ausführungen über diese, für die Autos mit dem Stern (und für mich) so bedeutende Zeit ausführlich berichtet. Ich fasse nur zusammen: 1952 die 300 SL Straßensportwagen, 1954 die Rennwagen, das 300 SL Flügeltüren-Coupé, 1957 der 300 SL Roadster. In Summa: Faszination über Faszination.

W 120 und W 180, die neuen, modernen Limousinen mit selbsttragender Karosserie und in der zeitgemäßeren Pontonform sind auch Produkte dieser Zeit, die Faszination

1. Les voitures de course victorieuses de 1914 ont constitué le premier jalon de toute une série de voitures de sport racées qui, au fil du temps, c'est-à-dire jusqu'aux environs de 1939, se sont muées graduellement en d'imposantes voitures de tourisme. Je fais allusion ici aux S, K, SSK, SSKL, ainsi qu'aux séries 500K et 540K. Pour ces voitures, on peut parler de fascination par la force et la beauté froide. Quelques 500K avec la « carrosserie de Sindelfingen » comptent parmi les voitures qui remportent le plus souvent des distinctions lors des concours d'élégance les plus prestigieux du monde.

2. Daimler-Benz est devenu l'un des rares spécialistes pour la conception et la construction de voitures de représentation. La Stuttgart aux lignes plutôt bourgeoises a été suivie par la légendaire Nürburg (les Nürburg du pape Pie XII et de l'empereur Hirohito peuvent être admirées au musée Daimler-Benz de Stuttgart). Mais la gamme 770K, aussi, a été une base idéale pour les voitures de représentation. Pour cette catégorie de « monuments automobiles », je parlerai de « fascination par l'autorité ».

3. À quiconque prétend que la voiture de course victorieuse de 1914 est le précurseur des voitures de sport routières, on pourrait rétorquer que sa conception n'était pas parfaite au point de donner naissance, par simple perfectionnement, aux spectaculaires W25, W125 et W154. Il a fallu pour cela accomplir des efforts difficilement imaginables de développement et de recherche. Ici, on peut parler de « fascination par la volonté de vaincre, avec comme facteur concomitant le leadership technologique acquis ». De 1935 à 1940, elles furent de grands acteurs sur les circuits d'Europe. Cette ère s'acheva brutalement lorsque éclata la Seconde Guerre mondiale, en 1939.

Après 1945, il a fallu s'adapter aux nouvelles donnes du marché. Les hostilités et leurs séquelles traumatiques mirent un point final aussi définitif que brutal à l'ère de la 540K. Faisant feu de tout bois, Daimler-Benz a redémarré sur la base d'une voiture d'avant-guerre, une berline à quatre portes appelée 170v. Elle reçut différentes variantes de carrosserie et des gammes nouvelles (220, 300) vinrent compléter le programme. La 300 était la *high status car* (nouvelle voiture de haut standing) de l'Allemagne. On en construisit aussi de magnifiques dérivés en tant que cabriolets et coupés. Esthétiquement encore très proches des voitures de l'avant-guerre, ces automobiles fascinent essentiellement par leur solidité et leur fiabilité. Pour Mercedes et ses voitures, 1952 est l'année inaugurale d'une ère nouvelle. Résumons : en 1952, les 300SL, de sport pour la route ; en 1954, les voitures de course, le coupé 300SL à ailes papillon et, en 1957, la 300SL Roadster. *Summa summarum :* fascination et encore fascination.

Les W120 et W180, les nouvelles limousines modernes à carrosserie autoporteuse et à la forme ponton plus moderne sont aussi des produits de cette époque, mais la fascination n'atteint bien évidemment pas les sommets de celle des voitures de sport. Toutefois, avec ces limousines, Daimler-Benz a pu encore cimenter sa réputation de constructeurs

C111/II, the Wankel prototypes; R and C107, the SL Roadster and Coupé; the W116 as the new S-class; the W123 with its coupé and station wagon variants.

A long period, from 1959 to 1977. What is the fascination of the cars from this period based on? One thing is certain: Daimler-Benz was able to further consolidate, expand and indeed claim as its own the role of the developer and manufacturer of unique cars in terms of safety, reliability and stability of value. The fascination of mastery of its art?

The 1977 C111/III prototype had been developed as a design study in aerodynamics. The W126, the S-class of 1979 and a number of other cars developed subsequently, such as the 1981 S-class coupé (the SEC), the 1983 190 series (W201), and the W124 (the "mid-range" series with all its variants) from 1985 onwards, profited from this. This period would be summed up for me by "the fascination of a perfect marriage of function and form."

The "fascination of a successfully interpreted myth" characterized the new SL (R129) in 1989. No more needs to be said.

The "fascination of authority" already encountered with reference to the Nürburg and 770K models also applies to the S-class and the S-class coupé of 1991/92. With regard to the C-class and the station wagon derived from it, I would refer to the "fascination of restraint." With the E-class, by contrast, I would prefer to speak of the "fascination of freshness and innovation."

SLK, CLK and A-class: three very different cars but which have one thing in common, the "fascination of design."

Bruno Alfieri wrote: "Mercedes-Benz cars can irrefutably be considered the most recent, and the most exciting, metamorphosis of the Classicist idea, even though viewed in a global creative scenario which includes art, architecture, photography, fashion, cinema, scenography and industrial design."[2]

[1] Leo Levine, head of press of Mercedes-Benz of North America in the 1980s (until 1989). Quote from an MBNA brochure, *Mercedes-Benz Design, by Bruno Sacco*, 1988.

[2] Bruno Alfieri, automobile historician, editor of automotive literature. Quote from *Form. Mercedes-Benz*, Automobilia, 1995, Milano.

[1] Leo Levine, Presseleiter von Mercedes-Benz of North America in den 80er Jahren (bis 1989). Das Zitat stammt aus einer Broschüre der MBNA, *Mercedes-Benz Design, by Bruno Sacco*, 1988.

[2] Bruno Alfieri, Automobilhistoriker, Herausgeber von Automobilliteratur. Zitat aus *Form. Mercedes-Benz*, Automobilia, 1995, Mailand.

[1] Leo Levine, attaché de presse de Mercedes-Benz of North America en 1980 (jusqu'en 1989). La citation est tirée d'une brochure de MBNA, *Mercedes-Benz Design, by Bruno Sacco*, 1988.

[2] Bruno Alfieri, historien de l'automobile, éditeur de livres sur l'automobile. Citation tirée de *Form. Mercedes-Benz*, Automobilia, 1995, Milan.

erreicht die Spitzen der Sportwagen nicht, begreiflicherweise. Aber mit dem W120 und dem W180 konnte Daimler-Benz seinen Ruf als Erbauer hochklassiger, hochwertiger Automobile weiter stärken. Faszination durch Festigung der Positionen.

1959 wird der W111 vorgestellt. Inzwischen als »die Heckflosse« besser bei Laien und Spezialisten bekannt. In der Tat die erste moderne Mercedes-Limousine der Oberklasse. Die wahre »Königin der Autobahn«. Zwei Jahre später kommt das Coupé: »The 1961 220 SE coupé is one of the most beautiful Mercedes ever designed, but not only that: it is one of the most beautiful cars ever designed anywhere«, sagte ich 1988 in Pebble Beach vor 20 fahrenden nordamerikanischen Journalisten, ohne auf irgendeinen Widerspruch zu stoßen. Dann kommt die »Pagode«, der W113. Danach der 600er (W100), wieder ein Auto für die große Repräsentation. Dann der W108, die stilistisch überzeugendere Ablösung er »Heckflosse«. W115/114; C111/I und C111/II, die Wankel-Prototypen; R und C107, die SL-Roadster und Coupé; der W116 als neue »S-Klasse«; der W123 mit seinen Varianten als Coupé und Stationswagen.

Eine lange Periode, von 1959 bis 1977. Worin besteht die Faszination, die aus den Automobilen dieser Zeit hervorgehen soll? Eines ist schon klar: Daimler-Benz konnte die Rolle des Entwicklers und Herstellers einzigartiger Fahrzeuge in Punkto Sicherheit, Zuverlässigkeit und Wertbeständigkeit weiter ausbauen, stärken und für sich in Anspruch nehmen. Faszination durch Beherrschung?

Der Prototyp C111/III von 1977 war als Aerodynamik-orientierte Designstudie entwickelt worden. Der W126, die s-Klasse von 1979 und mehrere danach entwickelten Autos, wie z.B. das Coupé der s-Klasse 1981 (der SEC), der 190er 1983 (W201), der W124 (die »Mittelklasse« mit allen Varianten) ab 1985, profitierten davon. Für diese Periode würde für mich gelten: »Faszination durch perfekte Abstimmung von Form und Funktion«.

»Faszination durch gelungene Interpretation eines Mythos« charakterisierte 1989 den neuen SL (R129). Weitere Worte wären hier überflüssig.

Die uns bereits bei den Nürburgs und 770K begegnete »Faszination durch Autorität« trifft auch für die s-Klasse und das Coupé der s-Klasse von 1991/92 zu. Bei der C-Klasse und dem davon abgeleiteten Stationswagen würde ich »Faszination durch Zurückhaltung« feststellen. Nicht so bei der E-Klasse, da möchte ich von »Faszination durch Frische und Innovation« sprechen.

SLK, CLK und A-Klasse: Drei sehr verschiedene Automobile. Eines haben sie gemeinsam: »Faszination durch Design«.

Zitat von Bruno Alfieri: »Es ist unwiderlegbar, dass Mercedes-Benz-Automobile als die jüngste und offensichtlichste Metamorphose der Klassik bezeichnet werden können; dies gilt auch, wenn man sie im Hinblick auf das gesamte kreative Umfeld betrachtet, das sich aus Kunst, Architektur, Fotografie, Mode, Film, Bühnenbild und Industriedesign zusammensetzt.«[2]

d'automobiles de très grande qualité et de très grande valeur. La fascination par la consolidation de sa réputation.

Année 1959 : présentation de la W111, entre-temps mieux connue des profanes et des spécialistes sous le surnom de « Mercedes à ailerons ». En fait, la première limousine Mercedes moderne du segment supérieur. La véritable « reine de l'autoroute ». Deux ans plus tard arrive le coupé : « The 1961 220SE coupé is one of the most beautiful Mercedes ever designed, but not only that: it is one of the most beautiful cars ever designed anywhere » (Le Coupé 220SE de 1961 est l'une des plus belles Mercedes jamais conçues, mais pas seulement : c'est l'une des plus belles voitures jamais conçues dans le monde), ai-je déclaré en 1988 à Pebble Beach devant vingt des plus grands journalistes automobiles d'Amérique du Nord, sans rencontrer la moindre contradiction. Vint ensuite la « Pagode », la W113. Et, après elle, la 600 (W100), encore une voiture de grand standing. Puis la W108, remplaçante, autrement plus séduisante sur le plan esthétique, de la « Mercedes à ailerons », et les W115/114, C111/I et C111/II ; les prototypes Wankel ; la R et la C107, la SL roadster et coupé ; la W116 comme nouvelle « Classe S » ; la W123 avec ses variantes coupé et break.

C'est une longue période, qui s'étend de 1959 à 1977. En quoi consiste la fascination censée émaner des voitures de cette époque ? Une chose est déjà claire : Daimler-Benz a pu accentuer, renforcer et revendiquer pour elle-même le rôle de concepteur et de constructeur de voitures uniques en leur genre en termes de sécurité, de fiabilité et de stabilité de leur valeur. Fascination par la maîtrise ?

Le prototype C111/III de 1977 a été conçu en tant qu'étude de style privilégiant l'aérodynamique. La W126, la Classe S de 1979 et plusieurs autres voitures mises au point plus tard, par exemple le coupé SEC de la Classe S de 1981, la 190 de 1983 (W201), la W124 (la « classe intermédiaire » avec toutes ses variantes) à partir de 1985 en ont profité. Pour cette période, j'invoquerais la devise : « Fascination par l'harmonie parfaite de la forme et de la fonction. »

« Fascination par l'interprétation réussie d'un mythe », voici ce qui caractérise, en 1989, la nouvelle SL (R129). Tout autre commentaire est ici superflu.

La « fascination par l'autorité » que nous avons déjà évoquée pour les Nürburg et 770K vaut aussi pour la Classe S et la version coupé de la Classe S de 1991-1992. Pour la Classe C et les breaks qui en sont les dérivés, je parlerais de « fascination par la discrétion ». Cela n'est pas le cas de la Classe E, pour laquelle je pense plutôt à la « fascination par la fraîcheur et l'innovation ».

SLK, CLK et Classe A : trois automobiles en aucun point comparables, sauf un : la « fascination par le design ».

Citons Bruno Alfieri : « Que les automobiles Mercedes-Benz puissent être considérées comme la métamorphose la plus récente et la plus manifeste de l'idée du classicisme ne peut guère être contesté, même si elles sont vues dans le panorama créateur global comprenant l'art, l'architecture, la photographie, la mode, le cinéma, la scénographie et le design industriel[2]. »

Glittering years – but not always:
A Mercedes-Benz chronicle

Lichtjahre – aber nicht immer:
Eine Chronik des Unternehmens Mercedes-Benz

Des années de lumière – mais avec des zones d'ombre :
une chronique de Mercedes-Benz

Pioneering deeds

Since time immemorial man has attempted to break free of the constraints imposed on him by his body and the limitations of his five senses. Human existence has been a constant struggle against the twin barriers of time and space within which man is destined to dwell. His motives and driving forces are imagination and a creative restlessness, aspirations to greater things, absolute dedication to progress. The myth of Icarus is a testament to this. He fashioned a pair of wings to help him fly and simply launched himself into the skies. But there was to be no happy ending: the wax holding his wings together melted in the sun like butter, and the courageous aviator died by plunging into the Aegean Sea. Icarus was guilty of the cardinal sin of hubris. He wanted to be like Zeus, and that did not please the ruler of Mount Olympus. Fear of divine indignation was less of a preoccupation in the second half of the 19th century when our story starts. In addition, many things had become technically feasible: machines of every kind were performing tasks previously undertaken by heads, hands, and feet and, following the invention of James Watt's steam engine in 1784 and Edmund Cartwright's mechanical loom in 1785, bringing social turmoil in their wake. The fact that from a very early stage the railway was regarded as a suitable subject for artistic endeavor is borne out by *Rain, Steam and Speed,* the early English Impressionist J.M.W. Turner's 1844 painting of the Great Western Railway. Alexander Graham Bell gave birth to the electromagnetic telephone as an extension of the voice and ear in 1876, while Samuel Thomas von Sömmering (1809) was the father of the electric telegraph which enabled the immediate transmission of ideas across the globe. Telephone and telegraph – the new names were cobbled together almost as awkwardly as the objects they represented: in their etymologies half looking backwards, half forwards, like the terms television, radio, or airplane.

As the *fin de siècle* approached, however, the time was right for the motor car, the automobile, the self-moving vehicle. The choice of names is indicative that this invention actually had two fathers, Gottlieb Daimler, born the

Pionier-Taten

Immer schon hat sich der Mensch bemüht, den Käfig zu sprengen, in den ihn sein Körper und die Begrenztheit seiner fünf Sinne einsperren. Seit jeher revoltiert er gegen die Doppelschranke von Raum und Zeit, in die er verwiesen ist. Seine Motive und Motoren: Phantasie und kreative Unruhe, ein hoher Anspruch, Hingabe an den Fortschritt schlechthin. Der Mythos vom Ikarus bezeugt es: Der baut sich ein Fluggerät und erhebt sich frech in die Lüfte. Aber die Sache geht nicht gut aus: Das Wachs, das seine Flügel zusammenhält, schmilzt in der Sonne wie Butter, und der kühne Flieger stirbt beim harten Aufprall auf die Ägäis. Ikarus hat sich der Kardinalsünde der Hybris schuldig gemacht. Er wollte sein wie Zeus, und das nahm der Chef des Olymps übel. In der zweiten Hälfte des 19. Jahrhunderts hat die Furcht vor der Empörung der Götter entschieden abgenommen. Dafür ist manches machbar geworden: Schon entlasten Maschinen aller Art Kopf, Hand und Fuß und sorgen für soziale Gärung seit 1784 James Watts Dampfmaschine, seit 1785 Edmund Cartwrights mechanischer Webstuhl. Dass die Eisenbahn schon frühzeitig sogar künstlerisch hoffähig geworden ist, bezeugt bereits 1844 das Gemälde *Regen, Dampf, Geschwindigkeit – Der große Westzug* des englischen Frühimpressionisten William Turner. Das elektromagnetische Telephon als Verlängerung von Stimme und Ohr wird 1876 von Alexander Graham Bell in die Welt gesetzt, der elektrische Telegraph zur umgehenden Vermittlung von Ideen überallhin schon 1809 durch Samuel Thomas von Sömmering. Fernsprecher und Fernschreiber – die neuen Namen sind genauso unbeholfen zusammengeschustert wie die neue Sache selbst: halb nach rückwärts, halb schon nach vorne gewandt wie später Fernsehen, Rundfunk oder Flugzeug.

Gegen das Fin de siècle aber ist die Zeit reif für das Automobil, den Selbstbeweger, auch Kraftwagen genannt. Deshalb hat es gleich zwei Väter, Gottlieb Daimler, am 17. März 1834 in Schorndorf als Sohn eines Bäckermeisters geboren, und Karl Benz, geboren am 25. November 1844 in Karlsruhe als Spross eines Lokomotivführers. Aus dem gleichen schwäbisch-alemannischen Sprachraum stammend,

Les pionniers

Dès sa création, l'homme s'est efforcé de briser la cage dans laquelle l'emprisonnent le corps et les limites de ses cinq sens. Depuis toujours, il se révolte contre le double obstacle de l'espace et du temps dans lequel il est contenu. Ses motifs et ses moteurs : l'imagination et le bouillonnement créateur, des ambitions élevées, une foi dans le progrès par excellence. Le mythe d'Icare en est la preuve : il se façonne des ailes et s'élève témérairement dans les airs. Mais son initiative se termine mal : la cire avec laquelle il a enduit ses ailes fond comme neige au soleil et le courageux aéronaute meurt en percutant brutalement les vagues de la mer Égée. Icare a commis le péché mortel de celui qui se veut hybride. Il a voulu être l'égal de Zeus et cela, le dieu de l'Olympe ne lui a pas pardonné. Dans la seconde moitié du XIXe siècle, l'homme craignait beaucoup moins la colère des dieux, et bien des choses sont devenues possibles : déjà, des machines en tout genre facilitent le travail intellectuel et physique, mais sont à l'origine d'une fermentation sociale depuis que, en 1784, James Watt a inventé la machine à vapeur et, en 1785, Edmund Cartwright, la machine à tisser mécanique.

Le tableau *Pluie, vapeur, vitesse* de l'impressionniste anglais William Turner, de 1844, prouve déjà que le chemin de fer a, très tôt, recueilli l'attention des artistes. En 1876, Alexander Graham Bell met au monde le téléphone électromagnétique comme prolongement de la voix et de l'oreille tandis que le télégraphe électrique de Samuel Thomas von Sömmering permet de transmettre instantanément des idées dès 1809. Téléphone et téléscripteur – néologismes aussi frustes que les nouveaux objets eux-mêmes : encore un peu antiques et pourtant déjà très novateurs comme, plus tard, la télévision, la radio ou l'avion.

Mais, dès la fin du siècle, les temps sont mûrs pour l'automobile. Une automobile qui peut revendiquer une double paternité, celle de Gottlieb Daimler, né le 17 mars 1834 à Schorndorf comme fils de boulanger, et de Karl Benz, né le 25 novembre 1844 à Karlsruhe, fils d'un conducteur de locomotive. Bien qu'originaires de la même aire linguistique souabe alémanique, les deux hommes ne se sont

son of a master baker on 17 March 1834 in Schorndorf, Germany, and Karl Benz, born on 25 November 1844 in Karlsruhe, Germany, the son of a train driver. Although both came from the same region of Swabia, they never met, but the history of the company that was to bear their names is at the very heart of the history of the motor car and personal mobility.

Others, of course, also claim paternity of the autonomous child; following a period which witnessed the creation of enormous, inelegant steam-powered dinosaurs, the Swiss Major Isaac de Rivaz made the first attempt to use a gas-powered engine to drive a vehicle in 1806. Although it did not manage more than a single lurch forward, in which the garage wall was demolished, the officer was granted a patent for a "motorized vehicle driven by a gas engine." In 1860 the Frenchman Etienne Lenoir designed a gas power unit that was the first to run properly, but it was rather rickety because of its size. In 1876 Nikolaus August Otto (1832–1891), the founder of Gasmotorenfabrik Deutz, appeared on the scene with a four-stroke engine that had a greater power output and consumed less coal gas than other engines had up to this point. His trick was to pre-compress the gas/air mixture. The electric ignition patented by Otto in 1884 made the use of liquid fuels possible. But his creation was too large and too bulky, and was therefore condemned to a stationary existence.

The French regard the engineer Edouard Delamare-Deboutteville as the inventor of the motor car. He too was granted a patent in 1884, but his creation fell victim to an explosion. Delamare in the meantime, a true polymath, turned in his dismay to other peaceful pursuits, viz. oyster farming and translation from Sanskrit. The Italians too claim copyright on the new invention of the car. Enrico Bernardi, a professor at the Institute for Applied Mechanics in Verona, applied for a patent for a gasoline engine in 1882 and installed it two years later in a cumbersome three-wheeler. The little engine, named after Bernardi's favorite daughter Pia, developed a feeble 0.024 bhp and probably never took a single breath of its own.

While the spirit was undoubtedly willing in all these early attempts, the flesh was weak in terms of their practicability. To succeed, four criteria had to be met: the design had to be documented; the vehicle had to work; it had to be tested; and the invention had to progress to further developments. And so it was that the Germans saw their hour come, combining as they did (and do) solidity, persistence verging on stubbornness, and a tendency to missionary zeal.

One such German was Karl Benz, a caring provider for his family of seven, a man with real staying power, even when life treated him roughly. In early photographs he cut a determined figure, what-you-see-is-what-you-get, with a visionary gaze fixed on the future of the car. On 29 January 1886 he was granted German Imperial Patent no. 37435 by the relevant authority in Berlin for a "vehicle powered

sind die beiden einander nie begegnet, aber Historie und Ursprung des Unternehmens, das ihre Namen tragen wird, werden zum Herzstück der Geschichte des Autos, der individuellen Beweglichkeit.

Die Vaterschaft des eigenständigen Kindes reklamieren natürlich auch andere: Nach einer Phase unförmiger und ungeschlachter Dampf-Dinosaurier unternimmt 1806 der Schweizer Major Isaac de Rivaz den ersten Versuch, ein Fahrzeug mit einem Gasmotor anzutreiben. Obwohl das Vehikel nur einen einzigen Sprung macht und dabei die Garagenwand zum Einsturz bringt, erhält der Offizier ein Patent auf ein »durch Gasmaschine angetriebenes Kraftfahrzeug«. 1860 konstruiert der Franzose Etienne Lenoir ein Gas-Triebwerk, das zum erstenmal richtig läuft, angesichts seiner Größe aber etwas rachitisch auf der Brust ist. 1876 meldet sich dann Nikolaus August Otto (1832–1891) zu Wort, Gründer der Gasmotorenfabrik Deutz, mit einem Viertaktmotor, der mehr leistet und weniger Leuchtgas konsumiert als die bisherigen Maschinen. Sein Trick: die Vorverdichtung des Gas-Luft-Gemischs. Die von Otto 1884 angemeldete elektrische Zündung macht die Verwendung flüssiger Kraftstoffe möglich. Aber sein Geschöpf ist zu groß und zu klobig und folglich zu stationärem Dasein verurteilt.

Die Franzosen halten den Ingenieur Edouard Delamare-Deboutteville für den Erfinder des Motorwagens. 1884 erhält auch er ein Patent, nur fällt seine Kreation einer Explosion zum Opfer. Delamare indessen, fürwahr vielseitig, wendet sich bestürzt anderen, friedlichen Steckenpferden zu, der Austernzucht und einer Übersetzung des

Berta Benz stopping to refuel at a drugstore in Wiesloch during her long journey in 1888.

Während ihrer Fernfahrt 1888 legt Berta Benz an einer Apotheke in Wiesloch einen Tankhalt ein.

Durant son excursion de 1888, Berta Benz refait le plein devant une pharmacie de Wiesloch.

jamais rencontrés, mais l'histoire et l'origine de l'entreprise qui portera leurs noms deviendront le synonyme de l'histoire de l'automobile, de la mobilité individuelle.

Bien d'autres réclament aussi la paternité de cet enfant qui grandira vite : après les dinosaures à vapeur aux formes bizarres et inesthétiques, le major suisse Isaac de Rivaz tente, en 1806, de faire avancer un véhicule propulsé par un moteur à gaz. Bien que le véhicule ne fasse qu'un seul et unique bond, faisant s'écrouler à cette occasion le mur du garage, l'officier obtient un brevet pour un « véhicule propulsé par un moteur à gaz ». En 1860, le Français Étienne Lenoir construit un moteur à gaz qui fonctionne pour la première fois correctement, mais qui, compte tenu de sa taille, développe une puissance plutôt ridicule. En 1876, un certain Nikolaus August Otto (1832–1891), fondateur de l'usine de moteurs à gaz de Deutz, fait parler de lui avec un moteur à quatre temps plus puissant et consommant moins de gaz d'éclairage que les moteurs connus à ce jour. Il a trouvé une parade : le mélange de gaz et d'air est précomprimé. L'allumage électrique breveté par Otto en 1884 permet d'utiliser des carburants liquides. Mais, trop grande et trop encombrante, sa création est logiquement condamnée à un destin stationnaire.

Pour les Français, l'ingénieur Édouard Delamare-Deboutteville est l'inventeur de l'automobile. En 1884, lui aussi obtient un brevet, mais sa création est victime d'une explosion. Delamare, homme vraiment éclectique, se tourne alors par dépit vers d'autres violons d'Ingres plus pacifiques : l'ostréiculture et la traduction du sanscrit. Les Italiens aussi revendiquent un droit de propriété intellectuelle sur l'automobile. Enrico Bernardi, professeur à l'Institut de mécanique appliquée de Vérone, dépose en 1882 un brevet pour un moteur à essence qu'il monte, deux ans plus tard, sur un tricycle bizarre. Ce petit moteur développe la puissance effrayante de 0,024 ch, est baptisé Pia d'après le nom de sa fille favorite, et n'a vraisemblablement jamais poussé le moindre soupir de sa propre force.

Désir et volonté sont à l'origine de tous ces premiers pas, mais leur praticabilité est une tout autre affaire. Qui se mesure à l'aune de quatre critères : la construction doit être documentée. Le véhicule doit fonctionner. Il doit avoir été essayé en public. L'invention doit représenter un progrès. Et c'est alors que sonne l'heure des Allemands, qui ont en commun le goût du travail et un acharnement têtu ainsi qu'un penchant pour l'esprit missionnaire.

Il y a là Karl Benz, père attentif d'une famille de sept personnes, un homme plein de patience, endurant, même si la vie n'est pas toujours tendre avec lui. Des portraits précoces le représentent comme un homme déterminé et sans fioritures, le regard missionnaire résolument tourné vers l'avenir de l'automobile. Le 29 janvier 1886, les autorités de tutelle de Berlin lui accordent le brevet du Reich impérial allemand numéro 37435 pour un « véhicule à propulsion par moteur à gaz dont le gaz est produit à partir de substances gazeuses par un appareil embarqué ». Ce carburant a pour nom ligroïne et est en vente en pharmacie.

Gottlieb Daimler (1834–1900) testing a "first practicable four-wheeled automobile" in 1886.
Gottlieb Daimler (1834–1900) erprobt 1886 ein »erstes vierrädriges gebrauchsfähiges Automobil«.
Gottlieb Daimler (1834–1900) expérimente en 1886 une « première automobile viable à quatre roues ».

by a gas engine whose gas is produced by fuel gasification by means of a device carried on the vehicle." The fuel was called ligroin and was available from the chemist's. Although the German term *(Benzin)* for gasoline as used later might lead people to think it is named after Karl Benz, this is not the case. Rather its name derives from the African port of Bizerte via which benzoin resin was exported as far back as the Middle Ages and which was used to manufacture volatile substances (benzenes).

The appearance of Benz's "Patent-Motorwagen" on 5 September of that year was officially documented and widely reported. The Mannheim-based newspaper, the *Generalanzeiger,* for example, wrote: "A velocipede powered by ligroin gas and designed by Benz & Co.'s Rheinische Gasmotorenfabrik… was test-driven this morning on the Ringstraße." The paper revealed its awareness of the significance of this moment, prophetically envisaging good times ahead for this tinny-sounding new arrival on the roads: "We believe that this vehicle will have a promising future because it can be used without any great fuss and because, assuming its speed increases, it will become the cheapest means of transport for company representatives and possibly also for tourists." The original version of this three-wheeled steel vehicle, which was dismantled shortly after granting of the patent, then later reassembled and made roadworthy again, was personally donated by Benz to the Deutsches Museum in Munich in 1906. It is a unique, absolutely irreplaceable witness of the age and an index fossil from the sediments of man's motorized origins.

Sanskrit. Auch die Italiener erheben Copyright-Ansprüche auf die Novität Automobil. Enrico Bernardi, Professor am Institut für angewandte Mechanik in Verona, meldet 1882 einen Benzinmotor zum Patent an und montiert ihn zwei Jahre später in ein ungefüges Dreirad. Das Maschinchen leistet matte 0,024 PS, wird nach Bernardis Lieblingstochter Pia benannt und hat vermutlich aus eigener Kraft nie einen einzigen Schnaufer getan.

Hinter all diesen Gehversuchen lassen sich Wunsch und Wille ausmachen, aber mit ihrer Praktikabilität steht es nicht zum besten. Diese muss sich an vier Kriterien messen lassen: Die Konstruktion muss dokumentiert werden. Das Fahrzeug muss funktionieren. Es muss öffentlich erprobt sein. Die Erfindung muss die weitere Entwicklung vorantreiben. Und damit schlägt die Stunde der Deutschen, die Solidität und Beharrlichkeit bis hin zur Sturheit sowie eine Neigung zum Missionarischen verbindet.

Da ist Karl Benz, seiner siebenköpfigen Familie ein treusorgender Vater, ein Steher, auch wenn das Leben rauh mit ihm umspringt. Frühe Abbildungen zeigen ihn entschlossen, einen Mann ohne Schnickschnack, den visionären Blick unbeirrt in die automobile Zukunft gerichtet. Am 29. Januar 1886 wird ihm von der zuständigen Behörde in Berlin das Kaiserliche Deutsche Reichspatent (DRP) Nummer 37435 zugeteilt, für ein »Fahrzeug mit Gasmotorenbetrieb, dessen Gas aus vergasenden Stoffen durch einen mitzuführenden Apparat erzeugt wird«. Der Kraftstoff heißt Ligroin und ist in Apotheken erhältlich. Das spätere Benzin, obwohl es der Name vermuten lassen würde, geht nicht auf Karl Benz zurück: Der Saft, aus dem die Kraft kommt, verdankt seinen Namen dem afrikanischen Hafen Bizerta (Benzert), über den das Benzoe-Harz schon im Mittelalter eingeführt und zur Herstellung flüchtiger Substanzen (Benzine) verarbeitet wurde.

Die Ausfahrt des Benzschen »Patent-Motorwagens« am 5. September jenes Jahres zum Beispiel ist verbrieft und verbürgt und wird ausführlicher Berichterstattung gewürdigt. So schreibt der *Generalanzeiger* der Stadt Mannheim: »Ein mittelst Ligroin-Gas zu treibendes Veloziped,… in der Rheinischen Gasmotorenfabrik von Benz & Co konstruiert …, wurde heute früh auf der Ringstraße probiert.« Das Blatt zeigt sich der Bedeutsamkeit des Augenblicks durchaus bewusst und mutmaßt seherisch künftige rosige Zeiten für den dünn knatternden Neuankömmling im Straßenverkehr: »Wir glauben, daß dieses Fuhrwerk eine gute Zukunft haben wird, weil dasselbe ohne viel Umstände in Gebrauch gesetzt werden kann und weil es, bei möglicher Schnelligkeit, das billigste Beförderungsmittel für Geschäftsreisende, eventuell auch für Touristen werden wird.« Benz übergibt die Originalversion seines dreirädrigen Stahlwagens, das bald nach der Patenterteilung zerlegt, später indes wieder komplettiert und lauffähig gemacht wird, im Jahre 1906 persönlich dem Deutschen Museum in München, Unikat, schier unersetzlicher Zeitzeuge und Leitfossil aus den Sedimenten des motorisierten Aufbruchs der Menschheit.

Contrairement à ce que pourrait faire croire son nom, le futur benzène n'est pas une invention de Karl Benz : le liquide dont provient la puissance doit son nom au port tunisien de Bizerte (Benzert), d'où l'on introduisait, dès le Moyen Âge, la résine de Benzoë que l'on utilisait alors pour fabriquer des substances volatiles (benzènes).

Les premiers tours de roue de la « Patent-Motorwagen » de Benz, le 5 septembre 1886, dûment certifiés et attestés, font l'objet d'amples reportages élogieux. Ainsi le journal *Generalanzeiger* de Mannheim écrit-il : « Un vélocipède propulsé à l'aide de gaz à la litrone […] construit dans l'usine de moteurs à gaz rhénane de Benz & Co […] a aujourd'hui été essayé, tôt ce matin, sur la Ringstrasse. » La gazette est parfaitement consciente de l'importance de l'événement et, prophète en son pays, prédit un avenir prometteur à ce nouveau protagoniste pétaradant de la circulation routière aux allures de sauterelle : « Nous croyons que ce véhicule aura un grand avenir parce qu'il peut être utilisé sans difficulté et parce que, à condition d'être suffisamment rapide, il pourra devenir le moyen de transport le moins coûteux pour les hommes d'affaires et, éventuellement aussi, pour les touristes. » En 1906, Benz remet personnellement la version originale de son tricycle en acier – qui sera vite démonté après l'octroi du brevet, mais, plus tard, de nouveau complété et remis en état de fonctionner – au Deutsches Museum de Munich, spécimen unique, témoin absolument irremplaçable des premières tentatives de motorisation de l'humanité.

Ayant fait ses études à l'École polytechnique de Karlsruhe, il a, contrairement à Daimler, d'emblée considéré l'automobile comme une entité. Il a mis au point sa propre préparation du mélange, et une espèce d'ancêtre du carburateur à flotteur. Comme il n'y a pas encore de réservoir, il faut toujours malheureusement, au bout de quelques kilomètres déjà, reverser du benzène dans la chambre du flotteur. Il a imaginé un allumage à haute tension dont le circuit de courant primaire est fermé en permanence lorsque le moteur fonctionne. Enfin, il n'a pas, contrairement à d'autres, transformé une calèche, mais construit un véhicule conçu spécialement pour le nouveau propulseur. Le cadre tubulaire simple, mais d'une solidité étonnante est originaire des usines de cycles Adler ; il est en quelque sorte l'ancêtre préhistorique de la construction allégée. L'idée d'une direction à deux roues acceptable techniquement est tout d'abord rejetée. Il choisit comme compromis une seule roue avant articulée à l'aide d'une manivelle de commande.

Karl Benz est parti de rien. Avec la Rheinische Gasmotorenfabrik, une société commerciale, il produit également des moteurs à deux temps stationnaires qui remportent un grand succès. Le marché automobile, en revanche, est extrêmement précaire. Il semblerait que Benz ait créé un objet pour lequel il existe encore peu de demande en 1886. On se déplace à pied ou en calèche à cheval. Le réseau ferroviaire couvre déjà 40 000 km, mais le réseau routier est dans un état déplorable. Et, de plus, cet objet novateur coûte cher, on parle de 3000 marks.

As a graduate of Karlsruhe's Polytechnic College, from the very beginning Benz, unlike Daimler, had a complete vision of the car as a whole. He designed his own fuel/air mixture processing system, a forerunner of the float-type carburetor. Since there was still no fuel tank, however, the float chamber had to be repeatedly topped up with fuel after the vehicle had traveled a short distance. He developed a high-voltage ignition system the primary circuit of which was permanently closed when the engine was running. And significantly he did not simply remodel a coach, but rather specifically built a vehicle around the new power unit. The simple, extremely robust tubular frame, in some senses a prehistoric form of lightweight design, was supplied by the Adler cycle factory. The concept of a technically acceptable two-wheel steering system was postponed for the moment. Compromise came in the form of a single front wheel operated by a steering shaft.

Karl Benz worked his way up from humble beginnings. At Rheinische Gasmotorenfabrik, a general partnership, he also produced successful two-stroke stationary engines. The motor car business, however, was very slow to pick up at this time. Benz, it would appear, had produced an article for which there was little demand in 1886. People either walked or rode in a horse-drawn carriage. The railway network already covered 40,000 km (24,850 miles), while the road network was in a wretched state. Moreover, at a rumored cost of 3000 marks, the new invention was decidedly expensive.

In 1888 Benz's industrious and energetic wife Berta, née Ringer, decided on a spectacular publicity stunt, which featured the first appearance of a woman at the wheel. Benz was still dozing when, at 5 am on a beautiful August morning, Berta and her sons Eugen (15) and Richard (14) fetched the "Patent-Motorwagen" from the outbuilding. This was already the third version, a somewhat modified product featuring wooden-spoke wheels, a slightly more powerful engine and two gears. The three intended visiting Granny in Pforzheim, a trip of 180 km (112 miles) on roads which hitherto had only seen horse-drawn traffic, accompanied by the wild barking of terrified dogs. At first everything went smoothly. However, the meager one-and-a-half horsepower of the chugging velocipede found the inclines after Wiesloch tough going. Richard got behind the wheel, while Berta and Eugen pushed. The downhill section almost proved too much for the wooden brake blocks which exerted their gentle braking action directly on the rear wheels. When the drive belt snapped after they had passed through Bruchsal, a local cobbler got them moving again. A blockage in the fuel line was overcome with the aid of Berta's hat pin, and a worn-through ignition cable was insulated with her garter. In the evening the conspirators telegraphed the extremely anxious head of the family to let him know that the long haul had gone well. Encouraged by this, he resolved the problems listed in Berta's test report. At the Engine and Machinery Exhibition in Munich in September he demonstrated his car daily between 2 pm and

Als Absolvent des Polytechnikums in Karlsruhe hat er, im Gegensatz zu Daimler, von vornherein das Automobil als Ganzes im Visier. Er hat seine eigene Gemischaufbereitung entwickelt, eine Urform des Schwimmer-Vergasers. Da es noch keinen Tank gibt, muss allerdings nach kurzer Strecke immer wieder Benzin in die Schwimmerkammer nachgefüllt werden. Er hat eine Hochspannungszündung ausgetüftelt, deren Primärstromkreis bei laufendem Motor permanent geschlossen ist. Er hat schließlich nicht etwa eine Kutsche umgemodelt, sondern ein Fahrzeug gebaut, das auf das neue Triebwerk abgestimmt ist. Von den Fahrradwerken Adler stammt der einfache, ungemein stabile Rohrrahmen, gewissermaßen eine prähistorische Form des Leichtbaus. Der Gedanke an eine technisch akzeptable Zweiradlenkung wird zunächst zurückgestellt. Als Kompromiss bietet sich das vermittels einer Steuerkurbel bewegte Einzelrad vorn an.

Karl Benz hat sich aus dürftigen Anfängen hochgerappelt. In der Rheinischen Gasmotorenfabrik, einer offenen Handelsgesellschaft, produziert er ebenfalls erfolgreiche stationäre Zweitakt-Triebwerke. Die Autokonjunktur indessen läuft ungemein schleppend an. Benz hat, so scheint es, einen Artikel auf die Räder gestellt, für den 1886 wenig Bedarf besteht. Man läuft oder nimmt die Pferdedroschke. Das Eisenbahnnetz ist bereits 40 000 Kilometer lang, das Straßennetz in miserabler Verfassung. Und überdies ist das neue Ding teuer, man spricht von 3000 Mark.

1888 entschließt sich Benz' tüchtige und energische Frau Berta, geborene Ringer, zu einer spektakulären Werbeaktion, Premiere zugleich der Dame am Steuer. Benz schlummert noch, da holt sie um fünf Uhr früh eines schönen Augustmorgens mit ihren Söhnen Eugen (15) und Richard (14) den »Patent-Motorwagen« aus der Remise. Es handelt sich bereits um die dritte Variante, ein Produkt sanfter Modellpflege mit Holzspeichenrädern, einem etwas stärkeren Motor sowie zwei Fahrstufen. Die drei wollen der Großmutter in Pforzheim einen Besuch abstatten, 180 Kilometer auf Straßen, über die bislang lediglich Pferdefuhrwerke geschwankt sind, begleitet vom rasenden Gebell einer erschreckten Hundepopulation. Der Start klappt reibungslos. Doch die Steigungen hinter Wiesloch sind zuviel für die anderthalb mageren Pferdestärken des tuckernden Velozipeds. Richard setzt sich hinters Steuer, Berta und Eugen schieben. Die Talfahrt überfordert schier die Holzklotzbremsen, die mild mäßigend unmittelbar auf die Hinterräder wirken. Hinter Bruchsal reißt der Antriebsriemen. Ein lokaler Schuster schafft Abhilfe. Als die Benzinleitung verstopft ist, hilft sich Berta mit ihrer Hutnadel. Ein durchgescheuertes Zündkabel wird mit ihrem Strumpfband isoliert. Am Abend telegraphieren die Verschwörer dem aufs höchste beunruhigten Familienvorstand, die Fernfahrt sei gut verlaufen. Er schöpft neuen Mut, behebt die in Bertas Testbericht aufgelisteten Mängel. Anlässlich der »Kraft- und Arbeitsmaschinenausstellung« in München im September demonstriert er täglich zwischen 14 und 16 Uhr seinen Wagen einem staunenden, aber nicht unbedingt kaufwilli-

The genius who preferred to stay out of the limelight: Wilhelm Maybach (1846–1929).

Der Genius, der lieber im Hintergrund wirkt: Wilhelm Maybach (1846–1929).

Le génie qui ne s'est jamais placé sous les feux de la rampe: Wilhelm Maybach (1846–1929).

En 1888, Berta, l'épouse ingénieuse et énergique de Benz, décide de faire une spectaculaire action publicitaire. C'est aussi la première d'une femme au volant. Alors que Benz est encore au pays des songes, elle sort la «Patent-Motorwagen» de la remise à cinq heures du matin d'une belle journée d'août avec ses fils, Eugen (15 ans) et Richard (14 ans). Il s'agit déjà de la troisième variante, un produit timidement modernisé avec des roues à rayons en bois, un moteur un peu plus puissant et deux vitesses. Les trois complices veulent rendre visite à la grand-mère des enfants, à Pforzheim: 180 km à couvrir sur des routes qui n'avaient jusque-là vu que des attelages à cheval, accompagnés par les aboiements furieux d'une meute de chiens effrayés. Le départ s'effectue sans difficulté. Mais les côtes derrière Wiesloch sont trop escarpées pour le rachitique 1,5 cheval du vélocipède pétaradant. Richard prend place au volant tandis que Berta et Eugen poussent la voiture. Les descentes mettent rudement à contribution les freins à plaquette en bois qui n'exercent qu'un effet relatif sur les roues arrière. Après avoir passé Bruchsal, la courroie d'entraînement se rompt. Un cordonnier de l'endroit procède à la réparation. Lorsque la conduite d'essence se bouche, Berta a l'idée d'utiliser son épingle de chapeau. Elle isole ensuite avec sa jarretière un câble d'allumage mis à nu par les frictions. Le soir, les conjurés envoient un télégraphe au chef de famille à bout de nerfs, lui disant que le voyage s'était bien passé. Cela lui donne un courage nouveau et il pallie les défauts énumérés dans le bilan du voyage dressé par Berta. À l'occasion du Salon des moteurs et machines de travail, à Munich, en septembre, il fait, de quatorze à seize heures, une démonstration quotidienne de sa voiture devant un public étonné, mais pas prêt pour autant à l'acheter.

4 pm to an astonished public, though one that showed little inclination to buy. Nonetheless, press reports and morale were good, and the trend was upwards.

Another whose hour had come was Gottlieb Daimler, a gunsmith and a hands-on type with a raging thirst for theoretical knowledge which he attempted to quench by studying at Stuttgart Polytechnic. His typically Swabian attitude to money and financial matters benefited not only his large family – Daimler married twice and had seven children in total – but also his friend and partner Wilhelm Maybach (1846–1929). He was scarcely any less brilliant and innovative though he had a tendency to hide his light discreetly under the proverbial bushel. Others were less reserved, and dubbed him the "King of the Designers" even during his lifetime.

In 1882 a homesick and rather angry Daimler left Nikolaus August Otto's Gasmotorenfabrik Deutz after ten years as one of its senior staff. He took with him shares with a nominal value of 112,000 marks. Furthermore, he ensured a generous settlement for Maybach who moved with him to pastures new in Bad Cannstatt. Nonetheless, conditions there were modest, and the greenhouse of his property in the Taubenheimstraße was where they put their heads together to cultivate new ideas. The outcome of their deliberations in 1884 was first a horizontal engine and then an upright engine developing half a horsepower. It ran at 600 rpm in contrast to the sluggish 180 rpm of Otto's engines, and was therefore much smaller and lighter. Daimler developed a new valve timing gear and a hot-tube ignition system which was patented in late 1883. Maybach contributed the surface carburetor which provided a fuel/air mixture by means of evaporation.

In August 1885 a patent was submitted for a "Reitwagen", a two-wheeled velocipede which had to withstand a suspension-free *tour de force* over the three kilometers (1.9 miles) from Cannstatt to Untertürkheim three months later. The two had just invented the motorcycle, but the idea withered on the vine ending as a mere subsidiary product.

One year later, Daimler's fast-running internal combustion engine, patent number 28022, was installed in a boat and then finally, in the autumn of 1886, in a four-seater car with four wheels. The chassis came from an Americain carriage commissioned at a cost of 795 marks from "By Royal Appointment" suppliers W. Wimpff & Sohn in Stuttgart. By this time Benz's three-wheeler had already stolen the show, the headlines and the distinctive charm of the first-born automobile from Daimler's motor carriage – the exponent of the car as an organic unit had taken a lead over the exponent of the engine. Nonetheless, for Daimler there was the excitement of a move ahead: in July 1887 he bought a 2900 sq m (31,216 sq ft) property with workshops in the Ludwigstraße in Cannstatt where a two-cylinder unit in the form of a v for victory was created in 1889. Wilhelm Maybach was the brains behind the "Stahlradwagen", a vehicle with a tubular steel frame and wire wheels, in which

gen Publikum. Presse und Moral sind dennoch gut, die Tendenz ist steigend.

Da ist Gottlieb Daimler, gelernter Büchsenmacher und Praktiker mit einem ausgeprägten Bedürfnis nach Theorie, das er mit einem Studium an der Polytechnischen Schule in Stuttgart zu stillen versucht. Von seinem schwäbisch-sensiblen Gespür für Geld und Geldeswert profitiert nicht nur seine umfangreiche Familie – Daimler heiratet zweimal und hat insgesamt sieben Kinder –, sondern auch sein Freund und Partner Wilhelm Maybach (1846–1929), der kaum weniger genial und innovativ ist, aber dazu neigt, sein Licht diskret unter den Scheffel zu stellen. Andere sind weniger zurückhaltend: Schon zu Lebzeiten nennen sie ihn den »König der Konstrukteure«.

Als Daimler Nikolaus August Ottos Gasmotorenfabrik Deutz 1882 nach zehn Jahren Zusammenarbeit in leitender Stellung voll Heimweh und nicht ohne Groll verlässt, nimmt er Aktien im Wert von nominell 112 000 Mark mit auf den Weg. Überdies sorgt er für eine großzügige Alimentierung Maybachs, der mit ihm zusammen nach Bad Cannstatt zu neuen Ufern aufbricht. Die Verhältnisse sind gleichwohl bescheiden: Man steckt dort die klugen Köpfe im Gewächshaus seines Anwesens in der Taubenheimstraße zusammen. Was dabei 1884 herauskommt: zuerst ein liegender, dann ein stehender Motor mit einer halben Pferdestärke. Er läuft mit 600/min, wo sich Ottos Maschinen lediglich zu müden 180 aufschwangen, ist deswegen viel kleiner und leichter. Daimler entwickelt eine neue Ventilsteuerung und eine Glührohrzündung, die Ende 1883 patentiert wird. Maybach steuert den Oberflächenvergaser bei, der ein Gemisch von Luft und Kraftstoff durch Verdunstung liefert.

Im August 1885 reicht man die Patentschrift für einen »Reitwagen« ein, ein zweirädriges Veloziped, das ein Vierteljahr später herhalten muss für eine ungefederte Tour de Force über die drei Kilometer von Cannstatt nach Untertürkheim. Die beiden haben soeben das Motorrad erfunden, aber es verkümmert zum Nebenprodukt.

Ein Jahr später ist Daimlers schnelllaufender Verbrennungsmotor, Patent Nummer 28 022, in ein Boot eingebaut, im Herbst 1886 schließlich in einen Viersitzer mit vier Rädern. Das Fahrgestell stammt von einer Kutsche Typ Americain, die für 795 Mark beim Königlichen Hoflieferanten W. Wimpff & Sohn in Stuttgart in Auftrag gegeben wurde. Da hat der Daimler Motorkutsche bereits das Benz-sche Dreirad die Schau, die Schlagzeilen und den aparten Charme des automobilen Erstgeborenen gestohlen, der Exponent des Kraftwagens als organisch zusammengewachsener Einheit dem Exponenten des Motors. Gleichwohl herrscht Aufbruchstimmung: Im Juli 1887 erwirbt man ein 2900 Quadratmeter großes Grundstück mit Werkstätten in der Cannstatter Ludwigstraße und bringt 1889 einen Zweizylinder zum Laufen, in der Form eines v wie Victory. Wilhelm Maybach ist der Kopf hinter dem Stahlradwagen, bei dem die Symbiose zwischen Trieb- und Fahrwerk bereits sehr weit gediehen ist. Als Exponat auf der

Malgré tout, la presse et le moral sont bons et la tendance est à l'optimisme.

Gottlieb Daimler, ajusteur et praticien, mais aussi très porté sur la théorie, étudie à l'École polytechnique de Stuttgart. Il est père d'une famille nombreuse – marié deux fois, il a au total sept enfants. Il a pour ami et associé Wilhelm Maybach (1846–1929), qui s'il ne lui cède en rien pour le génie et le caractère novateur, est plutôt réservé, peu enclin à occuper le devant de la scène. Tous profitent du sens typiquement souabe de Daimler pour la valeur de l'argent. D'autres collaborateurs, moins réservés, le portent aux nues : de son vivant, ils le surnomment « le roi des constructeurs ».

Lorsque Daimler quitte l'usine de moteurs à gaz de Nikolaus August Otto, en 1882, après dix ans de coopération à un poste de directeur, plein de nostalgie mais non sans ressentiment, il emmène avec lui des actions pour une valeur nominale de 112 000 marks. Il veille en outre à ce que Maybach obtienne une pension généreuse lorsqu'il part avec lui pour Bad Cannstatt où ils décident de repartir d'une feuille blanche. Les débuts n'en sont pas moins modestes. Là, les deux esprits inventifs se creusent les méninges dans la serre de sa propriété de la Taubenheimstrasse. Mais qu'en ressort-il en 1884 ? Tout d'abord un moteur horizontal, puis un moteur vertical d'un demi-cheval qui tourne à 600 tr/min alors que le moteur d'Otto atteignait péniblement 180 tr/min parce qu'il était beaucoup plus petit et plus léger. Daimler met au point une nouvelle distribution des soupapes et un allumage à tube incandescent breveté fin 1883. Maybach apporte une contribution sous la forme d'un carburateur de surface qui fournit par évaporation un mélange d'air et de carburant.

En août 1885, les deux hommes déposent un brevet pour une « Reitwagen » (voiture à chevaucher), un vélocipède à deux roues qui sert, trois mois plus tard, pour un tour de force sans suspension sur les trois kilomètres séparant Bad Cannstatt d'Untertürkheim. Les deux hommes viennent d'inventer la moto, mais elle devra se contenter d'un destin secondaire.

Un an plus tard, le moteur à combustion à régime rapide de Daimler, brevet numéro 28 022, est monté sur un bateau et, finalement, à l'automne 1886, dans une voiture à quatre places et à quatre roues. Le châssis provient d'une calèche type Américain commandé pour 795 marks auprès du fournisseur royal de la Cour, W. Wimpff & Sohn, à Stuttgart. La calèche à moteur de Daimler a déjà volé au tricycle de Benz la vedette, les grands titres des journaux et le charme indéniable du premier-né automobile, création parachevée en tant qu'ensemble organique de châssis et de moteur. Il règne à cette époque une ambiance de pionniers : en juillet 1887, les deux hommes acquièrent un terrain de 2900 mètres carrés avec des ateliers dans la Ludwigstrasse de Bad Cannstatt et font tourner, en 1889, un bicylindre en v, un v comme victoire. Wilhelm Maybach est le génie inventeur qui a engendré la voiture à roues en acier pour laquelle la symbiose de moteur et de châssis est déjà très

the symbiosis between the power plant and chassis was already very well developed. When exhibited at the World Exhibition in Paris in the same year, however, the filigree four-wheeler from Swabia was overshadowed by a static construction made of the same material, the Eiffel Tower. *La grande nation* creates its own legends, if you don't mind.

In 1890 Daimler, Max Duttenhofer and Wilhelm Lorenz founded Daimler-Motoren-Gesellschaft (DMG) "for the purpose of exploiting and utilizing Gottlieb Daimler's gasoline and gas engine inventions." 123 staff (89 more than in the preceding year) worked "at Daimler" – a formulation that gradually gained currency and which was never said without an undertone of pride.

Marching to separate tunes

Laurels (Benz & Cie. AG) 1899–1926

For Karl Benz too 1890 was a watershed. Partners Friedrich Wilhelm Eßlinger and Max Rose left his company to be replaced by Friedrich von Fischer (1845–1900) and Julius Ganß (1851–1905) who were very receptive to the idea of the automobile and were quite convinced that this "invention of the century" would turn a handsome profit in the long term. In 1899 Benz & Co. changed its company structure from a general partnership (OHG) to a stock corporation (AG) with Ganß and Benz himself on the board of management and Josef Brecht and Eugen Benz as authorized officers. The younger generation was pushing into positions of responsibility.

In addition to countless stationary engines, the company sold 603 motor vehicles in 1900, 341 of which went abroad. Benz & Cie. Rheinische Gasmotorenfabrik AG was the largest car factory in the world. Scarcely had this status been achieved, however, than it began to fade away. In 1901 sales fell to 385 vehicles, then to 226 in 1902, and in 1903 they dropped as low as 172. The company had been on the wrong track, and Karl Benz showed himself to be a remarkably hesitant businessman. He seemed almost timorous as he observed the restrictions on increases in the power and speed of his products, a primeval fear against which the car had been fighting from the very beginning. As late as the 1900–1901 annual report there was sharp criticism of "the recently emerging obsession for competitive racing at ever greater speeds." At the same time Daimler was becoming a threatening competitor and demonstrating an early awareness of the culture of *Vorsprung durch Technik* in the attractive form of the first Mercedes models. Faced with this situation, the progressively inclined sales director Julius Ganß remembered a Benz saying that although Germany was the father of the car, France was the mother, and consequently he hired the Frenchman Marius Barbarou from the Paris-based car company Clément-Bayard together with five other engineers.

Pariser Weltausstellung im gleichen Jahr steht der filigrane vierrädrige Selbstbeweger aus dem Schwabenland allerdings im Schatten einer anderen, statischen Konstruktion aus dem gleichen Werkstoff, des Eiffelturms. Die Grande Nation schafft sich ihre Mythen bitteschön selbst.

1890 gründen Daimler, Max Duttenhofer und Wilhelm Lorenz die Daimler-Motoren-Gesellschaft (DMG) »zum Zweck der Ausbeutung und Verwertung der von Gottlieb Daimler gemachten Petroleum- und Gasmotoren-Erfindungen«. 123 Angestellte (89 mehr als im Jahr zuvor) stehen in Brot und Lohn »beim Daimler« – eine Formulierung, die sich einschleifen und nie ohne einen Unterton von Stolz gesagt werden wird.

Getrennt marschieren

Lorbeer (Benz & Cie. AG) 1899–1926

Auch für Karl Benz gerät das Jahr 1890 zur Zäsur: Die Gesellschafter Friedrich Wilhelm Eßlinger und Max Rose verlassen seine Firma; an ihrer statt kommen Friedrich von Fischer (1845–1900) und Julius Ganß (1851–1905) an Bord, durch und durch offen für die Idee des Automobils und fest davon überzeugt, dass die Jahrhundert-Erfindung auf Dauer deftigen Gewinn abwerfen wird. 1899 wechselt die Benz & Co. (OHG) den Aggregatzustand und mutiert zur Aktiengesellschaft, mit Ganß und Benz selbst im Vorstand und Josef Brecht sowie Eugen Benz als Prokuristen – die junge Generation drängt in die Verantwortung.

1900 setzt man neben zahlreichen stationären Motoren 603 Fahrzeuge ab, 341 davon ins Ausland. Die Benz & Cie. Rheinische Gasmotorenfabrik AG ist die größte Autofabrik der Welt. Doch kaum errungen, wird dieser Nimbus bereits angenagt: 1901 stürzen die Verkäufe auf 385 Automobile ab, 1902 auf 226, 1903 gar auf 172. Weichen wurden falsch gestellt: Als merkwürdig zögerlich erweist sich Karl Benz. Fast furchtsam sieht er Grenzen des Wachstums hinsichtlich Stärke und Tempo seiner Produkte, eine Urangst, gegen die das Phänomen Auto von Anbeginn anrannte. Noch im Geschäftsbericht für das Jahr 1900/1901 rügt man säuerlich »die neuerdings hervortretende Sucht, sich bei Wettfahrten in immer größeren Schnelligkeiten zu überbieten«. Zugleich droht der Konkurrent Daimler und sichert sich einen Vorsprung durch Technik in der attraktiven Gestalt der ersten Mercedes-Modelle. In dieser Situation entsinnt sich der progressiver gesonnene Verkaufschef Julius Ganß eines Benz-Diktums, dass Deutschland der Vater des Automobils sei, die Mutter hingegen Frankreich, und heuert den Franzosen Marius Barbarou von der Pariser Autofirma Clément-Bayard sowie fünf weitere Ingenieure an.

Die ingeniöse Gallier-Riege bringt als Mitgift und Probe ihrer Kunst eine Reihe von fast fertigen Fahrzeugen mit, die mit Ideengut aus dem hauseigenen Konstruktions-

avancée. Présentée à l'Exposition universelle de Paris de la même année, l'automobile à quatre roues du pays souabe souffre toutefois de l'ombre d'une autre construction statique du même matériau, la tour Eiffel. La Grande Nation tient en effet à se donner ses mythes elle-même.

En 1890, Daimler, Max Duttenhofer et Wilhelm Lorenz fondent la société Daimler-Motoren-Gesellschaft (DMG) « afin d'exploiter et de valoriser les inventions de moteurs à pétrole faites par Gottlieb Daimler ». Cent vingt-trois employés (89 de plus que l'année précédente) figurent sur les fiches de salaire « chez Daimler » – un constat qui perdurera et ne s'entendra jamais prononcé sans un soupçon de fierté.

Marcher séparément

Les lauriers (Benz & Cie. AG) 1899–1926

Pour Karl Benz aussi, 1890 est une césure : ses associés Friedrich Wilhelm Esslinger et Max Rose quittent sa société que viennent rejoindre Friedrich von Fischer (1845–1900) et Julius Ganss (1851–1905), une société à l'esprit grand ouvert aux idées de l'automobile et fermement convaincue que l'invention du siècle finira par produire des bénéfices lucratifs. En 1899, Benz & Cie. (OHG) change de statut juridique et se mue en société anonyme, avec Ganss et Benz lui-même au directoire et Josef Brecht et Eugen Benz en tant que fondés de pouvoir – la jeune génération éprise de responsabilités rue déjà dans les brancards.

En 1900, outre de nombreux moteurs stationnaires, elle produit aussi 603 véhicules, dont 341 sont exportés. La Benz & Cie. Rheinische Gasmotorenfabrik AG est la plus grande usine automobile du monde. Mais, à peine obtenue, cette position est déjà en danger : en 1901, les ventes de voitures retombent à 385 exemplaires, à 226 en 1902 et même à 172 en 1903. Outre quelques erreurs de parcours, Karl Benz s'avère étonnamment hésitant. Presque craintif, il est réticent à accroître la puissance et la vitesse de ses voitures, une frilosité originale contre laquelle les tenants de l'automobile ont dû se battre dès les débuts. Dans le rapport d'exercice 1900–1901, encore, il critique avec amertume « la nouvelle manie de vouloir se surclasser en roulant toujours plus vite lors de courses ». Simultanément, son concurrent Daimler devient une menace d'autant plus sérieuse qu'il s'assure une avance mécanique avec ses premiers modèles Mercedes, aux formes attrayantes. Dans cette situation, le directeur des ventes, Julius Ganss, esprit progressiste, invente la formule selon laquelle l'Allemagne est le père de l'automobile alors que la France en est la mère ; il recrute donc le Français Marius Barbarou auprès du constructeur automobile parisien Clément-Bayard ainsi que cinq autres ingénieurs.

As their dowry and a taster of their skills, the ingenious Gallic team brought with them a range of almost finished vehicles which were combined with ideas from the in-house design office led by Georg Diehl and Fritz Erle. The result was the Parsifal range launched in 1903 which fortunately borrowed only its name from the Arthurian legends and not the association of sheer folly: upright four-cylinder engines and a cardan-shaft drive undoubtedly represented state-of-the-art automotive engineering. Marius Barbarou was revealed in the meantime as their spiritual father. This annoyed Karl Benz who left the board of management and resigned his executive directorship of the company in April 1903, although he remained a shareholder and joined the supervisory board in the summer of 1904.

But the turbulence, the comings and goings, and the tremors continued at Benz & Cie. Raging in his broken German, Barbarou disappeared back to the motherland of the car, while Julius Ganß left the board of management, disappointed by the unexpectedly poor response to the Parsifal. Josef Brecht and Fritz Hammesfahr took over the running of the company, while Diehl and Erle thoroughly revamped the range of models. It paid off: 1904–1905 saw a return to modest profitability, with the gap between Benz and Daimler closing. In 1908 Benz & Cie. even sporadically had its nose in front.

The Blitzen-Benz (1909), a beautiful, wild monster of a car built all in white with a massive 21.5-liter engine developing 200 bhp and capable of 228 kph (142 mph), was impossible to miss. The man behind this rugged machine which flaunted the German imperial eagle on its sides during record-breaking runs at Daytona was Hans Nibel (1880–1934) who was the senior designer as early as 1908, and a member of the board of management from 1917 onwards. Another up-and-coming man at Benz was Friedrich Nallinger (1880–1937) who was a member of the board of management of Daimler-Motoren-Gesellschaft at the tender age of 21 years and in 1912 replaced Fritz Hammesfahr on the board of management of Benz & Cie. Rheinische Automobil- und Motorenfabrik AG, which was the name under which the company had been trading since

Finishing shop at Benz & Cie.'s Mannheim factory, around 1910.

»Fertigmacherei« der Firma Benz & Cie. um 1910 im Werk Mannheim.

Montage final de la firme Benz & Cie., vers 1910 à l'usine de Mannheim.

büro unter Georg Diehl und Fritz Erle kombiniert werden. Resultat ist ab 1903 die Typenreihe Parsifal, die dem Artus-Mythos lediglich den Namen, nicht aber die Vorstellung der reinen Torheit entlehnt: stehende Vierzylinder-Motoren und Kardanantrieb repräsentieren durchaus Autobau *state of the art*. Als geistiger Vater wird indessen Marius Barbarou herausgestellt. Dies vergrätzt Karl Benz, der sich im April 1903 aus Vorstand und Geschäftsleitung zurückzieht, aber Teilhaber bleibt und im Sommer 1904 in den Aufsichtsrat eintritt.

Doch Turbulenzen, Stühlerücken und tektonische Beben innerhalb der Benz & Cie. halten an: In gebrochenem Deutsch zürnend, verschwindet Barbarou wieder im Mutterland des Autos, während Julius Ganß sich aus dem Vorstand verabschiedet, enttäuscht über das unerwartet dürftige Echo auf den Parsifal. Die Leitung des Hauses übernehmen Josef Brecht und Fritz Hammesfahr, während Diehl und Erle die Modell-Palette gründlich überarbeiten und retuschieren. Das zahlt sich aus: 1904/1905 beginnen sich sanfte Gewinne einzustellen, die Defizite gegenüber Daimler abzunehmen. 1908 hat man sogar hier und da die Nase vorn.

Ein unüberhörbares und unübersehbares Zeichen setzt der Blitzen-Benz von 1909, ein schönes, wildes Auto-Tier ganz in Weiß mit brutalen 21,5 Liter Hubraum, 200 PS stark und 228 Stundenkilometer schnell. Der Mann hinter dieser knorrigen Maschine, die bei Rekordfahrten in Daytona demonstrativ den deutschen Reichsadler auf den Flanken trägt: Hans Nibel (1880–1934), bereits 1908 Chefkonstrukteur, ab 1917 Vorstandsmitglied. Andere Coming Men bei Benz: Friedrich Nallinger (1880–1937), der schon im zarten Alter von 21 Jahren Angehöriger des Vorstands bei der Daimler-Motoren-Gesellschaft war und 1912 Fritz Hammesfahr ersetzt im Vorstand der Benz & Cie. Rheinische Automobil- und Motorenfabrik AG, als die das Unternehmen seit 1911 firmiert. Und, als dritter im Bunde, Wilhelm Kissel (1885–1942), 1904 Korrespondent, 1917 Prokurist und in den Gründerjahren 1925 und 1926 im Vorstand der »Interessengemeinschaft Daimler-Benz«.

Schon 1907 hat man trotz einer weltweiten Wirtschaftsflaute gegen eigene Aktien im Wert von 350 000 Mark einen früheren Konkurrenten adoptiert, die Süddeutsche Automobil-Fabrik Gaggenau, huldigt einem milden Polyzentrismus: Die Akquisition im badischen Murgtal soll ausschließlich dem Lastwagenbau dienen. Schon 1908 hat man die komplette Automobilproduktion in einem brandneuen Fabrikkomplex (Aufwand insgesamt 600 000 Mark) im Mannheimer Ortsteil Waldhof angesiedelt. 1909 ist Benz & Cie. für ein halbes Jahr mit Aufträgen ausgelastet. 1910 fertigen 2500 Mitarbeiter in Mannheim 1340 Personenwagen, die 840 Benz-Kostgänger in Gaggenau 381 Nutzfahrzeuge.

Das Durchschnittseinkommen liegt bei rund 1800 Mark, die Sozialleistungen suchen ihresgleichen: Es gibt einen Hilfs-Fonds für Arbeiter, eine »Beamten«-Unterstützungskasse als Pendant für die Büroangestellten sowie eine

En tant que dot et preuve de son savoir-faire, l'astucieuse équipe de Gaulois amène avec elle une série de voitures presque terminées qui sont combinées à quelques idées produites par le bureau d'ingénieurs maison dirigé par Georg Diehl et Fritz Erle. Le résultat en est, à partir de 1903, la série Parsifal, qui ne reprend du mythe du roi Arthur que le nom, mais non l'idée de la pure folie : le moteur à quatre cylindres verticaux et l'entraînement par cardan témoignent de l'art automobile. Marius Barbarou est qualifié de père intellectuel de ces inventions. Vexé, Karl Benz se retire du directoire et de la direction de l'entreprise en avril 1903, mais reste associé et entre au conseil de surveillance durant l'été 1904.

Mais les turbulences, les remaniements et les remplacements à la Benz & Cie. perdurent : exprimant sa fureur dans un allemand chaotique, Barbarou retourne chez la mère de l'automobile tandis que Julius Ganss démissionne du directoire, déçu du peu de succès remporté par la Parsifal. Josef Brecht et Fritz Hammesfahr prennent la direction de la maison tandis que Diehl et Erle retravaillent et retouchent en profondeur la gamme de production. Le travail porte ses fruits : en 1904–1905, ils commencent à engranger de légers bénéfices alors que les déficits vis-à-vis de Daimler diminuent. En 1908, ils parviennent même à surpasser leur concurrent dans certains domaines.

La Blitzen-Benz de 1909, une belle mais sauvage et bestiale voiture blanche avec l'énorme cylindrée de 21,5 litres, 200 ch et capable d'atteindre 228 km/h pose des jalons historiques. L'homme qui a dessiné cette imposante machine qui arbore démonstrativement l'aigle du Reich allemand sur ses flancs lors des tentatives de record à Daytona, s'appelle Franz Nibel (1880–1934), déjà chef constructeur en 1908 et membre du directoire à partir de 1917. Autre homme en devenir chez Benz : Friedrich Nallinger (1880–1937), membre du directoire de la Daimler-Motoren-Gesellschaft dès le jeune âge de 21 ans et qui remplace, en 1912, Fritz Hammesfahr au directoire de la Benz & Cie., Rheinische Automobil- und Motorenfabrik AG, nom que se donne l'entreprise en 1911. Troisième mousquetaire, Wilhelm Kissel (1885–1942), correspondant en 1904, fondé de pouvoir en 1917 et membre du directoire lors des années de fondation de 1925 et 1926 de l'« Interessengemeinschaft Daimler-Benz » (communauté d'intérêts).

Dès 1907, malgré un marasme économique mondial, l'équipe reprend, contre des actions d'une valeur de 350 000 marks, un ancien concurrent, la Süddeutsche Automobil-Fabrik Gaggenau, et fait preuve à cette occasion d'un polycentrisme de bon aloi : la société de Murgtal construira exclusivement des camions. Dès 1908, on a installé toute la production automobile dans un nouveau complexe industriel (qui a coûté la somme totale de 600 000 marks) dans un quartier de Mannheim, à Waldhof. En 1909, Benz & Cie. possède un carnet de commandes qui représente six mois de travail. En 1910, 2500 collaborateurs fabriquent à Mannheim 1340 voitures de tourisme et leurs 840 collègues de Gaggenau, 381 véhicules utilitaires.

1911. And the third in the group was Wilhelm Kissel (1885–1942) who rose from the position of clerk in 1904 via authorized officer in 1917 to become a member of the board of management of "Interessengemeinschaft Daimler-Benz" (the community of interest set up to merge the two companies) in its founding years of 1925 and 1926.

As early as 1907, despite a worldwide economic slump, Benz & Cie. took over a former competitor, Süddeutsche Automobil-Fabrik Gaggenau, in exchange for shares in Benz to the value of 350,000 marks. The aim was to expand the company's interests somewhat, as the acquisition in Murgtal in Baden was intended to be devoted solely to truck production. The entire car production operations had been transferred in 1908 to a brand-new factory complex (at a total cost of 600,000 marks) in Waldhof, a suburb of Mannheim. In 1909 Benz & Cie.'s order books were full for six months ahead. In 1910 2500 employees in Mannheim produced 1340 cars, while the 840 "adopted" Benz staff in Gaggenau completed 381 commercial vehicles.

The average income at this time was around 1800 marks, and the social welfare provisions were unparalleled. There was a benefit fund for workers, a salaried-staff relief fund, and a foundation which enabled employees in need of convalescence to be sent away on holiday. The company had concentrated on relatively large cars since 1901. Sales were running like clockwork, but there were still niche markets to be developed and gaps to be closed. It was decided to produce a mid-range car. In the summer of 1910 Benz's strategic planners took the unconventional step of launching an internal competition with a first prize of 3000 marks. This was won by the engineer Karl Ketterer for his praiseworthy design of an 8/18 bhp model, of which a series of 1000 units soon went into production. This became an 8/20 bhp type in 1912 and remained in continual production until 1921.

Net profits of 4.4 million marks were recorded in fiscal year 1911–1912, and this had risen to 6.3 million just a year later reflecting production figures of 2706 and 3664 vehicles respectively. In 1913 the share capital was increased to 22 million marks, and in March 1914 Benz shares were floated on the stock exchange and promptly traded at 226 per cent in free transactions. The cautious Friedrich Nallinger was not keen on the watering-can principle of offering eight different models simultaneously. However, his attempt to have the Benz range reduced to just two types was defeated by the sales department and the supervisory board which ruled that there had to be an appropriate Benz for every potential customer.

Paralysis followed, however. The post-1914 years also brought a halt to any technical developments except those with a direct bearing on improvements to the war machine. Large luxury cars were no longer required. On the other hand, the army did have a demand for medium-sized vehicles, even those in an out-and-out civil guise: when German forces advanced on the French capital on 1 September 1914, General Galliéni had 700 Parisian taxis requisitioned

Stiftung, deren Leistungen es möglich machen, erholungsbedürftige Werktätige in Urlaub zu schicken. Seit 1901 hat man sich auf größere Autos verlegt. Der Absatz läuft wie am Schnürchen, und dennoch sind noch Nischen und Spielräume auszureizen. Ein Mittelklassewagen muss her. Im Sommer 1910 greifen die Benz-Strategen zum unkonventionellen Mittel eines internen Ausschreibens, loben einen ersten Preis von 3000 Mark aus. Den sichert sich der Ingenieur Karl Ketterer mit der preiswürdigen Konstruktion eines Modells von 8/18 PS, von dem alsbald eine Serie von 1000 Einheiten aufgelegt wird, 1912 verbessert zum Typ 8/20 PS und Konstante in der Palette bis 1921.

Im Geschäftsjahr 1911/1912 können 4,4 Millionen Mark Reingewinn ausgewiesen werden, ein Jahr später gar 6,3 Millionen, bei einer Produktion von jeweils 2706 und 3664 Fahrzeugen. 1913 wird das Grundkapital auf 22 Millionen Mark aufgestockt, im März 1914 an der Börse die Benz-Aktie eingeführt, die bereits im freien Verkehr für 226 Prozent gehandelt wird. Das Gießkannen-Prinzip, acht Modelle nebeneinander auf dem Markt anzubieten, missfällt dem behutsamen Friedrich Nallinger. Sein Vorstoß, das Benz-Spektrum auf zwei Typen zu verengen, wird allerdings von Verkauf und Aufsichtsrat abgeschmettert: Es müsse für jeden potentiellen Kunden einen geeigneten Benz geben.

Dann folgt Lähmung: Die Jahre nach 1914 schneiden eine Zäsur auch in die technische Entwicklung, es sei denn, sie sind der Optimierung des Kriegswerkzeugs unmittelbar zuträglich. Nicht länger gefragt sind große Luxuswagen. Dafür besteht Heeresbedarf nach Mittelklassefahrzeugen, selbst in durch und durch bürgerlichem Habitus: Als am 1. September 1914 deutsche Streitkräfte gegen die französische Hauptstadt vorstoßen, lässt General Galliéni kurzerhand 700 Pariser Taxis requirieren, mit denen 3000 Soldaten an die Marne-Front reisen. Viele der 64 000 Autos, die im August 1914 deutsche Straßen bevölkern, verglühen im Inferno des Ersten Weltkrieges. Auch die Benz-Produktion knickt ein, Akzente verlagern sich: Zwischen 1914 und 1918 werden 3777 PKW hergestellt, dazu 6150 LKW und Busse. Der Krieg, angeblich Vater aller Dinge, erweist sich als reichlich stiefväterlich.

Das gilt auch für seine Nachwehen: Man kämpft, wie Don Quijote gegen die Windmühlenflügel, gegen die Inflation. 1920 hat die Reichsmark, ausgemergelt durch Krieg und Wiedergutmachung, zu siechen begonnen. Bald wird aus dem Trab der Geldentwertung ein halt- und zügelloser Galopp: »Die gewaltige Erhöhung der Produktionskosten hat die Unzulänglichkeit der eigenen Mittel in Erscheinung treten lassen«, beschwert sich der Vorstand der Benz & Cie. im August jenes Jahres in nüchternbekömmlichem Understatement.

Zwei neue Denkansätze missraten zum Flop: ein sportlicher kleiner Benz 6/18 PS mit einem Königswellen-Triebwerk von mimosenhafter Anfälligkeit sowie die Lizenznahme auf den »Tropfenwagen« des Flugzeugbauers Dr. Edmund Rumpler 1921. Dieser bringt Fortschrittliches

A Benz racing car from 1922, based on Dr. Edmund Rumpler's "Tropfenwagen" (Teardrop).

Dem »Tropfenwagen« Dr. Edmund Rumplers nachempfunden: ein Benz-Rennwagen aus dem Jahre 1922.

Réplique de la « Tropfenwagen » (voiture en goutte d'eau) d'Edmund Rumpler: une Benz de compétition de 1922.

Le salaire moyen est d'environ de 1800 marks et les prestations sociales sont inégalées: il existe un fonds de secours pour les ouvriers, une caisse de soutien de «fonctionnaires », son homologue pour les employés de bureau, ainsi qu'une fondation dont les prestations permettent d'envoyer en vacances les ouvriers ayant besoin de repos. Depuis 1901, l'usine fabrique surtout des voitures de plus grandes dimensions. Elles se vendent sans difficulté et, pourtant, il y a encore des créneaux et des zones grises à exploiter. Il faut donc fabriquer une voiture de classe moyenne. Durant l'été 1910, les stratèges de Benz recourent au moyen peu conventionnel d'un appel d'offres interne et décernent un premier prix de 3000 marks. C'est un ingénieur, Karl Ketterer, qui le remporte avec la construction, digne du prix, d'un modèle de 8/18 ch, dont une série de mille exemplaires sera bientôt fabriquée et qui sera améliorée, en 1912, pour donner naissance au type 8/20 ch et continuera à figurer au programme jusqu'en 1921.

Pour l'exercice 1911–1912, le bilan fait état de 4,4 millions de marks de bénéfices nets et même, un an plus tard, de 6,3 millions, pour une production respective de 2706 et 3664 véhicules. En 1913, le capital social est majoré à 22 millions de marks et l'action Benz est émise à la Bourse en mars 1914 alors qu'elle est déjà négociée en vente libre à 226 % de sa valeur. Le principe de l'arrosoir qui consiste à proposer simultanément huit modèles déplaît au prudent Friedrich Nallinger. Cette tentative de limiter le programme Benz à deux modèles se voit toutefois opposer une fin de non-recevoir par la direction des ventes et le conseil de surveillance: chaque client potentiel doit pouvoir choisir la Benz qui lui convient.

C'est alors que se produit une période de paralysie: les années postérieures à 1914 représentent également une césure dans le développement technique à moins qu'il ne soit directement compatible avec l'optimisation du matériel de guerre. Les grandes voitures de luxe cessent d'avoir la cote. En revanche, l'armée a besoin de véhicules de taille intermédiaire, même si elles sont d'un aspect tout à fait bourgeois: lorsque, le 1er septembre 1914, les forces allemandes se mettent en marche en direction de la capitale française, le général Gallieni fait réquisitionner immédiatement 700 taxis parisiens qui transportent 3000 soldats sur

there and then to transport 3000 soldiers to the Marne front. Many of the 64,000 cars on German streets in August 1914 were burnt out in the inferno of the First World War. Benz's production also responded to the call, shifting the thrust of its manufacturing effort. Between 1914 and 1918 3777 cars were produced, plus 6150 trucks and buses. The war, supposedly the war to end all wars, proved to be anything but that.

And then, of course, there were the after-effects. The battle against inflation was reminiscent of Don Quixote tilting at windmills. By 1920 the reichsmark, emaciated by war and reparations, was ailing. The trot of currency devaluation soon became an all-out gallop: "The huge increase in production costs has highlighted the inadequacy of the company's resources," the Benz & Cie. board of management complained in August of that year with sober understatement.

Two new ventures flopped, a small, sporty Benz of 6/18 bhp with a vertical-shaft drive of mimosa-like sensitivity, and a license in 1921 to produce the "Tropfenwagen", the "Teardrop" designed by the aeronautical engineer Dr. Edmund Rumpler. This brief association resulted in the introduction by Rumpler of advanced features such as aerodynamic design, a rear-mounted engine, and a swing axle, though without these elements becoming standard features of the company's production cars, as originally was hoped by Friedrich Nallinger and Hans Nibel.

Three factors, however, proved helpful: a car with the renown of a Benz was recognized as a safe investment to counteract the effects of inflation; the demand for the cars from outside Germany where currencies had remained comparatively stable continued unabated; and it was decided to face present and future perils purely as a motor vehicle factory. So on 27 February 1922 a consortium led by Deutsche Verkehrsbank in Berlin took over the old factory in Mannheim's Waldhofstraße where it ran what had been the "Stationary Gas Engine Department" as Motoren-Werke Mannheim AG (MWM).

But then Germany became the country of the poor millionaires. In June 1923 an Opel 6/16 bhp, for which you would have had to pay a still modest 115,000 marks in January 1921, cost a whacking 156 million marks. On 18 September the publishing house Ullstein-Verlag, for example, informed its staff that it would be charging 500,000 marks for a private telephone call. The price tag of a reasonable suit was around a billion, double the salary of a senior teacher. And the books of Benz & Cie. show that in July 1924 the total value of the assets had swollen, depending on whether you prefer the British or American numbering system, to over 5 trillion or quintillion marks (either way it's a five followed by 18 zeros!).

This is the grim background to the rise of Jakob Schapiro, an adventurer from Odessa. While others played safe by putting their money in material assets such as paintings, carpets, or property, and left it at that, Schapiro was a virtuoso speculator, a Mozart of devaluation. His first

Daytona Beach, 1910: Barney Oldfield setting a world record at a speed of 211.4 kph (132.1 mph) in the "Blitzen-Benz."

Daytona Beach anno 1910: Barney Oldfield fährt auf dem Blitzen-Benz mit 211,4 km/h Weltrekord.

Daytona Beach en 1910: Barney Oldfield établit un record mondial avec 211,4 km/h au volant de la « Blitzen-Benz ».

wie aerodynamisches Design, Heckmotor und Pendelachse mit in die kurze Ehe, ohne dass sich diese Detaillösungen, wie ursprünglich von Friedrich Nallinger und Hans Nibel erhofft, so ohne weiteres in die Serien einspeisen lassen.

Drei Dinge erweisen sich andererseits als hilfreich: Den Irrungen und Wirrungen der Inflation trotzt ein Automobil vom Renommee eines Benz als sichere Kapitalanlage. Die Nachfrage von jenseits der Grenzen, wo sich Währungen vergleichsweise stabil erhalten haben, dauert ungebrochen an. Und überdies ringt man sich dazu durch, den Fährnissen der Zeit und der Zukunft als reine Autofabrik zu begegnen: Am 27. Februar 1922 übernimmt ein Konsortium unter der Führung der deutschen Verkehrsbank in Berlin das alte Werk an der Mannheimer Waldhofstraße und führt die bisherige »Abteilung stationärer Gasmotorenbau« als Motoren-Werke Mannheim AG (MWM) weiter.

Dann aber wird Deutschland zur Nation der armen Millionäre. Im Juni 1923 kostet ein Opel 6/16 PS, für den man im Januar 1921 noch bescheidene 115000 Mark hatte entrichten müssen, bereits stramme 156 Millionen. Am 18. September setzt etwa der Ullstein-Verlag seine Mitarbeiter davon in Kenntnis, für ein privates Telefongespräch müssten 500000 Mark entrichtet werden. Ein brauchbarer Anzug schlägt mit einer runden Milliarde zu Buche, dem doppelten Gehalt eines Oberlehrers. Und als im Juli 1924 die Bilanz der Benz & Cie. vorgelegt wird, ist die Summe der Aktiva zu über 5 Trilliarden Mark aufgequollen, eine Zahl mit 19 Stellen.

Dies ist der düstere Hintergrund, vor dem sich der Aufstieg des Jakob Schapiro vollzieht, Glücksritter aus Odessa.

le front de la Marne. Beaucoup des 64 000 voitures qui sillonnent les routes allemandes en août 1914 disparaissent dans l'enfer de la Première Guerre mondiale. La production de Benz, également, s'effondre et les priorités diffèrent: entre 1914 et 1918, on produit 3777 voitures de tourisme, mais 6150 camions et bus.

La guerre n'est pas favorable au commerce: tel Don Quichotte se battant contre les moulins de la Manche, on se bat contre l'inflation. En 1920, le reichsmark, dévalorisé par la guerre et les réparations, a commencé à se déprécier. Bientôt, le trot de la dévalorisation de l'argent fait place à un galop irrésistible: «l'augmentation considérable des coûts de production a mis en évidence l'insuffisance de nos propres ressources», se plaint la direction de la Benz & Cie. en août 1920, en un bel euphémisme.

Les nouvelles tentatives, une sportive petite Benz 6/18 ch avec un moteur à arbre de renvoi d'une vulnérabilité maladive ainsi que la licence prise pour la « Tropfenwagen » (voiture goutte d'eau) du constructeur d'avions Edmund Rumpler en 1921, se soldent par un échec. Pourtant, cette voiture représente un grand progrès avec son design aérodynamique, son moteur arrière et son essieu brisé, mais le mariage est de courte durée et ses solutions de détail ne peuvent pas être transférées sans autre forme de procès dans la série, comme l'avaient espéré initialement Friedrich Nallinger et Hans Nibel.

Trois atouts s'avèrent bien utiles: malgré les incertitudes et les aléas de l'inflation, une voiture aussi réputée qu'une Benz est un placement sûr. La demande émanant des pays étrangers, où les monnaies jouissent d'une stabilité relative, ne se dément pas. Et, de plus, les décisions nécessaires pour parer aux difficultés de cette époque et de l'avenir en tant qu'usine purement automobile sont arrêtées: le 27 février 1922, un consortium sous l'égide de la Deutsche Verkehrsbank, à Berlin, reprend l'ancienne usine de la Waldhofstrasse à Mannheim et conserve l'ancien « Service de constructions de moteurs à gaz stationnaires » sous le titre de Motoren-Werke Mannheim AG (MWM, usine de moteurs de Mannheim).

Et l'Allemagne devient la nation des millionnaires pauvres. En juin 1923, une Opel 6/16 ch qui avait encore coûté la somme modique de 115 000 marks en janvier 1921 coûte dorénavant pas moins de 156 millions. Le 18 septembre, la maison d'édition Ullstein informe ses collaborateurs qu'ils devront désormais débourser 500 000 marks pour une communication téléphonique privée. Un costume de bon faiseur ne coûte pas moins d'un milliard de marks, le double du salaire d'un professeur de l'enseignement supérieur. Et, en juillet 1924, lorsque est présenté le bilan de la Benz & Cie., la somme des actifs se monte à plus de 5 milliards de milliards de marks, un nombre avec 19 chiffres.

Tel est le sombre contexte dans lequel s'effectue l'essor d'un certain Jakob Schapiro, opportuniste d'Odessa. Quand d'autres se réfugient dans les valeurs matérielles sûres – tableaux, tapis, biens immobiliers – et s'en con-

principle was: goods immediately, payment as late as possible, using bills that were extended *ad infinitum*. His second dubious dictum was: contracts are there to be ignored when times are bad, and it was rumored that he was the originator of that contemptible quotation.

And yet he retained a completely untainted view of the soundness of his business partners. In 1921 Schapiro bought 200 Benz chassis of type 8/20 bhp in the name of his company Carosserie Schebera AG in Berlin Tempelhof, and in 1922 he acquired Benz ordinary shares for around 40 million marks. By 1924, with 60 per cent of the Benz shares and 25 per cent of the Daimler shares in his possession, he had cheated his way into the position of a major shareholder.

It was only once the ghost of inflation had receded, with only occasional fleeting nightmare reappearances, that Wilhelm Kissel realized that his company did not have the strength alone to free itself from the speculator's all-embracing tentacles. The former competitor Daimler put itself forward as a partner of equivalent standing. At a time when companies were supporting one another to prevent themselves from collapse, such advances certainly did not fall on deaf ears. In May 1924 the companies formed a community of interests. The appropriate committee was chaired by Dr. h.c. Emil Georg von Stauß, who was both the chairman of the board of management of Deutsche Bank and chairman of the supervisory board of Daimler-Motoren-Gesellschaft (DMG). The groundwork was therefore already done for the hyphen that was permanently to join the life's work of Messrs. Gottlieb Daimler and Karl Benz. The agreed community quota negotiated with regard to the conversion of the balance sheets to gold marks showed DMG, which had been domiciled in Berlin since 1922, to be the stronger of the companies – it was assigned 654, and Benz & Cie. 346. They handled each other rather with kid gloves: "We regard ourselves as having been particularly fortunate to have secured your company as an ally whose glorious past offers the best guarantee for successful future cooperation," Benz & Cie. wrote in a thank-you letter for the Daimler presents given to the Mannheim company to mark its 25th anniversary as a public limited company.

Nevertheless past resentments and rivalries lingered, in the form of metaphorical punches on the nose and carefully placed kicks to the shin. When Wilhelm Kissel, a member of the board of management of both companies since June 1925 and the executive entrusted with preparations for the merger, arrived to take up his post in Stuttgart-Untertürkheim, he was collected from the station in the smallest available Benz. He was also given only a very small office in the administrative building, one which he pointedly kept long after he had risen to far greater things as the chairman of the board of management between 1930 and July 1942. In an understandable expression of self-interest Jakob Schapiro initially professed himself to be very pleased about the merger of the two companies. Then, however, Kissel, von Stauß, and Dr. Carl Jahr, the head of

Wo andere sich in der Geborgenheit des Sachwerts kuscheln, des Bildes, des Teppichs, der Immobilie, und es dabei bewenden lassen, beherrscht dieser virtuos die Spielregeln der Spekulation, ein Mozart der Geldentwertung. Sein Grundsatz Nummer eins lautet: Ware sofort, Bezahlung so spät wie möglich, mit Wechseln, die bis zum Es-geht-nicht-mehr prolongiert werden. Seine dubiose Devise Nummer zwei: Verträge sind dazu da, in schlechten Zeiten nicht eingehalten zu werden, ein schnödes Originalzitat, wie man munkelt.

Dabei bewahrt er sich einen durch nichts getrübten Blick für die Solidität seiner Geschäftspartner. 1921 ersteht Schapiro namens seiner Carosserie Schebera AG in Berlin Tempelhof 200 Benz-Fahrgestelle des Typs 8/20 PS, 1922 Benz-Stammaktien in Höhe von rund 40 Millionen Mark. 1924 hat er sich, mit 60 Prozent der Benz und 25 Prozent der Daimler-Anteile in seinem Besitz, zum Großaktionär emporgemogelt.

Spätestens jetzt, da der Inflations-Spuk verflogen ist und nur noch als Alptraum nachwirkt, ist Wilhelm Kissel klar, dass sich sein Unternehmen nicht aus eigener Kraft aus den alles umschlingenden Krakenarmen des Spekulanten befreien kann. Als Ansprechpartner gleichen gewichtigen Formats bietet sich der einstige Marktgegner Daimler an. In einer Zeit, da sich Firmen aneinanderlehnen, um einzeln nicht umzufallen, stoßen seine Avancen keineswegs auf taube Ohren. Im Mai 1924 findet man sich zusammen zu einer Interessengemeinschaft. Vorsitzender des entsprechenden Ausschusses wird Dr. h.c. Emil Georg von Stauß, in Personalunion Vorstandssprecher der Deutschen Bank und Aufsichtsratsvorsitzer der Daimler-Motoren-Gesellschaft (DMG). Der Bindestrich, der das Lebenswerk der Herren Gottlieb Daimler und Karl Benz dauerhaft aneinanderknüpfen wird, ist somit im Konzept bereits vorgezeichnet. Die vereinbarte Gemeinschaftsquote, die im Hinblick auf die Umstellung der Bilanzen auf Goldmark ausgehandelt wird, weist die aus steuerlichen Gründen seit 1922 in Berlin sesshafte DMG als den stärkeren Konzern aus – auf sie entfallen 654, auf die Benz & Cie. 346. Man geht gewissermaßen mit Glacéhandschuhen miteinander um: »Wir halten es für ein besonderes Glück, gerade Ihr Unternehmen als Bundesgenossen gefunden zu haben, dessen ruhmreiche Vergangenheit die schönste Gewähr für weiteres erfolgreiches Zusammenarbeiten bietet«, heißt es in einem Benz-Bedankemichbrief für die Daimler-Aufmerksamkeiten, die den Mannheimern zum 25jährigen Bestehen als Aktiengesellschaft zuteil wurden.

Dennoch schwingen die Ressentiments und Rivalitäten der Vergangenheit nach – in Nasenstübern und behutsamen Tritten gegen das Schienbein: Als Wilhelm Kissel, seit dem Juni 1925 Vorstandsmitglied beider Gesellschaften und mit der Vorbereitung der Fusion betraut, zum Dienstantritt in Stuttgart-Untertürkheim eintrifft, wird er mit dem kleinsten verfügbaren Benz am Bahnhof abgeholt und erhält auch nur ein ganz kleines Büro im Verwaltungsgebäude, das er demonstrativ behält, als er längst zu höchsten

tentent, lui maîtrise avec virtuosité les règles du jeu de la spéculation, véritable Mozart de la dévalorisation de l'argent. Principe numéro un : la marchandise immédiatement, le paiement aussi tard que possible, à l'aide de traites qui sont prorogées jusqu'à une date impossible. Douteuse devise numéro deux : les contrats sont là pour ne pas être respectés quand les temps sont durs, maxime dont la rumeur lui attribue la paternité.

À ce propos, il fait ses preuves dans un discernement que rien ne trouble en ce qui concerne la qualité de ses ex-partenaires commerciaux. En 1921, Schapiro acquiert au nom de sa société, la Carrosserie Schebera AG, à Berlin-Tempelhof, 200 châssis Benz du type 8/20 ch et, en 1922, des actions Benz pour un montant d'environ 40 millions de marks. En 1924, avec 60 % des actions de Benz et 25 % des actions de Daimler en sa possession, il s'est mué avec rouerie en actionnaire majoritaire.

Maintenant que le spectre de l'inflation s'est dissipé et n'est plus qu'un cauchemar dans les mémoires, Wilhelm Kissel est conscient que son entreprise ne pourra pas se libérer à elle seule des tentacules du spéculateur. L'ancien concurrent, Daimler, est tout désigné comme interlocuteur d'envergure comparable. À une époque à laquelle des firmes se rapprochent pour ne pas disparaître l'une après l'autre, ses avances ne peuvent pas résonner dans le vide. En mai 1924, les partenaires contractent une communauté d'intérêt. Le président de la commission est Emil Georg von Stauss, à la fois porte-parole du directoire de la Deutsche Bank et président du conseil de surveillance de la Daimler-Motoren-Gesellschaft (DMG). Le trait d'union qui va désormais lier durablement l'œuvre des deux partenaires Gottlieb Daimler et Karl Benz est donc, dès le début, présent dans le concept. Le taux communautaire convenu, négocié dans la perspective du passage des bilans au mark or, fait état de la DMG, qui a son siège à Berlin depuis 1922 pour des motifs fiscaux, comme le groupe le plus puissant – elle représente 654/1000, contre 346 pour la Benz & Cie. Mais les deux partenaires se regardent tout d'abord en chiens de faïence : « Nous considérons que c'est un bonheur tout particulier d'avoir trouvé justement comme confédérée votre entreprise dont le prestigieux passé est la plus belle garantie pour une coopération couronnée de succès à l'avenir », peut-on lire dans une lettre de remerciements écrite par Benz pour les attentions de Daimler et envoyée aux hommes de Mannheim pour le 25e anniversaire de leur société anonyme.

Et pourtant, les ressentiments et les rivalités du passé se font encore sentir avec des rosseries et des crocs-en-jambe discrets : lorsque Wilhelm Kissel, membre du directoire des deux sociétés depuis juin 1925 et chargé de préparer la fusion, arrive à Stuttgart-Untertürkheim pour prendre ses fonctions, on passe le prendre à la gare avec la plus petite Benz disponible ; il n'a également qu'un tout petit bureau dans l'immeuble administratif, qu'il conserve démonstrativement alors qu'il assume depuis longtemps les fonctions les plus élevées en tant que président du

Rheinische Creditbank AG in Mannheim and the chairman of the supervisory board of Benz & Cie. AG, checkmated him in a clever and tough move over his iniquitous use of bills. Schapiro was forced to leave the supervisory board of Daimler-Benz AG in June 1929, three years after its establishment. He disappeared into obscurity and emigrated to Paris in 1933.

The star (Daimler-Motoren-Gesellschaft AG) 1890–1926

The history of Daimler-Motoren-Gesellschaft in the first decade of its existence bears all the hallmarks of an ancient tragedy with shining lights and rogues, rises, falls, and delays, with intrigues, disputes, and anguish for the protagonist leading ultimately to his terrible death in the fifth act of the drama.

Gottlieb Daimler's early work was particularly admired abroad. The French rights to his engine patents were held by Madame Louise Sarazin, the widow of Edouard Sarazin, the lawyer who had initiated this business and who had died in 1887. Madame Sarazin sold the licenses to Société Anonyme Panhard & Levassor which had hitherto made its money by manufacturing woodworking machines. She also sealed the transaction privately in 1890 by marrying Emile Levassor, the head of the company. Before this French connection bore fruit, Levassor, who was known as the *"chevalier sans cheval,"* the horseless rider, and his partner René Panhard let several months pass. They wanted to give the car, that curious mutation of the carriage with its mishmash of old and new technology, its own identity. And indeed, the company's first-born in May 1891 showed evidence of a unified design. Daimler's v engine was mounted imperiously over the front axle, and its 2.5 bhp were transmitted to the 3-speed gearbox via a clutch and from there to the rear wheels by chains. Up to 1896 Peugeot only fitted Daimler engines manufactured at Panhard & Levassor in its own vehicles. The same year saw the establishment of Daimler Motor Ltd. in Coventry which, as result of the First World War, was to sever its links from the parent company and lead a separate existence for a long period. In the USA the piano mogul William Steinway represented Daimler in Bowery Bay, although there were financial disagreements. Österreichische Daimler-Motoren-Gesellschaft was set up in Wiener Neustadt outside Vienna in 1899; from 1906 onwards this company changed its name to Austro-Daimler and became renowned in its own right.

At home, in the meantime, the indications all pointed towards a coming storm, with ammunition and explosives aplenty available from the moment of the establishment of the parent company in Cannstatt. Founding father Max

Weihen aufgestiegen ist, als Vorstandsvorsitzer zwischen 1930 und Juli 1942. Jakob Schapiro zeigt sich zunächst in wohlverstandenem Eigennutz sehr angetan von der Verschmelzung der Konzerne. Dann aber bereiten Kissel, von Stauß sowie Kommerzienrat Dr. jur. Carl Jahr, Direktor der Rheinischen Creditbank AG Mannheim und geschäftsführendes Aufsichtsratsmitglied der Benz & Cie. AG, der unguten Wechselbeziehung in einem klugen und zähen Schachspiel ein Ende. Schapiro muss im Juni 1929 den Aufsichtsrat der Daimler-Benz AG drei Jahre nach deren Gründung verlassen, verblasst bis hin zur Bedeutungslosigkeit und emigriert 1933 nach Paris.

Stern (Daimler-Motoren-Gesellschaft AG) 1890–1926

Die Geschichte der Daimler-Motoren-Gesellschaft in der ersten Dekade ihres Daseins trägt alle Züge einer antiken Tragödie mit Lichtgestalten und Schurken, Aufstieg, Fall und retardierenden Momenten, mit Intrigen, Querelen und Qualen für den Protagonisten sowie dessen beklagenswertem Tod im fünften Akt.

Vor allem im Ausland findet Gottlieb Daimlers Frühwerk Anklang: Die französischen Rechte auf seine Motor-Patente befinden sich im Besitz von Madame Louise Sarazin, Witwe des 1887 verblichenen Rechtsanwalts Edouard Sarazin, der das Geschäft angebahnt hat. Diese verkauft die Lizenzen an die Société Anonyme Panhard & Levassor, die bislang ihr Geld mit der Herstellung von holzverarbeitenden Maschinen verdient hat, und besiegelt die Transaktion auch privat, indem sie 1890 den Firmenchef Emile Levassor ehelicht. Ehe diese French Connection Früchte zeitigt, lassen Levassor, den sie »Chevalier sans cheval« nennen, den Reiter ohne Pferd, und sein Teilhaber René Panhard etliche Monate verstreichen. Man möchte dem Auto, jener merkwürdigen Mutation der Kutsche mit ihrem Mischmasch aus alt und neu, eine eigene Identität geben. In der Tat wird der Erstling vom Mai 1891 ein Ding aus einem Guss. Daimlers v-Motor thront über der Vorderachse, und seine 2,5 PS werden über eine Kupplung an das Dreiganggetriebe und von dort mit Ketten an die Hinterräder weitervermittelt. Bis 1896 baut Peugeot in seine eigenen Fahrzeuge ausschließlich Daimler-Maschinen ein, die bei Panhard & Levassor gefertigt werden. Im gleichen Jahr etabliert sich in Coventry die Daimler Motor Ltd., die sich als Folge des Ersten Weltkriegs vom Mutterhaus lösen und lange Zeit ein selbständiges Dasein führen wird. In den USA nimmt der Piano-Mogul William Steinway an der Bowery Bay Daimlers Interessen wahr, nur dass man sich über Finanzielles nicht so recht einigen mag. In der Wiener Neustadt siedelt sich 1899 die Österreichische Daimler-Motoren-Gesellschaft an, die es ab 1906 als Austro-Daimler zu Ruhm und Renommee aus eigenem Recht bringen wird. Daheim stehen indessen die Zeichen auf Sturm: Sprengstoff und Munition werden bereits mit der Gründung der Muttergesellschaft in Cannstatt abgelagert: Grün-

directoire entre 1930 et juillet 1942. Conscient de l'utilité que cela peut avoir pour lui-même, Schapiro se révèle tout d'abord ravi de la fusion des deux groupes. Mais c'est alors que Kissel, von Stauss et Carl Jahr, respectivement docteur en droit, directeur de la Creditbank AG Mannheim et membre du conseil de surveillance de Benz & Cie. AG en tant qu'administrateur gérant, mettent un terme à ces relations commerciales risquées, par le biais d'une stratégie astucieuse. En juin 1929, Schapiro doit finalement quitter le conseil de surveillance de la Daimler-Benz AG trois ans après sa création ; il finit par sombrer dans l'anonymat et émigre à Paris en 1933.

L'étoile (Daimler-Motoren-Gesellschaft AG) 1890–1926

L'histoire de la Daimler-Motoren-Gesellschaft AG durant la première décennie de son existence affiche tous les traits caractéristiques d'une tragédie antique avec des personnages de lumière et des forbans, un essor, une chute et des moments de suspense, avec des intrigues, des querelles et des souffrances pour le protagoniste ainsi que sa mort regrettable au cinquième acte.

C'est surtout à l'étranger que l'œuvre précoce de Gottlieb Daimler a été plébiscitée : les droits français pour ses brevets de moteurs se trouvent en possession de madame Louise Sarazin, veuve de l'avocat Édouard Sarazin décédé en 1887, qui a présidé à cette opération. Sa veuve vend les licences à la société anonyme Panhard & Levassor, qui a jusqu'ici gagné son argent avec la fabrication de machines de traitement du bois, et scelle aussi la transaction, à titre privé, en épousant en 1890 le chef de la firme, Émile Levassor. Ce Levassor, que l'on avait surnommé « chevalier sans cheval », et son associé René Panhard laissent passer de nombreux mois avant que cette *French connection* ne porte ses fruits. Ils veulent donner sa propre identité à la voiture, cette mutation bizarre de calèche avec un mélange d'ancien et de nouveau. Et, de fait, le premier modèle présenté en mai 1891 est conçu d'un seul jet. Le moteur en v de Daimler trône au-dessus de l'essieu avant et ses 2,5 ch sont transmis à la boîte à trois vitesses à l'aide d'un embrayage et, de là, par chaînes aux roues arrière.

Jusqu'en 1896, Peugeot monte dans ses propres voitures exclusivement des moteurs Daimler qui sont fabriqués chez Panhard & Levassor. La même année s'établit à Coventry la Daimler Motor Ltd., qui se séparera de la maison mère après la Première Guerre mondiale et mènera longtemps un destin autonome. Aux États-Unis, le pape du piano, William Steinway représente les intérêts de Daimler à la Bowery Bay, à ceci près que l'on ne parvient pas à se mettre vraiment d'accord sur les questions financières. À Wiener Neustadt s'établit, en 1899, la Österreichische Daimler-Motoren-Gesellschaft qui connaîtra prestige et renommée sous son propre nom en tant qu'Austro-Daimler à partir de 1906.

À domicile, par contre, le baromètre annonce la tempête : explosifs et munitions se sont déjà accumulés dès

Duttenhofer, head of the Vereinigte Köln-Rottweiler Pulverfabriken explosives factory, and founding father Wilhelm Lorenz, head of the Deutsche Metallpatronenfabrik ammunition factory in Karlsruhe, were associated with the country's most powerful banker Dr. Kilian Steiner, the head of Württembergische Vereinsbank. The go-getting banker was in the process of gathering a large number of companies under his control. He had long cast a covetous eye on Daimler's achievements where he felt that there was a gaping chasm between technical potential and commercial exploitation. Backed up by appropriately large investments, the task of curtailing founding father Gottlieb Daimler's influence and engineering his own involvement, even in technical matters, began immediately.

Daimler, however, held to the view later articulated by Ernest Hemingway that a man can be destroyed but not defeated. Angered but resolute, Daimler himself and his closest commercial adviser Karl Linck together with Wilhelm Maybach and twelve hand-picked staff retired in 1893 to a "Research Center" for an annual rent of 1800 marks in part of the Hotel Hermann in Bad Cannstatt. Distanced from political complaints and carping crossfire, Daimler's team were soon engaged in fruitful work which yielded the so-called Phoenix engine with two inline cylinders and an atomizing carburetor, one of Maybach's developments, and the "Riemenwagen", the belt-driven car, which was the backbone of Daimler's production for a long time. In the actual factory, meanwhile, the company's designers tried this and that in an attempt to breathe life back into hopeless projects. The engineer Max Schroedter, whom Duttenhofer had hired as Technical Director, launched variants of the "Stahlradwagen" which proved to be congenitally flawed designs that failed to sell more than a dozen models in two years.

No wonder that the balance sheet revealed a less than encouraging picture. In 1894 DMG was 385,000 marks in the red at Württembergische Vereinsbank and was facing bankruptcy by the middle of the following year. Since salvation could only come from the Hotel Hermann think tank, Duttenhofer and Lorenz were forced to approach Daimler, though not before influential associates of the company had exerted great pressure on the board. One of these was the Briton Frederick Richard Simms who authorized large license payments only on condition that Daimler and Maybach were restored to their old positions. A reconciliation agreement was signed. The luckless and lackluster Schroedter sank into oblivion, the hotel-based "branch" was dissolved in November 1895, and Gottlieb Daimler was placated – for the moment – with compensation to the tune of 200,000 marks.

The problems appeared to have been resolved. In the years of the schism (1892–1895) only 15 motor cars were assembled in total, but this was followed by a gentle explosion of production: in 1896 there were 24, in 1897 26, in 1898 57, in 1899 108 and at the turn of the century in 1900 the figure was 96. The work force grew in the same period from

dervater Max Duttenhofer, Chef der Vereinigten Köln-Rottweiler Pulverfabriken, und Gründervater Wilhelm Lorenz, Boss der Deutschen Metallpatronenfabrik zu Karlsruhe, sind Männer des mächtigsten Bankiers im Lande, des Leiters der Württembergischen Vereinsbank Dr. Kilian Steiner. Der umtriebige Banker ist dabei, eine Vielzahl von Firmen unter sein Kuratel zu zwingen. Schon lange hat er ein begehrliches Auge auf Daimlers Errungenschaften geworfen, weit genug klafft für ihn die Schere zwischen technischem Potential und kaufmännischer Nutzung auseinander. Abgestützt durch entsprechend dimensionierte Einlagen, beginnt man umgehend, Gründervater Gottlieb Daimlers Einfluss zu schmälern und selbst in technische Dinge hineinzureden.

Der indes hält es mit dem späteren Diktum Ernest Hemingways, dass ein Mann zwar zerstört, nicht jedoch vernichtet werden könne. Man zieht sich 1893 vergrämt, aber zu allem entschlossen, für 1800 Mark Jahresmiete in ein »Entwicklungszentrum« im Gartensaal des Hotels Hermann in Bad Cannstatt zurück, Daimler selbst und sein kaufmännischer Intimus Karl Linck sowie Wilhelm Maybach und zwölf handverlesene Mitarbeiter. Dort wird alsbald fernab politischer Quengeleien und Querschüsse fruchtbare Arbeit geleistet, die einmündet in den sogenannten Phoenix-Motor mit zwei parallelen Zylindern und Spritzdüsenvergaser, einer Entwicklung Maybachs, und den »Riemenwagen«, für lange Zeit das Rückgrat der Daimler-Produktion. In der eigentlichen Werkstatt wandert man unterdessen auf konstruktive Irrwege ab in dem Versuch, längst Abgelebtes wieder zu reanimieren: Der Ingenieur Max Schroedter, den Duttenhofer als technischen Direktor angestellt hat, setzt mit Varianten des Stahlradwagens automobile Kretins in die Welt, die über die dürftige Verbreitung von einem Dutzend in zwei Jahren nicht hinauskommen.

Kein Wunder, dass es mit den Bilanzen nicht zum besten steht. 1894 findet sich die DMG bei der Württembergischen Vereinsbank mit 385000 Mark in der Kreide und Mitte des folgenden Jahres vor dem Bankrott. Da das Heil nur aus der Ideenfabrik im Hotel Hermann kommen kann, suchen Duttenhofer und Lorenz notgedrungen die Nähe Daimlers, nicht ohne dass einflussreiche Freunde des Hauses massiven Druck ausgeübt haben. Unter ihnen findet sich der Brite Frederick Richard Simms, der hohe Lizenzzahlungen nur unter der Bedingung lockermacht, dass Daimler und Maybach in ihre alten Rechte eingesetzt werden. Man unterschreibt einen »Wiedervereinigungs-Vertrag«. Der glück- und glanzlose Schroedter verschwindet in der Versenkung, die Hotel-Filiale wird im November 1895 aufgelöst, Gottlieb Daimler mit einer Entschädigung von 200000 Mark bei Laune gehalten – vorerst.

Der Knoten scheint geplatzt: In den Jahren des Schismas 1892–1895 werden lediglich insgesamt 15 Motorwagen zusammengeschraubt, dann kommt es zu einer milden Explosion: 1896 sind es 24, 1897 26, 1898 57, 1899 108 und im Jahr der Jahrhundertwende 1900 96. Im gleichen Zeitraum

la fondation de la société mère à Bad Cannstatt : le fondateur Max Duttenhofer, chef des Vereinigte Köln-Rottweiler Pulverfabriken, et le fondateur Wilhelm Lorenz, chef de la Deutsche Metallpatronenfabrik de Karlsruhe, sont les hommes du plus puissant banquier du pays, le directeur de la Württembergische Vereinsbank, le Dr Kilian Steiner. L'infatigable banquier est en passe de regrouper sous sa tutelle une multitude de firmes. Il y a longtemps déjà qu'il a jeté un œil avide sur les acquis de Daimler et il estime trop profond le fossé entre son potentiel technique et son profit commercial. À l'aide de placements d'envergure, il commence immédiatement à saper l'influence du

92 to 344 employees. Racing cars, trucks and buses left the factory. The old premises on Bad Cannstatt's Seelberg, which operated in a state of semi-ordered chaos, were bursting at the seams, and with great foresight, therefore, Daimler purchased a 185,000 sq m (1,991,400 sq ft) plot in Untertürkheim. What had appeared to be the end of the war, however, turned out to be merely a treacherous cease-fire as Kilian Steiner and his accomplices had never given up their plan of completely annexing DMG. In the summer of 1897 the stubborn automotive pioneer faced another challenge: Lorenz and Duttenhofer set up a new company Allgemeine Motorwagen GmbH, as a cheeky competitor with licenses that had never received Daimler's blessing. In November 1898 Motorfahrzeug- and Motorenfabrik Berlin AG (MMB), whose products resembled and were passed off as Daimler motor cars, was established. These pirate copies

A girl named Mercedes

The driving force behind Wilhelm Maybach's first creation in the early part of the century was Emil Jellinek (1853–1917). He had been born in Leipzig, brought up in Vienna, and had made his money as a merchant in North Africa. Hence the pith helmet which he particularly liked to wear, even in places where tropical heat was unlikely to be experienced. He was then based in Nice where he was the imperial and royal Austro-Hungarian Consul-General, an enigmatic society figure with fingers in all the Riviera pies. The new car had to be light, fast, and beautiful, he stipulated, and he backed up his ideas accordingly with a blanket order for 36 cars with a total value of 550,000 gold marks. Daimler's "35 bhp sports and touring car" met Jellinek's specifications in every respect. Its pressed sheet-steel chassis was some 25 per cent lighter than previous designs which were made of wood and angle iron. The straight-four engine of the four-seater "Phaeton" with its rugged 5.9 liters weighed only 350 kg (772 lb) – its block was made of alloy. The honeycomb radiator, a mass of almost 9000 small tubes was positioned ahead of the front axle. An atomizing carburetor provided the necessary fuel, and the 4-speed gearbox had a gate-change gear.

On 25 March 1901 Maybach's creation, finished in snowy-white, stood on the start line for the Nice-Salon-Nice race. Symbolically it also stood on the dividing line between yesterday and tomorrow. Baron Henri de Rothschild was the owner of this young automotive hero, Wilhelm Werner the driver. And with an average speed of 51 kph (32 mph) it made all its rivals look precisely what they were – absolutely outdated. Two days later Werner covered the flying kilometer along the Promenade des Anglais to the tumultuous applause of the beautiful people at a speed of 86.1 kph (53.5 mph). "We have entered the Mercedes era," stated Paul Meyan, General-Secretary of the Automobile-Club de France. Mercedes was the name of Jellinek's 11-year-old daughter, a cute child, but otherwise of no great significance. When Papa insisted that the attractive new Daimler should be called after her, he also guaranteed her a touch of immortality. The sonorous name gained immediate acceptance.

wächst die Belegschaft von 92 auf 344 Werktätige. Rennautos, Lastwagen und Busse entstehen. Die alten Räumlichkeiten am Cannstatter Seelberg mit ihrem halb geordneten Chaos platzen aus allen Nähten, sodass Daimler in weiser Voraussicht in Untertürkheim ein 185 000 Quadratmeter großes Grundstück anschafft. Was Kriegsende zu sein schien, entpuppt sich allerdings als trügerischer Waffenstillstand: Nie haben Kilian Steiner und seine Hilfstruppen und Helfershelfer den Plan aufgegeben, die DMG gänzlich zu annektieren. Im Sommer 1897 schleudert man dem widerspenstigen Auto-Pionier einen neuen Fehdehandschuh ins Gesicht: Lorenz und Duttenhofer rufen in Berlin die keck konkurrierende Allgemeine Motorwagen GmbH ins Leben, mit Lizenzen, die von Daimler nie abgesegnet wurden. Im November 1898 gründet man die Motorfahrzeug- und Motorenfabrik Berlin AG (MMB), deren Produkte als Daimler-Motorwagen angeboten und ausgeführt werden. Diese Raubkopien sind von minderer Qualität, nicht einmal austariert von ihren aufs knappste kalkulierten Kampfpreisen.

Für den herzkranken Daimler werden die hemdsärmeligen Methoden seiner Widersacher zur vitalen Bedrohung. Im Herbst 1899, eben von einer Kur zurückgekehrt, bricht er bei einer Probefahrt mit einem neuen Modell zusammen und fällt aus dem Wagen. Ein letztes Gespräch mit Duttenhofer am 10. Januar 1900 verkraftet er nicht mehr und stirbt am 6. März des Jahres. Sogar Madame Levassor, verwitwete Sarazin, zählt zur Trauergemeinde auf dem Cannstatter Uff-Friedhof, nicht aber Duttenhofer, der dringende Dienstgeschäfte vorschützt. Das Kapital der DMG, bewusst verknappt, um Gottlieb Daimler kurzzuhalten, beträgt 900 000 Mark. Auf drei Millionen belaufen sich die Rücklagen der missliebigen, aber flott florierenden Filiale in Berlin. Mit dem Ableben Daimlers hat diese gleichwohl Stoßrichtung und Sinn verloren, wird auf Beschluss der Generalversammlung im Juni 1902 zur Zweigniederlassung degradiert und am 29. Juli vom Mutterhaus übernommen. Im Aufsichtsrat der DMG sitzen Isidor Loewe, ein Vertrauter von Lorenz und Duttenhofer, Hermann Steiner, ein Neffe des Bankiers, sowie Alfred von Kaulla für die Württembergische Vereinsbank. Die Familie Daimler ist nachhaltig entmachtet: Ihr gehören nur noch drei Prozent der Firma, die ihren guten Namen trägt.

Allerdings ticken die DMG-Uhren nicht unbedingt im Takt der Zeit: Gemessen etwa an den fortschrittlicheren Benz-Mobilen aus Mannheim wirkt ihre Palette altertümlich, angerostet von der würdigen Patina des just verstrichenen Säkulums. Zum Zeitpunkt von Daimlers Tod ist Wilhelm Maybach 54 Jahre alt und von rastlos-ungebrochenem Schaffensdrang. Innerhalb von zehn Monaten stellt er ein völlig neues Modell auf die Räder, das Nimbus und Namen der Marke prägen wird (vgl. Kasten S. 24). Der spektakuläre Riviera-Coup des ersten Mercedes zeitigt ebenso spektakuläre Erfolge, weckt einen veritablen Heißhunger auf Mercedes, vor allem die verbesserte Baureihe Simplex: 1903 werden 232, ein Jahr später 698, 1905 gar

fondateur Gottlieb Daimler et à le remettre en question même sur le plan technique.

Quant à lui, il fera sienne avant la lettre ce qui sera plus tard la devise d'Ernest Hemingway, à savoir qu'un homme peut, certes, être détruit, mais jamais anéanti. Vexé, mais résolu à tout, Daimler lui-même se retire, en 1893, pour 1800 marks de loyer annuel, dans un « centre de développement », installé dans la salle du jardin de l'hôtel Hermann à Bad Cannstatt, avec son intime, le conseiller commercial Karl Linck ainsi que Wilhelm Maybach et douze collaborateurs triés sur le volet. Là, loin des querelles et divergences de vues politiques, ils fournissent vite un travail fertile qui se traduit par le moteur Phoenix à deux cylindres parallèles et carburateur à injecteur, une invention de Maybach, et la « Riemenwagen » (voiture à courroie) qui sera longtemps l'épine dorsale de la production de Daimler. Dans l'atelier proprement dit, on commet cependant aussi des erreurs de conception avec la tentative de réanimer des solutions depuis longtemps démodées : l'ingénieur Max Schroedter, que Duttenhofer a recruté comme directeur technique, met au monde, avec des variantes de la voiture à roues d'acier, des automobiles qui ne seront heureusement pas produites à plus d'une douzaine d'exemplaires en deux ans.

Rien d'étonnant à ce que les bilans ne soient pas particulièrement brillants. En 1894, la DMG a 385 000 marks de dettes auprès de la Württembergische Vereinsbank et, à la mi-1895, la faillite est inéluctable. Comme le salut ne peut provenir que du brain-trust de l'hôtel Hermann, Duttenhofer et Lorenz recherchent bon gré mal gré la proximité de Daimler, non sans que des amis influents de la maison n'aient exercé une pression massive. Parmi eux se trouve le Britannique Frederick Richard Simms, qui n'accepte de verser des licences élevées que si Daimler et Maybach sont restaurés dans leurs anciens droits. On signe alors un « contrat de réunification ». Le malheureux Schroedter sombre dans l'anonymat, la filiale de l'hôtel est fermée en novembre 1895 et Gottlieb Daimler est maintenu avec une indemnité de 200 000 marks – dans un premier temps.

Le nœud gordien semble tranché : durant les années du schisme, de 1892 à 1895, seules 15 voitures à moteur auront été montées au total, puis il se produit un sursaut : en 1896, leur nombre passe à 24, à 26 en 1897, à 57 en 1898, à 108 en 1899 et à 96 en 1900 pour la charnière du nouveau siècle. Pendant la même période, les effectifs passent de 92 à 344 ouvriers. Ils produisent des voitures de course, des camions et des bus. Les vieux locaux du Seelberg à Bad Cannstatt, avec leur chaos à moitié ordonné, craquent de toutes les coutures, et Daimler, clairvoyant – il allait en être récompensé –, acquiert à Untertürkheim un terrain de 185 000 m². Ce qui semble être la fin de la guerre s'avère en réalité un cessez-le-feu trompeur. Jamais Kilian Steiner ainsi que ses auxiliaires et bras tutélaires n'ont abandonné l'idée d'annexer totalement la DMG. Au cours de l'été 1897, ils jettent de nouveau le gant à l'intraitable pionnier de l'automobile : Lorenz et Duttenhofer créent, à Berlin, une

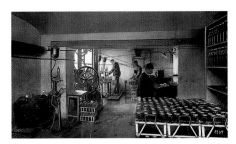

Lemonade factory at Daimler-Motoren Gesellschaft in 1913.

Limonadenfabrik der Daimler-Motoren-Gesellschaft 1913.

La fabrique de limonade de la Daimler-Motoren-Gesellschaft en 1913.

were of inferior quality, not even compensated for by the cut-throat prices.

The casual methods adopted by Daimler's adversaries became life-threatening in view of his weak heart. In the autumn of 1899, having just returned from a cure, he collapsed during a test drive in a new model and fell out of the car. He was unable to cope with a final discussion with Duttenhofer on 10 January 1900, and died on 6 March of that year. Even Madame Levassor, Sarazin's widow, was among the mourners at the Uff Cemetery in Cannstatt, though Duttenhofer, pleading urgent business, was a notable absentee. DMG's capital, which had deliberately been kept at a low level to restrict Gottlieb Daimler's ambitions, was 900,000 marks. The unpopular but flourishing branch in Berlin had reserves totaling three million. With Daimler's death this branch lost both its direction and its purpose, and the AGM in June 1902 downgraded it to a sub-branch before it was taken over by the parent company on 29 July. Isidor Loewe, a confidant of Lorenz and Duttenhofer, Hermann Steiner, a nephew of the banker, and Alfred von Kaulla representing Württembergische Vereinsbank now had seats on DMG's supervisory board. The Daimler family had lost its power for good: it now owned only three per cent of the company that bore its good name.

However, DMG was not necessarily marching in time with modern developments. Compared with the more progressive Benz cars from Mannheim, for example, its range seemed old-fashioned, lightly brushed with the patina of the century which had just passed. At the time of Daimler's death, Wilhelm Maybach was 54 years old and still filled with the creative urge. Within 10 months he had built a completely new model that was to play a decisive role in the make's image and name (see box p 22). The spectacular Riviera coup of the first Mercedes yielded equally spectacular successes and made Mercedes cars a very hot property, especially the improved Simplex range: in 1903 232 cars were manufactured, one year later 698, and in 1905 as many as 863. Compared with what had gone before, they were low, wide, powerful, and fast – the first "real" cars. Even Kaiser Wilhelm was chauffeured around in a "By Imperial Appointment" Daimler.

863 Exemplare hergestellt, vergleichsweise flach, breit, stark und schnell – schon richtige Autos. Auch Kaiser Wilhelm lässt sich in Wagen des Hoflieferanten Daimler chauffieren.

1903 gerät zur Gelenkstelle in der Vita des Unternehmens. In der Nacht zum 10. Juni geht, niemand weiß, wie es kam, die Montagehalle in Cannstatt in Flammen auf. Von 100 Autos, drei von ihnen sorgsam präpariert für das prestigeträchtige Gordon-Bennett-Rennen, bleiben nur noch verbogene und ausgeglühte Reste. Bei Daimler begreift man das Inferno als Chance, beschleunigt die Übersiedelung nach Untertürkheim, wo bereits 1904 munter weiterproduziert wird. In der neuen Heimat waltet zeitgemäße Humanität am Arbeitsplatz, mit erquicklichen Folgen für das Betriebsklima. Da sind lichte Hallen, zahlreiche elektrische Werkzeugmaschinen, die 54-Stunden-Woche, hochbezahlte Akkordleistungen. Man gönnt sich sogar den Luxus einer eigenen Limonadenfabrik mit einer Kapazität von 4000 Flaschen täglich, auf dass etwa die 3260 Mitarbeiter im Jahre 1905 vom Genuss geistiger Getränke abgehalten werden. Im Krankheitsfall wird der Daimler-Kostgänger der Leistungen einer Arbeiter-Unterstützungskasse teilhaftig. In einem riesigen Speisesaal lassen sich von zu Hause mitgebrachte Lebensmittel aufwärmen. 1906 bauen 3030 Beschäftigte bei neuneinhalb Stunden am Tag in zwei Schichten 546 Fahrzeuge, davon 437 für den Export.

Max Duttenhofer, inzwischen geadelt, ist am 14. August 1903 einem Herzschlag erlegen. Friktionen zwischen Wilhelm Lorenz und Wilhelm Maybach, ein anhaltender Klein- und Guerilla-Krieg, zermürben den Daimler-Getreuen der ersten Stunde, so dass dieser am 15. Februar 1907 den Dienst quittiert. Sein Nachfolger wird Paul Daimler, der 1908 als Konstruktionsleiter den Sieg beim Großen Preis von Frankreich an seine Fahnen und die der DMG heftet. Seine eigenen Frühwerke waren in den Neunzigern des vorigen Jahrhunderts als automobile Mauerblümchen verdorrt, intern Pauline, Paul-Daimler- oder kurz PD-Wagen geheißen. Ein Intermezzo hat ihn 1902 zur österreichischen Daimler-Dependance geführt. Seine Amtszeit lässt sich nicht sonderlich gut an: Eine internationale Flaute lastet auch lähmend auf den Bilanzen in Untertürkheim. Der alte Konkurrent Benz erstarkt. Und die Demission Maybachs hinterlässt deutliche Schrammen, selbst im Zwischenmenschlichen: Die ihm unterstellten Meister zum Beispiel sehen ihn nur höchst ungern scheiden.

Dass Daimler 1910 die Patente des Amerikaners Knight ersteht und dessen Ideengut umgehend in drei Modelle einspeist, leitet lediglich eine ebenso interessante wie kostspielige Episode in der Chronik des Hauses ein. Knights Hülsenschieber-Motoren glänzen zwar durch einen für die Zeit ganz ungewöhnlich kultivierten Lauf, neigen indessen zu Infarkten und gestatten überdies nur weitaus niedrigere Drehzahlen als vergleichbare Triebwerke mit Ventilen. Dennoch gehen die Geschäfte gut. Zwischen 1910 und 1913 wird ein Reingewinn von 8,66 Millionen Mark erwirtschaftet, 70 Prozent aller Mercedes werden exportiert. Längst ist der wohltönende Name der jungen Dame aus

société concurrente, la Allgemeine Motorwagen GmbH, avec des licences jamais approuvées par Daimler. En novembre 1898 est fondée la société Motorenfahrzeug- und Motorenfabrik Berlin AG (MMB), dont les produits sont proposés et exécutés en tant que voitures à moteur Daimler. Ces plagiats sont de moins bonne qualité, ce que ne compense même pas leur prix calculé au plus juste.

Pour Daimler, malade du cœur, les méthodes brutales de ses adversaires représentent une menace mortelle. À l'automne 1899, tout juste revenu d'une cure, il s'effondre lors de l'essai d'un nouveau modèle et tombe de la voiture. Un dernier entretien avec Duttenhofer, le 10 janvier 1900, lui porte un coup fatal et il meurt le 6 mars de cette année-là. Même Mᵐᵉ Levassor, veuve Sarazin, est présente au cimetière d'Uff de Bad Cannstatt, mais non Duttenhofer, qui prend pour prétexte d'importants rendez-vous. Le capital de la DMG, volontairement maintenu au plus juste pour museler Gottlieb Daimler, est de 900 000 marks. Les réserves de la douteuse mais florissante filiale de Berlin s'élèvent à trois millions de marks. Avec la disparition de Daimler, cette dernière a perdu sa justification et elle est dégradée au rang de succursale lors de l'assemblée générale de juin 1902 et reprise par la maison mère le 29 juillet. Au conseil de surveillance de la DMG, siègent Isidor Loewe, un homme de confiance de Lorenz et Duttenhofer, Hermann Steiner, un neveu du banquier, ainsi qu'Alfred von Kaulla, pour la Württembergische Vereinsbank. La famille Daimler est désormais définitivement réduite à l'impuissance : elle ne possède plus que 3 % de la firme qui porte son nom prestigieux.

Les horloges de la DMG ne fonctionnent toutefois pas absolument selon le rythme normal : par rapport aux Benz de Mannheim, bien plus modernes, son programme est démodé et arbore déjà la digne patine du siècle qui vient de s'achever. Au moment du décès de Daimler, Wilhelm Maybach a 54 ans et bouillonne d'énergie et d'idées. En dix mois, il réalise, en partant d'une feuille blanche, un tout nouveau modèle qui marquera l'aura et le nom de la marque (voir encadré p. 21). Le spectaculaire coup de la Riviera avec la première Mercedes se solde par des succès tout aussi spectaculaires et l'on s'arrache les Mercedes, notamment la série Simplex améliorée : en 1903, 232 exemplaires sont fabriqués, 698 un an plus tard et même 863 en 1905, voitures relativement basses, larges, puissantes et rapides – de vraies voitures, donc. L'empereur Guillaume lui aussi se fait conduire dans des voitures de Daimler, le fournisseur de la Cour.

1903 est une année charnière dans la généalogie de l'entreprise. Durant la nuit du 9 au 10 juin, nul ne sait pourquoi, le hall de montage de Bad Cannstatt s'embrase. Des 100 voitures, dont trois préparées minutieusement pour la prestigieuse course Gordon-Bennett, il ne reste plus que des vestiges tordus et calcinés. Pour Daimler, cet enfer est interprété comme une chance qui accélère le déménagement à Untertürkheim, où l'on continue de produire à un rythme soutenu dès 1904. Dans ce nouveau foyer

1903 was to be a defining moment in the company's history. No one knows how it happened, but on the night of 9 June the assembly works in Cannstatt went up in flames. Only twisted, burnt-out remains were left of 100 cars, three of which had been carefully prepared for the prestigious Gordon Bennett Trophy. At Daimler the inferno was seen as an opportunity which hastened the move to Untertürkheim, where production happily resumed as early as 1904. The new site was a haven of humane working practices, with pleasant consequences for the working environment. There were light-filled buildings, numerous electric machine tools, a 54-hour week, and high piecework rates. The company even allowed itself the luxury of its own lemonade factory with a daily capacity of 4000 bottles, in order perhaps to prevent the 3260 staff in 1905 from partaking of more potent drinks. If ill, a Daimler employee was eligible for benefits from a workers' relief fund. Food brought from home could be heated up in a huge dining hall. In 1906 3030 employees working for nine and a half hours a day in two shifts built 546 vehicles, of which 437 were for export.

Max Duttenhofer, by then ennobled, had died of a heart attack on 14 August 1903. The running guerrilla warfare between Wilhelm Lorenz and Wilhelm Maybach, who had been Daimler's faithful lieutenant from the earliest days, wore the latter down so much that he resigned on 15 February 1907. His successor was Paul Daimler, who in 1908 as chief engineer and designer celebrated victory in the French Grand Prix on his own account and that of DMG. His own early creations, known in-house as the Pauline, Paul-Daimler-Wagen or, for short, PD-Wagen, had withered away in the 1890s like so many wheeled wallflowers. An intermezzo had taken him to Daimler's Austrian subsidiary in 1902. His period of office there had a rather inauspicious beginning: international economic stagnation was also having a paralyzing effect on the balance sheet in Untertürkheim. The old enemy Benz was gaining in strength. And Maybach's departure left clear scars, even at the interpersonal level: the foremen under him, for example, were loath to see him go.

When Daimler acquired the patents of the American Knight in 1910 and immediately set about incorporating his ideas in three models, this marked the start of an episode in the history of the company that was as interesting as it was costly. Although an excellent feature of Knight's sleeve-valve engines was their very smooth running for the time, they tended to seize and furthermore could only produce far lower engine speeds than comparable power units with valves. Nonetheless, business was good. Between 1910 and 1913 net profits of 8.66 million marks were recorded, and 70 per cent of all Mercedes were exported. The melodious name of the young lady from Nice had long since become a byword for quality. The 1-2-3 for the Mercedes 18/100 in the French Grand Prix in Lyon on 4 July 1914 with Christian Lautenschlager, Louis Wagner, and Otto Salzer at the wheel was like an exclamation mark emphasizing something that everyone knew anyway.

Ein Mädchen namens Mercedes

Als treibende Kraft hinter Wilhelm Maybachs Erstgeborenem in den Anfängen des Jahrhunderts wirkt Emil Jellinek (1853–1917), gebürtig in Leipzig, erzogen in Wien, als Kaufmann zu Geld gekommen in Nordafrika. Daher rührt der Tropenhelm, den er mit Vorliebe trägt, auch wo keine Tropenhitze zu erwarten ist. Als k. u. k. österreichisch-ungarischer Generalkonsul ist er in Nizza ansässig, ein schillernder Gesellschaftslöwe und Hansdampf in allen Rivieragassen. Leicht und schnell und schön müsse er sein, der Neue, hat er sich ausbedungen und seinen Vorstellungen mit einer Blanko-Sammelbestellung über 36 Exemplare zu insgesamt 550 000 Goldmark gehörigen Nachdruck verliehen. Daimlers »Sport- und Tourenwagen 35 PS« entspricht den Vorgaben Jellineks in allen Punkten. Sein aus Stahlblech gepresster Rahmen ist gegenüber den bisherigen Gebilden aus Holz- und Winkeleisen um ein Viertel abgemagert. Der Vierzylinder-Reihenmotor des viersitzigen »Phaetons« mit seinen urigen 5,9 Litern wiegt lediglich 350 Kilogramm – sein Block ist aus Leichtmetall. Der Bienenwabenkühler, ein Dickicht aus fast 9000 Röhrchen, steht vor der Vorderachse. Ein Spritzdüsen-Vergaser spendet das Lebenselixir, das Vierganggetriebe hat eine Kulissenschaltung.

Am 25. März 1901 steht Maybachs reife Leistung in schneeigem Weiß am Start zum Rennen Nizza-Salon-Nizza und zugleich an der Scheidelinie zwischen gestern und morgen. Henri Baron de Rothschild ist der Besitzer dieses Jung-Siegfrieds in Autogestalt, Wilhelm Werner der Fahrer. Und der lässt mit einem Schnitt von 51 km/h alles andere, was da fleucht und kreucht, so aussehen, wie es wirklich ist – ganz alt. Zwei Tage später fährt Werner auf der Promenade des Anglais unter dem rauschenden Applaus der Schickeria den Kilometer mit fliegendem Start mit 86,1 km/h. »Wir sind in die Ära Mercedes eingetreten«, konstatiert Paul Meyan, Generalsekretär des Automobile-Club de France. Mercedes – so heißt Emil Jellineks elfjährige Tochter, niedlich, ansonsten aber völlig unbedeutend. Als Papa darauf besteht, der attraktive neue Daimler solle ihren Namen tragen, hat er auch sie ein bisschen unsterblich gemacht. Das volltönende Logo bürgert sich umgehend ein.

Nizza zum Inbegriff für Qualität an sich geworden. Der Dreifach-Sieg der Mercedes 18/100 am 4. Juli 1914 beim Grand Prix de France in Lyon mit Christian Lautenschlager, Louis Wagner und Otto Salzer wirkt da wie ein Ausrufezeichen unter etwas, das ohnehin schon jedermann weiß.

Den Ersten Weltkrieg überdauert man nicht nur ungeschoren, sondern – ausgelastet durch Heeresbedarf – in schier ungehemmtem Wachstum: Zwischen 1914 und 1918 entstehen 3643 Autos (1918 nur noch 108) sowie 3679 Lastwagen und Busse (1918 allein 996). Die Belegschaft allein in Untertürkheim steigt von 4717 anno 1914 auf 16 000 im Herbst 1918. Dazu kommen noch einmal 5450 Daimler-Schaffende im neuen Werk Sindelfingen, wo man 1916 für 320 000 Mark ein 500 000 Quadratmeter großes Terrain gekauft und sich auf Flugmotoren verlegt hat, sowie 3240 Beschäftigte in Berlin-Marienfelde. Dem deutschen Flugwesen werden mit dem Kriegsende die Flügel beschnitten, die Anlagen der Filiale Sindelfingen zur Karosseriefabrik

règne un humanisme moderniste dont les conditions favorisent une bonne atmosphère de travail: des halls clairs, de nombreuses machines-outils électriques, la semaine de 54 heures et des primes élevées pour le travail au rendement. On se paie même le luxe de sa propre usine à limonade avec la capacité quotidienne de 4000 bouteilles pour éviter aux 3260 collaborateurs, en 1905, de succomber à la tentation des boissons alcoolisées. En cas de maladie, le personnel bénéficie des prestations d'une caisse d'aide aux ouvriers. Dans une gigantesque salle à manger, ils peuvent réchauffer les aliments apportés de chez eux. En 1906, 3030 salariés construisent 546 voitures, dont 437 pour les exportations, à raison de neuf heures et demie de travail par jour en deux équipes.

Max Duttenhofer, entre-temps anobli, a succombé, le 14 août 1903, à un infarctus du myocarde. Des frictions entre Wilhelm Lorenz et Wilhelm Maybach épuisent ce cadre de la première heure de Daimler, si bien que ce dernier démissionne le 15 février 1907. Son successeur sera Paul Daimler, qui a inscrit à son fanion et à celui de la DMG la victoire au Grand Prix de France 1908 comme directeur de la construction. Ses œuvres personnelles précoces n'ont connu, dans les années 1890, qu'un destin automobile anonyme, surnommées, à l'usine, Pauline, voitures Paul Daimler ou, en abrégé, voitures PD. Un intermède l'a mené, en 1902, à la dépendance autrichienne de Daimler. Mais ses fonctions n'ont pas commencé sous de bons auspices: un marasme international paralyse aussi les bilans à Untertürkheim. Le vieux concurrent Benz reprend du poil de la bête. Et la démission de Maybach laisse un vide incommensurable, même dans les relations personnelles: les maîtres dont il était le supérieur hiérarchique, par exemple, sont très tristes de le voir partir.

En 1910, Daimler acquiert les brevets de l'Américain Knight et transpose immédiatement ses idées dans trois modèles, mais cela n'est qu'un épisode, aussi intéressant que coûteux, dans la chronique de la maison. Les moteurs à chemise tiroir de Knight brillent, certes, par une douceur de fonctionnement inédite à cette époque, mais ont en revanche un penchant pour les pannes et n'autorisent en outre que des régimes nettement inférieurs aux moteurs comparables à soupapes. Et pourtant, les affaires sont florissantes. De 1910 à 1913, les bénéfices nets s'élèvent à 8,66 millions de marks et 70 % de la production de Mercedes sont exportés. Il y a longtemps que le prénom mélodieux de la jeune dame de Nice (voir encadré p. 21) est devenu synonyme de qualité. Le triplé des Mercedes 18/100, le 4 juillet 1914 au Grand Prix de France, à Lyon, avec Christian Lautenschlager, Louis Wagner et Otto Salzer ne fait que souligner ce qui est déjà de notoriété publique.

Non seulement la firme survit fort bien à la Première Guerre mondiale, mais celle-ci, par suite des besoins de l'armée, lui vaut une croissance absolument inimaginable: de 1914 à 1918, elle construit 3643 voitures (contre seulement 108 en 1918) ainsi que 3679 camions et bus (pas moins

The company not only survived the First World War unscathed but – with full order books because of demand from the military – saw almost unrestrained growth. Between 1914 and 1918 3643 cars rolled out of the factory (compared with only 108 in 1918) together with 3679 trucks and buses (996 of them in 1918). The work force in Untertürkheim alone increased from 4717 in 1914 to 16,000 by the autumn of 1918. To this must be added the 5450 Daimler workers in the new Sindelfingen works where a 500,000 sq m (5,382,000 sq ft) plot had been bought for 320,000 marks in 1916 to produce aircraft engines, and 3240 employees in Berlin-Marienfelde. At the end of the war the German aviation industry had its wings clipped, and the Sindelfingen plant was converted into a coachwork factory. In the early Twenties diversification was in vogue at Daimler. It was decreed that typewriters and bicycles would also reflect the good name and image of the Stuttgart star. Not every decision proved inspired: the supercharged models favored by Paul Daimler and Ferdinand Porsche (1875–1951), his successor from 1922 onwards, part of their ongoing flirtation with the monumental, simply failed to meet the demands of a market that had been completely drained by the blood-letting of a lost war and the economic whirlpool that followed in its wake. Large cars like the 15/70/100 bhp Pullman limousine of 1924 were similar to a lovely pub sign in at least one respect: they were good publicity, but not revenue earners in their own right.

In the narrow target group, however, there was sufficient purchasing power, often of dubious origin in the aftermath of the Great War. The July 1919 issue of *Motorfahrer*, a publication by Germany's automobile club, the ADAC, complained that it often seemed "incomprehensible how many extremely large luxury cars were registered." And smart adverts in fashionable magazines showed enormous cabriolets in which mature and happy couples were almost lost against carefully selected Ticino panoramas. In other adverts, by contrast, families of five were squeezed like sardines into tiny vehicles – the social pyramid was also exemplified by the motoring hierarchy of the Roaring Twenties.

By the end, DMG was also greatly in need of a crutch. It was not just the hyphen that sealed the marriage of the two weakened companies on 28 June 1926 after a two-year engagement, but also the joint emblem formed by the fusion of the two formerly independent symbols. The Benz laurel which enclosed the new company name Mercedes-Benz now surrounded the Daimler star which represented the power of man over air, water, and land, an emblem which incidentally had only been registered as a trademark since 1911. The experts might not have taken much time to merge the company symbols, but the two independent microcosms Daimler-Motoren-Gesellschaft AG and Benz & Cie. Rheinische Automobil- and Motoren-Fabrik AG with all their egoisms, idiosyncrasies, and vanities still needed a little longer.

Daimler L 11 military single-seater from 1918.
Kampfeinsitzer Daimler L 11 von 1918.
L'avion de chasse monoplace Daimler L 11 de 1918.

umgewidmet. Anfang der Zwanziger ist bei Daimler Diversifikation angesagt. Auch Schreibmaschinen und Fahrräder sollen guter Ruf und Aureole des Stuttgarter Sterns beglänzen. Nicht immer beweist man ein geschicktes Händchen, plant gar mit Kompressormodellen, wie sie Paul Daimler und in seiner Nachfolge ab 1922 Ferdinand Porsche (1875– 1951) in ihrem Dauerflirt mit dem Monumentalen favorisieren, ungeschickt an einem Markt vorbei, der durch die Aderlässe eines verlorenen Krieges und die Strudel in seinem Kielwasser ausgeblutet ist. Karossen wie die 15/70/100 PS Pullman-Limousine von 1924 ähneln einem schönen Wirtshausschild zumindest in einem Punkt: Sie werben, bringen jedoch selbst nichts ein.

In der angepeilten schmalen Zielgruppe allerdings gibt es Kaufkraft genug, im Windschatten des Weltkriegs häufig dubiosen Ursprungs. Im Juli 1919 nörgelt denn auch das ADAC-Organ *Motorfahrer*, es erscheine »oft unverständlich, wie viele besonders große Luxuswagen dem Verkehr freigegeben sind«. Und schmucke Inserate in fashionablen Zeitschriften zeigen vor ausgewählten Tessiner Panoramen enorme Cabriolets, in denen sich reife und glückliche Paare schier verlieren. Auf anderen Anzeigen hingegen klemmen fünfköpfige Familien in winzigen Vehikeln wie Ölsardinen – auch in der Auto-Hierarchie der Roaring Twenties bildet sich die soziale Pyramide ab.

Am Ende ist auch die DMG stark anlehnungsbedürftig. Nicht nur der Bindestrich besiegelt nach zweijähriger Verlobungszeit die Hochzeit der geschwächten Elefanten am 28. Juni 1926, sondern auch das gemeinsame Emblem, zu dem die einst eigenständigen Markenzeichen verschmelzen: Der Daimler-Lorbeer, in den der neue Firmenname Mercedes-Benz eingelassen ist, umkränzt nun den Benz-Stern, der für die Macht des Menschen über Luft, Wasser und Erde steht, Warenzeichen übrigens erst seit 1911. Womit die Heraldiker rasch bei der Hand sind, dazu benötigen allerdings die beiden Mikrokosmen Daimler-Motoren-Gesellschaft AG und Benz & Cie. Rheinische Automobil- und Motoren-Fabrik AG mit all ihren Egotrips, Eigenheiten und Eitelkeiten noch ein bisschen länger.

de 996 rien qu'en 1918). Le seul personnel d'Untertürkheim passe de 4717 en 1914 à 16000 à l'automne 1918. À cela s'ajoutent 5 450 salariés de Daimler dans la nouvelle usine de Sindelfingen, où l'on a acheté, en 1916, un terrain de 500 000 m² pour 320 000 marks et où l'on s'est spécialisé dans les moteurs d'avion, ainsi que 3240 employés à Berlin-Marienfelde. Avec la fin de la guerre, l'aviation allemande se voit les ailes coupées et les équipements de la filiale de Sindelfingen sont transformés en une usine de carrosserie. Au début des années 1920, la diversification figure à l'ordre du jour chez Daimler. Des machines à écrire et des bicyclettes peuvent aussi fort bien faire briller l'étoile de Stuttgart. On n'a pas toujours fait preuve de clairvoyance dans le choix des priorités et l'on projette même des modèles à compresseur comme ceux de Paul Daimler que favorise, à partir de 1922, son successeur Ferdinand Porsche (1875–1951) dans son flirt permanent avec le monumental, en ignorant un marché exsangue par suite du tribut prélevé par la guerre perdue et de ses séquelles. Des limousines comme la 15/70/100 ch Pullman de 1924 ressemblent à une belle enseigne de restaurant, au moins sur un point : elles font de la publicité, mais ne rapportent elles-mêmes absolument rien !

La maigre clientèle visée bénéficie d'un pouvoir d'achat suffisant, d'origine souvent douteuse dans le sillage de la guerre mondiale. En juillet 1919, l'organe de l'ADAC lui-même, *Motorfahrer*, critique, ne cache pas son étonnement : « […] il est incompréhensible de voir le nombre de voitures de luxe particulièrement grandes à circuler sur nos routes ». Et de décoratifs placards publicitaires dans des journaux à la mode présentent, devant des panoramas tessinois spectaculaires, d'énormes cabriolets dans lesquels se fondent littéralement des couples mûrs et heureux. Sur d'autres annonces, par contre, des familles avec trois enfants s'entassent, telles des sardines, dans de minuscules véhicules – dans la hiérarchie automobile des *Roaring Twenties*, se constitue aussi une pyramide sociale.

À la fin, la DMG elle-même a besoin d'un solide partenaire. Le trait d'union n'est pas le seul à sceller, après deux ans de fiançailles, le mariage des deux éléphants affaiblis, le 28 juin 1926, qui associe aussi en un emblème commun les deux logos jadis autonomes : les lauriers de Daimler dans lesquels est inscrit le nouveau nom de la firme, Mercedes-Benz, cernent désormais l'étoile Benz qui est synonyme de la puissance de l'homme, dans les airs, sur l'eau et sur terre, marque de fabrique depuis 1911 seulement. Si cela ne demande pas beaucoup de temps aux spécialistes de l'héraldique, il en faut par contre beaucoup plus pour les deux microcosmes Daimler-Motoren-Gesellschaft AG et Benz & Cie. Rheinische Automobil- und Motoren-Fabrik AG, avec toute leur fierté, tous leurs particularismes et toutes leurs susceptibilités.

All for one

A period of adjustment 1926–1933

There can be no doubt: the lifelong bond into which former competitors Daimler and Benz had entered was certainly not forged in the smoldering heat of passion – it was a marriage of convenience, not an eternal love match. And so the universal truth of two axioms was demonstrated. The first, blithely ignored in popular literature and light comedies, is that things don't really begin until after the happy ending. The second, maliciously exploited by despots for their own dubious ends, is that pressure from without accelerates consolidation within. Wilhelm Kissel (1885–1942), the architect of integration, a charismatic, brusque man, who would have made the ultimate sacrifice for the Mercedes-Benz cause, steered the twin-headed company defiantly out into the heavy seas in which businesses were bobbing, tossing, and lurching in the second half of the Twenties.

Daimler-Benz AG owed the bank 28 million marks at the end of 1926. Of 86 German car factories operating in 1924, by 1927 a staggering 67 had disappeared. The magic word was rationalization, and Kissel, sympathetically supported by his right-hand man Wilhelm Haspel, applied the principle again and again. The regiment of 18,124 employees at the company in 1927 had shrunk to a troop of 8850 by 1932. Car production had long since been concentrated in Untertürkheim, truck production in Gaggenau, and coach-building in Sindelfingen. Just one year after the merger the factory in Berlin-Marienfelde had been reduced to a mere repair workshop and parts store. At the same time, after an incubation period of more than a decade since Henry Ford's first production lines had sprung into action, the company adopted "American production practices" which DMG itself had wholeheartedly endorsed shortly before the merger. The adjustment from the variety of tasks that had characterized old-fashioned craftsmanship to the monotony of the assembly lines "at Daimler" (or, for card-carrying Baden people, "at Benz") took time and was only completed in 1936, even though, for example, savings of 600 marks had quickly been calculated for a 2-liter model. An important step in this direction, which also symbolized the change from traditional construction methods using wood to the use of steel, was taken in 1928 with the installation of knuckle-joint drawing presses in Sindelfingen. Until then the customer had tended to have a bespoke body mounted on his Untertürkheim chassis by a coachbuilder of his own choice. The sales and service network was spruced up: 31 wholly-owned sales outlets and repair workshops with 2100 staff were complemented by 14 independent major representatives and 183 dealers and agents in 1928. The lines of command were clearly defined, and the squad of core troops operating away from the parent company was deliberately kept on a short leash. The range was also slimmed down, at

Vereint schlagen

Gewöhnungs-Phase 1926–1933

Kein Zweifel: Der Bund fürs Leben, zu dem sich die einstigen Kontrahenten Daimler und Benz gefunden haben, wurde keineswegs in lodernder Leidenschaft geschmiedet – er ist Zweckehe und kein immerwährendes Liebeslager. Und so lässt sich an ihm die universelle Anwendbarkeit zweier Binsenweisheiten festmachen. Die eine, von der Trivialliteratur und der Boulevardkomödie gerne ignoriert: dass es nach dem Happy-end erst so richtig losgeht. Die andere, von Despoten tückisch für ihre fragwürdigen Zwecke missbraucht: dass Druck von außen die innere Konsolidierung beschleunigt. Unter dem Architekten der Integration Wilhelm Kissel (1885–1942), einem Mann mit Ausstrahlung, schroff, loyal gegenüber der Sache Mercedes-Benz bis hin zur Selbstaufgabe, steuert das Doppel-Unternehmen trotzig in die rauhe See, in der die Wirtschaft in der zweiten Hälfte der zwanziger Jahre dümpelt, stampft und schlingert.

Die Bankverbindlichkeiten der Daimler-Benz AG belaufen sich Ende 1926 auf 28 Millionen Mark. Von 86 deutschen Autofabriken 1924 sind 1927 stramme 67 auf der Strecke geblieben. Das Zauberwort heißt Rationalisierung, und Kissel, kongenial unterstützt durch seine rechte Hand Wilhelm Haspel, spricht es wieder und wieder aus. Die Phalanx von 18124 Beschäftigten der Firma im Jahre 1927 schrumpft bis 1932 zum Fähnlein von 8850. Da sind längst die PKW-Produktion in Untertürkheim, die LKW-Fertigung in Gaggenau, der Karosseriebau in Sindelfingen konzentriert. Das Werk Berlin-Marienfelde verkümmert bereits im Jahr eins nach der Fusion zum Reparaturbetrieb und Ersatzteillager. Zugleich macht man sich am Ende einer Inkubationszeit von über einem Jahrzehnt nach Henry Fords ersten Fließbändern »amerikanische Fertigungsmethoden« zu eigen, was bereits die DMG kurz vor der Vereinigung vollmundig für sich in Anspruch nahm. Die Umstellung von der Mannigfaltigkeit urtümlichen Handwerks zur Monotonie der Montagelinien gerät »beim Daimler« (für bekennende Badenser »beim Benz«) schleppend und ist erst 1936 abgeschlossen, obwohl man etwa bei einem Zweiliter der Marke frühzeitig eine Ersparnis von 600 Mark errechnet. Ein wichtiger Schritt in dieser Richtung, sinnbildlich zugleich für den Wandel von der traditionellen Holz- zur Stahlbauweise, geschieht 1928 mit dem Aufstellen von Kniehebel-Ziehpressen in Sindelfingen. Bis dato ließ der Kunde sein Chassis aus Untertürkheim gerne von einem Karosserie-Schneider eigener Wahl bekleiden. Neu gespannt wird das Netz von Absatz und Service: 31 eigenen Verkaufsstellen und Reparaturwerkstätten mit 2100 Arbeitsplätzen steht 1928 ein Aufgebot von 14 eigenständigen Großvertretern und 183 Händlern und Vermittlern gegenüber. Die Kommandowege sind klar definiert, eine Kader- und Kerntruppe außerhalb der Zentrale wird ganz

Se battre en commun

La phase d'accoutumance 1926–1933

Il n'y a pas de doute : le mariage pour la vie qu'ont conclu les deux anciens adversaires Daimler et Benz n'a absolument pas été forgé dans une passion enflammée – c'est un mariage de raison qui n'a rien d'un amour éternel. Et c'est ainsi que l'on peut constater avec lui l'applicabilité universelle de deux règles d'airain. L'une, que la littérature triviale et les comédies de boulevard ignorent volontiers, est que c'est après le happy end que tout commence véritablement. L'autre, dont abusent ignoblement des despotes pour leurs visées contestables, est que la pression exercée de l'extérieur accélère la consolidation intérieure. Parmi les architectes de l'intégration figure Wilhelm Kissel (1885–1942), un homme charismatique, brusque, mais loyal envers la cause Mercedes-Benz jusqu'à l'abnégation, qui pilote courageusement la double entreprise dans la mer agitée au milieu de laquelle l'économie de la seconde moitié des années 1920 tangue, roule et menace de couler.

Fin 1926, les dettes de la Daimler-Benz AG envers les banques s'élèvent à 28 millions de marks. Des 86 usines automobiles allemandes de 1924, pas moins 67 ont disparu en 1927. Le mot

magique est rationalisation et Kissel, avec l'appui génial de son bras droit Wilhelm Haspel, ne cesse de recourir à cette méthode. La phalange des 18 124 salariés de la firme en 1927 s'est réduite jusqu'en 1932 pour devenir une petite légion de 8850 hommes. Il y a longtemps que la production de voitures de tourisme est concentrée à Untertürkheim, celle de camions à Gaggenau et la construction de carrosseries à Sindelfingen. Un an après la fusion, déjà, l'usine de Berlin-Marienfelde est dégradée au rang d'entreprise de réparations et de magasin de pièces détachées. En outre, à l'issue d'une période d'incubation de plus de dix ans, on reprend les « méthodes de fabrication américaines » avec les premières chaînes de montage à la Henri Ford, ce que la DMG avait déjà revendiqué ambitieusement pour elle-même avant la fusion des deux firmes. « Chez Daimler » (ou « chez Benz » pour les Badois professants), le passage de la diversité de l'artisanat original à la monotonie des chaînes de montage s'effectue de façon hésitante et n'est achevé qu'en 1936 bien que l'on ait, par exemple, pour une deux litres de la marque, calculé très tôt une économie de 600 marks. Une étape importante à ce point de vue, symbole également d'une mutation, est le passage de la construction traditionnelle en bois à la construction en acier, réalisée, en 1928, avec la mise en place de presses à emboutir à genouillères à Sindelfingen. Jusque-là, le client faisait volontiers habiller son châssis d'Untertürkheim par un carrossier de son propre choix. Le réseau de distribution et d'entretien est réorganisé : 31 succursales de vente et ateliers de réparations avec 2100 emplois font pièce, en

the expense of the Benz dowry which completely disappeared. Professor Ferdinand Porsche in the meantime was anything but a compliant accomplice to the management. He was brilliant, grumpy, and not one to look after the pennies. Rather, his penchant was for the six-cylinder models of 2 (later 2.6) and 3 (later 3.3 and 3.5) liters. The smaller models, built in Stuttgart, were launched with premature haste and were unreliable, a fact which caused the factory a lot of problems and costs. In creating the larger ones, manufactured in Mannheim and launched at the Berlin Motor Show in October 1926, Porsche had given birth to a race of hulking, lumbering giants. The Sudetenland German Porsche's retaliation against the Horch 8 of his predecessor Paul Daimler was the eight-cylinder type Nürburg 460 which was finally launched at the Paris Salon in the autumn of 1928. It was so named because a test car had been subjected to a two-week baptism of fire for 20,000 km (12,400 miles) around the "green hell" of the Nürburgring, a track which had opened in 1927.

The supercharged cars were kept in the range for prestige reasons. Porsche was fascinated by supercharging, but recognized at the same time that it was only practicable for racing cars and large-engined road cars. In 1928 he left Daimler-Benz in high dudgeon, as angry as the planning chief Paul Daimler had been and for very similar reasons. In addition, Kissel had accused his "38" model of not starting in the cold and of therefore being useless. His legacy included the supercharged 400 and 630 K as well as the celebrated s, ss, ssk and sskl ("Super Sport Kurz Leicht" – Super Sport Short Light) range, all symbols and embodiments of what a car should be and the ultimate advert for the make, despite there being only 290 of them to go round.

This was just what the ideology doctor ordered. In view of the unequal trade balance between imports and exports – in 1927 Germany imported 11,400 cars and exported only 2700, hindered by the USA, for example, with its hefty protectionist import duties – the company used the glamor of the star badge to symbolize the quality of the product, even if it was somewhat more expensive to drive a Mercedes. The banking and automotive sectors of the economy were, of course, closely interwoven. Scarcely anyone bought a car without taking out a loan. Manufacturers courted customers' favor with discounts and generous part-exchange deals. And with price reductions: in 1929 the cheapest Opel was yours for only 2100 marks; the open-top BMW Dixi cost 2200 marks; the Fiat 509 Roadster was listed at 3780 marks. A limousine in the lower mid-range built by Adler or Brennabor cost around 5000 marks. For the same money, however, you could get a Chevrolet or Opel with six cylinders, whereas a buyer had to place 7000 marks on the table to drive away an Adler Standard 6 or a Mercedes Stuttgart 200. The cheapest eight-cylinder limousines were the Röhr 2.3 for 8400 marks and the Stoewer S10 for 8950 marks. A Horch cost 13,250 marks, and the Mercedes Nürburg 460 went for 14,500 marks, while the 710 ss left no change from a handsome 35,000 marks. Lovers of Ameri-

bewusst an der kurzen Leine gehalten. Auch das Sortiment wird verschlankt, zu Lasten der Benz-Mitgift, die vollständig in der Versenkung verschwindet. Professor Ferdinand Porsche indessen ist dem Management alles andere als ein willfähriger Helfershelfer, genial, grantig-cholerisch, aber keiner, der die Mark noch einmal umdreht, bevor er sie ausgibt. Eher Pflicht- und Fingerübungen sind für ihn die Sechszylinder von zwei (später 2,6) und drei (später 3,3 und 3,5) Litern. Die kleineren Modelle, in Stuttgart gebaut, kommen überhastet auf den Markt und sind von delikater Konstitution, was das Werk Ärger und Geld kostet. Mit den größeren, auf der Berliner Automobil-Ausstellung im Oktober 1926 vorgestellt und in Mannheim gefertigt, hat Porsche ein Geschlecht von ungeschlachten und schwerfälligen Riesen in die Welt gesetzt. Zum Gegenschlag gegen den Horch 8 seines Vorgängers Paul Daimler holt der querköpfige Sudetendeutsche schließlich auf dem Pariser Salon im Herbst 1928 mit dem Achtzylinder Typ Nürburg 460 aus. Der heißt so, weil ein Versuchswagen in der ein Jahr zuvor eröffneten »grünen Hölle« des Rings einer zweiwöchigen Feuertaufe über 20 000 km unterzogen wurde.

Aus Prestigegründen in der Palette belassen werden die Kompressorwagen. Porsche ist von der Druck-Sache fasziniert, erkennt aber zugleich, sie tauge nur für Rennwagen und großkalibrige Straßenautos. 1928 verlässt er Daimler-Benz, wütend wie einst der Baurat Paul Daimler und aus ganz ähnlichen Gründen. Überdies hat ihn Kissel bezichtigt, sein »38er« springe bei Kälte nicht an und sei daher eine Niete. Als sein Vermächtnis bleiben unter anderem die aufgeladenen Modelle 400 und 630 K sowie die gefeierte Typenreihe s, ss, ssk und sskl (für Super Sport Kurz Leicht), allesamt Sinn- und Standbilder des Automobils und trotz ihrer dünnen Verbreitung von 290 Exemplaren dem höheren Ruhm der Marke bestens dienlich.

Das passt ideologisch genau ins Konzept: Angesichts einer schrägen Balance von Import und Export – 1927 werden 11 400 Autos nach Deutschland ein- und nur 2700 ausgeführt, von den USA zum Beispiel mit deftigen Schutzzöllen behindert – baut man auf die Strahlkraft des Sterns als Brandzeichen des besseren Produkts, auch wenn es etwas teurer ist, einen Mercedes zu fahren. Dabei sind das Bankgeschäft und das Autogeschäft eng miteinander verwoben. Kaum jemand gönnt sich einen Kraftwagen, ohne einen Kredit aufzunehmen. Die Hersteller buhlen um die Gunst der Kundschaft mit Rabatten und der generösen Inzahlungnahme von Gebrauchten. Und mit sinkenden Preisen: 1929 ist der billigste Opel schon für 2100 Mark zu haben. Der offene BMW Dixi kostet 2200 Mark, und der Fiat 509 Roadster steht mit 3780 Mark in der Liste. Eine Limousine der unteren Mittelklasse von Adler oder Brennabor kostet rund 5000 Mark. Für das gleiche Geld bekommt man aber schon einen Chevrolet oder Opel mit sechs Zylindern, während ein Adler Standard 6 oder ein Mercedes Stuttgart 200 für knapp 7000 Mark seiner Käufer harrt. Die billigsten Achtzylinder-Limousinen sind der Röhr 2,3 für 8400

1928, à un réseau de 14 concessionnaires indépendants et à 183 représentants ou agents. Les voies hiérarchiques sont clairement définies et une troupe de cadres en dehors de la centrale est sciemment dirigée selon des principes très stricts. De plus, le programme est élagué au détriment de la dot de Benz, qui disparaît complètement dans l'oubli. Pour la direction, par contre, le professeur Ferdinand Porsche est tout sauf un employé obéissant ; génial, rustre et colérique, ce n'est cependant pas un homme qui retourne encore une fois le mark avant de le dépenser. Pour lui, les six-cylindres de 2 litres (plus tard, 2,6 litres) et 3 litres (plus tard, 3,3 litres et 3,5 litres) sont plutôt des exercices de style. Les modèles de plus petites dimensions construits à Stuttgart arrivent trop tôt sur le marché et sont d'une faible constitution, ce qui coûte à l'usine bien des problèmes et beaucoup d'argent. Avec les plus grosses voitures, présentées à l'Exposition automobile de Berlin en octobre 1926 et fabriquées à Mannheim, Porsche a engendré une race de pachydermes aux lignes frustes. Le têtu Allemand des Sudètes prépare enfin une réplique à la Horch 8 de son prédécesseur Paul Daimler pour le Salon de Paris, à l'automne 1928, avec la Nürburg 460 à moteur huit cylindres. Qu'elle porte ce nom est dû à ce qu'une voiture expérimentale ait, un an plus tôt, inauguré « l'Enfer vert » du Nürburgring avec un baptême du feu de deux semaines durant lesquelles elle a couvert plus de 20 000 kilomètres.

Pour des raisons de prestige, les voitures à compresseur continuent de figurer au catalogue. Porsche est fasciné par le compresseur, mais reconnaît simultanément qu'il n'est intéressant que pour les voitures de course ou les routières de gros calibre. En 1928, il quitte Daimler-Benz, aussi furieux que, jadis, Paul Daimler et pour des raisons similaires. En outre, Kissel lui a reproché sa « 38 » ne démarrait pas par temps froid et qu'elle ne valait rien. Il laisse notamment en héritage les modèles turbocompressés 400 et 630K comme la fameuse série s, ss, ssk et sskl (pour « Super Sport Kurz Leicht » – Super Sport Courte Légère), modèles d'exception dans l'histoire de l'automobile et qui, malgré leur faible diffusion de 290 exemplaires, ont joué le rôle d'ambassadeurs pour accroître la célébrité de la marque.

Sur le plan idéologique, l'esprit de la firme s'en trouve conforté : compte tenu du déséquilibre entre les importations et les exportations – 11 400 voitures sont importées en Allemagne en 1927, mais seulement 2700 exportées, résultat entre autres d'une politique protectionniste des États-Unis, qui imposent des droits de douane élevés – on mise sur le prestige de l'étoile comme symbole emblématique du meilleur produit, même s'il coûte un peu plus cher de conduire une Mercedes. Ce faisant, opérations bancaires et opérations automobiles sont étroitement liées les unes aux autres. Presque personne ne peut s'acheter une voiture sans obtenir un crédit. Les constructeurs briguent les faveurs des clients avec des ristournes et la reprise généreuse de leurs voitures d'occasion. Et avec des prix revus à la baisse :

1909

can luxury limousines, who were not troubled by prohibitive rates of duty, could choose between the Cadillac at 22,600 marks and the Lincoln at 27,825 marks, both in the Pullman finish. A very few could acquire the new Rolls-Royce Phantom II at 46,000 marks – though that figure only covered the chassis.

No price category of car, however, saw a real boom in sales. The world economic crisis – the stock exchanges collapsed on 25 October 1929 – was paralyzing business. Of the 27.3 million people of working age in the German Reich three million were unemployed in 1930, and a further 1.8 million were on short-time work. 50,000 new cars were stockpiled, including 25 per cent of the 7820 Mercedes produced. 35,000 of the 90,000 workers employed in the automotive sector had been made redundant since 1927.

At the beginning of 1930 there were only 650,000 cars registered in Germany – one for every 97 inhabitants. In Sweden, on the other hand, the figure was one for every 45, in France and the UK one for every 32. And in the USA every fifth person owned a car. Amidst the general misery, Mercedes-Benz went relatively unscathed. In 1927, for example, when only three per cent of German cars were exported, Mercedes was responsible for 10 per cent of them and achieved sales of 130 million marks in 1928 (and repeated this in 1929). The diesel truck was ready for mass production in the same year though it promptly found itself faced with declining demand, since hardly anyone wanted to invest in commercial vehicles. 1930 saw the market for trucks halved, while production in Gaggenau, on the other hand, fell by only 41 per cent. By now every tenth car in Germany was a Mercedes.

The deaths of two car pioneers hit the headlines in 1929. Karl Benz died in April, and Wilhelm Maybach in December. Their passing marked the end of an era. New people advanced into positions of responsibility and into the ranks of the better-paid, such as Hans Nibel, an old Benz campaigner where he had become the head of design as early as 1911. He filled the vacancy left by Ferdinand Porsche, with Fritz Nallinger, the son of the supervisory board member Dr. Friedrich Nallinger, coming in his wake. Nibel, for example, developed the SSK into the SSKL with which Rudolf Caracciola won the Mille Miglia in 1931.

In October 1931 Nibel's new creation, the 170, was premièred at the Paris Salon. It was positioned at the lower end of the product range and, in terms of its revolutionary impact, was comparable with the 180 which was launched in 1953. The former saw the introduction of independent suspension, and the latter the monocoque design. Hitherto all Mercedes and their illustrious forebears under the Daimler and Benz names had taken to the road in ponderous majesty on rigid axles. The independently suspended wheel was not just a remarkable example of automotive innovation, it was also an absolute necessity, even at this stage, as the road network was almost as wretched as it was in the historic Germany of the minor princes. Those who left the partially leveled roadways of the towns found that

und der Stoewer S10 für 8950 Mark. Ein Horch kostet 13 250 Mark, und der Mercedes Nürburg 460 schlägt mit 14 500 Mark zu Buche, während der 710 SS gar nach der stattlichen Investition von 35 000 Mark verlangt. Liebhaber amerikanischer Luxus-Limousinen, denen sich kaum abwehrende Zölle in den Weg stellen, können zwischen dem Cadillac für 22 600 und dem Lincoln für 27 825 Mark wählen, beide in der Pullman-Variante. Für 46 000 Mark vermögen einige wenige den neuen Rolls-Royce Phantom II zu erstehen – allerdings nur das Fahrgestell.

Rechte Kauflust mag sich indessen in keiner Preisklasse einstellen. Die Weltwirtschaftskrise – am 25. Oktober 1929 kollabieren die Börsen – lähmt das Geschäft. Von 27,3 Millionen Erwerbstätigen im Deutschen Reich sind 1930 drei Millionen arbeitslos, weitere 1,8 Millionen müssen kurzarbeiten. 50 000 Neuwagen stehen auf Halde, unter ihnen 25 Prozent der 7820 produzierten Mercedes. Seit 1927 fielen 35 000 von 90 000 Auto-Werkern dem Rotstift zum Opfer.

Anfang 1930 sind in Deutschland erst 650 000 Automobile zugelassen – auf eines kommen 97 Einwohner. In Schweden sind es dagegen 45, in Frankreich und Großbritannien 32. Und in den USA hat bereits jeder fünfte ein Auto. Mercedes-Benz lässt inmitten der allgemeinen Misere relativ wenig Federn: 1927 zum Beispiel, als nur drei Prozent der deutschen Autos exportiert werden, bringt man es auf zehn Prozent davon und weist 1928 (wie auch 1929) einen Umsatz von 130 Millionen Mark aus. Im gleichen Jahr ist der Diesel-LKW serienreif, nagelt allerdings flugs in eine abebbende Nachfrage hinein, da kaum jemand in Nutzfahrzeuge investieren will. 1930 hat sich der Markt für Lastkraftwagen um die Hälfte verkleinert, die Produktion in Gaggenau dagegen nur um 41 Prozent. Jeder zehnte Wagen im Reich ist indessen ein Mercedes.

1929 macht der Tod zweier Auto-Pioniere Schlagzeilen. Karl Benz stirbt im April, Wilhelm Maybach im Dezember, mit ihnen eine Ära. Neue Leute drängen in die Verantwortung und auf die Gehaltslisten der Besserverdienenden, Hans Nibel zum Beispiel, ein alter Benz-Kämpe und dort 1911 schon Leiter des Konstruktionsbüros. Er füllt die Vakanz, die Ferdinand Porsche hinterlassen hat, in seinem Kielwasser Fritz Nallinger, der Sohn des Aufsichtsratsmitglieds Dr. Friedrich Nallinger. Nibel sublimiert beispielsweise den SSK zum SSKL, mit dem Rudolf Caracciola 1931 die Mille Miglia gewinnt.

Im Oktober des gleichen Jahres hat auf dem Pariser Salon die Nibel-Neuschöpfung Typ 170 Premiere, am unteren Rand der Produkt-Palette angesiedelt und an revolutionärem Impetus dem Typ 180 von 1953 vergleichbar: Jener inauguriert die Pontonkarosserie, dieser die Schwingachse. Bislang kamen alle Mercedes und ihre illustren Vorfahren namens Daimler und Benz in schwerfälliger Majestät auf Starrachsen dahergerollt. Das unabhängig aufgehängte Rad – nicht nur ein Vorzeige-Artikel automobiler Innovation, sondern auch bitter nötig, immer noch: Das Straßennetz ist fast so jämmerlich wie im Deutschland der Duodezfürsten.

1916

en 1929, l'Opel la moins chère est déjà disponible pour 2100 marks. La BMW Dixi décapotable coûte 2200 marks et la Fiat 509 Roadster figure au catalogue au prix de 3780 marks. Une berline du segment intermédiaire inférieur comme l'Adler où la Brennabor coûte environ 5000 marks. Mais, pour la même somme, on peut déjà obtenir une Chevrolet ou une Opel à six cylindres alors qu'une Adler Standard 6 ou une Mercedes Stuttgart 200 exigent de leur acheteur près de 7000 marks. Les berlines à huit cylindres les moins coûteuses sont la Röhr 2,3 pour 8400 marks, et la Stoewer S10 pour 8950 marks. Une Horch coûte 13 250 marks et la Mercedes Nürburg 460 est facturée 14 500 marks, alors que la 710 SS demande un investissement, considérable, de 35 000 marks. Les amateurs des luxueuses limousines américaines, pour lesquelles sont prélevées des droits de douane quasi astronomiques, peuvent choisir entre la Cadillac à 22 600 marks et la Lincoln à 27 825 marks, toutes les deux en exécution Pullman. Pour 46 000 marks, quelques rares heureux pourront acquérir la nouvelle Rolls-Royce Phantom II – et encore seulement le châssis!

Aucune catégorie de prix ne peut cependant se targuer de drainer les acheteurs. La crise économique mondiale – le 25 octobre 1929, les Bourses se sont effondrées – paralyse les affaires. Sur les 27,3 millions d'actifs dans le Reich allemand, 3 millions de personnes sont sans emploi en 1930 et 1,8 million au chômage partiel. Près de 50 000 voitures neuves sont en stock, dont 25 % des 7820 Mercedes produites. Depuis 1927, 35 000 des 90 000 ouvriers de l'industrie automobile ont perdu leur emploi.

Début 1930, 650 000 voitures seulement sont immatriculées en Allemagne – une pour 97 habitants. En Suède, à titre comparatif, ce taux est de 45 ou de 32 en France et en Grande-Bretagne. Aux États-Unis, un habitant sur cinq a déjà une voiture. Au cœur de cette misère générale, Mercedes-Benz perd relativement peu de plumes : en 1927, par exemple, alors que 3 % seulement des voitures allemandes sont exportées, elle en exporte 10 % et réalise en 1928 (comme aussi en 1929) un chiffre d'affaires de 130 millions de marks. La même année, le camion à moteur Diesel est mûr pour la série, mais ses claquements le desservent ; de plus, la demande est en baisse car presque personne ne veut investir dans des véhicules utilitaires. En 1930, le marché des camions a diminué de moitié, mais la production à Gaggenau de 41 %. Une voiture sur dix dans le Reich est, par contre, une Mercedes.

En 1929, le décès de deux pionniers de l'automobile défraie la chronique. Karl Benz meurt en avril et Wilhelm Maybach, en décembre. Avec eux, c'est une ère qui se termine. Des personnalités, anciennes et nouvelles, sont impatientes d'occuper des postes de responsabilité – et de profiter des avantages afférents – arrivent sur le devant de la scène : Hans Nibel, un vieux fidèle de Benz où il était déjà, en 1911, directeur du bureau d'études. Il comble la place laissée vacante par Ferdinand Porsche avec, dans son sillage, Fritz Nallinger, le fils du membre du conseil de

Joint advertising by Daimler and Benz.
Gemeinsame Werbung von Daimler und Benz.
Publicité commune de Daimler et Benz.

they had mistakenly wandered back to the Middle Ages on a tangle of narrow and severely cambered highways with crushed stone or cobbled surfaces, covered if you were lucky with a cracked and crumbling coating of macadam. Honorable local councilors seldom looked beyond the boundaries of their little world. The Avus (its name is a German acronym indicating a road and car test track) was a notable exception among this botched patchwork. This was a crossroads-free stretch of highway that was begun in 1912 along the Berlin-Wannsee railway line with private funding and then, having degenerated into a ruin during the war, was completed in 1921 by the industrialist Hugo Stinnes. The 170 was no people's car, though at a purchase price in 1931 of 4400 marks for the four-door model (with room for the luggage outside) it was nevertheless an attractive proposition to the less well off among the make's friends. Up to 1936 13,775 customers had taken advantage of it.

In the depression years of 1931 and 1932 motoring had become an expensive luxury. "German purchasing power has been laid low," ADAC-Motorwelt bitterly declared and it also knew who was to blame: the "excessive taxation and muddled administration of motoring." Vehicle tax, benzene tax, fuel tax, supplementary tax – an endless spiral of taxes was squeezing motorists completely dry. The total taxes levied per year per car were 798 reichsmarks, compared with 376 in France and a mere 128 in the USA. In the land of poets and philosophers the state issued emergency decrees and intervened in a partisan way in the competition between road and rail traffic in favor of the railway, the Reichsbahn.

Crisis manager Kissel had, however, planned cleverly and had fitted the company's trucks and buses almost exclusively with diesel engines. He was a tactician and strategist

Wer die halbwegs geebneten Rollbahnen der Ballungszentren verlässt, findet sich unversehens im Mittelalter wieder, auf einem Gewürm von schmalen und stark gewölbten Chausseen mit Schotter- und Kopfsteinbelag, bestenfalls von brüchigem und bröckelndem Makadam oder Teerbeton überzogen. Selten sehen die Gemeindeväter über den kommunalen Tellerrand hinaus. Eine rühmliche Ausnahme inmitten von Patchwork und Flickschusterei bildet die Avus (für Automobil-, Verkehrs- und Übungsstraße), ein kreuzungsfreier Autobahnstummel, der 1912 entlang der Eisenbahnstrecke Berlin-Wannsee mit privaten Mitteln begonnen und, während des Krieges zur Bauruine verödet, 1921 von dem Industriellen Hugo Stinnes vollendet wird. Ein Volks-Wagen ist der 170 nicht, gegen einen Kaufpreis von 4400 Mark für den Viertürer (Koffer freistehend) 1931 gleichwohl ein freundliches Angebot an die minder Bemittelten unter den Freunden der Marke. Bis 1936 wissen das 13775 Kunden zu würdigen.

In den Jahren der Dürre 1931 und 1932 ist Autofahren zum teuren Spaß geworden: »Die deutsche Kraftfahrt liegt darnieder«, konstatiert die ADAC-Motorwelt bitter und weiß auch, wer schuld ist: die »steuerliche Überlastung und umständliche Verwaltung des Kraftfahrwesens«. Kfz-Steuer, Benzolzoll, Betriebsstoffsteuer, Zusatzsteuer – eine Steuerschraube ohne Ende quetscht den Autofahrer nach allen Regeln der Kunst aus. Auf 798 Reichsmark beläuft sich die Gesamtbelastung pro Jahr und Wagen, in Frankreich sind es 376, in den USA lediglich 128. Im Lande der Dichter und Denker erlässt der Staat Notverordnungen, greift etwa parteilich in den Wettbewerb von Schiene und Straße zugunsten der Reichsbahn ein.

Dabei hat Krisen-Manager Kissel klug vorgebaut, stattet Lastwagen und Busse fast durchweg mit Diesel-Triebwerken aus. Als Taktiker und Stratege führt er einen Vielfronten-Krieg, nicht zuletzt gegen die Allianzen und Bündnisse, in denen sich faktische und potentielle Gegner aneinanderkuscheln: Seit 1929 schmückt sich die amerikanische Auto-Hydra General Motors mit ihrer deutschen Adoptivtochter Opel. 1932 finden sich mit DKW, Audi, Horch und Wanderer zumindest drei Konkurrenten unter dem schützenden Dach der Auto Union zusammen. So knirscht auch in Untertürkheim Sand im Getriebe: Mit 3084 Lohnempfängern ist dort der untere Totpunkt erreicht, der Erlös je PKW, 1925 noch bei 13590 Mark, auf weniger als 5000 Mark abgesunken. Im August des Vorjahres gab es die 16-Stunden-Woche, allerdings der Not gehorchend und nicht dem eigenen Triebe. Ende 1932 weist man Verluste von 13,4 Millionen aus, rund ein Drittel des Grundkapitals.

Aber die schlechte Nachricht ist auch die gute: Längst haben Miteinander und Gewöhnung Profilneurosen und partikulares Denken mit dem Tenor hier Daimler, da Benz nachhaltig therapiert und ein wohliges Wir-Bewusstsein bewirkt, längst hat die Not der Gründerjahre die Tugend der Kreativität geboren.

surveillance, le Dr Friedrich Nallinger. Nibel sublime par exemple la SSK en SSKL, avec laquelle Rudolf Caracciola remportera, en 1931, les Mille Miglia.

En octobre de la même année, au Salon de Paris, est présentée la création de Nibel, la 170. C'est un modèle bas de gamme qui donnera une impulsion révolutionnaire comparable à celle qu'aura la 180 en 1953 : celle-ci introduira la carrosserie ponton, celle-là, l'essieu oscillant.

Jusqu'à ce jour, toutes les Mercedes et leurs illustres ancêtres arborant le nom Daimler ou Benz roulaient, dans leur impériale majesté, sur des essieux rigides. La suspension à roues indépendantes – ce n'était pas seulement un exemple éminent d'innovation dans l'automobile, elle était aussi impérieusement nécessaire : le réseau routier en Allemagne est presque aussi misérable qu'à l'époque médiévale. Quiconque quitte les routes à peu près carrossables des grandes agglomérations se retrouve instantanément dans le Moyen Âge, dans un embrouillamini de chaussées étroites et fortement galbées avec un revêtement de cailloux et de pavés ou, dans le meilleur des cas, de macadam truffé de nids-de-poule et s'effritant sous les roues ou de béton goudronné.

Il est rare que les édiles regardent plus loin que leur clocher respectif. Mais il y a une célèbre exception à cette règle de patchworks et de mosaïques : l'Avus (abréviation signifiant route de circulation et d'essais pour l'automobile), un embryon d'autoroute sans carrefour qui voit le jour en 1912, le long de la voie ferrée Berlin-Wannsee, avec des crédits privés ; durant la guerre, il est laissé à l'abandon, avant d'être achevé en 1921 par l'industriel Hugo Stinnes. Si la 170 n'atteindra pas la popularité de la Volkswagen, son prix d'achat de 4400 marks pour la quatre-portes (avec malle séparée) en 1931 la met cependant à la portée des moins riches parmi les amis de la marque. D'ailleurs, jusqu'en 1936, 13775 clients sauront apprécier ce coût à sa juste valeur.

Durant les années de marasme de 1931–1932, conduire est devenu un coûteux plaisir : « L'automobile allemande est à l'agonie », constate amèrement l'ADAC-Motorwelt, qui cite dans la foulée le coupable : « La ponction fiscale exagérée et les complications administratives du secteur automobile. » Impôt sur l'automobile, droits de douane sur le benzène, impôt sur les combustibles, impôt supplémentaire – une ponction fiscale interminable presse l'automobiliste comme un citron. Les charges totales par voiture et par an s'élèvent à 798 reichsmarks, contre 376 en France et seulement 128 aux États-Unis. Au pays des poètes et des philosophes, l'État adopte des décrets d'urgence et intervient, par exemple, de façon partisane dans la concurrence entre le rail et la route en faveur de la compagnie ferroviaire nationale, la Reichsbahn.

Et pourtant, Kissel, qui gère la crise, a pris ses précautions et dote les camions et les bus presque exclusivement de moteurs Diesel. En bon technicien et stratège, il mène une guerre sur tous les fronts, aussi et surtout contre les alliances et fédérations au sein desquelles les adversaires actuels et potentiels se ménagent mutuellement : en 1929,

1926

directing a war on many fronts, not least against the alliances and coalitions in which actual and potential competitors were cozying up to one another. In 1929 the American car giant General Motors had taken over the German company Opel. 1932 saw DKW, Audi, Horch and Wanderer, at least three of whom were competitors, seek shelter together under the protective umbrella of Auto Union. In Untertürkheim too things were not firing on all cylinders. With its work force of 3084, rock bottom was reached when the revenue per car, which had been as high as 13,590 marks in 1925, fell to less than 5000 marks. August of the previous year had seen the adoption of a 16-hour week, a decision taken as a necessity rather than a simple matter of inclination. At the end of 1932 the company had recorded losses of 13.4 million marks, around a third of the stock capital.

But every cloud has a silver lining. Proximity and increasing familiarity had had a lasting therapeutic effect on the image neuroses and separatist leanings of the Daimler or Benz camps, and produced a cozy "We" feeling. The necessity of the early years had long since given way to the virtue of joint creativity.

Ferdinand Porsche was chief designer at Daimler-Benz between April 1923 and December 1928.

Ferdinand Porsche ist zwischen dem April 1923 und dem Dezember 1928 Chefkonstrukteur bei Daimler-Benz.

Ferdinand Porsche aura été chef constructeur chez Daimler-Benz d'avril 1923 à décembre 1928.

l'hydre automobile américaine General Motors a englouti Opel. En 1932, avec DKW, Audi, Horch et Wanderer, au moins trois concurrents sont regroupés dans le giron d'Auto Union. Et du sable fait grincer les engrenages à Untertürkheim également : avec 3084 salariés, on y a atteint le point mort inférieur et la recette par voiture de tourisme, qui était encore de 13 590 marks en 1925, est retombée à moins de 5000 marks. Le mois d'août de l'année précédente avait vu l'introduction de la semaine de seize heures, mais pour répondre à une nécessité et non pas de gaieté de cœur. Fin 1932, les pertes s'élèvent à 13,4 millions, soit environ un tiers du capital social.

Mais le revers s'accompagne d'une richesse : il y a longtemps que la coexistence et l'accoutumance ont mis un terme durable aux susceptibilités et à l'idéologie égoïste symbolisée par la devise : « ici Daimler, là Benz », et ont engendré un sentiment positif d'appartenance mutuelle ; la détresse des années de fondation s'est muée en une qualité, la créativité.

A nationalized company 1933–1945

Daimler-Benz and the Third Reich, the German marque with its special charisma and the dictator – that is a chapter in itself and yet only one part of a complex network of issues. Totalitarian states do not tolerate idylls, and the Nazi cartographers did not stand for any white patches on their maps. There were simply degrees of dependence, from toeing the party line, via lip service, to outright resistance – with its familiar consequences. Three examples can be quoted. Hermann Koehler, a member of the supervisory board since 1928, publicly criticized the regime, for which he was convicted by the "People's Court" and executed in 1943. Chairman of the board of management Wilhelm Kissel was a party member and belonged to the SS and the NSKK ("Nationalsozialistisches Kraftfahrt-Korps" or National Socialist Motorized Corps), but his brown façade was probably simply a tactical ploy to assist the company, a calculated cuddling-up as a means of mimicry. There is, though, no doubting director Jakob Werlin's conviction that salvation lay in Hitler. As a dyed-in-the-wool Nazi, he was behind the "Führer" right from the start in his Munich period and ensured access to the corridors of power for himself, and therefore the company, right to the end.

The seizure of power by Hitler, a car enthusiast, on 30 January 1933 heralded a boom in car sales which was fanned by tax breaks, sports promotion, and the prospect of a major road-building program. As early as March the rate of vehicle registrations in Germany had more than doubled, and the Mercedes work force, 14,003 by the end of the year, had almost regained its 1929 level. Sales of 100.9 million marks were recorded. In 1934 Sindelfingen was work-

Staats-Betrieb 1933–1945

Daimler-Benz und das Dritte Reich, die deutsche Marke mit dem besonderen Charisma und der Diktator – das ist ein Kapitel für sich und doch nur Teil eines komplexen Geflechts von Motiven. Totalitäre Staaten dulden keine Idylle, die Landvermesser der Nationalsozialisten keine weißen Flecken auf ihren Karten. Es gibt lediglich Schattierungen der Hörigkeit, von der Linientreue über das Lippenbekenntnis bis hin zum Widerstand – mit den bekannten Folgen. Drei Exponenten: Hermann Koehler, im Aufsichtsrat seit 1928, kritisiert das Regime öffentlich, wird 1943 vom »Volksgerichtshof« abgeurteilt und hingerichtet. Vorstandsvorsitzer Wilhelm Kissel ist Parteimitglied und Angehöriger der SS sowie des NSKK (für Nationalsozialistisches Kraftfahrt-Korps), aber die braune Fassade deckt wohl nur Taktik und Kalkül zum Wohle der Firma – der kalkulierte Schmusekurs als Mittel des Mimikry. Kein Zweifel indessen besteht hinsichtlich der Überzeugung von Vorstandsmitglied Jakob Werlin, das Heil liege in Hitler: In der Wolle gefärbter Nationalsozialist und Mann der ersten Stunde in des »Führers« Münchener Zeit, bewahrt er sich und damit dem Unternehmen bis zum Ende einen guten Draht zu den Schaltstellen der Macht.

Mit der Machtergreifung am 30. Januar 1933 beginnt der Boom, von Auto-Freund Hitler mit Steuervergünstigungen, Sportförderung und dem Ausblick auf üppigen Straßenbau angefacht. Bereits im März hat sich die Rate der Kraftfahrzeug-Zulassungen im Reich mehr als verdoppelt, die Arbeitnehmerschaft bei Mercedes am Ende des Jahres mit 14003 fast wieder die Stärke von 1929 erreicht. Ein Umsatz von 100,9 Millionen Mark wird ausgewiesen. Noch 1934 werden die Möglichkeiten in Sindelfingen zusätzlich

L'entreprise d'État 1933–1945

Daimler-Benz et le IIIe Reich, la marque allemande au charisme particulier et le régime dictatorial – est tout un chapitre en soi et, pourtant, seulement une partie d'un faisceau complexe de motifs. Les États totalitaires ne tolèrent pas d'idylle, les géomètres nationaux-socialistes, pas de taches blanches sur leurs cartes.

Il y a seulement des apparences d'obéissance, de la fidélité au système à la résistance en passant par les promesses faites du bout des lèvres – avec les conséquences bien connues. Trois noms sont révélateurs à ce point de vue : Hermann Koehler, membre du conseil de surveillance depuis 1928, critique publiquement le régime, est condamné en 1943 par la « Cour de justice populaire » et exécuté. Wilhelm Kissel, président du directoire et membre du parti appartient à la SS ainsi qu'à la NSKK (le corps automobile national-socialiste), mais sa façade brune ne dissimule que tactique et calcul pour le bien-être de la firme – flirt bien simulé comme un moyen de composer avec l'ennemi. Il n'y a aucun doute, par contre, en ce qui concerne la conviction de Jacob Werlin, pour qui c'est Hitler qui représente le salut : en tant que national-socialiste bon teint et recrue de l'époque munichoise du « Führer », il entretient jusqu'à la fin, pour lui-même et pour la firme, de bonnes relations avec les dirigeants.

Avec l'arrivée au pouvoir des nazis, le 30 janvier 1933, commence le boom déclenché par l'ami de l'automobile qu'est Hitler avec des allégements fiscaux, une promotion du sport et la perspective d'un réseau routier bien structuré. Dès mars, le taux des immatriculations automobiles dans le Reich a plus que doublé et, fin 1933, avec 14 003 salariés, les effectifs de Mercedes sont presque

ing at full capacity on the production of mass-produced bodies for Wanderer and BMW (Bayerische Motoren Werke), which did not fly the nest and operate as independent car factories until 1935.

By this time Daimler-Benz had long since needed all its available capacity for itself. It revived the Mannheim factory, where it manufactured bodies for luxury cars other than the major production cars. For the first time since the merger dividends were paid, five per cent on the ordinary shares and four per cent on the preference shares. And the annual report rejoiced in the required manner: "It is thanks to the personal initiative of our *Führer* and *Reichskanzler* that this business sector … has become a defining factor in our overall economy." Adolf Hitler was a genuine fan of the make with the star emblem, and a Mercedes was his preferred official car. This sent out an obvious signal to those exercising political power and all those who so wished to do so.

On 20 April 1939, the "Führer's" 50th birthday, Untertürkheim reciprocated with a small gift in the form of an open-top Großer Mercedes type 770, as that was how the birthday boy liked to appear in public. 46,000 marks was the price of the Cabriolet D with four doors, 47,500 for the Cabriolet F with six seats. Modesty forbids any mention of the cost of the special bullet-proof version that looked like a monument in itself. Its bodywork made of 18-mm-thick armor plate steel, 40-mm-thick windows, explosion-proof 20-chamber cellular tires, and side-mounted spare wheels which also functioned as armoring gave those in high office in the Third Reich and their colleagues in friendly countries abroad a comfortable feeling of security. Attempts had been made from 1934 onwards to win over new customers at the lower end of the range, with vehicles aimed at the man in the street. However, the project which consisted of rear-engined 1.3-, 1.5- and 1.7-liter cars turned into something of a Cinderella. The same fate was shared by the bold creations of designer Gustav Röhr between 1935 and 1937, with front-wheel drive, flat four- and eight-cylinder engines, and a V8 engine. None of them made it beyond the prototype stage, just as their spiritual father, a Rhinelander, never really settled in Untertürkheim, the epitome of Swabia. The car had become a political tool, caught up in the system: cars for the masses was the byword.

The Beetle was also harnessed as part of the state-organized scheme to generate a feel-good factor – KdF (standing for "Kraft durch Freude" or strength through joy), a phantom akin to the apples that constantly moved out of reach of the hungry and tormented Tantalus in Greek mythology. "What's happened to the Volkswagen?" was the question asked by impatient readers in the summer of 1935 of the editor of *Motorwelt*, by now the official publication of the unified DDAC ("Der Deutsche Automobil Club" – The German Automobile Club), the organization into which Hitler's old comrade Adolf Hühnlein as the leader of the NSKK had merged the many and varied German automobile clubs. They did not realize that they would have to wait for the end of the thousand-year Reich for an answer.

mit Serienkarosserien für Wanderer und die Bayerischen Motoren Werke ausgelastet, die sich erst 1935 freischwimmen und als Autofabrik autark werden.

Da braucht Daimler-Benz alle verfügbaren Kapazitäten schon lange selbst, hat das Werk Mannheim reanimiert und stellt dort Aufbauten für Luxuswagen abseits der großen Serien her. Erstmals nach der Vereinigung gibt es Dividende, fünf Prozent auf die Stamm- und vier Prozent auf die Vorzugsaktien. Und der Geschäftsbericht frohlockt in systemkonformer Prosa: »Der persönlichen Initiative unseres Führers und Reichskanzlers ist es zu danken, dass dieser Wirtschaftszweig … heute zu einem maßgebenden Faktor unserer gesamten Wirtschaft geworden ist.« Adolf Hitler schätzt die Marke mit dem Stern in der Tat besonders und tritt seine Dienstfahrten vorzugsweise in Mercedes-Wagen an, mit einer entsprechenden Signalwirkung auf die politische Nomenklatura und alle, die so gerne dazugehören würden.

Am 20. April 1939, des »Führers« Geburtstag jährt sich zum fünfzigsten Male, revanchiert man sich in Untertürkheim mit einer kleinen Aufmerksamkeit in Gestalt des Großen Mercedes Typ 770, offen, denn das kommt der Neigung des Jubilars zu öffentlichen Auftritten entgegen. 46 000 Mark kostet das Cabriolet D mit vier Türen, 47 500 das Cabriolet F mit sechs Sitzen. Über den Preis der kugelfesten Sonderausführung, die ausschaut wie ihr eigenes Denkmal, schweigt indessen des Sängers Höflichkeit. Mit ihrer Karosserie aus Panzerstahl von 18 Millimetern Stärke, 40 Millimeter dicken Scheiben, beschusssicheren 20-Kammer-Zellenreifen und seitlichen Ersatzrädern als Panzerschild vermittelt sie hohen Würdenträgern des Dritten Reichs und ihren Kollegen im befreundeten Ausland ein Gefühl der Geborgenheit. Schon ab 1934 hat man versucht, am unteren Ende des Typen-Spektrums Neuland zu besiedeln, gedacht für den kleinen Mann. Allerdings missrät das Projekt, Heckmotor-Autos mit 1,3, 1,5 und 1,7 Litern, zum Aschenbrödel. Das gleiche Los wird den Geschöpfen des wagemutigen Konstrukteurs Gustav Röhr zwischen 1935 und 1937 zuteil, mit Frontantrieb, Boxer-Triebwerken von vier und acht Zylindern und einer V8-Maschine. Allesamt kommen sie über das Stadium von Prototypen nicht hinaus, wie auch ihr geistiger Vater, ein Rheinländer, in der Schwaben-Hochburg Untertürkheim nie so recht heimisch wird. Da ist das Kraftfahrzeug schon zur politischen Größe geworden, in den Sog des Systems geraten: Autos für die Massen, heißt die Devise.

Auch der Käfer wird in das Geschirr der staatlich organisierten Volksbeglückung KdF (für Kraft durch Freude) gespannt, ein Phantom wie die Äpfel, die sich im griechischen Mythos dem hungrigen Tantalos immerfort entziehen. »Wo bleibt der Volkswagen?« fragen im Sommer 1935 ungeduldige Leser die Redaktion der *Motorwelt*, inzwischen Organ des Einheitsvereins DDAC (Der Deutsche Automobil Club), zu dem Hitlers alter Kampfgenosse Adolf Hühnlein als Führer des NSKK die bunte Vielfalt der deutschen Autoclubs zusammengefasst hat. Sie ahnen nicht,

revenus à leur niveau de 1929. Mercedes réalise un chiffre d'affaires de 100,9 millions de marks. En 1934 encore, les capacités de Sindelfingen sont également mises à contribution avec des carrosseries de série pour Wanderer et les Bayerische Motoren Werke, qui ne deviendront définitivement indépendants qu'en 1935.

À ce moment-là, il y a longtemps que Daimler-Benz a besoin elle-même de toutes les capacités disponibles : elle réactive l'usine de Mannheim et fabrique des carrosseries pour des voitures de luxe assemblées en marge des grandes séries. Des dividendes sont versés pour la première fois depuis l'unification des deux firmes, 5 % pour les actions normales et 4 % pour les actions privilégiées. Et le rapport d'exercice peint les choses en rose selon la prose conforme au système : « C'est à l'initiative personnelle de notre Führer et chancelier du Reich que l'on doit que ce secteur économique […] soit aujourd'hui devenu un facteur déterminant de toute notre économie. » De fait, Hitler apprécie particulièrement la marque à l'étoile et accomplit ses voyages de service par prédilection dans des Mercedes, qui fascinent aussi la caste politique et tous ceux qui en feraient si volontiers partie.

Le 20 avril 1939, cinquantième anniversaire du « Führer ». Untertürkheim exprime ses remerciements avec la Grosser Mercedes 770, décapotable qui va au-devant du penchant du bénéficiaire pour les manifestations publiques. Le Cabriolet D à quatre portes coûte 46 000 marks, et 47 500 le Cabriolet F à six places. Le chantre de l'opinion publique tait le prix de la version blindée. Avec sa carrosserie en acier blindé de 18 mm, ses vitres de 40 mm, ses pneus à cellules à vingt chambres increvables et ses roues de secours latérales comme bouclier supplémentaire, elle donne une sensation de sécurité aux grands dignitaires du IIIe Reich et à leurs homologues des pays étrangers amis. Dès 1934, on a tenté de coloniser des terres vierges à l'autre extrémité de la hiérarchie automobile, pensant à l'homme de la rue. Le projet de voiture à moteur arrière de 1,3, 1,5 et 1,7 litre de cylindrée se solde par un échec. Ce sera aussi le destin des créations du courageux constructeur Gustav Röhr, entre 1935 et 1937, avec traction avant, moteur boxer à quatre et huit-cylindres et moteur V8. Aucune ne dépasse le stade de prototype et leur père intellectuel, un Rhénan, ne se sentira jamais chez lui à Untertürkheim, localité souabe par excellence. Là, l'automobile est déjà devenue un paramètre politique qui est attiré dans le sillage du système : des voitures pour les masses, telle est la devise.

La Coccinelle est intégrée dans le système de bonheur populaire imposé par l'État, mais c'est un fantôme comme la pomme qui échappe toujours, dans la mythologie grecque, à Tantale affamé au moment où il veut la saisir. « Que devient la Volkswagen ? » demandent, en été 1935, les lecteurs impatients de la *Motorwelt*, entre-temps devenue l'organe du club unifié DDAC (Der Deutsche Automobil Club), au sein duquel un vieux complice de Hitler, Adolf Hühnlein, en tant que dirigeant du NSKK, a regroupé tout le gratin des automobiles clubs allemands.

And yet everything had looked so promising at the beginning. The car, according to Hitler in 1934, had to be relieved of its "class-dividing character" and it had to be made into a "source of a hitherto unknown, joyful happiness for millions of worthy, hard-working and good fellow citizens particularly on Sundays and public holidays." In the same year Ferdinand Porsche submitted a "memo relating to the construction of a German *Volkswagen* (people's car)" to the Imperial Ministry of Transport. In June 1935 Porsche GmbH in Stuttgart-Zuffenhausen was commissioned by the "Imperial Association of the Automobile Industry" to design an appropriate vehicle. After a number of prototypes, the VW 30 pilot series of 30 cars was produced in 1936 at Daimler-Benz in Sindelfingen, though not without technical reservations and misgivings about the professor who was still remembered by the older members among his staff at Mercedes as a stubborn negotiating partner. Wilhelm Kissel was positively disposed towards the project in principle, since the planned price for the Beetle of a laughably low 900 marks would establish a minimum level and therefore bring calm to the market. In fact the upstart automobile was met with complete disinterest by the established markets and was finally placed under the protection of Dr. Robert Ley at the "Deutsche Arbeitsfront."

The two new stars in the Mercedes range at the Berlin motor show in February 1936 were also targeted at a wider market: they were the rather robustly designed 170 V, which in all its variants sold 86,615 examples up to 1941, and the equally rugged 260 D. The reason for this was that patent 67207, granted in 1892 to Mr. Rudolf Diesel, was finally deemed suitable for the car – a mere 50 years after its birth. However, the 260 D shared the headlines of the show with the Hanomag Rekord Diesel. The path from concept to reality had been bumpy, with Robert Bosch's high-pressure injection pump of 1927 having been a milestone along the way.

Daimler-Benz's diesel debutante was still rough around the edges, but it was modest and tough, and therefore ideal for use as a taxi, like many of its successors. Its ancestry can be traced right back to its origins. And they remained basically in-house: on 26 June 1896 entry number 1329 in Daimler-Motoren-Gesellschaft's order book recorded an order for a Victoria motor car with a taximeter. The order was placed by Friedrich August Greiner, a haulage contractor in Stuttgart. He founded the Daimler-Motorwagen-Kutscherei coach company, put the first motorized cab into service in 1897 and became the first taxi operator in the world to use motor vehicles.

The design of the 260 D still bore all the hallmarks of Hans Nibel who had died in 1934. He was succeeded by Max Sailer, a legendary former Mercedes racer known for his spectacular starring roles such as in the 1914 French Grand Prix in Lyon or the 1922 Targa Florio. And the arrival of Gustav Röhr signaled the departure of Fritz Nallinger as head of testing, though he stayed at the company with responsibility for developing large engines.

dass sie erst das Ende des Tausendjährigen Reichs abwarten müssen.

Dabei hat alles vielversprechend begonnen. Man müsse, spricht Hitler bereits 1934, dem Automobil den »klassenspaltenden Charakter nehmen«, es »Millionen braver, fleißiger und tüchtiger Mitmenschen vor allem an Sonn- und Feiertagen zur Quelle eines unbekannten, freudigen Glücks« machen. Im selben Jahr übergibt Ferdinand Porsche dem Reichsverkehrsministerium ein »Exposé, betreffend den Bau eines deutschen Volkswagens«. Die Porsche GmbH in Stuttgart-Zuffenhausen wird im Juni 1935 vom »Reichsverband der Automobilindustrie« beauftragt, ein geeignetes Fahrzeug zu konzipieren. Nach etlichen Prototypen entsteht 1936, bei Daimler-Benz in Sindelfingen gefertigt, die Vorserie VW 30 in 30 Exemplaren, nicht ohne technische Bedenken und Vorbehalte gegen den Professor, den älteren unter seinen Mitarbeitern bei Mercedes noch als störrischer Verhandlungspartner bekannt. Wilhelm Kissel steht dem Projekt grundsätzlich positiv gegenüber, da der für den Käfer ins Visier genommene Spottpreis von 900 Mark eine untere Grenze abstecken und somit Ruhe in den Markt bringen würde. Im übrigen stößt der automobile Emporkömmling auf zähes Desinteresse seitens der etablierten Marken und wird schließlich 1937 in die Obhut der »Deutschen Arbeitsfront« unter Dr. Robert Ley gegeben.

Auch die beiden neuen Stars im Mercedes-Sortiment auf der Berliner Automobil-Ausstellung im Februar 1936 geben sich volksnah: der eher derb gewirkte 170 V, der bis 1941 in allen seinen Varianten 86 615 mal unter die Leute gebracht werden wird, und der gleichermaßen knorrige 260 D. Denn pünktlich zum 50. Jubiläum des Automobils ist dem Patent 67 207, erteilt 1892 an Herrn Rudolf Diesel, das Zeugnis der PKW-Reife zuerkannt worden. Der 260 D teilt sich die Schlagzeilen zu der Show allerdings mit dem Hanomag Rekord Diesel. Der Weg vom Prinzip zur Realisierung ist holprig gewesen, ein Meilenstein Robert Boschs Hochdruck-Einspritzpumpe von 1927.

Der Diesel-Debütant von Daimler-Benz ist noch immer ein rauher Bursche, aber schon genügsam und zählebig und damit ein Gewinn für das Taxi-Gewerbe, wie viele seiner Nachfahren. Nach hinten lässt sich seine Ahnenreihe bis zu den Ursprüngen verfolgen. Und die bleiben gewissermaßen im Hause: Am 26. Juni 1896 verzeichnet das »Commissionsbuch« der Daimler-Motoren-Gesellschaft unter der Nummer 1329 die Bestellung eines Motorwagens Typ Victoria mit Taxameter. Auftraggeber ist Friedrich August Greiner, Pferdefuhrunternehmer zu Stuttgart. Er gründet die Daimler-Motorwagen-Kutscherei, stellt 1897 die erste Motordroschke in Dienst und wird zum ersten Taxi-Unternehmer der Welt mit Automobilen.

Der 260 D trägt noch die konstruktiven Fingerabdrücke von Hans Nibel, der 1934 gestorben ist. Sein Nachfolger wird Max Sailer, ein firmeneigenes Renn-Denkmal mit spektakulären Einsätzen wie beim Grand Prix de France in Lyon 1914 oder der Targa Florio 1922 in der Stammrolle. Und als Gustav Röhr kommt, geht Versuchschef Fritz Nal-

Nul ne se doute qu'il va falloir attendre la fin du Reich de mille ans.

Et pourtant, tout a commencé de façon prometteuse. Il faut, a déjà dit Hitler en 1934, « ôter tout caractère distinctif de classe » à l'automobile, en faire « pour des millions de concitoyens courageux, zélés et travailleurs (surtout pour les dimanches et jours de fêtes) la source d'un bonheur inconnu et joyeux ». La même année, Ferdinand Porsche remet au ministère des Transports du Reich un « Exposé concernant la construction d'une voiture populaire (Volkswagen) allemande » et, en juin 1935, la Porsche GmbH, à Stuttgart-Zuffenhausen, reçoit de la « Fédération du Reich de l'Industrie automobile » l'ordre de concevoir une voiture appropriée. Après d'innombrables prototypes apparaît, en 1936, fabriquée chez Daimler-Benz à Sindelfingen, la présérie VW30 construite à 30 exemplaires, non sans remises en cause et réserves techniques contre le professeur, bien connu encore des plus vieux de ses collaborateurs de Mercedes comme interlocuteur intraitable. Wilhelm Kissel est, par principe, favorable au projet, car on a calculé pour la Coccinelle un prix théorique dérisoire de 900 marks qui ferait immédiatement régner le calme sur le marché. Pour le reste, la « voiture du peuple » suscite le plus vif désintérêt de la part des marques établies et sa fabrication est finalement confiée, en 1937, aux bons offices du « Front Ouvrier allemand » sous la direction du Dr Robert Ley.

Les deux nouvelles stars du programme Mercedes au Salon de l'Automobile de Berlin de février 1936 se veulent elles aussi à la portée du peuple : ce sont la 170 V, à l'allure plutôt fruste, qui trouvera tout de même preneur 86 615 fois dans toutes ses variantes jusqu'en 1941, et la tout aussi anguleuse 260 D. En effet, ponctuellement, pour le 50e anniversaire de l'automobile, le brevet nº 67207, décerné en 1892 à monsieur Rudolf Diesel, s'est vu accorder la mention de « maturité automobile ». La 260 D doit toutefois partager les grands titres des journaux avec la Hanomag Rekord Diesel. La route a été longue du principe à la réalisation avec, en 1927, une borne milliaire sous la forme de la pompe à injection à haute pression de Robert Bosch.

La diesel débutante de Daimler-Benz est encore un énergumène aux mœurs frustes, mais elle est déjà sobre et indestructible, ce qui la prédestine aux sociétés de taxi comme beaucoup de ses successeurs. On peut encore décrire avec précision sa galerie des ancêtres. Elle reste en quelque sorte dans la famille : le 26 juin 1896, le « Livre de Commissions » de la Daimler-Motoren-Gesellschaft note sous le nº 1329 la commande d'une voiture à moteur type Victoria à taximètre. L'acheteur est Friedrich August Greiner, voiturier de Stuttgart. Il fonde la Daimler-Motorwagen-Kutscherei, met en service le premier taxi à moteur en 1897 et se trouve donc être le premier entrepreneur de taxis du monde.

La 260 D porte encore, sur le plan mécanique, l'empreinte de Hans Nibel, décédé en 1934. Son successeur est Max Sailer, légendaire ex-pilote Mercedes qui s'est illustré au Grand Prix de France à Lyon en 1914 et à la Targa

The Treaty of Versailles had long bound and gagged the German aircraft industry. Now, however, state-of-the-art engines were emerging in the form of the DB 600, a 1000 bhp, water-cooled, supercharged twelve-cylinder engine from 1935 – and the DB 601 with fuel injection from 1936, tailored as it was for the Messerschmitt Me 109 fighter, the commonest aircraft in the Second World War. The post-war period had suddenly turned into the pre-war period again, though the shadows of war were foreseen by many. The 100 individual buildings of the new aero-engine factory in Genshagen (Teltow district), for example, were scattered over four million square meters (43 million sq ft) which lengthened distances for staff, but made pinpointing the exact target more difficult in air raids.

In 1938, on the threshold of the century's second cataclysm, 42,687 Mercedes vehicles left the assembly lines; sales were just below the 400 million barrier that was to be exceeded in all the war years between 1939 and 1944, and Mercedes-Benz had a work force of 35,123. 21,000 new registrations in Germany represented a 10 per cent share of the domestic market. Germany was still a developing country in terms of car ownership with one car for every 44 inhabitants compared with 19 in France and the UK, and four in the United States, which as long ago as 1932 had seen a car population of 23 million pouring onto its 500,000 km (310,700-mile) road network.

Export was the order of the day and also of the government. The country needed hard currency simply because raw materials such as rubber or aluminum were becoming rare. The glittering aura of the swastika was now dulling the glamor of the star. What had previously been regarded as the embodiment of German quality craftsmanship and had contributed to converting the "Made in Germany" origin label from a warning to a recommendation, was meeting with growing resistance.

Many cars were also exported without tires to guarantee continuity of supplies for the domestic market. In 1938 Daimler-Benz had to accept a loss of six million marks on its foreign business. At the same time the work force saw itself cushioned by a raft of attractive social benefits, although, having been termed a "retinue" in Nazi-speak, it had also seen itself become part of an army of millions of willing vassals. To the wage bill of 100 million marks had to be added statutory and voluntary benefits costing around ten million each, plus money for a "Work force Relief Fund" which had been set up in 1935, in recognition of similar social benefits in the past of the illustrious forebears Daimler and Benz. In the Gaggenau plant, for example, a "House of Cleanliness" was set up in all its splendor to underline the importance of hygiene.

But the writing was already on the wall, and the portents for *Führer,* people, and fatherland were already looming. At 4.45 AM on 1 September 1939 Hitler gave the order to invade Poland. With effect from the same day petrol was only available on coupons. Cars were called up for military service just like recruits, and private sales were banned

linger, bleibt allerdings dem Unternehmen als Leiter der Großmotoren-Entwicklung erhalten.

Der Vertrag von Versailles hat die deutsche Flugzeugindustrie auf lange Sicht geknebelt und verkrüppelt. Nun aber sind Triebwerke auf dem letzten Stand der Dinge im Werden, der DB 600, ein 1000 PS starker wassergekühlter Zwölfzylinder mit Aufladung von 1935 – und der DB 601 mit Einspritzung von 1936, maßgeschneidert etwa für die Me 109, das meistgebaute Flugzeug des Zweiten Weltkriegs. Denn unversehens ist die Nachkriegszeit wieder in die Vorkriegszeit umgeschlagen, und mancher scheint das zu ahnen: Die 100 einzelnen Gebäude des neuen Flugmotorenwerks in Genshagen (Kreis Teltow) sind über vier Millionen Quadratmeter verstreut, was die Dienstwege verlängert, bei Luftangriffen indessen die genaue Zielansprache erschwert.

1938, an der Schwelle zum Jahrhundert-Desaster Nummer zwei, verlassen 42 687 Mercedes-Fahrzeuge die Bänder, liegt der Umsatz knapp unter der 400-Millionen-Grenze, die in allen Kriegsjahren zwischen 1939 und 1944 überschritten werden wird, sind 35 123 Mitarbeiter für den Stuttgarter Star-Betrieb tätig. Mit 21 000 Neuzulassungen deckt man zehn Prozent des heimischen Markts ab. Noch ist das Reich mobiles Entwicklungsland mit einem Auto auf 44 Einwohner gegenüber 19 in Frankreich und Großbritannien und vier in den Vereinigten Staaten, wo sich schon 1932 eine PKW-Population von 23 Millionen über ein Straßengeflecht von 500 000 Kilometern ergoss.

Export ist das Gebot der Stunde und der Staatsführung. Man benötigt Devisen, schon weil Rohstoffe wie Kautschuk oder Aluminium rar werden. Die Glitzer-Aureole des Hakenkreuzes trübt indessen den Glamour des Sterns: Was draußen als Inkarnation deutscher Wertarbeit geschätzt wird und dazu beitrug, die Herkunftsbezeichnung »Made in Germany« von einer Warnung in eine Empfehlung umzumünzen, stößt zunehmend auf Widerwillen.

Viele Autos werden zudem ohne Reifen ausgeführt, damit die heimische Versorgung sichergestellt ist. 1938 hat sich Daimler-Benz mit einem Verlust von sechs Millionen Mark aus dem Auslandsgeschäft abzufinden. Auf den Rosen attraktiver Sozialleistungen gebettet sieht sich zugleich die Belegschaft, die sich nun als sogenannte »Gefolgschaft« einem Millionenheer williger Vasallen einverleibt sieht. Zu einer Lohnsumme von 100 Millionen Mark addieren sich gesetzliche und freiwillige Leistungen von jeweils rund zehn Millionen sowie Gelder aus einem »Unterstützungsfonds für die Gefolgschaft«, der, 1935, eingedenk ähnlicher sozialer Schmankerl in der Vergangenheit der illustren Ahnen Daimler und Benz, angelegt wurde. Im Werk Gaggenau etwa dient ein »Haus der Sauberkeit« in rundlicher Pracht hygienischen Zwecken.

Doch schon erscheint die Schrift an der Wand, bahnt sich das Menetekel an für »Führer«, Volk und Vaterland. Am 1. September 1939 gibt Hitler um 4.45 Uhr den Befehl zum Angriff auf Polen. Mit Wirkung vom gleichen Tage wird Benzin nur noch gegen Bezugsschein ausgegeben.

Florio en 1922 dans le rôle de leader. Et, lorsque Gustav Röhr arrive, le chef des essais Fritz Nallinger démissionne, mais reste toutefois à la disposition de l'entreprise en tant que directeur du développement pour les gros moteurs.

Le traité de Versailles muselle et va paralyser à long terme l'industrie aéronautique allemande qui bénéficie pourtant de moteurs à la pointe de la technique avec le DB 600, un douze-cylindres de 1000 ch refroidi par eau et avec suralimentation, de 1935, et le DB 601, de 1936, à injection, taillé sur mesure pour le Me 109, l'avion le plus construit de la Seconde Guerre mondiale. En effet, sans que l'on s'en aperçoive, l'après-guerre s'est de nouveau mué en avant-guerre et beaucoup semblent le deviner : les cent différents édifices de la nouvelle usine de moteurs d'avion de Genshagen (circonscription de Teltow) sont disséminés sur quatre millions de mètres carrés, ce qui allonge les trajets pour le travail, mais diminue en revanche le risque d'être touché en cas de bombardements aériens.

En 1938, à l'orée de la Seconde Guerre mondiale, 42 687 Mercedes sortent des chaînes de montage ; le chiffre d'affaires frôle les 400 millions, seuil qui sera dépassé durant toutes les années de guerre entre 1939 et 1944 ; et 35 123 collaborateurs travaillent pour l'entreprise vedette de Stuttgart. Avec 21 000 immatriculations de voitures neuves, on couvre 10 % du marché domestique. Le Reich est encore un pays en développement en matière de construction automobile, avec une voiture pour 44 habitants, contre 19 en France et en Grande-Bretagne ou 4 aux États-Unis, où l'on compte déjà, en 1932, un parc automobile de 23 millions de voitures roulant sur un réseau routier de 500 000 km.

Exporter est le mot d'ordre du moment et des gouvernants. On a besoin de devises, entre autres parce que des matières premières comme le caoutchouc et l'aluminium se raréfient. L'auréole scintillante de la croix gammée fait en revanche de l'ombre au brillant de l'étoile : ce qui, à l'extérieur, était apprécié comme une incarnation du savoir-faire allemand et a contribué à métamorphoser de mise en garde en recommandation la dénomination d'origine « Made in Germany » suscite désormais un rejet croissant.

En outre, de nombreuses voitures sont exportées sans pneumatiques pour garantir l'approvisionnement domestique. En 1938, Daimler-Benz doit prendre son parti des pertes de six millions de marks engendrées par les opérations à l'étranger. Les membres du personnel, désormais assimilés à des millions de vassaux sous le nom de « Gefolgschaft », voient miroiter devant eux un paradis de prestations sociales attrayantes. Aux cent millions de marks de salaires s'ajoutent des prestations, obligatoires et volontaires, d'environ dix millions de marks ainsi que les subventions au titre d'un « fonds de soutien pour la Gefolgschaft », institué en 1935 à l'instar des récompenses sociales similaires décernées au cours du passé par deux illustres ancêtres, Daimler et Benz. À l'usine de Gaggenau, par exemple, une « Maison de la

from 3 September onwards. Developments took their course, culminating five years later in a dreadful punchline: in 1944 Daimler-Benz AG saw precisely one car roll off the production line. Anyone who had ordered a Mercedes in 1939 had to be patient: the delivery time was one world war.

Production soon covered the whole gamut of military craftsmanship: pick-ups and trucks, aircraft and rocket components, propulsion units for spotlights, boats, and aircraft. Between 1936 and 1945 80,000 aero-engines were produced, mainly in the Genshagen and Berlin-Marienfelde factories. Daimler-Benz developments did not always lead the way. The company fell behind MAN in developing a battletank and was reduced to producing a copy of the rival product in Marienfelde. The three-ton LGF diesel had scorn heaped upon it even within the company. It was so heavy, they said, that it was all it could do to carry its own weight, let alone also carry a payload.

Opel, a competitor, was then awarded the contract. Rüsselsheim-based Opel's "Blitz" design, a gasoline-engined vehicle, but light and nimble and highly suitable for active service, was built in accordance with American methods in Mercedes' Mannheim factory, though not until 1944. The ambitious Wilhelm Kissel found it hard to overcome this double disgrace. Already in poor health, he died in July 1942. His successor was Wilhelm Haspel (1898–1952), head of the Sindelfingen factory since 1932, a deputy member of the board of management since 1935, and a full member since 1941.

Although he was married to a "half-Jew," the "inspired management" (in a direct quotation from the 1941 annual report) gave its explicit blessing to his election. In many respects Haspel was a complementary figure to the rigidly Prussian disposition of his predecessor, equally merciless in his goals but more reliable in his method, artistic and with a tendency to charmingly glossed-over unpunctuality. He had inherited a tough job. Although, as one of the main pillars of the German arms industry, the company was in extremely buoyant shape – after all a dividend was still paid out in 1943, and a total of 23 million marks were paid out in the first four years of the war – this good news was bad news at the same time. Since the German offensive had become bogged down on the Eastern front, there were all kinds of resupply problems. A Daimler-Benz branch had been opened in Königsberg (now better known as Kaliningrad) as early as 1938. The DB 603 aero-engine was also assembled near Cracow and in Vienna. 1942 saw the establishment of the military factory in Minsk. And since 300,000 vehicles were damaged in the East alone, a logistic interface reaching almost to the front lines was required, a huge organizational puzzle with countless disparate pieces.

On the other hand increasing raw materials shortages and an enormous lack of qualified manpower were becoming all too apparent. In the first year of the war the "retinue" was literally decimated: 10 per cent were called up for active service, and the ever more frequent and gaping vacancies which appeared were later more or less filled with

Autos werden zum Wehrdienst eingezogen wie Rekruten, private Verkäufe vom 3. September an untersagt. Entwicklungen nehmen ihren Lauf, die fünf Jahre später in einer schlimmen Pointe münden: 1944 wird sich die PKW-Produktion der Daimler-Benz AG auf ein Fahrzeug belaufen. Wer vor 1939 einen Mercedes bestellt hat, muss sich in Geduld fassen: Die Lieferfrist beträgt einen Weltkrieg.

Schon bald deckt die Fertigung die ganze Klaviatur des Kampfhandwerks ab: Kübel- und Lastkraftwagen, Flieger- und Raketenteile, Triebwerke für Scheinwerfer, Boote und Flugzeuge – zwischen 1936 und 1945 entstehen vornehmlich in den Werken Genshagen und Berlin-Marienfelde 80 000 Flugmotoren. Nicht immer schlagen Daimler-Benz-Entwicklungen die Konkurrenz aus dem Felde: Hinsichtlich eines Kampfpanzers gerät man gegenüber MAN ins Hintertreffen und muss das Fremdprodukt sogar in Marienfelde nachbauen. Der Diesel-Dreitonner LGF wird selbst im eigenen Hause mit Hohn überhäuft: Er sei so schwer, dass er mit sich selbst genug zu tun habe und nicht auch noch Lasten herumschleppen könne.

Folglich erhält Wettbewerber Opel den Zuschlag. Das Modell »Blitz« der Rüsselsheimer, ein Benziner, aber leicht und flink und ungewöhnlich kriegsverwendungsfähig, wird nach amerikanischen Methoden im Mercedes-Werk Mannheim auf die Räder gestellt, allerdings erst 1944. Diese Doppel-Schmach ist für den ehrgeizigen Wilhelm Kissel nur schwer zu verwinden. Er stirbt, ohnehin angeschlagen, im Juli 1942. Sein Nachfolger wird Wilhelm Haspel (1898–1952), seit 1932 Chef des Werks Sindelfingen, seit 1935 stellvertretendes und seit 1941 ordentliches Mitglied des Vorstands.

Obwohl er mit einer »Halbjüdin« verheiratet ist, wird seine Wahl ausdrücklich abgesegnet von der »genialen Führung« (Originalzitat aus dem Geschäftsbericht von 1941). Haspel ist in vieler Hinsicht eine Komplementärgestalt zu seinem rigide preußisch gesonnenen Vorgänger, ebenfalls unnachsichtig in der Sache, aber verbindlicher in der Methode, musisch und mit einer Tendenz zu charmant verbrämter Unpünktlichkeit. Er tritt ein schweres Erbe an. Zwar geht es dem Unternehmen als Hauptpfeiler der deutschen Rüstungsindustrie wirtschaftlich blendend – noch 1943 wird Dividende ausgezahlt, insgesamt 23 Millionen Mark während der ersten vier Kriegsjahre.

Aber wieder ist die gute Nachricht identisch mit der schlechten: Spätestens seitdem sich die deutsche Offensive an der Ostfront verzettelt, stellen sich vielfältige Nachschubprobleme ein. Schon 1938 gibt es eine Daimler-Benz-Filiale in Königsberg. Das Flugzeugtriebwerk DB 603 wird auch in der Nähe von Krakau und in Wien montiert. 1942 wird das K- (für Kriegs-) Werk Minsk eingerichtet. Und da allein im Osten 300 000 Fahrzeuge beschädigt sind, bedarf es einer logistischen Unterfütterung bis nahe an die Frontlinien, ein organisatorisches Riesen-Puzzle mit unzähligen disparaten Bausteinen.

Andererseits machen sich der zunehmende Rohstoffmangel und ein immenser Bedarf an qualifiziertem Perso-

propreté » est vouée à des fins hygiéniques où l'on ne tolère pas le moindre écart.

Mais déjà les choses se gâtent et la déchéance s'annonce pour le « Führer », le peuple et la patrie. Le 1er septembre 1939, Hitler donne, à quatre heures quarante-cinq, l'ordre d'attaquer la Pologne. Mesure prenant effet le même jour, l'essence n'est plus vendue que contre des tickets de rationnement. Les voitures sont réquisitionnées pour l'armée comme des recrues, et, à partir du 3 septembre, les ventes par des particuliers sont interdites. C'est alors que prennent cours des événements qui, cinq ans plus tard, atteindront un paroxysme dramatique : en 1944, la production de voitures de tourisme de Daimler-Benz AG s'élèvera à une voiture. Qui aura commandé une Mercedes avant 1939 devra faire preuve de patience : le délai de livraison est d'une guerre mondiale !

Très vite, la fabrication couvre tout le registre de l'art de la guerre : voitures et camions tout-terrain, pièces d'avions et de fusées, moteurs pour projecteurs, bateaux et avions – de 1936 à 1945, les usines de Genshagen et de Berlin-Marienfelde produisent surtout 80 000 moteurs d'avion. Les produits de Daimler-Benz ne battent pas toujours ceux de la concurrence : pour un blindé de combat, par exemple, elle doit s'avouer vaincue par rapport à MAN et même fabriquer une copie de ce produit à Marienfelde. Dans ses propres rangs, un camion diesel de trois tonnes, le LGF, fait l'objet de sarcasmes : il est si lourd, dit-on, qu'il a suffisamment à faire avec lui-même et ne peut pas, en plus, transporter des charges.

Logiquement, c'est un concurrent, Opel, qui obtient l'adjudication. Le « Blitz » de Opel à Rüsselsheim, un camion à essence, mais léger, vif et d'une polyvalence inhabituelle pour la guerre, est construit selon des méthodes américaines à l'usine Mercedes de Mannheim, mais seulement à partir de 1944. Ce double camouflet est difficile à assimiler pour l'ambitieux Wilhelm Kissel. Déjà affaibli, il meurt en juillet 1942. Son successeur sera Wilhelm Haspel (1898–1952), depuis 1932 chef de l'usine de Sindelfingen et, depuis 1935, membre adjoint du directoire dont il deviendra membre ordinaire en 1941.

Bien qu'il soit marié avec une « demi-juive », son choix reçoit la bénédiction expresse de la « direction géniale » (citation originale du rapport d'exercice de 1941). Haspel est, à de nombreux points de vue, aux antipodes de son rigide prédécesseur à l'esprit prussien ; tout aussi intraitable que lui sur la cause, il est bien plus souple dans la méthode, et d'un esprit plus ouvert ; toutefois, il fait preuve d'un manque de ponctualité aussi désarmant que charmant. Il doit reprendre un lourd héritage. Certes, sur le plan économique, l'entreprise va extrêmement bien en tant que pilier principal de l'industrie militaire allemande – en 1943 encore, des dividendes sont versés aux actionnaires, au total 23 millions de marks durant les quatre premières années de la guerre.

Une fois encore, l'industrie militaire « profite » des faiblesses de l'armée : à partir du moment où l'offensive

Untertürkheim factory after the air raid on 5 September 1944.

Werk Untertürkheim nach dem Angriff am 5. September 1944.

L'usine d'Untertürkheim après les bombardements du 5 septembre 1944.

"foreign workers," concentration camp inmates, and POWs – and with women who held their own everywhere.

In addition there was pressure from above – in both senses. The Allies' air supremacy increased until they enjoyed almost total dominance in the skies over Germany. The government consequently ordered that key positions should be evacuated.

Daimler-Benz complied, and took on the anonymity of inconspicuous cover addresses, stuffy caves, clammy galleries, or dark tunnels like the newly-completed "Lämmerbuckel" tunnel on the Geislingen Rise section of the highway. The final collapse of this coordinated chaos eventually occurred when total war was declared, and low-flying attack aircraft prevented all movements by road. In 1943 the Allied squadrons had a star in their sights: in April the Mannheim factory was attacked for the first time, in August Berlin-Marienfelde, in October Sindelfingen.

Initially it was possible, as it were, to staunch the cut eyes or bloody noses. In the second half of 1944, however, the knockout blow came: while Mannheim and Genshagen escaped the worst, Untertürkheim, Sindelfingen, and Marienfelde were razed to the ground. On 10 September, for example, American aircraft dropped 800 high-explosive bombs and 30,000 incendiary bombs on Daimler-Benz's Gaggenau factory with lethal precision and turned it into a smoldering ruin. Times such as these call for cunning. Wilhelm Haspel, together with a team of like-minded men with their gaze fixed beyond the current horrors of war, had long since been planning for peacetime. Orders to greet the victors with the consequences of a scorched earth policy were ignored or secretly sabotaged. When General Jodl signed the surrender document in Reims on 7 May 1945, German industry's pampered favorite was virtually in need of a life-support machine. The war had cost the lives of 2483 employees, and a further 816 were missing. Assets to the value of half a billion marks had been destroyed.

The rise and fall of Daimler-Benz AG had taken less than 20 years.

nal dringlich bemerkbar: Bereits das erste Jahr des Krieges dezimiert die »Gefolgschaft« buchstäblich: Zehn Prozent werden zum Dienst an der Waffe herangezogen, die immer wieder und immer weiter aufreißenden Vakanzen später notdürftig mit »Fremdarbeitern«, KZ-Häftlingen und Kriegsgefangenen gefüllt – und mit Frauen, die überall ihren Mann stehen.

Dazu kommt Druck von oben – im doppelten Sinne. Die Lufthoheit der Alliierten nimmt zu bis hin zur totalen Beherrschung des Himmels über Deutschland. Als Konsequenz daraus befiehlt die Führung, Schlüsselpositionen auszulagern.

Daimler-Benz pariert, bezieht die Anonymität unauffälliger Tarnadressen, stickiger Höhlen, klammer Stollen oder finsterer Röhren wie des just vollendeten Autobahntunnels »Lämmerbuckel« im Zuge der Geislinger Steige. Die Koordination des Chaos kollabiert spätestens, als der totale Krieg ausgerufen wird und Tiefflieger jegliche Bewegung auf den Straßen unterbinden. Ab 1943 finden sich die Geschwader der Verbündeten zum Stern-Flug zusammen: Im April wird das Werk Mannheim erstmalig heimgesucht, im August Berlin-Marienfelde, im Oktober Sindelfingen.

Für diesmal können die Blessuren gleichsam ambulant behandelt werden. In der zweiten Hälfte des Jahres 1944 folgt jedoch das Knockout: Während Mannheim und Genshagen halbwegs ungeschoren davonkommen, werden Untertürkheim, Sindelfingen und Marienfelde in Schutt und Asche gelegt. Am 10. September etwa verwandeln amerikanische Flugzeuge das Daimler-Benz-Werk Gaggenau vermittels 800 Sprengbomben und 30 000 Brandbomben mit letaler Sorgfalt in eine schwelende Trümmerwüste. In Zeitläuften wie diesen schlägt die Stunde des Schlitzohrs: Längst plant Wilhelm Haspel mit einem verschworenen Team von Männern, die über den Tellerrand der schlimmen Tagesaktualität hinausblicken, für den Frieden. Viele Befehle, die Angriffsspitzen der Sieger mit den Folgen einer Politik der verbrannten Erde zu konfrontieren, stoßen ins Leere oder werden listig konterkariert. Als Generaloberst Jodl am 7. Mai 1945 in Reims die Kapitulationsurkunde unterschreibt, ist der deutschen Wirtschaft gehätschelter Liebling ohnehin schwer zur Ader gelassen: Der Krieg hat 2483 Mitarbeiter das Leben gekostet, 816 werden vermisst. Sachwerte in Höhe von einer halben Milliarde sind vernichtet.

Zwischen Aufstieg und Fall der Daimler-Benz AG haben nicht einmal zwanzig Jahre gelegen.

allemande se dissémine sur le front de l'Est, se posent les problèmes d'approvisionnement les plus divers. Dès 1938, se crée une filiale de Daimler-Benz à Königsberg. Le moteur d'avion DB 603 est monté près de Cracovie et de Vienne. En 1942, c'est au tour de l'usine d'équipements militaires de Minsk de voir le jour. Et, comme 300 000 voitures sont endommagées rien qu'à l'Est, il faut un ravitaillement logistique jusqu'à proximité du front, gigantesque puzzle aux innombrables pièces disparates.

On enregistre une dramatique et croissante pénurie de matières premières et des besoins immenses en matière de personnels qualifiés : la première année de la guerre, déjà, décime littéralement le personnel : 10 % sont envoyés au front et les places vacantes seront plus tard comblées, plutôt mal que bien, avec des « ouvriers étrangers », des détenus de camps de concentration et prisonniers de guerre – et des femmes qui doivent partout jouer le rôle des hommes.

À cela s'ajoute une pression qui vient d'en haut – dans le double sens du terme. La souveraineté aérienne des Alliés augmente jusqu'à devenir une maîtrise totale du ciel au-dessus de l'Allemagne. Par conséquent, les gouvernants ordonnent de transférer les positions clés.

Daimler-Benz prend ses précautions, recherche l'anonymat de banales adresses, de cavernes étouffantes, de souterrains poisseux ou de sombres refuges comme le tunnel autoroutier du « Lämmerbuckel » qui vient d'être achevé à Geislingen. Coordonner le chaos devient impossible dès que la guerre totale est proclamée et que les vols d'avions en rase-mottes interdisent tout mouvement sur les routes. À partir de 1943, les escadrilles des Alliés se concertent pour attaquer l'Allemagne : en avril, l'usine de Mannheim est bombardée pour la première fois, en août, celle de Berlin-Marienfelde et en octobre, celle de Sindelfingen.

Au début, on peut panser ses blessures. Mais, durant la seconde moitié de 1944, le chaos est fatal : tandis que Mannheim et Genshagen s'en tirent à peu près bien, Untertürkheim, Sindelfingen et Marienfelde sont réduites en cendres. Le 10 septembre, des avions américains transforment l'usine Daimler-Benz de Gaggenau en un désert de ruines après avoir largué 800 bombes explosives et 30 000 bombes incendiaires. C'est à une époque comme celle-là que sonne l'heure des rusés : il y a longtemps que Wilhelm Haspel prend ses mesures en vue de la paix, avec une équipe soudée d'hommes qui voient plus loin que la grave actualité quotidienne. De nombreux ordres donnés pour confronter les premières troupes des vainqueurs aux conséquences d'une politique de la terre brûlée ne sont pas exécutés ou astucieusement pris à contre-pied. Lorsque le général Jodl signe le traité de capitulation, le 7 mai 1945 à Reims, l'enfant favori de l'économie allemande est pratiquement exsangue : la guerre a coûté la vie à 2483 collaborateurs et 816 sont portés disparus. Des équipements pour un montant d'un demi-milliard de marks ont été anéantis.

Entre l'essor et la décadence de la Daimler-Benz AG, il ne s'est même pas écoulé vingt ans.

Back to the future 1945–1952

It was meant to last a thousand years, but was in ruins after only twelve: Germany was poor as never before. People foraged and hoarded, pinched coal, and paid huge sums on the black market for half a pound of real coffee or a carton of Lucky Strike.

While Wolfgang Borchert's Beckmann was *The Man Outside* and a thin-as-a-rake Gerd Fröbe was starving as Joe Bloggs, the German automotive industry began the job of rising from the ruins. There was a lot to be done: in 1946 there were only 192,000 cars left in the West zones (not including Berlin). The statistics show the response: in 1956 there were 2.1 million, in 1966 10.3 million, and by 1976 18.9 million. 26 million cars occupied the roads of the Federal Republic in 1986. In 1949 Carl-Otto Windecker stated in ADAC *Motorwelt* that Germans needed vehicles "with at least as much comfort, convenience and taste as our homes". However, the entry into the motorized world was via the motorcycle, scooter and the bubble car made by the likes of Champion, Maico, Fulda- and Goggomobile, Victoria Spatz, Heinkel and Kleinschnittger until well into the Fifties.

The traditional Mercedes catchment area was and is far removed from this domain of automobile gnomes. Furthermore, after the severe illnesses of the last years of the war, Daimler-Benz was declared clinically dead. From his office in Untertürkheim Mercedes boss Wilhelm Haspel looked out on a scene of staggeringly thorough destruction in which scarcely one stone had been left standing on another. This was exactly the sort of surly vision hatched up by Henry Morgenthau Jr. at the second Quebec conference in September 1944. His remarkable paper called for the Germans to be turned into a nation of farmers when they were emerging from the "blood and soil" frenzy of the Third Reich, and colored American occupation policy until mid-1947 via Directive ICS 1067. In line with this dismal plan, former company employees under Albert Friedrich, one-time head of the aeroengine department, created a customized vehicle in Schwäbisch-Gmünd, the Unimog (standing for Universelles Motor Gerät or universal motorized device), a fantastically versatile companion in forest and field as a tractor, a transport vehicle and an almost indestructible workhorse. It was initially built at Erhardt & Söhne who also took care of the funding together with Friedrich and the shoe manufacturer Cotta in Faurndau. The castings came from Gebrüder Boehringer in Göppingen, the engines from Mercedes, from the 170 V originally and then, from 1947 onwards, from the 170 D. In October 1946 a chassis was ready and in December a cab. The Unimog was premiered at the exhibition of the German Agricultural Society (DLG) in Frankfurt in August 1948 and received such positive reviews that in September 1950 Daimler-Benz decided to manufacture and distribute the surrogate offspring. In June 1950 the Unimog bore the star

Zurück in die Zukunft 1945–1952

Tausend Jahre hat es halten sollen, aber schon nach zwölfen liegt es in Scherben: Das Reich ist arm wie nie zuvor. Man »fringst« und hamstert, der Kohlenklau geht um, und auf dem schwarzen Markt werden Unsummen für ein halbes Pfund Bohnenkaffee oder eine Stange Lucky Strike lockergemacht.

Während Wolfgang Borcherts Beckmann *Draußen vor der Tür* wartet und ein klapperdürrer Gerd Fröbe als Otto Normalverbraucher darbt, rappelt sich die deutsche Autoindustrie aus Ruinen auf. Es gibt viel zu tun: 1946 beträgt der Bestand an Personenwagen in den Westzonen (ohne Berlin) 192 000. Wie man es anpackt, belegt die Statistik: 1956 sind es 2,1 Millionen, 1966 zählt man 10,3 Millionen, 1976 bereits 18,9 Millionen. 1986 bevölkern 26 Millionen Autos die Republik. Noch 1949 fordert Carl-Otto Windecker in der ADAC *Motorwelt*, der Deutsche brauche Fahrzeuge, »die zum mindesten soviel Komfort, Bequemlichkeit und Geschmack aufweisen wie unsere Wohnungen«. Bis weit in die fünfziger Jahre findet indes der Einstieg in die Motorisierung über das Motorrad, den Roller und das Bubble Car vom Schlage der Champion, Maico, Fulda- und Goggomobile, Victoria Spatz, Heinkel und Kleinschnittger statt.

Von dieser Domäne automobiler Gnome ist der traditionelle Mercedes-Einzugsbereich weit entfernt. Überdies bescheinigt man dem Patienten Daimler-Benz nach dem schweren Siechtum der letzten Kriegsjahre gleichsam den klinischen Tod. Von seinem Büro in Untertürkheim schaut Direktor Wilhelm Haspel auf ein Szenario penibel perfektionierter Zerstörung: kaum dass ein Stein auf dem anderen liegt. So etwas passt genau in die unwirschen Visionen von Henry Morgenthau dem Jüngeren, ausgeheckt auf der zweiten Konferenz von Quebec im September 1944: Dessen bemerkenswerte Denkschrift sieht vor, die Deutschen aus dem Kater nach dem Blut- und Bodenrausch des Dritten Reichs als Volk von Ackerbauern und Viehzüchtern erwachen zu lassen, und färbt über die Direktive ICS 1067 bis Mitte 1947 die amerikanische Besatzungspolitik. Für dieses triste Konzept schaffen ehemalige Mitarbeiter des Konzerns um Albert Friedrich, einst Leiter der Flugmotorenabteilung, in Schwäbisch Gmünd ein Mobil nach Maß, den Unimog (für Universelles Motor Gerät), Tausendsassa und Multitalent in Wald und Flur als Schlepper, Transportfahrzeug und schier unverwüstliches Arbeitstier. Stätte der Fertigung ist anfänglich die Firma Erhardt & Söhne, die zusammen mit Friedrich und dem Schuhfabrikanten Cotta zu Faurndau auch für die Finanzierung sorgt. Die Gussteile stammen von den Gebrüdern Boehringer in Göppingen, die Motoren von Mercedes, zunächst vom 170 V, ab 1947 vom 170 D. Im Oktober 1946 ist ein Fahrgestell fertig, im Dezember ein Fahrerhaus. Premiere hat der Unimog bei der Ausstellung der Deutschen Landwirtschafts-Gesellschaft (DLG) im August 1948 in Frankfurt und heimst der-

Retour vers le futur 1945–1952

Il était censé durer mille ans, mais au bout de douze ans, déjà, il était réduit en cendres : le Reich est pauvre comme jamais auparavant dans son histoire. On « truande » et fait des stocks, le vol de charbon est une pratique répandue et, sur le marché noir, on débourse des sommes inimaginables pour une livre de café moulu ou une cartouche de Lucky Strike.

Tandis que le Beckmann de Wolfgang Borchert attend *Dehors devant la porte* et qu'un Gerd Fröbe, maigre comme un clou, joue des rôles d'Allemand moyen, l'industrie automobile allemande se relève de ses décombres. Et il y a du pain sur la planche : en 1946, le parc automobile des zones occidentales (sans Berlin) compte 192 000 voitures. Les statistiques prouvent que l'on s'est rapidement attelé à la tâche : en 1956, leur nombre est de 2,1 millions, de 10,3 millions en 1966 et déjà de 18,9 millions en 1976. En 1986, 26 millions de voitures roulent sur les routes allemandes. En 1949 encore, Carl-Otto Windecker rappelle, dans l'ADAC-*Motorwelt*, que les Allemands ont besoin de voitures « qui offrent au minimum autant de confort, de chaleur et de goût que nos appartements ». Jusqu'à une date avancée des années 1950, l'accès à la motorisation s'effectue pourtant par le biais de la moto, du scooter et des voiturettes du gabarit des Champion, Maico, Fuldamobil et Goggomobil ou autres Victoria Spatz, Heinkel et Kleinschnittger.

Les sphères dans lesquelles Mercedes recrute traditionnellement sa clientèle sont à des années-lumière de ces gnomes à roulettes. En outre, après la longue agonie des dernières années de guerre, on diagnostique simultanément au patient Daimler-Benz la mort clinique. De son bureau d'Untertürkheim, son directeur Wilhelm Haspel embrasse un scénario de destruction mis en œuvre avec une perfection de fonctionnaire : il n'y a pratiquement plus aucune pierre debout. Ce qui concorde exactement avec les brutales visions d'un certain Henry Morgenthau junior, concoctées lors de la deuxième conférence de Québec, en septembre 1944 : son mémorandum historique prévoit de guérir les Allemands de la terreur sanguinaire du IIIe Reich en en faisant un peuple de paysans et d'éleveurs, et il dictera la politique d'occupation américaine par le biais de la directive ICS 1067 jusqu'à l'été 1947. Prenant acte, d'anciens collaborateurs du groupe réunis autour d'Albert Friedrich, autrefois directeur du département moteurs d'avion, réalisent à Schwäbisch Gmünd un véhicule taillé sur mesure, l'Unimog (acronyme de « appareil à moteur universel »), véritable bête de somme aux multiples talents en forêt et en campagne comme tracteur, véhicule de transport et portefaix absolument indestructible. Il est initialement fabriqué par la firme Erhardt & Söhne, qui en assume aussi le financement conjointement avec Friedrich et le fabricant de chaussures Cotta zu Faurndau. Les pièces en fonte sont fournies par les frères Boehringer à Göppingen, les moteurs par Mercedes. Ce sont tout d'abord

badge for the first time, showing that it had finally been adopted. And there is still no end in sight for this most special of post-war careers.

Another thing that Haspel saw was that clearing-up and building work were going on in front of his window. Faced with the imposing size of the rubble heap which recognized no classes, positions in society vanished. The simple manual wage-earner with the most rudimentary of tools worked side-by-side with the salaried office worker. And as Mr. Morgenthau's twilight of the gods vision faded, a rosy dawn glow appeared on the horizon. On 6 September 1946 the American Secretary of State James Francis Byrnes delivered a speech in Stuttgart in which he gave German industry the green light for peaceful activities.

That was a sign of encouragement, as were the proposals of his compatriot George Catlett Marshall relating to containing the Eastern bloc by strengthening the resistance of European states. The Marshall Plan became law on 3 April 1948 three months after Haspel had become chairman of the board of management again after a brief exile. The situation was as follows: in a capital questionnaire "Fragebogen" action in July 1945 the Americans investigated the political past of the Daimler-Benz management. The outcome was that almost the entire management of the company had to go, a severe case of blood-letting. Haspel remained initially until Hans Rummel, the chairman of the supervisory board, received a plain letter from the military government on 25 October of the same year. The content was short and painful: "As a result of the *Fragebogen* action you are hereby directed to dismiss Dr. ing. Wilhelm Haspel from employment in the services of the Daimler-Benz AG." Haspel, who had headed the special committee for aero-engines during the war and had come to the attention of the denazification authorities for this reason, needed two years to regain his lost honor. During this interregnum the company was managed by a triumvirate: Carl Jahr, Otto Hoppe and Walter Kaufmann. In the same period the work force of the company's five factories in the West, i.e. in Untertürkheim, Sindelfingen, Mannheim, Gaggenau and Berlin-Marienfelde grew from 12,849 (at the end of 1945) to 20,241 (at the end of 1947) while sales fell from 130.4 million to 99 million Reichsmarks. Money! This was not just a subject to talk about; the company had plenty of it too. 250 million Reichsmarks were piled up in accounts in Stuttgart banks at the time of the surrender. To this must be added revenue from the repair workshop for US Army vehicles in Untertürkheim. Spares were manufactured in Marienfelde for Soviet Army vehicles, and the sale of a plot of land in the Buckower Chaussee to the city authorities in Berlin also yielded a certain amount. In advance of the currency reform of 21 June 1948 the Reichsmark looked good, but in the harsh light of the restructuring of the German monetary system Mercedes' balance fell from 108 million old marks to 13 million new German marks.

There were shortages of skilled workers, coal, electricity, production equipment, rolling mill products, textiles,

Wilhelm Haspel, chairman of the board of directors from 1942 to 1945 and from 1948 to the beginning of 1952.
Wilhelm Haspel, Vorstandsvorsitzender zwischen 1942 und 1945 und von 1948 bis Anfang 1952.
Wilhelm Haspel, président du directoire de 1942 à 1945 et de 1948 au début de 1952.

artig positive Rezensionen ein, dass sich Daimler-Benz im September 1950 zu Herstellung und Vertrieb des extern aufgewachsenen Sprösslings entschließt. Im Juni 1950 führt der Unimog zum erstenmal den Stern im Schilde und ist damit endgültig adoptiert, eine Nachkriegskarriere der besonderen Art, deren Ende noch heute nicht abzusehen ist.

Was Haspel auch sieht: dass vor seinem Fenster aufgeräumt und aufgebaut wird. Angesichts der klassenübergreifenden Majestät des großen Schutthaufens schwinden die Standesunterschiede. Der einfache Arbeiter schuftet mit simpelstem Werkzeug neben dem höheren Angestellten. Und in dem Maße, in dem die Götterdämmerung des Mister Morgenthau verblasst, zeigt sich am Horizont rosige Morgenröte. Am 6. September 1946 hält der amerikanische Außenminister James Francis Byrnes in Stuttgart eine programmatische Rede, in welcher er der deutschen Industrie grünes Licht gibt für friedfertige Aktivitäten.

Das ermutigt, ebenso wie die Vorstellungen seines Landsmanns George Catlett Marshall, die Eindämmung des Ostblocks durch Stärkung der Widerstandskraft der europäischen Staaten betreffend. Am 3. April 1948 wird der Marshall-Plan Gesetz, drei Monate, nachdem Haspel nach kurzem Exil wieder den Vorstandsvorsitz übernommen hat. Das aber kommt so: In einer hochnotpeinlichen Fragebogenaktion durchleuchten die Amerikaner im Juli 1945 die politische Vergangenheit des Daimler-Kaders. Konsequenz: Fast die gesamte Führung der Firma muss gehen, ein schwerer Aderlass. Haspel bleibt zunächst, bis den Vorsitzenden des Aufsichtsrats Hans Rummel am 25. Oktober desselben Jahres ein schmuckloses Schreiben der Militärregierung ereilt. Die Botschaft ist knapp und schmerzlich:

ceux de la 170 V et, à partir de 1947, de la 170 D. En octobre 1946, un châssis est terminé et, en décembre, une cabine. L'Unimog fête sa première lors du Salon de la Société allemande de l'agriculture (DLG) en août 1948 à Francfort et remporte un tel succès d'estime que Daimler-Benz décide, en septembre 1950, de fabriquer et distribuer le « rejeton », ainsi conçu en dehors de la famille. En juin 1950, l'Unimog arbore pour la première fois l'étoile sur son capot et est donc définitivement adopté ; une carrière d'après-guerre d'un genre tout particulier et dont la fin n'est pas encore prévisible aujourd'hui.

Mais Haspel voit aussi autre chose : devant sa fenêtre, on dégage et reconstruit. Compte tenu de la majesté du gigantesque tas de décombres échappant à toute classification, les différences de classe disparaissent elles aussi. Le simple ouvrier travaille avec l'outillage le plus fruste à côté de l'employé supérieur. Et, au fur et à mesure que pâlit le crépuscule des dieux dépeint par Mister Morgenthau, on voit apparaître à l'horizon de premières lueurs d'argent. Le 6 septembre 1946, le ministre américain des Affaires étrangères, James Francis Byrnes, tient, à Stuttgart, une allocution programmatique dans laquelle il donne à l'industrie allemande le feu vert pour des activités pacifiques.

Cela est encourageant, au même titre que les conceptions de son compatriote George Catlett Marshall concernant l'endiguement du bloc oriental en renforçant la capacité de résistance des États européens. Le 3 avril 1948, le plan Marshall prend force de loi, trois mois après que Haspel, à l'issue d'un bref exil, a de nouveau été nommé à la présidence du directoire. Que s'était-il passé ? À l'issue d'une enquête par questionnaires extrêmement pénible, les Américains passent au criblent, en juillet 1945, le passé politique des cadres de Daimler-Benz. Conséquence : presque toute la direction de la firme doit démissionner, une grave hémorragie. Haspel reste tout d'abord jusqu'à ce que le président du conseil de surveillance, Hans Rummel, reçoive, le 25 octobre de la même année, une brève lettre du gouvernement militaire l'enjoignant de démettre Haspel. Sa teneur est concise, mais douloureuse : « As a result of the *Fragebogen* action you are hereby directed to dismiss Dr ing. Wilhelm Haspel from employment in the services of the Daimler-Benz AG. » Ayant été, durant la guerre, directeur de la division spéciale pour les moteurs d'avion et, à ce titre, pris dans le collimateur des « dénazificateurs », celui-ci aura besoin de deux ans pour restaurer son honneur perdu. Durant cet interrègne, un triumvirat dirige l'entreprise : Carl Jahr, Otto Hoppe et Walter Kaufmann. Durant la même période, les effectifs des cinq usines occidentales du groupe – à Untertürkheim, Sindelfingen, Mannheim, Gaggenau et Berlin-Marienfelde – passent de 12 849 (fin 1945) à 20 241 (fin 1947) alors que le chiffre d'affaires chute de 130,4 millions à 99 millions de reichsmarks. On ne parle pas seulement de cet argent, on l'a bel et bien : 250 millions de reichsmarks sont déposés sur des comptes à Stuttgart au moment de la capitulation. À cela s'ajoutent les recettes des entreprises de réparation

and raw materials such as rubber. Potential customers were still requested for a long time to obtain their tires elsewhere. Production of the third-party product, the Opel Blitz, in Mannheim only paused for a short time. The contract with the Rüsselsheim-based General Motors subsidiary was even repeatedly extended until mid-1949 while one of the company's own projects for a three-and-a-half-ton diesel vehicle had to be shelved until then.

Permission was granted as early as November 1945 to build the 170 v again, though only the commercial vehicle version, and then in the spring of 1946 this was extended to include the four-door saloon. Even so, a meager 214 units were sold in that year. Even prominent people such as the Speaker of the Lower Saxony State Parliament, Karl Olfers, only received their 170 v after presenting the necessary coupon. It was only in October 1947 that production of the 1000th car after the war was celebrated, and not until February 1949 that 1000 cars were manufactured in a month.

By this time Haspel, who never stopped shaping the company's fortunes as an éminence grise in the wings, had gathered some hand-picked staff around him. Fritz Nallinger had returned from France where his experience in building turbines was being used. Otto Jacob was poached from Opel as the Purchasing Manager and Heinrich Wagner as the head of the Mannheim and Gaggenau factories. Haspel confidant Rolf P. G. Staelin took responsibility for distribution. For a while (1947–1951) Reinhold Maier, the respected Prime Minister of Württemberg-Baden remained an honorary member of the supervisory board and prevented what was charmingly termed "reallocation" in the linguistic usage of the time, i.e. the transfer of individual divisions to new companies. Haspel steered the company magnificently through the reefs and rocks of the monetary markets of those years: a bridging loan of ten million marks from Deutsche Bank, Dresdner Bank and Commerzbank was matched by finance from the insurance industry. Later, once money started flowing more freely again, funding was also provided by Kreditanstalt für Wiederaufbau (the Reconstruction Loan Corporation) and Württembergische Girozentrale.

Wilhelm Haspel lived to see two conspicuous successes: the 170 s and 170 D models and the L 3500 truck proved real winners in the eyes of the public both during and after their launch at the International Export Fair in Hanover in May 1949. This showed that the company was on the right path.

"A little over?" was the oft-heard refrain of the time to tempt customers at the butcher's, grocer's or greengrocer's, and the ever more common answer was "yes". A brisk breeze began to fill the sails of the economy, and Daimler-Benz also joined the fleet. The six-cylinder 220 and 300 models at the 1951 Frankfurt International Motor Show were some of the eminent fixtures of the budding economic miracle.

Just a short time later, however, the pilot who had steered Daimler-Benz safely through the choppy seas of the immediate post-war period left the ship when Wilhelm

»As a result of the *Fragebogen* action you are hereby directed to dismiss Dr. ing. Wilhelm Haspel from employment in the services of the Daimler-AG.« Zwei Jahre benötigt dieser, während des Krieges Leiter des Sonderausschusses für die Flugmotoren und deshalb ins Visier der Entnazifizierer geraten, seine verlorene Ehre wiederherzustellen. Während dieses Interregnums leitet ein Triumvirat das Unternehmen: Carl Jahr, Otto Hoppe und Walter Kaufmann. Im gleichen Zeitraum wächst die Belegschaft der fünf West-Werke des Konzerns in Untertürkheim, Sindelfingen, Mannheim, Gaggenau und Berlin-Marienfelde von 12 849 (Ende 1945) auf 20 241 (Ende 1947), während der Umsatz von 130,4 Millionen auf 99 Millionen Reichsmark sinkt. Geld – davon spricht man nicht nur, sondern man hat es auch: 250 Millionen Reichsmark liegen zum Zeitpunkt der Kapitulation auf Stuttgarter Konten. Dazu kommen Einnahmen aus dem Reparaturbetrieb für Fahrzeuge der US-Armee in Untertürkheim. In Marienfelde werden Ersatzteile für Mobile der Sowjet-Armee hergestellt, und auch der Verkauf eines Grundstücks an der Buckower Chaussee an die Stadt Berlin wirft einiges ab. Im Vorfeld der Währungsreform vom 21. Juni 1948 sitzt die Reichsmark locker: Im scharfen Licht der Neuordnung des deutschen Geldwesens welkt das Mercedes-Altgeldguthaben von 108 Millionen zu 13 Millionen neudeutschen Mark.

Woran es mangelt: Facharbeiter, Kohle, Strom, Produktionseinrichtungen, Walzwerkerzeugnisse, Textilien, Rohmaterialien wie Gummi. Noch lange ersucht man potentielle Kunden, sich ihre Reifen anderswo zu beschaffen. Nur kurz ruht die Herstellung des Fremd-Produkts Opel Blitz in Mannheim. Der Vertrag mit der Rüsselsheimer General-Motors-Filiale wird sogar sukzessive bis Mitte 1949 verlängert, während ein eigenes Projekt, ein Dreieinhalbtonner-Diesel, bis dahin auf Eis gelegt werden muss.

Schon im November 1945 wird die Genehmigung erteilt, den 170 v wieder zu bauen, allerdings lediglich in seinen Nutz-Varianten, und im Frühjahr 1946 auf den viertürigen Innenlenker erweitert. Gleichwohl bleibt es in jenem Jahr bei kargen 214 Einheiten. Selbst Prominenz wie der Präsident des niedersächsischen Landtags Karl Olfers erhält ihren 170 v nur gegen einen Bezugschein. Erst im Oktober 1947 feiert man das Wiegenfest des 1000. Personenwagens nach dem Krieg, erst im Februar 1949 die Herstellung von 1000 Autos in einem Monat.

Da hat Haspel, der ohnehin nie aufhörte, als graue Eminenz hinter den Kulissen die Geschicke der Firma mitzugestalten, bereits handverlesene Mitarbeiter um sich geschart: Aus Frankreich, wo man seine Erfahrungen im Turbinenbau anzuzapfen wusste, ist Fritz Nallinger zurückgekehrt. Von Opel abgeworben wurden Otto Jacob als Leiter des Einkaufs und Heinrich Wagner als Chef der Werke Mannheim und Gaggenau. Haspel-Intimus Rolf P. G. Staelin kümmert sich um den Vertrieb. Eine Zeitlang (1947–1951) verweilt Reinhold Maier, der allgemein geschätzte Ministerpräsident von Württemberg-Baden, ehrenamtlich im Aufsichtsrat und verhindert, was im

pour les véhicules de l'armée américaine à Untertürkheim. À Marienfelde, on fabrique des pièces de rechange pour les véhicules de l'armée soviétique, et même la vente d'un terrain sur la Buckower Chaussee à la ville de Berlin procure une somme non négligeable. En amont de la réforme monétaire du 21 juin 1948, le reichsmark n'a pas un très grand avenir : à la lumière brutale de la réorganisation du système monétaire allemand, le trésor de guerre de Mercedes voit sa valeur chuter de 108 millions à 13 millions de nouveaux deutsche marks.

Mais on manque de tout : d'ouvriers spécialisés, de charbon, de courant électrique, d'équipements de production, de produits de laminage, de textiles, de matériaux bruts comme le caoutchouc. Pendant longtemps, on recommande encore aux clients potentiels de se procurer ailleurs leurs pneumatiques. La fabrication de l'Opel Blitz, ce produit étranger, n'est interrompue que brièvement à Mannheim. Le contrat signé avec la filiale de General Motors à Rüsselsheim est même prorogé successivement jusqu'à la mi-1949 tandis qu'un projet maison, un diesel de 3,5 tonnes, doit être mis au placard jusqu'à cette date.

Dès novembre 1945, Mercedes obtient l'autorisation de construire de nouveau la 170 v, mais seulement dans ses variantes utilitaires et, au printemps 1946, cette autorisation est étendue à la conduite intérieure à quatre portes. Néanmoins, on n'en construit cette année-là, en tout et pour tout, que 214 exemplaires. Même des personnalités comme le président de la Diète régionale de Basse-Saxe, Karl Olfers, n'obtiennent leur 170 v que contre un ticket d'approvisionnement. Ce n'est qu'en octobre 1947 que l'on fête la naissance de la 1000ᵉ voiture de tourisme de l'après-guerre et il faudra attendre février 1949 pour que l'on fabrique 1000 voitures par mois.

À ce moment-là, Haspel, qui n'a de toute façon jamais cessé de continuer à présider aux destinées de la firme en tant qu'éminence grise, a déjà réuni autour de lui des collaborateurs triés sur le volet : Fritz Nallinger est revenu de France, où l'on avait su mettre à profit ses expériences dans la construction de turbines. Il a recruté chez Opel Otto Jacob comme directeur des achats et Heinrich Wagner comme chef des usines de Mannheim et de Gaggenau. Un intime de Haspel, Rolf P. G. Staelin, se charge de la distribution. Pendant un certain temps (1947–1951), Reinhold Maier, ministre président du Bade-Wurtemberg, apprécié de tous, est membre à titre bénévole du conseil de surveillance et empêche ce que dans le jargon de cette époque on nomme par un bel euphémisme, le « démembrement » : la réaffectation de secteurs particuliers d'une entreprise à de nouvelles sociétés. Haspel gouverne souverainement l'entreprise à travers les récifs et les tourbillons du marché monétaire de ces années-là : à un crédit de transition de dix millions de marks accordé par la Deutsche Bank, la Dresdner Bank et la Commerzbank s'ajoutent des ressources d'un même montant fournies par des compagnies d'assurances. Plus tard, lorsque les sources d'argent sont de nouveau plus généreuses, il met à profit les crédits de

Haspel died of the effects of a brain hemorrhage on 6 January 1952. Reconstruction had been a joint effort, an interplay between the individual and the collective determined by necessity, and his loss was therefore deeply felt.

A gentle flow of exports first had to pass through the eye of the Allied monitoring agencies' needles identified by their acronyms JEA (Joint Export Agency) and OFFICOMEX (Office du Commerce Extérieur) until things became a little easier after the dismantling of the barriers between the French and British occupation zones on 1 August 1948. A further obstacle came in the form of the unfavorable exchange rate with the dollar, initially DM 3.33, rising to DM 4.20 with effect from 28 September 1949.

This changed and still-changing background and the popularity of the new models formed a fertile soil from which Mercedes exports ran wild, from sales of 6.1 million marks in 1949 to 66.6 million marks in 1950. The man with his hand on the tiller now was Arnold Wychodil, Haspel's right-hand man from 1949 and a member of the board of management between 1952 and 1972. 1950 was a key year in which spectacular successes were recorded. More than a quarter of the export revenue came from Sweden where the go-getting agent Gunnar Valfried Philipson was active on the company's behalf. Moritz Straus, a former board of management member at Horch AG, set up an import company in Zurich.

As early as October 1949 a three-million-dollar deal with Brazil came up for the supply of 1000 unassembled truck chassis. This was followed a year later by a further large-scale order for 2000 trucks, 500 buses and 1500 cars. During a visit to Stuttgart the Argentinian Jorge Antonio presented a license from the Perón government for the import of 100 cars (40 of which were diesel taxis, the first of the famous gasoleros in Buenos Aires) together with five buses and five trucks and in July he founded Mercedes-Benz Argentina which originally had the status of a limited liability company before becoming a public limited company in 1952. Its most famous board of management member a few years later was the five-times world racing champion Juan Manuel Fangio.

By this time India had already displaced Argentina as the no. 1 market for Mercedes. The first moves in this direction went down in the Untertürkheim in-house jargon as the "Birla-Keil tragedy". An emissary of the Hindustan Motors Company, a subsidiary of the Birla Group, claimed that his company was interested in importing Daimler-Benz trucks in disassembled form. Hans Hugo Keil, a childhood friend of Wilhelm Haspel, traveled to Calcutta to check the situation. There was to be no happy ending, however, as the Indian Army had no such requirement for the ordered diesel trucks as claimed.

There was successful cooperation, on the other hand, with the "Indian Krupp", J.R.D. Tata, whose Tata Engineering and Locomotive Company Ltd. (Telco) manufactured Mercedes-Tata trucks in Jamshedpur between 1954 and 1969, 60,000 up to 1962, and 21,000 in 1968 alone. The care-

Sprachgebrauch der Zeit charmant »Entflechtung« genannt wird: die Zuordnung einzelner Teilbereiche zu neuen Gesellschaften. Souverän laviert Haspel das Unternehmen durch die Riffs und Klippen des monetären Markts jener Jahre: Zu einem Überbrückungskredit der Deutschen Bank, Dresdner Bank und Commerzbank von zehn Millionen Mark addieren sich Mittel aus dem Versicherungswesen in gleicher Höhe. Später, als die Geldquellen wieder ergiebiger sprudeln, kommen Darlehen der Kreditanstalt für Wiederaufbau und der Württembergische Girozentrale hinzu.

Zwei besondere Triumphe sind Wilhelm Haspel vergönnt: Die Modelle 170 S und 170 D sowie der Lastkraftwagen L 3500 erweisen sich während und nach ihrer Präsentation auf der Internationalen Exportmesse Hannover im Mai 1949 als wahre Renner in der Gunst des Publikums. Das zeigt, dass man auf dem rechten Wege ist.

»Darf es ein bisschen mehr sein?« kommt es damals lockend vom Schlachter, Kolonialwaren- oder Südfrüchtehändler, und immer häufiger heißt die Antwort ja. Eine flotte Brise beginnt die Segel des Konjunkturschiffs zu blähen, und dem mag man sich auch bei Daimler- nicht entziehen: Die Sechszylinder 220 und 300 auf der Frankfurter IAA von 1951 gehören schon zu den gehobenen Requisiten des knospenden Wirtschaftswunders. Wenig später aber geht der Lotse von Bord, der das Unternehmen Daimler- sicher durch die ruppige See der unmittelbaren Nachkriegszeit geleitet hat: Am 6. Januar 1952 stirbt Wilhelm Haspel an den Folgen einer Gehirnblutung. Der Wiederaufbau war eine konzertierte Aktion, ein von der Not abgestimmtes Wechselspiel zwischen dem einzelnen und dem Kollektiv. Und so ist die Anteilnahme groß.

Ein gemächlich anlaufender Export muss sich zunächst durch das Nadelöhr alliierter Kontrollinstanzen mit den klingenden Kürzeln JEA (für Joint Export Agency) und OFFICOMEX (für Office du Commerce Extérieur) quetschen, bis nach der Demontage der Schlagbäume zwischen dem französisch besetzten Teil und der anglophonen Bizone am 1. August 1948 mehr Freiheit gelassen wird. Ein anderes Hindernis: der ungünstige Wechselkurs zum Dollar, zunächst 3,33 Mark, vom 28. September 1949 an 4,20 Mark.

Dieses gewandelte und sich wandelnde Umfeld und die Popularität der neuen Modelle bilden einen Nährboden, auf dem die Mercedes-Ausfuhren förmlich ins Kraut schießen, von einem Umsatz von 6,1 Millionen Mark 1949 auf 66,6 Millionen Mark 1950. Mann an den Hebeln ist Arnold Wychodil, Haspels rechte Hand ab 1949 und zwischen 1952 und 1972 Mitglied des Vorstands. An das Schlüsseljahr 1950 knüpfen sich spektakuläre Erfolge. Mehr als ein Viertel der Exporterlöse stammt aus Schweden, wo der umtriebige Agent Gunnar Valfried Philipson zum Wohle der Firma wirkt. In Zürich gründet Moritz Straus, ein ehemaliges Vorstandsmitglied der Horch AG, eine Importgesellschaft.

Schon im Oktober 1949 bahnt sich ein Drei-Millionen-Dollar-Deal mit Brasilien an, 1000 LKW-Chassis in Teilen.

l'Office de crédit à la reconstruction (KfW/Kreditanstalt für Wiederaufbau) et de la Württembergische Girozentrale.

Wilhelm Haspel a le plaisir d'assister à deux triomphes particuliers : durant et après la présentation au Salon international des exportations de Hanovre, en mai 1949, les modèles 170 S et 170 D ainsi que le camion L 3500 remportent un immense succès auprès du grand public, ce qui prouve que l'on est sur la bonne voie.

« Voulez-vous que je vous en mette un peu plus ? », s'entend-on dire alors fréquemment par le charcutier ou l'épicier en produits coloniaux et fruits exotiques. Et, de plus en plus souvent, la réponse est oui. Une bonne brise commence à gonfler les voiles du bateau de la conjoncture et chez Daimler-Benz non plus on ne veut pas y échapper : les six-cylindres 220 et 300 présentés à l'IAA de Francfort en 1951 appartiennent déjà aux accessoires de haut niveau d'un miracle économique encore bourgeonnant. Mais, un peu plus tard, le pilote qui a gouverné l'entreprise de Daimler-Benz en toute sécurité à travers la mer déchaînée de l'immédiate après-guerre quitte le bord : le 6 janvier 1952, Wilhelm Haspel décède des suites d'une hémorragie cérébrale. La reconstruction était une action concertée, une interaction bien coordonnée par la détresse entre l'individu et la collectivité. Et cela explique les nombreuses marques de sympathie.

Les rares produits d'exportation doivent tout d'abord franchir le chas d'aiguille des instances de contrôle alliées aux abréviations aussi ronflantes que JEA (Joint Export Agency) et OFFICOMEX (Office du commerce extérieur) en attendant que, après le démontage des barrières mobiles, la zone d'occupation française et la bizone anglophone, le 1er août 1948, autorisent une plus grande liberté. Autre obstacle : le taux de change défavorable par rapport au dollar, tout d'abord de 3,33 marks, puis de 4,20 marks à partir du 28 septembre 1949.

Cet environnement inhabituel et toujours en mutation ainsi que la popularité des nouveaux modèles constituent les étincelles grâce auxquelles les exportations de Mercedes explosent littéralement, le chiffre d'affaires passant de 6,1 millions de marks en 1949 à 66,6 millions en 1950. L'homme aux commandes est Arnold Wychodil, le bras droit de Haspel depuis 1949 et membre du directoire de 1952 à 1972. 1950, année clé, en est une de succès spectaculaires. Plus du quart des recettes d'exportations provient de Suède, où l'infatigable agent Gunnar Valfried Philipson œuvre pour le bien-être de la firme. À Zurich, Moritz Strauss, un ancien membre du directoire de Horch AG, fonde une société d'importation.

Dès octobre 1949 s'esquisse un contrat de trois millions de dollars avec le Brésil portant sur 1000 châssis de camion en pièces détachées. Il donne lieu, un an plus tard, à une autre commande géante : 2000 camions, 500 bus, 1500 voitures de tourisme. Lors d'une visite à Stuttgart, l'Argentin Jorge Antonio présente une autorisation du gouvernement Perón portant sur l'importation de 100 voitures de tourisme (dont 40 taxis diesel, les premiers des célèbres « Gasoleros »

Chancellor Konrad Adenauer on the Mercedes stand at the IAA in Frankfurt in 1951. To his right stands Wilhelm Haspel.

Bundeskanzler Konrad Adenauer auf dem Mercedes-Stand bei der IAA in Frankfurt 1951. Rechts neben ihm Wilhelm Haspel.

Le chancelier fédéral Konrad Adenauer sur le stand Mercedes à l'IAA de Francfort 1951. À droite, à côté de lui, Wilhelm Haspel.

fully negotiated Technical Aid Agreement (TAA) laid down the framework and procedures. Nine-tenths of the vehicle components were sourced within India. Director Sumant Moolgoakar was in charge on the Tata side, and the German project manager was Mercedes man Hans Stoehr who took 50 Daimler-Benz staff with him and set up an ex-pat village far from home with Swabian as the lingua franca and a corresponding infrastructure. There were periods when every second commercial vehicle in the Indian part of the sub-continent bore the Mercedes star–throughout its long, hard and deprived life.

When the agreement ended, the right to carry the Mercedes insignia also expired. Nonetheless, the joint venture with Stuttgart gave Tata such a start that it has continued to operate successfully as a company in its own right. The Mercedes connection is still remembered today with affection and nostalgia.

Er zieht ein Jahr später eine weitere Großbestellung nach sich: 2000 LKW, 500 Busse, 1500 PKW. Bei einem Besuch in Stuttgart legt der Argentinier Jorge Antonio eine Genehmigung der Regierung Perón zur Einfuhr von 100 PKW (davon 40 Diesel-Taxis, die ersten der berühmten »Gasoleros« in Buenos Aires) und je fünf Bussen und LKW vor und initiiert im Juli die Mercedes-Benz Argentina, welche ursprünglich den Status einer GmbH und ab 1952 einer Aktiengesellschaft hat. Ihr berühmtestes Vorstandsmitglied ein paar Jahre später: der fünffache Automobilweltmeister Juan Manuel Fangio.

Da hat bereits Indien Argentinien als Markt Nummer 1 für Mercedes abgelöst. Ein erster Anlauf in dieser Richtung geht in den Untertürkheimer Hausjargon als die »Birla-Keil-Tragödie« ein. Ein Emissär der Hindustan Motors Company, Subunternehmen der Birla-Gruppe, gibt vor, seine Firma sei daran interessiert, LKW von Daimler-Benz in zerlegter Form einzuführen. Als Gewährsmann reist Hans Hugo Keil nach Kalkutta, ein Jugendfreund Wilhelm Haspels. Aber die Sache geht schief: Für die bestellten Diesel-LKW besteht bei der indischen Armee überhaupt kein Bedarf, wie ursprünglich vorgeschützt.

Unter einem günstigen Vorzeichen steht hingegen die Kooperation mit dem »indischen Krupp« J.R.D. Tata, dessen Tata Engineering and Locomotive Company Ltd. (Telco) zwischen 1954 und 1969 in Jamshedpur Mercedes-Tata-LKW herstellt, 60 000 bis 1962, 1968 allein 21 000. Das sorgfältig ausgehandelte Abkommen TAA (für Technical Aid Agreement) regelt Rahmen und Prozedere. Neun Zehntel der Fahrzeugteile stammen aus dem Inland. Zuständig auf Tata-Seite ist Direktor Sumant Moolgoakar, deutscher Projektleiter der Mercedes-Mann Hans Stoehr, der 50 Daimler-Benz-Bedienstete mitnimmt und fern der Heimat ein Diaspora-Dorf mit der Verkehrssprache Schwäbisch und einer entsprechenden Infrastruktur gründet. Zeitweise trägt jedes zweite Nutzfahrzeug auf dem indschen Teil des Subkontinents den Stern – ein langes, hartes und entbehrungsreiches Autoleben lang.

Mit dem Auslaufen des Vertrages entfällt auch das Recht, die Mercedes-Insignien zu führen. Immerhin hat das Joint Venture mit den Stuttgartern der attraktiven Tata-Tochter einen solchen Drall mit auf den Weg gegeben, dass sie künftig als erfolgreiches Unternehmen eigenen Rechts weiterexistiert. An die Mercedes-Connection erinnert man sich noch heute mit Wohlwollen und Wehmut.

de Buenos Aires) et sur respectivement cinq autobus et camions. En juillet, il fonde Mercedes-Benz Argentina, qui a tout d'abord un statut de SARL et, à partir de 1952, de société anonyme. Le membre le plus célèbre de son directoire sera, quelques années plus tard, le quintuple champion du monde Formule 1 Juan Manuel Fangio.

Mais l'Inde a déjà supplanté l'Argentine comme marché numéro 1 pour Mercedes. Dans le jargon maison d'Untertürkheim, une première tentative faite dans cette direction porte le surnom de « tragédie de Birla Keil ». Un émissaire de Hindustan Motors Company, sous-entreprise du groupe Birla, prétend que sa firme souhaite importer des camions Daimler-Benz sous forme de pièces détachées. Comme homme de confiance, on envoie à Calcutta Hans Hugo Keil, un ami d'enfance de Wilhelm Haspel. Mais tout se termine mal : contrairement à ce qui avait été prétendu initialement, il n'existe aucun besoin au sein de l'armée indienne pour les camions diesel commandés.

La coopération avec le « Krupp indien », J.R.D. Tata, dont la société Tata Engineering and Locomotive Company Ltd. (Telco) fabrique des camions Mercedes Tata à Jamshedpur entre 1954 et 1969, 60 000 jusqu'en 1962 et 21 000 rien qu'en 1968, se présente sous des auspices bien plus favorables. L'accord TAA (pour Technical Aid Agreement) minutieusement négocié régit le cadre et la procédure. Les neuf dixièmes des pièces des véhicules proviennent du pays. Le responsable pour Tata est le directeur Sumant Moolgoakar, le chef allemand du projet est un homme de Mercedes, Hans Stoehr, qui emmène avec lui 50 collaborateurs de Daimler et, loin de sa patrie, fonde un village de diaspora avec le souabe comme langue officielle et une infrastructure correspondante. Pendant un certain temps, la moitié des véhicules utilitaires circulant dans la partie indienne du subcontinent arborent l'étoile – durant une longue vie d'automobile, mais une vie dure et riche en privations.

Avec l'arrivée à expiration du contrat, devient aussi caduc le droit d'arborer les emblèmes Mercedes. Au moins le joint-venture avec le constructeur de Stuttgart aura-t-il donné à l'attrayante filiale de Tata une telle impulsion pour le futur qu'elle poursuivra sur cette lancée en tant qu'entreprise indépendante, et qui remportera de grands succès. Aujourd'hui encore, on se rappelle avec bienveillance et nostalgie la liaison avec Mercedes.

Upward mobility and turbulence 1952–1959

The year of Wilhelm Haspel's death and also year seven after the end of the war–1952–proved to be a watershed between reconstruction and a massively escalating economic miracle. In the Golden Fifties the gross national product doubled, unemployment turned into over-full employment, everyone started to look beyond just

Steigflug und Turbulenzen 1952–1959

Das Jahr von Wilhelm Haspels Tod und zugleich das Jahr sieben nach Kriegsende – 1952 – wird zur Wasserscheide zwischen Wiederaufbau und wuchernd ausferndem Wirtschaftswunder. In den Golden Fifties verdoppelt sich das Bruttosozialprodukt, schlägt Arbeitslosigkeit um in Überbeschäftigung, beginnt jeder-

Envol météorique et turbulences 1952–1959

L'année du décès de Wilhelm Haspel, sept ans après la fin de la guerre – 1952 –, est une césure entre la reconstruction et la véritable explosion du miracle économique. Durant les Golden Fifties, le produit national brut double, le chômage fait place au suremploi et chacun commence à regarder plus loin que le

getting by and to busily fill the vacuum where furniture and a car belonged.

Thoughts turned to the European or even global stage, contracts raised the barriers at national frontiers and in heads – at least as far as our pockets and budgets were concerned. GATT, the General Agreement on Tariffs and Trade, had been helping economic relations between its 23 signatory states since 1 January 1948, culminating in updates such as the Dillon Round of 1960 and 1961 and the Kennedy Round (1964–1967) which brought about a 35 per cent reduction in duty for industrial products. 1 January 1958 saw the enactment of the Treaty of Rome which established the European Economic Community (EEC). The German mark became a fully convertible currency as 1959 was ushered in. However, it was not to be Haspel's heir Heinrich Wagner who led Daimler-Benz AG into the promised land. Almost exactly a year to the day after Haspel's demise, Wagner died prematurely.

Fritz Könecke, who had been Wagner's deputy since 1 June 1952 and had already been chairman of the board of management at Continental-Gummiwerke in Hanover, was appointed to succeed him. In that year Mercedes had branches in 79 countries, and by 1959 in 143 countries. It was not always easy to make headway against dominant competitors such as British Leyland in the UK.

At the end of the Fifties the United States had just become the major market. As almost always, the initial thrust was provided by the creativity and initiative of one man, the Austrian Maximilian ("Maxi") Hoffman, born near Vienna on 12 November 1904. Hoffman imported quite a number of makes into the USA and was the man behind legendary cars such as the Porsche Speedster. Mercedes' successes, for example at the 1952 Carrera Panamericana, thrilled him, and so he pressed for domestic counterparts of the racing 300 SL such as the 300 SL Roadster and the 190 SL. Daimler-Benz were happy to listen to

Now we are someone again: the Mercedes range of 1952 also reveals growing prosperity.

Wir sind wieder wer: Die Mercedes-Palette von 1952 bildet auch wachsenden Wohlstand ab.

Nous sommes de nouveau quelqu'un : le programme Mercedes 1952 est aussi le reflet d'une prospérité croissante.

mann über den Tellerrand der Fresswelle zu schielen und emsig das Vakuum im Wohnzimmer und unter der Laternengarage zu füllen.

Man denkt europäisch oder gar global, Verträge lupfen die Barrieren an den Landesgrenzen und in den Köpfen – zumindest wenn es ums Portemonnaie und ums Budget geht: Seit dem 1. Januar 1948 erleichtert das Allgemeine Zoll- und Handelsabkommen GATT (für General Agreement on Tariffs and Trade) die Wirtschaftsbeziehungen zwischen seinen 23 Signatarstaaten, gipfelnd in Updates wie der Dillon-Runde von 1960 und 1961 und der Kennedy-Runde (1964–1967), die eine Zollsenkung von 35 Prozent für Industrieerzeugnisse mit sich bringt. Am 1. Januar 1958 treten die Römischen Verträge in Kraft, in denen die Europäische Wirtschaftsgemeinschaft (EWG) wurzelt. Um die Jahreswende 1958/1959 ist die Mark voll konvertierbar. Es ist allerdings nicht Haspels Thronerbe Heinrich Wagner, der die Daimler-Benz AG in diese üppig aufblühende Konjunkturlandschaft führen darf. Er wird fast auf den Tag genau ein Jahr später als dieser früh vollendet aus dem Leben gerissen.

Zum Nachfolger bestellt man Fritz Könecke, Wagners Stellvertreter seit dem 1. Juni 1952 und schon einmal Vorstandsvorsitzender bei den Continental-Gummiwerken in Hannover. In diesem Jahr unterhält Mercedes Niederlassungen in 79 Ländern, 1959 in 143 Ländern. Nicht immer ist es einfach, sich durchzuboxen gegen Platzhirsche wie etwa British Leyland in Großbritannien.

Ende der fünfziger Jahre sind die Vereinigten Staaten just zum wichtigsten Markt geworden. Am Anfang stehen – wie fast immer – die Kreativität und Initiative eines Mannes, des Österreichers Maximilian (»Maxi«) Hoffman, am 12. November 1904 in der Nähe von Wien geboren. Hoffman ist US-Importeur so mancher Marke und der Mann hinter automobilen Legenden wie dem Porsche Speedster. Die Mercedes-Erfolge zum Beispiel bei der Carrera Panamericana 1952 begeistern ihn, und so regt er domestizierte Pendants des Renn-300 SL wie den 300 SL Roadster und den 190 SL an. Bei Daimler-Benz glaubt man Hoffmans Erzählungen gerne – keiner kennt wie er die Gegeben- und Eigenheiten in seiner Wahlheimat. 1952 macht man ihn für sechs Jahre zum Agenten, ursprünglich für die Region ostwärts des Mississippi, später für die gesamten USA.

Doch seinen unbestreitbaren Verkaufserfolgen fehlt der Unterbau einer soliden Infrastruktur. Neue Wege sind gefragt, und so gründet man im April 1955 in Delaware die DBNA (für Daimler-Benz of North America Inc.). Auf der Suche nach einem Händlernetz wird man bei der Studebaker-Packard Corporation fündig und ist sich im April 1957 handelseinig, trotz etlicher Bedenken wegen des unvermeidlichen Niveaugefälles. Diese bewahrheiten sich in der Tat. Importiert wird fleißig, aber viele Autos verharren immobil auf Halde – unter ihnen der 300 SL Roadster, längst ein Mythos im fernen Europa. Am Ende einigt man sich darauf, Studebaker vorzeitig aus dem Vertrag zu entlassen, versüßt durch eine Abfindung von 3,75 Millionen

bord de son assiette en se ruant sur les restaurants de toute nationalité et en comblant avec zèle le moindre vide dans son salon et son garage.

On pense en termes d'Europe, voire de monde, les contrats font tomber les barrières aux frontières des pays et dans les esprits – tout au moins en ce qui concerne le porte-monnaie et le budget : depuis le 1er janvier 1948, le GATT (Accord général sur les tarifs douaniers et le commerce) facilite les relations économiques entre ses 23 États signataires – dont les cycles de négociations les plus importants seront le Dillon-Round de 1960 et 1961 et le Kennedy-Round de 1964–1967 –, qui entraîne une diminution des droits de douane de 35 % pour les produits industriels. Le 1er janvier 1958 voit l'entrée en vigueur du traité de Rome, qui donnera plus tard naissance à la Communauté économique européenne (CEE). Fin 1958/début 1959, le mark peut être converti à volonté. Ce n'est toutefois pas l'héritier du trône de Wilhelm Haspel, Heinrich Wagner, qui sera habilité à présider aux destinées de la Daimler-Benz AG dans ce paysage conjoncturel en plein essor. À peu près un an jour pour jour après celui-ci, il meurt subitement.

Pour lui succéder, on nomme Fritz Könecke, adjoint de Wagner depuis le 1er juin 1952 et, une fois déjà, président du directoire des Continental-Gummiwerke à Hanovre. Cette année-là, Mercedes possède des filiales dans 79 pays et, en 1959, dans 143 pays. Il n'est pas toujours facile d'obtenir gain de cause contre des firmes nationales bien établies telles que British Leyland en Grande-Bretagne.

À la fin des années 1950, les États-Unis sont devenus le marché le plus important. Au début – comme presque toujours – cela est dû à la créativité et à l'initiative d'un homme, l'Autrichien Maximilian (« Maxi ») Hoffman, né le 12 novembre 1904 à proximité de Vienne. Hoffman est l'importateur pour les États-Unis d'un certain nombre de marques et l'homme qui a engendré des légendes automobiles comme le Speedster Porsche. Les succès remportés par Mercedes lors de la Panamericana de 1952, par exemple, l'enthousiasment et ainsi suggère-t-il d'extrapoler des modèles domestiqués de la 300 SL de course comme la 300 SL Roadster et la 190 SL. Chez Daimler-Benz, on croit volontiers à ce que raconte Hoffman – nul ne connaît mieux que lui les particularismes et les habitudes de sa patrie d'adoption. En 1952, on le nomme agent pour une durée de dix ans, initialement pour la région se situant à l'est du Mississippi et, plus tard, pour la totalité des États-Unis.

Mais l'absence d'une solide infrastructure comme base fait obstacle à un succès commercial incontesté. Il faut donc innover et c'est ainsi que l'on fonde, en avril 1955 à Delaware, la DBNA (pour Daimler-Benz of North America Inc.). À la recherche d'un réseau de distribution, on trouve un partenaire avec la Studebaker-Packard Corporation et on signe les contrats en avril 1957 malgré certaines réserves en raison de l'inévitable différence de standing. Et celles-ci se vérifient dans les faits. D'innombrables voitures sont importées, mais beaucoup restent garées sur les parkings

Group photo with the 300S. To the right of the Mercedes stands Maxi Hoffman, the inspiration behind some important models.

Gruppenbild mit 300S. Rechts neben dem Mercedes Maxi Hoffman, der wichtige Modelle anregt.

Photo de groupe avec la 300 S. À droite, à côté de la Mercedes, Maxi Hoffman, initiateur de modèles importants.

Hoffman's tales – his knowledge of the conditions and peculiarities in his adopted country was unmatched. In 1952 he was appointed as the agent for six years, originally for the region to the east of the Mississippi, later for the entire USA.

Nevertheless, his incontrovertible sales successes lacked the support of a solid infrastructure. A new beginning was called for, and so DBNA (Daimler-Benz of North America Inc.) was founded in April 1955 in Delaware. The search for a dealer network ended at the Studebaker-Packard Corporation, and terms were agreed in April 1957, despite considerable reservations regarding the inevitable difference in standing. These proved well-founded. A great deal of cars were imported, but many were simply stockpiled – including the 300 SL Roadster, long since a legend in distant Europe. In the end it was agreed to release Studebaker prematurely from the agreement, with a 3.75 million dollar settlement to sweeten the pill. MBNA (Mercedes-Benz of North America) came into being on 14 December 1964 and supplied cars to 198 painstakingly selected dealers from 1 January 1965 onwards.

This was the signal for a marked upturn. In 1967 more than 20,000 cars were exported to the USA, in 1970 more than 30,000, and in 1985 more than 85,000. This meant that an endearing tradition of American customers – collecting their new Mercedes themselves from Sindelfingen and then, fitted out with the oval license plates issued by the German customs authorities, running it in during a trip through the Old World – was a thing of the past.

Those who bought Daimler-Benz shares in this decade saw a reliable increase in their wealth. Shares with a nominal value of 100 marks still cost 130 marks in 1953, though this had risen to 250 marks in 1954, 940 marks in 1958 and finally 2650 marks in 1959. This spiral was, however, also being affected by powerful men such as the industrialists

Dollar. Am 14. Dezember 1964 wird die MBNA (für Mercedes-Benz of North America) ins Leben gerufen, die vom 1. Januar 1965 an 198 penibel ausgesuchte Händler beliefert.

Von nun an geht's bergauf, und zwar kräftig: 1967 werden mehr als 20 000 Autos in die USA ausgeführt, 1970 mehr als 30 000, 1985 mehr als 85 000. Da gehört eine liebenswerte Gepflogenheit amerikanischer Kunden schon der Vergangenheit an: sich ihren Mercedes selbst in Sindelfingen zu holen und ihn, ausgestattet mit der ovalen Zollnummer, bei einem Trip durch die Alte Welt einzufahren.

Wer in dieser Dekade Daimler-Benz-Aktien kauft, mehrt damit sein Vermögen zuverlässig: Bei einem Nennwert von 100 Mark kosten sie 1953 noch 130 Mark, 1954 immerhin schon 250 Mark, 1958 bereits 940 Mark und 1959 schließlich 2650 Mark. An dieser Schraube drehen allerdings auch Männer mit Macht, wie die Konzern-Herren Friedrich Flick und Herbert Quandt, scharf beobachtet von Fritz Könecke und Hermann J. Abs, Vorsitzender des Aufsichtsrats zwischen 1955 und 1970 in der Nachfolge von Hans Rummel. Seit 1952 beschafft sich der Unternehmer Friedrich Flick mit seinem wachen Blick für blue chips massiv Mercedes-Anteile und drückt somit ihren Kurs in die Höhe. Auf der Hauptversammlung der Daimler-Benz AG im Juli 1955 tut Flicks Verwaltungsgesellschaft kund, sie besitze Aktien im Gegenwert von 18 Millionen Mark – ein Viertel des Stammaktienkapitals von 72 Millionen Mark, das seit der Währungsreform konstant geblieben ist. Mit diesem massiven Polster im Rücken meldet Flick seinen Anspruch auf einen Platz im Aufsichtsrat an, ebenso wie die Quandt-Gruppe, die 3,5 Prozent angibt. Auf der Hauptversammlung vom 25. Juni 1956 wird den beiden Großaktionären zugestanden, was sie fordern: drei Sitze für Flick und die Position des ersten Stellvertreters, zwei Sitze für die Gebrüder Quandt sowie den Posten des zweiten Stellvertreters für Herbert Quandt, den älteren der beiden. Das ist die Geburtsstunde des Dreigestirns Abs, Flick und Quandt an der Spitze des Aufsichtsrats – künftig ein potentes Äquivalent zum Vorstand und nicht so leicht zu überzeugen.

Durchaus wechselhaft verlaufen unterdessen die Viten der Mercedes-Töchter im fernen Südamerika, ehe sie jenseits der Krisen Tritt fassen. Vor allem bereiten die Schlüsselfiguren Kopfzerbrechen, eigenwillige Charaktere, die in den Prozess der Filiation eine nicht immer gewünschte und geheure Eigendynamik einbringen.

Beispiel Brasilien: Ansprechpartner ist dort der Exilpole Alfred Jurzykowski, ein Mann mit mancherlei Talenten, in dem sich unternehmerische Initiative mit einem Hang zum Risiko verquicken. Im April 1952 wird ein Vertrag hinsichtlich der Gründung der Mercedes-Benz do Brasil (MBB) abgeschlossen, ein Jahr später von Fritz Könecke und Arnold Wychodil vor Ort der Kauf eines Grundstücks in São Bernardo do Campo unweit São Paulo in die Wege geleitet, im Oktober 1953 die MBB ins Leben gerufen.

Aber der Segen der Regierung Getulio Vargas bleibt aus, selbst nachdem man einen detaillierten Marschplan vorgelegt hat, wie Teile und Aggregate von Daimler-Benz

des concessionnaires – parmi elles, la 300 SL Roadster, qui est depuis longtemps un mythe en Europe. En fin de compte, un accord est passé pour libérer prématurément Studebaker du contrat, dénonciation adoucie par une indemnité de 3,75 millions de dollars. Le 14 décembre 1964 est fondée la MBNA (pour Mercedes-Benz of North America), qui, à partir du 1er janvier 1965, approvisionne en voiture 198 concessionnaires triés sur le volet.

Cette fois, la cause est entendue : en 1967, plus de 20 000 voitures sont exportées aux États-Unis, plus de 30 000 en 1970 et plus de 85 000 en 1985. À ce moment-là, déjà, une bonne vieille coutume des clients américains appartient déjà au passé : l'habitude d'aller chercher soi-même sa Mercedes à Sindelfingen et, avec la plaque d'immatriculation douanière ovale, de la roder en partant en voyage à travers le Vieux Continent.

Quiconque achète des actions de Daimler-Benz à cette époque multiplie son patrimoine avec un zèle de fourmi : pour une valeur nominale de 100 marks, elles coûtent encore 130 marks en 1953, mais déjà 250 en 1954, 940 en 1958 et, enfin, 2 650 marks en 1959. Il faut avouer que des hommes de pouvoir tirent aussi les ficelles en coulisse, par exemple les présidents des groupes Friedrich Flick et Herbert Quandt, épiés d'un œil d'Argus par Fritz Könecke et Hermann J. Abs, président, de 1955 à 1970, du conseil de surveillance où il a pris la succession de Hans Rummel. À partir de 1952, l'industriel Friedrich Flick, qui a toujours du flair pour les « blue chips », achète systématiquement des actions de Mercedes, ce qui fait exploser leur cours. Lors de l'assemblée générale de Daimler-Benz AG, en juillet 1955, la société d'administration de biens de Flick annonce qu'elle possède des actions pour une valeur de 18 millions de marks – un quart du capital d'actions ordinaires de 72 millions de marks, qui est resté constant depuis la réforme monétaire. Avec un tel trésor de guerre, Flick réclame une place au conseil de surveillance, au même titre que le groupe Quandt, qui revendique 3,5 % des actions. Lors de l'assemblée générale du 25 juillet 1956, les deux gros actionnaires obtiennent gain de cause : on accorde trois sièges et le poste de premier adjoint à Flick, deux sièges aux frères Quandt et le poste de deuxième adjoint à Herbert Quandt, le plus âgé des deux. C'est l'acte de naissance de la Trinité Abs, Flick et Quandt à la tête du conseil de surveillance – qui sera à l'avenir un interlocuteur puissant du directoire et ne se laissera pas convaincre aisément.

La carrière des filiales de Mercedes sur le lointain continent sud-américain connaît bien des hauts et des bas avant de se stabiliser une fois les crises franchies. Certains personnages clés, notamment, causent des migraines, fortes têtes qui engendrent, dans le processus d'affiliation, une dynamique endogène pas toujours souhaitée et parfois gênante.

Par exemple au Brésil : l'interlocuteur dans ce pays est un Polonais exilé, Alfred Jurzykowski, un homme non dénué de talents, mais chez lequel l'initiative entrepreneuriale est mâtinée d'un certain goût du risque. En avril 1952,

Friedrich Flick and Herbert Quandt, carefully watched by Fritz Könecke and Hermann J. Abs who succeeded Hans Rummel as chairman of the supervisory board between 1955 and 1970. Businessman Friedrich Flick with his watchful eye for blue chips had been buying Mercedes shares heavily since 1952, thereby forcing their price up. At Daimler-Benz AG's Annual General Meeting in July 1955 Flick's management company announced that it owned shares with a present value of 18 million marks – a quarter of the ordinary share capital of 72 million marks that had remained constant since the currency reform. With this huge cushion behind him, Flick registered a claim for a place on the supervisory board, as did the Quandt Group which declared ownership of 3.5 per cent. The AGM of 25 June 1956 met the demands of these two major shareholders, granting Flick three seats and the position of the first deputy, and the Quandt brothers two seats and the post of second deputy for Herbert Quandt, the older of the brothers. This was the birth of the triumvirate of Abs, Flick and Quandt at the head of the supervisory board – which was to be a powerful counterpoint in future to the board of management and one that was not so easily persuaded.

Mercedes' subsidiaries in far-off South America meanwhile weathered many storms before they found their feet again. The key figures, strong-willed characters who brought to the process of setting up a subsidiary a level of momentum that was sometimes undesirable or scary, were the source of many of the headaches.

Take Brazil, for example, where the company's contact was the ex-pat Pole Alfred Jurzykowski, a man of multiple talents, in whom entrepreneurial initiative was mixed with a tendency to take risks. In April 1952 a contract for the formation of Mercedes-Benz do Brasil (MBB) was concluded, one year later the purchase of a plot of land in São Bernardo do Campo not far from São Paulo was initiated by Fritz Könecke and Arnold Wychodil during a local visit, and in October 1953 MBB came into being.

But the blessing of Getulio Vargas' government was not forthcoming, even when the company had submitted a detailed business plan showing how Daimler-Benz components and units could gradually be replaced by Brazilian-manufactured products. In July 1954 the project was rejected, though was then green-lighted by Vargas' successor Café Filho following the personal intervention of Germany's Federal Minister for Economic Affairs Ludwig Erhard. Filho's period in office was brief, only just a year, and so it was President Juscelino Kubitschek who was in power when the new factory complex was opened on 28 September 1956. The Governor of São Paulo Province, Quarros, had himself photographed in populist pose at the wheel of the first truck to leave the production line in São Bernardo do Campo.

This was followed by an ice-cold shower 30 months later, in stark contrast to the financial hot water in which an ailing MBB found itself. Investigations by the auditors Deutsche Treuhand-Gesellschaft unearthed a lot of dubi-

allmählich durch Produkte aus brasilianischer Fertigung ersetzt werden können. Im Juli 1954 wird das Projekt abgeschmettert, bekommt indessen durch Vargas' Nachfolger Café Filho grünes Licht, als sich Bundeswirtschaftsminister Ludwig Erhard persönlich einschaltet. Filhos Amtszeit ist kurz, gerade mal ein Jahr, und so ist es Präsident Juscelino Kubitschek, der die Einweihung des neuen Werkkomplexes am 28. September 1956 zur Chefsache macht. In populistischer Pose lässt sich der Gouverneur der Provinz São Paulo, Quarros, am Lenkrad des ersten LKW ablichten, der in São Bernardo do Campo gebaut wurde.

Eine eisige Dusche folgt 30 Monate später: Die MBB wird von Liquiditätsproblemen gebeutelt, und Recherchen der Deutschen Treuhand-Gesellschaft fördern so manches Windige und Ungereimte zutage. Das Mercedes-Management nimmt daraufhin den agilen Alfred Jurzykowski an die kurze Leine, der inzwischen zum Präsidenten des Aufsichtsrats der Problem-Filiale avanciert ist: Er muss die deutsche Zentrale in allen wichtigen Fragen schriftlich zu Rate ziehen und Rapport erstatten. Von nun an herrscht Ruhe an der brasilianischen Front, zumal sich die Untertürkheimer auf dornigen Wegen Schritt für Schritt das gesamte Aktienkapital der MBB aneignen – ein Prozess, der erst 1970 abgeschlossen ist.

Beispiel Argentinien: Die Mercedes-Benz Argentina S.A. gerät zunehmend in die Strudel, die die Wechselfälle des Peronismus und damit Aufstieg und Fall des Stern-Statthalters Jorge Antonio aufwerfen. Gewiss schichten sich die Lieferungen nach Buenos Aires zwischen 1952 und 1955 auf zum Gegenwert von 215 Millionen Mark. Gewiss beläuft sich der Exporterlös dorthin etwa 1953 auf 26 Prozent der Ausfuhren insgesamt. Andererseits wird die MBA politisch eingenordet, während sich Antonio, Mitglied von Juan Domingo Peróns Partido Laborista, zum Boss über einen

The inauguration of the Brazilian factory in September 1956. At the wheel of the L312 is Governor Quarros of São Paulo province.

Einweihung des brasilianischen Werks im September 1956. Am Lenkrad des L312 der Gouverneur der Provinz São Paulo, Quarros.

Inauguration de l'usine brésilienne, en septembre 1956. Au volant du L312 se trouve le gouverneur de la province de São Paulo, M. Quarros.

un contrat est signé en vue de la fondation de Mercedes-Benz do Brasil (MBB); un an plus tard, Fritz Könecke et Arnold Wychodil ouvrent, sur place, la voie à l'achat d'un terrain à São Bernardo do Campo, non loin de São Paulo, et, en octobre 1953, MBB est fondée.

Mais le gouvernement de Getulio Vargas refuse de donner sa bénédiction même après que l'on a présenté un échéancier détaillé expliquant comment les pièces et organes de Daimler-Benz pourront graduellement être remplacés par des produits de fabrication brésilienne. En juillet 1954, le projet sombre aux oubliettes avant de recevoir le feu vert du successeur de Vargas, Café Filho, lorsque le ministre fédéral de l'Économie Ludwig Erhard intervient personnellement. La législature de Filho est de courte durée, tout juste un an, et c'est donc le président Juscelino Kubitschek qui fait accélérer l'inauguration, le 28 septembre 1956, du nouveau complexe industriel. Dans une pose démagogique, le gouvernement de la province de São Paulo, Quarros, se fait photographier au volant du premier camion construit à São Bernardo do Campo.

Une douche froide survient trente mois plus tard: MBB est ébranlée par des problèmes de liquidités et des recherches de la Deutsche Treuhand-Gesellschaft font apparaître au grand jour bien des choses mystérieuses et illogiques. La direction de Mercedes contrôle désormais de plus près le dangereux Alfred Jurzykowski qui a entre-temps fait carrière comme président du conseil de surveillance de cette filiale à problèmes: il doit demander conseil par écrit à la centrale allemande pour toutes les questions importantes et rendre rapport. Dès lors, le calme revient sur le front brésilien, d'autant plus qu'Untertürkheim est parvenue non sans mal, étape après étape, à s'approprier la totalité du capital d'actions de MBB – un processus qui n'est achevé qu'en 1970.

Exemple Argentine: Mercedes-Benz Argentina S.A. est de plus en plus ballottée par les tourbillons qu'engendrent les aléas du péronisme et, par voie de conséquence, l'essor et la chute du représentant de la marque à l'étoile, Jorge Antonio. Certes, de 1952 à 1955, les livraisons à Buenos Aires s'additionnent pour représenter une contre-valeur de 215 millions de marks. Certes, les recettes réalisées aux exportations vers ce pays s'élèvent vers 1953 à 26% des exportations totales. Mais, d'un autre côté, MBA se politise à partir du moment où Antonio, membre du Partido Laborista de Juan Domingo Perón, s'élève au rang de chef par le truchement d'un groupe de firmes fidèle au gouvernement. Lorsque Perón est renversé en septembre 1955 lors d'un putsch militaire, cela signifie aussi la chute de son bras droit Antonio. La junte dirigée par le général Pedro Eugenio Aramburu laisse tout d'abord entendre qu'elle est prête à discuter, mais fait en réalité exproprier MBA en 1957 par une «Commission pour la récupération du patrimoine populaire» en reprenant exactement le capital d'actions accumulé par Jorge Antonio: 46%.

En octobre 1958, un tribunal argentin reconnaît les 54% restants comme propriété de Mercedes, entre-temps

ous deals and inconsistencies. The Mercedes management therefore decided to keep the sharp Alfred Jurzykowski, who was by now the chairman of the supervisory board of the problem subsidiary, on a short lead. He was required to consult and report to the German parent company in writing on all important issues. From this point on all was quiet on the Brazilian front, especially as Daimler-Benz, in a process which was not completed until 1970, gradually acquired MBB's entire share capital despite the difficulties inherent in such a move.

Or take Argentina: Mercedes-Benz Argentina S.A. found itself caught up more and more in the turbulence created by the vicissitudes of Peronism and thus the rise and fall of the Mercedes chief Jorge Antonio. It's true that deliveries to Buenos Aires between 1952 and 1955 were worth 215 million marks. It's true that export revenues to Argentina in 1953, for example, represented 26 per cent of the company's total exports. On the other hand, MBA was seen as politically aligned when Antonio, a member of Juan Domingo Perón's Partido Laborista, set himself up as a member of a company group which toed the party line. When Perón was ousted by a military coup in September 1955, his sidekick Antonio was also toppled. The junta under General Pedro Eugenio Aramburu initially declared itself prepared to talk, but then a "Commission for the Reacquisition of Public Wealth" expropriated MBA in 1957 of precisely the share capital – 46 per cent – that Jorge Antonio had accumulated.

The remaining 54 per cent were confirmed as the property of Mercedes, now under President Arturo Frondizi, by an Argentinian court in October 1958. Skillful maneuvering had added a further 37 per cent to that by 1962. The balance of nine per cent was acquired in July 1969 by Inval S.R.L., a limited liability company which had been importing production equipment from Stuttgart since 1959 under the Mercedes umbrella as a hedge against recourse claims and leasing it to MBA. In this way the Argentinian subsidiary's affiliation to the parent company's group had been lastingly cemented.

The company ideologues' product philosophy is based on two principles: whereas the commercial vehicle range covers the full spectrum from the light van to the heavy goods vehicle, the car range is aimed at the upper mid-range and the top of the range. Between 1950 and 1960 car production rose from 33,906 to 122,684 units while the work force grew in the same period from 30,846 to 67,521. Demand nonetheless outstripped supply.

The market below the Mercedes level was meanwhile threatening to become a playground for the EEC partners: Fiat and Renault, for instance, were looking longingly for the opportunity of a little cherry-picking next-door. It therefore made sense to build a stronghold in this sector, for example by merging with a company which occupied a lower position in the car make hierarchy.

The former competitor Auto Union was an obvious target. It had suffered a tough post-war fate since all of its factories were in the Soviet-occupied zone of Germany:

linientreuen Firmen-Verbund aufwirft. Als Perón im September 1955 durch einen Militärputsch gestürzt wird, strauchelt auch sein Palladin Antonio. Die Junta unter General Pedro Eugenio Aramburu verheißt zunächst Gesprächsbereitschaft, enteignet aber 1957 die MBA durch eine »Kommission zur Wiedergewinnung von Volksvermögen« just um jenes Aktienkapital, das Jorge Antonio angehäuft hat – 46 Prozent.

Die verbleibenden 54 Prozent werden im Oktober 1958 von einem argentinischen Gericht als Mercedes-Eigentum abgesegnet, inzwischen unter Präsident Arturo Frondizi. Dazu kommen durch geschicktes Taktieren bis 1962 weitere 37 Prozent. Die restlichen neun Prozent ersteht im Juli 1969 die Inval S.R.L., eine Gesellschaft mit beschränkter Haftung, die unter dem Mercedes-Dach seit 1959 als Schutz gegen Regressforderungen Produktionseinrichtungen aus Stuttgart einführt und an die MBA verpachtet. Damit ist die Zugehörigkeit der argentinischen Tochter zum Konzernverbund des Mutterhauses dauerhaft zementiert.

Die Produktphilosophie der Firmen-Ideologen ruht auf zwei Säulen: Während man bei den Nutzfahrzeugen die ganze Bandbreite zwischen dem Leicht-Laster und dem Schwertransporter bespielt, hat man bei den Personenwagen die obere Mittelklasse und die Oberklasse im Visier. Zwischen 1950 und 1960 – die Zahl der Mitarbeiter nimmt im gleichen Zeitraum von 30 846 auf 67 521 zu – steigt die PKW-Produktion von 33 906 auf 122 684 Einheiten. Die Nachfrage ist gleichwohl stärker als das Angebot.

Der Markt unterhalb der Mercedes-Ebene droht unterdessen zu Spielwiese und Tummelplatz der EWG-Partner zu werden: Schon schauen etwa Fiat und Renault begehrlich nach den Kirschen in Nachbars Garten. Da macht es Sinn, eine Bastion in diesem Segment zu errichten, zum Beispiel durch die Fusion mit einem Unternehmen, das in der Hierarchie der Automarken weiter unten angesiedelt ist.

Der einstige Konkurrent Auto Union bietet sich an, gebeutelt durch ein hartes Nachkriegsschicksal, da alle Werke im sowjetisch besetzten Teil Deutschlands liegen: demontiert schon 1946, enteignet 1948, aus den Handelsre-

The Mercedes-Benz Argentina S.A. factory in Buenos Aires.
Werk der Mercedes-Benz Argentina S.A. in Buenos Aires.
L'usine de Mercedes-Benz Argentina S.A. à Buenos Aires.

sous la présidence d'Arturo Frondizi. À cela s'ajoutent grâce à d'astucieuses manœuvres jusqu'en 1962 37 % supplémentaires. Les 9 % restants sont acquis, en juillet 1969, par Inval S.R.L., une société à responsabilité limitée qui, sous le toit de Mercedes, importe depuis 1959, en guise de protection contre les droits de recours, des équipements de production de Stuttgart qu'elle loue à MBA. Dorénavant, l'appartenance de la filiale argentine à la nébuleuse du groupe souabe est cimentée durablement.

La philosophie commerciale des idéologues de la firme repose sur deux axes : si, pour les utilitaires, on joue sur tous les registres, de la camionnette légère au gros poids lourd, pour les voitures particulières (VP), on se concentre sur les segments des moyennes supérieures et des voitures de luxe. Entre 1950 et 1960 – période pendant laquelle les effectifs passent de 30 846 à 67 521 – la production de VP augmente de 33 906 à 122 684 unités. Et encore la demande est-elle plus forte que l'offre.

Mais le marché du niveau inférieur à celui choisi par Mercedes risque alors de devenir la chasse gardée de ses concurrents de la CEE : Fiat et Renault, par exemple, louchent déjà avec envie sur ce gâteau appétissant. Il serait donc judicieux d'ériger un bastion dans ce segment, par exemple par la fusion avec une entreprise située un peu plus bas dans la hiérarchie automobile.

L'ancien concurrent Auto Union semble prédestiné, réduit à presque rien par le dur destin de l'après-guerre dès lors que toutes ses usines se trouvent dans la zone d'occupation soviétique de l'Allemagne : usines démontées dès 1946, expropriées en 1948, radiées des registres du commerce en 1949, reconstituées – mais tout en bas de l'échelle sociale – à Ingolstadt, le 3 septembre de la même année, avec un capital social de trois millions de marks. Tandis que là on s'y concentre sur la production d'utilitaires légers et de motos, à Düsseldorf, sur un terrain loué à Rheinmetall-Borsig AG, on entame en 1950 la fabrication de voitures de tourisme. Un peu plus tard pétarade la première DKW d'après-guerre avec ses fumerolles bleues typiques des moteurs deux temps : la F-89-P, baptisée Meisterklasse (classe des maîtres) au mépris de toute modestie, qui aura déjà été produite à 1000 exemplaires en décembre 1950.

Au Salon de Francfort du printemps de 1953, la bicylindre est suivie par la Sonderklasse (classe spéciale) à trois cylindres. Et, à l'automne 1955, Auto Union commercialise sa « grosse DKW 3=6 », élargie de dix centimètres. La dénomination a pour but d'inculquer aux snobs parmi les disciples de la marque que le moteur deux temps à trois cylindres comble ses passagers avec la douceur de fonctionnement d'un quatre-temps à six cylindres. Dès janvier 1955, Fritz Könecke se montre disposé à une adoption. Friedrich Flick possède en 1958 plus de 40 % des actions d'Auto Union, autant que son représentant général suisse Ernst Göhner. Lorsque les usines Ford de Cologne commencent elles aussi à manifester de l'intérêt pour l'entreprise d'Ingolstadt, on saisit l'occasion avant qu'il ne soit trop tard, le 1er janvier 1958 : Daimler-Benz reprend la

dismantled in 1946, expropriated in 1948, deleted from the company registers in 1949, resurrected, even if in reduced circumstances, in Ingolstadt on 3 September of the same year, with a share capital of three million marks. While this factory took up production of light-duty commercial vehicles and motorcycles, the company started manufacturing cars in 1950 on the site leased from Rheinmetall-Borsig AG in Düsseldorf. It wasn't long before the first post-war DKW, the F-89-P, also known in a complete reversal of understatement as the Meisterklasse (master class), put-putted its way off the assembly line with a blue puff of two-stroke exhaust, and had already sold 1000 units by December 1950.

The two-cylinder model was followed by the Sonderklasse (special class) model with three cylinders, launched at the Frankfurt Motor Show in the spring of 1953. And in the autumn of 1955 Auto Union brought its ten-centimeter-wider "large DKW 3=6" to market. The type designation was intended to suggested to the snobs amongst the make's disciples that the three-cylinder two-stroke model was spoiling its occupants with the driving properties of a six-cylinder four-stroke engine. Fritz Könecke had shown himself keen to adopt in January 1955. Friedrich Flick owned more than 40 per cent of Auto Union's shares in 1958, the same amount as the company's Swiss general agent Ernst Göhner. When the Cologne-based Ford also began showing an interest in the Ingolstadt company, Daimler-Benz stepped in and took over a majority share in Auto Union GmbH with effect from 1 January 1958. The cost was 47 million marks, payable in three annual installments.

It appeared to be a sound investment: The DKW Junior, manufactured from 1959 onwards in the new factory in Ingolstadt, proved a winner in the targeted market sector, just like its further developments the Junior de Luxe, F 12 and F 11. And the mid-range model DKW F 102 from 1963 with its sloping monocoque also attracted a considerable number of buyers. Between 1958 and 1960 sales rose from 500 to around 750 million marks. But at the beginning of the new decade the gnawing question of what exactly was the point became ever more pressing. There were four reasons against continuing this connection with Auto Union in its new Bavarian home. Firstly, there were glaring differences between Auto Union's product and branding ideology and Mercedes' noble image. In particular, the three-cylinder two-stroke engines which could not shake off the hint of "poor people's cars" were looked down on. Moreover, the harsh winter of 1962/1963 mercilessly exposed weaknesses in the much-vaunted performance of the automatic lubrication system: below minus 30 degrees the lubrication system failed, just as it did when driving happily at full speed, resulting in engine seizures. Secondly, Mercedes was loath to make the investment necessitated by the lively competition in the DKW class. Thirdly, the company needed money itself for the new truck production site in Wörth. Fourthly, DKW was beginning to run up losses – 60 million marks already by 1964.

gistern getilgt 1949, wiederauferstanden, wenn auch sozial abgesunken, in Ingolstadt am 3. September des gleichen Jahres, mit einem Stammkapital von drei Millionen Mark. Während man sich dort auf die Produktion von Leichtlastwagen und Motorrädern verlegt, wird in Düsseldorf 1950 auf dem gepachteten Gelände der Rheinmetall-Borsig AG die Fertigung von Personenautos aufgenommen. Wenig später klötert und ningelt der erste Nachkriegs-DKW mit blauem Zweitakt-Fähnlein am Auspuff vom Band, der F-89-P, jenseits allen Understatements auch Meisterklasse genannt, und bringt es schon im Dezember 1950 auf eine Verbreitung von 1000 Exemplaren.

Dem Zweizylinder folgt auf dem Frankfurter Salon im Frühjahr 1953 das Modell Sonderklasse mit drei Töpfen. Und im Herbst 1955 speist die Auto Union den »großen DKW 3=6« in den Markt ein mit seiner um zehn Zentimeter gewachsenen Wagenbreite. Die Typenbezeichnung soll den Snobs unter den Jüngern der Marke suggerieren, der Dreizylinder-Zweitakter verwöhne die Insassen mit der Laufkultur eines Sechszylinder-Viertakters. Schon im Januar 1955 zeigt sich Fritz Könecke geneigt zu einer Adoption. Friedrich Flick besitzt 1958 mehr als 40 Prozent der Anteile der Auto Union, ebenso viele wie deren Schweizer Generalvertreter Ernst Göhner. Als sich die Kölner Ford-Werke ebenfalls für das Ingolstädter Unternehmen interessieren, greift man mit Wirkung vom 1. Januar 1958 zu: Daimler-Benz übernimmt die Auto Union GmbH mehrheitlich. 47 Millionen Mark sind zu entrichten, zahlbar in drei Jahresraten.

Die Sache scheint sich zu lohnen: Der DKW Junior, ab 1959 schon hergestellt in der neuen Fabrik in Ingolstadt, kommt im angepeilten Marktsegment gut an, ebenso seine Extrapolationen Junior de Luxe, F 12 und F 11. Und auch das Mittelklasseangebot DKW F 102 von 1963 mit seiner gefällig geformten Pontonkarosserie weiß durchaus zu gefallen. Zwischen 1958 und 1960 erhöht sich der Umsatz von 500 auf rund 750 Millionen Mark. Aber Anfang des neuen Jahrzehnts stellt sich immer bohrender die Sinnfrage. Vier Gründe sprechen dagegen, an der neubayerischen Connection festzuhalten: Zum einen schrille Dissonanzen zwischen deren Produkt- und Markenideologie und dem Edel-Image von Mercedes. Vor allem schaut man scheel auf die Dreizylinder-Zweitaktmaschinen, denen selbst in ihrer sublimierten Form ein sanfter Arme-Leute-Mief anhaftet. Überdies legt der scharfe Winter 1962/1963 erbarmungslos Schwächen der vielgerühmten Errungenschaft Frischölautomatik bloß: Bei unter 30 Grad minus versagt die Schmierung ebenso wie bei lustvollen Vollgasfahrten, und es kommt zu ärgerlichen Motorinfarkten. Zum anderen scheut man die Investitionen, die der flotte Wettbewerb in der DKW-Klasse erfordert. Zum dritten braucht man selber Geld für die neue LKW-Produktionsstätte Wörth. Zum vierten beginnt DKW Verluste einzufahren – bis 1964 bereits 60 Millionen Mark.

Des einen Eule, des anderen Nachtigall: Die Volkswagenwerk AG hält Ausschau nach neuen Kapazitäten, und

Fritz Könecke, chairman of the board of directors from 1953 to 1960.

Fritz Könecke, Vorstandsvorsitzender 1953 bis 1960.

Fritz Könecke, président du directoire de 1953 à 1960.

majorité d'Auto Union GmbH. Prix: 47 millions de marks, déboursés en trois traites annuelles.

La cause semble valoir la peine: la DKW Junior fabriquée dès 1959 dans la nouvelle usine d'Ingolstadt marche bien dans son segment, à l'instar de ses extrapolations, la Junior de Luxe, la F 12 et la F 11. La DKW F 102 de 1963, une moyenne inférieure, plaît elle aussi avec sa charmante carrosserie ponton. De 1958 à 1960, le chiffre d'affaires passe de 500 à environ 750 millions de marks. Mais, au début de la nouvelle décennie, se pose, de plus en plus cruciale, la question du bien-fondé de ce rachat. Quatre arguments sont défavorables à la liaison néo-bavaroise: premièrement, le profond clivage entre son idéologie de produit et de marque et l'image de prestige de Mercedes. On regarde surtout d'un œil condescendant les moteurs trois-cylindres qui équipent ce que l'on considère alors comme « la voiture du pauvre ». De plus, le rude hiver de 1962–1963 met cruellement à jour les points faibles de la célèbre boîte automatique à huile fraîche: par moins 30 degrés, la lubrification s'interrompt, de même que lorsque l'on roule à fond, ce qui engendre d'irréparables pannes de moteur. On hésite également à investir autant que l'exigerait la forte concurrence dans le segment de la DKW; on a soi-même besoin d'argent pour construire la nouvelle usine de camions de Wörth. Enfin, DKW commence à générer des pertes – déjà 60 millions de marks accumulés en 1964.

Ce qui est pour l'un un inconvénient est pour l'autre un avantage: Volkswagenwerk AG recherche en effet de

One man's trash is another man's treasure. Volkswagenwerk AG was on the lookout for new capacity, and in a complicated transaction the adopted daughter changed parent, name and engineering base. At the beginning of 1965 50.28 per cent (corresponding to 80.452 million marks) of the share capital was transferred to VW, and the rest by the end of 1966. In a sudden rush of tradition the Sleeping Beauty of the old Auto Union logo "Audi" was awakened from its slumber, while the reflagged F 102 took with it as its dowry from Mercedes the "medium-compression engine", 1.7 liters, compression 11.2 : 1 – a four-stroke.

If Friedrich Flick was the architect of the Auto Union deal, Herbert Quandt was a strong proponent in May 1958 of affiliation with Bayerische Motoren Werke, in which he had an eight per cent share. BMW had also found it very hard to pick itself up after the war. The Iron Curtain had come down on the wrong side of the BMW enclave of Eisenach, and parts of the production plant had been carried off home as souvenirs by the victors. The baroque splendors of the 501 and 502 with their six- and eight-cylinder engines from 1952 to 1963 were just what the doctor had not ordered to meet the needs of the average German.

This applied even more so for the magnificently inefficient 503 and 507 sports models (1955–1959) which managed to find only 413 and 252 well-heeled buyers, respectively. The rounded Isetta was motoring at its most basic, while the kindest thing you can say about the thudding 600 and 700 models is that they were motorcycles with full rain protection for the passengers.

Fritz Könecke dispatched Paul Heim, a former head of the Sindelfingen factory, to Munich to take a look. Heim was married to one of the daughters of BMW chief executive Franz Josef Popp. His investigations yielded a lack of enthusiasm on the whole, especially as the acquisition of Auto Union had caused a considerable burden. The matter was shelved although even the Bavarian state government approached Daimler-Benz and requested it to give the ailing Munich company a helping hand.

An article in the Munich-based *Süddeutsche Zeitung* of 11 November 1959 entitled "The Fate of BMW" summed up the problems. "The company has advised that it has suffered losses of 49 million marks in the last ten years. The short-term debts have now reached around 60 million marks. In the management's view, liquidation of the company, if not even more serious action, seems inevitable if the restructuring plan proposed by the supervisory board is not accepted by the Annual General Meeting on 9 December. … The restructuring plan is based primarily on the fact that profitable use of BMW's production capacity will be guaranteed by orders from Daimler-Benz and funding will be ensured by a consortium made up of Deutsche Bank, Bayerische Staatsbank, Bayerische Landesanstalt für Aufbaufinanzierung and Daimler-Benz AG. The logical conclusion of this restructuring plan, of course, is … to affiliate Bayerische Motoren Werke with Daimler-Benz AG which is controlled by Flick. Sooner or later 75 per cent of

in einer komplizierten Transaktion wechselt die Adoptivtochter Besitzer, Namen und technische Grundlage. Anfang 1965 gehen 50,28 Prozent (entsprechend 80,452 Millionen Mark) des Stammkapitals auf VW über, der Rest bis Ende 1966. Da hat man in jäh aufbrechendem Traditionsbewusstsein das alte Auto-Union-Logo Audi aus seinem Dornröschenschlaf wachgeküsst, während der umgeflaggte F 102 als Mercedes-Mitgift den »Mitteldruckmotor« in die Zukunft mitnimmt, 1,7 Liter, Verdichtung 11,2 : 1 – einen Viertakter.

Ist Friedrich Flick der Architekt des Auto-Union-Deals, macht sich Herbert Quandt im Mai 1958 stark für eine Angliederung der Bayerischen Motoren Werke, an denen er Anteile von acht Prozent besitzt. Auch die Bajuwaren sind nach dem Krieg nur sehr schwer aus den Startlöchern gekommen: Vor der BMW-Enklave Eisenach hat sich der Eiserne Vorhang gesenkt, und Teile der Fertigungsanlagen in München haben die Sieger als Souvenirs mit nach Hause genommen. Die barocken Prunk-Produkte 501 und 502 mit ihren Sechs- und Achtzylindermaschinen von 1952 bis 1963 sind souverän an den Bedürfnissen des Durchschnitts-Deutschen vorbeigeplant. Das gilt erst recht für die prächtig-unrationellen Sportmodelle 503 und 507 (1955–1959), die sich an lediglich 413 beziehungsweise 252 Gutbetuchte absetzen lassen. Die kugelige Isetta sorgt für elementarste Motorisierung, während es sich bei den bollernden Modellen 600 und 700 allenfalls um Motorräder mit Regen-Vollschutz für die Passagiere handelt.

Fritz Könecke schickt Paul Heim, einen früheren Leiter des Werks Sindelfingen, nach München, um sich ein Bild zu machen. Heim ist mit einer Tochter von BMW-Generaldirektor Franz Josef Popp verheiratet. Das Ergebnis seiner Ermittlungen erzeugt eher Unlust, zumal man sich mit der Akquisition von Auto Union beträchtliche Belastungen aufgebürdet hat. Die Angelegenheit wird auf Eis gelegt, obwohl selbst die bayerische Landesregierung an Daimler-Benz mit der Bitte herantritt, der maroden Münchner Firma unter die Arme zu greifen.

Ein Artikel in der *Süddeutschen Zeitung* vom 11. November 1959, Titel: Das Schicksal der BMW, bringt die Problematik auf den Punkt: »Wie die Verwaltung mitteilt, hat das Unternehmen in den letzten zehn Jahren einen Geschäftsverlust von 49 Millionen Mark erlitten. Die kurzfristigen Schulden haben ein Ausmaß von rund 60 Millionen Mark angenommen. Eine Liquidation der Gesellschaft, wenn nicht noch schwerwiegendere Maßnahmen, erscheinen nach Ansicht der Verwaltung unvermeidlich, wenn der vom Aufsichtsrat vorgelegte Sanierungsplan von der am 9. Dezember stattfindenden Generalversammlung der Aktionäre nicht angenommen wird. … Der Sanierungsplan baut im wesentlichen darauf auf, dass eine rentable Auslastung der Produktionskapazitäten von BMW durch Aufträge von Daimler-Benz garantiert und die Finanzierung durch ein Konsortium gesichert wird, dem die Deutsche Bank, die Bayerische Staatsbank, die Bayerische Landesanstalt für Aufbaufinanzierung und die Daimler-Benz AG angehören. Dieser Sanierungsplan läuft freilich

nouvelles capacités et, à l'issue d'une transaction compliquée, la filiale adoptive change de parents, de nom et de base technique. Début 1965, 50,28 % du capital social (soit 80,452 millions de marks) passent à VW, le reste devant suivre jusqu'à fin 1966. Le sens de la tradition reprenant vigueur, on a réveillé de son sommeil de Belle au bois dormant l'ancien nom d'Auto Union, Audi, tandis que la voiture rebaptisée F 102 emmène comme dot de Mercedes le « moteur à pression intermédiaire », un quatre-temps de 1,7 litre à taux de compression de 11,2 : 1.

Si Friedrich Flick est l'architecte de la cession d'Auto Union, c'est Herbert Quandt qui se fait l'avocat, en 1958, d'une intégration des Bayerische Motoren Werke, dont il détient 8 % des actions. Après la guerre, les Bavarois aussi ont eu beaucoup de mal à sortir des starting-blocks : le rideau de fer s'est abaissé devant l'enclave BMW d'Eisenach pendant que les vainqueurs emmenaient avec eux comme souvenir certaines parties des équipements de Munich. Les baroques et luxueuses 501 et 502 à moteur à six et huit cylindres produites de 1952 à 1963 méprisent souverainement les besoins de l'Allemand moyen, ce qui vaut *a fortiori* pour les modèles sportifs, magnifiques mais totalement déplacés, la 503 et la 507 (1955–1959), que peuvent seulement s'offrir respectivement 413 et 252 amateurs aisés. La boulotte Isetta permet la motorisation la plus élémentaire que l'on puisse imaginer. Quant aux pétaradantes 600 et 700, il s'agit au mieux de motos avec un parapluie pour les passagers.

Fritz Könecke envoie Paul Heim, un ex-directeur de l'usine de Sindelfingen, à Munich pour se faire une idée de la situation. Heim est marié à une fille de Franz Josef Popp, le directeur général de BMW. Le résultat de son enquête est plutôt décourageant, d'autant plus que, avec l'acquisition d'Auto Union, on a déjà un lourd boulet à traîner. La question est classée immédiatement, bien que le gouvernement régional bavarois lui-même ait fait des démarches auprès de Daimler-Benz pour qu'elle vienne en aide à la firme munichoise malade.

Un article publié dans la *Süddeutsche Zeitung* du 11 novembre 1959 intitulé « Le destin de BMW » décrit bien la situation : « Comme l'administration l'a communiqué, l'entreprise a subi, ces dix dernières années, 49 millions de marks de pertes. Les dettes à court terme s'élèvent à environ 60 millions de marks. Une liquidation de la société, sinon des mesures plus graves encore, semblent inévitables, de l'avis de l'administration, si le plan d'assainissement présenté par le conseil de surveillance n'est pas accepté par les actionnaires lors de l'assemblée générale du 9 décembre. [...] Le plan d'assainissement mise essentiellement sur le fait qu'une exploitation rentable des capacités de BMW pourrait être garantie par des commandes de Daimler-Benz et que le financement en serait assuré par un consortium regroupant la Deutsche Bank, la Bayerische Staatsbank, le Bayerische Landesanstalt für Aufbaufinanzierung et Daimler-Benz AG. Ce plan d'assainissement équivaut évidemment, en dernier ressort, à intégrer les Bayerische Motoren Werke à une Daimler-Benz AG dominée par

the capital of BMW will belong to the Flick Group. The question is to what extent BMW's independence can be retained in this."

In early December the Mercedes board of management sent a circular to 63,000 staff which betrayed the Stuttgarters' intentions: "In recent weeks an opportunity was presented from outside which required careful examination. You will yourself have heard news of how Bayerische Motoren Werke AG has tried to find a way out of its long-term crisis. It has become clear in the last few months that this company is no longer able to secure its future by its own efforts. The view has long been expressed by the business community and the German public that a tie-up between the well-known Bavarian car maker and Daimler-Benz AG could represent a solution. When BMW and the Bavarian state government requested us … to help in the restructuring, the supervisory board and board of management of our company were unable to refuse. Such assistance with restructuring would give our company the opportunity to use the free capacity at Bayerische Motoren Werke AG for ourselves and in so doing to ensure full employment for the work force of some 6000. After a necessary start-up time, this will enable us to shorten our delivery times in the most economical way for us."

9 December 1959 was therefore the fateful day for the proud white-and-blue make and its shareholders: an ultimatum for restructuring and therefore sale, or bankruptcy and thus the devaluation of all shares – whatever happened, however, it involved a loss of face and identity.

The general mood was not necessarily favorable: a *Simplicissimus* caricature with the caption "Abs-olutism" showed the chairman of the Mercedes supervisory board enthroned and wearing a lavishly curled long wig while a wretched creature labeled "Industry" cowered humbly in the dust before him. What particularly incensed the old BMW shareholders was that they were not to receive any new shares. The plan was almost brought down at the 39th AGM in the history of Bayerische Motoren Werke, not least by the rhetorical force and tactical skill of the Frankfurt lawyer Dr. Friedrich Mathern and the Darmstadt coal merchant Erich Nold.

However, Daimler-Benz AG gained control of its keenest competitor.

letztlich darauf hinaus, die Bayerischen Motoren Werke der von Flick beherrschten Daimler-Benz AG … anzugliedern. Über kurz oder lang würden wohl 75 Prozent des Kapitals von BMW dem Flick-Konzern gehören. Die Frage ist, wie weit dabei die Eigenständigkeit der BMW erhalten werden kann.«

Anfang Dezember verschickt der Mercedes-Vorstand ein Rundschreiben an 63 000 Mitarbeiter, der die Optik der Stuttgarter verrät: »In den vergangenen Wochen bot sich von außen eine Gelegenheit an, die einer gewissenhaften Prüfung unterzogen werden musste. Sie selbst haben in der letzten Zeit verfolgt, wie sich die Bayerische Motoren Werke AG bemühte, aus ihrer langjährigen Krise herauszufinden. In den letzten Monaten wurde klar, dass dieses Unternehmen nicht mehr in der Lage ist, aus eigener Kraft wieder sicheren Boden zu gewinnen. In Kreisen der Wirtschaft und der deutschen Öffentlichkeit wurde schon seit längerem die Meinung vertreten, dass eine Verbindung des bekannten bayerischen Automobilwerks mit der Daimler-Benz AG einen Ausweg darstellen könnte. Als sich BMW und der bayerische Staat um Mitwirkung bei der Sanierung… an uns wandten, konnten sich Aufsichtsrat und Vorstand unserer Gesellschaft dem nicht verschließen. Mit einer solchen Sanierungshilfe würde sich für unsere Gesellschaft die Möglichkeit ergeben, die freie Kapazität der Bayerische Motoren Werke AG für uns auszunützen und damit die rund 6000 Mitarbeiter zählende Belegschaft voll zu beschäftigen. Dadurch können wir nach einer notwendigen Anlaufzeit unsere Lieferfristen auf die für uns wirtschaftlichste Weise verkürzen.«

Der 9. Dezember 1959 wird also zum Schicksalstag für die stolze weißblaue Marke und ihre Aktionäre: Sanierung in ultimativer Verpackung und damit praktisch Verkauf, oder Konkurs und somit Entwertung aller Anteile – in jedem Falle aber Verlust von Gesicht und Identität.

Die allgemeine Stimmung ist nicht unbedingt günstig: Eine Karikatur des *Simplicissimus* mit der Bildunterschrift »Abs-olutismus« zeigt den Mercedes-Aufsichtsratsvorsitzenden hoch thronend mit üppig sich ringelnder Allonge-Perücke, während vor ihm eine armselige Kreatur mit der Aufschrift »Industrie« demütig im Staube kauert. Vor allem ergrimmt die Alt-Aktionäre von BMW, dass sie keine jungen Aktien erhalten sollen. Auf der 39. Hauptversammlung in der Geschichte der Bayerischen Motoren Werke wird der Plan praktisch zu Fall gebracht, nicht zuletzt wegen Wortgewalt und taktischem Geschick des Frankfurter Rechtsanwalts Dr. Friedrich Mathern und des Darmstädter Kohlenhändlers Erich Nold.

Der Daimler-Benz AG aber bleibt der liebste Konkurrent erhalten.

Flick… À court ou à long terme, 75 % du capital de BMW appartiendraient sans aucun doute au groupe Flick. La question est de savoir jusqu'à quel point on pourrait alors préserver l'indépendance de BMW. »

Début décembre, le directoire de Mercedes envoie à 63 000 collaborateurs une circulaire qui indique le point de vue du constructeur de Stuttgart : « Ces dernières semaines, une occasion méritant d'être examinée consciencieusement nous a été offerte. Ces derniers temps, vous avez vous-mêmes suivi comment les Bayerische Motoren Werke AG s'efforçaient de sortir de leur longue crise. Ces derniers mois, il est apparu clairement que cette entreprise n'était plus en mesure de se rétablir de ses propres forces. Les milieux économiques et l'opinion publique allemande sont depuis longtemps d'avis qu'une liaison entre le célèbre constructeur automobile bavarois et Daimler-Benz AG pourrait constituer une issue. Lorsque BMW et l'État bavarois se sont adressés à nous […] pour participer à cet assainissement, le conseil de surveillance et le directoire de notre société n'ont pas pu faire la sourde oreille. Cette aide à l'assainissement donnerait à notre société la possibilité d'exploiter pour nous les capacités vacantes des Bayerische Motoren Werke AG et, ainsi, d'employer à temps complet les quelque 6000 collaborateurs du personnel. Cela nous permettrait en outre, après la période de lancement nécessaire, de réduire nos délais de livraison de la façon la plus économique pour nous. »

Le 9 décembre 1959 est un bien mauvais cadeau de Noël anticipé pour la fière marque à l'emblème bleu et blanc et ses actionnaires : assainissement sous forme d'ultimatum équivalant *de facto* à une vente ou faillite et, donc, à une perte sèche pour tous les actionnaires – mais, dans tous les cas, cela signifierait aussi perdre la face et son identité.

L'atmosphère générale n'est pas vraiment favorable : une caricature de la revue satirique *Simplicissimus* avec la légende « Abs-olutisme » représente le président du conseil de surveillance de Mercedes tout en haut de son trône avec une perruque à la Louis XIV tandis qu'une misérable créature portant l'inscription « industrie » se jette à ses pieds. Les anciens actionnaires de BMW sont surtout furieux parce qu'ils n'obtiendraient pas de nouvelles actions. Lors de la 39e assemblée générale dans l'histoire des Bayerische Motoren Werke, le plan capote, aussi et surtout à cause du réquisitoire et de la bonne tactique de l'avocat francfortois Friedrich Mathern et d'un marchand de charbon de Darmstadt, Erich Nold.

Daimler-Benz AG conserve donc son rival favori.

Diastole and systole 1959–1969

While the Fifties were paved with the gold of growth, progress, perhaps even with the advance of collective reason as proposed by Immanuel Kant and with the innocent belief that things would always continue like this, many a dream, vision and illusion went into a spin in the Sixties.

Fate crystallizes into dates, and dates make history. 1961 saw the building of the Wall as a horribly-German metastasis of the Iron Curtain. The Cuban crisis of 1962 revealed the red-hot magma below the solidified lava of the Cold War. In 1963 the world became a little colder and a bit darker after the assassination of John Fitzgerald Kennedy, and the end of the Adenauer era also marked the end of the charming Rhenish Gemütlichkeit in Rhöndorf which rapidly disappeared into the twilight of history with the Grand Coalition of 1966 and the Social Democrat/Liberal coalition of 1969.

However, the student revolution of 1968 not only broke down crumbling and decrepit structures, but also caused incalculable damage itself and created uncertainty without offering any actual new sense of direction. And while other currencies stumbled and fell, the German mark survived the decade in the rudest of health and was even twice revalued, in March 1961 by five per cent and in October 1969 by 9.3 per cent with the familiar consequences for business and its ability to export.

This caused a lot of problems, even around the car industry, particularly in 1967, the year of the economic blip. Daimler-Benz AG, on the other hand, skated almost unscathed over the raging waters. Domestic sales grew from 1.444 billion marks in 1960 (with a capital stock of 270 million) to 6.473 billion marks in 1970 (when the capital stock had been increased to 761 million), foreign sales grew from 1.027 billion to 5.202 billion, production from 174,908 to 397,122 units (not including component sets), and the work force from 67,521 to 116,985. However, Daimler-Benz the truck producer felt the keen wind of competition much more than the manufacturer of luxury cars. Here, demand always exceeded supply, an equation that was always consciously and carefully cultivated by Fritz Könecke and his successor, the Austrian honorary planning and construction official Walter Hitzinger. They believed that if a thing was worth having, it was worth being rare and not cheap. In November 1960 Könecke voluntarily requested the supervisory board to relieve him of his duties. Friedrich Flick put forward Hitzinger, the head of the steel group Vereinigte Österreichische Eisen- and Stahlwerke (VÖEST) in Linz, who was appointed chief executive and chairman of the board of management with effect from 10 February 1961.

A five-year period was scheduled and was not extended since Hitzinger had an unfortunate touch in many respects and loyalty towards him soon crumbled. During this period Joachim Zahn, doctor of law, financial expert and member

Diastole und Systole 1959–1969

Sind die fünfziger Jahre übergoldet von Wachstum, Fortschritt, vielleicht sogar durch ein Voranschreiten der kollektiven Vernunft im Sinne Immanuel Kants, sowie durch den blauäugig-pausbäckigen Glauben, das alles werde immerfort so weitergehen, geraten in den Sechzigern so manche Träume, Visionen und Illusionen ins Trudeln.

Das Schicksal kristallisiert sich in Daten, und Daten machen Geschichte: 1961 errichtet man die Mauer als ekligdeutsche Metastase des Eisernen Vorhangs. 1962 lässt die Kuba-Krise jäh das rotglühende Magma unter der erstarrten Lava des Kalten Krieges durchscheinen. 1963 wird die Welt nach der Ermordung John Fitzgerald Kennedys ein wenig kälter und ein bisschen dunkler, und das Ende der Ära Adenauer markiert auch das Ende der rheinisch-charmanten Rhöndorfer Gemütlichkeit, die mit der Großen Koalition von 1966 und der sozialliberalen Koalition von 1969 hurtig im Halbdämmern der Historie verschwindet.

Die Studentenrevolution von 1968 aber bricht nicht nur verharschte und verkrustete Strukturen auf, sondern richtet ihrerseits unübersehbaren Flurschaden an, schafft Verunsicherung ohne wirkliche Neuorientierung. Und während andere Währungen wanken und straucheln, übersteht die Deutsche Mark die Dekade strahlend stark und unversehrt, wird gar zweimal aufgewertet, im März 1961 um fünf Prozent, im Oktober 1969 um 9,3 Prozent mit den bekannten Konsequenzen für die Wirtschaft und ihre Exportfähigkeit.

Das macht so manchem zu schaffen, selbst im Umfeld der Autoindustrie, vor allem im Jahr der konjunkturellen Kerbe 1967. Die Daimler-Benz AG hingegen schwebt fast unversehrt über den wogenden Wassern. Der Inlandumsatz wächst von 1,444 Milliarden Mark 1960 (bei einem Grundkapital von 270 Millionen) auf 6,473 Milliarden Mark 1970 (als sich das Grundkapital auf 761 Millionen beläuft), der Auslandsumsatz von 1,027 Milliarden auf 5,202 Milliarden, die Produktion von 174 908 auf 397 122 Einheiten (ohne Teilesätze), die Zahl der Mitarbeiter von 67 521 auf 116 985. Dabei bläst dem LKW-Produzenten Daimler-Benz der schneidende Wind des Wettbewerbs viel heftiger ins Gesicht als dem Hersteller gehobener Automobile. Immer übersteigt da die Nachfrage das Angebot, eine Relation, die von Fritz Könecke und seinem Nachfolger im Amt, dem österreichischen Baurat honoris causa Walter Hitzinger, bewusst und sorgsam kultiviert wird: Was gut ist, soll auch rar und nicht billig sein. Könecke ersucht den Aufsichtsrat im November 1960 aus freien Stücken um seine Entlassung. Friedrich Flick lanciert Hitzinger, Chef der Vereinigten Österreichischen Eisen- und Stahlwerke (VÖEST) in Linz, der mit Wirkung vom 10. Februar 1961 zum Generaldirektor und Vorsitzenden des Vorstands ernannt wird.

Eine Verweildauer von fünf Jahren wird vorgesehen und nicht verlängert, da Hitzinger in vielen Dingen eine unglückliche Hand hat und die Loyalität ihm gegenüber rasch bröckelt. In dieser Phase gewinnt Joachim Zahn an

Diastole et systole 1959–1969

Après des années 1950 ripolinées à l'or de la croissance, du progrès et, peut-être aussi, d'une propagation de la raison collective dans le sens d'Emmanuel Kant ainsi que d'une croyance un peu naïve que tout continuerait ainsi, les années 1960 voient s'effondrer nombre de rêves, de visions et d'illusions.

Le destin se matérialise dans des dates et ce sont les dates qui marquent l'histoire : en 1961 s'élève le mur de Berlin en tant que repoussante métastase allemande du rideau de fer. En 1962, la crise de Cuba fait jaillir brutalement le magma brûlant sous la lave solidifiée de la guerre froide. En 1963, après l'assassinat de John Fitzgerald Kennedy, le monde se refroidit et s'assombrit quelque peu alors que la fin de l'ère Adenauer symbolise aussi l'achèvement de la bonne humeur au charme rhénan régnant à Rhöndorf, qui disparaît brutalement dans les oubliettes de l'histoire avec la grande coalition de 1966 et la coalition sociale-libérale de 1969.

Quant à la révolution estudiantine de 1968, elle ne fait pas seulement éclater les structures rigidifiées et encroûtées. Elle cause elle aussi des dommages irréparables et fait naître l'incertitude sans donner une réelle réorientation. Et, tandis que d'autres monnaies vacillent et s'effondrent, le deutsche Mark franchit la décennie rayonnant et invulnérable, et est même réévalué à deux reprises (en mars 1961 de 5 % et de 9,3 % en octobre 1969), avec les conséquences bien connues sur l'économie et les industries exportatrices.

Il en résulte bien des difficultés, même dans l'environnement de l'industrie automobile, notamment en 1967, année de baisse conjoncturelle. Daimler-Benz AG, par contre, semble surfer sur cette mer agitée. Le chiffre d'affaires domestique passe de 1,444 milliard de marks en 1960 (pour un capital social de 270 millions) à 6,473 milliards en 1970 (pour un capital social de 761 millions) ; le chiffre d'affaires à l'étranger augmente de 1,027 milliard à 5,202 milliards, la production, de 174 908 à 397 122 exemplaires (sans les kits de pièces détachées) et les effectifs croissent de 67 521 à 116 985. Simultanément, Daimler-Benz constructeur de camions doit faire face à une concurrence beaucoup plus vive en tant que fabricant de voitures de luxe. Dans ce segment, en effet, la demande est toujours supérieure à l'offre, une demande que Fritz Könecke et son successeur, l'Autrichien Walter Hitzinger, cultivent sciemment et avec minutie : ce qui est bon doit aussi être rare, mais surtout pas bon marché. En novembre 1960, Könecke demande de son propre chef au conseil de surveillance d'accepter sa démission. Pour le remplacer, Friedrich Flick avance le nom de Hitzinger, P.-D.G. des usines sidérurgiques autrichiennes VÖEST à Linz, qui est nommé directeur général et président du conseil de surveillance avec effet au 10 février 1961.

Ses fonctions prévues pour cinq ans ne sont pas prorogées, car, sur certaines questions, les choix de Hitzinger ont été malheureux, et la loyauté à son égard se dissipe

of the board of management since October 1958, increased his standing and, with his skillful arguments, became a beneficiary of the difficult interplay between the respected senior ranks of his colleagues such as Arnold Wychodil, Fritz Nallinger and Hanns Martin Schleyer, and the unpopular Austrian. On the latter's departure, no one was surprised when the choice fell on Zahn, who became the chief executive from 1 November 1965 onwards and was chairman of the board of management between 1971 and 1979.

He found himself faced by the contemporary equivalent of the eternal double-headed challenge: to rationalize and expand capacity. Even the founding fathers Daimler and Benz had been hemmed in by organic structures. After the Second World War too groundwork was needed, for example when car production was shifted in its entirety from the extremely cramped conditions in Untertürkheim to the more spacious accommodation offered by Sindelfingen. This would anyway have been necessary at the latest with the 1953 launch of the 180 model with its monocoque design. Between 1949 and 1958 15 million marks were invested here on average annually, and 45 million marks on average up to 1968.

The most sought-after – and most difficult to obtain – were, of course, plots and premises directly adjacent to or close to the head office in Untertürkheim. In 1955 Daimler-Benz acquired a plot to the north-west as part of an exchange deal with the Stuttgart city authorities and then in the Sixties purchased further land along the River Neckar towards the south-east, in Stuttgart-Hedelfingen (previous owner: Schaudt Maschinenbau), in Brühl (previous owner: Württembergische Baumwoll-Spinnerei and -Weberei) and in Esslingen-Mettingen (previous owner: Maschinenfabrik Esslingen), which at 550,000 square meters in total was only 10,000 less than the area of the Untertürkheim works.

The chronic shortage of space at Mercedes inevitably gave rise to a policy of far-flung multi-centrism. In 1960 it

Showing the way: Friedrich Flick (left) and Joachim Zahn (right).
Richtungsweisend: Friedrich Flick (links) und Joachim Zahn (rechts).
Prophètes en leur pays : Friedrich Flick (à gauche) et Joachim Zahn (à droite).

Profil, Doktor der Rechte, Finanzexperte und Mitglied des Vorstands seit Oktober 1958, wird gewandt argumentierend zum Nutznießer im schwierigen Widerspiel zwischen der gestandenen Seniorenriege seiner Kollegen, wie etwa Arnold Wychodil, Fritz Nallinger und Hanns Martin Schleyer, und dem ungeliebten Österreicher. Als dieser geht, fällt die Wahl zu niemandes Überraschung auf Zahn, ab 1. November 1965 »Sprecher« und zwischen 1971 und 1979 Vorsitzender des Vorstands.

Er sieht sich der zeitgenössischen Variante einer ewigen Doppel-Herausforderung gegenüber: Rationalisierung und Erweiterung der Kapazitäten – schon die Firmenväter Daimler und Benz wurden ja von historisch gewachsenen Strukturen eingezwängt. Auch nach dem Zweiten Weltkrieg gibt es Vorarbeit, als etwa die komplette PKW-Fertigung aus der qualvollen Enge von Untertürkheim in die freiere Luft von Sindelfingen ausgesiedelt wird. Spätestens der Typ 180 von 1953 mit seiner selbsttragenden Karosserie hätte ohnehin kategorisch nach einem gemeinsamen Dach verlangt. Zwischen 1949 und 1958 werden hier jährlich im Schnitt 15 Millionen Mark, bis 1968 durchschnittlich 45 Millionen Mark investiert.

Am begehrtesten – und am schwierigsten zu haben – sind naturgemäß Grundstücke und Komplexe, die sich unmittelbar an die Zentrale in Untertürkheim anlagern oder benachbart. 1955 erwirbt Daimler-Benz im Zuge eines Tauschs mit der Stadt Stuttgart ein Gelände nordwestlich davon und verleibt sich in den sechziger Jahren entlang des Neckars in Richtung Südosten weitere Liegenschaften ein, in Stuttgart-Hedelfingen (Vorbesitzer: Schaudt Maschinenbau), in Brühl (Vorbesitzer: die Württembergische Baumwoll-Spinnerei und -Weberei) und in Esslingen-Mettingen (Vorbesitzer: die Maschinenfabrik Esslingen), zusammen mit 550 000 Quadratmetern nur 10 000 weniger als die Grundfläche des Werks Untertürkheim.

Die chronische Raumnot der Marke mit dem Stern gebiert unausweichlich einen weitläufigen Polyzentrismus: 1960 übernimmt man den moribunden Zweiradhersteller Horex KG in Bad Homburg, pachtet 1962 das Gelände der Auto Union in Düsseldorf, deren Produktion inzwischen nach Ingolstadt verlegt worden ist, kauft sich 1968 mit 92 Prozent bei der Ernst Heinkel AG in Stuttgart-Zuffenhausen ein, übernimmt im gleichen Jahr die Hanomag-Werke in Hannover, Bremen und Hamburg-Harburg sowie das Henschel-Werk in Kassel und ersteht 1969 die Werkzeugmaschinenfabrik Köngen.

Beklemmend beengt sind auch die Verhältnisse in Mannheim und Gaggenau. Die LKW-Produktion dort birst aus allen Nähten, und Abhilfe tut not. Entlastung winkt gewissermaßen von der grünen Wiese in Wörth, in Rheinnähe westlich von Karlsruhe, wo die Gemeinde ein 1,5 Millionen Quadratmeter großes Baugelände feilbietet. Der Vorteile sind viele: Straßen- und Bahnanbindungen sowie ein Rheinhafen sind unschwer herzustellen, die Mercedes-Standorte Stuttgart, Mannheim und Gaggenau liegen nicht weit, die Anreisewege für Pendler aus benachbarten Bal-

rapidement. C'est alors que se profile un certain Joachim Zahn, docteur en droit, expert financier et membre du directoire depuis octobre 1958, dont les solides arguments font de lui le bénéficiaire des oppositions entre des rivaux tels qu'Arnold Wychodil, Fritz Nallinger et Hanns Martin Schleyer, d'une part, et l'Autrichien peu aimé, d'autre part. Au départ de celui-ci, nul n'est surpris de voir Zahn élu « porte-parole », le 1er novembre 1965, avant de devenir, de 1971 à 1979, président du directoire.

Il se voit confronté à la nouvelle version d'un éternel double défi : rationalisation et extension des capacités – les pères fondateurs de la firme, Daimler et Benz, ont, en leur temps déjà, été confrontés aux contraintes de structures historiques. Même après la Seconde Guerre mondiale le travail ne manque pas puisque l'on transfère par exemple le montage complet des voitures particulières de l'étouffant corset d'Untertürkheim vers les grands espaces de Sindelfingen. La 180 de 1953 à la carrosserie autoporteuse aurait de toute façon imposé catégoriquement une usine unique. De 1949 à 1958, on y investit chaque année en moyenne 15 millions de marks et même 45 millions jusqu'en 1968.

Les plus recherchés – mais aussi les plus difficiles à obtenir – sont notamment les terrains et complexes contigus ou proches de la centrale à Untertürkheim. En 1955, en un échange avec la ville de Stuttgart, Daimler-Benz acquiert un terrain au nord-ouest d'Untertürkheim et s'approprie, dans les années 1960, d'autres terrains longeant le Neckar en direction du sud-est, à Stuttgart-Hedelfingen (ancien propriétaire : Schaudt Maschinenbau), à Brühl (ancien propriétaire : la Württembergische Baumwoll-Spinnerei und -Weberei) et à Esslingen-Mettingen (ancien propriétaire : Maschinenfabrik Esslingen) ; au total 550 000 m², à peine 10 000 de moins que la superficie de l'usine d'Untertürkheim.

Le manque d'espace chronique de la marque à l'étoile génère inéluctablement un polycentrisme tous azimuts : en 1960, elle reprend le moribond fabricant de motos Horex KG à Bad Hombourg, loue en 1962 le terrain d'Auto Union à Düsseldorf, dont la production a entre-temps été transférée à Ingolstadt, reprend, en 1968, 92 % du capital d'Ernst Heinkel AG à Stuttgart-Zuffenhausen, achète la même année les usines Hanomag de Hanovre, de Brême et de Hambourg-Harbourg ainsi que l'usine Henschel de Kassel, et acquiert en 1969 l'usine de machines-outils de Köngen.

Elle est tout aussi à l'étroit à Mannheim et à Gaggenau. Là, la production de camions requiert des infrastructures plus vastes et il est urgent d'y remédier : la solution s'offre dans la verdure à Wörth, non loin du Rhin, à l'ouest de Karlsruhe, où la commune propose un terrain à bâtir de 1,5 million de mètres carrés. Les avantages sont nombreux : il n'est pas difficile d'établir les liaisons routières et ferroviaires nécessaires ainsi qu'avec le port du Rhin, les sites de Mercedes – Stuttgart, Mannheim et Gaggenau – ne sont pas éloignés et les trajets à couvrir par les ouvriers des agglomérations voisines ne sont pas trop longs. En outre,

took over the moribund bicycle manufacturer Horex KG in Bad Homburg, in 1962 took on the lease of the Auto Union site in Düsseldorf whose production had by then been transferred to Ingolstadt, purchased a 92 per cent holding in Ernst Heinkel AG in Stuttgart-Zuffenhausen in 1968, in the same year took over the Hanomag works in Hanover, Bremen and Hamburg-Harburg and the Henschel works in Kassel, and in 1969 acquired Werkzeugmaschinenfabrik Köngen.

The premises in Mannheim and Gaggenau were also claustrophobically cramped. Truck production there was bursting at the seams, and a solution was urgently needed. Relief was at hand, as it were, in the form of a green field in Wörth, to the west of Karlsruhe and close to the Rhine, where the local council was offering a 1.5 million square meter building plot for sale. The advantages were legion: road and rail connections and a Rhine barge harbor could easily be built, the Mercedes sites in Stuttgart, Mannheim and Gaggenau were not far away, the travel distances for commuters from adjacent population centers were not excessive. Furthermore, the state government under Prime Minister Peter Altmeier was prepared to offer all kinds of inducements to tempt an attractive Daimler-Benz project to this out-of-the-way corner of the Rhineland-Palatinate.

On 21 June 1960 Joachim Zahn and Hanns Martin Schleyer attended a meeting in Mainz and took the good news back with them that the state government intended building a flood prevention scheme for the Rhine and also a rail connection. On 2 August a contract was negotiated at the council offices in Germersheim which specified a price of 1.40 marks per square meter. This agreement, which incorporated an option on further land, was signed in Untertürkheim on 17 November. However, no firm decision had yet been taken on what exactly to do with this acquisition on the left bank of the Rhine, although it was linked with all sorts of speculation. Finally in the 1964 annual report it was announced that Wörth would be used for the central assembly of trucks. Suddenly everything seemed perfectly logical: a scheme for the division of labor like that between Untertürkheim and Sindelfingen could be implemented. Mannheim was responsible for building buses, and so the engines came from there. Gaggenau remained the center for Unimog production and supplied individual assemblies, gearboxes and axles.

The first trucks left the new assembly lines on 14 July 1965, by which time the latest branch already employed 2600 staff. An expansion of capacity by a quarter to 48,000 units was aimed at, almost achieved in 1968 and then rapidly exceeded. Wörth became the largest truck assembly plant in Europe.

Volume production on this scale cut overheads dramatically. The separation of unit manufacturing from assembly also allowed a more flexible reaction to changing market demands. The net was cast wide. Hardly any further domestic growth could be expected, and so the increased production went for export, in 1985, for example, 76,200 of the 220,500 commercial vehicles produced – not

Hanns Martin Schleyer with Ulrich Raue, member of the board of management between 1966 and 1974.
Hanns Martin Schleyer mit Ulrich Raue, Vorstandsmitglied zwischen 1966 und 1974.
Hanns Martin Schleyer, avec Ulrich Raue, membre du directoire de 1966 à 1974.

lungszentren halten sich in Grenzen. Überdies lockt die Landesregierung unter Ministerpräsident Peter Altmeier mit Wohlwollen sowie allerlei Vergünstigungen für ein attraktives Vorhaben von Daimler-Benz in diesem entlegenen Winkel von Rheinland-Pfalz.

Am 21. Juni 1960 werden Joachim Zahn und Hanns Martin Schleyer in Mainz vorstellig und nehmen die frohe Botschaft mit nach Hause, das Land werde den Rheindamm hochwassersicher ausbauen und auch einen Gleisanschluss herstellen. Am 2. August handelt man auf dem Landratsamt in Germersheim ein Vertragswerk aus, das einen Preis von 1,40 Mark pro Quadratmeter vorsieht. Am 17. November wird die Vereinbarung in Untertürkheim unterzeichnet, eine Option auf weiteres Gelände eingebaut. Nur: Was man mit der Anschaffung am linken Rheinufer eigentlich anfangen will, steht noch nicht fest, eine Dispositionsmasse, die in vielerlei Zusammenhänge gestellt wird. Erst 1964 steht im Geschäftsbericht, Wörth werde der zentralen Montage von Lastwagen zugeführt. Auf einmal erscheint alles ganz logisch: Ein arbeitsteiliges Verhältnis bietet sich an, wie zwischen Untertürkheim und Sindelfingen. Mannheim obliegt der Bau von Bussen, von dort kommen die Motoren. Gaggenau bleibt Garnison für die Herstellung des Unimog und liefert Einzelaggregate, Getriebe und Achsen.

Am 14. Juli 1965 – die jüngste Filiale beschäftigt bereits 2600 Mitarbeiter – verlässt der erste LKW eines der neuen Bänder. Eine Erweiterung der Kapazität um ein Viertel auf 48 000 Einheiten wird angestrebt, ist 1968 fast erreicht und wird dann zügig überschritten. Wörth ist das größte LKW-Montagewerk in Europa.

Die großen Serien schmelzen die Kosten ab. Die Abtrennung der Aggregate-Fertigung von der Montage gestattet auch eine flexible Anpassung an die wechselnden Bedürfnisse des Markts. Man streut weit: Im Inland sind kaum noch Zuwächse zu verzeichnen, also wird das Mehr an Produktion in den Export gelenkt, 1985 zum Beispiel 76 200 von den 220 500 produzierten Nutzfahrzeugen

le gouvernement régional dirigé par le ministre président Peter Altmeier fait miroiter des avantages en tout genre pour un attrayant projet de Daimler-Benz dans ce coin un peu isolé de Rhénanie-Palatinat.

Le 21 juin 1960, Joachim Zahn et Hanns Martin Schleyer, après une réunion à Mayence, rapportent la bonne nouvelle selon laquelle le Land rendrait la digue du Rhin à l'épreuve des inondations et réaliserait aussi un raccordement ferroviaire. Le 2 août, ils négocient avec le conseil régional de Germersheim un contrat prévoyant un prix de 1,40 mark au m². Le 17 novembre, l'accord est signé à Untertürkheim avec une option pour un autre terrain. Seul bémol : on ne sait pas encore comment disposer de l'acquisition sur la rive gauche du Rhin, terrain vacant qui peut se prêter à de nombreux usages. Ce n'est qu'en 1964, dans le rapport d'activités, qu'il est dit que Wörth serait le site du montage central des camions. D'un coup, tout cette opération s'inscrit dans la plus parfaite logique : c'est le reflet du partage du travail tel qu'il est pratiqué entre Untertürkheim et Sindelfingen. L'usine de Mannheim est chargée de construire les autobus et de fournir les moteurs. Gaggenau reste le berceau de l'Unimog et livre les différents organes, les boîtes de vitesses et les essieux.

Le 14 juillet 1965 – la nouvelle filiale emploie déjà 2600 collaborateurs – le premier camion sort des nouvelles chaînes. On envisage une augmentation des capacités de 25 %, à 48 000 unités, ce qui est presque atteint en 1968 puis dépassé rapidement. Wörth est la plus grande usine de montage de camions d'Europe.

Les économies d'échelle favorisent la diminution des coûts. La séparation entre la fabrication des organes et leur montage permet aussi de réagir avec plus de souplesse aux fluctuations du marché. On pratique la politique de l'arrosoir : puisque l'on ne peut plus guère enregistrer de taux de croissance en Allemagne, l'excédent de production est dirigé vers les marchés étrangers : en 1985, cet excédent correspond à 76 200 des 220 500 véhicules utilitaires produits – compte non tenu des 26 400 kits de véhicules prévus pour le montage à l'étranger. Jusqu'à cette date, on a investi au total 1,3 milliard de marks à Wörth, notamment dans plus de 500 000 m² de terrains supplémentaires.

Une autre question trouve également sa réponse : où installer la fabrication de gros moteurs ? C'est l'occasion pour des personnages qui sont des constantes dans la généalogie récente de Daimler-Benz de réapparaître. C'est de nouveau Friedrich Flick qui pose les premiers jalons en offrant à Mercedes, en juillet 1960, ses actions dans Maybach Motoren AG à Friedrichshafen, offre que l'équipe de Fritz Könecke accueille les bras ouverts. Par le biais d'une holding intermédiaire, ils possèdent bientôt pour 8,8 millions de marks d'actions, près des trois quarts du capital social, et l'on fabrique déjà, l'année suivante, les premiers moteurs Diesel à hautes performances dans l'ancienne usine mère de Maybach. Si c'est un progrès, ce n'est pas encore une solution définitive. Une seconde chance s'offre durant l'été 1963, lorsque l'on peut louer pour cinq ans le terrain

including the 26,400 vehicle kits for assembly abroad. Up to that year a total of 1.3 billion marks had been invested in Wörth, including further plots of 500,000 square meters.

When the question was then asked of where the manufacture of large engines should be based, the names mentioned included those steeped in resonances of the past which had helped to shape Daimler-Benz's early corporate history. In June 1960 Friedrich Flick again set the future course by offering Mercedes his shares in Maybach Motoren AG in Friedrichshafen, and Fritz Könecke's advisers were keen to accept. Through an intermediate holding company, Daimler-Benz soon held shares to the value of 8.88 million marks, almost three-quarters of the stock capital, and by the following year was already manufacturing the first high-performance diesel engines in the former headquarters of Maybach's company. This was a step forward, but still not the ultimate solution. A second chance came up in the summer of 1963 when Mercedes was able to lease the premises of Porsche-Diesel Motorenbau GmbH in the Friedrichshafen suburb of Manzell for five years, and the construction of special large engines began in August. Two years before expiry of the contract these two branches beside Lake Constance found themselves under the umbrella of the new company name Maybach Mercedes-Benz Motorenbau GmbH. In 1968 Daimler-Benz bought the property in Manzell on the banks of the lake for 17.1 million marks which, even when added to the leasing costs up to this point of 12.5 million, still represented good value as an acquisition.

At this point talks were being held with Maschinenfabrik Augsburg-Nürnberg (MAN) with the aim of achieving a merger of the new Daimler subsidiary and the MAN subsidiary Turbo GmbH in Munich on a parity basis. At the heart of the joint venture was the shared manufacture of jet engines and gas turbines. The corresponding contract was signed in Munich in July 1969, and the two partners were converted into Motoren- und Turbinen-Union Friedrichshafen GmbH and Motoren- und Turbinen-Union München GmbH. A star, MTU, was born, which enjoys worldwide renown as a producer of high-tech units. Following the transfer of MAN's 50 per cent holding in 1985 Daimler-Benz AG has been the sole partner, "a consistent step towards the target of diversification of the corporate base to include new, sophisticated technologies" as expressed in such a factual paean in company literature. The fate of the "component agreement" between the two corporations, by means of which truck engines developed by Daimler-Benz were to be supplied to both partners and were to enable economies of scale, was less profitable and also regarded with suspicion by Germany's Federal Cartel Office since it was in a competitive gray area. But its the small things that cause the problems. Furthermore, neither partner wished to endanger the shared fruit of their loins, MTU, and so the problem child was buried in December 1981 on expiry of the originally contracted period of ten years.

– nicht eingerechnet die 26 400 Fahrzeugsätze für die Montage im Ausland. Bis zu jenem Jahr hat man in Wörth insgesamt 1,3 Milliarden Mark investiert, unter anderem in weitere Grundstücke über 500 000 Quadratmeter.

Einer Antwort zugeführt wird unterdessen auch die Frage, wo die Fertigung von Großmotoren untergebracht werden soll, und dabei begegnet man Namen, die als Mitgestalter der frühen Firmengeschichte von Daimler-Benz mit der Patina würdigen Alters behaftet sind. Wieder stellt Friedrich Flick Weichen, offeriert Mercedes im Juni 1960 seine Anteile an der Maybach Motoren AG in Friedrichshafen, und die Männer um Fritz Könecke gehen bereitwillig darauf ein. Über eine Zwischenholding besitzt man bald Aktien im Wert von 8,88 Millionen Mark, fast drei Viertel des Stammkapitals, und fertigt schon im folgenden Jahr die ersten Hochleistungs-Dieselmaschinen im ehemaligen Maybach-Stammwerk. Das ist ein Schritt voran, aber noch keine Lösung. Eine zweite Chance bietet sich im Sommer 1963, als man das Gelände der Porsche-Diesel Motorenbau GmbH im Friedrichshafener Vorort Manzell für fünf Jahre pachten kann, wo bereits im August der Bau von Spezial-Großmotoren beginnt. Zwei Jahre vor dem Ablaufen des Vertrags finden sich die beiden Bodensee-Filialen unter dem Dach des neuen Firmennamens Maybach Mercedes-Benz Motorenbau GmbH zusammen. 1968 kauft Daimler-Benz das Manzeller Anwesen am Ufer des Sees für 17,1 Millionen Mark, die sich zum bisherigen Pachtzins von 12,5 Millionen addieren – noch immer eine preiswürdige Anschaffung.

Zu diesem Zeitpunkt laufen schon Gespräche mit der Maschinenfabrik Augsburg-Nürnberg, Ziel: ein Zusammengehen der neuen Daimler-Dependance mit der MAN-Tochter Turbo GmbH in München auf paritätischer Basis. Herzstück des Joint Venture ist die gemeinsame Fertigung von Strahltriebwerken und Gasturbinen. Im Juli 1969 unterzeichnet man in der bayerischen Metropole einen entsprechenden Vertrag, widmet die beiden Teil-Firmen um zur Motoren- und Turbinen-Union Friedrichshafen GmbH und Motoren- und Turbinen-Union München GmbH. Ein Stern wird geboren, die MTU, die weltweites Ansehen genießt als Produzent von High-Tech-Aggregaten. Seit der Übertragung der 50 Prozent MAN-Anteile 1985 ist die Daimler-Benz AG alleinige Gesellschafterin, »ein konsequenter Schritt zur angestrebten Verbreiterung der Unternehmensbasis in Richtung auf neue anspruchsvolle Technologien«, wie es sich sachlich-hymnisch in der Firmenliteratur liest. Weniger ersprießlich und überdies vom Kartellamt misstrauisch beäugt, da im Graubereich des Wettbewerbs angesiedelt, ist das Schicksal des »Komponenten-Vertrags« zwischen den beiden Konzernen: Von Daimler-Benz entwickelte LKW-Aggregate sollen beiden Partnern zugänglich gemacht, beträchtliche Stückzahlen ermöglicht und die Kosten verringert werden. Aber der Teufel steckt im Detail. Überdies möchte man den gemeinsamen Spross MTU nicht gefährden und trägt so das Problemkind mit dem Ablaufen der ursprünglich vereinbarten Frist von zehn Jahren im Dezember 1981 auch tatsächlich zu Grabe.

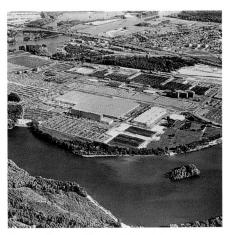

Mercedes-Benz-on-Rhine: the Wörth plant.
Mercedes-Benz in Rhein-Kultur: Werk Wörth.
Mercedes-Benz au vert: l'usine de Wörth, sur le Rhin.

de Porsche-Diesel Motorenbau GmbH à Manzell, dans la banlieue de Friedrichshafen, où, dès août, commence la fabrication de gros moteurs spéciaux. Deux ans avant l'arrivée à expiration du contrat, les deux filiales du lac de Constance fusionnent dans le giron de la firme, rebaptisée Maybach Mercedes-Benz Motorenbau GmbH. En 1968, Daimler-Benz achète le terrain de Manzell sur la rive du lac pour 17,1 millions de marks qui s'ajoutent aux 12,5 millions de loyer payés jusque-là – ce qui est encore une bonne affaire.

À cette époque, on mène déjà des entretiens avec la Maschinenfabrik Augsburg-Nürnberg (MAN), avec pour objectif une alliance entre la nouvelle filiale de Daimler et celle de MAN, Turbo GmbH, à Munich, sur une base paritaire. La clef du joint-venture est la fabrication en commun de moteurs à réaction et de turbines à gaz. En juillet 1969, le contrat correspondant est signé dans la métropole bavaroise et les deux branches sont rebaptisées en Motoren- und Turbinen-Union Friedrichshafen GmbH et Motoren- und Turbinen-Union München GmbH. Une étoile est née, MTU, qui jouit d'un prestige mondial en tant que fabricant de moteurs à haute technologie. Depuis la reprise des 50 % d'actions de MAN en 1985, Daimler-Benz AG est seul maître à bord, « un progrès décisif vers la diversification souhaitée de l'entreprise en direction de nouvelles technologies de pointe », selon la dialectique sobre mais néanmoins élogieuse de la firme. Le destin du « contrat de composants » passé entre les deux groupes est moins productif et regardé d'un œil méfiant par l'Office des fusions, car situé dans la zone grise de la concurrence : des organes de camion fabriqués par Daimler-Benz auraient été mis à la disposition des deux partenaires, ce qui aurait permis de produire à un rythme élevé et de comprimer les dépenses. Mais l'imperfection réside dans les détails. En outre, on ne souhaite pas mettre en danger la filiale commune MTU et, après l'arrivée à expiration de la durée initialement convenue de dix ans, on enterre en catimini le projet en décembre 1981.

Omnipresence, a flirt and a flop 1969–1973

At the beginning of the Seventies Daimler-Benz had a full range of commercial vehicles from vans to heavy goods vehicles, making it the unchallenged world market leader, plus buses of every size. This pleasing news was preceded by tough battles for markets, power and money, and Ulrich Raue in particular, a member of the board of management with responsibility for commercial vehicles since 1966, proved a cunning player. Two of his moves were triggered by the blip in the business cycle which hit the entire trucks sector hard at this time. The constellations showed remarkable parallels since in both cases foreign manufacturers were attempting to gain a foothold in the German market, and decisive action was called for. When Krupp finally decided to pull the plug on its loss-making truck production in 1967, the associated sales organization became redundant. Fiat was waiting in the wings, but Daimler-Benz pounced. Decent conditions were negotiated in a contract dated 28 February 1968, and the Krupp sales force merged seamlessly into the new structures.

A short time later the commercial vehicles section of Rheinstahl AG was up for sale, comprising Henschel in Kassel and Hanomag in Hanover, Hamburg-Harburg and Bremen. Another potential foreign partner in the form of British Leyland was lying in wait. Again, the strategists in Untertürkheim carried out a preemptive strike, offered satisfactory conditions to wrap the matter up and, following an audience with chairman of the supervisory board Hermann J. Abs in the evening of Christmas Eve because of the urgency of the matter, Hanomag-Henschel-Fahrzeugwerke GmbH (or HHF for short) was born.

The name was revealing because the new creation was promised a large degree of autonomy. The stock capital was 40 million marks. A transitional phase of six years was set, but an already ailing Rheinstahl AG transferred its 49 per cent holding in HHF to Daimler-Benz in 1970. The latter had already taken over Hanomag's and Henschel's distribution networks in 1969 and invested 580 million marks in updating the existing factories in Kassel, Harburg and Bremen. At the end of 1977 HHF was incorporated into the parent company.

In the no-man's-land between the systems, and also in the twilight world between politics and business and thus actually on fertile ground was a project that at the same time carried the seed of failure with it from the very start: in the late Sixties USSR was planning a huge plant on the Kama, the largest of the Volga's tributaries, in order to increase truck production capacity within five years from 500,000 to treble that figure. Daimler-Benz was asked whether, on account of its background of experience in Wörth, it wished to be involved in helping the Soviets in an advisory and hands-on capacity. Delegations were exchanged right up to ministerial level, negotiations were

Flächendeckende Präsenz, ein Flirt und ein Flop 1969–1973

Zu Beginn der siebziger Jahre bietet Daimler-Benz ein lückenloses Sortiment an zwischen dem Leichttransporter und dem Schwerlastwagen, wo man eine unangefochtene Spitzenstellung in der Welt einnimmt, dazu Busse jeglichen Formats. Dieser erquicklichen Kunde geht ein zähes Schach um Märkte, Macht und Mammon voraus, und vor allem Ulrich Raue, seit 1966 im Vorstand für das Ressort Nutzfahrzeuge, erweist sich dabei als raffinierter Spieler. Zwei seiner Züge werden angestoßen durch den Konjunktur-Knick, der um diese Zeit der gesamten LKW-Branche wehtut. Die Konstellationen weisen bemerkenswerte Parallelen auf, da in beiden Fällen ausländische Hersteller versuchen, den deutschen Markt zu kolonisieren, und entschlossenes Handeln angesagt ist. Als sich Krupp 1967 dazu durchringt, die Verlustquelle LKW-Produktion versiegen zu lassen, wird die dazugehörige Absatzorganisation redundant. Als Interessent antichambriert Fiat, aber Daimler-Benz reagiert umgehend. In einem Vertrag vom 28. Februar 1968 werden anständige Bedingungen ausgehandelt, und die Krupp-Außenstellen fügen sich geschmeidig in die neuen Strukturen.

Wenig später steht die Sektion Nutzfahrzeuge der Rheinstahl AG zur Disposition, Henschel in Kassel und Hanomag in Hannover, Hamburg-Harburg und Bremen. Wieder liegt mit British Leyland ein potentieller Partner von jenseits der Grenzen auf der Lauer. Erneut holen die Untertürkheimer Strategen zu einem Präventivschlag aus, bringen die Angelegenheit mit zufriedenstellenden Konditionen unter Dach und Fach, und noch in der Christnacht wird nach einer Audienz beim Aufsichtsratsvorsitzenden Hermann J. Abs wegen der Dringlichkeit der Sache die Hanomag-Henschel-Fahrzeugwerke GmbH (kurz HHF) aus der Taufe gehoben.

Der Name ist zugleich Programm, wird dem neuen Firmengebilde doch weitgehende Eigenständigkeit zugebilligt. Das Stammkapital beträgt 40 Millionen Mark. Eine Übergangsphase von sechs Jahren wird terminiert, aber schon 1970 überlässt eine bereits marode Rheinstahl AG Daimler-Benz ihre 49 Prozent Beteiligung an der HHF. Diese hat bereits 1969 die Vertriebsnetze von Hanomag und von Henschel übernommen und 580 Millionen Mark in die Anpassung der vorgefundenen Werke in Kassel, Harburg und Bremen gesteckt. Ende 1977 wird die HHF in den Mutterkonzern eingegliedert.

Im Niemandsland zwischen den Systemen, zugleich im Halbdunkel der Zone zwischen Politik und Wirtschaft und somit eigentlich auf ergiebigem Nährboden angesiedelt ist ein Projekt, das gleichwohl den Keim des Scheiterns von vornherein in sich trägt: Die UdSSR planen Ende der Sechziger ein riesiges Werk an der Kama, dem größten Nebenfluss der Wolga, um die Kapazitäten für die LKW-Fertigung binnen fünf Jahren von 500 000 auf das Dreifache

Présence tous azimuts, un flirt et un échec 1969–1973

Au début des années 1970, Daimler-Benz offre une gamme sans lacunes de la fourgonnette légère au gros poids lourd, domaine où elle est leader mondial incontesté, sans oublier les autobus de tous gabarits. Mais cette bonne nouvelle a été précédée par une lutte acharnée pour les marchés, le pouvoir et l'argent au cours de laquelle Ulrich Raue, notamment, depuis 1966 membre du directoire au titre des utilitaires, s'est révélé être un joueur rusé. Deux de ses scoops mettent à profit un effondrement de la production qui affecte alors tout le secteur des véhicules industriels. Les constellations présentent des parallèles remarquables : en effet, dans les deux cas, des constructeurs étrangers tentent de prendre pied sur le marché allemand. Il faut donc réagir, et vite. En 1967, Krupp se résout à suspendre sa production de camions, qui ne génère que des pertes ; son réseau de distribution devient donc superflu. Lorsque Fiat se déclare intéressée, Daimler-Benz réagit immédiatement. Des conditions acceptables sont négociées dans le contrat du 28 février 1968 et le réseau de distribution de Krupp s'intègre harmonieusement dans les nouvelles structures.

Un peu plus tard, le département Utilitaires de Rheinstahl AG est remis en question avec les usines Henschel à Kassel et Hanomag à Hanovre, Hambourg-Harbourg et Brême. Cette fois aussi, avec British Leyland, un puissant partenaire étranger est à l'affût. Une fois de plus, les stratèges d'Untertürkheim ne se laissent pas prendre de cours, règlent la question à des conditions satisfaisantes et, la nuit de Noël même, en raison de l'urgence de la cause, après une audience auprès du président du conseil de surveillance Hermann J. Abs, Hanomag-Henschel-Fahrzeugwerke GmbH (abrégée HHF) est portée sur les fonts baptismaux.

Le nom a aussi valeur de programme puisque l'on accorde l'indépendance presque totale à la nouvelle firme. Son capital social est de 40 millions de marks. Une phase de transition de six ans est prévue, mais, dès 1970, Rheinstahl AG, déjà à l'agonie, cède à Daimler-Benz sa participation de 49 % à HHF. Celle-ci a repris dès 1969 les réseaux de distribution de Hanomag et de Henschel et a investi 580 millions de marks dans la modernisation des usines de Kassel, Harbourg et Brême. Fin 1977, HHF est intégrée au groupe.

Il est alors un projet qui se situe dans le no man's land entre des systèmes et, simultanément, dans la zone grise entre la politique et l'économie – autrement dit, donc, sur un sol fertile – mais c'est aussi un projet qui mûrit en lui le germe de l'échec : à la fin des années 1960, l'URSS projette d'édifier une usine gigantesque sur la Kama, le plus grand affluent de la Volga, pour y faire passer, en cinq ans, les capacités de fabrication de camions de 500 000 à 1,5 million. Avec les expériences faites à Wörth, Daimler-Benz ne pourrait-elle pas, incognito, aider les Soviétiques

going well until just before contracts were to be signed, and even the Social Democrat/Liberal coalition were well disposed towards the project. But the smiles masked an explosive situation: Mercedes requested that the Kama products should not be allowed to be exported, always an unpopular stipulation. Furthermore, there was a huge gulf between the payments proposed and expected: the Soviets offered 100 million marks, while Daimler-Benz demanded 220 million which even then was regarded as being cut to the bone. When Daimler-Benz then had to up this figure because the number of licenses had been underestimated, a sharp telex was received from the Kremlin stating that any further negotiations were futile. Much ado about nothing: the only outcome of the Kama drama was costs, expenses and work.

Nonetheless fruitful contacts were retained. In November 1971 Alexei Nikolaievich Kossygin's son-in-law Gvishiani, Vice-President of the "State Committee for Science and Technology" visited senior Mercedes managers and advised them that Mercedes could, if it so wished, exhibit its products at a trade fair in Moscow from 28 February to 9 March 1973. The shining status symbols of the class enemy met with an enormous response. And in addition to the mere PR effect there was also a concrete outcome with an agreement on cooperation in the scientific-technical fields and a contract to set up a service center for cars in Moscow in collaboration with VW and BMW. Up till then, local Mercedes drivers – without exception high-up political functionaries – had always had to make the short trip to the subsidiary in Helsinki, Finland for servicing or in the event of a major fault.

In the meantime, what had begun from very humble origins in sheds and barns was now on its way to becoming a worldwide commercial empire. The 1983 annual report unashamedly stated that it was the company's intention "to be represented not just in major markets but in every country". At that time this was still half a statement of intent and half established fact: two years later the Stuttgart star was represented in 200 states, 123 general agents were working on the company's behalf and for its greater good, there were 21 wholly-owned sales companies in markets with a high Mercedes density, assembly companies in 24 countries, mainly in the Third World, and 25 factories manufacturing independently. In 1973 for the first time foreign sales outstripped those on the domestic market. The diplomatic finesse and the tact of a Talleyrand are sometimes required when dealing with the company's foreign outlets, especially when their sales impact tangibly on the overall production volume. While being partially independent units, they are nonetheless part of an empire that operates a centralist – though gentle – policy: often a minority holding and an appropriate management presence are enough to lend emphasis to the parent company's requirements. Thus the parent company took a holding in 1949 in Handelsgesellschaft für Daimler-Benz-Erzeugnisse in Zurich (HGZ for short), in 1958 in Mercedes-Benz (Australia) Pty. Ltd. in Mulgrave near Melbourne, and in 1966

auszubauen. Ob Daimler-Benz mit der in Wörth erworbenen Erfahrung im Hintergrund den Sowjets mit Rat und Tat zur Seite stehen wolle? Delegationen werden ausgetauscht bis hinauf in die Ministerebene, die Verhandlungen gedeihen bis in die unmittelbare Nähe der Unterschriften, und auch die sozialliberale Koalition nimmt sich des Projekts liebevoll an. Doch lächelnde Mienen kaschieren Zündstoff: Von Mercedes-Seite aus bittet man sich aus, die Kama-Produkte dürften nicht exportiert werden, allemal eine missliebige Klausel. Überdies klaffen die Vorstellungen über das Honorar weit auseinander: Die Sowjets bieten 100 Millionen Mark, Daimler-Benz fordert knapp kalkulierte 220 Millionen. Als man von Daimler-Benz-Seite wegen zu niedrig eingeschätzter Unterlizenzen noch einmal draufsatteln muss, trifft ein säuerliches Fernschreiben aus dem Kreml ein, weitere Verhandlungen seien witzlos. Viel Lärm um nichts: Das Kama-Drama hat nur Kosten, Spesen und Arbeit gemacht.

Dennoch bleiben fruchtbringende Kontakte erhalten: Im November 1971 stattet Aleksej Nikolajewitsch Kossygins Schwiegersohn Gwischiani, Vizepräsident des »Staatskomitees für Wissenschaft und Technik«, den Mercedes-Oberen einen Besuch ab: Wenn man wolle, könne man seine Erzeugnisse auf einer Messe in Moskau vom 28. Februar bis zum 9. März 1973 präsentieren. Die schimmernden Statussymbole des Klassenfeindes lösen dort eine enorme Resonanz aus. Über den bloßen Schau-Effekt hinaus indes springt Konkretes heraus: Es kommt zu einem Abkommen über eine Zusammenarbeit im wissenschaftlich-technischen Bereich und zu einer Vereinbarung hinsichtlich eines Stützpunktes für PKW in Moskau, gemeinsam mit VW und BMW. Bis dato bedurfte es für lokale Mercedes-Lenker – durchweg gehobene Nomenklatura – zu Wartung und Pflege sowie bei größeren Defekten einer kleinen Reise zu der Niederlassung im finnischen Helsinki.

Unterdessen wächst sich, was einst aus winzigen Anfängen in Schuppen und Scheunen begann, aus zum merkantilen Weltreich. Durchaus nicht verschämt, merkt der Geschäftsbericht von 1983 an, man wolle »nicht nur auf Schwerpunktmärkten, sondern in allen Ländern … vertreten sein«. Dergleichen ist um diese Zeit halb noch Programm und schon halb Zustand: Zwei Jahre später wird der Stuttgarter Stern in 200 Staaten repräsentiert, schaffen 123 Generalvertreter zum Wohle und zum höheren Ruhme der Firma, gibt es 21 eigene Vertriebsgesellschaften in Märkten mit hoher Mercedes-Dichte und Montagebetriebe in 24 Ländern vornehmlich der Dritten Welt sowie 25 Werke, die eigenständig produzieren. 1973 ist der Auslandsumsatz zum erstenmal höher als der im Inland. Im Umgang mit Außenposten rund um den Globus sind dabei manchmal die diplomatische Finesse und das Fingerspitzengefühl eines Talleyrand gefragt, vor allem, wenn ihr Absatz den Produktionsumfang insgesamt spürbar beeinflusst. Teils selbständige Einheiten, sind sie doch Teil eines Imperiums, das eine zentralistisch orientierte Politik betreibt – eine sanfte Politik: Oft genügen ein Minderheitsanteil und eine ent-

en actes et en paroles? Des délégations sont échangées qui vont jusqu'au niveau ministériel, les négociations se déroulent si bien que l'on est près de signer les contrats et la coalition sociale-libérale elle-même se montre séduite par le projet. Mais, derrière les sourires, le conflit couve déjà: une condition posée par Mercedes est que les produits de la Kama ne soient pas exportés, clause évidemment guère appréciée. En outre, les concessions relatives aux honoraires divergent diamétralement les unes des autres: les Soviétiques proposent 100 millions de marks alors que Daimler-Benz, magnanime, en réclame 220 millions. Quand Daimler-Benz doit encore réviser cette somme en raison de sa licence calculée trop bas, le Kremlin adresse un télex amer pour déclarer que toute autre négociation serait vaine. Beaucoup de bruit pour rien: le drame de la Kama n'aura coûté qu'argent, déplacements et travail.

Mais les contacts noués à cette occasion n'auront pas été inutiles: en 1971, Alexeï Nikolaïevitch Gvichiani, gendre de Kossyguine, vice-président du Comité d'État pour la Science et la Technique, rend une visite à la direction de Mercedes: si celle-ci le souhaitait, elle pourrait exposer ses produits lors d'un salon organisé à Moscou du 28 février au 9 mars 1973. Les brillants symboles du prestige de l'ennemi de classe suscitent dans ce pays un énorme intérêt. Outre le simple effet médiatique, tout cela donne aussi des résultats concrets: un accord est passé sur une coopération dans les domaines scientifique et technique et l'on signe une convention concernant une antenne pour les voitures de tourisme à Moscou, conjointement avec VW et BMW. Jusque-là, en effet, les conducteurs locaux de Mercedes – presque tous membres des hautes sphères de la nomenclature – devaient, pour faire entretenir leur voiture ou réparer les pannes, faire un « petit » voyage à la succursale finlandaise de Helsinki.

Entre-temps, ce qui avait débuté modestement dans les granges et garages commence à se muer en un empire commercial mondial. Faisant fi de toute modestie, le rapport d'activités de 1983 déclare que l'on voulait « non seulement opérer sur les marchés prioritaires, mais aussi être représenté dans tous les pays ». À ce moment-là, tout cela est encore pour moitié programme et, déjà, pour moitié réalité: deux ans plus tard, l'étoile de Stuttgart brille dans 200 pays, 123 importateurs œuvrent pour la prospérité et la gloire de la firme et il existe 21 sociétés de distribution propres à la marque sur les marchés à forte densité de Mercedes ainsi que des entreprises de montage dans 24 pays, essentiellement du tiers-monde, auxquelles s'ajoutent 25 usines qui produisent en toute autonomie. En 1973, le chiffre d'affaires à l'étranger dépasse pour la première fois celui de l'Allemagne. Dans les rapports avec les antennes extérieures tout autour du globe, il faut parfois faire preuve du sens diplomatique et du doigté d'un Talleyrand, notamment lorsque leurs débouchés influencent globalement et de façon sensible le volume de production. Bien que parfois unités autonomes, elles font tout de même partie d'un empire qui mène une politique centraliste – une politique

in United Car & Diesel Distributors (abbreviated to UCDD) in Pretoria, South Africa. In April 1984 Daimler-Benz owned 50.1 per cent of UCDD's share capital, and its name was then changed to Mercedes-Benz of South Africa.

The UCDD branch Car Distributors Assembly Ltd. in East London is a model example of the company's development policy. Initially this company simply assembled vehicles from components supplied by Stuttgart, but gradually became more and more of a production company as more and more components were manufactured on the domestic market. But an exception that proves the rule can also be found. The rule states that Mercedes cars are built exclusively in Germany. The exception is that this rule is broken in South Africa – and also in Indonesia where German Motor Manufacturing in Wanaherang assembles mid-range cars, bang in the middle of an area that the Japanese claim for themselves.

Commercial vehicles sporting the star symbol are now built all round the world, sometimes with a certain coincidental symmetry. Three out of a total of 15 associated companies are located in South America, one in Argentina, and the other two in Brazil; in addition to the factory in São Bernardo do Campo there has been another since 1979 in nearby Campinas for the production of buses and as a spare parts warehouse. Three other factories service the North American continent, one in Canada near Vancouver,

sprechende Präsenz in den Führungsgremien, um den Ansprüchen des Mutterhauses Nachdruck zu verleihen. Dessen Beteiligung fließt schon 1949 in die Handelsgesellschaft für Daimler-Benz-Erzeugnisse in Zürich (kurz HGZ), 1958 in die Mercedes-Benz (Australia) Pty. Ltd. in Mulgrave unweit Melbourne, ab 1966 in die United Car & Diesel Distributors (abgekürzt UCDD) im südafrikanischen Pretoria. Im April 1984 ist man im Besitz von 50,1 Prozent des Aktienkapitals der UCDD, die fortan Mercedes-Benz of South Africa heißt.

Zum Modellfall für die Entwicklungspolitik des Hauses erblüht der UCDD-Zweig Car Distributors Assembly Ltd. in East London. Anfänglich baut dieser lediglich aus Stuttgart Geliefertes zusammen, wandelt sich jedoch stetig zur Produktionsgesellschaft, als immer mehr Komponenten im Lande selbst gefertigt werden. Aber auch auf der Suche nach dem Sonderfall, der die Regel bestätigt, wird man fündig. Die Regel: dass Mercedes-PKW ausschließlich in Deutschland hergestellt werden. Die Ausnahme: dass sie in Südafrika durchbrochen wird – und in Indonesien, wo die German Motor Manufacturing in Wanaherang Mittelklassewagen montiert, mitten hinein in ein Territorium, das die Japaner für sich beanspruchen.

Nutzfahrzeuge mit dem Stern-Zeichen indes entstehen in aller Welt, gelegentlich in der Symmetrie des Zufalls: Drei von insgesamt 15 Beteiligungsgesellschaften finden

douce : il suffit souvent d'une participation minoritaire et d'une présence correspondante dans les organes de gestion pour donner du poids aux exigences de la maison mère. Dès 1949, cette participation est matérialisée par la Handelsgesellschaft de Daimler-Benz Erzeugnisse, à Zurich (abrégée HGZ), en 1958, dans la Mercedes-Benz (Australie) Pty. Ltd. à Mulgrave, non loin de Melbourne, à partir de 1966, dans la United Car & Diesel Distributors (abrégée UCDD) à Pretoria, en Afrique du Sud. En avril 1984, on détient 50,1 % du capital d'actions de l'UCDD, qui s'appelle désormais Mercedes-Benz of South Africa.

Un cas particulier illustrant la politique de développement de la maison est donné par une filiale de l'UCDD, Car Distributors Assembly Ltd., à East London. Au début, celle-ci assemblait exclusivement des pièces fournies par Stuttgart avant de se muer de plus en plus en société de production à partir du moment où elle fabriqua elle-même de plus en plus de composants domestiques. Mais il y a aussi l'exception qui confirme la règle. La règle est que les Mercedes de tourisme sont construites exclusivement en Allemagne. Toutefois, l'Afrique du Sud fait figure d'exception – tout comme l'Indonésie, où German Motor Manufacturing, à Wanaherang, monte des voitures du segment intermédiaire au cœur même d'un territoire que les Japonais revendiquent comme leur chasse gardée.

Les utilitaires à l'étoile, par contre, sont fabriqués dans le monde entier, parfois même avec la symétrie du hasard : trois d'un total de quinze sociétés de participation se trouvent en Amérique du Sud, une en Argentine et les deux autres au Brésil : outre l'usine de São Bernado do Campo, édifiée en 1979, une autre se trouve non loin de là, à Campinas, pour la production d'autobus et comme stock de pièces de rechange. Trois autres desservent le continent nord-américain, l'une au Canada, à proximité de Vancouver, et deux aux États-Unis, à Portland et à Mount Holly. Les ondes sismiques déclenchées par les crises pétrolières de 1973 et 1979 épargnent Untertürkheim et ses satellites. Il y a même deux bonnes nouvelles simultanées. Bien que son programme soit affecté par une consommation élevée des modèles, Daimler-Benz AG ne perd malgré tout pas de plumes. Bien au contraire, en 1973, le groupe fabrique 331 682 voitures de tourisme et 215 935 véhicules utilitaires. Le chiffre d'affaires est de 13,799 milliards de marks. En 1974, ces chiffres étaient de 340 006 VP, 205 344 utilitaires et 15,283 milliards de marks de chiffre d'affaires. Mercedes verse même 15 % de dividendes, pour un capital social qui a augmenté de 951,3 à 1189,1 millions de marks, et la réaction des actionnaires lors de l'assemblée générale va des louanges à l'émerveillement.

Plus la prospérité augmente, plus la demande émanant des pays exportateurs de pétrole, avides des luxueuses voitures de Stuttgart, connaît une croissance exponentielle. De 1974 à 1977, par exemple, le chiffre d'affaires réalisé en Irak et en Arabie saoudite est multiplié par onze par rapport à 1973. Une usine construite à Tabriz et où l'Iranian Diesel Manufacturing Company fabrique sous licence des

An S-class Mercedes (116 series) at the show in Moscow in March 1973.
Ein Mercedes der S-Klasse (Baureihe 116) bei der Ausstellung in Moskau im März 1973.
Une Mercedes Classe S (Série 116) lors d'un salon organisé à Moscou en mars 1973.

and two in the USA, in Portland and Mount Holly. The tremors following on from the oil shocks of 1973 and 1979 did not touch Untertürkheim and its satellites. There were even two pieces of good news. Although the company's range has a high fleet consumption, i.e. it is, as it were, a thirsty family with liberal drinking habits, Daimler-Benz AG suffered no ill effects. On the contrary, in 1973 the group manufactured 331,682 cars and 215,935 commercial vehicles, and sales totaled 13.799 billion marks. The comparable figures for 1974 were: 340,006 cars, 205,344 commercial vehicles, sales of 15.283 billion marks. There was even a 15 per cent dividend, on a capital stock which increased from 951.3 million to 1189.1 million marks, and the responses of the shareholders at the AGM ranged from praise to astonishment.

With increasing prosperity, the demand from the oil-exporting regions for Stuttgart's noble products experienced exponential growth. Between 1974 and 1977, for example, sales in Iraq and in Saudi Arabia were eleven times higher than in 1973. A factory in Tabriz, in which the Iranian Diesel Manufacturing Company (IDEM) has been manufacturing engines since 1970 under license has proved to be an ideal route into the Middle East. Business links with Iran have operated to mutual satisfaction since the Fifties when the transport authority in Teheran purchased a total of 1350 Mercedes buses. When Shah Mohammed Resa Pahlevi left in 1979 to be replaced by the Ayatollah Khomeini, the relationship was in crisis for a time especially as the factories of the two general importers had been confiscated on the spot. But by 1983 even the best sales figures achieved during the Shah's reign were surpassed again when Iran was in 4th place in the export revenue list.

In dealings with the sales and service organizations in Europe which Mercedes would like to see under its own direction, the way in which Mercedes-Benz of North America (MBNA) was set up in 1965 serves as a model. In the hierarchy of European dealers the French company SOFIDEL (Société Financière des Etablissements Ch. Delecroix S.A.) is clearly in the lead with sales equivalent to about half of those transacted in the USA. In January 1969 all available shares were purchased, and since 1970 SOFIDEL's subsidiary Mercedes-Benz de France S.A. has been responsible for distribution in France. A similar situation preceded the establishment of Mercedes-Benz (United Kingdom) Ltd. in Brentford on 1 January 1974, before its later move to Milton Keynes. Mercedes-Benz Italia S.p.A. was set up in Rome, with responsibility only for the import of commercial vehicles from 1973 onwards, but then also for car sales from 1982. A similarly cautious approach was adopted in converting the branches in Switzerland, Belgium, the Netherlands or Austria into Daimler subsidiaries.

sich in Südamerika, eine in Argentinien, zwei weitere in Brasilien: neben dem Werk in São Bernardo do Campo seit 1979 ein weiteres im nahegelegenen Campinas für die Produktion von Bussen und als Ersatzteillager. Drei weitere verpflegen den nordamerikanischen Kontinent, eines in Kanada in der Nähe von Vancouver, zwei in den USA, und zwar in Portland und Mount Holly. Die Erschütterungen, die von den Öl-Schocks der Jahre 1973 und 1979 ausgehen, lassen Untertürkheim und seine Trabanten unbehelligt. Es gibt sogar gleich zwei gute Nachrichten. Obwohl ihre Palette einen hohen Flottenverbrauch entwickelt, das heißt gleichsam als durstige Familie liberale Trunkgewohnheiten an den Tag legt, muss die Daimler-Benz AG keine Federn lassen. Im Gegenteil: 1973 stellt der Konzern 331 682 PKW und 215 935 Nutzfahrzeuge her. Der Umsatz beträgt 13,799 Milliarden Mark. Die Vergleichszahlen für 1974: 340 006 PKW, 205 344 Nutzfahrzeuge, 15,283 Milliarden Mark Umsatz. Es gibt sogar 15 Prozent Dividende, bei einem von 951,3 Millionen auf 1189,1 Millionen Mark erhöhten Grundkapital, und die Rückmeldungen der Aktionäre auf der Hauptversammlung reichen von Lob bis Bewunderung.

Mit wachsendem Wohlstand schwillt auch die Nachfrage aus den erdölexportierenden Regionen nach den Stuttgarter Edel-Erzeugnissen in exponentiellem Wachstum. Zwischen 1974 und 1977 zum Beispiel beläuft sich der Umsatz im Irak und in Saudi-Arabien auf das Elffache von 1973. Als wahre Einfallstraße in den Nahen und Mittleren Osten erweist sich seit 1970 ein Werk in Täbris, in dem die Iranian Diesel Manufacturing Company (IDEM) in Lizenz Maschinen herstellt. Die Geschäftsverbindungen zum Iran verlaufen zu wechselseitiger Zufriedenheit seit den Fünfzigern, als die Verkehrsbetriebe in Teheran insgesamt 1350 Mercedes-Busse beziehen. Als Schah Mohammed Resa Pahlevi 1979 geht und der Ayatollah Khomeini kommt, kriselt es eine Zeitlang, zumal die Werke der beiden General-Importeure kurzerhand konfisziert werden. Aber schon 1983 sind die stolzesten Umsätze der Schah-Ära wieder überschritten, als der Iran in der Hitliste der Exporterlöse auf Platz vier liegt.

Im Umgang mit den Organisationen für Vertrieb und Service im europäischen Umfeld, die man gerne in eigener Regie sehen möchte, dient die Mercedes-Benz of North America (MBNA) von 1965 zum Pilot-Projekt. In der Hierarchie der Europa-Händler thront die französische SOFIDEL (für Société Financière des Etablissements Ch. Delecroix S.A.) mit ungefähr der Hälfte des USA-Umsatzes ganz oben. Im Januar 1969 hat man alle greifbaren Aktien an sich gezogen, und seit 1970 trägt die SOFIDEL-Tochter Mercedes-Benz de France S.A. den Vertrieb in Frankreich. Nach einem ähnlichen Vorspiel kommt es am 1. Januar 1974 zur Gründung der Mercedes-Benz (United Kingdom) Ltd. in Brentford, heute in Milton Keynes. In Rom entsteht die Mercedes-Benz Italia S.p.A., ab 1973 lediglich für den Import von Nutzfahrzeugen, ab 1982 auch für den Vertrieb von Personenkraftwagen. Ähnlich behutsam macht man etwa die Niederlassungen in der Schweiz, Belgien, den Niederlanden oder Österreich zu Daimler-Domänen.

The diesel engine plant in Tabriz (Iran): gateway to the new markets in the East.
Das Dieselmotorenwerk in Täbris (Iran): Portal zu neuen Märkten im Osten.
L'usine de moteurs Diesel de Tabriz (Iran): la voie royale vers les nouveaux marchés du Moyen-Orient.

machines depuis 1970 constitue une véritable porte d'entrée vers le Proche et le Moyen-Orient. Les relations commerciales avec l'Iran font l'objet d'une satisfaction réciproque depuis les années 1950, époque à laquelle les transports municipaux de Téhéran ont acheté au total 1350 autobus Mercedes. Lorsque le shah Mohammad Reza Pahlavi est chassé en 1979, évincé par l'ayatollah Khomeyni, une crise éclate, d'autant plus que les usines des deux importateurs du pays ont été confisquées sans préavis. Mais, dès 1983, on dépasse déjà de nouveau les plus brillants chiffres d'affaires de l'ère du Shah puisque l'Iran figure au quatrième rang du classement pour les recettes aux exportations.

Mercedes-Benz of North America (MBNA), fondée en 1965, sert de projet-pilote dans les rapports avec les organisations de vente et de service dans les pays d'Europe, que Daimler aimerait bien voir passer sous sa propre régie. La SOFIDEL française (Société financière des établissements Ch. Delecroix s.a.), dont le chiffre d'affaires équivaut environ à la moitié de celui des États-Unis, figure tout en haut de la hiérarchie des importateurs européens. En janvier 1969, le maximum d'actions a été récupéré et, depuis 1970, Mercedes-Benz France s.a., filiale de SOFIDEL, se charge de la distribution en France. Après une escarmouche similaire, Mercedes-Benz Ltd. (United Kingdom), avec siège à Brentford et, aujourd'hui, à Milton Keynes, est fondée le 1er janvier 1974. À Rome est créée Mercedes-Benz Italia S.p.a., chargée seulement, à partir de 1973, des importations d'utilitaires et aussi, à partir de 1982, de la vente des voitures de tourisme. Avec la même diplomatie, les succursales de Suisse, de Belgique, des Pays-Bas et d'Autriche sont transformées en dépendances de la Daimler.

Changing times 1973–1985

A chapter has always been given over to the battle against crises and catastrophes in the military theory books of Mercedes generals – just as with the verdigris-covered Daimler and Benz monuments in their time. In the Seventies the apocalypse of individual mobility, tried out in Germany in the form of a ban on Sunday driving between 25 November 1973 and 6 January 1974, was grinning on the horizon. There were many reasons for the fact that Mercedes was unaffected by the pressure waves of the two cleverly planned oil shocks. One of these was the oft-cited creed that the company's growth was only moderate but constant and that it was not prey to the short-term highs and lows of the economy. Not only were long delivery times accepted, necessity was turned into a virtue – anticipation increases the appetite and makes the final enjoyment all the more intense. Moreover, the desire for Mercedes was fanned by innovations such as the s-class from September 1972. The 240 D launched in August 1973, and available as a 3.0 with five cylinders from July 1974 onwards, seemed tailor-made for this miserable period: there were no restrictions at all on the availability of diesel oil and it was cheap, and so production of these tough and economical cars with their characteristic engine noise rose within one year from 116,000 to 147,000. On the other hand, bad news arrived from Dusseldorf and Bremen. Short-time working was reported in the sensitive field of van production, and there was stagnation also in the bus market which was subject to its own laws anyway and was traditionally "difficult" simply because of fierce competition.

But these negative aspects were balanced out by the lively demand for heavy goods vehicles from the Middle East. Trucks with a protruding bonnet built in the former Henschel works in Kassel experienced a renaissance and later a boom, culminating in 1975 in 12,750 units. Arab drivers did not like the way flat cabs simply fell steeply away – they preferred to have a solid lump of engine in front of them.

In its dealings with its staff Daimler-Benz uses the family principle even in hard times, although in 1975, for example, no fewer than 149,742 employees earned their living "at

High-powered guest: Germany's President Heinemann, 1971.

Hoher Gast: Bundespräsident Heinemann, 1971.

Un hôte de marque : le président fédéral Heinemann, 1971.

Dauer im Wechsel 1973–1985

Der Kleinkrieg gegen Krisen und Katastrophen gehört seit jeher in den Clausewitz der Mercedes-Generäle – wie einst der längst von Grünspan übersponnenen Monumente Daimler und Benz. In den siebziger Jahren grinst am Horizont bereits die Apokalypse der individuellen Beweglichkeit, geprobt in den sonntäglichen Fahrverboten zwischen dem 25. November 1973 und dem 6. Januar 1974. Dass man von den Druckwellen der zwei clever inszenierten Öl-Schocks nicht erschüttert wird, hat viele Gründe. Einer davon ist das vielfach formulierte Credo, dem Unternehmen bekomme nur ein maßvolles, stetiges Wachstum, das sich nicht an den Hochs und Tiefs der Tageskonjunktur verzettelt. Lange Lieferfristen nimmt man dafür nicht nur in Kauf, sondern sublimiert die Not zur Tugend – Vorfreude ist halt die schönste Freude und steigert den Appetit. Die Lust auf Mercedes wird überdies angefacht durch Novitäten wie die s-Klasse vom September 1972. Der 240 D vom August 1973, als 3.0 mit fünf Zylindern ab Juli 1974, scheint gar wie gemacht für die Misere: Dieselöl ist schier unbegrenzt zu haben und billig, und so steigt die Auflage der zählebigen und genügsamen Nagler innerhalb eines Jahres von 116 000 auf 147 000. Andererseits treffen Hiobsbotschaften ein aus Düsseldorf und Bremen: Dort meldet man Kurzarbeit auf dem sensiblen Feld der Transporter-Fertigung, und lustlos ist auch die Tendenz auf dem Bus-Markt, der ohnehin seinen eigenen Gesetzmäßigkeiten unterworfen und traditionell »schwierig« ist, schon wegen des scharfen Wettbewerbs.

Aber diese Mankos werden ausgewuchtet durch die lebhafte Nachfrage nach Schwerlastwagen aus dem Nahen Osten. Renaissance und später Boom, kulminierend 1975 mit 12 750 Einheiten, widerfahren dabei dem Hauben-LKW, gebaut in der einstigen Henschel-Garnison Kassel: Seinen arabischen Lenkern ist der Steilabfall flacher Fahrerhäuser nicht geheuer – sie haben lieber einen robusten Motorentrakt vor sich.

Im Umgang mit den Mitarbeitern hegt Daimler-Benz dabei selbst in Zeiten der Dürre das familiäre Prinzip, obwohl zum Beispiel 1975 nicht weniger als 149 742 Werktätige »beim Daimler«, »beim Benz« oder in ihrem Einzugsbereich in Nähe und Ferne ihr Geld verdienen. Zur Bibel zeitgemäßer Menschenführung wird die Broschüre *Leitsätze zur Führung und Zusammenarbeit* von 1979, in der man dem Prinzip der vertikalen Kooperation huldigt. Entlassungen sind unüblich. Dafür erwartet man von den Mitgliedern der Mercedes-Großfamilie eine gewisse Bereitschaft zur Mobilität, etwa von einem Standort mit Überbeschäftigung in ein Notstandsgebiet.

Aber auch aus dem Inneren des Mikrokosmos Mercedes dringen tektonische Beben, die die Oberfläche der Bulletins und Kommuniqués kräuseln und dann von dem lärmenden Chor der Interpreten aufgenommen werden, der stets neugierig auf der Lauer liegt. Sie kommen in zwei

Pérennité dans le changement

La lutte aux crises et aux catastrophes a toujours compté comme une arme majeure dans l'arsenal des généraux de Mercedes – aussi ancienne que les monuments de Daimler et de Benz depuis longtemps rongés par le vert-de-gris. Dans les années 1970, on croit déjà voir se profiler à l'horizon l'apocalypse de la mobilité individuelle, mise à l'essai dans les interdictions de circuler dominicales entre le 25 janvier 1973 et le 6 janvier 1974. Si l'on ne se laisse pas ébranler par les ondes de choc des deux crises pétrolières mises astucieusement en scène, c'est qu'il y a de nombreuses raisons. L'une est le credo, souvent formulé, selon lequel l'entreprise ne bénéficiera d'une croissance modérée mais permanente que si elle ne se laisse pas distraire par les hauts et les bas de la conjoncture. À cette fin, on ne prend pas seulement son parti de longs délais de livraison, on élève même cette nécessité au rang de qualité – la joie anticipée est toujours la plus grande joie, qui donne de l'appétit. Un appétit chez Mercedes qui est aiguisé par des nouveautés comme la Classe s de septembre 1972. La 240 D d'août 1973, avec un cinq-cylindres de 3 litres à partir de juillet 1974, cible un large marché : le gazole se vend à bon prix, si bien que, en l'espace d'un an, les ventes de cette infatigable et sobre diesel passent de 116 000 à 147 000 exemplaires. En revanche, de mauvaises nouvelles arrivent de Düsseldorf et de Brême : ces deux usines doivent instaurer le chômage technique dans le domaine sensible des camionnettes et l'ambiance n'est guère plus gaie sur le marché des autobus, qui possède de toute façon ses propres lois et est traditionnellement « difficile », ne serait-ce qu'en raison de l'âpreté de la concurrence.

Mais ces défaillances sont compensées par les camions de gros gabarit, que l'on s'arrache au Proche-Orient. Les camions à capot, construits dans l'ancienne usine de Kassel, connaissent un regain de popularité dans le sillage d'un boom qui culminera en 1975 avec 12 750 unités : leurs conducteurs arabes n'ont pas confiance dans les cabines avancées à capot moteur vertical – ils préfèrent le sentiment de sécurité que donne un compartiment moteur bien visible.

Dans les rapports avec le personnel, Daimler-Benz met toujours en pratique les principes familiaux, même en période de difficultés, bien que, par exemple en 1975, pas moins de 149 742 salariés gagnent leur pain « chez Daimler », « chez Benz » ou dans leur environnement plus ou moins proche.

Des mouvements tectoniques qui laissent un frémissement dans les bulletins et les communiqués avant d'être repris par le chœur bruyant des interprètes curieux toujours à l'affût se produisent en deux vagues, tel un suspense à la Hitchcock. Une information qui filtre le 28 novembre 1974 est un scoop qui se transforme vite en scandale : le groupe Quandt aurait vendu à l'étranger, pour environ un milliard de marks, ses 14 % d'actions représentant une valeur nominale de 166,5 millions de marks du capital social de

Daimler", "at Benz" or at one of its suppliers near or far. The bible of modern man management is the brochure *Principles of Management and Cooperation* from 1979 which subscribes to the principle of vertical cooperation. Dismissals are unusual. In return, however, a certain willingness to be mobile is expected of the members of the extended Mercedes family, for example from a site with over-full employment to an area where there is an urgent need for staff.

But earthquakes also emerge from inside the Mercedes microcosm which wrinkle the surface of the bulletins and communiqués and are then picked up by the noisy chorus of inquisitive commentators who are always lying in wait. The best ones come in pairs as if scripted by a master of the whodunit. A scoop report from 28 November 1974 caused a scandal when it stated that the Quandt Group had sold its 14 per cent holding, nominally 166.5 million marks of the company's 1189.1 million marks of capital stock, for around a billion to a foreign investor. The identity of the buyer who was asserting his claims via Dresdner Bank, remained discreetly veiled and was only revealed a week later to be the Emirate of Kuwait. At the same time, it was stressed that there was no intention to exert any influence on company policy or to claim a seat on the supervisory board.

The Grail keepers of a German purity law had just regained their composure when the second episode was played out. Friedrich Karl Flick too was proposing to sell his holding, a small matter of 39 per cent of Daimler's share capital. The Shah of Iran was interested. Franz Heinrich Ulrich, who was both chairman of the board of management at Deutsche Bank and had been the successor to Hermann J. Abs as chairman of the supervisory board at Daimler-Benz since 1970, intervened in this affair. He persuaded Flick to

Lest we forget: even 50 years after the death of the founding father, it was a privilege to work "at Benz."

In wacher Erinnerung: Noch 50 Jahre nach dem Tod des Gründervaters ist es ein Privileg, »beim Benz« zu arbeiten.

Toujours présent dans les esprits : 50 ans encore après la mort du père fondateur, c'est un privilège que de travailler « chez Benz ».

Schüben, wie inszeniert nach einer Krimi-Dramaturgie von Meisterhand. Zu Scoop und Skandal gerät bereits eine Meldung vom 28. November 1974: Die Quandt-Gruppe habe ihre 14 Prozent Anteile, nominell 166,5 Millionen Mark von den 1189,1 Millionen Mark Grundkapital des Unternehmens, für rund eine Milliarde ins Ausland verkauft. Wer der Kunde ist, der seine Ansprüche über die Dresdner Bank geltend macht, bleibt diskret im dunkeln und kommt erst eine Woche später ans Tageslicht: das Scheichtum Kuwait. Zugleich wiegelt man ab, man wolle keinerlei Einfluss ausüben auf die Firmenpolitik und beanspruche auch keinen Sitz im Aufsichtsrat.

Die Gralshüter eines deutschen Reinheitsgebotes haben just ihre Fassung zurückgewonnen, da folgt der zweite Streich. Auch Friedrich Karl Flick gedenke sein Scherflein von 39 Prozent Daimler-Aktienkapital zu veräußern. Interessent sei der Schah von Persien. In dieses Szenario hinein interveniert Franz Heinrich Ulrich, in Personalunion Vorstandssprecher der Deutschen Bank und seit 1970 Vorsitzender des Aufsichtsrats bei Daimler-Benz als Nachfolger von Hermann J. Abs. Er wirkt auf Flick ein, zehn Prozent zu behalten und den Rest für zwei Milliarden Mark der Deutschen Bank zum zeitweiligen Verbleib zu überlassen. Diese schickt sich umgehend an, ihre Flick-Anteile nach dem Gießkannenprinzip unter die Leute zu bringen, um künftig massive Ballungen zu verhindern und damit Möglichkeiten des Hereinredens von außen oder gar absoluter Mehrheiten zu mindern. Man gründet die Mercedes Automobil-Holding AG (kurz MAH) und hält im Januar 1976 ein Drittel von deren Anteilen an der Börse feil, nominell 100 Millionen Mark zum Kurswert von 305 Mark für die 50-Mark-Aktie. 50 Millionen sind über die Ausgabe von Schuldverschreibungen der Deutschen Bank verfügbar. Der Rest wird zu jeweils 50 Prozent bei den beiden MAH-Töchtern Stern- und Stella-Automobil-Beteiligungs-GmbH unter Ausnutzung des Schachtel-Privilegs untergebracht. Anschließend ist das Grundkapital von Daimler-Benz weit gefächert – wie gewünscht: Deutsche Bank 28 Prozent, MAH 26 Prozent, Kuwait 14 Prozent, Flick 10 Prozent (die er 1985 an die Deutsche Bank verkauft), Bosch und Siemens jeweils zwei Prozent. In die verbleibenden 18 Prozent teilen sich 60 000 Kleininhaber. Mit diesem Akt gezielter Zerstreuung bläst man zugleich das Halali über den Großaktionären, was sich auch in einer geänderten Zusammensetzung des Aufsichtsrats abbildet: Herbert Quandt und Friedrich Karl Flick verschwinden aus dem Präsidium, in dem ihre Dynastien Sitz und Stimme gleichsam in Erbpacht gehalten haben, und verlieren insgesamt fünf Mandate. Das neue Mitbestimmungsgesetz vom Mai 1976 wirft bereits seine Schatten: In vorauseilendem Gehorsam reduziert man die Repräsentanten der Aktionäre von zwölf auf zehn. Diese werden paritätisch austariert durch zehn Vertreter der Arbeitnehmer, und so kommt man auf die 20 Mitglieder, die für große Unternehmen vorgesehen sind.

Mit wachsenden Produktionszahlen und einer filigran sich verästelnden Typenvielfalt bleibt unterdessen die

We made a good team: Daimler-Benz pensioners on a visit to their former workplace.

In alter Verbundenheit: Senioren von Daimler-Benz bei einem Besuch ihrer früheren Arbeitsstätte.

Toujours attachés à leur employeur : retraités de Daimler-Benz en visite dans leur ancienne usine.

l'entreprise, de 1189,1 millions de marks. Le nom du client, qui fait valoir ses droits par le biais de la Dresdner Bank, reste tout d'abord inconnu et n'est publié qu'une semaine plus tard : c'est l'émirat du Koweït. Simultanément, celui-ci s'empresse d'ajouter qu'il n'a pas l'intention d'exercer la moindre influence sur la politique de la firme et ne réclame pas non plus de siège au conseil de surveillance.

À peine les gardiens du Saint-Graal qu'est le commandement de la pureté allemande ont-ils retrouvé leur contenance qu'éclate le second coup de tonnerre : Friedrich Karl Flick lui aussi envisage de céder son portefeuille de 39 % du capital d'actions de Daimler. Un intéressé serait le shah d'Iran. Un scénario que vient contrecarrer Franz Heinrich Ulrich, à la fois porte-parole du directoire de la Deutsche Bank et, depuis 1970, président du conseil de surveillance de Daimler-Benz en tant que successeur de Hermann J. Abs. Il fait pression sur Flick pour qu'il conserve 10 % et remette le reste, pour deux milliards de marks, à la Deutsche Bank à titre provisoire. Celle-ci s'empresse immédiatement de distribuer ses actions de Flick à des investisseurs selon le principe de l'arrosoir pour éviter à l'avenir la formation de tout noyau dur et, ainsi, atténuer le risque de devoir subir une prise d'influence extérieure, voire que se constituent des majorités absolues. C'est ainsi qu'est fondée Mercedes Automobil-Holding AG (abrégée MAH), dont un tiers des actions sont introduites à la Bourse en janvier 1976 pour une valeur nominale de 100 millions de marks à un cours de 305 marks pour l'action de 50 marks. Cinquante millions sont disponibles par l'émission d'obligations de la Deutsche Bank. Le reste est placé à hauteur de 50 % auprès des deux filiales de MAH, Stern- et Stella-Automobil-Beteiligungs-GmbH, en utilisant le privilège de la participation croisée. À la suite de cela, le capital social de Daimler-Benz est réparti de façon équilibrée – tel que souhaité : 28 % pour la Deutsche Bank, 26 % pour MAH, 14 % pour le Koweït, 10 % pour Flick (qu'il revendra en 1985 à la Deutsche Bank) et respectivement 2 % pour Bosch et Siemens. Soixante mille petits actionnaires se partagent les 18 % restants. Par cette mesure de dissémination

retain ten per cent and to transfer the balance temporarily for two billion marks to Deutsche Bank. The bank then immediately set about selling its Flick shares in accordance with the watering can principle to prevent huge future concentrations and therefore to reduce the chances of external influence being exerted or even of absolute majorities. Mercedes Automobil-Holding AG (abbreviated to MAH) was set up, and a third of its shares were floated on the stock exchange in January 1976, nominally 100 million marks at a list price of 305 marks for the 50-marks share. 50 million were available via the issue of Deutsche Bank bonds. The rest was placed in the form of 50 per cent in each of the two MAH subsidiaries, Stern- and Stella-Automobil-Beteiligungs-GmbH using the affiliation privilege. Daimler-Benz's stock capital was then well spread out – as was the intention: Deutsche Bank 28 per cent, MAH 26 per cent, Kuwait 14 per cent, Flick 10 per cent (which he sold to Deutsche Bank in 1985), Bosch and Siemens two per cent each. The remaining 18 per cent was shared among 60,000 small investors. This act of intentional scattering also sounded the mort over the major shareholders which was also reflected in a changed composition on the supervisory board: Herbert Quandt and Friedrich Karl Flick disappeared from this board in which their dynasties had had a hereditary leasehold on seats and votes and lost a total of five seats. Germany's new co-determination law of May 1976 was already casting a shadow, and in an advance show of obedience the shareholders' representatives were cut from twelve to ten. These were balanced out by ten workers' representatives, thereby arriving at the figure of 20 members as planned for large companies.

In the light of increased production figures and a multiplying range of types, the question of space remained a permanent topic for discussion by the board of management and the supervisory board. However, within the Daimler-Benz archipelago was the island of Bremen-Sebaldsbrück, at one time the stage for the life's work of the tragically failed local politician Dr. Carl F. W. Borgward until all of his production equipment was shipped off to Mexico on 63 vessels in 1963. Bremen was certainly not working to full capacity on vans from the former Hanomag range. An expert's report in August 1973 showed that up to

Franz Heinrich Ulrich, chief executive of Deutsche Bank, and Friedrich Karl Flick, 1974.
Franz Heinrich Ulrich, Vorstandssprecher der Deutsche Bank, und Friedrich Karl Flick, 1974.
Franz Heinrich Ulrich, porte-parole du directoire de la Deutsche Bank, et Friedrich Karl Flick, 1974.

Joachim Zahn, chairman of the board of management 1971–1979.

Joachim Zahn, Vorstandsvorsitzender 1971–1979.

Joachim Zahn, président du directoire de 1971 à 1979.

Enge Dauerthema der Gespräche in Vorstand und Aufsichtsrat. Da gibt es im Archipel Daimler-Benz das Eiland Bremen-Sebaldsbrück, einst Bühne für das Lebenswerk des tragisch gescheiterten Konsuls Dr. Carl F.W. Borgward, bis 1963 dessen gesamte Produktionseinrichtungen auf 63 Schiffen gen Mexiko verfrachtet wurden. Bremen ist mit Leichtlastern noch aus Hanomag-Provenienz durchaus nicht ausgelastet. Eine Expertise im August 1973 ergibt, dass in dem nordwestlichen Satelliten bis zu 500 PKW montiert werden könnten. Zur Vorsicht gemahnt durch die Wiener OPEC-Beschlüsse, legt man die Angelegenheit zunächst auf Eis.

Aber die Garnison Bremen rückt wieder ins Blickfeld, als Mitte der siebziger Jahre die Baureihe T (für Touristik und Transport) aktuell wird. Auch an dieser scheiden sich die Geister: Wie steht es um die Billigung des geneigten Publikums? Ist das Blaumann-Image eines Kombinationskraftwagens voller Lacke, Lumpen und Leitern und mit einem roten Fähnchen hinter dem halboffenen Heck vereinbar mit der Nobel-Aureole, welche die Stern-Marke umgibt? Und lässt sich das Fluidum von knorriger Solidität, im Kaufpreis für die Produkte aus dem schwäbischen Standort Stuttgart gewissermaßen mit einbegriffen, so ohne weiteres nordwärts verpflanzen? 1977 gibt auch der Aufsichtsrat grünes Licht und läutet damit zugleich eine grundsätzliche Neuordnung ein: PKW sollen in Sindelfingen und Bremen, LKW in Wörth und Düsseldorf gebaut werden, Omnibusse in Mannheim und Unimog sowie dessen Agrar-Derivat MB-trac in Gaggenau.

Zugleich nimmt ein Projekt Gestalt an, das seit 1972 als Gedankenexperiment durch die Diskussion geistert und

systématique, on sonne simultanément l'hallali contre les gros actionnaires, ce qui se traduit aussi par une nouvelle composition du conseil de surveillance : Herbert Quandt et Friedrich Karl Flick disparaissent du bureau présidentiel, où leurs dynasties avaient pour ainsi dire un droit héréditaire sur sièges et voix, et perdent au total cinq mandats. La nouvelle loi sur la cogestion de mai 1976 se profile déjà à l'horizon : par obéissance anticipée, on réduit le nombre des représentants de l'actionnariat de douze à dix. Ceux-ci font face paritairement à dix représentants du personnel et ainsi obtient-on les vingt membres prévus pour les grandes entreprises.

Au fur et à mesure qu'augmentent les chiffres de production et que la diversité des modèles croît comme les rameaux d'un arbre, l'étroitesse reste naturellement un thème récurrent des entretiens au directoire et au conseil de surveillance. Or il y a, dans l'archipel Daimler-Benz, la petite ville de Brême-Sebaldsbrück, l'ancienne scène sur laquelle s'est joué le drame de l'échec du consul Carl F. W. Borgward dont la totalité des équipements de production a été expédiée par 63 bateaux au Mexique jusqu'en 1963. Brême est loin d'être totalement exploitée avec les petites camionnettes encore d'origine Hanomag. Une expertise d'août 1973 révèle que l'on pourrait y monter jusqu'à 500 VP. Incité à la prudence par des résolutions prises à Vienne par l'OPEP, on laisse tout d'abord cette question en suspens.

Mais la question de Brême revient à l'ordre du jour lorsque, au milieu des années 1970, est créée la gamme T (pour tourisme et transport). Et, une fois de plus, les esprits sont partagés sur celle-ci : qu'en pensera le cher public ? L'image de conducteur en salopette du break plein de pots de peinture, de pinceaux et d'échelles avec un petit chiffon rouge flottant derrière le hayon à demi-ouvert est-elle compatible avec le prestige que diffuse la marque à l'étoile ? Et peut-on aussi délocaliser sans état d'âme vers le Nord-Ouest le modèle de solidité indestructible, véritable marque de commerce des produits du site souabe de Stuttgart ? En 1977 aussi, le conseil de surveillance donne le feu vert et déclenche ainsi une réorientation fondamentale : les VP seront fabriquées à Sindelfingen et à Brême, les camions à Wörth et à Düsseldorf, les autobus et autocars à Mannheim et les Unimog ainsi que leur dérivé agricole le MB-trac, à Gaggenau.

Simultanément prend forme un projet que l'on ne cesse d'évoquer depuis 1972 en tant qu'expérience intellectuelle et que le chef du développement Hans Scherenberg a présenté au directoire en 1974 : la classe compacte, avec le nom de code interne W201. Mais ce sont les événements de l'actualité qui accélèrent la conception et déterminent l'accueil réservé à une petite Mercedes. Le renchérissement du carburant déclenche une nouvelle prise de conscience favorable aux voitures moins encombrantes et plus économiques, chose à laquelle contribue aussi énergiquement la législation sur l'important marché nord-américain. Les mesures restrictives avec lesquelles le président James Earl Carter, dès sa prise de fonctions en 1977, veut s'attaquer à

500 cars could be assembled in the north-west satellite. In view of the OPEC resolutions announced in Vienna, it was decided to shelve the matter for the moment.

But attention focused on Bremen again when the T range (for Tourism and Transport) was under consideration in the mid-Seventies. But here too opinions were divided. What would be the response of the interested public? Was the boiler-suited image of an estate car full of paint, rags and ladders and with a red cloth behind the half-open tailgate compatible with the aura of nobility surrounding the star make? And could the air of rugged solidity, which was basically included in the purchase price for the Swabian products from Stuttgart, simply be transferred northwards? In 1977 the supervisory board also gave the green light, thereby ushering in at the same time a fundamental reorganization: cars were to be built in Sindelfingen and Bremen, trucks in Wörth and Dusseldorf, buses in Mannheim, and the Unimog and its agricultural derivative MB-trac in Gaggenau.

At the same time a project was taking shape that had been discussed since 1972 before being submitted to the board of management in 1974 by R&D boss Hans Scherenberg: the compact class, termed W 201 in-house. The design and acceptance of a small Mercedes were encouraged by contemporary events. The increase in oil prices brought about a change in attitude towards less polluting and more economical cars, and this was also given a strong boost by legislation in the important US market. The restrictive measures implemented by President Jimmy Carter with the aim of reducing automotive fuel consumption and emissions right from the start of his administration in 1977 cut Mercedes to the quick. And even in the land of 60 mph limits the S-class, for example, which was a readily worn symbol of elevated status and standards not just in Denver and Dallas, was not the type to hold back. Its racy consumption drove the Daimler-Benz fleet consumption into the red. Help was needed at the other end of the spectrum.

As a first aid measure Scherenberg partially plugged this gap with the 300 SD turbo diesel (which celebrated its debut at the 1977 Frankfurt International Motor Show). The compact design was officially sanctioned in March 1979 when Werner Breitschwerdt, who had replaced Hans Scherenberg in the meantime, presented a model of the Baby Benz. It had a friendly reception all round as it had obviously retained the Mercedes charisma while appealing to the new market segment. The necessary new buildings in Bremen met with political approval there, but were then faced with the angry resistance of a well-prepared public once the first of the three buildings housing the bodyshop, paintshop and assembly lines was already finished.

Production of the W 201 in the old Hanseatic city of Bremen was linked to that in Sindelfingen in accordance with the law of communicating pipes: the plan provided for a potential volume of 120,000 vehicles per year each, with components exchanged back and forth. However, the Swabians had their noses in front. The 190 and 190 E started rolling off their assembly lines in the autumn of 1982,

1974 von Entwicklungsboss Hans Scherenberg dem Vorstand vorgestellt wird: die Kompaktklasse, intern W 201 genannt. Konzeption und Akzeptanz eines kleinen Mercedes werden durch die Ereignisse der Zeit befeuert. Die Ölteuerung bewirkt einen Wandel des Bewusstseins in Richtung auf weniger ausladende und sparsamere Autos, und überdies hilft die Gesetzgebung auf dem wichtigen US-Markt energisch nach. Die restriktiven Maßnahmen, mit denen Präsident James Earl Carter vom Jahre eins seiner Amtszeit 1977 an automobile Trunksucht und Emissionen in den Griff bekommen möchte, treffen Mercedes ins Mark. Auch im Land der 60-Meilen-Limits ist etwa die S-Klasse, gerne zur Schau getragenes Symbol für gehobenen Status und Standard nicht nur in Denver und Dallas, kein Kostverächter. Ihr flotter Verbrauch treibt den Flottenverbrauch der Daimler-Benz-Armada in den roten Bereich. Abhilfe am anderen Ende des Spektrums tut not.

Dorthin plaziert Scherenberg als Erste Hilfe den Turbodiesel 300 SD (Debüt 1977 auf der IAA in Frankfurt). Der offizielle Segen wird dem Kompakt-Konzept im März 1979 zuteil. Da zeigt Werner Breitschwerdt, der inzwischen Hans Scherenberg abgelöst hat, ein Modell des Baby-Benz vor. Es stößt allenthalben auf freundliche Akklamation, bewahrt es doch das Mercedes-Charisma offensichtlich auch im Umfeld des neuen Markt-Segments. Die nötigen Neubauten in Bremen finden dort politische Zustimmung, stoßen indessen auch dann noch auf den wütenden Widerstand wehrhafter Bürger, als die erste der drei Hallen für Karosserie, Lackierung und Montage bereits fertiggestellt ist.

Die Produktion des W 201 in der Hansestadt ist nach dem Gesetz der kommunizierenden Röhren vernetzt mit der in Sindelfingen: mögliches Volumen jeweils 120 000 pro Jahr, dazu Austausch von Komponenten von hüben und drüben, so die Planung. Allerdings haben die Schwaben die Nase vorn: Hier rollen 190 und 190 E seit dem Herbst 1982 vom Band, gefolgt vom 190 D im Dezember 1983. In Bremen läuft die Produktion 1984 an.

Seit dem Mai dieses Jahres empfiehlt sich der knuffigwieselflinke 190 E 2.3-16 den Sportsfreunden unter den Jüngern der Marke, wie etwa dem Formel-1-Weltmeister von 1964 John Surtees, als erstrebenswerter Besitz, eine gezielte

The wide-ranging 190 fleet from the 190 Diesel to the 190E 2.3-16.
Breites Angebot: die Flotte der 190er vom 190 Diesel bis zum 190E 2.3-16.
Pour tous les goûts: la flotte de la 190, de la 190 Diesel à la 190E 2.3-16.

la boulimie automobile et aux émissions de polluants touchent Mercedes en plein cœur. Même dans le pays de la limite à 60 miles, la Classe S, par exemple, est un symbole de réussite sociale que l'on affiche volontiers, mais qui n'a rien d'un ascète. Gourmande en carburant, elle augmente dangereusement la consommation de l'armada de Daimler-Benz. Il faut donc impérativement y remédier à l'autre extrémité de l'échelle.

Pour parer au plus pressé, Scherenberg y place la Turbodiesel 300SD (présentée en 1977 à l'IAA de Francfort). Le concept W 201 obtient la bénédiction officielle en mars 1979. Werner Breitschwerdt, qui a entre-temps remplacé Hans Scherenberg, présente alors une maquette de la Baby-Benz. Elle est immédiatement plébiscitée d'autant plus qu'elle préserve bel et bien le charisme de Mercedes même dans l'environnement de son nouveau segment de marché. Le projet de nouveaux édifices nécessaires à Brême obtient l'aval des politiques, mais est néanmoins confronté à l'opposition furieuse de citoyens énergiques quand le premier des trois ateliers pour la carrosserie, la peinture et le montage est déjà achevé.

Selon le principe des vases communicants, la production de la W 201 dans la ville hanséatique est interconnectée avec celle de Sindelfingen: un volume respectif possible de 120 000 exemplaires par an, plus un échange de composants dans les deux sens, tels sont les projets. Ce sont toutefois les Souabes qui inaugurent les festivités: là-bas, les 190 et 190 E sortent des chaînes à partir de l'automne 1982, suivies par la 190 D en décembre 1983. À Brême, la production débute en 1984.

À partir de mai 1984, l'adorable et ultrarapide 190 E 2.3-16 cherche à séduire les amateurs de sport parmi les disciples de la marque, par exemple le champion du monde de Formule 1 de 1964, John Surtees, qui s'en est offert une immédiatement, réplique cinglante aux reproches de lourdeur bourgeoise que l'on a toujours adressés aux berlines d'Untertürkheim. Avec la parution de la sportive seize-soupapes, cette tare génétique s'est évanouie comme par enchantement, d'autant plus qu'elle a fait sensation, en août 1983, avec des résultats aussi médiatiques que trois records du monde d'endurance sur des distances allant jusqu'à 50 000 kilomètres à Nardo, en Italie du Sud. Il faut investir pas moins de dix milliards de marks pour courir le risque de la W201. Mais le risque en vaut la chandelle. Certes, la réaction est tout d'abord hésitante: le standing Mercedes a, en effet, aussi une influence sur le prix d'achat d'une compacte. Et, en décembre 1982, par exemple, celui-ci est de pas moins de 25 600 marks pour le modèle d'appel, la 190, alors que pour la 200, le premier modèle de la gamme W123 qui la précède dans la hiérarchie, il ne faut débourser que 200 marks de plus. En outre, il faut payer contre espèces sonnantes et trébuchantes des options relativement banales.

Mais rien ne peut finalement entraver son succès: en 1988, la W201 a déjà été vendue à plus d'un million d'exemplaires (1 125 928), notamment à des automobilistes qui n'ont jamais possédé de Mercedes auparavant, dont environ

followed by the 190 D in December 1983, while production in Bremen only started in 1984.

Since May of that year, the lightning-fast 190 E 2.3-16 had appealed to the sportier amongst the make's disciples such as the 1964 Formula 1 world champion John Surtees as the car to own, a specific response to the charge of ponderous portliness which people had been so keen to level at Mercedes limousines since time immemorial. The launch of the nimble sixteen-valver simply blew this away, especially when, drum roll please, it set up three long-distance world records in August 1983 over distances up to 50,000 kilometers in Nardo in Southern Italy. Investments to the tune of ten billion had to be made available for the potentially speculative w 201. But it paid off. The initial response, admittedly, was hesitant. After all, the purchase price for the compact model also included Mercedes' famous standards. And this price for the entry-level model 190 in December 1982, for example, was a handsome 25,600 marks, while the 200, the lowest in the w 123 series which was actually superior in the hierarchy, cost only 200 marks more. In addition, relatively ordinary special trim levels came with a hefty surcharge.

But then things picked up. By 1988 over a million (1,125,928) w 201 models had already been sold, even to people who had never before owned a Mercedes, and around a third of them (413,905) were diesel-powered. In January 1984 journalists from a multitude of countries voted the 190 E World Car of the Year, and at the AGM in July of the same year Werner Breitschwerdt, chairman of the board of management since December 1983, expressed his satisfaction in well-chosen words at now being able to offer a top product in this sector too.

Credit for the fact that Mercedes could now fish in the turbulent waters of the world market with the trident of s-class, mid-range and compact class, went to Gerhard Prinz, Breitschwerdt's predecessor between January 1980 and October 1983, at the end of which month he died of heart failure. Prinz got two further projects underway: the modification of the Bremen site for car production and the advancement of powerful outposts in the North American truck market. The strong mark in 1973 made exports there impossible. Mercedes-Benz do Brasil leapt into the breech, supplying components to Mercedes-Benz Truck Co. in Hampton, Virginia not far from the Newport container port where the US subsidiary Mercedes-Benz of North America had erected an assembly plant for 6000 units annually at a cost of 14 million dollars. The problem was that this was for relatively light-duty trucks of between nine and 15 tons as required for short-distance haulage. What Mercedes could otherwise offer was the result of a pragmatic European approach and consequently completely incompatible with the American trucker's romantic notion of intimidatingly sized vehicles. To reach the heart of this different world, a native manufacturer had to be incorporated into the Mercedes empire – make mimicry was out of the question. This was carried out twice – with differing success. On 31 May 1977 Daimler-Benz AG acquired Euclid Incorporated

Replik auf den Vorwurf wogender Behäbigkeit, den man den Untertürkheimer Limousinen seit altersher gerne anlastet. Mit dem Erscheinen des agilen Sechzehnventilers ist dieser Mief wie weggeblasen, zumal er sich im August 1983 mit Paukenschlägen wie drei Langstrecken-Weltrekorden über Distanzen bis zu 50 000 Kilometer im süditalienischen Nardo einführt. Investitionen in Höhe von zehn Milliarden müssen für das Wagnis w 201 lockergemacht werden. Aber es lohnt sich. Zwar ist die Reaktion zunächst zögerlich: Mercedes-Standard hat nämlich auch der Kaufpreis für den Kompakten. Und der beträgt zum Beispiel im Dezember 1982 für das Einstiegsmodell 190 stattliche 25 600 Mark, während für den 200, den Geringsten unter der hierarchisch eigentlich übergeordneten Baureihe w 123, nur 200 Mark mehr zu entrichten sind. Überdies müssen relativ banale Sonderausstattungen heftig honoriert werden.

Aber dann kommen die Dinge in Schwung: Bis 1988 sind bereits über eine Million (1 125 928) w 201 selbst unter Leute gebracht worden, die nie zuvor einen Mercedes besaßen, rund ein Drittel davon (413 905) Diesel. Im Januar 1984 küren Journalisten aus vieler Herren Länder den 190 E zum World Car of the Year, und in der Hauptversammlung im Juli desselben Jahres bringt Werner Breitschwerdt, Vorstandsvorsitzender seit dem Dezember 1983, in wohl gewählten Worten seine Genugtuung zum Ausdruck, nun auch auf diesem Sektor ein Spitzenprodukt anbieten zu können.

Dass man nun in den bewegten Gewässern des Weltmarkts mit dem Dreizack s-Klasse, Mittelklasse und Kompaktklasse fischt, findet sich indes unter den Meriten von Gerhard Prinz, Breitschwerdts Vorgänger im Amt zwischen dem Januar 1980 und dem Oktober 1983, verstorben Ende jenes Monats an Herzversagen. Noch zwei weitere Projekte hat Prinz auf die richtige Schiene gesetzt: die Mutation des Standorts Bremen zur PKW-Manufaktur und das Vorantreiben starker Vorposten auf dem LKW-Markt in Nordamerika. 1973 macht die starke Mark dem Export dorthin den Garaus. Die Mercedes-Benz do Brasil springt in die Bresche, liefert Teile an die Mercedes-Benz Truck Co. in Hampton/Virginia unweit des Containerhafens Newport. Dort hat die US-Filiale Mercedes-Benz of North America für 14 Millionen Dollar ein Montagewerk für 6000 Einheiten jährlich errichtet. Der Haken: Es handelt sich um leichtere LKW zwischen neun und 15 Tonnen, wie sie im Einzugsbereich der Städte benötigt werden. Was Mercedes darüber hinaus anzubieten hätte, ist europäisch-pragmatisch gedacht und folglich durchaus nicht kompatibel mit der amerikanischen Trucker-Romantik, die sich um Fahrzeuge von bullig-einschüchternden Dimensionen rankt. Um ins Herz dieses Mythos zu gelangen, müsste man dem Stern-Imperium einen einheimischen Hersteller eingemeinden – ein Marken-Mimikry käme nicht in Frage. Dies geschieht zweimal – mit unterschiedlichem Erfolg. Am 31. Mai 1977 ersteht die Daimler-Benz AG für 56 Millionen Dollar die Euclid Incorporated in Cleveland/Ohio, ein Subunternehmen der White Motor Corporation, speziali-

Werner Breitschwerdt, Mercedes chairman 1983–1987.
Werner Breitschwerdt, Mercedes-Chef 1983–1987.
Werner Breitschwerdt, P.-D.G. de Mercedes de 1983 à 1987.

un tiers (413 905) de diesels. En janvier 1984, des journalistes d'un grand nombre de pays du monde sacrent la 190 E *World Car of the Year* et, lors de l'assemblée générale de la même année, Werner Breitschwerdt, président du directoire depuis décembre 1983, exprime en termes choisis sa satisfaction de pouvoir maintenant proposer aussi un produit de pointe dans ce segment.

C'est toutefois le mérite de Gerhard Prinz, prédécesseur de Breitschwerdt au directoire de janvier 1980 à octobre 1983 et décédé d'un infarctus cette même année, que Mercedes puisse pêcher dans les eaux agitées du marché mondial avec le trident Classe s, classe intermédiaire et classe compacte. Un Prinz qui a aussi engagé deux autres projets dans la bonne voie : la mutation du site de Brême en unité de production de VP et la mise en place de puissantes têtes de pont sur le marché nord-américain du camion. En 1973, la vigueur du mark étouffe les exportations vers ce continent. Mercedes-Benz do Brasil reprend le flambeau, fournit des pièces à Mercedes-Benz Truck Co. à Hampton/Virginie, non loin du port de conteneurs de Newport. La filiale américaine Mercedes-Benz of North America y a construit une usine de montage pour 6000 camions par an pour 14 millions de dollars. Mais il y a un bémol : il s'agit de camions légers de 9 à 15 tonnes comme on en a besoin dans les zones urbaines. Ce que Mercedes pourrait proposer au-dessus de ce segment est une conception pragmatique européenne et, logiquement, absolument pas compatible avec le romantisme des *truckers* (routiers) à l'américaine qui se nourrit de camions aux dimensions intimidantes. Pour parvenir au cœur de ce mythe, il faudrait que l'empire à l'étoile absorbe un constructeur autochtone – un plagiat n'entrant pas en ligne de compte. Cela s'effectue à deux reprises – avec un succès variable. Le 31 mai 1977, Daimler-Benz AG acquiert pour 56 millions de dollars Euclid Incorporated à Cleveland (Ohio), une firme du groupe White Motor Corporation

in Cleveland, Ohio for 56 million dollars, a subsidiary of White Motor Corporation, which specialized in the biggest of big trucks. Following a promising start. Cleveland returned red figures with depressing reliability, and so the disappointing US acquisition was sold on in early 1984.

A change of game brought a change of luck, and this time literally. In 1980 the ailing White Motor Corporation went bankrupt. In addition to Mercedes, the giant American trucking corporation Freightways was also interested in the assets. At the unavoidable meeting it was revealed that Freightways was looking to sell off its Freightliner subdivision which made high-quality heavy goods vehicles. This made the people in Untertürkheim sit up and then take action quickly. The usual signatures in Palo Alto, California on 31 July 1981 and the small matter of 260 million dollars meant that Daimler-Benz AG could call Freightliner Corporation its own and had thereby gained its target of access to the US markets. The White Motor deal never got off the ground. In early 1982 the North American Mercedes enclave was restructured. The newly established Daimler-Benz of North America Holding Company Inc. formed the umbrella under which sheltered the subsidiaries Freightliner and Mercedes-Benz Truck Co. Inc. on the one hand which jointly covered the trucks business, and Mercedes-Benz of North America on the other hand which handled the car side.

Diversification second time around, or the art of standing on several legs

A drawing by Walter Hanel, a caricaturist at the *Frankfurter Zeitung* succinctly summed it up: against the backdrop of a star-filled night sky, the two occupants of a Mercedes were looking in amazement at a UFO which was crowned by a gigantic antenna in the form of the make's familiar symbol. The guest from outer space's four thin legs terminated in discs with the Mercedes star and the inscriptions MTU, Dornier and AEG. This was a reference to what the powers-that-be in the group like to call the "tetrad" approach in their poetically transfigured wishful thinking – a kind of commercial harmony of the spheres. Diversification had been called for once before when Mercedes started up in the Twenties. It was not a success.

Then in the mid-Eighties, after reconstruction and takeovers and expansion of Mercedes provinces throughout the world, big was best, in line with the watchword of German classicism that isolation is reprehensible. The new acquisitions should form a colorful patchwork in their totality, be lucrative individually and promise a generous living for the future. The MTU leg: in February 1985 Daimler-Benz took over the shares of MAN in MTU München, thereby reinforcing its commitment to aeroengines and large engines. The Dornier leg: a little later Mercedes

siert auf schwerste LKW-Kaliber. Nach verheißungsvollem Start meldet Cleveland mit ermüdender Zuverlässigkeit rote Zahlen, und so stößt man die enttäuschende US-Akquisition Anfang 1984 wieder ab.

Neues Spiel, neues Glück, und diesmal buchstäblich: 1980 geht die kränkelnde White Motor Corporation bankrott. Neben Mercedes interessiert sich der amerikanische Speditions-Gigant Freightways für die Konkursmasse. Man begegnet einander zwangsläufig, und so bleibt nicht verborgen, dass dieser seine Subdivision Freightliner abzustoßen gedenkt. Diese stellt hochwertige Schwerlastwagen her. In Untertürkheim wird man hellhörig und greift zu. Nach den üblichen Unterschriften, im kalifornischen Palo Alto am 31. Juli 1981, und gegen einen Obolus von 260 Millionen Dollar nennt die Daimler-Benz AG die Freightliner Corporation ihr eigen und hat sich damit den gewünschten Zugriff auf die US-Märkte verschafft. Der White-Deal kommt nie zustande. Anfang 1982 wird die nordamerikanische Mercedes-Enklave neu gegliedert: Unter dem Dach der frisch gegründeten Daimler-Benz of North America Holding Company Inc. kuscheln sich die Stern-Töchter Freightliner und Mercedes-Benz Truck Co. Inc. einerseits, die gemeinsam die LKW-Seite abdecken, sowie MercedesBenz of North America andererseits, die das PKW-Geschäft besorgt.

Diversifikation zum zweiten, oder die Kunst, auf mehreren Standbeinen zu stehen

Eine Zeichnung von Walter Hanel, Karikaturist der *Frankfurter Zeitung,* bringt es auf den Punkt: Vor nächtlichem Sternenhimmel beäugen die beiden Insassen eines Mercedes verblüfft ein UFO, das von einer riesigen Antenne in der Form des vertrauten Marken-Emblems gekrönt wird. Die vier dünnen Beinchen des Gasts aus dem All fußen auf Scheiben mit dem Mercedes-Stern und den Aufschriften MTU, Dornier und AEG. Das ist eine Anspielung auf das, was die Konzern-Herren in poetisch verklärtem Wunschdenken »Vierklang« nennen – eine Art merkantile Sphären-Harmonie. Schon einmal, beim späten Daimler Anfang der zwanziger Jahre, war Diversifikation angesagt. Das Resultat war dürftig.

Nun, Mitte der Achtziger, nach dem Wiederaufbau und der Eroberung und dem Ausbau von Mercedes-Provinzen in aller Welt, will man's deftig, getreu der Devise der deutschen Klassik, alle Vereinzelung sei verwerflich. In ihrer Gesamtheit sollen die Neuerwerbungen ein buntes Patchwork bilden, einzeln lukrativ sein und für die Zukunft fette Pfründe verheißen. Standbein MTU: Im Februar 1985 übernimmt man die Anteile der MAN an der MTU München und verstärkt damit sein Engagement in Richtung Flugtriebwerke und Großmotoren. Standbein Dornier: Wenig später kauft

spécialisée dans les camions de très gros calibre. Après un départ prometteur, Cleveland annonce avec une régularité éprouvante des pertes qui incitent à se défaire à nouveau de la décevante acquisition américaine au début de 1984.

Nouveau jeu, nouvelle chance, ce qui s'entend cette fois-ci au sens propre : en 1980, à l'agonie, White Motor Corporation fait faillite. Outre Mercedes, le géant des transports américain Freightways s'intéresse également à l'actif de la faillite. On doit inévitablement aller au-devant l'un de l'autre et ainsi apprend-on que Freightways envisage de se séparer de sa division Freightliner. Celle-ci fabrique des poids lourds de haut niveau. À Untertürkheim, un déclic se produit et l'on saisit la balle au bond. Après les signatures de contrats traditionnelles, à Palo Alto en Californie, le 31 juillet 1981, et contre une obole de 260 millions de dollars, Daimler-Benz AG s'approprie Freightliner Corporation qui lui donne, comme souhaité, l'accès au marché américain. L'affaire avec White ne se fait pas. Début 1982, la tête de pont nord-américaine de Mercedes est réorganisée : sous le toit de la Daimler-Benz of North America Holding Company Inc. tout récemment fondée se regroupent les filiales à l'étoile Freightliner et Mercedes-Benz Truck Co. Inc., d'une part, qui couvrent à elles deux le marché des camions, ainsi que Mercedes-Benz of North America, d'autre part, qui se consacre aux opérations voitures de tourisme.

Diversification, première – ou l'art d'avoir plusieurs fers au feu

Un dessin de Walter Hanel, caricaturiste de la *Frankfurter Zeitung,* en dit plus que mille mots : devant la voûte céleste étoilée, deux passagers de Mercedes découvrent, étonnés, un ovni surplombé par une gigantesque antenne ayant la forme de l'emblème familier de leur marque. Les quatre minces pattes de l'inconnu venu de l'espace s'appuient sur des vitres avec l'étoile Mercedes et les inscriptions MTU, Dornier et AEG. C'est une allusion à ce que les maîtres du groupe appellent « quadrophonie » dans leur poétique désir pas encore devenu réalité – une espèce d'harmonie spatiale mercantile. Une fois déjà, dans la société Daimler du début des années 1920, la diversification avait été à l'ordre du jour. Avec les résultats que l'on connaît.

Et maintenant, au milieu des années 1980, après la reconstruction et la conquête ainsi que l'extension des filiales Mercedes dans le monde entier, on veut faire les choses correctement, fidèle à la devise du classicisme allemand selon laquelle tout isolement est condamnable. Dans leur complémentarité, les nouvelles acquisitions doivent constituer un patchwork haut en couleurs, être lucratives prises isolément et promettre de bons dividendes à l'avenir. Exemple MTU : en février 1985, Mercedes rachète les actions de MAN à MTU Munich et accentue ainsi son engagement

bought a majority holding with 65.5 per cent of the shares in Dornier GmbH, opening up its involvement in promising developments for the future in fields such as aeronautical engineering, space technology and medical technology through a company with a staff of 9000. The AEG leg: by February 1986 Daimler-Benz had accumulated 56 per cent of the capital of the electrical giant at a cost of 1.6 billion marks, one result of which was to give itself access to forward-looking high technology.

The expansion of the once pure-bred car maker into an integrated technology company with a new organizational structure, which had been forcefully promoted in particular by Edzard Reuter, Breitschwerdt's heir to the throne since September 1987, was crystallized on 29 June 1989. Daimler-Benz AG, which formed the umbrella and executive holding company in which the management functions and R&D were centralized, would in future rest on four columns – of extremely different solidity, as it later turned out. The traditional automotive division was now once again under the banner of Mercedes-Benz AG. The chairman of its board of management was Professor Werner Niefer who was then replaced with effect from 27 May 1993 by his hitherto deputy chairman Helmut Werner, a lively and highly qualified manager who had been brought in from outside. He had been the chairman of the board of management at the Hanover-based tire manufacturer Continental when he came to the attention of the then head of Deutsche Bank and chairman of the Daimler supervisory board Alfred Herrhausen who persuaded him to move to Stuttgart in 1987. Naturally the vehicle sector is seen as the icing on the cake of the other activities of the diversified Daimler-Benz Group. This is shown quite simply in the fact that use of the venerable star symbol is reserved only for this sector. Aerospace activities were brought together into Dasa, i.e. Deutsche Aerospace AG (renamed Daimler-Benz Aerospace with effect from 1 January 1995) which has also encompassed Messerschmitt-Bölkow-Blohm GmbH since late 1989. The decision to set up a further business unit to be known as Daimler-Benz Inter-

Trinity: Hermann J. Abs, Edzard Reuter and Werner Niefer.
Dreieinigkeit: Hermann J. Abs, Edzard Reuter und Werner Niefer.
La « Sainte Trinité » : Hermann J. Abs, Edzard Reuter et Werner Niefer.

Mercedes mit 65,5 Prozent die Mehrheit der Anteile bei der Dornier GmbH und erschließt sich zukunftsträchtige Felder wie Flugzeugbau, Raumfahrt und Medizintechnik auf dem Wege über ein Unternehmen mit 9000 Mitarbeitern. Standbein AEG: Bis Februar 1986 sammelt Daimler-Benz um 1,6 Milliarden Mark 56 Prozent vom Kapital des Elektro-Kolosses an und erarbeitet sich somit unter anderem einen Zugang zu nach vorn orientierten High-Tech-Technologien.

Am 29. Juni 1989 kristallisiert sich der vor allem von Edzard Reuter, Breitschwerdt-Thronerbe seit dem September 1987, mit Schwung vorangetriebene Ausbau der einst reinrassigen Auto-Manufaktur zum integrierten Technologiekonzern in einer neuen Organisationsform. Das Dach der Daimler-Benz AG als geschäftsführender Holding, in der Führungsfunktionen und Forschung gebündelt sind, ruht künftig auf vier Säulen – von höchst unterschiedlicher Solidität, wie sich herausstellen wird. Der traditionelle Automobil-Bereich findet sich nun im Gewand der Mercedes-Benz AG wieder. Ihr Vorstandsvorsitzender ist Professor Werner Niefer, ab 27. Mai 1993 dessen bisheriger Stellvertreter Helmut Werner, ein quirliger und hochqualifizierter Quereinsteiger. Als Vorstandchef des Hannoveraner Reifenherstellers Continental ist er dem damaligen Chef der Deutschen Bank und Daimler-Aufsichtsratsvorsitzenden Alfred Herrhausen aufgefallen, der ihn 1987 nach Stuttgart holt. Natürlich ist der Fahrzeug-Sektor als Sahnehäubchen über den weiteren Aktivitäten der Hydra Daimler-Benz gedacht. Dies zeigt sich bereits darin, dass ihm allein das altehrwürdige Stern-Zeichen als Symbol vorbehalten bleibt. Luft- und Raumfahrt werden in der Dasa zusammengefasst, der Deutschen Aerospace AG (ab 1. Januar 1995 Daimler-Benz Aerospace), die seit Ende 1989 auch die Messerschmitt-Bölkow-Blohm GmbH umspannt. Aus dem gleichen Jahr stammt der Entschluss, einen weiteren Unternehmensbereich zu errichten in Gestalt der Daimler-Benz InterServices (debis) AG. Diese bietet Dienstleistungen an wie Finanzierungen, Immobilienmanagement, Mobilfunkdienste oder Versicherungen. Indes: Nicht alle Blütenträume reifen, schon wegen der Klimaveränderungen in der Konjunkturlandschaft wie dem Versiegen der Nachfrage, welche die deutsche Wiedervereinigung ausgelöst hat. Spätestens nach dem Rekordverlust des Jahres 1995 von 5,7 Milliarden Mark zeigt sich, dass eine Integral-Rechnung à la Edzard Reuter nicht mehr aufgeht. Sein Nachfolger Jürgen E. Schrempp (im Amt seit dem Mai 1995) verordnet der Daimler-Benz AG eine drakonische Schlankheitskur. Verlust bringende Firmenteile wie AEG und Fokker werden abgestoßen, die Geschäftsfelder von 35 auf 23 verringert.

Während sich so die schlichte Weisheit zu bestätigen scheint, man dürfe auf nicht allzu vielen Hochzeiten gleichzeitig tanzen, wächst, blüht und gedeiht die Auto-Tochter Mercedes-Benz AG. Und da die Firmengeschichte ja zeitgleich verläuft mit dem Säkulum des Automobils, gerät der hundertste Geburtstag der Motorisierung 1986 gewissermaßen zur Familienfeier – mit Welt- Echo und Welt-Geltung. Weltweit mehren sich auch die Filialen im Zeichen

en direction des moteurs d'avion et des gros moteurs. Exemple Dornier : un peu plus tard, Mercedes achète, avec 65,5 % des actions, la majorité du capital de Dornier GmbH et a ainsi accès à des champs d'activités prometteurs pour l'avenir telles l'aéronautique, l'astronautique et la technique médicale, par le biais d'une entreprise de 9000 collaborateurs. Exemple AEG : jusqu'en février 1986, pour 1,6 milliard de marks, Daimler-Benz accapare 56 % du capital du géant de l'électronique qui lui ouvre ainsi les portes, notamment, de hautes technologies futuristes.

Le 29 juin 1989 se précise la transformation à marche forcée, voulue surtout par Edzard Reuter, héritier du trône de Breitschwerdt depuis septembre 1987, d'ex-manufacture exclusive d'automobiles en groupe technologique intégré avec une nouvelle forme d'organisation. Le toit de Daimler-Benz AG en tant que holding d'administration-gérance où sont regroupées les fonctions de direction et de recherche reposera à l'avenir sur quatre piliers – chacun d'une solidité extrêmement variable, comme on le constatera plus tard. Le bastion traditionnel de l'automobile a désormais pour nom Mercedes-Benz AG. Le président de son directoire est le professeur Werner Niefer, que son ancien adjoint, Helmut Werner, homme d'une grande intelligence et très qualifié qui ne provient pas du sérail remplace le 27 mai 1993. En tant que président du directoire de Continental, le fabricant de pneumatiques de Hanovre, il a attiré sur lui l'attention de l'ancien P.-D.G. de la Deutsche Bank et président du conseil de surveillance de Daimler, Alfred Herrhausen, qui l'a fait venir à Stuttgart en 1987. Naturellement, le secteur Automobile se conçoit comme la cerise sur le gâteau que sont les autres activités de l'hydre Daimler-Benz. Cela ressort déjà du fait que le traditionnel emblème à l'étoile lui est réservé exclusivement comme symbole. L'aéronautique et l'astronautique sont regroupées au sein de la Dasa, Deutsche Aerospace AG (rebaptisée en Daimler-Benz Aerospace le 1ᵉʳ janvier 1995), qui s'adjuge également Messerschmitt-Bölkow-Blohm GmbH fin 1989. La même année est prise la décision de constituer un autre secteur d'entreprise sous le nom de Daimler-Benz InterServices (debis) AG. Cette société offre des services tels que les financements, la gestion de parcs immobiliers, des services de téléphonie ou des assurances. Malheureusement, tous les rêves ne deviennent pas réalité, ne serait-ce que par suite des ruptures opérées par le cours de l'histoire qui grèvent la conjoncture économique, telle la diminution de la demande générée par la réunification de l'Allemagne. Après les pertes record de 1995 (5,7 milliards de marks), il apparaît qu'un concept intégral à la Edzard Reuter n'est plus viable. Son successeur, Jürgen E. Schrempp (entré en fonction en mai 1995), ordonne à Daimler-Benz AG une cure d'amaigrissement draconienne. On se sépare de firmes non rentables comme AEG et Fokker et le nombre des secteurs d'activités est réduit de 35 à 23.

Alors que semble se confirmer le proverbe dicté par le bon sens selon lequel il ne faut pas courir trop de lièvres à la fois, la filiale automobile Mercedes-Benz AG connaît un essor sans précédent. L'histoire de la firme concordant avec

Services (debis) AG also dated from the same year. This offered services such as finance, property management, mobile telephone services and insurance. However, not all dreams came to fruition, because of climate changes in the business landscape or a fall-off in the demand generated by the reunification of Germany. At the latest after the record losses of 5.7 billion marks in 1995 it was clear that an integrated system à la Edzard Reuter was no longer appropriate. His successor, Jürgen E. Schrempp (in office since May 1995), prescribed a drastic slimming course for Daimler-Benz AG. Loss-making parts of the group such as AEG and Fokker were hived off, and the number of business units was reduced from 35 to 23.

While the old saying seemed to be confirmed about spreading oneself too thinly, the automotive subsidiary Mercedes-Benz AG was growing and flourishing. And since the company's history was running on the same timescale as the century of the car, the 100th birthday of motorized transport in 1986 became a kind of family celebration – with a worldwide echo and worldwide prestige. The number of branches bearing the star sign also continued to multiply worldwide, a peaceful global offensive. In October of that year a commercial vehicle factory was opened in Aksaray, Turkey. Mercedes-Benz Asia was founded in 1990 to look after the markets in the east and south-east of the continent. In February 1991 a cooperation agreement was signed with the Korean SsanYong Motor Company. One month later Mercedes-Benz Danmark AS was established in Hillerød. The decision in February 1993 to build a bus factory in Monterrey, Mexico was immediately implemented, and this production center was opened as Mercedes-Benz Omnibuses Mexico S.A. in January 1995. In April 1993 the assembly of bus type O 303 at the Russian manufacturer AVTROCON began.

In July 1993 another holy cow was sacrificed on the altar of reason and progress when assembly of the E 420 went on-stream in Mexico too. The C 280 was scheduled to follow in the autumn of 1994, and the C 220 in January 1995. As Helmut Werner, chairman of the board of management, put it, the "Made in Germany" label must be replaced by the quality statement "Made by Mercedes" – and that can be done anywhere. February 1994 saw the beginning of the Swatch saga, a surprising sortie into the world of small cars, when talks were held with Schweizerische Gesellschaft für Mikroelektronik und Uhrenindustrie (SMH) AG with the aim of building a Micro Compact Car (MCC). Micro Compact Car AG was also the name of the company set up in April of that year in Bienne. The foundation stone for the assembly plant was laid in October 1995 in Hambach in France, to the accompaniment of countless good wishes for the future of the mini-mini.

A further joint venture in April 1994 strengthened the links to the old partner Tata Engineering and Locomotive Co. (Telco): Mercedes-Benz India began manufacturing E-class vehicles and engines for Telco. In May building work began in Tuscaloosa, Alabama where it is intended that a new market niche will be sounded from 1997 onwards with

Jürgen E. Schrempp, at the helm of Daimler-Benz since 1995.

Jürgen E. Schrempp führt Daimler-Benz seit 1995.

Jürgen E. Schrempp préside aux destinées de Daimler-Benz depuis 1995.

des Sterns, eine friedliche Global-Offensive. Im Oktober jenes Jahres wird ein Nutzfahrzeugwerk im türkischen Aksaray eröffnet. Die Mercedes-Benz Asia, 1990 gegründet, kümmert sich um Märkte im Osten und Südosten des Kontinents. Im Februar 1991 unterzeichnet man einen Kooperationsvertrag mit dem koreanischen Unternehmen SsanYong Motor Company. Einen Monat später wird die Mercedes-Benz Danmark AS in Hillerød ins Leben gerufen. Der Entscheidung für den Bau einer Omnibusfabrik in Monterrey/Mexiko im Februar 1993 folgt umgehend die Tat: Diese wird als Fertigungsstätte der Mercedes-Benz Omnibuses Mexico S.A. bereits im Januar 1995 eingeweiht. Im April 1993 läuft der Zusammenbau des Busses O 303 beim russischen Hersteller AVTROCON an.

Im Juli 1993 verblutet eine weitere heilige Kuh auf den Altären von Vernunft und Fortschritt, als der E 420 nun auch in Mexiko montiert wird. Im Herbst 1994 soll der C 280, im Januar 1995 der C 220 folgen. Das Prädikat »Made in Germany«, lehrt Vorstandvorsitzender Helmut Werner, sei zu ersetzen durch die Qualitätsformel »Made by Mercedes« – und das sei überall möglich. Im Februar 1994 beginnt die Swatch-Saga, ein überraschender Ausfallschritt in die Welt des Mobils in miniature: Man findet sich in unternehmerischem Tête-à-tête zusammen mit der Schweizerischen Gesellschaft für Mikroelektronik und Uhrenindustrie (SMH) AG mit dem Ziel, ein Micro Compact Car (MCC) zu bauen. Micro Compact Car AG heißt auch die Firma, die im April des Jahres in Biel gegründet wird. Den Grundstein für das Montagewerk, begleitet von vielen guten Wünschen für die Zukunft des Mini-Minis, versenkt man im Oktober 1995 im französischen Hambach.

le siècle de l'automobile, le centenaire de la motorisation, en 1986, est célébré en quelque sorte comme une fête de famille – avec un écho et une notoriété d'envergure mondiale. Tout comme se multiplient aussi à l'échelle mondiale les filiales arborant l'étoile, une pacifique offensive globale. En octobre de la même année, une usine de véhicules utilitaires est inaugurée à Aksaray, en Turquie. Mercedes-Benz Asia, fondée en 1990, dessert les marchés de l'est et du sud-est du continent. En février 1991 est signé un contrat de coopération avec l'entreprise coréenne Ssan Yong Motor Company. Un mois plus tard, Mercedes-Benz Danmark as est portée sur les fonts baptismaux à Hillerød. La décision de construire une fabrique d'autobus et d'autocars à Monterrey/Mexique, en février 1993, est transposée immédiatement dans les faits : celle-ci est inaugurée dès janvier 1995 comme unité de production de Mercedes-Benz Omnibuses Mexico S.A. En avril 1993 débute le montage du bus O 303 chez le constructeur russe AVTROCON.

En juillet 1993, on sacrifie une autre vache sacrée sur l'autel de la raison et du progrès : la E 420 est maintenant montée aussi au Mexique. Elle sera suivie, à l'automne 1994, par la C 280 et, en janvier 1995, par la C 220. Rien ne s'oppose, a enseigné le président du directoire Helmut Werner, à ce que l'on substitue au label « made in Germany » le label de qualité « made by Mercedes » – ce qui est, selon lui, possible partout. En février 1994 débute la saga de la Swatch, un écart de conduite surprenant en direction du monde de l'automobile miniature : on se retrouve en tête-à-tête entre industriels avec la Société suisse de Micro-électronique et d'Horlogerie (SMH) SA avec pour objectif de construire une Micro Compact Car (MCC). Micro Compact Car AG est aussi le nom de la firme qui est fondée en avril de cette année-là à Bienne. En octobre 1995, on pose à Hambach, en France, la première pierre de son usine de montage, accompagnée de tous les bons vœux pour l'avenir de la mini-mini.

Un autre *joint-venture* resserre, en avril 1994, les liens avec le vieux partenaire Tata Engineering and Locomotive Co. (Telco). Mercedes-Benz India fabrique des voitures de la Classe E et des moteurs pour Telco. En mai débutent à Tuscaloosa, dans l'État américain de l'Alabama, les travaux pour l'usine où sera construite à partir de 1997 l'All Activity Vehicle (AAV) appelée à combler une autre niche du marché. Depuis juin de la même année, il existe une Mercedes-Benz Sverige AB à Spanga, en Suède, et, depuis novembre, Mercedes-Benz Avtomobili AOST, à Moscou, comme société de distribution pour la Russie. En novembre 1995, le chancelier fédéral Helmut Kohl en personne pose la première pierre d'un centre de production de véhicules utilitaires et de VP à Hô Chi Minh-Ville, au Viêt-nam, et, un an plus tard déjà, les premiers modèles de la Classe E sortent de ses chaînes.

En 1996, l'offensive de la mondialisation se poursuit sur des fronts toujours nouveaux. Au Brésil, les conditions sont réunies pour produire la Classe A à raison de 70 000 unités par an qui iront se battre, dans des pays d'Amérique latine comme l'Argentine, le Brésil, le Chili, le Paraguay et l'Uruguay, contre l'inamovible best-seller de Volkswagen,

Pastures new: the Rastatt plant.
Auf zu neuen Ufern: Werk Rastatt.
Vers un nouvel avenir : l'usine de Rastatt.

the All Activity Vehicle (AAV). Mercedes-Benz Sverige AB began operating in Spanga, Sweden in June of the same year, and Mercedes-Benz Avtomobili AOST in Moscow in November as the distribution company for Russia. In November 1995 Federal Chancellor Helmut Kohl himself laid the foundation stone for a production plant for commercial vehicles and cars in Ho Chi Minh City in Vietnam, and just one year later the first E-class models came off the assembly line.

In 1996 the globalization offensive was extended to ever newer fronts. In Brazil the necessary steps were taken to enable 70,000 units of the A-class to be produced annually, with the intention of displacing Volkswagen's long-term bestseller, the Golf, and its current competitors in the Latin American countries of Argentina, Brazil, Chile, Paraguay and Uruguay. The Vitoria plant in Spain celebrated the production premiere of the V-class under southern sun. In the commercial vehicle sector, the assembly of Sprinter vans in Argentina and the Vito in Poland began. In September a contract was signed for the production of Mercedes buses in China with the local manufacturer Yangzhou Motor Coach Manufacturer General. In this way, according to Helmut Werner, it is possible not only to improve the company's market position in the relevant countries but also to safeguard jobs at Mercedes-Benz's German suppliers. After all, the company's internal and external policies have long since been intimately linked, two sides of the same coin.

Back in Germany too developments were quite dynamic in the gentle glow of the Swabian star. The stations of a never-ending story are set out below. In October 1990 a cooperation agreement was concluded with Automobilwerk Ludwigsfelde in Brandenburg where the first trucks of type LN 2 were assembled in the following year. In January 1994 this eastern satellite was taken over and placed under the wing of the parent company. In 1992 the choice fell on Papenburg as the site for a new test track. In May 1992 Helmut Kohl opened a third assembly plant in Rastatt where the new A-class is to be born. Noblesse – and a 110-year corporate history – oblige: when the Oldtimer Center was opened a year later, this meant that the maintenance and cultivation of tradition at Mercedes was based on three pillars. The other two were the museum and the archive.

Ein weiteres Joint Venture vertieft im April 1994 die Bande an den alten Partner Tata Engineering and Locomotive Co. (Telco): Mercedes-Benz India fertigt Fahrzeuge der E-Klasse und Motoren für die Telco. Im Mai beginnen Bauarbeiten in Tuscaloosa im amerikanischen Bundesstaat Alabama, wo man ab 1997 mit dem All Activity Vehicle (AAV) eine weitere Marktnische ausloten will. Seit dem Juni des gleichen Jahres gibt es die Mercedes-Benz Sverige AB in schwedischen Spanga, seit dem November die Mercedes-Benz Avtomobili AOST im Moskau als Vertriebsgesellschaft für Russland. Im November 1995 legt Bundeskanzler Helmut Kohl höchstselbst den Grundstein einer Produktionsstätte für Nutzfahrzeuge und PKW in Ho-Chi-Minh-Stadt in Vietnam, und bereits ein Jahr später laufen die ersten Modelle der E-Klasse vom Band.

1996 wird die Globalisierungsoffensive an immer neue Fronten vorangetragen. In Brasilien schafft man die Voraussetzungen, die A-Klasse in jährlich 70 000 Einheiten zu produzieren, welche in den lateinamerikanischen Ländern Argentinien, Brasilien, Chile, Paraguay und Uruguay dem Volkswagen-Dauerrenner Golf und seinen bereits real existierenden Konkurrenten den Rang ablaufen sollen. Im spanischen Werk Vitoria hat die V-Klasse Produktions-premiere unter südlicher Sonne. Im Segment Nutzfahrzeuge wird die Montage der Transporter Sprinter in Argentinien und des Vito in Polen angeschoben. Im September unterzeichnet man einen Vertrag über die Fertigung von Mercedes-Bussen in China mit dem einheimischen Hersteller Yangzhou Motor Coach Manufacturer General. Solchermaßen verbessere man nicht nur seine Marktposition in den jeweiligen Ländern, sagt Helmut Werner, sondern sichere auch die Arbeitsplätze in den deutschen Zulieferwerken von Mercedes-Benz. Denn längst sind Außen- und Innenpolitik der Firma aufs engste ineinander verwoben und vernetzt, zwei Seiten einer Münze.

Auch hierzulande entwickeln sich die Dinge durchaus dynamisch im milden Glanz des schwäbischen Sterns. Stationen einer unendlichen Geschichte: Im Oktober 1990 kommt es zu einem Kooperationsvertrag mit dem Automobilwerk Ludwigsfelde in Brandenburg, wo im folgenden Jahr bereits der erste LKW vom Typ LN 2 montiert wird. Im Januar 1994 überführt man den Ost-Trabanten in eigene Regie. 1992 fällt die Entscheidung für Papenburg als Standort für eine neue Teststrecke. Im Mai 1992 weiht Helmut Kohl ein drittes Montagewerk in Rastatt ein, das dereinst die neue A-Klasse in die Welt entlassen soll. Adel und eine Firmen-Historie von 110 Jahren verpflichten: Als ein Jahr später das Oldtimer-Center eröffnet wird, stützen sich Wartung und Pflege der Tradition bei Mercedes auf drei Pfeiler. Die beiden anderen: Museum und Archiv. Nur einen Steinwurf von der Zentrale in Untertürkheim entfernt gibt es im April 1994 den ersten Spatenstich für das Motorenwerk Bad Cannstatt, Geburtsstätte einer neuen Generation von V6- und V8-Maschinen vom Frühjahr 1997 an. Im September 1994 signiert man den Kaufvertrag zur Übernahme der Karl Käßbohrer GmbH, und als die EU-Kommission

la Golf, et ses concurrents d'ores et déjà sur le marché. Dans l'usine espagnole de Vitoria, la Classe V a fêté la première de sa production sous le soleil du Sud. Dans le segment des utilitaires, le montage des fourgonnettes Sprinter commence en Argentine et celles de la Vito, en Pologne. En septembre, on signe un contrat régissant la fabrication d'autobus Mercedes en Chine par le constructeur autochtone Yangzhou Motor Coach Manufacturer General. De cette manière, précise Helmut Werner, on n'améliore pas seulement la position sur le marché dans les pays respectifs, mais on assure aussi des emplois chez les sous-traitants allemands de Mercedes-Benz. En effet, il y a des lustres que la politique intérieure et la politique extérieure de la firme sont liées de la manière la plus étroite, telles les deux faces d'une pièce de monnaie.

En Allemagne aussi, les affaires connaissent un dynamisme certain sous la lueur tempérée de l'étoile souabe. Étapes d'une histoire sans fin, en octobre 1990 est signé un contrat de coopération avec l'usine automobile de Ludwigsfelde, dans le Brandebourg, où l'on monte dès l'année suivante le premier camion de la série LN 2 ; en janvier 1994, on reprend sous sa propre férule le satellite oriental ; en 1992 est prise la décision de choisir Papenbourg comme site d'un nouveau circuit d'essais ; en mai 1992, Helmut Kohl inaugure, à Rastatt, une troisième ligne de montage d'où partiront pour le monde entier les nouvelles Classe A.

Noblesse et une généalogie de 110 ans obligent : lorsque l'Oldtimer-Center est inauguré, un an plus tard, l'entretien et la culture de la tradition chez Mercedes s'appuient sur trois piliers. Les deux autres sont le musée et les archives. À un jet de pierres de la centrale d'Untertürkheim, on donne, en avril 1994, le premier coup de pioche pour l'usine de moteurs de Bad Cannstatt qui sera le berceau d'une nouvelle génération de moteurs V6 et V8 à partir du printemps 1997. En septembre 1994 est signé le contrat d'achat relatif à la reprise de Karl Käßbohrer GmbH et, après que la Commission de l'UE eut donné son feu vert à la fusion, est fondé, en 1995, EvoBus GmbH comme pure dépendance Mercedes, qui reprend toutes les activités Omnibus de la firme.

Et l'on enregistre record sur record : en février 1988, on célèbre la dix millionième Mercedes fabriquée depuis la fin de la guerre et, en mai 1990, la millionième fourgonnette construite à Düsseldorf depuis 1962. Mais il y a aussi des premières : en 1986, année centenaire de l'automobile, un pionnier prouve qu'il est aussi capable d'innovations en prise avec leur temps : Mercedes équipe tous ses modèles à essence d'un catalyseur à trois voies et, à partir du 1er octobre 1992, toute sa gamme de voitures, d'airbags et de l'ABS. Et il y a des distinctions : en 1990, la gamme de camions lourds est élue *Truck of the Year*, en 1995 le Sprinter et, en 1996, le Vito sont sacrés *Van of the Year*. La lecture d'un reportage destiné à la rédaction économique du 27 décembre 1996 est des plus édifiantes. Devise : nous allons bien, et comment ! En hausse, le chiffre d'affaires de Mercedes-Benz AG est passé à 77 milliards de marks (contre 72 en 1995). Avec les versions T des Classe C et E ainsi que la SLK et la Classe V,

The first sod for the Bad Cannstatt engine plant, destined to be the birthplace of a new generation of v6 and v8 engines from the spring of 1997 onwards, was cut in April 1994 just a stone's throw from the headquarters in Untertürkheim. In September 1994 the purchase agreement was signed to take over Karl Kässbohrer GmbH and, once the EU Commission had approved the merger, EvoBus GmbH was set up in 1995 as a wholly-owned Mercedes subsidiary to take over all the company's bus activities.

There were records: in February 1988 the ten millionth Mercedes car since the end of the war was celebrated, and in May 1990 the millionth van made in Düsseldorf since 1962. And premieres: in 1986, in the centenary of the car's invention, Mercedes showed itself to be a pioneer of appropriate innovation in series production when it began fitting all petrol models with a three-way catalytic converter, and its complete model range with an airbag and ABS with effect from 1 October 1992. And there were awards: in 1990 the Heavy Truck Class was voted Truck of the Year, in 1995 the Sprinter took Van of the Year and in 1996 it was the turn of the Vito. And so the annual report of 27 December 1996 which basically said "We're doing well, and how" made pleasant reading. Mercedes-Benz AG's sales rose to 77 billion marks (1995: 72 billion). With the T-models in the C- and E-classes and the SLK and the V-class four new car models were launched, flanked by the Vito and the Vario amongst the vans, the Actros in the heavy trucks and the new small Unimog UX 100 in the utility vehicles which also opened up new prospects for the Gaggenau site. EvoBus GmbH underlined its fighting strength with four new bus models. Never in the company's long history, Helmut Werner was able to report, had there been such a large number of major product launches. A new sales record was set when the company sold 345,000 commercial vehicles and 640,000 cars worldwide, with the E-class as the bestseller in the make's hierarchy and the SLK as everyone's favorite. The production target for the versatile sports car for 1997 was even increased from the originally planned 35,000 to 47,000 vehicles. Mercedes-Benz employs over 197,000 staff worldwide, 152,000 of them in the German factories, head office, branches and the consolidated domestic companies such as EvoBus GmbH and Micro Compact Car AG. There's also a red glow on the horizon signaling fair weather ahead for tomorrow. According to Werner, the A-class from Rastatt, the M-class from the USA and the new CLK coupé from Bremen will ensure access to further market segments for the company with good prospects for the future.

But there were soon dark clouds gathering over this entrepreneurial Arcadia, and trumpets sounding the praises of others but also of the trumpeters themselves. On 16 January 1997 Hilmar Kopper, head of Deutsche Bank and chairman of the Daimler-Benz AG supervisory board, opened a meeting of the board in Stuttgart-Möhringen with unusual formality. He read out a letter from Helmut Werner in which the latter asked to be released prematurely from his

dem Zusammenschluss zustimmt, entsteht 1995 die EvoBus GmbH als chemisch reine Mercedes-Dependance, die alle Omnibus-Aktivitäten des Unternehmens übernimmt.

Rekorde stellen sich ein: Im Februar 1988 begießt man den zehnmillionsten Mercedes-PKW seit Kriegsende, im Mai 1990 den millionsten Transporter Düsseldorfer Provenienz seit 1962. Und Premieren: 1986, im Jahre einhundert der Vita des Automobils, erweist man sich als Pionier von zeitgerecht-serienmäßiger Innovation: Mercedes rüstet alle Benziner mit Dreiwege-Katalysator aus, ab 1. Oktober 1992 seine komplette Modell-Palette mit Airbag und ABS. Und Ehrungen: 1990 wird die Schwere LKW-Klasse zum Truck of the Year gewählt, 1995 der Sprinter und 1996 der Vito zum Van of the Year. So liest sich ein Bericht für die Wirtschaftsredaktion vom 27. Dezember 1996 fürwahr erfreulich, Tenor: Uns geht's gut, und wie. Der Umsatz der Mercedes-Benz AG ist auf 77 Milliarden Mark (1995: 72 Milliarden) gestiegen. Mit den T-Modellen der C- und E-Klasse sowie dem SLK und der V-Klasse hat man vier neue PKW-Modelle in die Märkte eingespeist, flankiert von Vito und Vario bei den Transportern, dem Actros bei den schweren LKW und bei den Kommunalfahrzeugen den neuen kleinen Unimog UX 100, der zugleich dem Standort Gaggenau eine neue Perspektive gibt. Die EvoBus GmbH unterstrich ihre Kampfkraft mit vier neuen Omnibus-Modellen. Noch nie in der langen Geschichte der Firma, kann Helmut Werner berichten, habe es eine solche Fülle von wichtigen Produktvorstellungen gegeben. Weltweit hat man einen neuen Absatzrekord aufgestellt mit 345 000 Nutzfahrzeugen und 640 000 PKW, mit der E-Klasse als Bestseller in der Hierarchie der Marke und dem SLK als jedermanns Liebling: Das Produktionsziel für das sportive Multitalent wird gar für 1997 von ursprünglich geplanten 35 000 auf 47 000 Fahrzeuge angehoben. Weltweit sind bei Mercedes-Benz über 197 000 Mitarbeiter beschäftigt, in den deutschen Werken, der Hauptverwaltung, den Niederlassungen sowie den konsolidierten Inlandsgesellschaften wie EvoBus GmbH und Micro Compact Car AG 152 000 davon. Rosig-silbrig schimmern auch die Horizonte zum Morgen: Mit der A-Klasse aus Rastatt, der M-Klasse aus den USA und dem neuen Coupé CLK aus Bremen, so Werner, verschaffe man sich für 1997 Zugang zu weiteren, zukunftsträchtigen Marktsegmenten.

Doch schon ballt sich düsteres Gewölk über diesem unternehmerischen Arkadien, mischen sich schrille Töne in Lob und Eigenlob. Am 16. Januar 1997 eröffnet Hilmar Kopper, Chef der Deutschen Bank und Vorsitzer des Aufsichtsrats der Daimler-Benz AG, eine Zusammenkunft des Präsidiums in Stuttgart-Möhringen mit einer ungewöhnlichen Formalität. Er verliest ein Schreiben von Helmut Werner, in dem dieser um vorzeitige Auflösung seines Vertrags ersucht. Er werde sein Amt als Vorstandsmitglied der Holding-Gesellschaft anlässlich der außerordentlichen Daimler-Aufsichtsratssitzung am 23. des Monats und den Posten des Mercedes-Vorstandschefs am 6. Februar niederlegen. Kurz zuvor hat Werner, vom US-Magazin *Business Week* unlängst zu den 25 weltweit erfolgreichsten Konzern-

Showpieces such as this are mere extras. The real persuasion took place earlier.
Schaustücke wie diese sind nur Statisten. Die eigentliche Überzeugungsarbeit fand vorher statt.
Des voitures comme celle-ci ne jouent qu'un rôle de figurant. Le travail de persuasion proprement dit a déjà eu lieu auparavant.

Mercedes a lancé sur le marché quatre nouveaux modèles, escortés par le Vito et le Vario pour les fourgonnettes, l'Actros pour les camions lourds ainsi que, pour les véhicules communaux, par le nouveau petit Unimog UX 100, qui donne par la même occasion de nouvelles perspectives au site de Gaggenau. EvoBus GmbH prouve son agressivité avec quatre nouveaux modèles d'omnibus. Jamais encore dans la longue histoire de la firme, comme peut le communiquer Helmut Werner, on n'a présenté autant de produits d'une telle importance. À l'échelle mondiale, on a établi un nouveau record de ventes avec 345 000 utilitaires et 640 000 VP, avec la Classe E comme best-seller dans la hiérarchie de la marque, et le SLK comme coqueluche universelle : pour 1997, l'objectif de production pour ce multitalent sportif va même être majoré des 35 000 exemplaires prévus à l'origine à 47 000 voitures. Dans le monde entier, Mercedes-Benz emploie plus de 197 000 collaborateurs, dont 152 000 dans les usines allemandes, au siège social, dans les filiales ainsi que les sociétés consolidées allemandes comme EvoBus GmbH et Micro Compact Car AG. Et c'est plus qu'une lueur argentée qui pointe à l'horizon : avec la Classe A de Rastatt, la Classe M des États-Unis et le coupé CLK de Brême, a ajouté Helmut Werner, on aura accès, pour 1997, à d'autres segments prometteurs du marché.

Mais des nuages sombres ne tardent pas à s'accumuler dans un ciel jusque-là immaculé et des dissonances viennent troubler la mélodie. Le 16 janvier 1997, Hilmar Kopper, le P.-D.G. de la Deutsche Bank et président du conseil de surveillance de Daimler-Benz AG, ouvre une réunion du bureau présidentiel à Stuttgart-Möhringen avec un formalisme qui ne lui est pas coutumier. Il lit une lettre de Helmut Werner dans laquelle celui-ci demande que son contrat soit résilié prématurément. Il a l'intention de démissionner comme membre du directoire de la Holding à l'occasion de la réunion extraordinaire du conseil de surveillance de Daimler, le 23 du mois, et de remettre son poste de président du directoire de Mercedes le 6 février. Peu de temps auparavant, Werner, que la revue américaine *Business Week*

The Vito, manufactured in Vitoria Spain.

Im spanischen Vitoria hergestellt: der Vito.

Fabriqué à Vitoria, en Espagne : le Vito.

contract. He intended relinquishing his post as a member of the board of management of the holding company at an extraordinary meeting of the Daimler supervisory board on 23 January and leaving the post of chairman of the Mercedes board of management on 6 February. Werner, who had recently been listed as one of the 25 most successful corporate managers worldwide by the US magazine *Business Week*, had suffered a bitter defeat shortly before this. The Mercedes board of management had agreed unanimously on a resolution to build a luxury four-wheel-drive vehicle jointly with Porsche based on the M-class, but this had been dashed when the Daimler management stipulated that it would first have to take a financial holding in Porsche AG. Werner's resignation came at the end of months of battling with the chairman of the group's board of management, Jürgen Schrempp, who wished to merge the automotive side with the holding company which Mercedes man Werner opposed. This also put him in the firing line of the corporate supervisors who did actually decide on the merger on that Thursday in January. The reorganization was to be in place by 1 April, and it was to be made final by the Daimler AGM on 28 May of that year in Stuttgart. The fields of passenger cars, commercial vehicles, aerospace (Daimler-Benz Aerospace), services (debis), and also direct industrial investments are all progressing well. Daimler-Benz Aerospace comprises six lines of business: commercial aircraft and helicopters, military aircraft, space travel infrastructure, satellites, defense and civil systems, and also propulsion systems. The services sphere includes financial services and insurance, IT services, telecommunications and media services, and also trade and real estate management. Directly-controlled industrial investments encompass the railway systems including Adtranz (ABB Daimler-Benz Transportation GmbH), the diesel propulsion units branch (MTU) and also microelectronics (TEMIC). Aerospace AG in Munich and debis AG, whose new headquarters on Potsdamer Platz in Berlin was opened on 24 October remain legally autonomous, but their respective headquarters are being slimmed down. This leaner management structure comes at the usual human cost in terms of cuts in upper and middle management positions. At the same time, warns Manfred Göbels, chairman of the group's executive representation body, a great deal of hard work remains to be done: the shift in management and profit responsibilities to the

managern gerechnet, eine bittere Schlappe wegstecken müssen: Der bereits vom Mercedes-Vorstand einstimmig gefasste Beschluss, gemeinsam mit Porsche einen Luxus-Geländewagen auf der Basis der M-Klasse zu bauen, zerschellt am Postulat der Daimler-Führung, man müsse sich erst bei der Porsche AG finanziell beteiligen. Werners Demission steht am Ende eines monatelangen Tauziehens mit Konzern-Boss Jürgen Schrempp: Dieser will die schöne Autotochter mit der Holding verschmelzen, Mercedes-Mann Werner will das nicht. Er gerät damit auch in die Schusslinie der Kontrolleure des Unternehmens, die an jenem Donnerstag im Januar in der Tat die Fusion beschließen. Am 1. April soll der Umbau stehen. Rechtskräftig wird er durch die Daimler-Hauptversammlung am 28. Mai des Jahres in Stuttgart. Die Geschäftsfelder Personenwagen, Nutzfahrzeuge, Luft- und Raumfahrt (Daimler-Benz Aerospace), Dienstleistungen (debis) sowie direkt geführte industrielle Beteiligungen bilden sich aus. Die Daimler-Benz Aerospace umspannt sechs Bereiche: Verkehrsflugzeuge und Hubschrauber, Militärmaschinen, Raumfahrt-Infrastruktur, Satelliten, Verteidigung und Zivile Systeme sowie Antriebe. Das Geschäftsfeld Dienstleistungen fächert sich auf in das Spektrum Finanzdienstleistungen und Versicherungen, IT-Services, Telekommunikations- und Mediendienste, Handel und Immobilienmanagement. Die direkt geführten industriellen Beteiligungen sind die Bahnsysteme mit der Adtranz (ABB Daimler-Benz Transportation GmbH), der Zweig Dieselantriebe (MTU) sowie die Mikroelektronik (TEMIC). Die Aerospace AG in München und die debis AG, deren neuer Hauptsitz am Postdamer Platz in Berlin am 24. Oktober eingeweiht werden wird, bleiben rechtlich eigenständig, die Zentralen schrumpfen aber. Mit der strafferen Führungsstruktur ist Lean Management mit den üblichen Grausamkeiten angesagt: Abbau von Führungspositionen im oberen und mittleren Bereich. Zugleich, verkündet Manfred Göbels, Vorsitzer des Konzernsprecherausschusses, drohe Kärrnerarbeit: Die deutliche Verlagerung von Geschäfts- und Ergebnisverantwortung in die operativen Einheiten und die konsequente Aufgliederung des Konzerns in Divisionen müsse erst noch mit Geist erfüllt werden und setze eine viel kollegialere Zusammenarbeit voraus, als sie bislang praktiziert worden sei. Wie ein glückliches Omen wirkt da der Bilderbuchstart der 100. Ariane-Rakete vom Raumfahrtzentrum Kourou in Französisch-Guayana am 23. September. Auf ihrem Jubiläumsflug befördert sie den Kommunikationssatelliten Intelsat 803 in eine Erdumlaufbahn. Zu neuen Ufern lockt auch die Designstudie Mercedes-Benz Maybach auf der Tokyo Motor Show ab dem 24. Oktober, deren Bau vom Vorstand am 28. Juli des folgenden Jahres abgesegnet werden wird. Ein Statussymbol von gleichermaßen ausladenden wie einladenden Dimensionen, soll die klassisch geformte Limousine zum Ausbund strotzenden Komforts und innovativer Technik werden.

Kurz darauf besudelt ein hässlicher Fleck das funkelnde Firmenimage: Bei einem Versuch des schwedischen

vient de citer parmi les 25 meilleurs managers de groupe du monde entier, a dû subir une amère défaite : la décision, déjà prise à l'unanimité par le directoire de Mercedes, de construire conjointement avec Porsche une tout-terrain de luxe sur la base de la Classe M se voit opposer une fin de non-recevoir par la direction de Daimler, pour laquelle le préalable serait une participation financière de Mercedes à Porsche AG. La démission de Helmut Werner n'est que le point final d'un long duel contre le P.-D.G. du groupe, Jürgen Schrempp : celui-ci veut faire fusionner avec la holding la belle filiale automobile, chose que l'homme de Mercedes qu'est Werner cherche à empêcher à tout prix. Il se retrouve donc aussi dans le collimateur des contrôleurs de l'entreprise, qui optent de fait pour la fusion ce jeudi-là de janvier. La réorganisation doit être achevée le 1er avril. Elle entrera en vigueur à l'issue de l'assemblée générale de Daimler le 28 mai de cette même année à Stuttgart. Les secteurs d'activités Voitures de tourisme, Utilitaires, Aéronautique et espace (Daimler-Benz Aerospace), Services (debis) ainsi que les participations industrielles gérées directement se constituent. Daimler-Benz Aerospace comporte six secteurs : Avions civils et hélicoptères, Avions militaires, Infrastructure pour l'astronautique, Satellites, Défense et systèmes civils ainsi que Propulsions. Le secteur d'activités Services se subdivise en différentes catégories : Services financiers et assurances, Services informatiques, Services de télécommunications et de médias, Commerce et Management immobilier. Les participations industrielles gérées directement sont les systèmes ferroviaires avec Adtranz (ABB Daimler-Benz Transportation GmbH), la branche Motorisations diesel (MTU) ainsi que la Micro-électronique (TEMIC). Aerospace AG, à Munich, et debis AG, qui va emménager dans son nouveau siège social de la Potsdamer Platz à Berlin, le 24 octobre prochain, restent indépendantes sur le plan juridique, mais les centrales voient leur importance numérique diminuer. Avec un moins grand nombre de directeurs, le *Lean Management* et son train de mesures est à l'ordre du jour : suppression d'un certain nombre de postes directeurs aux échelons supérieurs et intermédiaires. Simultanément, Manfred Göbels, président de la commission des porte-parole du groupe, annonce qu'il reste encore beaucoup à faire : le transfert à grande échelle de la responsabilité des affaires et des résultats aux unités opérationnelles et la réorganisation systématique du groupe en divisions doivent

Far, fast, good: the heavy-duty Actros truck.

Fern, schnell, gut: der schwere Lastwagen Actros.

Loin, vite, bien : le gros poids lourd Actros.

operational units and the comprehensive reorganisation of the group into separate divisions must first be carried through with vigor, and this will require a much greater spirit of cooperation than has existed in the past. The copybook launch of the 100th Ariane rocket from Kourou Space Center in French Guyana on 23 September seemed like a lucky omen. On this anniversary flight Ariane was conveying the communication satellite Intelsat 803 into orbit.

The Mercedes-Benz Maybach concept car, presented at the Tokyo Motor Show starting on 24 October, also heralded new frontiers, and the executive board subsequently the following year gave their blessing to its production on 28 July. A status symbol par excellence with its sweeping and alluring lines, this classically-styled saloon car is the epitome of opulent levels of passenger comfort coupled with innovative technology.

Shortly afterwards, however, the company's glittering image was tarnished when, in a test carried out by the Swedish journal *Teknikens Värld* to simulate swerving to avoid an elk suddenly emerging from the undergrowth, an A Class Mercedes swayed and rocked wildly before finally toppling ignominiously onto its side. Matters were put right by modifying the suspension and equipping the car with the ESP dynamic drive system put matters right and made the mini Mercedes among the safest cars in its class. On 9 February 1998, after a three-month rethink and pause in production, the car again began to roll off the lines at Rastatt. Initial fears proved groundless and the A-class proved to be a winner with a year's production figure of 149,988 units. However, the expression 'elk test' has entered the language to express something worthy of ridicule.

Meanwhile, in the world of the automotive giants the company also made headlines when, on 7 May, Daimler-Benz AG and Chrysler Corporation signed a contract paving the way for a megamerger of unparalleled proportions between the two companies. The marriage was consecrated on 17 September at an extraordinary general meeting at the Hanns-Martin-Schleyer-Halle in Stuttgart, when 99.9 per cent of the shareholders approved the merger. Approval is almost as high at the future partner's meeting. Then on 26 October came the news that about 97 per cent of Daimler-Benz shares had been converted into DaimlerChrysler AG shares in line with the 30-day conversion offer. On 17 November the new DaimlerChrysler shares were traded for the first time on the New York, Frankfurt and 19 other stock exchanges, marking the beginning of a new era. The merger also meant that the subsidiaries Dasa and debis changed their names to DaimlerChrysler Aerospace AG and DaimlerChrysler Services (debis) AG respectively. At the supervisory board's constituting meeting on 16 December Hilmar Kopper was elected chairman, while the general committee appointed Jürgen E. Schrempp and Robert Eaton joint heads of the executive board. With the merger's entry in the Stuttgart Register of Companies on 21 December 1998 Daimler-Benz AG ceased to exist. Purists bitterly bemoaned the fact that

Heavyweight: Atego 1828.
Schwerkraft: Atego 1828.
Poids lourd: Atego 1828.

Journals *Teknikens Värld,* der das Umfahren eines jäh auftauchenden Elchs simuliert, wankt und schaukelt das examinierte Exemplar der A-Klasse und kippt schließlich schmählich auf die Seite. Mit einer geänderten Fahrwerksabstimmung und der Nachrüstung mit dem Fahrdynamiksystem ESP kriegt man die Sache in den Griff und erhebt den kleinen Mercedes zugleich in den Rang des Klassen-Primus in Sachen Sicherheit. Am 9. Februar 1998, nach einer Denk- und Produktionspause von einem Vierteljahr, wird die Fertigung in Rastatt wieder aufgenommen. Trotz anfänglichen Bangens gerät die A-Klasse zum Renner in einer Jahres-Population von 149 988 Einheiten. Die Vokabel Elchtest jedoch ist von nun an in aller Munde, zumeist zum Ausdruck für Humoriges verfremdet.

Auch im Makrokosmos der Auto-Größen tummelt man sich in den Schlagzeilen, als sich eine Elefantenhochzeit sondergleichen anbahnt. Am 7. Mai unterzeichnen die Daimler-Benz AG und die amerikanische Chrysler Corporation einen Vertrag, der den Boden zum Zusammenschluss vorbereitet. Szenen einer werdenden und schließlich vollzogenen Ehe: Am 17. September stimmen auf einer außerordentlichen Hauptversammlung in der Stuttgarter Hanns-Martin-Schleyer-Halle 99,9 Prozent der Aktionäre für die Fusion. Fast gleich hoch ist der Anteil beim künftigen Partner. Am 26. Oktober wartet man mit der frohen Botschaft auf, rund 97 Prozent der Daimler-Benz-Aktien seien im Rahmen des 30tägigen Umtauschangebots in Aktien der DaimlerChrysler AG umgetauscht worden. Am 17. November markiert der erste Handelstag der neuen DaimlerChrysler-Aktie an der New York Stock Exchange, der Frankfurter Börse sowie 19 weiteren Handelsplätzen den Beginn einer neuen Epoche. Mit dem Bund fürs Leben ändern auch die Töchter Dasa und debis ihre Namen in DaimlerChrysler Aerospace AG und DaimlerChrysler Services (debis) AG. Der Aufsichtsrat kürt auf seiner konstituierenden Sitzung am 16. Dezember Hilmar Kopper zum Vorsitzenden, der Präsidialausschuss bestallt die Doppel-Spitze Jürgen E. Schrempp und Robert Eaton zu Chefs des Vorstands. Mit dem Eintrag der Verschmelzung ins Stuttgarter Handelsregister am 21. Dezember 1998 ist die Daimler-Benz AG erloschen. Auf der Strecke bleibt, von Puristen bitterlich beweint, ein Mann der ersten Stunde: Karl Benz.

encore prendre vie, ce qui présuppose une coopération dans un esprit beaucoup plus collégial que par le passé. Le décollage d'anthologie de la 100e fusée Ariane du centre aérospatial de Kourou, en Guyane française, le 23 septembre 1997, apparaît comme un heureux présage. Lors de son vol-anniversaire, elle va placer sur orbite terrestre le satellite de communication Intelsat 803. Le prototype de style de la Mercedes-Benz Maybach dévoilé au Tokyo Motor Show le 24 octobre symbolise un départ vers de nouveaux horizons : le directoire a donné le feu vert pour sa construction le 28 juillet de l'année suivante. Cette limousine aux formes classiques, symbole de statut et voiture de représentation aux dimensions aussi imposantes qu'accueillantes, veut devenir une symbiose de confort dans tous les registres et de technique novatrice.

Peu de temps après, une tache hideuse vient ternir le blason scintillant de la firme : lors d'un essai de la revue spécialisée suédoise *Teknikens Värld* où l'on simule une manœuvre d'évitement d'un élan qui franchit la route de façon inattendue, la voiture d'essai, une Classe A, se dandine et se balance avant de basculer lamentablement sur le côté. Avec de nouveaux réglages de châssis et la greffe du système de contrôle dynamique ESP, on résout le problème et confère simultanément à la petite Mercedes la réputation de « forte en thème » en matière de sécurité. Le 9 février 1998, après trois mois d'interruption de la production mis à profit pour de longues réflexions, sa fabrication reprend à Rastatt. Malgré certaines hésitations initiales, la Classe A devient un bestseller et est produite à concurrence de 149 988 exemplaires en un an. Le « test de l'élan » est désormais sur toutes les lèvres et fournit souvent matière à d'innombrables plaisanteries.

Même dans le microcosme des géants de l'automobile, le constructeur de Stuttgart fait les grands titres lorsqu'un mariage éléphantesque s'annonce. Le 7 mai, Daimler-Benz AG et la Chrysler Corporation américaine signent un contrat qui aplanit la voie à leur fusion. Scènes d'un mariage annoncé et, finalement, consommé le 17 septembre, lors d'une assemblée générale extraordinaire à la Hanns-Martin-Schleyer-Halle de Stuttgart, où 99,9 % des actionnaires votent pour la fusion. Le scrutin est presque aussi consensuel chez son futur partenaire. Le 26 octobre, Stuttgart peut annoncer la bonne nouvelle selon laquelle environ 97 % des actions de Daimler-Benz ont été échangées contre des actions de DaimlerChrysler AG dans le cadre de l'offre de reprise de 30 jours. Le 17 novembre, premier jour de cotation de la nouvelle action DaimlerChrysler à la New York Stock Exchange, à la Bourse de Francfort ainsi que sur dix-neuf autres places boursières, marque le début d'une nouvelle époque. Avec cette union éternelle, les filiales Dasa et debis modifient également leurs noms en DaimlerChrysler Aerospace AG et DaimlerChrysler Services (debis) AG. Lors de sa réunion constitutive du 16 décembre, le conseil de surveillance élit Hilmar Kopper comme président alors que la commission de direction nomme le duo Jürgen E. Schrempp et Robert Eaton comme présidents du directoire. L'inscription de la fusion au registre du commerce de Stutt-

the new company's name left no room for a man from the dawn of automotive history: Karl Benz.

In 1999 business boomed: between January and the end of April the group sold 332,000 Mercedes passenger cars, 22 per cent more than the year before, and the sales forecast was upped to 140 billion euros. However, at the general meeting on 18 May there was sharp criticism from shareholders about the railway technology subsidiary Adtranz and the mini mobile Smart, which asserted itself despite being deeply in the red earlier on.

Putting the failing Chrysler Group back on its feet and repairing its market acceptability was a challenge the Mercedes men Dr. Dieter Zetsche and Dr. Wolfgang Bernhard were ready to meet. "Aha," the American critics of the merger prophesied gloomily, "it was just an unfriendly takeover." Little by little, the hostile voices were being silenced, for, in the fall of 2003, there were indications of the first operating profits. "Money making" is good and legitimate. Anyway, the sun of the 2004 automobile spring was shining over Detroit, and Chrysler – despite the previous discount battles in the US automobile industry.

Jürgen Schrempp's next steps were unexpectedly in the "World Corp." direction. Still beaming with delight, he shook the hand of Mitsubishi President Kawasoe in March 2000. DaimlerChrysler had just taken a stake in the in debt Japanese concern. Nissan had also been in discussion as an investment object. Of course, the globalization strategy demanded changes in personnel in this case as well: Rolf Eckrodt was chosen as the German boss of a Japanese concern, who, far from home, was to tackle the company's indigenous problems. The hoped-for financial injection from the Bank of Tokyo, also a part owner of Mitsubishi, to boost urgently needed projects did not materialize. The joint technical platform, such as that of the Mitsubishi Colt and the Smart Forfour, of which a new engine plant in Thuringia was a part, temporarily began to wobble. However, in the first quarter of 2004, there was also a crisis between Hyundai – here the stake was 10.5 percent – and DaimlerChrysler, which was in fact totally incomprehensible, as the Korean Hyundai-Kia concern had greatly improved its position between 1999 and 2003, and had entered the top ten of the world's major automobile producers.

626 bhp, 207 mph: the super sportsman 300 SLR McLaren
626 PS, 334 km/h: Supersportler 300 SLR McLaren
626 ch, 334 km/h : la supersportive 300 SLR McLaren

Anno 1999 laufen die Geschäfte glänzend: Vom Januar bis Ende April verkauft der Konzern 332 000 Mercedes-Personenwagen, 22 Prozent mehr als im Jahr zuvor. Prompt erhöht man die Umsatzprognose auf 140 Milliarden Euro. Kritik seitens der Aktionäre entzündet sich während der Hauptversammlung am 18. Mai an der Bahntechnik-Filiale Adtranz und dem Mini-mobil Smart, das sich nach anfänglich tiefroten Zahlen durchsetzt.

Die ziemlich angeschlagene Chrysler Group zu sanieren und salonfähig zu machen, ist eine Herausforderung, der sich die Mercedes-Mannen Dr. Dieter Zetsche und Dr. Wolfgang Bernhard stellen. »Aha«, unken sofort die Fusionskritiker in den USA, »es war eben doch eine feindliche Übernahme.« Nach und nach verstummen die bösen Stimmen, denn im Herbst 2003 deuten sich die ersten operativen Profite an. »Money making« ist gut und legitim. Jedenfalls scheint im Autofrühling 2004 über Detroit die Sonne, auch bei Chrysler – und trotz der vorangegangenen Rabatt-Schlachten der US-Autoindustrie.

Nicht erwartungsgemäß verläuft Jürgen Schrempps nächster Schritt in Richtung »Welt AG«. Im März 2000 schüttelt er noch freudestrahlend Mitsubishi-Präsident Kawasoe die Hand. Soeben ist DaimlerChrysler bei dem verschuldeten japanischen Konzern eingestiegen. Auch Nissan war als Investitionsobjekt im Gespräch gewesen. Natürlich verlangt die Globalisierungs-Strategie auch in diesem Falle nach personellen Veränderungen: Rolf Eckrodt heißt der Auserwählte, der sich fern der Heimat als deutscher Boss eines japanischen Konzerns mit einheimischen Problemen auseinandersetzen darf. So fehlen die erhofften Finanzspritzen der Bank of Tokyo, ebenfalls Anteilseigner von Mitsubishi, um dringend erforderliche Projekte anzukurbeln. Die gemeinsame technische Plattform, wie zwischen Mitsubishi Colt und Smart Forfour, zu der auch ein neues Motorenwerk in Thüringen gehört, gerät vorübergehend ins Wanken. Aber auch zwischen Hyundai – hier ist man mit 10,5 Prozent beteiligt – und DaimlerChrysler kriselt es im ersten Quartal 2004. Eigentlich völlig unverständlich, denn der koreanische Hyundai-Kia-Konzern hat zwischen 1999 und 2003 kräftig zugelegt und ist in die Top Ten der größten Auto-Hersteller der Welt eingedrungen.

»Das wichtigste Mittel, um den richtigen Weg zu finden, ist, den falschen zu vermeiden.« Dieser Satz von Manfred Rommel, Stuttgarts Oberbürgermeister zwischen 1974 und 1996, geistert durch die Führungsetage angesichts des verworfenen Nissan-Engagements. Globalisierung ist nur selten Glückssache, man muss in ihr aufgehen können. Mehrmals erhebt Dr. Manfred Gentz, Vorstand für Finanzen und Controlling, warnend den Finger und kritisiert das Fernost-Engagement wegen finanzieller Ungereimtheiten. Dennoch verliert Schrempp nicht seinen Optimismus. Nach anhaltenden, nervenaufreibenden internen Rangeleien auf höchster Ebene bittet der Aufsichtsrat der DaimlerChrysler AG zu einer Aussprache im vornehmen New Yorker Hotel Waldorf-Astoria. DaimlerChrysler-Boss und Querdenker Wolfgang Bernhard, eigentlich ab 1. Mai 2004 als Nachfolger des Mer-

gart, le 21 décembre 1998, signifie la dissolution de Daimler-Benz AG. Reste en chemin, faisant verser des larmes amères aux puristes, un homme de la première heure : Karl Benz.

En 1999, le succès commercial est exceptionnel : de janvier à fin avril, le groupe vend 332 000 Mercedes de tourisme, 22 % de plus qu'un an auparavant. Dans la foulée, on révise à la hausse les prévisions de chiffre d'affaires, annonçant 140 milliards d'euros. Les actionnaires ne ménagent cependant pas leurs critiques, lors de l'assemblée générale du 18 mai, au sujet de la filiale Technique ferroviaire Adtranz et de la mini Smart, qui finit par s'imposer après avoir engendré un certain déficit.

Remettre de l'ordre dans le Chrysler Group, plutôt malmené sur le plan économique, et le rendre de nouveau attrayant est un défi que s'attellent à relever deux fidèles de Mercedes, Dieter Zetsche et Wolfgang Bernhard. « Vous voyez, objectent immédiatement les détracteurs de la fusion aux États-Unis, il s'agissait bien d'une OPA hostile ». Peu à peu, les opposants doivent baisser de la voix, car, à l'automne 2003, les premiers signes de bénéfices opérationnels s'annoncent. « Money making » est une bonne chose, et légitime. Quoi qu'il en soit, au printemps de l'automobile 2004, le soleil brille au-dessus de Detroit, pour Chrysler aussi – et ce, malgré les campagnes de ristournes avec lesquelles cherchent à se surpasser les constructeurs automobiles américains.

Le prochain pas de Jürgen Schrempp vers la « SA Monde » ne se fait pas dans la direction escomptée. En mars 2000, encore rayonnant jusqu'aux oreilles, il serre chaleureusement la main du président de Mitsubishi, M. Kawasoe. Daimler-Chrysler vient de prendre une participation dans le groupe japonais profondément endetté. Nissan a aussi figuré dans son collimateur comme objet d'investissement. Naturellement, dans ce cas-là aussi, la stratégie de mondialisation exige des sacrifices personnels : Rolf Eckrodt est le nom de l'heureux élu qui va devoir, loin de sa patrie, s'attaquer aux problèmes endémiques en tant que patron allemand d'un groupe japonais. Bien qu'elle détienne elle aussi des actions de Mitsubishi, c'est peut-être pour cela que la Bank of Tokyo refuse, contrairement à ce que l'on avait espéré, d'injecter de l'argent frais, qui serait pourtant bien nécessaire pour financer la solution des problèmes urgents. La plate-forme technique commune, comme entre la Mitsubishi Colt et la Smart Forfour, dont fait aussi partie une nouvelle usine de moteurs en Thuringe, commence à vaciller, mais ce n'est que provisoire. Entre Hyundai – dont DC détient aussi une participation, de 10,5 % – et DaimlerChrysler, le torchon brûle au premier trimestre 2004. Il n'y a pourtant absolument aucun motif à cela, car le groupe coréen Hyundai-Kia a réalisé des progrès considérables entre 1999 et 2003 et a fait son apparition dans le top-ten des plus grands constructeurs automobiles du monde.

« Le meilleur moyen de trouver la bonne voie est d'éviter la fausse. » Cette sentence de Manfred Rommel, maire de Stuttgart de 1974 à 1996, ne cesse de tarauder les esprits des dirigeants de Mercedes, à la pensée qu'ils avaient abandonné l'idée de s'engager chez Nissan. La mondialisation n'est que rarement une affaire de chance, il faut savoir s'en pénétrer.

"The best means of finding the right path is to avoid the wrong one." This sentence by Manfred Rommel, the Lord Mayor of Stuttgart between 1974 and 1996, echoed through the corridors of management in the face of the rejected involvement with Nissan. Globalization is rarely a matter of luck, you have to work at it. Dr. Manfred Gentz, Director of Finance and Cost Control, raised his finger as a warning, and criticized the financial inconsistencies of the Far East engagement. However, Schrempp did not lose his optimism. After protracted, nerve-racking internal wrangling at the highest level, the DaimlerChrysler AG's supervisory board requested a meeting at the distinguished Waldorf-Astoria Hotel in New York. DaimlerChrysler's boss and open-minded thinker Wolfgang Bernhard, foreseen as successor as of 1st May 2004 to Mercedes boss Prof. Jürgen Hubbert, leant a little too far out of the window with his criticism, and in public at that! He kept his post on the board, although for the time being without concrete responsibilities. In this manner, his exile within the company's empire was discreetly achieved. Power and impotence lay close by another. While Hubbert again sat in the driving seat of the MercedesGroup, more firmly than ever, Schrempp sent Smart boss Andreas Renschler as a crisis manager to Japan to work out a new business plan, according to which the management, once again Japanese, could work. Eckrodt, who had been eagerly awaiting his well-earned retirement, resigned immediately.

In the meantime, the succession question has been solved: Eckhard Cordes, confidant of Schrempp and successful modernizer of the truck division, takes over the seat of Hubbert, while Renschler has taken over the truck division following the definitive termination of Daimler-Chrysler's involvement in Japan.

"After a century of Mercedes, and a decade of intensive 'genetic research' on our own account, we have come to the conclusion – in relation to the cars with the star – that a lot of potential is still to be found in the Mercedes-Benz DNA. But the right gene alone, or the dusting off of laurel leaves won long ago, is not sufficient in the competition of today. Whoever wishes to be successful has to manage to continuously update his products' relevancy," Hubbert declared at the Frankfurt IAA in 2001. And then proceeded to deliver the proof: ranging from the smallest model to the more than six-meter long cruise liner for the especially well-to-do, from the SLK to the SLR for the sport-minded, and from the A Class, rejuvenated in 2004, to the Viano for small families. Both the M and the G Class have also hit the mark – the latter for over 20 years.

Only the introduction of the HGV road toll system has put a strain on the technical performance. DaimlerChrysler has subscribed to the responsibility of developing Toll Collect, the German telematic registration system, which is slow to leave the starting blocks. Here a rash intuition has indeed led the way. Intuition – the Italian publication *Il Tempo* defined the word in a practical way: "Intelligence at too high a speed!"

Sally forth to the past: bosses Jürgen Schrempp and Robert Eaton on the Benz 3-wheeler.
Aufbruch in die Vergangenheit: Führungschefs Jürgen Schrempp und Robert Eaton auf dem benzschen Dreirad.
Retour dans le passé : les P.-D.G. Jürgen Schrempp et Robert Eaton sur le tricycle Benz.

cedes-Chefs Prof. Jürgen Hubbert vorgesehen, lehnte sich mit seiner Kritik ein wenig zu weit aus dem Fenster, zumal in der Öffentlichkeit. Er behielt seinen Vorstandsposten, zunächst jedoch ohne konkrete Befugnisse. So wird ihm die Verbannung innerhalb des Imperiums anheim gestellt. Macht und Ohnmacht liegen eben dicht beieinander. Während Hubbert wieder die MercedesGroup lenkt, fester als je zuvor, schickte Schrempp Smart-Chef Andreas Renschler als Krisenmanager nach Japan. Eckrodt, der schon sehnlichst auf den verdienten Ruhestand gewartet hatte, trat augenblicklich zurück.

Inzwischen ist die Nachfolge geregelt: Eckhard Cordes, Schrempp-Vertrauter und erfolgreicher Sanierer der LKW-Sparte, rückt auf den Hubbert-Stuhl, während Renschler nach dem definitiven Ende des Japan-Engagements von DaimlerChrysler den LKW-Bereich übernommen hat.

»Nach einem Jahrhundert Mercedes und einem Jahrzehnt intensiver ›Genforschung‹ in eigener Sache sind wir – was die Autos mit dem Stern angeht – zu der Erkenntnis gelangt, dass in der DNA von Mercedes-Benz noch jede Menge Potential steckt. Im heutigen Wettbewerb reichen aber nicht mehr allein die richtigen Gene, beziehungsweise das Abstauben gewonnener Lorbeerkränze. Wer erfolgreich sein will, muss es immer wieder schaffen, die Aktualität seiner Marke auf Touren zu halten«, verkündet Hubbert auf der Frankfurter IAA 2001. Und liefert den Beweis: Der reicht vom Kleinstwagen bis zum mehr als sechs Meter langen Traumschiff für besonders Wohlhabende, vom SLK bis zum SLR für sportlich Angehauchte und von der 2004 erneuerten A-Klasse bis zum Viano für kleine Familien. M- und G-Klasse – letztere schon seit 20 Jahren – sind ebenfalls Treffer.

Nur bei der Einführung des LKW-Mautsystems wird die technische Leistungsfähigkeit ziemlich strapaziert. Toll Collect, das telematische Erfassungssytem in Deutschland, an dessen Entwicklung DaimlerChrysler beteiligt ist, kommt nur langsam voran. Hier sind wohl voreilige Intuitionen vorausgegangen. Intuition – die italienische Publikation *Il Tempo* definiert sinnigerweise diesen Ausdruck wie folgt: »Intelligenz mit überhöhter Geschwindigkeit!«

Plusieurs fois, Manfred Gentz, membre du Directoire en charge des finances et du contrôle de gestion, élève un médium de censeur et critique l'engagement en Extrême-Orient en raison de ces inepties. Jürgen Schrempp ne se départit pas pour autant de son optimisme. Après de longues et fatigantes luttes intestines au plus haut niveau, le conseil de surveillance de DaimlerChrysler SA a convoqué les protagonistes pour un entretien au prestigieux hôtel Waldorf-Astoria de New York. Wolfgang Bernhard, patron de DaimlerChrysler qui n'a jamais fait mystère de ses opinions, pas toujours politiquement correctes, et qui était censé prendre la succession du professeur Jürgen Hubbert à la tête de Mercedes le 1er mai 2004, a formulé un peu trop ouvertement ses objections, et qui plus est, en public! Il a certes conservé son poste de membre du Directoire, mais, pour l'instant, sans prérogatives concrètes. Ainsi risque-t-il d'être banni aux confins de l'empire. Puissance et impuissance sont aussi proches l'une de l'autre que le Capitole et la Roche tarpéienne. Tandis que Jürgen Hubbert reprend les rênes du MercedesGroup, avec une main plus ferme que jamais, Jürgen Schrempp envoie Andreas Renschler, le patron de Smart, comme gestionnaire de la crise au Japon pour élaborer un nouveau business plan en vertu duquel le management à l'avenir de nouveau japonais pourra travailler. Rolf Eckrodt, qui attendait avec une nostalgie de plus en plus visible une retraite bien méritée, a immédiatement démissionné. Entre-temps, la question de la succession est réglée: Eckhard Cordes – le confident de Schrempp – qui a remis sur les rails la division Poids lourds, occupe désormais les fonctions de Jürgen Hubbert tandis Renschler reprend la division Poids lourds après que DaimlerChrysler ait définitivement mis un terme à son engagement au Japon.

«Après un siècle de Mercedes et une décennie de "recherche génétique intensive" *pro domo*, nous avons conclu – en ce qui concerne les autos à l'étoile – que l'ADN de Mercedes-Benz renferme encore un immense potentiel. Mais, dans la concurrence d'aujourd'hui, les bons gènes à eux seuls ne suffisent plus et l'on ne peut plus se contenter de dépoussiérer ses vieilles couronnes de laurier. Quiconque veut connaître le succès doit toujours maintenir sa marque sous les feux de la rampe», a déclaré Jürgen Hubbert lors de l'IAA de Francfort en 2001. Et il en administre la preuve: cela va de la citadine à la limousine de prestige de plus de six mètres de long pour les nantis, de la SLK à la SLR pour les amateurs de conduite sportive et de la Classe A remise à niveau en 2004 à la Viano pour les familles nombreuses. Quant aux Classe M et Classe G – cette dernière depuis vingt ans déjà – elles sont et restent également des best-sellers.

Il n'y a que pour l'introduction du système de péage pour les poids lourds que la compétence technique de Mercedes est mise à rude épreuve. Toll Collect, le système de saisie télématique allemand pour le développement duquel DaimlerChrysler a assumé la régie, ne progresse que lentement. Dans ce domaine, on s'est manifestement un peu trop vite fié à ses intuitions. Intuition – un terme que le journal italien *Il Tempo* définit, non sans ironie, en ces termes: «Intelligence alliée à une vitesse supérieure!»

A century in white and silver: The history of Mercedes motorsport
Ein Säkulum in Weiß und Silber: Geschichte des Mercedes-Motorsports
Un siècle aux couleurs blanc et argent : l'histoire de la compétition chez Mercedes

Motors and motives –
a synopsis

There are many facets to the Mercedes phenomenon. Motor racing is one of these. Although Gottlieb Daimler and Karl Benz themselves had a rather indifferent or even disapproving attitude to racing, the history of motorsport at Daimler and Benz and at Daimler-Benz is almost as old as the history of the marque itself.

The proudest chapters, of course, are those dealing with the Silver Arrows of the years 1934 to 1939 and 1952 to 1955. And with the men who drove them, such as Rudolf Caracciola, Manfred von Brauchitsch, or Hermann Lang in the Thirties and Juan Manuel Fangio, Stirling Moss, or Karl Kling in the Fifties. And with those who built them, such as Hans Nibel, Rudolf Uhlenhaut, and Fritz Nallinger. And with the powerful person who managed the whole enterprise, racing director Alfred Neubauer. He spanned both periods and left his mark on both, a man of quality, even if not necessarily of the stature of one of Frederick the Great's generals.

For many, Mercedes-Benz quick-silver still outshines Italian racing red, British racing green, and all that motley assortment of sponsors' colors that have proliferated since the end of the Sixties. And however simple the meaning of abbreviations such as SSKL, 300 SL and SLR or W196 may seem, apparently naked combinations of letters and numbers, when used in connection with the Stuttgart star they are magical symbols for all those to whom this sport means something.

The strange feature of the Silver Arrow legend is that it never dies, nor does it sleep; it merely slumbers. Even when a period of abstinence has been officially declared, everyone looks forward to the renaissance of the racers from Stuttgart, and it is a fair bet that the company always keeps up with the latest technical developments behind the scenes.

Sport always draws together the strengths in a company, and often throws up good ideas that can be fed into production cars. It also always serves to bolster the fame of the company – and of the fatherland. But that consequence has also been misused.

Motoren und Motive –
eine Synopse

Das Phänomen Mercedes hat viele Facetten. Eine davon: der Rennsport. Obwohl die Denkmäler Gottlieb Daimler und Karl Benz dem Wettkampf mit Wagen eher indifferent bis ablehnend gegenüberstehen, ist seine Geschichte bei Daimler und Benz und bei Daimler-Benz fast ebensolang wie die Geschichte der Marke selbst.

Natürlich handeln die stolzesten Kapitel von den Silberpfeilen der Jahre 1934 bis 1939 und 1952 bis 1955. Und von den Männern, die sie lenken, etwa Rudolf Caracciola, Manfred von Brauchitsch oder Hermann Lang in den Dreißigern und Juan Manuel Fangio, Stirling Moss oder Karl Kling in den Fünfzigern. Und von denen, die sie machen, wie Hans Nibel, Rudolf Uhlenhaut und Fritz Nallinger. Und auch von der wuchtigen Persönlichkeit, die ihren Einsatz dirigiert: Rennleiter Alfred Neubauer. Er überdauert beide Etappen und drückt beiden seinen Stempel auf, ein Kerl vom Format, wenn auch nicht unbedingt von der Statur eines friderizianischen Generals.

Quick-Silber von Mercedes-Benz: Für viele überstrahlt das noch immer italienisches Rennrot, British Racing Green und jegliches Sponsor-Kunterbunt seit dem Ende der sechziger Jahre. Und mag die Botschaft von Kürzeln wie SSKL, 300 SL und SLR oder W196, nackten Kombinationen von Buchstaben und Zahlen, wie es scheint, noch so schlicht sein: Im Zeichen des Sterns von Stuttgart sind sie magische Größen für alle, denen dieser Sport etwas bedeutet.

Das Ungewöhnliche am Mythos vom Silberpfeil: Er stirbt nie, er schläft nicht einmal, sondern schlummert nur. Selbst wenn offiziell Enthaltsamkeit angesagt ist, hofft jedermann auf die Renaissance der Renner aus Stuttgart, und hinter den Kulissen bleibt man technisch wohl stets auf der Höhe der Zeit.

Immer bindet der Sport die besten Kräfte des Hauses, und häufig setzt er gute Ideen für die Serie frei. Immer dient er auch dem höheren Ruhme des Unternehmens – und des Vaterlands. Aber das ist auch missbraucht worden.

Moteurs et motifs
– une rétrospective

Le phénomène Mercedes présente de nombreuses facettes, dont une, primordiale : la compétition. Bien que les deux monuments, Gottlieb Daimler et Karl Benz, aient plutôt fait preuve d'indifférence, voire d'aversion, à l'égard de la compétition automobile, son histoire chez Daimler et Benz ainsi que Daimler-Benz est presque aussi riche que l'histoire de la marque elle-même.

Naturellement, les chapitres les plus honorables sont ceux des Flèches d'argent écrits de 1934 à 1939 et de 1952 à 1955. Et c'est aussi l'histoire des hommes derrière leur volant, par exemple Rudolf Caracciola, Manfred von Brauchitsch ou Hermann Lang, dans les années 1930, et de Juan Manuel Fangio, Stirling Moss ou Karl Kling, dans les années 1950. Et c'est aussi l'histoire de ceux qui les ont faits, comme Hans Nibel, Rudolf Uhlenhaut et Fritz Nallinger. Sans oublier la personnalité imposante dans tous les sens du terme, qui a orchestré leurs démonstrations : le directeur de course Alfred Neubauer. Il a été la figure de proue de ces deux périodes, qu'il a marquées de son sceau, un homme d'envergure, même s'il n'avait pas tout à fait la stature d'un général frédéricien.

Le vif-argent Mercedes-Benz : pour beaucoup, il surclasse encore et toujours le rouge corsa italien, le *British Racing Green* et toutes les couleurs bigarrées des sponsors qui sont apparues à partir de la fin des années 1960. Et si le message véhiculé par des abréviations comme SSKL, 300 SL et SLR ou W196 se réduit à de sèches combinaisons de lettres et de chiffres, peu évocatrices, sous l'emblème de l'étoile de Stuttgart, ce sont des paramètres magiques pour tous ceux qui nourrissent ne serait-ce qu'un soupçon de passion pour ce sport.

Il y a quelque chose d'inhabituel au mythe des Flèches d'argent : il ne meurt jamais, il ne dort même pas, il sommeille seulement. Même si l'abstention figure officiellement à l'ordre du jour, chacun espère en la renaissance des bolides de Stuttgart et, dans les coulisses, on se maintient au top du savoir-faire technique.

Le sport focalise toujours les forces vives de la maison et, fréquemment, il donne naissance à de bonnes idées pour la série. Il contribue également au prestige de l'entreprise – et de la patrie. Et Dieu sait si l'on en a abusé pour celle-ci.

Racing colors of white: The early years 1894–1933

The Olympic ideal that "Taking part is everything" has undoubtedly never reflected reality, but it was always an appropriate sentiment with which to console the losers. The real trinity is not "Faster, higher, further" but "Gold, silver, and bronze" because that is what competition is all about, and nothing more. Why, in a world where Darwinism is an everyday fact of life, should the car driver (of all people) be any different, especially given the fact that he has the opportunity to get his nose in front of the opposition with the minimum of effort leaving the others empty-handed?

The first car race was presumably never documented. Let us suppose that a Benz Patent-Motorwagen model 3, built in 1888, was driving at 20 kph (12 mph) as it came up behind an 1892 Daimler "Schroedter-Wagen" pottering along at 18 kph (11 mph). While one overtook the other, the drivers perhaps courteously raised their hats, inquired after the health of their respective good ladies, and exchanged further pleasantries. Then, however, the Benz accelerated unstoppably away, and satisfaction could be seen on its driver's face while the Daimler driver's smile froze.

And so it was that an event that the Parisian *Petit Journal* of 1894 had announced for "voitures sans chevaux" got completely out of hand. The occasion in question was a journey from Paris to Rouen, 126 km (78 miles) along the Seine, up hill and down dale through Normandy. The terms "horseless carriages" covered a multitude of sins. A strange collection of vehicles therefore gathered on 22 July at Porte Maillot – electromobiles and hydromobiles, cars with compressed air engines and electropneumatic drives, and cars

Christian Werner with the Mercedes 35 PS, winning the Nice-Salon-Nice race on 25 March 1901.

Christian Werner mit dem Mercedes 35 PS als Gewinner des Rennens Nizza-Salon-Nizza am 25. März 1901.

Christian Werner, au volant de la Mercedes 35 ch victorieuse de la course Nice-Salon-Nice le 25 mars 1901.

Rennfarbe vorwiegend weiß: Die frühen Jahre 1894–1933

Kein Zweifel: Das olympische Postulat »Dabeisein ist alles« hat nie die Realität abgebildet, sondern war stets die gefällige Formel des Trostes für die Unterlegenen. In Wirklichkeit hat man sich der Dreiheiligkeit schneller, höher und weiter verschrieben, geht es um Gold, Silber und Bronze und sonst nichts. Warum soll in einer Welt des alltäglich praktizierten Darwinismus ausgerechnet der Autofahrer eine Ausnahme machen, überdies mit der Möglichkeit ausgestattet, mit einem Minimum an Mühe die Nase vorn zu haben und den anderen das Nachsehen zu geben?

Und so ist das erste Autorennen vermutlich gar nicht dokumentiert: Da nähert sich, sagen wir, ein Benz Patent-Motorwagen Modell 3 Baujahr 1888 mit Tempo 20 von hinten einem »Schroedter-Wagen« von Daimler Jahrgang 1892, der mit 18 Stundenkilometern betulich dahinrollt. Beim Vorüberziehen lupft man höflich die Hüte, erkundigt sich nach dem Befinden der werten Frau Gemahlin und tauscht weitere Gemeinplätze aus. Dann jedoch enteilt der Benz unaufhaltsam, und Genugtuung kräuselt die Lippen seines Lenkers, während das Lächeln des Daimler-Piloten gefriert.

Und so gerät auch eine Veranstaltung völlig aus der Fasson, die das Pariser *Petit Journal* 1894 für »voitures sans chevaux« ausgeschrieben hat, eine Reise von Paris nach Rouen, 126 Kilometer längs der Seine durch die Normandie über Stock und Stein. »Wagen ohne Pferde« – das ist ein weiter Rahmen. Deshalb stellt sich am 22. Juli an der Porte Maillot ein sonderbares Sammelsurium von Vehikeln ein, Elektro- und Hydromobile, Autos mit Pressluftmotoren und elektropneumatischem Antrieb, Wagen mit Benzinmotoren. Die Attraktion: eine fahrbare Dampfmaschine mit neun Personen an Bord. Sie thronen unter einem rotweiß gefältelten Baldachin, an dessen Borte unzählige Glöcklein bimmeln. Nach dem Start gegen acht Uhr übernimmt indes der Ehrgeiz der Konkurrenten die Regie.

Die 21 Selbst-Beweger sollen ihre Zuverlässigkeit unter Beweis stellen. Aber daraus entsteht ein Gerangel Rad an Rad. Um zehn vor fünf trifft der Dampftraktor des Marquis de Dion als erster in Rouen ein, mit einer Victoria-Kutsche im Schlepptau. In Minutenabstand folgen ein Panhard-Levassor (Durchschnitt 20,5 Stundenkilometer), dann ein Peugeot, beide mit Daimler-Maschinen. Sie sind die Sieger, denn »die Wagen entsprachen den Bestimmungen des Wettbewerbs am besten, so dass ihnen der erste Preis gebührt«. Pierre Giffard, Chefredakteur des *Petit Journal*, hat den Beweis – die »voitures sans chevaux« rollen, vorzugsweise mit einem Motor von »Monsieur Daimler, de Wurttemberg«.

Zum ersten wirklichen Rennen wird die Wettfahrt Paris–Bordeaux–Paris vom 11. bis zum 14. Juni 1895. Denn

Couleur course essentiellement blanche : les premières années 1894–1933

C'est l'évidence : le postulat olympique, « l'essentiel est de participer », n'a jamais concordé avec la réalité, mais a toujours été un mot de consolation bienvenue pour les vaincus. En réalité, on s'est voué à une trinité – plus vite, plus haut et plus loin – et il n'y a qu'un seul enjeu – l'or, l'argent et le bronze – sinon rien. Pourquoi, dans un monde qui réserve ses honneurs aux meilleurs, l'automobiliste devrait-il justement faire exception à cette règle, lui qui a la possibilité, pour un minimum de peine, de s'adjuger la victoire et de surclasser ses concurrents ?

Et si l'on détenait quelques documents photographiques, ou mieux, des images filmées sur la première course automobile du monde, on pourrait y voir s'approcher une Benz Patent-Motorwagen modèle 3, année 1888, à 20 km/h, d'une « Schroedter-Wagen » de Daimler, millésime 1892, roulant paisiblement à la vitesse de 18 km/h. Au moment de doubler, les conducteurs relèvent poliment leur chapeau, s'enquièrent de la santé de la chère épouse et échangent d'autres platitudes. Puis la Benz s'échappe irrésistiblement et un frisson de satisfaction fait frémir les lèvres de son conducteur tandis que se gèle le sourire du pilote de la Daimler.

Et c'est ainsi que se termine aussi dans le désordre une manifestation organisée par le *Petit Journal* de Paris, en 1894, pour des « voitures sans chevaux », un voyage de Paris à Rouen sur 126 kilomètres le long de la Seine sur les routes cahoteuses de la Normandie. « Voiture sans chevaux » – le cadre est bien vaguement défini. Cela explique que se rassemble, le 22 juillet à la porte Maillot, une cohorte de véhicules, électromobiles et hydromobiles, voitures avec moteur à air comprimé et entraînement électropneumatique, voitures avec moteur à essence. Avec une attraction : une machine à vapeur roulante sur laquelle ont pris place neuf passagers. Ils trônent sous un baldaquin rouge et blanc plié le long des bordures duquel sonnent d'innombrables clochettes. Après le départ, vers huit heures du matin, l'intérêt de la course elle-même prend le pas sur tout le reste.

Les 21 auto-mobiles sont censés administrer une preuve de fiabilité, pour eux-mêmes et leur véhicule. Mais c'est en réalité un duel acharné que se livrent les concurrents. À cinq heures moins dix, c'est le tracteur à vapeur du marquis de Dion qui arrive à Rouen le premier, talonné par une calèche Victoria. Quelques minutes plus tard arrivent une Panhard-Levassor (à une moyenne de 20,5 km/h), puis une Peugeot, toutes deux avec un moteur Daimler. Ce sont elles qui sont sacrées vainqueur, car « les voitures correspondaient le mieux aux dispositions du règlement, si bien que c'est à l'une d'elles que revient le premier prix ». Pierre Giffard, le rédacteur en chef du Petit Journal, détient la

with gasoline engines. The most visible attraction was a mobile steam engine with nine people on board. They sat in state beneath a red and white canopy, trimmed with countless tiny tinkling bells. But once the event started at around eight o'clock, the competitors' ambition took over.

The 21 self-propelled vehicles were simply expected to prove their mechanical reliability. But the result was a wheel-to-wheel scrap. At ten to five the Marquis de Dion's steam tractor was the first to arrive in Rouen with a Victoria coach in tow. There then followed at minute intervals a Panhard-Levassor (average speed 20.5 kph, 12.7 mph), then a Peugeot, both powered by Daimler engines. They were declared the winners because "the cars best met the competition rules, so they deserve the first prize." Pierre Giffard, editor-in-chief of the *Petit Journal* had the proof – the "voitures sans chevaux" run preferably with an engine from "Monsieur Daimler, de Wurttemberg."

The first real race was the Paris-Bordeaux-Paris race from 11 to 14 June 1895; the winner was to be the first person to reach the finish. The competitors had a maximum of 100 hours to cover the 1,192 km (741-mile) route. 22 vehicles set off on the arduous journey on 11 June. Only nine returned unscathed. The winner was Emile Levassor who was dubbed the "chevalier sans cheval." And how: the "horseless rider" won in 48 hours and 47 minutes, six hours ahead of the next car. To prevent himself from falling asleep, he reported, he chatted to his car on the second night. His engine would definitely have had a word or two to say: it was from Monsieur Daimler, de Wurttemberg.

It was also sport which defined the car's eventual layout, its future outline, perfectly coincident with the principle of expediency that form follows function. Wilhelm Maybach's 35 bhp sports and touring car which won the Nice-Salon-Nice race on 25 March 1901 had everything: a stretched, low-slung steel frame, a front-mounted multi-cylinder engine, and a gearbox using toothed wheels offering several gears mounted behind the engine and clutch.

The suspicion that the opposition was playing with marked cards, lightening the chassis and reboring the engine first raised its head in 1897. An engine size restriction – to 4.5 liters – was first imposed, meanwhile, in 1914. The stipulations for 1921 conformed to the Indianapolis ruling and specified 3-liter engines and a minimum weight of 800 kg (1,765 lb). In 1922 the sports authorities decided to cull the dinosaurs, stating that 2 liters and 650 kg (1,435 lb) were sufficient. As late as 1924 Grand Prix drivers still always started with accompaniment, i.e., with a passenger who trustingly placed himself at the mercy of the skills and wiles of the ace at the wheel. Up to 1925 events were dominated by Fiat, Alfa, Delage, Bugatti, and Sunbeam, while the 1.5-liter restriction of 1926 and 1927 was tailored to suit the blue of the Delage with its supercharged eight-cylinder engine. Alfa Romeo and Bugatti made best use of the latitude offered by semi-free formulas at the end of the decade. The only specification for 1931 was a limit of at least

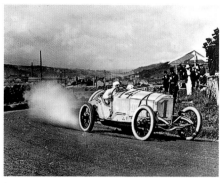

One-two-three in the 1914 French Grand Prix in Lyon, with Max Sailer setting the fastest lap.

Dreifacherfolg beim Grand Prix de France 1914 bei Lyon. Max Sailer fährt die schnellste Runde.

Triplé au Grand Prix de France de 1914 à Lyon. Max Sailer signe le record du tour.

Sieger soll sein, wer als erster das Ziel erreicht. Die 1192 Kilometer lange Strecke muss in maximal 100 Stunden bewältigt werden. 22 Fahrzeuge begeben sich am 11. Juni auf die beschwerliche Reise. Nur neun kehren ungeschoren zurück. Gewinner ist Emile Levassor, den sie den »Chevalier sans cheval« nennen. Und wie: Der »Reiter ohne Pferd« siegt in 48 Stunden und 47 Minuten, mit sechs Stunden Vorsprung vor dem nächsten Wagen. Um nicht einzuschlafen, berichtet er, habe er sich in der zweiten Nacht mit seinem Auto unterhalten. Ein Wörtchen mitzureden hat dabei gewiss dessen Maschine: von Monsieur Daimler, de Wurttemberg.

Der Sport ist es auch, der dem Automobil das endgültige Layout, die künftige Silhouette spendet, ganz im Sinne des Zweckmäßigkeitssatzes, die Form folge der Funktion. Wilhelm Maybachs Sport- und Tourenwagen 35 PS, der am 25. März 1901 das Rennen Nizza–Salon–Nizza gewinnt, hat schon alles: einen gestreckten, niederen Stahlrahmen, einen vorn liegenden Motor mit mehreren Zylindern, ein Zahnrad-Getriebe mit mehreren Gängen hinter Motor und Kupplung.

1897 keimt zum ersten Mal der schnöde Verdacht, der Gegner spiele mit gezinkten Karten, erleichtere sein Fahrgestell, bohre seine Triebwerke auf. Eine Hubraumbegrenzung wird indessen erst 1914 verordnet: 4,5 Liter. Die Bestimmungen für 1921 entsprechen dem Indianapolis-Reglement und sehen 3-Liter-Maschinen sowie 800 Kilo Minimalgewicht vor. 1922 entscheidet die Sportbehörde im Kampf gegen die Dinosaurier, 2 Liter und 650 Kilo seien genug. Stets in Begleitung starten übrigens noch 1924 die Grand-Prix-Piloten, mit einem Beifahrer, der sich den Künsten und Kapriolen des Asses am Volant gläubig ausliefert. Bis 1925 dominieren die Fiat, Alfa, Delage, Bugatti und Sunbeam, während die 1,5-Liter-Grenze von 1926 und 1927 den Delage mit ihren aufgeladenen Achtzylindern wie auf den blauen Leib geschnitten ist. Den Spielraum halbfreier Formeln gegen Ende des Jahrzehnts nutzen Alfa

preuve – «les voitures sans chevaux» sont capables de rouler, de préférence quand elles sont propulsées par un moteur de «Monsieur Daimler, de Wurtemberg».

La première compétition digne de ce nom est le Paris-Bordeaux-Paris, du 11 au 14 juin 1895. En effet, vainqueur sera celui qui atteindra l'arrivée le premier. Le trajet de 1192 kilomètres doit être couvert en un maximum de 100 heures. Le 11 juin, vingt-deux véhicules prennent le départ de ce pénible voyage. Neuf seulement reviennent sans mal à destination. Le vainqueur est Émile Levassor, que l'on surnomme «le chevalier sans cheval». Et sa victoire est sans appel: «le chevalier sans cheval» gagne en 48 heures et 47 minutes, avec une avance de 6 heures sur son rival le plus proche. Pour ne pas s'endormir, racontera-t-il plus tard, il s'est entretenu avec sa voiture au cours de la seconde nuit. Et son moteur avait sans aucun doute quelques mots à lui dire également: il était l'œuvre de monsieur Daimler, de Wurtemberg.

Et c'est aussi le sport qui modèle définitivement les lignes de l'automobile, lui donne sa silhouette future, tout à fait dans l'esprit du principe de la fonctionnalité selon lequel la forme se plie à la fonction. La voiture de sport et de tourisme de Wilhelm Maybach de 35 ch qui gagne la course Nice-Salon-Nice le 25 mars 1901 a déjà tout cela: un cadre en acier bas et tout en longueur, un moteur avant à plusieurs cylindres, une boîte de vitesses à engrenages à plusieurs rapports derrière le moteur et l'embrayage.

En 1897 naissent les premiers soupçons selon lesquels l'adversaire jouerait avec des cartes truquées, allégerait son châssis, réaléserait son moteur. Et pourtant, une limitation de la cylindrée n'est imposée qu'en 1914: 4,5 litres. Les dispositions pour 1921 correspondent au règlement d'Indianapolis et prévoient des moteurs de 3 litres ainsi qu'un poids minimal de 800 kg pour les voitures. En 1922, les autorités sportives décident de condamner les dinosaures, précisant que 2 litres et 650 kg sont suffisants. En 1924, les pilotes de Grand Prix ont d'ailleurs toujours un coéquipier, un passager qui se livre pieds et poings liés au savoir-faire et aux humeurs de l'as au volant. Jusqu'en 1925 dominent les Fiat, Alfa, Delage, Bugatti et Sunbeam alors que la limitation de cylindrée à 1,5 litre en 1926 et 1927 est comme taillée sur mesure pour les Delage à huit cylindres suralimentés et élégante carrosserie bleue. Alfa Romeo et Bugatti sont les deux marques qui exploitent le mieux la marge laissée par les formules semi-libres vers la fin de la décennie. Pour 1931, on impose seulement une limite de temps d'au minimum dix heures, ramenée à cinq à dix heures en 1932 et à 500 km en 1933.

Mercedes, pendant ce temps, pose des jalons, écrit des chapitres de lumière dans la jeune histoire des fanatiques de la vitesse, déjà assombrie par de nombreux drames. Le 2 juillet 1903, Camille Jenatzy, à Ballyshannon, en Irlande, gagne la quatrième édition d'une course créée par James Gordon Bennett, le propriétaire du *New York Herald*. C'est un triomphe de la lutte contre les aléas de la compétition: les trois Daimler de course préparées avec une minutie

One against all others: Rudolf Caracciola's greatest race

What was to end as a success story began as a farce. In the run-up to the 1931 Mille Miglia Rudolf Caracciola stopped over briefly in Milan and, together with friends, took a taxi. The driver recognized his famous passenger and felt encouraged to demonstrate his own skills, racing and skidding, and overtaking with millimeters to spare – and all this during the Milan rush hour which even then was notorious. Caracciola asked the man to be careful and finally insisted that he should stop immediately. He obeyed resentfully, grumbling about the German: "And he claims to be a racing driver."

A few days later, in the early hours of 12 April, the unknown taxi driver must have been making his apologies, the aura around his famous passenger was restored and shining with even greater brilliance. Rudolf Caracciola had just won the fifth Mille Miglia in a new record time, and he was the first foreigner to do so to boot. The initial situation looked completely hopeless, Mission Impossible, Goliath faced by a veritable army of Davids. Even the people in Untertürkheim smiled at the cheek of the tiny raiding party setting off impudently to Italy. In the aftershocks following the Wall Street Crash of 1929 Mercedes-Benz had radically reduced its racing budget. Director Wilhelm Kissel informed Caracciola that his contract was not being extended for 1931.

So began the reign of chief engineer Alfred Neubauer, like Caracciola himself a man on a fast track to legendary status. He set up a small team around Caracciola with Wilhelm Sebastian as a technically skilled co-driver and Willy "Fridolin" Zimmer as mechanic. With the aid of a friendly discount on the normal price of 40,000 Reichsmarks, he acquired an SSK (Super Sport Kurz, i.e., a short-wheelbase version of the Super Sport). This was a very special car, with an inline six-cylinder engine of 7065 cc developing 240 bhp This increased to 300 bhp once the Roots compressor kicked in. Engineers Hans Nibel and Max Wagner took a drill to solve the problem of chronic overweight and drilled out 200 kg (441 lb) from places where the "White Elephant's" strength would not be compromised, just as had been done with the *Tropfenwagen* previously. SSKL was the name given to this pinnacle of the range, where L stood for Leicht or light. Even so the car still weighed in at a formidable 1,500 kg (3,307 lb).

At the 1,000 Miles of Brescia a nation rejoiced, an entire country indulged in the feverish rapture of celebrating its ethnic identity. The Great White from the north was about as welcome as a nudist in a nunnery. Alfa Romeo had got wind of the German plan and countered with a huge input of equipment and logistics. 17 transporters rolled out to strategically significant sites, manned by 90 fitters. In addition, an army of volunteer accomplices lined the 1,635-km-long route with petrol cans and tires, local lads driven not by the desire to make a quick buck but by their love for *il duce*, their fatherland, and by the Olympic ideal that taking part is what matters. 30 of the 99 cars at the start in Brescia were Alfa Romeos. Interest and concern centered on the two Tipo 8C 2300 works cars – eight cylinders, 2336 cc, supercharged, developing 150 bhp at 5000 rpm. Although they had been hastily called up for active service to repel the Teutonic attack, they were at a very advanced level of development. One problem was, however, already becoming apparent: the marriage of the cars with the Pirelli tires which had been specially developed for them was not working. The Alfa engineers were still groping in the dark. Was the test phase too short? Was there sufficient traction? Was the weight distribution in need of improvement?

Alfa also had the pick of the drivers. Caracciola was faced with the *crème de la crème* of Italian drivers, each of them revered as the greatest, all apparently predestined to win, all avowed enemies of one another. There was, for example, the previous year's winner Tazio Nuvolari, known as the "Red Devil" or the "Flying Mantuan," who had spent his entire life either at the edge or beyond it – there was scarcely a bone in his body that he had not already broken. Then there was the former motorcycle champion Luigi Arcangeli who knew the route like the back of his hand and feared neither hell nor high water. Or take Giuseppe Campari, a polymath who excelled in three fields, as a racing driver, an opera singer, and a chef of fine Italian cuisine. And then there was Baconin Borzacchini, later immortalized by a statue erected in his home town of Terni, and a legend in his own lifetime. Danger also threatened from Nuvolari's favorite enemy Achille Varzi, a gentleman at the wheel and an elegant stylist, the only drawback being that his Bugatti with its eight-cylinder, 5-liter engine was not one of the more conspicuous successes of the Molsheim magician, Ettore Bugatti. Those in the know, and that applied to almost every Italian, were tipping the team of Giuseppe Morandi and Archimede Rosa in their O.M. *(officine meccaniche)* – the duo from Brescia were significantly faster than their aging car.

To face the might of this armored column in Italian racing red Mercedes-Benz could only muster a raiding party of seven upright souls who unobtrusively camped down in the Albergo Brescia: Rudolf Caracciola and his wife Charlotte, Alfred Neubauer, Wilhelm Sebastian, "Fridolin" Zimmer, and mechanics Heinrich Kühnle and Karlo Kumpf, who had married into the *Zur Sonne* pub in Untertürkheim but could not live without the atmosphere of the tracks. The party was also accompanied by Caracciola's dachshund Moritz, half member of the family, half mascot, and plagued by an inexplicable loss of appetite around this time. In strategy talks in front of a large-scale map of Italy, Neubauer demonstrated the qualities which were to make him famous in the course of that decade: knowledge and authority, together with a genius for dealing with emergencies. Like all the other competitors, Caracciola was required to stop at seven checkpoints to ensure that everyone followed the right route. The interim stops were documented by means of a stamp in a log book, and in addition a lead seal was crimped onto the steering column. The SSKL's average consumption per 100 km was 30 liters (7.8 mpg), and its rear-mounted tank had a capacity of 120 liters (32 gal). It followed therefore that a fuel depot had to be set up every 400 km (248 miles), near the Black Eagle Hotel in Siena, in Terni between Rome and the Adriatic, in Bologna, used on both the outward and the return legs, and in Feltre at the northernmost point of the route.

However, Neubauer only had three men available. The solution to the dilemma was that Karlo Kumpf would wait for Caracciola in Siena, then immediately strike camp and head for Bologna, 200 km (124 miles) away. The map was studied thoroughly because traffic jams caused by the magnetic attraction of the Mille Miglia were inevitable. Heinrich Kühnle was responsible for the stop in Terni, and "Fridolin" Zimmer for Feltre. Since the race car only arrived from Stuttgart at the last moment, there was only time for a single practice session in a rented car. But Caracciola knew his way round a little, as he had reconnoitered the course in 1930 in accordance with a tried-and-tested Mercedes practice, finishing sixth in an SSK. On 11 April former

minister Turati flagged off the race from Brescia, lowering the *tricolore* at one-minute intervals starting from 1 PM. The first to set off on their Mille Miglia adventure were the small cars. The elite class with its star drivers followed later. Only the final competitor to start had a complete overview of his position and the way the race was shaping up. Caracciola began the long journey through the millions lining the Italian roads at 3.12 PM, after a last cigarette and a passionate farewell from Charlotte. For Neubauer, a man of action, there was nothing left now but to drum his fingers and twiddle his thumbs. He had, so to speak, wound up the watch that would then count itself down in accordance with its own laws in the next 16 hours and 10 minutes.

1931 – all information was transmitted via one-way channels, by radio, telephone, telegraph, and huge illuminated boards which displayed the latest state of play with light bulbs. They reported Caracciola in the lead in Bologna where he had built up a cushion of seven minutes over the O.M. with an average speed of 154 km/h (96 mph) on fast roads. Campari and his co-driver Attilio Marinoni were one minute back, while Borzacchini and Nuvolari with passenger Giovanni Battista Guidotti were a further two back in one of the two Alfa 8C 2300s. The other had been entrusted to Arcangeli. 11 km (7 miles) into the race and Achille Varzi had already dropped out – fuel pump, the Bugatti people said. But then the landscape changed to one in which Nuvolari and the agile Alfa were really in their element, through the Apennines, for example, over the Raticosa and the Futa Passes. By Siena the "Flying Mantuan" was in the lead and he also took the Coppa Mussolini, the half-distance trophy which *il duce* had offered as the prize for the leading driver into Rome on time classification. The white Mercedes reached the checkpoint at the Milvio Bridge over the Tiber just ahead of him, although beaten on time by one and a half minutes. The patriotic crowd was rigid with anxiety and excitement. The Alfa drivers swapped the lead on the eastern section of the course. It was held first by Borzacchini, then Campari, and finally Arcangeli. But Caracciola inexorably swallowed up the opposition in the flat-out sections in Northern Italy like a pike in a carp pond. He took the lead in Treviso and did not relinquish it again. Shortly after seven in the morning on 12 April, aircraft signaled his arrival. At 7.22 am the high-pitched singing of the compressor fell silent as the SSKL crossed the finishing line, with Campari second and the O.M. third.

No one had escaped unscathed. Nine tire changes hindered the works Alfas' daring dash between Brescia and Rome alone. Arcangeli and Nuvolari went off the road near Verona. The "Red Devil" was leaking blood but still finished ninth. After Siena the Mercedes' exhaust was scraping along the ground. Sebastian tore it off manually, the hot metal blistering his hands. Caracciola had long since had blisters of his own on his right foot as the accelerator pedal transmitted heat from the engine. Near Viterbo the Germans were faced by a small oncoming group on their side of the road – the local car club was returning home from its favorite spectator spots. Near Terni the throttle linkage jammed. 30 km (18.5 miles) from the finish a rear tire on the Mercedes with start number 87 punctured – Wilhelm Sebastian slaved away to change it but kept his cool. The press releases of the Daimler-Benz Publicity Department praised the Mille Miglia victory of the "White Elephant" as a "quite exceptional success" and as a "fantastic performance by both driver and car." And so it was. But the furrowed brows of just a few days earlier told their own story.

ten hours, which was reduced to five to ten hours in 1932, and changed to 500 km (310 miles) in 1933.

Mercedes meanwhile was setting trends and guaranteeing excitement in the foot-flat-to-the-floor field which was never short of dramas anyway. On 2 July 1903 in Ballyshannon, Ireland, Camille Jenatzy won the fourth running of an event set up by James Gordon Bennett, the owner of the *New York Herald*. Mercedes won despite the fact that its three meticulously prepared Daimler racing cars had perished in the inferno of a factory fire during the night of 10 June. American millionaire Gray Dinsmore lent the Belgian Jenatzy, whom the crowd had demonized as the "Red Devil" because of his flaming hair and beard, his white Mercedes 60 bhp touring car. And that did the business, especially as the new tires from Continental-Caoutchouc-und-Gutta-Percha-Compagnie of Hanover lasted longer than all others. The most precious jewels in the crown of Daimler driver Christian Lautenschlager were his first places in the two French Grands Prix of 1908 at Dieppe (ahead of the Benz drivers Hémery and Hanriot) and in 1914 in Lyon, where the laurels for the second and third places were taken by the Mercedes musketeers, Louis Wagner and Otto Salzer. The singing of the four cylinders of his 18/100, Lautenschlager enthused, was the sweetest music he had ever heard. However, Wagner's car was shipped to the United States on 25 July on the ss *Vaterland*. War had long since prevented any motorsport activities in Europe when the good news arrived from the New World that the American Ralph de Palma had won the Indianapolis 500 with the old warrior.

Salzer's car also led a successful and fulfilled automotive life. In 1919 the Targa Florio was resurrected in Madonie, Sicily on a very hilly, 108-km (67-mile) long course which was without equal. The driving force behind this event was the wealthy shipping magnate and merchant Vincenzo Florio. The 1922 race was won by Count Giulio Masetti from Florence driving Salzer's veteran racer. The two principal new features were that four brakes had been fitted instead of the previous two, and, in order to protect the car against the stones of violent fans and against attacks by greedy brigands, that Italian racing red had replaced the

Count Giulio Masetti in the victorious Mercedes 18/100 at the 1922 Targa Florio.

Conte Giulio Masetti auf dem siegreichen Mercedes 18/100 bei der Targa Florio 1922.

Le comte Giulio Masetti dans sa Mercedes 18/100 victorieuse à la Targa Florio de 1922.

Romeo und Bugatti am besten. Für 1931 verfügt man lediglich ein Zeitlimit von mindestens zehn Stunden, verkürzt 1932 auf fünf bis zehn Stunden und 1933 auf 500 Kilometer.

Mercedes indessen setzt Akzente, sorgt für Highlights und Höhepunkte in der an Dramen ohnehin nicht armen Bleifuß-Branche. Am 2. Juli 1903 gewinnt Camille Jenatzy im irischen Ballyshannon die vierte Auflage einer Veranstaltung, die James Gordon Bennett ins Leben gerufen hat, Besitzer des *New York Herald*. Es ist ein Triumph des Trotzdem: Die drei pingelig präparierten Daimler-Rennautos sind in der Gluthitze des Werksbrandes in der Nacht vom 10. Juni verschmort. Der amerikanische Millionär Gray Dinsmore leiht dem Belgier, den die Menge wegen seines flammenden Haupt- und Barthaars zum »Roten Teufel« dämonisiert hat, seinen weißen Mercedes Tourenwagen 60 PS. Und der tut's auch, zumal die neuen Reifen der Continental-Caoutchouc-und-Gutta-Percha-Compagnie Hannover länger halten als alle anderen. Als die schönsten Perlen in der Krone von Daimler-Fahrer Christian Lautenschlager schimmern seine ersten Plätze bei den beiden Großen Preisen von Frankreich 1908 bei Dieppe (vor den Benz-Piloten Hémery und Hanriot) und 1914 in Lyon, wo der Lorbeer für den zweiten und dritten Rang die Stirnen der Mercedes-Musketiere Louis Wagner und Otto Salzer umkränzt. Der Gesang der vier Zylinder seines 18/100, schwärmt Lautenschlager, sei die süßeste Musik, die er je gehört habe. Wagners Wagen aber wird am 25. Juli auf der ss *Vaterland* in die Vereinigten Staaten verschifft. Längst haben Kampfhandlungen jegliche Motorsportaktivitäten in Europa unterbunden, da dringt aus der Neuen Welt die frohe Botschaft, der Amerikaner Ralph de Palma habe mit dem alten Recken die 500 Meilen von Indianapolis gewonnen.

Auch Salzers Fahrzeug ist ein erfülltes Autoleben beschieden. 1919 wird auf einer Berg- und Talbahn sondergleichen von 108 Kilometern in der sizilianischen Madonie die Targa Florio wiederbelebt, hinter der als treibende Kraft der wohlhabende Reeder und Handelsherr Vincenzo Florio wirkt. Sieger ist 1922 der florentinische Conte Giulio Masetti mit dem Salzer-Veteranen. Neu sind im wesentlichen zwei Dinge: Im Werk hat man ihn mit vier Bremsen anstelle der bisherigen zwei versehen. Und damit ihm die Steinwürfe von gewalttätigen Fans und der Zugriff gieriger Briganten erspart bleiben, ersetzt italienisches Rot das deutsche Weiß. Sechster und Gewinner der Coppa Florio für den schnellsten Serienwagen wird Max Sailer mit einem Mercedes 28/95, der sich im Jahr zuvor mit einem zweiten Platz insgesamt diesen Pokal schon einmal geholt hat. 1924 schließlich fegt Christian Werner in Ferdinand Porsches Zweiliter-Vierzylinder mit Kompressor in beängstigenden Driftwinkeln über die staubige Strecke und lässt dennoch alles so absurd einfach aussehen.

Im gleichen Jahr gewinnt der Remagener Rudolf Caracciola im Berliner Stadion ein Kleinstwagenrennen auf einem Ego. Der Rennfahrer Alfred Neubauer indessen, auf der Targa Florio 1922 mit einem Sascha nur Neun-

The 18/100 of Ralph de Palma, also a veteran of Lyon in 1914, during his Indy victory in 1915.

Der 18/100 von Ralph de Palma, ebenfalls Veteran von Lyon 1914, auf seiner Siegesfahrt in Indianapolis 1915.

La 18/100 de Ralph de Palma, un autre vétéran de Lyon en 1914, en route vers la victoire à Indianapolis en 1915.

inimaginable ont disparu dans l'incendie qui a ravagé l'usine durant la nuit du 10 juin. Le millionnaire américain Gray Dinsmore prête sa voiture de tourisme, une Mercedes blanche de 60 ch, au Belge que la foule a surnommé le « diable rouge » en raison de sa chevelure et de sa barbe rouge feu. Et c'est lui qui est sacré vainqueur, d'autant plus que les nouveaux pneus de la Continental-Caoutchouc-und-Gutta-Percha-Compagnie, de Hanovre, résistent mieux que ceux de ses concurrents. Les plus belles perles dans la couronne de succès remportés par le pilote de Daimler, Christian Lautenschlager, sont ses premières places lors des deux Grands Prix de France, en 1908 à Dieppe (devant les pilotes Benz, Hémery et Hanriot) et, en 1914, à Lyon, où les lauriers de la seconde et troisième places sont ceints par les mousquetaires de Mercedes, Louis Wagner et Otto Salzer. « Le chant des quatre-cylindres de la 18/100, déclare, élogieux, Lautenschlager, est la musique la plus douce que j'ai jamais entendue. » Mais, le 25 juillet, la voiture de Wagner est expédiée aux États-Unis avec le bateau ss *Vaterland*. Il y a longtemps que la guerre a suspendu toute activité en matière de compétition automobile en Europe lorsque arrive du Nouveau Monde la nouvelle que l'Américain Ralph de Palma a remporté avec cette voiture les 500 Miles d'Indianapolis.

La voiture de Salzer aura, elle aussi, vécu une vie d'automobile bien remplie. En 1919, sur l'incomparable circuit de montagnes russes de 108 kilomètres des Madonies en Sicile, la Targa Florio renaît de ses cendres grâce à la passion de Vincenzo Florio, un riche armateur et négociant italien. En 1922, le vainqueur est le comte florentin Giulio Masetti avec le bon vieux bolide de Salzer. Deux choses, essentiellement, sont nouvelles : à l'usine, on lui a maintenant greffé quatre freins au lieu de deux auparavant. Et, pour lui épargner les jets de pierres des *tifosi* violents ou les attaques de brigands de grand chemin, le rouge

Allein gegen alle: Rudolf Caracciolas größtes Rennen

Was als Erfolgsstory enden wird, beginnt als Farce: Im Vorfeld der Mille Miglia 1931 macht Rudolf Caracciola kurz Station in Mailand, vertraut sich dort, zusammen mit Freunden, einem Taxichauffeur an. Dieser erkennt den Passagier und fühlt sich ermuntert, rasend und driftend und mit millimeterknappen Überholmanövern Proben seines eigenen Könnens abzuliefern – am untauglichen Objekt der Mailänder Rush Hour, die schon damals gut ausgebildet ist. Caracciola bittet um Mäßigung, besteht schließlich darauf, der Mann solle sofort anhalten. Der gehorcht grollend, grantelt dem Deutschen hinterher: »Und sowas will Rennfahrer sein.«

Ein paar Tage später, in den Morgenstunden des 12. April, leistet der unbekannte Wagenlenker gewiss innere Abbitte, ist für ihn der Nimbus seines berühmten Fahrgasts restauriert und leuchtet mit zusätzlicher Strahlkraft: Da hat Rudolf Caracciola die fünfte Mille Miglia in neuer Rekordzeit gewonnen, als erster Ausländer zumal. Die Ausgangssituation ist völlig hoffnungslos, Mission Impossible, die eines Goliaths, der ganzen Horden von Davids ausgeliefert ist. Sogar in Untertürkheim lächelt man über die Keckheit des winzigen Rollkommandos, das da unverfroren nach Italien aufbricht. In den Nachbeben des Wall Street Crash von 1929 hat Mercedes-Benz das Renn-Budget radikal gekürzt. Direktor Wilhelm Kissel teilt Caracciola mit, sein Vertrag werde für 1931 nicht verlängert.

Damit schlägt die Stern-Stunde des Oberingenieurs Alfred Neubauer, wie Caracciola selbst auf dem Eilmarsch in die Legende. Er gründet um diesen und Wilhelm Sebastian als technisch versierten Beifahrer und Willy »Fridolin« Zimmer als Mechaniker ein kleines Team und ersteht mit einem freundlichen Rabatt auf den normalen Preis von 40 000 Reichsmark einen SSK (für Super Sport Kurz). Es ist ein sehr besonderes Auto, mit einem Reihensechszylinder von 7065 ccm und 240 PS. Daraus werden 300 PS, sowie sich das Roots-Gebläse zugeschaltet hat. Die Ingenieure Hans Nibel und Max Wagner sind seiner chronischen Übergewichtigkeit mit dem Bohrer zu Leibe gerückt und haben an Stellen, wo die Statik des »Weißen Elefanten« nicht leidet, 200 Kilo herausgedrillt wie einst am »Tropfenwagen«. SSKL heißt diese höchste Sublimationsstufe der Baureihe, mit L für Leicht – trotzige 1500 Kilogramm bringt sie noch immer auf die Waage.

Auf den 1000 Meilen von Brescia zelebriert eine Nation sich selbst, schwelgt ein ganzes Land in Rausch und Taumel ethnischer Identität. Da stört der Große Weiße aus dem Norden wie ein Nudist im Nonnenkloster. Bei Alfa Romeo hat man von der Sache Wind bekommen, kontert mit einem Riesenaufwand von Material und Logistik. 17 Transporter rollen an strategisch wichtige Punkte, bemannt mit 90 Monteuren. Ein Heer von freiwilligen Helfershelfern säumt zusätzlich die 1635 Kilometer lange Strecke mit Benzinkanistern und Reifen, Bengels aus der Umgebung, die nicht die Lust auf die schnelle Lira umtreibt, sondern die Liebe zu Duce, Volk und Vaterland sowie das olympische Reinheitsgebot, dass Dabeisein alles ist. 30 der 99 Wagen beim Start in Brescia sind Alfa Romeo, im Zentrum des Interesses und der Fürsorge: die beiden Werkswagen Tipo 8C 2300, Achtzylinder von 2336 ccm mit Kompressor, die 150 PS bei 5000/min mobilisieren. Obwohl sie angesichts der teutonischen Attacke hastig ins Gefecht geworfen werden, ist ihr Entwicklungsstand durchaus fortgeschritten. Ein Problem indessen deutet sich bereits an: Die Symbiose mit den eigens für sie geschaffenen Pirelli-Pneus klappt nicht. Die Alfa-Ingenieure tappen noch im dunkeln: War die Erprobungsphase

zu kurz? Lässt die Traktion zu wünschen übrig? Stimmt die Gewichtsverteilung nicht?

Die Auswahl der Piloten ist jedenfalls vom Feinsten. Caracciola bekommt es mit der Crème de la Crème unter den italienischen Fahrern zu tun, jeder der Größte, alle prädestiniert zum Siegen, einer dem anderen spinnefeind. Da ist Tazio Nuvolari, der Vorjahressieger, genannt der »Rote Teufel« oder auch der »Fliegende Mantuaner«, der sein ganzes Leben am Limit zugebracht hat und häufig auch jenseits des Limits – kaum ein Knochen, den er sich noch nicht gebrochen hat. Da ist der frühere Motorradchampion Luigi Arcangeli, der die Strecke kennt wie seine linke Westentasche und weder Tod noch Teufel scheut. Da ist Giuseppe Campari, ein Multitalent, Weltspitze gleich in drei Feldern, als Rennfahrer, Opernsänger und Koch feiner italienischer Küche. Da ist Baconin Borzacchini, später in seiner Heimatstadt Terni auf ewig in Metall gegossen, ein Monument schon zu Lebzeiten. Gefahr droht auch von Nuvolaris Intimfeind Achille Varzi, einem Gentleman am Volant und eleganten Stilisten, nur dass sein Bugatti mit seinem Achtzylinder-Triebwerk von fünf Litern nicht zu den großen Würfen des Zauberers von Molsheim Ettore Bugatti zählt. Als Geheimtip unter den Insidern, und fast jeder Italiener ist einer, wird das Gespann Giuseppe Morandi und Archimede Rosa gehandelt mit seinem O.M. (für *officine meccaniche*) – die Pilotenriege aus Brescia ist entschieden schneller als ihr betagtes Automobil.

Dieser Armada in italienischem Rennrot hat Mercedes-Benz nur ein Fähnlein von sieben Aufrechten entgegenzusetzen, das unauffällig sein Quartier im Albergo Brescia bezieht: Rudolf Caracciola und Gattin Charlotte, Alfred Neubauer, Wilhelm Sebastian, »Fridolin« Zimmer sowie die Mechaniker Heinrich Kühnle und Karlo Kumpf, der zwar in den Gasthof »Zur Sonne« in Untertürkheim eingeheiratet hat, ohne das Aroma der Pisten aber nicht leben kann. Mit von der Partie ist Caracciolas Dackel Moritz, halb Mitglied der Familie, halb Maskottchen und in diesen Tagen von unerklärlicher Appetitlosigkeit heimgesucht. Im Strategiegespräch vor einer Italien-Karte in großem Maßstab beweist Neubauer die Qualitäten, die ihn im Verlauf jenes Jahrzehnts berühmt machen werden: Durchblick und Autorität sowie Genialität bei der Verwaltung des Notstands. Auf sieben Stationen muss Caracciola sich pflichtgemäß einstellen wie alle anderen, damit niemand von rechten Wegen abkommt. Die Zwischenstopps werden dokumentiert durch Stempel in einem Bordbuch, überdies wird eine Plombe an der Lenksäule gezackt. Knapp 30 Liter schluckt der SSKL im Schnitt, 120 Liter fasst sein Tank im Heck. Folglich muss man alle 400 Kilometer ein Depot anlegen, nahe dem Hotel Schwarzer Adler in Siena, in Terni zwischen Rom und der Adria, in Bologna, das auf der Hin- und auf der Rückfahrt angelaufen wird, in Feltre am nördlichsten Punkt des Parcours.

Nur: Neubauer gebietet lediglich über drei Männer. Die Lösung des Dilemmas: Karlo Kumpf wird Caracciola in Siena erwarten, dann schleunigst seine Zelte abreißen und ins 200 Kilometer entfernte Bologna aufbrechen. Man studiert die Landkarte gründlich, denn der Stau im Spannungsfeld des Magneten Mille Miglia ist unvermeidlich. Für die Station in Terni ist Heinrich Kühnle zuständig, für die in Feltre »Fridolin« Zimmer. Da das Einsatzauto erst im letzten Augenblick aus Stuttgart eintrifft, reicht es lediglich zu einer einzigen Trainingsrunde in einem Mietwagen. Aber Caracciola kennt sich ein bisschen aus: 1930 hat er gemäß einer bewährten Mercedes-Praktik das Terrain

sondiert und ist in einem SSK sechster geworden. Am 11. April senkt der ehemalige Minister Turati in Brescia ab 13 Uhr im Minuten-Rhythmus die Tricolore. Als erste stürzen sich die kleinen Wagen in das Abenteuer Mille Miglia. Die automobile Oberklasse mit ihren Star-Piloten folgt später. Nur wer ganz am Schluss startet, hat einen gewissen Überblick über seine Position und den Verlauf des Rennens. Caracciola tritt den langen Marsch durch den italienischen Stiefel im Spalier der Millionen um 15.12 Uhr an, nach einer letzten Zigarette und innigem Lebewohl von Charlotte. Neubauer, diesem Mann der Tat, bleiben nur noch Fingertrommeln und Daumendrehen. Er hat gewissermaßen die Uhr aufgezogen, die in den folgenden 16 Stunden und zehn Minuten nach ihren eigenen Gesetzen abschnurren wird.

1931 – da läuft noch alle Information durch Einbahnkanäle, über Radio, Telefon, Telegraf und riesige Tafeln, auf denen der letzte Stand der Dinge mit Glühbirnen angezeigt wird. Sie melden Führung für Caracciola in Bologna, wo er sich mit einem Schnitt von 154 Stundenkilometern auf schnellen Straßen ein Sicherheitspolster von sieben Minuten auf den O.M. erarbeitet hat. Eine Minute Rückstand hat Campari mit seinem Copiloten Attilio Marinoni, zwei weitere Borzacchini und Nuvolari mit Beifahrer Giovanni Battista Guidotti, die den einen der beiden Alfa 8C 2300 bemannen – den anderen hat man Arcangeli anvertraut. Elf Kilometer nach dem Start auf der Strecke geblieben: Achille Varzi – die Benzinpumpe, sagen die Bugatti-Leute. Doch dann folgt Terrain, in dem sich Nuvolari und der wendige Alfa förmlich tummeln, der Appenin zum Beispiel mit dem Raticosa- und dem Futa-Pass. Schon in Siena führt der »Fliegende Mantuaner«, gewinnt auch die Coppa Mussolini, die Halbzeit-Trophäe, die der Duce für den Fahrer ausgelobt hat, der als erster in der Zeitwertung Rom erreicht hat. Knapp vor ihm, gleichwohl um anderthalb Minuten geschlagen, trifft der weiße Mercedes am Kontrollpunkt an der Milvio-Brücke über den Tiber ein. Die patriotisch bewegte Menge ist starr vor Schreck und vor Staunen. Im Ostteil der Strecke geben sich die Alfa-Piloten gleichsam die Stafette in die Hand. Erst führt Borzacchini, dann Campari, schließlich Arcangeli. Aber schier unaufhaltsam macht Caracciola in Nacht und Nebel Boden, ein Hecht im Karpfenteich auf den Vollgas-Passagen Norditaliens, hat in Treviso die Spitze übernommen und gibt sie nicht mehr ab. Am 12. April kurz nach sieben signalisieren Flugzeuge seine Ankunft. Um 7.22 Uhr verstummt das helle Singen des Kompressors nach der Zieldurchfahrt des SSKL, Campari wird zweiter, über den O.M. dritter.

Federn lassen mussten sie alle: Neun Reifenwechsel behindern die verwegene Fahrt der Werks-Alfa allein zwischen Brescia und Rom. Bei Verona kommen Arcangeli und Nuvolari von der Strecke ab. Der »Rote Teufel« blutet, wird aber noch neunter. Hinter Siena schleift der Auspuff des Mercedes am Boden. Sebastian reißt ihn ab und zieht sich Brandblasen an den Händen zu. Caracciola hat schon längst welche am rechten Fuß, da das Gaspedal die Hitze des Triebwerks überträgt. Bei Viterbo kommen dem Deutschen ein Grüppchen Geisterfahrer entgegen – der lokale Autoclub kehrt von bevorzugten Zuschauerplätzen nach Hause zurück. Bei Terni klemmt das Gasgestänge. 30 Kilometer vor dem Ziel platzt ein Hinterreifen des Mercedes mit der Startnummer 87 – Wilhelm Sebastian schuftet und schindet sich und bleibt dennoch gelassen. Als »Erfolg von ganz besonderem Ausmaße« preisen die Informationsbriefe der Werbeabteilung von Daimler-Benz den Mille-Miglia-Sieg des »Weißen Elefanten«, als »phantastische Leistung für Fahrer und Wagen«. So ist es. Aber ein paar Tage vorher hat man noch die Brauen gerunzelt.

Seul contre tous : la plus grande course de Rudolf Caracciola

Ce qui se terminera comme une « success story » aura tout d'abord commencé comme une farce : se rendant aux Mille Miglia 1931, Rudolf Caracciola fait brièvement étape à Milan et, là, en compagnie de quelques amis, il hèle un chauffeur de taxi. Celui-ci reconnaît son passager et se croit encouragé à lui donner un échantillon de son propre savoir-faire, roulant comme un fou et dérapant en doublant des voitures frôlées au millimètre près – au moment bien mal choisi de l'heure de pointe de Milan avec ses embouteillages alors déjà insurmontables. Caracciola demande à l'homme de se calmer et exige finalement qu'il s'arrête immédiatement. Il obéit de mauvais gré et ricane lorsque l'Allemand descend de voiture : « Et ça prétend être pilote de course ! »

Quelques jours plus tard, aux premières heures du 12 avril, le chauffeur de taxi inconnu aura sans aucun doute fait acte de contrition, le prestige de son célèbre passager aura sans doute été restauré pour briller avec d'autant plus de rayonnement : Rudolf Caracciola a en effet gagné les cinquièmes Mille Miglia en un temps record et, qui plus est, en tant que premier vainqueur étranger. La situation initiale est totalement désespérée, mission impossible, celle d'un Goliath livré à toute une horde de David. Même à Untertürkheim, l'effronterie du minuscule commando qui part vers l'Italie sans états d'âme fait sourire. Dans les remous du krach de Wall Street de 1929, Mercedes-Benz a considérablement amputé le budget du service Course et le directeur Wilhelm Kissel informe Caracciola que son contrat ne sera pas reconduit en 1931.

Et c'est alors que sonne l'heure de l'ingénieur en chef, Alfred Neubauer, qui, comme Caracciola lui-même, s'engage à grands pas dans la légende. Il réunit une petite équipe autour de lui, avec Wilhelm Sebastian comme copilote et mécanicien émérite, Willy « Fridolin » Zimmer comme mécanicien et, avec une ristourne bienvenue sur le prix d'achat normal de 40 000 reichsmarks, il se procure une SSK (pour Super Sport Courte), une voiture très particulière avec un six-cylindres en ligne de 7065 cm³ et 240 ch. La puissance est de 300 ch dès que le turbocompresseur Roots entre en action. Les ingénieurs Hans Nibel et Max Wagner se sont attaqués à son embonpoint chronique avec une perceuse et, là où cela ne portait pas préjudice à la solidité de l'« éléphant blanc », ils ont économisé 200 kg à coups de perforations comme avec la « voiture goutte d'eau » de jadis. SSKL est le nom donné à cette évolution ultime de la série, L étant l'abréviation de légère – ce qui ne l'empêche pas d'accuser encore tout de même 1500 kg.

Lors des Mille Miglia de Brescia, c'est une nation qui se célèbre elle-même, c'est un pays entier qui sombre dans l'enivrement et l'allégresse de l'identité ethnique. Et, là, l'éléphant blanc du Nord est aussi déplacé qu'un nudiste dans un couvent. Alfa Romeo a entendu parler de ce qui se trame et réplique avec une débauche de matériel et de logistique. Dix-sept camions sont placés aux endroits stratégiques importants avec une équipe de 90 mécaniciens. Une légion d'auxiliaires volontaires est, en outre, échelonnée le long des 1635 km du parcours, armée de jerricans d'essence et de pneus, gamins des environs qui ne sont pas animés par le plaisir de la lire gagnée rapidement, mais par l'amour du Duce, du peuple et de la patrie ainsi que par la devise olympique selon laquelle l'essentiel est de participer. Trente des 99 voitures qui s'alignent au départ à Brescia sont des Alfa Romeo avec, à l'épicentre de l'intérêt et de toutes les attentions, les deux voitures d'usine : des Tipo 8C 2300, huit-cylindres de 2336 cm³ à compresseur développant 150 ch à 5000 tr/min. Bien qu'on les ait jetées dans le feu de la bataille prématurément pour contrer l'attaque des Teutons, leur niveau de développement est tout à fait flatteur. Mais un problème s'esquisse d'ores et déjà : la symbiose avec les pneus Pirelli réalisés spécialement pour elles n'est pas parfaite. Les ingénieurs d'Alfa Romeo tâtonnent encore : la phase d'essais a-t-elle été trop courte ? La motricité laisse-t-elle à désirer ? Est-ce la répartition du poids qui n'est pas correcte ?

Pour le choix des pilotes, non plus, rien n'est laissé au hasard. Caracciola est confronté au gratin des pilotes italiens, chacun étant le plus grand et tous prédestinés pour vaincre, mais chacun étant aussi l'ennemi juré de l'autre. On y trouve Tazio Nuvolari, le vainqueur de la dernière édition, surnommé le « Diable rouge » ou encore le « Mantouais volant », qui, sa vie entière, a flirté avec la limite et a parfois aussi fréquemment dépassé celle-ci – il n'a presque plus un os qui ne soit pas encore brisé. On y trouve aussi l'ancien champion de moto Luigi Arcangeli, qui connaît le circuit comme sa poche et ne craint ni le diable ni la mort. Ou encore Giuseppe Campari, un multitalent qui pourrait être champion du monde dans trois registres simultanément, comme pilote de course, chanteur d'opéra et cuisinier de gastronomie italienne de haut vol. Il y a aussi Baconin Borzacchini, auquel sa ville natale de Terni élèvera plus tard une statue de bronze, à lui qui était déjà un monument de son vivant. Mais une menace émane aussi de l'ennemi intime de Nuvolari, Achille Varzi, un *gentleman* au volant et styliste élégant, à ceci près que sa Bugatti, avec son huit-cylindres de 5 litres, ne compte pas parmi les plus grandes réussites du sorcier de Molsheim, Ettore Bugatti. Comme tuyau parmi les initiés, et presque chaque Italien en est un, on se murmure les noms du duo Giuseppe Morandi et Archimede Rosa avec son O.M. (pour Officine meccaniche) – la paire de pilotes de Brescia étant beaucoup plus rapide que sa vieille voiture.

Face à cette armada en rouge course italien, Mercedes-Benz ne peut aligner qu'une troupe de sept mercenaires qui est descendue dans l'anonymat à l'Albergo Brescia : Rudolf Caracciola et son épouse Charlotte, Alfred Neubauer, Wilhelm Sebastian, « Fridolin » Zimmer ainsi que les mécaniciens Heinrich Kühnle et Karlo Kumpf, qui s'est certes marié tout récemment, mais ne peut vivre sans le parfum des pistes. Un autre qui est de la partie est le chien de Caracciola, Moritz, à moitié membre de la famille et à moitié mascotte, qui, ces jours-ci, souffre d'un inexplicable manque d'appétit. Lors des entretiens stratégiques devant une carte de l'Italie à grande échelle, Neubauer révèle les qualités qui l'ont rendu célèbre au cours de la décennie : maîtrise de la situation et autorité ainsi que génie dans la gestion de la crise. Conformément au règlement, Caracciola doit, comme tous les autres, passer à sept points de contrôle pour que nul ne prenne un raccourci. Les passages sont documentés par des cachets dans un livre de bord et, en outre, un plomb placé sur la colonne de direction est gravé. La SSKL consomme en moyenne près de 30 litres aux 100 kilomètres et son réservoir arrière a une capacité de 120 litres. Il faut donc logiquement prévoir un dépôt tous les 400 kilomètres, près de l'hôtel du Schwarzer Adler à Sienne, à Terni, entre Rome et l'Adria, à Bologne, où l'on passe à l'aller et au retour, ainsi qu'à Feltre, au point le plus septentrional du parcours.

Le seul problème est que Neubauer n'a que trois hommes sous ses ordres. Solution du dilemme : Karlo Kumpf attendra Caracciola à Sienne puis il fera ses bagages le plus rapidement possible pour se rendre à Bologne, à 200 kilomètres de là. Il faut étudier la carte minutieusement, car les embouteillages sont inévitables dans le sillage des Mille Miglia qui sont un immense succès populaire. Heinrich Kühnle est compétent pour l'étape de Terni et « Fridolin » Zimmer pour celle de Feltre. Comme la voiture de course n'arrive de Stuttgart qu'au dernier moment, la courageuse équipe ne peut couvrir qu'un seul tour d'essai dans une voiture de location. Mais Caracciola s'y connaît un peu : en 1930, selon une pratique éprouvée chez Mercedes, il a sondé le terrain et a terminé sixième au volant d'une SSK. Le 11 avril, le ministre de cette époque, M. Turati, abaisse le drapeau tricolore à Brescia, libérant les voitures à partir de 13 heures à un rythme d'une par minute. Les premières à se jeter dans la bataille des Mille Miglia sont les petites voitures. Le gratin automobile avec ses pilotes vedettes ne démarrera que plus tard. Seuls ceux qui prennent le départ tout à la fin ont une certaine idée de leur position et du déroulement de la course. Caracciola prend le départ de la longue marche à travers la botte italienne, au milieu d'une haie de millions de personnes à 15 h 12, après une ultime cigarette et une tendre étreinte de Charlotte. Neubauer, cet homme d'action, ne peut plus que croiser les doigts et se tourner les pouces. Il a en quelque sorte remonté la pendule qui, pendant les 16 heures et dix minutes suivantes, va battre à son propre rythme.

En 1931, toutes les informations arrivent encore en sens unique, par la radio, le téléphone, le télégraphe et les gigantesques tableaux sur lesquels des ampoules affichent le classement actuel. Elles indiquent que Caracciola est en tête à Bologne, où, avec une moyenne de 154 km/h sur les routes rapides, il a grignoté une petite avance de sept minutes sur l'O.M. Campari et son copilote Attilio Marinoni ont une minute de retard ; deux minutes plus loin, on trouve Borzacchini ainsi que Nuvolari avec son copilote Giovanni Battista Guidotti, qui conduisent l'une des deux Alfa 8C 2300 – l'autre ayant été confiée à Arcangeli. Achille Varzi a déjà abandonné onze kilomètres après le départ : la pompe à essence, déclarent les mécaniciens de Bugatti. Mais vient alors une région dans laquelle Nuvolari et la maniable Alfa Romeo s'ébattent littéralement comme un poisson dans l'eau : les Apennins, par exemple, avec les cols de Raticosa et de Futa. À Sienne, déjà, le « Mantouais volant » est en tête et il remporte aussi la Coppa Mussolini, le trophée de la mi-course que le Duce décerne au pilote qui atteint le premier le point de contrôle de Rome. Juste devant lui et pourtant battue d'une minute et demie, la Mercedes blanche franchit le point de contrôle du pont de Milvio sur le Tibre. La foule agitée de sentiments patriotiques est paralysée de frayeur et d'étonnement. Sur la portion orientale du parcours, les pilotes d'Alfa se passent pour ainsi dire le relais en tête. C'est tout d'abord Borzacchini qui se porte en tête, suivi de Campari et, enfin, d'Arcangeli. Mais, dans un élan irrésistible, Caracciola regagne du terrain à travers la nuit et le brouillard, roulant comme un fou sur les passages du nord de l'Italie. À Trévise, il a repris la tête et ne la cédera plus. Le 12 avril, peu après 7 h, des avions signalent son arrivée. À 7 h 22, le chant clair du compresseur s'éteint après le passage de la ligne d'arrivée par la SSKL. Campari termine deuxième, l'O.M., troisième.

Tous ont perdu des plumes dans la bataille : neuf changements de pneumatiques entravent la course échevelée des Alfa usine rien qu'entre Brescia et Rome. À Vérone, Arcangeli et Nuvolari sortent de la piste. Le « Diable rouge » est en sang et termine pourtant neuvième. Derrière Sienne, le pot d'échappement de la Mercedes traîne sur le sol. Sebastian l'arrache et se brûle gravement les mains. Caracciola a depuis longtemps déjà des brûlures au pied droit parce que l'accélérateur transmet la chaleur du moteur. Près de Viterbe, l'Allemand croise un petit groupe de voitures arrivant en sens inverse – l'automobile-club local rentre chez lui après avoir quitté les endroits favoris des spectateurs. À Terni, la timonerie d'accélérateur se bloque.

À trente kilomètres de l'arrivée, un pneu arrière de la Mercedes au numéro 87 éclate – Wilhelm Sebastian s'acharne et s'époumone et reste pourtant décontracté. Les lettres d'information du service publicitaire de Daimler-Benz qualifient la victoire de « l'éléphant blanc » aux Mille Miglia de « succès d'une beauté tout à fait particulière », de « performance fantastique pour les pilotes et la voiture ». C'est bien vrai. Mais, quelques jours plus tôt, on fronçait encore les sourcils.

Christian Werner in the two-liter supercharged car in which he won the Targa and Coppa Florio in 1924.

Christian Werner im Zweiliter mit Kompressor, mit dem er Targa und Coppa Florio 1924 gewinnt.

Christian Werner avec la deux-litres à compresseur avec laquelle il a gagné la Targa et la Coppa Florio en 1924.

German white livery. Sixth place and with it victory in the Coppa Florio for the fastest production car was taken by Max Sailer in a Mercedes 28/95. Sailer had already won this cup before with his second overall position the previous year. And finally in 1924 Christian Werner drove Ferdinand Porsche's supercharged 2-liter, four-cylinder car at worrying angles of drift over the dusty course, but he still managed to make everything seem absurdly simple.

In the same year Rudolf Caracciola from Remagen won a small car race in the Berlin Stadium in an Ego. Racing driver Alfred Neubauer meanwhile, no better than nineteenth in the 1922 Targa Florio in a Sascha, and only in an ominous thirteenth place in the 1924 race in a Mercedes, finally recognized that his talents lay more with direction and management. An ego trip and a change of post were to have lasting consequences. Caracciola's first great Mercedes victory was at the 1926 German Grand Prix held at the Avus in the 2-liter, eight-cylinder car which had been converted to a four-seater to comply with the rules. This was an early Neubauer production and came about because, following confusion and muddle in the international ruling body, the German Grand Prix had suddenly been declared a sports-car race.

And so began the almost never-ending story of the s series and its metamorphoses right up to the ssKL, as a foreword to the saga of the Silver Arrows. Driving the s model, Caracciola won the opening race at the Nürburgring on 19 June 1927. At the German Grand Prix on the same track and just one month later Otto Merz, Christian Werner, and Willy Walb, all in s models, produced a storming one-two-three. And because that sounded so good, a repeat performance was conjured up the following year in the ss under a burning sun. A prize of 18,000 marks had been put up for the winners, and these turned out to be the elderly Christian Werner and the young Rudi Caracciola,

zehnter, 1924 mit einem Mercedes lediglich auf dem ominösen Rang dreizehn, ringt sich zu der Erkenntnis durch, die Regie und das Regieren lägen ihm eigentlich mehr. Ego-Trip und Stellungs-Wechsel sollen nachhaltige Folgen zeitigen. Eine Neubauer-Inszenierung ist bereits Caracciolas erster großer Mercedes-Sieg beim Großen Preis von Deutschland 1926 auf der Avus mit dem Zweiliter-Achtzylinder, der sich reglementskonform zum Viersitzer gewandelt hat. Angesichts von Konfusion und Kuddelmuddel im internationalen Regelwerk hat man nämlich die deutschen Grand Prix kurzerhand für »Sportwagen« ausgeschrieben.

Und damit beginnt die schier unendliche Geschichte von der Baureihe s und ihren Metamorphosen bis hin zum ssKL, als Prolegomenon gewissermaßen für die Saga von den Silberpfeilen. Auf dem s gewinnt Caracciola das Eröffnungsrennen auf dem Nürburgring am 19. Juni 1927. Beim Großen Preis von Deutschland, am gleichen Ort und nur einen Monat später, greifen die s-Piloten Otto Merz, Christian Werner und Willy Walb gar zu einem Dreifach-Akkord in die Tasten. Und weil der so schön klingt, kommt es im folgenden Jahr zu einer Reprise mit dem ss in einer Sonnenschlacht sondergleichen. 18 000 Mark sind für die Sieger ausgelobt, den alten Christian Werner und den jungen Rudi Caracciola, wie sich erweist, trotz eines ausgekugelten Arms (Werner), Hitzschlags und versengter Fußsohlen (Caracciola). Auf den Plätzen folgen der bärige Merz, der die fünf Hitzestunden durch die grüne Hölle alleine durchsteht, und Walb, der Werner in dessen eigenem Fahrzeug abgelöst hat. Der Ring scheint dem »Weißen Elefanten« geradezu auf den 33 Zentner schweren Leib geschneidert zu sein.

Zwei seiner spektakulärsten Erfolge indessen erringt er woanders und viel später: bei der Mille Miglia 1931 (vgl. Kasten s. 75) und am 22. Mai 1932 auf der Avus. Der Freiherr Reinhard von König Fachsenfeld hat einem ssKL ein wunderlich geformtes Stromlinien-Habit verpasst, mit dem bekleidet sich der archaisch anmutende Urklotz förmlich in den Fahrtwind schmiegt. »Zigarre« oder gar »Zeppelin« tauft ihn der Volksmund. Damit siegt der 27jährige Manfred von Brauchitsch mit einem Durchschnitt von 194,4 Stundenkilometern vor ausverkauftem Haus. Alfa-

Caracciola winning the 1926 German Grand Prix at the Avus.

Caracciola gewinnt 1926 den deutschen GP auf der Avus.

En 1926, Caracciola gagne le Grand Prix d'Allemagne sur l'Avus.

Opening race at the Nürburgring in 1927: Caracciola and Rosenberger in an S type, von Mosch in the 630K.

Eröffnungsrennen 1927 am Ring: Caracciola und Rosenberger auf dem Typ S, von Mosch auf dem 630K.

La course inaugurale du Nürburgring en 1927: Caracciola et Rosenberger sur la type S, von Mosch sur la 630K.

italien a remplacé le blanc allemand. Le sixième et vainqueur de la Coppa Florio pour la voiture de série la plus rapide est Max Sailer, avec une Mercedes 28/95 qui avait déjà remporté cette coupe un an auparavant en terminant à la seconde place. En 1924, finalement, Christian Werner, au volant de la 2-litres quatre-cylindres à compresseur de Ferdinand Porsche, couvre le circuit poussiéreux dans d'impressionnants dérapages contrôlés alors que tout semble pourtant d'une si flagrante simplicité.

La même année, Rudolf Caracciola, de Remagen, gagne dans le stade de Berlin une course de voiturettes sur une Ego. Pendant ce temps, le pilote de course Alfred Neubauer, qui termine seulement dix-neuvième de la Targa Florio 1922 sur une Sascha et à la place porte-malheur de treizième avec une Mercedes en 1924, prend conscience que jouer les hommes-orchestres lui conviendrait à proprement parler beaucoup mieux. Cette prise de conscience et ce passage de l'autre coté de la barrière auront des conséquences durables. La première grande victoire de Caracciola sur Mercedes, lors du Grand Prix d'Allemagne 1926 sur l'Avus, avec la 2-litres huit-cylindres qui s'est transformée en une quatre places par conformité envers le règlement, est déjà une mise en scène de Neubauer. Vu la confusion et les tricheries permises par les règlements internationaux, on a, en effet, tout simplement organisé les Grands Prix d'Allemagne pour les « voitures de sport ».

Et c'est alors que commence l'histoire interminable de la série s et de ses métamorphoses jusqu'à la ssKL, qui est en quelque sorte les prolégomènes pour la saga des Flèches d'argent. Sur une s, Caracciola gagne la course inaugurale du Nürburgring le 19 juin 1927. Lors du Grand Prix d'Allemagne, au même endroit et seulement un mois plus tard, les pilotes de s, Otto Merz, Christian Werner et Willy Walb, signent même un historique triplé. Et, comme la mélodie est si belle, elle est rejouée l'année suivante, avec la ss, sous un soleil torride. Près de 18 000 marks sont remportés par les vainqueurs, le vieux Christian Werner et le jeune Rudi Caracciola, qui souffraient, comme on l'apprit plus tard, d'une épaule foulée pour Werner et d'une insolation

victorious despite a dislocated arm (Werner) and heat-stroke and singed soles (Caracciola). The other places were taken by the amazing Merz who drove alone for the entire five hours of heat through the green hell, and Walb who had replaced Werner in the latter's own car. The Ring seemed tailor-made for the "White Elephant" with its 33-hundredweight body.

Two of its most spectacular successes meanwhile were achieved elsewhere and at a much later date – in the 1931 Mille Miglia (see box p 73) and on 22 May 1932 at the Avus. Baron Reinhard von König Fachsenfeld had designed a marvelously streamlined body for an SSKL, clad in which the seemingly archaic contraption simply cut through the airstream. The nicknames "Cigar" and even "Zeppelin" stuck. It was this car that the 27-year-old Manfred von Brauchitsch drove to victory at an average speed of 194.4 kph (120.8 mph) before a sell-out crowd. Caracciola, meanwhile, who was guesting in an Alfa Romeo, was booed by the angry Berliners. But the potential of the SSKL was not enough to see it through another year. On 21 March 1933 von Brauchitsch was only sixth in the equivalent race. Half the government dressed in Nazi brown was in the Avus grandstand to see the fall of a legend. They felt that the side had been let down. The dawn of a new era was steadily approaching.

Manfred von Brauchitsch winning the 1932 Avus Race in a streamlined SSKL.

Manfred von Brauchitsch siegt im Avus-Rennen 1932 auf einem SSKL mit Stromlinien-Karrosserie.

Manfred von Brauchitsch gagne la course de l'Avus 1932 sur une SSKL à carrosserie aérodynamique.

Romeo-Gastpilot Caracciola wird indessen von erbosten Berlinern ausgebuht. Doch für ein weiteres Jahr reicht das Potential des SSKL nicht mehr. Am 21. März 1933 wird von Brauchitsch am gleichen Platz nur noch sechster. Auf der Avus-Tribüne verfolgt die halbe Reichsregierung in Nazi-Braun den Absturz einer Legende. Man empfindet ihn als Blamage für das System. Da dämmert bereits eine neue Ära herauf.

et des plantes de pieds brûlées pour Caracciola. Leurs dauphins sont le bourru Merz, qui s'est battu tout seul pendant cinq heures dans la chaleur mortelle de l'« Enfer vert », et Walb, qui a remplacé Werner dans sa propre voiture. Le « Ring » semble absolument taillé sur mesure pour les « éléphants blancs » et leurs 1650 kg. C'est toutefois ailleurs et beaucoup plus tard qu'ils remporteront deux de leurs succès les plus spectaculaires : lors des Mille Miglia de 1931 (voir encadré p. 76) et, le 22 mai 1932, sur l'Avus. Le baron Reinhard von König Fachsenfeld a affublé une SSKL d'une carrosserie pseudo-aérodynamique aux formes bizarres avec laquelle le monstre aux lignes archaïques fend littéralement le vent. Le bon sens populaire l'a surnommé « le cigare » ou même « Zeppelin ». Avec elle, Manfred von Brauchitsch, âgé de 27 ans, gagne à une moyenne de 194,4 km/h une course disputée à guichets fermés. Rudolf Caracciola, recruté cette année-là par Alfa Romeo, est sifflé par les Berlinois furieux de cette défection. Mais le potentiel de la SSKL ne suffit plus l'année suivante. Le 21 mars 1933, sur la même scène, von Brauchitsch ne termine plus que sixième. Dans les tribunes de l'Avus, la moitié du gouvernement du Reich, en chemise brune, assiste à l'effondrement d'une légende. Ce qui est ressenti comme un camouflet pour le système. Mais une ère nouvelle est d'ores et déjà en train de s'ouvrir.

A boost to the company: The supercharger era 1934–1939

An excessively permissive regime often yields the same results as an anti-authoritarian upbringing; in other words, give someone enough rope and he may just hang himself. In the early Thirties racing cars were in danger of becoming too fast, as their specifications were almost unrestricted by the proliferation of semi-free formulas. In response, motorsport's ruling body AIACR (Association Internationale des Automobile Clubs Reconnus) announced on 1 October 1932 to the applause of the constructors that, with effect from the 1934 season, Grand Prix cars must not exceed 750 kg (1,655 lb) without tires, fuel, and driver. The minimum racing distance was to be 500 km (310 miles). This ruling was initially valid for three years, though it was later extended until 1937.

Any initial reluctance – initiatives were still wilting in the long shadows of the world economic crisis – was counteracted by the financial incentives offered by the German government. State grants of 450,000 marks per year were made to the two German teams, Daimler-Benz and Auto Union, plus 20,000, 10,000, and 5,000 marks for first, second, and third places. In the seven years between 1933 and 1939 the cars with the star received 2.78 million marks in subsidies and the four-ringed fireballs 2.58 mil-

Geladene Gesellschaft: Die Kompressor-Ära 1934–1939

Allzu permissive Gesetzgebung zeitigt die gleichen Ergebnisse wie antiautoritäres Erziehen: Die an der langen Leine Gelassenen bestimmen ihre Spiel-Räume selbst. Vom Wildwuchs halbfreier Formeln fast unbehindert, drohen Rennautos Anfang der dreißiger Jahre zu schnell zu werden. Da interveniert die Motorsport-Legislative AIACR (für Association Internationale des Automobile Clubs Reconnus) unter dem Applaus der Konstrukteure mit einem neuen Reglement, verkündet am 12. Oktober 1932: Grand-Prix-Wagen dürfen von der Saison 1934 an nicht schwerer sein als 750 Kilogramm ohne Reifen, Betriebsstoffe und Fahrer. Die Renn-Distanz muss bei mindestens 500 Kilometern liegen. Die Bestimmung ist zunächst für drei Jahre gültig, wird aber später auf 1937 ausgeweitet.

Eventuell aufkeimender Unlust – noch verwelken Initiativen im langen Schlagschatten der Weltwirtschaftskrise – begegnet die Reichsregierung mit finanziellen Anreizen: 450 000 Mark staatliche Beihilfe pro anno werden für die beiden deutschen Protagonisten Daimler-Benz und Auto Union ausgeworfen, dazu 20 000, 10 000 und 5000 Mark für die Plätze eins bis drei. In den sieben Jahren zwischen 1933 und 1939 werden die Wagen mit dem Stern mit 2,78 Millionen Mark bezuschusst, die Boliden im Zeichen der vier

Une compagnie qui ne manque pas d'air : l'ère des compresseurs 1934–1939

Une législation trop permissive induit les mêmes résultats qu'une éducation antiautoritaire : en l'absence de sévérité, chacun cherche à déterminer jusqu'où il peut aller trop loin. Par suite de l'anarchie des formules semi-libres, les voitures de course du début des années 1930 risquent de devenir trop rapides. L'AIACR (pour Association internationale des Automobiles-Clubs reconnus), le pouvoir législatif de la compétition automobile, intervient alors avec l'appui des constructeurs et adopte un nouveau règlement, promulgué le 12 octobre 1932 : pour la saison 1934, les voitures de Grand Prix ne devront pas peser plus de 750 kg, pneus, carburant, fluides et pilote non compris. Les courses doivent avoir une longueur minimale de 500 kilomètres. Adopté tout d'abord pour une durée de trois ans, le règlement sera ensuite prorogé jusqu'en 1937.

Pour parer à tout risque de désaffection – les initiatives sont encore peu nombreuses dans le sillage de la grave crise économique mondiale des années 1930 – le gouvernement du Reich a l'idée d'incitations financières : 450 000 marks de subventions publiques par an sont votés pour les deux protagonistes allemands, Daimler-Benz et Auto Union, ainsi que 20 000, 10 000 et 5 000 marks quand ils termineront aux

lion, further sweetened by 330,000 and 217,000 marks respectively in prize money. Given the stiff increases in costs, however, this was not a vast sum, initially 30 and later only 10 per cent of the development costs.

The Stuttgart team immediately rolled up its sleeves. Hans Nibel was the chief designer. Max Wagner designed the chassis, and Albert Hees, assisted by Otto Schilling, the engine. Nibel's confidant, Fritz Nallinger, was responsible for assembly. Otto Weber took charge of engine assembly, and Jakob Krauss of the running gear. Vehicle preparation was in the hands of Max Sailer. As racing director, Alfred Neubauer was in charge at the track. Testing of the w25, the company's first real Grand Prix car for nine years, was completed in May 1934. Its straight-eight engine, a four-valve design, was supercharged by a Roots compressor which charged two pressure carburetors and initially developed 354 bhp. Its innovative front axle with short wishbones soon proved to be a trendsetter for production cars too, while the rear axle used the same configuration

A martyr at the wheel: Rudolf Caracciola (1901–1959)

Even as late as 1955 when Rudi Caracciola turned up for the Swedish Grand Prix as part of the Mercedes circus, the autograph hunters surrounded him. Three tumultuous decades had passed since his first victory in the German Grand Prix at the Avus in 1926, 17 years since his last European championship. But time had not dimmed the radiance of this sporting icon. Nor did the fact that his best years were spent driving not only for the Mercedes star that represented human dominance on land, on water, and in the skies, but also under the banner of the swastika which, according to Bert Brecht, was a large hook for the small man.

And yet the smile on the face of Caracciola the victor hid the anguish of a man in pain, a St. Sebastian figure, stigmatized and martyred for his sport. Since an accident in practice in Monaco in April 1933 Caracciola had been missing the ball joint at the top of his left femur. He had fought against opponents like Stuck, von Brauchitsch, Rosemeyer, and Nuvolari, against the clock and against constant pain. The second of his personal stations of the cross was the result of an accident – again in practice – in 1946 in Indianapolis where he fractured his skull. The third and last came on 18 May 1952 at the Bremgarten track near Berne. On lap 13 Caracciola's 300 sl left the track and demolished a tree. The driver was extricated from the car with compound fractures of his right femur.

He spent the remaining years of his life drifting between alertness and a strange state of somnolence in glamorous exile in his house in Ruvigliana on Lake Lugano. His second wife Alice cared for him, as his first wife Charlie had done after the Monaco disaster. If true heroism consists in overcoming a serious handicap, then Rudolf Caracciola, known for being a supreme driver in the rain, the winner of 27 major races, was a genuine hero.

Ringe mit 2,58 Millionen, versüßt durch 330 000 beziehungsweise 217 000 Mark Preisgelder. Angesichts munter kletternder Kosten ist das nicht viel, anfänglich dreißig, später nur noch zehn Prozent des Aufwands für die Entwicklung.

In Stuttgart krempelt man umgehend die Ärmel hoch. Für das Design zuständig zeichnet Hans Nibel. Max Wagner konzipiert das Chassis, Albert Hees, unterstützt von Otto Schilling, die Maschine. Verantwortlich für den Zusammenbau ist Nibel-Intimus Fritz Nallinger. Otto Weber kümmert sich um die Montage der Motoren, Jakob Krauss um die Konstruktion des Fahrwerks. Die Vorbereitung der Fahrzeuge liegt in den Händen von Max Sailer. Als Regisseur vor Ort wirkt Rennleiter Alfred Neubauer. Im Mai 1934 sind die Versuche mit dem w25 abgeschlossen, dem ersten richtigen Grand-Prix-Wagen des hohen Hauses seit neun Jahren. Sein Reihen-Achtzylinder, ein Vierventiler, wird zwangsbeatmet von einem Roots-Kompressor, der zwei Druckvergaser beschickt, und leistet zu Beginn 354 ps. Seine innovative Vorderachse mit kurzen Querlenkern entpuppt sich umgehend als Trendsetter auch für die Serie, während die Hinterachse die gleiche Konfiguration aufweist wie einst der Tropfenwagen: pendelnde Achsarme, am Differential aufgehängt. Gewichtsproblemen rückt man mit bewährten Praktiken zu Leibe: Löcher überall, sogar in den Radnaben vorne.

Es reicht dennoch nicht: Bei der Abnahme zum Eifelrennen am 3. Juni, seiner Premiere, bringt der w25 zwei Kilo zuviel auf die Waage des Nürburgrings. Indes ist guter Rat billig: »Die Karosserie bestand aus per Hand gehämmerten Aluminiumblättern mit vielen Unebenheiten«, wird die Geburt der Rennfarbe Silber später von Hermann Lang beschrieben, damals noch Mechaniker des Werks-Piloten Luigi Fagioli. »Wir kratzten einfach den weißen Lack und die stellenweise dicke Schicht von Bleispachtel darunter weg. Das Resultat: genau 750 Kilogramm.« Als Gold-Stück erweist sich indessen der w25 – zunächst: Der Erfolg von Manfred von Brauchitsch am Ring ist der erste von fünf Siegen in dieser Saison. Und Rudi Caracciola sattelt noch drauf: Für Rekordversuche wird einem auf 430 ps erstarkten w25 eine Art Hardtop aufgestülpt, und mit dieser »Renn-Limousine«, wie er sie nennt, fährt er zum Beispiel am 10. Dezember mit fliegendem Start einen Rekord von 311,98 Stundenkilometern über die Meile. Auch im folgenden Jahr hält man bei zehn Starts mit neun Siegen, fünf davon im Doppel, den Rivalen Auto Union nieder. Caracciola aber avanciert zum Superstar und wird Europameister. Diesen höchsten Titel, der damals zu vergeben ist, wird er 1937 und 1938 zwei weitere Male einheimsen (vgl. Kasten oben).

1936 indessen gerät zum Jahr der Krise und der Neuorientierung. Die Auto Union mit ihren Mittelmotoren von 16 Zylindern, Copyright Professor Ferdinand Porsche, sind einfach nicht zu halten. Mit sieben Siegen, drei davon bei Großen Preisen, greift allein der Senkrechtstarter Bernd Rosemeyer nach den Sternen. Das Mercedes-Imperium

Martyr au volant : Rudolf Caracciola (1901–1959)

Lorsqu'il arrive au Grand Prix de Suède avec l'équipe Mercedes en 1955, il est talonné par les chasseurs d'autographes. Trois décennies riches en événements se sont écoulées depuis sa première victoire lors du Grand Prix d'Allemagne sur l'Avus en 1926 et dix-sept ans ont passé depuis son dernier titre de champion d'Europe. Mais le temps n'a pas fait perdre sa splendeur au rayonnement de l'illustrissime sportif Rudi Caracciola. Ni au fait que, à la période de son apogée, il n'ait pas seulement pris le départ sous l'emblème de l'étoile, synonyme de la maîtrise de l'homme sur la terre, dans les airs et sur l'eau, mais aussi au nom de cette croix – gammée – qui, selon Bertolt Brecht, a un grand défaut pour l'homme de la rue.

Et pourtant, derrière le sourire de vainqueur de Caracciola, se dissimule un homme qui sait ce qu'est la douleur, à l'image de saint Sébastien, stigmatisé et torturé par son sport. Depuis un accident aux essais de Monaco en avril 1933, il lui manque l'articulation de la cuisse gauche et Caracciola se bat contre des concurrents ayant pour nom Stuck, von Brauchitsch, Rosemeyer et Nuvolari, mais aussi chronomètre et douleur. Seconde station de son calvaire : accident – à nouveau lors des essais – en 1946 à Indianapolis, fracture du crâne. Et la troisième, enfin : le 18 mai 1952 sur le circuit de Bremgarten, près de Berne. Dans le 13e tour, la 300 sl de Caracciola sort de la route et fauche un arbre. Le pilote est dégagé avec des fractures compliquées à la cuisse droite.

Les dernières années de sa vie, il les passe entre l'éveil et un bizarre état d'hébétude dans le luxueux exil de sa propriété de Ruviglina, sur le lac de Lugano. Sa seconde épouse, Alice, le soigne comme l'a fait sa première femme Charlotte, jadis, après la catastrophe de Monaco. Si le véritable héroïsme consiste à se battre contre un handicap insurmontable, alors, Rudolf Caracciola, surnommé le «champion de la pluie», vainqueur de 27 courses importantes, est réellement un héros.

rangs 1 à 3. Pendant sept ans, de 1933 à 1939, les voitures à l'étoile recevront 2,78 millions de marks de subventions alors que les bolides avec l'emblème aux quatre anneaux en engrangeront 2,58 millions, sommes auxquelles se sont respectivement ajoutées 330 000 et 217 000 marks de prix versés par les organisateurs. Vu l'explosion des coûts, cela n'est pas beaucoup et représente au début 1930, puis, plus tard, seulement 10 % des crédits consacrés au développement.

À Stuttgart, on relève immédiatement ses manches. Hans Nibel est nommé responsable de la carrosserie. Max Wagner conçoit le châssis, Albert Hees, soutenu par Otto Schilling, dessine le moteur. Le responsable du montage est un intime du Nibel, Fritz Nallinger. Otto Weber se charge de l'assemblage des moteurs et Jacob Krauss, de la construction des châssis. La préparation des voitures a été confiée à Max Sailer. Le metteur en scène sur les circuits est le directeur de course Alfred Neubauer. En mai 1934, on en termine avec les essais de la w25, qui est la première

as previously used in the "Tropfenwagen": swing axles mounted on the differential. Weight problems were dealt with by using a tried-and-tested method: holes were drilled everywhere, even in the front wheel hubs, in order to save weight.

But it was still not enough. During scrutiny of the cars for the Eifel Race on 3 June, its première, the Nürburgring weighbridge revealed that the w 25 was two kilos (4.4 lb) overweight. The solution was ingeniously simple: "The bodywork consisted of very uneven hand-beaten aluminum panels," recalled Hermann Lang, at that time still a mechanic for the works driver Luigi Fagioli, when later describing the birth of silver as the racing color. "We simply scraped off the white paint and the sometimes thick layer of lead filler underneath it. The result: 750 kilos exactly." The w 25 then proved to be worth its weight in gold – initially. Manfred von Brauchitsch's success at the Ring was the first of five victories in that season. And Rudi Caracciola did his bit too. A kind of hardtop was tacked on to a w 25 whose power output had been upgraded to 430 bhp for record attempts, and Caracciola drove this "racing limousine," as he dubbed it, at record speeds. For example on 10 December, he clocked a record speed of 311.98 kph (193.86 mph) over a flying mile. With nine victories (including five races with a one-two finish for the team) from ten starts the next year, too, Mercedes remained on top of arch rival Auto Union. Caracciola went on to become a superstar and European champion. He was to take this title, the pre-eminent one at this time, twice more in 1937 and 1938 (see box p 79).

1936 meanwhile developed into a year of crisis and restructuring. Auto Union with its 16-cylinder rear engines, copyright Professor Ferdinand Porsche, was simply unstoppable. New kid on the block Bernd Rosemeyer with seven personal victories, three of them in Grands Prix, was reaching out for the stars. The Mercedes empire struck back by engineering a reshuffle. The Research Department had an autonomous Racing Department added to it. Rudolf Uhlenhaut, just 30, employed at Daimler-Benz for five years and blessed with the unique talent of being able to push a Grand Prix car to the limit equally as well as the star drivers employed specially to do so, was appointed to head this department. He hounded and harried the w 25 for a thousand kilometers (621 miles) over the hummocks and dips of the Nürburgring.

His findings were shattering. The car lifted from the track, and not just at the usual places, the chassis twisted longitudinally, the steering was jerky, its road position was a cause for concern. Uhlenhaut drew on this information when designing the w 125, and produced a new single-seater paragon, which understeered slightly as required and was given to a gentle four-wheel drift when pushed to the edge. Its front axle had been copied from the 500 K and 540 K production models. At the rear a de Dion axle was used, and so was soft damping and hard springing, in contrast to the previous philosophy. The improved handling was

Märtyrer am Volant: Rudolf Caracciola (1901–1959)

Noch als er 1955 auf dem Grand Prix von Schweden im Mercedes-Tross aufkreuzt, bedrängen ihn die Autogrammjäger. Drei tosende Jahrzehnte sind seit seinem ersten Sieg beim Großen Preis von Deutschland auf der Avus 1926 ins Land gegangen, 17 Jahre seit seiner letzten Europameisterschaft. Doch die Zeit hat die Leuchtkraft der Sport-Ikone Rudi Caracciola nicht verschlissen. Und auch nicht, dass er in seiner besten Zeit nicht nur im Zeichen des Sterns startet, der für die Herrschaft des Menschen über Land, Luft und Wasser steht, sondern auch im Namen jenes Kreuzes, das laut Bert Brecht für den kleinen Mann einen großen Haken hat.

Dabei verbirgt sich hinter dem Lachen des Siegers Caracciola ein Schmerzensmann, eine Sebastians-Gestalt, stigmatisiert und gemartert durch seinen Sport. Seit einem Trainingsunfall in Monaco im April 1933 fehlt die Gelenkkugel an seinem linken Oberschenkel, kämpft Caracciola gegen Konkurrenten wie Stuck, von Brauchitsch, Rosemeyer und Nuvolari, die Uhr und die Qual. Die zweite Station auf seinem Passionsweg: Unfall – wieder beim Training – 1946 in Indianapolis, Schädelbruch. Die dritte schließlich: der 18. Mai 1952 auf dem Bremgartenkurs bei Bern. In der 13. Runde kommt Caracciolas 300 SL von der Strecke ab und fällt einen Baum. Der Fahrer wird mit komplizierten Brüchen im rechten Oberschenkel geborgen.

Die verbleibenden Jahre seines Lebens verbringt er zwischen Wachheit und einem eigentümlichen Dämmerzustand im Edel-Exil seines Hauses in Ruvigliana am Luganer See. Seine zweite Gattin Alice umsorgt ihn, wie es seine erste Frau Charlie einst nach dem Monaco-Desaster getan hat. Wenn wahrer Heroismus darin besteht, ein schlimmes Handicap niederzuringen, dann ist Rudolf Caracciola, der »Regenmeister« genannt, Gewinner von 27 bedeutenden Rennen, in der Tat ein Held.

schlägt zurück mit Rochade und Revirement. Man fügt der Versuchsabteilung eine selbständige Rennabteilung hinzu. Leiter wird Rudolf Uhlenhaut, gerade 30, seit fünf Jahren bei Daimler-Benz und begnadet mit dem einzigartigen Talent, mit einem Grand-Prix-Wagen ebenso am Limit tasten zu können wie die eigens dafür bestallten Stars. Er scheucht und schindet den w 25 tausend Kilometer über die Buckel und Rinnen des Nürburgrings.

Der Befund ist fürwahr niederschmetternd: Das Auto hebt zu Sprüngen ab, nicht nur an den üblichen Stellen, der Rahmen verwindet sich in Längsrichtung, die Lenkung stößt, die Straßenlage ist bedenklich. Diese Erkenntnisse bringt Uhlenhaut in die Konzeption des w 125 ein, macht einen Musterknaben aus dem neuen Monoposto, der wunschgemäß leicht untersteuert und sich im Grenzbereich in einem sanften Four-Wheel-Drift bewegt. Seine Vorderachse ist den Produktionsmodellen 500 K und 540 K abgeschaut. Hinten wählt man eine de-Dion-Auslegung, dämpft weich und federt hart, entgegen der bisherigen Philosophie. Zum besseren Handling gesellt sich bullige

véritable voiture de Grand Prix de cette célèbre maison depuis neuf ans. Son huit-cylindres en ligne à quatre soupapes est suralimenté par un compresseur Roots qui fait respirer deux carburateurs sous pression et développe initialement 354 ch. Son essieu avant novateur avec deux courts bras transversaux s'avère si efficace qu'il est immédiatement repris aussi pour la série alors que l'essieu arrière présente la même configuration que celui de la voiture aérodynamique de jadis : avec des bras d'essieu oscillants ancrés sur le différentiel. On s'attaque aux problèmes de poids avec des solutions éprouvées : on fait des trous partout, même dans les moyeux de roues avant.

Et pourtant, cela ne suffit pas : lors du contrôle technique pour la course de l'Eifel, le 3 juin, sa première, la w 25 pèse 2 kg de trop sur la balance du Nürburgring. Que faire ? « La carrosserie était en tôle d'aluminium martelée à la main avec de nombreuses bosses », déclare plus tard Hermann Lang au sujet de la naissance de la couleur course argent, alors qu'il était encore mécanicien du pilote d'usine Luigi Fagioli. « Nous avons tout simplement gratté la peinture blanche et la parfois épaisse couche de mastic de plomb sous celle-ci. Résultat : exactement 750 kg. » La w 25 vaut entre-temps plus qu'une tonne d'or – tout d'abord : le succès remporté par Manfred von Brauchitsch au Ring est la première de cinq victoires signées cette saison. Et Rudi Caracciola y met encore un point d'orgue : pour des essais de record, une w 25 au moteur à la puissance majorée à 430 ch reçoit une espèce de hard-top et, avec cette « berline de course », comme il l'a surnommée lui-même, il signe par exemple, le 10 décembre, un record de 311,98 km/h pour le mile départ arrêté. L'année suivante, aussi, elle remporte, sur dix départs, neuf victoires, dont cinq doublés, battant à plate couture sa rivale l'Auto Union. Caracciola, quant à lui, devient une super-star et est sacré champion d'Europe. C'est le titre suprême que l'on peut remporter à cette époque-là et il le remportera encore à deux reprises en 1937 et 1938 (voir encadré p. 79).

1936, en revanche, est une année de crise et de changement de cap. L'Auto Union avec son moteur central à seize cylindres, copyright professeur Ferdinand Porsche, est tout simplement imbattable. Avec sept victoires, dont trois lors de Grands Prix, le jeune Bernd Rosemeyer à la carrière météorique se rend immortel. L'empire Mercedes réplique avec sa détermination légendaire. Le département Essais est complété par un service Courses autonome. Le directeur en est Rudolf Uhlenhaut, tout juste âgé de trente ans et depuis cinq ans chez Daimler-Benz, doué d'un talent absolument unique lui permettant de piloter une voiture de Grand Prix de façon aussi artistique que les vedettes engagées spécialement à cette fin. Il cravache et donne les éperons à la w 25 sur des milliers de kilomètres du Nürburgring.

Et son bilan est véritablement édifiant : la voiture a tendance à s'envoler même aux endroits les plus inhabituels, le châssis se tord dans le sens longitudinal, la direction transmet des chocs, la tenue de route est précaire. Uhlenhaut tient compte de ces conclusions lors de la

accompanied by huge power: a new 5.7-liter engine delivered 646 bhp. One horsepower only had to shoulder the weight of 1.16 kg (2.56 lb) of car. Of the ten Grands Prix, the W125 took five, finishing first and second twice (Germany and Italy) and one-two-three twice (Monaco and Switzerland). The race on the Avus in the capital of the Reich, and thus in the Reich's showcase, was a veritable pedal-to-metal affair won at an average speed of 261.7 kph (162.6 mph) by Hermann Lang in the streamlined Mercedes. The political implication was unmistakable: the system was paying homage to itself as it had in the Olympic Games of the previous year.

Yet again the AIACR had to step in to ensure that the product marketed by the Grand Prix sector – speed – did not get out of control. This time the chosen tool was the engine size: 3 liters for blown or 4.5 liters for unblown engines had to suffice to prevent excursions into the gray area beyond 300 kph (186 mph). In Spa, for example, Hermann Lang's car was clocked at 310 kph (193 mph) in 1937 on the descent before the Masta kink. Mercedes had taken the precaution of commissioning a 4.5-liter unblown engine from the Porsche design house, but it then opted for a blown power unit following encouraging results on the test rig. This time the preference was for a V12, as it was easier to control overheating problems than with an eight-cylinder. In its first season it achieved 450 bhp, and in 1939 30 bhp more. It is not surprising that Rudolf Uhlenhaut became hard of hearing over the years: the primeval scream of the 12-cylinder engine was blood-curdling. It was as loud as five of the ERAS which he used to drive, joked Mercedes driver Dick Seaman who won the XIth German Grand Prix at the Nürburgring on 23 July 1938 in the W154, on the same occasion that saw Manfred von Brauchitsch's car engulfed in a gasoline fire in the pits for a few dreadful seconds. The chassis was the same as that of the W125 apart from hydraulic shock absorbers whose hardness could be adjusted from the cockpit. The engine was canted so that the cardan shaft could pass through the left side of the cockpit. The driver sat to the right, almost 13 cm (5 in) lower than in the preceding model. This was the formula with which Mercedes won six races in 1938, four of them Grands Prix, and seven events in 1939, again including four Grands Prix. Hermann Lang was the 1939 European champion.

The career of the W154, a born winner, ended on a discordant and bad-tempered note when the Belgrade City Race, the last Grand Prix before the war, was won by the "Flying Mantuan" Tazio Nuvolari on 3 September 1939 in an Auto Union. Alfred Neubauer was livid when Manfred von Brauchitsch threw away his chances with some wild driving. And it led to a farce when the old warriors were called out of retirement for two non-formula races organized in Argentina in February 1951. The course design told against the silver-gray visitors right from the start. In addition, cement dust caused problems for the W154's sensitive engines, and so they only took second and third places in

1938 star team: von Brauchitsch, Seaman, Lang, Caracciola at the German Grand Prix.

Star-Aufgebot 1938: von Brauchitsch, Seaman, Lang, Caracciola beim Großen Preis von Deutschland.

Une belle brochette de pilotes pour 1938: von Brauchitsch, Seaman, Lang, Caracciola lors du Grand Prix d'Allemagne.

Kraft: 646 PS bringt ein neues Triebwerk mit 5,7 Litern Hubraum auf die Bremse. Eine Pferdestärke hat nur noch 1,16 Kilogramm Auto zu schultern. Von zehn Großen Preisen holt sich der W125 fünf, landet zwei Doppelerfolge (Deutschland und Italien) und zwei Dreifachsiege (Monaco und Schweiz). Zu einer wahren Vollgas-Messe mit einem Schnitt von 261,7 Stundenkilometern für den Sieger Hermann Lang im Stromlinien-Mercedes gerät das Rennen auf der Avus im Weichbild der Reichshauptstadt, gleichsam im Schaukasten des Reichs. Die politische Implikation ist unverkennbar: Da huldigt sich das System selbst – wie bei den Olympischen Spielen im Jahr zuvor.

Und wieder muss sich die AIACR darum kümmern, dass das Produkt nicht außer Kontrolle gerät, das die Grand-Prix-Branche vermarktet – Tempo. Diesmal rückt man dem Hubraum zu Leibe: drei Liter mit oder 4,5 Liter ohne Kompressor müssen genügen als Prophylaxe gegen Ausflüge in den Graubereich jenseits von 300. In Spa misst man zum Beispiel 1937 für den Wagen von Hermann Lang 310 Stundenkilometer auf dem Gefälle vor dem Masta-Schlängel. Vorsichtshalber hat Mercedes im Konstruktionsbüro Porsche einen 4,5-Liter Saugmotor in Auftrag gegeben, votiert wegen ermutigender Ergebnisse auf dem Prüfstand dann jedoch für ein aufgeladenes Triebwerk.

conception de la W125 et transforme en élève modèle la nouvelle monoplace, qui, comme il le désire, sous-vire légèrement et, quand elle flirte avec la limite, affiche un léger dérapage contrôlé. Son train avant est copié sur les modèles de série, les 500 K et 540 K. À l'arrière, il opte pour un essieu de Dion qui amortit en douceur mais avec des ressorts d'une certaine fermeté, contrairement à la philosophie pratiquée jusque-là. Le comportement amélioré va de pair avec une puissance généreuse : son nouveau moteur de 5,7 litres développe 646 ch au frein à rouleaux. Un cheval n'a plus qu'1,16 kg à mouvoir. Sur dix Grands Prix, la W125 en gagne cinq, signe deux doublés (en Allemagne et en Italie) et deux triplés (à Monaco et en Suisse). La course de l'Avus, dans la banlieue de la capitale du Reich, et simultanément une vitrine du Reich lui-même, est une véritable orgie de vitesse avec une moyenne de 261,7 km/h pour le vainqueur Hermann Lang au volant de la Mercedes aérodynamique. L'implication politique est incontestable : le système se célèbre lui-même – au même titre que lors des jeux Olympiques, un an auparavant.

Et, une fois de plus, l'AIACR doit veiller à ce que n'échappe pas au contrôle le produit que commercialise la branche des Grands Prix – la vitesse. C'est à la cylindrée que l'on s'attaque : 3 litres avec compresseur ou 4,5 litres sans compresseur doivent suffire comme prophylaxie contre les excursions dans la zone trouble au-delà des 300 km/h. À Spa en 1937, par exemple, on mesure une vitesse de 310 km/h dans la descente précédant les esses de Masta pour la voiture de Hermann Lang. À titre préventif, Mercedes a commandé au bureau d'études de Porsche un moteur atmosphérique de 4,5 litres. Mais, malgré les résultats encourageants au banc d'essais, elle opte cependant pour un moteur suralimenté. Cette fois-ci, on donne la préférence à un V12, qui permet de mieux maîtriser les problèmes thermiques qu'un huit-cylindres. À sa première saison, il développe 450 ch, et 30 ch de plus dès 1939. Il n'y a rien d'étonnant à ce que Rudolf Uhlenhaut finisse par devenir sourd au fil des années : le hurlement bestial du douze-cylindres vous brise les tympans. Dick Seaman, qui remporte le onzième Grand Prix d'Allemagne au Nürburgring au volant d'une W154, le 23 juillet 1938, alors que Manfred von Brauchitsch voit sa voiture brûler pendant de douloureuses secondes devant les stands, déclare que le V12 était aussi bruyante que les cinq ERA qu'il avait pilotées auparavant. Le châssis est identique à celui de la W125, hormis les amortisseurs hydrauliques dont la fermeté peut être réglée depuis le cockpit. Le moteur est monté en diagonale de façon que l'arbre de transmission puisse traverser le cockpit sur le côté gauche. Le conducteur est assis à droite, près de treize centimètres plus bas que dans l'ancien modèle. C'est la recette qui permet à Mercedes de remporter six courses en 1938, dont quatre Grands Prix, et sept manifestations en 1939, parmi lesquelles, de nouveau, quatre Grands Prix. Le champion d'Europe 1939 est Hermann Lang.

La carrière de la W154, un vainqueur né, se termine dans les malentendus et la cacophonie : la course sur le circuit

Poster to celebrate the triumph in the Swiss GP, 1939.
Das Plakat würdigt den Triumph beim Schweizer GP 1939.
L'affiche fête le triomphe remporté au GP de Suisse, 1939.

both races. However, the message delivered in a far-off land by their v12 engines about the great racing days of 12 years previously was just as piercing as ever. But only Buenos Aires' sizable German colony really understood it.

The situation was very similar in another distant land on 15 May 1939, the date announced by the Italian sports authorities for the Tripoli Grand Prix for racing cars of up to 1.5 liters. This engine formula was a clear foul committed against the team from Stuttgart. Libya was an Italian colony, and the Italians wanted the field to themselves with their 1.5-liter cars. No serious competition could be expected from the few Englishmen who were prepared to make the trip to the fast desert track at El Mehalla.

But then followed the "Tripoli miracle" as Alfred Neubauer called it in his autobiography *Männer, Frauen und Motoren* (Men, Women and Engines). Mercedes accepted the challenge and just eight months later pulled the w165 from the hat with a compact v8, whose cylinder banks were 90 degrees offset, displacement: 1.5 liters, output: 254 bhp. A short road test at Hockenheim did not reveal any shortcomings, on the contrary the car "seemed capable of moving forwards, sideways and probably backwards too without any problems," mused the British racing expert Laurence Pomeroy. The hopelessly estranged drivers Rudolf Caracciola and Hermann Lang mainly moved it forwards, and at high speed, and Lang won at an average speed of 197.8 kph (122.9 mph) ahead of his illustrious teammate while the track temperature measured 52°C (126°F). 28 Italian, French and English racing cars either crashed out or otherwise failed to finish the race.

Diesmal gibt man einem v12 den Vorzug, denn thermische Probleme lassen sich besser in den Griff bekommen als an einem Achtzylinder. Schon in seiner ersten Saison leistet er 450 PS, 1939 bereits 30 PS mehr. Kein Wunder, dass Rudolf Uhlenhaut mit den Jahren schwerhörig wird: Der Urschrei des Zwölfzylinders ist markerschütternd. So laut sei er gewesen wie fünf der ERA, die er früher gefahren habe, scherzt Mercedes-Pilot Dick Seaman, der am 23. Juli 1938 mit dem w154 den XI. Großen Preis von Deutschland auf dem Nürburgring gewinnt, während Manfred von Brauchitschs Fahrzeug vor den Boxen für qualvolle Sekunden von einem Benzinfeuer flambiert wird. Das Chassis gleicht dem des w125, abgesehen von hydraulischen Dämpfern, deren Härte vom Cockpit aus zu regulieren ist. Die Maschine ist schräg eingebaut, so dass die Kardanwelle das Cockpit links durchqueren kann. Der Fahrer sitzt rechts daneben, fast 13 Zentimeter tiefer als im Vorgängermodell. Das ist das Rezept, mit dem Mercedes 1938 sechs Rennen gewinnt, davon vier Große Preise, 1939 sieben Veranstaltungen, unter ihnen wiederum vier Grand Prix. Europameister 1939 ist Hermann Lang.

Die Karriere des w154, eines geborenen Siegers, endet in Missklang und Unmut: Das Stadtrennen in Belgrad am 3. September 1939, den letzten Großen Preis vor dem Weltkrieg, gewinnt der »fliegende Mantuaner« Tazio Nuvolari auf Auto Union. Alfred Neubauer schimpft wie ein Rohrspatz, weil Manfred von Brauchitsch in wüster Fahrt alles verspielt hat. Und sie mündet in einer Farce: Für zwei formelfreie Rennen in Argentinien im Februar 1951 werden die alten Kämpen reaktiviert. Aber die Piste wurde von vornherein gegen die silbergrauen Besucher aus Übersee geplant. Überdies macht Zementstaub den sensiblen Triebwerken der w154 zu schaffen: Sie belegen zweimal den zweiten und dritten Platz. Ungebrochen aber ist das Donnerwort, mit dem ihre v12 von der guten alten Zeit zwölf Jahre zuvor künden – in einem fernen Land. Und so recht versteht sie nur die umfangreiche deutsche Kolonie von Buenos Aires.

Ganz ähnlich ist die Ausgangslage am 15. Mai 1939 in einem anderen fernen Land: Die italienische Sportbehörde hat den Grand Prix von Tripolis zu diesem Termin für Rennwagen bis 1,5 Liter ausgeschrieben. Das ist ein klares Foul gegen das Team aus Stuttgart. Libyen ist italienische Kolonie, die Italiener möchten mit ihren Anderthalblitern unter sich sein. Von den paar Engländern, die die Exkursion zu der schnellen Wüstenpiste El Mehalla nicht scheuen, ist keine ernsthafte Konkurrenz zu erwarten.

Dann aber nimmt seinen Lauf, was Alfred Neubauer in seiner Autobiographie *Männer, Frauen und Motoren* das »Wunder von Tripolis« nennt. Mercedes stellt sich der Herausforderung und zaubert in nur acht Monaten den w165 aus dem Hut mit einem kompakten v8, dessen Zylinderbänke sich im Winkel von 90 Grad auftun, Hubraum: 1,5 Liter, Leistung: 254 PS. Ein kurzer Funktionstest in Hockenheim deckt keinerlei Blößen auf, im Gegenteil: »Es schien, als ob man ihn ungestraft vorwärts, seitwärts

urbain de Belgrade, le 3 septembre 1939, le dernier Grand Prix avant la guerre mondiale, est remporté par le « Mantouais volant » Tazio Nuvolari, sur Auto Union. Alfred Neubauer est rouge de fureur parce que Manfred von Brauchitsch a gâché toutes ses chances par sa conduite échevelée. Et cette carrière se termine par une farce : les bons vieux bolides sont réactivés pour deux courses de formule libre en Argentine, en février 1951. Mais le circuit avait été tracé d'emblée pour désavantager les bolides gris argentés d'outre-mer. En outre, la poussière de ciment étouffe les sensibles moteurs de la w154 : elle termine à deux reprises aux deuxième et troisième rangs. Rien de changé, par contre, au bruit de tonnerre que font résonner leurs v12 comme au bon vieux temps, douze ans auparavant – dans un pays étranger. Et c'est ainsi que seule la riche colonie allemande de Buenos Aires les comprend vraiment bien.

La situation initiale le 15 mai 1939, dans un autre pays étranger, est tout à fait similaire : les autorités sportives italiennes ont organisé le Grand Prix de Tripoli de ce jour-là pour les voitures de course jusqu'à 1,5 litre de cylindrée. C'est un véritable coup de poignard dans le dos de l'écurie de Stuttgart. La Libye est une colonie italienne et les Italiens souhaitent être entre eux avec leurs voitures de 1500 cm³. Il ne faut, en effet, pas s'attendre à une concurrence sérieuse de la part de quelques Anglais qui n'ont pas hésité à faire le long voyage jusqu'au rapide circuit désertique d'El Mehalla.

C'est alors que prend son cours ce que, dans son autobiographie *Männer, Frauen und Motoren* (Hommes, femmes et moteurs), Alfred Neubauer nomme le « miracle de Tripoli ». Mercedes relève le défi et sort de son chapeau, en huit mois seulement, la w165 et son compact v8 à 90°, d'une cylindrée de 1,5 litre et d'une puissance de 254 ch. Un bref essai à Hockenheim ne dévoile aucune maladie de jeunesse, bien au contraire : « On a l'impression qu'on aurait pu la faire rouler en avant, sur le côté et, vraisemblablement aussi, en arrière sans la moindre punition », se perd en conjectures le pape de la compétition automobile britannique, Laurence Pomeroy. Ennemis jurés bien que coéquipiers, Rudolf Caracciola et Hermann Lang la déplacent surtout en avant, et plutôt vite : Lang gagne à une moyenne de 197,8 km/h devant son illustre équipier malgré une température au sol de 52°C. Vingt-huit voitures de courses italiennes, françaises et anglaises sont battues à plate couture ou ne rallient même pas l'arrivée.

Le programme de mondanités, lui non plus, ne laisse rien à désirer : le gouverneur général Italo Balbo a préparé pour ses rapides invités un véritable festin avec, comme toujours, des excursions dans l'intérieur du pays, de luxueuses réceptions et un gala des vainqueurs au superlatif.

Tout cela est conçu, à proprement parler comme un cadre pour les héros italiens. Or, à ce point de vue, il n'a pas de très bonnes cartes : depuis 1935, Mercedes-Benz a pris un abonnement pour la première place en Libye, à l'exception de 1936, année durant laquelle Achille Varzi, dans le duel interne à son écurie contre Hans Stuck, a

And the occasion boasted all the trimmings too. Governor-general Italo Balbo laid on a veritable land of milk and honey for his high-speed guests, consisting as always of excursions up-country, lavish receptions, and a dazzling victory celebration.

This was all actually intended to fête Italian heroes. However, things did not turn out as planned. Mercedes-Benz had exercised its option on the number one spot in Libya every year since 1935, with the exception of 1936 when Achille Varzi got the nose of his Auto Union ahead of teammate Hans Stuck. Caracciola won once, and Hermann Lang three times in succession. For the w165, meanwhile, the Tripoli miracle remained a great episode, a footnote to a glorious past. The two race cars were soon retired and are still on display in the museum today.

und wahrscheinlich auch rückwärts bewegen konnte«, mutmaßt der britische Rennsport-Kundige Laurence Pomeroy. Die unter sich heillos zerstrittene Piloten-Riege Rudolf Caracciola und Hermann Lang bewegt ihn vor allem vorwärts, und zwar zügig: Lang siegt mit einem Schnitt von 197,8 Stundenkilometern vor seinem illustren Stallgefährten bei einer Bodentemperatur von 52 Grad. 28 italienische, französische und englische Rennwagen bleiben abgeschlagen oder havariert auf der Strecke.

Auch das Drumherum stimmt: Generalgouverneur Italo Balbo bereitet seinen schnellen Gästen ein wahres Schlaraffenland, wie immer mit Ausflügen ins Landesinnere, üppigen Empfängen und einer Siegerehrung der Superlative.

All das ist eigentlich als Rahmen um italienische Helden herum gedacht. Aber in dieser Hinsicht sieht es ganz schlecht aus: Seit 1935 hält Mercedes-Benz Platz eins in Libyen in Erbpacht, mit Ausnahme von 1936, als Achille Varzi im stallinternen Duell gegen Hans Stuck die Nase seines Auto Union vorn hat. Einmal gewinnt Caracciola, dreimal hintereinander Hermann Lang. Für den w165 indes bleibt das Wunder von Tripolis Episode, Fußnote unter glorreicher Vergangenheit. Die beiden Einsatzwagen wandern umgehend aufs Altenteil und sind noch heute im Besitz des Museums.

Lift-off: Hermann Lang really flying in the Belgrade City Race on 3 September 1939.

Flugeinlage: Hermann Lang hebt ab beim Stadtrennen von Belgrad am 3. September 1939.

Rase-mottes : Hermann Lang s'envole lors de la course sur le circuit urbain de Belgrade, le 3 septembre 1939.

rallié le premier la ligne d'arrivée avec son Auto Union. Caracciola gagne une fois et Hermann Lang, trois fois consécutives. Pour la w165, par contre, le miracle de Tripoli n'aura été qu'un épisode, une note en bas de page dans un passé glorieux. Les deux voitures de course sont envoyées immédiatement à la retraite et se trouvent aujourd'hui dans la collection du musée.

Renaissance of a legend: the triumphal march of the injection engines 1952–1955

Daimler-Benz's resumption of activities after the zero hour of 1945 can be compared with driving a car: the company looked firmly forward, but without losing sight of what was going on in the rear-view mirror. This applied to the marque's philosophy. It applied to the products, once innovative, but now with a tendency towards the conservative, though still in keeping with their time. It applied to the sport: what seemed to be a vision of the future just before the Second World War brought everything to a halt, should not be regarded as outmoded in 1951. And so it was decided at the board of management meeting on 15 June to build five more w165s, the sensation of Tripoli in 1939.

However, this decision was subsequently circumvented and finally rejected. After all, the design was 12 years old, new makes such as Ferrari had appeared on the scene, and furthermore the 1.5-liter blown (or 4.5-liter unblown) formula was due to expire at the end of the 1951 season. Building a new single-seater would tie up too many resources which were needed more urgently elsewhere. A trip into new

Renaissance eines Mythos: Siegeszug der Einspritzmotoren 1952–1955

Der Neubeginn nach der Stunde Null von 1945 vollzieht sich bei Daimler-Benz so, wie man Auto fahren sollte: Den Blick fest nach vorn, ohne die Botschaft des Rückspiegels aus den Augen zu verlieren. Das gilt für die Markenphilosophie. Das gilt für die Produkte, innovativ einst, jetzt eher konservativ, aber noch keineswegs unzeitgemäß. Das gilt für den Sport: Was in die Zukunft wies, unmittelbar bevor der Zweite Weltkrieg alles lahmlegte, dürfte 1951 nicht zum alten Eisen gehören. Und so beschließt man auf der Vorstandssitzung vom 15. Juni, den w165 noch einmal in fünf Exemplaren aufzulegen, die Sensation von Tripolis 1939.

Aber dann wird der Beschluss unterlaufen und schließlich verworfen: Das Konzept des Wagens ist eben doch zwölf Jahre alt, neue Marken wie Ferrari sind auf der Bildfläche erschienen, überdies läuft die Formel 1,5 Liter mit Kompressor (oder 4,5 Liter ohne) mit dem Ende der Saison 1951 aus. Einen neuen Monoposto zu bauen würde zu viele Kräfte binden, die anderswo dringender benötigt werden. Weniger aufwändig wäre ein Ausflug in Neuland. Könnte man nicht,

Renaissance d'un mythe : le triomphe des moteurs à injection 1952–1955

Le nouveau départ, en 1945, s'effectue, chez Daimler-Benz, comme le fait tout bon conducteur au moment de démarrer : le regard résolument tourné vers l'avant sans perdre de vue pour autant ce qui se passe dans le rétroviseur. Cela vaut pour la philosophie de la marque. Cela vaut pour les produits, jadis novateurs, maintenant plutôt conservateurs, mais absolument pas démodés. Et cela vaut pour le sport : ce qui annonçait l'avenir avant que la Seconde Guerre mondiale ne paralyse tout ne devait pas être mis au placard en 1951. Et c'est ainsi que, lors de la réunion du Directoire du 15 juin, on décide de produire à nouveau cinq exemplaires de la w165, la sensation de Tripoli en 1939.

Mais la décision n'est pas respectée et, finalement, elle est abandonnée : il a fallu admettre que le concept de la voiture avait tout de même déjà douze ans, que de nouvelles marques comme Ferrari étaient apparues sur la scène de la compétition et que, en outre, la formule 1,5 litre à compresseur (ou 4,5 litres sans compresseur) arrivait à expiration à la fin de la saison 1951. La construction d'une

territory would be less costly. Would it not be possible, mused the technical director Fritz Nallinger, to create a sports car from the Mercedes 300, the star of the Frankfurt Motor Show in April of that year? The 300 SL (standing for Sport, Light) was on the track within just nine months under project manager Rudolf Uhlenhaut. The complete drive train came from the 300 model, together with the independent front suspension on parallel wishbones and the low-slung swing axle at the rear, a Mercedes standard right up to 1968. The power unit was fed by 3 Solex downcraft carburetors. It delivered 175 bhp, 60 more than the solid roadgoing saloon, and was canted at an angle of 50 degrees to the left in the multi-tubular spaceframe chassis. Keeping this torsion-resistant filigree structure flat involved an unorthodox solution to problem of allowing access to the coupé. Gullwing doors were chosen, consisting of the windows and part of the roof and, from Le Mans onwards, also of a section from the flanks of the car. This sytem was used later in the 300 SL production sports car of 1954.

A completely naked chassis had been spotted in November 1951 driving at high speed on the Solitude test track, and on 12 March 1952 the finished car was presented to the press. "We are opening a small window on the racing scene," said Fritz Nallinger modestly.

And how: the 300 SL came, saw – and conquered. Admittedly, not immediately, but in due course all the more lastingly. At the 19th Mille Miglia on 2 May, Karl Kling, a newcomer to the team though already 41 years old, finished second behind local hero Giovanni Bracco in the Ferrari 250 s. At the Grand Prix de Berne, Kling won ahead of his team-mates Hermann Lang and Fritz Rieß. But the race also stays in the memory as the swan-song of the great Rudolf Caracciola whose red 300 SL went off the track at the Forsthaus bend on the ominous 13th lap and demolished a tree, condemning him to spend the next two years in a wheelchair. Le Mans saw a one-two for Lang/Rieß and Theo Helfrich/Helmut Niedermayr, obviously a surprise result as the band at the victory celebration had not brought the music for the German national anthem with them. At the main sports-car race at the Nürburgring meeting the Mercedes team took the first three places with 300 SL roadsters, Lang winning ahead of Kling and Rieß.

Proof that the 300 SL could be both a sprinter and a long-distance runner was provided in particular by the IIIrd Carrera Panamericana in Mexico starting on 19 November 1952. The race was a marathon ordeal run over 3,113 km (1,935 miles) through the swamps of the south, tropical jungles, sweltering marshes by the Pacific coast, up into the desolate wasteland of the Sierra Madre, over the fertile high plateau of Mexico City, past extinct volcanoes, cities full of skyscrapers, and deprived Indian settlements. It lasted five days and covered eight stages. The race was won by Karl Kling, although after only 300 km (186 miles) a vulture taking off rather lazily went through the windscreen into the cockpit, hitting co-driver Hans Klenk smack in the face. Hermann Lang finished second.

sinniert der technische Direktor Fritz Nallinger, aus dem Mercedes 300, Star der Frankfurter Autoausstellung im April jenes Jahres, einen Sportwagen sublimieren? In nur neun Monaten entsteht der 300 SL (für Sport, Leicht) unter dem Projektleiter Rudolf Uhlenhaut. Der komplette Antriebsstrang stammt vom Modell 300, dazu die Einzelradaufhängung vorn an Parallelquerlenkern und die tief angesetzte Pendelachse hinten, Mercedes-Standard noch bis 1968. Das Triebwerk, gespeist von drei Solex-Fallstrom-Vergasern, gibt 175 PS ab, 60 mehr als in der behäbigen Staatslimousine, und ist im Winkel von 50 Grad nach links geneigt in den Gitterrohrrahmen eingelassen. Dass man dieses verwindungssteife Filigranwerk flach halten möchte, bedingt eine unorthodoxe Lösung für den Zutritt zum Coupé: via Flügeltüren, bestehend aus den Fenstern und einem Teil des Dachs und, ab Le Mans, zusätzlich einem Ausschnitt aus den Flanken – wie später am Seriensportwagen 300 SL von 1954.

Bereits im November 1951 wird ein splitternacktes Chassis in zügiger Fahrt auf der Solitude gesichtet, am 12. März 1952 das komplette Auto der Presse präsentiert. »Wir öffnen ein Fensterchen zur Rennszene hin«, sagt Fritz Nallinger bescheiden.

Und wie: Der 300 SL kommt, sieht – und siegt zwar nicht sofort, dann dafür aber umso nachhaltiger. Auf der 19. Mille Miglia am 2. Mai wird Karl Kling, neu im Team, aber schon 41 Jahre alt, zweiter hinter Lokalheros Giovanni Bracco auf dem Ferrari 250 s. Beim Großen Preis von Bern gewinnt Kling vor seinen Teamgefährten Hermann Lang und Fritz Rieß. Aber das Rennen haftet auch im Gedächtnis als Schwanengesang des großen Rudolf Caracciola, der in der ominösen 13. Runde mit seinem roten 300 SL in der Forsthauskurve von der Bahn abkommt, einen Baum fällt und die beiden nächsten Jahre im Rollstuhl verbringen muss. In Le Mans gibt es einen Doppelerfolg für Lang/Rieß und Theo Helfrich/Helmut Niedermayr, offenbar überraschend, denn die Kapelle hat für die Siegerehrung die Noten der deutschen Nationalhymne nicht mitgebracht. Beim Großen Jubiläumspreis für Sportwagen auf dem Nürburgring ist die Mercedes-Riege mit dem 300 SL Roadster auf den ersten drei Plätzen unter sich, Lang vor Kling und Rieß.

Dass der 300 SL ein Stürmer und ein Steher sein kann, zeigt sich vor allem bei der III. Carrera Panamericana in Mexiko vom 19. November 1952 an, einem Marathon und Martyrium über 3113 Kilometer durch die Fiebersümpfe des Südens, tropische Urwälder, glutkochende Niederungen am Pazifik, bergauf in die trostlose Öde der Sierra Madre, über die fruchtbare Hochebene von Mexico City, vorbei an erloschenen Vulkanen, Städten voller Wolkenkratzer und ärmlichen Indiosiedlungen, in fünf Tagen und acht Etappen. Karl Kling gewinnt, obwohl nach den ersten 300 Kilometern ein schwerfällig aufflatternder Aasgeier durch die zersplitternde Scheibe ins Cockpit eindringt, mitten ins Gesicht von Beifahrer Hans Klenk. Hermann Lang wird zweiter. Die Werbewirkung des mexikanischen Abenteuers ist enorm, vor allem auf dem amerikanischen Kontinent.

nouvelle monoplace aurait concentré beaucoup trop d'énergies, des énergies nécessaires de façon impérieuse ailleurs. Il serait moins onéreux de se lancer dans un domaine mieux connu. Ne pourrait-on pas, s'est en effet demandé le directeur technique Fritz Nallinger, extrapoler une voiture de sport à partir de la Mercedes 300, la vedette du Salon de l'Automobile de Francfort d'avril de la même année ? Et c'est ainsi qu'en seulement neuf mois naît la 300 SL (pour Sport, Légère), sous la férule de Rudolf Uhlenhaut comme directeur de projet. Toute la chaîne cinématique au grand complet provient de la 300 dont on reprend également la suspension à roues indépendantes à l'avant avec bras transversaux parallèles et l'essieu oscillant arrière surbaissé, qui fut encore la norme chez Mercedes jusqu'en 1968. Alimenté par trois carburateurs Solex inversés, le moteur développe 175 ch, soit 60 de plus que dans les lourdes limousines de représentation, et est inséré dans le châssis tubulaire en étant incliné de 50 degrés vers la gauche. Les ingénieurs veulent que cette structure filigrane d'une très grande rigidité torsionnelle soit la plus basse possible, ce qui impose une solution peu orthodoxe pour l'accès au coupé : par des portes en ailes de papillon se composant de la fenêtre et d'une partie du toit ainsi que, à partir du Mans, d'une découpe supplémentaire dans les flancs – comme, plus tard, pour la voiture de sport de série 300 SL de 1954.

Dès novembre 1951, des passants voient un châssis non carrossé tourner à bride abattue sur le circuit de Solitude et, le 12 mars 1952, la voiture terminée est présentée à la presse. « Nous ouvrons une petite fenêtre sur les milieux de la compétition », déclare modestement Fritz Nallinger.

Et comment ! La 300 SL arrive, regarde – et gagne. Certes pas immédiatement, mais, en revanche, d'autant plus durablement. Pour les 19e Mille Miglia, le 2 mai, Karl Kling, un néophyte dans l'écurie bien que déjà âgé de 41 ans, termine deuxième derrière le régional de l'étape, le héros Giovanni Bracco, sur Ferrari 250 s. Lors du Grand Prix de Berne, Kling gagne devant ses coéquipiers Hermann Lang et Fritz Riess. Mais la course est gravée dans les mémoires par le grave accident du grand Rudolf Caracciola qui donne son chant du cygne lorsque, au cours du fatal 13e tour, il sort de la route avec sa 300 SL rouge dans le virage de la maison forestière, fauche un arbre et doit passer les deux années suivantes dans un fauteuil roulant. Au Mans, Mercedes signe un doublé avec Lang/Riess et Theo Helfrich/ Helmut Niedermayr, victoire avec laquelle personne n'avait apparemment compté puisque l'orchestre n'avait même pas amené avec lui la partition de l'hymne national allemand pour la remise des coupes. Lors du Grand Prix anniversaire pour voitures de sport, sur le Nürburgring, l'écurie Mercedes monopolise les trois premières places avec la 300 SL Roadster : dans l'ordre, Lang devant Kling et Riess.

Ses qualités de sprinter, mais peut aussi être de coureur d'endurance, la 300 SL les prouve surtout lors de la IIIe Carrera Panamericana, au Mexique, le 19 novembre 1952 : un marathon et calvaire de 3113 kilomètres à travers les marais

The publicity impact of the Mexican adventure was enormous, particularly on the American continent.

4 July 1954 became a key date for the German sporting community, though the arenas in which the achievements took place were in neighboring countries. In Berne the national football team won the World Cup, while in Reims Daimler-Benz AG took to the track for its first post-war Grand Prix – in accordance with the new 2.5-liter formula. The date was indeed symbolic – precisely 40 years earlier Daimler drivers Christian Lautenschlager, Louis Wagner, and Otto Salzer had been traditionally crowned with laurel leaves for their one-two-three in the French Grand Prix in their Mercedes 18/100s.

The team was, of course, conscious of its duty to live up to the fame of the earlier victory, and at first it looked as though history really would repeat itself. 22 cars lined up for the start, with 61 laps ahead of them over a total of 506 km (314 miles). After 100 km (62 miles) the three fully enclosed Mercedes W 196s were in the lead, flashing down the straights at up to 262 kph (163 mph). At the front Karl Kling was involved in a duel to the finish with the great Juan Manuel Fangio and he probably felt that he could match the maestro. But the Argentinian won by one-tenth of a second. Hans Herrmann, however, who set the fastest lap, dropped out with a damaged fuel tank. Additional tanks had been made in Untertürkheim on the Friday night, and Rudolf Uhlenhaut had personally delivered them to the Champagne region, adopting in the process a very liberal interpretation of all the speed limits en route. Thus no refueling stop was needed, no tires had to be changed, the bonnets remained closed. Fangio received 120,000 marks in prize money, Kling 60,000 marks. But the signal sent out by this event was priceless.

In a sense, the idea behind the 300 SL had been taken to its logical conclusion in the abstraction of the W 196 formula car. It too was based on a multi-tubular spaceframe, weighing only 36 kg (79 lb), but 30 per cent stiffer than in the sports car. Its powerplant was also canted (at an angle of 60 degrees), so that the front end and the center of gravity were low. With regard to the timing gear, designer Hans Gassmann used an idea which came to him during a tram journey in Stuttgart: the inlet and outlet valves were operated desmodromically, i.e., via two cams. The best drivers had also been engaged. Apart from the Reims drivers, Hermann Lang also saw service in the cockpit of the W 196, though only once, the last time, at the familiar Nürburgring. Fangio, who had driven for Maserati in 1953 and in the early part of the 1954 season, only gradually gave into Alfred Neubauer's wooing. But in the end the old fox knew how to bring the superstar round to his way of thinking with all kinds of gifts and tokens.

As in 1951, the British Grand Prix was won by Fangio's compatriot Froilán González in a Ferrari. The W 196 in its original streamlined form proved to be the wrong car for this race, simply because the drivers could not line up exactly on the gasoline drums which marked out the course

Victory for Karl Kling/Hans Klenk at the III. Carrera Panamericana in 1952. The windscreen is protected by bars after the incident with the vulture.

Sieg für Karl Kling/Hans Klenk bei der III. Carrera Panamericana 1952. Die Windschutzscheibe ist nach der Geier-Episode hinter Gittern.

Victoire pour Karl Kling/Hans Klenk à la IIIe Carrera Panamericana de 1952. Après l'anecdote du vautour, le pare-brise est protégé par de petits barreaux.

Zum Schlüsseltag für den deutschen Sport wird der 4. Juli 1954, nur dass sich die Schauplätze jeweils in Anrainerstaaten finden. In Bern holt sich die Nationalelf die Fußballweltmeisterschaft, in Reims tritt die Daimler-Benz AG zu ihrem ersten Grand Prix nach dem Krieg an – nach der neuen 2,5-Liter-Formel. Das Datum ist fürwahr symbolträchtig: Vor genau 40 Jahren wurden die Stirnen der Daimler-Lenker Christian Lautenschlager, Louis Wagner und Otto Salzer für ihren Tripel-Triumph mit dem Mercedes 18/100 beim Großen Preis von Frankreich nach antikischer Sitte mit Lorbeer umkränzt.

Natürlich verpflichtet der Ruhm der frühen Jahre, und zunächst scheint es, als sei Geschichte in der Tat wiederholbar. 22 Wagen sind am Start, 61 Runden zu fahren über insgesamt 506 Kilometer. Nach 100 Kilometern sind die drei voll verkleideten Mercedes W 196 vorn, huschen die Geraden mit bis zu 262 Stundenkilometern herunter. An der Spitze liefert Karl Kling dem großen Juan Manuel Fangio ein Gefecht bis aufs Messer, gelangt wohl auch zu der Überzeugung, er könne es dem Maestro gleichtun. Der Argentinier gewinnt mit einer Zehntelsekunde Vorsprung, Hans Herrmann jedoch, der die schnellste Runde gefahren ist, scheidet wegen eines Schadens am Tank aus. Noch in der Nacht vom Freitag auf den Samstag wurden in Untertürkheim Zusatzbehälter angefertigt. Rudolf Uhlenhaut hat sie als Eilkurier persönlich ins Champagnerland spediert, in freier Interpretation sämtlicher Geschwindigkeitsbegrenzungen. So kommt man ohne Tankhalt aus, kein Reifen muss gewechselt werden, alle Hauben bleiben geschlossen. Fangio erhält 120 000, Kling 60 000 Mark Preisgeld. Unbezahlbar aber ist die Signalwirkung des Ereignisses.

Mit dem W 196 wird gewissermaßen die Idee hinter dem 300 SL auf die Spitze getrieben bis hinein in die Abstraktion des Formelautos. Auch sein Rückgrat bildet

du Sud, les forêts vierges tropicales, la chaleur torride des vallées le long du Pacifique, dans les lacets du sinistre désert de la sierra Madre, à travers le fertile haut plateau de Mexico City, le long de volcans éteints, de villes pleines de gratte-ciel et de misérables bidonvilles peuplés d'Indiens, en cinq jours et huit étapes. Karl Kling gagne bien qu'après les premiers 300 kilomètres, un vautour volant trop bas ait pénétré dans le cockpit après avoir fait voler en éclats le pare-brise, frappant en plein visage son coéquipier Hans Klenk. Hermann Lang termine deuxième. L'effet médiatique de l'aventure mexicaine est énorme, notamment sur le continent américain.

Le 4 juillet 1954 entrera dans l'histoire comme journée à marquer d'une pierre blanche pour le sport allemand, à cela près que les théâtres se trouvent respectivement dans des pays contigus. À Berne, l'équipe nationale de football remporte la coupe du monde et, à Reims, la Daimler-Benz AG s'aligne pour son premier Grand Prix de l'aprèsguerre – selon la nouvelle formule 2,5 litres. Cette date a en effet une portée symbolique : il y a exactement quarante ans, les fronts des pilotes Daimler Christian Lautenschlager, Louis Wagner et Otto Salzer furent ceints de lauriers selon une coutume antique pour leur triomphal triplé avec la Mercedes 18/100 lors du Grand Prix de France 1914.

Naturellement, la gloire des années passées oblige, pourtant au premier abord, il semble que l'histoire puisse réellement bégayer. Vingt-deux voitures s'alignent au départ pour couvrir 61 tours de circuit, soit un total de 506 km. Au bout de cent kilomètres, les trois Mercedes W 196 complètement carénées sont en tête et dévalent les lignes droites à une vitesse qui atteint jusqu'à 262 km/h. En tête, Karl Kling se bat le couteau entre les dents contre le grand Juan Manuel Fangio et parvient même à se convaincre qu'il pourrait être l'égal du maître. Mais c'est pourtant l'Argentin qui gagne avec un dixième de seconde d'avance alors que Hans Herrmann, qui a signé le meilleur tour en course, doit abandonner sur fuite de réservoir. Durant la nuit du vendredi au samedi, encore, des réservoirs supplémentaires avaient été fabriqués à Untertürkheim et Rudolf Uhlenhaut faisant office de coursier express les avait transportés personnellement au pays du champagne au mépris le plus total de toutes les limitations de vitesse. Ainsi put-on couvrir la distance sans devoir ravitailler et sans changer les pneus, tous les capots restant fermés. Fangio se voit remettre 120 000 marks de récompense et Karl Kling, 60 000 marks. Mais l'effet publicitaire de l'événement est d'une tout autre ampleur que la valeur de l'argent.

Avec la W 196, on pousse en quelque sorte au paroxysme la philosophie de la 300 SL, jusqu'à l'abstraction de la monoplace. Elle aussi comporte un filigrane châssis tubulaire pesant seulement 36 kg, mais de 30 % plus rigide que celui de la voiture de sport. Son moteur est également monté incliné (selon un angle de 60 degrés) pour réduire le maître couple et abaisser le plus possible le centre de gravité. Pour la commande des soupapes, l'ingénieur Hans Gassmann a eu une idée géniale en se rendant à son bureau

The start of the 1954 French Grand Prix in Reims.
Next to the Mercedes is Alberto Ascari in the Maserati.

Start zum Grand Prix de France in Reims 1954.
Neben den beiden Mercedes Alberto Ascari auf Maserati.

Départ du Grand Prix de France à Reims en 1954.
À côté des deux Mercedes, Alberto Ascari sur Maserati.

on the airfield at Silverstone. Then, however, Fangio heaped victory upon victory – at the Nürburgring where the single-seater was first available with open wheels, at the Bremsgarten course in Berne, and at Monza. In the final race in Pedralbes not far from Barcelona, his w196 scraped across the line in only third place, crippled by an oil leak and an overheating engine. When the points were totaled up at the end of the season, it emerged that Fangio was champion for the second time, following his first win in 1951. Karl Kling took advantage of the situation and won the Avus Race, which was not part of the Grand Prix circus, at an average speed of 213.5 kph (132.6 mph).

During the winter break, which scarcely merited its name even then, work concentrated on the running gear. A new racing tire, developed in November and December 1954 by Continental, played its part in increasing the possible transverse acceleration from a moderate 0.7 g to 1 g. Alfred Neubauer's shopping list for drivers was headed by the young Englishman Stirling Moss. He hesitated initially; he did not like the idea of being the clear number two behind Fangio. Nonetheless, he found the contract that he was offered "fantastic." On 3 December Moss drove a Mercedes 220 and then a production 300 SL to get to know the Hockenheim course, and then he climbed into the w196 without further ado to demonstrate his genius, and on a wet track at that.

The Briton's first race was in the inferno of the Argentinian Grand Prix on 16 January. The track was blistering in the searing heat of that Sunday. Moss stopped. When he fainted, he was pulled from the car and taken off to hospital, regardless of his protests. Once there, he was able to make himself understood in English, returned to the track with a police escort, took over Hans Herrmann's car and still finished fourth. The race was won by Fangio, whom no one had considered capable of such an ascetic performance. He was the only driver to last the full three

Simply the best: Juan Manuel Fangio (1911–1995)

»Der Mann ist wie ein Magnet. Sobald er einen Raum betritt, auch voller Leute, ist ihm alles zugeordnet«, sagt Phil Hill, Weltmeister von 1961, und seine tiefe und erdige Stimme wird ganz spröde vor lauter Ehrfurcht. Das ist 1991 im Londoner Dorchester Hotel, und man feiert in großem Stil Juan Manuel Fangios 80. Geburtstag, und der Argentinier kommt herein, und es ist wirklich so. Vermutlich liegt darin das Geheimnis hinter seiner Größe: Autorität, gegenüber sich selbst, gegenüber anderen. Zwei Bilder des Schweizer Fotografen Yves Debraine, 1957 aufgenommen beim Großen Preis von Deutschland an der gleichen Stelle des Nürburgrings, berichten von einem Drama: Herausforderer Mike Hawthorn, knabenhaft verloren im Cockpit des Ferrari, voll Angst vor der eigenen Courage, eher Passagier als Pilot, und dann Fangio, gesammelt und doch eiskalt gelassen, im Gesicht den unerbittlichen Willen zum Sieg. Zuchtmeister und Zögling... Natürlich ist das auch das Generationenkonflikt, der da ausgefochten wird. »Jugend stürmt gegen Fangio«, lautet das Motto, das man für den deutschen Grand Prix 1956 ausgegeben hat. Aber dieser Mittvierziger schlägt sie alle, Hawthorn und Stirling Moss, Eugenio Castellotti und Luigi Musso, Peter Collins und Tony Brooks, ein Übervater von einschüchternder Statur. Bis ihm 1958 auf der endlos langen Zielgeraden von Reims, wo man viel Zeit hat zum Nachdenken, Bedenken kommen: Was machst du eigentlich? Du hast doch alles erreicht, und mehr. Da habe er sich entschlossen aufzuhören, jetzt und hier – diesen Einblick in sein sonst sorgfältig umfriedetes Innenleben eröffnet er der überraschten Geburtstagsparty im Dorchester. Und die Jugend von damals? Im Auto gestorben, wie Castellotti, Musso, Collins und Hawthorn. Oder auch schon ein bisschen alt und ein bisschen grau, wie Brooks und Stirling Moss. »Fangio«, lächelt der und zuckt mit den Achseln, »war unschlagbar.« Dass dieser Mann seinen eigenen Blütentraum zerstört hat, selber einmal Weltmeister zu werden, trägt er ohne Groll.

ein filigranes Gitterwerk, nur 36 Kilogramm schwer, aber um 30 Prozent steifer als im Sportwagen. Sein Triebwerk wird schräg eingebaut (im Winkel von 60 Grad), damit die Frontfläche niedrig und der Schwerpunkt tief ist. Was die Ventilsteuerung anbelangt, so hat sich Konstrukteur Hans Gassmann während einer Fahrt in der Stuttgarter Straßenbahn etwas einfallen lassen: Ein- und Auslassventile werden desmodromisch zur Arbeit angehalten, das heißt über zwei Nocken. Vom Feinsten ist auch die Fahrerausstattung. Außer den Piloten von Reims tut Hermann Lang Dienst im Cockpit des w196, allerdings nur einmal, das letzte Mal: auf dem vertrauten Nürburgring. Fangio, 1953 und zu Beginn der Saison 1954 noch auf Maserati, folgt den buhlenden Rufen Alfred Neubauers nur zögerlich. Aber der alte Fuchs versteht es, sich den Superstar mit allerlei Geschenken und Aufmerksamkeiten schließlich geneigt zu machen.

dans un tramway de Stuttgart: les soupapes d'admission et d'échappement seraient actionnées par une commande desmodromique, c'est-à-dire à l'aide de deux cames. L'équipe de pilotes est également des plus relevées. Outre les pilotes de Reims, Hermann Lang officie également dans le cockpit de la w196, mais une fois seulement, et ce sera la dernière: sur le Nürburgring qui lui est familier. Fangio, qui conduit encore pour Maserati en 1953 et au début de la saison 1954, ne répond qu'avec hésitation aux appels de sirène d'Alfred Neubauer. Mais le vieux renard sait s'y prendre et obtient finalement l'accord de la superstar avec des cadeaux en tout genre et de nombreuses attentions.

Comme en 1951 déjà, c'est son compatriote Froilán González, sur Ferrari, qui remporte le Grand Prix d'Angleterre. Avec sa carrosserie aérodynamique initiale, la w196 s'avère déjà déplacée, ne serait-ce que parce que les pilotes ne peuvent pas viser avec précision les fûts d'essence qui longent le tracé sur l'aéroport de Silverstone. Mais, une fois cette lacune corrigée, Fangio accumule victoire sur victoire: au Ring, où il dispose pour la première fois de la monoplace dans son exécution à roues non carénées, sur le circuit de Bremgarten à Berne et à Monza. Lors de la finale, sur le circuit espagnol de Pedralbes, non loin de Barcelone, sa w196 rallie péniblement l'arrivée au troisième rang, handicapée par une fuite d'huile et un moteur surchauffé. Mais lorsque l'on fait les comptes, à la fin de la saison, Fangio est champion pour la seconde fois, après 1951. Karl Kling a sauvé l'honneur lors de la course de l'Avus, qui ne compte pas pour le classement des Grands Prix, avec une vitesse moyenne de 213,5 km/h.

Durant la pause hivernale qui, à cette époque déjà, ne méritait pas son nom, on se concentre sur le châssis. Un nouveau pneu course mis au point par Continental en novembre et décembre 1954 contribue à faire passer les accélérations latérales possibles d'un modeste 0,7 à 1 g. Tout en haut sur la liste des préférences d'Alfred Neubauer pour les pilotes figure le jeune Anglais Stirling Moss. Celui-ci hésite tout d'abord: être sans équivoque le numéro deux derrière Fangio ne lui plaît guère. Il trouve pourtant

Juan Manuel Fangio during his victorious drive at the Nürburgring on 1 August 1954.

Juan Manuel Fangio während seiner Siegesfahrt am Nürburgring am 1. August 1954.

Juan Manuel Fangio en route vers la victoire au Nürburgring, le 1er août 1954.

hours despite being practically barbecued by the tubes in the spaceframe. He won a further race in Argentina with a 3-liter engine at the front of the w196, followed by the Grands Prix of Belgium, Holland, and Italy – all stepping stones to his third championship. Moss was left with his home Grand Prix at Silverstone as a consolation prize. The Briton was already creating his reputation of being the greatest driver never to have been world champion. His way was blocked, and he soon had to recognize this with a shrug of resignation and growing respect, by that man Fangio.

The Argentinian was beatable, however, in sports cars. And Mercedes gave Moss a sympathetic tool in the form of the 300 SLR (standing for Super, Light, Racing). Its in-house type designation w196s betrayed its closeness to the successful formula racing car. One of the absolute highlights in the sport's history was the sensational drive by Moss and his red-bearded passenger Denis Jenkinson through the

Simply the best: Juan Manuel Fangio (1911–1995)

"The man is like a magnet. As soon as he enters a room, even when it's full of people, he becomes its focal point," said Phil Hill, 1961 world champion, and his deep, earthy voice almost cracked with sheer respect. The year was 1991, the location London's Dorchester Hotel, and the occasion a grand celebration for Juan Manuel Fangio's 80th birthday. The Argentinian entered the room, and that's precisely how it was. Presumably that was the secret of his greatness: authority over himself and others. Two photos taken in 1957 by Swiss photographer Yves Debraine at the German Grand Prix at the same point on the Nürburgring reveal the drama of the occasion: challenger Mike Hawthorn, lost like a small boy in the cockpit of the Ferrari, fearful of his own courage, more a passenger than a driver, and then Fangio, collected, ice-cool, yet relaxed, his face showing his relentless desire for victory. Master and pupil... there was also a battle of the generations going on out there, of course. "Youth attacks Fangio" was the motto of the 1956 German Grand Prix. But Fangio in his mid-forties beat them all, Hawthorn and Stirling Moss, Eugenio Castellotti and Luigi Musso, Peter Collins and Tony Brooks, an overlord of intimidating proportions. That was the case until the first doubts entered his mind in 1958 on the seemingly endless finishing straights in Reims which left ample time for reflection. "What are you actually doing here? You've done everything, and then some." There and then the decision to retire was made – this insight into his otherwise carefully concealed inner life was revealed to the surprised birthday party guests at the Dorchester. And what of the youth of that era? Dead in crashes, like Castellotti, Musso, Collins and Hawthorn. Or also a little old and a little gray by then, like Brooks and Stirling Moss. "Fangio," smiled Moss and shrugged his shoulders, "was unbeatable." And there was no trace of resentment that this man had destroyed his own dreams of one day being world champion himself.

Beim Großen Preis von England gewinnt wie schon 1951 sein Landsmann Froilán González auf Ferrari. Der w196 erweist sich in seiner ursprünglichen Stromlinienform als Fehlbesetzung, schon weil die Fahrer die Benzinfässer nicht exakt anpeilen können, die die Strecke auf dem Flugplatz von Silverstone markieren. Dann aber häuft Fangio Sieg auf Sieg, auf dem Ring, wo zum erstenmal der Monoposto mit seinen freistehenden Rädern zur Verfügung steht, auf dem Berner Bremgartenkurs, in Monza. Beim Finale im spanischen Pedralbes unweit Barcelona schleppt sich sein w196 nur als dritter ins Ziel, verkrüppelt durch Ölverlust und eine überhitzende Maschine. Als am Ende zusammengezählt wird, ist Fangio Champion, zum zweiten Mal nach 1951. Karl Kling hält sich schadlos beim Avus-Rennen, das nicht zum Grand-Prix-Zyklus zählt, mit einem Schnitt von 213,5 Stundenkilometern.

Während der Winterpause, die schon damals ihren Namen nicht verdient, konzentriert man sich auf das Fahrwerk. Ein neuer Rennreifen, von Continental im November und Dezember 1954 entwickelt, tut das seinige, die mögliche Querbeschleunigung von moderaten 0,7 g auf

The dynamic director responsible for the success of the Silver Arrows: team manager Alfred Neubauer.

Der dynamische Regisseur hinter den Erfolgen der Silberpfeile: Rennleiter Alfred Neubauer.

Metteur en scène infatigable derrière les succès des Flèches d'argent : le directeur de course Alfred Neubauer.

1 g zu steigern. Hoch oben auf Alfred Neubauers Einkaufsliste für die Piloten steht der junge Engländer Stirling Moss. Der zaudert zunächst: Eindeutig die Nummer zwei hinter Fangio zu sein, behagt ihm nicht. Den Kontrakt, den man ihm anbietet, findet er gleichwohl »phantastisch«. Am 3. Dezember macht sich Moss in einem Mercedes 220 und dann mit einem 300 SL aus der Serie mit dem Hockenheimring vertraut und stellt anschließend sein Fahrgenie

L'as des as : Juan Manuel Fangio (1911–1995)

« L'homme est comme un aimant. Dès qu'il pénètre dans une pièce, même si elle est bondée, tout le monde a le regard tourné vers lui », déclare Phil Hill, champion du monde en 1961, et sa voix basse et caverneuse se charge d'un respect absolu. La scène se passe en 1991, à l'hôtel Dorchester de Londres, où l'on fête de la façon la plus solennelle le 80e anniversaire de Juan Manuel Fangio et, lorsque l'Argentin fait son entrée, tous les regards se fixent sur lui. Il se dégage de son visage une autorité, envers lui-même, envers autrui, qui est sans doute le secret de sa grandeur. Deux clichés du photographe suisse Yves Debraine, pris en 1957 lors du Grand Prix d'Allemagne au même endroit du Nürburgring, sont les témoignages d'un drame : le challenger Mike Hawthorn, perdu tel un gamin dans le cockpit de la Ferrari, complètement effrayé par son propre courage, plutôt passager que pilote, et, de l'autre côté, Fangio, concentré et pourtant d'une décontraction glaciale, avec, inscrite sur le visage, la volonté intraitable de vaincre. Le maître et son élève... Naturellement, l'écart qui sépare deux générations est parfaitement illustré. « La jeunesse s'attaque à Fangio », est la devise que l'on a choisie pour le Grand Prix d'Allemagne de 1956. Et pourtant, c'est cet homme de quarante-cinq ans qui les battra tous, Mike Hawthorn et Stirling Moss, Eugenio Castellotti et Luigi Musso, Peter Collins et Tony Brooks, un père censeur à la stature intimidante. Jusqu'à ce jour de 1958, sur les interminables lignes droites du circuit de Reims où l'on a beaucoup de temps pour réfléchir, il commence à se poser des questions : que fais-tu là à proprement parler ? Tu as déjà tout gagné, et plus encore. Et c'est alors qu'il décide de raccrocher, maintenant et ici – ce coin du voile sur sa vie privée sinon défendue bec et ongles, il le soulève aux invités surpris de la fête anniversaire du Dorchester. Et la jeunesse d'alors ? Morte au volant, comme Castellotti, Musso, Collins et Hawthorn. Ou bien, déjà un peu vieillie et grisonnante, comme Brooks et Stirling Moss, qui déclare : « Fangio était imbattable ». Il accepte sans arrière-pensée que cet homme ait détruit son propre rêve de devenir un jour champion du monde.

« fantastique » le contrat qui lui est présenté. Le 3 décembre, Moss se familiarise avec le circuit de Hockenheim au volant d'une Mercedes 220 puis d'une 300 SL de série et administre ensuite d'emblée la preuve de son génie de la conduite avec la w196, qui plus est, sur un circuit humide.

Le Britannique subit son baptême du feu lors du Grand Prix d'Argentine, le 16 janvier. La chaleur de ce dimanche est si torride que l'asphalte est boursouflé. Mais Moss résiste. Victime d'une insolation, on doit l'extirper de sa voiture et le transporter contre son gré à l'hôpital. Là, il peut s'exprimer en anglais, est ramené au circuit par une voiture toutes sirènes hurlantes, reprend la monoplace de Hans Herrmann et termine encore quatrième. Le vainqueur est Fangio, que personne n'aurait cru capable

Possibly the greatest ever: Juan Manuel Fangio, World Champion with Mercedes in 1954 and 1955.

Vielleicht der Größte: Juan Manuel Fangio, Weltmeister auf Mercedes 1954 und 1955.

Peut-être le plus grand de tous : Juan Manuel Fangio, champion du monde sur Mercedes en 1954 et 1955.

boot of Italy during the 22nd Mille Miglia on 30 April 1955, a thousand miles (1,610 km) in ten hours, seven minutes, and 48 seconds, a record that will never be touched. And then the 300 SLR simply could not stop winning, in the Eifel Race, the Swedish Grand Prix, the Tourist Trophy, and the Targa Florio. Daimler-Benz also won the European touring car championship with Werner Engel alternating between a 300 SL and a 220 A, and the American sports car championship (driver: Paul O'Shea). Daimler's dominance on all fronts was total.

But the writing was already on the wall. At the Le Mans 24 Hour Race on 11 June the 300 SLR of Frenchman Pierre Levegh (alias Pierre Bouillon) crashed into the crowd like a rocket. A figure of 90 dead was given, though the exact number will never be known. Mercedes withdrew its remaining cars as a mark of respect for the dead. When Alfred Neubauer returned to his hotel room after the Targa Florio on 16 October, a letter from chief engineer Professor Nallinger was waiting for him. Its contents were brief but significant: "After careful consideration the board of management has decided… to withdraw definitively from racing for a number of years." The Le Mans disaster was only the trigger for this decision, while its underlying cause was quite different. "In the interests of the further development

mit dem W 196 auf Anhieb unter Beweis, auf feuchter Strecke zumal.

Seinen Einstand gibt der Brite im Fegefeuer des Großen Preises von Argentinien am 16. Januar. In der Gluthitze dieses Sonntags wirft der Asphalt Blasen. Moss hält. Als ihm die Sinne schwinden, zerrt man ihn aus dem Wagen, befördert den Widerstrebenden ins Hospital. Dort kann er sich auf englisch verständlich machen, wird mit Blaulicht zur Piste zurückgebracht, übernimmt den Wagen von Hans Herrmann und wird noch vierter. Sieger ist Fangio, dem keiner eine solche asketische Leistung zugetraut hätte. Er hält als einziger drei Stunden durch, obwohl ihn die glühenden Röhren des Rahmens förmlich grillen und gewinnt ein weiteres Rennen in Argentinien mit einer Dreiliter-Maschine im Bug des W 196, dann die Großen Preise von Belgien, Holland und Italien als Aufbauarbeit für sein drittes Championat. Moss bleibt sein heimischer Grand Prix in Silverstone als Ehrentreffer. Der Brite feilt bereits emsig an seinem Ruf, der größte Fahrer zu sein, der es nie zum Weltmeister brachte. Im Wege steht, das muss er bald in achselzuckender Resignation und wachsender Verehrung erkennen, dieser Mann Fangio.

Schlagbar ist der Argentinier indessen im Rennsportwagen. Und da gibt Mercedes Moss ein kongeniales Arbeitsgerät an die Hand mit dem 300 SLR (für Super, Leicht, Rennen). Schon das hausinterne Typen-Sigel W 196 S verrät seine Nähe zu den erfolgreichen Formelwagen der Marke. Zu den absoluten Highlights in der Historie des Sports zählt die Sensationsrunde von Moss und seinem rotbärtigen Begleiter Denis Jenkinson durch den italienischen Stiefel anlässlich der 22. Mille Miglia am 30. April 1955, tausend Meilen (1 610 km) in zehn Stunden, sieben Minuten und 48 Sekunden, ein Rekord, den niemand mehr antasten wird. Und dann hört der 300 SLR nicht mehr auf zu siegen, beim Eifelrennen, beim Grand Prix von Schweden, bei der Tourist Trophy, bei der Targa Florio. Daimler-Benz gewinnt auch die Europameisterschaft für Tourenwagen mit Werner Engel abwechselnd im 300 SL und im 220 A und die amerikanische Sportwagenmeisterschaft (Fahrer: Paul O'Shea). Die Daimler-Dominanz an allen Fronten ist total.

Aber schon erscheint die Schrift an der Wand: Beim 24-Stunden-Rennen von Le Mans am 11. Juni ist der 300 SLR des Franzosen Pierre Levegh (alias Pierre Bouillon) wie ein Geschoss in die Menge eingeschlagen. Von 90 Opfern ist die Rede, die genaue Zahl wird man nie erfahren. Mercedes zieht die restlichen Wagen als Tribut an die Toten zurück. Als Alfred Neubauer am Abend nach der Targa Florio am 16. Oktober in sein Quartier zurückkehrt, erwartet ihn ein Schreiben von Chefingenieur Professor Dr. Ing. E. H. Nallinger. Der Inhalt ist knapp und inhaltsschwer: »Der Vorstand hat sich nach reiflicher Überlegung entschlossen, … sich endgültig für einige Jahre vom Rennsport … fernzuhalten.« Das Desaster von Le Mans ist nur der Anlass für die Entscheidung, die Ursache liegt ganz woanders: »Die Weiterentwicklung unseres Produktionsprogramms lässt es

d'une telle performance d'ascétique. Il est le seul à tenir le coup pendant trois heures bien que les tubulures brûlantes du châssis l'aient littéralement rôti. Il gagnera encore une autre course en Argentine avec un moteur de 3 litres sous le capot de la W 196. Il remporte ensuite la victoire aux Grands Prix de Belgique, de Hollande et d'Italie et jette ainsi les bases pour son troisième titre de champion du monde. Moss sauve l'honneur en remportant son Grand Prix national à Silverstone. Le Britannique cimente déjà ardemment sa réputation de plus grand pilote qui n'aura jamais été champion du monde. Il y a un obstacle sur sa route, il doit bientôt l'admettre dans un haussement d'épaules résigné et teinté d'une admiration croissante, et cet obstacle a pour nom Fangio.

Mais l'Argentin n'est pas imbattable, notamment au volant d'une voiture de sport. Et, pour cela, Mercedes donne à Stirling Moss un instrument de travail absolument génial avec la 300 SLR (pour Super, Légère, Course). Le nom de code interne, W 196 S, trahit déjà irrémédiablement sa proximité avec la monoplace de la marque croulant sous les lauriers. Parmi les points d'orgue absolus dans l'histoire de la compétition automobile figure le sensationnel record de Stirling Moss et de son copilote à la barbe rousse, Denis Jenkinson, à travers la botte italienne, à l'occasion des 22e Mille Miglia, le 30 avril 1955, mille miles (1610 km) couverts en 10 heures, 7 minutes et 48 secondes, un record qui restera inégalé. Puis la 300 SLR n'arrête plus de vaincre, à la Course de l'Eifel, au Grand Prix de Suède, au Tourist Trophy, à la Targa Florio. Daimler-Benz remporte aussi le championnat d'Europe des voitures de tourisme avec Werner Engel, alternativement avec la 300 SL et la 220 A, ainsi que le championnat d'Amérique des voitures de sport avec comme pilote Paul O'Shea. La domination de Daimler sur tous les fronts est absolue.

Mais, déjà, la catastrophe s'annonce : lors des 24 heures du Mans, le 11 juin 1955, la 300 SLR du pilote français Pierre Levegh (alias Pierre Bouillon) trace un sillon sanglant à travers la foule des spectateurs. On parle de 90 victimes, mais on n'apprendra jamais le nombre exact de morts. Par égard envers les disparus, Mercedes retire le reste de ses voitures. Lorsque Alfred Neubauer, le soir de la Targa Florio, le 16 octobre, rentre chez lui, il y trouve une lettre de l'ingénieur en chef, le professeur ingénieur *honoris causa* Nallinger. Sa teneur est concise, mais d'une portée inouïe : « Après mûres réflexions, le Directoire a décidé… de se retirer totalement de la compétition automobile pendant quelques années. » Le désastre du Mans n'est que le prétexte de cette décision, car sa cause est totalement différente : « Le perfectionnement de notre programme de production nous incite à faire que ces spécialistes très qualifiés (les constructeurs et les ingénieurs) se consacrent désormais au champ d'activité qui est le plus intéressant pour notre nombreuse clientèle dans le monde entier, à savoir la construction de voitures de série », déclare Nallinger lors de la cérémonie traditionnelle de clôture de la saison et de récompense des vainqueurs, le 22 octobre.

of our production range it seems advisable to us to have these highly-qualified staff (the designers and engineers) work solely in that field which is of most interest to our numerous customers around the world, i.e., in the field of production car manufacturing," explained Nallinger at the company's traditional end-of-season victory celebrations on 22 October.

As Hans Stuck Senior once said, you should stop when things taste their best. Or quit at the top because your reputation then shines at its brightest.

Sport with touring cars: from the Herkomer Trials to a high-tech happening 1956–2004

The development of touring-car racing since the car's adolescence at the start of the century has been an inexorable journey from reality to illusion. To explain: initially competing machines were actual production cars, now they just appear to be so. The German portrait painter Hubert von Herkomer, living in England, endowed a prize in 1905 for a competition named after himself. It was his dearest wish "that as practical and reliable a touring car as possible should emerge at a price that is widely affordable." Both the Daimler and Benz factories had such cars available, and they each took one of the three Herkomer Trials held between 1905 and 1907. In 1905 Daimler won, and in 1907 Benz, when designer Fritz Erle personally drove his 50 bhp car to victory.

In the Thirties rally-like reliability trials were thick on the ground – the Winter Rally, Brandenburg Rally, East Prussian Rally, Alpine Rally, 2,000 Kilometer Rally through Germany and so on. These were all but handed on a plate to Daimler-Benz's "off-road team" which could also boast

Ewy Rosquist at the 1963 Monte Carlo Rallye.
Ewy Rosquist bei der Rallye Monte Carlo 1963.
Ewy Rosquist lors du rallye de Monte Carlo 1963.

uns ratsam erscheinen, nunmehr diese hochqualifizierten Kräfte (die Konstrukteure und Ingenieure) allein auf jenem Gebiet tätig werden zu lassen, das für unsere zahlreiche Kundschaft in aller Welt am interessantesten ist, nämlich auf dem Gebiete des Serienwagenbaus«, sagt Nallinger auf der traditionellen Schluss- und Siegesfeier des Hauses am 22. Oktober.

Man sollte, hat Hans Stuck der Ältere einmal gesagt, dann aufhören, wenn es am besten schmeckt. Oder ungeschlagen abtreten, denn dann strahlt der Nachruhm am hellsten.

Sport mit Tourenwagen: Von der Herkomer-Fahrt zum High-Tech-Happening 1956–2004

Die Entwicklung des Tourenwagensports seit den Flegeljahren des Automobils Anfang des Jahrhunderts führt unaufhaltsam vom Sein zum Schein: Am Anfang sind die Protagonisten lupenreine Serienautos, am Ende sehen sie nur noch so aus. Der deutsche Porträtmaler Hubert von Herkomer, wohnhaft in England, setzt 1905 einen Preis aus für einen nach ihm benannten Wettbewerb. Sein Herzenswunsch: »Daß sich ein möglichst praktischer und zuverlässiger Reisewagen einstelle, dessen Preis für weitere Kreise erschwinglich sei.« Solche Autos halten die Manufakturen Daimler und Benz bereit, und so gewinnen sie zwei der drei Herkomer-Fahrten zwischen 1905 und 1907 brüderlich-paritätisch: 1905 Daimler, Benz 1907, als Konstrukteur Fritz Erle seinen Wagen mit 50 PS höchstpersönlich zum Sieg lenkt.

In den Dreißigern schießen rallyeähnliche Zuverlässigkeitsprüfungen förmlich ins Kraut, die Winterfahrt, Brandenburgische Geländefahrt, Ostpreußenfahrt, Alpenfahrt, 2 000-Kilometer-Fahrt durch Deutschland und dergleichen, ein gefundenes Fressen für die »Geländemannschaft« von Daimler-Benz, welche ganz abseits von Glanz, Glamour und Glorie der Silberpfeile ebenfalls üppge Erfolgsbilanzen vorweisen kann.

Auf diese Weise verdient sich etwa der spätere Grand-Prix-Star Karl Kling seine Sporen. 1959 kehrt er gewissermaßen zu den Ursprüngen zurück, als er zusammen mit dem Journalisten Rainer Günzler die Rallye Mediterranée-le Cap gewinnt. Sein Arbeitsgerät, untauglich nur scheinbar: der 190 D. Ein gutes Stück heißer mochten's 1956 Walter Schock und Rolf Moll: Sie wurden Rallye-Europa-Meister mit einem 300 SL und werden es vier Jahre später wieder mit dem vergleichsweise kommoden 220 SE, mit dem Sieg bei der Rallye Monte Carlo als Sahnehäubchen auf der Erfolgstorte. Nirgends werden zwischen 1961 und 1964 Limousinen brutaler geschunden als beim Gran Premio in Argentinien, und immer ist das Mürbemacher-

Comme Hans Stuck père l'a dit un jour, il est préférable de raccrocher quand le moment vous convient le mieux. Ou de se retirer invaincu, car c'est alors que la gloire rayonne avec le plus de clarté.

Sport avec les voitures de tourisme: de la Course Herkomer à la débauche de haute technologie 1956–2004

Depuis les balbutiements de l'automobile, au début du siècle, le développement des compétitions de voitures de tourisme passe irrémédiablement de l'être au paraître: au début, les protagonistes sont de pures voitures de série et, à la fin, elles n'en ont plus que l'apparence, et encore. Le portraitiste allemand Hubert von Herkomer, qui a son domicile en Angleterre, crée en 1905 un prix pour une compétition qui porte son nom. Son désir le plus cher: «Une voiture de voyage dont le prix soit à portée de larges couches de la population et qui s'avère aussi pratique et fiable que possible.» Les manufactures Daimler et Benz proposent de telles voitures et c'est ainsi qu'elles gagnent deux des trois courses Herkomer entre 1905 et 1907 dans une conviviale fraternité: Daimler en 1905, Benz en 1907, années où le constructeur Fritz Erle mène personnellement à la victoire sa voiture de 50 chevaux.

Dans les années 1930, on assiste littéralement à une explosion du nombre d'épreuves de fiabilité rappelant les rallyes, le Rallye d'hiver, le Rallye tout-terrain du Brandebourg, le Rallye de Prusse Orientale, le Rallye des Alpes, le Rallye des 2000 km à travers l'Allemagne et bien d'autres encore, une bonne aubaine pour l'«équipe de tout-terrain» de Daimler-Benz qui, à des années-lumière des paillettes, du champagne et des mondanités des Flèches d'argent, peut également se targuer d'une brochette de succès des plus flatteuses.

C'est par exemple ainsi que la future vedette des Grands Prix, Karl Kling, gagne ses premiers galons. En 1959, il retourne en quelque sorte à la source lorsque, faisant équipe avec le journaliste Rainer Günzler, il remporte le Rallye Méditerranée-Le Cap. Leur destrier n'est mal choisi qu'en apparence: c'est le 190 D. Ce n'est pas tout à fait la pointure choisie en 1956 par Walzer Schock et Rolf Moll: ils ont été sacrés champions d'Europe des rallyes avec une 300 SE et le seront de nouveau, quatre ans plus tard, avec la relativement confortable 220 SE, en remportant la victoire

an extremely successful record far away from the glitter, glamor, and glory of the Silver Arrows.

This is how the later Grand Prix star Karl Kling, for example, won his spurs. In 1959 he returned to his roots in a sense when he won the Rallye Mediterranée-le Cap together with the journalist Rainer Günzler. His chosen tool, which was obviously more suitable than it first appeared, was the 190 D. Walter Schock and Rolf Moll liked it a good deal hotter in 1956 when they became European Rally Champions in a 300 SL, and then repeated the feat four years later with the comparatively comfortable 220 SE, victory in the Monte Carlo Rally being the icing on the cake of their success. Nowhere were cars subjected to more brutal treatment between 1961 and 1964 than in the Argentine Gran Premio, and Mercedes carried off the prize in this war of attrition every time. Ewy Rosqvist and Ursula Wirth's 1962 victory in a 220 SE gave the lie to the stupid but persistent prejudice against women drivers. In that year Eugen Böhringer won the European Rally Championship with the same model, and shone in 1964 with strong performances on the track in a 300 SE. In the Nürburgring Touring-Car Race in particular, Böhringer demonstrated that this category too was by no means the last bastion of gentlemanly conduct: "Six hours of battering," was the headline of the German magazine *auto motor and sport* over its report. And in a letter to the editor, a bitter opponent complained that the bald Stuttgart hotelier had simply rammed weaker competitors such as the Steyr Puch from the track "with his big Merc" when they impeded his high-speed charge.

Between 1965 and 1967 the company took a break to recharge its batteries, returning (even if only briefly) in 1968 like a phoenix from the ashes, when Erich Waxenberger, later to be the marque's racing director, won the Macao Six-Hour Race, in a 300 SEL 6.3. It was not until the victory of the team of Cowan/Malkin/Broad in the 1977 London-Sydney Rallye in a 280 SE that the company's return to rallye sport was celebrated, firstly with private teams and then, from 1978 onwards, under the aegis of a works team. Their two most spectacular successes again had a touch of the exotic about them. In 1979 the team took the first four places in the Bandana Rallye in the Ivory Coast, and 12 months later finished first and second in the same event – in the first year with the 450 SLC 5.0, and in the second with the 500 SLC. Three landmarks celebrated their birthdays on 5 May 1984: the new Nürburgring; the Brazilian Mozart of speed, Ayrton Senna; and the Daimler-Benz 190 E 2.3-16 with which the make intended to tackle the chronic issue of the advancing age of its clientele. The average Mercedes buyer was 50. In a show of absolute disdain for the slippery track and legendary speedsters such as Hans Herrmann, James Hunt, Niki Lauda, Alain Prost, Keke Rosberg, and John Surtees, Senna won the opening race in the freshly renovated "green hell" driving the sixteen-valver. One year later the nimble Baby Benz was homologated for Group A, signaling the start of a wonderful career which saw 50 victories in German Touring Car

Hannu Mikkola/Arne Hertz with their 450 SLC 5.0 at the Argentinian Rallye in 1980.

Hannu Mikkola/Arne Hertz mit dem 450 SLC 5.0 bei der Argentinien-Rallye 1980.

Hannu Mikkola/Arne Hertz avec la 450 SLC 5.0 lors du rallye d'Argentine de 1980.

Marathon eine Beute der Mercedes. 1962 widerlegen dort die Damen Ewy Rosqvist und Ursula Wirth mit ihrem Sieg im 220 SE das dümmlich-hartnäckige Vorurteil, Frau am Steuer, das sei nicht geheuer. In jenem Jahr erringt Eugen Böhringer die Rallye-Europameisterschaft mit dem gleichen Modell und glänzt 1964 mit starken Auftritten auf der Rundstrecke im 300 SE. Vor allem beim »Großen Preis der Tourenwagen« auf dem Nürburgring erbringt Böhringer den Beweis, dass es auch in dieser Kategorie nicht sonderlich gemütvoll hergeht: »Sechs Stunden gebolzt« meldet das Fachblatt *auto motor und sport* in der Überschrift zu seinem Report. Und in einem Leserbrief beschwert sich ein verbitterter Konkurrent, der kahlköpfige Stuttgarter Hotelier habe »mit seinem dicken Mercedes« schwächliche Mitbewerber wie die Steyr Puch einfach hemdsärmelig von der Piste gestoßen, als sie seine rasende Fahrt behinderten.

Zwischen 1965 und 1967 legt man eine schöpferische Pause ein und kehrt 1968 wie Phönix aus der Asche zurück, wenn auch nur kurz: Das 6-Stunden-Rennen von Macao gewinnt Erich Waxenberger, zukünftiger Rennleiter der Marke, in einem 300 SEL 6.3. Erst der Sieg der Dreier-Riege Cowan/Malkin/Broad 1977 bei der Rallye London-Sydney auf einem 280 SE stößt ein Comeback im Rallyesport an, zunächst mit Privatteams, ab 1978 unter der Ägide des Werks. Die zwei spektakulärsten Erfolge umfächelt wiederum eine Aura des Exotischen: Vierfachsieg an der Elfenbeinküste bei der Rallye Bandana 1979, Doppelsieg bei der gleichen Veranstaltung zwölf Monate später, im ersten Jahr mit dem 450 SLC 5.0, im zweiten mit dem 500 SLC. Der 5. Mai 1984 wird zum Geburtstag dreier Karrieren, des neuen Nürburgrings, des brasilianischen Bleifuß-Mozarts Ayrton Senna, des Daimler-Benz 190 E 2.3-16, mit dem die Marke der chronischen Überalterung ihrer Klientel zu Leibe rücken will: Der durchschnittliche Mercedes-Käufer ist 50. Ohne den geringsten Respekt vor der rutschigen

au Rallye de Monte-Carlo comme cerise sur le gâteau du succès. Nulle part ailleurs les berlines ne seront plus brutalement cravachées qu'entre 1961 et 1964 lors du Gran Premio d'Argentina et cet éprouvant marathon sera toujours un butin des Mercedes. En 1962, les dames Ewy Rosqvist et Ursula Wirth, avec leur victoire au volant d'une 220 SE, prouvent l'absence de fondement du ridicule mais indéracinable préjugé selon lequel, avec une femme au volant, c'est la mort au tournant. Cette année-là, Eugen Böhringer gagne le championnat d'Europe des rallyes avec la même voiture et se distingue en 1964 avec d'admirables démonstrations en circuit au volant d'une 300 SE. Lors du « Grand Prix des Voitures de tourisme » sur le Nürburgring, notamment, Böhringer prouve que même dans cette catégorie, la course n'a rien d'une promenade : « Six heures à fond la caisse », titre la revue spécialisée *auto motor und sport* dans son reportage sur la course. Et, dans une lettre de lecteur, un concurrent amer se plaint que l'hôtelier chauve de Stuttgart, « avec sa grosse Mercedes », aurait tout simplement bousculé de la piste des concurrents aux voitures moins puissantes telles les Steyr Puch comme si elles avaient fait obstacle à sa course échevelée.

De 1965 à 1967, Mercedes fait une pause et revient sur les pistes en 1968, comme le phénix renaissant de ses cendres, mais ce n'est qu'un bref intermède : Erich Waxenberger, futur directeur de course de la marque gagne les Six Heures de Macao au volant d'une 300 SEL 6.3. Il faudra attendre le triplé de Cowan/Malkin/Broad, en 1977 lors du Rallye Londres-Sydney, sur 280 SE pour un véritable retour en rallye, tout d'abord avec des écuries privées et, à partir de 1978, aux couleurs de l'usine. Les deux succès les plus spectaculaires donnent à leur tour une touche d'exotisme : quadruplé en Côte d'Ivoire lors du Rallye du Bandana en 1979 et doublé lors de la même épreuve, un an plus tard, la première année avec une 450 SLC 5.0 et, la seconde, avec une 500 SLC. Le 5 mai 1984 est l'anniversaire de l'éclosion de trois carrières : celle du nouveau Nürburgring, celle du Mozart du volant, le Brésilien Ayrton Senna, et celle de la Daimler-Benz 190 E 2.3-16 avec laquelle la marque veut remédier à la sénescence chronique de sa clientèle. L'acheteur de Mercedes moyen est en effet âgé de cinquante ans. Sans le moindre respect envers une piste glissante et des monuments de la course automobile aussi historiques que rapides comme Hans Herrmann, James Hunt, Niki Lauda, Alain Prost, Keke Rosberg ou John Surtees, Senna gagne au volant de la seize-soupapes la course inaugurale de l'« Enfer vert » tout fraîchement rénové. Un an plus tard, la rapide Baby-Benz est homologuée pour le Groupe A, commencement d'une carrière au superlatif à l'issue de laquelle, fin 1993, se seront accumulées cinquante victoires dans le cadre du DTM, le championnat d'Allemagne des voitures de tourisme. La version originale avec ses 255 ch a déjà été suivie par les deux évolutions, la 2,5-16 Evo I en 1989, avec 330 ch, et l'Evo II (à partir de Diepholz 1990), avec 373 ch, et, après des années de travail, les succès se sont accumulés : en 1991, Mercedes remporte le classement Marques ainsi

Championship (DTM) races by the time it retired from the scene in 1993. The original version which developed 255 bhp was followed by the two development stages of 2.5-16 Evo I from 1989 with 330 bhp and Evo II (from Diepholz in 1990) with 373 bhp. After years finding its feet, the team was on track for success. In 1991 Mercedes won the constructors' competition and also the team competition for its Affalterbach-based partner AMG. Mercedes driver Klaus Ludwig was in the lead until the final round at Hockenheim, but finally had to give best to Audi man Frank Biela.

In 1992 the Stuttgart star team made the DTM its own: the speed trio of Kurt Thiim, Klaus Ludwig, and Bernd Schneider played leapfrog at the head of the table, but it was Ludwig who had his nose in front at the end. Mercedes won 16 of the 24 races, and Ellen Lohr secured a notable first, namely the first victory for a woman in the DTM, when she won at Hockenheim in May. The slight downturn in the following season – runner-up position for Roland Asch behind the four-wheel-drive, six-cylinder Alfa Romeos – was merely a valley between two peaks. 1994 saw the introduction of a new regulation: 2.5-liter limit, six cylinders that could also be derived from a production engine by the addition or subtraction of two cylinders. In just eight months Mercedes engineers conjured a thoroughbred racing engine delivering more than 400 bhp at over 11,000 rpm from the V8 of the 420 SE, and it was this engine that was fitted to the new C-class. The proof of the pudding is in the eating: Klaus Ludwig was German champion again, with Jörg van Ommen as runner-up and winner of the Gold Cup classification, which also included the placings in the invitation races in Mugello and Donington. In addition, Mercedes won the constructors' championship for the third time after previous wins in 1991 and 1992.

1995 saw the unveiling of an engineering marvel: "The car transports the driver to a surreal world in which the laws of physics seem to have been revoked," enthused for-

Battle of the giants during the opening race on the new Nürburgring in 1984.

Zweikampf der Denkmäler beim Eröffnungsrennen auf dem neuen Nürburgring 1984.

Duel de deux géants de la compétition automobile lors de la course inaugurale du nouveau Nürburgring en 1984.

A home race for Bernd Schneider in the AMG-Mercedes at Hockenheim in 1996.

Heimspiel für Bernd Schneider mit dem AMG-Mercedes in Hockenheim 1996.

Match à domicile pour Bernd Schneider avec la Mercedes AMG à Hockenheim en 1996.

Fahrbahn und rasenden Naturdenkmälern wie Hans Herrmann, James Hunt, Niki Lauda, Alain Prost, Keke Rosberg und John Surtees gewinnt Senna auf dem Sechzehnventiler das Eröffnungsrennen in der frisch renovierten »Grünen Hölle«. Ein Jahr später wird der flinke Baby-Benz für die Gruppe A homologiert, Startschuss in eine Laufbahn der Superlative, an deren Ende 1993 sich 50 Siege in Läufen um die DTM (für Deutsche Tourenwagen-Meisterschaft) angesammelt haben. Da sind der Ur-Version mit ihren 255 PS bereits die beiden Entwicklungsstufen 2,5-16 Evo I von 1989 mit 330 PS und Evo II (ab Diepholz 1990) mit 373 PS gefolgt, und nach Jahren der Orientierung hat sich üppiger Erfolg angebahnt: 1991 erringt man die Markenwertung sowie die Teamwertung für den in Affalterbach ansässigen Mercedes-Partner AMG. Bis zum Finale in Hockenheim führt Benz-Pilot Klaus Ludwig, muss sich aber schließlich dem Audi-Bediensteten Frank Biela beugen.

1992 wird die DTM zur Domäne der Stuttgarter Stern-Fahrer: die Tempo-Trinität Kurt Thiim, Klaus Ludwig und Bernd Schneider spielt gleichsam Bäumchen-wechsel-dich an der Spitze der Wertung, wobei Ludwig am Ende die Nase vorn hat. 16 von 24 Rennen gewinnen die Mercedes, und Ellen Lohr sorgt für ein Novum: erster Sieg für eine Dame bei der DTM, in Hockenheim im Mai. Der sanfte Abschwung in der nächsten Saison – Vizemeisterschaft für Roland Asch hinter den starken allradgetriebenen Sechszylindern von Alfa Romeo – führt indes lediglich in ein Tal zwischen zwei Wellenbergen. 1994 gilt ein neues Reglement: 2,5 Liter Limit, sechs Zylinder, die aus einem Serientriebwerk auch durch Addition oder Substraktion von zwei Verbrennungseinheiten hergestellt werden können. In nur acht Monaten sublimieren die Mercedes-Techniker aus dem V8 des 420 SE eine reinrassige Rennmaschine mit mehr als 400 PS bei über 11 000/min, die in die neue C-Klasse installiert wird. Die Rechnung geht auf: Klaus Ludwig bringt es erneut zum deutschen Meister, Jörg van Ommen wird zweiter im Championat und Sieger in der

que le classement Écuries pour son partenaire AMG, qui a son siège à Affalterbach. Jusqu'à la finale de Hockenheim, Klaus Ludwig, le pilote Mercedes, est en tête, mais il doit finalement céder aux assauts du mercenaire d'Audi, Frank Biela.

En 1992, le DTM devient la chasse gardée des voitures étoilées de Stuttgart : comme une trinité des pistes, Kurt Thiim, Klaus Ludwig et Bernd Schneider se relaient en tête du classement avant que Ludwig ne finisse par remporter le titre. Les Mercedes gagnent 16 courses sur 24 et Ellen Lohr est l'auteur d'une grande nouveauté : première victoire d'une femme au DTM, à Hockenheim en mai. La légère baisse de tension durant la saison suivante – Roland Asch termine deuxième au championnat derrière les puissantes six-cylindres à traction intégrale d'Alfa Romeo – n'est en réalité qu'un creux entre deux vagues à la hauteur impressionnante. En 1994 entre en vigueur un nouveau règlement : cylindrée limitée à 2,5 litres, six-cylindres dérivé d'un moteur de série ou auquel on aura ajouté ou amputé deux cylindres. En huit mois seulement, les techniciens de Mercedes transforment le V8 de la 420 SE en un moteur de course pur et dur développant plus de 400 ch à plus de 11 000 tr/min et qui est placé sous le capot de la nouvelle Classe C. À la fin de la saison, les comptes sont bons : Klaus Ludwig est de nouveau sacré champion d'Allemagne, Jörg van Ommen termine deuxième au championnat, mais premier au classement de la Gold Cup, qui tient également compte des places obtenues lors des courses d'invitation de Mugello et de Donington. En outre, Mercedes termine premier au classement Marques, pour la troisième fois depuis 1991 et 1992.

En 1995, les pilotes découvrent un chef-d'œuvre mécanique : « La voiture transpose le pilote dans un monde surréaliste où les lois de la physique semblent ne plus être en vigueur », déclare l'ancien pilote de Grand Prix John Watson dans une envolée lyrique. Métamorphosée en version course par AMG, la nouvelle Classe C est plus puissante, plus légère, plus rigide et plus rapide. Un *gentlemen agreement* passé entre les écuries ne peut même pas mettre un terme à sa marche triomphale : après la course de Donington, elles signent un accord destiné à compenser le clivage entre les voitures à quatre roues motrices et celles à propulsion à l'arrière. Les premières embarquent 20 kg de plus et les secondes peuvent s'alléger de 20 kg, poids unitaire de 1040 kg. Le champion sera cependant le pilote Mercedes Bernd Schneider – aussi bien pour le DTM et ses 13 manches que pour l'ITC (International Touring Car Series), qui comprend également cinq autres courses disputées à l'étranger. Les voitures avec l'étoile sur le capot remportent aussi les championnats respectifs des marques.

L'attrait du DTM n'a pas échappé à la Fédération internationale de l'Automobile qui fait cependant sonner le glas de l'ex-championnat d'Allemagne en 1996 et exporte la série dans le monde entier sous le label ITC. Jusqu'à l'avant-dernière manche sur le circuit d'Interlagos, dans la banlieue de São Paulo, l'issue du championnat reste ouverte entre

mer Grand Prix driver John Watson in his paean of praise. The new C-class, race-prepared by AMG, had become more powerful, lighter, stiffer, and faster. Even a self-imposed act of denial could not hold back this successful formula. After the Donington race an agreement was signed which was intended to provide an even playing field on which the four-wheel-drive and rear-wheel-drive cars could compete on equal terms. This amounted to a 20 kg (44 lb) allowance for the former and a 20 kg penalty for the latter with reference to the unified weight of 1,040 kg (2,293 lb). Despite this, Mercedes man Bernd Schneider took the championship – both for the 13 DTM races and also in the ITC (International Touring Car) Series in which a further five races abroad were included. The cars with the star also won the constructors' championship in both series.

The attraction of the DTM did not escape the FIA (Fédération Internationale de l'Automobile) which then sounded the death knell in 1996 for the one-time German domestic championship and exported the series as an ITC event worldwide. Up to the penultimate round on the Interlagos track outside São Paulo in Brazil the championship was between Bernd Schneider in a Mercedes and the Opel exponent Manuel Reuter. Schneider chose the wrong tires for the wet track in the second heat, and Reuter was the champion. The season's end was marked by a dispute and by the sudden death of the ITC, the FIA's baby, when rivals Alfa Romeo and Opel withdrew from the competition in a barely disguised joint action.

Four years later Schneider has his revenge: the DTM – now called Masters Touring Car – celebrates its renaissance and the Saarland driver steals the title from Reuter. The rules are fine-tuned in 2001 to achieve better equality of prospects. Mercedes increases its driver contingent as a precaution, and assembles such a concentration of quantity and quality that the competition is reduced to battling for the fifth place. Moreover, Bernd Schneider dominates once again. These great moments are suddenly interrupted in 2002 by the Frenchman Laurent Aiello in his Abt-Audi.

This "faux pas" allows the AMG technicians and the HWA team no rest: they go into the 2003 season well armed. Four of the nine Mercedes victories can be booked to the account of the young Swiss driver Marcel Fässler, two are won by Jean Alesi, but in the end, the master is once again Schneider: the fourth title for the old man of the pack. In 2004, it is especially the youngsters who romp around the track with vigor. The talented Briton Gary Paffet took the cup at the prelude in Hockenheim marking Mercedes' 97th DTM victory, while the young Dutchman Christijan Albers achieves victory number 98 at Estoril despite strengthened opposition from Audi.

Wertung für den Gold Cup, die auch die Plazierungen bei den Einladungsrennen in Mugello und Donington einbezieht. Überdies ist Mercedes Marken-Bester, zum dritten Mal seit 1991 und 1992.

1995 tritt man mit einem technischen Wunderwerk an: »Das Auto transportiert den Fahrer in eine surreale Welt, in der die Gesetze der Physik aufgehoben zu sein scheinen«, schwärmt der frühere Grand-Prix-Pilot John Watson geradezu hymnisch. Von AMG in Renntrimm versetzt, ist die neue C-Klasse stärker, leichter, steifer und schneller geworden. Dem Erfolgsrezept tut sogar eine selbst auferlegte Grausamkeit keinen Abbruch: Nach dem Rennen in Donington unterzeichnet man eine Vereinbarung, die das Gefälle zwischen Allradlern und heckgetriebenen Autos ausgleichen soll: 20 Kilogramm minus für jene, 20 Kilogramm plus für diese, Einheitsgewicht 1040 Kilogramm. Dennoch wird Mercedes-Mann Bernd Schneider Meister – sowohl bei den 13 DTM-Läufen als auch in der ITC (für International Touring Car Series), in der fünf weitere Rennen im Ausland einbegriffen sind. Die Wagen mit dem Stern gewinnen auch das jeweilige Championat der Marken.

Die Attraktivität der DTM ist der FIA (für Fédération Internationale de l'Automobile) nicht entgangen, die gleichwohl für 1996 das Sterbeglöcklein für die einst national-deutsche Meisterschaft bimmeln lässt und die Serie als ITC weltweit exportiert. Bis zum vorletzten Lauf auf dem Kurs von Interlagos unweit São Paulo bleibt das Championat unentschieden zwischen Bernd Schneider auf Mercedes und dem Opel-Exponenten Manuel Reuter. Schneider verwachst, falsche Reifen auf der nassen Strecke im zweiten Lauf, Reuter wird Champion. Ende der Saison kommt es zum Eklat und zum plötzlichen Kindstod des FIA-Säuglings ITC, als sich die Konkurrenten Alfa Romeo und Opel in einer kaum kaschierten konzertierten Aktion aus dem Wettbewerb zurückziehen.

Vier Jahre später revanchiert sich Schneider: Die DTM – jetzt Tourenwagen Masters genannt – feiert ihre Renaissance, und der Saarländer schnappt Reuter den Titel weg. 2001 wird das Reglement verfeinert, um noch mehr Chancengleichheit zu erreichen. Vorsichtshalber stockt Mercedes sein Fahrerkontingent auf und tritt mit einer derartigen Konzentration von Masse und Klasse an, dass die Konkurrenz um den fünften Platz kämpfen darf. Und wieder dominiert Bernd Schneider. Die vielen Sternstunden unterbricht 2002 jäh der Franzose Laurent Aiello mit seinem Abt-Audi.

Dieser Fauxpas lässt die AMG-Techniker und die HWA-Truppe nicht ruhen: Bestens gerüstet gehen sie in die Saison 2003. Vier der neun Mercedes-Siege gehen auf das Konto des jungen Schweizers Marcel Fässler, zwei fährt Jean Alesi ein, doch am Schluss heißt der Master wieder Schneider: Vierter Titel für den Senior im Feld. In diesem tummeln sich 2004 besonders stark die Youngster. Beim Auftakt in Hockenheim holt der talentierte Brite Gary Paffet den Pokal für den insgesamt 97. DTM-Sieg von Mercedes, und in Estoril lässt der junge Holländer Christijan Albers trotz erstarkter Audi-Konkurrenz Nummer 98 folgen.

Le Mans 1991: the Mercedes C11 of Dickens/Palmer/Thiim.
Le Mans 1991: der Mercedes C11 von Dickens/Palmer/Thiim.
Le Mans 1991: la Mercedes C11 de Dickens/Palmer/Thiim.

Bernd Schneider, sur Mercedes, et Manuel Reuter, son adversaire de chez Opel. Schneider commet une erreur en faisant monter les mauvais pneus sur le circuit humide lors de la deuxième manche et Reuter est sacré champion. La fin de la saison est marquée par un coup d'éclat qui se traduit par la mort instantanée de l'ITC, le rejeton de la FIA, lorsque les concurrents Alfa Romeo et Opel décident, dans le cadre d'une action manifestement concertée, de se retirer de la compétition.

Quatre ans plus tard, Bernd Schneider tient sa revanche : le DTM – désormais appelé Tourenwagen Masters – fête sa renaissance et le Sarrois chipe le titre à Manuel Reuter. En 2001, le règlement est peaufiné pour instaurer une encore plus grande égalité des chances. Prudent, Mercedes augmente son contingent de pilotes et s'aligne au départ du championnat avec une telle concentration de quantité et de qualité que la concurrence ne peut plus espérer qu'en la cinquième place. Et, de nouveau, Bernd Schneider impose sa domination. Seul le Français Laurent Aiello, avec son Abt-Audi, interrompt en 2002 l'épopée du constructeur de Stuttgart.

Ce faux pas stimule les techniciens d'AMG et les mercenaires de HWA : ils sont parfaitement armés lorsqu'ils s'alignent pour la saison 2003. Quatre des neuf victoires de Mercedes sont à porter à l'actif du jeune pilote suisse Marcel Fässler, Jean Alesi en engrange deux, mais, quand on fait les comptes, Schneider coiffe de nouveau la couronne du Masters : quatrième titre pour le doyen du plateau. Un plateau où apparaissent, en 2004, de nombreux jeunes loups aux dents longues. Lors de l'ouverture du championnat, à Hockenheim, le Britannique Gary Paffet au talent avéré signe la 97e victoire de Mercedes au DTM et, à Estoril, le jeune Néerlandais Christijan Albers, malgré les Audi rivales qui se sont renforcées, ajoute la 98e.

Revival of the legend – as a *joint venture*

Sauber marvels: Mercedes engines – powerful hearts in Group C 1985–1991

The first official contact between Daimler-Benz AG and Peter Sauber's Swiss racing car workshop is documented on 28 October 1983. This took place at the Sauber premises in Hinwil near Zurich. However, their paths had crossed before. The Swiss built Group C racing sports cars (introduced in 1982, minimum weight initially 800 kg/1,764 lb, 100-liter/26.4 gal tank, maximum fuel consumption 60 liters over 100 km/3.9 mpg, engine from a recognized manufacturer). Mercedes technicians had assisted with the development of previous Sauber Group C creations in the form of some official moonlighting – on the C6 which combined BMW elements in the chassis and the Cosworth DFL engine, and on the C7 which used the comparatively weak but reliable engine of the BMW M1. In addition, Sauber was allowed to use the Mercedes wind tunnel in Sindelfingen for testing. It was not just that the powers-that-be turned a blind eye to this; rather, they also discovered that the small entrepreneur's name (meaning gleaming in German) was reflected in his cars, which were also absolutely fantastic. The meeting in Hinwil did not bear real fruit until 1985 when a Mercedes product occupied the engine compartment of the Sauber C8: the M117 HL V8 with two KKK turbochargers, 4973 cc and 700 bhp, based on the production engine of the 450 SLC 5.0.

The sponsor, arranged by motorsport do-it-all Jochen Neerpasch who was engaged by Mercedes as a consultant, was Yves Saint-Laurent. The win by Sauber's Mike Thackwell and Henri Pescarolo in the 1,000-kilometer race at the Nürburgring in 1986 turned out to be the one swallow that did not make a summer. It was only in 1988, now with the C9, that further dividends were reaped with first places in five races. Daimler-Benz had by then decided on an official return to racing, provided Sauber with comprehensive backup, and also brought in its AEG subsidiary as a sponsor.

AEG's dark blue gave way to the traditional silver in 1989, a visual reference to past glories stipulated personally by Werner Niefer, the chairman of the board of directors of the newly founded Mercedes-Benz AG. The car immediately picked up where the 300 SLR had left off in 1955. Of the 18 races in which the Sauber-Mercedes C9 and C11 started in 1989 and 1990 they won 16, including the one-two at Le Mans in 1989, an accolade for the deep-throated, high-speed German-Swiss coproduction. Mercedes boycotted the Sarthe course in 1990 in protest at the endless quarreling between motorsport's ruling body FISA and the organizers of the 24-Hour Race about the status of that year's event. In Dijon in 1989 the Michelin tires of the Sauber Silver Arrows wore too quickly, and a Goodyear-shod Joest-Porsche won ahead of the helplessly sliding C9. At Silver-

Reanimation der Legende – als *joint venture*

Sauber-Kunststücke: Mercedes-Maschinen als starke Herzen in der Gruppe C 1985–1991

Der erste offizielle Kontakt zwischen der Daimler-Benz AG und der Schweizer Rennwagen-Schmiede von Peter Sauber ist belegt für den 28. Oktober 1983. Schauplatz ist die Sauber-Garnison Hinwil bei Zürich. Doch schon vorher hat man einander umspielt: Der Eidgenosse baut Rennsportwagen der Gruppe C (1982 eingeführt, Mindestgewicht zunächst 800 kg, 100-Liter-Tank, Maximalverbrauch 60 Liter auf 100 Kilometer, Maschine von einem anerkannten Hersteller). Mercedes-Techniker haben gewissermaßen als Feierabend-Aktivität bei der Entwicklung früherer Sauber-Kreationen für die Gruppe C mitgewirkt – beim C6, der BMW-Elemente im Chassis und das Cosworth-Triebwerk DFL miteinander vereint, und beim C7, in dem die vergleichsweise schwächliche, aber zuverlässige Maschine des BMW M1 Dienst tut. Überdies darf man den Mercedes-Windtunnel in Sindelfingen benutzen. Nicht nur, dass die Konzern-Oberen dazu ein Auge zudrücken, sie stellen zugleich fest, dass der Name des kleinen Unternehmers programmatisch ist: Blitzsauber sind auch seine Produkte. Das Meeting von Hinwil trägt erst 1985 reale Früchte, als im Maschinenraum des Sauber C8 ein Mercedes-Erzeugnis Einzug hält: der M117 HL V8 mit zwei KKK-Ladern, 4973 ccm und 700 PS, basierend auf dem Serienmotor des 450 SLC 5.0.

Sponsor, vermittelt von Rennsport-Faktotum Jochen Neerpasch, für Mercedes als Berater tätig, ist Yves Saint-Laurent. Der Sieg der Sauber-Männer Mike Thackwell und Henri Pescarolo beim 1000-Kilometer-Rennen auf dem Nürburgring 1986 entpuppt sich indes als Einzelschwalbe, die noch keinen Sommer macht. Erst 1988, nun schon mit dem C9, stellt sich mit ersten Plätzen in fünf Rennen weitere Erfolgsdividende ein. Da hat Daimler-Benz bereits seine offizielle Rückkehr in den Rennsport beschlossen, lässt Sauber eine umfassende Betreuung angedeihen und bringt auch gleich die Konzerntochter AEG als Mäzen mit.

Deren Dunkelblau weicht 1989 dem traditionellen Silber, eine Anspielung auf große Vergangenheit, die sich Werner Niefer, Vorstandsvorsitzender der neu gegründeten Mercedes-Benz AG, persönlich ausbedungen hat. Man fährt gleichsam da fort, wo die 300 SLR 1955 aufgehört haben: Von den 18 Läufen, in denen die Sauber-Mercedes C9 und C11 in den Jahren 1989 und 1990 starten, gewinnen sie 16 – inklusive des Doppelsiegs in Le Mans 1989 als Ritterschlag für die rasende und sonor grollende deutschschweizerische Koproduktion. 1990 bleibt Mercedes dem Sarthe-Kurs fern, als Protest gegen die endlose Querele zwischen der Motorsport-Legislative FISA und den Organisatoren des 24-Stunden-Rennens über den Status der Veranstaltung in diesem Jahr. In Dijon 1989 nutzen sich die Michelin-Pneus der

Une légende revit – sous forme de *joint-venture*

Sauber le sorcier : des moteurs de Mercedes pour le Groupe C 1985–1991

Les premiers contacts officiels entre la Daimler-Benz AG et le constructeur suisse Peter Sauber remontent au 28 octobre 1983. La scène se passe dans les ateliers de Sauber à Hinwil. Mais les protagonistes ont déjà joué au chat et à la souris auparavant : l'Helvète construit des voitures de course pour le Groupe C (institué en 1982, poids minimum initial 800 kg, réservoir de 100 litres, consommation maximale 60 litres aux 100 km, moteur construit par un fabricant connu). En perruque, si l'on peut dire, des techniciens de Mercedes ont contribué au développement des anciens bolides de Sauber pour le Groupe C – par exemple la C6, qui combine fraternellement des éléments de BMW pour le châssis et un moteur Cosworth DFL, ou la C7 sous le capot de laquelle officie le moteur un peu faible mais fiable de la BMW M1. Ils sont en outre autorisés à utiliser la soufflerie Mercedes de Sindelfingen. Les dirigeants du groupe ne se contentent pas de tolérer avec bienveillance ces activités, il ne leur échappe pas non plus que le nom de la firme a aussi valeur de programme : les produits Sauber font honneur à leur nom, ils brillent par leur propreté et leur qualité de finition. La réunion de Hinwil ne porte ses premiers fruits officiels qu'en 1985 lorsque l'on soulève le capot moteur de la Sauber C8 et y découvre un moteur Mercedes : le M117 HL V8 avec deux turbocompresseurs KKK, une cylindrée de 4973 cm³ et 700 ch, dérivé du moteur de série de la 450 SLC 5.0.

Le sponsor, déniché par Jochen Neerpasch, mentor de la compétition automobile en Allemagne et consultant de Mercedes, est Yves Saint Laurent. La victoire remportée par les pilotes Sauber, Mike Thackwell et Henri Pescarolo, à la course des 1000 km du Nürburgring en 1986, est en réalité une hirondelle qui ne fait pas le printemps. Ce n'est qu'en 1988, déjà avec la C9, que l'on encaisse d'autres dividendes du succès avec cinq premières places. Mais Daimler-Benz a déjà annoncé son retrait officiel de la compétition automobile tout en faisant bénéficier Sauber d'une assistance tous azimuts et, en retour, entraînant AEG, filiale du groupe, comme sponsor.

En 1989, leur bleu marine disparaît au profit de l'argent traditionnel, une allusion à un grand passé, que Werner Niefer, président du Directoire de la nouvelle firme Mercedes-Benz AG, a imaginée personnellement. On reprend son ouvrage là où on l'avait interrompu en 1955 avec la 300 SLR : sur les 18 manches auxquelles les Sauber-Mercedes C9 et C11 participent en 1989 et 1990, elles en gagnent seize – y compris le doublé du Mans en 1989 qui donne ses lettres de noblesse à la coproduction germano-suisse aussi bruyante que performante. En 1990, Mercedes reste absente du circuit de la Sarthe en signe de protestation contre les interminables querelles entre les autorités fédérales, la FISA, et les organi-

stone in 1990 one C11 was disqualified for using outside assistance, and the other dropped out with mechanical failure. The 1989 world sports car champion was Jean-Louis Schlesser, and in 1990 Schlesser shared the title with Mauro Baldi.

The 1991 season acted as a counterpoint to this. A new regulation for Group C specified 3.5-liter aspirated engines and a dry weight of at least 750 kg (1,653 lb). Mercedes-Benz responded with a V12 of 3492 cc and 700 bhp at over 13,000 rpm, and Sauber with the C291 chassis. But the 12-cylinder was plagued by numerous faults, and Jaguar won the world championship.

Nonetheless, the season ended on a conciliatory note for Sauber-Mercedes at the "Autopolis" track in Japan where the C291 crew of Michael Schumacher/Karl Wendlinger earned the right to spray the winners' champagne and notched up further good marks for themselves in Mercedes-Benz's "flying classroom." After such high-flying, everyone was quickly brought down to earth again by the decision of the board of management on 26 November 1991 to withdraw from Group C racing. The three C292s which had already been prepared for the following season shared the fate of many other rockets: they looked promising but they never went into action.

Symbioses: engine supplier for Formula 1 and IndyCar since 1994

After the withdrawal from the sports-car field half of the five-year contract with Peter Sauber still remained to run. The names of Mercedes and Sauber were still joined, both legally and morally. Since July 1991 Harvey Postlethwaite, a doctor of philosophy, and also one of the most renowned designers in the field, had been working in Hinwil on a Formula 1 chassis for 1993. He had signed up in anticipation of Mercedes playing a full part in future. Sauber retained access to Postlethwaite's creation, and also to a V10 from his Swiss compatriot Mario Illien, a partner in the engine-builder Ilmor which was based in Brixworth in the English county of Northamptonshire. He was also provided with 30 million marks a year as a starter, with the proviso that he had to find the balance of the necessary funding for himself. Jochen Neerpasch was entrusted with this task, though he left a disappointed man in mid-1992 after his attempts to mine the ever more meager sponsorship fields failed to locate any sources of funding which could be tapped. Postlethwaite also departed. His work was continued by Leo Ress. The Sauber C12 for 1993, however, had to make do without the threatened weapon of an active suspension, and so, an underdog, it faded from serious competition.

A new leaf seemed to have been turned over on 3 November 1993 when the Mercedes management

Sauber-Silberpfeile zu rasch ab, und ein Goodyear-besohlter Joest-Porsche kommt vor den hilflos umherrutschenden C9 ins Ziel. In Silverstone 1990 wird ein C11 wegen Inanspruchnahme fremder Hilfe disqualifiziert, der andere fällt mit einem mechanischen Schaden aus. Sportwagenweltmeister 1989 wird Jean-Louis Schlesser, 1990 wiederum Schlesser ex aequo mit Mauro Baldi.

Da wirkt die Saison 1991 als Kontrapunkt: Ein neues Regelwerk für die Gruppe C sieht Saugmotoren von 3,5 Litern und ein Trockengewicht von mindestens 750 Kilogramm vor. Mercedes-Benz antwortet mit einem V12 von 3492 ccm und 700 PS bei über 13 000/min, Sauber mit dem Chassis C291. Aber der Zwölfzylinder wird heimgesucht von zahlreichen Defekten. Weltmeister werden die Jaguar.

Dennoch klingt die Saison aus mit einem versöhnlichen Akkord für die Sauber-Mercedes im japanischen »Autopolis«: Den Champagner für die Sieger versprüht die C291-Crew Michael Schumacher/Karl Wendlinger und holt sich damit weitere gute Noten im »fliegenden Klassenzimmer« von Mercedes-Benz. Dem Höhenflug folgt der Absturz: Am 26. November 1991 entschließt sich der Vorstand, künftig der Gruppe C fernzubleiben. Die drei C292 aber, die bereits für die nächste Saison vorbereitet worden sind, teilen das Los der meisten anderen Raketen: Sie sehen vielversprechend aus, kommen aber nie zum Einsatz.

Symbiosen: Motorenlieferant für Formel 1 und IndyCar seit 1994

Was nach dem Rückzug von der Sportwagen-front bleibt, ist ein nur zur Hälfte aufgebrauchter Fünf-Jahres-Vertrag mit Peter Sauber. Man steht gleichsam doppelt im Wort, legal und moralisch. Seit dem Juli 1991 arbeitet in Hinwil Harvey Postlethwaite, seines Zeichens Doktor der Philosophie, aber auch einer der renommiertesten Designer der Branche, an einem Formel-1-Chassis für 1993. Er hat angeheuert im Vertrauen auf ein zukünftiges volles Mercedes-Engagement. Sauber behält den Zugriff auf Postlethwaites Kreation ebenso wie auf einen V10 seines Schweizer Landsmanns Mario Illien, Partner und Teilhaber an der Motoren-Manufaktur Ilmor in Brixworth in der englischen Grafschaft Northamptonshire. Überdies greift man ihm mit 30 Millionen Mark pro anno unter die Arme, mit der Maßgabe, sich den Rest der nötigen Mittel selbst zu besorgen. Damit betraut ist Jochen Neerpasch, der sich indes Mitte 1992 enttäuscht absetzt, weil sich bei seinem Wünschelrutengang über die karger werdenden Sponsor-Gründe keine Geldquellen anzapfen lassen. Auch Postlethwaite geht. Seine Arbeit wird von Leo Ress fortgesetzt. Der Sauber-C12 für 1993 muss allerdings ohne die in jenem Jahr ultimative Raffinesse eines aktiven Fahrwerks auskommen und verkümmert deshalb zum Underdog.

Das Blatt scheint sich zu wenden, als das Mercedes-Management am 3. November 1993 den künftigen Sport-

sateurs des 24 heures quant au statut de l'épreuve. À Dijon en 1989, les pneus Michelin des Flèches d'argent s'usent trop rapidement et une Joest-Porsche chaussée par Goodyear passe la ligne d'arrivée avant les C9 à l'agonie. À Silverstone en 1990, une C11 est disqualifiée pour avoir fait appel à une aide extérieure et l'autre abandonne sur panne mécanique. En 1989, le champion du monde des voitures de rallye est Jean-Louis Schlesser, qui réédite sa performance en 1990, année où il termine ex aequo avec Mauro Baldi.

Qui aurait cru que la saison 1991 s'inscrirait alors en contrepoint? Un nouveau règlement pour le Groupe C impose des moteurs atmosphériques de 3,5 litres et un poids à sec minimal de 750 kg. Mercedes-Benz réplique avec un V12 de 3492 cm³ et 700 ch à plus de 13 000 tr/min et Sauber, avec le châssis C291. Mais les V12 ne sont pas fiables et Jaguar est sacré champion du monde. La saison se termine pourtant sur une note plus gaie pour l'équipe Sauber-Mercedes sur le circuit d'« Autopolis », au Japon : l'équipage de la C291, Michael Schumacher/Karl Wendlinger, fait pétiller le champagne des vainqueurs, obtenant ainsi un prix d'excellence supplémentaire dans la « salle de classe volante » de Mercedes-Benz. Mais plus dure sera la chute : le 26 novembre 1991, le Directoire décide de ne plus participer désormais au Groupe C. Les trois C292, partagent le destin de la majorité des autres fusées à quatre roues : elles sont prometteuses, mais ne subiront jamais leur baptême du feu.

Symbioses : motoriste pour la Formule 1 et l'IndyCar depuis 1994

Ce qui reste après le retrait du championnat des voitures de sport, c'est un contrat de cinq ans avec Peter Sauber qui n'a été honoré qu'à moitié. Mercedes est en quelque sorte obligée à un double point de vue, sur le plan légal et sur le plan moral. Depuis juillet 1991, un certain Harvey Postlethwaite, titulaire d'un doctorat en philosophie, mais aussi l'un des designers les plus réputés de ce secteur, travaille à Hinwil à un châssis de Formule 1 pour 1993. Il a été recruté, confiant en un engagement total de Mercedes à l'avenir. Sauber pourra continuer d'utiliser la création de Postlethwaite ainsi que le V10 concocté par son compatriote suisse Mario Illien, partenaire et associé de la manufacture de moteurs Ilmor à Brixworth, dans le comté anglais du Northamptonshire. On lui accorde en outre un budget de 30 millions de marks par an à la condition qu'il se procure lui-même le reste des crédits nécessaires. On fait appel pour cela à Jochen Neerpasch, qui démissionne cependant à la mi-1992, déçu, parce qu'il ne parvient à découvrir aucune source d'argent dans le cadre de sa quête de sponsors potentiels. Harvey Postlethwaite démissionne lui aussi. Son travail est repris par Leo Ress. Pour 1993, la Sauber C12 doit toutefois renoncer au châssis actif, raffinement technique dont l'absence la condamne à végéter dans les milieux de peloton.

La situation semble devoir s'améliorer, le 3 novembre 1993, lorsque la direction de Mercedes annonce l'engage-

announced the company's future sporting involvement in three fields: Formula 1, IndyCar, and DTM. The Sauber-C13 for the 1994 season was now adorned with the slogan "Concept by Mercedes" and the Mercedes logo appeared on the cylinder head covers of the compact, lightweight type 2175 B V10 developed by Ilmor. The C13 remained pitch black. According to a pensive Peter Sauber, the color of fibers which had been charred to pure carbon was a technical sort of color that was every bit as beautiful as the silver of times gone by. However, the fortunes of his team also remained black. The season was overshadowed by Sauber driver Karl Wendlinger's serious accident on 12 May in Monaco. Team-mate Heinz-Harald Frentzen also failed to impress with his 13th place in the world championship. The main feature of the season, though, was the failure to attract the hoped-for sponsorship, and so the Sauber-connection came to an end on 31 December 1994.

This left the way clear for what the well-known Swiss journalist Adriano Cimarosti, writing in *Automobil Revue*, called "a second Mercedes marriage", driven by the compulsion for success. The other partner this time, McLaren International, was one of the most eligible of all, a team that commanded attention with 104 Grand Prix wins and seven world championship titles in the previous 11 years to their name, though one which had been relegated to the slow lane of success in the post-Ayrton Senna era. The intention was to finish among the top four teams in 1995, promised director Jürgen Hubbert with moderate confidence when the five-year agreement with the Britons was announced in the museum in Untertürkheim on 28 October 1994. And that's exactly what happened – that, but no more than that. The team with the McLaren MP4/10 chassis and the Mercedes-Benz FO 110 V10 3-liter engine completed by Ilmor in just 19 weeks finished fourth in the Constructors' Championship. The highlights of a season dominated by Benetton, Williams, and Ferrari were two second places for McLaren-Mercedes driver Mika Hakkinen. During practice for the Australian Grand Prix the Finn suffered almost fatal head injuries but was back in the cockpit and as fast as ever the following year after a miraculous recovery. However, the apprenticeship of 1995 was by no means a prelude to a year of mastery in 1996. Although four-times world champion Alain Prost had been engaged as a consultant and test driver to back up the driving team of Hakkinen and David Coulthard, although the difficult MP4/11 chassis was improved continuously, and although the Mercedes engine was regarded as one of the most powerful in Formula 1, the team had to be content with strong performances on tracks which favored fast, fluent driving. It took some satisfaction from tantalizingly close finishes when victory was within reach three times. Ultimately, however, it was only enough for fourth place again in the Constructors' Championship.

Silver was predominant in the mix of gleaming colors of the new MP4/12 model at its unveiling at London's Alexandra Palace in front of 4,500 invited guests in February 1997. But this visual reference to the past was played

Einsatz der Firma auf drei Feldern verheißt: Formel 1, Indy-Car, DTM. Den Sauber-C13 für die Saison 1994 schmückt nun der Slogan »Concept by Mercedes« und das Mercedes-Logo auf den Zylinderkopfdeckeln des kompakten und leichten V10 Typ 2175 B, den Ilmor entwickelt hat. Der C13 bleibt sargschwarz: Die Farbe von zu reinem Kohlenstoff verglühten Fasern, sagt Peter Sauber versonnen, sei eine technische Couleur, genauso schön wie das Silber von damals. Schwarz bleiben indessen auch die Geschicke seines Teams. Die Saison wird überschattet vom schweren Sturz des Sauber-Piloten Karl Wendlinger am 12. Mai in Monaco. Auch Teamgefährte Heinz-Harald Frentzen vermag sich mit Rang 13 in der Weltmeisterschaft nicht so recht in Szene zu setzen. Vor allem aber bleiben die erhofften Sponsor-Zuwendungen aus. Und so lässt man die Sauber-Connection am 31. Dezember 1994 ausklingen.

Da ist bereits angebahnt, was der bekannte Schweizer Journalist Adriano Cimarosti in der *Automobil Revue* »eine zweite Mercedes-Ehe« nennt, gestiftet vom Zwang zum Erfolg. Diesmal hat man sich an eine der besten Adressen im Geschäft gewendet, McLaren International, ein Team, das sich mit 104 gewonnenen Grand Prix und sieben Weltmeistertiteln innerhalb der letzten elf Jahre der Aufmerksamkeit empfohlen hat, in der Ära nach Ayrton Senna allerdings auf die Kriechspur des Erfolgs abgedrängt worden ist. Man wolle 1995 unter den vier Top-Teams sein, verspricht Vorstandsmitglied Jürgen Hubbert in moderater Zuversicht, als der Fünfjahres-Pakt mit den Briten am 28. Oktober 1994 im Museum in Untertürkheim verkündet wird. Genau dies trifft ein – aber auch nicht mehr: Mit dem Chassis McLaren MP4/10 und der von Ilmor in nur 19 Wochen fertiggestellten Dreiliter-Maschine Mercedes-Benz FO 110 V10 wird man vierter im Championat der Konstrukteure. Highlights in einer Saison, die von Benetton, Williams und Ferrari beherrscht wird: zwei zweite Plätze für McLaren-Mercedes-Pilot Mika Hakkinen. Beim Training zum Grand Prix von Australien zieht sich der Finne fast letale Kopfverletzungen zu, sitzt jedoch nach wundersamer Heilung im nächsten Jahr wieder im Cockpit, schnell wie eh und je. Gleichwohl

It's all there in black and white: Barcelona 1993.
Urheberschaft weiß auf schwarz: Barcelona 1993.
Copyright noir sur blanc : Barcelone 1993.

ment futur de la firme dans son domaine : la Formule 1, le championnat IndyCar et le DTM. La Sauber C13 pour la saison 1994 arbore désormais fièrement sur son capot le slogan « Concept by Mercedes » et le logo Mercedes sur les culasses du compact et léger V10, type 2175 B mis au point par Ilmor. La C13 reste d'un noir de corbillard : la couleur des fibres que la cuisson a transformées en carbone pur, déclare Peter Sauber dans un clin d'œil, est une couleur technique qui est aussi belle que l'argent de jadis. Mais le noir sera aussi la couleur de la chronique de son écurie. La saison est en effet ombragée par le grave accident du pilote Sauber Karl Wendlinger, le 12 mai à Monaco. Son coéquipier Heinz-Harald Frentzen, quant à lui, ne parvient pas à vraiment se mettre en valeur et termine 13e au championnat du monde. Mais le pire est que les crédits espérés des sponsors se font attendre. Et c'est ainsi que la liaison avec Sauber arrive à expiration le 31 décembre 1994.

Pendant ce temps s'esquisse déjà ce que le célèbre journaliste suisse Adriano Cimarosti nomme, dans la *Revue Automobile*, un « second mariage Mercedes », initié par la contrainte du succès. Cette fois-ci, Mercedes a choisi l'un des noms les plus illustres du plateau, McLaren International, une écurie qui s'est recommandée à son attention en remportant 104 Grands Prix et sept titres de champion du monde au cours des onze dernières années, mais qui, après le départ d'Ayrton Senna, n'a toutefois plus remporté de victoire. Terminer parmi les quatre top teams en 1995 est l'objectif proclamé, avec une confiance empreinte de modestie, par le membre du Directoire Jürgen Hubbert lorsque le contrat de cinq ans avec les Britanniques est annoncé, le 28 octobre 1994, au musée de Untertürkheim. Le contrat est rempli – mais rien de plus : avec le châssis McLaren MP4/10 et le moteur Mercedes-Benz FO 110 V10 de trois litres réalisé par Ilmor en 19 semaines seulement, le couple termine quatrième au championnat Constructeurs. Les temps forts d'une saison dominée par Benetton, Williams et Ferrari sont deux secondes places pour le pilote Mercedes McLaren Mika Hakkinen. Lors des qualifications pour le Grand Prix d'Australie, le Finlandais se blesse très gravement à la tête, mais, après une guérison presque miraculeuse, retrouve l'année suivante son cockpit, aussi rapide que toujours. Et pourtant, l'année d'apprentissage de 1995 ne sera en aucun cas suivie par une année 1996 comblée de succès. Certes, on a donné au duo de pilotes Mika Hakkinen et David Coulthard le quadruple champion du monde Alain Prost comme consultant et pilote d'essais ; certes, le châssis MP4/11 difficile à régler est amélioré en permanence ; certes, le moteur Mercedes a la réputation d'être l'un des plus puissants de la Formule 1, mais l'on doit se contenter de démonstrations prometteuses sur les circuits rapides et fluides, et la seule consolation que l'on puisse tirer du supplice de Tantale est d'avoir eu à trois reprises la victoire à portée de la main. En fin de compte, il faudra se contenter à nouveau d'une quatrième place au classement Marques.

L'argent prédomine dans le cocktail de couleurs, grâce auquel le nouveau modèle MP4/12 brille lors de sa présen-

Banned smoke signals: Mika Hakkinen at the 1996
European Grand Prix at the Nürburgring.

Verbotene Rauch-Zeichen: Mika Hakkinen beim Großen
Preis von Europa 1996 auf dem Nürburgring.

Mika Hakkinen, au Grand Prix d'Europe, en 1996,
sur le Nürburgring.

down by McLaren boss Ron Dennis who said this was just
a question of the overall effect of the color composition.
And Mercedes' head of motorsport Norbert Haug seconded
him cautiously: "Before a car becomes a Silver Arrow, it first
has to win." This happened much sooner than he
could have dared to hope when David Coulthard, driving
the McLaren MP4/11, won the Australian Grand Prix on
9 March 1997, the first of the new season. There was instant
success too on another front, in Indianapolis on 29 May
1994, 79 years after the Daimler success of Ralph de Palma
in the holiest-of-holies of American motorsport. Mercedes
supplied the Penske team with turbocharged v8 engines for
the Stock Block category, in accordance with the USAC
(United States Auto Club) rules: 3.43 liters, only two valves
per cylinder operated by a single camshaft rotating in the
engine block, 1024 bhp. Ilmor required 23 weeks to turn the
concept into reality. Penske driver Emerson Fittipaldi led
for 144 laps and then scraped the outside wall 16 laps before
the finish and had to drop out. The race was won by Penske
driver Al Unser Junior, known affectionately in the Indy-
Car world as Little Al. He finished the 1995 IndyCar Series
in second place with a new 2.65-liter engine, behind Jacques
Villeneuve in a Reynard-Ford.

In 1996 the solid Canadian Paul Tracy joined the existing team of drivers. The season reached its punchline, but
no one at Roger Penske found it funny. Up to the final
round in Laguna Seca Al Unser's hopes of the title were still
alive. However, everything went wrong there, and ultimately the youngest scion of one of the leading racing families in the country was relegated to fourth place by Lady
Luck of the Tracks.

folgt dem Lehrjahr 1995 keineswegs ein Herrenjahr 1996.
Zwar hat man der Piloten-Combo Hakkinen und David
Coulthard Vierfach-Champion Alain Prost als Berater und
Testfahrer zur Seite gestellt, zwar wird das diffizile Chassis
MP 4/11 kontinuierlich verbessert, zwar gilt der Mercedes-
Motor als einer der stärksten in der Formel 1, aber man muss
sich mit starken Auftritten auf zügig und flüssig zu fahrenden Kursen bescheiden und zieht eine kleine Befriedigung
aus dem Tantalus-Effekt, der Sieg sei dreimal in Reichweite
gewesen. Am Ende langt es wieder nur zum vierten Platz in
der Markenwertung.

In der Farben-Melange, in der das neue Modell MP 4/12
bei seiner Präsentation im Londoner Alexandra Palace vor
4500 geladenen Gästen im Februar 1997 erglänzt, überwiegt
Silber. Nur: Das sei, wiegelt McLaren-Chef Ron Dennis ab,
allein eine Frage der Gesamtwirkung der Komposition.
Und Mercedes Motorsport-Boss Norbert Haug sekundiert
ihm behutsam: »Ehe man ein Silberpfeil wird, muss man
erst einmal gewinnen.« Dies geschieht viel schneller, als
es zu träumen gewagt hätte: Beim Grand Prix von Australien am 9. März 1997, dem ersten der neuen Saison, siegt
David Coulthard auf McLaren MP 4/12. Auch an einer anderen Front stellt sich auf Anhieb Erfolg ein, in Indianapolis
am 29. Mai 1994, 79 Jahre nach dem Daimler-Erfolg von
Ralph de Palma im Allerheiligsten des amerikanischen
Motorsports. Mercedes hat das Penske-Team mit aufgeladenen v8-Triebwerken im Rahmen der Stock-Block-Kate-
gorie ausgestattet, konform mit den Spielregeln des USAC
(für United States Auto Club): 3,43 Liter, nur zwei Ventile
je Zylinder, die über eine einzige im Motorblock rotierende
Nockenwelle zur Arbeit angehalten werden, 1024 PS. Für
die Wegstrecke vom Konzept zum Produkt benötigt Ilmor
23 Wochen. 144 Runden führt Penske-Pilot Emerson Fittipaldi, streift 16 Runden vor Schluss die Begrenzungsmauer
und muss aufgeben. Sieger wird Penske-Pilot Al Unser der
Jüngere, in der Branche liebevoll Little Al genannt. Die
IndyCar-Serie 1995 schließt Little Al mit einem neuen
Triebwerk von 2,65 Litern als zweiter ab, hinter Jacques
Villeneuve auf Reynard-Ford.

1996 gesellt sich der bullige Kanadier Paul Tracy zu der
vorhandenen Fahrerausstattung. Die Saison mündet in

Spa 1994: Heinz-Harald Frentzen in a Sauber-Mercedes
C13 at the Eau Rouge chicane.

Spa 1994: Heinz-Harald Frentzen auf dem Sauber-
Mercedes C13 in der Schikane bei Eau Rouge.

Spa 1994 : Heinz-Harald Frentzen, sur la Sauber-
Mercedes C13 dans la chicane de l'Eau Rouge.

tation à l'Alexandra Palace de Londres devant 4500 invités
triés sur le volet, en février 1997. Prudent, le P.-D.G. de
McLaren Ron Dennis précise que c'est exclusivement une
question d'effet global de la composition. Et Norbert Haug,
directeur des activités de compétition de Mercedes, abonde
dans son sens : « Avant d'être une Flèche d'argent, il faut
d'abord savoir gagner. » Or cela se produit beaucoup plus
rapidement qu'il n'aurait jamais osé l'espérer : lors du Grand
Prix d'Australie, le 9 mars 1997, le premier de la nouvelle
saison, David Coulthard remporte la victoire avec la
McLaren MP4/12. Dans un autre registre, aussi, la marque
remporte d'emblée un succès, à Indianapolis, le 29 mai 1994,
79 ans après le succès de Daimler remporté par Ralph de
Palma dans le saint des saints de la compétition automobile
américaine. Mercedes a équipé l'écurie Penske de moteurs
v8 suralimentés dans le cadre de la catégorie Stock-Block
conformément aux règles du jeu de l'USAC (United States
Auto Club) : 3,43 litres de cylindrée, seulement deux
soupapes par cylindre, qui sont actionnées par un seul
arbre à cames tournant dans le bloc moteur, et 1024 ch.
Partant d'une feuille blanche, Ilmor aura eu besoin de
23 semaines pour présenter son nouvel enfant. Emerson
Fittipaldi, pilote de Penske, est en tête pendant 144 tours,
mais percute le mur à 16 tours de l'arrivée et doit abandonner. C'est ainsi que gagne le pilote Penske Al Unser
junior, que l'on surnomme affectueusement Little Al dans
le milieu. Little Al termine la série Indy-Car 1995 avec un
nouveau moteur de 2,65 litres au deuxième rang, derrière
Jacques Villeneuve sur Reynard-Ford. En 1996, le corpulent
canadien Paul Tracy vient compléter l'équipe de pilotes. La
saison se termine sur une pointe d'ironie qui ne fait rire
personne chez Roger Penske : jusqu'à la finale à Laguna
Seca, Al Unser est encore en position de remporter le
titre. Mais, là, tout va de travers et, au final, le benjamin de
l'une des grandes dynasties de la compétition automobile
américaine est relégué au quatrième rang par la (mauvaise)
fortune des circuits.

Il faudrait plus de trois hirondelles pour annoncer le
printemps au championnat CART de la saison 1997. Avec des
victoires à Nazareth, Rio de Janeiro et Madison, Paul Tracy
semble pourtant gagner ses galons pour sa promotion. Et
pourtant, en une saison qui vaudra aux pilotes Mercedes
neuf succès en 17 courses avec, à la clef, tout de même, le
championnat Constructeurs, il voit s'envoler ce qu'il croyait
avoir bien en main. La saison se termine malgré tout sur
une note réjouissante lorsque Mark Blundell, le pilote de
PacWest, signe son premier succès sur un ovale au California
Speedway de Fontana. Après sa victoire, le jovial Britannique se réjouit comme un gamin : qu'y a-t-il de plus beau,
dans ce sport, que de pouvoir déclarer pendant des mois
que l'on a gagné la dernière course ?

C'est aussi ce que peut se dire – et plus encore – Bernd
Schneider, sacré champion FIA-GT. Il lui aura toutefois fallu
attendre l'ultime manche, lors de la finale de Laguna Seca,
pour s'assurer le titre des Pilotes avec l'aide compétente de
Klaus Ludwig. Avec six victoires en onze courses et le titre

Not even three swallows made the 1997 CART Summer. With victories in Nazareth, Rio de Janeiro and Madison Paul Tracy at first looked destined to go on to greater things, but after initially appearing irresistible, the car failed to completely live up to expectations, scoring nine wins from 17 races and thus at least securing the Constructors' Championship. The season then ended on an optimistic note as PacWest driver Mark Blundell scored his first success on an Oval track at the California Speedway in Fontana. The jovial Briton was as happy as a sandboy at the end – after all, what better feeling is there in this game than being able to tell people for months on end that you won the last race?

FIA GT Champion Bernd Schneider can say the same – and more. He finally secured the Drivers' Championship in the last race of the season at Laguna Seca, with the able assistance of Klaus Ludwig. With six victories in eleven races and the Constructors' Championship to its name, the CLK-GTR carried on where the 300 SLR had left off way back in 1955. Despite the fact that it was still awaiting homologation and the development of the street version, and that the ideal car set up had not yet been found, the car made a copybook start to the season at the Nürburgring in June with a one-two for the two line-ups Schneider/Ludwig and Alessandro Nannini/Marcel Tiemann, both recording lap times almost a second faster than those of their nearest rivals.

The great success of Laguna Seca was to be repeated on 26 October, by which time Mercedes' cup was positively brimming over, as Daimler-Benz boss Jürgen Schrempp, head of motorsport Haug and engine Guru Mario Illien were popping champagne corks in celebration amidst clouds of fragrant smoke from the finest Brazilian cigars. Formula 1 team Hakkinen and Coulthard had just secured first and second places, in that order, at the European Grand Prix, with a little calm but energetic help from their friends in the pit team. It was the Finn's turn to win after Coulthard had prevailed in Monza, 42 years almost to the day after the previous Mercedes victory there, chalked up by one Juan Manuel Fangio.

1998 was to demonstrate that Hakkinen could also do the business all by himself, as the McLaren powered by the Mercedes MP4/13 proved itself a superb Formula 1 package.

Hakkinen's personal training times duel with his Scottish teammate ended with a telltale 13:3 superiority for the Finn. Indeed, Coulthard, who recorded just one victory (at Imola) generally appeared not to do himself justice. The unassuming Finn, on the other hand, having scored his first victory the year before in Jerez after seven years without a win, scored nine pole positions, eight first, three second and four third places, and in so doing acceded to the pantheon reserved for the motorsport greats. Just when many were writing off the season as the story of one man, Michael Schumacher, against Mercedes, Hakkinen simply left the Ferrari superstar floundering in his wake at the Nürburgring – just where it would hurt his rival the most and give his own ego the biggest boost.

einer Pointe, nur dass bei Roger Penske niemand darüber zu lachen vermag: Bis zum Finallauf in Laguna Seca kann sich Al Unser noch Hoffnungen auf den Titel machen. Dort jedoch läuft alles verquer, und am Ende findet sich der jüngste Spross einer der ersten Renn-Familien des Landes von der Fortuna der Pisten auf den vierten Rang relegiert.

Nicht einmal drei Schwalben machen den CART-Sommer 1997. Mit Siegen in Nazareth, Rio de Janeiro und Madison scheint sich Paul Tracy anfänglich für höhere Weihen zu empfehlen. Doch allzu hoch gespannte Erwartungen zerschellen an einer sich dynamisch entwickelnden Realität. Immerhin beschert die Saison den Mercedes-Fahrern neun Erfolge in 17 Läufen und damit das Markenchampionat. Sie endet überdies mit einer erfreulichen Perspektive, als Pac-West-Pilot Mark Blundell seinen ersten Erfolg auf einem Oval in den Makadam des California Speedway in Fontana radiert. Der joviale Brite frohlockt anschließend wie ein Kind: Was gäbe es Schöneres in diesem Sport, als monatelang sagen zu können, man habe das letzte Rennen gewonnen?

Dergleichen kann auch FIA-GT-Champion Bernd Schneider von sich behaupten – und mehr. Allerdings ist ihm der Fahrertitel erst nach dem Finale in Laguna Seca sicher, mit kompetenter Hilfe von Klaus Ludwig. Mit sechs Siegen in elf Rennen und der Teammeisterschaft knüpft der CLK-GTR da an, wo der 300 SLR 1955 aufgehört hat. Obwohl seine Homologation noch abgeschlossen, die Straßenversion entwickelt und die beste Abstimmung gefunden werden müssen, kommt es bereits beim Auftakt auf dem Nürburgring im Juni zu einem Start nach Maß: Zweifachsieg für Schneider/Ludwig und Alessandro Nannini/Marcel Tiemann, mit Rundenzeiten, die fast eine Sekunde unter denen der besten Gegner liegen.

Die frohe Botschaft von Laguna Seca ist am 26. Oktober gerade aktenkundig geworden, da hängt der Mercedes-Himmel auch anderswo voller Geigen: Im Fahrerlager von Jerez beraten Daimler-Benz-Boss Jürgen Schrempp, Rennsportchef Haug und Motoren-Guru Mario Illien inmitten des schwärzlichen Gewölks edler Brasilzigarren, Champagnerkelche in der Rechten. Denn just hat die Riege Hakkinen und Coulthard beim Großen Preis von Europa die Ränge eins und zwei belegt, in dieser Reihenfolge. Die Boxenregie half sanft, aber energisch etwas nach. Der Finne war dran, nachdem Coulthard auch in Monza gewonnen hatte, fast auf den Tag 42 Jahre nach dem letzten Mercedes-Sieg dort durch Juan Manuel Fangio.

Dass Hakkinen auch alleine klarkommt, zeigt sich 1998, als McLaren Mercedes mit dem MP4/13 exzellentes Arbeitsgerät bereitgestellt hat.

13:3 steht schließlich das stets verräterische Trainingsduell gegen seinen schottischen Teamkollegen, der sich im übrigen mit nur einem Sieg in Imola unter seinem Wert zu verkaufen scheint. Der scheue Blonde aus Helsinki jedoch, in den sieben Jahre vor Jerez 1997 sieglos und nun plötzlich Champion, verschafft sich mit neun Pole Positions, acht ersten, drei zweiten und vier dritten Plätzen Zutritt zu der Loge, die den Großen seines Sports vorbehalten ist. Schon

Town traffic: Mika Hakkinen in his McLaren MP4/12 at Monaco 1997.

Stadtverkehr: Mika Hakkinen im McLaren MP4/12, Monaco 1997.

Tourniquet: Mika Hakkinen sur McLaren MP4/12 à Monaco en 1997.

des Constructeurs, la CLK-GTR fait revivre la tradition là où elle s'était interrompue en 1955 avec la 300SLR. Bien que son homologation doive encore être obtenue, et que sa version routière reste à concrétiser, et malgré une mise au point et des réglages imparfaits, elle ne fait déjà pas les choses à moitié lorsqu'elle s'aligne pour la première fois au départ du Nürburgring, en juin : doublé pour Schneider/Ludwig et Alessandro Nannini/Marcel Tiemann, avec des temps au tour inférieurs de près d'une seconde à ceux de leurs adversaires directs.

À peine a-t-on pris connaissance de la bonne nouvelle de Laguna Seca, le 26 octobre, que les hommes de Mercedes sont aux anges sous d'autres latitudes également : au paddock de Jerez, Jürgen Schrempp, le président de Daimler-Benz, Norbert Haug, directeur des activités de compétition, et Mario Illien, le gourou des moteurs, célèbrent une nouvelle victoire, la tête dans les nuages de fumée de gros cigares brésiliens, une coupe de champagne à la main droite. En effet, le duo Hakkinen/Coulthard vient de rafler la première et la deuxième place, dans cet ordre, au Grand Prix d'Europe. La stratégie des stands n'y a pas été pour rien – main de fer dans un gant de velours. Mais c'était bien le tour du Finlandais après la victoire de Coulthard à Monza, près de 42 ans jour pour jour après la dernière victoire de Mercedes sur ce circuit avec Juan Manuel Fangio.

Mais, en 1998, on constatera que Hakkinen peut fort bien se débrouiller tout seul au volant de la MP4/13, l'excellent outil de travail mis à sa disposition par McLaren.

Toujours révélateur, le duel des qualifications se solde par un 13 à 3 aux dépens de son coéquipier écossais, qui,

Success…: Victory for Greg Moore in his Player's/
Forsythe Mercedes-Reynard at the opening race of the
1999 FedEx ChampCar Series at Homestead, Florida.

Des einen Nachtigall: Sieg für Greg Moore im Mercedes-
Reynard des Player's/Forsythe-Teams beim Auftaktrennen
zur FedEx ChampCar-Serie 1999 in Homestead, Florida.

Le bonheur de l'un…: victoire pour Greg Moore, sur la
Mercedes-Reynard du team Player's/Forsythe, lors de la
course en lever de rideau du championnat FedEx
ChampCar 1999, à Homestead, en Floride.

While the red of Ferrari sullied the picture somewhat in the Formula 1 scene, the FIA GT series turned into a veritable procession for the silver arrows of Mercedes. Ten victories from ten races: a rare 100 per cent success rate. The CLK-GTR from the previous year had to contest the first two races at Oschersleben and Silverstone before being replaced by the CLK-LM, which took things to a new level. With five victories apiece, the two teams of Bernd Schneider/Mark Webber and Klaus Ludwig/Ricardo Zonta practiced share-and-share alike throughout the season before the balance finally tipped in the favor of the German-Brazilian pairing in the last race of the season, once again at Laguna Seca. One sour note, however: in the 24-hour marathon at Le Mans, the eponymous Mercedes LM failed, with Schneider dropping out due to engine failure just one hour after the start, while Christophe Bouchut lasted three hours before the same fate befell him too.

In contrast, the CART season was a tale of mediocrity. Over the 19 races of the 1998 ChampCar series six training best times were converted into two first, four second and three third places for the eight men powered by Mercedes engines. In the final analysis the best of these, the Forsythe driver Greg Moore, came just fifth, after having become at 22 the youngest CART winner of all time in 1997.

In contrast, the GTR's appearance on 12 June 1999 at Le Mans proved to be a more dramatic flop, though miraculously one which the drivers escaped without injury. At around 9 pm the car driven by the Scot Peter Dumbreck literally took off from the track shortly before the Indianapolis corner at a speed of 300 kph (190 mph), and somersaulted off the track in terrifying fashion. A similar fate had already befallen his teammate Mark Webber during the warm-up, so the third car was immediately withdrawn from the race. However, happier news was to arrive from far-off Montreal a day later, as Mika Hakkinen won the Canadian Grand Prix, after arch-rival Michael

munkeln manche, die Saison missrate zum Duell des Mannes Michael Schumacher gegen die Marke Mercedes, da fährt Hakkinen dem Ferrari-Superstar auf dem Nürburgring kurzerhand weg – da, wo es dem anderen am wehesten tut und dem eigenen Ego am ehesten schmeichelt.

Sprenkeln sich in der Formel 1 noch störende rote Tupfen ins Bild, mutiert die GT-Serie der FIA gänzlich zur Sinfonie in Silber: zehn Siege in zehn Rennen. Für die ersten beiden Läufe in Oschersleben und Silverstone muss noch der CLK-GTR vom Vorjahr herhalten, dann sorgt der CLK-LM für zeitgemäße Fortbewegung. Mit je fünf Erfolgen gehen die beiden Teams Bernd Schneider/Mark Webber und Klaus Ludwig/Ricardo Zonta durchaus brüderlich miteinander um. Erst beim letzten Rennen, erneut in Laguna Seca, neigt sich die Waagschale zugunsten des deutsch-brasilianischen Duos. Beim Marathon von Le Mans hingegen, dessen Namen er trägt, versagt der LM: Aus für Schneider in der Stunde eins nach dem Start, Motorschaden, Aus für Christophe Bouchut in Stunde drei, gleiche Diagnose.

Eher mäßig liest sich die CART-Bilanz: In den 19 Raten des ChampCar-Championats 1998 sechs Trainingsbestwerte, zwei erste, vier zweite, drei dritte Plätze für die acht Männer mit Mercedes-Motoren im Nacken. Unter dem Strich nur fünfter wird der erste unter ihnen, Forsythe-Fahrer Greg Moore, 1997 im zarten Alter von 22 Jahren jüngster CART-Sieger aller Zeiten.

Als Flip-Flop hingegen, wundersamerweise ohne Personenschäden, entpuppt sich der Einsatz des GTR am 12. Juni 1999 in Le Mans. Gegen 21 Uhr segelt das Exemplar des Schotten Peter Dumbreck kurz vor der Indianapolis-Kurve bei Tempo 300 in einer eindrucksvollen Flugbahn von der Strecke. Ähnliches widerfuhr bereits seinem Teamgefährten Mark Webber während des Warmups. Daraufhin wird der dritte Wagen umgehend via Funk aus dem Rennen genommen. Aus dem fernen Montreal trifft einen Tag später weitaus erfreulichere Kunde ein: Sieg für Mika

avec une seule victoire à Imola, semble ne pas avoir été à la hauteur de sa réputation. Avec neuf pole positions, huit premières places, trois deuxièmes et quatre troisièmes places, le timide blondinet d'Helsinki, qui n'a pas remporté la moindre victoire en sept ans avant Jerez 1997 et qui devient brusquement champion du monde, accède à la loge qui est réservée aux grands de son sport. Alors que certains chuchotent déjà que la saison est en passe de se transformer en un duel de l'homme Michael Schumacher contre la marque Mercedes, Hakkinen réplique en dominant de la tête et des épaules la superstar de Ferrari au Nürburgring – là où il était sûr que cela lui ferait le plus mal et là où cela flatterait le plus son propre ego.

Alors que le rouge de Ferrari vient encore éclabousser le monde de la Formule 1, la série GT de la FIA cultive la monochromie du gris argenté. Dix victoires en dix courses – un tel taux de réussite de cent pour cent est d'une extrême rareté. Pour les deux premières manches, à Oschersleben et Silverstone, la CLK-GTR de l'année précédente doit encore reprendre du service avant que la CLK-LM plus moderne ne puisse s'aligner au départ. Avec chacun cinq succès, les deux équipages Bernd Schneider/Mark Webber et Klaus Ludwig/Ricardo Zonta se partagent équitablement les victoires. Il faudra attendre la dernière course, une fois de plus à Laguna Seca, pour que le fléau de la balance penche en faveur de l'équipage germano-brésilien. Mais Mercedes aussi doit mettre de l'eau dans son vin. Lors des deux tours d'horloge du Mans, dont elle porte le nom, la LM connaît un échec: abandon pour Schneider moins d'une heure après le départ sur panne de moteur et abandon pour Christophe Bouchut à la troisième heure: même motif, même punition.

Le bilan du championnat CART n'est pas vraiment enthousiasmant: à l'issue des 19 manches du championnat ChampCar 1998, les huit pilotes avec des moteurs Mercedes sous le capot doivent se contenter de six pole positions,

… and failure: seventh place only for Moore's teammate Patrick Carpentier in the same race. A stop-and-go penalty robbed him of any chance of victory.

Des anderen Eule: nur Platz sieben für Moores Teamkollegen Patrick Carpentier beim gleichen Rennen. Eine Stop-and-Go Strafe beraubt ihn aller Chancen.

… fait le malheur de l'autre: septième place seulement pour le coéquipier de Moore, Patrick Carpentier, lors de la même course. Une pénalité de stop-and-go lui a ôté toute chance.

Bernd Schneider in his Mercedes CLR during training for the Le Mans 24 hour race. The car's future did not look rosy.

Bernd Schneider auf Mercedes CLR beim Training zum 24-Stunden-Rennen von Le Mans. Mit der Zukunft seines Wagens stand es nicht zum besten.

Bernd Schneider, sur Mercedes CLR, lors des essais des 24 Heures du Mans. L'avenir de sa voiture s'avère sombre.

Schumacher's Ferrari regrettably ended up squashed against a wall.

The British at first held their breath as Michael Schumacher crashed in Silverstone, then went on to celebrate a Scotsman: David Coulthard had boxed his way through his own team colleagues to the top step of the victors' platform. Mika still took it calmly, but as tire damage forced him into the gravel at Hockenheim the path to his title defense began to get stony – even in the absence of the Ferrari star. With his victory in front of Coulthard in Hungary, the competitors presumed the silver arrows were once again flying in the usual order. No way: Coulthard turned the tables in Belgium, and Mika had to leave his arrows in its quiver at Monza. A silly gear-change mistake stalled the engine. A second title receded into the distance as Michael Schumacher most impressively reported back again at the Grand Prix premiere at Sepang in Malaysia. Everything or nothing: at the final in Suzuka, Mika managed to keep Schumacher's and Irvine's Ferraris off his back and toasted his second title – rather often as fellow revelers reported.

In 2000, the Mercedes duo managed together seven victories, while Michael Schumacher notched up nine alone. There was no ground for celebration 2001 either: "DC" second and Mika only fifth. Hakkinen let his young fellow compatriot Kimi Räikkönen have the cockpit after this not exactly enthralling season's result. Following a careful acclimatization in 2002, Kimi 2003 gained the title of runner-up in the world championship – only two points behind "Schumi" himself. The meager McLaren-Mercedes harvest of the first half of the 2004 season is enough to put anyone off, and that after seven years of relative abundance!

Hakkinen beim Grand Prix von Kanada, nachdem Erzfeind Schumacher seinen Ferrari an der Mauer zerquetscht hat.

Als Michael Schumacher in Silverstone verunglückt, stockt den Briten der Atem, doch dann feiern sie einen Schotten: David Coulthard hat sich gegen den eigenen Teamkameraden auf die oberste Stufe des Siegespodestes durchgeboxt. Noch trägt es Mika mit Fassung, doch als ihn in Hockenheim ein Reifenschaden ins Kiesbett befördert, beginnt der Weg zur Titelverteidigung – auch in Absenz des Ferrari-Stars – steinig zu werden. Sieg in Ungarn vor Coulthard, die Silberpfeile fliegen in Order, mutmaßt die Konkurrenz. Denkste: In Belgien dreht Coulthard den Spieß um, und in Monza muss Mika seine Pfeile im Köcher lassen. Ein dummer Schaltfehler würgt den Motor ab. Der zweite Titel rückt in weite Ferne, denn bei der Grand-Prix-Premiere von Sepang in Malaysia meldet sich mehr als eindrucksvoll Michael Schumacher zurück. Alles oder nichts: Mika hält sich beim Finale in Suzuka die Ferrari von Schumacher und Irvine vom Hals und darf auf den zweiten Titel anstoßen – ziemlich oft, wie Mittrinker berichten.

Im Jahr 2000 fährt das Mercedes-Duo zusammen sieben Siege ein, doch Michael Schumacher holt allein deren neun. Kein Grund zum Feiern gibt es 2001: »DC« Zweiter und Mika nur Fünfter. Nach dieser nicht gerade berauschenden Saisonbilanz überlässt Hakkinen das Cockpit seinem jungen Landsmann Kimi Räikkönen. Nach vorsichtigem Eingewöhnen 2002, sichert sich Kimi 2003 den Titel eines Vize-Weltmeisers – nur um zwei Punkte von »Schumi« distanziert. Eher zum Abgewöhnen für McLaren-Mercedes ist die kärgliche Ernte der ersten Saisonhälfte 2004. Und das nach sieben ziemlich fetten Jahren!

de deux premières places, quatre deuxièmes et trois troisièmes. Au décompte final, le premier d'entre eux, le pilote Forsythe Greg Moore, le plus jeune vainqueur de la série CART de tous les temps en 1997 à l'âge tendre de 22 ans, doit se contenter d'une cinquième place.

Le circuit des 24 heures du Mans, le 12 juin 1999, voit s'envoler la GTR et, avec elle, tous les espoirs de Mercedes – miraculeusement, sans causer de victimes. Vers 21 heures, la voiture de l'Écossais Peter Dumbreck s'envole peu avant le virage d'Indianapolis, à 300 km/h, virevoltant dans les airs avant de s'écraser dans une clairière. Lors du *warm-up*, son coéquipier Mark Webber avait déjà connu une telle mésaventure. Par radio, Norbert Haug donne immédiatement à la troisième voiture l'ordre de rentrer aux stands – fin d'un intermède qui aura coûté 200 millions de marks. D'outre-Atlantique, en l'occurrence de Montréal, arrive, un jour plus tard, une nouvelle beaucoup plus réjouissante: Mika Hakkinen remporte la victoire au Grand Prix du Canada.

Les Britanniques ont le souffle coupé quand Michael Schumacher est victime d'un accident à Silverstone. Mais, dans la foulée, ils fêtent la victoire d'un des leurs: l'Écossais David Coulthard est parvenu, en jouant des coudes, à grimper sur la plus haute marche du podium au détriment de son propre coéquipier. Mika Hakkinen ne se fait pas encore de soucis mais, quand lui-même se retrouve dans un bac à gravier à Hockenheim suite à un déchapage, la défense de son titre – même en l'absence de la vedette de Ferrari – commence à devenir difficile. Victoire en Hongrie devant Coulthard, les Flèches d'argent gagnent en respectant les ordres de l'équipe, pensent leurs concurrents. Mais en Belgique, Coulthard lui rend la monnaie de sa pièce et, à Monza, Hakkinen doit laisser ses flèches dans son carquois. Un changement de vitesse loupé de manière stupide signe l'arrêt de mort de son moteur. Le second titre semble devoir lui échapper car, lors de la première du Grand Prix de Sepang, en Malaisie, Michael Schumacher remet les pendules à l'heure dès son retour. Quitte ou double: lors de la finale à Suzuka, Hakkinen parvient à se débarrasser des Ferrari de Schumacher et d'Irvine pour savourer le champagne de la victoire et son second titre – au grand dam de ses rivaux qui fêtent avec lui.

En l'an 2000, les deux mercenaires de Mercedes engrangent de nouveau sept victoires à eux deux, mais Michael Schumacher, à lui seul, pas moins de neuf. Aucun motif de réjouissances en 2001: «DC» (David Coulthard) finit deuxième et Hakkinen, seulement cinquième. À l'issue du bilan de cette saison qui n'a rien d'enthousiasmant, le Finlandais cède son cockpit à son jeune compatriote Kimi Räikkönen. Après avoir cherché ses marques en 2002, Kimi s'assure le titre de vice-champion du monde en 2003 – à seulement deux points de «Schumi». La récolte de la première moitié de la saison 2004 est encore une plus grande désillusion pour McLaren-Mercedes. Et ce, après sept années plutôt fastes!

The essential factor that made this vehicle worthy of the German Imperial Patent 37435, dated 29 January 1886, was its sheer functionality. The first motor car ever, designed by Karl Benz, was not simply a carriage with an engine bolted to it. Instead the motor, chassis, and drive train formed an integrated unit. Its first public appearance – on Mannheim's "Circular Road" which was constructed on the fragments of the earlier city wall – certainly disturbed the quiet of that Sunday: 3 July 1886.

Any onlookers had a treat. The passengers sat on a double bench seat perilously exposed to the vagaries of the weather. Those first spectators also had a clear view of the technology that was at work. The heart of the car was a compact, fast-running four-stroke engine, which, much later, was evaluated at the Technical University of Stuttgart and found to produce 0.9 bhp at 400 rpm. A water boiler projecting above the engine was Benz's solution to the problem of the single cylinder overheating – the effect of evaporation cooling prevented it.

Ligroin bought direct from the chemist's was used as the fuel, but no tank was provided for it. The surface carburetor held 1.5 liters (0.4 gal) and to replenish it Benz's son, Eugen, had to trot alongside the vehicle and top it up from a bottle every 10–15 km (6–9 miles). The flywheel on the original model rotated horizontally. Benz believed that a vertical arrangement would adversely affect the steering of the vehicle due to gyrostatic effect.

Sadly Model 1 saw out the remainder of the century in a dismantled and neglected condition, and it was immaculately restored only as a result of Daimler-Motoren-Gesellschaft's claim to have produced the world's first motor car. Initially Model 2 received similarly neglectful treatment but it then served as a four-wheeled test vehicle for the investigation of swiveling-axle, and later stub-axle, steering. Model 3 (from 1886 onwards) was very advanced, having two forward gears, a more powerful engine with a vertical flywheel, wooden-spoke wheels and solid rubber tires (first only on the front but later also on the rear wheels). It was available in a half-roof and dickey-seat version.

Evidence of Benz's pride in this vehicle can be found in a brochure which stated that the third-generation car should be benevolently regarded as a "pleasing carriage and mountain climbing machine."

Was ihn des Deutschen Reichs-Patents 37435 vom 29. Januar 1886 würdig macht, ist seine Funktionalität: Der automobile Erstling von Karl Benz ist keine Kutsche, in die man ein Triebwerk hineingeschraubt hat, sondern Motor, Fahrgestell und Antrieb finden sich zu einem Guss zusammen. Sein erstes Erscheinen auf einer öffentlichen Straße, dem Mannheimer »Ring« auf den Parzellen des früheren Stadtwalls, stört indes erst die sonntägliche Ruhe des 3. Juli 1886.

Der spärliche Zuschauerflor bekommt einen Fall für zwei zu sehen: Auf einer Doppelbank sind die Passagiere den Wechselfällen der Witterung schutzlos preisgegeben. Durch nichts behindert wird auch der Blick des neugierigen Betrachters auf die Technik hinter ihnen, Herzstück: ein kompakter, schnellaufender Viertakter. Viel später misst man an der Technischen Hochschule Stuttgart 0,9 PS bei 400/min. Über der Maschine ragt ein Wasserkessel auf: Möglicher Überhitzung des Einzylinders hat Karl Benz mit Kühlung durch Verdampfung vorgebeugt.

Für den Treibstoff Ligroin, erhältlich in Apotheken, findet sich indes kein Behältnis: 1,5 Liter fasst der Oberflächenvergaser, und notfalls muss Benz' Filius Eugen das väterliche Fahrzeug in lockerem Trab begleiten und alle zehn bis 15 Kilometer aus einer Flasche nachfüllen. Das Schwungrad rotiert am Ur-Typ horizontal. Senkrechte Anordnung, meint Benz, würde wegen unerwünschter Kreiselwirkung die Lenkbarkeit beeinträchtigen.

Modell 1 erlebt den Rest des Jahrhunderts zerlegt und vernachlässigt und wird erst dann untadelig restauriert, als auch die Daimler-Motoren-Gesellschaft den Anspruch darauf erhebt, das erste Auto in die Welt gesetzt zu haben. Ein Modell 2 erfährt zunächst ebenfalls stiefväterliche Behandlung, dient aber dann mit vier Rädern als Versuchsträger für eine Drehschemel- und später für eine Achsschenkellenkung. Das Modell 3 (ab 1886) gibt sich durchaus fortschrittlich, mit zwei Vorwärtsgängen, stärkerem Motor mit vertikalem Schwungrad, Holzspeichenrädern, Vollgummireifen erst vorn und später auch hinten. Es ist lieferbar mit Halbverdeck und Notbank als Option.

In einem Prospekt artikuliert sich verschämt Vaterstolz: Der Motorwagen der dritten Generation wird der geneigten Aufmerksamkeit als »gefälliges Fuhrwerk und als Bergsteigeapparat« empfohlen.

Ce qui la rend digne du brevet du Reich allemand 37435 du 29 janvier 1886, c'est son caractère fonctionnel : la première création automobile de Karl Benz n'est pas une calèche sur laquelle on a greffé un moteur. Châssis, moteur et chaîne cinématique constituent une entité. Cela n'empêche pas que sa première apparition sur une route publique, sur le « ring » de Mannheim, ait troublé le calme dominical du 3 juillet 1886.

Peu nombreux, les spectateurs découvrent deux courageux pionniers : juchés sur une banquette double, les passagers sont exposés sans la moindre protection aux aléas des intempéries. Rien n'entrave, non plus, la vue du curieux sur la mécanique derrière eux avec, comme morceau de bravoure, un compact moteur à quatre temps à régime rapide. Beaucoup plus tard, à l'université technique de Stuttgart, on mesurera une puissance de 0,9 ch à 400 tr/min. Un réservoir d'eau trône sur le moteur : Karl Benz a paré à toute éventualité de surchauffe du monocylindre avec un refroidissement par vaporisation.

Pour le carburant, de la ligroïne en vente en pharmacie ; on ne trouve pas en revanche de réservoir : le carburateur de surface a une capacité de 1,5 litre et, en cas de besoin, le fils de Benz, Eugen, doit accompagner le véhicule de son père en le suivant au pas de course pour refaire le plein, tous les dix à quinze kilomètres, à l'aide d'une bouteille. Sur le modèle original, le volant-moteur est horizontal. Une position verticale, pense Benz, porterait préjudice à la maniabilité en raison de la force centrifuge indésirable.

Le modèle 1 vécut le reste du siècle démonté et abandonné dans un coin et il n'est alors restauré à la perfection que lorsque la Daimler-Motoren-Gesellschaft revendique pour elle le statut d'avoir construit la première voiture du monde. Un modèle 2 est tout d'abord, lui aussi, traité en cousin pauvre avant de servir ensuite de véhicule expérimental à quatre roues pour une direction à boggie et, plus tard, à fusée. Le modèle 3 (à partir de 1886) comporte déjà de nombreux progrès avec deux rapports avant, un moteur plus puissant à volant-moteur vertical, des roues à rayons en bois, des pneus en caoutchouc plein tout d'abord à l'avant et, plus tard, aussi à l'arrière. Il est livrable avec une demi-capote et une banquette de dépannage en option. La fierté paternelle transparaît à deux niveaux dans un prospectus : la voiture à moteur de la troisième génération est recommandée aux intéressés potentiels comme « véhicule séduisant ou appareil à escalader les montagnes ».

Benz Patent-Motorwagen 1886

Great things cast long shadows. The overhead view reveals the compact dimensions and the strict functionalism of the Benz three-wheeler. Nothing was ornamental: everything served a purpose.

Große Dinge werfen ihre Schatten voraus: Der Blick von oben zeigt die kompakten Dimensionen und die strenge Zweckmäßigkeit des Benzschen Tricycles: Alles ist Funktion, nichts Ornament.

Les grands événements jettent leur ombre longtemps à l'avance : compacité et fonctionnalité sévère du tricycle de Benz vu d'en haut : tout est fonction, rien n'est fioriture.

Before automobiles were shrouded in bodywork, their technical workings were plain for all to see. It is astounding how Karl Benz had already achieved such a harmonious design.

Bevor Automobile von Karosserien umhüllt werden, treten die technischen Details noch nackt zutage. Erstaunlich, wie Karl Benz bereits ihr Zusammenspiel arrangiert hat.

Les automobiles ne sont pas encore carrossées et les détails techniques sont encore exposés au regard. Elle est étonnante, l'harmonie avec laquelle Karl Benz a déjà organisé leur coexistence.

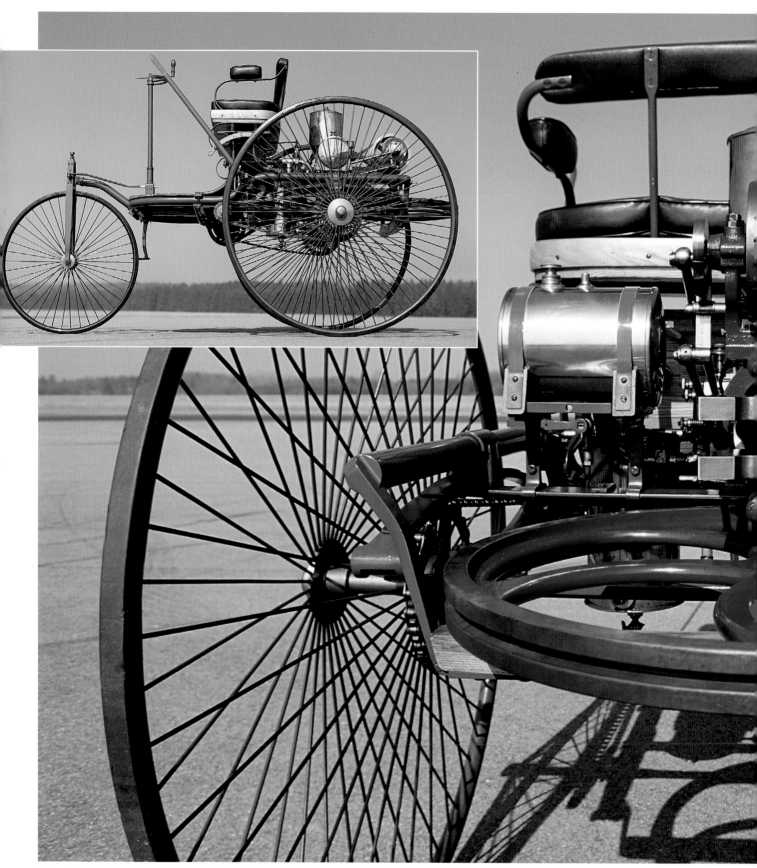

Benz Patent-Motorwagen 1886

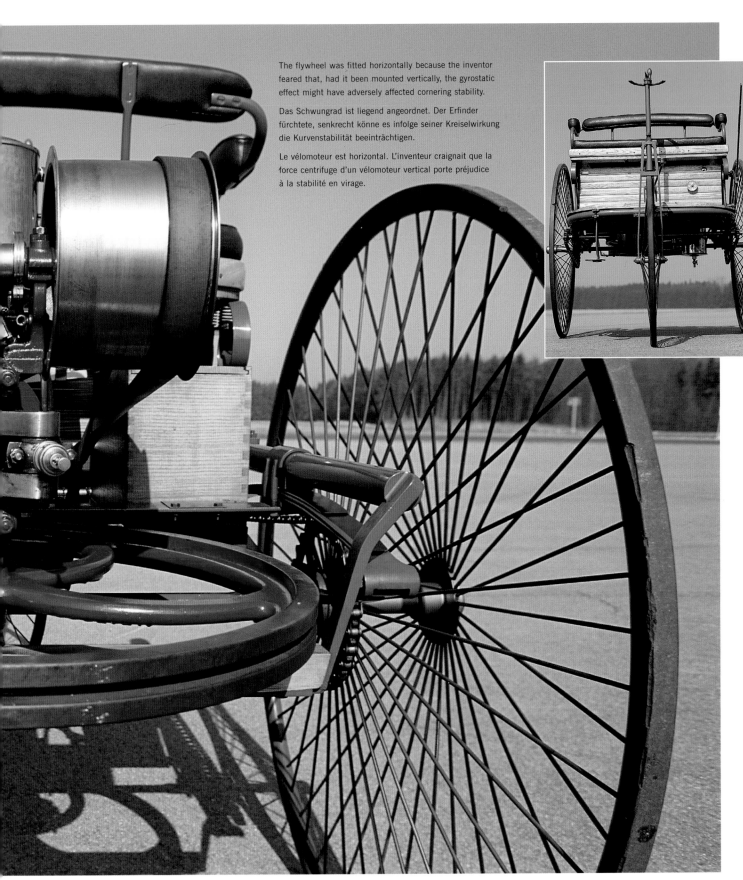

The flywheel was fitted horizontally because the inventor feared that, had it been mounted vertically, the gyrostatic effect might have adversely affected cornering stability.

Das Schwungrad ist liegend angeordnet. Der Erfinder fürchtete, senkrecht könne es infolge seiner Kreiselwirkung die Kurvenstabilität beeinträchtigen.

Le vélomoteur est horizontal. L'inventeur craignait que la force centrifuge d'un vélomoteur vertical porte préjudice à la stabilité en virage.

On 8 March 1886 Gottlieb Daimler ordered an Americain carriage from coachbuilder Wilhelm Wimpff & Sohn in Stuttgart. It was delivered in August at a price of 795 Goldmarks. The manufacturer generously guaranteed the axles, springs, and wheels for two years.

What seems to have been conceived as a present for the approaching birthday of Daimler's wife, Berta, meanwhile developed its own dynamic – literally. The carriage was taken to the Maschinenfabrik Esslingen where, under Daimler's precise guidance, it developed into the automobile. First of all, the shaft was removed – an act of historical significance. The passengers in the second row of seats had to share footspace with Daimler's fast-running combustion engine which developed 1.1 bhp at 650 rpm. The unit functioned proudly and efficiently, and was nicknamed the "grandfather clock" in company parlance because of its resemblance to that stately timepiece. The single cylinder was fired by glow-tube ignition, a system protected by German Imperial Patent 28022 of 16 December 1883. A small externally-heated tube projected into the combustion chamber. The piston compressed the gas mixture until it ignited at the correct moment, so avoiding misfires which would cause the piston to blow back before it reached the cylinder's top dead center. This was a provision that the man who operated the starting handle could be profoundly grateful for – a misfire could have easily resulted in a broken arm.

The "grandfather clock" was fed by Wilhelm Maybach's surface carburetor. The carburetor float ensured that the air was continuously mixed with a consistent quantity of fuel and so the composition of the resulting mixture remained constant. A multi-plate cooler of tinplate behind the rear seat kept the engine operating at a comfortable and stable temperature. Swiveling-axle steering, actuated by a toothed quadrant, ensured that the front wheels of the motor carriage pointed in the required direction. The driver had two gears available. The belt pulley of the engine drove differently sized pulleys on a countershaft, which drove the rear wheels through pinion crown gears on both sides of the vehicle. Gear changing was performed manually and required the belts to be changed over while the vehicle was stationary.

The horseless four-seater managed a bare 20 kph (12.5 mph). The first excursion in it of the creative team of Gottlieb Daimler and Wilhelm Maybach in April 1887 was greeted with mixed emotions by the citizens of Esslingen, Bad Cannstatt, and Untertürkheim. Popular opinion held that it was the work of the devil and general bewilderment reigned.

Am 8. März 1886 bestellt Gottlieb Daimler bei der Wagenbaufabrik Wilhelm Wimpff & Sohn in Stuttgart eine Kutsche vom Typ Americain, die im August um den Preis von 795 Goldmark geliefert wird. Der Hersteller gewährt generös eine Zweijahres-Garantie auf Achsen, Federn und Räder.

Was ein Geschenk zum bevorstehenden Geburtstag von Daimlers Gattin Berta zu sein scheint, entwickelt indes seine eigene Dynamik – buchstäblich. Die Kutsche wird nämlich zur Maschinenfabrik Esslingen gebracht und mutiert dort nach Daimlers genauer Anleitung zum Automobil. Als erstes entfernt man die Deichsel – eine Tat von historischer Tragweite. Die Passagiere in der zweiten Reihe müssen sich den Fußraum mit Daimlers schnell laufendem Verbrennungsmotor von 1,1 PS bei 650/min teilen, der dort seiner Tätigkeit stolz und aufrecht nachgeht, im Hausjargon wegen der unverkennbaren Ähnlichkeit die »Standuhr« genannt. Befeuert wird der Einzylinder von einer Glührohrzündung, urheberrechtlich geschützt durch das Deutsche Reichspatent 28022 vom 16. Dezember 1883. Ein von außen erhitztes Röhrchen ragt in den Verbrennungsraum. Der Kolben quetscht das Gasgemisch zusammen, bis es termingerecht entflammt. Fehlzündungen, die ihn vor dem Erreichen des oberen Totpunkts zurückwerfen würden, werden solchermaßen vermieden. Es dankt der Mann an der Anlasserkurbel – ihm könnte das schon mal den Arm brechen.

Verpflegt wird die »Standuhr« durch Wilhelm Maybachs Oberflächenvergaser. Dessen Schwimmer gewährleistet, dass die Luft eine ständig gleich dicke Kraftstoffschicht durchmisst und das entstehende Gemisch konstant zusammengesetzt bleibt. Ein Lamellenkühler aus Weißblech hinter dem Rücksitz hält die Maschine bei Laune und bei angenehmen Betriebstemperaturen, eine Drehschemellenkung, betätigt über ein Zahnbogensegment, sorgt dafür, dass die Vorderräder der Motorkutsche in die gewünschte Richtung zeigen. Ihr Lenker gebietet über zwei Gänge: Die Riemenscheibe des Motors treibt verschieden große Scheiben einer Vorlegewelle an. Diese bewegt durch beidseitige Ritzel Zahnkränze an den Hinterrädern. Per Handarbeit wird der Gangwechsel vorgenommen – das Umlegen der Riemen bei stehendem Fahrzeug.

Der pferdelose Viersitzer läuft knapp 20 Stundenkilometer, und erste Ausfahrten der kreativen Herren-Riege Gottlieb Daimler und Wilhelm Maybach im April 1887 nehmen die Bürger von Esslingen, Bad Cannstatt und Untertürkheim mit gemischten Gefühlen zur Kenntnis. Der Gedanke an Teufelswerk drängt sich auf, so dass Bestürzung überwiegt.

Le 8 mars 1886, Gottlieb Daimler commande à l'usine de construction de voitures Wilhelm Wimpff & Sohn à Stuttgart une calèche type Américain qui lui est livrée en août au prix de 795 marks or. Le fabricant accorde généreusement une garantie de deux ans sur les essieux, les ressorts et les roues.

Ce que l'on croit être un cadeau pour l'anniversaire imminent de Berta, l'épouse de Daimler, génère en réalité sa propre dynamique – au sens propre du mot. La calèche est en effet amenée à l'usine de machines d'Esslingen où elle se mue, selon les instructions exactes de Daimler, en une automobile. On commence par éloigner le timon – une action d'une portée historique. Les passagers de la deuxième rangée doivent partager l'espace pour les jambes avec le moteur thermique à régime rapide de Daimler, qui développe 1,1 ch à 650 tr/min et s'attelle là à la tâche verticalement et avec fierté, ce qui lui a valu dans le jargon maison, en raison d'une évidente similitude, le surnom d'« horloge ». Le monocylindre est actionné par un allumage à tube incandescent, système déposé par le brevet du Reich allemand 28022 du 16 décembre 1883. Un petit tube chauffé de l'extérieur fait saillie dans la chambre de combustion. Le piston comprime le mélange gazeux jusqu'à ce qu'il s'enflamme au bon moment. Cela permet d'éviter tout raté d'allumage qui le ferait revenir en arrière avant qu'il n'ait atteint le point mort supérieur. Cela épargne un retour de manivelle à l'homme qui démarre le moteur – cela pourrait lui briser net le bras.

L'« horloge » est alimentée par le carburateur à surface de Wilhelm Maybach. Son flotteur garantit que l'air traverse toujours une couche de carburant à l'épaisseur identique et que le mélange ainsi formé reste d'une composition constante. Un radiateur à lamelles en tôle étamée derrière le siège arrière maintient le moteur de bonne humeur et à une température de fonctionnement agréable, une direction à boggie actionnée par un secteur denté garantissant que les roues avant de la calèche à moteur sont orientées dans la direction souhaitée. Son conducteur est maître de deux rapports : le disque de courroie du moteur entraîne les disques de diamètre différent d'un arbre intermédiaire. Grâce à des pignons des deux côtés, celui-ci entraîne des couronnes dentées se trouvant sur les roues arrière. Le changement de vitesses s'effectue à la main – on déplace les courroies une fois la voiture arrêtée.

Cette quatre-places sans chevaux frise les 20 km/h et les premières excursions des ingénieux Gottlieb Daimler et Wilhelm Maybach, en avril 1887, suscitent des sentiments mitigés parmi les citoyens d'Esslingen, Bad Cannstatt et Untertürkheim. Ils y voient surtout une machine infernale et c'est donc l'effroi qui prédomine.

DAIMLER MOTORKUTSCHE 1886

The resemblance of the motor carriage to its horse-drawn antecedent was unmistakable, though the shaft, like the horse itself, had become redundant, and horsepower was generated by the vehicle itself.

An der Verwandtschaft der Motorkutsche zum Pferdefuhrwerk kommt kein Zweifel auf. Nur: Wie das Pferd selbst ist auch die Deichsel entbehrlich geworden, und die Pferdestärken erzeugt das Fahrzeug selbst.

La parenté est évidente entre la calèche à moteur et le char à bancs. À cela près que, avec le cheval, le timon lui aussi est devenu superflu et que les chevaux sont produits par le véhicule lui-même.

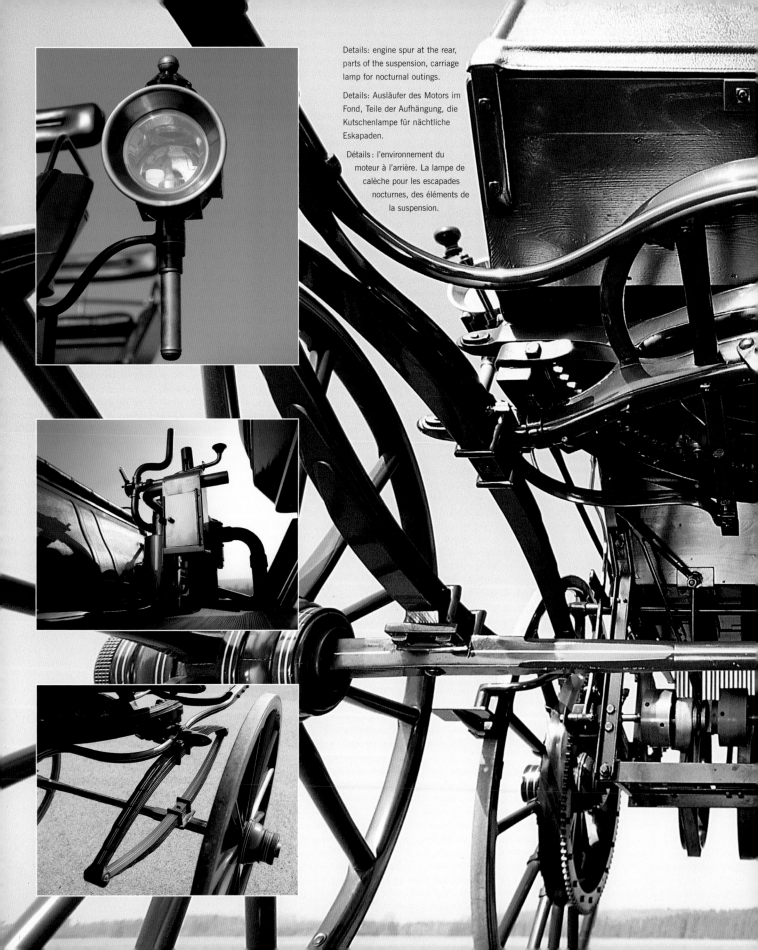

Details: engine spur at the rear, parts of the suspension, carriage lamp for nocturnal outings.

Details: Ausläufer des Motors im Fond, Teile der Aufhängung, die Kutschenlampe für nächtliche Eskapaden.

Détails: l'environnement du moteur à l'arrière. La lampe de calèche pour les escapades nocturnes, des éléments de la suspension.

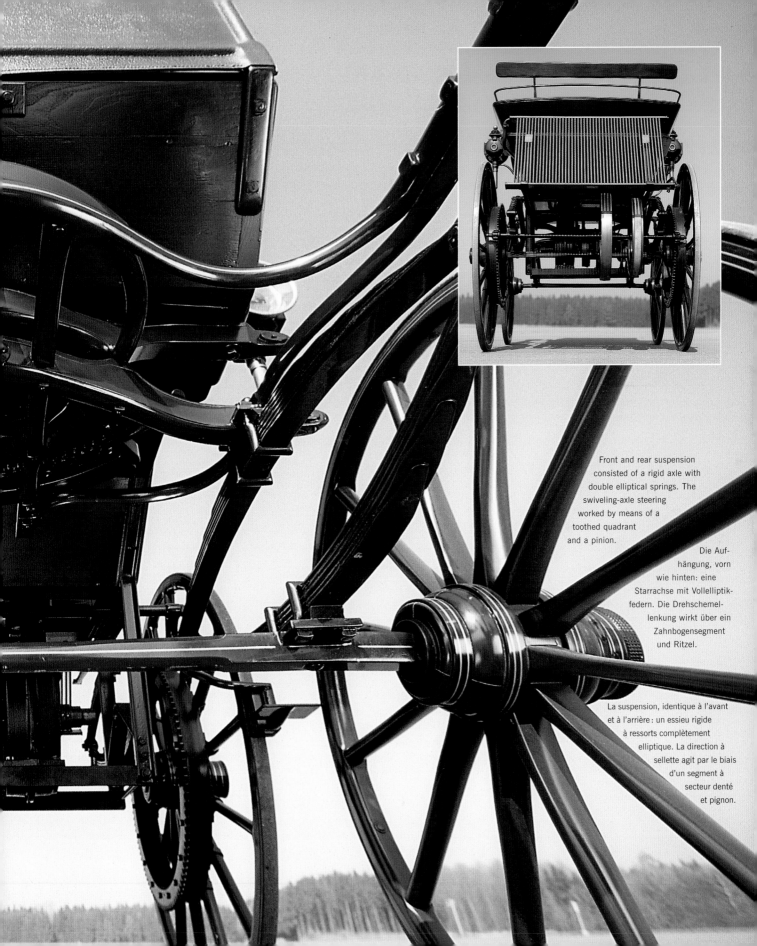

Front and rear suspension
consisted of a rigid axle with
double elliptical springs. The
swiveling-axle steering
worked by means of a
toothed quadrant
and a pinion.

Die Auf-
hängung, vorn
wie hinten: eine
Starrachse mit Vollelliptikfedern. Die Drehschemel-
lenkung wirkt über ein
Zahnbogensegment
und Ritzel.

La suspension, identique à l'avant
et à l'arrière : un essieu rigide
à ressorts complètement
elliptique. La direction à
sellette agit par le biais
d'un segment à
secteur denté
et pignon.

The 89 million visitors to the World Exhibition in Paris in 1889 gazed in wonder at the Eiffel Tower, showed polite interest in two boats powered by Daimler engines plying the Seine, but frankly regarded the steel-wheel car from the same company as a bizarre detour into a technical no-man's-land. However, the graceful conveyance did have something to offer because, like Benz's three-wheeler, the sum of its parts amounted to a complete automobile.

Because Gottlieb Daimler was a man of enduring convictions, his partner Wilhelm Maybach had to exert all his persuasive powers to convince him of the worth of new ideas. While Daimler liked to feel that his engines were suitable for all kinds of applications and was content with a quiet evolution of the carriage, Maybach opted for a tubular steel frame which also served as a duct for cooling water. The front wheels ran in bicycle-wheel forks which were aligned by means of a common steering rod. The chassis was manufactured by Neckarsulmer Strickmaschinen-Fabrik AG, a company which later became famously known as NSU. Where Daimler considered the belt drive of the motor car of 1886 still capable of development and advancement, Maybach pointed the way to the future with a 4-speed transmission. A relaxed journey to Paris, a bold adventure undertaken without any unbecoming fuss, was convincing proof of the validity of this solution. At a top speed of 18 kph (11 mph), the beauty and variety of the French landscape could really be appreciated.

The steel-wheel car was of two-cylinder type with the v-engine set at an angle of 17 degrees, configured – as usual – vertically under the driver and the front passenger seat, a double "grandfather clock" so to speak. Careful examination of this rare powerplant in 1961 showed that its designer had managed to extract 1.65 bhp at 920 rpm from a cubic capacity of 565 cc. The surface carburetor also acted as a reservoir holding two liters (0.53 gal) of fuel. An enclosed bevel gear differential was mounted in the rear axle next to the right-hand wheel and the left-hand rear wheel was provided with an external band brake that was operated from the driver's seat.

This development ended after two show models had been built; Gottlieb Daimler simply lost all interest in the project. A further twelve vehicles, known as Schroedter cars, were sold by the Daimler-Motoren-Gesellschaft between 1892 and 1895. They were named after the new Technical Director of the company as by this time both creators of the Paris model had temporarily turned their backs on the business in disgruntlement. What had been hailed as the latest craze had simply become antiquated. One particular feature of the original is absent from the reconstructed model – its wheels are made of wood, not steel.

Die 89 Millionen Besucher der Pariser Weltausstellung von 1889 bestaunen den Eiffelturm, zollen zwei Booten auf der Seine mit Motoren von Daimler höfliches Interesse, tun jedoch den Stahlradwagen aus dem gleichen Hause als skurrilen Abstecher in technisches Niemandsland ab. Dabei hat das grazile Gefährt einiges zu bieten: Auch in ihm bildet wie am Dreirad von Benz die Summe der Teile ein automobiles Ganzes.

Da Gottlieb Daimler ein Mann bewahrender Denkungsart ist, hat Partner Wilhelm Maybach streckenweise echte Überzeugungsarbeit zu leisten. Wo jener seine Motoren allen möglichen Verwendungen zugeführt sehen und sich mit einer sanften Evolution der Kutsche begnügen möchte, setzt dieser auf einen Rahmen aus Stahlrohren, durch die zugleich das Kühlwasser strömt. Die Vorderräder laufen in Fahrradgabeln, welche mittels einer gemeinsamen Lenkstange gleichgerichtet werden. Gefertigt wird das Chassis von der Neckarsulmer Strickmaschinen-Fabrik AG, die später unter dem Namen NSU firmieren wird. Wo jener meint, das Riemengetriebe des Motorwagens von 1886 sei noch durchaus entwicklungs- und ausbaufähig, zeigt dieser mit einem Viergang-Zahnradgetriebe den Weg in die Zukunft. Von den Qualitäten dieser Lösung überzeugt man sich bereits schmunzelnd anlässlich der Anreise nach Paris, einem Unterfangen ohne ungebührliche Hektik: Bei Tempo 18 Spitze kommen Schönheit und Vielfalt französischer Landschaften noch so recht zur Geltung.

Der Stahlradwagen ist ein Zweizylinder: Unter der Sitzbank für Fahrer und Beifahrer steht gewohnt aufrecht ein v-Motor im Winkel von 17 Grad, eine doppelte »Standuhr« gewissermaßen. Eine penible Prüfung dieses Leitfossils ergibt 1961, dass seine Väter aus 565 ccm Hubraum 1,65 PS bei 920/min mobilisiert haben. Der Oberflächenvergaser bildet zugleich ein Reservoir für zwei Liter Kraftstoff. Neben dem rechten Rad findet sich in der Hinterachse ein gekapseltes Kegelrad-Differential, im linken Hinterrad eine Außenbandbremse, vom Fahrersitz aus zu betätigen.

Zunächst hat es mit zwei Show-Exemplaren sein Bewenden, wohl auch, weil Gottlieb Daimler dem Projekt mit zäher Unlust begegnet. Weitere zwölf werden von der Daimler-Motoren-Gesellschaft zwischen 1892 und 1895 vertrieben, bekannt als Schroedter-Wagen. Sie heißen so nach dem neuen Technischen Direktor der Firma, denn die beiden Schöpfer des Pariser Exponats haben dem Unternehmen zeitweise verstimmt den Rücken gekehrt. Was damals der letzte Schrei war, ist indessen nun einfach alt. Unter anderen charakteristischen Merkmalen des Originals fehlt der Kopie vor allem eines: Ihre Speichen sind aus Holz.

Les 89 millions de visiteurs de l'Exposition universelle de Paris, en 1889, admirent bouche bée la tour Eiffel, portent un intérêt poli à deux bateaux à moteurs Daimler se trouvant sur la Seine, mais considèrent en revanche la voiture à roues d'acier de la même maison comme un bizarre représentant de la technique. Et pourtant, le gracile engin ne manque pas d'élégance : comme le tricycle de Benz, lui aussi constitue, avec la somme de ses pièces, une entité automobile.

Comme Gottlieb Daimler est un homme à l'esprit conservateur, son associé Wilhelm Maybach doit parfois faire preuve d'un grand pouvoir de persuasion. Là où le premier préférerait voir ses moteurs affectés à toutes les utilisations possibles et souhaiterait se contenter d'une évolution modérée de la calèche, le second impose un cadre en tubes d'acier à travers lesquels circule l'eau de refroidissement. Les roues avant sont montées dans des fourches de vélo qui sont orientées dans la même direction grâce à une bielle de direction commune. Le châssis est fabriqué par la Neckarsulmer Strickmaschinen-Fabrik AG, qui deviendra plus tard célèbre sous l'abréviation NSU.

Là où le premier pense que la boîte de vitesses à courroies de la voiture à moteur de 1886 mériterait encore parfaitement d'être perfectionnée, le second s'engage dans la voie de l'avenir avec une boîte de vitesses à engrenages à quatre rapports. On peut déjà se convaincre en souriant des qualités de cette solution à l'occasion du voyage à Paris, entreprise exempte de toute nervosité : à 18 km/h, on peut encore vraiment admirer la beauté et la diversité des paysages français.

La voiture à roues d'acier est une bicylindre : sous la banquette du conducteur et du passager se trouve – à la verticale comme d'habitude – un moteur en v à 17 degrés, une « double horloge », en quelque sorte. Un examen minutieux de ce fossile a révélé en 1961 que ses pères avaient mobilisé 1,65 ch à 920 tr/min à partir d'une cylindrée de 565 cm³. Le carburateur à surface constitue simultanément un réservoir pour deux litres de carburant.

À côté de la roue droite se trouve, dans le train arrière, un différentiel à roue conique encapsulé et, dans la roue arrière gauche, un frein à bande extérieur, à actionner depuis le siège conducteur.

Il en exista tout d'abord seulement deux exemplaires de démonstration, pour une bonne partie parce que Gottlieb Daimler ne s'attaqua à ce projet qu'avec un empressement mitigé. Douze autres modèles seront vendus par la Daimler-Motoren-Gesellschaft entre 1892 et 1895, sous le nom de voiture de Schroedter. Elles portent le nom du nouveau directeur technique de la société, car les deux créateurs de la voiture exposée à Paris ont provisoirement quitté l'entreprise par suite de divergences de vues. Ce qui était alors le dernier cri est maintenant tout simplement démodé. Entre autres caractéristiques de l'original, on déplore, sur la copie, surtout l'absence d'une chose : leurs rayons sont en bois.

DAIMLER STAHLRADWAGEN 1889

The Stahlradwagen or steel-wheel car was a light four-wheeled carriage with its engine located in front of the rear axle underneath the seat. After its première at the Paris World Fair in 1889, it remained in France.

Der Stahlradwagen: eine leichte Vierradkutsche mit Motor vor der Hinterachse stehend unter dem Sitz. Nach seiner Premiere auf der Pariser Weltausstellung 1889 bleibt er in Frankreich.

La Stahlradwagen ou la voiture à roues en acier: une légère calèche à quatre roues avec moteur vertical sous le siège devant le train arrière. Après sa première à l'Exposition universelle de Paris en 1889, elle reste en France.

The drive came via gear wheels in direct
contact with the rear axles, and the
V-engine's power was transmitted by a
4-speed gear mechanism. The two-liter
(0.53-gal) fuel supply in the surface carburetor
was soon exhausted.

Der Antrieb erfolgt über Zahnräder direkt auf die
Hinterachse. Vermittelt wird die Kraft des V-Motors
durch ein Viergang-Zahnradgetriebe. Der Kraftstoff-
vorrat von zwei Litern im Oberflächenvergaser ist rasch
aufgezehrt.

L'essieu arrière est entraîné directement via des
engrenages. La puissance du moteur en V est transmise
par une boîte de vitesses à engrenages à quatre
rapports. La réserve de carburant, de deux litres, dans
le carburateur à surface, est rapidement consommée.

"Victoria" is what Karl Benz is supposed to have rejoiced in Latin when he invented stub-axle steering. In the winter of 1892–93 he patented it as a "car steering device with steering circles to be set tangential to the wheels." The main advantage of this innovation was that the front wheels on the inside and the outside of the curve could now run at different angles to the direction of travel. On 28 February 1893 he was awarded Imperial Patent 73151 for this invention.

With a jubilant cry of relief Benz at the same time celebrated victory over the three-wheeler – from now on four wheels were to be the norm on a motor car. Many doubt this etymology of the car's name – Victoria is also understood to have been the name of an ordinary carriage with two seats. Nevertheless, whatever the derivation, this is what Karl Benz named his first four-wheeler, which progressively became more powerful and faster. In 1893 the rear-mounted, single-cylinder engine with its vertical flywheel produced 3 bhp from 1730 cc, in 1894 4 bhp from 1990 cc, 5 bhp from 2650 cc in 1895 and 6 bhp from 2915 cc from 1898 onwards.

Despite its heavy appearance, the Victoria was in fact quite light, weighing not more than 610 kg (1,345 lb) in total. The flat belt drive had two gears, sometimes with a supplementary planetary gear, and from 1896 onwards it had three forward gears and one reverse. The gears were changed by shifting the belts from one of the two stepped pulleys of the engine to the fixed pulleys or idling pulleys of the countershaft to which the differential was also connected. The rear wheels were driven by chains. The family resemblance to the carriage was always evident, whether the Victoria was a Two-seater, Vis-à-Vis, Phaeton or Landau. At first only the small front wheels bore solid rubber tires but later they were also fitted to the large rear wheels. Of all Benz's creations, the Victoria was his favorite, "because its solid tires gave it protection from the normal tire defects and the high seating position was clear of road dust." Pride in the product was evident in the advertising literature produced by the very successful French Benz agent Emile Roger. It described it as "horseless carriage driven by a special petroleum engine … elegance, solidity, comfort, great simplicity, no shaking, upkeep with ease."

But the reality was not quite so rosy. The car required 20 liters (5.28 gal) of gasoline and 160 liters (42.3 gal) of water every 100 km (62 miles) to keep going. This did not deter Theodor Freiherr von Liebig from covering the considerable distance from Reichenberg in Bohemia via Mannheim to Reims in France and back in 1894 in a Victoria. Although the look on the nobleman's face when he reached his destination was one of quiet dignity, it is likely that among his circle of close friends he would also have admitted to a feeling of relief.

Victoria« soll Karl Benz auf lateinisch frohlockt haben, als er die Achsschenkellenkung erfand. Im Winter 1892/93 meldet er sie zum Patent an, als »Wagenlenkvorrichtung mit tangential zu den Rädern zu stellenden Lenkkreisen«. Hauptvorteil dieser Novität: Kurveninneres und kurvenäußeres Vorderrad können nun in unterschiedlichen Winkeln zur bisherigen Fahrtrichtung laufen. Am 28. Februar 1893 wird ihm dafür das Reichspatent 73 1 5 1 zugeteilt.

Mit dem Jubelschrei der Erleichterung feiert Benz zugleich den Sieg über das Dreirad – vier Räder sind von Stund an die Norm. Manche zweifeln diese Etymologie aus dem Hochgefühl des glücklichen Augenblicks heraus an – Victoria habe auch ein landläufiger Kutschentyp mit zwei Sitzen geheißen. Immerhin nennt Karl Benz seinen ersten Vierradler so, der im Laufe seiner Modellgeschichte immer kräftiger und immer schneller wird: Drei Pferdestärken und 1730 ccm hat der hinten liegend eingebaute Einzylinder mit stehendem Schwungrad 1893, vier PS aus 1990 ccm 1894, fünf PS aus 2650 ccm 1895 und sechs PS aus 2915 ccm ab 1898. Der Victoria sieht klobig aus, ist aber leicht: ganze 610 Kilogramm. Zwei Gänge hat sein Flachriemengetriebe, gegebenenfalls mit zusätzlichem Planetengetriebe, drei Fahrstufen vorwärts und eine rückwärts ab 1896. Der Wechsel der Gänge vollzieht sich durch Verschieben der Riemen von den beiden Stufenscheiben des Motors zu den Festscheiben oder Leerscheiben der Vorgelegewelle, auf der auch das Differential angesiedelt ist. Die Hinterräder werden durch Ketten in Marsch gesetzt und am Laufen gehalten.

Immer präsent ist die Familienähnlichkeit zur Kutsche, ob der Victoria nun als Zweisitzer, Vis-à-Vis, Phaeton oder Landauer daherkommt. Erst sind nur die kleinen Vorderräder vollgummibereift, später auch die großen Hinterräder. Von all seinen Kreationen ist Karl Benz der Victoria die liebste, »da seine Vollreifen vor den üblichen Reifendefekten schützten und durch den hohen Sitz der Straßenstaub abgehalten wurde«. Der Stolz auf das Produkt schlägt sich etwa in den Werbetexten des sehr erfolgreichen französischen Benz-Agenten Emile Roger nieder. Er verheißt »pferdelose Wagen, durch Spezial-Petroleum-Motoren angetrieben. … Eleganz, Solidität, Bequemlichkeit, große Einfachheit, keine Erschütterungen, große Leichtigkeit der Unterhaltung«.

Ganz so rosig sehen die Dinge jedoch realiter nicht aus: Das Auto möchte immerhin mit 20 Litern Benzin und 160 Litern Wasser je hundert Kilometer bei Laune gehalten werden. Das bringt Theodor Freiherr von Liebig indes nicht davon ab, 1894 mit einem Victoria die beträchtliche Entfernung von Reichenberg in Böhmen über Mannheim nach Reims und retour zurückzulegen. Obwohl die Gesichtszüge des Edelmannes bei der Zieldurchfahrt eine Art verklärter Würde ausdrücken, wird er in kleinem Kreise auch Erleichterung eingestanden haben.

Victoria» se serait écrié Karl Benz en latin, après avoir découvert la direction à fusée de roue. Durant l'hiver 1892–1893, il fait déposer pour elle un brevet en tant que « dispositif de braquage de voiture avec cercles de braquage tangentiels aux roues ». Avantage majeur de cette innovation : la roue intérieure au virage et la roue extérieure au virage peuvent désormais tourner en prenant des angles différents par rapport à direction initiale. Le 28 février 1893, on lui décerne le brevet du Reich 73151.

Avec ce cri de joie et de soulagement, Benz fête simultanément la victoire sur le tricycle – dorénavant, quatre roues sont la norme. Certains mettent en doute l'étymologie et son lien à l'instant de bonheur – il y aurait aussi eu un type de calèches à deux sièges répandu appelé Victoria. C'est en tout cas ainsi que Karl Benz baptise sa première voiture à quatre roues qui, au cours de son histoire, devient de plus en plus puissante et de plus en plus rapide : le monocylindre en position horizontale à l'arrière avec volant-moteur vertical de 1893 a trois chevaux et une cylindrée de 1730 cm³ ; celui de 1894 en tire quatre à partir de 1990 cm³, celui de 1895, cinq de 2650 cm³ et celui de 1898, six chevaux à partir de 2915 cm³. La Victoria a l'air massif, mais c'est trompeur : elle ne pèse que 610 kg. Sa boîte de vitesses à deux rapports plate, parfois avec engrenage planétaire supplémentaire, trois rapports avant et une marche arrière à partir de 1896. Le changement des rapports s'effectue en déplaçant les courroies de la poulie étagée du moteur vers les disques fixes ou disques vides de l'arbre intermédiaire, sur lequel se trouve aussi le différentiel. Les roues arrière sont entraînées par chaînes.

La Victoria présente encore une similitude avec la calèche, qu'elle soit carrossée en Biplace, Vis-à-Vis, Phaeton ou Landau. Au début, seules les petites roues avant ont des bandages à caoutchouc plein. Ce ne sera, aussi, le cas des grandes roues arrière que plus tard. De toutes ses créations, c'est la Victoria que Karl Benz préfère, « car ses pneus pleins ne sont pas sujet aux défaillances des pneus courants et que, grâce aux sièges élevés, la poussière de la route n'est pas soulevée ». L'agent de Benz en France, Émile Roger, remporte un très grand succès en faisant de la fierté du propriétaire un argument de vente. Il évoque dans ses publicités « des voitures sans chevaux, propulsées par des moteurs à pétrole spécial … Élégance, solidité, confort, grande simplicité, pas de secousses, entretien d'une grande facilité ».

Dans la réalité, les choses ne sont pourtant pas tout aussi simples : la voiture tient tout de même à se sustenter avec 20 litres d'essence et 160 litres d'eau tous les 100 km. Cela n'empêche pas le comte Theodor von Liebig de couvrir, en 1894, avec une Victoria, la distance considérable de Reichenberg, en Bohème, à Reims, en passant par Mannheim et retour. Bien que les traits du visage du noble aient traduit une espèce de dignité rayonnante lors de son arrivée, il n'en aura sans doute pas moins exprimé son soulagement à huis clos.

BENZ VICTORIA & VICTORIA-FAMILIE 1893

The seat backs in the front of the car and the armrests reveal that in the Vis-à-Vis you sat face to face, just as Karl Benz and his wife Berta once did.

Die Rücklehne vorn und die Armstützen zeigen es: Im Vis-à-Vis sitzt man einander Auge in Auge gegenüber wie einst Karl Benz und Gattin Berta.

Le dossier du siège avant et les accoudoirs le prouvent: dans la Vis-à-Vis, on se fait face comme jadis Karl Benz et son épouse Berta.

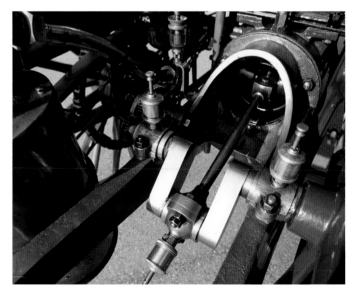

Benz Victoria & Victoria-Familie 1893

A technical puzzle made up of components which, working in unison, made it possible for people to travel under their own steam, albeit slowly and not exactly in comfort. The steering wheel crank sat on a vertical steering column in the middle of the vehicle, leading to an innovative stub-axle steering system. Karl Benz is said to have shouted "Victoria!" when the idea came to him. As at the rear, the front wheels were suspended from a rigid axle by double elliptical springs. The bodywork was wooden and frameless. Parts of the stub-axle steering can clearly be seen.

Ein technisches Puzzle aus Teilen, die in ihrer Summe menschliche Fortbewegung aus eigener Kraft ermöglichen, gemächlich noch und wenig komfortabel, aber immerhin. Die Lenkradkurbel auf einer senkrechten Säule in der Wagenmitte führt zu der innovativen Achsschenkellenkung, deren Erfindung Karl Benz den Freudenschrei »Victoria« entlockt haben soll. Wie auch hinten sind die Räder vorn an einer Starrachse mit Vollelliptikfedern aufgehängt. Der Aufbau: rahmenlos aus Holz. Deutlich zu erkennen sind Elemente der Achsschenkellenkung.

Un vrai puzzle technique qui permet à l'homme de se mouvoir de sa propre force, lentement encore et de façon peu confortable, certes. La manivelle de volant sur une colonne verticale au centre de la voiture entraîne une direction novatrice à fusée, dont la découverte aurait fait pousser à Karl Benz le cri de joie « Victoria ! » À l'arrière, comme à l'avant, les roues sont suspendues à un essieu rigide avec ressorts complètement elliptiques. La carrosserie, tout en bois, ne comporte aucun cadre. On reconnaît aisément les éléments de la direction à fusée.

The top speed of the Benz-Laudaulet was 30 kph, making the horn an important supplement to the driver's shouts. With its modern-looking folding roof, the Landaulet could be used both as a coupé and as a cabriolet – a sensible concession to the German climate. The doors and roof could be completely removed.

Das Benz-Laudaulet von 1898 läuft bis zu 30 Stundenkilometern. Da ist die Hupe schon eine willkommene Ergänzung zu den Zurufen des Fahrers. Mit seinem modern anmutenden Klappverdeck ist das Landaulet als Coupé wie als Cabriolet universell verwendbar – eine kluge Konzession an deutsche Witterungsverhältnisse. Türen und Dach lassen sich komplett herausnehmen.

Le Landaulet-Benz de 1898 peut rouler jusqu'à 30 km/h. Le klaxon est donc un complément bienvenu aux cris du conducteur. Avec sa capote rabattable d'allure moderne, le Landaulet peut se présenter en coupé comme en cabriolet – une concession intelligente aux aléas du temps en Allemagne. Les portières et le toit se démontent complètement.

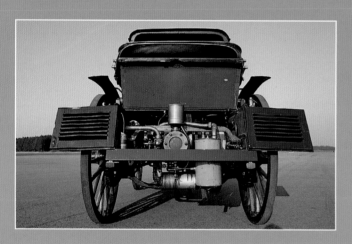

Benz Victoria & Victoria-Familie 1893

The vertically-mounted steering of the Landaulet seen from below and above. While the passengers can protect themselves against the weather somehow or other, the driver is entirely at the mercy of the elements. Parts of the engine housing and drip feed lubricators.

Die steil stehende Lenkung des Landaulet aus der Frosch- und aus der Vogelperspektive. Während sich die Passagiere so oder so auf das Wetter einrichten können, verrichtet der Fahrer seine Arbeit in jedem Fall im Freien. Teile der Motorabdeckung und Tropföler für die Schmierung der Maschine.

La direction verticale du Landaulet vue du dessous et du dessus (page de gauche). Alors que les passagers pouvaient se protéger des intempéries d'une manière ou d'une autre, le conducteur n'avait d'autre issue que d'officier à l'air libre. Parties du capot moteur et du graisseur à gouttes pour la lubrification du moteur.

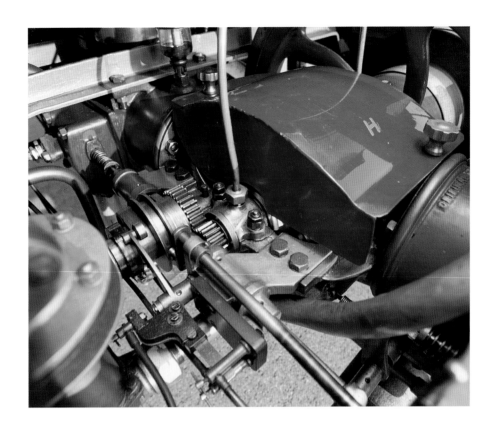

The impetus for the development of this light, inexpensive vehicle came from Josef Brecht who was Karl Benz's business advisor. The Benz Velociped, known as Velo for short, was built with that specification in mind. The melodious and unassuming name is a reminder of the origins of the self-propelled vehicle.

That was exactly what its inventor had in mind, as was its silhouette that recalled a carriage with its small front wheels and large rear wheels. Even up to the mid 1890s, Benz stressed the kinship of his creation with the horse-drawn carriage in his advertising literature, until Benz cars took the lead in emancipated design. The Velo was in fact very light and at 280 kg (127 lb) a seductive offer, even to the many doubters of the day. According to a contemporary brochure, the Velociped cost 2,000 marks "complete with the finest fittings with lamps, or 2,200 marks fitted out with a half roof and grained leather." Customers flocked to buy it in huge numbers. Between October 1894 and October 1895, 125 Velos were sold. Together with the improved Comfortable version from 1898 (available with pneumatic tires), 1,200 cars were sold. Thus the production car was born. One third of this number went to customers in Germany and France (under the name Eclair, "lightning" in English) and the remainder to other countries.

Initially, the single-cylinder engine produced 1.5 bhp at 450 rpm from a good 1-liter capacity, and 3.5 bhp at 800 rpm by the end of its production in 1901. Benz never tired of making changes to the Velociped, first offering it with flat belt gearing and later with planetary gears – three forward gears and one reverse. An unusually advanced detail was its float carburetor. A gas-air quantity regulator on the inlet manifold operating together with a throttle valve and adjustment of the ignition produced more flexible engine running.

The advanced variant, the Ideal, whose cooling-water tank somewhat resembled an engine bonnet, and its offshoots, the Duc and Charette, proved difficult to sell. In 1902, its last year of production, the Ideal was offered with a commanding 8 bhp powerplant. Lateral thinker Benz had fitted it with a special kind of two-cylinder engine which he called the Contra Engine. In fact this was none other than a flat boxer engine which gave the "small two-seater car" a powerful advantage. Although Karl Benz had a healthy aversion to power and speed, the last generation Ideal was capable of up to 50 kph (31 mph).

Die Anregung für ein leichtes und preiswürdiges Fahrzeug kommt von Josef Brecht, der Karl Benz in kaufmännischen Dingen beratend zur Seite steht. Nach diesen Parametern entsteht das Benz Velociped, kurz Velo geheißen. Der Name ist klangvoll und bescheiden, und er gemahnt an die Ursprünge des Selbstbewegers.

Das ist ganz im Sinne des Erfinders, ebenso wie die kaum verhohlene Kutschen-Silhouette mit kleinen Rädern vorn und großen Rädern hinten. Noch bis Mitte der Neunziger des vorigen Jahrhunderts hebt Benz in den Werbeschriften der Firma die Affinität seiner Kreationen zum Pferde-Fuhrwerk hervor, bis Benz-Automobile führend werden in emanzipatorischem Design. Ein Leichtgewicht ist der Velo in der Tat mit seinen 280 Kilogramm und ein verführerisches Angebot dazu, selbst an die zahlreichen Auto-Muffel der Zeit: »Preis komplett in feinster Ausstattung mit Laternen Mark 2000. Mit Halbverdeck und Spritzleder ausgestattet kostet das Velociped Mark 2200«, steht in einem zeitgenössischen Prospekt zu lesen. Kunden in ungewöhnlicher Zahl wissen das zu würdigen. Zwischen dem Oktober 1894 und dem gleichen Monat im folgenden Jahr allein werden 125 Velos verkauft. Zusammen mit der verbesserten Version Comfortable ab 1898 (mit Luftreifen) bringt man 1200 Exemplare unter die Leute: Soeben ist das Serienauto geboren worden. Je ein Drittel geht nach Deutschland, Frankreich (unter dem Namen Eclair, zu deutsch Blitz) und ins restliche Ausland.

1,5 PS bei 450/min leistet der Einzylinder von reichlich einem Liter Inhalt am Anfang, 3,5 PS bei 800/min am Ende seiner Produktion 1901, und auch sonst unterzieht Benz das Velociped nimmermüder Modellpflege, bietet es etwa zunächst mit Flachriemengetriebe und später mit einem Planetengetriebe an, mit drei Fahrstufen und einem Rückwärtsgang. Ein ungemein fortschrittliches Detail ist sein Schwimmervergaser. Ein Gas-Luft-Mengenregler am Ansaugrohr reguliert gemeinsam mit einer Drosselklappe und einer Verstellung des Zündzeitpunkts den Motorlauf flexibler.

Schwer verkäuflich bleiben die Sublimationsstufe Ideal, deren Umkleidung für den Kühlwasserbehälter vorn den Anschein erweckt, es handele sich um eine Motorhaube, und ihre Varianten Duc und Charette. Im letzten Jahr seiner Fertigung 1902 kommt der Ideal mit stattlichen acht PS daher. Querdenker Benz hat ihm einen Zweizylinder der besonderen Art spendiert. Was er Contra-Motor nennt, ist nichts anderes als ein Boxertriebwerk, das dem »Kleinen zweisitzigen Kutschierwagen« mächtig auf die Sprünge hilft: Obwohl Karl Benz eine gesunde Abneigung gegen Kraft und Tempo hegt, ist der Ideal der letzten Generation fähig zu Tempo 50.

C'est Josef Brecht, le conseiller de Karl Benz pour les questions commerciales, qui suggéra de produire un véhicule léger et peu coûteux. C'est selon ce cahier des charges que naît le vélocipède Benz, familièrement appelé Velo. Le nom sonne bien, est modeste, et il rappelle les origines de l'automobile.

Cela est tout à fait dans l'esprit de l'inventeur, au même titre que la silhouette à peine masquée de calèche avec de petites roues à l'avant et de grandes à l'arrière. Jusque vers le milieu des années 1890, encore, Benz souligne, dans les prospectus de la firme, l'affinité de ses créations avec les calèches jusqu'à ce que ses voitures deviennent les pionniers d'un design émancipateur. Avec ses 280 kg, le Velo est vraiment un poids plume et, qui plus est, une nouvelle option, même pour les nombreux adversaires de l'automobile de cette époque : « Prix complet en finition de luxe avec lanternes, 2000 marks. Avec semi-capote et cuir antiprojections, le Vélocipède coûte 2200 marks », peut-on lire dans un prospectus de cette époque. Un nombre inhabituel de clients l'auront apprécié personnellement. D'octobre 1894 à octobre 1895, Benz ne vend pas moins de 125 véhicules. Conjointement avec la version améliorée, baptisée « Comfortable » à partir de 1898 (avec pneus à chambre à air), ce ne sont pas moins de 1200 exemplaires qui trouvent preneur : le véhicule de série venait de naître. Un tiers a été vendu en Allemagne et en France (sous le nom d'Éclair), le reste, dans les autres pays étrangers.

Le monocylindre d'un bon litre de cylindrée développe au début 1,5 ch à 450 tr/min puis 3,5 ch à 800 tr/min, à la fin de sa production, en 1901. D'ailleurs, Benz ne ménage aucun effort pour maintenir son vélocipède toujours au goût du jour. Ainsi le propose-t-il tout d'abord avec une boîte de vitesses à courroies plates et, plus tard, avec une boîte de vitesses planétaire à trois rapports avant et une marche arrière. Son carburateur à flotteur est une caractéristique qui représente un très grand progrès. Conjointement avec une vis papillon et un décalage de l'allumage, un régulateur du volume gaz-air dans le tube d'aspiration rend plus harmonieux le fonctionnement du moteur.

Ultime extrapolation, l'Ideal, dont le carénage du réservoir d'eau de refroidissement à l'avant incite à penser qu'il s'agit d'un capot moteur, avec ses variantes Duc et Charette qui s'avèrent difficiles à vendre. Lors de sa dernière année de production, en 1902, l'Ideal a la puissance respectable de huit chevaux. Esprit fertile, Benz l'a doté d'un bicylindre d'un type particulier. Ce qu'il appelle moteur Contra n'est rien d'autre qu'un moteur à plat qui donne des ailes à la « petite calèche à deux places » : bien que Karl Benz nourrisse une profonde méfiance à l'égard de la puissance et de la vitesse, l'Ideal de la dernière génération est capable d'atteindre le 50 km/h.

The small Comfortable, manufactured from 1898, was technically the same as the Velo. As the name suggests, however, it offered greater comfort and had a nicely rounded hood.

Der kleine Comfortable ab 1898 entspricht technisch dem Velo. Er bietet aber, wie der Name sagt, mehr Komfort und hat eine gefällig gerundete Motorhaube.

La petite Comfortable, construite à partir de 1898, correspond techniquement au Velo. Mais, comme son nom l'indique, elle offre plus de confort et un élégant capot moteur arrondi.

Benz Velo 1894

The Veloziped Comfortable was driven by a four-stroke single cylinder engine with an upright flywheel. It first justified its name in 1896 with the addition of pneumatic tires. The family resemblance to the horse-drawn carriage is still clearly apparent.

Angetrieben wird das Veloziped Comfortable durch einen Viertakt-Einzylinder mit stehendem Schwungrad. Luftreifen gereichen seinem Namen erst ab 1896 zur Ehre. Die Familienähnlichkeit zur Kutsche ist immer noch deutlich.

Le vélocipède Comfortable est propulsé par un monocylindre à quatre temps avec volant-moteur vertical. Il ne mérite son nom qu'en 1896 avec l'adjonction de pneus. La parenté avec la calèche est encore manifeste.

Parts of the front suspension and the mountain safety bar which could be let down to brake the car on steep roads, a necessary precaution since the outer band brakes only worked when moving in a forward direction.

Teile der Vorderradaufhängung und die Bergstütze. Sie muss den Wagen an Steigungen halten, weil die Außenbandbremsen nur in Vorwärtsfahrt greifen.

Parties de la suspension avant et du frein de montagne que l'on peut faire descendre sur les routes escarpées. Le système retient la voiture en montée car le frein courroie extérieur agit seulement en marche avant.

Benz Velo 1894

The next evolutionary development, the Velo Ideal, proved hard
to sell despite the obvious
advances. The bodywork was now
mounted on a sectional steel
frame, whereas its forerunner still
used wood.

Als schwer verkäuflich erweist
sich die Velo-Evolutionsstufe Ideal
trotz manifester Fortschritte:
Die Karosserie lagert nun auf
einem Rahmen aus Profilstahl,
wo beim Vorgänger noch Holz
herhalten musste.

Le Velo Ideal s'avère difficilement
vendable malgré des progrès
manifestes: la carrosserie repose
maintenant sur un cadre en profilé
d'acier là où sa devancière
comportait encore du bois.

Benz Velo 1894

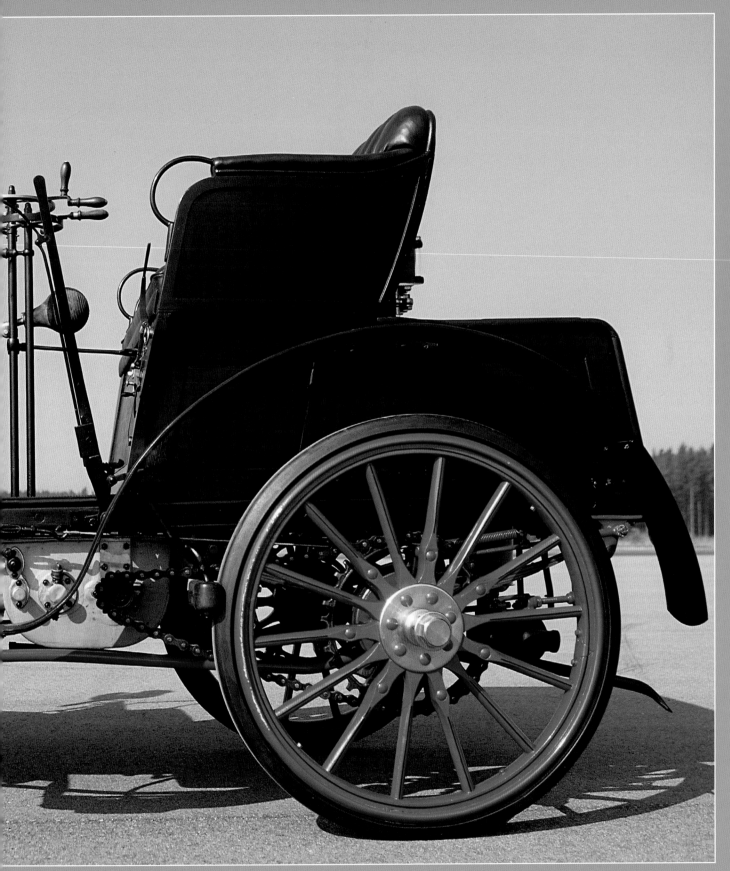

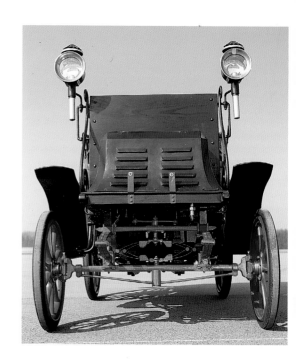

The hood opened in one piece from above to reveal the four-stroke, one cylinder engine. Under the front lid with the ventilation slits was the cooling water tank.

Aus einem Stück: die nach oben zu öffnende Motorhaube über dem Viertakt-Einzylinder. Unter dem vorderen Deckel, durch Luftschlitze aufgebrochen, verbirgt sich der Behälter für das Kühlwasser.

D'un seul jet : le capot moteur s'ouvrant vers le haut au-dessus du monocylindre à quatre temps. Sous le carénage avant, interrompu par des fentes d'aération, se trouve le réservoir d'eau de refroidissement.

Benz Velo 1894

Details of the driver's cockpit. The photographs show the oil supply and the drip-feed lubricator with the outlets to the lubrication points (right), and the accelerator handle, ignition timing handle, and mixture controller (left).

Details aus dem Führerstand. Ölvorrat und Tropfölerapparat mit Abgängen an die Schmierstellen (rechts), Handgashebel, Zündverstellhebel und Gemischregler (links).

Détails du poste de pilotage. À droite, le réservoir à huile et ses sorties vers les points de lubrification ; à gauche, l'accélérateur à main et le levier de réglage de l'allumage et la régulation du mélange.

In the early years of motoring history, it was not just the silhouettes of vehicles which provided a reminder of their lineage, it was also their names. A Phaeton, named after the son of Helios, the sun god in Greek mythology, was originally a light, four-wheeled carriage, a Tonneau was a two-wheeled bassinet with a pair of shafts which you entered from the rear, a Break was a light, open carriage.

The terms Vis-à-Vis and Dos-à-Dos refer to the arrangement of the passengers relative to one another, a situation that also determined the degree of sociability which travelers could enjoy as a consequence. In the Vis-à-Vis the occupants sat facing one another – in early cars of this type a stoical composure was always clearly maintained by the passengers as numerous contemporary pictures show. The driver was somewhat handicapped in having to look past the passengers in the front row. In the Dos-à-Dos the occupants sat back to back, an arrangement which helped the driver to concentrate on the road ahead, but made conversation between the occupants of the two rows of seats rather difficult.

In 1899 the Benz range was extended by the Mylord, Break and Dos-à-Dos model types all equipped with opposed two-cylinder flat engines (in company jargon: Contra Engines). The first of these cars had 5 bhp, 1710 cc engines which doubled the top speed of the Mannheim cars from a sluggish 25 to a brisk 50 kph (15.5 to 31 mph). The most powerful of these boxer engines, a 20 bhp unit, was produced in 1901 but was never actually installed. In that year the standard Dos-à-Dos had a 10 bhp, 2690 cc engine, and, depending on its equipment, it was available for up to 7,800 marks. The power was transmitted via a 3-speed box with reverse gear, through a belt to the countershaft and by chains to the rear wheels.

From 1897 onwards, pneumatic tires promised a more comfortable ride but they were not without their problems. A journey might frequently be interrupted by the explosive hiss of suddenly escaping air, much to the annoyance of the chauffeur who at that time could still be readily recognized by his dirty hands. A tire change required tedious dismantling work. It was not until 1908 that the first removable rims appeared, and not until just before the First World War that wheel changing became relatively straightforward. But by this time the principle of the Dos-à-Dos was outmoded. It did not surface again until after the Second World War – this time in the form of the poor man's car, the Zündapp Janus.

Nicht nur die Silhouette erinnert in den Baby-jahren des Automobils an die Mutter Kutsche, sondern auch die Namensgebung. So ist ein Phaeton, benannt nach dem Sohn des Sonnengotts im griechischen Mythos, ursprünglich ein leichter vierrädriger Kutschwagen, ein Tonneau ein zweirädriger Korbwagen mit Gabeldeichsel sowie Einstieg von hinten, ein Break ein leichter, offener Wagen.

Die Begriffe Vis-à-Vis und Dos-à-Dos bezeichnen die Anordnung der Passagiere zueinander und umreißen zugleich das Maß an Geselligkeit, die diese Gefährte gestatten: Im Vis-à-Vis sitzt man einander Auge in Auge gegenüber, in frühen Autos dieses Typs offenbar stets in stoischer Gelassenheit, wie zahlreiche zeitgenössische Abbildungen bezeugen. Leicht behindert wird der Fahrer, der an den Reisenden im ersten Glied vorbeischauen muss. Im Dos-à-Dos indessen kehrt man einander den Rücken zu, was der Konzentration des Piloten auf den Weg vor ihm förderlich ist, aber die Kommunikation zwischen Reihe eins und Reihe zwei erschwert.

Im Jahre 1899 wird die Benz-Palette erweitert um die Modellfamilien Mylord, Break und Dos-à-Dos, allesamt ausgestattet mit Zweizylinder-Flachtriebwerken (Haus-jargon: Contra-Motoren) von zunächst 1710 ccm und fünf Pferdestärken, was die Spitzengeschwindigkeit der Mobile aus Mannheim umgehend von müden 25 auf muntere 50 Stundenkilometer verdoppelt. Die mit 20 PS stärkste dieser Boxermaschinen entsteht 1901, gelangt indes wohl nie zum Einbau. In jenem Jahr hat der Dos-à-Dos à la carte, je nach Ausstattung feil für bis zu 7800 Mark, bereits 2690 ccm und zehn Pferdestärken. Sie werden vermittelt über ein Dreiganggetriebe mit Rückwärtsgang – per Riemen auf das Vorgelege, via Ketten zu den Hinterrädern.

Für vermehrten Fahrkomfort sorgen ab 1897 Luft-reifen. Aber sie gereichen nicht nur zu ungetrübter Freude: Häufig unterbricht das Zischen schlagartig entweichender Luft die Fahrt, zum Leidwesen der Chauf-feure, die man zu jener Zeit noch an ihren schwärzlichen Händen erkennen kann. Umständliche Demontage-arbeiten sind die Folge, erst 1908 gibt es abnehmbare Felgen, erst kurz vor dem ersten Weltkrieg vergleichsweise bequem zu entfernende Räder. Da aber gehört das Prinzip Dos-à-Dos längst der Vergangenheit an und feiert erst nach dem zweiten Weltkrieg fröhliche Urständ – in der Form des Armeleute-Autos Zündapp Janus.

Lors des premiers pas de l'automobile, il n'y a pas que la silhouette, mais aussi le nom qui rappelle ses origines, la calèche. Ainsi un Phaeton, nommé d'après le fils du dieu du Soleil dans la mythologie grecque, est-il à l'origine une légère calèche à quatre roues alors qu'une Tonneau est une voiture compacte à deux roues à carrosserie tressée et brancard à fourche ainsi qu'accès depuis l'arrière, un Break étant une voiture légère et découverte.

Les dénominations Vis-à-Vis et Dos-à-Dos font allusion à l'agencement des sièges passagers et donnent simultanément un aperçu de la convivialité autorisée par ces véhicules : dans la Vis-à-Vis, on peut se regarder les yeux dans les yeux ; dans les premières voitures de ce type apparemment toujours avec une décontraction stoïque ainsi que le prouvent d'innombrables illustrations con-temporaines. Le conducteur est légèrement handicapé, car le passager assis devant lui se trouve exactement dans son champ de vision. Dans la Dos-à-Dos, si la position conforme au nom est bénéfique à la concentration du pilote, elle l'est beaucoup moins à la communication.

En 1899, la gamme Benz s'enrichit de la famille Mylord, Break et Dos-à-Dos, toutes propulsées par des moteurs bicylindriques à courroies plates (en jargon maison : moteurs Contra) de tout d'abord 1710 cm³ de cylindrée et 5 chevaux, ce qui fait instantanément passer la vitesse de pointe des automobiles de Mannheim d'un lymphatique 25 km/h à un fringant 50. Le 20 ch, le plus puissant de ces moteurs boxer, naît en 1901, mais ne sera en réalité jamais installé dans une voiture. Cette année-là, la Dos-à-Dos proposée à un prix pouvant aller jusqu'à 7800 marks selon son équipement à la carte, a déjà une cylindrée de 2690 cm³ et 10 ch. Ceux-ci sont transmis à la route via une boîte à trois vitesses avec marche arrière – par courroies à l'arbre intermédiaire et par chaînes aux roues arrière.

À partir de 1897, les pneus à chambre à air confèrent un meilleur confort. Mais ils ne sont pas toujours une source de plaisir sans faille : il est fréquent que le siffle-ment de l'air qui s'échappe inopinément interrompe le voyage, au grand dam des chauffeurs que l'on peut recon-naître encore à cette époque à leurs mains noires. Cela impose de laborieux travaux de démontage, car la pre-mière jante interchangeable n'apparaît qu'en 1908 et les roues relativement faciles à remplacer, tout juste avant la Première Guerre mondiale. Mais, à ce moment-là, le principe de la Dos-à-Dos appartient depuis longtemps à une époque révolue et il ne connaîtra un regain de popularité qu'après la Seconde Guerre mondiale – sous la forme de la Zündapp Janus, voiture pour conducteurs à revenus modestes.

Benz Dos-à-Dos 1899

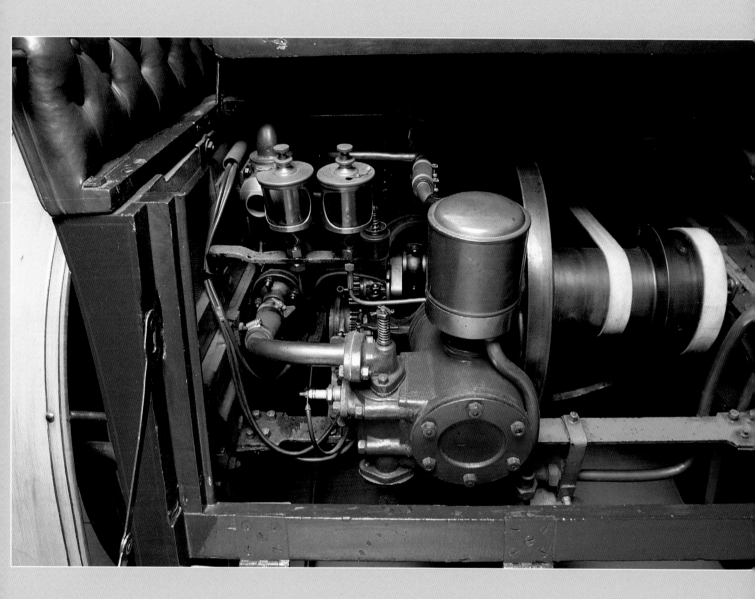

The Benz Dos-à-Dos (French for back to back) demonstrated that carmakers at that time were still experimenting with seating arrangements. It was not until the turn of the century that today's well-nigh universal arrangement became customary.
Above: a view of parts of the power train with the seats and floor removed.

Der Benz Dos-à-Dos (für Rücken an Rücken) zeigt, dass man noch mit der Sitzanordnung experimentiert. Erst im neuen Jahrhundert setzt sich die bis heute übliche Verteilung durch. Oben: Unter der entfernten Sitzfläche Teile der Kraftübertragung.

La Benz Dos-à-Dos montre que l'on fait encore des expériences avec l'agencement des sièges à cette époque. Il faudra attendre le XXᵉ siècle pour que la répartition aujourd'hui courante s'impose. Ci-dessus : sous les sièges, des parties de la transmission.

As the nineteenth century drew to a close the new cult word "vitesse" (or speed) rang out from France; the yardstick for the progress of the car was marked in meters and seconds. Karl Benz was at the same time bemoaning the lamentable state of the network of roads and tracks, an impossible situation for vehicles capable of 50 kph (31 mph). Nevertheless, the tracks on which the new fashionable sport of car racing took place were packed with onlookers, half of them curious, half apprehensive. What they saw came to outpace even the speed of runaway horses. There were clear advantages for manufacturers in racing their cars. The severity of the test was undeniable and the car quietly came to be accepted by the general public, while the effectiveness of the sport as a means of advertising surpassed newspaper advertisements and all other kinds of printed promotion.

Even Karl Benz could no longer hold out against the trend of the time and in 1899 he built a racing car with a 2280 cc opposed-cylinder engine producing 8 bhp at 750 rpm. The top of the range was a 2827 cc machine which produced 16 bhp at 1000 rpm. The engine was cooled by evaporation which required regular replenishment of the water reservoir – and also of the oil which was dripped on the crankshaft for lubrication and then leaked away into the dust of the track. A flat belt which absorbed many impact loads and considerable vibration connected the engine to the 4-speed gearbox. The robust vehicle rode on stout wooden wheels, such as those used by artillery of the time. Both front lanterns were removed as a precaution when racing. Fritz Held, proprietor of Held-Automobile in Mannheim and a close friend of the family, won early racing fame by winning the 193.2-km (120-mile) Frankfurt to Cologne rally in a Benz racing car at an average speed of 22.5 kph (14 mph). Meanwhile, with the engine increased to 12 bhp, he took second in the Innsbruck–Munich race and the Berlin–Leipzig race, together with Richard Benz, with the shortest run time.

In 1900 a 16 bhp production racing car with a top speed of 65 kph (40 mph), derived from this car, was available for a hefty 15,000 marks. When raced for the first time by Fritz Scarisbrick on the Eisenach–Oberhof–Meiningen–Eisenach mountain rally, it took second place at an average speed of 30.1 kph (18.7 mph) – so bearing out the truth of Benz advertising claim that the car could climb any gradients.

Mit dem Ausgang des 19. Jahrhunderts kommt aus Frankreich der neue Kultbegriff Tempo, entdeckt man die Messbarkeit automobilen Fortschritts in Metern und Sekunden. Zugleich beschwert sich Karl Benz, das Straßen- und Wegenetz befinde sich in verheerendem Zustand, eine Zumutung für Fahrzeuge, die 50 Stundenkilometer liefen. Gleichwohl sind die Rollbahnen, auf denen sich der neue Modesport Autorennen abwickelt, dicht gesäumt mit Zuschauern, neugierig halb, halb beklommen. Denn was sie zu sehen bekommen, übersteigt allmählich entschieden die Geschwindigkeit selbst durchgehender Pferde. Ihre Wagen in Rennen einzusetzen hat für die Hersteller manifeste Vorteile: Der Härtetest ist unvergleichlich, das Auto wird klammheimlich in der allgemeinen Gunst verankert, die Werbewirksamkeit des Sports sticht alle Zeitungsanzeigen sowie sonstige gedruckten Lobhudeleien jeglicher Art aus.

Dem Zug der Zeit mag sich auch Karl Benz nicht mehr entziehen und baut 1899 einen Rennwagen mit einem Contra-Motor von 2280 ccm mit acht Pferdestärken Leistung bei 750/min, in seiner schärfsten Variante von 2827 ccm und 16 PS bei 1000/min. Gekühlt wird er durch Verdunstung, so dass ab und an Wasser nachgefüllt werden muss ebenso wie Öl, denn das träufelt tröpfchenweise auf die Kurbelwelle und verschwindet dann auf ewig im Staub der Piste. Ein Flachriemen, der so manchen Stoß und manche Erschütterung abfängt, verbindet das Triebwerk mit dem Vierganggetriebe. Das robuste Fahrzeug steht auf trotzigen hölzernen Rädern, wie sie die zeitgenössische Artillerie verwendet. Die beiden Frontlaternen werden für den Rennbetrieb vorsorglich entfernt. Fritz Held, Inhaber der Firma Held-Automobile in Mannheim und enger Freund der Familie, erringt frühen Renn-Ruhm, als er mit dem Benz-Boliden die Fernfahrt Frankfurt–Köln über 193,2 Kilometer mit einem Schnitt von 22,5 km/h gewinnt. Inzwischen von zwölf Pferdestärken beflügelt, legt er gleich noch mit einem zweiten Rang bei der Fahrt Innsbruck–München und Berlin–Leipzig nach, zusammen mit Richard Benz Sieger mit der kürzesten Fahrzeit.

Aus diesem Auto abgeleitet wird 1900 ein Produktionsrennwagen mit 16 PS und 65 km/h Spitze, zu haben um deftige 15 000 Mark. Beim ersten Einsatz unter Fritz Scarisbrick bei der Gebirgsfahrt Eisenach–Oberhof–Meiningen–Eisenach stellt er mit einem zweiten Platz und einem Stundenmittel von 30,1 km/h auch gleich unter Beweis, dass die Benz-Werbung nicht lügt. Sie besagt nämlich, der Wagen überwinde alle Steigungen.

À la fin du XIXe siècle, un nouveau culte, originaire de France, la vitesse, fait son apparition et on est dorénavant capable de mesurer en mètres et secondes les progrès réalisés dans l'automobile. Simultanément, Karl Benz se plaint de l'état déplorable du réseau routier, trop dommageable aux véhicules roulant à 50 km/h. Cela n'empêche pas que les pistes sur lesquelles se déroule le nouveau sport à la mode, la compétition automobile, soient bordées d'une haie de spectateurs, moitié curieux, moitié intimidés. En effet, ce qui se passe sous leurs yeux finit par aller beaucoup plus vite qu'un cheval, même emballé. Pour les constructeurs, l'engagement de leurs voitures en compétition présente des avantages évidents : le test d'endurance est incomparable et procure à la voiture une grande notoriété.

Karl Benz lui-même ne peut se permettre de se tenir à l'écart de ces compétitions et construit en 1899 une voiture de course avec un moteur Contra de 2280 cm³ développant huit chevaux à 750 tr/min, et même 16 ch à 1000 tr/min dans sa version la plus poussée de 2827 cm³. Il est refroidi par évaporation et il faut donc rajouter de l'eau de temps à autre, ainsi que de l'huile, car celle-ci s'écoule goutte à goutte sur le vilebrequin et disparaît pour l'éternité dans la poussière de la piste. Une courroie plate qui absorbe une grande partie des chocs et des secousses relie le moteur à la boîte à quatre vitesses. Cette robuste voiture est campée sur d'imposantes roues en bois comme celles utilisées par l'artillerie de cette époque. Par mesure de prudence, on démonte les deux lanternes avant pour la course. Fritz Held, propriétaire de la société Automobiles Held à Mannheim et ami intime de la famille, acquiert une célébrité précoce en compétition en gagnant, avec une voiture de course Benz, la course Francfort–Cologne sur 193 km à une vitesse moyenne de 22,5 km/h. La puissance ayant été entre-temps majorée à douze chevaux, il réédite sa performance avec une deuxième place sur les courses Innsbruck–Munich et Berlin–Leipzig, avec Richard Benz, vainqueur avec le temps le plus rapide.

En 1900, Benz, s'inspirant de ce véhicule, crée une voiture de course de production de 16 ch atteignant 65 km/h en pointe, mais malheureusement coûteuse : pas moins de 15 000 marks. Lors de sa première participation à une course, pilotée par Fritz Scarisbrick pour le circuit de montagne Eisenach–Oberhof–Meiningen–Eisenach, il administre aussi immédiatement la preuve, avec une seconde place à une moyenne de 30,1 km/h, que la publicité de Benz ne ment pas. Elle promet en effet que la voiture est capable de franchir toutes les côtes.

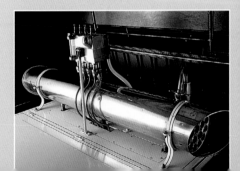

BENZ RENNWAGEN 1899

The tapered nose of the Benz racing car was lined with laminated vertical pipes in which the coolant water for the two-cylinder engine condensed.

Der spitze Bug des Benz-Renners ist mit vertikalen lamellierten Rohren bestückt, in denen das Kühlwasser für den Zweizylinder kondensiert.

La proue pointue de la voiture de course Benz est dotée de tubulures en lamelles verticales dans lesquelles se condense l'eau de refroidissement du bicylindre.

Phoenix was the name given to a mythical bird which repeatedly destroyed itself in the flames of its funeral pyre, only to rise again each time new-born from the ashes. Phoenix was also the name given by Gottlieb Daimler to an inline two-cylinder engine. Its combustion chambers were arranged parallel in a single block mounted on a spherical crankcase. It was initially known as the N-engine (N for new model), which was the company's working designation for it. Substantially improved as a 6 bhp, vertical, front-mounted engine, from 1897 onwards it was used to power a car called the Phoenix, the performance of which increased over time to 10 bhp.

For higher performance, Daimler preferred a four-cylinder engine of the same type which from 1899 boosted the Phoenix to 6, 8 or 10 bhp. It was first developed in 1890, weighed 150 kg (331 lb) and was originally intended for use on boats. At around the same time, Wilhelm Maybach had developed an enclosed cooling system consisting of an almost 4-meter (13-ft) long tube with an air-cooled surface area of more than 2 square meters (21.5 sq ft). An improved version, patented in 1895, meant that from 1898 onwards more power could be produced. The designer himself described it as an "apparatus for cooling the water flowing around the cylinders of internal combustion engines, consisting of a flat vessel through which passes a large number of tubes whereby the heat is drawn from the cooler by an airflow, generated by a suitable fan device, which passes constantly through the tubes."

Something else enabled the power level to be improved to around the 12 bhp mark, i.e., the low-voltage magneto ignition developed by Robert Bosch which in the autumn of that year replaced the Daimler glow-tube. Advance on all fronts was now unstoppable. Gone was the belt drive and in came the gearbox with four gears, mounted as a unit with a differential. Chains drove the rear wheels, a leather-lined cone had to serve as the clutch. The frame consisted of U-sections and the front and rear axles were carried by lengthwise leaf springs. Despite these advances in manufacture, the bodywork was still produced by hand-forming over wooden formers and the paintwork still took up to three weeks to finish. Also the car still had about 30 different lubrication points. This was truly an extended family covering Dog-car, Vis-à-Vis, Victoria, Phaeton, Coupé and Landauer on short and long chassis. And the prices were equally wide-ranging; the motorist had to lay out anything between 9,400 and 13,100 marks for his Phoenix.

Phoenix – so heißt im griechischen Mythos ein Vogel mit masochistischen Neigungen: Immer wieder verbrennt er sich selbstquälerisch, immer wieder klettert er wie neugeboren aus der Asche. Phoenix, so nennt Gottlieb Daimler ein Zweizylinder-Reihentriebwerk. Seine Verbrennungseinheiten sind parallel in einem Block zusammengegeben, der auf ein kugelförmiges Kurbelgehäuse geflanscht ist. Als er seinen ersten Schnaufer tut, lautet sein firmeninterner Arbeitstitel noch N-Motor (für neues Modell). Erheblich verbessert, mit sechs PS vorn stehend eingebaut, treibt er ab 1897 ein Auto namens Phoenix an, steigert sich im Laufe der Zeit auf zehn PS.

Für höhere Leistung bevorzugt Daimler einen Vierzylinder nach dem gleichen Baumuster, der dem Phoenix ab 1899 auf die Sprünge hilft, mit sechs, acht oder zehn PS. Er stammt aus dem Jahr 1890 und ist, drei Zentner schwer, ursprünglich für Boote vorgesehen. Um die gleiche Zeit hat Wilhelm Maybach ein geschlossenes Kühlsystem entwickelt: ein fast vier Meter langes Rohr mit mehr als zwei Quadratmetern luftberührter Kühlfläche. In verbesserter Form, 1895 patentiert, gestattet es ab 1898 mehr Kraft, ein »Apparat zum Kühlen des die Zylinder von Explosionsmotoren umströmenden Wassers, bestehend aus einem flachen Gefäß, welches von einer großen Anzahl von Röhren durchzogen wird, wobei ein die Röhren beständig durchziehender, von einer geeigneten Ventilationseinrichtung erzeugter Luftstrom dem Kühler die Wärme entzieht«, beschreibt es der Konstrukteur selbst.

Und noch etwas macht es möglich, dass sich die Pferdestärken zügig dem Dutzend nähern: die Niederspannungs-Magnetzündung von Robert Bosch, die vom Herbst jenes Jahres an das Daimlersche Glührohr ersetzt. Überhaupt ist der Fortschritt an allen Fronten nicht mehr aufzuhalten. Abschied gibt es vom Riemengetriebe, Willkommen für das Zahnrad-Wechselgetriebe mit vier Fahrstufen, verblockt mit dem Differential. Ketten treiben die Hinterräder, ein Lederkonus muss als Kupplung herhalten. Der Rahmen besteht aus Blechen im U-Profil, Vorder- und Hinterachse sind an längs angeordneten Blattfedern aufgehängt. Noch werden indessen die Karosserien mit der Hand über Holzformen gezogen, noch dauert die Lackierung bis zu drei Wochen, noch muss das Automobil an ungefähr dreißig Punkten abgeschmiert werden. Eine veritable Großfamilie umspannt Dog-car, Vis-à-Vis, Victoria, Phaeton, Coupé und Landauer auf kurzem und langem Fahrgestell. Und auch die Preisentwicklung ist stürmisch: Zwischen 9400 und 13100 Mark muss der Automobilist schon anlegen für seinen Phoenix.

Phoenix, tel est le nom, dans la mythologie grecque, d'un oiseau fabuleux: le seul de son espèce, il vivait plusieurs siècles, brûlait, et renaissait de ses cendres, ce qui en fit le symbole de l'immortalité. Phoenix, c'est le nom donné par Gottlieb Daimler à un bicylindre en ligne. Ses chambres de combustion sont placées parallèlement dans un bloc qui trône sur un carter moteur de forme sphérique. À ses débuts, son code de développement, interne à la firme, est encore moteur N (pour Nouveau modèle). Considérablement amélioré et monté en position verticale avec 6 ch, ce moteur propulse à partir de 1897 la Phoenix et voit sa puissance croître au fil du temps pour atteindre 10 ch.

Pour obtenir plus de puissance, Daimler préfère un quatre-cylindres à l'architecture identique, qui donne des ailes à la Phoenix à partir de 1899 avec 6, 8 ou 10 ch. Il remonte à l'année 1890, pèse 150 kg et était conçu initialement pour des bateaux. À la même époque, Wilhelm Maybach a mis au point un système de refroidissement à circuit fermé: un tube de près de quatre mètres de long avec une surface de refroidissement exposée au vent de plus de 2 m². Amélioré et breveté en 1895, il génère plus de puissance à partir de 1898. La description est du constructeur lui-même: «Appareil pour refroidir l'eau baignant les cylindres de moteurs à explosion, se composant d'un récipient plan sillonné par un grand nombre de tubulures, à l'occasion de quoi un courant d'air produit par un dispositif de ventilation approprié et franchissant en permanence les tubulures évacue la chaleur du radiateur.»

Et une autre innovation permet aux chevaux d'atteindre rapidement la douzaine: l'allumage magnétique à basse tension de Robert Bosch qui, à partir de l'automne de cette année-là, remplace le tube à incandescence de Daimler. D'ailleurs, dans tous les domaines, on ne peut plus arrêter le progrès. On prend congé de la boîte de vitesses à courroies, évincée par la boîte à engrenages à quatre rapports qui fait bloc avec le différentiel. Des chaînes entraînent les roues arrière, un cône de cuir sert d'embrayage. Le châssis se compose de tôles en U, les trains avant et arrière sont suspendus à des ressorts à lames longitudinaux. En revanche, les carrosseries doivent encore être martelées à la main sur des formes en bois, la peinture dure encore jusqu'à trois semaines, et l'automobile doit encore être graissée à une trentaine de points. Une véritable grande famille vient de naître: Dog-car, Vis-à-Vis, Victoria, Phaeton, Coupé et Landau à empattement court ou long. Mais l'évolution des prix, elle aussi, suit ce rythme: l'automobiliste doit déjà débourser entre 9400 et 13100 marks pour s'offrir sa Phoenix.

The strange fate of a motor vehicle: Count Zborowski used the car illustrated to win the Nice mountain rally in 1902. Later it was used for 31 years to power a circular saw. At the driver's knee level, a battery of inspection tubes showed the oil flowing to the numerous lubrication points.

Kurioses Autoschicksal: Mit dem abgebildeten Fahrzeug gewinnt Graf Zborowski 1902 das Bergrennen in Nizza. Später dient es 31 Jahre lang als Antrieb einer Kreissäge. Auf Höhe der Fahrerknie: eine Batterie von Schauröhrchen, durch die das Öl für die vielen Schmierstellen träufelt.

Curieux destin d'une automobile : avec la voiture représentée ici, le comte Zborowski remporte la course de côte de Nice en 1902. Plus tard, elle servira pendant 31 ans d'entraînement pour une scie circulaire. À hauteur du genou du conducteur, une batterie de tubulures de contrôle à travers lesquelles s'écoule l'huile vers les innombrables points de lubrification.

Daimler Phoenix 1899

The visitors to the fifth Automobile and Bicycle exhibition in the Paris Grand Palais were witnesses to the first instance of mass imitation in the history of the car. The Mercedes Simplex was the original and there was an abundance of copies. No manufacturer was able to resist the trend towards a modern car which now bore less and less resemblance to the original carriage. Mercedes has revolutionized the world of the car intoned the chorus of reviewers of the show, while some cheeky individuals among them dared to ponder the question "can the car really be further improved?" "But of course" was the response from Wilhelm Maybach who, since the death of Gottlieb Daimler in March 1900, was solely responsible for engineering at Daimler-Motoren-Gesellschaft. He indicated those areas which still offered room for improvement. Tire technology was one example. The 60 kph (37 mph) barrier had long been passed but motor journeys were still bedevilled by irritating punctures with depressing regularity. Meanwhile, engines had not only become more powerful, they had also grown louder.

The Mercedes Simplex really did have something to offer. The Daimler cars had been called Mercedes ever since Emil Jellinek had so named them after his favorite daughter, and he used them in a positively imperial round of presentations of the company to potential customers in Austria-Hungary, France, Belgium, and the United States. Jellinek was the driving force behind the 35 PS sports and touring car of 1901, which, between 1901 and 1905, became the basis of the multi-variant Simplex dynasty with engines ranging from 28 bhp (at 5315 cc capacity) to 60 bhp (at 9235 cc capacity) with various wheelbases and bodies. The cars were called Simplex because of the simplicity with which they could be operated.

The outstanding features of these cars were their long shape, low center of gravity, and light weight. No effort had been spared on the four-cylinder engine which now weighed 185 kg (408 lb). It was constructed of alloy and the cylinders consisted of two units each of two cylinders in a single casting. The cylinder head and block were cast as one unit. The chassis of the first Simplex weighed only 1,000 kg (2,205 lb). Maybach's honeycomb radiator consisted of rectangular tubes and it enabled the power of the engine to increase as required while at the same time substantially reducing the amount of cooling water it needed. In 1898 a 5 bhp car required 18 liters (4.75 gal) of cooling water; the winning car at Nice in 1901 still required 9 liters (2.4 gal), whereas a Simplex 28/32 bhp of the same year required a mere 7 liters (1.8 gal).

The numerical code forming part of the car's name in those days provided two pieces of information. The numbers before the slash showed the rated horsepower of the engine, while the actual power was shown after the slash. Power was to increase rapidly – in the second decade of Maybach's leadership "at Daimler" it increased sixtyfold.

Die Besucher der v. Automobil- und Fahrrad-ausstellung im Pariser Grand Palais werden zu Augenzeugen des ersten Massen-Mimikrys der Autogeschichte. Original ist der Mercedes Simplex, Kopien gibt es in Hülle und Fülle. Kein Hersteller mag sich dem Zug der Zeit zum modernen Mobil entziehen, das sich auch visuell immer mehr von der Mutter Kutsche entfernt. Mercedes, so intoniert der Chor der Rezensenten der Show, habe die Autowelt umgekrempelt. Und kecke Solisten wagen die nachdenkliche Frage: »Kann das Kraftfahrzeug überhaupt noch verbessert werden?« »Aber gewiss«, antwortet ihnen Wilhelm Maybach, der seit dem Tod Gottlieb Daimlers im März 1900 die alleinige technische Verantwortung in der Daimler-Motoren-Gesellschaft trägt, und nennt auch gleich Felder, auf denen dem Fortschritt noch Spielräume offenstehen. In der Reifentechnik zum Beispiel: Die 60-Stundenkilometer-Mauer ist längst geschleift, und ärgerliche Pneu-Pannen säumen nach wie vor den Pfad der Automobilisten mit bedrückender Regelmäßigkeit. Und die Motoren sind nicht nur immer stärker, sondern auch immer lauter geworden.

Der Mercedes Simplex indes hat in der Tat einiges zu bieten. Mercedes heißen die Daimler-Wagen, seitdem Emil Jellinek ihnen den Namen seiner Lieblingstochter gegeben hat und sie in ein regelrechtes Imperium von Vertretungen der Firma ausführt, nach Österreich-Ungarn, Frankreich, Belgien und den Vereinigten Staaten. Jellinek ist der Anreger hinter dem Daimler Sport- und Tourenwagen 35 PS von 1901, und dieser wird zum Vorbild der weitverzweigten Simplex-Dynastie zwischen 1901 und 1905 mit Maschinen zwischen 28 PS (bei 5315 ccm Hubraum) und 60 PS (Hubraum: 9235 ccm) mit diversen Radständen und Aufbauten, Simplex geheißen, weil ihre Bedienung so simpel ist.

Markante Merkmale sind die gestreckte Form, der niedrige Schwerpunkt, die Leichtigkeit: Vor allem an den nun 185 Kilo schweren Vierzylindern hat man abgespeckt. Sie bestehen aus Leichtmetall, und jeweils zwei Zylinder sind zusammengegossen. Kopf und Block bilden eine Einheit. Das Fahrgestell des ersten Simplex wiegt nur noch 1000 Kilogramm. Maybachs Bienenwabenkühler ist komponiert aus eckigen Röhrchen und erlaubt, die Kraft der Maschinen nach Belieben zu steigern sowie die Kühlwassermenge erheblich zu reduzieren: 1898 werden für einen Wagen mit fünf Pferdestärken noch 18 Liter benötigt, für den Siegerwagen von Nizza 1901 noch neun Liter, für einen Simplex 28/32 PS aus dem gleichen Jahr lediglich sieben.

Der Zahlencode, der die Autonamen in dieser Zeit begleitet, enthält eine doppelte Information: vor dem schrägen Querstrich die Steuer-PS, abgeleitet vom Hubraum, dahinter die tatsächliche Leistung. Sie eskaliert zügig: In den zwei Jahrzehnten von Maybachs Stabführung »beim Daimler« auf das Sechzigfache.

Les visiteurs du 5e Salon de l'Automobile et du Cycle, au Grand Palais de Paris, sont témoins du premier plagiat industriel dans l'histoire de l'automobile. L'original est la Mercedes Simplex et il en existe des copies par dizaines. Aucun constructeur ne peut se payer le luxe de négliger la mode de la voiture moderne, qui présente également de moins en moins de similitudes avec la calèche à ses origines. Mercedes, déclarent encore les journalistes présents à l'exposition, a révolutionné le monde de l'automobile. Et quelques plumes effrontées posent même une question qui fait réfléchir : « L'automobile peut-elle même être encore améliorée ? » « Mais bien sûr », leur répond Wilhelm Maybach qui, depuis la mort de Gottlieb Daimler en mars 1900, assume la responsabilité technique exclusive dans la Daimler-Motoren-Gesellschaft et cite aussi, immédiatement, des domaines dans lesquels il y a encore une certaine marge de progrès. Dans la technique des pneumatiques, par exemple : il y a des lustres que l'on a franchi le mur des 60 km/h et les ennuyantes crevaisons bornent toujours le sentier des automobilistes avec une déprimante régularité. Quant aux moteurs, ils ne sont pas seulement devenus toujours plus puissants, mais aussi toujours plus bruyants.

La Mercedes Simplex ne manque réellement pas d'atouts percutants. Les voitures de Daimler s'appellent Mercedes depuis qu'Emil Jellinek leur a donné le nom de sa fille préférée et les exporte pour les distribuer dans le véritable empire de concessions de sa firme en Autriche-Hongrie, France, Belgique et aux États-Unis. Jellinek est l'initiateur de la voiture de sport et de tourisme Daimler 35 ch de 1901, qui sert régulièrement d'exemple pour la généalogie Simplex, très ramifiée, entre 1901 et 1905 avec des moteurs allant de 28 ch (pour une cylindrée de 5315 cm³) à 60 ch (cylindrée : 9235 cm³) avec divers empattements et de multiples carrosseries, baptisées Simplex parce que leur maniement était d'une grande simplicité.

Parmi les caractéristiques marquantes, la forme allongée, le centre de gravité bas, la légèreté : ce sont surtout les quatre-cylindres, qui pèsent maintenant 185 kg, qui ont perdu du poids. Ils sont en alliage léger et deux cylindres sont respectivement coulés ensemble. La culasse et le bloc moteur constituent une entité. Le châssis de la première Simplex ne pèse plus qu'une tonne. Le radiateur Maybach à nid d'abeilles est une mosaïque de petites tubulures anguleuses qui permet de majorer à volonté la puissance des moteurs et de réduire considérablement la quantité d'eau de refroidissement : en 1898, il fallait encore 18 litres pour une voiture de 5 ch alors que la voiture victorieuse à Nice en 1901 se contente de 9 litres et qu'une Simplex de 28/32 ch de la même année n'en a besoin que de 7.

Signification du code numérique : les chevaux fiscaux, calculés sur la base de la cylindrée, précèdent la barre oblique, les deux autres chiffres indiquant la puissance réelle ; celle-ci est multipliée par soixante durant les vingt ans passés par Maybach à la direction « chez Daimler ».

Mercedes Simplex 1902

An emancipated car already – the large, long-wheelbase Simplex touring car of 1909. The roof is clearly tied down at the front.

Schon ein emanzipiertes Auto: Großer Simplex-Tourenwagen von 1909 mit langem Radstand. Das Verdeck ist auf einleuchtende Weise nach vorn verzurrt.

Déjà une voiture émancipée: la grosse Simplex de tourisme, de 1909, à empattement long. La capote est logiquement rattachée à l'avant.

The Simplex 26/45 was a straight four-cylinder engine with a piston carburetor and valves at the side in a T formation. The camshaft was driven by spur gears.

Die Maschine des Simplex 26/45: ein Vierzylinder-Reihenmotor mit Kolbenvergaser und seitlich stehenden Ventilen in T-Anordnung. Die Nockenwellen werden über Stirnräder angetrieben.

Le moteur de la Simplex 26/45: un quatre-cylindres en ligne avec carburateur à piston et soupapes latérales suspendues en T. Les arbres à cames sont actionnés par des pignons droits.

Mercedes Simplex 1902

The Mercedes Simplex 60 PS, 1903: undoubtedly an elegant motor vehicle which had shrugged off the past and which pointed the way far into the future, both as a complete design and in its details.

Der Mercedes Simplex 60 PS, 1903: zweifellos eine stattliche Auto-Erscheinung, die sich von der Vergangenheit gelöst hat und im Ganzen wie im Detail weit in die Zukunft weist.

La Mercedes Simplex 60 ch de 1903 : un modèle élégant et précurseur, aussi bien dans la ligne générale que dans les détails.

The view from above reveals
the character of the Simplex,
a machine that transported its
occupants in considerable comfort.

Die Perspektive von vorn
offenbart den Charakter des
Simplex: eine Maschine, die mit
elementarem Komfort aufwartet.

La vue de l'avant illustre le
caractère de la Simplex: un engin
présentant un grand confort.

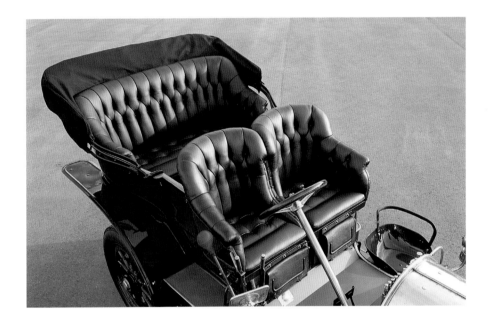

Variations on the seating theme:
the touring car's front passenger
seat opens a quarter turn outwards
to allow access to the rear seats.
The seats in the racing version of
the Simplex are relatively spartan,
and there is no rear seating.

Variationen: Der Beifahrersitz im
Tourenwagen eröffnet auf eine
Vierteldrehung hin den Zugang
nach hinten. Vergleichsweise
spartanisch sind die Schalen in der
Rennausführung des Simplex ohne
Aufsatz für die Fond-Passagiere.

Variations: le siège passager de
la voiture de tourisme libère en
un quart de tour l'accès à l'arrière.
Dans la version course de la
Simplex, les baquets dépourvus
de rembourrage pour les passagers
arrière sont plutôt spartiates.

What the driver sees – glass inspection panels for the drip-feed lubricators and a large glass oil jar for additional lubrication of the clutch and crankshaft. On the right next to the clock is the speedometer.

Im Blickfeld des Fahrers: Schaugläschen für die Tropföler, ein großes Ölglas für die Zusatzschmierung von Kupplung und Kurbelwelle. Rechts neben der Uhr der Tachometer.

Dans le champ de vision du conducteur : un petit voyant pour le graisseur à gouttes, un grand voyant pour la lubrification supplémentaire de l'embrayage et du vilebrequin. À droite, à côté de la montre, le tachymètre.

Left: a hefty oil tank for pressure feed lubrication. Right: the Simplex engine which consumed oil in copious quantities.

Links: voluminöser Vorratsbehälter für die Druckschmierung. Rechts das Triebwerk des Simplex, das Öl als Grundnahrungsmittel zu sich nimmt.

À gauche, le volumineux réservoir d'huile pour la lubrification sous pression. À droite, le gourmand moteur de la Simplex.

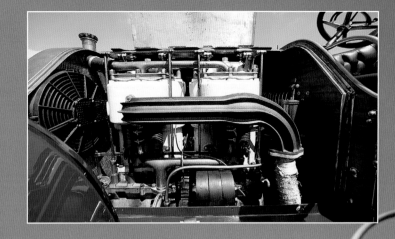

Bright yellow in color, it now stands in the Mercedes Museum in Stuttgart-Untertürkheim, a remarkable fossil that was literally dug out of the sediment of automobile history.

Its curiosity value begins with its name. Today we associate the word spider with cars that are low and wide and rounded, whereas this Benz is of a slender, angular build. But this is what open, two-seater vehicles were called at the turn of the century. In fact, by using suitable accessories, the Benz Spider could easily be converted into a four-seater that was available for 8,500 marks. It had a horizontal, opposed two-cylinder engine mounted in the front, unlike earlier practice, a configuration which is reminiscent of today's underfloor construction. With a capacity of 2945 cc, it produced 15 bhp at 1100 rpm, making it quite fast for its time. This yellow car could do 60 kph (37 mph) and take up to a 20 per cent gradient without the passenger having to get out and push.

There is also a certain romanticism attached to the history of the permanent exhibit in Stuttgart. For a long time the Spider slept under an Irish coalheap, jealously concealed from the eyes of the world. There it was discovered by an English enthusiast who kissed the sleeping beauty awake, fastidiously restored it and sold it to hotelier R.G. Sloan. He proved the unbroken roadworthiness of his acquisition by taking part in the veteran London to Brighton rally, where the short Benz car soon became a regular participant. When asked how long he intended to keep this gem of a car, Sloan would answer that it had become the love of his life. However, when he later had an opportunity to buy a larger hotel, he needed cash and agreed to sell the car to Daimler-Benz, being consoled by the knowledge that this slice of recovered automobile history was in good hands.

On 16 January 1969 the Benz Spider arrived in Stuttgart in a special waggon of the German Railways, in the illustrious company of an SSK. Since then many people have had the opportunity to see and marvel at what was once buried under a coalheap.

Poppig-postgelb steht er heute im Mercedes-Museum in Stuttgart-Untertürkheim, ein drolliges Leitfossil, das aus den Sedimenten der Automobilgeschichte gegraben wurde – buchstäblich.

Seine Kuriosität beginnt beim Namen: Mit dem Wort Spider verknüpfen wir heute Begriffe wie flach und breit und rundlich, wo doch dieser Benz von schmalem und eckigem Hochwuchs ist. Um die Jahrhundertwende nennt man so zweisitzige Fahrzeuge ohne Verdeck, nur dass der Benz Spider durch geeignete Anbauten ohne Schwierigkeiten in einen Vierplätzer verwandelt werden kann, der für 8500 Mark käuflich ist. Er hat einen liegend angeordneten Zweizylinder-Contra-Motor, entgegen früheren Gepflogenheiten im Wagenbug untergebracht in einer Art, die an die heutige Unterflurbauweise erinnert. Sein Hubraum beträgt 2945 ccm, und 15 Pferdestärken bei 1100/min machen ihn ganz schön flott: 60 Stundenkilometer läuft der Gelbe, und er steigt bis zu 20 Prozent, ohne dass der Beifahrer schieben muss.

Die Vita des Stuttgarter Dauer-Exponats trägt romanhafte Züge: Lange Zeit schlummert der Spider unter einer irischen Kohlehalde, von irgendjemand eifersüchtig versteckt vor dem Zugriff dieser Welt. Dort entdeckt ihn ein englischer Enthusiast, küsst ihn wach aus seinem Dornröschenschlaf, restauriert ihn pingelig und veräußert ihn an den Hotelier R.G. Sloan. Dieser bestätigt die ungebrochene Fahrtauglichkeit seiner Akquisition, indem er an der Veteranen-Rallye London–Brighton teilnimmt, wo der kurze Benz bald zum lebenden Inventar zählt. Auf die Frage, wie lange er diese automobile Gemme zu behalten gedenke, pflegt Sloan zu antworten, mit ihr verbinde ihn schon eine Liebe auf Lebenszeit. Schließlich wird ihm jedoch ein größeres Hotel zum Kauf angeboten. Er benötigt Bares, wird sich handelseinig mit Daimler-Benz und hat zugleich die tröstliche Gewissheit, die Fundsache komme in gute Hände.

Am 16. Januar 1969 trifft der Benz Spider in einem Spezialwagen der Bundesbahn in Stuttgart ein, in der illustren Begleitung eines SSK. Viele haben seitdem gesehen, was einst unter einem Haufen Kohle verborgen war.

Jaune bouton d'or, elle trône aujourd'hui au musée Mercedes de Stuttgart-Untertürkheim, étrange fossile exhumé – littéralement – des sédiments de l'histoire de l'automobile.

Les bizarreries commencent déjà avec son nom : par Spider, on entend aujourd'hui des qualificatifs comme bas, large et rond alors que cette Benz est de haute stature, étroite et anguleuse. À la charnière du siècle, c'est le nom que l'on donne aux véhicules biplaces sans capote, à cette différence près que la Benz Spider peut sans difficulté se transformer en une quatre places, facturée 8500 marks, grâce à des carrosseries appropriées. Elle possède un bicylindre à plat horizontal qui, contrairement à la coutume, est monté dans la proue de la voiture selon une architecture qui rappelle les moteurs sous plancher d'aujourd'hui. Sa cylindrée est de 2945 cm³ et ses 15 ch à 110 tr/min lui confèrent de bonnes performances : notre voiture jaune atteint le 60 km/h et est capable de grimper des pentes de 20 % sans que le passager n'ait à la pousser.

L'historique de cet hôte permanent du musée de Stuttgart a des caractères romanesques : longtemps, le Spider a croupi sous un tas de charbon irlandais. Jusqu'à ce qu'il soit découvert un jour par un Anglais enthousiaste qui le réveilla de son sommeil de Belle au bois dormant et le restaura avec une minutie incroyable avant de le céder à l'hôtelier R.G. Sloan. Celui-ci confirma la vitalité de sa nouvelle acquisition en participant au rallye de voitures anciennes Londres–Brighton, auquel la courte Benz participe régulièrement désormais. À ceux qui lui demandaient combien de temps il entendait conserver ce joyau automobile, Sloan avait coutume de répondre qu'il ressentait pour lui déjà un amour éternel. Finalement, on lui proposa l'achat d'un grand hôtel, pour lequel il manquait de liquidités : il passa un marché avec Daimler-Benz et eut simultanément la certitude consolante que son bijou serait désormais en de bonnes mains.

Le 16 janvier 1969, la Benz Spider arrive à Stuttgart dans un wagon spécial de la Bundesbahn avec l'illustre escorte d'une SSK. Depuis, beaucoup ont admiré ce que jadis un tas de charbon avait soustrait à la vue de tous.

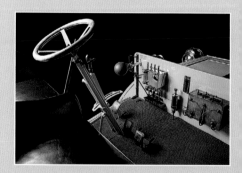

BENZ SPIDER 1902

Back in the light of day – this Benz Spider spent many years beneath a coalheap in Ireland. As can be seen, the car, now a museum piece, survived its ordeal in fine condition.

Durch Nacht zum Licht: Viele Jahre verbrachte der Benz Spider unter einer irischen Kohlehalde. Wie man sieht, hat das heutige Museumsstück das Exil glänzend überstanden.

La lumière au bout de la nuit : cette Benz Spider a passé de longues années sous un tas de charbon irlandais. Comme on peut le constater, ce véhicule exposé aujourd'hui dans un musée a fort bien survécu à cet enfouissement.

This was a solo competitor and a born winner, conquering with power and vigor while at the same time standing as an exemplar of what was then technically feasible. A record in itself, the snow-white racer established countless records, an ability embodied by its daunting appearance – rounded, with a bold nose of gleaming brass which formed part of the cooling system, and a pointed tapering tail.

Its heart, towering gothically under its slender hood, was the largest-capacity engine ever built by Daimler or Benz or Daimler-Benz, a monument of an engine weighing 470 kg (1,036 lb) and producing a powerful 200 bhp from its enormous capacity of 21.5 liters – almost fifteen times as much as the Tripoli Silver Arrow of 1939. The fuel mixture was ignited simultaneously by two Bosch spark plugs screwed in at opposite ends, which shortened the combustion time. Its chassis was similar to passenger cars of the time, but was perforated to save weight, making it look as though it had been riddled by machine gun fire. A cable handbrake acted on the rear wheels, both half-axles of the chain-drive shaft were fitted with band brakes each operated by a pedal.

The head of Benz was inspired to build such an elemental absurdity by two sporting successes achieved by the marque. These were second, third and fifth places in the French Grand Prix of 1908 in Dieppe, and first place in the Saint Petersburg to Moscow race in the same year, which Victor Hémery won at an average speed of 80 kph (50 mph). Hémery was then dispatched with the Benz racing car to the British racetrack at Brooklands, but on this occasion the narrowness of the course meant that running the car was like trying to race a juggernaut around country lanes.

This extremist among cars was then shipped to the United States where it could give full rein to its longing for freedom and adventure on the wide hard beaches of Daytona. This it did there, and at many other places, carrying the permanent starting number 19 and thereby becoming as well-known as a performing circus dog. Somehow the roaring, fire-breathing monster gave the impression of being typically German, and so it was decorated with the black imperial eagle and given the name "Blitzen-Benz" (Lightning Benz), so evoking images from

Er ist ein Solist und geborener Sieger, von strotzender Kraft und markiger Gesundheit, zugleich ein Musterbeispiel für das damals technisch Machbare. Selbst ein Rekord, ist der schneeweiße Renner zu unzähligen Rekorden fähig, von einschüchterndem Äußeren zumal: rundlich, mit einer kühnen Nase aus schimmerndem Messing, die ein Teil seines Kühlsystems ist, und spitz auslaufendem Heck.

Herzstück, gotisch aufstrebend unter seiner schlanken Motorhaube, ist das hubraumstärkste Triebwerk, das je von Daimler oder Benz oder Daimler-Benz gebaut wurde, ein Monument von einer Maschine, 470 Kilogramm schwer, 200 PS kräftig und mit dem enormen Volumen von 21,5 Litern versehen – fast fünfzehnmal soviel wie der Tripolis-Silberpfeil von 1939. Das Gemisch wird von je zwei an entgegengesetzten Enden eingeschraubten Bosch-Kerzen gleichzeitig entzündet, was die Verbrenndauer verkürzt. Sein Chassis entspricht den Personenwagen seiner Zeit, ist allerdings aus Gründen der Gewichtsersparnis durchlöchert, als sei eine MG-Garbe hindurchgefetzt. Eine Seilzug-Handbremse wirkt auf die Hinterräder, beide Halbachsen der Kettenantriebswelle sind mit Bandbremsen ausgestattet, die durch je ein Pedal betätigt werden.

Inspiriert wurden die Benz-Bosse zu dem urigen Un-Ding durch zwei Sporterfolge der Marke und deren Protagonisten: Platz zwei, drei und fünf beim Großen Preis von Frankreich 1908 in Dieppe, Rang eins beim Rennen Sankt Petersburg–Moskau im selben Jahr, das Victor Hémery mit einem Schnitt von 80 Stundenkilometern gewann. Hémery ist es auch, der mit dem Benz-Boliden auf die britische Rennstrecke von Brooklands geschickt wird, aber der wird von der Enge des Kurses eingezwängt wie ein Sperber von einem Käfig für einen Wellensittich.

Daraufhin verschifft man den automobilen Extremisten in die Vereinigten Staaten, damit er seinen Hang zu Freiheit und Abenteuer auf den weiten und harten Stränden von Daytona austoben kann. Dies tut er dort und an vielen anderen Plätzen, inzwischen bekannt wie ein bunter Hund, eine rasende Zirkusattraktion mit der permanenten Startnummer 19. Irgendwie erweckt das brüllende und feuerspuckende Monster den Eindruck, es sei typisch deutsch, und so versieht man es mit dem

C'est un soliste et un vainqueur-né, d'une force rayonnante et d'une santé éclatante, la parfaite illustration de ce qui était techniquement réalisable à cette époque. Elle-même un exploit, cette voiture de course blanche comme neige a signé d'innombrables records. Elle se signale aussi par ses formes: tout en rondeurs, avec un nez pointu en laiton scintillant, partie de son système de refroidissement, et une poupe acérée.

Le morceau de bravoure, véritable cathédrale gothique sous son étroit capot moteur, est le moteur de plus forte cylindrée que Daimler ou Benz ou Daimler-Benz aient jamais construit, un moteur monumental de 470 kg, 200 ch et avec l'énorme cylindrée de 21,5 litres – près de quinze fois celle de la Flèche d'argent victorieuse à Tripoli en 1939. Le mélange est allumé par deux bougies Bosch respectivement vissées face à face, ce qui raccourcit la durée de combustion. Son châssis est identique à celui des voitures de tourisme de son époque mais, pour des motifs d'économie de poids, il est perforé comme s'il avait reçu une salve de mitrailleuse. Le frein à main à câble agit sur les roues arrière et les deux demi-essieux de l'arbre d'entraînement de la chaîne comportent des freins à bande actionnés chacun par sa pédale respective.

La direction de Benz a trouvé l'inspiration pour cet étrange engin dans le succès en compétition de la marque et de leurs protagonistes: place deux, trois et cinq lors du Grand Prix de France de 1908 à Dieppe et première place lors de la course Saint-Pétersbourg–Moscou de la même année, remportée par Victor Hémery à une moyenne de 80 km/h. C'est aussi Hémery qui est envoyé avec le bolide Benz sur le circuit britannique de Brooklands, piste où sa voiture se sent aussi à l'étroit qu'un épervier dans une cage de perruche.

Sans perdre de temps, on envoie donc l'automobile aux États-Unis, où elle peut laisser libre cours à son penchant pour la liberté et l'aventure sur les larges et dures plages de Daytona. C'est ce qu'elle fait, ainsi que dans d'autres endroits, entre-temps connue comme le loup blanc, attraction de cirque itinérante avec le 19 comme invariable numéro de départ. D'une façon ou d'une autre, ce monstre pétaradant et crachant le feu donnait l'impression d'être typiquement allemand, raison pour laquelle

BLITZEN-BENZ 1909

folklore. The first owner was the cigar chain-smoker Barney Oldfield. Later, as many imagined that the speedy visitor was past its best, it passed into the hands of the young and daring Bob Burman. In 1911 he pushed it to 228.1 kph (141.7 mph) on a track between Daytona and Ormond Beach, twice as fast as aircraft of the time. This record remained as unassailable as a concrete bunker until 1919, and Kaiser Wilhelm congratulated the "valiant Yankee on a remarkable display in a German car."

schwarzen Reichsadler und dem folkloristischen Namen »Blitzen-Benz«. Besitzer ist zunächst Zigarren-Kettenraucher Barney Oldfield und später, als viele den flinken Importartikel schon beim alten Eisen wähnen, der junge und verwegene Bob Burman. Der hetzt ihn 1911 über eine Piste zwischen Daytona und Ormond Beach mit 228,1 Stundenkilometern, doppelt so schnell wie zeitgenössische Flugzeuge. Bis 1919 steht dieser Rekord wie ein Betonbunker, und Kaiser Wilhelm gratuliert »dem beherzten Yankee zu einer bemerkenswerten Vorstellung auf einem deutschen Auto«.

on y apposa l'aigle noir du Reich et lui donna le surnom folklorique de « Blitzen-Benz » (Éclair-Benz). Son premier propriétaire fut Barney Oldfield, fumeur invétéré de cigares, et, plus tard, alors que beaucoup croyaient le rapide produit d'importation déjà digne d'être mis au placard, le jeune et téméraire Bob Burman. En 1911, il le cravache à 228,1 km/h, deux fois plus vite qu'un avion de son époque, sur une piste entre Daytona et Ormond Beach. Ce record tient jusqu'en 1919 et l'empereur Guillaume félicite « le courageux Yankee pour sa remarquable performance sur une voiture allemande ».

In September 1913 the relevant Sports Commission approved a new Grand Prix Formula for cars of up to 4.5 liters in capacity and weighing less than 1,100 kg (2,425 lb). This favored the Sunbeam and Vauxhall and more especially the Peugeot, which was considered the favorite amongst the 32 starters lined up for the French Grand Prix in Lyon on 4 July 1914. Their engines had four valves per cylinder, operated by two camshafts; they had brakes on all four wheels, and were robust and sleek racing cars.

The five works Mercedes were considered the underdogs, but astonishingly three of them took the first three places at the finish. The winner was Christian Lautenschlager who hurtled through the race's 752 km (467 miles) in 7 hours, 8 minutes, and 18.4 seconds (averaging 105.6 kph/65.6 mph), followed by Louis Wagner and Otto Salzer. France was stunned. The fact was that the men from Mercedes had also had a couple of aces up their sleeves, the best of which was their 93654 racing engine. Its designation derived from a complicated numerical code, signifying its 93 mm stroke and 165 mm bore, with the 4 at the end indicating the number of cylinders. It had a capacity of 4483 cc producing 115 bhp at 3100 rpm, and a little more at maximum engine speed. Mercedes had also availed themselves of four-valve technology and used three ignition plugs for each combustion unit. The camshaft driven by a vertical shaft was mounted overhead as on the company's aero engines, a brainwave of Wilhelm Maybach which Paul Daimler, the head of R&D, was glad to adopt. Each pair of inlet valves was actuated by a forked rocker arm. The exhaust valves were timed by one rocker arm. Changing the four gears of the gear transmission was accomplished by Lautenschlager & Co. by means of an internal gate. A cardan shaft transmitted the power of the robust engine to the rear axle. After much flirting with the idea of using chains to save weight, it was finally decided to consign the chain drive to history.

The white 18/100 PS Mercedes left blue wisps of exhaust behind it like condensation trails, increasingly so towards the end of the Grand Prix. The passenger used a pump in the footwell to pump lubricant to sensitive points in the engine and, where necessary, also to drip lubricant on to vulnerable parts of the chassis. According to a company maxim, no opportunity should ever be missed because of a lack of oil.

The winning car from Lyon was shipped to England in the hope that it would achieve even greater fame for Daimler. However, the war intervened and the loaned car was taken into the guardianship of the British Admiralty. It was sent to Rolls-Royce at Derby where the 93654 engine was tested, dismantled, minutely examined and then copied – to become the pattern for all Rolls-Royce aero engines of the First World War.

Im September 1913 beschließt die zuständige Sportkommission eine neue Grand-Prix-Formel: bis zu 4,5 Liter, unter 1100 Kilogramm. Sie begünstigt die Sunbeam, Vauxhall, vor allem aber die Peugeot, die beim Großen Preis von Frankreich in Lyon am 4. Juli 1914 als Favoriten unter den 32 Konkurrenten an den Start gehen. Sie haben vier Ventile je Zylinder, zur Arbeit angehalten von zwei Nockenwellen, und Vierradbremsen, sind robust und liegen glänzend.

Die fünf Werks-Mercedes gelten als Underdogs, aber drei von ihnen sind am Ende vorn. Sieger ist Christian Lautenschlager, der sich über die 752 Kilometer des Rennens in sieben Stunden, acht Minuten und 18,4 Sekunden (Schnitt 105,6 Stundenkilometer) beeilt, gefolgt von Louis Wagner und Otto Salzer. Die Grande Nation ist wie versteinert. Auch die Mercedes-Männer haben nämlich ein paar Asse im Ärmel, das beste davon: ihren Rennmotor 93654, nach einem etwas komplizierten Schlüssel so benannt wegen seiner 93 Millimeter Hub und 165 Millimeter Bohrung, mit einer Vier am Schluss für die Anzahl der Zylinder. Das Volumen: 4483 ccm, die Leistung: 115 PS bei 3100/min, die Höchstdrehzahl: wenig darüber. Mercedes bedient sich ebenfalls der Vierventil-Technik, dazu dreier Zündkerzen je Verbrennungseinheit. Die Nockenwelle, angetrieben von einer Königswelle, rotiert oben wie bei den Flugmotoren der Firma, ein Denkanstoß von Wilhelm Maybach, auf den Entwicklungschef Paul Daimler gerne zurückgreift. Je ein gegabelter Kipphebel betätigt die beiden Einlassventile. Die Auslassventile werden von einem Kipphebel in Trab gehalten. Die vier Fahrstufen des Zahnradgetriebes wechseln Lautenschlager & Co. von einer innen liegenden Kulisse aus. Eine Kardanwelle vermittelt die Kraft des robusten Triebwerks zur Hinterachse. Lange hat man noch mit Ketten geliebäugelt, um Gewicht zu sparen, sich schließlich aber des Griffs in die Mottenkiste geschämt.

Die weißen Mercedes 18/100 PS ziehen blaue Fahnen hinter sich her wie Kondensstreifen, gegen Ende des Grand Prix immer mehr: Ihre Beifahrer verpflegen über eine Pumpe im Fußraum neuralgische Punkte des Motors mit Schmierstoff und können ihn bei Bedarf auch auf bedürftige Stellen des Chassis tropfen lassen. An mangelnder Ölversorgung, das ist eine Maxime des Hauses, soll die Angelegenheit keinesfalls scheitern.

Der Siegerwagen von Lyon wird nach England verfrachtet, um dort für den höheren Ruhm des Hauses Daimler zu werben. Doch dann interveniert der Krieg, und die Leihgabe gerät unter das Kuratel des britischen Marineministeriums. Man schickt es nach Derby zu Rolls-Royce, wo das Triebwerk 93654 getestet, zerlegt, genauestens untersucht und schließlich kopiert wird – Urbild sämtlicher Rolls-Royce-Flugmaschinen des Ersten Weltkriegs.

En septembre 1913, la commission sportive compétente adopte une nouvelle formule pour les courses de Grand Prix: une cylindrée maximale de 4,5 litres et un poids inférieur à 1100 kg. Elle favorise les Sunbeam, Vauxhall, mais aussi et surtout les Peugeot, qui prennent le départ du Grand Prix de France, à Lyon, le 4 juillet 1914, comme favorites parmi les 32 concurrents. Elles ont quatre soupapes par cylindre entraîné par deux arbres à cames et des freins sur les quatre roues, sont robustes et ont une excellente tenue de route.

Les cinq Mercedes d'usine sont considérées comme des outsiders, mais, quand on fait les comptes, il y en a trois en tête. Le vainqueur est Christian Lautenschlager, qui n'a pas traîné en route puisqu'il a couvert les 752 km de la course en 7 heures, 8 minutes et 18,4 secondes (moyenne de 105,6 km/h), suivi de Louis Wagner et Otto Salzer. Les Français sont ahuris. Les hommes de chez Mercedes ont en effet quelques atouts dans leurs manches, dont le meilleur: leur moteur de course 93654, ainsi nommé selon une clef un peu compliquée en raison de ses 93 mm de course et de ses 165 mm d'alésage, avec un 4 à la fin pour le nombre de cylindres. Cylindrée: 4483 cm³, puissance: 115 ch à 3100 tr/min, régime maxi: légèrement supérieur. Mercedes recourt également à la technique à quatre soupapes, mais avec respectivement trois bougies par chambre de combustion. L'arbre à cames, entraîné par un arbre de renvoi, a son centre de rotation en haut comme pour les moteurs d'avion de la firme, une idée de Wilhelm Maybach volontiers reprise par le chef du développement, Paul Daimler. Un culbuteur à fourche respectif actionne les deux soupapes d'admission. Les soupapes d'échappement suivent le rythme grâce à un culbuteur. Lautenschlager & Co. changent les quatre rapports de la boîte à engrenages à l'aide d'une coulisse intérieure. Un arbre-cardan transmet le couple du robuste moteur à l'essieu arrière. On avait longtemps envisagé d'utiliser encore des chaînes pour économiser du poids, mais, par dignité, finalement renoncé à cette solution dépassée.

Les Mercedes 18/100 ch blanches crachent derrière elles une fumée bleue comme les avions à réaction: grâce à une pompe à proximité des pieds, leurs passagers peuvent lubrifier les points névralgiques du moteur et, en cas de besoin, aussi faire tomber quelques gouttes aux endroits requis du châssis. Une pénurie d'huile ne doit en aucun cas être à l'origine d'une défaite.

La voiture victorieuse de Lyon est expédiée en Angleterre pour y battre les trompettes de la renommée en faveur de la maison Daimler. Mais la guerre éclate entretemps et ce prêt est placé sous la curatelle du ministère britannique de la Marine. On envoie les voitures à Derby, chez Rolls-Royce, où le moteur 93654 est testé, démonté, analysé minutieusement et, finalement, copié – c'est le père de tous les moteurs d'avion Rolls-Royce de la Première Guerre mondiale.

MERCEDES 18/100 PS GRAND PRIX 1914

The 1914 Mercedes Grand Prix Racing Car set the
absolute standards that the marque's future successes
would maintain. It was the three-time winner of the
French Grand Prix at Lyon.

Der Mercedes Grand-Prix-Rennwagen von 1914 setzt
absolute Maßstäbe, wie die Erfolge der Marke in Zukunft
auszusehen haben: Dreifachsieg beim Großen Preis von
Frankreich in Lyon.

La Mercedes du Grand Prix de 1914 pose des jalons
absolus indiquant ce que seront les succès de la marque
à l'avenir: triplé lors du Grand Prix de France à Lyon.

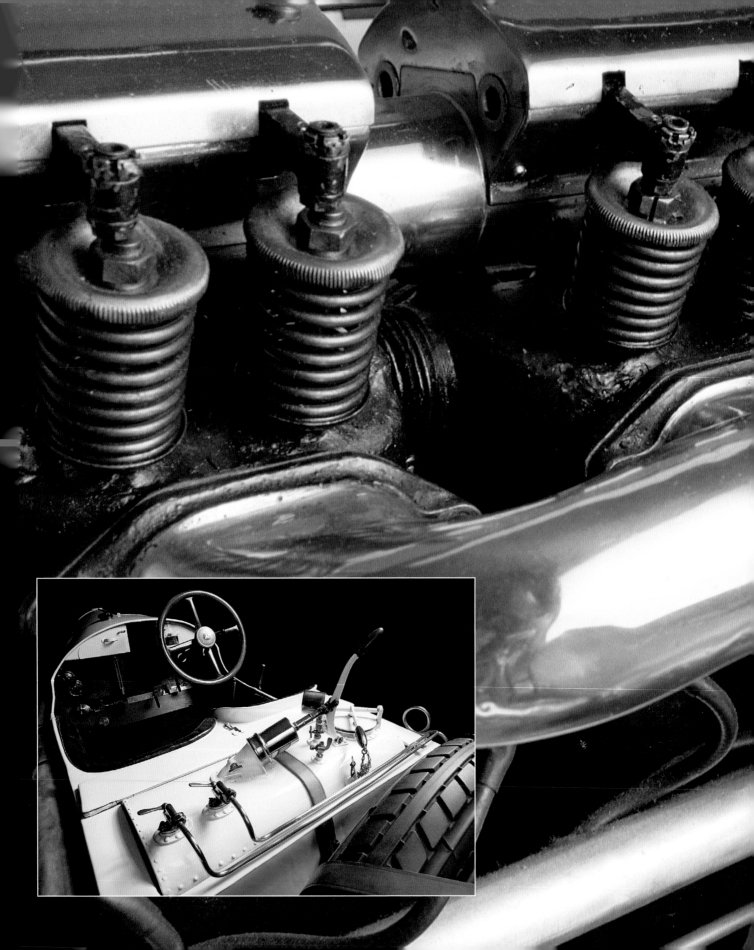

The slender two-seater's engine was based on a Daimler aero-engine, and generated 115 horsepower at an unusually high 3200 rpm. This was coupled with excellent reliability.

Die Maschine des schlanken Zweisitzers basiert auf einem Daimler-Flugtriebwerk und leistet bei der ungewöhnlich hohen Drehzahl von 3200/min 115 PS. Dazu gesellt sich urige Zuverlässigkeit.

Le moteur de cette masse biplace dérive d'un moteur d'avion Daimler et délivre 115 ch au régime inhabituellement élevé de 3200 tr/min. À cela s'ajoute une fiabilité à toute épreuve.

This was the first of an illustrious series of powerful and distinguished high-performance cars encompassing both sports cars and thoroughbred racers, a series which ranged from k through s, ss, ssk, sskl up to the 500 k and 540 k. Distinctive features of this model were the pointed radiator with its two star badges, and the exhaust routed externally on both the left and the right of the car with the exhaust pipes wrapped in metal hose. This had been an extra-cost option on Mercedes models from 1912, but it was now a standard feature for the first time. Displaying the exhaust prominently outside the car as a styling element was to become a feature of the supercharged cars from Stuttgart-Untertürkheim.

The distinctive image of the status-symbol 28/95 ps Mercedes hinted at its hidden qualities. This was particularly the six-cylinder 7280 cc engine which produced 90 bhp at 1800 rpm. It had an overhead camshaft driven by a vertical shaft. This engine had its origin in the Kaiser Prize, an award promised in May 1912 for the best aero engine. Such engines would have to be economical, powerful, and light. Paul Daimler responded with an engine which was intentionally lightweight, with pistons and crankcase made of aluminum. Steel pistons and a welded water jacket were employed. The valves were arranged in a v configuration.

First place went to Daimler's competitor, Benz. Daimler-Motoren-Gesellschaft had to be content with second place, but it still made the best of it. Of the four Mercedes on the starting line in the 1913 Sarthe Grand Prix in Le Mans two had the Kaiser Prize aero engines bearing the code DF80 under their bonnets. Suitably modified, this engine was also used in tourers and it drew remarkable performances from the 28/95 ps. To exploit these qualities fully required a driver with power, courage, and skill. The job was not easy in other respects also – the operating instructions warned that 23 lubrication points needed daily attention, and a further 10 needed similar treatment at the end of each week.

Only 25 production models were produced during the 1914 and 1915 war years, with a further 565 between 1920 and 1924. Anyone with the means to purchase a 28/95 ps was indeed faced with an agonizing choice. The model was available as a two-seater and sports and racing two-seater, as Phaeton and Sport-Phaeton, as a sedan, as a town coupé, a touring car or sport sedan. And added to this, it still held its own on dusty race tracks. Mercedes driver Max Sailer completed the first of the four 167-km (104-mile) long circuits of the 12th Targa Florio on 29 May 1921 in his white two-seater 28/95 ps, finishing second and having notched up the fastest lap.

Er steht am Anfang einer illustren Reihe von kraftvollen und vornehmen Spitzenautomobilen mit sportlichem Akzent einschließlich reinrassiger Rennfahrzeuge, vom k über die s, ss, ssk, sskl bis hin zu den 500 k und 540 k. Gattungsmerkmale sind der Spitzkühler mit den zwei Stern-Emblemen rechts und links sowie nach außen verlegte, mit Metallschläuchen umwundene Auspuffrohre, aufpreispflichtige Option bereits an Mercedes-Modellen von 1912, nun erstmals serienmäßig. Dass der Auspuff als Stilelement für jedermann sichtbar ausgelagert ist, gehört später zum Image der Kompressorwagen aus Stuttgart-Untertürkheim.

Das gediegene Erscheinungsbild des Status-Symbols Mercedes 28/95 ps lässt auf innere Werte schließen. Korrelat ist vor allem sein Sechszylinder mit 7280 ccm und 90 ps bei 1800/min, mit einer obenliegenden Nockenwelle, die von einer Königswelle angetrieben wird. Seine Genese: Im Mai 1912 wird der Kaiserpreis ausgelobt für den besten Flugmotor. Sparsam soll er sein und stark und leicht. Paul Daimler antwortet mit einem Triebwerk, das auf Leichtbau abgestellt ist: Kolben und Kurbelgehäuse sind aus Aluminium. Überdies verwendet man Stahlkolben und einen aufgeschweißten Kühlwassermantel. Die Ventile hängen v-förmig.

Den ersten Platz erringt Konkurrent Benz. Die Daimler-Motoren-Gesellschaft muss sich mit Rang zwei bescheiden, macht indessen das Beste daraus. Von den vier Mercedes, die 1913 beim Sarthe Grand Prix in Le Mans zum Start rollen, haben zwei das Kaiserpreis-Flugtriebwerk mit dem Code DF80 unter der Haube. Mit entsprechenden Modifikationen wird es auch für den Einsatz im Tourenwagen vorbereitet und beflügelt etwa den 28/95 ps zu bemerkenswerten Fahrleistungen. Diese voll auszuschöpfen erfordert einen Chauffeur, der Kraft, Mut und Können mitbringen muss. Auch sonst ist der Job nicht einfach: Die Gebrauchsanleitung mahnt an, 23 Schmierstellen bedürften täglicher Zuwendung, am Ende der Woche noch einmal zehn weitere.

Lediglich 25 Serienexemplare entstehen in den Kriegsjahren 1914 und 1915, weitere 565 zwischen 1920 und 1924. Wer sich für einen 28/95 ps entscheidet und die nötigen Mittel mitbringt, hat fürwahr die Qual der Wahl: Es gibt ihn als Zweisitzer und Sport- und Rennsport-Zweiplätzer, als Phaeton und Sport-Phaeton, als Limousine, Stadt-Coupé, Touring Car sowie Sport Sedan. Selbst auf staubigen Pisten steht er seinen Mann: Die erste von vier 167 Kilometer langen Durchgängen der 12. Targa Florio am 29. Mai 1921 führt Mercedes-Pilot Max Sailer mit seinem weißen zweisitzigen 28/95 ps, wird am Ende zweiter und fährt auch die schnellste Runde.

Elle est au début d'une illustre série de puissantes et prestigieuses voitures de très grand standing à l'accent sportif, y compris d'authentiques voitures de compétition, de la k aux 500 k et 540 k en passant par les s, ss, ssk et sskl. Une caractéristique génétique est le radiateur pointu avec deux étoiles servant d'emblème à droite et à gauche ainsi que les tuyaux d'échappement placés à l'extérieur du capot traversant des tubulures de métal, option matière à supplément de prix dès les modèles Mercedes de 1912, mais désormais proposée en série. Le pot d'échappement placé bien visible par chacun comme élément de style sera plus tard un signe distinctif des voitures à compresseur de Stuttgart-Untertürkheim.

La prestance imposante et luxueuse de la voiture phare qu'est la Mercedes 28/95 ch est le reflet de ce qui se cache sous son capot. Il s'agit surtout, en l'occurrence, de son six-cylindres de 7280 cm³ et 90 ch à 1800 tr/min, avec un arbre à cames en tête entraîné par un arbre à renvoi. Sa genèse est intéressante : en mai 1912, le Prix de l'Empereur est décerné pour le meilleur moteur d'avion. Il doit être économique, mais aussi puissant et léger. La réponse de Paul Daimler est un moteur dédié à la légèreté de construction : pistons et carter-moteur sont en aluminium. Il utilise en outre des pistons en acier et un manteau d'eau de refroidissement soudé. Les soupapes sont suspendues en v.

C'est le concurrent Benz qui remporte la première place. La Daimler-Motoren-Gesellschaft doit se contenter du rang de dauphin, mais en tire le meilleur profit. Sur les quatre Mercedes qui prennent le départ du Grand Prix de la Sarthe au Mans, en 1913, deux, avec le code DF80, ont sous le capot le moteur d'avion du Prix de l'Empereur. Il suffit de le modifier en conséquence pour l'installer aussi dans les voitures de compétition : il permet à la 28/95 ch d'afficher des performances enviables. Pour en exploiter à fond tout le potentiel, il faut un chauffeur qui possède force, courage et savoir-faire. Mais quoi qu'il en soit, le travail n'est pas simple : le mode d'emploi cite 23 points de graissage qui doivent recevoir leurs soins quotidiens, sans compter 10 autres échus à la fin de la semaine.

Vingt-cinq exemplaires de série seulement seront construits durant les années de guerre 1914 et 1915, suivis de 565 autres entre 1920 et 1924. Quiconque opte pour une 28/95 ch, à condition d'avoir les moyens, n'a vraiment que l'embarras du choix : elle est proposée en biplace ou biplace de sport et de compétition, en Phaeton et Phaeton-Sport, en limousine, coupé de ville, Touring Car et Sport Sedan. Même sur les pistes poussiéreuses, elle fait honneur à son nom : le 29 mai 1921, le pilote de Mercedes, Max Sailer, avec sa 28/95 ch biplace blanche, couvre en tête le premier des quatre tours de 167 km de long de la douzième Targa Florio. Finalement, il termine deuxième et signe aussi le meilleur tour.

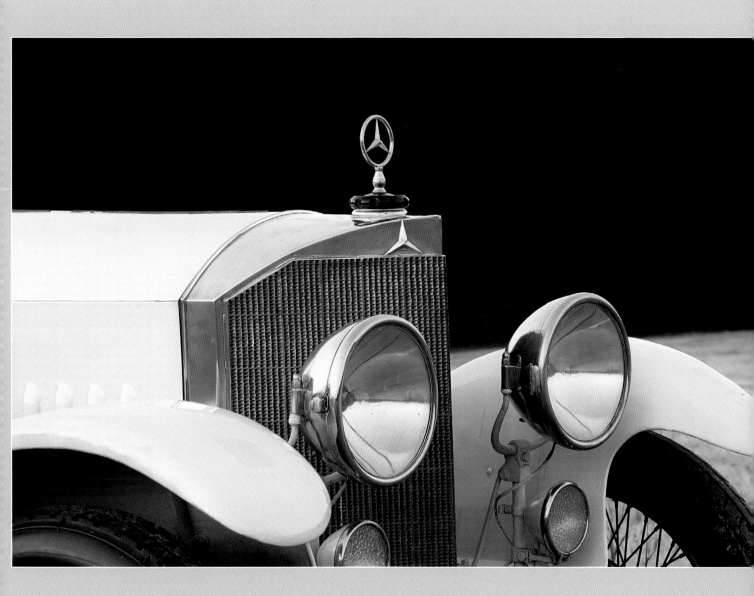

The front-mounted radiator of the 1922 Sport Phaeton contained square pipes soldered together. The metal used was still brass, though this was later replaced by nickel and chrome. Incidentally, this striking design has survived right up to the present day and has almost become part of the Mercedes-Benz emblem.

Im Spitzkühler des Sport Phaeton von 1922 sind quadratische Rohre miteinander verlötet. Noch ist das Material Messing. Es wird erst später durch Nickel und Chrom ersetzt. Das markante Design hat sich andeutungsweise bis auf den heutigen Tag erhalten und wurde praktisch Teil des Firmenemblems.

Des tubes de section carrée sont soudés les uns aux autres dans le radiateur du Phaeton-Sport de 1922. Le matériau est encore du laiton, mais il sera remplacé plus tard par du nickel et du chrome. Ce design spécifique a été en partie préservé jusqu'à aujourd'hui et est pratiquement devenu un élément constitutif de l'emblème de la firme.

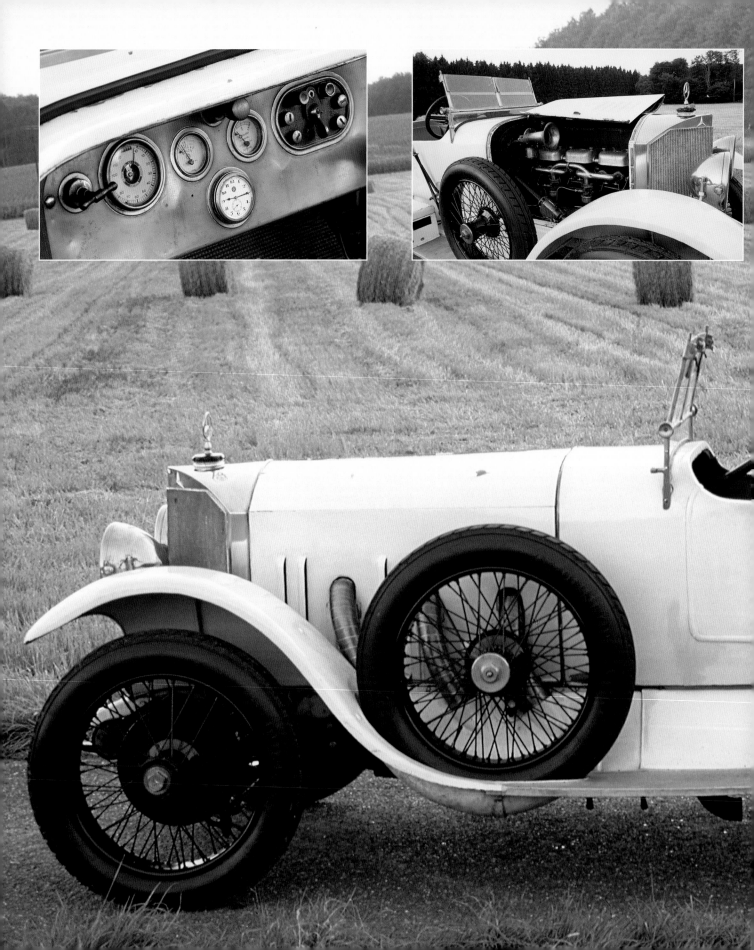

A blast from the past: on 23 March 1922 this 28/95 was despatched to one Señor Villota in Spain. However, it was ordered by Rudolf Ullstein of Berlin. Characteristic feature: the dashboard switch box for electrical instruments.

Zeichen aus der Vergangenheit: Am 23. März 1922 wurde dieser 28/95 an einen Señor Villota nach Spanien ausgeliefert. Besteller war allerdings Rudolf Ullstein in Berlin. Typisch: der Schaltkasten für elektrische Funktionen am Armaturenbrett.

Signe du passé : le 23 mars 1922, cette 28/95 a été livrée à un certain Señor Villota en Espagne. L'auteur de la commande était toutefois Rudolf Ullstein de Berlin. Caractéristique typique : le boîtier à fusibles pour les fonctions électriques au tableau de bord.

According to a British adage, "Racing improves the breed." But it also reveals how advanced matters are. Both these points were proved by the history of the Mercedes two-seater with its supercharged four-cylinder engine, in which Christian Werner won the Targa Florio on 27 April 1924. He was accompanied by Max Sailer whose particular task as co-driver was to make sure that the petrol tank was always pressurized and that lubrication was applied where and when it was required. The narrowness of the cockpit meant that this function had to be carried out in intimate shoulder-to-shoulder contact with the driver.

The Targa victory convincingly demonstrated that the supercharged engine had come of age. Daimler-Motoren-Gesellschaft had left nothing to chance. As early as January they had dispatched two cars to the labyrinthine bends in the mountainous Madonie. There the drivers could closely study the route and iron out a few bugs, for example, the fact that the plugs oiled up. As in 1922, the regulations of the motor sport ruling body, which stipulated that a German racing car had to be in the national color white at the start of the race, were violated. The Mercedes, still sporting their wings and number plates as required by Italian law, were taken to Sicily by road, but were painted in Italian red, a strategem designed to protect them against the wrath and stone-throwing of the angry *tifosi* (fans).

This machine was based on the Indianapolis car produced by the company in 1923, a legacy of the work of designer Paul Daimler who, in a display of anger, had resigned his post in 1922. The engine, with the works designation M7294, unmistakably showed his hand. It had a capacity of 1989 cc, four valves per cylinder, two overhead camshafts and a water jacket of pressed steel. All did not go well with the Indy mission, however. Although the engines proved stable, the extra power from the supercharger kicked in suddenly and only when the gas pedal was pushed to the floor. This led to spins and frequent accidents.

Ferdinand Porsche, who officially started at DMG on 1 April 1923 but who in actual fact began work somewhat earlier, re-engineered the M7294 carefully right down to the exhaust valves which he filled with mercury to improve heat dissipation. In Targa trim the engines produced 67.5 bhp unblown and 126 bhp (up to 150 bhp later in the season) blown. The maximum engine speed was 4500 rpm. This could be increased to 5000, but only for a short period, otherwise the conrods would break. And it wasn't just the power that was impressive, but also the way the engine produced it. According to the American publication *Motor Age*, the Mercedes had "a highly unusual sound."

Racing improves the breed«, lautet eine britische Bleifuß-Binsenweisheit – Rennen verfeinern die Rasse. Aber sie geben auch Auskunft über den letzten Stand der Dinge. Beides beweist die Geschichte des Mercedes-Zweiliters mit aufgeladenem Vierzylinder, mit dem Christian Werner am 27. April 1924 die Targa Florio gewinnt. Begleitet wird er von Beifahrer Max Sailer, der vor allem dafür zu sorgen hat, dass der Benzintank stets unter Druck gehalten wird und die Schmierung überall und zu jeder Zeit in Ordnung geht. Er tut das in innigem Schulterschluss mit dem Fahrer, denn im Cockpit geht es eng her.

Der Targa-Sieg stellt vor allem dem Kompressor das Zeugnis der Reife aus. Nichts hat die Daimler-Motoren-Gesellschaft dem Zufall überlassen: Schon im Januar entsendet sie zwei Wagen in das Kurvenlabyrinth der bergigen Madonie, lässt die Piloten den Streckenverlauf büffeln und bügelt ein paar Missstände aus, zum Beispiel, dass die Kerzen verölen. Wie 1922 unterläuft man die Vorschrift der Motorsport-Legislative, ein deutscher Rennwagen habe mit der Nationalfarbe weiß an den Start zu rollen. Die Mercedes, mit Kotflügeln und amtlichem Kennzeichen gesetzeskonform aufbereitet und auf Landstraßen nach Sizilien überführt, erscheinen in italienischem Rot, was sie gegebenenfalls vor der Wut und den Steinwürfen der gereizten Tifosi schützen soll.

Sie basieren auf den Indianapolis-Autos der Firma von 1923, einem Vermächtnis von Konstrukteur Paul Daimler, der 1922 voller Zorn gekündigt hat. Deren Triebwerke, intern M7294 genannt, tragen unverkennbar seine Handschrift: 1989 ccm, vier Ventile pro Zylinder, zwei obenliegende Nockenwellen, Kühlwassermantel aus Stahlblech. Die Indy-Mission verläuft wenig befriedigend: Die Maschinen erweisen sich als standfest. Probleme ergeben sich aber dadurch, dass die Mehrleistung durch den Kompressor erst dann schlagartig freigesetzt wird, wenn man das Gaspedal bis zum Bodenblech durchtritt. Dreher und Unfälle sind die Folge.

Ferdinand Porsche, der seinen Dienst bei der DMG offiziell am 1. April 1923, tatsächlich aber schon etwas eher beginnt, überarbeitet M7294 penibel bis hin zu Auslassventilen, die zur besseren Wärmeabführung mit Quecksilber gefüllt sind. Im Targa-Trimm leisten die Motoren 67,5 PS ohne und 126 PS (in der späteren Saison bis zu 150 PS) mit eingeschaltetem Gebläse. Die Höchstdrehzahl beträgt 4500/min, darf indes bis 5000 gesteigert werden – kurzfristig, damit die Pleuel nicht brechen. Eindrucksvoll ist nicht nur ihre Leistung, sondern auch die Art und Weise, wie sie produziert wird: Die Mercedes, schreibt die amerikanische Publikation *Motor Age,* hätten »höchst ungewöhnliche Töne« von sich gegeben.

Racing improves the breed» («la course affine la race»), est un proverbe bien connu des Britanniques fanatiques de vitesse. L'épreuve de la course est aussi riche d'enseignements sur les ultimes progrès de la technique. L'histoire de la Mercedes 2 litres à quatre cylindres suralimentés avec laquelle Christian Werner a remporté la Targa Florio le 27 avril 1924 confirme ces deux points de vue. Accompagné par son passager Max Sailer, il doit surtout veiller à ce que le réservoir d'essence soit toujours sous pression et que le graissage s'effectue bien partout et au bon moment. Il fait cela au coude à coude avec le pilote, car la place est vraiment comptée dans le cockpit.

La victoire à la Targa Florio démontre surtout la fiabilité du compresseur. La Daimler-Motoren-Gesellschaft n'a absolument rien laissé au hasard : en janvier, déjà, elle envoie deux voitures dans le labyrinthe de virages du circuit montagneux des Madonies. Elle fait apprendre aux pilotes le déroulement de la piste et permet d'éliminer quelques dysfonctionnements, par exemple les bougies souillées d'huile. Comme en 1922, on contourne les règlements des fonctionnaires de la compétition automobile en vertu desquels les voitures de course allemandes doivent prendre le départ avec la couleur nationale blanche. Les Mercedes, dotées d'ailes et de plaques d'immatriculation conformes à la loi et emmenées en Sicile par voie routière, apparaissent en rouge italien, ce qui a accessoirement pour avantage de les protéger de la fureur et des jets de pierre des *tifosi* excités.

Elles dérivent des voitures d'Indianapolis de 1923, un héritage du constructeur Paul Daimler qui, courroucé, a donné son congé en 1922. Leurs moteurs avec le code interne M7294 porte sa signature infalsifiable : 1989 cm³, quatre soupapes par cylindre, deux arbres à cames en tête, manteau de refroidissement en tôle d'acier. La mission Indy est une frustration : les moteurs s'avèrent fiables. Mais des problèmes se posent du fait que la puissance supplémentaire fournie par le compresseur n'est libérée totalement que lorsque l'on enfonce l'accélérateur jusqu'au plancher. Conséquences : tête-à-queue et accidents.

Ferdinand Porsche, qui prend officiellement ses fonctions à la DMG le 1er avril 1923, mais commence en réalité un peu plus tôt, révise complètement le M7294 jusqu'aux soupapes d'échappement qui sont remplies de mercure pour améliorer l'évacuation de la chaleur. En version pour la Targa Florio, les moteurs développent 67,5 ch sans compresseur et 126 ch avec (jusqu'à 150 ch un peu plus tard dans la saison). Si le régime maxi est de 4500 tr/min, il tolère néanmoins 5000 tours – mais pas trop longtemps, sinon les bielles se rompent. Impressionnantes, les voitures ne le sont pas seulement par leur puissance, mais aussi par leur moteur : les Mercedes, écrit la revue américaine *Motor Age,* auraient fait entendre « des sonorités pour le moins inhabituelles ».

MERCEDES TARGA FLORIO 1924

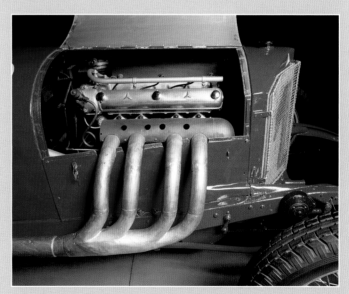

Mercedes Targa Florio 1924

Shake-ups and intrigue are not just a feature of the modern Formula One racing scene; they have been part of the history of the car right from the very start. Egos have always clashed. Both success and failure have always been embodied in one outstanding figure, and constructors' heads have invariably rolled as the price for the failure of designs and concepts.

And of course Daimler-Motoren-Gesellschaft was no Arcadian haven in this Darwinian jungle. After all one man's meat is another man's poison. Paul Daimler left the company in 1922 to build an eight-cylinder engine for competitor Horch, which the Daimler board, with an ever watchful eye trained on the average car buyer, had turned down. Ferdinand Porsche became equally obsessed with the idea of the supercharger. But he contented himself with the realization that supercharged engines were fit only for racing cars and one-offs. Two of these, 15/70/100 PS and the 24/100/140 PS, completed the DMG program after a gestation period of two years and were greeted by the chorus of critics as crowning works of world-class production. After the merger of Daimler and Benz in 1926, they were simply called the 400 and 630. The multiple-digit slash code indicated the rated horsepower and the power of the engine blown and unblown.

Many variants were derived from this single master. Some chassis were fitted with Sindelfingen bodies while others were fitted out by coachbuilders such as Erdmann & Rossi, Reutter, Papler, Balzer, Million Guiet, or the Farina stable to suit their customer's taste. The series was crowned by a third variant, the type K (*kurz*, for short wheelbase) in 1926. This came as sporty two- and four-seaters equipped with the 6.3-liter engine of the 24/100/140 PS and a wheelbase shortened from 3750 mm (12 ft 4 in) to 3400 mm (11 ft 2 in). The total length was reduced from 5320 mm (17 ft 5 in) to 4735 mm (15 ft 6 in) on the K variant, an abbreviation that did not detract from its stately appearance. The three hefty metal exhaust pipes sweeping extravagantly out of the right side of the bonnet were also incorporated in the autumn of 1927 in the sister models, the 400 and 630. In this configuration the 630 K was the fastest tourer in the world with a top speed of 145 kph (90 mph). In 1928 Porsche and his team went even further and produced the ultimate version of the K which delivered 110 bhp unblown and 160 bhp blown. The more powerful engine was still available as an option – even for the standard 630. An average fuel consumption of 25 liters (6.6 gal) was easily achieved and could be readily exceeded, but, after all, a good 2,000 kg (4,410 lb) of car had to be shifted. And in any case fuel economy mattered little to the well-heeled clientele of the Twenties – their small talk did not include money.

Revirement und Personal-Rochade gehören nicht erst ins Repertoire der modernen Formel 1, sondern begleiten die Geschichte des Automobils von Anbeginn an. Schon immer knirschen Egos aufeinander. Schon immer knüpfen sich Erfolg und Misserfolg an herausragende einzelne. Schon immer rollen Konstrukteurs-Köpfe für das Scheitern von Konstruktionen und Konzepten.

Die Daimler-Motoren-Gesellschaft bleibt da kein Arkadien inmitten eines darwinistischen Dschungels. Indes: Des einen Eule ist oft des anderen Nachtigall. Paul Daimler geht 1922, um für den Konkurrenten Horch die Achtzylinder zu bauen, die ihm der Daimler-Vorstand mit wachem Blick auf den Mittelstand der Autokäufer verwehrt. Ferdinand Porsche kommt, gleichermaßen besessen von der Idee des Kompressors. Aber er bescheidet sich: Aufgeladene Maschinen taugen nur für Rennfahrzeuge und Repräsentationswagen. Zwei von letzteren runden nach einer Inkubationszeit von zwei Jahren das DMG-Programm nach oben ab, vom Chor der Kritiker zugleich willkommen geheißen als Spitzen-Werke der Weltproduktion, der 15/70/100 PS und der 24/100/140 PS. Nach der Fusion von Daimler und Benz 1926 werden sie schlicht 400 und 630 genannt. Die dreiteiligen Schrägstrich-Kürzel geben Auskunft über Steuer-PS sowie die Leistung ohne und mit Kompressor.

Die Modellreihe wird zum Tummelplatz des Unikats: Viele Fahrgestelle sind mit Sindelfinger Aufbauten erhältlich, andere werden von Karosseriewerken wie Erdmann & Rossi, Reutter, Papler, Balzer, Million Guiet oder den Stabilimenti Farina eingekleidet, ganz nach Gusto ihrer Kunden. 1926 krönt eine dritte Variante die Baureihe, der Typ K (für kurzer Radstand). Sie umspannt sportive Zwei- und Viersitzer mit dem 6,3-Liter-Triebwerk des 24/100/140 PS, dessen Radstand von 3750 auf 3400 Millimeter verringert wird. Wo die Gesamtlänge sonst monumentale 5320 Millimeter betragen mag, tun es für den K deren 4735, ohne dass seinem stattlichen Auftritt Abbruch getan würde. Die drei fetten Metallschläuche, die aus der rechten Seite seiner Motorhaube wuchern, werden im Herbst 1927 auch den Schwestermodellen 400 und 630 spendiert. Bereits in dieser Form ist der 630 K mit einer Spitze von 145 Stundenkilometer der schnellste Tourenwagen der Welt. 1928 satteln Porsche & Cie. noch einmal drauf: 110 PS ohne und 160 PS mit Kompressor leistet der K in dieser ultimativen Version. Auf Wunsch ist die stärkere Maschine auch für den Normal-630 erhältlich. Ein durchschnittlicher Verbrauch von 25 Litern ist rasch erreicht und wird mühelos überschritten – immerhin wollen gut und gerne 2000 Kilogramm in Schwung und bei Laune gehalten werden. Für die verehrte Klientel gilt ohnehin, was im Small Talk der Zwanziger so locker dahingesagt wird: Geld, davon spricht man nicht, man hat es.

Les revirements et échanges de personnel ne figurent pas seulement au répertoire de la Formule 1 moderne. Ils ont accompagné l'histoire de l'automobile dès ses tout débuts. Les ego sont toujours entrés en collision. Succès et échecs ont toujours été liés à des personnalités individuelles éminentes. Des têtes d'ingénieurs sont toujours tombées lorsque les constructions et les concepts se sont soldés par un échec.

La Daimler-Motoren-Gesellschaft ne constitue pas un pays d'Arcadie au cœur d'une jungle darwinienne. Néanmoins, chacun voit midi devant sa porte. Paul Daimler s'en va en 1922 pour aller construire, chez le concurrent Porsche, le huit-cylindres que la direction de Daimler lui refuse, parfaitement consciente de ce que les acheteurs de voitures appartiennent le plus souvent aux classes moyennes. Ferdinand Porsche arrive, littéralement obsédé par l'idée du compresseur. Mais il fait preuve de modestie : selon lui, les moteurs suralimentés ne sont idéaux que pour les voitures de course ou de représentation. Après une période d'incubation de deux ans, deux de ces dernières couronnent le programme de la DMG, accompagnées par le chœur enthousiaste des critiques qui les classent parmi les meilleures réalisations de la production mondiale, la 15/70/100 ch et la 24/100/140 ch. Après la fusion de Daimler et de Benz en 1926, elles sont tout simplement rebaptisées 400 et 630. La kyrielle de chiffres indique les chevaux fiscaux ainsi que la puissance sans et avec compresseur.

La gamme se mue en royaume du spécimen unique : de nombreux châssis sont disponibles avec des carrosseries de Sindelfingen alors que d'autres sont habillés par des carrossiers tels Erdmann & Rossi, Reutter, Papler, Balzer, Million Guiet ou le Stabilimenti Farina. Le client est roi. En 1926, une troisième version couronne la gamme, la K (pour empattement court). Elle se compose de deux et quatre places sportives avec le moteur de 6,3 litres de la 24/100/140 ch, dont l'empattement est raccourci de 3750 à 3400 mm. Là où la longueur hors tout atteint, sinon, le chiffre monumental de 5320 mm, pour la K, 4735 « suffisent ». Les trois gros flexibles en métal dont est affublé le côté droit de son capot moteur font aussi leur apparition, à l'automne 1927, sur les modèles jumeaux, la 400 et la 630. Sous cette forme, déjà, la 630 K est, avec une vitesse de pointe de 145 km/h, la voiture de tourisme la plus rapide du monde. En 1928, Porsche & Cie ajoutent du piment : dans cette version ultime, la K développe 110 ch sans compresseur et 160 avec. Pour celui qui le désire, le moteur plus puissant est aussi disponible pour la 630 normale. Une consommation moyenne de 25 litres aux 100 km est tout à fait banale et facile à dépasser – il faut, en effet, faire conserver leur rythme et leur élan à deux bonnes tonnes. Pour l'honorable clientèle, la consommation de carburant est un sujet mineur dans les conversations des années 1920 puisque l'argent, si on n'en parle pas, ne manque pas.

MERCEDES 400–630 K 1924

A wide variety of functions were brought together on the steering wheel of the open-top 630 K tourer of 1926. Pressing the instrument ring sounded the horn, while lifting it activated the dipped beam, the handle on the left was a hand throttle, and the handle on the right operated the ignition. The gas pedal was in the middle, a characteristic feature of models K to SSKL.

Am Lenkrad des offenen Tourers 630 K von 1926 sind viele Funktionen versammelt. Das Drücken des Signalrings löst die Hupe aus, das Heben das Abblendlicht, der Hebel links Handgas, der Hebel rechts die Zündverstellung. Das Gaspedal steht in der Mitte, typisch für die Modelle K bis SSKL.

De nombreuses fonctions ont été rapprochées du volant de la Tourer 630K de 1926. Pour klaxonner, il faut appuyer sur l'anneau de signal et le relever pour enclencher les feux de croisement. Le levier à gauche est l'accélérateur manuel, le levier à droite, celui du réglage de l'allumage. L'accélérateur se trouve au centre, détail typique des modèles K à SSKL.

The 630 K still had separate lamps for main (the upper pair of lamps) and dipped headlights. The practical luggage compartment consisted of a detachable trunk. The spare canister on the running board was for oil, which early automobiles dripped over the countryside in copious amounts.

Für Fernlicht und Abblendlicht gibt es im 630 K noch verschiedene Leuchten. Das Gepäckabteil besteht praktischerweise aus einem abnehmbaren Koffer. Der Ersatzkanister auf dem Trittbrett ist vorzugsweise für den Transport von Öl gedacht, das die Automobile der Frühzeit noch liberal auf die Landschaft tröpfeln ließen.

La 630K comporte encore des phares différents pour les phares de route (en haut) et les feux de croisement. Le coffre à bagages consiste en une malle démontable, ce qui est bien pratique.
Le jerrican sur le marchepied est destiné de préférence au transport d'huile, que les voitures des débuts de l'automobile écoulaient encore avec libéralité sur les routes.

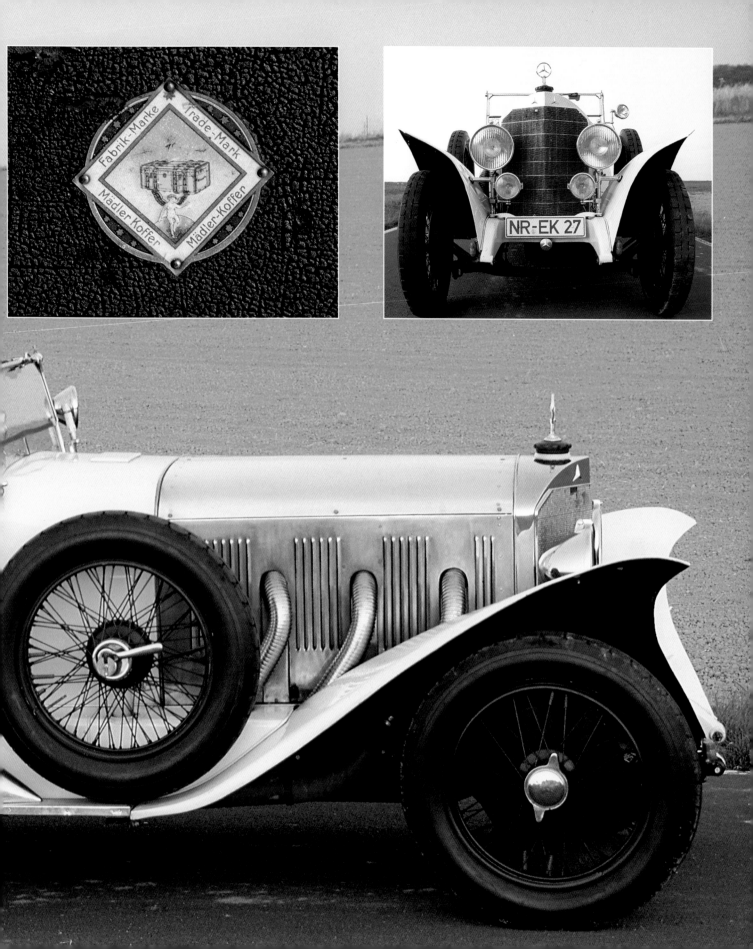

The day 19 June 1927 developed into a German festival of patriotic celebration. At the opening event on the Nürburgring, three Mercedes were lined up on the first row, two s-types driven by Rudolf Caracciola and Adolf Rosenberger and a 630 k with retired cavalry captain Mosch at the wheel.

The similarities between the cars were obvious, but there could be no doubt as to which model was the antecedent and which the successors. The s-type had the shortened chassis of the k, lowered between the axles and deeply curved over them. This lowered the center of gravity and improved roadholding. The engine was more powerful, constructed of silumin, an alloy of aluminum and 13 per cent silicon, with race linings and gray cast-iron cylinder heads. A two-vane supercharger geared to run at three times engine speed blew additional air as required through two pressure carburetors and boosted the power of the monumental six-cylinder engine from 60 to 70 bhp. It was activated by pressing the throttle hard to the floor – a professional signature of the men on the racetrack. The engines idled at a quiet rumble, punctuated by isolated gas surges, then at half-past ten the start of the race was signaled by a shattering crescendo of engine noise which died away as the cars went into the dip of the south loop. They swept into view again on the return straight and then all was stillness, broken 18 minutes later by the rising whine of compressors coming from the direction of Antoniusbuche. The Mercedes were in the lead. Their headlong speed, the blurred merging of the white bodywork into the red of the upholstery – this was the stuff of dreams.

The s model, the masterpiece of Professor Ferdinand Porsche during his time at Daimler-Benz, and its derivatives are among the cars of the century which still fascinate us to this day. One reason for this is their sheer size, the result solely of the massive size of the engine with its 6800 cc capacity, which was increased to 7065 cc from the ss onwards. Only half the 290 units were used for racing; others were acquired for everyday use taking advantage of their utterly solid and tractable engines which produced full power at low rpm. Their type codes mark their journey into legend and are themselves already legends. s for Sport, ss (from 1928) for Super Sport, ssk (also from 1929) for Super Sport Kurz (Short), because the wheelbase had been shortened from 3400 to 2950 mm (11 ft 2in to 9 ft 8 in), sskl (from 1931 onwards) for Super Sport Kurz Leicht (Short Light), so-called because engineers Hans Nibel and Max Wagner had drilled away material wherever possible to save weight. The combination of numbers associated with these magical letters denote the escalation of elegant, controlled power according to the established sequence of the rated horsepower/unblown horsepower/blown horsepower: 26/120/180 (s), 27/170/225 (ss), 27/180/250 (ssk), and 27/240/300 (sskl). It is sometimes difficult to identify exactly which was the original model. Older cars were frequently updated to the latest

Der 19. Juni 1927 wird zum Fest vaterländischen Hochgefühls: Bei der Eröffnungsveranstaltung auf dem Nürburgring stehen drei Mercedes in der ersten Reihe, die beiden s von Rudolf Caracciola und Adolf Rosenberger und ein 630 k, den der Rittmeister a. D. von Mosch lenkt.

Man sieht die Ähnlichkeit, kein Zweifel aber auch, welches Modell Vorgänger und welches Nachfolger ist: Der s hat den verkürzten Rahmen des k, näher zur Fahrbahn zwischen den Achsen, stärker hochgekröpft über ihnen. So liegt der Schwerpunkt tiefer, ist die Straßenlage besser. Noch kräftiger sind die Motoren, aus Silumin, einer Legierung aus Aluminium und 13 Prozent Silizium, mit Laufbüchsen und abnehmbaren Zylinderköpfen aus Grauguss. Ein Zweiflügel-Gebläse, das mit dreifacher Motordrehzahl läuft, beschickt bei Bedarf zwei Druckvergaser mit zusätzlicher Luft und bläst dem monumentalen Sechszylinder dann mehr Leistung ein, 60 bis 70 PS. Es wird aktiviert durch beherztes Durchtreten des Gaspedals, Berufsmerkmal der Männer am Ring. Maschinen grollen im Leerlauf, vereinzelte Gasstöße folgen. Schließlich, gegen halb elf, kündet wütendes Crescendo vom Start des Rennens, verebbt im Gefälle der Südschleife. Noch einmal erscheinen die Wagen auf der Gegengeraden, dann herrscht Stille, bis nach 18 Minuten aus Richtung Antoniusbuche das hohe Weinen der Kompressoren anschwillt. Die Mercedes führen. Ihre rasende Passage, das verschwimmende Ineinander vom Weiß der Karosserie und vom Rot der Polster, ist der Stoff, aus dem die Träume sind.

Der s, Meister-Stück des Professors Ferdinand Porsche während seiner Dienstzeit bei Daimler-Benz, und seine Derivate sind Jahrhundertautos, deren Faszination sich bis auf den heutigen Tag mitteilt. Ein Grund dafür liegt in ihrer schieren Größe, bedingt allein schon von der stattlichen Bauhöhe des Triebwerks mit seinen 6800 ccm, vom ss an 7065 ccm. Nur etwa die Hälfte der 290 Exemplare wird in Rennen eingesetzt, uneingeschränkt alltagstauglich, auch sie mit ursoliden und geschmeidigen Motoren, die ihre volle Leistung bei niedrigen Drehzahlen abgeben. Ihre Typenkürzel markieren ihren Weg in die Legende und sind selbst schon Legende: s steht für Sport, ss (ab 1928) für Super Sport, ssk (ebenfalls ab 1929) für Super Sport Kurz, denn der Radstand ist von 3400 auf 2950 Millimeter verknappt worden, sskl (ab 1931) für Super Sport Kurz Leicht, weil die Ingenieure Hans Nibel und Max Wagner Substanz herausgedrillt haben, wo immer das vertretbar war. Die Zahlenkombinationen aber, die diesen magischen Lettern zugeordnet sind, zeichnen die Eskalation elegant gebändigter Gewalt nach, jeweils in der Reihenfolge zu versteuernde PS, PS ohne Kompressor, PS mit Kompressor: 26/120/180 (s), 27/170/225 (ss), 27/180/250 (ssk) und 27/240/300 (sskl). Genau zu orten, um welches Modell es sich ursprünglich handelt, ist manchmal schwierig: Ältere Fahrzeuge wurden häufig auf den letzten Stand der Dinge gebracht, und der Typ sskl ist in den Kommissions-

Le 19 juin 1927 fait vibrer la fibre patriotique des spectateurs: lors de l'inauguration solennelle du Nürburgring, trois Mercedes figurent en première ligne au départ, les deux s de Rudolf Caracciola et Adolf Rosenberger et une 630 k, pilotée par le noble von Mosch.

On reconnaît la similitude, mais sans le moindre doute aussi la filiation entre chacun des modèles: la s a le cadre raccourci de la k avec moins de garde au sol entre les essieux, plus fortement galbé au-dessus de ceux-ci. Le centre de gravité est, ainsi, plus bas et la tenue de route, meilleure. Les moteurs sont encore plus puissants, en silumi, un alliage d'aluminium et de 13 % de silicium, avec des chemises et des culasses démontables en fonte grise. Un compresseur à doubles ailettes tournant à un régime triple de celui du moteur envoie en cas de besoin de l'air supplémentaire à deux carburateurs à pression et insuffle alors au monumental six-cylindres environ 60 à 70 chevaux supplémentaires. On actionne le compresseur en enfonçant brutalement l'accélérateur – déformation professionnelle des hommes forts du Nürburgring. Au ralenti, les moteurs émettent des borborygmes suivis de coups d'accélérateur nerveux. Enfin, vers 10 h 30, le crescendo furieux annonce le départ de la course avant de s'évanouir peu à peu dans la descente de la boucle Sud. Les voitures font leur réapparition, puis c'est le silence total jusqu'à ce que, 18 minutes plus tard, en direction d'Antoniusbuche, la plainte stridente des compresseurs reprenne de l'ampleur. Les Mercedes sont en tête. Leur passage météorique, la mosaïque floue des flancs de leur carrosserie et du rouge des capitonnages est la substance dont sont faits les rêves.

La s, chef-d'œuvre du professeur Ferdinand Porsche durant son passage chez Daimler-Benz, et ses dérivés sont des autos qui ont marqué leur siècle et à la fascination desquelles nous succombons aujourd'hui encore. L'un des motifs est leur taille inimaginable, due, déjà, à l'énorme encombrement en hauteur du moteur avec ses 6800 cm³ de cylindrée, ou 7065 pour la ss. La moitié seulement, environ, des 290 exemplaires a été engagée en course, sans la moindre restriction quant à une utilisation quotidienne, elles aussi avec des moteurs indestructibles et ronronnants qui délivrent toute leur puissance à bas régime. Les dénominations sont des étapes sur la route de la légende et elles font elles-mêmes déjà légende: s signifie Sport, ss (à partir de 1928) Super Sport, ssk (à partir de 1929) Super Sport Court, car l'empattement a été ramené de 3400 à 2950 mm, sskl (à partir de 1931) pour Super Sport Court Léger, parce que les ingénieurs Hans Nibel et Max Wagner ont fait la chasse aux kilogrammes superflus partout où cela était raisonnable. Mais les combinaisons de chiffres qui précèdent ces lettres magiques sont le symbole d'une course à la puissance maîtrisée avec élégance, toujours dans la chronologie des chevaux fiscaux, chevaux sans compresseur et chevaux avec compresseur: 26/120/180 (s), 27/170/225 (ss), 27/180/250 (ssk) et 27/240/300 (sskl). Il est parfois difficile de savoir avec exactitude de quel modèle il s'agissait à l'origine: les modèles anciens sont

MERCEDES-BENZ S—SSKL 1927

specification and the type SSKL is not to be found on the order books of Mercedes, even though at least one works car was built.

Even though the chassis of an SS cost 31,000 reichsmarks and the sports four-seater 44,000 reichsmarks, no profit was made from the construction of the series. Its function was rather that of an artistically-designed tavern sign. The car itself earned nothing, but its advertising value was considerable.

büchern von Mercedes nicht nachzuweisen, obwohl es mindestens einen Werkswagen gab.

Obwohl etwa das Fahrgestell eines SS 31 000 und der Sport-Viersitzer 44 000 Reichsmark kosten, ist mit der Baureihe kein Profit zu machen. Sie erfüllt eher die Funktion eines kunstvoll gestalteten Wirtshausschildes: Es bringt selbst nichts ein, aber die Werbewirkung ist beträchtlich.

fréquemment restaurés, au gré des évolutions techniques, mais la SSKL ne figure pas dans les livres de commissions de Mercedes bien qu'il en ait existé au moins une voiture d'usine.

Bien qu'un châssis de SS coûte 31 000 reichsmarks et la quatre-places Sport, 44 000 reichsmarks, il n'est pas possible de faire des bénéfices avec cette gamme. Elle a surtout pour fonction de donner un lustre supplémentaire à une marque dont l'image est déjà prestigieuse: elle ne rapporte rien elle-même, mais l'effet médiatique est considérable.

The lights were from Zeiss, and the horn from Bosch. The body of the four-seater S cabriolet from 1929 was the work of the Berlin-based coachbuilders Erdmann & Rossi. Only about half of all chassis had a works-built body.

Die Lampen kommen von Zeiss, das Horn steuert Bosch bei. Der Aufbau des viersitzigen S-Cabriolets aus dem Jahr 1929 stammt von der Berliner Karosseriefabrik Erdmann & Rossi. Nur etwa die Hälfte aller Chassis werden vom Werk eingekleidet.

Les phares sont signés Zeiss, le Klaxon est de Bosch. La carrosserie du cabriolet S à quatre places de 1929 est l'œuvre du styliste berlinois Erdmann & Rossi. Environ la moitié, seulement, de tous les châssis ont été habillés par l'usine.

It came, it saw – and it conquered: the winning car in the opening race at the Nürburgring on 19 June 1927, an S-model racing car. The small door ahead of the rear wheels was a concession to the rules and was not functional.

Er kam, sah – und gewann: Der Siegerwagen des Eröffnungsrennens am Nürburgring am 19. Juni 1927, ein S-Rennsport. Die kleine Tür vor den Hinterrädern ist ein Zugeständnis an das Reglement und wurde nicht benutzt.

Veni, vidi, vici: la voiture victorieuse de la course inaugurale du Nürburgring, le 19 juin 1927, un Cabriolet S. La petite porte devant les roues arrière est une concession au règlement qui n'était pas utilisable.

Mercedes-Benz S–SSKL 1927

This four-seater,
open-top S tourer from 1928 is
fitted with a body from Sindelfingen. At
the head of it all, the radiatior cap surmounted
by the Mercedes star with a thermometer in its base.

Dieser viersitzige offene S-Tourer von 1928 ist mit
einer Karosserie aus Sindelfingen bekleidet. Beherrschend der
Kühlerverschluss: der Mercedes-Stern mit einem Thermometer im Sockel.

Cette Tourer S
décapotable à quatre places
de 1928 possède une carrosserie
réalisée à Sindelfingen. Notez le magnifique
bouchon de radiateur : l'étoile Mercedes avec un
thermomètre dans le socle.

The stick-on cellophane side-screens hardly protected this sporting tourer against the rigors of the weather. It had a detachable trunk. Under the bonnet the two carburetors are visible, while the adjustable supercharger was mounted vertically at the front of the engine.

Selbst mit seitlichen Steckscheiben aus Zellophan ist der Tourer kaum gegen die Unbilden der Witterung gewappnet, ein sportliches Reisefahrzeug mit abnehmbarem Koffer. Jenseits der Motorhaube werden seine zwei Vergaser sichtbar. Der zuschaltbare Kompressor steht vorn senkrecht.

Même avec les vitres latérales démontables en Cellophane, la Tourer n'est presque pas protégée contre les aléas du temps. Elle possède une malle démontable à l'arrière. Sous le capot apparaissent, bien visibles, les deux carburateurs. Le compresseur débrayable se trouve à la verticale, à l'avant.

Mercedes-Benz S–SSKL 1927   173

Mercedes-Benz S–SSKL 1927

Another open-top tourer, this time an SS model, whose clean-lined Sindelfingen body suits it perfectly.

Ein weiterer offener Tourer, vom Typ SS, dem seine Sindelfinger Karosserie mit ihren klaren Linien trefflich steht.

Une autre Tourer décapotable, une SS, à laquelle sa carrosserie de Sindelfingen aux lignes claires sied extrêmement bien.

At the end of the Roaring Twenties the exuberance of the times demanded extravagant status symbols. The SS Tourer was a majestic motor vehicle which met this need to perfection, with its high radiator, masses of chrome, and impressive dimensions.

Am Ende der Roaring Twenties verlangt ein gesteigertes Lebensgefühl nach manifester Statussymbolik. Der SS-Tourer eignet sich glänzend dazu, ein majestätisches Automobil mit höherem Kühler, viel Chrom und einschüchternden Dimensionen.

À la fin des *Roaring Twenties,* années d'exubérance, les signes extérieurs de richesse sont essentiels. La SS Tourer, automobile majestueuse s'il en est, satisfait cette exigence de perfection, avec un radiateur plus élevé, des chromes omniprésents et de larges dimensions.

Mercedes-Benz S–SSKL 1927

After its win, with Rudi Caracciola at the wheel, in the 1929 Tourist Trophy, the SS Rennsport depicted here was purchased by wealthy amateur racing driver Earl Howe. He commissioned the English firm Barker to fit it with new bodywork which was fairly similar to the original works version. However, the ash frame was replaced by a light aluminum structure.

Nach seinem Sieg unter Rudi Caracciola bei der Tourist Trophy 1929 wird der abgebildete SS Rennsport von dem wohlhabenden Herrenfahrer Earl Howe erstanden. Der lässt ihm eine englische Barker-Karosserie verpassen, nicht unähnlich dem ursprünglichen Werksaufbau. Allerdings ersetzt man das Eschengestell durch eine leichte Aluminiumkonstruktion.

Après sa victoire avec Rudi Caracciola au Tourist Trophy de 1929, la SS Rennsport illustrée ici est achetée par un *gentleman driver* aisé, Earl Howe. Il la dote d'une carrosserie anglaise Barker, assez semblable à la carrosserie d'origine. Par contre, il fait remplacer le cadre en frêne par une construction plus légère, en aluminium.

The license plate is from the time of Earl Howe. However, the German origin of the vehicle is betrayed by its left-hand drive.

Das Kennzeichen stammt aus der Zeit des Earl Howe. Die deutschen Ursprünge des Autos verrät allerdings noch seine Linkslenkung.

La plaque minéralogique remonte à l'époque de Earl Howe. Sa direction à gauche trahit toutefois les origines allemandes de la voiture.

Record-breaking British driver
Malcolm Campbell was so taken
by Caracciola's success in the
1929 Tourist Trophy that he
ordered an SS for the following
year, with works bodywork and
right-hand drive. His GP 10 license
plate became famous, not least
because of his successes with the
car on the Brooklands racetrack.

Der britische Rekordfahrer
Malcolm Campbell ist so begeistert
von Caracciolas Erfolg bei der
Tourist Trophy 1929, dass er
sich fürs nächste Jahr einen
SS bestellt, mit Werkskarosserie
und Rechtslenkung. Nicht zuletzt
durch seine Erfolge auf der
Bahn von Brooklands wird sein
Nummernschild berühmt: GP 10.

Le pilote de record britannique
Malcolm Campbell est si
enthousiasmé par le succès
de Caracciola lors du Tourist
Trophy 1929 qu'il se commande
pour l'année suivante une SS avec
carrosserie d'usine et conduite
à droite. Sa plaque minéralogique
– GP 10 – deviendra célèbre,
notamment grâce à ses succès sur
les pistes de Brooklands.

Mercedes-Benz S–SSKL 1927

Mercedes-Benz S–SSKL 1927

The soft top of the SS Rennsport is a makeshift feature in a car lacking side windows. The mighty six-cylinder engine looks all the more impressive, a monument in itself. Loving details: Mercedes star with thermometer, adjustable windshield to reduce wind resistance.

Das Stoffverdeck des SS Rennsport ist fürwahr eine Notlösung. Nicht einmal Seitenscheiben sind vorgesehen. Um so eindrucksvoller der riesige Sechszylinder, ein Monument seiner selbst. Liebe zum Detail: Stern mit Thermometer, umlegbare Windschutzscheibe zur Verringerung des Luftwiderstands.

La capote en tissu de la SS Rennsport n'est qu'une solution de dépannage sur un véhicule qui ne comporte même pas de vitres latérales. D'autant plus impressionnant, le gigantesque six-cylindres, un monument dédié à lui-même. L'amour du détail : le bouchon de réservoir à l'anglaise, l'étoile avec thermomètre, le pare-brise rabattable pour diminuer la résistance aérodynamique.

Stylistically this two-seater SS cabriolet with in-house coachwork, the only one of its type, was a precursor of the future 500 series. Power and ambition are embodied in its aristocratic appearance.

Stilistisch weist dieses zweisitzige SS-Cabriolet, einziges seiner Art, bereits auf die zukünftige Baureihe 500 vor. Die Karosserie wurde im Werk geschaffen. In seinem aristokratischen Auftreten manifestieren sich Macht und Anspruch.

Sur le plan esthétique, ce cabriolet SS deux places, le seul en son genre, préfigure déjà la future série 500. La carrosserie a été réalisée à l'usine. Dans sa démarche aristocratique, elle incarne pouvoir et ambition.

Mercedes-Benz S–SSKL 1927

Enormous two-seater: the semi-circular wings merging with the running boards were a striking feature. Also noteworthy are the chrome-plated counterbalance weights. The characteristic instrument ring with throttle and ignition handles was still fitted on the steering wheel. The engine was identical to that of the racing version.

Monumentaler Zweisitzer mit markanten Radlaufkotflügeln. Bemerkenswert: die Chromhülsen der Auswuchtgewichte. Vor sich hat der Pilot aufwändige Armaturen. Auf dem Lenkrad sitzt wieder der typische Signalring mit Hebeln für Handgas und Zündverstellung. Der Motor ist identisch mit dem der Wettbewerbswagen.

Détail typique : les ailes qui couvrent un demi-cercle de la roue avant de se fondre dans les marchepieds. À remarquer : les manchons chromés des masses d'équilibrage. Le pilote a de quoi se distraire avec ces nombreux cadrans. Au volant, on retrouve le typique anneau avec leviers pour l'accélérateur manuel et le réglage de l'allumage. Le moteur est identique à celui de la version course.

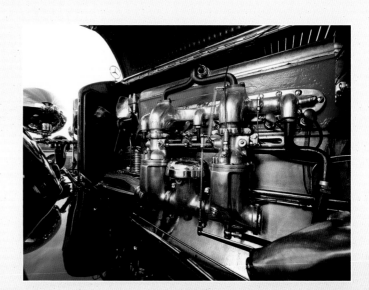

A lavish application of chrome: the Mercedes star, now without the thermometer, the characteristic central wheel fastener, and the decorative trim at the car door.

Üppige Chromapplikationen: Stern, nun ohne Thermometer, der charakteristische Zentralverschluss, die Zierleisten im Einstieg.

Généreuses applications de chrome : l'étoile, maintenant sans thermomètre ; le caractéristique verrouillage central des roues ; les joncs décoratifs du marchepied.

Mercedes-Benz S–SSKL 1927

The unmistakable SSK, the K standing for *kurz* (short). Note the two-seater sports-car bodywork without doors, wings housing the wheels, and the small windshield to which the roof attached by two cord loops.

Unverkennbar SSK, mit K für kurz: zweisitzige Sportkarosserie ohne Türen, Radlaufkotflügel, die kleine Windschutzscheibe, an der das Notdach nur mittels zweier Ösen festgezurrt werden kann.

Incontestablement une SSK, avec un K comme *kurz* (« court ») : carrosserie sport biplace sans portières, pare-boue enveloppants sur les roues, petit pare-brise sur lequel la capote de dépannage ne peut être attachée qu'à l'aide de deux œillets.

In order to assist "privateers" like Hans Stuck and Rudi Caracciola, Mercedes engineers Hans Nibel and Max Wagner reduced the weight of the SSK wherever possible. The result was the SSKL, of which there were probably only ever three examples.

Um »Privatfahrer« wie Hans Stuck und Rudi Caracciola zu unterstützen, erleichtern die Mercedes-Ingenieure Hans Nibel und Max Wagner den SSK, wo es geht. Das Ergebnis ist der SSKL. Wahrscheinlich gab es nicht mehr als drei.

Pour soutenir les pilotes « privés » comme Hans Stuck et Rudi Caracciola, les ingénieurs de Mercedes Hans Nibel et Max Wagner allègent autant que possible la SSK : cela donne la SSKL. Il n'y en aura vraisemblablement pas eu plus de trois exemplaires.

Mercedes-Benz S–SSKL 1927

Of course, large supercharged cars were the most glamorous exhibits at the Berlin Automobile Exhibition of October 1926, but for the ordinary man in the street they remained objects of pure platonic worship. The straight six, 2-liter Type 8/38 PS attracted far greater customer attention. Nevertheless, the angular mid-range Mercedes proved difficult to sell. The prices of 7,800 reichsmarks for the tourer and 8,600 reichsmarks for the two-door sedan were pitched far too high. The fact that the model was offered a year later for a good deal less led to the suspicion that it was being sold off cheaply because of numerous teething problems. In the end, even the designer Ferdinand Porsche came to grief over the 8/38 PS project and left Daimler-Benz AG in 1928 on the worst of terms.

His successor Hans Nibel, who did not become the technical director officially responsible for design and engineering until the beginning of 1929, gladly took the problem child under his wing. He ironed out problems in the detail and made it look more appealing. In the autumn of 1928 it was given the name Stuttgart 200, and in January 1929 it was fitted with a 2.6-liter engine under the designation of Stuttgart 260 (10/50 PS). Drawing on the company's good reputation, the price was set just a little higher than that of its competitors, such as the Adler Favorit and the Opel 8/40 PS. The gamble paid off and the Stuttgart type became the backbone of Mercedes production for years. It was manufactured exclusively in Unter-türkheim with the coachwork carried out in Sindelfingen. There were many variants: sedans, cabriolets and road-sters, a Pullman version with six seats and a stretched chassis, taxis and hire cars, and delivery vehicles for commercial purposes. In the first half of the Thirties, jeeps based on the Stuttgart 260, which were as solid, robust, and tough as the entire range, became standard equipment with the Reichswehr and Wehrmacht military forces.

And this was no surprise, as it was a classic example of conventional and well-tried vehicle construction. It had U-section framework, rigid axles with semi-elliptical springs and band shock absorbers front and rear, mechanical brakes on all four wheels, a cardan shaft with a centrally-mounted ball-joint gearshift, engines with seven-bearing crankshafts, vibration dampers, and three-point mounting, as well as upright valves controlled by a lateral camshaft. From the middle of 1930 onwards, a cruise or overdrive gear could be added to the existing three gears. But the performance remained rather sluggish – the Stuttgart 200 was capable of 80 kph (50 mph), but the Stuttgart 260 was 10 km (6 mph) faster.

Natürlich gereichen der Berliner Automobil-Ausstellung im Oktober 1926 vor allem die großen Kompressorwagen zur Zierde, für den normalen Bürger gleichwohl Gegenstände rein platonischer Anbetung. Aufsehen und wohlwollendes Interesse einer viel größeren Klientel erregt der Typ 8/38 PS mit einem Reihen-Sechszylinder von zwei Litern Inhalt. Der kantige Mittelklasse-Mercedes erweist sich indes als schwieriger Fall: Die Einstandspreise von 7800 Reichsmark für den Tourenwagen und 8600 Reichsmark für die zweitürige Limousine sind viel zu hoch angesiedelt, und als das Modell ein Jahr später ein gutes Stück billiger angeboten wird, keimt der Verdacht auf, es werde verramscht wegen seiner zahlreichen Kinderkrankheiten. Am Ende stolpert sogar Konstrukteur Ferdinand Porsche über das Projekt 8/38 PS und verlässt die Daimler-Benz AG 1928 in schlechtestem Einvernehmen.

Da hat sich bereits sein Nachfolger Hans Nibel, erst Anfang 1929 als technischer Direktor offiziell zuständig für Konstruktion und Technik, des Problemkinds liebevoll angenommen, Mängel im Detail ausgemerzt und für ein ansprechenderes Äußeres gesorgt. Im Herbst 1928 erhält es den Namen Stuttgart 200, im Januar 1929 ist es auch mit einem 2,6-Liter-Triebwerk als Stuttgart 260 (10/50 PS) zu haben. Man baut auf den guten Ruf des Hauses und setzt das Preisniveau nur unwesentlich über dem von Konkurrenten wie dem Adler Favorit und dem Opel 8/40 PS an. Das Kalkül geht auf: Der Typ Stuttgart wird auf Jahre zum Rückgrat der Mercedes-Produktion. Er wird ausschließlich in Untertürkheim hergestellt und in Sindelfingen karossiert. Seiner Varianten sind viele: Limousinen, Cabriolets und Roadster, eine Pullman-Version mit sechs Sitzen auf einem verlängerten Fahrgestell, Droschken und Mietwagen, Lieferwagen für gewerbliche Zwecke. In der ersten Hälfte der dreißiger Jahre gehören Kübelwagen auf der Basis des Stuttgart 260 zur Standardausstattung von Reichswehr und Wehrmacht, solide, robust und zählebig wie die gesamte Baureihe.

Kein Wunder – sie ist ein Muster konventionellen und erprobten Fahrzeugbaus: U-Profilrahmen, Starrachsen mit Halbelliptikfedern und Bandstoßdämpfern vorn und hinten, mechanische Vierradbremsen, Kardanrohr mit Kugelschaltung in der Mitte; Motoren mit siebenfach gelagerten Kurbelwellen mit Schwingungsdämpfern und Dreipunktaufhängung sowie stehenden Ventilen, die von einer seitlichen Nockenwelle gesteuert werden. Den drei Fahrstufen kann ab Mitte 1930 ein Schon- oder Schnellgang zugeschaltet werden. Die Fahrleistungen bleiben dennoch behäbig: 80 Stundenkilometer läuft der Stuttgart 200, zehn Kilometer schneller der Stuttgart 260.

Naturellement, les grosses voitures à compresseur sont une décoration idéale pour le Salon de l'Automobile de Berlin d'octobre 1926. Mais pour le citoyen moyen, elles ne sont que l'objet d'une adoration purement platonique. C'est la 8/38 ch, au six-cylindres en ligne de 2 litres, qui attire l'attention et le succès bienveillant d'une clientèle beaucoup plus vaste. L'anguleuse Mercedes du segment intermédiaire s'avère en réalité un cas difficile : les prix de base de 7800 reichs-marks pour la voiture de tourisme et de 8600 reichsmarks pour la berline à deux portes sont beaucoup trop élevés et lorsque, un an plus tard, ce modèle est proposé à une somme nettement inférieure, on a l'impression qu'on la solde en raison de ses nombreuses « maladies infantiles ». À la fin, le constructeur Ferdinand Porsche lui-même achoppe sur le projet 8/38 ch et quitte la Daimler-Benz AG en 1928, dans la mésentente.

Son successeur, Hans Nibel, qui ne deviendra directeur technique, en charge de la conception et de la construction qu'à partir de 1929, s'est penché avec amour sur ce modèle, l'a guéri de chacun de ses défauts et lui a redonné une constitution plus séduisante. À l'automne 1928, la voiture est baptisée Stuttgart 200 et, en janvier 1929, elle est aussi disponible avec un 2,6 litres sous le nom de Stuttgart 260 (10/50 ch). Les spécialistes du marketing misent sur la bonne réputation de la maison et adoptent une tarification à peine supérieure à celle de ses concurrentes comme l'Adler Favorit et l'Opel 8/40 ch. Et cela marche : durant des années, la Stuttgart devient l'épine dorsale de la production de Mercedes. Elle est fabriquée exclusivement à Untertürkheim et carrossée à Sindelfingen. Il en existe de nombreuses variantes : limousines cabriolets et roadsters, une version Pullman à six sièges sur un châssis à empattement allongé, taxis et voitures de location ou voitures de livraison pour le commerce et l'industrie. Durant la première moitié des années 1930, les voitures tout-terrain, inspirées de la Stuttgart 260, font partie de l'équipement normal de la Reichswehr et de la Wehrmacht, solides, robustes et résistantes comme toute la gamme.

Et ce n'est pas étonnant – c'est une référence de construction automobile conventionnelle éprouvée : cadre à profilés en U, essieux rigides avec ressorts semi-elliptiques et amortisseurs à bande à l'avant et à l'arrière, freins mécaniques sur les quatre roues, tubes de cardan avec changement de vitesses au centre ; moteur à vilebrequin à sept paliers avec amortisseurs d'oscillations et suspension trois points ainsi que soupapes suspendues commandées par un arbre à cames latéral.

À partir de 1935, une vitesse surmultipliée peut être utilisée en sus des trois rapports normaux. Les performances n'en restent pas moins médiocres : la Stuttgart 200 atteint 80 km/h alors que la Stuttgart 260 ne la bat que de 10 km.

MERCEDES-BENZ STUTTGART 1928

The Stuttgart was the first reasonably-priced mid-range Mercedes, and despite its largely rectangular lines it had a pleasing appearance. Its simple exterior concealed tried and tested technology.

Der Stuttgart wird zum ersten preiswürdigen Mercedes in der Mittelklasse, zumeist eine Domäne des rechten Winkels und gleichwohl gefällig anzusehen. Im schlichten Gewand verbirgt sich gestandene Technik.

La Stuttgart est la première Mercedes à prix calculé au plus juste dans le segment intermédiaire, un modèle caractérisé par l'angle droit mais néanmoins d'une allure assez séduisante. Une mécanique à toute épreuve se dissimule sous une présentation sobre.

Manufacturers and drivers alike have always used symbols or numbers
and letters to draw attention to features of their vehicles which are
not immediately apparent. In this case the logo boasted of the
mechanical four-wheel braking system (*Bremse* = brake).

Schon immer wiesen Werke oder Kunden durch Sigel oder Symbole
auf verborgene Errungenschaften ihrer Fahrzeuge hin. Hier
manifestiert sich der Stolz auf die mechanische Vierradbremse.

Depuis toujours, constructeurs et conducteurs ont attiré l'attention sur
les caractéristiques méconnues de leurs véhicules à l'aide de chiffres,
de lettres ou de symboles. Celui-ci représente la particularité du frein
mécanique sur les quatre roues (*Bremse* = « frein »).

It was remarkable how the careers of Ferdinand Porsche and Hans Nibel, his successor as technical director at Daimler-Benz, intersected. Nibel officially arrived on 1 January 1929, on the same day that Porsche became the overall technical director of Steyr-Werke. At the same time Nibel rented Porsche's villa in Feuerbacher Weg, Stuttgart.

The German had actually become involved somewhat earlier and had sorted out a couple of serious problems that he inherited from the grumpy Austrian genius, such as the model 8/38 PS which Nibel developed into the Stuttgart. The case of the structurally-similar, Porsche-designed, Mercedes-Benz 300, which was unveiled as an upper mid-range car at the 1926 Berlin Motor Show, turned out to be quite similar. Such terms are relative. Although this "stagecoach," which seemed massive and impractical, was equipped in rapid succession with large 3-, 3.2- and 3.5-liter six-cylinder engines, the favorites of the contemporary motoring upper-class, such as the types s and ss, simply had much more cubic capacity to offer.

Nibel gave Porsche's luckless and dull creation more sensible dimensions and an appealing appearance, and he named the remodeled and restyled version the Mannheim in honor of the old Benz team. The Mannheim 350 (or 14/70 PS) of 1929 was followed in the same year by the 370 (or 15/75 PS), and then a year later by the 370 K – for kurz (short) as the wheelbase had been reduced from 3200 mm (10 ft 6 in) to 3025 mm (9 ft 11 in) – and the 370 s (for Sport), with a wheelbase again reduced to a bare 2850 mm (9 ft 4 in).

The 370 s, exclusively built as a roadster and cabriolet, became the star of the series and, costed at 12,800 or 13,800 reichsmarks, was seen as a reasonably-priced alternative for those who could not afford the sinfully-expensive s models. With only 183 units built, it was neither particularly powerful nor particularly fast, however. With a top speed of 115 kph (71 mph), the 370 s still rolled along at a leisurely pace. In 1932 the 380 s (or 15/80 PS) was produced, again available only as a cabriolet. Production of the model was shared between the Daimler-Benz sites at Stuttgart and Mannheim. The 350 and 370 were produced in Mannheim, and the K and s versions in Stuttgart.

Merkwürdig, wie sich die Lebensläufe von Ferdinand Porsche und Hans Nibel, seinem Nachfolger als technischer Direktor bei Daimler-Benz, überkreuzen. Nibel tritt diese Stelle am 1. Januar 1929 an, am gleichen Tag wird Porsche technischer Gesamtleiter der Steyr-Werke. Zugleich pachtet Nibel Porsches Villa am Stuttgarter Feuerbacher Weg.

Schon vorher hat der Deutsche ein paar Hypotheken übernommen und abgetragen, die der grantig-geniale Österreicher hinterlassen hat, wie das Modell 8/38 PS, aus dem Nibel den Stuttgart sublimiert. Ganz ähnlich ist der Fall des konstruktiv fast gleichen Porsche-Opus Mercedes-Benz 300 gelagert, seit der Berliner Automobil-Ausstellung 1926 Offerte der Stuttgarter in der gehobenen Mittelklasse. Solche Begriffe sind relativ: Obwohl diese ein wenig klobig und unbeholfen wirkenden Karossen in rascher Folge mit voluminösen Sechszylindern von 3, 3,2 und 3,5 Litern ausgestattet werden, haben Exponenten der zeitgenössischen automobilen Oberkaste, wie etwa die Typen s und ss, einfach noch viel mehr Hubraum.

Nibel verhilft Porsches glück- und glanzloser Schöpfung zu vernünftigen Dimensionen und einem ansprechenderen Erscheinungsbild und nennt die überarbeitete und retuschierte Version Mannheim, zu Ehren der alten Benz-Garnison. Auf den Mannheim 350 (oder 14/70 PS) von 1929 folgt noch im gleichen Jahr der 370 (oder 15/75 PS), ein Jahr später der 370 K (für kurz: Der Radstand wurde von 3200 auf 3025 Millimeter zurückgenommen) und der 370 s (für Sport, mit nochmals auf 2850 Millimeter verknapptem Radstand).

Der 370 s, ausschließlich als Roadster und als Cabriolet gebaut, wird zum Star der Baureihe, für 12 800 beziehungsweise 13 800 Reichsmark eine preiswürdige Alternative für alle, die sich die sündhaft teuren s-Modelle nicht leisten können. In nur 183 Exemplaren hergestellt, ist er allerdings weder besonders stark noch sonderlich schnell: Mit 115 Stundenkilometern Spitzengeschwindigkeit rollt ein 370 s doch relativ gemächlich dahin. 1932 sattelt man noch mit dem 380 s (oder 15/80 PS) drauf, der wiederum lediglich als Cabriolet erhältlich ist. Die Fertigung des Modells schultern die Daimler-Benz Standorte Stuttgart und Mannheim arbeitsteilig: In Mannheim werden 350 und 370 hergestellt, in Stuttgart die Versionen K und s.

Il est étonnant de voir combien les vies de Ferdinand Porsche et de Hans Nibel, son successeur comme directeur technique chez Daimler-Benz, se recoupent. Nibel le remplace le 1er janvier 1929, jour même où Porsche est nommé directeur technique général des usines Steyr. Au même moment, Nibel loue la villa de Porsche située Feuerbacher Weg à Stuttgart.

Auparavant, déjà, l'Allemand a repris et payé quelques hypothèques laissées par le bourru mais génial Autrichien, par exemple la 8/38 ch que Nibel sublime pour donner naissance à la Stuttgart. Leurs carrières vont encore se croiser avec la Mercedes-Benz 300, œuvre de Porsche presque identique sur le plan mécanique à la Stuttgart, et qui sera présentée au Salon de l'Automobile de Berlin de 1926, lors duquel Nibel se présente en défenseur des voitures de classe moyenne supérieure. Toutefois, bien que ces limousines un peu imposantes et peu gracieuses se succèdent rapidement avec de volumineux six-cylindres de 3, 3,2 et 3,5 litres, les représentants de la classe automobile supérieure de cette époque, par exemple les types s et ss, ont tout simplement encore plus de cylindrée.

Nibel redonne des dimensions raisonnables à la création peu réussie et peu séduisante de Porsche. En l'honneur de la vieille ville de garnison de Benz, il donne à cette version retravaillée et retouchée, au style plus agréable, le nom de Mannheim. La Mannheim 350 (ou 14/70 ch) de 1929 est encore suivie, la même année, la 370 (ou 15/75 ch), un an plus tard par la 370 K pour kurz («court»: l'empattement a été ramené de 3200 à 3025 mm) et par la 370 s (pour sport, avec empattement encore raccourci à 2850 mm).

La 370 s, construite exclusivement en roadster et cabriolet, devient la vedette de la gamme, avec un prix respectif de 12 800 et 13 800 reichsmarks, un choix à la portée de tous ceux qui ne peuvent pas se payer le luxe des séries s, d'un coût astronomique. Construite à raison de seulement 183 exemplaires, elle n'est toutefois ni particulièrement puissante ni extrêmement rapide: avec une vitesse de pointe de 115 km/h, une 370 s est donc relativement lente. En 1932, elle est remplacée par la 380 s (ou 15/80 ch), qui est, elle aussi, disponible seulement en cabriolet. Les sites de production de Daimler-Benz, à Stuttgart et à Mannheim, se partagent le travail pour fabriquer ce modèle: Mannheim fabrique les 350 et 370 alors que Stuttgart se consacre aux versions K et s.

MERCEDES-BENZ MANNHEIM 1929

Despite its impressive size, the Mannheim was an upper
mid-range model.

Bei durchaus stattlichen Dimensionen zählt der Typ Mannheim
gleichwohl zur gehobenen Mittelklasse.

Malgré des dimensions assez imposantes, la Mannheim appartient
néanmoins au segment intermédiaire supérieur.

Views of the elegantly designed dashboard and the six-cylinder engine. The factory recommendation was that the pressure differential between the studded tires on the same axle "should not exceed 0.1 atmospheres."

Freier Durchblick auf das aufwändig gestaltete Armaturenbrett und den Sechszylinder. Das Werk schreibt vor, der Druckunterschied der Ballon-Stahlseilreifen auf einer Achse dürfe »nicht größer als 0,1 atm« sein.

Vue du tableau sophistiqué et du moteur six-cylindres. L'usine prescrit que la différence de pression entre les pneus ballons à fil d'acier d'un même essieu ne doit pas « être supérieure à 0,1 bar ».

The 1929 Mannheim 350 model touring car offers plenty of places in the sun.
The spare wheels on the right and left and the trunk were all situated outside the
passenger compartment and it was all just a little bit drafty.

Viel Platz an der Sonne: im Tourenwagen Typ Mannheim 350 von 1929. Kofferraum
sowie Reserveräder links und rechts sind ausgelagert, und es zieht schon mal ein
bisschen.

Beaucoup de place au soleil: dans la voiture de tourisme Mannheim 350 de
1929, les roues de secours placées sur les côtés à l'avant et le coffre
à l'arrière dégagent de l'espace. Seul défaut: on est parfois
exposé aux courants d'air.

Some of the visions which inspired Ferdinand Porsche during his six-year period as head of the design department of Daimler and Daimler-Benz seem to have belonged somewhat in the past. This applies to the 8/38 PS and 12/55 Type 300, as well as the 18/80 PS Type 460, also called the Nürburg, which occupied a slightly higher place in the automobile hierarchy. Even at its première in the autumn of 1928 it appeared quite old-fashioned, or classical if one preferred a more generous term. Classic in its form, classic in its chassis with a high framework of U-sections, rigid axles, and semi-elliptical springs. Nevertheless, the eight-cylinder inline engine was an innovation, similar in concept to the six-cylinder engines of both other models, with side-operated valves and cast-iron cylinders cast as a unit with the top section of the crankshaft housing. The alloy bottom section also served as the oil sump for the pressure-circulated lubrication system. The dynamic image conjured up by the name Nürburg turned out in reality to be mere sound and smoke. In its quickest version, the venerable two-tonner could not manage more than 110 kph (68 mph). It did however prove its durability in a two-week 13,000-km (8,080-mile) endurance marathon on the Eifel circuit.

By an irony of fate, Paul Daimler, who had broken away from the Daimler management because of a disagreement regarding an eight-cylinder engine, was now building the Horch 8 for manufacturing competitor Horch. And in this category the car was the benchmark, more than a match for Mercedes in all respects, attractive, outstandingly engineered, technically more advanced, and better priced. Even a total revamp from which the Nürburg 460 emerged visually rejuvenated and embellished was not enough to enable Hans Nibel to turn this situation around. His short-variant K with its 3430 mm (11 ft 3 in) – as opposed to the normal 3670 mm (12 ft 4 in) – wheelbase was designed principally as a four- to five-seater with production fittings and special bodywork. Numerous cabriolets tailored by fashionable coachbuilders such as Gläser, Papler, or Erdmann & Rossi were also available. Customers, however, almost always preferred the long version, simply because it was hardly any more expensive to buy.

The Nürburg 500 (or 19/100 PS), later simply called the Type 500, with an engine capacity of 4918 cc, followed in 1931. To the confusion of historians, a few examples of the 460 were fitted out as Pullman sedans with the coachwork of the Großer Mercedes 770. One of these became part of the Pope's automobile fleet, surely the equivalent of the elevation of an automobile to the peerage.

Einige der Visionen, die Ferdinand Porsche während seiner sechsjährigen Verweildauer als Chef der Konstruktionsabteilung von Daimler und von Daimler-Benz vorschweben, scheinen eher rückwärts gewandt. Das gilt für den 8/38 PS und den 12/55 Typ 300 sowie den 18/80 PS Typ 460, auch Nürburg geheißen, der in der automobilen Klassengesellschaft noch ein wenig höher angesiedelt ist: Schon bei seiner Premiere im Herbst 1928 sieht er ganz alt aus, oder klassisch, sofern man einen freundlicheren Begriff bevorzugt. Klassisch ist seine Form, klassisch sein Fahrwerk mit einem Hochrahmen aus U-Profilen, Starrachsen und Halbelliptikfedern. Eine Novität indessen stellt sein Achtzylinder-Reihenmotor dar, ganz ähnlich konzipiert wie die Sechszylinder der beiden anderen Modelle, mit seitengesteuerten Ventilen und Zylindern, die in einem Graugussblock mit dem Oberteil des Kurbelgehäuses zusammengegeben sind. Das Unterteil aus Leichtmetall dient zugleich als Ölwanne für die Druckumlaufschmierung. Die Dynamik, die der Name Nürburg verheißt, entpuppt sich übrigens als Schall und Rauch. In seiner flinksten Version läuft der knorrige Zweitonner nicht mehr als 110 Stundenkilometer. Ein Zweiwochen-Marathon über 13 000 Kilometer auf dem Eifelkurs hat vor allem seine Standfestigkeit erwiesen.

Ironie des Schicksals: Paul Daimler, der sich einst mit dem Daimler-Management wegen eines Achtzylinders überworfen hat, baut jetzt für den Konkurrenten Horch den Horch 8. Und der ist in dieser Kategorie das Maß aller Dinge, dem Mercedes in allen Punkten ebenbürtig oder überlegen, ansehnlich, hervorragend verarbeitet, technisch raffinierter – und preiswerter. Da kann auch Hans Nibel das Ruder nicht mehr herumwerfen mit einer weiteren Total-Retusche, aus der der Nürburg 460 optisch verjüngt und verschönert hervorgeht. Seine Kurz-Variante K mit ihren 3430 (sonst 3670) Millimetern Radstand ist vor allem für vier- bis fünfsitzige Serienaufbauten und Sonderkarosserien sowie zahlreiche Cabriolets gedacht, die meist bei Couturiers wie Gläser, Papler oder Erdmann & Rossi eingekleidet werden. Die Kundschaft schätzt indessen fast durchweg die Lang-Version mehr, schon weil sie kaum teurer ist.

1931 folgt der Nürburg 500 (oder 19/100 PS) mit 4918 ccm, später nur noch Typ 500 genannt. Zur Verwirrung der Chronisten werden ein paar Exemplare des 460 als Pullman-Limousinen mit der Karosserie des Großen Mercedes 770 versehen. Eines davon wird dem Fuhrpark des Papstes einverleibt – schon immer die Erhebung eines Automobils in den Adelsstand.

Quelques-unes des visions qu'eut Ferdinand Porsche durant les six années qu'il a passées comme chef du service de construction de Daimler et de Daimler-Benz semblent avoir été plutôt dépassées. Cela vaut pour la 8/38 ch et la 12/55 type 300 ainsi que pour la 18/80 ch type 460, appelée aussi Nürburg, qui se situe encore un peu plus haut dans le standing de la classe automobile: dès sa première, à l'automne 1928, elle semble déjà vieillotte, si tant est que l'on veuille utiliser un qualificatif bienveillant: sa forme est classique, son châssis également avec un cadre aux profilés en U, ses essieux sont rigides et ses ressorts, semi-elliptiques. Là où elle innove, par contre, c'est avec son huit-cylindres en ligne, à la conception analogue à celle des six-cylindres des deux autres modèles, avec soupapes à commande latérale et cylindres faisant bloc avec la partie supérieure du carter moteur dans un bloc en fonte grise. La partie inférieure en alliage léger sert également de carter d'huile pour la lubrification par circulation forcée. La dynamique que suscite le nom Nürburg, par ailleurs, s'avère vite une promesse sans fondement. Dans sa version la plus vive, l'anguleuse deux tonnes ne dépasse même pas les 110 km/h. Un marathon de quinze jours et de 13 000 kilomètres sur le circuit de l'Eifel aura tout au plus fourni la preuve de sa fiabilité.

Ironie du destin: Paul Daimler, qui s'est jadis brouillé avec la direction de Daimler à cause d'un huit-cylindres, construit maintenant la Horch 8 pour son concurrent Horch. Et, dans cette catégorie, c'est l'aune à laquelle se mesurent toutes les autres: égale ou supérieure à la Mercedes dans tous les registres, séduisante, d'une remarquable finition, d'un grand raffinement technique, elle est aussi moins chère. Même Hans Nibel ne peut pas renverser la situation avec une nouvelle refonte qui donne naissance à la Nürburg 460, plus jeune esthétiquement et aux lignes plus plaisantes. Sa version à empattement court, baptisée K avec son empattement de 3430 mm (sinon 3670), se conçoit surtout pour les carrosseries de série à quatre ou cinq places et les carrosseries spéciales ainsi que de nombreux cabriolets, qui sont habillés le plus souvent par des couturiers comme Gläser, Papler ou Erdmann & Rossi. La clientèle donne presque toujours la préférence à la version à empattement long, surtout qu'elle coûte à peine plus cher.

En 1931 est lancée la Nürburg 500 (ou 19/100 ch) de 4918 cm³, appelée plus tard uniquement type 500. Comme pour donner des cheveux gris aux historiens, quelques exemplaires de la 460 sont produits en version limousine Pullman avec la carrosserie de la Grosser Mercedes 770. L'une figure dans la flotte du pape – ce qui est toujours noble pour une automobile.

MERCEDES-BENZ NÜRBURG 1929

The Nürburg 500 Pullman sedan was certainly one of the most elegant motor cars to appear on German roads. This two-and-a-half ton giant's fuel tank needed refilling with 30 liters (7.9 gal) every 100 km (62 miles). The Nürburg depicted here, 5380 mm (17 ft 8 in) long by 1820 mm (6 ft) in height and width, was first delivered to the German Embassy in London in 1936, two years after its construction.

Die Pullman-Limousine vom Typ Nürburg 500 gehört gewiss zu den hochherrschaftlichen Auto-Erscheinungen auf deutschen Rollbahnen. Dafür möchte der Zweieinhalbtonner mit bis zu 30 Litern Treibstoff je 100 Kilometer bei Laune gehalten werden.
5380 Millimeter lang und mit 1820 Millimetern ebenso hoch wie breit, wurde der abgebildete Nürburg 500 erst 1936 zwei Jahre nach seinem Bau an die deutsche Botschaft in London ausgeliefert.

La limousine Pullman Nürburg 500 figure incontestablement parmi les voitures de très grand luxe les plus imposantes des routes allemandes. En revanche, ce pachyderme de 2,5 tonnes pouvait consommer jusqu'à 30 litres de carburant aux 100 km. 5380 mm de long pour 1820 mm de haut et de large : la Nürburg 500 représentée ici n'a été livrée qu'en 1936, deux ans après sa construction, à l'ambassade d'Allemagne à Londres.

The three rows of seats of this classy Mercedes offered varying degrees of comfort for six or seven passengers. The rear-view mirror was mounted on the spare wheel. The four-wheel-brakes logo on the trunk served the additional purpose of warning following drivers: don't mess with this car!

Auf drei Sitzreihen offeriert der Nobel-Mercedes durchaus unterschiedlichen Komfort für sechs bis sieben Passagiere. Der Rückspiegel thront auf dem Reserverad. Der Hinweis auf die Vierradbremse auf dem Koffer dient auch als Warnung an Nachfolgende: Mit diesem Auto ist nicht zu spaßen.

Sur trois rangées de sièges, cette Mercedes grand luxe offre un confort assez variable pour six ou sept passagers. Le rétroviseur trône sur la roue de secours. Sur la malle, le logo rappelant la présence de freins sur les quatre roues fait office de mise en garde pour les véhicules qui suivent : il est recommandé de se méfier de cette voiture.

At the start of his career with the company, chief designer Hans Nibel had been mainly engaged in sorting out his predecessor's creations and bringing them to a level which everyone expected of a Mercedes. At the Paris Automobile Exhibition in October 1931 he presented his own masterpiece. The new car, which fitted in well with the existing range of models, precisely matched the market conditions created by the world economic crisis. It was compact, economical, well built, and most reasonably priced for a six-cylinder vehicle. In the year in which it appeared, with standard production equipment, which even included an ignition steering lock as a precaution against theft, the 170 (or 7/32 PS) cost 4,400 reichsmarks, 1,580 marks less than the Stuttgart 200 from the same stable.

Nibel had also been working on independent suspension since 1924. The 170 with its front and rear independent suspension was the forerunner of what was to become a standard in future Mercedes and which established a new yardstick with regard to safer roadholding for many years to come. The front wheels were mounted on two transverse springs and the rear wheels on double coil springs. The engine delivered 32 bhp from 1692 cc and used an average of 11 liters (2.9 gal) of fuel per 100 km (62 miles) from its 33-liter (8.7-gal) tank. As the advertising proclaimed, such fuel consumption was assisted by its overdrive and economy gear in addition to the normal three gears. The concept was so successful and the technical standard of the 170 so high that a mere four major design changes were made in the six years of its production. It was first delivered with a separate trunk two centimeters (0.8 in) from the rear enclosure of the bodywork. This was followed in 1934 by a mounted trunk, and an integrated luggage compartment in 1935. In the same year, the U-section frame was replaced by a box-section, pressed-steel lower frame. A softly-angled wedge-shaped radiator replaced the previous flat radiator in February of the following year. A revised and updated instrument panel was also more ergonomical in design. The 170 was presented as a two-door model at the Berlin Automobile Exhibition in that month and this clearly anticipated the rounded lines of the 170 v of 1936.

The pretty cabriolet, a roadster and the Type L 300 delivery van, 126 of which were used mainly for commercial purposes from 1932 onwards, were also members of the family of the smallest Mercedes. It was not simply that the Type 170 was the right car for the Depression era after the Wall Street crash, it also carried Daimler-Benz AG through the lean years of the early Thirties. It was a favorite with the public and 4,481 of the models were sold in its first year, more than the complete production of the company in the previous year. A total of 13,775 of the first generation Mercedes 170s were produced, which set a new record.

Bisher ist Chefkonstrukteur Hans Nibel vor allem damit beschäftigt gewesen, die Kreationen seines Vorgängers formal zu entrümpeln und auf das Niveau zu heben, das jedermann von einem Mercedes erwartet. Auf der Pariser Autoschau im Oktober 1931 meldet er sich mit einem eigenen Meisterstück zu Wort. Der Neue, der sich von unten an die bestehende Modellpalette anlagert, passt genau in das Umfeld, das die Weltwirtschaftskrise geschaffen hat: kompakt, sparsam, von trotziger Qualität und höchst erschwinglich für einen Sechszylinder. Im Jahr seines Erscheinens kostet der 170 (oder 7/32 PS) mit einer Serienausstattung, die sogar ein Zünd-Lenkschloss als Diebstahlvorsorge umfasst, 4400 Reichsmark – 1580 Mark weniger als ein Stuttgart 200 aus demselben Hause.

Schon seit 1924 hat sich Nibel mit der Einzelradaufhängung beschäftigt. In dieser Hinsicht wird der 170 zum Pilotauto, mit Schwingachsen vorn und hinten, die künftig Mercedes-Norm werden und für lange Zeit neue Maßstäbe hinsichtlich hoher Fahrsicherheit setzen. Seine Vorderräder sind an zwei Querfedern, die Hinterräder an doppelten Schraubenfedern aufgehängt. Sein Triebwerk leistet 32 PS aus 1692 ccm und entzieht dem 33-Liter-Tank im Schnitt elf Liter Kraftstoff auf 100 Kilometer. Zu den Punkten, die die Werbung herausstellt, zählt sein Schnell- und Spargang zusätzlich zu den normalen drei Fahrstufen. So gelungen ist das Konzept, so hoch der technische Standard des 170, dass in den sechs Jahren seiner Fertigung lediglich vier größere Retuschen fällig werden. Er wird zunächst mit einem freistehenden Koffer ausgeliefert, zwei Zentimeter von der hinteren Karosseriewand entfernt. An diese schließt sich 1934 ein angebauter Koffer und 1935 ein integriertes Gepäckabteil an. Im gleichen Jahr ersetzt man den bisherigen U-Profilrahmen durch einen Kastenprofil-Pressstahl-Niederrahmen. Im Februar des folgenden Jahres findet sich ein Kühler in sanft gewinkelter Keilform an der Stelle des bisherigen Flachkühlers. Überarbeitet und auf den neuesten Stand gebracht bietet sich auch die Armaturentafel dem Auge und der Hand dar. Auf der Berliner Automobil-Ausstellung im selben Monat wird der 170 als Zweitürer präsentiert und nimmt bereits die rundlicheren Linien des 170 v von 1936 vorweg.

Zur Familie des kleinsten Mercedes gehören schmucke Cabriolets, ein Roadster sowie der Kastenwagen vom Typ L 300, der ab 1932 in 126 Exemplaren vornehmlich gewerblichen Zwecken dient. Nicht nur, dass der Typ 170 wie gemacht scheint für die Zeit der Flaute nach dem Wall Street Crash, er trägt die Daimler-Benz AG auch durch die mageren Jahre Anfang der Dreißiger hindurch, ein Liebling des Publikums: Schon im ersten Jahr seines Modell-Lebens wird er in 4481 Einheiten unter die Leute gebracht, mehr als die gesamte Produktion der Firma im Jahr vorher. Insgesamt entstehen 13 775 Mercedes 170 der ersten Generation – das ist eine neue Rekordmarke.

Jusque-là, le chef constructeur Hans Nibel s'est surtout consacré à épurer esthétiquement les créations de son prédécesseur et à les élever au niveau que chacun attend d'une Mercedes. Au Salon de l'Automobile de Paris, en octobre 1931, il fait pour la première fois parler de lui avec son propre chef-d'œuvre. Le nouveau modèle, qui s'ajoute au bas de gamme existant, intègre à la perfection l'environnement généré par la crise économique mondiale : compacte, économique, de très bonne qualité et d'un prix vraiment très bas pour une six-cylindres. L'année de sa sortie, la 170 (ou 7/32 ch) coûte, avec un équipement de série qui comporte même une clef de contact comme prévention antivol, 4400 reichsmarks – soit 1580 marks de moins qu'une Stuttgart 200 de la même écurie.

En 1924 déjà, Nibel s'était penché sur la suspension à roue indépendante. Dans cette perspective, la 170 jouait le rôle de voiture expérimentale, avec essieux oscillants à l'avant et à l'arrière qui allaient devenir la norme chez Mercedes à l'avenir et poser pendant longtemps de nouveaux jalons en ce qui concerne une sécurité de conduite optimale. Ses roues avant sont suspendues à deux ressorts transversaux et les roues arrière, à des ressorts hélicoïdaux doubles. Son moteur développe 32 ch à partir de 1692 cm³ et prélève en moyenne 11 litres de carburant aux 100 km dans le réservoir de 33 litres. Parmi les points mis en exergue par la publicité figure sa vitesse surmultipliée en sus des trois rapports avant normaux. Le concept est si bien étudié et le niveau technique de la 170 si sophistiqué que seules quatre retouches importantes seront nécessaires durant les six années de sa fabrication. Elle est tout d'abord livrée avec un coffre de malle séparé éloigné de la paroi de carrosserie arrière de 2 centimètres. En 1934, le coffre de malle est contigu à celle-ci et, en 1935, il est transformé en un coffre à bagages intégré.

La même année, le cadre profilé en U utilisé jusqu'ici est remplacé par un cadre bas en acier soudé à profilés en forme de caisson. En février 1936, un radiateur de forme légèrement cunéiforme remplace l'ancien radiateur plat. Le tableau de bord est, lui aussi, plus séduisant pour l'œil et plus pratique depuis qu'il a été retravaillé et incarne dès lors l'état de la technique. Au Salon de l'Automobile de Berlin, le même mois, la 170 est présentée en deux portes et anticipe d'ores et déjà les lignes plus arrondies de la 170 v de 1936.

La famille de la plus petite Mercedes comporte de jolis cabriolets, un roadster ainsi que la fourgonnette type L 300 fabriquée à 126 exemplaires à partir de 1932 et qui sert essentiellement d'utilitaire. Absolument idéale pour l'époque de marasme après le crack de Wall Street, la 170 aide aussi Daimler-Benz AG à franchir les années de vaches maigres du début des années 1930. Véritable coqueluche du public, dès sa première année, elle est vendue à 4481 exemplaires, soit plus que toute la production de la firme de l'année précédente. Au total, ce sont 13 775 Mercedes 170 de la première génération qui seront construites – et c'est un nouveau record.

MERCEDES-BENZ 170 1931

The long life of a motor vehicle has its highs and lows. During the 1960s this 1931 170 found itself serving as a chicken coop near the Czech town of Budweis.

Auch ein langes Autoleben hat seine Höhen und Tiefen: In den sechziger Jahren musste dieser 170 von 1931 in der Nähe des tschechischen Budweis als Hühnerstall herhalten.

Une longue vie de voiture a aussi ses hauts et ses bas: dans les années 1960, cette 170 de 1931 a servi de poulailler non loin de Budweis, en Tchéquie.

An open invitation: lit by its interior lights in twilight's last gleaming, the 170 seems to take on a life of its own.

Einladend geöffnet: Im letzten Licht des Abends und traulich illuminiert durch die Bordbeleuchtung scheint der 170 eigenes Leben zu entwickeln.

Accueillante : sous les derniers rayons du crépuscule et avec l'éclairage intime de bord, la 170 dévoile un habitacle cossu.

The 500 K and its derivatives are firmly rooted in the great tradition of supercharged Mercedes cars, of which the s to ssKL series was the first blossoming. While the latter certainly met the purpose of getting quickly from A to B, free of the need for unnecessary adornment and elaborate fittings, with form distinctly subordinate to function and (where necessary) race-winning performance, the 500 and its derivatives still displayed definite elements of the majestic, extravagant baroque styling, even the gigantic, reflecting the changed consciousness of Germany in the Thirties. A particular example of this was (in company jargon up to 1935) the "Chassis for sports cars" which later came to be known as the "Chassis with set-back engine." This had a standard wheelbase of 3290 mm (10 ft 10 in) and the radiator, engine and cockpit were moved back 185 mm (7 in), affording the mighty inline eight-cylinder engine its "Lebensraum" under the seemingly endless bonnet.

The series was to produce its most beautiful blossoms twice. One was the Special Roadster which cost 6,000 reichsmarks (the equivalent price of a four-door Type 230 sedan) over and above the generously priced 22,000 reichsmarks for most of the other models, and the other the Autobahnkurier at 24,000 reichsmarks which paid homage to the current vogue for pseudo-streamlining. These were dream cars and much talked-about spirits of their time. When the Second World War broke out, the series had made a great evolutionary leap, but had nowhere to go. The 5018 cc 500 K, which produced 100 bhp unblown or 160 bhp blown and was shown at the Berlin Motor Show in February 1934, was followed by the 540 K (115/180 bhp from 5401 cc) at the Paris Salon in October 1936. A 580 K (130/200 bhp from 5800 cc) was brought to production standard by 1940 but the project then petered out because new priorities had intervened. Max Sailer, manager of the Design Office of Daimler-Benz after the death of Hans Nibel, was already responsible for the 540 K. Only after a change in engine capacity did the showpiece Mercedes gain a power unit with the dynamism to match its visual appeal. Just the bare chassis alone weighed 1,800 kg (3,968 lb) and with bodywork it tipped the scales at a good 2,500 kg (5,511 lb), with the special armored type weighing even more at 3,100 kg (6,834 lb). Its fuel consumption resembled the appetite of a gluttonous Renaissance prince – 30 liters per 100 km (8 mpg) was quickly reached, and even exceeded if the 540 K's 170 kph (106 mph) top speed was attained.

Ten styles of bodywork were available ex-works, among them various tourers, sedans, coupés and cabriolets. The Sindelfingen stylists proved to be surprisingly imaginative and were willing to meet the special requirements of a distinctive clientele, provided they were ready to meet the extra cost. In all a total of 342 of the 500 K and 319 of the 540 K models were produced. This clientele included the famous and mighty from around the world. An Indian Maharajah used a 540 K to hunt tigers. And of

Gewiss stehen der 500 K und seine Derivate in einer Tradition von Mercedes-Kompressorwagen, in der die Baureihe s bis ssKL erste Gipfel aufwarf. Wo diese allerdings dem Ziel diente, frei von unnützem Zierat und Schnickschnack rasch von A nach B zu gelangen, wo Form allein der Funktion untertan war, schnell zu sein und notfalls auch mal ein Rennen gewinnen zu können, finden sich an jenen durchaus Elemente des Majestätischen, Barock-Überladenen, ja Gigantischen – Ausdruck auch eines gewandelten und sich wandelnden Bewusstseins im Deutschland der dreißiger Jahre. Besonders bietet sich für dergleichen an, was im Werksjargon bis 1935 »Fahrgestell für Sportwagen« und später »Fahrgestell mit zurückgesetztem Motor« genannt wird: Bei normalem Radstand von 3290 Millimetern werden Kühler, Antriebseinheit und Cockpit 185 Millimeter zurückgenommen, so dass der mächtige Reihenachtzylinder unter einer schier endlos langen Motorhaube an Lebensraum gewinnt.

Ihre schönsten Blüten treibt die Modellreihe zwiefach: im Spezial-Roadster, dessen Käufer auf den liberal kalkulierten Preis von 22 000 Reichsmark für die meisten anderen Modelle noch einmal 6000 Mark (den Gegenwert einer viertürigen Limousine vom Typ 230) zuzahlen muss, und im Autobahnkurier für 24 000 Mark, mit dem man einer zeitgemäßen Pseudo-Stromlinie huldigt. Sie sind Traumwagen und beredte Zeugnisse ihrer Epoche. Als der Zweite Weltkrieg ausbricht, hat die Serie einen evolutionären Dreisprung hinter sich – ohne Auslaufzone. Auf den 500 K mit 5018 ccm und 100 PS ohne oder 160 PS mit zugeschaltetem Kompressor, vorgestellt auf der Berliner Automobil-Ausstellung im Februar 1934, folgt auf dem Pariser Salon im Oktober 1936 der 540 K (115/180 PS aus 5401 ccm). Ein 580 K (130/200 PS aus 5800 ccm) wird bis 1940 zur Serienreife entwickelt. Dann versandet das Projekt, weil die Zeitläufte nach anderen Prioritäten verlangen. Für den 540 K ist bereits Max Sailer zuständig, Leiter des Konstruktionsbüros von Daimler-Benz nach dem Tode von Hans Nibel. Erst mit der Hubraum-Nachrüstung ist der Renommier-Mercedes angemessen motorisiert, finden sich optischer Anspruch und faktische Dynamik zum Gleichklang zusammen: Schon das splitternackte Fahrgestell bringt nämlich 1800 Kilogramm auf die Waage, mit Aufbau gut und gerne 2500 Kilogramm, in der gepanzerten Sonderausführung gar 3100 Kilogramm. In seinem Konsumverhalten ähnelt er lebens- und fresslustigen Renaissancefürsten: 30 Liter je 100 Kilometer werden rasch erreicht und überschritten, wenn man sich häufig den 170 Stundenkilometern annähert, zu denen ein 540 K fähig ist.

Zehn Karosserie-Varianten werden ab Werk angeboten, unter ihnen diverse Tourenwagen, Limousinen, Coupés und Cabriolets. Die Sindelfinger Couturiers erweisen sich als erstaunlich einfallsreich und gehen auf die Sonderwünsche einer überschaubaren Klientel – insgesamt entstehen 342 Exemplare des 500 K und 319 des 540 K – bereitwillig ein, vorausgesetzt, diese ist bereit,

La 500 K et ses sœurs s'inscrivent, certes, dans une longue tradition de voitures à compresseur de chez Mercedes où la gamme s à ssKL a été un premier sommet. Mais, alors que celles-ci, dépouillées de toutes fioritures et de tout superflu, avaient pour objectif d'aller rapidement de A à B, avec une forme seulement assujettie à la fonction, à savoir être rapides et, le cas échéant, gagner aussi une course, d'autres affichent par contre toujours quelque chose de majestueux, de baroque luxuriant, de gigantesque – l'expression d'un état d'esprit nouveau et en mutation dans l'Allemagne des années 1930. Un magnifique exemple en est donné par ce que, jusqu'en 1935, l'on a appelé dans le jargon d'usine le « châssis pour voitures de sport » et nommera plus tard « châssis avec moteur reculé » : sur un empattement normal de 3290 mm, le radiateur, le propulseur et le cockpit sont reculés de 185 mm, si bien que l'imposant huit-cylindres en ligne peut prendre toutes ses aises sous un capot moteur qui semble ne jamais vouloir se terminer.

Cette gamme atteint son apogée avec deux voitures : le Spezial-Roadster dont les acheteurs, en sus du prix vraiment « démocratique » de 22 000 reichsmarks, doivent débourser 6000 reichsmarks supplémentaires (la contrevaleur d'une berline à quatre portes type 230) pour la majorité des autres modèles, et l'Autobahnkurier à 24 000 reichsmarks, qui cultive le pseudo-aérodynamisme en vogue à cette époque. Ce sont des voitures de rêve et des témoins éloquents de leur époque. Lorsque la Seconde Guerre mondiale éclate, la série a fait un triple saut dans l'évolution – sans filet. La 500 K de 5018 cm³ et 100 ch sans compresseur ou 160 ch avec compresseur, présentée au Salon de l'Automobile de Berlin en février 1934, est suivie, au Salon de Paris en octobre 1936, par la 540 K (115/180 ch de 5401 cm³). Une 580 K (130/200 ch de 5800 cm³) est prête pour la série en 1940. Mais le projet capote. À ce moment-là, on avait en effet bien d'autres préoccupations. Max Sailer, directeur du bureau d'études de Daimler-Benz après le décès de Hans Nibel, est déjà compétent pour la 540 K. Ce n'est qu'après la course à la cylindrée que la Mercedes de prestige possède une motorisation digne de son rang et que l'exigence esthétique et la dynamique réelle contractent une symbiose harmonieuse : à lui seul, le châssis nu accuse en effet un poids de pas moins de 1800 kg, avec la carrosserie aisément 2500 kg et, en version spéciale blindée, jusqu'à 3100 kg. Très gourmande en carburant, sa consommation atteint des sommets : 30 litres aux 100 km sont vite atteints et dépassés si l'on flirte fréquemment avec les 170 km/h qu'une 540 K est capable d'atteindre.

Dix variantes de carrosserie sont proposées au départ de l'usine : voitures de tourisme, limousines, coupés et cabriolets. Les concepteurs de Sindelfingen ont une imagination débordante et exécutent les désirs particuliers d'une clientèle triée sur le volet – on comptera au total 342 exemplaires de la 500 K et 319 de la 540 K –, à condition que cette clientèle – célébrités et puissants de ce monde – soit disposée à payer les suppléments de prix exigés.

MERCEDES-BENZ 500K & 540K 1934

course the powerful charisma of this giant was not lost on the Nazi high command. After the attack on Reinhard Heydrich, Reichsprotector of Bohemia and Moravia, 20 Type 770 and 20 Type 540 K armored versions were ordered from Daimler-Benz for their protection and that of allies in other countries. Those who doubted their own popularity preferred, it seems, to ride in bullet-proof security.

entsprechende Aufpreise zu entrichten. Die Klientel: die Prominenten und Mächtigen dieser Welt. Ein indischer Maharadscha verwendet einen 540 K zur Tigerjagd. Natürlich bleibt auch der Nazi-Nomenklatura das robuste Charisma des Kolossalischen nicht verborgen. Nach dem Attentat auf Reinhard Heydrich zum Beispiel, Reichsprotektor über Böhmen und Mähren, gibt man bei Daimler-Benz 20 Einheiten des Typs 770 und 20 Exemplare des 540 K in Auftrag, gepanzert, zum eigenen Schutz und zu dem von Freunden im Ausland. Wo man an der eigenen Beliebtheit zweifelt, reist man doch lieber kugelfest.

Un maharadjah indien utilise une 540 K pour aller chasser le tigre! Le charisme indestructible de tout ce qui est colossal n'échappe pas non plus à la nomenklatura nazie. Après l'attentat perpétré contre Reinhard Heydrich, protecteur du Reich de Bohême et Moravie, par exemple, Daimler-Benz reçoit une commande pour vingt exemplaires de la 770 et vingt de la 540 K, blindés, pour la protection des dignitaires nazis et celle de leurs amis à l'étranger. Là où l'on doute que l'on soit populaire, il est en effet recommandé de bien se protéger.

The two-seater Cabriolet A was unmistakable with its low windshield, low waistline, and recessed radiator. The bodywork was that of the 500 K, the powerplant came from the 540 K, an interim model with only five units manufactured. The externally mounted spare wheels could be removed without tools thanks to the flanged retaining nut. The 5.4-liter, eight-cylinder engine with laterally actuated valves and horizontally mounted, two-stage Roots supercharger was the epitome of power and magnificence.

Unverkennbar das zweisitzige Cabriolet A: mit niedriger Windschutzscheibe, niedriger Gürtellinie, zurückgesetztem Kühler. Die Karosserie ist die des 500 K, das Triebwerk vom 540 K, ein Interimsmodell, in nur fünf Exemplaren gefertigt. Die hinten außen liegenden Reserveräder können dank einer Knebelmutter rasch und ohne Werkzeug entfernt werden. Der 5,4-Liter-Achtzylinder mit seitengesteuerten Ventilen und liegendem zuschaltbarem Zweiflügel-Roots-Gebläse ist Inbegriff von Macht und Herrlichkeit.

L'inconfondable Cabriolet A à deux places : avec un pare-brise bas, une ligne de ceinture basse et un radiateur reculé. La carrosserie est celle de la 500 K, le moteur celui de la 540 K, modèle intérimaire réalisé à cinq exemplaires seulement. À l'extérieur, à l'arrière, les roues de secours peuvent être démontées rapidement et sans outil grâce à un écrou papillon. Le huit-cylindres de 5,4 litres à soupapes à commande latérale et compresseur Roots à doubles ailettes horizontales débrayables est l'incarnation même de la puissance et de la magnificence.

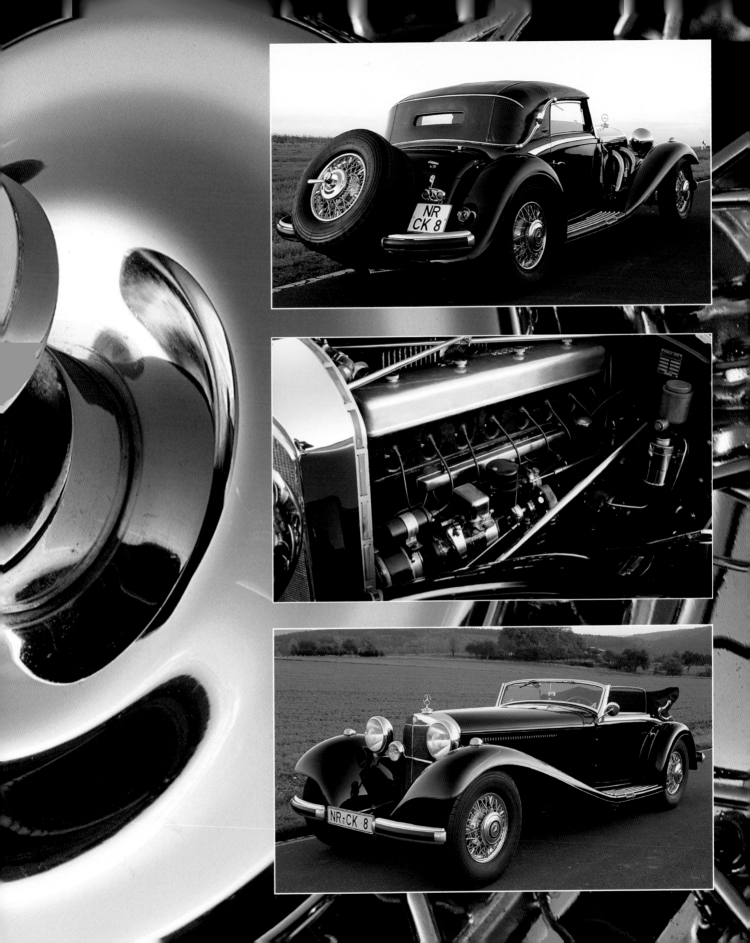

The cabriolet A of the 540K was a car of seductively virile beauty, acquisition and ownership of which was reserved for just a few lucky souls. The engine seemed to go on for ever. Characteristic were the two large front headlights and the central fog lamp. The license plate at the rear was mounted under a transparent cover.

Das Cabriolet A des 540K besticht mit viriler Schönheit, deren Erwerb und Besitz nur einigen wenigen Glücklichen vorbehalten war. Der Motortrakt scheint nicht zu enden. Typisch: die beiden großen Scheinwerfer vorn und die zentrale Nebellampe. Das Nummernschild hinten findet sich im Anschluss an eine transparente Abdeckung.

Le cabriolet A de la 540K séduit par sa beauté virile,
mais le posséder n'est l'apanage que d'un petit nombre
d'heureux élus. Le capot du moteur semble interminable.
Typique : les deux grands phares avant et le phare
antibrouillard central. La plaque minéralogique arrière
se trouve juste derrière une protection transparente.

Easy access: the impressive polished chrome mount for the spare wheel and the rear-view mirror mounted on top of the spare wheel, which was also finished in polished chrome.

Schnelle Lösungen: die einprägsam geformte Halterung für das Ersatzrad, der Rückspiegel rittlings auf diesem, Chromglanz hingegen wie für die Ewigkeit.

D'un accès aisé : le support de la roue de secours orné de l'emblème et le rétroviseur qui chevauche celle-ci, des chromes brillants pour l'éternité.

A shoe scraper was inset into the running board.

Auf ordentliche Leute warten Schuhabstreifer als Intarsien in den Trittbrettern.

Des gratte-pieds intégrés au marchepied incitent à la propreté.

Mercedes-Benz 500K & 540K 1934

The Bosch two-tone horn
underneath the huge hood also
helped establish the right tone.
The series' distinctive dashboard
was inlaid with mother-of-pearl.

Für den guten Ton sorgt ein
Bosch-Zweiklanghorn unter der
gewaltigen Haube. Das für die
Baureihe markante Armaturenbrett
ist mit Perlmutt hinterlegt.

Un Klaxon Bosch à deux tons sous
le gigantesque capot libère la voie
en fanfare. Le tableau de bord
spécifique de cette série est décoré
de nacre.

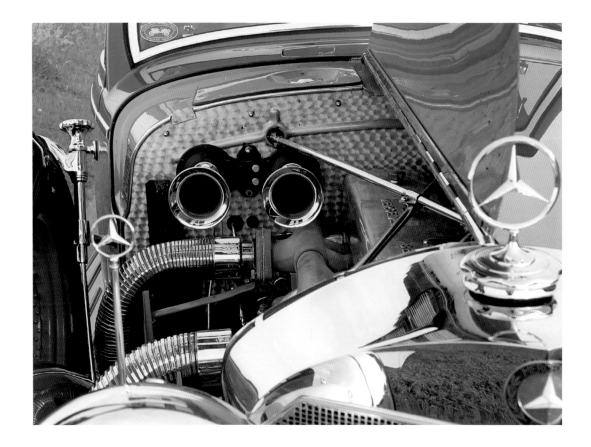

In the six years between 1934 and 1939, the Mercedes Racing Department had a reputation for being a breeding ground for expressions of speed. Never was the route between something being said and it being done shorter, and never was the saying, "The impossible is done immediately but miracles take a little longer" nearer to the truth. And in no activity was the claim of German superiority "Deutschland über alles" more peaceably and impressively demonstrated than on the racing front, before it was almost dashed to pieces within the space of a further six years.

Three racing formulas had to be addressed, and within two of the formulas the performances of the Mercedes single seaters ascended into the realms of the downright improbable. The w 165 of 1939, precisely set up for a single race, remains a one-off and a curiosity, but it was also the apotheosis of the drama surrounding the Silver Arrows racing team. There was little place for lady luck here. Victory in racing, according to chief engineer Nallinger, consisted of 95 per cent preparation and 5 per cent luck. The drivers were like the last runners in a long relay race, almost outshone by their cars which were the real stars of the show.

First came the w 25, Daimler-Benz's first response to the 750 kilo formula. Its frame with its longitudinal u-section members owed much to past models, but its suspension, independent at the front, swing axle at the back with leaf springing underneath and friction shock absorbers, was a pointer to the future. Four forward gears and reverse were available through a gate-type gearshift. The car had an inline eight-cylinder, four-valve-per-cylinder engine weighing 211 kg (456 lb) with four combustion units respectively welded to the cylinder head and water jackets. The supercharger was mounted at the front and supplied two pressure carburetors. Fuel consumption reached 98 liters per 100 km (2.4 mpg), drawn from a 215-liter (57 gal) tank.

Because only the car weight was officially stipulated, between 1934 and 1936 nothing stood in the way of engineering a rapid increase in engine capacity and therefore power – from 354 bhp at 5800 rpm produced by the original 3360 cc engine (works code m 25 a) to the 494 bhp at 5800 rpm from 4740 cc in 1936 – the year of the Silver Arrow crisis.

The w 125 of 1937, meticulously worked on by Rudolf Uhlenhaut, could be custom prepared for the particular circuit, with regard to gears, tank capacity, carburetors, turbochargers, rims and tire sizes, torque, and achievable speeds in the individual gears. Its oval tubular frame with four transverse members was made of special steel. The front wheels were suspended on wishbones with coil springs. The rear wheel arrangement was new, consisting of a double-jointed axle which guaranteed a constant camber angle with only a small change in track. Thrust and braking moments were transmitted to the chassis by side rods. Torsion bars were used for suspension. The

In den sechs Jahren zwischen 1934 und 1939 mutet die Mercedes-Rennabteilung an wie ein schneller Brüter für schnelle Redensarten: Nirgends sind die Wege kürzer zwischen Gesagt und Getan, nie bildet das Scherzwort, dass Unmögliches sofort erledigt werde, Wunder aber etwas länger brauchten, eine Wirklichkeit genauer ab. Und: An keiner Front lässt sich der hehre Anspruch »Deutschland über alles« friedfertiger und eindrucksvoller umsetzen als an der Rennfront, bevor weitere sechs Jahre alles in Scherben schlagen.

Mit drei Formeln muss man es aufnehmen, innerhalb zweier Formeln eskalieren die Leistungen der Mercedes-Monoposti und ihre Fähigkeit, diese auch auf den Boden zu bringen, bis hinein in den roten Bereich des geradezu Unwahrscheinlichen. Der w 165 von 1939, maßgeschneidert für ein einziges Rennen, bleibt Unikat und Kuriosum, wird aber auch zur Apotheose des Dramas um die Silberpfeile. Der Regisseur Zufall hat dabei kaum eine Chance: Rennsiege, sagt Chefingenieur Nallinger, bestehen zu 95 Prozent aus Vorbereitung und zu fünf Prozent aus Glück. Die Fahrer starten so als letzte Läufer in einer langen Stafette, fast überstrahlt von ihren Fahrzeugen, jenen silbernen Stars im Zeichen des Sterns.

Am Anfang steht der w 25, die erste Replik von Daimler-Benz auf die 750-Kilo-Formel. Sein Rahmen greift noch Baumuster aus der Vergangenheit auf: Längsträger im u-Profil. Schon in die Zukunft weist die Aufhängung: Einzelradaufhängung vorn, Pendelachse hinten mit untenliegender Blattfeder und Reibungsstoßdämpfern. Den Piloten stehen vier Fahrstufen sowie ein Rückwärtsgang zur Verfügung, zu schalten von einer Kulisse mit Verriegelung aus. 211 Kilogramm wiegt der Reihen-Achtzylinder, ein Vierventiler, an dem jeweils vier Verbrennungseinheiten zusammen mit dem Zylinderkopf und Kühlwassermänteln verschweißt sind. Der Kompressor ist vorn angeordnet und beschickt zwei Druckvergaser. Dem 215-Liter-Tank werden bis zu 98 Liter je hundert Kilometer entzogen.

Da nur das Fahrzeuggewicht vorgeschrieben ist, steht zwischen 1934 und 1936 einer zügigen Expansion des Hubraums und damit der Stärke nichts im Wege: von den 354 ps bei 5800/min, die das ursprüngliche Triebwerk von 3360 ccm (Werkscode m 25 a) abgibt, bis zu den 494 ps bei gleichgebliebener Drehzahl, aber aus 4740 ccm im Jahr der Silberpfeil-Krise 1936.

Der w 125 von 1937, akribisch überarbeitet von Rudolf Uhlenhaut, lässt sich bereits gezielt auf die jeweilige Rennstrecke einstellen, hinsichtlich Getriebe, Tankvolumen, Vergaser, Lader, Felgen und Reifengrößen, Drehmoment und erreichbaren Geschwindigkeiten in den einzelnen Gängen. Sein Ovalrohrrahmen mit vier Querträgern ist aus einem Spezialstahl, die Räder vorn sind an Dreiecklenkern mit Schraubenfedern aufgehängt. Neu ist die Führung der Hinterräder: eine Doppelgelenkachse, die einen konstanten Radsturz bei nur geringer Änderung der Spurweite garantiert. Schub- und Bremsmomente werden

Pendant six ans, de 1934 à 1939, le département Compétition de Mercedes se mue en une véritable ruche bourdonnante : nulle part ailleurs, il ne se passe aussi peu de temps entre ce qui est dit et ce qui est fait, jamais n'a été aussi proche de la réalité la plaisanterie selon laquelle ce qui est impossible est réalisé immédiatement, mais les miracles durent un peu plus longtemps. Et, sur nul autre front, la noble devise « Deutschland über alles » ne peut être mise en œuvre de façon plus pacifique et plus impressionnante que sur le front de la compétition, avant, de nouveau pendant six ans, que tout ne tombe en ruine.

Le règlement propose trois formules et, dans deux formules, la puissance des monoplaces Mercedes et leur aptitude à la traduire sur la route la conduisent jusque dans la zone rouge. La w 165 de 1939, taillée sur mesure pour une seule course, reste une pièce unique et une curiosité historique, mais elle est aussi l'apothéose du drame dont les Flèches d'argent sont les actrices principales. On ne laisse pratiquement plus aucune chance au hasard comme metteur en scène : les victoires en compétition, déclare l'ingénieur en chef Nallinger, sont pour 95 % le résultat de la préparation et pour 5 %, de la chance. Les pilotes sont donc les ultimes coureurs d'une longue chaîne de relayeurs, presque dans l'ombre de leur voiture, vedette d'argent sous le signe de l'étoile.

Tout a commencé avec la w 25, la première réplique de Daimler-Benz pour la formule de 750 kg. Son cadre reprend des solutions éprouvées du passé : longerons longitudinaux avec profilés en u. Mais la suspension, déjà, est futuriste : suspension à roue indépendante à l'avant, essieu brisé à l'arrière avec ressorts à lames inférieurs et amortisseurs à frictions. Les pilotes ont à leur disposition quatre rapports avant et une marche arrière, cette dernière avec verrouillage. Le huit-cylindres en ligne pèse 211 kg. C'est un quatre-soupapes où quatre chambres de combustion respectives sont soudées en bloc avec la culasse et les chemises d'eau de refroidissement. Le compresseur est placé à l'avant et actionne deux carburateurs à pression. Les 215 litres du réservoir d'essence ne sont pas de trop, car on y prélève jusqu'à 98 litres aux 100 km.

Comme le seul critère est le poids de la voiture, on assiste, entre 1934 et 1936, à une véritable explosion de la cylindrée et rien ne s'oppose donc plus à la course à la puissance : de 354 ch à 5800 tr/min obtenus avec le moteur original de 3360 cm³ (code m25a), la puissance passe à 494 ch à un régime identique, mais à partir d'une cylindrée de 4740 cm³, l'année de la crise des Flèches d'argent en 1936.

La w 125 de 1937, revue et corrigée jusque dans les moindres détails par Rudolf Uhlenhaut, peut déjà être réglée en fonction de chaque circuit en ce qui concerne la boîte de vitesses, le volume du réservoir, les carburateurs, les compresseurs, les jantes et les dimensions des pneumatiques ainsi que le couple et les vitesses respectivement possibles sur les différents rapports. Son châssis à tubes

MERCEDES-BENZ W25–W165 1934

A rear view of the W25 – the view that most of its opponents generally had of it during the years from 1934 to 1939.

Der W25 aus dem Blickwinkel, aus dem die meisten Konkurrenten in den Jahren zwischen 1934 und 1939 die Mercedes-Silberpfeile zu sehen bekommen: von hinten.

La W25 sous l'angle duquel la majorité de ses concurrents a vu entre 1934 et 1939 les Mercedes Flèches d'argent: de l'arrière.

handbrake had been dispensed with. At the time of the Gran Premio d'Italia, the car (code M125F) could produce 592 bhp from 5660 cc at 5800 rpm, which was close to its maximum speed. Its thirst also grew and the 222 kg (489 lb) power unit required on average up to 100 liters per 100 km (2.35 mpg).

Such figures are, however, comparatively moderate compared with the enormous thirst of the W154 of 1938 whose V12 required 180 liters of fuel (an explosive cocktail of 88 per cent methyl alcohol, 8.8 per cent acetone and trace elements of other substances) per 100 km (1.3 mpg), which sloshed about in a 233-liter (61.5-gal) tank. With a capacity of 2963 cc, the engine was almost at the stipulated limit of three liters, and at 253 kg (558 lb) weighed almost a quarter of the total vehicle weight of 981 kg (2,162 lb). The cylinders of the four-valve-per-cylinder engine with four overhead camshafts were forged in three-cylinder units from a block of chrome nickel steel with the head and cylinder cast in one piece. The crankcase was made of electrometal. A twelve-cylinder engine with relatively small combustion units was chosen in order to deal with thermal problems. The use of glycol as coolant allowed radiator temperatures to reach 125°C (257°F). An efficient pump forced 100 liters (53 gal) of lubricant per minute through bearings and shafts. Fed by two single-stage superchargers, the roaring power unit originally produced 468 bhp at 7800 rpm, and then in 1939 483 bhp at the same speed but with a two-stage supercharger. Because the weight of the car had now assumed secondary importance, the

durch seitliche Lenker auf das Fahrgestell übertragen. Zur Federung dienen Drehstäbe. Eine Handbremse gibt es nicht mehr. Zum Zeitpunkt des Gran Premio d'Italia mobilisiert die Maschine (Code M125F) 592 PS aus 5660 ccm Volumen, wie gehabt bei 5800/min ganz in der Nähe der Höchstdrehzahl. Ihr Durst ist leicht gestiegen: Nach 100 Litern verlangt es den 222 Kilo schweren Treibsatz im Schnitt.

Solche Werte nehmen sich allerdings noch vergleichsweise moderat aus neben der Trunksucht des W154 von 1938. Denn dessen V12 verlangt es je 100 Kilometer nach 180 Litern Kraftstoff – einem brisanten Cocktail aus 88 Prozent Methylalkohol, 8,8 Prozent Aceton und Spurenelementen anderer Substanzen, der in einem Tank von 233 Litern Inhalt schwappt. Mit 2963 ccm Hubraum ist die Maschine bis in die Nähe der vorgeschriebenen drei Liter ausgereizt und bringt mit 253 Kilogramm fast ein Viertel des Fahrzeuggewichts von 981 Kilogramm auf die Waage. Je drei Zylinder des Vierventilers mit vier obenliegenden Nockenwellen sind in einem Block aus Chromnickelstahl geschmiedet, Kopf und Zylinder in einem Stück. Das Kurbelgehäuse besteht aus Elektrometall. Für einen Zwölfzylinder mit seinen kleineren Verbrennungseinheiten entschied man sich, um thermische Probleme in den Griff zu bekommen. Die Verwendung von Glykol lässt Kühlertemperaturen bis zu 125 Grad zu. Eine effiziente Pumpe schickt je Minute 100 Liter Schmierstoff durch Lager und Wellen. Von zwei Einstufenkompressoren zwangsbeatmet, leistet das brüllende Triebwerk ursprüng-

ovales avec quatre poutres transversales est fabriqué dans un acier spécial et les roues avant sont articulées sur des triangles avec ressorts hélicoïdaux. Le guidage des roues arrière innove également: un essieu à double articulation garantit un déport constant des roues avec une très faible modification de la voie. Les couples de poussée et de freinage sont répartis sur le châssis grâce à des bras latéraux. La suspension est à barres de torsion. Il n'y a plus de frein à main. Pour le Gran Premio d'Italia, le moteur (code interne M125F) développe 592 ch à partir d'une cylindrée de 5660 cm³, comme de coutume à 5800 tr/min, soit à la limite de la zone rouge. Sa consommation a légèrement augmenté: le moteur de 222 kg engloutit en moyenne ses 100 litres aux 100 km.

Et encore de tels chiffres sont-ils modestes, comparés à la consommation de la W154 de 1938. Son V12 exige 180 litres aux 100 km – un cocktail explosif se composant de 88 % d'alcool de méthyle, de 8,8 % d'acétone et de traces d'autres substances qui remplissent un réservoir de 233 litres. Avec 2963 cm³, le moteur frôle la limite réglementaire de 3 litres et, avec 253 kg, représente près d'un quart du poids de la voiture, qui accuse 981 kg. Trois cylindres du moteur à quatre soupapes avec quatre arbres à cames en tête sont forgés en un seul bloc d'acier en chrome-nickel, culasses et cylindres faisant bloc. Le carter moteur est en électrométal. Priorité a été donnée à un douze-cylindres aux chambres de combustion respectives de plus petites dimensions pour éviter les problèmes thermiques. L'utilisation de glycol autorise des températures de

Until the turbocharged era of the 1980s, the W125 revelled in the distinction of being the most powerful Grand Prix racing car of all time.

Bis zur Turbo-Ära der achtziger Jahre war der W125 von der Gloriole umkränzt, der stärkste Grand-Prix-Wagen aller Zeiten zu sein. Man sieht es ihm an.

Jusqu'à l'ère du turbo dans les années 1980, la W125 a été nimbée de la gloire d'être la plus puissante voiture de Grand Prix de tous les temps. On s'en rend compte instantanément.

power of the w154 could be delivered to the rear axle via five gears. Nevertheless, the relationship of its transmission to that of its predecessor was unmistakable.

Compared with the majestic appearance of the 4250 mm (13 ft 11 in) long 3-liter car, the w165, the backbone of which was formed by an oval tubular framework with five transverse members, seemed positively dainty at 3680 mm (12 ft 1 in) in length. The front wheels were suspended on wishbones with vertical coil springs, the rear wheels on a swing axle pivoted at the center. Suspension was again provided by torsion bars. Its eight cylinders, whose banks were set at an angle of 90 degrees, produced 254 bhp at 8000 rpm from a capacity of 1495 cc and could be revved up to 9000 rpm. The w165 was light, weighing a mere 700 kg (1543 lb), of which the engine accounted for 195 kg (430 lb) despite its 5-speed transmission. This car certainly had a healthy appetite. Under the hot sun of Tripoli, Hermann Lang and Rudolf Caracciola burned up 137 liters of fuel in 100 km (1.7 mpg), thus rapidly emptying the 250-liter (66-gal) tank. One of the most impressive features of an impressive car was its enormous brake drums, which almost completely filled the inside of the wheels.

lich 468 PS bei 7800/min, 1939 mit einem Zweistufenkompressor 483 PS bei identischer Drehzahl. Da das Gewicht nun zweitrangig geworden ist, kann die Leistung des w154 mit fünf Fahrstufen an die Hinterachse vermittelt werden. Die Affinität seines Fahrwerks zu dem des Vorgängers ist indessen noch unverkennbar.

Vergleichsweise zierlich neben der Majestät des 4250 Millimeter langen Dreiliters wirkt mit 3680 Millimetern der w165, dessen Rückgrat ein Ovalrohrrahmen mit fünf Quertraversen bildet. Vorn sind seine Räder an Dreiecklenkern mit Vertikalschraubenfedern aufgehängt, hinten an einer Schwingachse, die an der Achsmitte angelenkt ist. Drehstäbe besorgen wiederum die Federung. Sein Achtzylinder, dessen Bänke sich im Winkel von 90 Grad spreizen, leistet mit 1495 ccm bei 8000/min 254 PS und lässt sich bereits bis 9000/min hochdrehen. Der w165 ist leicht, nur 700 Kilogramm, von denen 195 auf den Motor entfallen – trotz seines Fünfgang-Getriebes. Zum Kostverächter verkümmert jedoch auch er nicht: Unter der heißen Sonne von Tripolis verfeuern Hermann Lang und Rudolf Caracciola 137 Liter auf 100 Kilometer, so dass der zuständige 250-Liter-Behälter zügig geleert wird. Mit das eindrucksvollste Detail an einem eindrucksvollen Auto: seine riesigen Bremstrommeln, die fast das ganze Innere der Räder ausfüllen.

radiateur pouvant atteindre 125 degrés. Une pompe injecte 100 litres de lubrifiant par minute dans les paliers et les arbres. Deux compresseurs à un étage assurent la respiration forcée du moteur aux feulements de bête sauvage qui développe 468 ch à 7800 tr/min puis 483 ch à régime identique, en 1939, avec un compresseur à deux étages. Comme le poids n'est plus qu'un critère secondaire, la puissance de la w154 peut être transmise aux roues arrière par une boîte à cinq rapports. Son châssis est pratiquement calqué sur celui de sa devancière.

Avec ses 3680 millimètres, la w165, dont l'épine dorsale est un châssis en tubes ovales avec cinq poutres transversales, semble relativement frêle, comparée à la majesté de la 3 litres avec ses 4,25 m de long. Ses roues avant sont suspendues à des triangles avec ressorts hélicoïdaux verticaux et, à l'arrière, on trouve un essieu oscillant avec fixation au centre de l'essieu. Des barres de torsion assurent ici aussi la suspension. Son v8 à 90 degrés développe 254 ch à 8000 tr/min pour une cylindrée de 1495 cm³ et peut déjà monter jusqu'à 9000 tours. La w165 ne pèse que 700 kg, dont 195 pour le moteur – malgré sa boîte à cinq vitesses. Lui non plus, toutefois, n'est pas un ascète : sous le soleil ardent de Tripoli, Hermann Lang et Rudolf Caracciola brûlent 137 litres aux 100 km et le réservoir de 250 litres se vide donc rapidement. Détail parmi les plus impressionnants d'une voiture elle-même impressionnante : ses gigantesques tambours de freins qui occupent presque tout l'intérieur des roues.

The exhaust side of the huge eight-cylinder engine and the cranked gear lever in the middle of its gate. Thrust and braking moments were transmitted to the chassis by side-mounted suspension arms.

Die Auslassseite des Achtzylinders in seiner statuarischen Größe und der gekröpfte Schalthebel inmitten der Kulisse. Die Schub- und Bremsmomente werden durch seitliche Lenker auf das Fahrgestell übertragen.

Le côté échappement du huit-cylindres dans toute sa splendeur et le levier de commande coudé au centre de la grille. Les efforts de poussée et de freinage sont transmis au châssis par des bras latéraux.

The design of the 1939 W 154 was the result of wide-ranging testing during 1938 and the winter of 1938–39. One novelty was that the height of the sides was raised nearer to the level of the driver's shoulders.

In die Form des W 154 von 1939 fließen die Ergebnisse umfangreicher Tests im Jahr zuvor und im Winter ein. Eine Neuerung: die Seitenverkleidungen werden höher zu den Schultern des Fahrers emporgezogen.

Mercedes-Benz W25–W165 1934

La forme de la W154 de 1939 intègre les résultats de tests exhaustifs réalisés durant l'année 1938 et l'hiver suivant. Une innovation : les carénages latéraux sont relevés en direction des épaules du pilote.

The W154's V12 engine was obliquely mounted so that the driver could sit lower in the car with his legs alongside rather than on top of the drive shaft.

Der V12 des W154 ist schräg eingebaut. Damit kann der Fahrer neben statt über der Antriebswelle und folglich tiefer sitzen.

Le V12 de la W154 est monté en biais pour que le conducteur puisse s'asseoir à côté de l'arbre de transmission, donc plus bas.

Picture of a winner: the W165
is a curiosity of motorsport history.
It was built in just six months to
compete in a single race – the
Tripoli Grand Prix of May 1939.
It won.

Das Gesicht eines Siegers: Der
W165 ist ein Kuriosum in der
Motorsportgeschichte. Er wurde in
nur acht Monaten für nur ein
Rennen gebaut, den Großen Preis
von Tripolis im Mai 1939, und
das gewann er.

Un visage de vainqueur: la W165
est une curiosité dans l'histoire
de la compétition mécanique.
Elle n'a été construite qu'en huit
mois et pour une seule et unique
course, le Grand Prix de Tripoli,
en mai 1939, qu'elle a gagné.

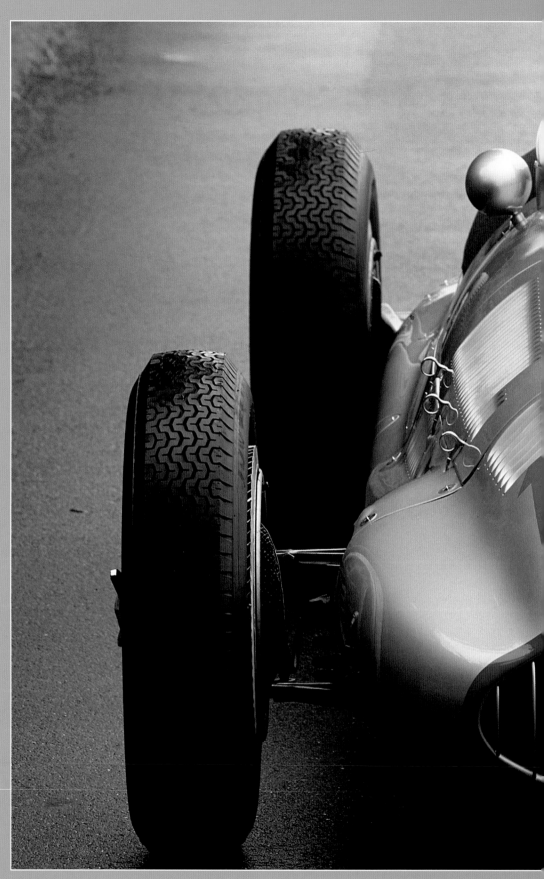

The W165 looked like a scaled-down version of the W154, especially of the 1939 version. It was 570 mm (22.5 in) shorter, 240 mm (9.5 in) narrower, and 60 mm (2.4 in) lower.

Der W165 wirkt wie ein maßstabsgerecht verkleinerter W154, vor allem in dessen Version von 1939. Er ist 570 mm kürzer, 240 mm schmaler und 60 mm niedriger.

La W165 ressemble à une W154 miniature, notamment dans sa version de 1939. Elle mesure 570 mm de moins en longueur, 240 mm en largeur et 60 mm en hauteur.

The winning car
at Tripoli was also the
embodiment of
contemporary notions
of streamlining.

Der Siegerwagen von
Tripolis ist auch
eine zeitgenössische
Interpretation dessen,
was man unter
Stromlinie verstand.

La voiture victorieuse
à Tripoli traduit
parfaitement ce que
l'on entendait alors par
« aérodynamique ».

The front wheels of the W 165 were mounted on wishbones with vertical coil springs. Like the W 154 on which it was based, the rear wheels were mounted on an independent swing axle, pivoted at the center, with torsion bar suspension.

Die Vorderräder des W 165 sind aufgehängt an Dreiecks-Querlenkern mit senkrecht stehenden Schraubenfedern. Die Hinterräder hängen wie am Vorbild W 154 an einer Schwingachse in Parallelradausführung, in Achsmitte angelenkt, mit Drehstabfederung.

Les roues avant de la W165 sont suspendues à des triangles transversaux avec des ressorts hélicoïdaux verticaux. Comme sur son modèle, la W154, les roues arrière sont montées sur un essieu oscillant en exécution à roues parallèles, articulées au centre de l'essieu, avec une suspension à barre de torsion.

This was an oddity, a strange model ill-suited to the Mercedes range, and one destined to have a short, unfulfilled lifespan. The Type 130 reflected the fashion of the time – streamlining, or what at that time passed for streamlining. The design created a lot of space at the back of the car so that it seemed appropriate to move the engine to the rear for the car's first trials. The fact that Daimler-Benz spent any time on it passed generally unnoticed. The forerunners of the 130, such as the w17 of 1931 with its 1.2-liter, four-cylinder boxer engine, or the w25D of 1933, which drew a passable performance from its three-cylinder, 30 bhp diesel engine flourished and disappeared unremarked. Consequently, the 130 attracted considerable attention at the Berlin Motor Show in February 1934 because of its shape and the technology it incorporated. Its backbone was a central supporting tube on which the wheels were independently suspended. Its 1308 cc, inline, four-cylinder engine produced 26 bhp and was supported on rubber mountings behind the rear axle.

But soon talk of flaws and handling problems emerged. Two thirds of the vehicle's weight was at the back and this meant that the little car was as treacherous as a roused rattlesnake, a backslider which could only be held in check by masterful driving, and, all in all, rather a handful. Six 1498 cc, 55 bhp Type 150 Sport Limousines prepared for the popular 2,000 km Rally of that year behaved rather more agreeably because their engines were relocated forward of the rear axle. This early interpretation of the mid-engine principle, however, meant that two seats were sacrificed. A sporty roadster built in 1935 on the same chassis, although clearly eye-catching and appealing, proved decidedly too expensive at a purchase price of 6,600 marks compared with 3,900 marks for a 130 cabrio sedan. It also already had a notorious reputation because of its difficult handling. Its trunk was barely worthy to bear the Mercedes name. The 150 therefore shared the fate of the 130 and disappeared from the sales catalogue in 1936.

Meanwhile the 170H had been developed in Untertürkheim in parallel with the 170V and was launched in February 1936. The 38 bhp car with a capacity of 1697 cc was distinctly more civilized than the earlier rear-engined models. And yet while the front-engined 170 blossomed in the market place, the 170H withered away like a wallflower and was deleted from the range in 1939. It did, however, achieve late honors after the war as some new (unused) examples were still available, only now they were as exclusive as they should have been when first marketed. In all a total of only 5,805 units of the 130 and 170 series were produced – it proved to be an excursion which ended in a cul de sac.

Er ist ein Sonderling, seltsam fehl am Platze im Mercedes-Sortiment, und deshalb ist ihm auch nur ein kurzes, unerfülltes Modellleben beschieden. Der Typ 130 wird aus einer Zeitmode heraus geboren, Stromlinie – oder was man damals dafür hält. Sie lässt viel Platz im Heck, so dass es sich anbietet, den Motor wieder nach hinten umzusiedeln wie einst, als das Auto seine ersten Gehversuche machte.

Dass sich Daimler-Benz mit dergleichen abgibt, bleibt gänzlich unbemerkt: Vorstufen des 130 wie der w17 von 1931 mit einem Vierzylinder-Boxertriebwerk von 1,2 Litern oder der w25D von 1933, dem ein Dreizylinder-Dieselmotor von 30 PS zu durchaus passablen Fahrleistungen verhilft, blühen und verblühen im stillen. Folglich erregt der 130 auf der Berliner Automobil-Ausstellung im Februar 1934 beträchtliches Aufsehen wegen seiner Form und seiner Technik. Als Rückgrat dient ein zentrales Tragrohr, an dem die Räder einzeln aufgehängt sind. Sein Reihenvierzylinder mit 1308 ccm Volumen gibt 26 PS ab und ist jenseits der Hinterachse in Gummi gelagert.

Doch bald sprechen sich seine Mucken und Macken herum. Zwei Drittel seines Gewichts konzentrieren sich hinten. Also ist das Wägelchen tückisch wie eine gereizte Klapperschlange, eine Heckschleuder, wie sie im Buche steht, nur durch Meisterhände wieder einzufangen und überdies ein reichlich ruppiger Geselle. Sechs Sportlimousinen vom Typ 150 mit 1498 ccm und 55 PS, für die populäre 2000-Kilometer-Fahrt jenes Jahres vorbereitet, geben sich weitaus verträglicher, da die Maschine einen neuen Standort vor der Hinterachse bezogen hat. Dieser frühen Interpretation des Mittelmotor-Prinzips müssen allerdings zwei Sitzplätze geopfert werden. Auf dem gleichen Fahrwerk entsteht 1935 ein sportiver Roadster, zweifellos Blickfang und Augenweide, aber mit einem Kaufpreis von 6600 Mark etwa gegenüber den 3900 Mark für eine Cabrio-Limousine des 130 entschieden zu teuer und bereits berüchtigt wegen schwierigen Handlings. Sein Kofferraum ist kaum der Bezeichnung wert. So teilt der 150 mit dem 130 das Los, 1936 aus dem Angebot zu verschwinden.

Inzwischen hat man in Untertürkheim parallel zum 170V den 170H entwickelt und im Februar 1936 vorgestellt, mit 1697 ccm und 38 PS und deutlich urbaner als die früheren Modelle mit der Maschine im Nacken der Passagiere. Doch während der Frontmotor-170 als Verkaufsschlager erblüht, verkümmert der 170H zum Mauerblümchen und wird 1939 aus dem Programm gestrichen. Zu späten Ehren gelangt er nach dem Krieg, als noch neuwertige Exemplare zu haben sind, erst jetzt so exklusiv, wie sie ursprünglich hatten sein sollen. Insgesamt bringen es die Baureihen 130 und 170 auf die dünne Population von 5805 Einheiten, ein Ausflug, der in einer Sackgasse endete.

C'est un engin bizarre, étonnamment déplacé dans le programme Mercedes, raison pour laquelle il n'aura droit qu'à une vie automobile courte et jamais assumée totalement. La 130 est l'enfant d'une mode temporelle, l'aérodynamique – ou ce que l'on entendait par là à cette époque. La place ne manque pas à l'arrière; il est donc logique que le moteur fasse sa réapparition là où il se trouvait jadis lorsque l'automobile en était à ses premiers balbutiements.

Le grand public n'a presque pas pris note des tentatives de Daimler-Benz dans ce domaine: les ancêtres de la 130, ainsi que la w17 de 1931 à quatre cylindres à plat de 1,2 litre ou la w25D de 1933, à laquelle un moteur Diesel à trois cylindres de 30 ch donnait des performances tout à fait suffisantes, naissent et disparaissent telle une bulle de savon. Par conséquent, la 130, lors de sa présentation au Salon de l'Automobile de Berlin en février 1934, stupéfie les visiteurs par sa forme et sa mécanique. Elle a pour épine dorsale une poutre transversale sur laquelle les roues sont fixées par une suspension indépendante. Le quatre-cylindres en ligne de 1308 cm³ délivre 26 ch et est monté loin derrière le train arrière sur des paliers en caoutchouc.

Mais ses défauts et insuffisances deviennent vite notoires. Les deux tiers de son poids sont concentrés sur l'arrière. Cette petite voiture se montre donc capricieuse sur route, avec une propension à chasser de l'arrière. Seul un très bon conducteur peut la maîtriser. C'est de plus une voiture dont la souplesse ne restera pas dans la légende. Six berlines de sport de la série 150, de 1498 cm³ et 55 ch, préparées spécialement pour la populaire Course des 2000 Kilomètres de cette même année, s'avèrent beaucoup plus civilisées: il est vrai que le moteur a été transposé devant l'essieu arrière. Cette interprétation précoce du concept du moteur central s'est toutefois soldée par la disparition de deux places. Sur un châssis identique est créé, en 1935, un roadster sportif qui attire immédiatement le regard par son esthétique réussie, mais qui est beaucoup trop cher par son prix d'achat de 6600 marks, alors qu'une version cabriolet limousine de la 130 en coûte 3900, et qui a déjà une mauvaise réputation en raison de son comportement problématique. Pratiquement inexistant, son coffre ne mérite même pas ce nom. Ainsi la 150 partage-t-elle le destin de la 130 et disparaît-elle du catalogue en 1936.

Entre-temps, Untertürkheim a préparé, profitant de la construction de la 170V, la 170H, dévoilée en février 1936, avec un moteur de 1697 cm³ et 38 ch, et nettement plus civilisée que les modèles précédents avec le moteur dans le dos des passagers. Mais, tandis que la 170 à moteur avant remporte un grand succès commercial, la 170H végète dans l'anonymat et est mise au placard en 1939. Elle connaîtra cependant une popularité tardive, après la guerre, quand certains exemplaires quasi neufs sont encore disponibles, obtenant l'exclusivité qu'elle était censée avoir à l'origine. Au total, les gammes 130 et 170 n'auront été produites qu'à 5805 exemplaires, une expérience qui ne sera terminée en queue de poisson.

MERCEDES-BENZ 130H–170H 1934

A short front and long rear with the 1.5-liter straight four breathing down the passengers' neck. The lines of the 150 type sport roadster conjured up speed, but due to its glaring faults, it enjoyed little success. The 150 was an eye-catching car, but its roadholding was diabolical.

Wenig Bug, viel Heck mit dem Reihenvierzylinder von 1,5 Litern im Nacken der Insassen. Die Silhouette des Sportroadsters Typ 150 mutet zwar rasant an, gleichwohl findet das Auto wenig Anklang wegen seiner evidenten Untugenden. Ein Blickfang ist der 150 gewiss. Aber seine Straßenlage ist teuflisch.

Une proue discrète, mais une poupe allongée avec les quatre-cylindres en ligne de 1,5 litre placés dans le dos des passagers. Le roadster sport 150 affiche une silhouette plutôt sportive, mais la voiture a cependant remporté peu de succès en raison de ses défauts. La 150 a certes fière allure, mais sa tenue de route est déficiente.

Mercedes-Benz 130H–170H 1934

When this model was shown at the Berlin Motor Show in February 1936 as a successor to the six-cylinder 170, it was already destined for a success which was to carry it through almost two decades. The 170 V was economical, and at a price of 3,750 reichsmarks for the two-door sedan it was unusually good value for money. It was as strong as a battletank, both as a unit and in its individual components, and it was designed to a technically conservative brief. It had an unobtrusive style, far removed from the contemporary fashion, in whichever variant it was offered, i.e., as a two- or four-door sedan, two- or four-seat cabriolet, roadster and cabrio-sedan, open tourer, delivery van – of either pickup or box type, and ambulance or patrol car. Such a great variety of types could be offered because of its mixed construction technique of steel sheet cladding over a wooden framework. When in 1946 the 170 V was reintroduced completely in steel, the options shrunk decidedly. Its construction was based on a cruciform oval tubular frame. The rear swing axle was supported on both sides by coil springs attaching it to the frame. The front wheels, as on its predecessor, were independently suspended on a pair of transverse leaf-springs. The 1697 cc engine was hardly overworked in producing just 38 bhp and, being resiliently-mounted at two points, was remarkable for its unprecedentedly quiet running. Initially only the two top gears were synchromeshed, but from 1940 all four were.

The concept was so comprehensively engineered and developed that very few changes were necessary. The star badge, first fixed to the radiator frame, again crowned the radiator cap from 1937 onwards. The structure of the Cabriolet B's top was changed in April 1937 and the additional pillars between the side windows were removed at the same time. The fuel tank in the engine compartment was first of 33-liter (8.7-gal) capacity. From 1939 this was increased by 10 liters (2.6 gal), which was quite enough for the thrifty 170 V with its average fuel consumption of 10 liters per 100 km (23.5 mpg).

Following contemporary practice, the model was used in several different guises for long distance events such as the 1938 Motor Vehicle Winter Rally. This was not so much because of sporting considerations, but so as to verify its suitability for war use. While the off-road 200 V two-seater of 1938 bore only a faint resemblance to the original, the jeep used by the Wehrmacht owed much to the series. The 16,315 examples amounted to one fifth of the total of 86,615 units produced between 1935 and 1942. This made the 170 V the most-produced Mercedes of this period, and it was also a step in the direction of the concept of "people's motoring" demanded by Adolf Hitler.

There is no doubt that in this respect the ruling regime performed a service for the common good.

Als er auf der Berliner Automobil-Ausstellung im Februar 1936 als Nachfolger des Sechszylinder-Modells 170 präsentiert wird, ist ein Erfolg bereits programmiert, der ihn durch fast zwei Jahrzehnte tragen wird: Der 170 V ist wirtschaftlich, mit 3750 Reichsmark für die zweitürige Limousine ungemein preiswert, als Ganzes und in seinen Komponenten stabil wie ein Panzer, technisch zurückhaltend konzipiert. Und er spricht eine unaufdringliche Formensprache jenseits der ausgeprägten Geschmäcker, in welcher Variante auch immer er angeboten wird, als zwei- oder viertüriger Innenlenker, zwei- oder viersitziges Cabriolet, als Roadster und Cabrio-Limousine, offener Tourenwagen, Lieferwagen mit Ladepritsche oder Kastenaufbau, Krankentransporter oder Streifenwagen. Was eine derartige Artenvielfalt gestattet, ist seine Gemischtbauweise: Stahlblechverkleidung über Holzgerippe. Als der 170 V 1946 ganz in Stahl neu ersteht, schrumpfen die Wahlmöglichkeiten entschieden. Sein Aufbau ruht auf einem x-förmigen Ovalrohrgebälk. Die hintere Pendelachse stützt sich beiderseits mit Schraubenfedern gegen den Rahmen ab. Die Vorderräder hängen wie beim Vorgänger unabhängig an einem Paar Querblattfedern. Das Triebwerk – mit 38 PS aus 1697 ccm nur gering ausgelastet – ist elastisch an zwei Punkten aufgehängt. Das führt zu einer Laufruhe, wie sie bislang für einen Vierzylinder unbekannt ist. Anfänglich sind lediglich die beiden oberen Fahrstufen synchronisiert, ab 1940 alle vier Gänge.

So schlüssig ist das ganze Konzept, dass es wenige Retuschen über sich ergehen lassen muss: Der Stern, erst in den Kühlerrahmen eingepflanzt, krönt ab 1937 wieder die Kühlerverschraubung. Das Cabriolet B erhält vom April 1937 an eine neue Verdeckstruktur, zugleich entfällt die zusätzliche Säule zwischen den Seitenscheiben. Der im Motorraum angesiedelte Tank fasst erst 33 Liter, ab 1939 zehn Liter mehr, mit denen der 170 V genügsam umgeht bei einem Durchschnittsverbrauch von 10 Litern auf 100 Kilometer.

Einer Usance der Zeit folgend, wird das Modell in etlichen Metamorphosen bei Langstreckenveranstaltungen wie der Kraftfahrzeug-Winterprüfung 1938 eingesetzt, allerdings weniger aus sportlichen Erwägungen als um seine Kriegsverwendungsfähigkeit nachzuweisen. Während etwa der Geländesport-Zweisitzer 200 V von 1938 nur noch eine schwache Ähnlichkeit mit dem Original aufweist, lehnt sich der Kübelwagen der Wehrmacht eng an die Serie an. Mit 16 315 Exemplaren macht er etwa ein Fünftel der Fertigung von 86 615 Einheiten insgesamt zwischen 1935 und 1942 aus. Damit wird der 170 V zum meistproduzierten Mercedes dieser Jahre, auch er ein Schritt in Richtung auf die »Volksmotorisierung«, wie sie Adolf Hitler gefordert hat.

Kein Zweifel – in diesem Punkt hat sich das Regime um das kollektive Wohl verdient gemacht.

Lors de sa présentation au Salon de l'Automobile de Berlin en février 1936 comme successeur de la 170 six-cylindres, son succès est déjà assuré, qui ne se démentira pas pendant près de vingt ans : la 170 V est économique, avec un prix très intéressant de 3750 reichsmarks pour la berline deux portes, solide comme un char d'assaut et d'une conception mécanique conservatrice. De plus, elle parle une langue formelle discrète convenant à tous les goûts, en conduite intérieure à deux ou quatre portes, cabriolet à deux ou quatre places, roadster, cabriolet limousine, voiture de tourisme ouverte, fourgonnette à plateau ou fourgon, ambulance ou voiture de police. C'est son architecture spécifique qui autorise une telle diversité de modèles : la carrosserie en tôle d'acier habille un squelette en bois. Lorsque la 170 V apparaît, en 1946, tout en acier, cette polyvalence appartient au passé. La carrosserie repose sur un châssis à tubes ovales en forme de x. L'essieu brisé arrière s'appuie, de chaque côté, sur des ressorts hélicoïdaux fixés au châssis. Comme sur le modèle précédent, les roues avant sont à suspension indépendante avec des ressorts à lames transversaux. Avec 38 ch pour une cylindrée de 1697 cm³, le moteur, qui n'est pas poussé dans ses derniers retranchements, repose sur deux paliers élastiques, ce qui lui donne une douceur de fonctionnement inconnue à ce jour pour un quatre-cylindres. Seuls les deux rapports supérieurs sont synchronisés puis, à partir de 1940, les quatre rapports.

Le concept dans son ensemble présente une grande homogénéité, si bien que peu de modifications ultérieures seront nécessaires : l'étoile, tout d'abord intégrée à l'encadrement de radiateur, couronne de nouveau le bouchon de radiateur à partir de 1937. En avril 1937, le cabriolet B reçoit une capote dont le profilé est nouveau, à l'occasion de quoi disparaît le montant supplémentaire entre les vitres latérales. Le réservoir placé dans le compartiment moteur a tout d'abord une capacité de 33 litres, qui augmente de 10 litres en 1939, que la 170 V digère avec modération puisque sa consommation moyenne est de 10 litres aux 100 km.

Selon une coutume de cette époque, la voiture subit d'innombrables métamorphoses pour participer à des courses d'endurance comme le rallye d'hiver de 1938, moins, toutefois, pour des considérations sportives que pour prouver son aptitude à des fins militaires. Contrairement à la 200 V biplace sport tout-terrain de 1938, qui ne présente plus qu'une vague similitude avec l'original, la tout-terrain destinée à la Wehrmacht reste proche de la série. Avec 16 315 exemplaires, elle représente environ un cinquième de la production des 86 615 voitures construites de 1935 à 1942. Cela fait de la 170 V la Mercedes la plus construite à cette époque, elle aussi contribuant à la « motorisation du peuple » exigée par Adolf Hitler.

Il n'y a pas de doute, sur ce point, la communauté allemande aura profité de cette politique gouvernementale.

MERCEDES-BENZ 170 V 1936

Its critics called it a little bit homespun, but there were some fine members of this series, such as the Cabriolet A, which featured nice design details, such as the spare-wheel cover.

Ihre Kritiker mäkeln, sie sei ein bisschen hausbacken. Aber die Modellfamilie hat auch schöne Angehörige wie das Cabriolet A mit schönen Details wie etwa der Abdeckung des Reserverads.

Ses détracteurs lui reprochent d'être un peu banale. Mais cette famille de modèles a aussi de beaux rejetons comme le Cabriolet A aux jolis détails, tel le carénage de la roue de secours.

Mercedes-Benz 170V 1936

Unlike the 170/6 series with its seven relatively similar models, the 1936 170 came in seven very different designs. The cabrio both drew on the past and pointed the way to the future. Generating just 38 bhp, the four-cylinder engine was a sedate performer, but with the top down and in a cozy twosome, the top speed of 108 kph (67 mph) was quite sufficient in those days, as it still is now.

Im Unterschied zum 170/6 mit seinen sieben ziemlich uniformen Varianten hat der 170 von 1936 sieben sehr verschiedene Karosserieformen zu bieten. Das Cabrio nimmt Motive von gestern auf und weist weit über morgen hinaus. Mit bescheidenen 38 PS ermöglicht der Vierzylinder geruhsame Fortbewegung. Aber bei offenem Verdeck und trauter Zweisamkeit sind 108 Stundenkilometer Spitze völlig ausreichend, damals wie heute.

À la différence de la 170/6 avec ses sept variantes plutôt similaires, la 170 de 1936 propose sept formes de carrosserie très différentes. Le Cabriolet reprend des motifs d'hier mais se montre tout autant avant-gardiste. Avec ses modestes 38 ch, le quatre-cylindres n'autorise qu'une mobilité décontractée. Mais, la capote ouverte et à deux, une vitesse de pointe de 108 km/h est tout à fait suffisante, hier comme aujourd'hui.

The chrome-trimmed dashboard
included (from left to right) fuel
and oil pressure gauges,
speedometer, and clock. The
external semaphore indicator is
only legally permitted today if
supplemented by normal turn-
signal lights. The two-tone
paintwork, almost the norm in
those days, was highly popular.

In Chrom gefasste Armaturentafel
mit Instrumenten für Benzin und
Öldruck, Tachometer und Zeituhr
(von links). Der Winker ist heute
nur zusätzlich zum Blinker erlaubt.
Sehr beliebt und fast schon die
Norm: die Zweifarbenlackierung.

Tableau de bord avec des cadrans
cernés de chromes pour les jauges
d'essence et d'huile, le tachymètre
et l'horloge (de gauche à droite).
Aujourd'hui, le bras de
changement de direction n'est
autorisé qu'en complément au
clignotant. Très populaire et déjà
presque la norme : la peinture
deux tons.

The spotlights-cum-rear-view mirrors (top photograph) and the additional brake lights (below) came as extras, while the white running lights were used in urban traffic.

Extras sind der Suchscheinwerfer mit Rückspiegel (oben) und die zusätzliche Bremsleuchte (unten), während die weißen Positionslampen für den Stadtverkehr benutzt wurden.

Le projecteur orientable avec rétroviseur (en haut) et le voyant de frein supplémentaire (en bas) sont facultatifs tandis que les feux de position blancs sont utilisés pour circuler en ville.

Among the Mercedes exhibits at the Berlin Motor Show of 1936, the one which particularly caught the public eye was the 260 D. Its message was that Daimler-Benz had managed to produce a diesel engine suitable for passenger cars. What no one could predict was that the company had at the same time laid the foundation stone of an empire that would dominate the market in hackney carriages, taxis, and hire cars from then until the present day.

But this achievement did not come easily, the road was rough, strewn with mantraps and pitfalls. The high compression of the diesel engine with its similarly sized combustion units gave rise to two problems. One was that the thicker cylinder walls meant more weight, and the other was that, compared with a gasoline engine, higher inertial forces at the same speed led to uneven engine running. This caused headaches for the engineers in the new Development Department in the Gaggenau Works, and gave one or two of them sleepless nights. In the autumn of 1933 two Mannheim-type diesel sedans were taken from production and mounted on a test rig. These had six-cylinder, 3.8-liter engines producing a stately 80 bhp at 2800 rpm. The tests showed that the transmission was being hammered by the vibration of the engine. A battle had been lost, but not the war.

Three things helped to solve the problem. The use of the Bosch injection pump meant that the path of the fuel up to the injection nozzle could be checked. An inlet chamber system divided the combustion process into two phases so that some of the impulse stressing of the bearings was removed. Then in November 1934 two cylinders were removed from the existing engine resulting in a 2.6-liter unit producing a modest 45 bhp at 3200 rpm which proved to be relatively quiet, smoke-free, and unusually tough and economical. It consumed an average of 9.5 liters (2.5 gal) of fuel compared with the 13 liters (3.4 gal) of a comparable 2300 cc gasoline engine. Furthermore, diesel fuel at that time cost 17 pfennigs per liter compared with 38 pfennigs for gasoline. A field trial for the new four-cylinder model was first run with 170 models clad in the unprepossessing habit of the type 200/230 landaulet six-seater, used almost exclusively as taxis. The new kid on the block was still rough, but the results were encouraging. The vehicles which had dominated the taxi business up to that point, the Adler Favorit and Adler Standard 6, were soon displaced, especially as their manufacturer Adler had no equivalent car to offer at the time. The second-generation 260 D, which was launched in 1937 in the guise of the type 230 as a six-seater with a wider body, was better behaved. A four-seater sedan and two cabriolets B and D then followed for private owners who wanted, one might say, the automotive equivalent of being seated in a box at the theater. Driving a diesel was a declaration of a certain world view, in addition to being a recognition of commercial utility; this view, however, was shared by only 2,000 customers between 1936 and 1940.

Zu den Mercedes-Exponaten, die sich auf der Berliner Automobil-Ausstellung 1936 der besonderen Aufmerksamkeit des Publikums empfehlen, zählt der 260 D. Seine Botschaft: dass es Daimler-Benz gelungen ist, dem Personenwagen den Dieselmotor zugänglich zu machen. Was noch niemand weiß: dass die Stuttgarter zugleich den Grundstein gelegt haben zu einer souveränen Herrschaft über den Markt im Droschken-, Taxi- und Mietwagengewerbe, die bis auf den heutigen Tag andauert.

Der Weg dorthin ist allerdings holprig gewesen, übersät gleichsam mit Fußangeln und Selbstschüssen. Die hohe Verdichtung am Diesel-Triebwerk bei gleichen Abmessungen der Verbrennungseinheiten wirft zweierlei Probleme auf. Zum einen führen dickere Zylinderwände zu mehr Gewicht. Zum anderen wirken bei gleichen Drehzahlen wie beim Benziner höhere Massenkräfte, was unruhigen Motorlauf zur Folge hat. Dies bereitet den Ingenieuren einer eigens ins Leben gerufenen Entwicklungsabteilung im Werk Gaggenau einiges Kopfzerbrechen und die eine oder andere schlaflose Nacht. Dort stehen seit dem Herbst 1933 zwei aus der Serie abgezweigte Limousinen vom Typ Mannheim dieselnd auf dem Prüfstand, mit Sechszylindern von 3,8 Litern, die bei 2800/min stattliche 80 PS leisten. Wie sich erweist, wird das Fahrwerk von den Schwingungen der Maschine zerrüttet und zermürbt. Man hat eine Schlacht, nicht aber den Krieg verloren.

Drei Dinge helfen: Durch die Verwendung der Bosch-Einspritzpumpe lassen sich die Wege des Kraftstoffs bis zur Einspritzdüse kontrollieren. Ein Vorkammer-System unterteilt den Verbrennungsablauf in zwei Phasen, so dass etwa die stoßweise Belastung der Lager entfällt. Und: Man amputiert im November 1934 zwei Zylinder aus dem bestehenden Triebwerk. Ein 2,6 Liter mit bescheidenen 45 PS bei 3200/min entsteht, der sich als relativ leise, rauchfrei, ungemein zählebig und sparsam erweist: Er verbraucht im Schnitt 9,5 Liter gegenüber den 13 Litern eines vergleichbaren Benzinmotors von 2300 ccm. Überdies kostet Dieselkraftstoff zu jener Zeit 17 Pfennige, Benzin aber 38 Pfennige pro Liter. Der neue Vierzylinder wird zunächst im unscheinbaren Habit des Landaulet Sechssitzers vom Typ 200/230 in 170 Exemplaren einem Feldversuch zugeführt, fast ausschließlich im Taxigewerbe. Noch immer gibt sich der Debütant knorrig und rauh, aber die Ergebnisse ermutigen. Rasch bleiben die bisherigen Platzhirsche im Taxigewerbe, Adler Favorit und Adler Standard 6, auf der Strecke, zumal der Konkurrent Adler im Augenblick nichts Gleichwertiges anzubieten hat. Schon feinere Manieren erzieht man dem 260 D der zweiten Generation an, der 1937 im Gewand des Modells 230 mit einem breiteren Aufbau als Sechssitzer präsentiert wird. Eine viersitzige Limousine und zwei Cabriolets B und D folgen als Offerte an eine private Kundschaft mit Logencharakter. Einen Diesel zu fahren, das verrät jenseits seiner kommerziellen Nutzbarkeit zugleich eine gewisse Weltanschauung, die zwischen 1936 und 1940 nur 2000 Kunden teilen.

L'une des Mercedes exposées au Salon de l'Automobile de Berlin de 1936 qui ont surtout attiré l'attention du public est la 260 D. Elle véhicule un message : que Mercedes a réussi à civiliser le moteur Diesel pour la voiture de tourisme. Mais nul ne sait encore que le constructeur de Stuttgart vient de poser la première pierre d'un monopole incontesté sur le marché des taxis et voitures de location, monopole qui perdure aujourd'hui encore.

Mais pour y parvenir, il aura fallu contourner de nombreux obstacles et pièges. Le taux de compression élevé des moteurs Diesel, pour des chambres de combustion aux cotes identiques, pose un double problème. Premièrement, les parois de cylindres, plus épaisses, sont aussi plus lourdes. Deuxièmement, à un régime identique à celui d'un moteur à essence, les masses en mouvement sont plus importantes et le moteur ne tourne donc pas aussi rond. Ce qui a occasionné bien des migraines et des nuits blanches aux ingénieurs du service de développement institué spécifiquement à cette fin à l'usine de Gaggenau. Depuis l'automne 1933, deux berlines Mannheim prélevées sur la série s'y trouvent au banc d'essais des moteurs Diesel, avec des six-cylindres de 3,8 litres développant la puissance respectable de 80 ch à 2800 tr/min. Comme prévu, le châssis ne résiste pas aux oscillations provenant du moteur et se brise. Si l'on a perdu une bataille, on n'a pas perdu la guerre pour autant.

Trois remèdes sont trouvés : l'utilisation de la pompe à injection Bosch permet de contrôler l'écoulement du carburant jusqu'aux injecteurs. Un système à préchambre subdivise le processus de combustion en deux phases distinctes, si bien que les charges brutales subies par les paliers disparaissent. Et, en novembre 1934, on ampute deux cylindres au moteur existant. On obtient ainsi un 2,6 litres à la puissance modérée de 45 ch à 3200 tr/min, relativement léger, peu polluant, d'une longévité incroyable et sobre : il consomme en moyenne 9,5 litres alors qu'un moteur à essence comparable de 2,3 litres en brûle 13 litres. En outre, à cette époque-là, le gazole coûte plus de deux fois moins cher que le litre d'essence. Le nouveau quatre-cylindres subit tout d'abord des premiers essais grandeur nature dans l'anonymat le plus complet du Landaulet six places de la série 200/230 avec 170 exemplaires, presque tous des taxis. Le moteur est encore rugueux et fruste, mais les résultats sont encourageants. Les anciennes dominatrices de l'industrie du taxi, l'Adler Favorit et l'Adler Standard 6, sont vite réduites à la défensive, d'autant plus qu'Adler n'a rien d'équivalent à opposer. La 260 D de la deuxième génération, présentée en 1937 sous la forme de la 230 à carrosserie plus large, a déjà affiné ses manières. Une berline à quatre places et deux cabriolets B et D la suivent pour briguer les faveurs d'une clientèle privée qui n'hésite pas à faire parler d'elle. Outre les aspects purement économiques, conduire un diesel à cette époque était aussi le symbole d'un certain état d'esprit qu'entre 1936 et 1940 ne partagent que 2000 clients.

MERCEDES-BENZ 260D 1936

The conventional appearance of the 260D masks a technical innovation: it was the first production car with a diesel engine. The use of diesel was particularly favourable in the mid-1930s: a litre of petrol cost 38 pfennigs, while a litre of diesel fuel was less than half that sum. This sturdy auto-igniting vehicle spoils its owners with its economical fuel consumption, roomy interior and high degree of comfort. These features made it ideal for the taxi trade.

Das eher biedere Gewand des 260D verhüllt eine technische Premiere: den ersten serienmäßigen Dieselmotor in einem PKW. Seine Genügsamkeit ist höchst willkommen. Ein Liter Benzin kostet Mitte der Dreißiger 38 Pfennige, ein Liter Dieselöl weniger als die Hälfte. Trotz kernigen Nagelns verwöhnt der stämmige Selbstzünder seine Besitzer, mit günstigem Verbrauch, viel Innenraum und hohem Komfort. Das prädestiniert ihn für das Taxigewerbe.

La robe plutôt banale de la 260D dissimule une première technique : le premier moteur Diesel équipant en série une voiture de tourisme. Sa sobriété est un atout bienvenu. Vers le milieu des années 1930, un litre d'essence coûte 38 pfennigs, alors qu'un litre de gazole n'en coûte que 17. Malgré les claquements, le vigoureux moteur à auto-allumage comble ses propriétaires par une consommation peu élevée, avantage qui s'ajoute à la grande habitabilité et au confort de son intérieur. Un véhicule prédestiné aux compagnies de taxis.

The 260D's
4-cylinder engine was
designed by Fritz Nallinger.
The fuel is delivered to the
combustion chamber via a pre-chamber.
The patent for this process was first issued to
Benz & Co. in March 1909.

Der Vierzylinder des 260D ist eine Konstruktion von Fritz
Nallinger. Der Kraftstoff gelangt über eine Vorkammer in den
Verbrennungsraum. Das Patent zu diesem Verfahren wurde bereits im
März 1909 an Benz & Co. erteilt.

Le quatre-cylindres de la 260D est l'œuvre de Fritz Nallinger. Le carburant
arrive dans la chambre de combustion après avoir transité par une préchambre.
Le brevet pour ce procédé a été décerné à Benz & Co. dès mars 1909.

Introduced in February 1937, the Mercedes-Benz 320 was a comfortable car available in a huge range of bodywork configurations, from a four-door saloon costing 8,950 marks, via a six-seater touring car, a number of cabriolets and a roadster, up to a streamlined saloon available for 14,550 marks.

The most distinctive form of this series, based on a shortened chassis, was a two-seater, like the 540 K in pocket-book format, which was available as a cabrio or a coupé whose solid top could be replaced by a light fabric hood. This was an early precursor of the hardtop. This Proteus in automobile form was termed a convertible coupé or convertible car by Mercedes. With only 5,097 cars sold, the 320 was never a particularly common car, and its performance was hardly electric: its inline six-cylinder engine developed 78 bhp but had to propel a vehicle weighing up to 1,950 kg (4,300 lb). Nonetheless, its running gear consisting of coil springs all round and a rear swing axle was a state-of-the-art design and coped wonderfully well even with difficult conditions.

In the autumn of 1938 its 3208 cc displacement was increased to 3405 cc to compensate for the deteriorating fuel quality. At the same time the Pullman version was fitted with a huge trunk as standard. The power output and the type designation of 320, which indicated a 3.2-liter engine, remained unchanged. The four gears provided hitherto were then supplemented by an overdrive from Zahnradfabrik Friedrichshafen so that the top speed of 126 kph (78 mph) was also the cruising speed. Owners appreciated this on the steadily growing motorway network which measured 2,100 km (1,305 miles) by the end of the war.

Im Februar 1937 eingeführt, ist der Mercedes-Benz 320 ein kommodes Reiseauto in den unterschiedlichsten Karosserie-Konfigurationen, von der viertürigen Limousine für 8950 Mark über einen sechssitzigen Tourenwagen, etliche Cabriolets und einen Roadster bis hin zu einer Limousine in aktueller Stromlinie für 14 550 Mark.

Die aparteste Ausformung der Baureihe, auf verkürztem Fahrgestell: ein Zweisitzer, gleichsam ein 540 K im Taschenbuchformat, als Cabrio zu haben oder als Coupé, dessen Festdach gegen ein leichtes Stoffverdeck ausgewechselt werden kann. Das Hardtop grüßt von ferne, aber die Namensgebung ist aus heutiger Sicht verwirrend – Kombinations-Coupé oder Kombinationswagen nennt man diesen automobilen Proteus bei Mercedes. Insgesamt bleibt der 320 mit 5097 Exemplaren recht schwach verbreitet. Ein Ausbund an Feuer ist er nicht: Sein Reihen-Sechszylinder mit 78 PS muss es mit bis zu 1950 Kilogramm Wagengewicht aufnehmen. Gleichwohl auf dem letzten Stand der Dinge, kommt sein Fahrwerk mit Schraubenfedern ringsum und Pendelachse hinten auch mit schwierigeren Umständen glänzend zurecht.

Im Herbst 1938 wird sein Hubraum von 3208 ccm auf 3405 ccm vergrößert, um mindere Treibstoffqualität aufzufangen. Zugleich erhält die Pullman-Version serienmäßig einen voluminösen Außenkoffer. Unverändert bleiben die Leistung und auch die Typenbezeichnung 320, die ja auf einen 3,2 Liter hinweist. Den vier Fahrstufen bisher kann indessen ein »Ferngang« der Zahnradfabrik Friedrichshafen zugeschaltet werden, so dass die Höchstgeschwindigkeit von 126 Stundenkilometern auch als Dauer-Tempo genutzt werden kann. Auf dem stetig sich erweiternden Autobahnnetz – bei Kriegsende 2100 Kilometer – wissen die Kunden das zu würdigen.

Présentée en février 1937, la Mercedes-Benz 32 est une confortable voiture de voyage dans l configurations de carrosseries les plus diverses, la berline à quatre portes pour 8950 marks à la limousi à carrosserie aérodynamique en vente pour 14 550 mar en passant par la voiture de tourisme à six places, nombreux cabriolets et un roadster.

Modèle le plus élégant de la gamme sur châss raccourci : une biplace, espèce de 540 K miniaturisé disponible en cabriolet ou coupé dont le toit en d peut être échangé contre une légère capote en tissu. C'e l'ancêtre du hard-top, mais son nom nous semble p approprié aujourd'hui. Mercedes baptise ce Prot « coupé convertible » ou « voiture convertible ». Avec total 5097 exemplaires, la 320 ne connaît pas une tr grande diffusion. Elle ne brille pas non plus particulièr ment par ses performances : son six-cylindres en ligne 78 ch doit en effet mouvoir jusqu'à 1950 kg. En revanch ses trains roulants à ressorts hélicoïdaux sur les quat roues et essieu brisé à l'arrière s'en tirent tout à le honneur même dans les circonstances difficiles.

À l'automne 1938, sa cylindrée est majorée de 3208 3405 cm³ pour compenser la moindre qualité de certai carburants. À cette occasion, la version Pullman reç en série un volumineux coffre à bagages extérieur. puissance et la dénomination, 320, qui indiquent l'exi tence d'un moteur de 3,2 litres, restent inchangées. Apr les quatre rapports actuels, on peut en revanche enclench une « surmultipliée » de Zahnradfabrik Friedrichshafe qui a l'avantage de transformer la vitesse maximale 126 km/h en une authentique vitesse de croisière. réseau autoroutier devient de plus en plus dense – compte 2100 km à la fin de la guerre – et les clie l'apprécient à sa juste valeur.

Mercedes-Benz 320 1937

The streamlined type 320 sedan used the same bodywork
and chassis as its predecessor, the type 290. Aerodynamic
lines were all the rage; streamlined 500 K and 540 K coupés
were also available.

Karosserie und Chassis übernimmt die Stromlinienlimousine
Typ 320 von ihrem Vorgänger Typ 290. Windschnittig zu sein
ist der letzte Schrei: Auch 500 K und 540 K gibt es als
Stromlinien-Coupés.

La limousine 320 aux lignes fluides reprend de sa devancière,
la 290, la carrosserie et le châssis. Son aérodynamisme est du
dernier cri. La 500 K et la 540 K sont aussi proposées en coupés
très profilés.

Before Professor Kamm's principle of the aerodynamic efficiency of the smallest possible cross-section became generally accepted, long sweeping curves were regarded as the ideal solution.

Bevor sich die Lehre des Professors Kamm von der Effizienz des kleinsten Abreißquerschnitts durchsetzt, gilt ein lang ausschwingendes Heck als der Weisheit letzter Schluss.

Avant que la doctrine du professeur Kamm ne s'impose (soit l'efficacité du moindre maître-couple), une longue poupe effilée était considérée comme le summum de l'aérodynamique.

The rear-hinged doors opened wide. The pursuit of an aerodynamic shape carried through to the smallest detail, as witness the rear lights and the enclosed rear wheels.

Weit lassen sich die hinten angeschlagenen Türen öffnen. Auf der Suche nach Windschlüpfigkeit hat man auch am Detail gefeilt, wie Rückleuchte und Abdeckung des Hinterrads belegen.

Les portières à charnières postérieures s'ouvrent largement. Dans une quête éperdue d'aérodynamisme, on a aussi affiné des détails comme le feu arrière et le carénage de la roue de secours.

Mercedes-Benz 320 1937

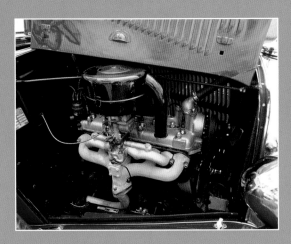

The 320 Cabriolet D with its characteristic wedge-shaped windshield. Its strengths were roominess and comfort. The exhaust side of the straight six-cylinder engine with its cleverly shaped exhaust manifolds. The front and rear doors on each side were both hinged on the central pillar.

Das 320 Cabriolet D mit seiner typischen keilförmig geteilten Windschutzscheibe. Seine Stärken: Geräumigkeit, Bequemlichkeit, Komfort. Die Auslassseite des Reihensechszylinders mit sinnreich geformten Auspuffkrümmern. Je zwei Türen sind an einer zentralen Säule angeschlagen.

La 320 Cabriolet D avec son typique pare-brise cunéiforme en deux parties. Ses atouts : elle est spacieuse et confortable. L'échappement du six-cylindres en ligne avec ses collecteurs d'échappement subtilement dessinés. Les charnières des portières sont ancrées sur un même montant central.

Mercedes-Benz 320 1937

Since 1971 an exhibit in the Mercedes Museum in Untertürkheim has borne witness to the presence of giants in the history of the car, namely a Pullman type 770 limousine from the Emperor of Japan's fleet whose emblem – a chrysanthemum – appears on its red doors. This species, manufactured from 1930 onwards in Stuttgart, would quickly have become extinct if it had not been kept alive by the excited interest of the leadership of Nazi Germany exhibiting its characteristic passion for the gigantic. So it was that a new edition even appeared in 1938. The 117 first-generation models were then followed by a further 88, including one chassis without bodywork.

The main features of the early "Großer Mercedes" were: it was, above all, big with an inline eight-cylinder engine of 7655 cc and 150 bhp without or 200 bhp with supercharger, a 3-speed gearbox with a semi-automatic overdrive, a pressed-steel low-frame chassis with U-sections and cross-bracing, rigid axles and semi-elliptic springs front and rear. The later models were the epitome of contemporary high-tech state-of-the-art manufacture. The alloy engine of unchanged capacity used a combination of battery and magneto ignition with two spark plugs per cylinder and developed 155 bhp without and 230 bhp with the fitted Roots supercharger, power which was transmitted to the rear axle via five synchromeshed gears. The chassis consisted of an oval-tube frame with double wishbones and coil springs at the front and a double-pivot axle with coil springs (from 1939 onwards interlocking double coil springs) at the rear. The ample power which was available even at a low engine speed had to shift a heavy load: the bare chassis weighed 2,100 kg (4,630 lb), while the complete car which was capable of 170 kph (106 mph) tipped the scales at up to 3,600 kg (7,936 lb).

The armor-plated special version of the 770 in which politicians of the time used to keep themselves far from the madding crowd weighed in at 4,800 kg (10,582 lb), as a result of the 40 mm-thick bulletproof glass and 18 mm-thick armor plate steel with which it was shielded. To make up for this, a slight weight saving was achieved on the wings which were constructed of aluminium. The factory recommended that this heavyweight should not be taken above 80 kph (50 mph) as it was possible that the tires might fail above this speed. This special version consumed 40 liters of fuel per 100 km (5.9 mpg) whereas the series version got by with 10 liters less (7.8 mpg). Would-be owners had to splash out 44,000 reichsmarks for the Pullman version, 46,000 reichsmarks for the four-door Cabriolet D, or 47,500 reichsmarks for the six-seater Cabriolet F. This pricing structure inevitably reduced the circle of potential purchasers of the "Großer Mercedes." In the end, interest in the armored version increased – in inverse proportion to the decreasing popularity of its occupants.

Seit 1971 kündet ein Exponat des Mercedes-Museums in Untertürkheim vom Vorkommen von Riesen in der Geschichte des Automobils, eine Pullman-Limousine des Typs 770 aus dem Fuhrpark des japanischen Kaisers, dessen Emblem sie auf den roten Türen trägt: eine Chrysantheme. Diese Spezies, in Stuttgart ab 1930 gefertigt, wäre schon bald ausgestorben, hätte sie nicht das lebhafte Interesse der politischen Führungskaste des nationalsozialistischen Deutschlands mit ihrer arteigenen Gigantomanie am Leben gehalten. So kommt es 1938 sogar zu einer Neuauflage: Auf 117 Exemplare der ersten Generation folgen noch einmal 88 weitere, davon ein unbekleidetes Fahrgestell.

Der frühe »Große Mercedes«: vor allem groß, mit einem Reihen-Achtzylinder von 7655 ccm und 150 PS ohne oder 200 PS mit Kompressor, Dreigang-Getriebe mit halbautomatischem Schnellgang, einem Pressstahl-Niederrahmen mit U-Profilen und Kreuzverstrebungen, Starrachsen und Halbfedern vorn und hinten. Der späte: ein Ausbund von High-Tech auf dem Stande der Zeit. Sein Leichtmetall-Triebwerk mit unverändertem Volumen, befeuert von einer kombinierten Batterie- und Magnetzündung mit zwei Kerzen je Zylinder, leistet 155 PS ohne und 230 PS mit zugeschaltetem Roots-Gebläse, die von fünf synchronisierten Fahrstufen an die Hinterachse vermittelt werden. Das Chassis: ein Ovalrohrrahmen mit Doppel-Querlenkern und Schraubenfedern vorn und einer Doppelgelenkachse mit Schraubenfedern (ab 1939 ineinanderliegenden Doppelschraubenfedern) hinten. Die üppig bemessenen und bereits bei niedrigen Drehzahlen verfügbaren Pferdestärken haben auch ordentlich zu schleppen: 2100 Kilogramm wiegt das bloße Fahrgestell, bis zu 3600 Kilogramm das ganze Auto, das zu 170 Stundenkilometern fähig ist.

In der gepanzerten Sonderausführung, mit der sich führende Politiker der Zeit vor dem Zugriff der Menge schützen, bringt der Typ 770 bis zu 4800 Kilogramm auf die Waage, bedingt durch Panzerglas von 40 Millimetern und Panzerstahl von 18 Millimetern Dicke. An den Kotflügeln hat man dafür leicht eingespart – sie sind aus Aluminium. Das Werk empfiehlt, diesem Schwergewichtler höchstens Tempo 80 zuzumuten, da darüber die Reifen nicht mehr mitspielen könnten. Ihn verlangt es nach 40 Litern Treibstoff je 100 Kilometer, wo sich die Serienausführung mit zehn Litern weniger begnügt. Für die Pullman-Version muss die Klientel 44000 Reichsmark auf den Tisch legen, für das viertürige Cabriolet D 46000, für das sechssitzige Cabriolet F 47500 Reichsmark. Diese Preisgestaltung engt den Kreis der Bezieher des »Großen Mercedes« zwangsläufig ein. Am Ende nimmt das Interesse an der Panzer-Variante zu – umgekehrt proportional zu der abnehmenden Popularität seiner Insassen...

Depuis 1971, une voiture exposée au musée Mercedes d'Untertürkheim témoigne de l'existence de titans dans l'histoire de l'automobile, une limousine Pullman 770 de la flotte de l'empereur japonais, dont elle arbore l'emblème sur ses portes rouges: un chrysanthème. Cette espèce fabriquée à Stuttgart à partir de 1930 se serait rapidement éteinte si le vif intérêt manifesté par la classe politique de l'Allemagne nazie, connue pour sa folie des grandeurs, ne l'avait pas maintenue en vie. Ainsi une nouvelle série en est même produite en 1938: les 117 exemplaires de la première génération sont suivis, un peu plus tard, par 88 autres, dont un châssis nu.

L'ancienne «Grosser Mercedes»: surtout grosse, avec un huit-cylindres en ligne de 7655 cm³ et 150 ch sans compresseur ou 200 ch avec boîte à trois vitesses avec surmultipliée semi-automatique, châssis surbaissé en acier extrudé avec profilés en U et renforts en X, essieux rigides et ressorts semi-elliptiques à l'avant et à l'arrière. La seconde «Grosser Mercedes»: un parangon de haute technologie qui tutoie les sommets de la technique. Son moteur en alliage léger, d'une cylindrée inchangée, alimenté par un allumage mixte à batterie et magnétique à deux bougies par cylindre développant 155 ch, et 230 ch avec le compresseur Roots en action, une cavalerie transmise aux roues arrière par cinq vitesses synchronisées. Le châssis est formé d'un cadre en tubes ovales doubles bras transversaux et ressorts hélicoïdaux à l'avant ainsi qu'essieu à double articulation et ressorts hélicoïdaux (à partir de 1939, avec doubles ressorts hélicoïdaux concentriques) à l'arrière. Pléthoriques et disponibles dès les bas régimes, les chevaux n'ont pas une tâche enviable: le châssis nu pèse déjà 2100 kg et la voiture peut atteindre jusqu'à 3600 kg alors qu'elle est capable de rouler 170 km/h.

Dans la version blindée spéciale, destinée principalement aux hommes politiques de leur temps lors de leurs déplacements, la 770 peut accuser jusqu'à 4800 kg, tribut du verre blindé de 40 mm et de l'acier blindé de 18 mm d'épaisseur. Économie symbolique de poids: les ailes sont en aluminium. L'usine recommande de ne pas faire rouler ce «poids lourd» à plus de 80 km/h, car, au-delà, les pneus risqueraient de ne plus jouer le jeu. Sa voracité est extraordinaire: 40 litres de carburant aux 100 km alors que la version de série se contente de 30 litres. Pour la version Pullman, la clientèle doit débourser 44000 reichsmarks, 46000 pour le cabriolet D à quatre portes et même 47500 pour le cabriolet F six places. Une telle tarification limite évidemment le nombre de clients potentiels de la «Grosser Mercedes». En fin de compte, l'intérêt suscité par la version blindée augmente – de façon inversement proportionnelle à la popularité en régression de ses passagers.

GROSSER MERCEDES 770 1938

...he many people who could not afford one nicknamed ...he Großer Mercedes "the express train of the roads." ...ardly surprising: no expense was spared in the ...manufacture of this prestige automobile.

Dem »Großen Mercedes« legen die vielen, die ihn sich nicht leisten können, den Spitznamen »D-Zug der Landstraße« bei. Kein Wunder: Er ist ein Prestige-automobil, das ohne Rücksicht auf Kosten gebaut wird.

Tous ceux qui ne pouvaient se l'offrir ont affublé la « Grosser Mercedes » du surnom de « train express de la route ». Ce n'est pas étonnant : c'est une voiture de prestige construite sans égard envers les coûts.

Open touring cars like this formed part of the Reich Chancellery's fleet. Somewhat illogically, the passengers of this 4.5-ton vehicle were protected by armor-plating – but only up to shoulder height. This rolling fortress was powered by an inline eight-cylinder engine with a fitted Roots supercharger and a colossal 7600 cc, generating 230 bhp a 3200 rpm.

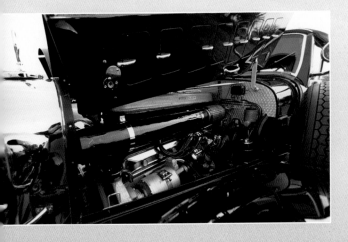

Offene Tourenwagen wie dieser zählen zum Fuhrpark der Reichskanzlei. Ein Widersinn ist, dass die Panzerung des 4,5-Tonners seine Insassen bestenfalls bis auf Schulterhöhe vor Unheil behütet. Für die Fortbewegung der rollenden Festung zuständig ist ein Achtzylinder-Reihenmotor mit zuschaltbarem Roots-Gebläse und dem kolossalen Hubraum von 7600 ccm. Er leistet 230 PS bei 3200/min.

Des voitures de tourisme décapotables comme celle-ci figuraient dans la flotte de la chancellerie du Reich. Erreur de conception? Le blindage de cette voiture de 4,5 tonnes protège au maximum ses passagers jusqu'à hauteur des épaules! Un huit-cylindres en ligne à turbocompresseur Roots débrayable avec la cylindrée colossale de 7600 cm³ assure la propulsion de cette citadelle roulante. Il développe 230 ch à 3200 tr/min.

Its appearance at the Berlin Automobile Exhibition seemed simultaneously to signal an investment in a great future, and a declaration of war. In the sophisticated mid-range market, the new Mercedes 230 with its 2.3-liter, straight six-cylinder engine generating 55 bhp was challenging tried and tested competition such as the Adler 2.5 liter and the Opel Kapitän. But it was not to be: against the ominous backdrop of the Second World War the latest creation from Stuttgart withered like a spring flower, and only 4,210 were ever produced. However, the Mercedes 230 sedan and its cabriolet A, B, and D variants did perform one service. Its design was so timeless and handsome, and its chassis with its cruciform oval tubular frame, as with the 170 v, was so modern, that 10 years later it formed their basis for the design of the post-war models 170 s and 220.

Seine Vorstellung auf der Berliner Automobil-Ausstellung wirkt wie eine Anzahlung auf eine schöne Zukunft und ist zugleich eine Kampfansage: In der gehobenen Mittelklasse stößt der neue Mercedes 230 mit seinem Sechszylinder-Reihenmotor von 2,3 Litern und 55 PS auf gestandene Konkurrenten wie den Adler 2,5 Liter und den Opel Kapitän. Aber es soll nicht sein: Vor dem Hintergrund des Zweiten Weltkriegs verkümmert die jüngste Kreation aus Stuttgart in einer Auflage von lediglich 4210 Exemplaren zum Mauerblümchen. Ein Verdienst indessen bleibt dem Mercedes 230 in den Varianten Limousine und Cabriolet A, B und D unbenommen: So schön und zeitlos sind seine Formen, so modern ist sein Fahrgestell mit einem x-förmigen Ovalrohrrahmen wie beim 170 v, dass man sich noch zehn Jahre später bei der Konzeption der Nachkriegsmodelle 170 s und 220 an ihnen orientiert.

Sa présentation au Salon de l'Automobile de Berli[n] fait figure d'acompte sur un futur tout en ros[e] mais est aussi, simultanément, une déclaratio[n] de guerre : dans le segment intermédiaire supérieur, [la] nouvelle Mercedes 230 doit faire face, avec son six[-] cylindres en ligne de 2,3 litres et 55 ch à une concurren[ce] aussi relevée que l'Adler 2,5 litres et l'Opel Kapitän. Ma[is] il n'en sera rien : dans l'ombre de la Seconde Guerr[e] mondiale, imminente, la toute dernière création de Stutt[-] gart connaîtra un destin peu enviable. Elle ne sera pro[-] duite qu'à 4210 exemplaires. Elle a en revanche des mérite[s] qu'on ne peut lui contester : en versions berline et cabrio[-] let A, B et D, ses formes sont si belles et si intemporelle[s,] son châssis est si moderne avec son cadre en tubes oval[es] en forme de x, comme pour la 170 v, que, dix ans plu[s] tard, pour la conception des modèles d'après-guerre, [la] 170 s et la 220, on s'en inspirera encore.

Mercedes-Benz 230   1938

The type 230 Cabriolet D began its long life in 1939 as a service vehicle for the NSFK (Nationalsozialistisches Flieger-Korps or National Socialist Flying Corps) at the Kassel garrison. After a long exile in Czechoslovakia, it finally returned to Germany in 1986.

Das abgebildete Cabriolet D vom Typ 230 beginnt sein langes Leben 1939 wie andere auch als Dienstfahrzeug beim NSFK (für Nationalsozialistisches Flieger-Korps) mit Garnison Kassel und kehrt 1986 nach langem Exil in der Tschechoslowakei nach Deutschland zurück.

Le Cabriolet D 230 représenté ici entame sa longue carrière en 1939 comme d'autres également en tant que voiture de fonction auprès du NSFK (Nationalsozialistisches Flieger-Korps ou corps d'aviateurs national socialiste) de la garnison de Kassel et reviendra en Allemagne en 1986 après un long exil dans la Tchécoslovaquie.

A glimpse under the bonnet and at the interior revealing the 2.3-liter, six-cylinder engine surrounded by auxiliary units, and the cockpit with its clock and a combined instrument dial including the speedometer and gauges for the water temperature, oil pressure, and fuel.

Einblicke unter die Haube und ins Innere:
Der 2,3-Liter Sechszylinder im Kreise
seiner Hilfsaggregate und das Cockpit
mit mechanischer Zeituhr, Kombi-
Instrument für Wassertemperatur,
Öldruck, Benzin und Tachometer.

Vue sous le capot et à l'intérieur:
le six-cylindres de 2,3 litres
au centre de ses organes
secondaires; le tableau de
bord avec une horloge,
un panneau combinant
température d'eau,
pression d'huile,
niveau d'essence,
et le tachymètre.

Mercedes-Benz 230 1938

With its rough, classless solidity, it was just made for difficult times. So it was that the Mercedes-Benz W136, better known by its model name, the 170V, ensured continuity for the star marque from the last years of peace, through the Second World War and the turmoil of reconstruction, to the burgeoning post-war economic miracle. And, with 169,805 units sold, it carried Daimler-Benz AG from catastrophe, with its nadir in corporate destruction, to resurrection at the beginning of the Fifties, as the bestseller up to that time in the company's history.

The new beginning started out modestly; in 1946 various small vans were produced using very crude bodies made by Hägele, a Stuttgart-based coachbuilder, simply because there was always something needing transport at that time. A four-door saloon built all of steel appeared in July 1947. In manufacturing this, the Mercedes engineers of the immediate post-war period were fortunate in that the large deep-drawing press in Sindelfingen had survived the war almost unscathed. At the Hanover Technical Export Fair in May 1949 the 170 D was introduced alongside the 170V. Like the 170V, this had a 1697 cc engine developing 38 bhp, but it used diesel fuel which was available everywhere without rationing. The characteristic feature of the 170 D was its robust, knocking engine sound. In May 1950 the twins were given a thorough makeover. This involved increasing the engine size (1767 cc) and the power (45 bhp for the gasoline model, 40 bhp for the diesel), modifications to the running gear in the form of telescopic shock absorbers, a broader rear track and better brakes, and greater comfort provided by wider seats and more elbow-room. A further facelift in May 1952 also brought about distinct changes: a further-increased rear track, one-piece bumpers, a larger windshield, and a few horizontally inset ventilation slits in the hood which had previously sported a number of vertically inclined vents.

7,358 chassis were exported throughout the world, for example to Argentina, where they were shipped in "ckd" (completely knocked down) form. The Bochum-based Daimler-Benz agent and coachbuilder Lueg fitted various special bodies to the chassis. In 1951 and 1952 the German Federal Border Guard took delivery of 530 units of the semi-military OTP version (Open-top Police Touring Car), a 170 D with four doors, a lightweight fold-down top, top-hung windows at the side, and a windshield that could pivot forwards. The collectible status later enjoyed by this model – many people think it is a relic from Hitler's army fleet – is not always justified.

In seiner knorrig-klassenlosen Solidität ist er wie geschaffen für schwierige Zeiten. Also sorgt der Mercedes-Benz W136, besser bekannt unter seinem Modellnamen, 170V, für Kontinuität im Zeichen des Sterns, von den letzten Friedensjahren über den Zweiten Weltkrieg und die Wirren des Wiederaufbaus bis hinein in das werdende Wirtschaftswunder. Und er trägt die Daimler-Benz AG vom Fall mit dem Tiefpunkt der Zerstörung des Konzerns in den Aufstieg Anfang der Fünfziger, als vorläufiger Bestseller in der Firmengeschichte mit 169 805 Exemplaren.

Der Neubeginn lässt sich indessen bescheiden an: 1946 entstehen mit reichlich kruden Aufbauten des Stuttgarter Karosseriefabrikanten Hägele diverse Kleinlaster, schon weil es in jenen Jahren immer irgend etwas zu transportieren gibt. Eine viertürige Limousine in Ganzstahlbauweise stellt sich im Juli 1947 ein, wobei den Mercedes-Männern der ersten Stunde zugute kommt, dass die große Tiefziehpresse in Sindelfingen den Krieg fast unversehrt überstanden hat. Auf der Technischen Exportmesse Hannover im Mai 1949 rollt dem 170V der 170 D zur Seite, wie dieser 38 PS stark bei einem Motorvolumen von 1697 ccm, aber mit Dieselkraftstoff gespeist, der überall uneingeschränkt gezapft werden kann. Der 170 D ist vor allem erkennbar durch kerniges Nageln. Im Mai 1950 lässt man den Zwillingen eine energische Modellpflege angedeihen. Sie umspannt mehr Hubraum (1767 ccm) und mehr Leistung (45 PS für den Benziner, 40 PS für den Diesel), Retuschen am Fahrwerk wie Teleskop-Stoßdämpfer, eine erweiterte hintere Spur und bessere Bremsen sowie ein Plus an Komfort durch breitere Sitze und zusätzliche Freiheit für den Ellenbogen. Auch ein weiteres Facelifting im Mai 1952 hinterlässt deutliche Veränderungen: noch mehr Spurweite hinten, einteilige Stoßstangen, eine größere Frontscheibe sowie wenige waagerecht eingeschnittene Lüftungsschlitze in der Motorhaube, die bislang schräg senkrecht vielfach aufgebrochen war.

7358 Fahrgestelle werden zum Teil in alle Welt exportiert, zum Beispiel nach Argentinien, wohin sie als Teilesätze (»ckd«, für completely knocked down) reisen. Zahlreiche Sonderaufbauten stülpt dem Chassis der Bochumer Daimler-Benz-Agent und Karosseriebauer Lueg über. 1951 und 1952 erhält der Bundesgrenzschutz 530 Einheiten der halbmilitärischen Version OTP (für Offener Polizei-Tourenwagen), ein 170 D mit vier Türen, einem leichten Klappverdeck, seitlichen Steckfenstern und einer Frontscheibe, die sich nach vorn umlegen lässt. Der Sammlerwert, der dieser Spezies später beigemessen wird, ist nicht immer gerechtfertigt: Viele halten sie für Relikte aus dem Fuhrpark der Wehrmacht.

Par ses lignes banales qui échappent à toute classification sociale, elle est comme prédestinée aux temps difficiles. La Mercedes-Benz W136, mieux connue sous son nom de série 170V, garantit donc la continuité sous l'emblème de l'étoile, des dernières années de paix en passant par la Seconde Guerre mondiale et les aléas de la reconstruction jusqu'aux débuts du miracle économique. Et elle porte Daimler-Benz AG depuis sa chute et la destruction du groupe jusqu'à son essor du début des années 1950, en tant que best-seller provisoire dans l'histoire de la firme avec 169 805 exemplaires.

Ces nouveaux débuts s'effectuent toutefois dans la plus grande modestie : en 1946 avec les carrosseries, dénuées de tout charme, du carrossier de Stuttgart, Hägele, Daimler-Benz produit divers petits camions car, au cours de ces années, le transport est une activité en plein essor. Une berline à quatre portes avec carrosserie tout acier n'apparaît qu'en juillet 1947. Les ouvriers de la première heure de chez Mercedes ont profité de ce que la grosse presse emboutisseuse de Sindelfingen a survécu à la guerre sans dommages notables. Lors du Salon des exportations techniques de Hanovre, en mai 1949, la 170V est rejointe par la 170 D, qui possède comme celle-ci un moteur de 38 ch et 1697 cm³, mais diesel, le gazole étant désormais un carburant que l'on peut se procurer sans restriction. La 170 D se reconnaît notamment à ses claquements marqués. En mai 1950, les deux jumelles bénéficient d'une modernisation poussée. Leur cylindrée augmente (1767 cm³) et leur puissance aussi (45 ch pour le moteur à essence, 40 ch pour le diesel), leur châssis est retouché avec des amortisseurs télescopiques, des voies plus larges à l'arrière et de meilleurs freins tandis que le confort s'améliore grâce à des sièges plus larges et à une plus grande liberté de mouvement à hauteur des coudes. Un nouveau lifting, en mai 1952, laisse lui aussi des traces sensibles : la voie arrière est encore élargie, les pare-chocs sont d'une pièce, le pare-brise de plus grandes dimensions et un petit nombre de fentes d'aération horizontales ornent le capot moteur à la place des multiples fentes diagonales de l'ancien modèle.

Sur 7358 châssis, une partie a été exportée dans le monde entier, par exemple en Argentine où ils s'en vont en pièces détachées. Lueg, concessionnaire Daimler-Benz et carrossier de Bochum, habille les châssis de nombreuses carrosseries spéciales. En 1951 et 1952, la Protection fédérale des frontières prend possession de 530 exemplaires de la version semi-militaire OTP (pour voiture de tourisme de police décapotée). Il s'agit d'une 170 D à quatre portes avec capote légère, fenêtres latérales à insérer et pare-brise rabattable vers l'avant. La valeur que les collectionneurs attacheront plus tard à cette espèce n'est pas toujours justifiée : beaucoup les considèrent comme des survivantes du parc automobile de la Wehrmacht.

MERCEDES-BENZ 170V 1946

The 170V's simple lines and, after a few teething troubles were sorted out, its virtual indestructibility ensured that one of the better products of pre-war Germany remained available for the first seven years after the war.

Eine schlichte Erscheinung und nach den Anlaufschwierigkeiten der Anfangsphase schier unzerstörbar, rettet der 170V ein gutes Stück Vorkriegsdeutschland in die ersten sieben Nachkriegsjahre hinüber.

D'une grande sobriété extérieure et, après correction de ses défauts de jeunesse, absolument indestructible, la 170V réincarne l'Allemagne de l'avant-guerre au cours des sept premières années de l'après-guerre.

The small Mercedes was also a symbol of the resurrection of Stuttgart's proud star. To own one of these cars during the turmoil of that time was a sure sign that you had arrived.

Der kleine Mercedes kündet zugleich von der Wiederauferstehung des stolzen Sterns von Stuttgart. Wer ihn in den Irrungen und Wirrungen jener Zeit besitzt, gilt durchaus als arriviert.

La petite Mercedes matérialise aussi la renaissance de la fière étoile de Stuttgart. Quiconque en possède une durant cette période troublée peut dire qu'il a réussi.

Mercedes-Benz 170V 1946

Even minor details like the windshield wipers, which worked from above, betray the pre-war provenance of the 170V. The trunk lid hinges together with the spare-wheel cover were at the bottom. Modest improvements in 1950 saw the seats increased in size, and the interior widened. The various switches, levers, handles, and other controls had a comfortingly solid feel to them.

Auch Kleinigkeiten wie die Scheibenwischer, die ihre Arbeit von oben verrichten, verraten die Vorkriegs-Provenienz des 170V. Die Scharniere des Kofferraumdeckels mit der Verkleidung des Reserverads sind unten angesiedelt. Im Zuge sanfter Modellpflege werden 1950 Sitze und Innenbreite vergrößert. Schalter, Hebel, Kurbeln und andere Bedienungselemente sind von knackiger Solidität.

De petits détails comme les essuie-glace articulés en haut du pare-brise trahissent que la 170V remonte à l'avant-guerre. Les charnières du couvercle de malle comportant le carénage de la roue de secours sont placées en bas. Au cours d'une remise au goût du jour modérée, en 1950, sièges et espace intérieur s'agrandissent. Les manettes, leviers et autres éléments de commande dégagent une impression de grande solidité.

Mercedes-Benz 170V 1946

It did not exactly flaunt its charms, but nonetheless it appealed to those who were enjoying the first blossoming of renewed affluence in Germany and were keen to show off what they had achieved. In its style and design the 170 s, which was launched at the Hanover Technical Export Fair in May 1949, was derived from the pre-war model 230, though two prestigious cylinders had been ditched en route. In engineering terms it was based on the 170 v whose power unit delivered 52 bhp in the smoother bodywork of the new car. An important innovation in the running gear revealed the hand of the gifted engineer Rudolf Uhlenhaut: forged double wishbones at the front with coil springs and an anti-roll bar.

The 170 s initiated the post-war tradition of the slightly more refined Mercedes whose special status was already hinted at in the simple suffix "s." Its introductory price (which was later to fall) was 9850 marks. That was already quite a sum. However, Joe Average did not have a hope of affording the two cabriolets – the B (four-seater, 12,850 marks) and A (a well-designed two-seater, 15,800 marks), 830 of which were sold alongside the sedan between 1949 and November 1951. In January 1952 the original version was replaced by the revamped 170 sb which can be recognized by its larger rear screen, internal hinges on the trunk lid, steering-column-mounted gear lever, hypoid rear axle, camshaft drive via a duplex chain, wider track, and more effective heating. It was in production until August 1953, matching the lifespan of the diesel model, which was slightly damaging to the supposed exclusivity of the series. Even more damaging was the despicable attempt to play the modular card in 1953 when the Mercedes strategists planned to help their ageing star stand out against the type 180 by means of lower prices. The s and ds were simply transplanted onto the 170 v and d chassis, giving birth to the 170 s-v and s-d hybrids. Most buyers opted for the diesel version whose 11,800 sales between 1953 and 1955 decisively outstripped the 3,002 gasoline-engined units. Connoisseurs recognize the two cut-down models by the lack of chrome trim strips on the air vents in the hood, a grab handle instead of a twist handle on the trunk lid, and the fact that the bumpers were no longer reinforced with overriders. And that put paid to the refined image of the 170 s, especially as all manner of third-party bodies were foisted upon it to allow it to be used for more mundane purposes than the transport of bosses, professors, and ministers.

Er versteckt seinen noblen Charme gewissermaßen in der hohlen Hand und kommt dennoch dem Wunsch des frühen bundesrepublikanischen Wohlstandsbürgers entgegen, Errungenes auch zur Schau zu stellen. Im Stil und seiner Konzeption nach leitet sich der 170 s, präsentiert auf der Technischen Exportmesse zu Hannover im Mai 1949, vom Vorkriegsmodell 230 her, nur dass zwei prestigeträchtige Zylinder auf der Strecke geblieben sind. Technisch fußt er auf dem 170 v, dessen Triebwerk sich im glatteren Gewande des Neuen zu 52 PS aufschwingt. Eine wichtige Innovation im Bereich des Fahrwerks verrät die Hand des begnadeten Ingenieurs Rudolf Uhlenhaut: geschmiedete Doppel-Querlenker vorn mit Schraubenfedern und einem Stabilisator.

Der 170 s begründet die Tradition der noch etwas feineren Mercedes nach dem Kriege, deren besonderer Status sich bereits an dem bloßen Buchstaben »s« kristallisiert. Sein Einstandspreis, der später nach unten tendiert: 9850 Mark. Das ist schon eine ganze Menge. Aber vollends unerreichbar für Otto Normalverbraucher sind die beiden Cabriolets B (mit vier Sitzen, 12 850 Mark) und A (ein wohlgeformter Zweisitzer, 15 800 Mark), welche die Limousine zwischen 1949 und dem November 1951 in einer Verbreitung von zusammen 830 Exemplaren flankieren. Im Januar 1952 wird die ursprüngliche Version abgelöst vom vielfältig retuschierten 170 sb, erkennbar an seiner größeren Heckscheibe, nach innen verlegten Scharnieren des Kofferraumdeckels, Lenkradschaltung, hypoidverzahnter Hinterachse, Nockenwellenantrieb durch Duplex-Rollenkette, breiterer Spur und wirksamerer Heizung. Er wird bis zum August 1953 gebaut, zeitgleich mit der Diesel-Variante, die der bisherigen Exklusivität der Baureihe ein wenig zum Schaden gereicht. Noch mehr tut dies ein schnöder Griff in die Baukästen, als die Mercedes-Strategen 1953 den alternden Star durch Minderpreise gegen den Typ 180 abheben wollen: s und DS werden kurzerhand auf die Fahrgestelle von 170 v und D gesetzt, so dass die Hybriden 170 s-v und s-D entstehen. Die Mehrzahl der Klientel entscheidet sich für den Diesel, der mit 11 800 Einheiten zwischen 1953 und 1955 gegenüber den 3002 Benzinern entschieden die Oberhand hat. Kundige erkennen die beiden Mager-Modelle daran, dass die Chromleisten an den Lüftungsschlitzen der Motorhaube fehlen, ein Haltebügel den Drehgriff am Kofferraumdeckel ablöst und die Stoßstangen nicht mehr mit Hörnern bewehrt sind. Um das feine Image des 170 s ist es damit endgültig geschehen, zumal er auch mit zahlreichen extern gefertigten Sonderaufbauten profaneren Verwendungen zugeführt wird als dem Transport von Bossen, Professoren und Ministern.

Elle incarne à sa manière le charme discret de la bourgeoisie et répond au désir du citoyen prospère d'Allemagne fédérale d'afficher sa réussite. Par son style et sa conception, la 170 s présentée lors du Salon des exportations techniques de Hanovre en mai 1949 dérive de la 230 d'avant-guerre. À cette différence près que deux cylindres, signe de prestige, lui ont été amputés. Sur le plan mécanique, elle est extrapolée de la 170 v, dont le moteur sous la carrosserie du nouveau modèle aux lignes plus lisses développe maintenant 52 ch. Une innovation importante dans le domaine des trains roulants porte la signature du talentueux ingénieur Rudolf Uhlenhaut : les doubles bras transversaux forgés à l'avant avec ressorts hélicoïdaux et barre antiroulis.

La 170 s instaure la tradition des Mercedes encore un peu plus luxueuses après la guerre, dont le statut particulier est déjà mis en exergue avec la simple lettre « s ». Son prix d'achat, qui sera plus tard revu à la baisse, est de 9850 marks, montant qui représente déjà une certaine somme pour l'époque. Mais les deux cabriolets, le B (quatre places, 12 850 marks) et le A (une biplace élégante, 15 800 marks) qui viennent épauler la berline de 1949 à novembre 1951, en étant diffusés à eux deux à 830 exemplaires, sont financièrement tout à fait hors de portée de l'Allemand moyen. En janvier 1952, la version originelle est remplacée par la 170 sb retouchée dans de nombreux domaines et reconnaissable à sa lunette arrière de plus grandes dimensions, aux charnières du coffre à bagages désormais placées à l'intérieur de la malle, au levier de changement de vitesses au volant, avec l'essieu arrière à engrenages hypoïdes, l'entraînement de l'arbre à cames par chaîne à rouleau double, les voies plus larges et un chauffage plus efficace. Elle sera construite jusqu'en août 1953, parallèlement à la version diesel qui – il faut bien l'avouer – entache un peu l'exclusivité qu'avait la gamme auparavant. En cette même année, les stratèges de Mercedes, souhaitant relooker le modèle, revoient à la baisse les prix de la star vieillissante qui doit faire face à la concurrence de la nouvelle 180 : les s et DS sont en un tour de main montées sur des châssis de 170 v et D, donnant naissance aux 170 s-v et s-D.

La majorité des acheteurs opte pour la diesel qui, avec 11 800 exemplaires vendus de 1953 à 1955, bat à plates coutures la version à essence vendue seulement 3002 fois. Les initiés reconnaissent les deux modèles économiques à l'absence de joncs chromés le long des ouïes d'aération du capot moteur, à l'étrier qui remplace la poignée tournante sur le couvercle de malle et au pare-chocs désormais sans cornes. L'image raffinée de la 170 s a donc totalement disparu, surtout à partir du moment où de nombreuses carrosseries spéciales fabriquées à l'extérieur lui donnent des applications beaucoup moins « nobles » que le transport de managers de l'économie, de professeurs et de ministres.

MERCEDES-BENZ 170S 1949

The 170S was available in Cabriolet A or B form from its launch year in 1949. It was time to live again, particularly when it only took a few movements to let in the summer sun.

Bereits in seinem Geburtsjahr 1949 ist der 170S als Cabriolet A oder B erhältlich. Die Lebensgeister erwachen wieder, vor allem, wenn man Sommer und Sonne mit ein paar Handgriffen Einlass verschaffen kann.

Dès sa naissance, en 1949, la 170S est disponible en Cabriolet A ou B. On commence à reprendre goût à la vie, notamment quand quelques gestes suffisent pour faire entrer à flots l'été et le soleil.

At a price of 15,800 marks (compared with 9,450 marks for the sedan), the 1950 Cabriolet A would remain a pipe dream for the man in the street. You can see why. The whitewall tires were a popular luxury accessory.

Mit einem Preis von 15 800 Mark (Limousine: 9450 Mark) ist das Cabriolet A anno 1950 ein Auto, an dem der Normalverbraucher allenfalls seine Wünsche und Träume festmachen kann. Man sieht warum. Ein beliebtes Luxus-Accessoire: die Weißwandreifen.

Avec un prix de 15 800 marks (9450 marks pour la berline), le Cabriolet A de 1950 est une voiture dont l'Allemand moyen ne peut, dans le meilleur des cas, que rêver. On voit pourquoi. Un accessoire de luxe apprécié à cette époque: les pneus à flancs blancs.

Mercedes-Benz 170S 1949

Before unit-body construction brought about uniformity in car body design, the sum of a vehicle's parts sometimes, as here, contributed to the beauty of the whole. An abundance of chrome trim was regarded as a sure sign of exalted taste and ambition. To some extent it was a reflection of the owner himself. It was only later realized that the engine too could be an object of beauty.

Mercedes-Benz 170S 1949

Bevor sich mit der Pontonkarosserie Monotonie unter den Autoformen breitmacht, fügt sich manchmal wie hier die Summe der Details zum schönen Ganzen. Chromapplikationen in Hülle und Fülle gelten als Indiz für einen gehobenen Geschmack und einen gehobenen Anspruch. In ihnen bespiegelt der Besitzer gewissermaßen sich selbst. Dass auch die Maschine eine Augenweide sein kann, entdeckt man indes erst später.

Avant que la monotonie ne s'instaure dans le style automobile avec la carrosserie ponton, la somme des détails concourt parfois, comme ici, à donner un bel ensemble. Une débauche de chromes est considérée comme un indice de bon goût et de standing. Des chromes qui reflètent en quelque sorte l'ambition du propriétaire lui-même. On ne s'apercevra par contre que plus tard que le moteur, lui aussi, mérite d'être admiré.

Mercedes-Benz 170S 1949

Six-cylinder engines have always been a defining feature of the company's history. The first record of such an engine at Daimler-Motoren-Gesellschaft came in 1906, and at Benz & Cie. in 1914. It was the six-cylinder engine in the Mercedes 220 which knocked the 170 s off its perch at the pinnacle of the company hierarchy when it was launched at the Frankfurt International Motor Show in April 1951.

It represented the latest in engine technology, and the racing input was unmistakable. It was an oversquare engine with valves operated by an overhead camshaft, with an oil cooler in the form of a cooling-water heat exchanger, thermostatic heating of the induction manifold and an "octane number compensator." Although the compression of 6.5 : 1 had deliberately been kept low because of the poor fuel quality, it was possible to adjust the ignition timing with a small hand lever. The 4-speed gearbox with its fashionable steering-column gearshift featured synchromesh on all gears. Its 80 bhp pushed the 220 to an impressive top speed of 140 kph (87 mph), exactly the same as its contemporary, the Porsche 356 A 1100, which was regarded as extremely fast, and 18 kph (11 mph) quicker than the 170 s. The 220 had inherited its running gear and internal dimensions from the latter model, and the main difference between it and this older model was a stylistic one: the headlights were inset in the front of the fenders, the result of very painstaking and patient work.

Following the example of the 170 s, three body types were initially available, the sedan and the two cabriolets B and A, the respective prices of which – 15,160 marks and 18,860 marks – had already secured them a niche in the elevated ranks of dream cars.

Pressure from prominent customers, as attested by a circular from the senior sales management, resulted in a coupé being added from May 1954 onwards which set its new owners back 22,000 marks if ordered with a sliding steel sunroof. With only 85 units sold, it remained a rarity, and its 85 bhp engine meant that, like the two contemporary cabriolets and the slightly later 220a version, it was not exactly overpowered. In November 1953 the cabriolet A was given a curved windshield which matched its gentle body curves. Despite the series' evident nobility, it could also be used for quite mundane tasks, as evidenced by the 41 open-top touring cars for the police manufactured between August 1952 and May 1953. These were not unlike the cabriolet B, though they had four doors and a top without storm stays. No wonder they were much in demand for official business.

Sechszylinder prägen die Historie des Hauses seit jeher. Für 1906 notiert der Chronist ein erstes Vorkommen bei der Daimler-Motoren-Gesellschaft, für 1914 bei der Benz & Cie. AG. Der Sechszylinder im Mercedes 220 ist es, der auf der ersten Internationalen Automobilausstellung in Frankfurt im April 1951 den 170 s vom Sockel seiner Spitzenstellung in der Firmen-Hierarchie kippt.

Es ist ein modernes Triebwerk, und unverkennbar ist die Rückkoppelung vom Rennsport: ein Kurzhuber, dessen Ventile von einer obenliegenden Nockenwelle zur Arbeit angehalten werden, mit einem Ölkühler in Gestalt eines Kühlwasser-Wärmeaustauschers, thermostatischer Beheizung des Ansaugrohrs sowie einem »Oktanzahlkompensator«: Obwohl die Verdichtung mit 6,5 : 1 bewusst niedrig gehalten wurde wegen der schlechten Treibstoffqualität, lässt sich der Zündzeitpunkt noch einmal mit einem kleinen Handknebel verstellen. Das Vierganggetriebe mit der modischen Lenkradschaltung ist voll synchronisiert. Seine 80 PS befähigen den 220 zu stattlichen 140 Stundenkilometern, genausoviel wie der als ausgesprochen flink geltende Zeitgenosse Porsche 356 A 1100 und 18 Stundenkilometer schneller als der 170 s. Von diesem hat der 220 Fahrwerk und Innenmaße übernommen und hebt sich im wesentlichen durch einen stilistischen Gag von dem älteren Modell ab: Die Scheinwerfer sind als Intarsien in die Spitzen der Kotflügel eingelassen, Ergebnis geduldiger Tüftelarbeit.

Nach dem Muster des 170 s werden zunächst drei Karosserievarianten angeboten: die Limousine und die beiden Cabriolets B und A, die durch ihren Preis von 15 160 Mark beziehungsweise 18 860 Mark bereits in die entlegene Sphäre der Traumwagen entrückt werden.

Auf Drängen prominenter Kunden, wie ein Rundschreiben der Verkaufsleitung ausweist, sattelt man ab Mai 1954 mit einem Coupé drauf, dessen Anschaffung mit 22 000 Mark zu Buche schlägt, wenn man ein Stahlschiebedach ordert. Es bleibt in 85 Exemplaren eine Rarität, mit 85 PS motorisch mild aufgerüstet wie auch die beiden Cabriolets um die gleiche Zeit und wenig später die Version 220a. Im November 1953 erhält das Cabriolet A eine gewölbte Frontscheibe, die mit seiner sanften Rundlichkeit harmoniert. Trotz der evidenten Noblesse der Baureihe kann sie auch durchaus profanen Alltagstätigkeiten zugeführt werden wie jene 41 offenen Tourenwagen für die Polizei, die zwischen dem August 1952 und dem Mai 1953 produziert werden, nicht unähnlich dem Cabriolet B, aber mit vier Türen und einem Verdeck ohne Sturmstangen. Kein Wunder, dass sie als Dienstwagen begehrt sind.

Les six-cylindres ont de tout temps ponctué la généalogie de la maison. Le chroniqueur relate leur première apparition à la Daimler-Motoren-Gesellschaft en 1906 et en 1914 pour la Benz & Cie. AG. C'est le six-cylindres de la Mercedes 220 qui, au premier Salon international de l'Automobile organisé à Francfort en avril 1951, fait perdre à la 170 s son statut de modèle haut de gamme dans la hiérarchie de la firme.

C'est un moteur moderne où l'on retrouve incontestablement les enseignements tirés de la compétition : un moteur à course courte dont les soupapes sont actionnées par un arbre à cames en tête, avec un radiateur d'huile sous la forme d'un échangeur thermique pour l'eau de refroidissement, un chauffage à thermostat du collecteur d'aspiration ainsi qu'un « compensateur d'octane » : bien qu'avec 6,5 : 1 le taux de compression ait été volontairement maintenu à un bas niveau à cause de la mauvaise qualité des carburants, il est encore possible de régler l'allumage à l'aide d'un petit levier manuel. La boîte à quatre vitesses avec la commande au volant alors à la mode est complètement synchronisée. Ses 80 ch permettent à la 220 d'atteindre la vitesse respectable de 140 km/h, soit autant que la Porsche 356 A 1100, considérée comme l'une de ses contemporaines particulièrement rapides, et 18 km/h de plus que la 170 s. De celle-ci, la 220 a d'ailleurs repris les trains roulants et les cotes intérieures et elle se distingue du modèle le plus ancien essentiellement par un gag esthétique : les phares sont intégrés comme une marqueterie dans la pointe des ailes, résultat d'un patient travail de réflexion.

À l'instar de la 170 s, Mercedes propose tout d'abord trois variantes de carrosserie : la berline et les deux cabriolets B et A, que le prix respectif de 15 160 et 18 860 marks situe déjà dans les sphères inaccessibles des voitures de rêve.

À la demande de clients célèbres, comme le fait savoir une circulaire émise par la direction des ventes, on y ajoute en mai 1954 un coupé dont le prix d'achat s'élève à 22 000 marks si l'on commande en plus un toit ouvrant en acier. Avec 85 exemplaires, il restera rarissime et, avec 85 ch, sa motorisation sera modeste, de même que celle des deux cabriolets de la même époque et, un peu plus tard, de la version 220 a. En novembre 1953, le cabriolet A reçoit un pare-brise galbé en parfaite harmonie avec ses lignes tout en rondeurs. Malgré l'évidente noblesse de la gamme, elle aussi peut parfaitement être consacrée à des activités quotidiennes banales comme le prouvent les 41 voitures de tourisme décapotables de la police produites d'août 1952 à mai 1953, des voitures semblables au cabriolet B, mais à quatre portes et une capote sans tiges de stabilisation. On envie les agents de la force publique.

MERCEDES-BENZ 220   1951

The 220 catered to the increased demand in West Germany for status symbols. Its powerful appearance and, in particular, the six-cylinder engine under the hood contributed to this effect.

Der 220 ist auf den vermehrten Bedarf der Bundesbürger nach Statussymbolik zugeschnitten. Dazu trägt sein stattliches Erscheinungsbild bei, vor allem aber der Sechszylinder unter der Haube.

La 220 va au-devant de l'Allemand qui veut donner une preuve de sa réussite. Sa stature déjà imposante y contribue encore plus quand un six-cylindres se trouve sous le capot.

The chassis and body came from the 170S, but this model's defining feature was new: its headlights were incorporated in the front fenders, a minor technical masterpiece.

Chassis und Karosserie stammen vom 170S, abgesehen von der Eigenheit, die dem Modell sein Profil gibt: Seine Scheinwerfer sind in die vorderen Kotflügel eingelassen, technisch eine kleine Meisterleistung.

Le châssis et la carrosserie sont ceux de la 170S, à l'exception du particularisme qui fait la spécificité de ce modèle : ses phares sont intégrés dans les ailes avant, un petit chef-d'œuvre mécanique.

Although the exterior design of the car was still largely classical, certain features were already reflecting the spirit of a new age, such as the column-mounted gearshift and the straight-six engine with its overhead camshaft.

Noch ist das Exterieur überwiegend klassisch, schon atmen bestimmte Requisiten den Geist der neuen Zeit, die Lenkradschaltung, der Reihensechszylinder mit einer obenliegenden Nockenwelle.

Son extérieur est, encore, essentiellement classique, mais certains détails reflètent déjà l'esprit d'une époque nouvelle, par exemple l'existence d'un levier de vitesses au sol ou le six-cylindres en ligne à arbre à cames en tête.

Mercedes-Benz 220 1951   283

It was either known as the "Adenauer Mercedes" after its most prominent customer, the German chancellor Konrad Adenauer, or simply as the "Three Hundred," and it represented much more than just a car. It was a metaphorical expression of an era, a symbol of the Federal Republic and its dignitaries. Like the 220, the 300 was also launched at the Frankfurt Motor Show in 1951, and its body was also mounted on a cruciform oval-tubed chassis. Like the 220 it had a twin-pivot swing axle with double coil springs at the rear, but also additional torsion bars for each wheel which could be actuated by a dashboard-mounted servo if heavy loads were being carried. Its shape already gave hints of future unit-construction designs. Its powerplant, 2996 cc and 115 bhp in original form, was an inline six-cylinder with an overhead camshaft. Apart from this, however, it had little in common with that of the 220 since its engine was rather longer in stroke and fed by two downdraft carburetors.

In its 11-year production life, the "Three Hundred," which was always very solidly equipped, underwent a comprehensive makeover. Three further generations emerged. In the 300b of March 1954 the power was increased to 125 bhp, and stronger brakes took the speedy heavyweight in hand. The 300c (from September 1955 onwards) had a single-pivot swing axle and a larger rear screen, and a Borg-Warner automatic gearbox was also available as an optional extra. From July 1956 there was a long version, made in response to a suggestion from Chancellor Adenauer, with a longer wheelbase (3150 instead of 3050 mm, 10 ft 4 in not 10 ft) and a longer rear section (length overall 5165 instead of 5065 mm, 16 ft 11 in not 16 ft 7 in), as a result of which 140 mm (5.5 in) more legroom was created in the back. The 300d of August 1957 with its substantially redesigned bodywork looked more angular when mounted on the long running gear of the Adenauer version, while a Bosch injection system helped the engine to develop 160 bhp.

A cabriolet D, which was offered alongside the sedan from the word go, disappeared from the range for a time, though it became available again from July 1958 onwards on special request – for a handsome 35,500 marks compared with the 27,000 marks of the basic 300 model. Three special stretched models dating from 1960 (wheelbase 3600 mm, 11 ft 10 in; overall length 5640 mm, 18 ft 6 in) revelled in their air of cultivated and lovingly celebrated overstatement. One was purchased by Pope John XXIII as his official car, while the other two could be hired by the day from Mercedes together with a chauffeur. Meanwhile collective prosperity had obviously spread pretty far and wide. This was clear from the fact that 11,430 original owners were not put off such a purchase and wanted to call a Mercedes 300 their own.

Sie nennen ihn den »Adenauer-Mercedes« nach seinem prominentesten Kunden oder schlicht den »Dreihunderter«, und er ist viel mehr als nur ein Auto: sinnbildliche Ausprägung einer Ära, Symbol auch der Bonner Republik und ihrer Würdenträger. Wie der 220 debütiert der 300 auf der Frankfurter Ausstellung 1951, und wie bei jenem ruht sein Aufbau auf einem x-förmigen Ovalrohrrahmen. Analog zum 220 hat er hinten eine Zweigelenk-Pendelachse mit doppelten Schraubenfedern, aber auch zusätzliche Drehstäbe für jedes Rad, vom Armaturenbrett elektrisch aktivierbar für höhere Zuladungen. Seine Formen zeigen bereits Anklänge an künftige Pontonkarosserien. Sein Triebwerk mit 2996 ccm und ursprünglich 115 PS ist ein Reihen-Sechszylinder mit einer obenliegenden Nockenwelle, im übrigen aber dem des 220 wenig verwandt, da eher langhubig konzipiert und von zwei Fallstromvergasern gespeist.

In den elf Jahren seiner Fertigung wird dem »Dreihunderter«, von Natur aus mit strotzender Robustheit ausgestattet, eine umfassende Modellpflege zuteil. Sie manifestiert sich in drei weiteren Generationen. Im 300b vom März 1954 wird die Leistung auf 125 PS angehoben, und größere Bremsen nehmen das flinke Schwergewicht an die Kandare. Der 300c (ab September 1955) hat eine Eingelenk-Pendelachse sowie eine größere Heckscheibe und wird wahlweise mit einer Automatik von Borg-Warner angeboten. Vom Juli 1956 an gibt es, einem Denkanstoß von Bundeskanzler Adenauer folgend, eine lange Variante mit mehr Radstand (3150 statt 3050 mm) und mehr Auto hinten (5165 statt 5065 mm), wodurch im Fond 140 mm Beinfreiheit gewonnen werden. Der 300d vom August 1957 kommt mit kräftig retuschierter Karosserie kantiger daher auf dem langen Fahrwerk der Adenauer-Version, während eine Bosch-Einspritzung der Maschine zu 160 Pferdestärken verhilft.

Ein Cabriolet D, der Limousine von Anbeginn an zur Seite gestellt, verschwindet eine Zeitlang aus dem Angebot, ist jedoch ab Juli 1958 auf besonderen Wunsch wieder erhältlich – für stramme 35 500 Mark gegenüber den 27 000 Mark des Basis-300. Drei extra lange Sonderausführungen von 1960 (Radstand 3600 mm, Gesamtlänge 5640 mm) umfächelt ein Hauch gepflegten und genüsslich zelebrierten Overstatements: Eine bezieht Papst Johannes XXIII. als Dienstfahrzeug, die beiden anderen können beim Werk tageweise mit Chauffeur angemietet werden. Der kollektive Wohlstand ist indessen schon wieder recht weit gediehen. Das kann man daran erkennen, dass immerhin 11 430 Erstbesitzer die Anschaffung nicht scheuen und einen Mercedes 300 ihr eigen nennen wollen.

Ils l'appellent la « Mercedes Adenauer » d'après so client le plus célèbre ou, simplement, la « Troi Cents », et elle est beaucoup plus qu'une simple voiture : c'est l'incarnation de toute une époque, le symbole, aussi, de la république de Bonn et de se dignitaires. À l'instar de la 220, la 300 fait ses débuts au Salon de l'Automobile de Francfort en 1951 et, comme celle-ci, sa carrosserie repose sur un châssis en tube ovales en forme de x. Toujours à l'instar de la 220, elle a, à l'arrière, un essieu brisé à double articulation avec doubles ressorts hélicoïdaux, mais aussi des barres de torsion supplémentaires pour chaque roue, que l'on peut actionner électriquement depuis le tableau de bord en cas de charges élevées. Ses formes annoncent d'ores et déjà celles des futures carrosseries ponton. Son moteur de 2996 cm³ développant initialement 115 ch est un six cylindres en ligne avec arbre à cames en tête, mais, pou le reste, il présente peu de similitudes avec celui de la 220, qui est plutôt à course longue et alimentée par deux carburateurs inversés.

Produite pendant onze ans, la « Trois Cents », doté par nature d'une forte constitution, a bénéficié de remise au goût du jour permanentes. Il y en a ainsi eu trois autre générations. La 300b de mars 1954 voit sa puissance majorée à 125 ch et reçoit de plus gros freins qui décélèren mieux cette voiture rapide, mais lourde. La 300c (à parti de septembre 1955) a un essieu brisé à une articulation ainsi qu'une lunette arrière de plus grandes dimension et est proposée avec une boîte automatique Borg-Warner À partir de juillet 1956, sur une idée du chancelier fédéral Adenauer, il en est lancé une variante à empattement long (de 3150 au lieu de 3050 mm) et également plus longue à l'arrière (5165 au lieu de 5065 mm), ce qui permet de gagner 140 mm à l'arrière pour les jambes. La 300 d d'août 1957 possède une carrosserie plus anguleuse et sérieusement redessinée sur le châssis long de la version Adenauer dont le moteur développe maintenant 160 ch grâce à une injection Bosch.

Le cabriolet D, qui a toujours été le compagnon de route de la limousine, disparaît un certain temps du catalogue, mais est de nouveau disponible à partir de juillet 1958 sur demande expresse – pour le prix farami neux de 35 500 marks alors que la 300 de base en coûte 27 000. Trois versions spéciales à empattement extrême ment long sont produites en 1960 (empattement 3600 mm longueur hors tout 5640 mm), d'apparence discrète e soignée : l'une est destinée au pape Jean XXIII comme voiture de service, les deux autres pouvant être louées à la journée avec chauffeur auprès de l'usine. Il est vra que la période est à la prospérité collective. Ce que l'on peut déjà constater au fait que pas moins de 11 430 acheteurs n'ont pas hésité à débourser la somme exigée pour devenir propriétaire d'une Mercedes 300.

MERCEDES-BENZ 300   1951

A familiar view for the political and financial elite of West Germany's early years: a Mercedes 300d from 1959 before the privileged classes took to the back seat and left the rest to the chauffeur.

Ein Anblick, welcher der Polit- und Geldaristokratie der frühen Bonner Republik vertraut ist: Ein Mercedes 300d von 1959, bevor man den Fond bezieht und sein bedeutendes Schicksal seinem Chauffeur anvertraut.

Une vue familière à l'élite politique et financière de l'ancienne république de Bonn : une Mercedes 300d de 1959 avant que l'on ne prenne place sur la banquette arrière et confie son destin à son chauffeur.

"If you've got something, you are something," was a well-known slogan of a bank group at the time, and those who owned this car really were something. The angular silhouette of the 300d from 1957 onwards was similar to contemporary unit-body types. The windows could be lowered almost completely.

»Hast du was, so bist du was«, besagte ein Slogan der Sparkassen, und wer ihn hatte, der war in der Tat etwas. Die kantige Silhouette des 300d ab 1957 nähert sich bereits zeitgenössischen Pontonformen an. Die Fenster lassen sich fast durchgehend versenken.

« Si tu as quelque chose, tu es quelqu'un ! » proclamait un slogan des caisses d'épargne à l'époque. Avoir ce modèle faisait de vous quelqu'un. La silhouette anguleuse de la 300d à partir de 1957 se rapproche déjà des carrosseries ponton contemporaines. Les fenêtres se baissent presque complètement.

The generously-appointed cockpit of the 300d with the chromed column-mounted gearshift and the ubiquitous Becker Mexico radio.

Das reich besiedelte Cockpit des 300d mit dem Chromhebel für die Lenkradschaltung und dem allgegenwärtigen Radio Becker Mexico.

Le tableau de bord richement décoré de la 300d, avec le levier de vitesses chromé au volant et l'omniprésent autoradio Becker Mexico.

This was the apotheosis of classic automotive engineering, a cultural event that harmoniously married swelling shapes with noble simplicity. The 300 s did not gradually develop this aura; it was there right from the very beginning when the attractive trinity of coupé, cabriolet, and roadster was launched into the world of the beautiful and rich at the Paris Salon in October 1951 to crown the Mercedes range.

Reviewers went into immediate raptures; they spoke of the "car of the world's elite" and reckoned that the 300 s now represented "the standard for what could be achieved today in car making," that is, in a "traditional and, in this case, particularly noble form… without recourse to aerodynamics." There was scarcely any difference between the cabriolet and the roadster – the latter had a lighter top which could be completely retracted without storm stays, while the cabrio had a more opulent design which gave the impression of lavish coziness. The 300 formed the basis of the design, but its wheelbase was reduced by 150 mm (6 in) to 2900 mm (9 ft 6 in). The three-liter engine's compression was increased from 6.4 : 1 to 7.8 : 1, and three Solex downdraft carburetors did their bit, with the result that its power output rose to 150 bhp. At 176 kph (109 mph), the 300 s was one of the fastest cars in Germany.

Since nothing and no-one is perfect, however, even the 300 s had to put up with its creators making further changes. The resulting 300 sc, which was shown together with the updated 300 c at the 1955 Frankfurt International Motor Show (IAA), had a single-pivot swing axle with a low center of gravity. With its Bosch direct injection system and a compression ratio which had been increased to 8.55 : 1, the six-cylinder engine developed 175 bhp, enough for a speed of 180 kph (112 mph). Outwardly a second-generation 300 s can be recognized by its perforated chrome-plated disc wheels, vent windows, larger turn signals front and rear, two cooling slits sporting horizontal chrome-plated strips above the front fender, and the "Einspritzmotor" (injection engine) badge on the trunk lid. The fact that the mixture was no longer provided by carburetors did not in any way reduce the engine's thirst which still had to be quenched with 16–20 liters per 100 km (12–15 mpg).

The appearance of the 300 SL Roadster in 1957 brought interest in the antique beau which had sold 760 units to a sudden end. Whereas the 300 s tended to look to the past, the 300 SL was a taste of the future. To this must be added the fact that at 32,500 marks the newer model was 4,000 marks cheaper than the old one. And even in the naturally limited circle of those who could afford such a price, this fact caught the attention.

Er ist die Apotheose klassischen Automobilbaus, ein Kulturereignis, das schwellende Formen in harmonischer Weise mit nobler Schlichtheit vermählt. Dieser Nimbus wächst dem 300 s nicht erst allmählich zu, sondern er ist sofort vorhanden, als er zur Krönung des Mercedes-Programms in der attraktiven Dreieinigkeit Coupé, Cabriolet und Roadster auf dem Pariser Salon im Oktober 1951 in die Welt der Schönen und der Reichen eingeführt wird.

Und so geraten seine Rezensenten umgehend ins Schwärmen, sprechen vom »Wagen der Weltelite« und davon, dass der 300 s nun »der Maßstab für das heute im Automobilbau Erreichbare« sei und zwar in einer »traditionellen und in diesem Fall besonders edlen Form… ohne Zuflucht zur Aerodynamik«. Cabriolet und Roadster unterscheiden sich kaum – letzterer hat ein leichteres und gänzlich versenkbares Verdeck ohne Sturmstangen, wo das Cabrio mit einer aufwändigeren Konstruktion den Eindruck üppiger Wohnlichkeit vermittelt. Basis ist der Typ 300, dessen Radstand um 150 mm auf 2900 mm zurückgenommen wird. Die Verdichtung des Dreiliter-Triebwerks wird von 6,4 : 1 auf 7,8 : 1 erhöht, und drei Solex-Fallstromvergaser tun das Ihrige, so dass seine Leistung auf 150 PS anwächst. Mit 176 Stundenkilometern Spitzengeschwindigkeit zählt der 300 s zu den Schnellsten im Lande.

Da aber nichts und niemand perfekt ist, muss selbst er sich gefallen lassen, dass seine Schöpfer noch einmal Hand an ihn legen: Der 300 sc, der zusammen mit dem überarbeiteten 300 c auf der Frankfurter IAA 1955 gezeigt wird, hat eine Eingelenk-Pendelachse mit tief liegendem Schwerpunkt erhalten, und mit einer Direkteinspritzung von Bosch sowie einer auf 8,55 : 1 gesteigerten Verdichtung gibt der Sechszylinder 175 PS ab, gut für Tempo 180. Nach außen hin verraten den 300 s der zweiten Generation verchromte Lochscheibenräder, Ausstellfensterchen, größere Blinkleuchten vorn und hinten, zwei mit Chromleisten verblendete waagerechte Kühlschlitze oberhalb der vorderen Kotflügel sowie der Schriftzug »Einspritzmotor« am Kofferraumdeckel. Dass die Gemischaufbereitung nicht länger von Vergasern besorgt wird, wirkt sich keineswegs mildernd auf den Durst des Motors aus, der allemal mit 16 bis 20 Litern verpflegt werden möchte.

Mit dem Erscheinen des 300 SL Roadsters 1957 lässt das Interesse an dem antikischen Beau, der es auf eine Verbreitung von 760 Exemplaren bringt, jäh nach: Die Vision 300 s ist doch eher nach hinten gewandt, die Vision 300 SL mehr nach vorn. Überdies kostet das neuere Modell mit 32 500 Mark 4000 Mark weniger als das alte. Und darauf achtet man selbst im naturgemäß begrenzten Kreis derer, die sich das alles leisten können.

C'est l'apothéose de la construction automobi classique, un événement culturel qui alli dans la plus grande harmonie, des forme exubérantes et une sobriété pleine de noblesse. C'est un aura que la 300 s n'acquiert pas graduellement, mais qu la caractérise immédiatement lorsqu'elle est présentée, a Salon de Paris d'octobre 1951, dans le monde des riches des célébrités pour couronner le programme Mercede sous la forme d'une attrayante trinité : coupé, cabriole et roadster.

Ainsi les critiques se répandent-elles immédiatemen en éloges, parlant de « voiture de l'élite mondiale » et d ce que la 300 s était désormais « le critère de ce qui es aujourd'hui réalisable en construction automobile », savoir dans une « forme traditionnelle et, dans le ca présent, particulièrement noble… sans fioritures aéro dynamiques ». Cabriolet et roadster sont presque iden tiques – ce dernier a une capote plus légère et totalemer escamotable sans barreaux de rigidification alors que cabriolet, au mécanisme plus sophistiqué, dégage un impression chaleureuse. Ils ont pour base la 300 d l'empattement a été raccourci de 150 mm, à 2900 mm Le taux de compression du moteur de 3 litres est major de 6,4 : 1 à 7,8 : 1 et trois carburateurs inversés Solex pe mettent à sa puissance de passer à 150 ch. Avec une vitess de pointe de 176 km/h, la 300 s est l'une des plus rapide voitures de son temps.

Mais comme rien ni personne n'est parfait, elle-mêm doit tolérer que ses créateurs lui fassent subir une cure c rajeunissement : la 300 sc, qui est dévoilée au Salon inte national de l'Automobile de Francfort (IAA) de 1955 simu tanément avec la 300 c retravaillée, possède un essieu bris à une articulation avec centre de gravité abaissé et, grâc à une injection directe Bosch ainsi qu'à un taux c compression majoré à 8,55 : 1, le six-cylindres déliv 175 ch qui lui permettent d'atteindre aisément 180 km/ Extérieurement, la 300 s deuxième génération se distingu à ses roues chromées à jantes perforées, aux peti déflecteurs, aux plus grands clignotants à l'avant et l'arrière, aux deux fentes de refroidissement horizontale décorées d'un jonc chromé au-dessus des ailes avant ain qu'à l'inscription « Einspritzmotor » (moteur d'injectior sur le couvercle de malle. Si la préparation du mélang n'est désormais plus assurée par des carburateurs, cel n'a en revanche absolument aucun effet bénéfique sur soif du moteur, qui engloutit toujours ses 16 à 20 litre aux 100 km.

Avec la parution du roadster 300 SL, en 1957, l'intéré manifesté à cette beauté antique diffusée à raison c 760 exemplaires s'évanouit instantanément : la visio 300 SL est, il faut l'avouer, plutôt orientée vers le pass alors que la vision 300 SL est résolument tournée ve l'avenir. De plus, le nouveau modèle, à 32 500 marks, coû 4000 marks de moins que l'ancien. Et c'est une somn non négligeable, même dans le gotha naturellement tr élitaire de ceux qui peuvent se permettre un tel achat.

MERCEDES-BENZ 300 S 1951

Before horizontal lines and right angles finally seized power, traditional design philosophy bore its most exquisite fruit in the Mercedes 300 S series. At the same time, however, it must be admitted that only very few people were fortunate enough to own such a car.

Vor der endgültigen Machtergreifung der Horizontale und des rechten Winkels treibt eine traditionell ausgerichtete Philosophie der Formen ihre schönste Blüte in der Mercedes-Baureihe 300 S. Kein Zweifel aber auch, dass solche Automobile einigen wenigen Glücklichen vorbehalten bleiben.

Avant la prise du pouvoir définitive par l'horizontale et l'angle droit, une philosophie des formes éprise de traditions connaît son apogée avec la série Mercedes 300 S. Le doute n'est pas permis : de telles automobiles seront restées l'apanage d'une élite.

Although the coupé was developed
from the 300 model, which was
the German government's official
car of choice, it nonetheless
evolved its own balanced
proportions in which tastefully-
rounded contours dominated.

Zwar wurde das Coupé aus der
Staatslimousine 300 sublimiert,
findet aber dennoch zu eigenständigen und ausgewogenen
Proportionen, in denen die
kunstvolle Rundung dominiert.

Bien qu'extrapolé de la limousine
d'apparat 300, le coupé possède
cependant des lignes personnelles
et des proportions équilibrées dans
lesquelles prédomine le galbe avec
toute son élégance.

Once its lightweight fold-down top had disappeared into its recess, the 300S Roadster was an open declaration of war on all other cars on the road.

Sowie sein leichtes Klappverdeck in der Versenkung verschwunden ist, wird der 300S Roadster zur offenen Kriegserklärung an den Rest der Auto-Welt.

Une fois sa légère capote rangée dans son compartiment, la 300S Roadster est une déclaration de guerre au reste du monde automobile.

Mercedes-Benz 300S 1951

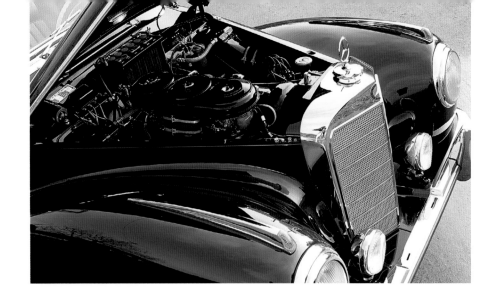

Elegance overall – elegant solutions in its details coupled with no-frills simplicity. It was not until September 1955 that side vent windows, solid rims with sporty holes, and more chrome appeared.

Eleganz im Ganzen, elegante Lösungen im Detail, gepaart mit schnörkelloser Schlichtheit. Erst im September 1955 stellen sich seitliche Ausstellfenster, Lochscheibenfelgen und mehr Chrom ein.

Élégance générale – élégance des détails, alliée à une sobriété sans fioritures. Les déflecteurs latéraux, les jantes perforées et des chromes supplémentaires ne sont apparus qu'en septembre 1955.

At the beginning of the Fifties Mercedes made its return to racing via the back door. The budget was small, and Formula 1 regulations were in constant flux. Re-entry into the world of sports car racing was the obvious solution. A number of people at Mercedes wanted to base the new car around the V12 engine of the W154 in the light of the spectacular successes of the pre-war Silver Arrows, but director Fritz Nallinger poured cold water on this idea. In his view the current production cars offered great potential, and the closeness of this type of racing to production models was always reckoned to be good for the image.

These talks went on in mid-1951. A team including Wolf-Dieter Bensinger, Franz Roller, Manfred Lorscheidt, and Ludwig Kraus, under the leadership of Rudolf Uhlenhaut, the head of passenger car development and himself a brilliant driver, immediately set to work. The six-cylinder engine which powered the type 300 official government cars was transformed into a racing engine with a removable aluminum cylinder head, three Solex downdraft carburetors, and 175 bhp. All four gears had synchromesh.

The engine and drivetrain were rather heavy, and weight therefore had to be saved on the chassis and body. The car weighed in at 870 kg (1918 lb) when the legendary 300 SL (3 liters Sports Light) was born nine months later. Of this, the engine alone was responsible for 265 kg (584 lb). Seven cars were planned and clad in aluminum, some as roadsters, others with gullwings that either ended below the side windows or intersected with the waist line, as with the three cars for Le Mans.

Upward-opening doors were chosen because the outer struts of an ingeniously conceived latticework of interwoven thin steel tubes which formed the SL's chassis were hidden immediately below the side door sills, a large number of interlinked triangles whose sides were subjected to compressive and tensile stresses. To keep the height to a minimum, the engine (affectionately known as "Schräger Otto" – "Sloping Otto") was canted at an angle of 50 degrees to the left when mounted in this latticework frame. The fitting of the suspension also caused few problems: parallel wishbones with coil springs at the front, a swing axle at the rear. Although the 300 SL was designed with the express purpose of winning races, its cockpit nonetheless welcomed the driver with elemental coziness. "The driver," said Rudi Uhlenhaut, "should feel comfortable in his workplace." The two main instruments, the speedometer and tachometer, were positioned under a small windshield which was intended to prevent glare above the detachable four-spoke steering wheel directly in the driver's field of vision. Four further pressure and temperature gauges were located to the left and right of the steering column. Even the luggage compartment was worthy of its name: during long-distance races, such as the Carrera Panamericana, the Mercedes cars carried two spare wheels with them.

Anfang der Fünfziger meldet sich Mercedes gleichsam durch die Hintertür im Rennsport zurück. Das Budget ist schmal, das Regelwerk der Formel 1 ständig in Bewegung. Da empfiehlt sich der Neueinstieg mit dem Sportwagen. Als einige Mitarbeiter eingedenk der spektakulären Erfolge der Vorkriegs-Silberpfeile das V12-Triebwerk des W154 zur technischen Grundlage machen möchten, wiegelt Direktor Fritz Nallinger ab: Es gebe durchaus Potential bei den gegenwärtigen Produktionswagen, und die Nachbarschaft zur Serie sei immer gut für das Image.

Solche Gespräche werden Mitte des Jahres 1951 geführt. Umgehend krempelt ein Team um Rudolf Uhlenhaut, Leiter der Personenwagenentwicklung und selbst ein glänzender Fahrer, die Ärmel hoch, unter anderen Wolf-Dieter Bensinger, Franz Roller, Manfred Lorscheidt und Ludwig Kraus. Aus dem Sechszylinder der Staatslimousine 300 sublimiert man eine Rennmaschine mit abnehmbarem Zylinderkopf aus Aluminium, drei Fallstromvergasern von Solex und 175 PS. Die vier Gänge sind voll synchronisiert.

Motor und Antriebsstrang bringen eine Menge Gewicht auf die Waage, also muss an Chassis und Karosserie gespart werden. 870 Kilogramm wiegt das Produkt, als der Mythos 300 SL (für drei Liter, Sport, Leicht) neun Monate später geboren wird. Davon entfallen allein auf das Triebwerk 265 Kilogramm. Sieben Exemplare werden geplant und in Aluminium eingekleidet, einige davon als Roadster, andere mit Flügeltüren, die entweder unterhalb der Seitenfenster enden oder in die Hüftlinie einschneiden, wie an den drei Wagen für Le Mans.

Den Weg nach oben hat man gewählt, weil sich unmittelbar unterhalb der seitlichen Bordkanten die äußeren Streben eines ingeniös ausgedachten Geflechts aus dünnen Stahlrohren verbergen, die den Rahmen des SL bilden, eine Vielzahl miteinander verknüpfter Dreiecke, deren Seiten auf Druck und Zug beansprucht werden. Um an Bauhöhe zu sparen, wird der Motor (Hausjargon: Schräger Otto) in dieses filigrane Fachwerk um 50 Grad nach links gekippt eingelassen. Wenig Schwierigkeiten bereitet auch das Einpflanzen der Aufhängung: Parallel-Querlenker mit Schraubenfedern vorn, eine Pendelachse hinten. Obwohl der 300 SL nüchtern auf seinen Zweck hin ausgerichtet ist, wartet sein Cockpit mit elementarer Wohnlichkeit auf: »Der Fahrer«, sagt Rudi Uhlenhaut, »soll sich wohlfühlen an seinem Arbeitsplatz.« Die beiden Hauptinstrumente, Tachometer und Drehzahlmesser, liegen unter einem kleinen Schirm als Blendschutz oberhalb des abnehmbaren Vierspeichen-Lenkrads genau im Blickfeld des Piloten. Vier weitere Uhren für Drücke und Temperaturen sind links und rechts der Lenksäule angesiedelt. Selbst das Gepäckabteil verdient seinen Namen: Auf Langstreckenrennen wie der Carrera Panamericana führen die Mercedes zwei Reserveräder mit.

Au début des années 1950, Mercedes revient à [la] compétition automobile par la petite port[e]. Le budget est réduit et les règlements de [la] Formule 1 sont en mutation permanente. Un engageme[nt] en catégorie Voitures de sport est donc prédestiné. Aya[nt] encore en mémoire les spectaculaires succès remport[és] par les Flèches d'argent d'avant-guerre, quelques collab[o]rateurs souhaitent utiliser le V12 de la W154 comme ba[se] mécanique, mais le directeur Fritz Nallinger s'y oppos[e] catégoriquement: les voitures de la production actuel[le] renferment un potentiel parfaitement suffisant, dit-il, [et] la proximité vis-à-vis de la série est toujours bonne pou[r] l'image de marque.

De tels entretiens sont menés vers la mi-195[1]. Immédiatement, une équipe regroupée autour de Rud[olf] Uhlenhaut, directeur du développement Voitures [de] tourisme et lui-même pilote émérite, retrousse se[s] manches, avec notamment Wolf-Dieter Bensinger, Fran[z] Roller, Manfred Lorscheidt et Ludwig Kraus. Ils sublime[nt] le six-cylindres de la 300, limousine de représentatio[n,] en un moteur de course avec culasse démontable en al[u]minium, trois carburateurs inversés Solex et 175 ch. L[es] quatre vitesses sont complètement synchronisées.

Il faut faire des économies de poids sur le châssis [et] la carrosserie. 870 kg est le poids de l'objet lorsque [le] mythe 300 SL (pour 3 litres, Sport, Légère) naît, neuf mo[is] plus tard. Le moteur à lui seul en représente 265. Se[pt] exemplaires sont projetés et habillés en aluminiu[m,] certains en roadster, d'autres avec des ailes papillon, do[nt] l'échancrure se termine en dessous des fenêtres latéral[es] ou descend jusqu'à hauteur des hanches comme pour le[s] trois voitures du Mans.

Immédiatement sous les arêtes latérales, se trouve[nt] les tubes extérieurs d'un ingénieux faisceau de minc[es] tubes d'acier qui constituent le châssis de la SL, une mul[ti]tude de triangles solidaires les uns des autres dont le[s] arêtes sont sollicitées en pression et en traction. Pou[r] économiser de la hauteur, le moteur (baptisé en jargo[n] maison *Schräger Otto* – «Otto le penché») est incliné d[e] 50 degrés vers la gauche dans cette toile d'araigné[e] filigrane. On rencontre aussi quelques difficultés lors d[u] montage de la suspension. Bras transversaux parallèle[s] avec ressorts hélicoïdaux à l'avant, essieu brisé à l'arrièr[e.] Bien que la 300 SL soit conçue en fonction d'un seul [et] unique but, à savoir gagner des courses, son cockpit e[st] d'une chaleur tout à fait acceptable: «Le pilote, déclar[e] Rudi Uhlenhaut, doit se sentir à l'aise à son poste d[e] travail.» Le tachymètre et le compte-tours prennent leur[s] aises sous une petite casquette antireflet au-dessus d[u] volant à quatre branches démontables, exactement dan[s] le champ de vision du pilote. Quatre autres cadrans pou[r] les pressions et les températures sont répartis à gauch[e] et à droite de la colonne de direction. Même le coffre [à] bagages mérite son nom: lors des courses d'enduranc[e] comme la Carrera Panamericana, les Mercedes emmène[nt] en effet avec elles deux roues de secours.

MERCEDES-BENZ 300SL (W194) 1952

Inspired by these designs, the North American Mercedes agent Maxi Hoffman suggested building a production car based on the 300 SL racing car. The motoring world is indebted to him for the 300 SL Coupé which took to the road two years later.

Begeistert von diesen Formen, regt der nordamerikanische Mercedes-Agent Maxi Hoffman an, auf der Basis des Rennsportwagens 300 SL eine Serienversion zu bauen. Ihm verdankt die Auto-Welt das 300 SL Coupé für die Straße zwei Jahre später.

Séduit par ses formes, l'importateur nord-américain de Mercedes, Maxi Hoffman, suggère de construire une version de série sur la base de la 300 SL de compétition. C'est à lui que le monde de l'automobile doit le coupé 300 SL pour la route qui apparaîtra deux ans plus tard.

Views of a victorious racer endowed with a veneer of comfort. The "D" badge also opened the trunk.

Aspekte eines Rennsiegers mit einem Firnis von Komfort. Das Kennzeichen D eröffnet auch den Zugang zum Kofferraum.

Vues d'un vainqueur avec un vernis de confort. La lettre D donne aussi accès au coffre.

Mercedes-Benz 300SL (W194) 1952

Progress sometimes took its time at Daimler-Benz. Thus it was that the watershed between tradition and modernity did not really reveal itself in Untertürkheim until 1953. The unit body design, based on the American three-box model of engine, passenger, and luggage compartments, had already been imported into Germany in 1949 by Borgward with the Hansa 1500. Opel and Ford, as subsidiaries of US corporations, followed suit. Despite the aesthetic sparseness of this concept, its benefits were obvious. While occupying the same floor area, it was much more economic than conventional bodies which squandered valuable space with generous fenders and wide running boards. Compared with the 170 s, the 180 had 20 per cent more cabin space and 75 per cent more luggage space. Its body, an absolute stronghold of the right angle, was still not a true monocoque; it provided support, combined with a sturdy floorpan chassis made of steel box sections with sheet metal welded between them, which was comparatively light and stiff. This helped the occupants in the event of an accident too as it had soft crumple zones positioned in front of and behind the rigid passenger cage.

An unusual feature of the 180, which was later to become standard, was that the engine, gearbox, steering gear, and the wishbones pressed from sheet metal were mounted at the front on a sub-frame that was connected to the rest of the running gear via three rubber bearings. Drivers of 180s were greeted by a welcome increase in visibility on all sides, and even the traditional imposingly gothic radiator grille was perfectly in keeping with the new design configuration. Other than this, the car was rather conventional. It was not until September 1955 that the usual twin-pivot swing axle with additional longitudinal swing arms was replaced by a counterpart in which the two halves of the axle simply moved about a common low pivot. Design-instigated changes in camber were kept to a manageable minimum in this way.

The 52 bhp side-valve engine from the 170 s was a real workhorse, reliable and rugged, even if it lacked any touches of brilliance. In August 1957 it gave way to the 1.9-liter unit from its sister model, the 190, with an overhead camshaft and a solid 68 bhp. As far as the popular diesel engines were concerned, which cost an extra 500 to 1,000 marks, the designers also opted for an in-house, off-the-shelf solution: the long-stroke engine from the 170 D was upgraded in 1955 to produce 43 bhp. A version with an overhead camshaft followed, and from 1962 onwards the 180 D used the engine from the 190 D which had been enlarged to a capacity of two liters. Mercedes diesel models still suffered from a high level of noise. Their life expectancy, however, had taken on almost biblical proportions, and it was not unusual to find taxis, for example, with half a million kilometers on the clock.

Der Fortschritt nimmt sich bei Daimler-Benz manchmal Zeit. So wölbt sich die Wasserscheide zwischen Tradition und Moderne in Untertürkheim eigentlich erst 1953. Die Pontonkarosserie, fußend auf der amerikanischen Three-Box-Bauweise Motorraum, Passagiertrakt und Gepäckabteil, wird von Borgward mit dem Hansa 1500 bereits 1949 in Deutschland eingeführt. Opel und Ford als Töchter von US-Konzernen ziehen nach. Trotz der ästhetischen Kargheit dieses Konzepts liegen seine Vorzüge auf der Hand. Bei gleicher Grundfläche ist seine Ökonomie viel besser als die herkömmlicher Aufbauten, die mit schwellenden Kotflügeln und ellbogenbreiten Trittbrettern kostbaren Platz liberal verschwenden: Gegenüber dem 170 s gewinnt der 180 um die 20 Prozent Wohnraum und 75 Prozent Gepäckvolumen. Noch ist seine Karosserie, eine unumschränkte Domäne des rechten Winkels, nicht selbsttragend: Sie trägt mit, verquickt mit einer fahrfähigen Rahmen-Bodengruppe aus stählernen Kastenträgern und dazwischen geschweißten Blechen, vergleichsweise leicht und steif. Bei einem Unfall kommt den Insassen auch zugute, dass sich an die rigide Passagierzelle vorn und hinten weiche Knautschzonen anlagern.

Eine Eigentümlichkeit des 180, aber zukünftiger Standard: dass Motor, Getriebe, Lenkung sowie die aus Blech gepressten Querlenker vorn auf einem »Fahrschemel« zusammengefasst sind, der über drei Gummilager mit dem Rest des Fahrwerks verbunden ist. Den 180-Lenker erwartet ein erfreulicher Zuwachs an Überblick nach allen Seiten, und selbst der traditionelle gotisch aufragende Kühlergrill verträgt sich durchaus mit der neuen Form. Im Übrigen geht es im zeitgemäßen Gewande eher konventionell zu. Die übliche Zweigelenk-Pendelachse mit zusätzlichen Längslenkern wird erst im September 1955 durch ein Pendant abgelöst, bei dem sich die Achshälften nur noch um einen gemeinsamen tief gelegten Drehpunkt bewegen. So lassen sich die konstruktionsbedingten Sturzänderungen auf ein erträgliches Maß reduzieren.

Ein wahres Urgestein ist das seitengesteuerte Triebwerk aus dem 170 s mit seinen 52 PS, brav und zählebig, wenn auch ohne Brillanz. Im August 1957 weicht es dem 1,9-Liter-Aggregat aus dem Schwestermodell 190, mit einer oben liegenden Nockenwelle und 68 soliden PS. Was die volkstümlichen, aber stets mit einem Aufpreis von 500 bis 1000 Mark zu honorierenden Diesel-Aggregate anbelangt, bedient man sich ebenfalls aus den Regalen des Hauses: Der Langhuber aus dem 170 D wird 1955 auf 43 PS Leistung nachgerüstet. Eine Version mit einer oben liegenden Nockenwelle folgt, und ab 1962 gibt es den 180 D mit dem auf zwei Liter Hubraum vergrößerten Motor des 190 D. Noch ist das Geräuschniveau der Benz-Selbstzünder hoch.

Geradezu biblisch mutet dafür ihre Lebenserwartung an: Im Taxigewerbe zum Beispiel sind Laufleistungen von einer halben Million Kilometern nicht unüblich.

Chez Daimler-Benz, le progrès prend parfoi[s] beaucoup de temps. C'est ainsi que la ligne d[e] partage entre la tradition et le modernisme n'es[t] tracée définitivement, à Untertürkheim, qu'en 1953. L[a] carrosserie ponton, qui reprend l'architecture *three-bo[x]* américaine avec compartiment moteur, cellule passager[s] et coffre à bagages, a déjà été introduite en Allemagn[e] par Borgward avec la Hansa 1500 de 1949. Opel et For[d] toutes deux filiales de groupes américains, suivent elle[s] aussi. Malgré l'aridité esthétique de ce concept, se[s] avantages sont patents. Pour un périmètre de sustentatio[n] identique, son économie est bien meilleure que celle de[s] carrosseries traditionnelles qui gaspillent avec prodigalit[é] une place précieuse : par rapport à la 170 s, la 180 offre u[n] espace habitable majoré de 20 %, et de 75 % pour l[e] volume de bagages. Sa carrosserie, domaine incontest[é] de l'angle droit, n'est pas encore autoporteuse ; elle es[t] semi-porteuse, conjointement avec une plate-form[e] châssis en longerons caissons en acier et tôles soudé[es] entre eux, à la fois relativement légère et rigide. Cela es[t] aussi tout bénéfice pour les passagers en cas d'accident à l'avant et à l'arrière, la cellule passagers rigide est pré[-] cédée par des zones de déformation programmée.

Particularisme de la 180 qui deviendra vite u[n] standard : le moteur, la boîte de vitesses, la directio[n] ainsi que les leviers transversaux avant en tôle d'acie[r] sont regroupés sur un «berceau auxiliaire» qui est reli[é] au reste du châssis à l'aide de trois paliers en caoutchouc[.] Le conducteur de la 180 jouit d'un champ de vision nette[-] ment amélioré dans toutes les directions et même l[a] calandre traditionnelle de style gothique est parfaiteme[nt] compatible avec la nouvelle forme. Pour le reste, sous un[e] robe conforme à l'air du temps, tout est plutôt conventio[n]nel. L'habituel essieu brisé à deux articulations avec levier[s] longitudinaux supplémentaires ne sera remplacé qu'e[n] septembre 1955 par un train arrière où les demi-essieux n[e] sont plus ancrés que sur un seul point de rotation commu[n] surbaissé. Cela permet de ramener à un niveau tolérable le[s] modifications de déport dues au système.

Le moteur à commande latérale issu de la 170 s[,] avec ses 52 chevaux, brave et indestructible, mais sans l[e] moindre prestige, est une véritable antiquité. En août 1957[,] il est donc évincé par le 1,9 litre de sa jumelle la 190, ave[c] un arbre à cames en tête et 68 ch de bonne constitution[.] En ce qui concerne les populaires moteurs Diesel, qu[i] sont toujours facturés avec un supplément de prix d[e] 500 à 1000 marks, on recourt aux ressources interne[s :] le course longue de la 170 D voit sa puissance augmente[r] à 43 ch en 1955. Il est suivi d'une version à arbre à came[s] en tête et, à partir de 1962, il existe une 180 D avec l[e] moteur majoré à deux litres de cylindrée de la 190 D. Le[s] moteurs à auto-allumage de chez Benz se font encor[e] entendre de loin. En revanche, leur espérance de vi[e] permet de tabler sur un âge absolument canonique : dan[s] l'industrie du taxi, par exemple, des kilométrages d'u[n] demi-million de kilomètres n'ont rien de spectaculaire.

MERCEDES-BENZ 180   1953

A far-reaching measure: the unit-body construction of the 180 with its mere hints of rear fenders made virtually optimum use of the footprint occupied by the first monocoque Mercedes.

Einschneidende Maßnahme: Die Pontonform des 180 mit nur noch angedeuteten Kotflügeln hinten nutzt fast optimal die Grundfläche, auf welcher der erste Mercedes mit einer selbsttragenden Karosserie steht.

Mesure décisive : la forme en ponton de la 180 aux ailes encore seulement esquissées à l'arrière exploite presque optimalement le périmètre de sustentation de la première Mercedes à carrosserie autoporteuse.

In contrast to the scarcely-rounded
tail, the vertical radiator grille was
a leftover from the past – a rather
unsuccessful feature in the eyes of
some critics.

Im Gegensatz zum nur sanft
gerundeten Heck wird als Relikt
aus der Vergangenheit das
senkrecht stehende Kühlergitter
beibehalten – in den Augen einiger
Kritiker eine wenig geglückte
Lösung.

Contrairement à l'arrière aux galbes
rares, on a conservé comme relique
du passé la calandre verticale –
solution peu réussie aux yeux de
quelques critiques.

Mercedes-Benz 180 1953

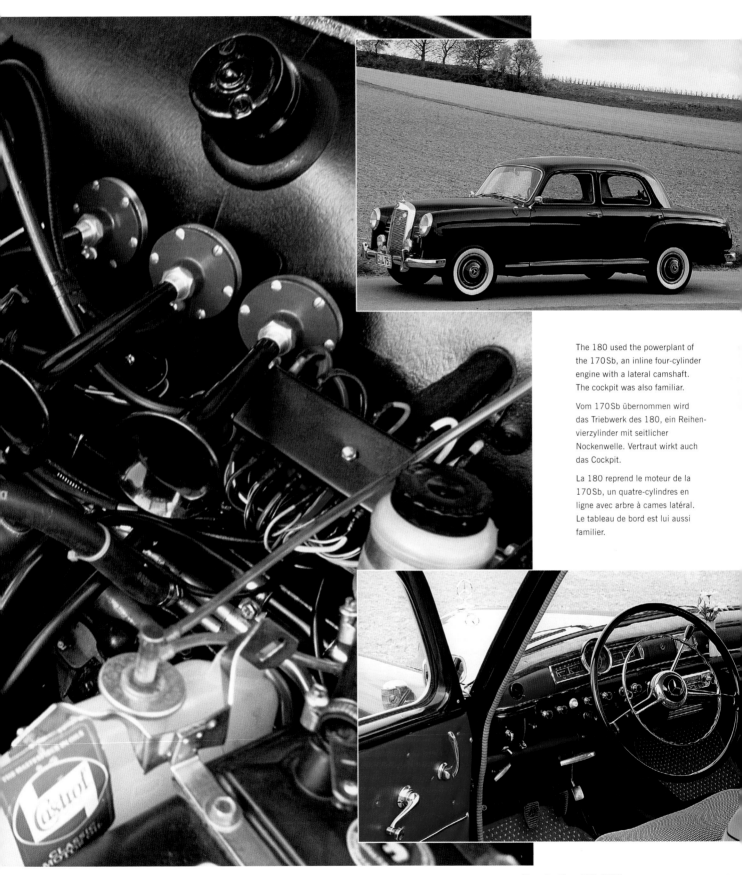

The 180 used the powerplant of
the 170Sb, an inline four-cylinder
engine with a lateral camshaft.
The cockpit was also familiar.

Vom 170Sb übernommen wird
das Triebwerk des 180, ein Reihen-
vierzylinder mit seitlicher
Nockenwelle. Vertraut wirkt auch
das Cockpit.

La 180 reprend le moteur de la
170Sb, un quatre-cylindres en
ligne avec arbre à cames latéral.
Le tableau de bord est lui aussi
familier.

Mercedes biographer Karl Ludvigsen called him the counterpart to Emil Jellinek. Max Hoffman, who had been the official Mercedes-Benz importer into the United States since 1952, was also Austrian and, like Jellinek, it was at his instigation – half a century later – that a model was created which caused a sensation. The dynamic businessman was highly impressed by the successes of the 1952 300 SL – and by its design. Something similar for the road, he told the Mercedes management in Stuttgart, could be just what was needed to open up the American market, and he put his money where his mouth was by ordering 1,000 gullwing models.

A charismatic product was unveiled to an eager motor industry and countless fans at the International Motor Sports Show in New York on 6 February 1954: the road-going 300 SL Coupé. That it had the SL racing car in its direct bloodline was undeniable, though, as was the case with this ancestor, a constructional necessity was turned into a positive virtue. The outer elements of the massive spaceframe, weighing in at a hefty 50 kg (110 lb), stood so high off the road as to make normal entry into the car impossible. Gullwings, which gave the car its name in the English-speaking world, were again the answer to the problem. And, as in the first-generation SL, the six-cylinder engine was canted to the left so that the front was low and streamlined.

Curiously the production engine delivered 40 bhp more than the racing engine. This was the result of the use for the first time by Mercedes of a high-pressure fuel-injection system developed by Dr. Hans Scherenberg, later the chief designer. The running gear was the same as that used on the 300 – without additional springs and set up for sporty performance. However, the dynamics of the rear twin-pivot swing axle called for expert handling when pushed to the limit – the track width and camber changed constantly. Between August 1954 and May 1957, 1,400 of the gullwinged coupés were sold, 29 of them with alloy bodies, and one with plastic bodywork.

As early as the summer of 1956 resourceful journalists at the German specialist publication *auto motor und sport* had tracked down a rolling chassis in the Stuttgart area which differed from the actual 300 SL only in respect of its low-slung longitudinal chassis tubes and a single-joint low-pivot swing axle à la 220. In October of that year the American sports-car champion Paul O'Shea unveiled the 300 SL Roadster at the Solitude track near Stuttgart. It was then officially launched at the 1957 Geneva Spring Motor Show with appropriate razzmatazz. The ball had again been set rolling by Maxi Hoffman who foresaw good sales prospects in the land of limitless opportunities for an open-top version of Stuttgart's finest. When production of the Roadster ceased in Sindelfingen on 8 February 1963, 1,858 cars had left the line.

Major events in the history of this model include: from October 1958 onwards, just in time for the approaching

Mercedes-Biograph Karl Ludvigsen nennt ihn das Pendant zu Emil Jellinek: Max Hoffman, seit dem September 1952 offizieller Daimler-Benz-Importeur in den Vereinigten Staaten, ist Österreicher wie jener, und wie Jellinek gibt er den Anstoß für ein Modell, das Aufsehen erregt – ein halbes Jahrhundert später. Der rührige Geschäftsmann zeigt sich sehr angetan von den Erfolgen der 300 SL – Jahrgang 1952 – und von ihrer Form. Etwas Vergleichbares für die Straße, trägt er dem Mercedes-Management in Stuttgart vor, könne dazu beitragen, den amerikanischen Markt zu erschließen, und bestellt zur Bekräftigung 1000 Flügeltürer.

Auf der International Motor Sports Show in New York ab 6. Februar 1954 erwartet eine aufhorchende Fachwelt und unzählige Fans ein charismatisches Produkt: das 300 SL Coupé für die Straße. Überhaupt nicht zu leugnen ist die Verwandtschaft zu den Renn-SL, wobei man wie bei diesen aus einer Not eine Tugend macht: Die Ausläufer des trutzigen Gitterrohrrahmens, ganze 50 Kilogramm schwer, liegen so hoch über der Fahrbahn, dass sich ein normaler Einstieg verbietet. Gullwings (zu deutsch Möwenflügel), die dem Wagen im anglophonen Bereich den Namen geben, sind erneut des Dilemmas Lösung. Und wie in den SL der ersten Generation ist der Sechszylinder schräg nach links installiert, damit die Front niedrig und strömungsgünstig in den Fahrtwind pfeilt.

Ein Kuriosum: dass das Serientriebwerk 40 PS stärker ist als der Rennmotor. Für dieses zuständig, erstmals in einem Produktionswagen des Hauses, ist eine Hochdruckeinspritzanlage, entwickelt vom späteren Chefkonstrukteur Dr. Hans Scherenberg. Das Fahrwerk entspricht dem des Typs 300 – ohne Zusatzfedern und sportlich abgestimmt. Allerdings verlangt die Eigendynamik der hinteren Zweigelenk-Pendelachse im Grenzbereich nach kundigen Händen – ständig ändern sich Spurweite und Radsturz. Zwischen August 1954 und Mai 1957 wird das geflügelte Coupé in 1400 Exemplaren aufgelegt, 29 davon mit Aufbauten aus Leichtmetall, eines mit einer Karosserie aus Kunststoff.

Bereits im Sommer 1956 machen die findigen Redakteure des Fachmagazins *auto motor und sport* im Großraum Stuttgart ein rollendes Chassis aus, das nur niedrig gehaltene Längsträger sowie eine Eingelenk-Pendelachse mit tiefgelegtem Schwerpunkt à la 220 von dem des real existierenden 300 SL unterscheidet. Im Oktober jenes Jahres stellt der amerikanische Sportwagenmeister Paul O'Shea auf der Solitude unweit der schwäbischen Metropole den 300 SL Roadster vor, der offiziell mit dem gebührenden Fanfarengeschmetter auf der Genfer Frühjahrsmesse 1957 präsentiert werden wird. Wieder hat den Stein Maxi Hoffman ins Rollen gebracht, der im Land der unbegrenzten Möglichkeiten gute Absatzchancen für eine offene Version des Stuttgarter Beaus wittert. Als am 8. Februar 1963 die Produktion des Roadsters in Sindelfingen versiegt, hat er es auf eine Verbreitung von 1858 Stück gebracht.

Pour le biographe de Mercedes, Karl Ludvigsen, il est l'homologue d'Emil Jellinek: Max Hoffman, depuis septembre 1952 importateur officiel de Daimler-Benz aux États-Unis, est autrichien comme celui-ci et comme Jellinek, il donne l'impulsion d'un modèle qui fera sensation – le tout un demi-siècle plus tard. Homme d'affaires avisé, il se montre séduit par le succès remporté par la 300 SL – millésime 1952 – et par sa forme. Une voiture comparable pour la route, confie-t-il à la direction de Mercedes à Stuttgart, serait tout à fait de nature à lui permettre de conquérir le marché américain et, pour confirmer ses dires, il commande 1000 «Ailes de mouette».

Lors de l'International Motor Sports Show de New York, le 6 février 1954, les milieux spécialisés impatients et d'innombrables fans attendent un produit charismatique: le coupé 300 SL pour la route. La parenté avec les SL de course est manifeste au premier coup d'œil et, comme pour celles-ci, on a fait de nécessité vertu: les éléments de l'encombrant châssis tubulaire, qui pèsent en tout et pour tout 50 kg, sont si élevés au-dessus de la route qu'un accès normal est absolument exclu. Les *gullwings* («ailes de mouette» en français), qui donneront à la voiture son surnom dans les pays anglophones, sont une fois de plus la solution pour échapper au dilemme. Et, comme dans les SL de la première génération, le six-cylindres est lui aussi incliné vers la gauche pour que la poupe basse et aérodynamique fende mieux le vent.

Curiosité en marge: le moteur de série développe 40 ch de plus que son homologue de compétition. Le «coupable» en est une pompe à injection à haute pression, qui fait sa première apparition dans une voiture de production de la maison et a été mise au point par le futur constructeur en chef, le Dr Hans Scherenberg. Le châssis est calqué sur celui de la 300 – sans ressorts supplémentaires et d'une fermeté sportive. Les sautes d'humeur de l'essieu brisé arrière à double articulation exigent toutefois encore un pilote émérite quand on flirte avec la limite d'adhérence – les voies et le déport changent en effet en permanence. D'août 1954 à mai 1957, le coupé aux ailes de mouette est produit à 1400 exemplaires, dont 29 avec une carrosserie en aluminium et un avec une carrosserie en matière plastique.

Dès l'été 1956, les rédacteurs de la revue spécialisée *auto motor und sport*, auxquels rien n'échappe, découvrent dans les environs de Stuttgart un châssis roulant que seuls des longerons longitudinaux surbaissés ainsi qu'un essieu brisé à une articulation avec centre de gravité abaissé à la 220 distinguent de la 300 SL qui existe réellement. En octobre de cette année-là, Paul O'Shea, le champion américain des voitures de sport, dévoile, sur le circuit de Solitude, à un jet de pierre de la métropole souabe, la 300 SL Roadster qui sera ensuite présentée officiellement en fanfare au Salon de printemps genevois de 1957. Maxi Hoffman voit, au pays des possibilités illimitées, de bons débouchés pour une version décapotable de la belle brute de Stuttgart. Quand la production du roadster sera arrêtée à Sindelfingen, le 8 février 1963, il aura été édité à 1858 exemplaires.

MERCEDES-BENZ 300SL (W198) 1954

Mercedes-Benz 300 SL Coupé 1955

winter, an attractive, removable coupé hardtop was available for an extra 1,500 marks; the already very effective bimetallic drum brakes, in which aluminum was coated with a thin layer of cast iron, gave way to Dunlop disc brakes in March 1961; and in March 1962 the SL was given a modified engine with an alloy block.

Einschneidende Vorkommnisse in der Modellgeschichte: Ab Oktober 1958, zeitgerecht zum nahenden Winter, ist ein attraktives abnehmbares Coupédach zum Mehrpreis von 1500 Mark erhältlich. Die bereits recht wirksamen Trommelbremsen in Verbundbauweise – Aluminium wird überzogen von einer dünnen Schicht aus Gusseisen – weichen im März 1961 Dunlop-Scheibenbremsen. Und noch im März 1962 spendiert man dem SL einen modifizierten Motor mit einem Block aus Leichtmetall.

Étapes décisives dans la généalogie du modèle: en octobre 1958, juste avant l'hiver menaçant, Mercedes propose un attrayant toit coupé démontable contre un supplément de prix de 1500 marks. Déjà assez efficaces avec leur structure mixte – aluminium recouvert d'une mince couche de fonte – les freins à tambours sont remplacés en mars 1961 par des freins à disques Dunlop. Et, dès mars 1962, la SL bénéficie d'un moteur modifié avec bloc en aluminium.

At sports-car races in the mid-fifties, drivers like the German Walter Schock, Swede Bengt Martenson, or Belgian Willy Mairesse drove to the start with the gullwings raised, to get as much fresh air into the cockpit as possible, but also, it should be said, to make an impression.

Bei den Sportwagenrennen der Mittfünfziger rollen seine Piloten wie der Deutsche Walter Schock, der Schwede Bengt Martenson oder der Belgier Willy Mairesse mit erhobenem Flügel-Werk an den Start, wegen der frischen Luft und wohl auch ein bisschen wegen des Show-Effekts.

Lors des courses de voitures de sport du milieu des années 1950, ses pilotes comme l'Allemand Walter Schock, le Suédois Bengt Martenson ou le Belge Willy Mairesse roulent jusqu'au départ avec les portières relevées. Pour avoir un peu d'air frais, mais aussi, sans aucun doute, pour épater la galerie.

Mercedes-Benz 300SL (W198) 1954

Chalk and cheese: the Roadster from 1959, with its comparitively gentle manners, and the Gullwing of 1955, a constant temptation to floor it – for those who could handle it...

Ungleiche Brüder: der Roadster von 1959, mit eher milden Manieren ausgestattet, vor dem Flügeltürer von 1955, einer ständigen Versuchung zum Schnellfahren – für den, der ihn beherrschte...

Des jumeaux bien dissemblables : le Roadster de 1959, aux manières plutôt policées, devant une « ailes de mouette » de 1955, une tentation permanente de conduire vite – pour celui qui savait la maîtriser...

Mercedes-Benz 300SL (W198) 1954

Mercedes-Benz 300SL (W198) 1954

imeless designs. A striking feature was the Talbot rear-view
mirror. The main feature that distinguished the roadster from
the coupé was its vertical light units.

ormen, denen die Zeit nichts anhaben kann. Ein markantes
Requisit: der Talbot-Rückspiegel. Das Gesicht des Roadsters
unterscheidet sich von dem des Coupés vor allem durch die
senkrechten Leuchteneinheiten.

Des formes à l'épreuve du temps. Un accessoire typique :
le rétroviseur Talbot. L'allure du roadster se distingue surtout
de celle du coupé par ses phares verticaux.

Mercedes-Benz 300SL (W198) 1954

When I finally got behind the wheel I was really excited. The car was a beauty, and from the first test drive onwards I had the unmistakable feeling of sitting in the perfect car, something that drivers dream of all their lives." This was how Juan Manuel Fangio, who won the 1954 and 1955 world championships in a Mercedes, later described the W196. A one-two finish in the French Grand Prix in Reims on 4 July 1954 would appear to back him up. But just a fortnight later in the British Grand Prix there was a rude awakening: the silver single-seater in its original streamlined form was simply unsuitable for some tracks. If he had not noticed it already, the Argentinian soon realized it when he hit a sand-filled marker drum at Beckett's Corner. He requested an urgent solution to fix the problem, and by the German Grand Prix on 1 August a single-seater with open wheels was available.

It was the first year of a new formula, 2.5 liters unblown or 750 cc blown. Rudolf Uhlenhaut, who was in charge of the project, and his team opted for the aspirated engine, a straight eight which was to be canted at an angle of 60 degrees in a spaceframe. A V12 in the pre-war tradition would have raised the center of gravity too high. Initially an embryonic experimental engine was developed, consisting of a single cylinder with a capacity of 310 cc and four valves. As with the engines from the Thirties, there were problems with valve timing at engine speeds above 8000 rpm until engineer Hans Gassmann came up with the solution of using a desmodromic system. This promised three benefits: higher engine speeds, higher power output, and greater reliability. When the company sought to patent his flash of inspiration, it found to its surprise that someone had already been there, done that, and possibly even got the T-shirt. Way back in the French Grand Prix of 1914, the Delage and the Schneider engines had used a similar principle which Gassmann had fortuitously rediscovered. Even relatively large and heavy valves could be actuated with the prescribed timing, so that there was no need for more than two valves per cylinder. The test embryo uttered its first cries in this configuration on 4 November.

Right from the outset, the racing engine was designed with fuel injection. The preliminary work was carried out by Karl-Heinz Göschel in collaboration with Bosch. Esso, the successor to Mercedes' pre-war supplier Standard Oil Company, offered 25 fuel blends. Seven were shortlisted. In the end blend R.D.1 was chosen: 45 per cent benzene, 25 per cent methyl alcohol, 25 per cent 110/130 octane gasoline, 3 per cent acetone, 2 per cent nitrobenzene.

The use of a single-pivot swing axle in contrast to Mercedes' competitors, who were using the de Dion system, caused surprise. But Uhlenhaut calmly responded by stating that his team were familiar with this principle and that furthermore there had not been adequate time to examine alternatives. On an icy December day in 1953 Karl Kling drove a totally bare rolling chassis out for a trial run

Als ich endlich hinter dem Lenkrad saß, war ich richtig aufgeregt. Der Wagen war schön, und vom ersten Test an hatte ich das untrügliche Gefühl, in dem perfekten Auto zu sitzen, von dem Fahrer ihr ganzes Leben träumen«, schreibt Juan Manuel Fangio, Weltmeister 1954 und 1955 auf Mercedes, später über den W196. Der Doppelerfolg beim Grand Prix von Frankreich in Reims in 4. Juli 1954 scheint ihm recht zu geben. Aber schon beim Großen Preis von England 14 Tage später geht eine eisige Dusche nieder: Für manche Kurse ist der silberne Einsitzer in seinem ursprünglichen Stromlinien-Gewand schlicht ungeeignet. Das merkt der Argentinier spätestens, als er in Beckett's Corner eines der mit Sand gefüllten Begrenzungsfässer umstößt. Er bittet dringlich um Abhilfe, und in der Tat steht schon beim deutschen Großen Preis am 1. August alternativ ein Monoposto mit freistehenden Rädern zur Verfügung.

Es ist das erste Jahr einer neuen Formel, 2,5 Liter ohne oder 750 ccm mit Kompressor. Rudolf Uhlenhaut, in dessen Obhut das Projekt gegeben ist, und die Männer um ihn votieren für den Saugmotor, einen Reihen-Achtzylinder, im Winkel von 60 Grad schräg in einen Gitterrohrrahmen einzubauen. Ein V12 in der Vorkriegs-Tradition würde den Schwerpunkt zu weit nach oben heben. Am Anfang steht indessen ein Versuchsaggregat mit einer einsamen Verbrennungseinheit in embryonalem Zustand gewissermaßen, mit 310 ccm und vier Ventilen. Wie bei den Maschinen der dreißiger Jahre stellen sich bei Drehzahlen über 8000/min Schwierigkeiten im Umkreis des Ventiltriebs ein, bis Ingenieur Hans Gassmann die rettende Idee der Zwangssteuerung hat. Sie verheißt dreierlei Vorteile: höhere Drehzahlen, höhere Leistung, höhere Sicherheit. Als man seinen Geistesblitz zum Patent anmelden will, macht man die überraschende Feststellung, dass es sich um einen alten Hut handelt: Schon beim Grand Prix de France 1914 arbeiteten die Triebwerke der Delage und der Schneider nach einem ähnlichen Prinzip, das Gassmann unversehens wiederentdeckt hat. Auch größere und schwerere Ventile lassen sich solchermaßen im vorgeschriebenen Rhythmus bewegen, so dass man es bei zwei Ventilen pro Zylinder belässt. Am 4. November gibt der Test-Embryo seinen ersten Brüller in dieser Konfiguration von sich.

Der Rennmotor ist von vornherein als Einspritzer konzipiert. Die Vorarbeit wird von Karl-Heinz Göschel geleistet im Zusammenwirken mit Bosch. 25 Treibstoff-Mixturen bietet Esso an, Nachfolger der Standard Oil Company, die Mercedes vor dem Krieg beliefert hat. Sieben kommen in die engere Wahl. Am Ende erhält Mischung R.D.1 den Zuschlag: 45 Prozent Benzol, 25 Prozent Methylalkohol, 25 Prozent Gasolin von 110/130 Oktan, 3 Prozent Aceton, 2 Prozent Nitrobenzol.

Überraschung löst die Verwendung einer Eingelenk-Pendelachse aus, wo die Konkurrenz im großen und ganzen auf die de-Dion-Auslegung setzt. Aber Uhlenhaut kontert gelassen, man kenne dieses Prinzip gut und habe

Quand je me suis enfin retrouvé derrière le volan j'étais vraiment excité. La voiture était belle et dès le premier essai, j'ai eu le sentiment qui n trompe pas d'être assis dans la voiture parfaite dont u pilote rêve sa vie entière », écrit plus tard Juan Manue Fangio, champion du monde en 1954 et 1955 sur Mercedes au sujet de la W196. Le doublé lors du Grand Prix de Franc à Reims, le 4 juillet 1954, semble lui donner raison. Mais dès le Grand Prix d'Angleterre, quinze jours plus tard, un douche écossaise lui dessille les yeux : sur certains circuits la monoplace argentée est tout simplement inconduisibl avec sa carrosserie aérodynamique originelle. L'Argenti s'en aperçoit au plus tard lorsque, dans Beckett's Corner, renverse l'un des fûts remplis de sable délimitant la pist Il prie instamment d'y remédier et, de fait, dès le Gran Prix d'Allemagne, le 1er août, on lui propose une mono place aux roues non carénées.

C'est la première année d'une nouvelle formule 2,5 litres sans compresseur ou 750 cm³ avec compresseu Rudolf Uhlenhaut, à qui l'on a confié le projet, et so équipe votent pour le moteur atmosphérique, un huit cylindres en ligne, qui est monté obliquement selon u angle de 60 degrés dans un châssis tubulaire. Un V12 dan la tradition de l'avant-guerre aurait eu un centre d gravité trop élevé. Tout a pourtant commencé avec u moteur expérimental à une seule chambre de combustio dans un état embryonnaire, en quelque sorte, avec 310 cm de cylindrée et quatre soupapes. Comme avec les moteur des années 1930, on rencontre des difficultés de distribu tion des soupapes dès que le régime dépasse 8000 tr/mi jusqu'à ce que l'ingénieur Hans Gassmann ait l'idé salvatrice de la distribution forcée. Elle présente troi avantages : des régimes supérieurs, une plus grande puis sance, une meilleure sécurité. La surprise est grand lorsque l'on veut faire breveter son idée de génie. O apprend en effet qu'il s'agit d'une bonne vieille recette au Grand Prix de France de 1914, déjà, les moteurs de Delage et des Schneider fonctionnaient selon un princip similaire que Gassmann a redécouvert sans le savoir Même des soupapes plus grosses et plus lourdes peuven ainsi être actionnées sur le rythme prescrit, et l'on peu donc se permettre de se contenter de deux soupapes pa cylindre. Le 4 novembre, le moteur embryon fait entendr ses premiers rugissements dans cette configuration.

Le moteur de course est conçu d'emblée avec l'injection Les travaux préliminaires sont pris en charge par Karl Heinz Göschel avec le concours de Bosch. Esso, le succes seur de la Standard Oil Company qui approvisionnai Mercedes avant la guerre, propose 25 cocktails de carbu rant. Sept sont sélectionnés pour les ultimes tests. Au bou du compte, c'est le mélange R.D.1 qui est choisi : 45 % d benzène, 25 % d'alcool de méthyle, 25 % de gazoline d 110/130 octanes, 3 % d'acétone, 2 % de nitrobenzène.

Mercedes défraye la chronique en utilisant un essieu brisé à une articulation alors que ses concurrents misen presque tous sur un essieu de Dion. Rudolf Uhlenhau

MERCEDES-BENZ W196R 1954

the works grounds in Untertürkheim. The first test drives at Hockenheim took place on 18 February 1954. These were followed by further tests, round and round the Baden racing circuit and at the Nürburgring, and finally also in Reims in advance of the great event of 4 July.

All this may account for the aura surrounding Mercedes, the still potent reputation for invincibility. However, it also underlines a more fundamental fact, great success is generally founded on meticulous preparation.

überdies nicht viel Zeit gehabt für andere Lösungen. An einem eisigen Dezembertag des Jahres 1953 reitet Karl Kling ein splitternacktes rollendes Chassis bei einem Probegalopp auf dem Werksgelände in Untertürkheim. Erste Versuchsfahrten in Hockenheim folgen am 18. Februar 1954. Weitere schließen sich an, immer wieder auf der alten Badischen Rennstrecke und auf dem Nürburgring, schließlich aber auch in Reims im Vorfeld des großen Ereignisses vom 4. Juli.

Dieses mag einen Nimbus begründen, den nie angetasteten Ruf der Unbesiegbarkeit. Es bezeugt aber auch eine tiefere Einsicht: dass hinter handfesten Erfolgen in der Regel penible Vorarbeit steckt.

réplique sans se démonter que l'on connaît bien ce principe et que l'on n'a d'ailleurs pas eu beaucoup de temps pour rechercher une autre solution. Par une froide journée de décembre 1953, Karl Kling fait subir un galop d'essai à un châssis roulant sans la moindre carrosserie dans l'enceinte de l'usine à Untertürkheim. De premiers essais ont ensuite lieu à Hockenheim le 18 février 1954. Puis d'autres sont organisés sur le vieux circuit du pays de Bade et sur le Nürburgring, mais aussi à Reims en amont du grand événement du 4 juillet.

Cela aura peut-être donné naissance à une légende, sa réputation jamais attaquée d'invincibilité. Mais c'est aussi le témoignage d'un enseignement plus profond: que tout succès est, en règle générale, le fruit d'un âpre travail préliminaire.

A retired warrior: even today there's no doubting that the W196R was perfectly designed for the job it had to do. The grille at the front right filtered the intake air fed to the engine.

Recke im Ruhestand: An der Zweckmäßigkeit seiner Formen lässt der W196R auch heute noch keinen Zweifel aufkommen. Das Gitternetz vorn rechts filtert die Atemluft des Motors.

Bolide à la retraite: aujourd'hui encore, la W196R ne laisse pas poindre le moindre doute quant à la fonctionnalité de ses formes. La grille à l'avant filtre l'air aspiré par le moteur.

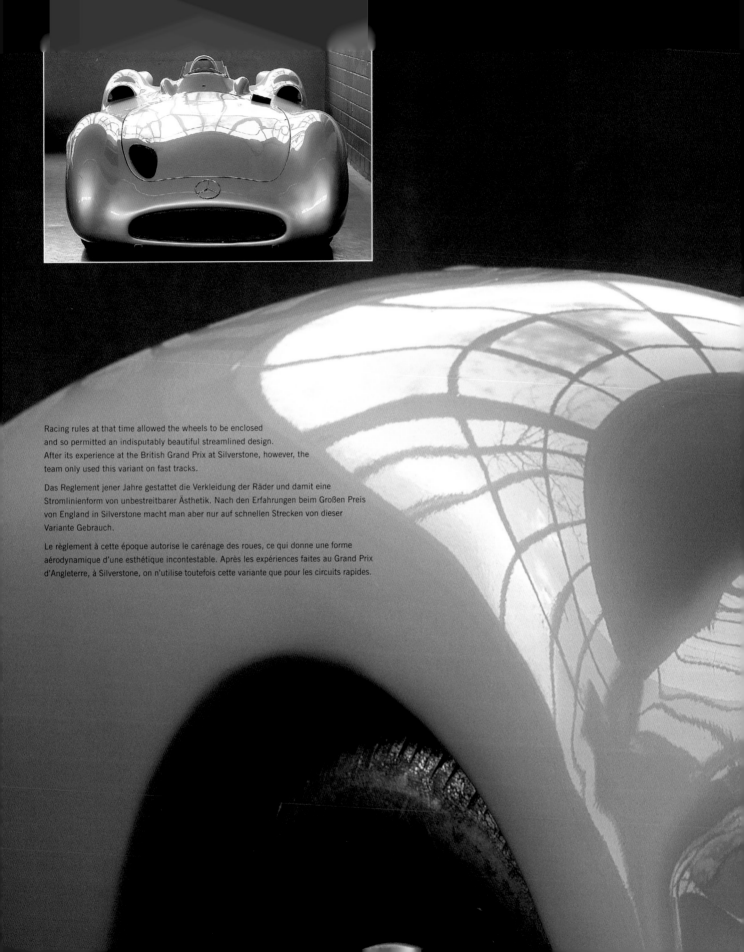

Racing rules at that time allowed the wheels to be enclosed
and so permitted an indisputably beautiful streamlined design.
After its experience at the British Grand Prix at Silverstone, however, the
team only used this variant on fast tracks.

Das Reglement jener Jahre gestattet die Verkleidung der Räder und damit eine
Stromlinienform von unbestreitbarer Ästhetik. Nach den Erfahrungen beim Großen Preis
von England in Silverstone macht man aber nur auf schnellen Strecken von dieser
Variante Gebrauch.

Le règlement à cette époque autorise le carénage des roues, ce qui donne une forme
aérodynamique d'une esthétique incontestable. Après les expériences faites au Grand Prix
d'Angleterre, à Silverstone, on n'utilise toutefois cette variante que pour les circuits rapides.

The fact that the 220a, launched in March 1954, and the 180 were closely related is unmistakable. Both were representatives of the new generation of unit-construction Mercedes. The difference, though, was that the 220 looked more stretched and elegant, while the 180, the unit body pioneer, came across as stocky and ungainly. Like the older model, the newer model's body was firmly welded to the floorpan chassis. The sub-frame and the front suspension using twin wishbones and coil springs were also re-employed. The rear axle, on the other hand, a single-joint low-pivot swing axle as fitted to the w196 Grand Prix car, represented the state of the art. It ensured that the driver was not caught out by severe changes in track widths and cambers. The extended wheelbase – lengthened by 170 mm (6.7 in) to 2820 mm (9 ft 3 in) – gave more legroom to the rear passengers and to the six-cylinder engine under the stretched bonnet – a well-known feature of the 220 from 1951. Higher compression, a more positive camshaft, and a larger carburetor helped the car achieve a power output of 85 bhp. Much attention had been lavished on the brakes, with strongly ribbed drums to which cooling air was ducted via slits in the hubs. From September 1955 onwards a servo brake fitted as standard relieved the load on the driver's right foot.

The successor 220s introduced in March 1956 was almost identical, though it developed 100 bhp, to which two governor carburetors contributed their mite. The engine now rested on four points on the sub-frame instead of two. An additional trim strip indicated the minor difference. At the same time the cut-down 219 was launched, a cross between the 190 and the engine of the 220a. It cost 2,000 marks less, and the clumsy type designation meant that it was already slightly devalued in the eyes of potential customers.

When Daimler-Benz decided in August 1957 to lavish free-of-charge upgrades on almost all the cars in its range, the main change to the 219 and 220s was an increase in power, one by 5 and the other by 6 bhp. A Hydrak hydraulically-operated automatic clutch was available as an option at an extra cost of 450 marks, and it was available also on the 220 SE of September 1958 which was powered to 115 bhp by an intermittent induction-manifold fuel-injection system. With only 1974 cars built in a 10-month period, this model remained rare and exclusive. Even more exclusive were the most exquisite models in the series, the sumptuously appointed cabriolet A/C, which appeared in the summer of 1956, and the coupé that followed in the autumn. Both underwent the same changes as the sedan and, although this was discontinued in August 1959, they were built for a little longer – though then fitted with the engine of the new 220 SEb.

Unverkennbar ist die nahe Verwandtschaft des 220a, vorgestellt im März 1954, zum 180: Beide sind Vertreter der neuen Mercedes-Generation in Pontongestalt. Nur wirkt der 220 gestreckter und eleganter, wo der Ponton-Pionier 180 gedrungen und ein wenig unansehnlich daherkommt. Wie bei dem etwas älteren Modell ist die Karosserie des etwas neueren fest verschweißt mit der Rahmenbodenanlage. Übernommen werden auch der Fahrschemel und die Vorderradaufhängung an Doppel-Querlenkern und Schraubenfedern. Den letzten Stand der Dinge hingegen verkörpert die Hinterachse: eine Eingelenk-Pendelachse mit tief liegendem Drehpunkt wie am Grand-Prix-Rennwagen w196. Sie gewährleistet, dass der Fahrer nicht mehr durch heftige Spur- und Sturzänderungen überrumpelt wird. Vom verlängerten Radstand – um 170 auf 2820 Millimeter – profitieren die Passagiere im Fond und der Sechszylinder unter der weit heruntergezogenen Motorhaube, ein alter Bekannter aus dem 220 von 1951. Eine höhere Verdichtung, eine schärfere Nockenwelle und ein größerer Vergaser verhelfen ihm indes zu 85 PS. Viel Sorgfalt hat man auf die Bremsen verwendet, mit stark verrippten Trommeln, die durch Schlitze in den Felgen mit Kühlluft beschickt werden. Ab September 1955 nimmt ein serienmäßiger Bremskraftverstärker dem rechten Fuß ein gutes Stück Arbeit ab.

Fast identisch ist der Nachfolger 220s ab März 1956 mit 100 PS, zu denen zwei Register-Vergaser ihr Scherflein beitragen. Der Motor ruht nun an vier anstatt bisher zwei Punkten auf dem Fahrschemel. Eine zusätzliche Zierleiste weist auf den kleinen Unterschied hin. Zugleich bringt man die Mager-Version 219 auf den Markt, eine Kreuzung des 190 mit der Maschine des 220a zum Minderpreis von 2000 Mark und bereits durch die unbeholfene Typenbezeichnung ein bisschen in der Gunst der Kundschaft geschmälert.

Als Daimler-Benz im August 1957 über fast allen Personenwagen seiner Palette das Füllhorn kostenloser Verbesserungen ausschüttet, gewinnen 219 und 220s vor allem an Stärke, der eine fünf, der andere sechs PS. Auf Wunsch und zum Mehrpreis von 450 Mark ist die hydraulisch-automatische Kupplung Hydrak zu haben, auch für den 220 SE vom September 1958, der durch eine intermittierende Saugrohr-Einspritzung zu 115 PS befähigt wird. Mit 1974 Exemplaren in zehn Monaten Bauzeit bleibt er rar und exklusiv. Das gilt erst recht für die schönsten Blüten der Baureihe, mit Prunk sanft überladen, das Cabriolet A/C, das im Sommer 1956 seine Aufwartung macht, und das Coupé, das im Herbst nachgereicht wird. Beide machen die verschiedenen Metamorphosen der Limousine mit und werden, nachdem diese im August 1959 verblichen ist, noch eine Zeitlang weitergebaut – allerdings schon ausgerüstet mit dem Triebwerk des neuen 220 SEb.

La 220a présentée en mars 1954 est incontestabl ment un parent tout proche de la 180 : elles so toutes les deux des représentantes de la nouve génération de Mercedes à carrosserie ponton. Sauf que 220 aux lignes plus allongées est plus élégante alors que pionnière du ponton, la 180, est plus trapue et, donc, u peu moins plaisante au regard. La carrosserie de la no velle est soudée à la plate-forme. Elle reprend aussi l'id du berceau auxiliaire et la suspension avant avec doubl bras transversaux et ressorts hélicoïdaux. Le train arrièr un essieu brisé à une articulation avec centre de gravi surbaissé comme pour la voiture de Grand Prix, la w19

Elle épargne désormais au conducteur les risqu inhérents aux brutaux changements de voie et de dépo Les bénéficiaires de l'empattement allongé – de 170 mm 2820 mm – sont les passagers de la banquette arrière ain que les six-cylindres qui prend ses aises sous le long cap moteur – une bonne vieille connaissance de la 220 de 19 Un taux de compression supérieur, un arbre à cames pl pointu et un plus gros carburateur lui donnent revanche une puissance de 85 ch. Les freins ont recuei une grande attention avec des tambours aux nombreus rainures qui sont refroidis par de l'air provenant de fent dans les jantes. À partir de septembre 1955, un servofre monté en série décharge le pied droit d'une bonne portic de travail.

Son successeur, la 220s présentée en mars 1956 av 100 ch auxquels les deux carburateurs à registre contr buent de façon notable, lui est presque identique. moteur repose maintenant sur le berceau auxiliaire av quatre et non plus deux paliers. Un jonc décora supplémentaire le long du bas de caisse souligne la pet différence. Mercedes commercialise également u version amaigrie, la 219, une version de la 190 avec moteur de la 220a à un prix inférieur de 2000 marks que la dénomination choisie sans bonheur handica quelque peu dans les faveurs de la clientèle.

Lorsqu'en août 1957, Daimler-Benz déverse sur presq toutes les voitures de tourisme de son programme le cor d'abondance d'améliorations gratuites, la 219 et la 22 gagnent surtout en puissance, la première avec cinq l'autre avec six chevaux. Sur demande et contre un supp ment de prix de 450 marks, on peut obtenir l'embraya hydraulique automatique Hydrak, ce qui vaut égalem pour la 220 SE de septembre 1958, qui est capable de dé lopper 115 ch grâce à une injection intermittente dans tubulures d'aspiration. Avec 1974 exemplaires produits dix mois, elle reste rare et exclusive. Cela vaut a fortic pour les plus belles fleurs de la gamme, d'un luxe de b aloi, le cabriolet A/C qui tire sa révérence au cours l'été 1956, et le coupé, qui vient le rejoindre à l'automr Eux aussi bénéficient des différentes métamorphos subies par la berline et, alors que celle-ci disparaîtra programme en août 1959, ils seront encore constru pendant un certain temps – mais déjà équipés du mote de la nouvelle 220 SEb.

e introduction of the Cabriolet A/C type 220S in
y 1956 represented in a sense the first appearance
unit-body construction with its associated problems.
the time being, the monocoque body required the
pport of a hardtop.

Mit der Einführung des Cabriolets A/C vom Typ 220S
im Juli 1956 findet gewissermaßen die erstmalige
Eröffnung des Pontonaufbaus statt mit den damit
verbundenen Schwierigkeiten: Die selbsttragende
Karosserie ist zunächst einmal auf die Unterstützung
des Festdachs angewiesen.

Avec l'introduction du Cabriolet A/C de la 220S, en
juillet 1956, la première ouverture d'une carrosserie
ponton a lieu avec les difficultés que cela implique:
la carrosserie autoporteuse ne peut pas, en effet,
se passer de la rigidité que confère un toit fixe.

Experiments with a new design – the relative proportions of the front and rear were not all they might have been, and the chrome trim was a little overdone. The wide doors also gave access to the rear bench seat. It was rather a squeeze in the back.

Experimente mit einer neuen Form: Nicht unbedingt ausgewogen sind die Proportionen von Bug und Heck, etwas zu dick aufgetragen die Chromapplikationen. Die breiten Türen geben auch den Zugang frei zur hinteren Sitzbank. Im Fond geht es leicht beengt zu.

Expériences avec une nouvelle forme : les proportions de la proue et de la poupe ne sont pas très équilibrées et les applications de chromes sont un peu trop appuyées. Les larges portières donnent aussi accès à la banquette arrière, où l'espace est cependant un peu compté.

This car shared the same fate as all those whom fortune has blessed with charismatic siblings. While purely at a visual level the 300 SL conjured up a hint of drama and adventure at the New York International Motor Sports Show in February 1954, the impression given by the 190 SL alongside it was neat, certainly sporty and with dashing lines supplied by Mercedes designers Karl Wilfert and Walter Häckert, but – well – a little bit conventional. The statistics, however, tell their own tale; between May 1955 and February 1963, 25,881 of these cars were sold – it was a success.

Before that, however, there was still work to be done. Many aspects of the model exhibited in New York had not been thoroughly thought-out, and it was not until the Geneva Spring Motor Show in 1955 that the smaller SL appeared in its final form. It was available as a roadster, which was actually a cabriolet with its wind-down windows and a tough fabric top, or as a coupé which was basically a hardtop version with a removable alloy roof. Many reliable features of other series were incorporated in the 190 SL, which was only available in silver-grey until the end of 1956. Its engine, four inline cylinders with a chain-driven overhead camshaft and two governor downdraft carburetors, was in effect a part of the straight six from the "Three Hundred," delivering a respectable 105 bhp, even if it was rather rough beyond 3000 rpm. Its all-steel body was of monocoque design, welded to the shortened floorpan chassis of the type 180.

The engine was mounted on the sub-frame initially only at the front, though from January 1956 there were two further support points at the back. As with the 220 a, a single-joint, low-pivot swing axle counteracted any particularly severe changes in camber. A racing variant with aluminum doors and a small windshield was dropped in great secrecy. A series of minor modifications punctuated the 190 SL's lifetime. In March 1956 wider chrome trim strips bordered the area above the door; in June of the same year it was given the larger tail-lights of the 220 a, 219, and 220 s sedans. In July 1957 the rear number-plate light was incorporated into the bumper overriders to make room for the larger number plates required by changes in legislation. And in October 1959 the coupé was given a new hardtop with an enlarged rear screen like those also found in the soft top of the roadster from this period.

The 190 SL's reputation was regrettably slightly tarnished. Admittedly it was regarded as an indispensable prop for films and fashion magazines. But the Frankfurt demi-mondaine Rosemarie Nitribitt also bought one to increase her appeal, and she enjoyed a rather dubious popularity in Germany which rubbed off on all the possessions with which she surrounded herself.

Er scheint das Los all derer zu teilen, denen das Schicksal charismatische Brüder und Schwestern an die Seite gestellt hat: Wo der 300 SL auf der New Yorker International Motor Sports Show im Februar 1954 schon rein visuell von einem Hauch von Drama und Abenteuer umgeben ist, wirkt der 190 SL neben ihm adrett, gewiss auch sportlich-schmissig mit seiner Silhouette, die die Mercedes-Mitarbeiter Karl Wilfert und Walter Häckert entworfen haben, aber eben ein bisschen bieder. Indessen sprechen Zahlen ihre eigene Sprache: Zwischen Mai 1955 und Februar 1963 bringt es das Modell auf eine Auflage von 25 881 Exemplaren – ein Erfolgstyp.

Bis dahin gibt es noch einiges zu tun: Vieles an dem New Yorker Exponat ist nicht ganz ins reine gedacht, und erst auf dem Genfer Frühlingssalon 1955 erscheint der kleinere SL in seiner endgültigen Form. Es gibt ihn als Roadster, der eigentlich ein Cabriolet ist mit seinen Kurbelfenstern und einem soliden Stoffverdeck, oder als Coupé, bei dem es sich im Grunde genommen um eine Hardtop-Version handelt, deren Leichtmetalldach man abnehmen kann. Viel Solides aus anderen Serien wird in den 190 SL eingespeist, der bis einschließlich 1956 nur in kleidsamem Silbergrau zu haben ist. Sein Motor, vier Verbrennungseinheiten in Linie mit einer kettengetriebenen obenliegenden Nockenwelle und zwei Register-Fallstromvergasern, ist praktisch ein Teil des Reihensechszylinders aus dem »Dreihunderter«, 105 anständige PS stark, wenn auch jenseits der 3000/min ein wenig knurrig. Sein Ganzstahlaufbau ist selbsttragend, verschweißt mit der verkürzten Rahmenbodengruppe des Typs 180.

Die Maschine ist auf dem Fahrschemel zunächst nur vorn gelagert, ab Januar 1956 gibt es zwei zusätzliche Auflagepunkte hinten. Wie am 220 a beugt eine Eingelenk-Pendelachse mit tiefgelegtem Drehpunkt allzu heftigen Sturzänderungen vor. Von einer Renn-Variante mit Aluminiumtüren und einer kleinen Windschutzscheibe nimmt man klammheimlich wieder Abstand. Die Modell-Vita des 190 SL ist gesäumt von sanften Retuschen: Im März 1956 fassen breitere Chromleisten den oberen Türabschluss ein, im Juni des gleichen Jahres erhält er die größeren Rückleuchten der Limousinen 220 a, 219 und 220 s. Im Juli 1957 wird die hintere Kennzeichenbeleuchtung in die Stoßstangenhörner eingelegt, so dass die vorgeschriebenen voluminöseren Nummernschilder Platz finden. Und im Oktober 1959 stülpt man dem Coupé ein neues Hardtop über mit einer vergrößerten Heckscheibe, wie sie von nun an auch im Stoffdach des Roadsters zu finden ist.

Da ist der Ruf des 190 SL schon leicht ramponiert. Gewiss muss er herhalten als schier unentbehrliches Requisit für Filme und Modejournale. Aber auch die Frankfurter Lebedame Rosemarie Nitribitt hat sich einen zum Kundenfang zugelegt, und die erfreut sich in Deutschland dubioser Popularität, mithin auch das Hab und Gut, mit dem sie sich schmückt...

Elle semble partager le sort de tous ceux auxquels destin a fait côtoyer des frères et sœurs charism tiques : alors que la 300 SL présentée au New Yo International Motor Sports Show de février 1954 était d nimbée, sur le seul plan visuel, d'une aura de drame d'aventure, la 190 SL semble comparativement jolie, cer sportive et élégante avec sa silhouette qui est l'œuvre deux collaborateurs de Mercedes, Karl Wilfert et Wal Häckert, mais malheureusement aussi un peu banale.

Les chiffres, par contre, parlent une toute au langue : de mai 1955 à février 1963, ce modèle a en effet produit à 25 881 exemplaires. Un succès sans appel.

Mais, avant d'en arriver là, il aura fallu bien du trava bien des détails du modèle exporté à New York restaie encore à régler et ce n'est qu'au Salon de printemps Genève, en 1955, que la petite SL paraît sous sa for définitive. Elle est proposée en roadster, mais c'est réalité un cabriolet avec ses fenêtres à manivelle e solide capote de toit, ou en coupé, qui est en réalité u version en *hard-top* dont on peut ôter le toit en aluminiu On greffe en revanche sur la 190 SL, qui n'est disponible jusqu'en 1956 compris – que dans un élégant gris métalli de nombreux organes solides provenant d'autres séri Son moteur, un quatre-cylindres en ligne avec arbre cames en tête entraîné par chaînes et deux carburateu inversés à registre est pratiquement un fragment du s cylindres en ligne de la « Trois Cents », avec 105 cheva piaffants quoique légèrement lymphatiques au-delà 3000 tr/min. Sa carrosserie tout acier est autoporteu et soudée sur la plate-forme à empattement raccourci la 180.

Le moteur reçoit, à partir de janvier 1956, deux pali supplémentaires à l'arrière. Comme sur la 220 a, un essi brisé à une articulation et ancrage surbaissé réprime modifications de carrosserie trop violentes. Une versi course avec portes en aluminium et petit pare-br coupe-vent disparaît discrètement aux oubliettes. curriculum vitae de la 190 SL est ponctué de discrèt retouches : en mars 1956, des joncs de chrome plus larg ornent l'arête de porte supérieure et, en juin de la mêm année, elle reçoit les feux arrière de plus grandes dime sions des berlines 220 a, 219 et 220 s. En juillet 1957, l'écla rage de la plaque signalétique arrière est placé dans l cornes de pare-chocs, ce qui permet de monter les plaqu minéralogiques de plus grandes dimensions désorma prescrites. Et, en octobre 1959, le coupé reçoit un nouvea *hard-top* avec une lunette arrière plus vaste identique celle du roadster.

Mais la réputation de la 190 SL est déjà légèrem entachée. Certes, elle a encore un beau rôle à jouer en ta qu'accessoire absolument indispensable pour les films revues de mode. Mais la prostituée de luxe francforto Rosemarie Nitribitt s'est aussi fait, avec elle, une jo clientèle et elle est victime en Allemagne d'une populari douteuse, ce qui vaut également pour ceux qui se pavan au volant de cette voiture...

MERCEDES-BENZ 190 SL   1955

he little brother. The similarity between the 190SL and the 300SL
clear to see. This too was a good-looking car and popular to boot.
owever, it did not find its way onto the racetracks.

leiner Bruder: Die Ähnlichkeit zum 300SL steht dem 190SL
s Gesicht geschrieben. Schön ist auch er und populär dazu.
as Ambiente der Pisten jedoch umfächelt ihn nicht.

etite sœur: la similitude de la 190SL avec la 300SL est
contestable. Tout aussi jolie et, ce qui ne gâte rien, populaire.
ais elle n'a jamais reniflé l'odeur d'huile des circuits.

Mercedes-Benz 190SL 1955

The 190 SL occupied the niche for
sporty touring car with good
driving performance within the
ever-expanding Mercedes range.
Caressed by the summer heat of an
Atlantic high, driving with the top
down was unalloyed pleasure.

In der sich immer ausweitenden
Typenpalette von Mercedes hat der
190 SL seinen Platz als sportliches
Reisefahrzeug mit guten Fahreigenschaften. Bei offenem
Verdeck in der Schmeichelwärme
des Azorenhochs wird der Ausflug
zum reinen Vergnügen.

Dans la gamme toujours plus
diversifiée des Mercedes, la
190 SL a sa place bien à elle
comme voiture de voyage sportive
et sûre. Avec la capote ouverte
pour accueillir les premières
chaleurs du printemps, une
excursion à la campagne est
un plaisir sans mélange.

The robust four-cylinder engine did not necessarily need to be monitored by the tachometer. But it was all part of the sporty image.

Nicht unbedingt bedarf der kernige Vierzylinder der Überwachung durch den Drehzahlmesser. Aber der gehört zum sportiven Image.

Le compte-tours n'est pas absolument nécessaire pour surveiller le quatre-cylindres à la rauque sonorité. Mais il contribue à lui donner une touche sportive.

The sum of its parts created a whole of naked aggression and captivating beauty, in which form coincided perfectly with function. However, the 1955 300 SLR drew on diverse components and elements, ideas from the racing SL of 1952 and the W196R Formula 1 car from 1954, and in particular tank-like stability teamed with surprisingly delicate touches. "Although Stirling and I honestly tried to wreck the car by leaping over chasms, charging through walls and bumping into other cars, it somehow survived," mocked Peter Collins after winning the Targa Florio on 16 October 1955 with Stirling Moss. It's true: during an excursion to Madonie in Sicily by Moss, the SLR of the two Britons landed astride a cliff edge, leaving the drive wheels turning in mid-air. Collins treated the Mercedes equally badly when he demolished a crumbling wall. And yet Moss was still squeezing lap records out of it at the end. The 300 SLR's engine delivered 296 bhp before Moss's victory in the Mille Miglia on 30 April of the same year, and it was still delivering 296 bhp afterwards when tested in the factory – the hood had not even been lifted during the thousand miles. Another one ran for 10,000 km (6,200 miles) in 32 hours at racing speed on the dynamometer, and the only intervention necessary was to replace the oiling rings at 6,000 km (3,730 miles). The engine was developed from its 2.5-liter counterpart in Formula 1, an inline eight-cylinder with two banks of four combustion units, with the heads and blocks in a housing in accordance with an ancient Mercedes custom. The cylinder linings were chrome-plated, the valves used a desmodromic system employing two overhead camshafts to operate them. An engine of this kind required 30 to 40 liters of fuel, delivered by a Bosch injection pump, per 100 km (6–8 mpg), whereas it had only a moderate thirst for oil. The tried-and-tested stiff spaceframe was used again, and it required all the team's ingenuity to fit in all the drive units and containers, such as the 265-liter (70-gal) fuel tank.

Stirling Moss admitted in honest amazement that his races had never been so thoroughly prepared. During practice for the Mille Miglia, for example, three cars were available to the drivers, while in the race itself they had four brand new cars at their disposal. The 300 SLR proved highly adaptable. At Le Mans and in the Swedish Grand Prix, airbrakes assisted the braking process. The drivers operated a lever to actuate the air brakes which could be hydraulically raised or lowered in the air flow with the aid of the engine oil. In two special variants of the 300 SLR, christened Uhlenhaut Coupés after the project leader, an attempt was made to blend the consistency of the series 300 SL with the power and agility of the racing car. The Swiss magazine *Automobil Revue* measured a top speed of 284 kph (176 mph) for one of these hybrids, but recommended at the same time that the occupants should always wear ear protection.

In that season the 300 SLRs were definitely not the fastest but they were certainly the best all-round sports cars, and so they maintained a slight points lead to win the

MERCEDES-BENZ 300 SLR   1955

The 300SLR was used in 1955 with this spoiler as an air brake at Le Mans and the Swedish Grand Prix in Kristianstad. Although it had to withstand substantial forces, it worked reliably.

Mit diesem als Luftbremse ausgebildeten Heckteil wird der 300SLR 1955 in Le Mans und beim Großen Preis von Schweden in Kristianstad eingesetzt. Obwohl erhebliche Kräfte auf sie einwirken, arbeitet sie zuverlässig.

La 300SLR est engagée en 1955 au Mans et au Grand Prix de Suède, à Kristianstad, avec ce frein aérodynamique arrière rétractable. Bien que l'énergie encaissée ait été considérable, il a toujours fonctionné.

championship. Their career ended on a somber note, however, because of the deaths at Le Mans on 11 June 1955 when Frenchman Pierre Levegh's car flew into the crowd and disintegrated. The accident occurred at half past six, two and half hours after the start. The Mercedes team of Juan Manuel Fangio and Stirling Moss had a two-lap lead. Shortly before two o'clock in the morning, the remaining cars were flagged into the pits on management orders from Stuttgart. The start at the Targa Florio after this was merely a case of going through the motions.

den Insassen, unter allen Umständen Ohrenschützer zur Hilfe zu ziehen.

In jener Saison sind die 300SLR keineswegs die schnellsten, aber die besten Sportwagen all round, und so gewinnen sie das Championat mit knappem Vorsprung. Ihre Karriere endet gleichwohl auf einer düsteren Note wegen der Toten von Le Mans am 11. Juni 1955, als der Wagen des Franzosen Pierre Levegh in die Zuschauerränge hinein zerplatzt. Um halb sieben ereignet sich der Unfall, zweieinhalb Stunden nach dem Start. Die Mercedes-Riege Juan Manuel Fangio und Stirling Moss führt mit zwei Runden Vorsprung. Kurz vor zwei Uhr nachts befolgt man eine Order des Managements in Stuttgart und flaggt die verbleibenden Wagen in die Box. Der Einsatz bei der Targa Florio bleibt da nur noch eine Pflichtübung.

Cette saison-là, les 300SLR sont loin d'être les plus rapides, mais elles sont globalement les meilleures voitures de sport et gagnent donc le championnat, quoique avec une avance mineure. Leur carrière se termine pourtant sur une note dramatique à cause de la catastrophe des 24 heures du Mans. Le 11 juin 1955, la voiture du Français Pierre Levegh sort de la piste après une collision et explose au milieu des spectateurs. L'accident se produit à six heures et demic, deux heures et demie après le départ. Les deux meilleurs pilotes de Mercedes, Juan Manuel Fangio et Stirling Moss, sont en tête avec deux tours d'avance. Peu avant deux heures du matin arrive un ordre de la direction de Stuttgart et on fait rentrer au drapeau les voitures au stand. La participation à la Targa Florio n'est alors plus qu'un exercice auquel l'on se plie à contrecœur.

Mercedes-Benz 300SLR 1955

The driver's head restraint was raised together with the air brake. The apertures were to enable the driver to see behind him and they had to be enlarged for Le Mans on the explicit instruction of the organizers.

Mit der Luftbremse richtet sich auch die Kopfstütze für den Piloten auf. Die Scharten dienen einer Sicht nach hinten und müssen für Le Mans auf eine ausdrückliche Weisung der Veranstalter hin vergrößert werden.

L'appuie-tête pour le pilote se met en place en même temps que le frein aérodynamique. Les meurtrières lui permettent de regarder vers l'arrière et doivent être agrandies pour Le Mans sur une instruction expresse des organisateurs.

Mercedes-Benz 300SLR 1955

Even though its hardtop protected
passengers from the vagaries of
the weather, the Uhlenhaut coupé
remained a barely-tamed racing
car, an audaciously beautiful
curiosity.

Auch wenn sein Festdach die
Passagiere vor den Schikanen
der Witterung schützt, bleibt
das Uhlenhaut-Coupé ein
kaum gezähmter Rennwagen,
ein Kuriosum von verwegener
Schönheit.

Même si son toit fixe protège les
passagers des aléas de la
météorologie, le coupé Uhlenhaut
reste une voiture de course à peine
civilisée, une curiosité d'une beauté
irrésistible.

Mercedes-Benz 300SLR 1955

Two features betrayed the Uhlenhaut coupé's origins: like the hardtop 300SL of 1952 it had gullwings, and the trunk was opened by means of the chrome-plated D. The powerplant of the 300SLR directly adjacent to the huge internal ribbed brake drums. At right, details of the spartan cockpit and the gate plus gearshift. The trunk could hold two spare tires.

Doppelzitat: Wie der geschlossene 300SL von 1952 hat das Uhlenhaut-Coupé Flügeltüren, und wie bei jenem lässt sich das Gepäckabteil durch Herunterklappen des verchromten D entriegeln. Das Kraftwerk des 300SLR in unmittelbarer Nachbarschaft der innenliegenden riesigen verrippten Bremstrommeln. Rechts das spartanische Cockpit und die Kulisse nebst Schaltknauf. Der Kofferraum kann mit zwei Reserverädern beladen werden.

Double réminiscence : comme la 300SL Coupé de 1952, le coupé Uhlenhaut a des portières en ailes de papillon et son coffre s'ouvre en levant le D chromé. Le propulseur de la 300SLR à proximité immédiate des gigantesques tambours de freins avec leurs rainures. À droite, le tableau de bord spartiate et la grille avec le levier de vitesses. Le coffre peut recevoir deux roues de secours.

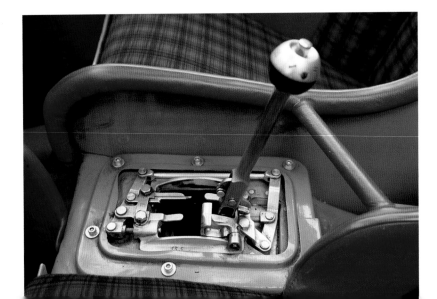

Design features sometimes inspire names that are much more memorable and enduring than the official company designations. Often they are vernacular terms that become part of the tradition. Thus it was that the earliest unit body type was known in German as the "Ponton"-Mercedes (or pontoon Mercedes), and this was followed in 1959 by the "Fin," so-called because of its gentle extensions at the upper ends of the rear fenders. These were concessions to contemporary taste that was greatly influenced by the United States, though they were much more restrained than, for example, the enormous protuberances of the Cadillac ("sharks fins") or Lincoln. And since Mercedes was determined that form should follow function, the new baby was given a matter-of-fact name: "Peilstege".

The motto for the 220 b, 220 sb and 220 seb was "The new six-cylinders – a class of their own." Their quality showed particularly in the safety features. For the first time ideas from Mercedes employee Béla Barényi had been implemented with all their implications. In the event of an accident, a tough passenger cage would be protected by deformable zones at the front and rear. Safety consciousness also extended to the interior design – a cushioned pad was added to the steering wheel, and the dashboard was also cushioned. Notorious slashers and stabbers among the operating levers were flexibly mounted and some were also recessed. Wedge-pivot door locks were steps in the same direction.

Outwardly the two s models differed in that the 220 sb had more lavish chrome trim, and its engine was fed by two Solex carburetors, resulting in a power output of 95 bhp. The injection engine of the seb was also retrofitted with linear induction manifolds, resulting in 120 bhp compared with its predecessor's 115 bhp. The subframe consisted of a simple cross-strut, flexibly connected to the chassis at two points. A compensating spring above the swing-axle pivot ensured even distribution of the axle load to the two drive wheels. Moving the four shock absorbers to the outside improved their accessibility and also their ability to damp vibrations. In April 1962 the s models were fitted with disc brakes. 16 months later so was the 220 b and a servo brake was fitted as standard at the same time. The Hydrak semi-automatic gearbox was an option until the beginning of 1962, when a fully automatic gearbox, a hydraulic clutch connected to a 4-speed planetary gear system, rendered it obsolete. This was available for the seb from April onwards and from August 1962 onwards for an extra 1,400 marks for the other two models. Like air suspension and power steering, this was fitted as standard from August 1961 onwards to the top-of-the-range model, the 300 se, which was then joined by a stretched version, launched at the Geneva Spring Motor Show in March 1963 with a 100-mm- (4-in-) longer wheelbase. When production of this series ended in the summer of 1965, the 230 s remained available for a time as a rebored derivative of the 220 b. However, the coupé, launched at

Manchmal regen Designmerkmale zu Namen an, die einprägsamer und dauerhafter sind als die offizielle Nomenklatur einer Firma. Der Volksmund prägt sie, und schließlich gehen sie ein in die Überlieferung. So folgt auf den »Ponton«-Mercedes 1959 die »Heckflosse«, so genannt nach sanften Auswüchsen an den oberen Enden der hinteren Kotflügel. Es sind Konzessionen an einen Zeitgeschmack, der aus den Vereinigten Staaten gespeist wird, gleichwohl viel zurückhaltender als etwa die enormen Protuberanzen der Cadillac (»Haifischflossen«) oder Lincoln. Und da man bei Mercedes darauf bedacht ist, dass die Form der Funktion zu folgen habe, bekommt das Kind auch gleich einen sachlichen Namen: Peilstege.

Das Motto über der Baureihe 220 b, 220 sb und 220 seb: Die neuen Sechszylinder – eine Klasse für sich. Das beginnt mit dem Bemühen um Sicherheit. Zum ersten Mal hat man Ideengut von Mercedes-Kostgänger Béla Barényi konsequent umgesetzt: Ein stabiler Passagiertrakt wird im Falle eines Unfalls abgefedert durch verformbare Zonen vorn und hinten. Mehr Sicherheit zugleich für den Innenraum: Auf das Lenkrad ist eine Polsterplatte gesattelt, auch das Armaturenbrett ist gepolstert. Notorische Schlitzer und Stecher unter den Bedienungselementen wurden elastisch und zum Teil versenkt angeordnet. Keilzapfen-Türschlösser sind Schritte in die gleiche Richtung.

Nach außen unterscheiden sich die beiden s-Modelle im wesentlichen durch üppigeren Chromzierrat vom 220 sb, dessen Triebwerk nun durch zwei Solex-Vergaser ernährt wird und 95 PS leistet. Auch beim Einspritzmotor des seb wurde nachgerüstet mit geraden Ansaugrohren: 120 PS gegenüber den 115 PS des Vorgängers. Der Fahrschemel besteht nur noch aus einem simplen Querträger, an zwei Stellen elastisch verbunden mit dem Rahmen. Eine Ausgleichsfeder oberhalb des Drehpunkts der Pendelachse sorgt für gleichmäßige Verteilung der Achslast auf die beiden Antriebsräder. Dass alle vier Stoßdämpfer ganz nach außen gelegt wurden, verbessert ihre Zugänglichkeit sowie die Schwingungsdämpfung. Im April 1962 erhalten die s-Modelle Scheibenbremsen, der 220 b zieht 16 Monate später nach und wird zugleich mit einem serienmäßigen Bremskraftverstärker ausgestattet. Der Halbautomat Hydrak ist noch bis Anfang 1962 zu haben, schon obsolet angesichts einer vollwertigen Automatik, die bereits seit dem April für den seb und ab August 1962 für einen Aufpreis von 1400 Mark für die beiden anderen erhältlich ist, eine hydraulische Kupplung mit nachgeschaltetem Viergang-Planetengetriebe. Sie gehört, wie Luftfederung und Servolenkung, zur Grundausstattung des Spitzenmodells 300 se ab August 1961, dem im März 1963 auf dem Genfer Frühlingssalon eine Lang-Version mit 100 Millimetern mehr Radstand zur Seite gestellt wird. Als die Baureihe im Sommer 1965 ausläuft, bleibt noch eine Zeitlang der 230 s als aufgebohrtes Derivat des 220 b. Es bleiben aber auch das Coupé, präsentiert bei der Eröffnung des Daimler-

Il arrive que des caractéristiques de style donnent une voiture un nom qui s'imprègne plus durablement dans les esprits que la nomenclature officielle d'une firme. Baptisées par le grand public, elles s'intègrent ensuite à la tradition de la marque. C'est ainsi que la Mercedes « Ponton » a été suivie, en 1959, par celle aux « dérives » ainsi nommée à cause des arêtes proéminentes de ses ailes arrière. Ce sont des concessions faites à la mode d'un moment en provenance des États-Unis, mais avec toutefois beaucoup plus de retenue que les énormes protubérances des Cadillac (« ailerons de requin ») ou Lincoln. Et comme, chez Mercedes, on aspire toujours à ce que la forme obéisse à la fonction, l'enfant reçoit vite son surnom : le collimateur.

Une devise préside à la gamme 220 b, 220 sb et 220 seb les nouveaux six-cylindres – une classe à part. Principal champ d'action : la sécurité. Pour la première fois, on a transposé systématiquement la philosophie de Béla Barényi, l'apôtre de la sécurité chez Mercedes : une solide cellule passagers est amortie, en cas d'accident, par des zones à déformation programmée à l'avant et à l'arrière. Plus de sécurité également pour l'habitacle : le moyeu du volant est rembourré et le tableau de bord est, lui aussi, capitonné. Toutes les manettes et commandes proéminentes sont montées élastiquement et, en partie, affleurantes. Les serrures de portières à tourillon conique sont un autre pas dans la même direction.

Extérieurement, les deux modèles s se distinguent essentiellement par des chromes plus généreux de la 220 sb, dont le moteur est maintenant alimenté par deux carburateurs Solex et développe 95 ch. Le moteur à injection de la seb fait, lui aussi, des progrès et, avec ses tubulures d'aspiration droites, développe 120 ch contre 115 pour l'ancien modèle. Le berceau auxiliaire ne consiste plus en une poutre transversale simple reliée élastiquement au cadre à deux endroits. Un ressort de compensation au-dessus du point de rotation de l'essieu brisé assure une répartition équilibrée de la charge d'essieu entre les deux roues motrices. Désormais placés tout à l'extérieur, les quatre amortisseurs sont plus accessibles, ce qui améliore aussi leur action. En avril 1962, les modèles s reçoivent des freins à disques, progrès dont bénéficie également, seize mois plus tard, la 220 b qui reçoit aussi en série un servofrein. La boîte semi-automatique Hydrak est proposée jusqu'au début de 1962, mais elle est déjà obsolète, compte tenu de la boîte complètement automatique déjà offerte depuis avril pour la seb et, à partir d'août 1962, contre un supplément de prix de 1400 marks pour les deux autres modèles, un embrayage hydraulique avec boîte planétaire à quatre rapports en aval. Comme la suspension pneumatique et la direction assistée, elle fait partie de l'équipement de série du navire amiral, la 300 se, à partir d'août 1961, voiture épaulée, en mars 1963, à partir du Salon de printemps de Genève, par une version à empattement long allongée de 100 mm. Lorsque la production de la gamme est suspendue durant l'été 1965

MERCEDES-BENZ 220b–300SE 1959

Mercedes-Benz 220Sb 1964

The 220 series had come of age, with a stretched body and a much greater window area. The headlights were mounted behind Plexiglas covers.

The opening of the Daimler-Benz Museum on 24 February 1961, and the cabriolet, first unveiled in August of the same year, were still built. Their shapes were so elegant and timeless that they housed the engines of later model generations right up to the beautiful twins of the 280 SE 3.5 of September 1969 with their silky-smooth 200 bhp v8 engines and which were only distinguishable from their predecessors by their flatter radiators.

Die Reihe 220 ist erwachsener geworden, mit einer gestreckten Karosserie und einer kräftig vergrößerten Verglasung. Die Scheinwerfer finden sich hinter Abdeckungen aus Plexiglas.

Benz-Museums am 24. Februar 1961, und das Cabriolet, zum erstenmal gezeigt im August desselben Jahres. So elegant und zeitlos sind ihre Formen, dass sie noch die Motoren späterer Modellgenerationen beherbergen bis hin zu den schönen Zwillingen 280 SE 3.5 vom September 1969 mit ihren seidig laufenden v8-Triebwerken von 200 PS, die sich ansonsten nur durch ihre flacheren Kühler von ihren Vorgängern unterscheiden.

La Série 220 agrandie, avec une carrosserie aux lignes étirées et des surfaces vitrées beaucoup plus généreuses. Les phares se trouvent derrière un carénage en Plexiglas.

seule la 230 s est encore proposée un certain temps en tant qu'extrapolation de la cylindrée majorée de la 220b. Mais il reste encore le coupé, présenté lors de l'inauguration du musée Daimler-Benz, le 24 février 1961, et le cabriolet, dévoilé en août de la même année. Leurs formes sont si élégantes et intemporelles qu'ils hébergeront encore les moteurs de générations ultérieures jusqu'aux admirables sœurs, les 280 SE 3.5 de septembre 1969 avec leurs moteurs v8 soyeux de 200 chevaux, qui ne se distinguent de leurs devancières que par leur seule calandre moins élevée.

The striking feature at the rear of the car – the wing extensions, popularly known as fins.

Markantes Merkmal am Heck: die Peilstege, im Volksmund Heckflossen geheißen.

Un arrière bien caractéristique : les ailes qui lui ont valu son surnom de « Mercedes à ailerons ».

The horn-ring, which was flattened out towards the top, was prone to breaking off if treated roughly. The straight-six fuel-injected engine of the 220SE was 10 bhp more powerful than the carburetor engine of the 220S. Note the permanent vent on the rear roof carrier.

Der nach oben abgeflachte Signalring bricht bei rüder Behandlung gerne ab. Der Reihensechszylinder des 220SE ist als Einspritzer zehn PS stärker als der Vergasermotor des 220S. Am hinteren Dachträger eine Dauerentlüftung.

L'anneau de signalisation à pan coupé en haut se brise volontiers si on le brutalise. Le six-cylindres en ligne de la 220SE à injection a dix chevaux de plus que le moteur à carburateur de la 220S. À l'extrémité supérieure du montant de pavillon arrière : une ouïe d'aération permanente.

The body and running gear of the type 200 corresponded to that of the 220S. However, the hood was shorter, the fenders were more simple, and the headlights were round.

Karosserie und Fahrwerk des Typs 200 entsprechen dem 220S. Allerdings ist die Haube kürzer, sind die Stoßstangen einfacher und die Scheinwerfer rund.

La carrosserie et le châssis de la 200 sont identiques à ceux de la 220S, mais le capot moteur est plus court, les pare-chocs sont plus simples et les phares ronds.

Mercedes-Benz 220b–300SE 1959

Mercedes-Benz 220b–300SE 1959

The fender extensions on the coupé and cabriolet in the series were discreetly rounded, which gave the design a certain timeless continuity.

An Coupé und Cabriolet der Baureihe sind die Peilstege dezent gerundet, was ihrer Formensprache eine gewisse zeitlose Beständigkeit verleiht.

Sur le coupé et le cabriolet de la gamme, les ailerons sont légèrement arrondis, ce qui confère à leur langage formel un certain caractère intemporel.

Mercedes-Benz 220b–300SE 1959

Mercedes-Benz 220b–300SE 1959

Mercedes-Benz 220b–300SE 1959

...e dashboard and steering wheel bore witness
...the importance now placed on safety:
...formability and a cushioned pad had arrived.

...maturenbrett und Lenkrad zeugen vom
...reben nach Sicherheit: Deformierbarkeit und
...olsternabe haben Einzug gehalten.

...tableau de bord et le volant témoignent
...désir de sécurité : ils sont déformables
...rembourrés.

Mercedes-Benz 220b–300SE 1959   349

It doesn't always go without saying – but even with the hood up the large cabriolet was a real looker. The front of the cabriolet was almost baroque in its splendor. The export model for the United States dropped the Plexiglas headlight cover. The radiator grille was made wider and lower from 1969 onwards.

Nicht immer selbstverständlich – auch mit geschlossenem Verdeck macht das große Cabriolet eine gute Figur. Von geradezu barocker Pracht: die Frontpartie des Cabriolets. In der Exportausführung für die Vereinigten Staaten entfällt die Plexiglasabdeckung der Scheinwerfer. Seit 1969 ist das Kühlergitter breiter und niedriger.

Pas toujours évident – mais même avec la capote fermée, le grand cabriolet fait bonne figure. Magnificence baroque: la proue du cabriolet. La version destinée aux États-Unis ne comporte pas le carénage en Plexiglas des phares. Depuis 1969, la calandre est plus large et plus basse.

Mercedes-Benz 220b–300SE 1959

Mercedes engineers were given three specifications in an attempt, as it were, to square the circle. A joint successor was sought for the very popular 190 SL and the 300 SL, which was a legend in its own lifetime. The design had to be absolutely contemporary. The new car had to be (1) bright, comfortable, and spacious, (2) use as many elements as possible of existing series, and (3) have a beautiful body.

The result, first seen at the Geneva Motor Show in March 1963, was what became popularly known as the "Pagoda" because of the concave bow in its roof. It was undoubtedly a gimmick with a touch of the avant-garde which cost the car a little in terms of top speed. However, it was also a safety factor which counteracted any possible instability caused by the lightweight construction. Safety was writ very large in the design of the 230 SL. The responsible expert, Béla Barényi, left his fingerprints all over this one – and more besides. Like modern-day sedans of the time, the new SL protected its occupants by means of a rigid cage with deformable sections to the front and rear.

Like the 190 SL, the 230 SL was available as a coupé with a removable roof and roadster top, or as a coupé with a removable roof, although four levers had to be released to remove the hardtop before two strong adults lifted it away. The elegantly flat body sat on the shortened, stiffened floorpan chassis of the 220 SEB, whose suspension was also used. Its engine had been rebored to increase its displacement by 100 cc, and increased compression and a Bosch six-stage pump also helped the luxury sports car to achieve 150 bhp. An automatic gearbox was available as an option, and a ZF 5-speed transmission from May 1966. The 230 SL proved its sporty qualities when the Stuttgart hotelier Eugen Böhringer, together with team-mate Klaus Kaiser, won the 1963 Liège-Sofia-Liège Rally in a well-prepared car.

On 27 February 1967 the 250 SL was launched as its replacement, unchanged outwardly, though fitted with elements from the 250 SE. Take the engine, for example: the SL's power output remained the same though it achieved 10 per cent more torque. Or its brakes: like the sedan, the 250 SL now had disc brakes all round, rather than the rear drum brakes that it had made do with up till then. In addition, the disc size had been increased, and a servo brake relieved the driver of some of the work. The fuel tank had also been enlarged by 17 liters (4.5 gal) to 82 liters (21.7 gal). A further version offered to customers who could count on reliably good weather came to be known as the California model. The top and its box were replaced by a rear seat, but anyone caught out in a cloudburst without a coupé roof had to make a quick dash for cover.

The 250 SL had only been on the market for about a year when the "Pagoda" was treated to the general upgrading that top-of-the-range cars often enjoy. An increase in engine size to 2.8 liters yielded 20 bhp more and a further 10 per cent more torque. The only external

Drei Vorgaben bekommen die Techniker von Mercedes-Benz, um gewissermaßen die Quadratur des Zirkels zu erfinden. Gesucht wird ein gemeinsamer Nachfolger für den 190 SL, der sich großen Anklangs erfreut, und den 300 SL, der schon zu Lebzeiten in die Legende eingegangen ist. Gefunden werden muss ein durch und durch zeitgemäßes Konzept. Der Neue soll 1. hell, bequem und geräumig sein, 2. möglichst viele Elemente aus den vorhandenen Serien übernehmen und 3. eine schöne Karosserie haben.

Heraus kommt dabei, erstmals zu besichtigen auf der Genfer Show im März 1963, was die Stimme des Volkes »Pagode« nennen wird wegen seines konkav eingewölbten Dachteils. Gewiss ist das ein avantgardistisch anmutender Gag, der das Auto ein bisschen von seiner Spitzengeschwindigkeit kostet. Es stellt aber auch einen Sicherheitsfaktor dar, durch den man mögliche Labilität durch Leichtbau austariert. Überhaupt wird Sicherheit am 230 SL großgeschrieben. Allenthalben hat der zuständige Experte Béla Barényi seine Fingerabdrücke hinterlassen – und mehr: Wie die aktuellen Limousinen schützt der neue SL seine Insassen durch eine rigide Zelle, an die verformbare Partien vorn und hinten angrenzen.

Wie den 190 SL gibt es den 230 SL als Coupé mit abnehmbarem Dach und Roadsterverdeck oder als Coupé mit abnehmbarem Dach, wobei zum Entfernen des Hardtops vier Hebel gelöst werden müssen, bevor zwei kräftige Erwachsene zupacken können. Der flächig-elegante Aufbau ruht auf dem verkürzten und verstärkten Rahmenboden des 220 SEB, von dem auch die Aufhängungen übernommen werden. Sein Triebwerk wurde um 100 ccm aufgebohrt, und erhöhte Verdichtung sowie eine Sechsstempelpumpe von Bosch tragen das Ihrige bei zu den 150 PS des Salon-Sportlers. Als Option ist eine Automatik verfügbar, ab Mai 1966 ein Fünfgang-Getriebe von ZF. Sportliche Qualitäten stellt der 230 SL unter Beweis, als der Stuttgarter Hotelier Eugen Böhringer mit Coéquipier Klaus Kaiser 1963 mit einem wohlpräparierten Exemplar das Marathon Lüttich-Sofia-Lüttich gewinnt.

Am 27. Februar 1967 wird als Ablösung der 250 SL präsentiert, formal unverändert, im übrigen aber ausgestattet mit Bauelementen des 250 SE. Etwa dem Motor: Die Leistung des SL bleibt gleichwohl unangetastet, während sich zehn Prozent mehr Drehmoment eingestellt haben. Und seiner Bremsanlage: Wie die Limousine hat der 250 SL nun Scheibenbremsen ringsum, wo das Modell bislang noch mit Trommelbremsen hinten auskommen musste. Überdies sind die Scheiben größer geworden, und ein Bremskraftverstärker nimmt dem Fahrer ein bisschen Arbeit ab. Um 17 Liter auf 82 Liter Kapazität vergrößert hat man auch den Tank. Für Landstriche mit zuverlässig heiterer Witterung bietet man nun als weitere Version die sogenannte California-Ausführung an: Verdeck und Verdeckkasten entfallen zugunsten einer hinteren Sitzbank, und wer ohne Coupédach in einen Wolkenbruch gerät, muss sich umgehend nach Schutz und Schirm umsehen.

Trois ordres sont donnés aux techniciens Mercedes-Benz pour résoudre la quadrature cercle. Il leur faut trouver un successeur à la f pour la 190 SL, qui jouit d'une grande popularité, et à 300 SL, qui est déjà entrée dans la légende de son viva Il leur faut trouver un concept moderne jusqu'au bc des roues. La nouvelle voiture doit être, d'abord, cla confortable et spacieuse ; elle doit aussi, ensuite, repren le plus grand nombre possible d'éléments des séries ex tantes et elle doit, enfin, posséder une belle carrosserie.

Le produit de leurs réflexions est exposé pour la p mière fois au Salon de l'Automobile de Genève en m 1963 et la voix du peuple le surnommera rapideme « pagode » en raison de la forme concave de son to Certes, il s'agit d'un gag plutôt avant-gardiste qui coût la voiture quelques kilomètres en vitesse de pointe. Ma représente aussi un facteur de sécurité, car l'on compe ainsi la fragilité éventuelle due à la légèreté. D'ailleurs, sécurité figure tout en haut du cahier des charges de 230 SL. L'expert en la matière, Béla Barényi, a laissé s empreinte dans tous les domaines – et plus encore : les berlines actuelles, la nouvelle SL protège elle aussi passagers par une cellule rigide avec des éléments déf mables à l'avant et à l'arrière.

Comme la 190 SL, la 230 SL est aussi proposée en cou avec toit escamotable et capote roadster, et en coupé av toit démontable (le démontage du hard-top suppos que l'on débloque quatre leviers, avant que deux adul costauds puissent l'ôter). La carrosserie très basse élégante repose sur la plate-forme raccourcie et renfor de la 220 SEB, dont elle reprend également les suspensio La cylindrée de son moteur a été majorée de 100 cm³, qui, conjointement avec l'augmentation du taux de co pression et une pompe Bosch à six pistons, contribue a 150 chevaux de cette sportive en smoking. Parmi options figurent une boîte automatique et, à partir mai 1966, une boîte ZF à cinq vitesses. La 230 SL adminis la preuve de ses qualités sportives lorsqu'un hôte de Stuttgart, Eugen Böhringer, avec Klaus Kaiser po coéquipier, remporte, en 1963, le marathon Liège-Sof Liège avec un exemplaire bien préparé.

Le 27 février 1967, elle est remplacée par la 250 extérieurement absolument identique, mais, pour le res dotée des composants de la 250 SE. Dont le moteur : puissance de la SL reste, certes, identique, mais elle gag 10 % en couple. Quant au freinage, comme la berline, 250 SL a maintenant des freins à disques sur les qua roues alors que sa devancière devait jusqu'ici se conten de tambours à l'arrière. Le diamètre des disques a, plus, augmenté et un servofrein facilite un peu la tâc du conducteur. Le réservoir d'essence voit sa capac augmenter de 17 à 82 litres. Pour les régions où l'on assuré qu'il fait beau temps, Mercedes propose maintena une version supplémentaire, baptisée California : cap et coffre à capote disparaissent en faveur d'une banque arrière et celui qui, sans toit, se retrouve inopiném

MERCEDES-BENZ 230 SL–280 SL 1963

Mercedes-Benz 250 SL 1967

ferences between the 280 SL and its predecessors
re its hub caps and the badge on the trunk. When pro-
action ceased in March 1971, this series had sold 48,912
rs in eight years. Although the challenge of squaring
e circle was still open, the sales statistics spoke volumes
r its success.

Nicht einmal ein Jahr ist der 250 SL im Angebot, dann
hat die »Pagode« teil an der allgemeinen Aufrüstung, die
den Wagen der Oberklasse widerfährt. Eine Hubraum-
vergrößerung auf 2,8 Liter bringt 20 PS und erneut zehn
Prozent mehr Drehmoment. Nur an seinen Radzierblenden und der üblichen Aufschrift auf dem Heck ist
der 280 SL von seinen Vorfahren zu unterscheiden. Als
die Produktion im März 1971 ausläuft, hat es die Baureihe
in acht Jahren auf 48 912 Exemplare gebracht. Die
Quadratur des Zirkels bleibt zwar nach wie vor eine
Herausforderung. Aber wenn es um Erfolg geht, sprechen
ja auch Zahlen Bände.

sous une averse doit immédiatement se mettre en quête
d'un abri.

La 250 SL n'aura même pas été produite pendant un an
puisque la « Pagode » participe à la course générale aux
améliorations dont bénéficient les voitures du segment
supérieur. L'accroissement de cylindrée à 2,8 litres lui donne
vingt chevaux de plus et, de nouveau, 10 % de couple
supplémentaire. La 280 SL ne se distingue de ses devancières
que par de nouveaux enjoliveurs de roues et le patronyme
traditionnel sur la malle arrière. Lorsque la production est
suspendue en mars 1971, la gamme a donné naissance en
huit ans à 48912 exemplaires. La quadrature du cercle n'a,
certes, toujours pas été résolue, mais, quand il est question
de succès, les chiffres disent parfois plus que mille mots.

As with the 190 SL, the 230 SL was also available as a coupé with a removable roof and roadster top, or simply with a removable top. To remove the hardtop four levers had to be released before two strong adults lifted the roof off.

Wie den 190 SL gibt es den 230 SL als Coupé mit abnehmbarem Dach und Roadster-verdeck oder lediglich mit abnehmbarem Dach. Zum Entfernen des Hardtops müssen vier Hebel gelöst werden, bevor zwei kräftige Erwachsene zupacken können.

Comme la 190 SL, la 230 SL est disponible en coupé à toit escamotable et capote roadster ou seulement avec toit démontable. Pour ôter le *hard-top*, il faut desserrer quatre leviers avant que deux adultes vigoureux puissent l'enlever.

Mercedes' interior stylists had a field day. The lavish interior trim and comprehensive instrumentation ensured that everything was taken care of.

Die Innenarchitekten von Mercedes haben es gut mit ihm gemeint: Üppige Innenausstattung und umfassende Instrumentierung sorgen für behagliche Solidität.

Les décorateurs intérieurs de Mercedes n'ont pas regardé à la dépense: équipement pléthorique et tableau de bord très complet donnent une impression de solidité accueillante.

You either love it or hate it. Some regarded this car as a crude lump, a dire apotheosis of the right angle, while others saw it as the prestige car. Whatever, the Mercedes 600, which made its debut at the Frankfurt International Motor Show in September 1963, was an impressive phenomenon, a synthesis of all that had been achieved in automotive engineering to date. Its engine was a first for the company: a v8 injection engine with a capacity of 6.3 liters, developing 250 bhp and a maximum torque of 51 mkg. It powered the two-and-a-half-ton vehicle, which could well have been sluggish, to a performance that would not have disgraced a lively sports car of the time. It had a top speed of 205 kph (127 mph), and 100 kph (62 mph) was reached in 10 seconds without the automatic transmission seeming to be unduly troubled. The driver could adjust the hardness of the shock absorbers using a lever on the steering column. Its dual-circuit brake system was assisted by compressed air, and the front disc brakes were operated by two brake calipers each.

All-round comfort was a priority: air suspension, a comprehensive servo system, and the electrically regulated heating and ventilation system represented 1963 state-of-the-art. A sophisticated hydraulic system ensured ride comfort in every conceivable way. It helped to adjust the front seats horizontally and vertically and also changed the tilt of the back rest at the relevant input. It moved the rear seat longitudinally, assisted with the opening and closing of the doors, the trunk lid and the (optional) sunroof, and also raised and lowered the side windows.

The most common model sold was the 3200-mm-(10 ft-6 in-) wheelbase sedan which seated up to six passengers. There were also three Pullman versions with up to eight seats; one four-door model with facing rear seats, one Pullman sedan with six doors and a rear bench seat together with additional folding seats facing the direction of travel, plus a Landaulet model which normally had four seats and luxury individual seats in which the passengers faced one another. A rarer version of the Landaulet had six doors, the middle ones of which were supplied on request without handles as in the corresponding Pullman versions.

In the 17 years of manufacture up to 16 June 1981, 2,677 Mercedes 600 units were built, including 429 Pullmans and 59 Landaulets. Highly customizable, hardly any two were identical. Nevertheless, three models stand out even from this host of individualists. In September 1965 a Pullman-Landaulet joined the Vatican fleet for Pope Paul VI, with four doors, individual rear seats, a raised roof, and a higher floor in the back which levelled out the transmission tunnel. It saw service for over 20 years, under two further Catholic pontiffs, before returning to Untertürkheim in 1985, its mission completed, and where it has been on display in the museum since February 1986. In May 1967 a sporty customer had the Landaulet body crossed with a chassis with the normal wheelbase. At the

An ihm scheiden sich die Geister: Die einen halten ihn für einen kruden Klotz, die schlimme Apotheose des rechten Winkels, die anderen für das repräsentative Automobil schlechthin. In jedem Fall ist der Mercedes 600, Debütant auf der Frankfurter IAA im September 1963, eine eindrucksvolle Erscheinung, zugleich ein Kompendium all dessen, was zu diesem Zeitpunkt im Autobau erreicht worden ist. Eine hauseigene Premiere: sein v8, ein Einspritzer mit 6,3 Litern Hubraum, 250 PS und einem maximalen Drehmoment von 51 mkg. Er animiert den träge anmutenden Zweieinhalbtonner zu den Fahrleistungen eines gut im Saft stehenden zeitgenössischen Sportwagens: Er läuft 205 Stundenkilometer Spitze, und Tempo 100 ist nach zehn Sekunden erreicht, ohne dass die Automatik den Eindruck erweckt, rüde gefordert zu werden. Sein Chauffeur kann während der Fahrt die Härte der Stoßdämpfer von der Lenksäule aus regeln. Seine Zweikreis-Bremsanlage wird unterstützt durch Luftdruck, und je zwei Bremszangen nehmen die vorderen Scheibenbremsen in den Griff.

Ein Maximum an Komfort allüberall: Luftfederung, ein umfassendes Servosystem sowie die elektrisch regulierte Heizungs- und Lüftungsanlage verkörpern *state of the art* anno 1963. Eine aufwändige Komfort-Hydraulik verästelt ihre Dienstleistungen in alle erdenklichen Richtungen. Sie hilft, die Frontsitze horizontal und vertikal einzurichten, und verändert auf einen diesbezüglichen Impuls hin auch die Neigung der Rücklehne. Sie verstellt die hintere Bank in Längsrichtung, unterstützt das Öffnen und Schließen der Türen, des Kofferraumdeckels und des Schiebedachs (Option) und hebt und senkt die Seitenfenster.

Die größte Verbreitung erfährt die Limousine mit ihren 3200 Millimetern Radstand, in der bis zu sechs Passagiere Platz nehmen können. Dazu gibt es drei Pullman-Versionen mit bis zu acht Sitzen: einen Viertürer, dessen Fondsitze vis-à-vis angeordnet sind, eine Pullman-Limousine, die via sechs Türen betreten werden kann und eine Sitzbank hinten sowie zusätzliches Klappgestühl in Fahrtrichtung anbietet, sowie eine Landaulet-Variante: normalerweise mit vier Sitzen und Fond-Fauteuils, auf denen die Reisenden einander von Angesicht zu Angesicht gegenüberlagern. Im selteneren Falle eröffnen den Zugang zu diesem Landaulet sechs Türen, die mittleren auf Wunsch ohne Griff wie bei den entsprechenden Pullman-Limousinen.

In den 17 Jahren seiner Fertigung bis zum 16. Juni 1981 entstehen 2677 Mercedes 600, davon 429 Pullman und 59 Landaulet. Kaum zwei sind je identisch. Gleichwohl heben sich drei Exemplare selbst von dieser Schar von Individualisten ab. Im September 1965 wird ein Pullman-Landaulet dem Fuhrpark des Vatikans eingegliedert für den damaligen Pontifex maximus Paul VI., mit vier Türen, einzelnen Sesseln hinten, einem erhöhten Dachaufbau und höherem Boden im Fond, der den Kardantunnel nach oben hin abdeckt. Über 20 Jahre tut er Dienst auch noch

S'il est une voiture qui a divisé les esprits, c'est b elle: les uns la considèrent taillée à la serpe, élo de l'angle droit poussé au paroxysme, les autr comme la limousine de représentation par excellen Quoiqu'il en soit, la Mercedes 600, qui a fait ses début l'IAA de Francfort en septembre 1963, est une voit impressionnante et, simultanément, le parangon de ce d est techniquement possible à cette époque en automob À commencer par son moteur: un v8 à injection de 6,3 lit de cylindrée, 250 ch et un couple maximum de 51 mkg confère à ce pachyderme de 2,5 t les performances d'u voiture de sport de son temps: elle atteint une vitesse pointe de 205 km/h et passe de 0 à 100 km/h en 10 second sans que la boîte automatique ne donne un seul insta l'impression d'avoir été mise à contribution plus qu'il convient. Tout en conduisant, son chauffeur peut régler fermeté des amortisseurs depuis le volant. Son dispos de freinage à double circuit possède une assistance pne matique, et deux étriers de freins respectifs s'attaquen chacun des freins à disque avant.

Le confort atteint un niveau inégalé: la suspensi pneumatique, un système d'assistance exhaustif q que le chauffage et la ventilation à régulation électriq incarnent une véritable avancée technique en cette ann 1963. Tout aussi sophistiqué, un système hydraulique grand confort assume toutes les fonctions que l'on puis imaginer. Il permet de déplacer les sièges avant dans sens horizontal et vertical et de modifier aussi, sur sim pression d'un bouton, l'inclinaison des dossiers. Il dépla la banquette arrière dans le sens longitudinal, facil l'ouverture et la fermeture des portières, du couver de malle et du toit ouvrant (proposé en option) et, bi évidemment, il lève et baisse les vitres latérales.

C'est avec son empattement de 3200 mm que ce imposante limousine, qui peut alors transporter jusqu six passagers, est la plus diffusée. Mais il en existe au trois versions Pullman avec jusqu'à huit sièges: u quatre-portes, dont les sièges arrière y sont placés vis-à-vis, une limousine Pullman à laquelle on accè grâce à six portières et qui propose une banquette arri et des strapontins supplémentaires dans le sens de marche, ainsi qu'une version Landaulet: normaleme avec quatre sièges et fauteuils arrière sur lesquels voyageurs se font face. Dans quelques cas plus rares, s portières donnent accès à ce Landaulet, celles du cent sur demande, sans poignée comme pour les limousin Pullman correspondante.

Aux cours des dix-sept ans de sa fabrication jusqu' 16 juin 1981, 2677 Mercedes 600 ont été construites, do 429 Pullman et 59 Landaulet. Il est pratiquement imp que deux soient identiques. Et pourtant, trois exemplair se distinguent même de ce groupe d'individualistes. septembre 1965, un Landaulet Pullman vient rejoindre flotte du Vatican pour Paul VI, avec quatre portières, d fauteuils individuels à l'arrière, une superstructure de to surélevée et un plancher plus haut à l'arrière qui dissimu

Mercedes-Benz 600 Pullman-Landaulet 1971

d of the Eighties this one-off was thoroughly restored
d is now in private ownership, as is the prototype of
two-door coupé which is enjoying a well-deserved
irement in the land of its fathers after an intermezzo
the United States.

bei zwei weiteren obersten Seelenhirten der katholischen
Christenheit und kehrt 1985 nach erfolgreicher Mission
nach Untertürkheim zurück, wo er seit dem Februar 1986
im Museum zu besichtigen ist. Im Mai 1967 lässt ein sportlicher Kunde den Landaulet-Aufbau mit einem Chassis
kreuzen, das den normalen Radstand aufweist. Ende der
achtziger Jahre wird dieses Unikat gründlich restauriert
und befindet sich heute in Privatbesitz ebenso wie der
Prototyp eines zweitürigen Coupés, das nach einem
Intermezzo in den Vereinigten Staaten im Land seiner
Väter den verdienten Ruhestand genießt.

l'arbre de transmission. Pendant plus de vingt ans, il
assume encore de bons et loyaux services pour deux autres
souverains pontifes de l'Église catholique avant, mission
accomplie avec succès, de rentrer en 1985 à Untertürkheim
où on peut l'admirer au musée depuis février 1986. En mai
1967, un client à la fibre sportive fait croiser une superstructure de Landaulet et un châssis possédant l'empattement normal.

À la fin des années 1980, ce spécimen unique est restauré minutieusement et se trouve depuis dans une collection privée, au même titre que le prototype d'un coupé
deux portes qui jouit d'une retraite bien méritée au pays
de ses ancêtres après un bref intermède aux États-Unis.

A monument to power – this four-door Pullman-Landaulet, half sedan, half cabriolet, belonged to the fleet of the State President of Senegal.

Monument der Macht: Dieses viertürige Pullman-Landaulet, halb Limousine, halb Cabriolet, gehörte zum Fahrzeugpark des Staatspräsidenten von Senegal.

Monument du pouvoir : ce Landaulet Pullman à quatre portes – semi-limousine, semi-cabriolet – a appartenu à la flotte du président de la république du Sénégal.

Living in style. A sophisticated hydraulic system helped to adjust the front seats of the 600 horizontally and vertically, changed the tilt of the back rest, moved the rear seat longitudinally, and assisted with the opening and closing of the doors.

Schöner Wohnen: Eine aufwändige Komfort-Hydraulik hilft unter anderem, die Frontsitze des 600 horizontal und vertikal einzurichten, verändert die Neigung der Rücklehne, verstellt die hintere Bank in Längsrichtung und unterstützt das Öffnen und Schließen der Türen.

Confort intégral: un système hydraulique sophistiqué permet notamment de déplacer horizontalement et verticalement les sièges avant de la 600, de changer l'inclinaison des dossiers, d'avancer ou de reculer la banquette arrière et d'ouvrir et fermer plus facilement les portières.

Mercedes-Benz 600 1963   363

While Mercedes made a passing nod to contemporary taste with the "Fin" car, the new version of the s-class, introduced in August 1965, made no such concession. Paul Bracq was the designer of this series, and the 250 s, 250 se, and 300 se had a restrained, timeless quality. The figures for the two smaller-engined models tell their story: their six-cylinder engines were of 2.5 liters, derived from the earlier 2.2-liter engines with a longer stroke and a larger bore. The injectors were fed by Bosch six-stage pumps.

The air suspension system of the 300 se was gone, and it only reappeared in the long-wheelbase 300 sel version from March 1966 onwards; its wheelbase was increased by 100 mm (4 in) to 2850 mm (9 ft 4 in). Like the other two members of the w108 model family, a hydropneumatic compensating spring on the rear axle ensured a constant ride level under changing loads and stresses. The 300 sel was given the in-house designation of w109, denoting its own series. Two cars, a Pullman and a Landaulet, graced the Vatican fleet which had long been a satisfied Mercedes customer, without any undue concern for Italian vanity.

The start of 1968 saw a changing of the guard with the introduction of the 280 s and the 280 se, in accordance with the time-honored maxim that there is only one thing better than a large engine, and that is an even larger engine. The carburetor engine now delivered 140 bhp, and the injection model 160 bhp, each 10 bhp more than previously, while the 170 bhp engine of the 280 sl replaced the expensive-to-manufacture 3-liter alloy engines in the 300 sel from January 1968 onwards. The series reached its zenith in March of the same year with the 300 sel 6.3. Connoisseurs guessed what was powering this car – the v8 from the luxury 600, coupled with its automatic 4-speed transmission. Despite its discreet appearance, this sedan could reach 221 kph (137 mph). Eight seconds was all it took for the speedometer needle to pass 100 kph (62 mph), and the 105-liter (27.7-gal) tank had to splash out 21 liters every 100 km (11.2 mpg). Many of its 6,526 owners took extra pleasure in helping this athlete of the automotive world take to the road like a wolf in sheep's clothing by completely removing any indications of its identity from the trunk, or by fitting misleading badges instead such as that for the 280 s.

From the autumn of 1969 onwards the 300 sel bore the suffix 3.5 on the trunk, an indication that a 3.5-liter v8 delivering 200 bhp had taken up residence. This powerplant, which was also the pilot for a new generation of engine, was available for the 280 se too from March 1971 and became the standard engine in the 280 sel as well as in the coupé and cabriolet. A further v8 of 4.5 liters was destined solely for the American market from May 1971 onwards, under the hoods of the 280 se and sel, and of the 300 sel.

The type designations had long since taken on a life of their own. Only the 280 s badge on the trunk lid of

Macht Mercedes mit der »Heckflosse« noch einen kleinen Ausfallschritt in Richtung auf den Zeitgeschmack, kommt die Neuauflage der s-Klasse vom August 1965 an gänzlich ohne dergleichen aus. Paul Bracq hat sie gezeichnet, und sie gibt sich zurückhaltend und mit zeitloser Würde, als 250 s, 250 se und 300 se. Die Zahlen-Sigel der beiden hubraumschwächeren Modelle verraten es: Ihre Sechszylinder haben 2,5 Liter, Derivate der früheren 2,2-Liter-Motoren mit mehr Hub und mehr Bohrung. Die Einspritzer werden beschickt von Sechsstempelpumpen von Bosch.

Verschwunden ist die Luftfederung des 300 se und kehrt erst zurück in der Lang-Version 300 sel vom März 1966, deren Radstand um 100 mm auf 2850 mm aufgestockt wurde. Dafür hält wie bei den beiden anderen Mitgliedern der Modell-Familie w108 eine hydropneumatische Ausgleichsfeder an der Hinterachse das Niveau bei unterschiedlichen Beladungen und Belastungen konstant. Dem 300 sel wird immerhin der werksinterne Name w109 für eine eigene Baureihe zuteil. Zwei Exemplare, ein Pullman und ein Landaulet, gereichen dem Fahrzeugpark des Vatikan zur Zierde, lange schon ohne übertriebene Rücksichten auf italienische Eitelkeiten ein zufriedener Kunde der Untertürkheimer.

Anfang 1968 findet eine Wachablösung statt getreu der bewährten Devise, besser als viel Hubraum sei noch mehr Hubraum, mit dem 280 s und dem 280 se. Die Vergasermaschine leistet nun 140 ps, der Einspritzer 160 ps, beide jeweils zehn ps mehr als zuvor, während im 300 sel vom Januar 1968 an das 170 ps starke Triebwerk des 280 sl den in der Fertigung teuren Leichtmetallmotor mit drei Litern verdrängt. Die Reihe gipfelt im März desselben Jahres im 300 sel 6.3. Die Kundigen ahnen, was diesem Auto so mächtig auf die Sprünge hilft: der v8 aus dem Renommier-Klotz 600, gepaart mit dessen Viergang-Automatik. 221 Stundenkilometer erreicht diese diskret auftretende Limousine, Tempo 100 ist nach acht Sekunden kein Thema mehr, und 21 Liter je 100 Kilometer werden ihrem 105-Liter-Tank mühelos entzogen. Viele seiner 6526 Besitzer finden ein zusätzliches Vergnügen daran, dass der Modell-Athlet wie ein Wolf im Schafspelz auftritt, indem sie jeglichen Hinweis am Heck gänzlich entfernen oder irreführende Verweisungszeichen wie 280 s anbringen lassen.

Ab Herbst 1969 trägt der 300 sel den Zusatz 3.5 am Heck, Hinweis darauf, dass nun ein v8 von 3,5 Litern mit 200 ps unter seiner vorderen Haube eingezogen ist. Dieses Triebwerk, Pilot gleichsam einer neuen Generation von Motoren, ist ab März 1971 auch für den 280 se verfügbar und wird Norm im 280 sel wie auch im Coupé und im Cabriolet. Nur für den amerikanischen Markt bestimmt ist ein weiterer v8 mit 4,5 Litern ab Mai 1971, zu bestellen im Gewande des 280 se und sel sowie des 300 sel.

Längst haben sich die Typenbezeichnungen verselbständigt. Zuverlässig Auskunft über das Volumen ihrer

Si, avec la Mercedes « à dérive », Stuttgart a enco fait une petite concession à une mode temporel la nouvelle version de la Classe s d'août 1965 totalement démunie de telles fioritures. Elle est l'œuvre Paul Bracq, toute de discrétion et parfaitement à l'épreu du temps en version 250 s, 250 se et 300 se. La nome clature des deux versions les plus faibles ne laissent pas moindre ambiguïté : leurs six-cylindres ont une cylindr de 2,5 litres, ils sont extrapolés des anciens moteurs 2,2 litres avec une course et un alésage accrus. Les inje teurs sont alimentés par des pompes Bosch à six pistons

La suspension pneumatique de la 300 se a disparu, e ne reviendra qu'avec la version à empattement long, 300 sel de mars 1966, dont l'empattement a été majo de 100 mm, à 2850 mm. En revanche, comme pour l deux autres membres de la famille de modèle w108, u ressort de compensation hydropneumatique à l'essi arrière maintient constant le niveau quels que soient chargement et les sollicitations. La 300 sel se voit mê accorder le nom de code interne w109, qui équivaut une série spécifique. Deux exemplaires, un Pullman et u Landaulet, viennent enrichir la flotte du Vatican, qui depuis longtemps cessé de tenir compte des susceptibilit italiennes et est depuis tout aussi longtemps un clie satisfait d'Untertürkheim.

Début 1968 s'effectue une relève de la garde selon ur devise éprouvée : on ne peut mieux remplacer beaucou de cylindrée que par encore plus de cylindrée, avec la 28 et la 280 se. Le moteur à carburateur développe mainte nant 140 ch, celui à injection, 160 ch, tous les deux ave respectivement 10 ch de plus qu'auparavant, alors qu dans la 300 sel, à partir de janvier 1968, le moteur d 170 ch de la 280 sl remplace le 3 litres en alliage lége beaucoup trop coûteux à fabriquer. La gamme atteint so paroxysme, en mars de la même année, avec la 300 sel 6.3 Les initiés se doutent de ce qui a donné des ailes à cet voiture : le v8 de l'aussi fameuse qu'anguleuse 600, coup à sa boîte automatique à quatre rapports. Cette limousin aux lignes discrètes croise à 221 km/h, abat sans difficul le 0 à 100 km/h en 8 secondes et prélève avec aussi peu d peine 21 litres de carburant aux 100 km dans son réservo de 105 litres. Beaucoup de ses 6526 propriétaires prenner en outre un malin plaisir à jouer, avec ce bel athlète, a loup dans la bergerie en ne faisant pas apposer le moindr sigle à l'arrière où en y faisant placer des patronyme fallacieux tel 280 s.

À partir de l'automne 1969, la 300 sel arbore le chiffr supplémentaire 3.5 à l'arrière, ce qui indique que, désor mais, un v8 de 3,5 litres et 200 ch a pris place sous so capot avant. Ce moteur, qui est aussi le précurseur d toute une nouvelle génération de moteurs, est disponibl à partir de mars 1971 pour la 280 se également et il devien la norme dans la 280 sel ainsi que dans le coupé et l cabriolet. Réservé exclusivement au marché américain, u autre v8, de 4,5 litres fait son apparition en mai 1971 et es disponible pour les 280 se et sel ainsi que la 300 sel.

MERCEDES-BENZ 250 S – 300 SEL 3.5   1965

Mercedes-Benz 300 SEL 3.5 1971

he carburetor version, which survived all these metamorphoses until 1972, gave any reliable information
bout its engine size.

Maschine gibt nur noch die Aufschrift 280 s auf dem
Kofferraumdeckel der Vergaser-Variante, die all diese
Metamorphosen bis 1972 überdauert.

Il y a des lustres que les dénominations de série ont
perdu toute signification véritable. Seule la mention 280 s
sur le couvercle de malle de la version à carburateur dit
encore la vérité quant à la cylindrée de son moteur, version
qui survivra à toutes ces métamorphoses jusqu'en 1972.

The 3.5-liter V8 filled the entire engine compartment. The dashboard sported circular instruments which superseded the vertical arrangement that was fashionable for a time.

Eingebettet in den Kreis seiner Domestiken nimmt der V8 von 3,5 Litern den gesamten Motorraum in Anspruch. In der Armaturentafel haben Rundinstrumente das eine Zeitlang modische Vertikal-Arrangement abgelöst.

Le V8 de 3,5 litres occupe la totalité du compartiment moteur. Sur le tableau de bord, les instruments circulaires ont remplacé leurs homologues verticaux qui n'auront été à la mode que très peu de temps.

Although production of the new generation of mid-range Mercedes began in 1967, they were popularly known as the /8 models after the year of their first public appearance. Yet there was nothing remotely revolutionary about the Daimler-Benz /8 models apart from the chaotic series of abbreviations that was prodigally applied to them over the years. A tiny palace revolution was caused simply by their diagonal swing axle which improved drive performance without making any concessions in terms of comfort.

Introduced in January 1968, the series initially encompassed six types from the 200 D with 55 bhp up to the 250 with a six-cylinder carburetor engine delivering 130 bhp. In November of that year the series was crowned by the two coupés, the 250 C and 250 CE. And this really was an innovation, as this was the first time that this body variant had been available in a mid-range series. It immediately generated lively interest, although to a degree less car was being offered for more money, for example, it was identical to the sedans up to the A-pillar, with a flatter windshield and a 45-mm- (1.8-in-) lower roof section, frameless and fully retractable side windows, and two large doors. The coupés from this series sold 67,048 units up to 1976. Another subsidiary line stands out because of the exclusivity of its lower sales figures: around 10,000 units were sold of models 220 D, 230, 240 D, and 230.6 with three rows of seats and eight places on a chassis which had been stretched by 650 mm (2 ft 1.5 in), a variant greatly welcomed by, for example, taxi companies and airlines.

In April 1972 the range was extended to include types 280 and 280 E and the corresponding coupés. Their new six-cylinder engines with double overhead camshafts delivered 160 bhp in the carburetor version and 185 bhp as injection engines, identifiable by the double bumpers at the front like the 250, and by rear bumpers that wrapped round as far as the wheel arches, as well as by twin muffler end pipes. At the same time the 250 and 250 C were fitted with the older 2.8-liter engine from the 280 s, reduced by 10 bhp to 130 bhp. The facelift that the series underwent in September 1973 was primarily concerned with safety considerations, involving movable external mirrors that could be adjusted from inside the car, trims on the A-pillars which kept dirt off the side windows, grooved tail-lights, and a gutter above the rear screen. Headrests, inertia-reel belts, and a four-spoke safety steering wheel had been standard equipment for six months.

The cosmetic revamps undertaken at the same time as those in the s-class did not always signal actual progress; for example the side vent windows had been discontinued or the hood had become lower and wider. Double bumpers were now a thing of the past, though to be honest they had always been a cosmetically effective and costly extra. At the same time two new four-cylinder cars were available, the 240 D as the largest diesel-engined model, and the 230/4 which replaced the 220. The 4 after the slash served to prevent confusion with the previous 230, a six-

Die Produktion der neuen Generation in der Mercedes-Mittelklasse beginnt zwar schon 1967, aber die Stimme des Volkes nennt sie Strich-Acht-Modelle nach dem Jahr ihres ersten öffentlichen Auftretens. Dabei haftet den Achtundsechzigern von Daimler-Benz so gar nichts Revolutionäres an, abgesehen von dem Kürzel-Chaos, das ihre verschwenderische Vielfalt im Lauf der Jahre entfachen wird. Eine winzige Palastrevolte wird lediglich angezettelt mit ihrer Diagonal-Pendelachse, die zu besserem Fahrverhalten beiträgt, ohne dass damit Abstriche beim Komfort gemacht werden müssen.

Eingeführt im Januar 1968, umspannt die Baureihe zunächst sechs Typen vom 200 D mit 55 PS bis zum 250 mit einem Sechszylinder-Vergasermotor von 130 PS. Im November des Jahres wird sie gekrönt durch die beiden Coupés 250 C und 250 CE, und das ist in der Tat neu: Zum ersten Mal gibt es diese Karosserievariante in der Mittelklasse. Sie stößt umgehend auf reges Interesse, obwohl gewissermaßen für mehr Geld weniger Auto angeboten wird, identisch mit den Limousinen bis zur A-Säule, mit einer flacheren Windschutzscheibe und einer um 45 Millimeter niedrigeren Dachpartie, rahmenlosen und voll versenkbaren Seitenfenstern sowie zwei großen Türen. Auf eine Verbreitung von 67 048 bringen es die Coupés der Baureihe bis 1976. Eine andere Seitenlinie zeichnet sich vor allem durch die Exklusivität der niedrigeren Zahl aus: etwa 10 000 Exemplare der Modelle 220 D, 230, 240 D und 230.6 mit drei Sitzreihen und acht Plätzen auf einem Fahrgestell mit 650 mm mehr Radstand, höchst willkommen etwa bei Taxiunternehmen und Fluggesellschaften.

Im April 1972 weitet sich die Palette aus mit den Typen 280 und 280 E und den entsprechenden Coupés. Ihre neuen Sechszylinder mit zwei oben liegenden Nockenwellen leisten 160 PS in der Vergaser-Version und 185 PS als Einspritzer, erkennbar an Doppelstoßstangen vorn wie bereits der 250 und Stoßstangen hinten, die bis zu den Radausschnitten vorgezogen sind, sowie zwei Auspuff-Endrohren. Zugleich erhalten 250 und 250 C den älteren 2,8-Liter-Motor aus dem 280 s, um zehn PS auf 130 PS gedrosselt. Das Facelifting, dem die Serie im September 1973 unterzogen wird, erstreckt sich in erster Linie auf Aspekte der Sicherheit, mit beweglichen, von innen einstellbaren Außenspiegeln, Blenden an den A-Säulen, die Schmutz von den Seitenscheiben fernhalten, profilierten Heckleuchten und einer Regenrinne über der Heckscheibe. Kopfstützen, Automatikgurte sowie ein Vierspeichen-Sicherheitslenkrad sind schon seit einem halben Jahr Standardausrüstung.

Nicht immer bedeuten die gleichzeitig vorgenommenen optischen Retuschen analog zu denen bei der s-Klasse faktischen Fortschritt, etwa dass die seitlichen Ausstellfenster fortgefallen sind oder dass die Motorhaube niedriger und breiter geworden ist. Doppelstoßstangen sind nun ein Ding der Vergangenheit, immer schon eher ein visuell wirksames und überdies kostspieliges Requisit. Zugleich werden zwei neue Vierzylinder angeboten, der 240 D als

La production de la nouvelle génération du segment intermédiaire chez Mercedes commence, certe dès 1967, mais la voix du peuple l'a surnommée / d'après l'année de sa première présentation en public. Ma les soixante-huitards de Daimler-Benz n'ont vraime rien de révolutionnaire, si ce n'est le fouillis de dénomina tions que leur prolifération va déclencher au fil des an Une bien modeste révolution de palais est seuleme déclenchée par son essieu brisé en diagonale, qui contribu à lui donner un meilleur comportement sans que ce n'aille au détriment du confort.

Introduite en janvier 1968, la gamme comporte to d'abord six modèles, de la 200 D de 55 ch à la 250 à mote six-cylindres à carburateur de 130 ch. En novembre de même année, la gamme est couronnée par les deux coup 250 C et 250 CE, et cela est vraiment nouveau : cette varian de carrosserie est proposée pour la première fois da le segment intermédiaire. Elle suscite immédiatement u très vif engouement bien que l'on ait en quelque sor moins de voiture pour plus d'argent, celle-ci étant ide tique aux berlines jusqu'au pied de pare-brise, avec un baie plus inclinée et un toit plus bas de 45 mm, les fenêtr latérales sans encadrement et totalement escamotabl ainsi que deux grandes portières. Jusqu'en 1976, les coup de la gamme sont diffusés à raison de 67 048 exemplaire Une autre lignée se distingue surtout par l'exclusivité sa production : quelque 10 000 exemplaires des modèl 220 D, 230, 240 D et 230.6 à trois rangées de sièges huit places sur un châssis allongé de 650 mm font plus grand bonheur, par exemple, des sociétés de tax et des compagnies aériennes.

En avril 1972, la gamme s'enrichit des modèles 280 280 E avec les coupés correspondants. Leurs nouveaux six cylindres à deux arbres à cames en tête développent 160 c en version carburateur et 185 ch en version injection. I sont reconnaissables au double pare-chocs à l'avan comme pour la 250 déjà, et au pare-chocs arrière, chacu étant prolongé jusqu'aux arches de roues (et pour l'arriè jusqu'aux doubles sorties d'échappement). Simultaném les 250 et 250 C reçoivent le moteur de 2,8 litres plus ancie de la 280 s, qui a perdu 10 ch et n'en développe plus que 130 La remise au goût du jour dont bénéficie la série e septembre 1973 concerne essentiellement des éléments d sécurité avec des rétroviseurs extérieurs mobiles et réglable de l'intérieur, des gouttières sur les montants de pare-bris qui dévient les saletés des vitres latérales, des feux arrière rainures et une gouttière au-dessus de la lunette arrière. L appuie-tête, les ceintures de sécurité automatiques ains qu'un volant de sécurité à quatre branches font déjà parti de l'équipement standard depuis six mois.

À l'instar de celles de la Classe s, les retouches esthé tiques ne représentent pas toujours un progrès réel, pa exemple la disparition des déflecteurs latéraux ou le capo moteur plus bas et plus large. Les doubles pare-choc appartiennent désormais au passé. Deux nouveaux quatre cylindres font leur apparition : le 240 D en tant que moteur

MERCEDES-BENZ 200—240D 3.0 1967

cylinder, which continued to be sold as the 230/6. In July 1974 there was another addition to the family in the form of the 240D 3.0, a five-cylinder 3-liter engine delivering 80 bhp. The new generation was now turning into the older generation, but although the successors, type W123, had already been unveiled in January 1976, these predecessors proved hardy – and most continued to be built until the end of the year.

hubraumstärkster Diesel und der 230/4, der den 220 ersetzt. Die Vier hinter dem Schrägstrich dient dazu, Verwechslungen mit dem früheren 230 vorzubeugen, einem Sechszylinder, der als 230/6 weiterhin im Angebot bleibt. Im Juli 1974 bekommt die Modellfamilie noch einmal Zuwachs in Gestalt des 240D 3.0, eines Fünfzylinders mit drei Litern und 80 PS. Da ist die neue Generation schon fast die alte Generation. Doch obwohl im Januar 1976 bereits die Nachfolger W123 vorgestellt werden, erweisen sich die Vorgänger als zählebig – die meisten werden noch bis Ende jenes Jahres weitergebaut.

Diesel ayant la plus forte cylindrée, et le 230/4 qui remplace le 220. Le 4 derrière la barre oblique a pour but d'éliminer toute confusion avec l'ancien 230, un six-cylindres qui reste toujours au programme en tant que 230/6. En juillet 1974, la famille s'enrichit encore avec un 240D 3.0, un cinq-cylindres de 3 litres développant 80 ch. Mais la nouvelle génération se confond presque déjà avec l'ancienne. En effet, bien que sa remplaçante la W123 ait déjà été présentée en janvier 1976, les anciens modèles semblent résister puisque la plupart sont encore construits jusqu'à la fin de cette année-là.

Mercedes-Benz 200–240D3.0 1967

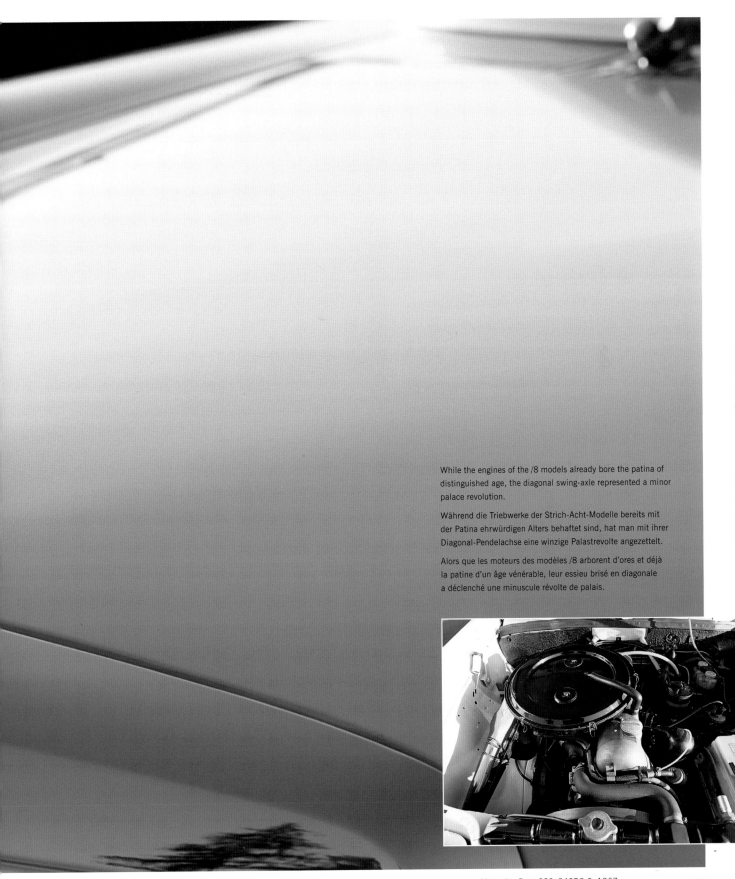

While the engines of the /8 models already bore the patina of
distinguished age, the diagonal swing-axle represented a minor
palace revolution.

Während die Triebwerke der Strich-Acht-Modelle bereits mit
der Patina ehrwürdigen Alters behaftet sind, hat man mit ihrer
Diagonal-Pendelachse eine winzige Palastrevolte angezettelt.

Alors que les moteurs des modèles /8 arborent d'ores et déjà
la patine d'un âge vénérable, leur essieu brisé en diagonale
a déclenché une minuscule révolte de palais.

From its very first appearance at the Frankfurt International Motor Show in September 1969 until some time in the Seventies, this car fed an appetite that was never genuinely satisfied. Although its makers marked it out from the very start as ourely and simply a research instrument, using intimidating and sobering descriptions such as "experimental vehicle" and "laboratory on wheels," public desire for the return of a Mercedes supersportscar was deep-seated. And so for a long time demand from potential purchasers refused to die. Some even tried to underline their case by writing a blank check. The C111 really was seductive, an 1125-mm- (3-ft-8-in-) low wedge, just a whisper higher than the 300 SLR Coupé of the time, with gullwings like the legendary 300 SL, finished in the rather garish orange that is known somewhat inexplicably at Mercedes as "rosé" and which acts as an ideal warning color for fast motorway journeys. Its uncompromising exterior was made of an unusual material: glass-fiber reinforced plastics as used in racing cars, bonded and riveted to a steel floorpan chassis. A spaceframe and a monocoque were also considered and rejected as unsuitable, which meant that the upwards-opening doors were nothing more than a stylistic feature. The suspension was also based on the racing car – double wishbones with torsion bars as anti-roll bars at the front, and three wishbones and two longitudinal swing arms for each rear wheel, with front and rear springing in the form of telescopic struts.

Meanwhile the heart of C111 and the real reason for its existence was its Wankel rotary engine, initially a three-rotor unit developing 280 bhp which drove the lightweight car (a mere 1,100 kg, 2,425 lb) at up to 270 kph (168 mph). The next evolutionary stage with four rotors and 350 bhp was even better. It powered the C111 Mark 2, which was unveiled to an enthusiastic and eager public at the Geneva Motor Show in March 1970, to phenomenal figures: 300 kph (186 mph), 0–100 kph (62 mph) in 4.9 seconds. It was also more attractive, with a more pleasing body, improved visibility, and more luggage space bringing it closer to everyday motoring. But the Not For Sale notices of its predecessor applied just as much to the Mark 2.

In 1976, the C111 was re-awoken with a kiss, like Snow White, when, against the background of the energy crisis, it became necessary to show the world that a diesel engine could also deliver high performance in a car. Consequently the five-cylinder engine from the 300 SD, beefed up to 190 bhp with a turbocharger and other refinements, took its place in the compartment behind the seats which had been vacated by the Wankel engine's demise. Love's labor was not lost: 13 diesel records fell to it in mid-June of that year on the high-speed track in Nardo, Southern Italy, plus three absolute records, including one over 5,000 miles (8,050 km) at an average speed of 252.54 kph (156.9 mph). And even then the pensioner was not left in peace. Instead it became ever longer and ever thinner, with all kinds of fins and spoilers added. On 30 April, again in Nardo, Mercedes set out to break all the records that could be

Von seinem ersten Auftreten bei der Frankfurter IAA im September 1969 an bis in die Siebziger erregt er einen Appetit, der nie gestillt wird. Zwar stempeln seine Väter den C111 von vornherein mit abschreckenden und ernüchternden Vokabeln wie »Experimentalfahrzeug« und »rollendes Versuchslabor« als reines Arbeitsgerät ab, aber der Wunsch nach der Wiederkehr der Mercedes-Supersportwagen sitzt tief. Und so reißt die Nachfrage potentieller Käufer über lange Zeit nicht ab. Manche versuchen gar, ihm mit einem Blankoscheck Nachdruck zu verleihen. Verführerisch ist der C111 in der Tat, ein 1125 mm flacher Keil, eine Idee höher als damals das 300 SLR Coupé, mit Flügeltüren wie der in die Legende abgewanderte 300 SL, in dem etwas schrillem Orange, das man bei Mercedes »weißherbst« nennt und als Signalfarbe für schnelle Autobahnfahrten empfiehlt. Sein militantes Äußeres ist modelliert aus ungewöhnlichem Material: glasfaserverstärktem Kunststoff wie im Rennsport, verklebt und vernietet mit einer stählernen Rahmenbodenanlage. Ein Gitterrohrrahmen und ein Monocoque werden ebenfalls erwogen und für ungeeignet befunden, was die nach oben öffnenden Türen zum bloßen Stilelement verfremdet. Am Rennwagen orientiert sich auch die Radaufhängung: Doppel-Querlenker mit Drehstab-Stabilisator vorn, hinten pro Rad drei Querlenker und zwei Längslenker, Federung vorn und hinten durch Federbeine.

Herzstück indes und der eigentliche Grund für das Dasein des C111 ist sein Wankelmotor, zunächst ein Dreischeiben-Aggregat mit 280 PS, welches das Leichtgewicht von 1100 Kilogramm auf bis zu 270 Stundenkilometer vorantreibt. Noch besser kann's die nächste Evolutionsstufe mit vier Scheiben und 350 PS. Sie befähigt den C111 Mark 2, einem begeisterten und begierigen Publikum auf dem Genfer Salon im März 1970 vor Augen gestellt, zu phänomenalen Werten: 300 Stundenkilometer, Sprint auf Tempo 100 in 4,9 Sekunden. Schöner ist er auch, mit einer gefälligeren Karosserie, besserer Sicht und mehr Kofferraum näher an den automobilen Alltag herangerückt und dennoch unverkäuflich wie sein Vorgänger.

Dann wird es still um den Kreiskolbenmotor. 1976 indes küsst man den C111 wieder wach aus seinem Dornröschenschlaf, als es darum geht, der Welt vor dem Hintergrund der Energiekrise zu zeigen, auch ein Dieselmotor könne ein Auto flottmachen. Folglich rückt der Fünfzylinder aus dem 300 SD, mit Hilfe eines Turboladers und flankierender Maßnahmen auf 190 PS erstarkt, in das Abteil hinter den Sitzen ein, das durch das Hinscheiden des Wankel-Triebwerks vakant geworden ist. Lohn der Liebesmüh: 13 Diesel-Rekorde Mitte Juni jenes Jahres auf der süditalienischen Tempo-Piste in Nardo, dazu drei absolute Bestwerte, einer davon über 5000 Meilen mit 252,54 Stundenkilometern. Und auch weiterhin kommt der Pensionär nicht zur Ruhe, der immer länger und immer schlanker wird und allerlei Flossen und Spoiler ansetzt. Am 30. April schickt man sich an, wieder in Nardo, alle Rekorde zu brechen, die sich innerhalb von

Dès sa première apparition, à l'IAA de Francfo en septembre 1969, et jusque dans les anné 1970, elle suscite un appétit qui ne sera jama assouvi. Certes, ses pères ont affublé d'emblée la C111 qualificatifs dissuasifs et démoralisants tels « voiture exp rimentale » et « laboratoire roulant », montrant bien qu s'agissait d'un pur engin de travail, mais le désir de vo renaître de ses cendres la super Mercedes de sport res profondément enraciné dans les esprits. Ce qui expliqu que la demande d'acheteurs potentiels ne se soit p démentie pendant longtemps. Certains n'hésitent mêm pas à donner du poids à leurs doléances en y joignant u chèque en blanc. Et, de fait, la C111 est bien séduisan avec ses 1125 mm de carrosserie cunéiforme, un soupço plus haute que le coupé 300 SLR de jadis et, avec des ail de mouette comme la 300 SL, depuis longtemps déjà entr dans la légende, dans un orange quelque peu criard, appe curieusement chez Mercedes « blanc automne » et recom mandé comme couleur voyante pour rouler rapidemen sur l'autoroute. Sa silhouette aux lignes fluides est mode lée dans un matériaux inhabituel : de la matière plastiqu renforcée de fibre de verre comme en compétition, coll et rivetée sur une plate-forme en acier. La suspension es aussi, directement inspirée de la compétition : doub triangulation transversale avec barre antiroulis à l'avan trois leviers transversaux et deux leviers longitudinaux pa roue à l'arrière, suspension à jambe élastique à l'avant et l'arrière.

Mais la raison d'être proprement dite de la C111 est so moteur Wankel, tout d'abord un tri-rotor de 280 ch qu catapulte ce poids plume de 1100 kg à 270 km/h. Mais ce n'est rien comparé à l'évolution suivante, un quadri-roto de 350 ch. Il permet à la C111 Mark 2, présentée à un publi enthousiasmé et avide de sensations au Salon de Genèv de mars 1970, d'atteindre des performances phénomé nales : 300 km/h et 4,9 secondes pour le 0 à 100 km/h. El est, aussi, plus belle, avec une carrosserie plus séduisante une meilleure visibilité et, avec plus de coffre, plus proch des considérations de la vie quotidienne dans l'auto mobile bien que tout aussi invendable que sa devancière.

Puis le rideau retombe sur le moteur rotatif. Un prin charmant réveille la C111, en 1976, de son sommeil de Bell au bois dormant lorsque, dans le contexte de la crise éner gétique, l'on veut montrer combien un moteur Diesel es capable de donner des ailes à une voiture. On place don dans le compartiment devenu vacant depuis le départ d moteur Wankel derrière les sièges, le cinq-cylindres de l 300 SD dont la puissance est majorée à 190 ch, un turbo compresseur et autres éléments mécaniques. Et la récom pense ne se fait pas attendre : 13 records diesel sont battu à la mi-juin de cette année sur la piste à haute vitesse d Nardo, dans le sud de l'Italie, plus trois records absolu dont l'un sur plus de 5000 miles à 252,54 km/h d moyenne. Décidément, le calme est refusé à cette retrait qui ne cesse de s'allonger et de s'amincir au fur et à mesur qu'elle se voit pousser des ailerons et becquets. Le 30 avri

ackled within twelve hours – with a car that by then elivered 231 bhp. The test engineers, who also doubled up s the drivers, covered 3,774 km (2,345 miles) in half a day ith an average consumption of less than 16 liters per 0 km (14.7 mpg). Engineer Hans Liebold did even etter, setting a lap record at 403.978 kph (251.05 mph) on May 1979 with the modified v8 from the 450 SE and 0 bhp – no-one had ever traveled so quickly from A A. The C111 had long since discarded any pretence of imilarity to the dream car of yore.

zwölf Stunden erledigen lassen – inzwischen mit 231 PS. Ingenieure des Versuchs, in Personalunion auch Piloten, legen an einem halben Tag 3774 Kilometer zurück, mit einem Durchschnitts-Konsum von weniger als 16 Litern. Noch besser kann es Ingenieur Hans Liebold, der am 5. Mai 1979 mit dem modifizierten v8 aus dem 450 SE und 500 PS eine Rekordrunde von 403,978 Stundenkilometern hinlegt – schneller reiste noch niemand von A nach A. Da hat der C111 schon längst jede Ähnlichkeit mit dem Traumwagen von einst verloren.

ainsi parée, on l'envoie de nouveau à Nardo pour battre tous les records que l'on peut battre en 12 heures avec 231 ch. Les ingénieurs, qui sont aussi les pilotes, couvrent 3774 km en consommant en moyenne moins de 16 litres aux 100 km. Mais l'ingénieur Hans Liebold fait encore mieux, le 5 mai 1979, avec le v8 modifié de la 450 SE déve-loppant 500 ch puisqu'il établit un record du tour à 403,978 km/h – personne n'est allé encore plus vite. Mais, la C111 a désormais, et depuis longtemps, perdu toute similitude avec la voiture de rêve qu'elle était jadis.

The C111 dream car bore all the hallmarks of almost everyday practicality. But the chance to buy one never became a reality, although some were prepared to offer huge sums for the privilege.

Der Traumwagen C111 wird ausgestattet mit allen Anzeichen alltagsnaher Praktikabilität. Nur: Zur käuflichen Realität wird er nie, obwohl man Unsummen für ihn bietet.

voiture de rêve, la C111 a aussi tout d'une voiture de tous les jours. Mais elle ne sera jamais mise en vente, bien que certains aient proposé des sommes astronomiques pour en offrir une.

Mercedes-Benz C111 1969

Mercedes-Benz C111 1969

spaceframe and a monocoque were also considered during the design of the C111, ut were rejected as unsuitable. This meant that its gullwing doors were nothing more han a stylistic element and in-house feature.

ei der Konzeption des C111 werden ein Gitterrohrrahmen und ein Monocoque rwogen und verworfen, was seine Flügeltüren zum bloßen attraktiven Stilelement nd Selbstzitat verfremdet.

ors de la conception de la C111, on envisage un châssis tubulaire et une monocoque, ue l'on rejette plus tard, ce qui fait de ses portières en ailes de mouette un banal mais ttrayant élément de style, ainsi qu'une citation de soi-même.

The launch of the 350 SL in April 1971 marked the beginning of the almost never-ending story of the 107 series. The fact that this spanned 18 years and a total of 237,387 cars was convincing evidence of the success of the design, and of the concept of a powerful and comfortable two-seater touring sports car with a convertible roadster top or a removable hardtop. The new car had only the abbreviation SL in common with the rugged gullwing coupé of earlier years, and even that was deceptive. It was nowhere near as sporty and at 1,560 kg (3,439 lb) it was certainly not light. After all, luxury and comprehensive protection had to be paid for in terms of weight.

Quite a number of the components again came from other series, for example the suspension from the /8 saloons, or the V8 from the 280 SE 3.5. The 350 SL was a safe car. The fuel tank was now in a protected position above the rear axle. The padded dashboard with its flexibly mounted or recessed switches and levers were safety features as was the four-spoke steering wheel with its baffle and wide cushioned pad. Cleverly designed wind deflector profiles on the A-pillars kept the side windows clear in rain. The turn-signal lights were wrapped around into the fenders and highly visible, while the tail-lights were large and their ribbed profile kept them clear of dirt. The Paris Salon in the autumn of 1971 saw the launch of the stylistically related 350 SLC, intended to an extent as a family car, a four-seater coupé with a fixed roof and a 360-mm- (14-in-) longer wheelbase. From April 1973 onwards both cars were available with a 4.5-liter V8, or, from July 1974 onwards in the shadow of the oil crisis, with a 2.8-liter six-cylinder with double overhead camshafts. The 280 SL could be recognized by its narrower tires, and the 450 SL by a front spoiler which also directed more air to the radiator. None was restrained in its drinking habits. The change to Bosch's mechanical K-Jetronic system at the beginning of 1975, which also entailed a slight drop in performance, made little change in this respect. At the same time a solid-state transistorized ignition system and a hydraulic compensator for valve play were introduced. The updated SL family was presented in Geneva in March 1980 with obvious influences in the interior deriving from the S-class. The 3-speed converter automatic transmission had now given way to a 4-speed variant, while the 280 SL retained a 5-speed manual gearbox, standard equipment since 1981.

The engine of the 450 SLC 5.0 of September 1977 also found its way into the 500 SL from March 1980 onwards. The "Last Post" was also played for the 350 SL, which was replaced by the 380 SL, like its sister model with an alloy hood and a discreet front spoiler. The unveiling of the 380 SEC and 500 SEC coupés at the 1981 Frankfurt International Motor Show meant the end of the road for the SLC. The SL remained, however, with regular updates. In the autumn of 1985 a thoroughly revamped version was even exhibited again at the Frankfurt show. The 2.8-liter engine was replaced by a 3-liter six-cylinder.

Als im April 1971 der 350 SL vorgestellt wird, beginnt die schier unendliche Geschichte der Baureihe 107. Dass diese achtzehn Jahre umgreift und insgesamt 237387 Fahrzeuge hervorbringt, beweist den Erfolg einer Form und eines Konzepts: des starken und kommoden Reisesportwagens für zwei, mit versenkbarem Roadsterverdeck oder abnehmbarem Hardtop. Mit dem rauhen Gullwing-Coupé von damals hat der Neue nur noch das Kürzel SL gemeinsam, und selbst das trügt: Er ist längst nicht so sportlich und mit 1560 Kilogramm Gewicht erst recht nicht leicht. Denn Luxus und ein umfassender Schutz im Falle eines Falles müssen mit zusätzlichen Pfunden erkauft werden.

Wieder stammen etliche Komponenten aus anderen Serien, etwa die Radaufhängungen aus den Strich-Acht-Limousinen, der V8 aus dem 280 SE 3.5. Der 350 SL ist ein sicheres Auto: Der Tank liegt jetzt geschützt über der Hinterachse. Das gepolsterte Armaturenbrett mit seinen elastischen oder versenkt eingebauten Schaltern und Hebeln bewahrt vor Unbill ebenso wie das Vierspeichen-Lenkrad mit Pralltopf und breiter Polsterplatte. Raffinierte Windleitprofile an den A-Säulen halten die Seitenfenster bei Regen frei. Weit in die Flanken gezogen und gut sichtbar sind die Blinker, üppig dimensioniert die Heckleuchte, deren geripptes Profil Schmutz fernhält. Auf dem Pariser Salon im Herbst 1971 folgt, gewissermaßen als Familienangebot, der stilistisch verwandte 350 SLC, ein viersitziges Coupé mit festem Dach und 360 mm mehr Radstand. Ab April 1973 gibt es beide Modelle mit einem V8 von 4,5 Litern, ab Juli 1974 im Schlagschatten der Ölkrise auch mit dem 2,8-Liter-Sechszylinder mit zwei oben liegenden Nockenwellen. Den 280 SL erkennt man an schmaleren Reifen, den 450 SL an einem Frontspoiler, der zugleich dem Kühler mehr Luft zuführt. Kostverächter sind sie alle nicht. Daran ändert auch die Umstellung auf die mechanische K-Jetronic von Bosch um die Jahreswende 1975 kaum etwas, die Hand in Hand geht mit geringen Leistungseinbußen. Zugleich werden die kontaktlose Transistorzündung und ein hydraulischer Ausgleich für Ventilspiel eingeführt. Im März 1980 präsentiert sich die SL-Familie in aktualisierter Form mit evidenten Einflüssen aus der S-Klasse im Interieur. Die Wandlerautomatik mit drei Fahrstufen hat nun Platz gemacht für eine Variante mit vier Gängen, beim 280 SL bleibt es indessen bei einem Fünfgang-Schaltgetriebe, Standard seit 1981.

Das Triebwerk des 450 SLC 5.0 vom September 1977 findet sich ab März 1980 auch im 500 SL. Zugleich bläst man das Halali über dem 350 SL, an dessen Stelle der 380 SL tritt, wie die Schwestermodelle mit einer Motorhaube aus Leichtmetall und einem dezenten Spoiler vorn. Das Erscheinen der Coupés 380 SEC und 500 SEC auf der Frankfurter IAA 1981 bedeutet das Aus für den SLC. Der SL aber bleibt, durch Retuschen immer wieder aufgewertet. Im Herbst 1985 wird er gar auf der Frankfurter Ausstellung noch einmal nachhaltig runderneuert gezeigt.

En avril 1971, date de présentation de la 350 SL, commence la généalogie véritablement interminable de la série 107. Celle-ci allait durer 18 ans et engendrer au total 237 387 voitures, preuve du succès d'une forme et d'un concept : celui de la voiture de sport de voyage, puissante et confortable pour deux personnes avec capote escamotable ou *hard-top* démontable. Avec viril coupé Gullwing de jadis, la nouvelle n'a plus en commun que l'abréviation SL, et même cela est trompeur : elle est loin d'être aussi sportive et, avec 1560 kg, *a fortiori*, loin d'être aussi légère. En effet, le luxe et une protection exhaustive en cas d'accident exigent leur tribut.

De nombreux composants proviennent d'autres séries, par exemple les suspensions, des berlines /8, le v8, de la 280 SE 3.5. La 350 SL est une voiture sûre : bien protégée le réservoir se trouve maintenant au-dessus de l'essieu arrière. Le tableau de bord rembourré avec ses manettes commandes affleurantes épargne des blessures, de même que le volant à quatre branches avec pot antichocs et large plaque capitonnée. Les gouttières raffinées le long des montants des pare-brise dévient l'eau des fenêtres latérales en cas de pluie. Les clignotants mordent largement sur les flancs et sont bien visibles. Quant aux feux arrière, au profil rainuré qui élimine les saletés, ils sont de grandes dimensions. Elle est suivie, au Salon de Paris de l'automne 1971, par un coupé à quatre places, avec 360 mm d'empattement supplémentaire : la 350 SLC, esthétiquement très proche et plutôt destinée aux pères de famille. À partir d'avril 1973, les deux modèles sont disponibles également avec un v8 de 4,5 litres et, à partir de juillet 1974 sous le choc de la crise pétrolière, également avec le six-cylindres de 2,8 litres à deux arbres à cames en tête. On distingue la 280 SL à ses pneus plus étroits et la 450 SL, un aileron avant qui canalise plus d'air vers le radiateur. Toutes deux n'ont rien d'ascétique. Et ce n'est pas l'adoption de l'injection mécanique K-Jetronic de Bosch, fin 1974 – qui voit disparaître quelques chevaux – qui y change grand-chose. Mercedes introduit par la même occasion l'allumage à transistor sans contact et le rattrapage hydraulique du jeu des soupapes. En mars 1980 à Genève, la famille SL se présente revue et corrigée avec des influences de la Classe S dans le cockpit. La boîte automatique à convertisseur et trois rapports a maintenant disparu au profit d'une transmission à quatre vitesses, 280 SL restant proposée avec une boîte manuelle à cinq vitesses qui est la norme depuis 1981.

Le moteur de la 450 SLC 5.0 de septembre 1977 propulse également la 500 SL à partir de mars 1980. Simultanément, il sonne le glas de la 350 SL, remplacée par la 380 SL avec comme ses sœurs, un capot moteur en alliage léger et un discret aileron à l'avant. L'arrivée des coupés 380 SEC et 500 SEC à l'IAA de Francfort en 1981 scelle le destin de la SLC. Mais la SL demeure au programme, toujours remis au goût du jour à l'aide de délicates retouches. À l'automne 1985, au Salon de Francfort, elle bénéficie même d'un profond lifting. Le 2,8 litres prend une retraite bien méritée.

MERCEDES-BENZ 350 SL – 560 SL   1971

Mercedes-Benz 500SL 1986

his then ushered in the renaissance of a legend – the
300 SL – though in name only. The 420 SL's badge tacitly
indicated that the previous 3.8-liter engine had been
rebored to 4.2 liters. Modifications had been made to
the 5-liter powerplant of the 500 SL, which developed
245 bhp with its Bosch KE-Jetronic electromechanical
injection system and electronic ignition (compared with
the previous 240 bhp). The 560 SL, whose potential was
reduced to a mere 230 SAE-bhp when trimmed by
the harsh regime of emissions legislation in some countries, was intended exclusively for export. Ultimately,
SL no longer meant quite what it had in the early
years. The rampant growth in engine size in the meantime
had revealed one simple fact: even in the latter stages
of the economic miracle, lots of people were still doing
very well.

Wachablösung gibt es für den 2,8 Liter: einen Dreiliter-
Sechszylinder. Damit kommt es zugleich zur Renaissance
einer Legende, aber nur, was den Namen anbelangt:
300 SL. Das Sigel 420 SL verrät implizit, dass der bisherige
3,8 Liter auf 4,2 Liter aufgebohrt wurde. Modifiziert
worden ist das 5-Liter-Triebwerk des 500 SL, das mit
der elektronisch-mechanischen Einspritzanlage Bosch
KE-Jetronic und elektronischer Zündung 245 PS leistet
(bisher 240). Nur für den Export bestimmt ist der 560 SL,
dessen Potential im scharfen Licht der Emissionsgesetz-
gebung einiger Länder auf lediglich 230 SAE-PS zusam-
menschmilzt. Am Ende heißt kein SL mehr so wie in
den frühen Jahren. Das Wuchern der Hubräume in der
Zwischenzeit verrät vor allem eines: Auch in der Spät-
phase des Wirtschaftswunders geht es noch sehr vielen
Leuten sehr gut.

est remplacé par un six-cylindres de 3 litres. Cela pourrait
faire croire à la renaissance d'une légende, mais n'est vrai
que pour le nom : 300 SL. Le sigle 420 SL induit que l'ancien
3,8 litres a vu sa cylindrée majorée à 4,2 litres. Le 5 litres de
la 500 SL bénéficie lui aussi de modifications puisqu'il reçoit
l'injection électronique mécanique Bosch KE-Jetronic et
un allumage électronique qui lui permet de développer
désormais 245 ch contre 240 auparavant. La 560 SL est
réservée aux exportations, mais sa puissance retombe à
230 ch SAE par suite des sévères législations écologiques
de certains pays. À la fin, aucune SL n'a plus le même nom
que quelques années auparavant. L'inflation des cylindrées
survenue entre-temps prouve surtout une chose : même
durant la phase ultime du miracle économique, il y a
encore énormément de gens qui n'ont pas le moindre
souci financier.

The series' comprehensive safety features included a dashboard on which you could not hurt yourself, together with a steering wheel with a baffle and cushioned pad. The turn signals and light units were ribbed to keep them clear of dirt. The roadster top disappeared completely under a metal cover. The rubber lip on the trunk was not to everyone's taste.

Zum umfassenden Sicherheitskonzept der Baureihe gehört ein Armaturenbrett, an dem man sich nicht wehtun kann, sowie das Lenkrad mit Pralltopf und Polsterplatte. Blinker und Leuchteneinheiten sind geriffelt, damit Schmutz von ihnen ferngehalten wird. Das Verdeck des Roadsters verschwindet zur Gänze unter einem metallenen Deckel. Die Gummilippe am Heck indessen trifft nicht jedermanns Geschmack.

Le concept de sécurité intégrale de la gamme comporte un tableau de bord parfaitement sécurisé ainsi qu'un volant à moyeu rembourré. Clignotants et feux arrière sont rainurés pour être moins sensibles à la saleté. La capote du roadster disparaît totalement sous un couvercle métallique. L'aileron arrière en caoutchouc n'est pas du goût de tous.

The SLC coupé was launched in October 1971 as a sister model to the SL.
Its extended wheelbase offered space for a growing family of four. The 280 SLC
owed its existence to the 1973 oil crisis. It proved a good buy, as its six-cylinder engine
delivered the same performance as the 3.5-liter V8 but with lower fuel consumption.

Das Coupé SLC wird im Oktober 1971 als Schwestermodell zum SL herausgebracht
und bietet über einem verlängerten Radstand Platz für eine knospende Familie von
vier Köpfen. Der 280 SLC verdankt seine Existenz der Ölkrise von 1973. Der Käufer
macht einen guten Fang: Bei geringerem Verbrauch schwingt sich sein Sechszylinder
zu den gleichen Fahrleistungen auf wie der V8 von 3,5 Litern.

Le coupé SLC vient épauler son jumeau le cabriolet en octobre 1971.
Grâce à un empattement allongé, il offre suffisamment de place pour une famille
de quatre personnes. La 280 SLC doit sa naissance à la crise pétrolière de 1973.
L'acheteur fait une bonne affaire: son six-cylindres affiche les mêmes performances
que le V8 de 3,5 litres, tout en consommant moins.

Mercedes-Benz 350SL–560SL 1971

The name had long since been accepted in common parlance, and then it was finally adopted by the manufacturer too; the w116 series officially became known as the s-class, launched in September 1972. The first models were the 280 s, 280 se, and 350 se. These were followed in March 1973 by the 450 se and the 450 sel which offered its rear passengers more space because of the 100 mm (4 in) increase in the wheelbase to 2965 mm (9 ft 9 in). Further long-wheelbase versions, which were popular as chauffeur-driven and company cars, appeared in November (350 sel) and in April 1974 (280 sel).

The front suspension had been inspired by the c111: double wishbones with a roll radius of 0 and an anti-dive mechanism. At the rear, tried-and-tested technology from the '68 saloons and the 350 sl – the tilted-shaft axle – was re-used. The standard set by the latter model was also applied to safety features too, both in detail and in overall design. The safety cage provided even greater protection for the occupants in the event of an accident, and the front and rear sections were even better at absorbing the kinetic energy of a collision. The 96-liter (25.4-gal) fuel tank was located above the rear axle. Wind deflectors on the a-pillars kept the side windows clear of water which might otherwise impair vision. The turn-signal lights wrapped round into the fenders, and the tail-lights were grooved as a protection against soiling. The series again found its finest expression in a real supercar, the 450 sel 6.9, unveiled in May, and produced from September 1975 onwards.

The engine, almost seven liters in displacement, developed 286 bhp. Even more impressive than its performance – top speed 225 kph (140 mph), 0–100 kph (62 mph) in 7.4 seconds – was the manner in which the top Mercedes of its time achieved this with supreme coolness. Its 3-speed automatic transmission and pneumatic springing with hydraulic level control also contributed to this effect. Central locking, air-conditioning, and headlight washers all came as standard. 7,380 owners of the 450 sel 6.9 appreciated all these features, even though at 73,100 marks in March 1977 it cost twice as much as a 350 se.

Towards the end of 1975 the electronic fuel supply of the injection versions was replaced by the mechanical k-Jetronic system. At the same time both v8 engines had a solid-state transistorized ignition system and hydraulic compensator for valve play fitted. Slight deteriorations in performance were cancelled out in the next two years.

Another new arrival joined the family in May 1978, and an innovation at that – the 300 sd was the first s-class diesel model. The powerplant was familiar from the 240 d 3.0 and the 300 d, a 3-liter five-cylinder. Supercharged by a turbocharger, it reached the unfamiliar territory of 115 bhp, though it did have to shift a dry vehicle weight of 1,815 kg (4,000 lb). However, only residents of Canada and the United States were able to enjoy these hybrids of luxury and economy. A tactical

Der Name hat sich längst eingebürgert, da wird er auch vom Hersteller selbst adoptiert: Mercedes-Benz s-Klasse heißt nun offiziell die Baureihe w116, Debüt im September 1972. Am Anfang stehen 280 s, 280 se und 350 se. Im März 1973 folgen der 450 se und der 450 sel, der den hinteren Passagieren mit seinem um 100 mm auf 2965 mm erweiterten Radstand mehr Lebensraum zugesteht. Als weitere Lang-Versionen, beliebt als Chauffeur- und Firmenwagen, werden im November der 350 sel und im April 1974 der 280 sel nachgereicht.

Die Aufhängung vorn zeigt sich inspiriert vom c111: Doppel-Querlenker mit Lenkrollradius 0 und Bremsnick-Abstützung. Hinten greift man auf Bewährtes aus den Strich-Acht-Limousinen und dem 350 sl zurück: eine Schräglenkerachse. In puncto Sicherheit gleicht man sich ebenfalls dem Standard an, den dieser gesetzt hat, im Detail wie in der Konzeption insgesamt. Noch massiver trotzt der Hochsicherheitstrakt für die Insassen etwaigen Unfällen, noch besser absorbieren die vorderen und hinteren Anbauten die Energie, die bei einem Aufprall auf sie einwirkt. Der 96-Liter-Tank reitet über der Hinterachse. Windleitprofile an den a-Säulen bewahren die Seitenscheiben vor trübem Wasser. In die Flanken gerundet sind die Blinker, die Leuchten hinten gerifft als Vorkehrung gegen Verschmutzung. Wieder findet die Baureihe ihre Apotheose in einem wahren Kraft-Wagen, dem 450 sel 6.9, vorgestellt im Mai, produziert ab September 1975.

Aus fast sieben Litern Hubraum hat man 286 ps sublimiert. Noch eindrucksvoller als seine Fahrleistungen – 225 Stundenkilometer Spitze, Sprint auf Tempo 100 in 7,4 Sekunden – ist die Art und Weise, wie der Top-Mercedes jener Jahre diese möglich macht: mit souveräner Gelassenheit. Auch seine Dreigang-Automatik und seine Gasfederung mit hydraulischer Niveau-Regulierung tragen dazu bei. Zu den guten Dingen der Serienausstattung zählen Zentralverriegelung, Klima- und Scheinwerfer-Waschanlage. 7380 Erstbesitzer des 450 sel 6.9 wissen das zu würdigen, obwohl er mit 73 100 Mark im März 1977 doppelt so teuer ist wie ein 350 se.

Gegen Ende 1975 wird die elektronische Kraftstoffversorgung der Einspritz-Versionen abgelöst von der mechanischen k-Jetronic. Zugleich erhalten beide v8-Maschinen eine kontaktlose Transistorzündung sowie hydraulischen Ausgleich für Ventilspiel. Geringe Leistungseinbußen sind nach zwei Jahren wieder ausgeglichen.

Im Mai 1978 stellt sich noch einmal Zuwachs ein, ein Novum zumal: Mit dem 300 sd bekommt die s-Klasse erstmals ein eigenes Diesel-Modell. Das Triebwerk ist bekannt aus dem 240 d 3.0 und dem 300 d, ein Dreiliter-Fünfzylinder. Von einem Turbolader zwangsbeatmet, schwingt er sich in ungewohnter Umgebung zu 115 ps auf, immerhin zuständig für den Transport von allein 1815 kg Wagengewicht. In den Genuss dieses Hybriden aus Luxus und Genügsamkeit kommen allerdings lediglich Kanadier und Bürger der Vereinigten Staaten. Dahinter steckt ein taktischer Schachzug: Der 300 sd soll helfen, den Flotten-

Le nom s'est établi depuis longtemps et le constr teur lui-même ne peut faire autrement que l'adopter: Mercedes-Benz – Classe s est désorm le nom officiel de la série w116 qui fait ses débuts en se tembre 1972. Trois modèles sont tout d'abord proposés 280 s, 280 se et la 350 se. Elles sont suivies, en mars 1973, la 450 se et la 450 sel, dont l'empattement est allongé 100 mm, à 2965 mm, et offre donc plus d'espace habita aux passagers des fauteuils arrière. Autres version empattement long appréciées comme voiture de chauffe et de société, la 350 sel, présentée en novembre, suivie la 280 sel en avril 1974.

À l'avant, la suspension est inspirée de la c111: dou bras transversaux avec déport nul de l'axe de pivot de fus et dispositifs évitant l'effet de révérence au freinage. Po l'arrière, Mercedes reprend les composants éprouvés d berlines /8 et de la 350 sl: un essieu à bras obliques. matière de sécurité, également, on s'aligne sur la nor que celui-ci a instaurée, pour les détails comme pour concept global. Encore plus rigide, la cellule passager haute sécurité pare encore mieux aux éventuels acciden tandis que les parties avant et arrière absorbent bien mie l'impact d'une éventuelle collision. Le réservoir de 96 litr est à cheval sur l'essieu arrière. Les gouttières profilées s les montants de pare-brise dévient l'eau de pluie des vitr latérales. Les clignotants débordent sur les flancs et l feux arrière sont rainurés pour offrir moins de prise à l salissures. Une fois de plus, la gamme est couronnée p une authentique voiture de grand prestige, la 450 sel 6 présentée en mai et produite à partir de septembre 1975.

De près de 7 litres de cylindrée, les motoristes ont sublir 290 ch. Chose plus impressionnante encore que ses perfo mances – vitesse de pointe 225 km/h et passage de 0 à 100 km en 7,4 secondes, la Mercedes la plus prestigieuse de ce époque les affiche dans la décontraction la plus souverain Il faut admettre que sa boîte automatique à trois rapports sa suspension à gaz avec correcteur d'assiette hydrauliqu contribuent de façon déterminante. Parmi les accessoir bienvenus de l'équipement de série figurent le verrouilla centralisé, la climatisation et les lave-phares. Les propri taires de 450 sel 6.9, au nombre de 7380, apprécient s qualités à leur juste valeur bien que, avec 73 100 marks, e coûte, en mars 1977, deux fois plus cher qu'une 350 se.

Vers la fin de 1975, l'alimentation électronique d versions à injection est remplacée par une k-Jetror mécanique. Par la même occasion, les deux moteurs reçoivent un allumage à transistor sans contact ainsi qu' rattrapage hydraulique du jeu des soupapes. Les faib baisses sont compensées deux ans plus tard.

En mai 1978, un rejeton vient agrandir la famille: av la 300 sd, la Classe s est, pour la première fois, dotée son propre modèle diesel. Le moteur est bien connu pu qu'il provient de la 240 d 3.0 et de la 300 d. C'est donc cinq-cylindres de 3 litres. Avec la respiration forcée d' turbocompresseur, il développe dans cet environneme inhabituel une puissance de 115 ch qui sont bien néce

Mercedes-Benz 350SEL 1979

e was behind this; it was intended that the 300 SD
ld help to reduce fleet fuel consumption, a figure
duced by the Carter administration. The average
umption of all a manufacturer's models was assessed
art of the authorization process for driving on
rican roads, and Mercedes had a little catching-up
. Of the 473,035 cars of the w116 series, 28,634 were
Ds, including the last one to roll off the assembly line
ndelfingen in September 1980.

verbrauch zu senken, eine Größe, die die Carter-Adminis-
tration eingeführt hat: Der Durchschnitts-Konsum aller
Modelle eines Herstellers ist Bestandteil ihrer Legitima-
tion auf amerikanischen Straßen, und da gibt es bei
Mercedes einigen Nachholbedarf. Immerhin sind 28 634
der 473 035 Exemplare der Serie w116 vom Typ 300 SD,
auch der letzte, der im September 1980 in Sindelfingen
vom Band rollt.

saires quand on sait que la voiture, à elle seule, accuse un
poids de 1815 kg. Seuls les Canadiens et les citoyens des
États-Unis profitent toutefois de cette symbiose de luxe et
de sobriété. La stratégie qui se dissimule derrière cette
décision est de bon aloi. La 300 SD a, en effet, pour but
de diminuer une allègre consommation, suivant un paramètre introduit par l'administration Carter : la consommation moyenne de tous les modèles d'un constructeur
conditionne son homologation pour circuler aux États-
Unis, et, dans ce domaine, Mercedes a fort à faire. Des
473 035 exemplaires de la série w116, 28 634 appartiennent
au type 300 SD, dont la dernière qui sort de chaîne à Sindelfingen en septembre 1980.

The 350SEL, clothed in its smooth, solid lines, was one of the best cars of its era for performance, comfort, quality, and durability. The cockpit also bore witness to the notion of unobtrusive objectivity where only function determined form. The wheelbase, rear footwell and rear doors were 10 cm (4 in) longer than in the standard version. It was decided to change the configuration of the lights from vertical to horizontal. The ribbed design of the tail-lights prevented dirt from sticking to them.

Von ruhiger und gediegener Linienführung, zählt der 350SEL zu den besten Autos seiner Zeit hinsichtlich Leistung, Komfort, Qualität und Langlebigkeit. Auch das Cockpit zeugt von jener unaufgeregten Sachlichkeit, bei der allein der Zweck die Formen bestimmt. Radstand, hinterer Sitzraum und hintere Türen sind zehn Zentimeter länger als bei der Normalversion. Bei der Anordnung der Lampen ist man von der Vertikalen zur Horizontalen übergegangen. Die Verrippung der hinteren Leuchten wirkt ihrer Verschmutzung entgegen.

La 350SEL aux lignes pures, mais élégantes est l'une des meilleures voitures de son temps pour la puissance, le confort, la qualité et la longévité. Le tableau de bord affiche lui aussi cette sobriété reposante en vertu de laquelle seule la fonction dicte les formes. L'empattement, l'espace et les portières arrière mesurent dix centimètres de plus que pour la version normale. Pour l'agencement des phares, on a abandonné la verticale pour l'horizontale. Les rainures des optiques arrière maintiennent les phares plus propres.

The transition was smooth – the /8 saloons were still rolling off the production line when the w123 series was introduced in January 1976, again a large family ranging from the rather rough-sounding 55 bhp 200 D to the powerful 280 E delivering 185 bhp. This was also mirrored by the price range, from 18,900 to 26,900 marks. The round lights, a main headlight located side-by-side with a small halogen light behind a common diffuser screen, were the most conspicuous external feature. The top-of-the-range models, the 280 and 280 E, were fitted with rectangular halogen wide-band headlights which were standard for the entire range from September 1982 onwards. The traditional sub-frame was dropped since the front wheels were now suspended from double wishbones with a roll radius of 0.

Furthermore, the Mercedes motto of "Safety First," which had been elevated to the status of a creed, was very much in evidence. Everyone is equal when faced with the trauma of a motor accident, and so passengers in Mercedes mid-range cars were not denied the safety features of the s and sl models. The passenger cage with its rigid roof frame, high-strength pillars, and reinforced doors had become even more stable, while the front and tail ends absorbed impacts more willingly thanks to "controlled deformability" as it was so inelegantly termed in the publicity literature. The safety steering column was an innovative feature. The steering linkage and steering column jacket were connected through a corrugated sleeve which reduced the risk of the steering column being thrust like a spear into the car interior in the event of an accident.

Initially there was little news to report in terms of the engines, except that the 250 was using a freshly developed 2.5-liter six-cylinder instead of the elderly 2.8 liters of previously. 1977 saw the range of bodies expanded with three new types. There was the coupé launched in Geneva in March as the 230 C, 280 C, and 280 CE. There was the stretched version of the 240, 240 D, and 250 with three rows of seats, and a 630-mm- (25-in-) longer wheelbase, unveiled in August. And there was the T sedan, a refined Mercedes term for a refined estate car, first shown at the Frankfurt International Motor Show in September. The following three years saw the engines progressively beefed up: 185 bhp (previously 177 bhp) for the 280 E in April 1978, 72 bhp (originally 65 bhp) for the 240 D in August 1978, 60 bhp (previously 55 bhp) for the 200 D in February 1979. In June 1980 the series was offered with three new engines. There was a 5-cylinder, three-liter diesel with an exhaust-driven turbocharger available initially only in the estate, though later also fitted to the saloon and coupé for export. There was a new 2-liter carburetor engine developing 109 bhp, to replace the earlier engines of the same size, and a corresponding 2.3-liter injection model delivering 136 bhp which was slightly canted to reduce the overall height. The 280 disappeared from the range in July 1981, as the 220 D had before it in February 1979.

Der Übergang vollzieht sich mit weichem Schnitt, noch rollen die Strich-Acht-Limousinen vom Band, da wird bereits im Januar 1976 die Baureihe w123 eingeführt, wie jene eine vielgliedrige Familie zwischen dem etwas rachitischen 200 D mit 55 PS und dem potenten 280 E mit 185 PS. Entsprechend ist die Preisspanne: zwischen 18 900 Mark und 26 900 Mark. Auffälligstes äußeres Merkmal sind die waagerecht hinter gemeinsamen Streuscheiben untergebrachten runden Lichtquellen, jeweils ein Hauptscheinwerfer neben einer kleineren Halogen-Lampe. Die Top-Typen 280 und 280 E sind mit rechteckigen Halogen-Breitbandscheinwerfern ausgerüstet – Standard für die gesamte Palette ab September 1982. Der traditionelle Fahrschemel entfällt, da die vorderen Räder nun an doppelten Querlenkern mit dem Lenkrollradius 0 aufgehängt sind.

Im Übrigen gilt die in den Rang eines Credos erhobene Daimler-Devise »Safety first«. Vor der Majestät des Unfalls sind alle gleich, und so mag man den Passagieren der Mittelklasse die Schutzvorkehrungen der s- und der sl-Modelle nicht vorenthalten. Überdies ist die Fahrgastzelle noch stabiler geworden mit ihrem steifen Dachrahmen, hochfesten Säulen und verstärkten Türen, während Bug und Heck einen Aufprall williger absorbieren dank »kontrollierter Deformationsfähigkeit«, wie es in den Werbeschriften der Firma so unschön heißt. Eine Novität: die Sicherheitslenksäule. Lenkaggregat und Mantelrohr sind verbunden durch ein Wellrohr, was die Gefahr mindert, dass bei einem Unfall die Lenksäule wie ein Speer ins Innere dringt.

Wenig Neues gibt es zunächst hinsichtlich der Motoren zu vermelden, nur dass im 250 ein frisch entwickelter 2,5-Liter-Sechszylinder Dienst tut anstatt des bisherigen ältlichen 2,8-Liters. Das Jahr 1977 bereichert das Spektrum um drei weitere Karosserievarianten. Da ist das Coupé, vorgestellt in Genf im März, als 230 C, 280 C und 280 CE. Da ist die Lang-Version von 240, 240 D und 250 mit drei Sitzreihen und 630 mm mehr Radstand, präsentiert im August. Und da ist die T-Limousine, ein vornehmer Mercedes-Begriff für einen vornehmen Kombinationskraftwagen, erstmalig gezeigt bei der Frankfurter IAA im September. In den folgenden drei Jahren ist mehr Muskel für die Motoren angesagt, 185 PS (vorher 177 PS) für den 280 E im April 1978, 72 PS (ursprünglich 65 PS) für den 240 D im August 1978, 60 PS (früher 55 PS) für den 200 D im Februar 1979. Im Juni 1980 wird die Baureihe mit drei neuen Maschinen angeboten. Da ist, zunächst nur in der T-Limousine, ein Fünfzylinder-Diesel von drei Litern mit Abgasturbolader, für den Export später auch in Limousine und Coupé eingebaut. Da ist, anstelle der früheren Maschinen mit dem gleichen Hubraum, ein neues Zweiliter-Vergasertriebwerk mit 109 PS und ein entsprechender Einspritzer von 2,3 Litern mit 136 PS, leicht geneigt zu implantieren, um Bauhöhe einzusparen. Im Juli 1981 verschwindet der 280 aus dem Programm wie schon der 220 D im Februar 1979.

La transition s'effectue en douceur – Les berlines sortent encore de chaîne que la série w123 est d présentée en janvier 1976, elle aussi une famille a nombreux membres allant de la plutôt lymphatique 20 de 55 ch à la puissante 280 E de 185 ch. La fourchette prix est à l'image de la plage de puissance : elle va de 18 9 à 26 900 marks. Signe distinctif extérieur le plus frappa elles possèdent deux phares ronds placés derrière un ve commun à rainures horizontales, respectivement un feu route contigu à un phare halogène de plus petit diamèt Les modèles haut de gamme, la 280 et la 280 E, ont phares rectangulaires à halogène – qui seront le standa pour toute la gamme à partir de septembre 1982. berceau auxiliaire a disparu, car les roues avant sont dés mais suspendues à des bras transversaux doubles a un déport nul de l'axe de fusée.

Pour le reste, elles professent elles aussi le credo de qui est devenu une devise chez Daimler-Benz : Safety f (« la sécurité d'abord »). On ne veut donc pas refuser a passagers des voitures du segment intermédiaire le nive de protection des Classes s et sl. De plus, la cellule pas gers a été considérablement rigidifiée avec son sol cadre de toit, ses montants de pavillon à haute résistance ses portières renforcées alors que la proue et la pou absorbent plus linéairement l'impact d'une collision gra à une « capacité de déformation contrôlée », comme proclament, avec peu d'élégance, les prospectus de marque. Une nouveauté : la colonne de direction sécurité. Le boîtier de direction et le tube sont reliés p un tube annelé qui diminue le risque de voir la colon de direction pénétrer telle une lance dans l'habitacle cas d'accident.

Il y a, par contre, tout d'abord bien peu de nouveau en ce qui concerne les moteurs, à part un tout nouve six-cylindres de 2,5 litres qui a remplacé le bon vie 2,8 litres dans la 250. L'année 1977 voit arriver trois aut variantes de carrosserie. La première est le coupé, prése à Genève en mars, en versions 230 C, 280 C et 280 CE. P vient la version à empattement long des 240, 240 D et 2 avec trois rangées de sièges et un empattement allon de 630 mm, présentée en août. Et arrive enfin la berline un néologisme plein d'élégance créé par Mercedes po un break tout aussi élégant qui est dévoilé lors de l'I de Francfort en septembre. Les trois années suivantes. gamme gagne en muscles, avec 185 ch (contre 177 aupa vant) pour la 280 E en avril 1978, 72 (initialement 65 pour la 240 D en août 1978 et 60 ch (55 ch auparavant) po la 200 D en février 1979. En juin 1980, trois nouvea moteurs sont proposés pour cette gamme. Le premier réservé tout d'abord aux breaks T, un diesel à c cylindres de 3 litres avec turbocompresseur, disponi aussi, plus tard, sur les marchés d'exportation pour berline et le coupé. Un nouveau 2 litres à carburat 109 ch remplace l'ancien moteur de même cylindrée e est accompagné par un moteur correspondant à inject de 2,3 litres et 136 ch, monté légèrement en biais po

Mercedes-Benz 200–300TD 1976

ercedes-Benz 280E 1983

profile there was little to distinguish the sedans of
e 123 series from those of the earlier /8 generation.
was the details that made them better cars.

In September 1982 all the models were fitted with new
ind deflectors on the A-pillars and power steering
ecame standard, while ABS and a driver's airbag were
ailable as options. When the W123 took its final bow
November 1985, 2,696,915 cars had left the factory
Sindelfingen, of which 2,375,440 had been sedans.
he 240D, whose purchase price brought with it a life
pectation of almost biblical proportions, alone sold
4,679 units.

Im Profil unterscheiden sich die Limousinen der
Baureihe 123 wenig von denen der Strich-Acht-
Generation zuvor. Es sind die Details, die sie zu
besseren Autos machen.

Im September 1982 erhalten alle Modelle neue Windleitprofile an den A-Säulen, und die Servolenkung wird
der Grundausstattung zugeschlagen, während als Option
ABS und Airbag auf der Fahrerseite zu haben sind. Als
der W123 im November 1985 das Zeitliche segnet, haben
2 696 915 Fahrzeuge die Werkshallen in Sindelfingen verlassen, davon 2 375 440 Limousinen. Der 240D allein hat
es auf eine Population von 454 679 gebracht, wobei eine
geradezu alttestamentarische Lebenserwartung im Kaufpreis mit einbegriffen ist.

Vues de profil, les berlines de la série 123 ne se
distinguent guère de la génération /8 précédente.
Ce sont des détails qui en font les meilleures voitures.

économiser de la hauteur. En juillet 1981, la 280 disparaît
du programme, comme déjà la 220 D en février 1979.

En septembre 1982, tous les modèles reçoivent de
nouveaux profilés déflecteurs sur les montants de pare-
brise et la direction assistée fait désormais partie de
l'équipement de série alors que l'abs et le coussin gonflable
côté conducteur sont proposés en option. Lorsque la W123
est retirée du marché en novembre 1985, 2 696 915 exemplaires sont sortis des chaînes de Sindelfingen, dont
2 375 440 berlines. À elle seule, la 240 D a été produite à
raison de 454 679 exemplaires avec une espérance de vie
absolument canonique comprise dans le prix d'achat.

More function than form, with the emphasis on unobstrusiveness. In addition the company-specific sales argument that solidness and a long service life were included in the price. The round headlights located horizontally behind common diffuser lenses were the most striking feature. However, the top-of-the-range models, the 280 and 280 E, were fitted with rectangular halogen wide-band headlights.

Mehr sein als scheinen: Formen und Funktionsträger fern jeglicher Aufdringlichkeit. Dazu das firmenspezifische Verkaufsargument, dass Solidität und ein langes Autoleben im Preis inbegriffen sind. Auffälligstes Merkmal sind die waagerecht hinter gemeinsamen Streuscheiben untergebrachten runden Lichtquellen. Die Top-Typen 280 und 280 E sind allerdings mit rechteckigen Halogen-Breitbandscheinwerfern ausgerüstet.

Être, plus que paraître : des formes et fonctions aux antipodes de l'arrogance. Avec, en prime, l'argument commercial, spécifique à la marque, que solidité et longévité sont comprises dans le prix de la voiture. Principal signe distinctif : les phares ronds placés verticalement derrière une plaque de diffusion unique. Les modèles haut de gamme, 280 et 280 E, possèdent quant à eux des phares à iode rectangulaires.

While the coupés of the '68 generation looked like sedans with part of the roof sliced off, the new C models stood out as a result of their original, balanced design.

Während die Coupés der Achtundsechziger-Generation wie Limousinen ausschauen, aus denen man ein Teil ihres Dachs tranchiert hat, bestechen die neuen C-Modelle durch eine eigenständige, ausgewogene Form.

Contrairement aux coupés de la génération de 1968, qui ressemblaient à des berlines auxquelles on aurait ôté une partie du toit, les nouveaux modèles C se distinguent par des lignes personnelles et une forme équilibrée.

Mercedes-Benz 200–300TD 1976

Mercedes-Benz 200–300TD 1976 393

The station-wagon, the T model,
built in the Bremen factory from
April 1978 onwards, combined an
impressive appearance, robust
practicality, and the prestige of the
star marque.

In der Kombilimousine T, ab April
1978 im Werk Bremen hergestellt,
verbinden sich Ansehnlichkeit,
robuste Praktikabilität und das
Prestige der Marke mit dem Stern.

Les breaks de la série T, fabriqués
à partir d'avril 1978 à Brême,
combinent l'élégance, un caractère
robuste et pratique, et le prestige
de la marque à l'étoile.

Mercedes-Benz 200–300TD 1976

In many respects the new s-class, premièred at the Frankfurt International Motor Show in September 1979, marked a watershed between the past and the future in its continued use of mature technology and its cautious acceptance of engineering innovations. Nevertheless, the w126 was a success, and the 818,036 units sold in 12 years have made it the bestselling large Mercedes to date.

The term s-class again covered a broad spectrum. Initially there were seven models with four engines, ranging from the 280s (six cylinders, carburetor, 156 bhp) to the 500 SEL (v8, injection, 240 bhp). As was by now a standard feature, two variants were available, a normal and a stretched version with its wheelbase extended by 140 mm (5.5 in). Again it was the passengers in the rear who benefited, where wider doors were also provided. The designers had to meet three main specifications: the new car should be more comfortable, safer, and more economical. s-class comfort has long been the benchmark worldwide. As far as safety was concerned too, this series was the result of state-of-the-art research and its passengers would survive unscathed even an oblique crash at a speed of 55 kph (34 mph).

There just remained the third specification: economy. Ten per cent lower fuel consumption was promised. The bodies were optimized in the wind tunnel, excess pounds were trimmed off wherever possible, for example by the use of plastics and alloy. These were the materials used for the crankcases of the two eight-cylinders, the 5-liter engine that had previously been used in the 450 SLC 5.0 and the 3.8-liter engine based on the previous 3.5-liter unit. The 2.8-liter six-cylinder engine with carburetor or injection system was unchanged for the moment.

The saloons on display at the 1981 Frankfurt International Motor Show shared the platform with a pleasingly shaped coupé which was only available with an eight-cylinder engine, which had again been made more economical as part of the Mercedes-Benz energy initiative for reducing consumption and pollution. It was again in Frankfurt, this time in September 1985, that a completely revamped s-class was unveiled. Changes started with the external appearance, with lower skirts to exert more downforce at the front and better channeling of the air at the back, together with smooth side protection strips. The engines were new or substantially modified. Two six-cylinder injection engines of 2.6 and 3 liters were borrowed from the mid-range w124 to replace the 2.8-liter engine which had done such sterling service. The 3.8-liter engine was rebored to 4.2 liters. The 5-liter engine now with electronic ignition and the electromechanical Bosch Jetronic system now delivered 245 bhp, five more than at its most powerful previously. The first appearance of the designations 560 SEL and SEC attest to the existence of a new v8 with a capacity of 5.6 liters and 272 bhp, or 300 bhp at a higher compression.

In vieler Hinsicht steht die neue s-Klasse, Premiere auf der IAA zu Frankfurt im September 1979, auf der Nahtstelle zwischen gestern und morgen im Rückgriff auf Gestandenes und im behutsamen Zugriff auf technisches Neuland. Gleichwohl ist der w126 ein Erfolgstyp und erweist sich in zwölf Jahren mit 818 036 Exemplaren als der auflagenstärkste große Mercedes bislang.

Wieder deckt der Begriff s-Klasse ein breites Spektrum ab: Am Anfang gibt es sieben Modelle mit vier Motoren, zwischen dem 280s (sechs Zylinder, Vergaser, 156 PS) und dem 500 SEL (v8, Einspritzer, 240 PS). Wie längst eingespielt, stehen zwei Varianten zur Verfügung, eine Normal- und eine Langversion mit 140 mm mehr Radstand. Wiederum profitieren die Reisenden im Fond, der überdies durch breitere Türen betreten werden kann. Drei Leitlinien wurden den Konstrukteuren mit auf den Weg gegeben: Der Neue soll komfortabler, sicherer und sparsamer sein. Der s-Komfort setzt längst weltweit Maßstäbe. Auch was die Sicherheit anbelangt, verkörpert die Typenreihe den letzten Stand der Forschung, da die Passagiere selbst einen versetzten Frontalaufprall (offset crash) bei Tempo 55 unversehrt überstehen.

Bleibt das dritte Gebot: Sparsamkeit. Zehn Prozent Minderverbrauch werden verheißen. Die Karosserien sind im Windkanal optimiert, überflüssige Pfunde abgespeckt, wo immer das geht, etwa durch die Verwendung von Kunststoff und Leichtmetall. Aus diesem bestehen die Kurbelgehäuse der beiden Achtzylinder, des Fünfliters, der bereits im 450 SLC 5.0 Dienst getan hat, und eines 3,8-Liters, der auf dem bisherigen Aggregat mit 3,5 Litern fußt. Zunächst unverändert: der 2,8 Liter Sechszylinder mit Vergaser oder Einspritzung.

Auf der IAA 1981 findet sich an der Seite der Limousinen ein wohlgeformtes Coupé, lediglich zu haben mit den Achtzylindern, denen man im Rahmen des Mercedes-Benz Energiekonzepts zur Reduzierung von Verbrauch und Schadstoff mehr Genügsamkeit anerzogen hat. Wieder in Frankfurt, im September 1985, präsentiert sich die s-Palette komplett renoviert. Das beginnt mit ihrem äußeren Erscheinungsbild, tiefer herabgezogenen Schürzen für mehr Abtrieb vorn und besserer Kanalisierung der Luft hinten sowie einem glatten Flankenschutz. Neu oder zumindest kräftig retuschiert sind die Maschinen. Zwei Sechszylinder-Einspritzer mit 2,6 und drei Litern werden der Mittelklasse w124 entlehnt und verdrängen den in Ehren ergrauten 2,8-Liter. Der 3,8-Liter wurde auf 4,2 Liter aufgebohrt. Der Fünfliter leistet nun mit elektronischer Zündung und der elektronisch-mechanischen Bosch-Jetronic 245 PS, fünf mehr als in seinen stärksten Zeiten zuvor. Das erstmalige Vorkommen der Bezeichnungen 560 SEL und SEC bezeugt die Existenz eines neuen v8 mit 5,6 Litern Volumen und 272 PS, mit höherer Kompression auch 300 PS.

Dass die Versorgung mit bleifreiem Benzin noch nicht flächendeckend ist, fängt man flexibel mit Zwischenlösungen auf. Erst im September 1986 haben alle Otto-

A de nombreux points de vue, la nouvelle Classe s qui fête sa première à l'IAA de Francfort en septembre 1979, à la ligne de césure entre hier et demain, recourt à des solutions éprouvées du passé et s'engage prudemment dans un no-man's-land technique. En fin de compte, la w126 sera un modèle largement plébiscité et, produite à 818 036 exemplaires en douze ans, ce sera le plus fort tirage de la grande Mercedes à ce jour.

La Classe s couvre de nouveau un large spectre : au début, il en existe sept modèles avec quatre moteurs allant de la 280s (six-cylindres, carburateur, 156 ch) à la 500 SEL (v8, injection, 240 ch). On a le choix entre deux variantes d'empattement, normal et long avec 140 mm de plus d'empattement. Une fois de plus, les bénéficiaires en sont les passagers de la banquette arrière à laquelle on accède, en outre, par des portes plus larges. Trois préceptes ont été inculqués aux ingénieurs pour sa conception : la nouvelle voiture doit être plus confortable, plus sûre et plus économique. En ce qui concerne la sécurité aussi, cette gamme incarne un sommet de la recherche puisque les passagers sont censés ne pas subir la moindre blessure même en cas de collision frontale décalée (offset crash) à une vitesse de 55 km/h.

Pour ce qui est du troisième commandement (économique), la sobriété. Mercedes revendique une diminution de la consommation de 10 %. Les carrosseries ont été optimisées en soufflerie, la guerre a été déclarée aux kilogrammes superflus partout où cela a été possible, par exemple grâce à l'utilisation de matière plastique et d'alliage léger. C'est d'ailleurs dans ce matériau qu'à été réalisé le carter-moteur des deux huit-cylindres, le 5 litres qui officiait d'ores et déjà dans la 450 SLC 5.0 et un 3,8 litres extrapolé de l'ancien moteur de 3,5 litres. Tout d'abord inchangé, le six-cylindres de 2,8 litres est proposé au choix avec carburateur ou injection.

À l'IAA de 1981, les limousines sont rejointes par un coupé aux lignes élégantes propulsé exclusivement par le huit-cylindres auxquels, dans le cadre du concept d'économie d'énergie de Mercedes-Benz visant à réduire la consommation et les rejets de polluants, on a inculqué une plus grande sobriété. Toujours à Francfort, en septembre 1985, la série s est rénovée de fond en comble. Les moteurs sont nouveaux ou, tout au moins, sérieusement retravaillés. Deux six-cylindres à injection, de 2,6 litres et 3 litres de cylindrée, sont repris de la classe intermédiaire, la w124, et évincent le 2,8 litres après des années de bons et loyaux services. La cylindrée du 3,8 litres a été majorée à 4,2 litres. Grâce à l'allumage électronique et à l'injection d'essence électro-mécanique Bosch-Jetronic, le 5 litres délivre désormais 245 ch, soit 5 de plus qu'à sa meilleure époque. Un néologisme dans la nomenclature de Mercedes, 560 SEL et SEC, témoigne de l'existence d'un nouveau v8 de 5,6 litres de cylindrée et d'une puissance de 272 ch, qui peut atteindre aussi 300 ch avec un taux de compression plus élevé.

L'approvisionnement en essence sans plomb n'étant pas encore garanti à l'échelle du territoire, Daimler-

Mercedes-Benz 300SEL 1986

Since lead-free gasoline could not be obtained everywhere, interim solutions were adopted to provide a flexible response. It was not until September 1986 that all Daimler-Benz gasoline engines had a regulated catalytic converter. The innovative impetus of those years also extended to the exotic member of the s-class family. The 300SD, a special model for the North American market, yielded the 300SDL with an extended wheelbase and a six-cylinder turbodiesel developing 150 bhp. After the Paris Salon a year later, the most powerful engine in the series was also available as a 560SE, while the 350SDL of June 1989 offered more capacity and better torque though delivering 14 bhp less, the victim of exhaust gas recycling and oxidizing catalytic converters. From June 1990 onwards the shortened form, the 350SD, was available as an alternative, the last link in an evolutionary chain which had, let it not be forgotten, produced 97,546 s-class diesels.

Motoren von Daimler-Benz den geregelten Katalysator. In den Innovationsschub jenes Jahres einbegriffen ist auch der Exot in der s-Familie: Aus dem 300SD, Sonderangebot für den nordamerikanischen Markt, ist der 300SDL geworden mit verlängertem Radstand und einem Turbodiesel mit sechs Zylindern, der 150 PS abgibt. Nach dem Pariser Salon ein Jahr später ist das stärkste Stück der Baureihe auch als 560SE erhältlich, während der 350SDL vom Juni 1989 mit mehr Hubraum und einem besseren Drehmoment, dafür aber mit 14 PS weniger aufwartet, die der Abgasrückführung und Oxidationskatalysatoren zum Opfer gefallen sind. Ab Juni 1990 gibt es als Alternative die Kurz-Form 350SD, letztes Glied in einer evolutionären Kette, aus der immerhin 97546 s-Diesel hervorgegangen sind.

compose tout d'abord avec cet aléa en proposant des solutions à la carte. Ce n'est qu'en septembre 1986 que tous les moteurs thermiques de Daimler-Benz posséderont un catalyseur réglé. Un modèle à part dans la famille s s'inscrit aussi dans la poussée d'innovation de cette année: la 300SD, modèle spécial pour le marché nord-américain, s'est muée en une 300SDL à empattement long et moteur turbodiesel six-cylindres développant 150 ch. Après le Salon de Paris, un an plus tard, le modèle le plus puissant de la gamme est aussi disponible en exécution 560SE tandis que la 350SDL de juin 1989 voit sa cylindrée et son couple majorés, mais sa puissance abaissée de 14 ch, victimes du recyclage des gaz d'échappement et des catalyseurs à oxydation. À partir de juin 1990, Mercedes propose à titre alternatif une version à empattement court, la 350SD, dernier maillon d'une chaîne évolutive qui a tout de même engendrée 97546 modèles s Diesel.

he bodies of the S-class of 1979 were optimized in the wind tunnel, and excess ounds were trimmed off wherever possible, for example by the use of plastics and lloys. Nonetheless, they had a defiantly solid air.

ie Karosserien der S-Klasse von 1979 sind im Windkanal optimiert, überflüssige funde abgespeckt, wo immer es geht, etwa durch die Verwendung von Kunststoff und eichtmetall. Dennoch umfächelt sie ein Ambiente von trotziger Robustheit.

es carrosseries de la Classe S de 1979 ont été optimisées en soufflerie et l'on a chassé s kilogrammes superflus, notamment en utilisant matières plastiques et alliages légers. ela n'empêche pas une solidité à toute épreuve.

The new family coupé replaced the previous SLC at the 1981 IAA. The latter had been based on the sporty SL, the former on the 1979 S-class sedan, a solid and dignified car.

Mit dem Erscheinen des neuen Familien-Coupés auf der IAA 1981 wird der bisherige SLC aus der Produktion genommen. Dieser leitete sich vom sportiven SL ab. Jener fußt auf der S-Limousine von 1979, eine stattliche und würdevolle Auto-Erscheinung.

La parution de la nouvelle famille de coupés à l'IAA 1981 sonne le glas de l'ancienne SLC. L'ancienne dérivait de la sportive SL. La nouvelle est extrapolée de la Classe S de 1979, une voiture imposante et pleine de dignité.

The driver of the top-of-the-range model, the 560SEC available from 1985, could call on 242 bhp of sheer power which delivered throughout the engine's performance range.

Im Spitzenmodell 560SEC ab 1985 gebietet der Lenker über 242 PS, urige Kraft, die in allen Lebenslagen bereitwillig zur Verfügung steht.

Avec la 560SEC haut de gamme de 1985, le conducteur est le maître de 242 ch, une force tranquille qui est docilement à sa disposition dans toutes les situations.

Mercedes-Benz 280S–350SD 1979

The level of comfort offered
by the SEC extended to the
seat-belt acceptors for the
front-seat occupants, a rather
complicated device that
occasionally went on strike.

Zum Komfort, den der SEC
offeriert, zählt für die vorderen
Passagiere der Gurtanreicher,
eine etwas komplizierte
Vorkehrung, die gelegentlich
in den Ausstand tritt.

L'un des accessoires de confort
offerts par la SEC est le
présentateur de ceintures pour
les passagers avant, dispositif
quelque peu compliqué qui a
parfois le mauvais goût de
ne pas fonctionner.

Mercedes-Benz 280S–350SD 1979   403

In February 1979 Mercedes positioned the G model at the fiercely competitive intersection between the tool and the leisure vehicle. Like the motorcycle and the station wagon, vehicles of this type have enjoyed an irresistible social rise which has considerably increased the range of their applications. The G (for *Gelände* or off-road) was an Austro-German co-production. The mechanical components came from Daimler-Benz's standard selection, while the chassis and bodywork were built by Steyr-Daimler-Puch AG. In Austria, Switzerland and in Eastern Europe it was known as a Puch. It started life as the Open-Top Car with a short wheelbase (2400 mm), and as a Station Wagon and a delivery truck, with either a long (2850 mm wheelbase) or a short chassis.

The four powerplants – 2.4-liter and 3-liter diesels and 2.3-liter and 2.8-liter gasoline engines – were taken off the 123 series shelves. Almost immediately the ongoing revisions started. The interior underwent constant upgrading, with ever more special trims being offered. But the engine range also changed. In April 1982 the 230 GE, an injection engine, replaced the 230 G with its carburetor engine, and in October 1987 the five-cylinder diesel 250 GD replaced the 240 GD. The introduction of the revamped 463 series alongside the existing 460 series in September 1989 represented a decisive innovation. In terms of comfort the G model had been brought closer to the marque's passenger cars, the front end had been discreetly remodeled, and permanent four-wheel drive and a (disengageable) ABS had been introduced. The smaller of the two diesels and the 2.3-liter injection engine had been carefully modified, while two six-cylinder models each of three liters – one gasoline-driven and one diesel-powered – rounded off the G series at the top end of the range. The delivery truck disappeared from the range, while the Open-Top Car was rebadged as the more aristocratic-sounding Cabrio.

Everything was also in flux in the 460 series. The 280 GE was dropped from the range. The two diesel variants were replaced by the 290 GD in early 1992 whose five cylinders delivered more power and, in particular, a better torque response. This model and the sole-surviving 230 GE were brought under the umbrella of the 461 series until the accountants drew a line under the latter in June 1996. Most professional users from whom the customer base was recruited had long preferred the more economical diesel version.

The 463 series had already undergone various metamorphoses. The 350 GD, a 136 bhp model with a four-speed automatic gearbox as standard, was unveiled at the 1991 Frankfurt International Motor Show and superseded the 250 GD. At the other end of the scale the 500 GE with its 5-liter V8 engine delivering 240 bhp has been serving up impressive performances since 1993. That same year the G types were rebadged like all the other passenger cars: the letters D and E which had long had such significance were dropped, and the G was used to prefix a three-digit numerical code. Also making its appearance in Frankfurt was the G 320 with its 24-valve, six-cylinder engine developing 210 bhp which was also transmitted to the axles via a four-speed automatic.

In die heftig umkämpfte Schnittzone von Arbeitsgerät und Freizeitmobil platziert Mercedes im Februar 1979 das G-Modell. Wie Motorrad und Kombinationskraftwagen haben Fahrzeuge dieses Schlages einen unaufhaltsamen sozialen Aufstieg hinter sich. Damit erweiterte sich das Spektrum ihrer Verwendungsmöglichkeiten beträchtlich. Der G (für Gelände) ist Deutsch-Österreicher. Die mechanischen Teile stammen aus den Baukästen von Daimler-Benz, Rahmen und Karosserie von der Steyr-Daimler-Puch AG. In Österreich, der Schweiz und in Osteuropa heißt er Puch. Ursprünglich gibt es den Offenen Wagen mit kurzem Radstand (2400 mm) und eine Kombi-Version, auch Station Wagon genannt, sowie einen Kastenwagen, mit jeweils langem Radstand (2850 mm) oder kurzem Fahrgestell.

Aus den Regalen der Baureihe 123 entnommen sind die vier Triebwerke, Diesel von 2,4 und 3 Litern, Benziner mit 2,3 und 2,8 Litern. Fast umgehend setzt kontinuierliche Modellpflege ein. Stetig wertet man das Interieur auf, bietet immer mehr Sonderausstattungen an. Aber auch die Motoren-Palette wandelt sich. Im April 1982 löst der 230 GE, ein Einspritzer, den 230 G mit seiner Vergasermaschine ab, im Oktober 1987 der 250 GD mit einem Fünfzylinder-Diesel den 240 GD. Ein entschiedener Innovationsschub wird sichtbar, als im September 1989 der bisherigen Baureihe 460 die energisch retuschierte Baureihe 463 an die Seite gestellt wird. In punkto Komfort hat man sich den Personenwagen der Marke angenähert, die Frontpartie dezent überarbeitet, permanenten Allradantrieb und (abschaltbares) ABS eingeführt. Sorgsam überarbeitet wurden der kleinere der beiden Diesel und der 2,3-Liter-Einspritzer, während zwei Sechszylinder mit jeweils drei Litern – ein Benziner und ein Selbstzünder – das G-Spektrum krönen. Der Kastenwagen entfällt ersatzlos, der Offene Wagen wird mit der Nobel-Vokabel Cabrio geschmückt.

Auch in der Baureihe 460 ist alles im Fluss: Aus dem Programm genommen wird der 280 GE. An die Stelle der beiden Diesel-Varianten tritt Anfang 1992 der 290 GD, dessen fünf Zylinder mit mehr Leistung und vor allem mit einem besseren Drehmoment aufwarten. In der Baureihe 461 zusammengefasst werden dieser und der als einziger überlebende 230 GE, bis letzteren im Juni 1996 der rote Ring des Kalkulators ereilt. Die meisten Profi-Benutzer, aus denen sich der Kundenkreis rekrutiert, haben seit langem der genügsameren Diesel-Version den Vorzug gegeben.

Da hat die Baureihe 463 bereits diverse Metamorphosen durchlaufen. Auf der Frankfurter IAA wird 1991 der 350 GD Turbo vorgestellt, 136 PS stark und serienmäßig mit einer Viergang-Automatik ausgestattet. Er verdrängt den 250 GD aus dem Sortiment. Am anderen Ende der Skala hält seit 1993 der 500 GE mit seinem V8 von fünf Litern und 240 PS eindrucksvolle Fahrleistungen bereit. Im gleichen Jahr erhalten die G-Typen wie auch das restliche PKW-Programm neue Namen: Die lange Zeit bedeutungsschwangeren Buchstaben D und E entfallen, das G wird dem dreistelligen Zahlen-Code vorangestellt. In Frankfurt macht der G 320 seine Aufwartung, mit sechs Zylindern

En février 1979, Mercedes lance son modèle G da[ns] un segment âprement disputé, celui des voitur[es] de travail et de loisirs. À l'instar des motos et d[es] breaks, une catégorie de voitures qui voit son prestige soc[ial] grimper irrésistiblement. Cela élargit le spectre de leu[rs] possibilités d'utilisation. La G (pour *Gelände*, « tout-terrain [»]) est austro-allemande. Les éléments mécaniques provienne[nt] de chez Daimler-Benz tandis que Steyr-Daimler-Puch A[G] fournit le châssis et la carrosserie. En Autriche, en Suisse [et] en Europe de l'Est, elle est baptisée Puch. Il en exis[te] initialement une version décapotable à empattement cou[rt] (2400 mm) et une version break, appelée aussi Static[n] Wagon, ainsi qu'un fourgon, tous deux à empattement lo[ng] (de 2850 mm) ou, au choix, court.

Les quatre moteurs – des diesels de 2,4 et 3 litres ain[si] que des moteurs à essence de 2,3 et 2,8 litres – provienne[nt] de la série 123. Un réaménagement permanent débu[te] presque immédiatement, avec un habitacle toujours am[é]lioré et un nombre toujours plus grand d'options. Mais l[es] motorisations évoluent elles aussi. En avril 1982, la 230 G[E] à injection, remplace la 230 G à carburateur et, en octob[re] 1987, c'est au tour de la 250 GD à diesel cinq-cylindr[es] d'évincer la 240 GD. Une vague d'innovations déferle [en] septembre 1989 lorsque l'ancienne gamme 460 est rejoin[te] par la 463 aux retouches beaucoup plus profondes. [En] termes de confort, elle se rapproche des voitures [de] tourisme de la marque, la proue a été retravaillée av[ec] discrétion, la traction intégrale devient permanente et u[n] ABS (débrayable) est introduit. Le plus petit des deu[x] moteurs Diesel et le 2,3 litres à injection ont été retravaill[és] tandis que les deux six-cylindres de 3 litres – à essence [et] à auto-allumage – couronnent la gamme G. Le fourg[on] disparaît du programme et la décapotable peut désorma[is] se parer du vocable prestigieux Cabriolet.

Mais l'évolution perdure dans la gamme 460 égale[ment: la 280 GE disparaît du programme. Début 1992, l[es] deux versions diesel sont remplacées par la 290 GD, dont [le] cinq-cylindres est plus puissant et délivre en particulie[r] un couple supérieur. Celle-ci et la seule 230 GE survivan[te] sont regroupées sous le vocable 461 jusqu'à ce que cet[te] dernière soit condamnée, en juin 1996, par le crayon roug[e] des spécialistes du marketing. La plupart des utilisateu[rs] professionnels avaient depuis longtemps déjà donné [la] préférence à la version diesel, plus sobre.

La Série 463 a déjà subi diverses métamorphoses. [À] l'IAA de Francfort de 1991, on assiste à la présentation [de] la 350 GD Turbo, de 136 ch et équipée en série d'une boî[te] automatique à quatre rapports. Elle fait disparaître l[a] 250 GD du programme. À l'autre extrémité de l'échelle, l[a] 500 GE apparue en 1993 peut se prévaloir de performance[s] impressionnantes avec son V8 de 5 litres et 240 ch. L[a] même année, les séries G sont rebaptisées tout comme l[e] reste du programme de voitures de tourisme : les abrévia[] tions D et E sont supprimées et le G est placé devant le cod[e] à trois chiffres. La G 320 fait son apparition à Francfort, ave[c] un moteur six-cylindres à 24 soupapes développant 210 c[h]

MERCEDES-BENZ 230 G – G 500 V8 1979

Mercedes-Benz G350 Turbodiesel langer Radstand 1996

The G230, G300 and G300 Diesel were consigned to the history books for the German market from June 1994 onwards, while the 3.6-liter G36 AMG was launched at the 1995 Geneva Motor Show and the G300 Turbodiesel in September 1996. With its four valves per cylinder and charge cooling, the latter – the successor to the G350 Turbodiesel – was 40 bhp more powerful at 177 bhp, had a 10 per cent better torque response, optimized combustion and reduced emissions of contaminants. The increase in comfort was due not least to the electronically controlled five-speed automatic gearbox with a slip-controlled converter clutch also fitted in the most recent offshoot of the G family, the 296 horsepower G500 V8, which first saw the light of day in Spring 1998.

und 24 Ventilen und 210 PS, die ebenfalls von einem Automaten mit vier Gängen an die Achsen vermittelt werden.

Ab Juni 1994 gehören G230, G300 und G300 Diesel im Inland der Vergangenheit an, während in Genf 1995 der G36 AMG mit 3,6 Litern und im September 1996 der G300 Turbodiesel präsentiert werden. Dieser ist Nachfolger des G350 Turbodiesel, ein Vierventiler mit Ladeluftkühlung, mit 177 PS 40 PS stärker und mit einem um zehn Prozent verbesserten Drehmoment, optimierter Verbrennung sowie verringerter Schadstoffemission. Für gesteigerten Komfort sorgt nicht zuletzt eine elektronisch gesteuerte Fünfgang-Automatik mit schlupfgesteuerter Wandler-Überbrückungskupplung. Sie findet sich auch im jüngsten und mit 296 PS stärksten Spross der G-Familie, gebürtig im Frühjahr 1998, dem G500 V8.

qui sont également transmis aux quatre roues motrices par une boîte automatique à quatre rapports.

À partir de juin 1994, la G230, la G300 et la G300 Diesel appartiennent au passé en Allemagne puis la G36 AMG de 3,6 litres est présentée à Genève en 1995 suivie, en septembre 1996, par la G300 Turbodiesel. Celle-ci succède à la G350 Turbodiesel: son moteur à quatre soupapes et échangeur d'air développe 177 ch, soit 40 ch de plus, et son couple s'est amélioré de 10 %, avec une combustion optimisée et de moindres émissions de polluants. Une boîte automatique à cinq vitesses et commande électronique avec embrayage de pontage du convertisseur à commande à patinage garantit un confort supplémentaire. Elle se retrouve dans la plus récente version de la famille G, née au printemps 1998, la G500 V8, qui est la plus puissante avec ses 296 ch.

Like the motorcycle and the station wagon, vehicles such as the G model have seen an irresistible social rise. An all-round vehicle was now called for, equally at home on the farm and in front of the opera house.

Wie Motorrad und Kombi haben Fahrzeuge vom Schlage des G-Modells einen unaufhaltsamen sozialen Aufstieg hinter sich. Heute ist ein Multi-Talent gefragt, vorzeigbar auf der Alm ebenso wie vor dem Opernhaus.

Comme les motos et les breaks, les voitures de l'acabit de la G tout-terrain connaissent une popularité sans précédent. Aujourd'hui, il faut être un multitalent qui ait sa place aussi bien dans les alpages que sur les Champs-Élysées.

Mercedes-Benz 230G–G500V8 1979

The members of the W201 compact class, launched on 8 December 1982, were undoubtedly compact, but also in a class of their own. Apart from smaller dimensions, however, they embodied very traditional Untertürkheim virtues such as reliability, low depreciation, and safety.

New suspension systems guaranteed excellent handling – the McPherson strut front axle with anti-dive mechanism, connected to individual triangular wishbones, the multi-link rear suspension, where each wheel was connected to five fixing points. Instead of Mercedes' typical foot-operated parking brake, there was a conventional handbrake in the center console. The new compact was initially offered as a 190 and a 190 E. Its powerplant came from the current type 200 with a carburetor, reduced to 90 bhp or with the Bosch KE-Jetronic system and increased to 122 bhp.

This base series was then extended in both directions in the autumn of 1983. This saw the introduction of the 190 D with 72 bhp whose engine was enclosed so that the familiar diesel knocking noise was reduced by a half, and of the sporty 190 E 2.3-16 with 185 bhp, a 16-valver with a wing spoiler on the trunk lid that sent shivers down the spine of even the most innocent observer. In 1985 the family grew by a further three models, the 190 D 2.5 with 90 bhp, very nimble with the five-cylinder engine from the 250 D, the 190 E 2.3 with the 136 bhp engine from the 230 E, and the aristocratic version, the 190 E 2.6, with a 166 bhp six-cylinder shoehorned into the engine compartment.

Various interim solutions were adopted to cope with the fact that unleaded fuel was not universally available until September 1985, when all Mercedes gasoline engines were supplied with a regulated catalytic converter. The 190 D 2.5 Turbo, whose 122 bhp powered the car to 190 kph (118 mph), could be recognized by the six gills at the front right between the turn signal and the wheel arch.

At the Paris Salon a year later, a considerably revamped series was exhibited with wide plastic side strips, lower front and rear skirts for improved air channeling, and wider fenders. The first generation of 16-valvers was replaced by the 190 E 2.5-16 with 195 bhp. Before this could form the basis of a Group A touring car for race purposes, further preliminary work was necessary. Its long-stroke engine was not capable of further development. Consequently a new oversquare engine of the same volume was built, the power source for the 190 E 2.5-16 Evolution, which looked decidedly rough when unveiled at the Geneva Motor Show in March 1989. Stage II, which was revealed on the same occasion a year later, looked even more of a mess. Nevertheless, buyers were quickly found for the 500 units of each as required for homologation purposes. The young dynamic image was also served by two special editions, the Sportline package of June 1989 and the Avantgarde trim of March 1992, though these stood out more because of their fashionably weird design than any increased performance.

Kompakt sind sie, aber auch eine Klasse für sich, die Exponenten der Kompaktklasse W201, eingeführt am 8. Dezember 1982. Denn neben geringen Abmessungen bringen sie durchaus traditionelle Untertürkheimer Tugenden mit, Zuverlässigkeit, Wertbeständigkeit und Sicherheit.

Neue Lösungen bei der Aufhängung gewährleisten glänzende Fahreigenschaften: die Dämpferbein-Vorderachse mit Bremsnick-Abstützung, geführt an einzelnen Dreieck-Querlenkern, die Raumlenkerachse hinten, wo jedes Rad an fünf Stablenkern geführt wird. Anstelle der Mercedes-typischen Feststellbremse, die per Fußtritt aktiviert wird, findet sich eine normale Handbremse rechts neben dem Fahrer. Zunächst wird der neue Kompakte als 190 und als 190 E angeboten. Sein Triebwerk: das des aktuellen Typs 200 mit Vergaser und auf 90 PS gedrosselt oder mit der KE-Jetronic von Bosch und auf 122 PS gesteigert.

Im Herbst 1983 wird dieses Rumpfprogramm nach beiden Seiten ausgebaut. Da ist der 190 D mit 72 PS, dessen Motor so eingekapselt ist, dass das vertraute Diesel-Nageln um die Hälfte gedämpft wird. Und da ist die sportliche Offerte 190 E 2.3-16 mit 185 PS, ein Sechzehnventiler mit einem Flügelspoiler auf dem Kofferraumdeckel, bei dessen Anblick selbst dem arglosen Betrachter Unheil schwant. 1985 wächst die Kompakt-Familie um drei weitere Modelle, den 190 D 2.5 mit 90 PS, durchaus agil mit dem Fünfzylinder aus dem 250 D, den 190 E 2.3 mit der 136 PS starken Maschine aus dem 230 E und die Nobel-Variante 190 E 2.6, in deren Motorenabteil man einen 166 PS leistenden Sechszylinder gezwängt hat.

Dem Nebeneinander von verbleitem und bleifreiem Kraftstoff begegnet man mit diversen Zwischenlösungen, bis im September 1985 alle Mercedes mit Otto-Motoren mit geregeltem Katalysator geliefert werden. Den 190 D 2.5 Turbo, 122 PS kräftig und 190 Stundenkilometer schnell, erkennt man an sechs Kiemen vorn rechts zwischen Blinkleuchte und Radausschnitt.

Auf dem Pariser Salon ein Jahr später erscheint die Baureihe energisch retuschiert, mit breiten seitlichen Leisten aus Kunststoff, tiefer hängenden Bug- und Heckschürzen zu besserer Luftführung und voluminöseren Kotflügeln. Die erste Generation von Sechzehnventilern wird abgelöst vom 190 E 2.5-16 mit 195 PS. Bis dieser zur Basis eines Renntourenwagens der Gruppe A werden kann, ist indes noch Vorarbeit notwendig: Sein Triebwerk ist als Langhuber nicht entwicklungsfähig. Folglich konstruiert man einen neuen Kurzhuber mit gleichem Volumen, Kraftquelle des 190 E 2.5-16 Evolution, der sich auf der Genfer Show im März 1989 in entschieden halbstarkem Habitus präsentiert. Noch wüster treibt es visuell die Stufe II, die ein Jahr später bei der gleichen Gelegenheit gezündet wird. Gleichwohl finden sich rasch die Käufer für die jeweils 500 Exemplare, welche die Homologation fordert. Dem Image junger Dynamik sind auch zwei Sonderausstattungen dienlich, das Sportline-Paket vom

Tout aussi compactes qu'elles soient, elles n'en c pas moins une grande classe, les « petites » de gamme compacte W201 introduite le 8 décemb 1982. En effet, malgré leur faible encombrement, elles po sèdent les qualités que l'on attribue traditionnellement a voitures d'Untertürkheim, fiabilité, stabilité et sécurité.

Des solutions inédites pour la suspension garantisse un comportement inégalé à ce jour : l'essieu avant à jam élastique avec dispositif antiplongée au freinage, guidée p un triangle transversal respectif, et l'essieu arrière mul bras où chaque roue est guidée par cinq tirants. À la pla du typique frein de stationnement Mercedes à pédale, « trouve un frein à main normal situé à droite du conducter La nouvelle compacte est tout d'abord proposée en exéc tions 190 et 190 E. Son moteur est celui de l'actuelle sé 200 à carburateur, dont la puissance a été abaissée à 90 ou, avec l'injection KE-Jetronic Bosch, majorée à 122 ch.

À l'automne 1983, ce programme embryonnaire s'en chit dans les deux directions. Vers le bas, avec la 190 D 72 ch dont le moteur a été si bien encapsulé que les claqu ments familiers du diesel ne sont plus perceptibles qu moitié. Et, vers le haut, avec une version sportive, 190 E 2.3-16 de 185 ch, un seize-soupapes avec un becqu sur le couvercle de malle qui laisse entrevoir, même au pl profane des observateurs, ce dont est capable cette voitu En 1985, la famille des compactes s'enrichit de trois autr modèles, la 190 D 2.5 de 90 ch, à laquelle le cinq-cylindr de la 250 D confère une agilité surprenante, la 190 E 2.3 av le moteur de 136 ch de la 230 E, et une version luxueuse, 190 E 2.6 dont le compartiment moteur héberge à gran peine un six-cylindres de 166 ch.

Après septembre 1985, Mercedes ne fabrique plus q des moteurs thermiques à catalyseurs réglés. On reconna la 190 D 2.5 Turbo, avec ses 122 ch et ses 190 km/h, à s fentes d'aérations à l'avant droit entre le clignotant l'arche de roue.

Pour le Salon de Paris, un an plus tard, la gamme a é profondément retravaillée avec de larges panneaux de ca rosserie en matière plastique protégeant les portières, d boucliers avant et arrière descendant plus bas pour mie canaliser l'air et des ailes plus volumineuses. La premiè génération de seize-soupapes est remplacée par u 190 E 2.5-16 de 195 ch. Mais bien du travail attend enco les ingénieurs avant que celle-ci puisse servir de base une voiture du tourisme du Groupe A : à course longu son moteur n'offre aucune perspective de développemen Logiquement, on construit donc un nouveau moteur course courte de cylindrée identique, qui propulse 190 E 2.5-16 Evolution, laquelle est présentée dans u accoutrement pour le moins tape-à-l'œil au Salon l'Automobile de Genève en mars 1989. L'Evolution présenté un an plus tard lors du même Salon, pous le bouchon encore plus loin sur le plan « esthétique Cela n'empêche pas qu'elle trouve rapidement les 500 pr neurs nécessaires pour son homologation. Deux éditio spéciales sont très bénéfiques à son image de jeunesse et

Mercedes-Benz 190 E 2.5-16 Evolution II 1991

By March 1990 the 190 E 1.8 had replaced the original 190 which was the last Mercedes with a carburetor engine. And from January 1991 on the entire w201 range, apart from the entry models 190 E 1.8 and 190 D, had ABS brakes, a center console, and body-colored housings for the external mirrors. The designation 190 E had had a 2.0 added to it, and the car it referred to had become 4 bhp more powerful, as had the 190 E 2.3.

Juni 1989 sowie die Avantgarde-Ausrüstung vom März 1992, die allerdings eher durch poppig-ausgefallenes Design glänzt als durch vermehrte Funktionalität.

Da hat bereits – im März 1990 – der 190 E 1.8 den ursprünglichen 190 abgelöst, mithin den letzten Mercedes mit einem Vergasermotor. Und seit dem Januar 1991 hat das gesamte w201-Spektrum außer den Einstiegstypen 190 E 1.8 und 190 D das Antiblockiersystem, eine Mittelkonsole und in Wagenfarbe lackierte Gehäuse der Außenspiegel. Die Bezeichnung 190 E hat ein 2.0 angesetzt, und das dazugehörige Auto ist um vier PS stärker geworden, ebenso wie der 190 E 2.3.

dynamisme, le pack Sportline de juin 1989 ainsi que la version Avantgarde de mars 1992, qui se distingue toutefois plus par son style coloré et tape-à-l'œil que par une fonctionnalité améliorée.

Pendant ce temps, en mars 1990, la 190 E 1.8 a déjà remplacé la 190 originelle, la dernière Mercedes à moteur à carburateur. Et, depuis janvier 1991, toute la série w201, sauf les modèles d'appel 190 E 1.8 et 190 D, possèdent le système d'antiblocage, une console médiane et des rétroviseurs extérieurs peints dans la couleur de la carrosserie. La dénomination 190 E a été complétée par un 2.0 et le moteur de la voiture correspondante a vu sa puissance augmenter de quatre chevaux, au même titre que celui de la 190 E 2.3.

The 190 E 2.5-16 Evolution II was the wildest of the 190 models, offering 235 bhp and 250 kph (155 mph). The combative look derived mainly from the huge rear spoiler. Inside, however, it was perfectly civilized as drivers expected to find almost all the comforts offered by the 201 series. The powerful engine – quite a dish.

Der 190 E 2.5-16 Evolution II ist der Wildeste unter den Hundert-neunzigern, 235 PS stark und 250 Stundenkilometer schnell. Der martialische Eindruck rührt vor allem vom riesigen Luftleitwerk am Heck her. Drinnen geht es hingegen durchaus gesittet her: Da erwarten den Piloten fast ungeschmälert die Annehmlichkeiten, welche die Baureihe 201 zu bieten hat. Kulinarisch aufbereitet: das potente Triebwerk.

La 190 E 2.5-16 Evolution II est la plus sauvage des 190 avec ses 235 ch et ses 250 km/h. C'est surtout son gigantesque aileron arrière qui lui donne son air martial. L'intérieur, en revanche, est beaucoup plus conventionnel : ses pilotes y retrouvent presque tout le confort qu'offre la gamme 201. Revu par les hommes de l'art : le puissant moteur.

Cosmetically and technically the new Mercedes W124 mid-range series, launched in the final two months of 1984, revealed the influence of the company's compact cars. Nevertheless, it retained an individual profile, nowhere more noticeable than in the rounded tapering tail with a low loading edge below the trapezoidally extended trunk lid.

The four-cylinder engines came from the W123 series, and the diesel engines were also existing models, a four-cylinder of 2 liters, a five-cylinder of 2.5 liters and a six-cylinder of 3 liters. Two further six-cylinder gasoline engines were new, with displacements of 2.6 and 3 liters respectively. The T model made its debut at the 1985 Frankfurt International Motor Show. At the same time the 4matic system was introduced as an optional extra for the six-cylinder engines and convertibles. This was an automatically actuatable four-wheel-drive system of subtle refinement, the front differential of which was an integral part of the oil sump.

March 1987 saw the launch of a coupé in Geneva, and six months later, in Frankfurt, the turbo version of the 300 D, also available as a 4matic and identifiable by the five air-inlet slits in the right front fender. The range was further extended in September 1988 in Paris with the 200 E and the 250 D Turbo, effectively detoxified by the use of precombustion chambers with inclined injection like their old and bigger brother, the 300 D Turbo; each was 4 bhp more powerful as a result. Five months later the diesels with aspirated engines followed, again with a slight increase in power as a bonus. The most conspicuous external features of the cosmetic finish of the cars at the International Motor Show in the autumn of 1989 were the plastic side-protection strips and the restrained use of chrome trim. All three body types were available with a 3-liter six-cylinder engine whose 24 valves produced a hefty 220 bhp, together with stretched versions with an 800-mm- (31.5-in-) longer wheelbase, six doors, and three rows of seats for the 250 D and 260 E.

The series reached its culmination in October 1990 in Paris with the 500 E, whose 5-liter v8 served up 326 bhp – at the handsome price initially of 134,520 marks. The construction of the body shell and the final assembly were handled by Porsche in Stuttgart-Zuffenhausen, while Mercedes in Sindelfingen was responsible for the paintwork and delivery. The significant features of this powerhouse were: lowered by 23 mm (0.9 in), wider fenders, foglights in the front skirt, 16-inch wheels with wide tires of specification 225/55 ZR16.

In Frankfurt in 1991 the four-seater 300 CE cabriolet was added to the series, while the revamping of the range a year later concentrated in particular on the engines. Four valves per cylinder became standard for all the gasoline engines, and two new six-cylinder engines of 2.8 and 3.2 liters were introduced which replaced the previous 3-liter units with the exception of the cabriolet and the four-wheel-drive version. The 400 E, which was available

Formal wie technisch lehnt sich die neue Mercedes-Mittelklasse W124, eingeführt in den beiden letzten Monaten des Jahres 1984, an die Kompakten aus dem gleichen Hause an. Sie bewahrt sich dennoch ein individuelles Profil, nirgends augenscheinlicher als am rundlich sich verjüngenden Heck mit tiefer Ladekante unterhalb des trapezförmig heruntergezogenen Kofferraumdeckels.

Vom W123 übernommen werden die Vierzylinder, und auch die Dieseltriebwerke stammen aus dem Repertoire: ein Vierzylinder mit zwei, ein Fünfzylinder mit 2,5 und ein Sechszylinder mit drei Litern. Neu sind zwei weitere Sechszylinder, Benziner mit 2,6 und drei Litern Hubraum. Auf der Frankfurter IAA 1985 debütierte das T-Modell. Zugleich stellt man als Option für die Sechszylinder und Kombinationslimousinen das System 4matic vor, einen automatisch zuschaltbaren Vierradantrieb von subtiler Raffinesse, dessen vorderes Differential in die Ölwanne integriert ist.

Im März 1987 folgt in Genf ein Coupé, auf der IAA ein halbes Jahr später die Turboversion des 300 D, auch als 4matic zu haben und zu identifizieren an fünf Lufteinlassschlitzen im rechten vorderen Kotflügel. Weiterer Nachwuchs stellt sich im September 1988 in Paris ein, der 200 E und der 250 D Turbo, wirksam entgiftet durch Vorkammern mit Schrägeinspritzung wie auch der größere und ältere Bruder 300 D Turbo, wobei jeweils vier weitere Pferdestärken herausgesprungen sind. Fünf Monate später sind die Selbstzünder mit Saugmotoren nachgezogen, wiederum mit einem sanften Gewinn an Kraft als Zugabe. Auffälligste äußere Merkmale der Modell-Kosmetik bei der IAA im Herbst 1989 sind der seitliche Flankenschutz aus Kunststoff sowie zurückhaltend aufgetragener Chromschmuck. Zugleich gibt es alle drei Karosserievarianten mit einem Sechszylinder von drei Litern, dessen 24 Ventile ihn zu 220 PS ermuntern, sowie Langversionen mit 800 mm mehr Radstand, sechs Türen und drei Sitzbänken für 250 D und 260 E.

Ihre Apotheose erfährt die Baureihe im Oktober 1990 in Paris mit dem 500 E, dessen Fünfliter-v8 mit 326 PS aufwartet – um den stolzen Preis von anfänglich 134 520 Mark. Den Aufbau der Rohkarosserie und die Endmontage besorgt Porsche in Stuttgart-Zuffenhausen, Lackierung und Auslieferung Mercedes in Sindelfingen. Markante Merkmale dieses Kraft-Fahrzeugs: Absenkung um 23 mm, breitere Kotflügel, Nebelscheinwerfer in der Bugschürze, 16-Zoll-Räder mit Breitreifen des Kalibers 225/55 ZR16.

In Frankfurt 1991 fügt man der Palette das viersitzige Cabriolet 300 CE an, während die Runderneuerung des Programms ein Jahr später vor allem bei den Motoren ansetzt: durchgehend Vierventil-Technik bei den Benzinern, dazu zwei neue Sechszylinder mit 2,8 und 3,2 Litern, welche die bisherigen Dreiliter-Aggregate ersetzen mit Ausnahme des Cabrios und der Allrad-Spielart. Eher im finanziellen Einzugsbereich der Klientel als der 500 E liegt der 400 E ab Oktober 1992. Immerhin 50 000 Mark

Aussi bien sur le plan esthétique que mécaniq la nouvelle classe intermédiaire de chez Merced Benz, la W124 présentée lors des deux derniers m de l'année 1984, s'inspire des compactes de la même m son. Elle n'en possède pas moins un profil très personne

Les quatre-cylindres sont facturés au prix de la sé W123 et les moteurs Diesel, eux aussi, sont bien connus : quatre-cylindres de 2 litres, un cinq-cylindres de 2,5 lit et un six-cylindres de 3 litres. Deux autres six-cylind sont, par contre, nouveaux : à essence de 2,6 litres et 3 lit de cylindrée. Le break T fait ses débuts à l'IAA de Francf en 1985. À titre alternatif, Mercedes propose aussi option, pour les six-cylindres et les breaks, le systè 4matic, une traction intégrale s'embrayant automatiqu ment d'un grand raffinement et dont le différentiel ava est intégré au carter d'huile.

En mars 1987, un coupé est présenté à Genève et, mois plus tard, à l'IAA de Francfort, la version turbo 300 D, disponible aussi en 4matic et que l'on peut identif à ses cinq prises d'air d'admission dans le capot ava droit. D'autres nouveautés font leur apparition en se tembre 1988 à Paris, la 200 E et la 250 D Turbo, efficacem dépolluée grâce à ses antichambres avec injection en d gonale comme pour sa sœur plus grande et plus ancien la 300 D Turbo, ce qui lui fait bénéficier accessoirem de 4 ch supplémentaires. Cinq mois plus tard, les mote atmosphériques à auto-allumage suivent cet exemple bénéficient également de quelques chevaux supplémé taires. La manifestation extérieure de cette remise au go du jour, lors de l'IAA à l'automne 1989, sont les pannea de protection latéraux en matière plastique ainsi qu'u plus grande retenue dans la décoration de chrome. De pl chacune des trois variantes de carrosserie est disponib au choix avec un six-cylindres de 3 litres auquel les 24 so papes confèrent une puissance de 220 ch, ainsi qu' version à empattement long allongé de 800 mm, avec portières et trois rangées de sièges pour la 250 D et la 260

La gamme atteint son apogée, en octobre 1990 à Pa avec la 500 E dont le v8 de 5 litres développe 326 ch et c est facturée au prix initial non négligeable de 134 520 mar La construction de la carrosserie blanche et le monta final sont pris en charge par Porsche à Stuttgart-Zuffe hausen, la peinture et la livraison étant réalisées par M cedes à Sindelfingen. Caractéristiques extérieures de ce voiture de sport en robe de berline : abaissement de carrosserie de 23 mm, ailes plus larges, phares an brouillard intégrés à l'aileron avant, roues de 16 pou avec larges pneus de 225/55 ZR16.

À Francfort en 1991, la gamme s'enrichit du cabrio à quatre places 300 CE, alors qu'en 1992, la remise goût du jour du programme profite essentiellement a moteurs : les moteurs à essence sont tous à culasse à qua soupapes et ils sont rejoints par deux nouveaux si cylindres, de 2,8 litres et 3,2 litres, qui remplacent anciens moteurs de 3 litres sauf pour le cabriolet et version à quatre roues motrices. La 400 E présentée

Mercedes-Benz 200–E420 1984

Mercedes-Benz 300 E 4matic 1986

om October 1992, was more within the financial
each of customers than the 500 E. It was 50,000 marks
heaper than the latter, but its 278 bhp meant that it
vas still agile enough, especially as both engines had a
oluntary self-limiter system which intervened at a speed
f 250 kph (155 mph).

The diesel models with aspirated engines also began
o go over to four-valve-per-cylinder technology provided
hey had more than four cylinders. In June 1993 this series
vas also stylistically updated in line with the marque's
ther models, with radiator badges, for example, in the
orm of narrow chrome strips, and new lights. The
nomenclature was tidied up; the D was superfluous
ecause only injection models were now manufactured,
nd c and T were dropped because the body shape was
elf-explanatory. The D was replaced by the terms Diesel
nd Turbodiesel. The Daimler-Benz mid-range was now
alled E-class, however, with an E before the numerical
ymbol in contrast to previous practice.

billiger als jener, gibt er sich mit 278 PS noch immer
agil genug, zumal sich die Maschine bei Tempo 250 in
beiden Fällen ohnehin in freiwilliger Selbstkontrolle
einen Riegel vorschiebt.

Um die gleiche Zeit beginnen auch die Diesel-Modelle
mit Saugmotoren ihren Stoffwechsel über vier Ventile
zu vollziehen, sofern sie mehr als vier Zylinder haben.
Im Juni 1993 präsentiert sich die Reihe stilistisch aktuali-
siert analog zu den anderen Modellen der Marke, mit
Plakettenkühlern zum Beispiel, paspelliert von schmalen
Chromstreifen, sowie neuen Leuchten. Zugleich entrüm-
pelt man die Nomenklatur: das E erübrigt sich, denn es
gibt nur noch Einspritzer, und c und T entfallen, weil die
Karosserieform ja für sich spricht. Das D wird ersetzt
durch die Begriffe Diesel und Turbodiesel. Der Mittelstand von Daimler-Benz aber nennt sich jetzt E-Klasse,
mit einem E vor dem Zahlenkürzel im Gegensatz zur
Praxis bisher.

octobre 1992 coûte 50 000 marks de moins que la 500 E
et, avec 278 ch, elle est presque aussi sportive que
celle-ci, d'autant plus que la vitesse de pointe est de toute
façon limitée dans les deux cas à 250 km/h en vertu
d'un *gentleman's agreement* conclu entre les principaux
constructeurs allemands.

À la même époque, les moteurs Diesel atmosphériques
commencent à bénéficier eux aussi d'une alimentation
à quatre soupapes à condition d'avoir plus de quatre
cylindres. En juin 1993, la gamme est remise au goût du
jour sur le plan esthétique avec une calandre modifiée
soulignée de minces bandes chromées et de nouveaux
phares. Parallèlement, la nomenclature est élaguée : le E est
devenu superflu dès lors qu'il n'existe plus que des moteurs
à injection, ce qui est aussi le cas du c et du T, pour lesquels
la forme de carrosserie ne prête pas à confusion. Le T est
remplacé par les notions Diesel et Turbodiesel. Le segment
intermédiaire de chez Daimler-Benz se nomme dorénavant
Classe E, avec un E précédant la série de chiffres contrairement à la pratique ancienne.

How times change: what was regarded as the non plus ultra amongst status symbols in the Fifties ranked only as an upper mid-range model in the Eighties – a Mercedes 300. The Mercedes-coined term "4matic" represented a four-wheel-drive system that engaged as soon as the car detected that it was required. In March 1987 the first six-cylinder cars were supplied with this system. Demand remained relatively low.

Wie sich die Zeiten ändern: Was in den fünfziger Jahren als Nonplusultra unter den Statussymbolen galt, wird in den Achtzigern der gehobenen Mittelklasse zugeordnet – ein Mercedes 300. Hinter dem kuriosen Kunstwort »4matic« verbirgt sich ein Vierradantrieb, der sich zuschaltet, sofern das Auto den Bedarf dazu verspürt. Im März 1987 werden die ersten Sechszylinder mit diesem System ausgeliefert. Der Bedarf bleibt relativ gering.

Comme les temps changent : ce qui était considéré comme le *nec plus ultra* parmi les symboles de réussite des années 1950 n'appartient plus, dans les années 1980, qu'au segment intermédiaire supérieur – une Mercedes 300. Derrière l'hermétique néologisme « 4matic » se dissimule quatre roues motrices qui s'enclenchent dès que la voiture en ressent le besoin. Les premières six-cylindres sont équipées de ce système en mars 1987, mais son écho est décevant.

The most powerful car in the series, assembled at Porsche: a 500E with lowered chassis, the V8 of the new S-class with four valves per cylinder, brakes from the SL, and 16-inch wheels. Owners of the high-speed eight-cylinder could expect to find tactile and visual treats both in the cockpit and under the hood. After all, if it is good, it should also look good.

Das stärkste Stück der Baureihe, bei Porsche montiert: ein 500E mit tiefer gelegtem Fahrwerk, dem V8 der neuen S-Klasse mit vier Ventilen je Zylinder, den Bremsen des SL und 16-Zoll-Rädern. Handschmeichler und Augenweiden erwarten den Eigner des hurtigen Achtzylinders im Cockpit und unter der Motorhaube. Was gut ist, soll schließlich auch schön sein.

Le modèle le plus puissant de la gamme, monté chez Porsche : la 500E à châssis surbaissé, avec le V8 de la nouvelle Classe S à quatre soupapes par cylindre, les freins de la SL et des roues de 16 pouces. Dans l'habitacle et sous le capot moteur, une main de fer dans un gant de velours attend les propriétaires de la puissante huit-cylindres. Ce qui est bon doit évidemment être également beau.

Mercedes-Benz 200–E420 1984

The second-generation T model, unveiled at the 1985 Frankfurt International Motor Show, was closely related to the series 124 sedan. However, the running gear, brakes, and other units were adapted to the higher payload, and the tail was designed to comply with the latest safety standards. The E250T Diesel from 1993 underwent a facelift to incorporate the latest features. The radiator grille, for example, was designed to match that of the S-class, and the star was included separately on the hood.

Auf der Frankfurter IAA 1985 vorgestellt, lehnt sich das T-Modell der zweiten Generation eng an die Limousine der Baureihe 124 an. Allerdings sind Fahrwerk, Bremsanlage und Aggregate der höheren Nutzlast angepasst, und das Heck wird enstprechend dem neuesten Sicherheitsstandard gestaltet. Der E250T Diesel von 1993 wurde dem jüngsten Facelifting unterzogen. Die Kühlermaske zum Beispiel ist analog zur S-Klasse gestaltet, der Stern separat in die Motorhaube eingepflanzt.

Présenté pour l'IAA 1985, le modèle T deuxième génération est étroitement dérivé des berlines de la série 124. Les trains roulants, le système de freinage et divers organes sont toutefois adaptés à la charge utile supérieure et l'arrière a été repensé en fonction des normes de sécurité les plus récentes. La E250T Diesel de 1993 vient de bénéficier de la dernière remise au goût du jour. La calandre, par exemple, s'inspire de celle de la Classe S et l'étoile, dissociée, est maintenant placée sur le capot moteur.

Mercedes-Benz 200–E420 1984

Mercedes-Benz 200–E420 1984

other four-seater: the series 124 coupé was essentially based on the template drawn up at Mercedes the head of an aspirational family. The rear part of the roof merged gently with the midline.

Noch ein Fall für vier: Das Coupé der Baureihe 124 folgt grundsätzlich dem Baumuster, das man bei Mercedes für den Vater einer aufstrebenden Familie vorgesehen hat. Der hintere Teil des Dachs mündet dabei in sanfter Schräge in die Gürtellinie ein.

Encore une quatre-places : le coupé de la série 124 s'inspire par principe de l'architecture prévue par Mercedes pour le père d'une jeune famille en plein essor. La partie postérieure du toit se fond en une harmonieuse diagonale avec la ligne de ceinture.

Mercedes-Benz 200–E420 1984

Mercedes-Benz 200–E420 1984

An open invitation: like all four-seater cabriolets, however, the E200 version catered rather more for its front-seat occupants. It could be a little drafty in the back. A semi-automatic system to open the top was available as an optional extra. It concertina-ed backwards with much rustling and whirring until finally a solid metal cover descended with a definitive plop over the fabric.

Einladend geöffnet: Wie alle viersitzigen Cabriolets nimmt sich allerdings das vom Typ E200 der Passagiere in der ersten Reihe behutsamer an. Hinten pfeift bald ein strammes Lüftchen. Eine Halbautomatik übernimmt gegen Aufpreis das Öffnen des Verdecks, das raschelnd und knisternd seinen Weg nach hinten antritt, bis sich am Ende ein Deckel aus dickem Blech mit ultimativem Plopp über allem Stofflichen senkt.

Ouverte et accueillante : comme tous les cabriolets à quatre places, la E200 privilégie nettement les passagers des fauteuils avant. En effet, une brise fraîche ne tarde pas à se faire sentir à l'arrière. En option, un système semi-automatique se charge d'ouvrir et de fermer la capote qui se rabat presque silencieusement avant de disparaître dans un bruit distingué sous un épais capot de tôle.

Mercedes-Benz 200–E420 1984

When the Group c was introduced in 1982, fundamentally liberal new regulations came into force. The constants were that the fuel tank capacity was to be 100 liters (26.4 gal) and consumption was not allowed to exceed 60 liters per 100 km (3.92 mpg). The vehicle weight, on the other hand, was a movable feast: originally 800 kg (1764 lb), it was increased to 850 kg (1874 lb) in 1984, and then finally to 900 kg (1984 lb) from 1989 onwards. During his joint venture with Daimler-Benz, the racing car constructor Peter Sauber from Hinwil in Switzerland produced three models, the c8 (weighing 870 kg, 1918 lb) from 1985 to mid-1987, the c9 (905 kg, 1995 lb) which ran until the first race of the championship in Suzuka, Japan, and the c11 (again 905 kg) until the end of that season. The monocoque for the first two was made of aluminum, while the third was made of carbon fiber. The engines, supplied by Mercedes-Benz, were developed from production engines, although each also had two turbochargers. These engines were originally based on the M117 unit, then from 1989 onwards on the four-valve-per-cylinder M119 developed from this which could deliver up to 925 bhp for brief periods if required. Power outputs increased continually, from 700 bhp in the c8, via 720 bhp in the c9, up to 730 bhp in the c11. The success curve, meanwhile, showed a rapid upward trend: victory in one race in 1986, five race wins in 1988, eight each in 1989 and 1990, culminating in the constructor's championship for the team and the driver's championship for Jean-Louis Schlesser in the first year and Schlesser and Mauro Baldi in the second year.

1991 was a counterpoint with a downward slide, though there was a happy ending with the solitary victory for the Mercedes team of Michael Schumacher and Karl Wendlinger in the last race of the season at Autopolis in Japan. What had happened was that a new regulation called for normally aspirated engines with a volume of 3.5 liters as in Formula 1 and a dry weight of at least 750 kg (1653 lb). The c291 carbon-fiber chassis was provided by Sauber in collaboration with Mercedes, and the M291 engine, a 700 bhp V12 whose cylinder banks were offset at an extreme angle of 180 degrees, came from Daimler-Benz. On paper everything was perfect, and no-one was in any doubt that the c291 was a born winner. Like newcomers Peugeot, however, the Sauber-Mercedes team then had to sit out its time on the substitute's bench of success. The beautiful 12-cylinder engines had the life expectancy of a rocket on Guy Fawkes Night, while the TWR-Jaguars with their tried-and-tested Cosworth HB Grand Prix engines showed a clean pair of heels to the competition and divided the spoils in-house.

The c291 was therefore a one-season car. Its successor, the c292, never saw action. The victory at Autopolis was bitter-sweet as the team had won a battle, but lost the war. And Mercedes-Benz had never liked that.

Mit der Einführung der Gruppe c im Jahre 1982 tritt ein grundsätzlich liberales neues Regelwerk in Kraft. Die Konstanten: dass das Tankvolumen 100 Liter, der Verbrauch 60 Liter je 100 Kilometer nicht überschreiten darf. Im Fluss hingegen das Wagengewicht: anfänglich 800 kg, 1984 angehoben auf 850 kg, ab 1989 schließlich 900 kg. Während seines Joint Ventures mit Daimler-Benz antwortet der Rennwagenkonstrukteur Peter Sauber im schweizerischen Hinwil mit drei Modellen, dem c8 (870 kg schwer) von 1985 bis Mitte 1987, dem c9 (905 kg) bis hin zum ersten Meisterschaftslauf 1990 im japanischen Suzuka, dem c11 (905 kg) bis zum Ende jener Saison. Das Monocoque der ersten beiden besteht aus Aluminium, das des dritten aus Kohlefaser. Die Motoren, Mitgift von Mercedes-Benz, werden aus Serientriebwerken sublimiert, allerdings zusätzlich von zwei Turboladern beatmet. Basis ist zunächst das Aggregat M117, ab 1989 der aus diesem entwickelte Vierventiler M119, der sich bei Bedarf kurzfristig zu 925 PS aufschwingt. Im übrigen steigt die Leistung kontinuierlich, von 700 PS im c8 über 720 PS im c9 bis 730 PS im c11. Zügig nach oben zeigt indessen die Kurve des Erfolgs: Sieg in einem Rennen 1986, fünf gewonnene Läufe 1988, je acht 1989 und 1990, einmündend in die Markenmeisterschaften für das Team und die Fahrer-Championate für Jean-Louis Schlesser im ersten und Schlesser und Mauro Baldi im zweiten Jahr.

1991 folgen Kontrapunkt und Absturz, vergütet durch ein Happy-end mit dem einzigen Sieg der Mercedes-Riege Michael Schumacher und Karl Wendlinger beim letzten Lauf auf dem japanischen Kurs von Autopolis. Was geschehen ist: Ein neues Reglement sieht Saugmotoren mit einem Volumen von 3,5 Litern wie in der Formel 1 sowie das Trockengewicht von mindestens 750 kg vor. Von Sauber im Zusammenwirken mit Mercedes stammt das Karbonfiber-Chassis c291, von Daimler-Benz der Motor M291, ein 700 PS starker V12, dessen Zylinderbänke sich im Extremwinkel von 180 Grad spreizen. Auf dem Papier stimmt alles, und dass der c291 ein geborener Gewinner sei, auch darüber besteht kein Zweifel. Dann aber muss man, wie Klassen-Neuling Peugeot, seine Zeit auf der Reservebank des Erfolgs absitzen. Die schönen Zwölfzylinder haben die Lebenserwartung einer Silvesterrakete, bevor sie in kostspieligen Platzern verröcheln, während die TWR-Jaguar mit ihren gestandenen Cosworth HB Grand-Prix-Triebwerken der Konkurrenz leichtfüßig enteilen und die Dinge unter sich ausmachen.

So bleibt der Mercedes-Benz c291 ein Wagen für eine Saison. Sein Nachfolger c292 kommt nie zum Einsatz. Denn der Erfolg von Autopolis ist bittersüß: Man hat eine Schlacht gewonnen, den Krieg aber verloren. Und eine solche Bilanz hat Mercedes-Benz noch nie behagt.

Avec l'introduction du Groupe c en 1982, en en vigueur un nouveau règlement par princi libéral. Les constantes : le volume du réservoir doit pas dépasser 100 litres et la consommation, 60 lit aux 100 km. Ce qui fluctue, par contre, c'est le poids de voiture, avec 800 kg au début avant de passer à 850 kg 1984 et de se stabiliser enfin à 900 kg à partir de 198 Durant son *joint-venture* avec Daimler-Benz, le constru teur de voitures de course Peter Sauber, qui a son atelie Hinwil en Suisse, répond avec trois armes, la c8 (870 kg de 1985 à la mi-1987, la c9 (905 kg) jusqu'à la premiè manche du championnat 1990 à Suzuka au Japon et la c (905 kg) jusqu'à la fin de cette saison-là. Alors que monocoque des deux premiers modèles était en alum nium, celle du troisième était en fibre de carbone. L moteurs, dot de Mercedes-Benz, sont extrapolés d groupes de série, mais respirent mieux grâce à de turbocompresseurs. La base en est tout d'abord le mote M117 et, à partir de 1989, le M119 à quatre soupapes extr polé de celui-ci et qui, en cas de besoin, délivre tempora rement jusqu'à 925 ch. D'ailleurs, la puissance augmen en permanence, de 700 ch dans la c8 en passant à 720 ch la c9 puis 730 dans la c11. La courbe du succès est, quan elle, plus escarpée que celle de la puissance : victoire lo d'une course en 1986, cinq manches remportées en 1988 respectivement 8 en 1989 et 1990, ce qui est sanctionné p le titre de champion du monde constructeurs et pilot pour Jean-Louis Schlesser la première année et Schlesser Mauro Baldi la deuxième année.

L'année 1991 est aux antipodes des deux précédente toute de zones d'ombres avec pour seule lueur d'espoir l'horizon une unique victoire des deux pilotes Mercede Michael Schumacher et Karl Wendlinger, lors de dernière manche sur le circuit japonais d'Autopolis. L nouveau règlement impose des moteurs atmosphériqu d'une cylindrée de 3,5 litres comme en Formule 1 ain qu'un poids à sec de 750 kg. Avec le concours de Mercede Sauber réalise le châssis en fibre de carbone c291, Daimle Benz fournissant le moteur M291, un V12 de 700 ch don les bancs de cylindres décrivent un angle de 180 degré Sur le papier, tous les arguments sont réunis et nul n doute que la c291 soit un vainqueur-né. D'autant plu grande est alors la surprise de devoir patienter un certai temps sur le banc de réserve du succès. Les magnifiqu douze-cylindres ont l'espérance de vie d'une fusée de Saint-Sylvestre avant de se désintégrer en un feu d'artifi d'un coût astronomique alors que les TWR Jaguar ave leurs Cosworth HB à l'épreuve des Grands Prix dominer la concurrence de la tête et des épaules et se partage les victoires entre elles.

Ainsi la Mercedes-Benz c291 aura-t-elle seulemen été la voiture d'une saison. Sa remplaçante, la c292, n sera jamais engagée. En effet, le succès d'Autopol laisse un goût amer : si l'on a gagné une bataille, o a perdu la guerre. Or un tel bilan n'a jamais été du goû de Mercedes-Benz.

Sauber-Mercedes c8 –
Mercedes-Benz c291 1985

The winning car at Le Mans in 1989, a Sauber-Mercedes C9 driven
by the team of Mass/Reuter/Dickens. It covered 389 laps of the Sarthe
course in 24 hours.

Der Siegerwagen von Le Mans 1989, ein Sauber-Mercedes C9
mit den Piloten Mass/Reuter/Dickens. Er absolviert in 24 Stunden
389 Runden des Sarthe-Kurses.

La voiture victorieuse au Mans en 1989, une Sauber-Mercedes C9
pilotée par Mass/Reuter/Dickens. En 24 heures, elle a bouclé
389 fois le circuit de la Sarthe.

The victorious C9 during
its last and decisive pitstop.

Der siegreiche C9 beim
letzten und entscheidenden
Boxenhalt.

La C9 victorieuse lors de
son dernier et décisif arrêt
aux stands.

re and beautiful: the 720 bhp V8 of the Le Mans winner, a front view showing the large pipe
cool the interior in the middle, and the engine from the side flanked by the horizontal units of
rings and shock absorbers.

schöner Nacktheit: der 720 ps starke V8 des Le-Mans-Siegers, eine Frontalansicht mit dem
ten Rohr für die Kühlung des Innenraums in der Mitte, das Triebwerk von der Seite, flankiert
n den horizontalen Einheiten von Federn und Dämpfern.

auté de la nudité : le V8 de 720 ch du vainqueur du Mans, vue frontale avec la grosse
se d'air pour l'aération du cockpit ; le moteur vu de côté, flanqué par les combinés
rizontaux ressorts-amortisseurs.

Sauber-Mercedes C8 – Mercedes-Benz C291 1985

A C11 during a pitstop at the 1991 Le Mans. Almost invincible the previous year, Mercedes-Benz dominated for 21 of the 24 hours, but minor problems forced the team to drop out. The cockpit cover was narrower than that of the C9, which improved the airflow over the rear spoiler.

Ein C11 beim Boxenstopp in Le Mans 1991. Fast unschlagbar im Vorjahr, dominieren die Mercedes-Benz für 21 der 24 Stunden, fallen aber wegen Kleinigkeiten aus. Ihr Dachpavillon ist schmaler als bei den C9, wodurch der Fahrtwind den Heckflügel besser anströmen kann.

Une C11 arrêtée aux stands au Mans en 1991. Presque imbattables l'année précédente, les Mercedes-Benz dominent pendant 21 des 24 heures, mais sont contraintes à l'abandon pour des bagatelles. Leur pavillon de toit est plus étroit que celui de la C9, ce qui favorise l'écoulement de l'air vers l'aileron arrière.

The Mercedes-Benz C11 with its 730 bhp V8, turbocharged by two KKK units. The 5-speed racing gearbox had its own oil cooler.

Der Mercedes-Benz C11 mit seinem V8 von 730 PS, zwangsbeatmet von zwei KKK-Turboladern. Das Fünfgang-Renngetriebe hat seinen eigenen Ölkühler.

La Mercedes-Benz C11 et son V8 de 730 ch avec, comme *pacemaker,* deux turbocompresseurs KKK. La boîte course à cinq vitesses possède son propre radiateur d'huile.

Sauber-Mercedes C8 – Mercedes-Benz C291 1985

A C291 won at Autopolis in Japan
in 1991 with Michael Schumacher
and Karl Wendlinger at the wheel.
But that was to be the only success
of the season. The 700 bhp V12 from
Mercedes-Benz looked good but was
unreliable.

Ein C291, siegreich auf der japanischen Piste
von Autopolis 1991 unter Michael Schumacher
und Karl Wendlinger. Dabei bleibt es in jener
Saison: Der V12 von Mercedes-Benz, 700 PS
stark, ist zwar schön, aber fragil.

La C291 victorieuse sur le circuit japonais
d'Autopolis en 1991 avec Michael Schumacher
et Karl Wendlinger. Ce sera tout pour cette saison :
la fiabilité du V12 Mercedes-Benz, de 700 ch, n'est
en effet pas à la hauteur de sa beauté.

The fourth-generation SL, a star attraction at the Geneva Motor Show in March 1989 where it appeared as a 300 SL, 300 SL-24, and 500 SL, surpassed its predecessor in three aspects: assuredness of design, safety, and comfort.

The design, half with an eye to past tradition, half forward-looking, had found a way back to a beautiful simplicity. Safety levels for the occupants matched those of the sedans, despite the lack of a roof. Many factors combined to ensure this; the rigid floorpan chassis, for example, with its high-strength panels and generously sized beam sections. The doors with their cleverly designed inner beading structure also made a contribution. A spectacular innovation was the automatic roll-bar made of high-tensile steel. At rest it was hidden in front of the box for the top, tensioned by springs, ready for action should the worst come to the worst. In that event, an electromagnetic system triggered deployment, ensuring that it was vertical within one-third of a second and locked in place with safety catches. Since the A-pillars were also solid pieces of high-tensile steel plate, reinforced with solid tubes, the SL formed a survival cell for its passengers in the event that the car should overturn.

The coupé roof, which had become 10 kg (22 lb) lighter despite the large window area, thus had no load-bearing role any more. Opening and closing the electrohydraulic top, however, merely required a switch to be pressed. Everything else was taken care of within 30 seconds by 17 limit switches, 15 pressure cylinders, and 11 solenoids in movement sequences that were marvellously choreographed by microprocessors.

The suspension – McPherson strut front axle and multi-link suspension rear axle – corresponded to that of the 210 and 124 series, and was tailored to the special requirements of the roadster. It was backed up by state-of-the-art supplementary systems such as a speed-dependent level control system and the ADS adaptive damping system, adjustable shock absorbers under electronic control which adapted them extremely rapidly to changes in the road surface under the wheels. The six-cylinder engines of the two 3-liter models came from existing engines but had undergone detailed modifications. The four-valve-per-cylinder system of the 300 SL-24, for example, had ignition-map-controlled adjustment of the inlet camshaft as did each cylinder bank of the 5-liter v8 in the 500 SL, at 326 bhp the most powerful Mercedes production engine.

This figure was surpassed by a 6-liter v12 in the 600 SL available from October 1992 onwards which developed 394 bhp. What buyers of this model received for their 60,000 marks was scarcely any increase in drive performance, but instead the turbine-like quietness of the 12-cylinder and a rather more abstract quality – considerable social prestige.

From June 1993 onwards, the two top models were rebadged as the SL 500 and SL 600 during the Mercedes name reform, and the 3-liter engine models were replaced by an SL 280 and an SL 320, both using four-valves-per-

In drei Punkten überbietet der SL der vierten Generation, Attraktion des Genfer Salons im März 1989 als 300 SL, 300 SL-24 und 500 SL, seinen Vorgänger: hinsichtlich formaler Schlüssigkeit, Sicherheit und Komfort.

Das Design, halb der Tradition verpflichtet, halb nach vorn gewandt, hat zu einer schönen Schlichtheit zurückgefunden. Der Schutz der Insassen entspricht den Limousinen – trotz des fehlenden Dachs. Viele Faktoren wirken da zusammen, die rigide Bodenanlage zum Beispiel mit hochfesten Blechen und üppigen Trägerquerschnitten. Auch die Türen mit ihrer raffiniert ausgetüftelten inneren Sickenstruktur werden in das Konzept eingebunden. Eine spektakuläre Novität: der automatische Überrollbügel aus hochfestem Stahl. Im Ruhestand lagert er verborgen vor dem Verdeckkasten, von Federn vorgespannt für den Fall eines Falles. Tritt dieser ein, so schnellt er, elektromagnetisch ausgelöst, innerhalb einer Drittelsekunde in die Vertikale und wird durch Sperrklinken arretiert. Da auch die A-Säulen starke Stücke sind aus hochfestem Stahlblech, bewehrt mit massiven Rohren, schafft der SL bei einem Überschlag so einen Überlebensraum für seine Passagiere.

Keine tragende Rolle mehr fällt damit dem Coupédach zu, das trotz größerer Fensterfläche um zehn Kilogramm leichter geworden ist. Zum Öffnen und Schließen des elektrohydraulischen Verdecks genügt es, einen Schalter zu betätigen. Alles andere besorgen binnen einer halben Minute 17 Endschalter, 15 Druckzylinder sowie elf Magnetventile in Bewegungsabläufen, die durch Mikroprozessoren prächtig organisiert werden.

Die Aufhängung – Dämpferbein-Vorderachse und Raumlenker-Hinterachse – entspricht der der Baureihen 210 und 124, ist indes auf die besonderen Bedürfnisse des Roadsters zugeschnitten. Sie wird ergänzt durch Zusatzsysteme auf dem letzten Stand, eine geschwindigkeitsabhängige Niveauregulierung und das Adaptive Dämpfungs-System ADS, verstellbare Stoßdämpfer mit elektronischer Steuerung, die diese blitzschnell einem veränderten Untergrund anpasst. Die Sechszylinder der beiden Dreiliter stammen aus den Baukästen, wurden jedoch einer pingeligen Feinarbeit unterzogen. So verfügt etwa der Vierventiler des 300 SL-24 über eine kennfeldgesteuerte Verstellung der Einlassnockenwelle ebenso wie jede Zylinderbank des Fünfliter-v8 am 500 SL, dem stärksten Daimler-Serienmotor mit 326 PS.

Noch besser kann es ein Sechsliter-v12 von 394 PS im 600 SL vom Oktober 1992 an. Dessen Käufer handelt sich für 60 000 Mark mehr kaum höhere Fahrleistungen ein, dafür aber die turbinenartige Laufruhe des Zwölfzylinders sowie einen eher abstrakten Wert: viel Sozialprestige.

Ab Juni 1993 heißen die beiden Top-Modelle im Zuge der Mercedes-Namenreform SL 500 und SL 600, und die Dreiliter werden ersetzt durch einen SL 280 und einen SL 320, beide mit Vierventil-Technik. Nur noch der SL 280 hat ein Fünfgang-Schaltgetriebe. Auf der IAA im September 1995 zeigt sich die Baureihe technisch und

La SL de la quatrième génération, l'attraction salon de Genève de mars 1989, en versions 300 s 300 SL-24 et 500 SL, surclasse sa devancière à tr points de vue : par son homogénéité esthétique, sa sécur et son confort.

Le design, à la fois pétri de tradition et tourné v l'avenir, est l'émanation d'une magnifique sobriété. protection des passagers est égale à celle qu'offrent l berlines – malgré l'absence de toit. Mais cela est le fru de nombreux facteurs, la plate-forme rigide, par exemp aux tôles à haute résistance et aux généreuses poutr transversales. Nouveauté spectaculaire : l'arceau de sécu rité automatique en acier à haute résistance. Comme l montants de pare-brise sont également en tôle d'acier haute résistance, la SL offre donc un espace de survie ses passagers même en cas de tonneau.

Le toit coupé n'assume plus aucun rôle structurel e malgré des surfaces vitrées plus généreuses, il pèse 10 kg d moins. Pour ouvrir et fermer la capote électro-hydrau lique, en revanche, il suffit d'appuyer sur un bouton. Tou le reste, ce sont 17 commutateurs de fin de course, 15 vérin hydrauliques et 11 électrovannes qui s'en chargent, e 30 secondes et en un processus admirablement orchestr par une ribambelle de microprocesseurs.

La suspension – avec essieu avant à jambes élastique et essieu arrière multibras – correspond à celle des série 210 et 124, mais toutefois adaptée aux besoins particulier du roadster. Elle est complétée par des systèmes addi tionnels très en pointe, une correction d'assiette asservi à la vitesse et un système d'amortissement adaptatif AD avec des amortisseurs réglables à commande électroniqu qui l'adapte instantanément à toute modification d revêtement. Les six-cylindres des deux 3 litres proviennen de chez Mercedes, mais ils ont été retravaillés dans le moindres détails. À titre d'exemple, le quatre-soupape de la 300 SL-24 possède un variateur cartographique d l'arbre à cames d'admission au même titre que chaqu banc de cylindres du v8 de 5 litres de la 500 SL, le moteu de série le plus puissant de chez Daimler-Benz avec 326 ch

Mais tous ces chiffres font bien pâle figure comparé au v12 de 6 litres et 394 ch de la 600 SL présentée e octobre 1992. Pour un supplément de prix de 60 000 marks, ses acheteurs ne bénéficient guère de performance supérieures, mais, en revanche, de la montée en puissanc du douze-cylindres digne d'une turbine ainsi que d'un valeur plutôt abstraite : un prestige social inégalable.

À partir de juin 1993, les deux modèles haut de gamm sont rebaptisés SL 500 et SL 600 tandis que les 3 litres sont remplacés par une SL 280 et une SL 320, toutes deux à culasse à quatre soupapes. Seule la SL 280 possède encor une boîte manuelle à cinq vitesses. À l'IAA, en septembr 1995, la gamme bénéficie des retouches mécaniques et esthétiques avec de nouveaux pare-chocs ainsi que des panneaux de carrosserie latéraux peints couleur carrosse rie. Celui qui le désire peut obtenir à la place du hard-top en aluminium un toit en verre avec store pare-soleil et des

MERCEDES-BENZ 300 SL – SL 600   1988

Mercedes-Benz SL 500 1995

linder technology. The SL 280 was the only model still to ...e a 5-speed manual gearbox. At the International Motor ...ow in September 1995 a technically and cosmetically ...dated series was unveiled with new bumpers which, like ...e side strips, were body-colored. On request buyers ...uld have a glass roof with a sunblind in place of the ...minum hardtop, and xenon gas lamps with double the ...minous efficiency. A cruise control for 30 kph zones ...lped avoid confrontations with the law.

The same month saw the replacement of the automatic ...arbox used until then in the SL 500 and SL 600 by a com-...ct, lightweight, 5-speed automatic transmission using a ...nverter clutch and electronic transmission control. If the ...iver made errors while driving, the ESP electronic stabil-...y program, an optional extra in the SL 500 and fitted as ...andard to the SL 600, provided assistance. From June 1996 ...wards the new automatic transmission was also available ...r the six-cylinders and it could be combined with the ESP ...om December 1996 onwards. In addition, SL drivers had ...e BAS brake assistance system. In 1998 the previous ...raight cylinder engines were replaced by v6 and v8 power ...nits which are more compact, albeit not entirely refined.

optisch retuschiert, mit neuen Stoßfängern wie auch den seitlichen Verkleidungen in Wagenfarbe. Wer das möchte, bekommt anstelle des Aluminium-Hardtops ein Glasdach mit Sonnenrollo und Xenon-Gaslampen mit doppelter Lichtausbeute. Ein Tempomat für 30-Kilometer-Zonen beugt Konflikten mit dem Gesetz vor.

Im gleichen Monat wird im SL 500 und SL 600 der bis-herige Getriebeautomat ersetzt durch eine kompakte und leichte Fünfgang-Automatik mit Wandler-Überbrückungs-kupplung und elektronischer Getriebesteuerung. Bei Fahrfehlern geht dem Lenker das Fahrstabilitätspro-gramm ESP zur Hand, Option beim SL 500, Serie am SL 600. Ab Juni 1996 ist die neue Automatik auch für die Sechszylinder verfügbar und kann vom Dezember des gleichen Jahres an mit dem Fahrdynamik-System ESP kombiniert werden. Zusätzlich greift nun dem SL-Piloten der Bremsassistent BAS unter die Arme. 1998 ersetzen v6- und v8-Triebwerke die bisherigen Reihenmotoren, kompakter, wenn auch nicht unbedingt kultivierter.

phares à décharge de gaz au xénon avec double rendement lumineux. Un régulateur de croisière pour les zones à 30 km/h prévient tout conflit avec les forces de l'ordre.

Le même mois, la boîte automatique équipant jusque-là la SL 500 et la SL 600 est remplacée par une nouvelle transmission automatique compacte et légère avec embrayage de pontage du convertisseur et commande de boîte électronique. En cas d'erreur de conduite, le pro-gramme de stabilité dynamique ESP vient au secours du conducteur, dispositif proposé en option pour la SL 500 et offert en série sur la SL 600. À partir de juin 1996, la nouvelle boîte automatique est aussi disponible pour les six-cylindres et peut être combinée, à partir de décembre de la même année, au système ESP. Les pilotes de SL peuvent désormais compter sur l'aide supplémentaire du dispositif d'assistance au freinage BAS. En 1998, des moteurs v6 et v8, plus compacts, mais pas nécessairement plus perfectionnés, remplacent les anciens 6 et 8 en ligne.

The SL was at its best when completely open to the elements. However, to insure against the uncertainty of central European weather, occupants could have a top securely over their heads within 30 seconds – automatically.

Am liebsten präsentiert sich der SL in kompromissloser Offenheit. Den Wechselfällen und Schikanen mitteleuropäischer Witterung ausgeliefert, haben die Insassen indessen binnen 30 Sekunden ein Dach über dem Kopf – automatisch.

C'est décapotée que la SL fait la meilleure figure. Pour faire face aux aléas de la météorologie en Europe, les passagers peuvent refermer le toit en 30 secondes – automatiquement.

The cockpit of the SL 500 with perfectly-designed seats under the steeply-inclined windshield, and its 326 bhp V8 engine which helped the roadster to deliver amazing performance figures.

Cockpit des SL 500 mit perfekt sitzendem Gestühl unter der starken Schräge der Windschutzscheibe und sein V8 von 326 PS, der dem Roadster zu souveränen Fahrleistungen verhilft.

L'habitacle de la SL 500, avec ses fauteuils parfaits derrière le pare-brise fortement incliné et son V8 de 326 ch qui confère au roadster des performances souveraines.

The appearance of the latest s-class at the Geneva Motor Show in March 1991 was not greeted exclusively by paeans of praise. Great lumps, moaned some, too large for most garages and many parking spaces. Future modifications were, therefore, often designed to correct this impression. The question of sheer size still remained, however: 5110 x 1890 x 1490 mm (16 ft 9 in x 6 ft 2 in x 4 ft 11 in) for the standard version, 100 mm (4 in) more length and wheelbase for the longer version, and a thumping 6213 mm (20 ft 4.5 in) for the Pullman from September 1995.

In Germany the 140 series was initially offered with a choice of four engines, the first production v12 in the company's history at 6 liters and 408 bhp, the familiar 5-liter v8, and two other engines developed from existing units, a v8 of 4.2 liters and a six-cylinder of 3.2 liters. All used four-valves-per-cylinder technology and adjustable inlet camshafts and were fitted with state-of-the-art electronics: electronic injection and an ignition system that calculated the optimum ignition point for each cylinder individually from 300 ignition maps. The control modules of the engine and drive management system communicated with each other via a joint data channel.

The standard series was sumptuously appointed, including special features such as retractable external mirrors and a 65-mm- (2.6-in-) long reversing antenna at the rear which extended within two seconds once reverse gear was selected. The range was expanded at the Paris Show in October 1992 by the inclusion of the entry models 300 SE 2.8 and 350 SD. At the same time the eight- and twelve-cylinder engines had been made more economical, a development for which slight concessions had had to be made. The v12 now stood just under the magical 400 bhp threshold at 394 bhp. From May 1995 onwards the Parktronic system signaled distances at the front and rear ultrasonically; it was fitted as standard on the v12 and was available as an optional extra on the others.

From September of the same year onwards the previous 4-speed automatic gearbox was replaced by a 5-speed automatic transmission with a converter clutch that smoothly adapted to every driving situation, and that was also more compact and lighter. The ESP electronic stability program, which was fitted as standard in the s600 or was an optional extra for the eight-cylinder models, used a sensor-controlled system to brake when required to counteract moments of instability. From June 1996 onwards the new automatic transmission was also available for the six-cylinder engines, as an optional extra in the s280. Other new features included the front sidebags and a rain sensor which adjusted the wipe intervals to the amount of rain experienced. The side strips which had previously been in contrasting colors were now body-colored, though in a silk finish. A changing of the guard also took place in the s-class diesels, from the s350 Turbo-diesel with 150 bhp to the s300 TD, a four-valves-per-

Nicht nur wohlwollende Kommentare begleiten das Erscheinen der jüngsten s-Klasse auf dem Genfer Salon im März 1991. Klötze seien das, grollen manche, zu groß für etliche Garagen und viele Parklücken. Und so dient künftige Modellpflege häufig dazu, diesen Eindruck zu verwischen. Dennoch bleibt schiere Größe: 5110 x 1890 x 1490 mm für die Normalversion, 100 mm mehr Länge und Radstand für die lange Variante, das Gardemaß von 6213 mm für den Pullman ab September 1995.

In Deutschland wird die Baureihe 140 zunächst mit vier Triebwerken angeboten, dem ersten serienmäßigen v12 in der Geschichte des Hauses mit sechs Litern und 408 PS, dem bekannten Fünfliter-v8 sowie zwei Maschinen, die aus existierenden Motoren entwickelt worden sind, einem v8 von 4,2 Litern und einem Sechszylinder mit 3,2 Litern. Sie alle haben Vierventil-Technik sowie verstellbare Einlassnockenwellen und sind mit den neuesten Segnungen der Elektronik versehen: elektronischer Einspritzung und einer Zündung, die den optimalen Zündzeitpunkt für jeden Zylinder einzeln aus 300 Kennfeldern errechnet. Die Steuermodule des Motor- und Antriebsmanagements kommunizieren über einen gemeinsamen Datenkanal miteinander.

Die Serienausstattung ist üppig und umspannt Besonderheiten wie abklappbare Außenspiegel und einen 65 mm langen Peilstab hinten, der binnen zwei Sekunden ausgefahren wird, nachdem der Rückwärtsgang eingelegt wurde. Auf der Pariser Show im Oktober 1992 wird die Palette bereichert um die Einstiegsmodelle 300 SE 2.8 und 350 SD. Zugleich hat man den Acht- und Zwölfzylindern mehr Genügsamkeit anerzogen, was mit geringen Aderlässen erkauft wird: Der v12 bleibt nun mit 394 PS knapp unter der magischen 400-PS-Grenze. Vom Mai 1995 meldet die Einparkhilfe Parktronic per Ultraschall die Abstände nach vorn und hinten, serienmäßig beim v12, auf Wunsch und gegen Mehrpreis bei den anderen.

Ab September des gleichen Jahres findet sich an der Stelle des bisherigen Viergang-Automaten eine Fünfgang-Automatik mit Wandler-Überbrückungskupplung, die sich schmiegsam in jede Fahrsituation einpasst und überdies kompakter und leichter ist. Als Grundausrüstung der s600, Option bei den Achtzylindern, wirkt nun das Elektronische Fahrstabilitäts-Programm ESP bei Fahrfehlern sensorgesteuert durch gezielten Bremseingriff dem instabilen Moment entgegen. Ab Juni 1996 tut die neue Automatik auch in den Sechszylindern Dienst, beim s280 auf Wunsch. Neu sind ebenfalls die vorderen Sidebags sowie ein Regensensor, der die Wischintervalle auf die Niederschlagsmenge abstimmt. Die seitlichen Anbauteile, vorher in Kontrastfarbe gehalten, schimmern jetzt in der Couleur des Wagenkörpers, allerdings seidig glänzend. Zugleich findet ein Wachwechsel bei den s-Dieseln statt, vom s350 Turbodiesel mit 150 PS zum s300 TD, einem Vierventiler mit Ladeluftkühlung und 177 PS, welche von der Fünfgang-Automatik an die

La présentation de la dernière Classe s, au Salon d Genève de mars 1991, ne recueille pas que d commentaires bienveillants. Quels horribles pach dermes, grognent certains, trop grands pour de nombre garages et beaucoup de créneaux. Par la suite, Merced s'efforcera de dissiper cette impression. Imposante, e l'est en effet: 5110 mm de long sur 1890 mm de large 1490 de haut pour la version normale, 100 mm de plus longueur et en empattement pour la version allong et pas moins de 6213 mm pour la Pullman à partir septembre 1995.

En Allemagne, la série 140 est tout d'abord propose avec quatre moteurs, le premier v12 de série dans l'histoi de la maison, avec 6 litres et 408 ch, le v8 de 5 litres bie connu ainsi que deux nouveaux moteurs extrapolés d groupes préexistants, un v8 de 4,2 litres et un six-cylindr de 3,2 litres. Tous ont une culasse à quatre soupapes ain que des arbres à cames d'admission à décalage et so dotés des dernières bénédictions de l'électronique: u injection électronique et un allumage qui calcule moment optimal pour l'allumage de chaque cylindre partir d'une cartographie à trois cents paramètres. l module de commande du moteur et de la chaîne cinéma tique communiquent entre eux grâce à un bus de donnée

L'équipement de série est de grand luxe et compor des particularismes comme des rétroviseurs extérieu rabattables et une barre de visée de 65 mm à l'arrière q se met en place en deux secondes dès que l'on enclench la marche arrière. Au Salon de Paris, en octobre 1992, gamme s'enrichit de deux modèles d'appel, la 300 SE 2.8 la 350 SD. Pendant ce temps, on a inculqué plus de sobriét aux huit et douze-cylindres: avec 394 ch, le v12 rest désormais juste au-dessous du seuil magique des 400 c À partir de mai 1995, le système d'aide au stationnemer Parktronic communique par ultrasons la distance vis-à vis des obstacles à l'avant et à l'arrière, dispositif propos en série pour la v12, mais sur demande et contre supplé ment de prix pour les autres modèles.

À partir de septembre de la même année, l'ancienn boîte automatique à quatre rapports disparaît au pro d'une transmission à cinq vitesses avec embrayage d pontage du convertisseur qui s'adapte aux différente situations respectives et possède en outre l'avantage d'êt plus compacte et plus légère. En équipement de base pou la s600 et en option pour les huit-cylindres, le dispositif d stabilité dynamique électronique ESP gomme les erreu de conduite à l'aide de capteurs qui répriment toute inst bilité en freinant de façon ciblée une ou plusieurs roues. partir de juin 1996, la nouvelle boîte automatique est aus en service pour les six-cylindres, en option pour la s28 Autres nouveautés, les airbags latéraux à l'avant ain qu'un détecteur de pluie qui calcule le rythme d'essuyag en fonction de la densité des précipitations. Les panneau de protection latérale, autrefois ton sur ton, sont désorma dans la couleur de la carrosserie, mais avec une nuance plu soyeuse. Pour les Classe s à moteur Diesel, une relève de

Mercedes-Benz 300 se – s 300 td 1991

Mercedes-Benz S320 1996

linder model with charge-cooling and 177 bhp which
s transmitted to the rear axle by the 5-speed automatic
arbox. From December 1996 onwards all s280 and s320
odels with automatic transmission were fitted as stan-
rd with the ESP electronic stability program and, in line
th the other models in the 129 and 140 series, with the
s braking assistance system which cleverly detected
ergency braking operations and determined the short-
t braking distance. Although stylistically very much its
n boss, the coupé, which was unveiled at the Motor
ow in Detroit in January 1992 as the 500 SEC and
o SEC, was greatly indebted in engineering terms to the
class sedans. The above models were joined by the s420
upé, launched in Geneva in 1994 for the slightly less
ll-off. All three were rebadged as CL420, CL500, and
600 in June 1996 and fitted with modified bumpers with
egral sensors for the Parktronic system, which was
ed as standard. Other new standard features were
e xenon lights and a cruise control with a limiter for
kph zones.

Hinterachse vermittelt werden. Vom Dezember 1996 an
werden alle s280 und s320 mit Getriebeautomaten ausgestattet mit dem Fahrdynamik-System ESP sowie, analog
zu den übrigen Modellen der Reihen 129 und 140, mit dem
Bremsassistenten BAS, der Notbremsungen klug erkennt
und den kürzesten Bremsweg ermittelt. Bei relativ großer
formaler Eigenständigkeit technisch weitgehend den
s-Limousinen verpflichtet ist das Coupé, im Januar 1992
bei der Motor Show zu Detroit eingeführt als 500 SEC
und 600 SEC. Dazu gesellt sich in Genf 1994 das s420
Coupé für die etwas weniger Wohlhabenden. Im Juni 1996
werden alle drei umbenannt in CL420, CL500 und CL600
und ausgestattet mit überarbeiteten Stoßfängern, in die
man die Sensoren für das serienmäßige System Parktronic
integriert hat. Ebenfalls neu, aber im Grundpreis
enthalten: Xenon-Licht sowie ein Tempomat mit einem
Begrenzer auf 30 Stundenkilometer.

garde a lieu puisque la s350 turbo diesel de 150 ch fait place
à une s300 TD, avec un quatre-soupapes à échangeur d'air
développant 177 ch qui sont transmis à l'essieu arrière
par une boîte automatique à cinq rapports. À partir de
décembre 1996, toutes les s280 et s320 à boîte automatique
reçoivent aussi le dispositif de stabilité dynamique ESP
ainsi que, par analogie aux autres modèles des séries 129 et
140, le dispositif intelligent d'assistance de freinage bas qui
reconnaît les freinages d'urgence et calcule la distance de
freinage la plus courte. Le coupé, qui se distingue par une
personnalité esthétique relativement grande, mais est,
techniquement, très proche des limousines de la Classe s,
est présenté en janvier 1992 au Detroit Motor Show en
versions 500 SEC et 600 SEC. Pour le Salon de Genève de
1994, ils sont rejoints par le coupé s420 destiné à ceux qui
ne sont pas tout aussi aisés. En juin 1996, tous trois sont
rebaptisés en CL420, CL500 et CL600 et reçoivent des pare-
chocs d'une forme nouvelle dans lesquels on a intégré les
capteurs pour le système Parktronic offert en série. Autres
nouveautés toutefois comprises dans le prix de base, les
phares au xénon ainsi qu'un régulateur de croisière avec
un limiteur à 30 km/h.

Although of extremely solid proportions, the S-class series 140 also proved surprisingly nimble. Steps were taken in 1994 to brighten up previously bare surfaces, so that the sedan did not look quite so imposing.

Von ungemein stattlichen Proportionen, gibt sich die S-Klasse Baureihe 140 gleichwohl erstaunlich behende. 1994 werden vormals kahle Flächen visuell belebt, so dass die Limousine weniger monumental erscheint.

Bien qu'extrêmement imposante, la Classe S série 140 n'en est pas moins étonnamment maniable. En 1994, les panneaux de carrosserie jusque-là lisses sont rainurés pour donner plus de légèreté à la limousine.

Mercedes family traits were evident in the S320 – the trapezoidal rear section of the trunk lid, the 1994 modification of the radiator grille, and the star set back on the hood. The bumpers housed the sensors for the Parktronic system.

Merkmale der Mercedes-Familie am S320: der trapezförmige hintere Teil des Kofferraumdeckels, der 1994 modifizierte Kühlergrill und der auf der Motorhaube zurückgesetzte Stern. In den Stoßstangen die Sensoren der Parktronic.

Signes génétiques de la famille Mercedes sur la S320 : la partie arrière du couvercle de malle découpée en trapèze, la calandre modifiée de 1994 et l'étoile reportée sur le capot moteur. Dans les pare-chocs, les capteurs du système Parktronic.

Mercedes-Benz 300SE–S300TD 1991

The entry-level model: a CL 420 from 1997 wearing the face adopted from the SL. The coupé did not attempt to hide its size, and offered its rear-seat passengers a comfortable ride below its broad C-pillars.

Einstiegsmodell: ein CL 420 von 1997 mit seinem vom SL übernommenen Gesicht. Das Coupé mag seine Größe ebenfalls nicht verhehlen und gestattet unter seinen breit ausgeprägten C-Säulen auch den hinten Sitzenden bequemes Reisen.

Modèle d'« appel » : une CL 420 de 1997 avec sa proue inspirée de la SL. Le coupé ne cherche pas, lui non plus, à dissimuler sa grandeur et permet aussi aux passagers de l'arrière de voyager avec tout le confort dû à leur rang.

...e exemplary neatness of the interior and engine compartment. The engine had long since ...come a style element. There was hardly any room for improvement in terms of comfort, ...onomics, and looks. Double-glazed windows made of safety glass provided thermal ...ulation and kept noise out.

...enraum und Motorabteil zeigen sich mustergültig aufgeräumt. Schon lange ist die ...aschine« zum Stilelement geworden. Was Komfort, Ergonomie und Ästhetik anbelangt, ...t es kaum noch etwas zu verbessern. Doppelscheiben aus ESG-Sicherheitsglas dienen ... Wärmedämmung und halten Lärm fern.

...abitacle et le capot moteur sont d'une clarté exemplaire. Il y a longtemps que le moteur est ...enu un élément de style. Il n'y a pratiquement plus rien à améliorer en ce qui concerne le ...fort, l'ergonomie et l'esthétique. Un double vitrage en verre de sécurité Triplex protège de ...chaleur et du bruit.

Like the s-class models, the second generation of compact Mercedes, launched in May 1993, was given its own name. It was now known as the c-class, with the c preceding the three-digit numerical code in accordance with the new Mercedes system. For about the same amount of money as for the w201 predecessor, the customer now got more car: more space, more safety, more comfort. A driver's airbag, integrated side-impact protection, ABS, power steering, 5-speed transmission, and central locking were included in the standard package. In addition to the standard version, there were also three special versions of the w202 that were obviously aimed at a younger clientele. The Esprit sat 25 mm (1 in) lower and had a brightly colored interior; the Elegance was sumptuously appointed inside, and bore protective strips in contrasting colors, various chrome trims, and different lights; and the Sport, also with a lowered suspension, had harder running gear, wide tires and alloy wheels. Those whose thirst for a dynamic look was still not satisfied could turn to the AMG variant which offered a lowered sports suspension, different skirts, and side panels.

Four gasoline engines were available, the four-valves-per-cylinder types familiar from the 124 series and a new 1.8-liter engine with electronic injection, together with three diesel powerplants, the two-liter from the preceding model, and 2.2-liter and 2.5-liter engines, both using four-valves-per-cylinder technology for the first time. At the International Motor Show in September 1993, collaboration with dynamic partner AMG in Affalterbach reached high c, as it were, with the C36 AMG, which contributed a powerful helping hand in the form of a six-cylinder, 4-valve, 3.6-liter engine which delivered 280 bhp.

There were quite a number of innovations in the 202 series to report from the Frankfurt International Motor Show in the autumn of 1995. The standard model was now called Classic, and had new lights plus an updated interior, the whole series had been shod with 195/65 R15 tires and its front track had been increased by 6 mm (0.24 in). Two new variants were pressurized in different ways: the C230 Kompressor had a Roots supercharger that coaxed 193 bhp from its four-cylinder engine, and the C250 Turbodiesel with four valves per cylinder by an exhaust-driven turbocharger that helped it to 150 bhp and so to a lively performance. Both engines offered a good torque response over a wide engine speed range. The introduction of their turbocharged counterpart signaled the disappearance without trace of the C200 Diesel and the C250 Diesel, while the C220 was replaced in August 1996 by the C230. From then on the whole range was available on request, and at an extra charge, with a 5-speed automatic transmission which reduced fuel consumption, noise, and also maintenance costs.

Three months earlier Mercedes had entered the sporty compact estate-car sector with the T model which had nevertheless proved to be unusually spacious. Measured

Analog zu den s-Modellen bekommt die zweite Generation der kompakten Mercedes, vorgestellt im Mai 1993, einen eigenen Namen. Sie heißt nun c-Klasse, mit dem c vor dem dreistelligen Zahlencode nach neuem Benz-Brauch. Für ungefähr das gleiche Geld wie für den Vorgänger w201 erwirbt der Kunde mehr Auto: mehr Raum, mehr Sicherheit, mehr Komfort. Ins Serienpaket geschnürt sind Fahrer-Airbag, integrierter Seitenaufprallschutz, Servolenkung, Fünfgang-Getriebe, ABS sowie Zentralverriegelung. Neben der Standardausführung bietet man den w202 in drei Sonderversionen an, die offensichtlich an eine jüngere Klientel adressiert sind, als Esprit 25 mm tiefer und mit farbig-frohem Interieur, als Elegance mit üppiger Innenausstattung, Schutzleisten in Kontrastfarben, diversen Chromintarsien und anderen Leuchten und als Sport, wiederum tiefer gelegt, mit härterem Fahrwerk, Breitreifen und Leichtmetallfelgen. Wen es nach noch mehr visueller Dynamik dürstet, der kann mit der AMG-Variante zufriedengestellt werden, die mit einem abgesenkten Sportfahrwerk, anderen Schürzen und seitlichen Schwellern daherkommt.

Vier Ottomotoren stehen zur Verfügung, die aus der Baureihe 124 bekannten Vierventiler und ein neuer 1,8-Liter mit elektronischer Einspritzung, dazu drei Dieseltriebwerke: der Zweiliter aus dem Vorgänger sowie ein 2,2-Liter und ein 2,5-Liter, beide erstmals mit Vierventiltechnik. Auf der IAA im September 1993 zeitigt die Zusammenarbeit mit dem dynamischen Partner AMG in Affalterbach gewissermaßen das hohe c mit dem C36 AMG, dem ein Sechszylinder-Vierventiler mit 3,6 Litern und 280 PS mächtig auf die Sprünge hilft.

Auf der Frankfurter Ausstellung im Herbst 1995 gibt es mancherlei Neues zu berichten von der Baureihe 202: das Standardmodell heißt nun Classic und hat neue Leuchten sowie ein aktualisiertes Interieur, die ganze Reihe ist mit Reifen des Formats 195/65 R15 besohlt und hat sechs Millimeter mehr Spurweite vorn. Zwei neue Spielarten werden auf unterschiedliche Weise unter Druck gesetzt: der C230 Kompressor von einem Roots-Gebläse, das seinem Vierzylinder 193 PS einhaucht, der C250 Turbodiesel mit vier Ventilen je Zylinder von einem Abgaslader, der ihm zu 150 PS und damit ebenfalls zu munteren Fahrleistungen verhilft. Beide Maschinen warten mit einem guten Drehmoment über ein weites Drehzahlband auf. Mit dem Erscheinen ihres zwangsbeatmeten Pendants verschwinden der C200 Diesel und der C250 Diesel sang- und klanglos aus dem Programm, während der C220 im August 1996 durch den C230 abgelöst wird. Vom gleichen Zeitpunkt an gibt es die gesamte Palette auf Wunsch und gegen Aufpreis mit einer Fünfgang-Automatik, die Verbrauch und Geräuschemission ebenso mäßigt wie die Kosten für ihre Wartung.

Ein Vierteljahr vorher sind die Untertürkheimer in das Segment der sportlich-kompakten Kombis mit dem T-Modell vorgestoßen, das sich gleichwohl als

À l'instar des modèles de la Classe s, la deuxi génération de la compacte Mercedes prése en mai 1993 se voit dotée d'un nom spécifi Elle s'appelle Classe c, le c se trouvant devant le co trois chiffres selon les us et coutumes désormais en vigu chez Mercedes. Pour une somme sensiblement ident à celle qu'il fallait débourser pour sa devancière la w le client en a maintenant plus pour son argent : d'espace, plus de sécurité, plus de confort. L'équipem de série comporte l'airbag conducteur, une protec intégrée anticollision latérale, l'ABS, la direction assistée, boîte à cinq vitesses ainsi que le verrouillage centra Outre l'exécution standard, la w202 est proposée en t versions spéciales destinées à une clientèle plus je l'Esprit à châssis surbaissé de 25 mm et habitacle h en couleur, l'Elegance à l'aménagement intérieur généreux, avec bandes de protection latérales de cou contrastée, diverses applications de chrome et d'au optiques, et, enfin, la Sport, elle aussi à châssis surba avec trains roulants plus fermes, pneus larges et jan alliage. Celui qui souhaite plus d'esthétisme peut être co avec la version AMG caractérisée par un châssis sport s baissé, d'autres boucliers et des jupes de bas de caisse.

La motorisation consiste en quatre moteurs à esse les quatre-soupapes connus de la série 124 et un nouv 1,8 litre à injection électronique, plus trois moteurs Die le deux litres de l'ancien modèle ainsi qu'un 2,2 litre un 2,5 litres, dotés d'une culasse à quatre soupapes. À l'I de septembre 1993, la coopération avec le partenaire Mercedes-Benz, AMG, à Affalterbach, porte ses fruits a la C36 AMG. Un six-cylindres à quatre soupapes de 3,6 li et 280 ch lui confère des performances hors du commu

Lors du Salon de Francfort, à l'automne 1995, les n veautés ne manquent pas en ce qui concerne la gamme 2 le modèle standard s'appelle Classic et a de nouveaux ph ainsi qu'un intérieur remis au goût du jour, toute la gam étant chaussée de pneus de 195/65 R15 avec des voies é gies de 6 mm à l'avant. Deux nouvelles variantes sont m sous pression de façon différente : la C230 Kompressor a un compresseur Roots qui confère 193 ch à son qua cylindres, ainsi que la C250 Turbodiesel à quatre soupa par cylindre avec un turbocompresseur qui lui insuffle 15 et la rend plus performante que la moyenne. Les d moteurs se distinguent par un couple généreux sur une l plage de régime. L'apparition de son homologue tur chargé signifie pour la C200 Diesel et la C250 Diesel disparition du programme alors que la C220 est rempla en août 1996, par la C230. Toute la gamme est dispon sur demande et contre supplément avec une bo automatique à cinq rapports qui tempère aussi bien la c sommation et le niveau sonore que les coûts d'utilisati

Trois mois plus tôt, le constructeur de Stuttgart s lancé dans le segment des breaks sportifs et comp avec le modèle T qui se signale par une habitabilité g reuse : avec un coffre de 1510 litres de capacité selo norme VDA en étant chargé jusque sous le toit et a

MERCEDES-BENZ C 200 – C 43 AMG 1993

cedes-Benz C180 1996

accordance with the VDA norm, it had a capacity of liters if loaded right up to roof level or 465 liters in normal luggage compartment. Initially two diesel nes and three gasoline engines could be ordered, the ner being a four-cylinder, 2.2-liter model and the liter turbodiesel with five cylinders, and the gasoline dels of 1.8, 2.0, and 2.3 liters which were also fitted to sedans in slightly modified form.

This illustrates a time-honored Daimler-Benz prin e – a development spawns more offspring that in advance further development. 1997 saw quite far ching changes in the engine sector when tried- tested old friends were ditched to be replaced by v6 engines with 18 valves, a 2.4-liter model to ace the previous inline four-cylinder in the C230 , almost at the same price, a 2.8-liter model in the o. And for those who like it hot, the AMG high-per mance subsidiary in Affalterbach presented the top del in the series at the Frankfurt Motor Show in umn 1997: the C43 AMG, powered by a 4.3 liter v8 ducing 306 horsepower.

ungewöhnlich geräumig erweist: mit 1510 Litern nach VDA-Norm bei Beladung bis unters Dach, mit 465 Litern, die sich im normalen Gepäckabteil verstauen lassen. Zunächst können zwei Diesel- und drei Otto-Aggregate geordert werden, die Selbstzünder mit einem Vierzylinder von 2,2 Litern und dem 2,5-Liter Turbodiesel mit fünf Verbrennungseinheiten, die Benziner mit 1,8, 2,0 und 2,3 Litern, die etwas modifiziert und in ihrer überarbeiteten Form wieder in die Limousinen eingebracht werden.

So entlässt die Evolution ihre Kinder, die ihrerseits die Evolution vorantragen, Daimler-Benz-Prinzip von altersher. Massivere Eingriffe gibt es indessen 1997 im Motorensektor, als man Gestandenes und längst Bewährtes über Bord wirft und neue v6-Maschinen mit 18 Ventilen einführt, mit 2,4 Litern anstatt des bisherigen Reihen-Vierzylinders im C230 und fast um den gleichen Preis, mit 2,8 Litern im C280. Für alle aber, die es heiß mögen, hält die Hochleistungs-Filiale AMG in Affalterbach seit der Frankfurter Ausstellung im Herbst 1997 gleichsam das hohe C bereit: den C43 AMG, in dessen Motorenabteil sich ein v8 von 4,3 Litern für 306 PS stark macht.

465 litres en configuration normale. On a le choix entre deux diesels et trois moteurs à essence, les moteurs à autoallumage étant un quatre-cylindres de 2,2 litres et le 2,5 litres Turbodiesel à cinq-cylindres, alors que les moteurs à essence ont une cylindrée de 1,8, 2 et 2,3 litres et sont proposés pour les berlines avec de légères modifications.

C'est ainsi que l'évolution engendre ses enfants qui, quant à eux, font progresser l'évolution, principe cultivé de tout temps par Daimler-Benz. Des interventions plus significatives en ce qui concerne les moteurs sont à l'ordre du jour en 1997, année qui voit l'abandon de solutions depuis longtemps éprouvées et l'apparition d'un moteur v6 à 18 soupapes, avec 2,4 litres pour l'ancien quatre-cylindres en ligne de la C230 et, presque pour le même prix, avec 2,8 litres dans la C280. Mais, pour tous ceux qui n'ont jamais assez de chevaux sous le pied, les ateliers d'AMG, le service Course, à Affalterbach, proposent aussi, depuis le Salon de l'Automobile de Francfort, à l'automne 1997, une version C transcendée: la C43 AMG dans le compartiment moteur de laquelle se trouve un v8 de 4,3 litres délivrant 306 ch.

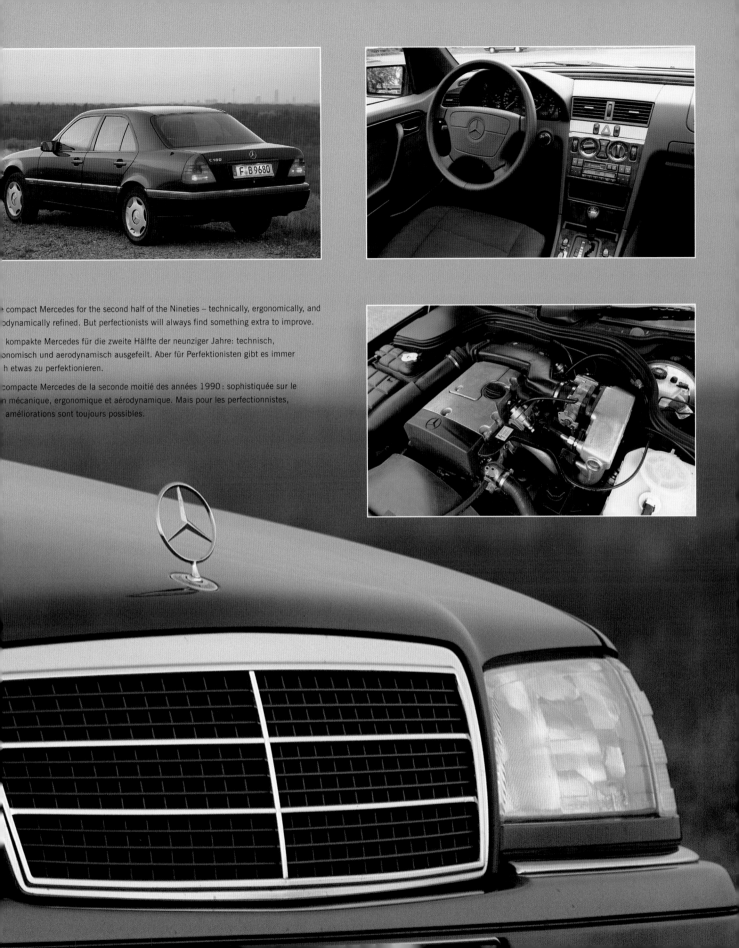

compact Mercedes for the second half of the Nineties – technically, ergonomically, and odynamically refined. But perfectionists will always find something extra to improve.

kompakte Mercedes für die zweite Hälfte der neunziger Jahre: technisch, onomisch und aerodynamisch ausgefeilt. Aber für Perfektionisten gibt es immer h etwas zu perfektionieren.

compacte Mercedes de la seconde moitié des années 1990: sophistiquée sur le n mécanique, ergonomique et aérodynamique. Mais pour les perfectionnistes, améliorations sont toujours possibles.

Mercedes-Benz C200–C43 AMG 1993

T time again: the C-class station wagon was light and sporty, and intentionally so. Station wagons had long since rid themselves of the reputation of being merely functional.

Kennzeichen T: Der Kombi im C-Format gibt sich leicht und sportlich. Das ist beabsichtigt. Denn längst haftet dem Kombinationskraftwagen nicht mehr das Odium kühler Nützlichkeit an.

Sous le signe du T: le break de la Classe C se veut léger et sportif. Ce n'est pas le fait du hasard. En effet, il y a longtemps que le break a cessé d'être dédié exclusivement à des affectations professionnelles.

Following the abrupt end to the Group C joint venture at the end of 1991, Mercedes boss Werner Niefer offered the Swiss Sauber racing team the opportunity to become involved in the Grand Prix world using Ilmor engines built by Peter Sauber's compatriot Mario Illien in Brixworth in the English county of Northamptonshire. The contract still had three years to run.

Eight chassis were produced from 1992 onwards for the C12, funded by Mercedes. Its design was the work of Dr. Harvey Postlethwaite, one of the select band of Formula 1 chassis builders. When the Briton left the team that same year, Sauber engineer Leo Ress was given responsibility for continuing the development work. The material used was carbon fiber, the black gold of the Nineties, baked into a low and compact form at DPS Components in England. The suspension was conventional, even classical: wishbones and enclosed units of springs and dampers, with drag struts front and rear. On the other hand, the layout of the six-speed box, a semi-automatic with gear shifting by means of two levers underneath the steering wheel, was unusual in that it was positioned longitudinally between the engine and the differential while others preferred a transverse configuration.

The brief was for a light, compact design, and that matched the philosophy of Mario Illien whose V10 was no heavier and required no more space than a comparable V8. The Ilmor 2175 A, whose cylinder banks were at an angle of 72 degrees to each other, weighed 126 kg, and back in 1991 it was amongst the most powerful engines in its field delivering 685 bhp at 13,100 rpm. The initial signs were promising: during winter testing the Saubers returned impressive times. In the 1993 season's opening grand prix at Kyalami Sauber driver J.J. Lehto finished fifth. Lehto finished in thirteenth place in the drivers' championship, while teammate Karl Wendlinger was eleventh. The team had had access to the Ilmor 2175 B producing 730 bhp at 13,500 rpm, or 745 bhp at 14,000 rpm in practice, with a greater bore and shorter stroke than its predecessor since the Italian Grand Prix on 12 September. 25 engines were built, 20 of them with conventional valve timing. The remaining five incorporated a pneumatically controlled system.

That year the Sauber engines bore the Mercedes-Benz badge after the management in Stuttgart had announced its decision on 3 November of the previous year to return to Formula 1 and to supply its Swiss protégé with the Brixworth-built engines free of charge. The Technical Director was André de Cortanze who oversaw the development of the Sauber C13 by Leo Ress, though Harvey Postlethwaite's original design was undeniably visible in the finished car. The monocoques were again sourced in England, from specialist supplier Ian Thomson. Seven were purchased, each weighing 40 kg.

But the season was overshadowed by accidents. One befell the Sauber team itself when Karl Wendlinger crashed badly in Monaco during practice. Roland Ratzenberger and

Nach dem abrupten Ende des Joint Ventures Gruppe C Ende 1991 stellt Mercedes-Chef Werner Niefer dem Schweizer Sauber-Rennstall anheim, sich im Grand-Prix-Geschäft zu engagieren, mit den Ilmor-Motoren, die Peter Saubers Landsmann Mario Illien in Brixworth in der Grafschaft Northamptonshire herstellt. Noch ist man für drei Jahre vertraglich aneinander gebunden.

Mit Mercedes-Mitteln entsteht ab 1992 in einer Auflage von acht Chassis der Sauber C12. Sein Design stammt aus der Feder von Dr. Harvey Postlethwaite, aus der kleinen, aber feinen Zunft derer, die Fahrwerke für die Formel 1 in die Welt setzen. Als der Brite das Team noch im gleichen Jahr verlässt, wird Sauber-Ingenieur Leo Ress zuständig für die weitere Entwicklungsarbeit. Werkstoff ist Kohlefaser, jenes schwarze Gold der neunziger Jahre, in eine niedrige und kompakte Form gebacken bei DPS Components in England. Konventionell, ja klassisch die Aufhängung: Dreiecks-Querlenker und innenliegende Einheiten von Federn und Dämpfern sowie Schubstreben vorn und hinten. Ungewöhnlich hingegen das Layout des Sechsgang-Getriebes, eines Halbautomaten, der vermittels zweier Hebel unterhalb des Lenkrads geschaltet wird: längs zwischen Motor und Differential, wo andere der Anordnung quer den Vorzug geben.

Leicht und von knappen Ausmaßen soll alles sein, und das deckt sich mit der Philosophie Mario Illiens, dessen V10 nicht schwerer ist und auch nicht mehr Platz in Anspruch nimmt als ein vergleichbarer V8. 126 kg wiegt der Ilmor 2175 A, dessen Zylinderbänke im Winkel von 72 Grad zueinander stehen, und schon 1991 zählt er mit bis zu 685 PS bei 13100/min zu den Stärksten im Lande. Die Anfänge machen Mut: Bei den Wintertests fahren die Sauber gute Zeiten. Im ersten Grand Prix der Saison 1993 in Kyalami wird Sauber-Pilot J.J. Lehto fünfter. Lehto landet in der Fahrermeisterschaft jedoch nur auf Platz 13, sein Teamkollege Karl Wendlinger auf Rang elf. Seit dem Großen Preis von Italien am 12. September hat man Zugang zum Ilmor-Opus 2175 B, bei 13500/min 730 PS stark, im Training 745 PS bei 14000/min, mit mehr Bohrung und weniger Hub als der Vorgänger. 25 Motoren werden gebaut, 20 davon mit herkömmlichem Ventiltrieb. In den restlichen fünf wird der Stoffwechsel pneumatisch geregelt.

In dieser Saison tragen die Sauber-Maschinen das Logo Mercedes-Benz: Am 3. November des Vorjahres hatte das Stuttgarter Management seine Entscheidung kundgetan, in der Formel 1 präsent zu sein und den Schweizer Schützling gratis mit den Motoren aus Brixworth zu verpflegen. Technischer Direktor ist jetzt André de Cortanze, unter dessen Stabführung Leo Ress den Sauber C13 entwickelt, ohne dass dieser seine Affinität zu dem ursprünglichen Konzept von Harvey Postlethwaite verleugnen könnte. Wieder kommen die Monocoques aus England, bezogen vom Spezialisten Ian Thomson, sieben an der Zahl, jedes 40 kg schwer.

Aber die Saison wird überschattet von Unfällen. Einer betrifft das Sauber-Team selbst, als beim Training

Le joint-venture contracté pour le Groupe C ay[ant] capoté brutalement fin 1991, Werner Niefer, P.-D.G. de Mercedes, recommande à l'écurie sui[sse] Sauber de s'engager en Grands Prix avec les moteurs Ilm[or] que fabrique à Brixworth, Northamptonshire, un co[m]patriote de Peter Sauber, Mario Illien. Les conjoints so[nt] encore liés contractuellement l'un à l'autre pour une du[rée] de trois ans.

Avec les crédits de Mercedes, huit châssis Sauber [C12] sont réalisés à partir de 1992. Ils sont l'œuvre de Harv[ey] Postlethwaite, membre de l'élitaire groupe d'ingénie[urs] triés sur le volet qui réalisent des châssis pour la Formule [1]. Le Britannique ayant quitté l'écurie la même année, l'ing[é]nieur Sauber Leo Ress reprend le flambeau pour po[ur]suivre les travaux de développement. Le matériau cho[isi] est de la fibre de carbone qui permet de concocter [des] coques basses et compactes, mais extrêmement résistan[tes] commandées, en l'occurrence, à DPS Components [en] Angleterre. La suspension est conventionnelle, voire cla[s]sique: triangles transversaux avec combinés ressor[ts]-amortisseurs in-board, poussoirs à l'avant et à l'arrière.

La boîte à six vitesses, par contre, l'est moins: il s'ag[it] d'une transmission semi-automatique avec deux leviers [de] commande derrière le volant; elle est placée longitudina[le]ment entre le moteur et le différentiel alors que les aut[res] donnent la préférence à une boîte transversale.

Tout est conçu pour être léger et compact, ce qui es[t] aussi la philosophie de Mario Illien dont le V10 n'est pas pl[us] lourd ni plus encombrant qu'un V8 comparable. L'Ilm[or] 2175 A, dont les bancs de cylindres décrivent un angle [de] 72 degrés, pèse 126 kg et, dès 1991, avec jusqu'à 685 ch [à] 13100 tr/min, c'est l'un des plus puissants du plateau. L[es] débuts sont encourageants: lors des tests hivernaux, l[es] Sauber font de bons temps. Lors du premier Grand Prix [de] la saison 1993, à Kyalami, J.J. Lehto, le pilote Sauber, termi[ne] cinquième. Au classement Pilotes, Lehto termine 13e [et] son coéquipier Karl Wendlinger, 11e. Depuis le Grand Pr[ix] d'Italie, le 12 septembre, elles sont propulsées par un nouv[eau] moteur Ilmor, le 2175 B qui développe 730 ch à 13500 tr/m[in] et 745 ch à 14000 tr/min en qualifications, avec alésa[ge] agrandi, mais course raccourcie par rapport à son prédéce[s]seur. Vingt-cinq exemplaires sont construits, dont 20 av[ec] une distribution de soupapes conventionnelle. Pour les cin[q] derniers, les échanges de gaz sont à commande pneumatiqu[e].

Cette saison-là, les monoplaces Sauber arborent [le] logo de Mercedes-Benz: le 3 novembre de l'année précé[de]nte, la direction du constructeur de Stuttgart ava[it] annoncé sa décision de s'engager en Formule 1 et de fourni[r] gratuitement à son protégé suisse les moteurs de Brixwort[h]. Le directeur technique est maintenant André de Cortanz[e] sous la direction duquel Leo Ress conçoit la Sauber c[13] qui ne renie toutefois pas ses affinités avec le concept ori[i]ginal de Harvey Postlethwaite. Les monocoques vienne[nt] de nouveau d'Angleterre, mais elles sont cette fois-[ci] signées par le spécialiste Ian Thomson, au nombre de sep[t], chacune pesant 40 kg.

Sauber-Mercedes C13 1994

great Ayrton Senna died at Imola. All continuity was ought to a halt when the governing body of motorsport, e FIA (*Fédération Internationale de l'Automobile*) ordered anges to wings and undersides with the intention of proving safety. These were expensive to implement. en without these, Peter Sauber's small company was boring under a chronic shortage of finance since the ped-for sponsorship had failed to materialize. The result as the lukewarm bath of mediocrity: eighth position the constructors' championship, while the Sauber ivers had to be satisfied with places 13 (Heinz-Harald entzen), 18 (Karl Wendlinger and Andrea de Cesaris) and (J.J. Lehto). Sauber was delivered an ultimatum in ptember: either the Swiss-based junior partner ensured equate third-party funding or Mercedes would not new the contract when it expired in 1994.

In a scene reminiscent of many a marriage, divorce came absolute on 31 December 1994 when no cash was rthcoming.

in Monaco Karl Wendlinger schwer verunglückt. In Imola sterben Roland Ratzenberger und der große Ayrton Senna. Jegliche Kontinuität reißt ab, als die Motorsport-behörde FIA (für *Fédération Internationale de l'Automobile*) Änderungen an Flügeln und Unterböden verordnet, die für mehr Sicherheit sorgen sollen. Diese sind kost-spielig. Ohnehin laboriert das kleine Unternehmen Peter Saubers an chronischem Geldmangel, da sich die erhofften Sponsor-Zuwendungen nicht einstellen. Da bleibt wieder nur das lauwarme Bad im Mittelmaß: Position acht in der Wertung der Konstrukteure, während sich die Sauber-Riege mit den Plätzen 13 (Heinz-Harald Frentzen), 18 (Karl Wendlinger und Andrea de Cesaris) und 24 (J.J. Lehto) bescheiden muss. Im September ergeht ein Ultimatum an Sauber: Entweder sorgt der eidgenössische Junior-Partner für ausreichende finanzielle Zuwendungen von außen, oder Mercedes lässt den Kontrakt fristgemäß 1994 auslaufen.

Szenen einer Ehe: Das Geld bleibt aus, und so kommt es am 31. Dezember 1994 zur Scheidung.

Mais la saison est assombrie par une série d'accidents. L'un concerne l'écurie Sauber elle-même lorsque, aux essais du Grand Prix de Monaco, Karl Wendlinger se blesse grièvement. À Imola, Roland Ratzenberger et l'inoubliable Ayrton Senna se tuent en course. La règle de la continuité est rendue caduque lorsque la FIA impose des modifica-tions des ailerons et du fond plat pour garantir une plus grande sécurité. Or ces modifications sont coûteuses.

A fortiori pour la petite entreprise de Peter Sauber qui souffre d'un manque chronique d'argent. Et c'est ainsi qu'elle ne peut s'extirper des milieux de peloton : huitième rang au classement Constructeurs alors que les mercenaires de Sauber doivent se contenter de la 13e place pour Heinz-Harald Frentzen, de la 18e pour Karl Wendlinger et Andrea de Cesaris ainsi que de la 24e pour J.J. Lehto. En septembre, Sauber reçoit un ultimatum : soit l'écurie suisse garantit des rentrées d'argent suffisantes à l'aide de sponsors, soit Mercedes laisse expirer le contrat en 1994.

Scènes d'un mariage : l'argent n'arrive pas et l'on divorce donc le 31 décembre 1994.

The V10, codenamed 2175B,
was developed by Ilmor, and the
C13 chassis by Sauber. However,
there was no doubting the role
also played by Mercedes-Benz
in its pedigree.

Der V10 namens 2175B ist von
Ilmor entwickelt, das Chassis C13
von Sauber. Kein Zweifel wird
allerdings gelassen an der Eltern-
schaft von Mercedes-Benz.

Le V10 version 2175B a été mis
au point par Ilmor, le châssis C13,
par Sauber. Aucun doute ne plane,
par contre, en ce qui concerne la
paternité de Mercedes-Benz.

Sauber-Mercedes C13 1994

The new mid-range Mercedes, launched as the 210 series in June 1995, was unmistakably an Untertürkheim product. Stylistically, however, there were hints of independence; for example, the rear light assemblies which were parabolically rounded into the sides, and in particular the anatomic peculiarity of its four-eyed face, four discrete elliptical lights flanking the radiator grille.

The customer had the choice of eight powerplants, five gasoline and three diesel engines. The gasoline engines were as follows: four-cylinder with 2 liters (136 bhp) and 2.3 liters (150 bhp), six-cylinder with 2.8 liters (193 bhp) and 3.2 liters (220 bhp), a v8 of 4.2 liters (279 bhp), all with four valves per cylinder. Two of the diesels were old friends, the 2.2-liter model delivering 95 bhp and the turbocharged 3-liter with 177 bhp. A new five-cylinder engine of 2.9 liters delivering 129 bhp, with a turbocharger, charge-cooling and direct injection represented the state of the art. In one respect progress involved reverting to technology that was thought to have passed its sell-by date – the E 290 Turbodiesel's metabolism was controlled by only two valves per cylinder.

The more difficult market situation that obtained in the mid-Nineties meant that the basic price had long since become inclusive of a number of useful and desirable features, such as an electronic driver authority system, the ETS electronic traction system, electrically operated windows front and rear, a third brake light on the parcel shelf, seat-belt load limiters and sidebags. Making their first appearance in the 210 model line were a rain sensor, which adjusted wiper speed in accordance with the amount of rain, and the Parktronic ultrasonic parking aid.

The control of the injection, ignition, and exhaust gas functions was in the hands of the Bosch Motronic 1.0. Engine management in the E 420 also entailed electronic transmission control of the 5-speed automatic gearbox. Six months after the series launch, the E 500 was succeeded by the E 50 AMG, with a 5-liter v8 developing 347 bhp whose external appearance and suspension setup also betrayed that it was obviously on the warpath. Its gearbox was a new automatic 5-speed transmission that reduced fuel consumption, noise emissions, and the number of gear changes, while also being more robust and durable than in earlier generations. From June 1996 onwards, this was also available either as an optional extra or as standard equipment in the models with four, five, and six cylinders. The T model, based on the sedan but with massively reinforced structures particularly in the tail end where the fuel tank was located under the luggage compartment and behind the axle, had made its appearance one month previously. Apart from offering more comfort and freedom of movement for the occupants than its predecessor, this star-badged aristocrat among estate cars also offered an additional 70 liters of load capacity. This was also available in three trim versions (Classic, Elegance, and Avantgarde) with the full range of engines of the sedans

Gewiss ist der neue Mittelklasse-Mercedes, vorgestellt als Baureihe 210 im Juni 1995, unverkennbar ein Produkt aus Untertürkheim. Aber er gibt sich auch stilistisch eigenmächtig, mit parabolisch in die Seiten gerundeten Leuchten-Ensembles hinten zum Beispiel, vor allem jedoch durch die anatomische Absonderlichkeit seines Vier-Augen-Gesichts, vier elliptischen Scheinwerfern, die getrennt voneinander den Kühlergrill flankieren.

Der Kunde hat die Wahl zwischen acht Triebwerken, fünf Otto- und drei Dieselmotoren. Die Benziner: Vierzylinder mit zwei (136 PS) und 2,3 Litern (150 PS), Sechszylinder von 2,8 (193 PS) und 3,2 Litern (220 PS), ein v8 von 4,2 Litern (279 PS), allesamt Vierventiler. Zwei der Selbstzünder sind alte Bekannte, der 2,2-Liter von 95 PS, der aufgeladene Dreiliter mit 177 PS. Neu und auf dem letzten Stand der Wissenschaft: ein Fünfzylinder mit 2,9 Litern und 129 PS, mit Turbolader, Ladeluftkühlung und Direkteinspritzung. In einem Punkt besteht der Fortschritt im Rückgriff auf scheinbar Überholtes: Der Stoffwechsel des E 290 Turbodiesel vollzieht sich über je zwei Ventile.

Auf dem schwieriger gewordenen Markt der Mittneunziger ist der Grundpreis längst zum Inklusivpreis für viel Nützliches und Erstrebenswertes geworden, wie ein elektronisches Fahrberechtigungssystem, das Elektronische Traktions-System ETS, elektrische Fensterheber vorn und hinten, eine dritte Bremsleuchte auf der Hutablage, Gurtkraftbegrenzer und Sidebags. Ihren Einstand geben in der Modellinie 210 ein Regensensor, der die Aktivität der Scheibenwischer gemäß der Menge an Niederschlag dosiert, und die Ultraschall-Einparkhilfe Parktronic.

Die Steuerungsfunktionen für Einspritzung, Zündung und E-Gas sind in der Bosch Motronic 1.0 zusammengefasst. Das Motor-Management umgreift im E 420 zusätzlich die elektronische Getriebesteuerung des Fünfgang-Automaten. Ein halbes Jahr nach der Einführung der Reihe wird als Nachfolger des E 500 der E 50 AMG inthronisiert, mit einem v8 von fünf Litern und 347 PS, der auch hinsichtlich seiner Optik und Fahrwerkstechnik manifest auf dem Kriegspfad wandelt. Sein Getriebe: eine neue Automatik mit fünf Gängen, die den Verbrauch ebenso reduziert wie die Geräuschemissionen und die Anzahl der Schaltvorgänge, robuster und langlebiger zumal als frühere Generationen. Ab Juni 1996 hält sie als Option oder serienmäßig auch Einzug in die Spielarten mit vier, fünf und sechs Zylindern. Einen Monat zuvor ist das T-Modell erschienen, auf der Basis der Limousine, aber mit massiv verstärkten Strukturen vor allem im Heckbereich, wo der Tank hinter der Achse unterhalb des Gepäckabteils untergebracht ist. Neben mehr Komfort und Bewegungsfreiheit für die Insassen als sein Vorgänger bietet der Edel-Kombi im Zeichen des Sterns zusätzlich 70 Liter Ladevolumen. Auch er ist in den drei Attraktivitäts-Stufen Classic, Elegance und Avantgarde erhältlich, mit dem Motorenspektrum der Limousinen

Certes, la nouvelle classe intermédiaire de Mercedes, présentée en tant que série 210 en juin 1995, est incontestablement un produit d'Untertürkheim. Mais elle n'en fait pas moins preuve d'une grande personnalité par son style, par exemple avec des feux arrière paraboliques débordant sur les côtés, mais surtout de par son visage à quatre yeux, avec quatre phares elliptiques individuels ponctuant la grille de calandre.

Le client a le choix entre huit moteurs, cinq à essence et trois diesels. Les moteurs essence : des quatre-cylindres de 2 litres (136 ch) et 2,3 litres (150 ch), des six-cylindres de 2,8 litres (193 ch) et 3,2 litres (220 ch), un v8 de 4,2 litres (279 ch), tous à quatre soupapes. Deux des moteurs à auto-allumage sont de bonnes vieilles connaissances, il s'agit du 2,2 litres de 95 ch et du 3 litres suralimenté de 177 ch. Mais il existe aussi un nouveau moteur de cinq cylindres de 2,9 litres et 129 ch, avec turbocompresseur, échangeur d'air et injection directe. Ici, le progrès consiste en la résurgence d'une solution apparemment démodée : les échanges de gaz de la E 290 Turbodiesel s'effectuent grâce à deux soupapes.

Sur un marché devenu plus difficile au cours du milieu des années 1990, le prix de base est depuis longtemps devenu un prix net, qui inclut de nombreux accessoires intéressants tels que le système électronique d'habilitation à la conduite, le système de régulation électronique de la motricité ETS, les vitres électriques à l'avant et l'arrière, un troisième feu de frein sur la lunette arrière, des limiteurs de tension de la ceinture et des coussins gonflables latéraux. La série 210 est le théâtre de plusieurs premières : le capteur de pluie qui règle le rythme d'essuyage du pare-brise et le système d'aide au stationnement à ultrasons Parktronic.

Les fonctions de commande pour l'injection, l'allumage et l'accélérateur électronique sont regroupées dans la centrale Bosch Motronic 1.0. Dans la E 420, la gestion moteur comporte à titre supplémentaire la commande électronique de la boîte automatique à cinq vitesses. Six mois après la présentation de la gamme, la E 50 AMG est intronisée comme remplaçante de la E 500. Avec un v8 de 5 litres et 347 ch, elle s'est manifestement engagée sur le sentier de la guerre, notamment sur le plan esthétique et par ses impressionnants trains roulants. Sa boîte de vitesses, une nouvelle transmission automatique à cinq rapports, réduit la consommation, le niveau sonore et le nombre de changements de rapports. À partir de juin 1996, elle fait aussi son apparition en option ou de série dans les variantes à quatre, cinq et six-cylindres. Un mois plus tôt a eu lieu la présentation du modèle T, break dérivé de la berline, mais avec des structures sérieusement renforcées, notamment à l'arrière. Ce break de luxe sous le signe de l'étoile offre 70 litres de volume de chargement supplémentaire. Le break aussi est proposé dans trois niveaux de finition, Classic, Elegance, et Avantgarde, avec les mêmes motorisations que les berlines et des boîtes manuelles à cinq vitesses pour les quatre et cinq-cylindres

Mercedes-Benz E 270 CDI 1999

and 5-speed manual gearboxes in the four- and five-cylinder models. The automatic transmission with its slip-controlled converter clutch was fitted as standard to the top models with six or eight cylinders, and was otherwise available as an optional extra. 1997 saw novel features appear under the hood where newly developed v6 engines replaced the previous straight-six engines in two cases, namely in the E 280 with 204 bhp and in the E 320 with 224 bhp. At the same time these models saw the resurrection of the 4matic principle, though as a permanent four-wheel-drive with automatic braking of spinning wheels, instead of the conventional differential locks. According to the specialist publication *auto motor und sport*, there was no better system.

und Fünfgang-Schaltgetrieben an den Vier- und Fünfzylindern. Die Automatik mit schlupfgesteuerter Wandler-Überbrückungskupplung bleibt als Serienausstattung den Top-Typen mit sechs oder acht Verbrennungseinheiten vorbehalten und ist ansonsten aufpreispflichtig. Das Jahr 1997 beschert Novitäten unter der vorderen Haube, wo in zwei Fällen neu entwickelte v6-Triebwerke die bisherigen Reihen-Sechszylinder verdrängen, im E 280 mit 204 PS, im E 320 mit 224 PS. Zugleich feiert in diesen Modellen das Prinzip 4matic Urständ, allerdings als permanenter Allradantrieb mit automatischem Bremseingriff an durchdrehenden Rädern statt der üblichen Differentialsperren. Ein besseres System, bescheinigt das Fachblatt *auto motor und sport*, gebe es nicht.

La transmission automatique avec embrayage de pontage du convertisseur commandé par patinage reste proposée en série uniquement pour les modèles haut de gamme à six ou huit-cylindres et est, sinon, facturée contre supplément. L'année 1997 se traduit par des nouveautés sous le capot moteur où, dans deux cas, de nouveaux moteurs v6 remplacent les anciens six-cylindres en ligne, dans la E 280 avec 204 ch et dans la E 320 avec 224 ch. Simultanément, le système 4matic fait sa réapparition sur ces modèles, mais en tant que traction intégrale permanente avec intervention automatique par freinage des roues qui patinent à la place des blocages de différentiel conventionnels. Selon la revue spécialisée *auto motor und sport*, il n'y a pas de meilleur système.

he beauty of individual details can create a pleasing interplay of forms, one of the arameters in the design of the E-class. Striking features included the four-eyed look, nd the light units which extended into the trunk lid.

chöne Details finden sich zum Zusammenspiel der Formen, einem der Parameter bei er Konzeption der E-Klasse. Auffällig das Vier-Augen-Gesicht und die bis in den offerraumdeckel hineingezogenen hinteren Leuchten-Ensembles.

e jolis détails illustrent le jeu des formes, l'un des paramètres qui a présidé à la onception de la Classe E. Spectaculaires: son visage à quatre yeux et les optiques rrière qui se poursuivent jusque sur le couvercle de malle.

The tail section of the new mid-range Mercedes – represented here by the E230 – was reminiscent of the marque's coupés. Attractive plane-wood trim was included as standard.

Die Heckpartie des neuen Mercedes für die Mittelklasse – hier vertreten durch den E230 – erinnert an die Coupés der Marke. Schmucke Intarsien aus Platanenholz gehören zur Serienausstattung.

La partie arrière de la nouvelle Mercedes du segment intermédiaire – ici celle de la E230 – rappelle les coupés de la marque. Les élégantes applications de platane font partie de l'équipement de série.

...ter the July 1999 facelift we see indicators in the wing mirrors, lower wings, flatter ...adlights, an altered radiator grille and integrated bumpers. The program now comprises ...e six petrol engine models, the E200, E240, E280, E320, E430 and E55AMG plus ...e four common rail diesels, the E200CDI, E220CDI, E270CDI, and E320CDI.

...ach dem Facelift im Juli 1999: Blinker in den Außenspiegeln, niedrigere Kotflügel, ...chere Scheinwerfer, veränderter Kühlergrill und integrierte Stoßfänger. Das Programm ...nspannt jetzt die sechs Benziner E200, E240, E280, E320, E430 und E55AMG sowie ...e vier Common Rail-Diesel E200CDI, E220CDI, E270CDI und E320CDI.

...orès le lifting de juillet 1999: clignotants intégrés aux rétroviseurs extérieurs, ailes ...aissées, phares plus minces, nouvelle calandre et pare-chocs intégré. La gamme se ...mpose maintenant de six versions à essence – E200, E240, E280, E320, E430 et ...55 AMG – ainsi que de quatre diesels à rampe commune: E200 CDI, E220 CDI, ...270 CDI et E320 CDI.

The alliance between the Formula 1 team McLaren and Mercedes, who supply the engines, was forged on 28 October 1994 with the signing of a five-year contract, repeatedly extended since 1998. However, 33 Grands Prix were to pass before the partnership yielded its avowed goal: the first victory.

The hope was that a new body, the McLaren MP4-12, and a new power unit, the Mercedes Benz FO110E (standing for Formula One, Series 1, 10 cylinders, version E) would guarantee this for the 1997 season. The body is attractive in appearance with its trim, sleek lines, and the nose now dropping markedly, in sharp contrast to the shark nose of the year before. The driver's position is 35 mm lower, making the side impact protectors lower in turn and so more aerodynamic, guiding the airstream into the engine air inlet and towards the rear assembly. The water cooler vents are narrower and higher, also in the interests of improved aerodynamics.

The engine is of conventional design: a V10 with cylinder banks at an angle of 75 degrees (72 degrees from version F onwards), four overhead camshafts and four valves per cylinder. The bore and stroke have been chosen so as to allow the steel crank shaft to reach 16,000 rpm. It is now 5 mm lower, and the whole engine is two centimeters flatter, leading to a corresponding lowering of the McLaren MP4-12's center of gravity. The overall weight of the power unit is 126 kg (277 lb). The complex drive management function is performed by the TAG 2000 combined computer system. This product of McLaren subsidiary TAG Electronics also controls the semi-automatic transmission system.

No sooner had the MP4-12 gone into service than work began on its successor. The most drastic changes in Formula 1 regulations for 15 years were impending: the maximum width of a Formula 1 car was to be reduced from 2000 mm to 1800 mm, while the width of the front wheels would have to be at least 305 mm, and of the rear wheel at most 380 mm. On top of this, three grooves were to be added to the tires in order to reduce the grip through corners. McLaren Mercedes' answer to this challenge was the MP4-13, a sleek projectile which was to prove every inch a winner. It had its premiere on 5 February 1998 at McLaren's headquarters in Woking. To improve the weight distribution, the cockpit had been shifted towards the rear, and the wheelbase had been increased from 2930 mm to 3100 mm. The fact that the FO110G power unit and its auxiliary equipment weighed just 107 kg (236 lb) provided some highly welcome room for maneuver: the shortfall with respect to the minimum permitted weight of 600 kg (1323 lb) has to be made good by the addition of ballast, which can be transferred to the rear of the car on slow circuits such as Monaco, or to the front of the car on fast circuits such as Silverstone or Monza.

The comparatively minor changes in the 1999 regulations allowed the engineers to fine tune the details. Changes include four grooves per tire instead of three,

Seit dem 28. Oktober 1994 ist die Allianz des Formel-1-Rennstalls McLaren mit Mercedes als Motorenlieferant verklammert durch einen Bindestrich, den Händedruck der Bosse sowie einen Vertrag über fünf Jahre, seit 1998 mehrmals verlängert. 33 Grand Prix lässt indes das erklärte Nahziel auf sich warten: der erste Sieg.

Den soll 1997 ein neues Chassis garantieren, der McLaren MP4-12, und ein neues Triebwerk, der Mercedes-Benz FO110E (für Formula One, Baureihe 1, 10 Zylinder, Ausbaustufe E). Das Chassis: schön anzusehen und von properer Verarbeitung. Deutlich abgesenkt ist die Nase, die im Vorjahr noch hoch getragen wurde. Der Pilot sitzt 35 Millimeter tiefer. Der seitliche Aufprallschutz wird dadurch niedriger und windschlüpfiger. Das glättet die Führung des Lebenselixiers Luft zum entsprechenden Einlass der Maschine und zum Heckleitwerk. Schmaler und höher sind die Öffnungen zu den Wasserkühlern, auch dies im Dienst der Aerodynamik.

Die Maschine: von konventioneller Architektur, ein V10 mit Zylinderbänken im Winkel von 75 Grad (ab Stufe F noch im gleichen Jahr 72 Grad), vier oben liegenden Nockenwellen und vier Ventilen pro Brennraum. Bohrung und Hub sind so gewählt, dass die stählerne Kurbelwelle Drehzahlen von über 16 000/min erreicht. Sie liegt fünf Millimeter tiefer, der ganze Motor wurde um 20 Millimeter flacher, was den Schwerpunkt des MP4-12 entsprechend absenkt – ein deutlicher Trend auch bei künftigen Modifikationen. Samt seinen Anbauten wiegt das Aggregat 126 kg. Das komplexe Antriebsmanagement übernimmt die kombinierte Rechnereinheit TAG 2000, Produkt des McLaren-Satelliten TAG Electronics. Sie steuert auch die Funktionen der halbautomatischen Schaltung.

Kaum steht der MP4-12 auf den feisten Rädern, da beginnt bereits die Arbeit am Nachfolger. Dramatische Änderungen des Regelwerks stehen an, die drastischsten seit 15 Jahren. Die maximale Breite eines Formel-1-Wagens wird von bislang 2000 auf 1800 Millimeter begrenzt. Die Reifen vorn müssen mindestens 305, die hinteren dürfen höchstens 380 Millimeter breit sein. Drei Rillen durchfurchen jeweils die Laufflächen, um ihre Haftung in Kurven zu verringern. McLaren-Mercedes antwortet mit dem MP4-13, einem schlanken Projektil, jeder Zoll ein Sieger, wie sich erweisen wird. Premiere ist am 5. Februar 1998 am McLaren-Standort Woking. Zur besseren Gewichtsverteilung wurde das Cockpit nach hinten verlagert, der Radstand von 2930 auf 3100 Millimeter verlängert. Dass das Triebwerk FO110G nebst Trabanten nur noch 107 Kilogramm auf die Waage bringt, schafft höchst willkommene Spielräume. Das Minus gegenüber dem vorgeschriebenen Mindestgewicht von 600 Kilogramm muss durch Ballast austariert werden, der sich verschieben lässt, auf langsamen Kursen wie Monaco nach hinten, auf schnellen wie Silverstone oder Monza nach vorn.

Vergleichsweise behutsam retuschiert, lässt das Reglement für 1999 die Ingenieure eher am Detail feilen: Vier

Depuis le 28 octobre 1994, l'alliance entre l'écu… de Formule 1 McLaren et Mercedes en tant q… motoriste est scellée par un trait d'union, … poignée de mains des managers et un contrat qui porte s… cinq ans, contrat prorogé, depuis 1998, plusieurs fois. … leur faut toutefois attendre 33 Grands Prix pour attein… leur objectif à court terme avoué : la première victoire.

Pour cela, ils jettent de nouveaux arguments da… la bataille en 1997 : la McLaren MP4-12, et un nouvea… moteur, le Mercedes-Benz FO110E (pour Formula On… série 1, 10 cylindres, évolution E). Le châssis : d'une gran… beauté et, comme toujours chez McLaren, d'une finiti… parfaite. Le mufle qui, l'an dernier, se dressait enco… dans le vent, a été nettement abaissé. Le pilote est ass… 35 mm plus bas, ce qui a permis d'abaisser aussi l… pontons latéraux, qui sont donc d'autant plus aérodyn… miques. Cela favorise l'écoulement de l'air vers la pri… d'air moteur et l'aileron arrière. Les ouvertures des radi… teurs d'eau sont plus étroites et plus hautes – toujours … diktat de l'aérodynamique.

Le moteur : d'une architecture conventionnelle, il s'ag… d'un V10 à 75 degrés (qui passera à 72 avec l'évolution F a… cours même de la saison), avec quatre arbres à cames e… tête et quatre soupapes par cylindre. La course et l'alésa… ont été ainsi calculés afin que le vilebrequin en acier puis… dépasser des régimes de 16 000 tr/min. Il a été abaissé … cinq mm et le moteur a perdu 20 mm en hauteur, ce qui… permis d'abaisser en conséquence le centre de gravité … la MP4-12 – une tendance qui se poursuivra aussi avec l… modifications ultérieures. Avec toute sa périphérie, … moteur pèse 126 kg. La complexe gestion moteur est assure… par la centrale combinée TAG 2000, un produit de TAG Ele… tronics, une filiale de McLaren. Elle gère également l… fonctions de la transmission semi-automatique.

La MP4-12 a à peine fait ses premiers tours de rou… que ses ingénieurs préparent déjà la naissance de sa rem… plaçante. Des modifications draconiennes du règlemen… sont annoncées, les plus profondes depuis 15 ans. D… 2000 mm jusqu'à présent, la largeur maximale d'un… Formule 1 va être limitée à 1800 mm. Les pneus avan… devront avoir au minimum 305 mm de large et ceux … l'arrière, au maximum 380 mm. Trois rainures respective… sont prévues dans leur surface de roulement afin de dim… nuer l'adhérence en virage. McLaren-Mercedes répliqu… avec la MP4-13, un projectile effilé comme une fusée, conç… dans les moindres détails pour gagner, comme on le consta… tera par la suite. Elle est dévoilée le 5 février 1998 à l'usin… McLaren de Woking. Pour améliorer la répartition d… poids, le cockpit a été reculé et l'empattement, allongé d… 2930 à 3100 mm. Le moteur FO110G avec ses organes a… pèse plus que 107 kg, ce qui donne une marge de manœuvr… bienvenue aux ingénieurs. La MP4-13 est inférieure au poid… réglementaire de 600 kg. On la dote donc d'un ballas… que l'on peut déplacer : vers l'arrière sur les circuits len… comme Monaco, vers l'avant sur les circuits rapides comm… Silverstone ou Monza.

McLaren-Mercedes
MP 4-10—MP 4-19B 1995

McLaren-Mercedes MP4-14 1999

ats that can be lifted out of the car along with the
river in the event of an accident, and wheels that are
tained on the car by polymer belts after a collision. As a
sult, the MP4-14 resembled its predecessor. However,
s streamlined contours concealed a number of further
finements. Among them was a seven-speed gearbox in a
agnesium housing, which is lighter than the previous
x-speed version, while the suspension, still involving
elical springs on the MP4-12, was now provided by
rsion bar stabilizers all round. Engine boss Mario Illien's
en's main focus, though, was on the driveability of the
version of the V10 over a useable engine speed range
f almost 10,000 rpm. That almost sounds like they're
lking about driver comfort.

Rillen je Reifen sind angesagt, Sitze, die sich nach einem
Unfall mitsamt dem Piloten aus dem Cockpit hieven
lassen, Räder, die bei einer Kollision von Polymergurten
am Fahrzeug festgehalten werden. Folglich ähnelt der
MP4-14 dem Vorgänger. Allerdings sieht unter seinen
flüssigen Formen manches anders aus: Das neue Sieben-
gang-Getriebe, untergebracht in einem Gehäuse aus
Magnesium, ist leichter als das frühere mit sechs Fahrstufen. Die Federung, im MP4-12 noch durch Schraubenfedern besorgt, übernehmen nun Drehstäbe ringsum.
Das besondere Augenmerk der Männer um Motorenchef
Mario Illien aber richtete sich auf die *driveability* der
Version H des V10, der Umgänglichkeit über ein nutzbares
Drehzahlband von fast 10 000/min. Das grenzt schon fast
an Komfort.

Les modifications de règlement pour 1999 sont
mineures et obligent les ingénieurs à travailler sur les
détails: quatre rainures par pneu sont imposées, un siège
que l'on peut extraire du cockpit avec son pilote en cas
d'accident, des roues qui sont maintenues au châssis par
un câble en polymère en cas de collision. Logiquement, la
MP4-14 est très proche de sa devancière. Et pourtant, sous
sa carrosserie aux lignes fluides, bien des choses sont différentes: la nouvelle boîte à sept vitesses, dans un carter en
magnésium, est plus légère que l'ancienne version à six
rapports. La suspension, encore avec ressorts hélicoïdaux
dans la MP4-12, est maintenant assurée par des barres de
torsion. Mais l'équipe de motoristes réunie autour de
Mario Illien a surtout fait porter son attention sur la
« driveability » de la version H du V10, dont la plage de
régime utile est de presque 10 000 tr/min. On pourrait
presque parler de confort.

Congested area: after the chaos of the start of the 1998 Monaco Grand Prix the two Mercedes have already put some distance between themselves and the opposition by the first corner, Sainte Dévote. While everyone can judge for themselves the skills of the driver, a veil of secrecy has long since obscured the skills and technology that go into the car itself.

McLaren-Mercedes MP4-10–MP4-19B 1995

Blaubereich: Aus dem Getümmel beim Start zum Grand Prix de Monaco 1998 haben sich die beiden McLaren-Mercedes an der ersten Kurve Sainte Dévote bereits etwas abgesetzt. Von der Technik der Piloten kann sich jeder ein Bild machen. Über die Technik der Wagen dessen werden längst Schleier des Geheimnisses und graue Tücher gebreitet.

Bouchon: après le départ fulminant du Grand Prix de Monaco de 1998, les deux McLaren-Mercedes ont pris une légère avance dès la sortie du premier virage, à Sainte-Dévote. Chacun peut se faire une idée de la technique des pilotes. Mais celle des voitures, en revanche, reste depuis longtemps dissimulée sous le manteau du secret et des bâches grises.

McLaren-Mercedes MP4-10–MP4-19B 1995 471

1995   1996   1997

(Above) 1995 was a lean year for the MP 4-10: second place for Hakkinen in Monza; the following year was no better for the team, and saw the end of the "Marlboro era".
(Right) 1997: After Hakkinen's victory in Suzuka at the end of a long Grand Prix season the defeated Michael Schumacher congratulates him warmly.

(Oben) 1995 –mageres Jahr für den MP 4-10: ein zweiter Platz für Hakkinen in Monza; im Folgejahr sah es für das Team nicht besser aus, zugleich das Ende der »Marlboro-Ära«.
(Rechts) Nach Hakkinens Sieg in Suzuka am Ende der langen Grand-Prix-Tournee 1997 gratuliert der unterlegene Michael Schumacher dem neuen Weltmeister Mika Hakkinen fair.

(Ci-dessus) 1995 – saison décevante pour la MP 4-10 avec une deuxième place pour Hakkinen à Monza ; l'année suivante, les choses ne s'améliorent guère et l'on assiste aussi à la fin de l'« ère Marlboro ».
(Ci-contre) 1997 : Après la victoire de Hakkinen, à Suzuka, à la fin de la longue tournée mondiale des Grands Prix, son dauphin, Michael Schumacher, félicite loyalement le nouveau champion du monde.

98   1999

(above and below) Masterful: 1998 world champion Mika Hakkinen in the McLaren-Mercedes MP4-13.

(oben und unten) Meisterlich: Mika Hakkinen auf McLaren-Mercedes MP4-13, Champion 1998.

(ci-dessus et ci-dessous) Magistral : Mika Hakkinen sur la McLaren-Mercedes MP4-13, champion du monde 1998.

In 1999, the Finn took the title once again, the MP4-14 chalked up 2659 lead kilometers, eleven pole positions, and seven victories.

1999 holt der Finne erneut den Titel, und der MP4-14 bringt es auf 2659 Führungskilometer, elf Pole-Positionen und sieben Siege.

En 1999, le Finlandais décroche de nouveau le titre et la MP4-14 peut se prévaloir d'avoir couvert 2659 kilomètres en tête, avec onze pole positions et sept victoires à la clef.

2000   2001   2002

Die Siegbilanz des Vorjahres wiederholt sich auch 2000, trotzdem müssen sich McLaren-Mercedes und Mika der Kombination Schumacher-Ferrari in dieser Saison geschlagen geben.

2001 holt sich David Coulthard den Lorbeer eines Vizeweltmeisters, während sich Häkkinen mit 37 Punkten bescheiden muss. Nach seinem Rücktritt übernimmt Landsmann Kimi Räikkönen das vakante McLaren-Cockpit und verfehlt 2003 mit 91 WM-Punkten nur knapp den Titel.

2002 und 2003 muss sich McLaren-Mercedes mit dem dritten Platz der Konstrukteurs-WM begnügen. Und auch 2004, nach anfänglichen Problemen mit dem MP4-19, deutet sich erst in Silverstone mit dem Einsatz des MP4-19B wieder eine Sternstunde des Teams an.

Multifunktions-Lenkrad und Auspuff-Krümmer – die Einblicke, die dem Fotografen zuteil werden, wenn er auf die Technik zielt, sind streng kontrolliert; eine Innovation kann über Sieg oder Niederlage entscheide

The success story of the previous year repeated itself in 2002. Nevertheless, McLaren-Mercedes and Mika had to accept defeat at the hands of the Schumacher-Ferrari combination.

In 2001, David Coulthard took the vice champion's laurels, while Hakkinen had to make do with 37 championship points. Following his retirement, his fellow Finn Kimi Räikkönen took over the vacant cockpit and with 91 points only just failed to take the championship title in 2003.

In 2002 and 2003, McLaren-Mercedes had to make do with third place in the team championship. And in 2004, after early problems with the MP4-19, it was only with the introduction at Silverstone of the MP4-19B that the team again began to shine.

Multi-functional steering wheel and exhaust manifold – the insights allowed the photographer with technology in his viewfinder are strictly controlled; an innovation can be decisive for victory or defeat.

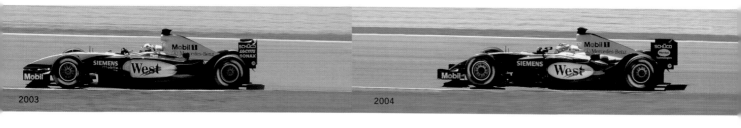

En l'an 2000, le nombre de victoires est le même que celui de l'année précédente, mais, cette saison-là, McLaren-Mercedes et Mika doivent tout de même s'avouer vaincus par le duo Schumacher-Ferrari.

En 2001, David Coulthard coiffe la couronne de laurier du vice-champion tandis que Hakkinen ne compte que 37 maigres points. Après que ce dernier ait raccroché son casque, son compatriote Kimi Räikkönen se glisse dans le cockpit vacant de la McLaren et, avec 91 points au championnat du monde, rate de peu le titre en 2003.

En 2002 et 2003, McLaren-Mercedes doit se contenter de la troisième place au championnat des constructeurs. Et, en 2004 également, après un début de saison calamiteux avec la MP4-19, l'horizon s'éclaircit de nouveau à partir de Silverstone avec l'arrivée de la MP4-19B.

Volant multifonctions et collecteur d'échappement – le photographe n'a que très rarement le droit de braquer son objectif sur les détails techniques, une innovation étant souvent synonyme de victoire ou de défaite.

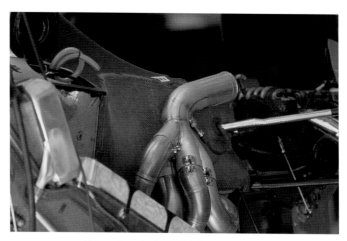

McLaren-Mercedes MP4-10–MP4-19B 1995

David Coulthard study driving the MP4-19 in Monte Carlo 2004: this time the 2002 Monaco victor 2002 did not have the McLaren-Mercedes nose up front.

Fahrstudie von David Coulthard mit dem MP4-19 in Monte Carlo 2004: Diesmal hatte der Monaco-Sieger von 2002 nicht die McLaren-Mercedes-Nase vorn.

Étude de pilotage de David Coulthard avec la MP4-19 à Monte Carlo en 2004 : cette fois-ci, le vainqueur de Monaco en 2002 n'a pas pu tirer son épingle du jeu avec sa McLaren-Mercedes.

With this car we are experiencing a renaissance of automobile aesthetics," declared Helmut Werner, chairman of the executive board of Mercedes Benz AG, ignoring the hurricane of the wind tunnel resounding in everyone's ears.

"In a car like this the journey is the end in itself," added Jürgen Hubbert, board member and head of the sedan car section.

Of course all this is corporate hype to woo waverers and entice new customers. However, the SLK has no need of any such assistance. Launched at the Turin Exhibition in April 1996, it is half young Siegfried and half Don Juan reborn in the guise of a motor vehicle, the sweetest temptation to come out to Untertürkheim in living memory. It is love at first sight, as you gaze on the low windshield, the long hood, the wide doors and the defiant tail, with short valances at front and rear and a comparatively long wheelbase of 2400 mm (7 ft 10.5 in), plus of course that certain indefinable something.

And then there's the price, throwing down the gauntlet to its competitors in this difficult market sector: precisely calculated at 60,950 marks for the more expensive of the two 2.3-liter models, with its supercharger generating 193 bhp. The version with the normally aspirated engine generating 136 bhp costs a modest 54,150 marks, and for this price the lucky owner gets two cars: press a little red button and in 25 seconds the SLK coupé you drove away from the show room retracts its roof to become a roadster. All material that could flap, flutter, judder, get wet, or spoil the elegant lines simply disappears.

Before the SLK reveals itself to the sun, moon, or stars, six precisely coordinated operations take place, all controlled by five hydraulic cylinders, two to drive the retractable roof, two for the loading action of the trunk lid, and one to fasten the roof when it is put up again. When the operation is complete the carefully folded hardtop is fully hidden from view in the trunk. That's the good news. The bad news is that this complex operation reduces the volume of the trunk from a reasonable 348 liters to a somewhat miserly 145 liters, so that for long journeys with plenty of luggage the roof has to stay up. Two steps have been taken in the factory to combat this problem: the fuel tank holds just 53 liters (14 gal) and a spare wheel has been completely omitted (though a collapsible compact spare tire is available as an option): if the worst comes to the worst and you do have a puncture, and statistically this happens only once every 150,000 km (c. 90,000 miles), a Tirefit tire repair kit, consisting of sealant and an electric pump, provides first aid.

SLK is a blend of well-known Mercedes designations of the past, and stands for *Sport, Leicht, Kurz* (Sport, Light, Short). "Light," as always with Mercedes, is somewhat economical with the truth: the SLK230 Kompressor weighs in at 1325 kg (2921 lb). "Short" is true enough,

---

Wir erleben mit ihm eine Renaissance automobiler Ästhetik«, sagt Helmut Werner, Vorstandsvorsitzer der Mercedes-Benz AG, so als sei die im alles glättenden Orkan des Windkanals verlorengegangen.

Und: »In einem solchen Automobil ist der Weg das Ziel«, sekundiert ihm Jürgen Hubbert, Mitglied des Vorstands und zuständig für das Geschäftsfeld PKW.

Das ist natürlich Konzernlyrik, Buhlen um Zaudernde, dazu bestimmt, neue Kunden zu betören. Nur: So was hat der SLK, vorgestellt auf dem Turiner Salon im April 1996, gar nicht nötig, halb Jung Siegfried, halb Don Juan in Autogestalt und die süßeste Verlockung aus Untertürkheim seit Menschengedenken. Liebe geht durch das Auge, und das sieht eine niedrige Frontscheibe, lange Motorhaube, breite Türen und ein trotziges Heck, dazu kurze Überhänge vorn und hinten und den vergleichsweise langen Radstand von 2400 Millimetern, versetzt mit einer Riesenportion gewisses Etwas.

Dazu der Preis, ein frecher Fehdehandschuh mitten ins Gesicht der Konkurrenten im fraglichen Marktsegment: laserscharf kalkulierte 60950 Mark für die teurere der beiden Versionen mit 2,3 Liter-Triebwerk und Kompressor, 193 Pferdestärken stark. Die andere, mit einem Zweiliter-Saugmotor und 136 PS, kostet gar nur bescheidene 54510 Mark. Um diesen Betrag kriegt der glückliche Besitzer zwei Autos: Ein Druck auf eine kleine rote Taste, und das Coupé, als das man den SLK vielleicht noch beim Händler abgeholt hat, weil das Wetter einfach unausstehlich war, wechselt in 25 Sekunden seinen Aggregatzustand und wird zum Roadster. Jegliches Stoffliche entfällt, mithin alles, was flattern, knattern, frösteln machen, durchnässen oder eine schöne Form schnöde verstümmeln könnte.

Bevor Sonne, Mond und Sterne Zugang zum Inneren des SLK haben, laufen sechs penibel koordinierte Arbeitsgänge ab, angezettelt und durchgeführt von fünf Hydraulikzylindern, zwei für den Antrieb des Variodachs, zwei für die einladende Bewegung des Kofferraumdeckels, ein weiterer für die Verriegelung des Dachs am Scheibenrahmen, wenn die Sache wieder rückgängig gemacht wird. Am Ende ruht das Hardtop sorgfältig zerknickt und dem neugierigen Blick radikal entzogen im Kofferraum. Soweit die gute Nachricht. Die schlechte: Dass sich durch dieses singuläre technische Prozedere das Gepäckvolumen von passablen 348 Litern auf dürftige 145 verringert – längere Reisen in angemessenem Outfit wird man hochgeschlossen antreten müssen. Mit zwei Maßnahmen ist man der Raumnot hinten bereits werksseitig begegnet: Das Tankvolumen beträgt lediglich 53 Liter, und auf ein Reserverad (ein Faltrad gibt es als Option) wird gänzlich verzichtet. Im Falle jenes Falles, der laut Statistik nur alle 150000 Kilometer eintritt, leisten das Reifendichtmittel Tirefit und eine elektrische Luftpumpe erste Hilfe.

SLK, ein Mix aus bedeutsamen Mercedes-Kürzeln der Vergangenheit, bedeutet Sportlich, Leicht, Kurz. »Leicht«

Nous assistons avec elles à une renaissance de l'esthétique dans l'automobile », déclare Helmut Werner, président du directoire de Mercedes-Benz AG, comme s'il y avait eu un risque que l'on oublie tout cela dans l'ouragan dévastateur de la soufflerie.

Et, « dans une telle automobile, la route est la destination, » lui réplique Jürgen Hubbert, membre du directoire au titre du secteur d'activité Voitures de tourisme.

Ce n'est naturellement qu'un plaidoyer *pro domo* pour rallier les faveurs des hésitants, pour séduire de nouveaux clients. Sauf qu'elle n'a vraiment pas besoin de cela, la SLK, présentée au Salon de Turin en avril 1996, semi jeune Siegfried, semi Don Juan sous les traits d'une voiture et, de mémoire d'homme, la tentation la plus irrésistible en provenance d'Untertürkheim : un pare-brise peu élevé, un long capot moteur, deux larges portes et une poupe rectiligne, avec de faibles porte-à-faux à l'avant et à l'arrière pour un empattement relativement long de 2400 mm, tout assaisonné d'un certain « je-ne-sais-quoi ».

Surtout par son prix, qui est une véritable gifle pour ses concurrents : 60950 marks, prix calculé au plus juste pour la plus coûteuse des deux versions, à moteur de 2,3 litres et compresseur développant 193 ch. L'autre, avec moteur atmosphérique de 2 litres et 136 ch, ne coûte même que la somme modeste de 54510 marks. Et, qui plus est, pour cette somme, l'heureux propriétaire a deux voitures en une : une simple pression sur un petit bouton rouge et le coupé SLK que l'on vient d'acquérir se métamorphose en un roadster en 25 secondes. En l'absence de tout tissu disparaît aussi tout ce qui peut claquer, vibrer, engendrer des courants d'air, laisser passer la pluie où faire perdre tout son charme à une forme séduisante.

Avant que le soleil, la lune et les étoiles n'aient librement accès au cockpit de la SLK, se déroulent six processus minutieusement coordonnés, déclenchés et exécutés par cinq vérins hydrauliques, deux pour le mécanisme de toit escamotable, deux pour l'ouverture accueillante du couvercle de malle et un cinquième pour le verrouillage du toit sur le cadre du pare-brise lorsque se termine la procédure dans le sens inverse. À l'issue du processus, le *hardtop* disparaît aux regards curieux, dissimulé dans le coffre. Voilà pour les bonnes nouvelles. Quant à la mauvaise, ce processus technique unique au monde ramène la capacité du coffre, *a priori* acceptable, de 348 à 145 litres – on ne peut donc partir en voyage prolongé avec une certaine quantité de bagages qu'avec le toit fermé. Deux mesures sont censées pallier le manque d'espace à l'arrière : la capacité du réservoir n'est que de 53 litres et il n'y a pas la moindre roue de secours (une roue galette est proposée en option) : en cas de malheur – ce qui, selon les statistiques, ne se produit que tous les 150000 km – la bombe anticrevaison Tirefit et une pompe à air électrique permettent de porter les premiers secours.

SLK, un cocktail d'abréviations Mercedes riches en tradition, signifie Sportive, Légère, Courte. « Légère » est

Mercedes-Benz slk 200 – slk 230 1996

ercedes-Benz SLK 230 Kompressor 1996

ough: this mini Mercedes needs less parking space than
vw Golf. And it is definitely sporty, with a top speed
231 kph (144 mph), 0–100 kph (62 mph) in 7.5 seconds,
d with agile, quicksilver steering, while remaining,
ether the roof is up or down, as rigid and solid as the
ost stable Mercedes Benz sedan.

And everybody wants one: "I've already ordered
ne," declared Fritz B. Busch, the eloquent doyen of
erman automobile journalists, a man hardened and
ured to anything that goes on four wheels, "I wasn't
ing to hang about." And no wonder: the demand
outstrips supply, despite the fact that the production
nt in Bremen quickly took on 600 new employees. By
e beginning of October 1996 41,300 German slk fans
d ordered one.

ist, wie schon immer in der Geschichte der Marke, eine
charmante Schwindelei: Der slk 230 Kompressor bringt
immerhin 1325 Kilogramm auf die Waage. »Kurz« trifft
zweifellos zu: Der Baby-Benz nimmt weniger Parkraum
in Anspruch als ein vw Golf. Und sportlich ist er auch,
231 Stundenkilometer schnell, in 7,5 Sekunden auf
Tempo 100 und wieselflink zu lenken, dabei offen wie
geschlossen steif und rigide wie die stabilste Limousine
aus dem gleichen noblen Hause.

Und so wollen ihn alle haben: »Ich habe mir gleich
einen bestellt«, sagt etwa Fritz B. Busch, wortgewaltiger
Nestor unter den deutschen Motor-Schreibern, mit
allen Wassern gewaschen und abgebrüht gegen alles,
was vier Räder hat, »da gab es überhaupt kein Vertun.«
Kein Wunder: Die Nachfrage übersteigt entschieden
das Angebot, obwohl im Produktionswerk Bremen
flugs 600 neue Arbeitsplätze eingerichtet werden. Anfang
Oktober 1996 haben bereits 41300 deutsche Mitbürger
und slk-Beflissene einen Kaufvertrag in der Tasche.

comme toujours dans l'histoire de la marque, un euphémisme: la slk 230 Kompressor accuse tout de même un
poids de 1325 kg. «Courte» est sans aucun doute vrai: la
mini-Mercedes a besoin de moins d'espace pour se garer
qu'une vw Golf. Et, sportive, elle l'est bel et bien avec une
vitesse de pointe de 231 km/h, un temps de 7,5 secondes
pour le 0 à 100 km/h et une maniabilité de feu follet, tout
en étant tout aussi ferme et rigide, ouverte ou fermée, que
la berline la plus solide de la même noble maison.

Et c'est pourquoi tous veulent en avoir une. «Je m'en
suis commandée une tout de suite» déclare par exemple
Fritz B. Busch, plume prestigieuse s'il en est parmi les
journalistes spécialisés allemands, qui en a vu de toutes les
couleurs et a pris le volant de tout ce qui a quatre roues.
«On ne risque absolument pas de se tromper.» Et ce n'est
pas un miracle: la demande est très largement supérieure
à l'offre bien que 600 nouveaux emplois aient été créés
spécialement pour sa ligne de production à Brême. Début
octobre 1996, 41300 Allemands et adorateurs de slk avaient
d'ores et déjà un contrat en poche.

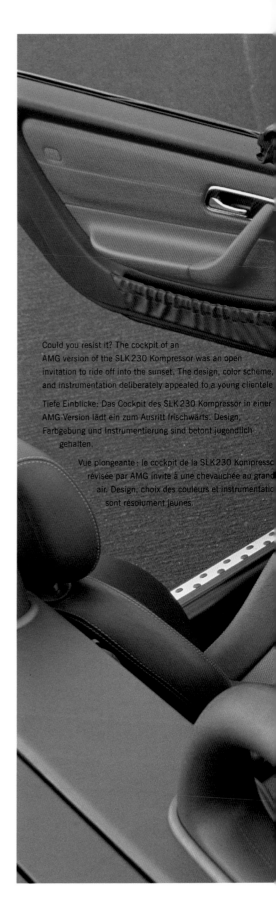

Could you resist it? The cockpit of an
AMG version of the SLK 230 Kompressor was an open
invitation to ride off into the sunset. The design, color scheme,
and instrumentation deliberately appealed to a young clientele

Tiefe Einblicke: Das Cockpit des SLK 230 Kompressor in einer
AMG-Version lädt ein zum Ausritt frischwärts. Design,
Farbgebung und Instrumentierung sind betont jugendlich
gehalten.

Vue plongeante: le cockpit de la SLK 230 Kompressor
révisée par AMG invite à une chevauchée au grand
air. Design, choix des couleurs et instrumentation
sont résolument jeunes.

The aerodynamically-polished skirts and five-spoke wheels were specific to the AMG model. It took just 25 seconds before the mobile hardtop disappeared from view into its recess.

Spezifisch für die AMG-Variante sind die aerodynamisch durchgefeilten Schweller und fünfzackige Felgen. Bevor das mobile Hardtop von der Bildfläche und in der Versenkung verschwunden ist, vergehen 25 Sekunden.

Les bas de caisse aérodynamiques et les jantes en étoile sont caractéristiques de la version AMG. Il faut 25 secondes seulement pour voir le *hard-top* disparaître dans son compartiment où il sait se faire oublier.

Appearances can be deceptive, and in this case they are intended to be: the visual resemblance of the AMG Mercedes designed for the 1996 International Touring Car Series (ITC) to the road car conceals state-of-the-art racing car technology which is only distantly related to the mass-market product.

It starts with the power unit, a 500 bhp, 110 kg (243 lb), 2.5-liter V6 engine, the cylinder banks of which are set at an angle of 90 degrees, thus allowing plenty of space for the induction system. It was developed from the V8 engine of the E 420 and S 420 models, though the generous regulations allow two cylinders to be dispensed with before the Mercedes and AMG (Mercedes' partner in the power department) engineers get expertly to work on the job of fine tuning and adjustment. The work includes increasing the rigidity of the cast components so that they can withstand the pressures and G-forces of racing conditions, and also the replacement of the usual steel valve springs with a pneumatic closing mechanism à la Formula 1.

Like the engine the drivetrain to the rear axle had to be shifted a little to the right, and the transmission (sequential, with six gears operated by buttons on the steering wheel) had to be be tilted at a right angle to the longitudinal direction. The reason for these changes was that the driver sat in a carbon-fiber composite seat almost in the middle of the car, protected against the massive side impact of an accident by the space between him and the side of the car, by head rests with forward projecting cheek pieces, by padding and robust longitudinal bracing, and also by crashpads in the door area. Safety first was the watchword, just as with the road cars. The same purpose was served by the improved airbag, wide safety belt, and a highly effective roll cage, the strength of which was the product of an investment by the technicians of over 800 working hours per vehicle.

The suspension incorporated classic racing technology: double suspension arms and units composed of gas pressure shock absorbers and coil springs, operated by diagonal ties. The driver could personally fine-tune the roll steer effect, since the stabilizers were hydraulically adjustable during the race. The doors – steel plate at the front, carbon fiber at the rear – only reach down as far as the middle of the wheel. This was also permitted under the race regulations, which additionally raised no objection to the modular design of the Mercedes Class 1 Racing Car. The car was composed of three maintenance-friendly elements: after releasing four screw joints and a small number of connections the engine, front axle, steering and radiator could be detached from the middle part of the bodywork, and at the rear the same went for the rear axle and the differential.

Clearly a born winner, just like the C Class Mercedes of the two previous years. But the fortunes of the race track also play their part: another team won the 1996 ITC.

Der Schein trügt, und das soll er auch: Das visuell seriennahe Gewand des AMG-Mercedes für die International Touring Car Series (ITC) 1996 verhüllt hohe Renn-Technologie vom Edelsten, mit dem Fließband-Produkt allenfalls entfernt verwandt.

Das beginnt mit der treibenden Kraft, einem 500 PS starken und 110 kg leichten kompakten V6 von 2,5 Litern, dessen Bänke sich im weiten Winkel von 90 Grad öffnen und somit viel Freiraum für die Ansauganlage lassen. Abgeleitet ist er vom V8 der Modelle E 420 und S 420. Allerdings – so gestattet es das liberale Reglement – bleiben zwei Zylinder auf der Strecke, ehe sich die Motor-Chirurgen von Mercedes und AMG, Partner in Potenz-fragen, mit kundigen Händen an die Feinarbeit machen. Dazu gehört, dass man die Steifigkeit der Gussteile steigert, um den hohen Arbeitsdrücken und Massen-kräften des Rennbetriebs zu begegnen. Dazu zählt ebenso die Umstellung von herkömmlichen Ventilfedern aus Stahl auf einen pneumatischen Schließmechanismus – analog zur Formel 1.

Wie die Maschine muss auch der Antriebsstrang zur Hinterachse ein Stück nach rechts ausweichen, das Getriebe (sequentiell, mit sechs Gängen, die mit Tasten am Lenkrad geschaltet werden) in Längsrichtung im rechten Winkel gedreht werden. Der Grund: Der Pilot lagert in einer Sitzschale aus Kohlefaser-Verbundwerkstoff fast in der Mitte, gegen gewaltsame Einwirkungen von der Seite bei einem Unfall durch viel Raum, Kopfstützen mit nach vorne gezogenen Wangen, Polsterungen und robuste Längsverstrebungen sowie Crashpads im Türbereich abgesichert. Safety first – wie in der Serie, so auch im Sport. Dem gleichen Ziel dienen ein verbesserter Airbag, breite Gurte und ein trotziger Überrollkäfig, in dessen Widerstandsfähigkeit die Techniker seit dem Vorjahr 800 Arbeitsstunden pro Auto investiert haben.

Die Aufhängungen verkörpern klassische Renntech-nik: doppelte Querlenker, Einheiten aus Gasdruck-Stoß-dämpfern und Schraubenfedern, die über Zugstreben betätigt werden. In die Feinabstimmung des Eigenlenk-verhaltens kann der Fahrer persönlich eingreifen, denn die Stabilisatoren sind während der Fahrt hydraulisch verstellbar. Die Türen – vorn aus Stahlblech, hinten aus Karbon – reichen nur noch bis auf die Höhe der Radmitte nach unten. Auch das gestattet das Regelwerk, das überdies gegen die Modulbauweise des Klasse-1-Rennwagens von Mercedes nichts einzuwenden hat. Dieser ist wartungs-freundlich aus drei Elementen komponiert: Nach dem Lösen von vier Schraubverbindungen und wenigen Anschlüssen kann der Motor nebst Vorderachse, Lenkung und Kühlern nach vorn aus dem Karosserie-Mittelteil herausgefahren werden. Achtern gilt für die Hinterachse mit dem Differential das gleiche Prinzip.

Offenbar hat man da einen geborenen Sieger in die Welt gesetzt wie mit den C-Klasse-Mercedes der beiden Vorjahre. Aber dann mischt sich die Fortuna der Renn-strecken ein – Gewinner der ITC 1996 wird jemand anders.

L'habit ne fait pas le moine, mais cela est voul[u] visuellement proche de la série, la robe de l'AM[G] Mercedes pour l'International Touring Car Seri[es] (ITC), en 1996, incarne le haut de gamme en matière [de] technologie de compétition, à des années-lumière de [la] production à la chaîne.

Cela commence par le groupe propulseur, un V6 [de] 2,5 litres développant 500 ch, compact et léger avec 110 k[g] dont les bancs de cylindres décrivent un angle de 90° [et] laissent ainsi suffisamment d'espace pour les collecteu[rs] d'admission. Il est dérivé du V8 de la E 420 et de la S 42[0]. Mais – le règlement libéral l'autorise – il a été amputé [de] deux cylindres avant que les chirurgiens motoristes de ch[ez] Mercedes et AMG ne s'attaquent aux ultimes travaux. Il [a] fallu pour cela accroître la rigidité des éléments en fon[te] pour encaisser les pressions de travail et forces de mas[se] énormes de la compétition et remplacer les ressorts [de] soupapes traditionnels en acier par un système de ferm[e]-ture pneumatique copié sur la Formule 1.

Comme le moteur, il a aussi fallu décaler légèreme[nt] vers la droite la chaîne de transmission, et la boîte [de] vitesses (séquentielle, avec six rapports actionnés par d[es] touches au volant) a été retournée de 90° dans le se[ns] longitudinal. Explication: le pilote prend place dans u[n] baquet en fibre de carbone et matériau composite presqu[e] au centre de la voiture, parfaitement protégé de l'impa[ct] d'une collision violente par beaucoup d'espace, un appui-tête avec des joues latérales proéminentes, des rembou[r]-rages et de robustes renforts longitudinaux ainsi que d[es] coussins anticollision dans les portières. Safety first – [en] série comme en compétition. Tel est aussi l'objectif d'u[n] airbag amélioré, de larges ceintures et d'un imposa[nt] arceau-cage de sécurité dans la résistance de laquelle l[es] techniciens ont investi 800 heures de travail par voiture.

Les suspensions représentent une technique de comp[é]-tition classique: doubles triangles transversaux, combin[és] amortisseurs à gaz et ressorts hélicoïdaux actionnés p[ar] tirants. Le pilote peut intervenir personnellement dans [la] répartition du comportement, car les barres antirou[lis] sont réglables hydrauliquement pendant la conduite. L[es] portières – en tôle d'acier et en carbone – ne descende[nt] plus que jusqu'à mi-hauteur des roues. Cela aussi est aut[o]-risé par le règlement qui n'a, en outre, rien à dire cont[re] la construction modulaire de la voiture de course de [la] Classe 1 de Mercedes qui se compose de trois élément[s]: après avoir déverrouillé quatre fixations rapides [et] démonté quelques branchements, le moteur peut êt[re] extrait de la partie centrale de la carrosserie avec l'essie[u] avant, la direction et les radiateurs. À l'arrière, il en va c[e] même pour l'essieu avec le différentiel.

Apparemment, on a engendré un vainqueur-né av[ec] la Mercedes Classe C les deux années précédentes. Ma[is] rien n'est moins sûr que le succès sur les circuits du mon[de] – la victoire au championnat ITC 1996 aura été remport[ée] par quelqu'un d'autre.

AMG Mercedes c-Klasse (Klasse 1) 1996

Even the solid tail of a C-class Mercedes, dominated by a projecting spoiler, appeared to symbolize the determination to win.

Selbst das stämmige Heck des Mercedes der C-Klasse, beherrscht von einem ausladenden Luftleitwerk, scheint die Entschlossenheit zum Sieg auszudrücken.

Même la poupe râblée de la Mercedes Classe C dominée par son imposant becquet semble exprimer la volonté de vaincre.

The front and rear sections could be completely removed. In compliance with racing rules, the doors reached only to the level of the wheel hubs. They were made of sheet steel at the front and carbon fiber at the rear.

Front- und Heckteil sind komplett abnehmbar. Die Türen reichen reglementskonform nur bis zur Höhe der Radnaben. Sie sind vorne aus Stahlblech und hinten aus Kohlefaser.

Les parties avant et arrière sont totalement démontables. Conformément au règlement, les portières ne descendent que jusqu'à hauteur des moyeux de roues. Elles sont en acier à l'avant et en fibre de carbone à l'arrière.

AMG Mercedes C-Klasse (Klasse 1) 1996

The sturdy V6 derived from a placid eight-cylinder production engine and weighed only just over two hundredweight. Nonetheless, enhanced rigidity in the castings increased its durability.

Der gedrungene V6 stammt von einem friedfertigen Serientriebwerk mit acht Zylindern ab und wiegt nur knapp über zwei Zentner. Dennoch steigert erhöhte Steifigkeit der Gussteile seine Standfestigkeit.

Le compact V6 dérive d'un pacifique huit-cylindres de série et pèse un peu plus de 100 kg. La rigidité accrue des pièces en fonte augmente cependant sa fiabilité.

In scouring the market for new customer base, the Untertürkheim strategists have struck gold in the 1990s not only with previously peripheral socio-economic groups as regards Mercedes ownership, but also with once atypical age groups. Thus the CLK, launched in Detroit in January 1997, offers a perfectly-targeted status symbol for upwardly-mobile thirty-somethings. As the company literature movingly puts it, it is aimed at "the young and the young at heart." But they really go a little too far in that direction with the so-called Carbon look of the interior – the color combinations are unconventional, almost garish, while the pale instruments seem bland by comparison. In fact the CLK does not need such gimmicks. It is an elegant well-proportioned machine with softly curving lines, both classless and coming between two classes, in that the underbody and chassis come from the C-class, while the "four-eyed face" was borrowed from the E-class. In size too it is intermediate, being 8 cm (3.1 in) longer than the C-class but 23 cm (9 in) shorter than the E-class. However, it does not seem small – after all, a Mercedes coupé must have a certain presence.

As you would expect from a car of this type, both the sense of space and the actual space available are much greater in the front seats than in the rear. Access to the two individual rear seats is made easier by the so-called Easy Entry system: operating a handle makes the front seat slide forwards while its back folds down. The attractively carpeted trunk has a storage capacity of 420 liters, and the backs of the rear seats can be folded from one third to two thirds of the way forwards to provide additional space. The regular version of the CLK, the Sport, offers a long list of standard features from automatic childseat sensors to green-tinted heat-insulating glass. The more expensive Elegance adds such features as five-spoke alloy wheels.

Both versions use the new "access and authorization system," using an electronic fob with no key bit instead of the old ignition key not only to unlock the doors, but also to lock them all automatically when driving off. It is inserted and turned in the usual way to start the car. The CLK 200 is a four-cylinder, 136 bhp, fuel-injection engine, while the CLK 230 Kompressor's supercharger generates 193 bhp. The CLK 320's power unit is Mercedes' latest six-cylinder engine, in V configuration, with three-valve technology producing 218 bhp, and also the CLK 430's v8, generating 279 horsepower. Both are equipped as standard with an excellent automatic transmission with five drive positions. At first the introduction of the v6 engine caused concern among the experts: would it provide the same silky drive as the old straight six? The answer: not quite, and yet … although the sound of the engine is not quite the same, it still bespeaks sonorous power, while the actual drive quality is more or less identical.

The decision to buy a CLK will come from the heart, but with the head also playing a part, in the judgement of the trade magazine *auto motor und sport*. Not the worst compromise.

Beim Ausleuchten des Markts nach neuer Klientel werden die Untertürkheimer Strategen in den Neunzigern bei den sozialen Randgruppen der bisherigen Mercedes-Welt ebenso fündig wie in bislang untypischen Altersstufen. So stellt man mit dem CLK, der im Januar 1997 in Detroit debütiert, dem dynamisch-arrivierten Mittdreißiger ein schmuckes Statussymbol in die Garage. Er sei, preist ihn die Firmenliteratur mit bewegten Worten, ein Angebot für »junge und junggebliebene Menschen«. Zugleich schießt man mit der so genannten Karbon-Optik des Interieurs fast schon ein bisschen über das Ziel hinaus: Da finden sich unkonventionelle, fast schon fetzige Farbkombinationen, während die Instrumente den Fahrer gewöhnungsbedürftig bleich anschauen. Dabei hätte der CLK dergleichen gar nicht nötig, eine automobile Schönheit mit weich geschwungenen Linien und wohlproportionierten Formen, im Grunde klassenlos und zwischen den Klassen: Bodengruppe und Fahrwerk entsprechen der C-Klasse, das Vier-Augen-Gesicht wurde von der E-Klasse übernommen. Auch was seine Dimensionen anbelangt, liegt er zwischen den Marken-Kollegen, acht Zentimeter über dem C-Modell, 23 Zentimeter kürzer als ein E. Gleichwohl wirkt er nicht klein – eine gewisse Statur muss ein Mercedes-Coupé schon mitbringen.

Was sich bei Autos dieser Spezies eigentlich von selbst versteht: Raumgefühl und faktisches Platzangebot sind vorne ungleich üppiger als hinten. Der Zugang zum Fond mit seinen beiden Einzelsitzen wird einem durch eine Einstieghilfe mit Namen Easy Entry erleichtert. Nach Betätigung eines Hebels an der vorderen Sitzlehne wird nicht nur diese selbst nach vorne geklappt, sondern via Federkraft der komplette Fauteuil nach vorn gefahren. Das Kofferabteil mit seiner attraktiven Teppichauskleidung, 420 Liter geräumig, mag man gar nicht beschmutzen. Die Rückenlehnen der hinteren Sitze lassen sich im Verhältnis ein Drittel zu zwei Drittel umlegen, was zusätzliches Stauvolumen schafft. Schon in der Basis-Linie, Sport genannt, bietet der CLK eine lange Liste Nützliches und Erstrebenswertes, von der automatischen Kindersitzerkennung (AKSE) bis hin zu grünem Wärme dämmendem Glas rundum. Die teurere Elegance-Linie sattelt da in mancher Hinsicht drauf, mit Leichtmetallrädern im Fünfloch-Design zum Beispiel.

Beiden gemeinsam: das neue »Zugangs- und Berechtigungssystem«. Mit einem bartlosen Elektronikkästchen statt des herkömmlichen Zündschlüssels verschafft man sich nicht nur den Zutritt zum CLK. Es sorgt auch für die automatische Verriegelung der Türen nach dem Anfahren. Indem es wie gewohnt eingeführt und zum Starten gedreht wird, lässt sich schließlich auch der Motor anlassen, im CLK 200 und CLK 230 Kompressor Vierzylinder-Einspritzer ohne oder mit Aufladung und 136 PS beziehungsweise 193 PS. Im CLK 320 meldet sich dann der jüngste Sechszylinder des Hauses zu Wort, in V-Form, 218 PS stark und mit Dreiventiltechnik wie auch der v8 im CLK 430, der 279 PS leistet. Beide sind serienmäßig zusam-

En quête de segments du marché pas encore défri chés, les stratèges de Untertürkheim des année 1990 voient leurs recherches couronnées de succè dans des groupes marginaux de la société du monde Me cedes conventionnel ou encore dans des tranches d'âg jusque-là atypiques. Ainsi, avec la CLK qui fait ses débu à Detroit en janvier 1997, ils proposent aux moins d quarante ans dynamiques et argentés un joli symbole d réussite. Il s'agit, déclarent en termes éloquents les public taires de la marque, d'une offre pour « les jeunes et ceux qu le sont restés ». Simultanément, avec le pack carbone pro posé pour le cockpit, ils en font déjà peut-être un pe trop : on y trouve des combinaisons de coloris non conven tionnels, presque tape-à-l'œil, alors que les instrument regardent le conducteur d'un œil blafard. Et pourtant, l CLK n'aurait pas besoin de tous ces artifices, car c'est un beauté automobile avec ses lignes au galbe élégant et se formes bien proportionnées, en quelque sorte inclassable e entre les classes : la plate-forme et les trains roulants son ceux de la Classe C alors que le visage aux quatre yeux a ét repris de la Classe E. En ce qui concerne ses dimension également, elle se situe entre ses deux sœurs, huit cent mètres plus longue que la C, mais 23 centimètres plus court que la E. Elle n'a pourtant rien d'une petite voiture – un coup Mercedes doit en effet en imposer avec une certaine statur

Chose qui va vraiment de soi pour les voitures de cett catégorie, la sensation d'espace et l'habitabilité réelle son incomparablement plus généreuses à l'avant qu'à l'arrièr L'accès à l'arrière avec ses deux fauteuils individuels es facilité par un dispositif baptisé *Easy Entry*. Un levier plac sur le dossier de siège avant ne permet pas seulement d rabattre celui-ci, mais aussi, grâce à des ressorts, de fair avancer le fauteuil dans son ensemble. Avec son attrayan moquette, le coffre d'une capacité de 420 litres est s luxueux que l'on a peur de le salir. Les dossiers des sièg sont rabattables symétriquement à raison de deux tiers-u tiers, ce qui crée un volume de chargement supplémen taire. La finition de base de la CLK, baptisée Sport, off une longue liste d'accessoires utiles et enviés, de la recon naissance automatique d'occupation du siège enfant au vitres de couleur verte réfléchissant la chaleur. Un peu plu coûteuse, la ligne Elegance en rajoute encore, notammen avec des jantes alliage à cinq trous.

Les deux versions ont en commun le nouvea « système d'habilitation à la conduite ». Une bizarre cle électronique sans panneton à la place de la clef de contac traditionnelle ne permet pas seulement d'accéder à la CL Elle assure aussi le verrouillage automatique des portière après le démarrage. Il suffit de l'introduire et de la tourne comme une clef classique pour faire ensuite démarrer l moteur, dans la CLK 200 et la CLK 230 Kompressor, de quatre-cylindres à injection sans ou avec suralimentatio développant respectivement 136 ou 193 ch. Sous le capot d la CLK 320, on trouve le tout dernier six-cylindres maiso en V, délivrant 218 ch, à culasse à trois soupapes comm pour le v8 de la CLK 430, qui développe 279 ch. Ils son

Mercedes-Benz CLK 200–CLK 430 1997

Mercedes-Benz CLK 320 1997

mengespannt mit einer Fünfstufen-Automatik, mit der sie sich prächtig verstehen. Das Erscheinen der v6-Triebwerke löste zunächst Unruhe unter den Kennern aus: Würden sie mit der gleichen Seidigkeit aufwarten wie die Reihensechszylinder der Vergangenheit? Nicht ganz, und doch: Das Klangbild ist anders als früher, aber von sonorer Kräftigkeit. Und ein Unterschied in der Laufkultur ist kaum festzustellen.

Der CLK sei ein Auto, das mit Emotionen gekauft werde, die Ratio aber nicht unberücksichtigt lasse, wertet das Fachmagazin *auto motor und sport*. Das ist nicht der schlechteste Kompromiss.

accolés de série à une boîte automatique à cinq vitesses avec laquelle ils s'entendent à la perfection. L'annonce des moteurs v6 a tout d'abord déclenché des remous parmi les initiés: seraient-ils aussi soyeux que les six-cylindres du passé? Pas tout à fait, et pourtant: leur chant est différent de jadis, mais d'une vigueur bien sonore. Et l'on ne constate pratiquement aucune différence en ce qui concerne la douceur de fonctionnement.

La CLK est une voiture que l'on achète avec le cœur, mais qui ne laisse pas de côté la raison, a écrit un jour la revue spécialisée *auto motor und sport*. Et ce n'est pas le pire des compromis.

The CLK320's
powerplant: a V6 with
three valves per
cylinder and double
overhead camshafts.
In performance terms
it was scarcely inferior
to a straight-six.

Das Triebwerk des
CLK320: ein V6 mit
drei Ventilen je Zylinder
und zwei oben liegenden
Nockenwellen. In seiner
Laufkultur steht es
einem Reihensechs-
zylinder kaum nach.

Le moteur de la
CLK320: un V6 à trois
soupapes par cylindre
et deux arbres à cames
en tête qui ne le cède
pratiquement en rien
aux six-cylindres en
ligne par sa douceur
de fonctionnement.

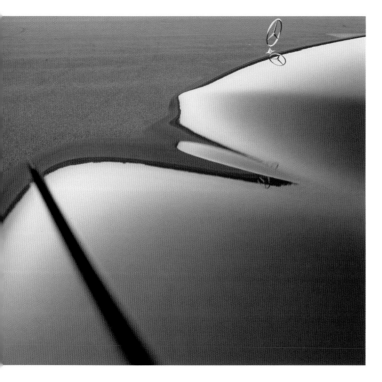

Mercedes-Benz CLK200–CLK430 1997

The CLK was the embodiment of the company's new maxim, namely that the combination of beautiful parts inevitably creates a beautiful whole.

Auch für den CLK gilt das neue Prinzip des Hauses, dass das schöne Ganze aus dem Miteinander schöner Teile erwächst.

Pour la CLK aussi, prévaut le nouveau principe de la maison selon lequel la beauté de l'ensemble résulte de la coexistence de jolis composants.

Beautiful: the CLK cabriolet was launched in 1998 as an open declaration of war on the rest of the cabriolet sector. When you pull a lever on the mid console the tight, firm cabriolet top conceals itself beneath a solid metal lid within 30 seconds.

Schöne Windsbraut: 1998 erscheint das CLK-Cabriolet als offene Kriegserklärung an den Rest der Cabrio-Welt. Das straff sitzende Verdeck verkriecht sich innerhalb von 30 Sekunden unter einem festen Deckel, nachdem man an einem Schalter auf der Mittelkonsole gezogen hat.

La jolie fiancée du vent : en 1998 paraît le cabriolet CLK – déclaration de guerre ouverte au reste du monde des cabriolets. La capote bien tendue disparaît en 30 secondes dans un compartiment étanche après que l'on a actionné une commande sur la console médiane.

Where there's a will, there's a way: when the world motor sport organizing body Fédération Internationale de l'Automobile decreed that the production car championship for 1997 would be staged as the new FIA GT championship, Mercedes took just 128 days to come up with the CLK-GTR, the top model in the CLK range. In December 1996 the Mercedes motor sports subsidiary AMG of Affalterbach began to design and build a suitable vehicle, and by the end of March driver Bernd Schneider was testing the finished product in Jarama in Spain – with encouraging results.

The CLK-GTR is the first mid-engined Mercedes production racing car. It is based on a road car for somewhat higher income groups, for people who are not put off by the massive price tag of 2,640,000 marks for each specimen of this limited edition vehicle. A clause in the sport's homologation rules leaves a back door open for the road version of the GTR to be completed somewhat later: as required under the regulations, the racing variant met just 16 of the 34 conditions laid down for homologation in the European Community.

While the racing version's six liter engine with twelve cylinders generates 600 horsepower, the road version's 6.9 liter engine produces 560 bhp. The engine is based on the S 600. A Bosch-Motronic serves as a control center for ignition and fuel injection. The power unit, which is fastened to the back of the monocoque, has a supporting function, as does the axle drive and transmission unit, and the rear wheel suspension is attached to their housing.

The power of the twelve cylinder engine is transmitted by a transversely-mounted six-speed aluminum gearbox. The driver changes gear sequentially using a gear lever. The chassis geometry is taken from the previous year's racer, and features double suspension arms at front and rear and springs controlled by diagonal ties. The front wheel's suspension is attached directly to the monocoque, which also encases the 100 liter petrol tank. In tandem with the steel roll cage this ensures a high degree of rigidity and passive safety. Like the front and side crash boxes, the passenger safety cage and the projecting rear spoilers, the bodywork is made of carbon fiber composite. The windshield is laminated glass and the other windows are polycarbonate. The only things remaining from the original road car are the general outline, the radiator grill, the four-eyed look – and the name.

The GTR was put out to grass after the first two races of the 1998 season. A wooden board 30 mm thick has now been installed between the axles at the FIA's behest, increasing the minimum ground clearance and preventing the chassis from coming into contact with the ground.

The next staging post in the evolution of the racing version of the CLK is the LM (standing for Le Mans), which is similar in appearance, has a marginally smaller cubic capacity and the same performance. However, behind the driver now is a V8 engine derived from the M119 production power unit which also does service on the S and SL, as

Wo ein Wille ist, werden die Wege kurz: Auf das Dekret der Weltmotorsportbehörde Fédération Internationale de l'Automobile hin, den Wettbewerb mit Produktionswagen 1997 auf der neuen Bühne der FIA-GT-Meisterschaft zu inszenieren, zaubert Mercedes in nur 128 Tagen den CLK-GTR aus dem Hut, die höchste Ausbaustufe der CLK-Serie. Im Dezember 1996 beginnt die Rennsportfiliale AMG in Affalterbach mit Entwurf und Herstellung eines geeigneten Fahrzeugs. Ende März 1997 testet Pilot Bernd Schneider das fertige Auto im spanischen Jarama – mit ermutigenden Ergebnissen.

Der CLK-GTR ist der erste Produktionsrennwagen der Marke mit Mittelmotor. Er basiert auf einer bürgerlichen Version für Besserverdiener, die sich selbst durch den monumentalen Preis von 2 640 000 Mark je Exemplar aus einer limitierten Edition von 25 nicht einschüchtern lassen. Eine Klausel in der Sporthomologation lässt das Hintertürchen offen, die zivile Fassung des GTR gewissermaßen nachreichen zu dürfen. Denn die scharfe Variante erfüllt reglementskonform 16 der 34 Bedingungen, die zu einer Typengenehmigung in der Europäischen Gemeinschaft verlangt werden.

Während der Zwölfzylinder auf der Rennstrecke rund 600 PS aus nur sechs Litern schöpft, mobilisiert sein Pendant für den öffentlichen Straßenverkehr aus 6,9 Litern Hubraum 560 PS. Basis ist der Motor aus dem S 600. Als Steuerungszentrale für Zündung und Einspritzung dient eine Bosch-Motronic. Die Maschine, mit der Rückwand des Monocoques verschraubt, hat tragende Funktion wie auch die Einheit aus Achsantrieb und Schaltgetriebe. An deren Gehäuse ist die hintere Radaufhängung befestigt.

Die Potenz des Zwölfzylinders vermittelt ein quer eingebautes Sechsgang-Getriebe aus Aluminium. Der Fahrer wechselt die Fahrstufen sequentiell mit der Hand am Schalthebel. Von dem Renntourenwagen der C-Klasse in Vorjahr übernimmt man die Fahrwerksgeometrie: Doppelquerlenker vorn und hinten, Federn, die über Zugstreben betätigt werden. Die Aufhängung der Vorderräder ist direkt am Monocoque befestigt, das auch den 100-Liter-Tank umschließt. Zusammen mit dem Überrollkäfig aus Stahl sorgt es für hohe Steifigkeit und viel passive Sicherheit. Wie die Crash Boxes vorn und in den Flanken, die Fahrgastzelle und der ausladende Heckflügel ist die Karosserie aus Kohlefaser-Verbundstoff gefertigt. Die Frontscheibe besteht aus Verbundglas, der Rest der Fenster aus Polycarbonat. Von dem Basis-Produkt bleiben eigentlich nur die vagen Umrisse, der Kühlergrill, der Vieraugen-Look – und der Name.

Aufs verdiente Altenteil abgeschoben wird der GTR erst nach den ersten beiden Rennen der Saison 1998. Eine 30 Millimeter starke Holzplatte zwischen den Achsen – so will es die FIA – vergrößert inzwischen die Mindestbodenfreiheit und wirkt dem Aufsetzen des Chassis auf dem Asphalt entgegen.

An der nächsten Gelenkstelle in der Evolution des Renn-CLK findet sich der LM (für Le Mans) mit ähnlicher

Qui veut la fin veut les moyens : à la suite d[...] décret publié par la Fédération internationa[...] de l'automobile, l'autorité de tutelle pour l[...] sports mécaniques, qui met en scène les courses de voitur[...] de production en 1997 dans le cadre du championn[...] FIA-GT, le magicien Mercedes sort de son chapeau, e[...] seulement 128 jours, la CLK-GTR, l'évolution la plus pou[...] sée de la série CLK. En décembre 1996, le compte à rebou[...] commence au service course AMG, à Affalterbach, avec le[...] plans et la fabrication d'une voiture appropriée. Fin ma[...] 1997, le pilote Bernd Schneider teste la voiture sur le ci[...] cuit espagnol de Jarama – les résultats sont encourageant[...]

La CLK-GTR est la première voiture de course de pr[...] duction de la marque à l'étoile qui possède un moteu[...] central. Elle est extrapolée d'une version civile destiné[...] aux nantis qui ne se laissent pas effrayer par le prix d[...] 2 640 000 marks pour chaque exemplaire d'une éditio[...] limitée à 25 unités. Une clause de l'homologation laisse un[...] porte entrouverte pour présenter a posteriori la versio[...] civile de la GTR. La variante de course s'avère conforme a[...] règlement en remplissant 16 des 34 conditions exigées pou[...] une homologation dans la Communauté européenne.

Le douze-cylindres de circuit fournit environ 600 ch[...] partir de 6 litres. Son homologue pour la circulation rou[...] tière en délivre 560 ch à partir d'une cylindrée de 6,9 litre[...]

La base en est le moteur de S 600. La centrale de gestio[...] de l'allumage et de l'injection est une Bosch-Motronic[...] Boulonné à la paroi postérieure de la monocoque, l[...] moteur est porteur, au même titre que le bloc demi-arbres[...] boîte de vitesses, dont le carter sert de fixation pour l[...] suspension arrière.

Une boîte à six vitesses transversale en aluminium[...] transmet la puissance du douze-cylindres aux roues arrière[...] Le pilote change de rapport avec une commande séquen[...] tielle et garde la main au volant. Les épures de suspensio[...] sont les mêmes que pour les voitures de course qui on[...] disputé le championnat de tourisme de la saison précédent[...] les Classe C : double triangulation transversale à l'avant e[...] à l'arrière, ressorts actionnés par tirants. La suspension de[...] roues avant est fixée sur la monocoque, qui englobe aussi le[...] réservoir de 100 litres. Avec l'arceau-cage de sécurité e[...] acier, elle est garante d'une grande rigidité torsionnelle e[...] d'une sécurité passive optimale. Comme les crash boxes[...] l'avant et sur les côtés, la cellule de pilotage et l'ailero[...] arrière, la carrosserie est fabriquée en matériaux composite[...] et fibre de carbone. Le pare-brise est en verre triplex, le[...] autres vitres étant en polycarbonate. Du produit de base, i[...] ne reste plus que les contours de la carrosserie – et encore ! –[...] la calandre, le look à quatre yeux et le nom.

La GTR ne prendra une retraite méritée qu'à l'issue de[...] deux premières courses de la saison 1998. Un sabot de bois[...] de 30 mm d'épaisseur entre les essieux – imposé par la FIA[...] – accroît entre-temps la garde au sol minimale et empêche[...] le châssis de frotter sur l'asphalte. Le prochain maillo[...] dans la chaîne de la CLK de course est incarné par la LM[...] (pour Le Mans), de forme similaire avec une cylindrée à[...]

Mercedes-Benz CLR 1999

well as the E class. This power plant remained a constant factor in the development of the CLR which contested Le Mans on 12 June 1999, featuring a smaller frontal area and a 10 centimeter reduction in height from its predecessor. The spectacular aerial crashes there have now revealed the fatal shortcomings in the overall aerodynamic design, which sails too close to the wind and, on the Sarthe course at any rate, is clearly not a practical proposition.

Form, kaum weniger Hubraum und gleicher Leistung. Allerdings sitzt dem Piloten nun ein V8 im Nacken, sublimiert aus dem Serienaggregat M119, wie es in den Typen S und SL sowie in der E-Klasse Dienst tut. Dieses Triebwerk bleibt als Konstante, als für den Einsatz in Le Mans am 12. Juni 1999 der CLR entwickelt wird, mit einer geringeren Stirnfläche und zehn Zentimeter niedriger als der Vorgänger. Die spektakulären Flugnummern dort indessen decken die fatalen Defizite eines aerodynamischen Gesamtkonzepts auf, das zu hart an die Grenzen geht: Es ist zumindestens auf dem Sarthe-Kurs nicht praktikabel.

peine inférieure et une puissance identique. Mais le pilote a dans le dos un moteur V8, sublimé à partir du groupe de série qui accomplit de bons et loyaux services sous le capot des Mercedes S et SL ainsi que de la Classe E. Ce moteur est déclaré bon pour le service et est perfectionné pour propulser la CLR au Mans, le 12 juin 1999, CLR qui possède un moindre maître-couple et est 10 cm plus basse que sa devancière. Les spectaculaires envols sur le circuit manceau mettent en revanche à jour le déficit d'un concept aérodynamique qui flirte trop avec la limite : il est impraticable, tout au moins sur le circuit de la Sarthe.

The same proviso applied to the shape of the GTR as to its overall design: any connections with the friendly CLK on which it was based were tenuous. The generously formulated rules made this possible.

Für die Form des GTR gilt das gleiche wie für seine Konstruktion insgesamt: Die Anklänge an das freundliche Basisprodukt CLK sind nur zart und vage. Ein freizügiges Regelwerk macht's möglich.

La même chose vaut autant pour la forme de la GTR que pour sa construction dans son ensemble : les réminiscences de la CLK comme pacifique produit de base sont peu nombreuses et très vagues. Le règlement est en effet très libéral.

The mid-mounted and longitudinally configured engine of the CLK-GTR was derived from the V12 of the S600 and SL600. The rear suspension was attached to the gearbox casing.

Abgeleitet vom V12 des S600 und SL600, ist die Maschine des CLK-GTR in Mittelmotoranordnung längs mittragend angeordnet. Die hintere Radaufhängung ist am Getriebegehäuse befestigt.

Dérivé du V12 de la S600 et de la SL600, le moteur de la CLK-GTR est placé en position longitudinale, au centre. La suspension arrière est ancrée sur le carter de boîte de vitesses.

A special solution for the car of Italian driver Alessandro Nannini who could hardly move his right hand following a helicopter accident: two large levers for changing up and down.

Besondere Lösung für den Wagen des Italieners Alessandro Nannini, der seit einem Hubschrauber-Unfall seine rechte Hand kaum bewegen kann: zwei massive Hebel für das Herauf- und das Herunterschalten.

Solution particulière pour la voiture de l'Italien Alessandro Nannini qui, depuis son accident d'hélicoptère, ne peut pratiquement plus mouvoir sa main droite : deux massifs leviers pour monter et descendre les vitesses.

Red faces: at the 1998 Le Mans 24-hour race both the
CLK-LMs retired early. Since then, however, all obstacles
to a successful run have been removed.

Rote Ohren: Beim 24-Stunden-Rennen von Le Mans 1998
fallen die beiden CLK-LM frühzeitig aus. Damit sind
indessen alle Hindernisse für eine glänzende Karriere aus
dem Wege geräumt.

Le rouge de la honte: aux 24 Heures du Mans 1998,
les deux CLK-LM abandonnent prématurément. Mais elles
ont, dès lors, mangé leur pain noir et rien ne s'oppose plus
à une carrière brillante pendant le reste de la saison.

Mercedes-Benz CLK-GTR–CLR 1997

Literally true: the Mercedes-Benz CLR was billed as a "one day flier" in the March 1999 edition of *Mercedes-Magazin,* and so it turned out: on the second weekend in June they caused alarm by taking spectacularly to the air before being withdraw from the event, where not already destroyed in any case.

Beim Wort genommen: Als »Eintagsflieger« werden die Mercedes-Benz CLR im *Mercedes-Magazin* vom März 1999 angekündigt. In der Tat – am zweiten Wochenende im Juni überraschen sie durch spektakuläre Flugeinlagen und werden dann, soweit nicht bereits zerstört, aus dem Verkehr gezogen.

Pris au mot : dans la revue *Mercedes-Magazin* de mars 1999, les Mercedes-Benz CLR étaient qualifiées d'« éphémères ». De fait, le second week-end de juin, les coléoptères argentés surprennent le monde entier par leurs envols spectaculaires et, dans la mesure où ils n'ont pas déjà été endommagés à cette occasion, déclarent ensuite forfait.

The launch of the smallest Mercedes yet was prepared as carefully as the staged entrance of a superstar. Four years earlier, market research at the Frankfurt IAA tested public reactions, and two years before the launch all relevant dates and details had, seemingly against Mercedes' will, been revealed. Then in the final year the show "A-Motion" toured Germany. Snappy brochures and advertising material heightened public interest, with specially set-up hotlines receiving 375,000 calls, and 75,000 prospective purchasers swept up in the carefully prepared marketing net. The motoring press was unanimous: the mini Mercedes is a winner.

It is a compact 3570 mm (11 ft 8 in) four-door car drawing together features previously considered incompatible: normal Mercedes safety standards and fuel economy, the maneuverability of a town car and the roominess of a family sedan, the comfort of a limousine and the versatility of a van. And you can pick and choose from 72 variants. These take into account the fact that the asymmetrically arranged rear seats may be adjusted, folded, or quickly removed, as can the front passenger seat as an optional extra, increasing storage space to 1740 liters. Even with all the seating in, the boot still provides 350 liters of storage space, plus a further 40 liters if the Tirefit repair kit is chosen instead of a spare wheel.

With this car the squaring of the circle becomes a reality through the crossing of one box and sandwich design: axles, petrol tank, battery, and also a large part of the engine and transmission are fitted below the floor of the vehicle, so that the passengers sit slightly higher than in a conventional car. In the event of a head-on collision the engine is forced completely underneath the car, an additional safety measure supplementing the robust frame, four airbags, safety belt tighteners and tensioners, and ABS.

The chassis, on the other hand, is largely conventional, with front-wheel drive, wishbones and McPherson struts at the front, and longitudinal control arms at the rear. The four cylinders, though, are completely new, and are designed to guarantee the car the maximum possible agility. Initially two models were launched: the 1.4-liter, twin-valve, 82 bhp A140 and the 1.6-liter, twin-valve, 102 bhp A160. In 1998 come the 1.7-liter Turbo Diesels with either 60 or 90 bhp and direct fuel injection, a charge cooler and four valves. A new feature is the common rail injection, whereby the fuel passes through a joint duct which acts as an accumulator before distributing the fuel into the jets. An electronic device controls the timing of injection and the amount entering each cylinder according to the load and revs in order to achieve optimum combustion and even performance. In June 1999 the A190, offering a robust 125 bhp, comes onto the market. As an alternative to the 5-speed manual gearbox, an automatic version with five drive positions and an automatic clutch is available.

Der Markt-Start des vorerst kleinsten Autos mit dem Stern wird vorbereitet wie der Auftritt eines Superstars: Vier Jahre zuvor treibt man eine Studie auf der Frankfurter IAA wie eine Sonde in die Gunst des Publikums voran. Zwei Jahre vorher sind alle Daten und Details scheinbar widerstrebend enthüllt. Im letzten Jahr tingeln Gaukler mit der Show A-Motion durch deutsche Lande. Poppiges Prospektmaterial steigert den Appetit zum Heißhunger: 375000 Neugierige rufen auf eigens eingerichteten Hotlines an, und 75000 verfangen sich vorab als Käufer im fein gewobenen Marketingnetz. Der Winzling, meldet die Fachpresse unisono, ist eine Wucht.

Der Winzling: ein 3,57 Meter kurzer Viertürer, der die Koexistenz des Unvereinbaren möglich macht: Sicherheit auf Mercedes-Niveau und günstiger Verbrauch, Wendigkeit eines Stadtwagens und Raumangebot eines Familienautos, Komfort einer Limousine und Variabilität eines Vans. Man hat die Qual der Wahl zwischen 72 Varianten. Sie ergeben sich etwa dadurch, dass sich die asymmetrisch geteilten Rücksitze getrennt verstellen, umklappen und flugs herausnehmen lassen wie gegen Aufpreis auch der Beifahrersitz, was das Ladevolumen auf 1740 Liter erweitert. Selbst bei voller Bestuhlung lassen sich im Kofferraum noch immer 350 Liter bewegliche Habe verstauen, dazu weitere 40 Liter, wenn anstelle eines Reserverads das Reparaturset Tirefit gewählt wurde.

Die Quadratur des Zirkels, hier wird sie Ereignis, durch eine Kreuzung von One-Box-Design und Sandwich-Bauweise: Achsen, Tank, Batterie sowie eine größere Portion von Motor und Getriebe sind unter dem Wagenboden angeordnet, wodurch die Insassen leicht erhaben über dem Normal-Niveau thronen. Bei einer Frontalkollision taucht die Antriebseinheit gänzlich nach unten ab, eine Sicherheitsmaßnahme wie der robuste Rahmen oder die Anwesenheit von vier Airbags, Gurtstraffern und Gurtkraft-Begrenzern sowie ABS.

Eher konventionell gibt sich sein Fahrwerk, mit Frontantrieb, Dreieckslenkern und McPherson-Federbeinen vorn und Längslenkern hinten. Völlig neu konstruiert hingegen sind die Vierzylinder, allesamt dazu angetan, den Kleinen mit wieselflinker Agilität auszustatten. Am Anfang stehen die beiden Modelle A140 und A160 mit Zweiventilern von 1,4 Litern und 82 PS und 1,6 Litern und 102 PS. 1998 folgen die Turbodiesel mit 1,7 Litern und 60 beziehungsweise 90 PS, Direkteinspritzer mit Ladeluftkühlung und Vierventiltechnik. Neu ist die Common-Rail-Einspritzung: Der Kraftstoff wird den Düsen über eine gemeinsame Leitung zugeführt, die als Druckspeicher dient und ihn verzweigt. Ein elektronischer Rechner steuert Zeitpunkt und Dosierung für jeden Zylinder gemäß Last und Drehzahl im Dienst von optimaler Verbrennung und gleichmäßiger Leistungsentfaltung. Mit urigen 125 PS wartet der A190 ab Juni 1999 auf. Als Alternative zum Fünfgang-Getriebe gibt es eine Automatik mit derselben Anzahl von Fahrstufen und eine automatische Kupplung.

La commercialisation de la plus petite voiture à l'étoile à ce jour est préparée comme le show d'u superstar : quatre ans auparavant, un prototyp été présenté à l'IAA de Francfort afin de sonder les réactio du public. Deux ans plus tard, on commence à dévoi toutes les données et tous les détails. Et, enfin, l'an derni des artistes ont fait une tournée à travers l'Allemag avec le Show A-Motion. Des prospectus hauts en coule aiguisent les appétits : 375 000 curieux téléphonent sur d lignes créées spécialement à cette fin et 75 000 achete potentiels restent prisonniers des rets tissés avec astuce p les spécialistes du marketing. La petite, déclare à l'uniss la presse spécialisée, « va faire un carton ».

La petite, une quatre-portes de 3,57 mètres de lor rend possible la coexistence d'antagonismes : sécurité consommation réduite, maniabilité de citadine et habita lité de voiture familiale, confort de berline et polyvalen de monospace. On a l'embarras du choix entre 72 variant En effet, les sièges arrière asymétriques peuvent être dép cés séparément, rabattus ou enlevés de la voiture en un ir tant, au même titre que, en option, le siège passager, ce q fait passer le volume de chargement à 1740 litres. Même av tous les fauteuils, le coffre a encore une capacité de 350 litr auxquels on peut ajouter 40 litres si, à la place d'une roue secours, on choisit le kit de réparation Tirefit.

La quadrature du cercle élevée au rang d'événeme grâce à une symbiose de design monocorps et de constru tion en sandwich : les essieux, le réservoir, la batterie ai qu'une grande partie du moteur et de la boîte de vitess sont placés sous le plancher de la voiture, grâce à quoi passagers sont assis à une hauteur légèrement supérieu à la normale. En cas de collision frontale, toute la chaî cinématique glisse sous le plancher, mesure qui contribu la sécurité au même titre que le solide châssis ou la présen de quatre airbags, de tendeurs de ceinture et de limiteurs tension de ceinture ainsi que de l'ABS.

Ses trains roulants sont plutôt conventionnels av traction avant, triangles transversaux et jambes élastiqu McPherson à l'avant ainsi que bras longitudinaux l'arrière. Les quatre-cylindres, par contre, sont inédits tous destinés à donner à cette compacte une vivac enviable. La commercialisation commencera avec les de modèles A140 et A160 propulsés par des moteurs à de soupapes de 1,4 litre et 82 ch ainsi que de 1,6 litre et 102 c Ils seront suivis, en 1998, par un turbo diesel de 1,7 litre 60 ou 90 ch à injection directe, échangeur d'air et culass quatre soupapes. Une nouveauté est l'injection Commo Rail : le carburant est envoyé aux injecteurs par une Du commune qui sert de réservoir à pression et répartit le pr cieux liquide. Un calculateur électronique gère le mome et le dosage cylindre par cylindre en fonction de la char et du régime de façon à garantir une combustion optima et une montée en puissance linéaire. La A190, avec 1 vaillants ch, est présentée en juin 1999. En option à la boî à cinq vitesses, une boîte automatique également à ci vitesses et un embrayage automatique.

Mercedes-Benz A 160 1997

The A-class is fresh and innovative in a number of other ways too. For example, for a few marks more you can two built-in rear childrens' seats or a steel retractable tional sunroof which can be opened at the press of a ton so that the passenger seat too becomes a sun nger. The standard equipment of the regular model, Classic, includes all the important features, such as trically operated rear view mirrors and central lock- , while, as in the E-class, the luxury version Elegance is ailable, as is the sporty Avantgarde. The A-class is small perfectly formed, in the best traditions of Mercedes.

Auch sonst zeigt sich die A-Klasse keck und innovativ, gegebenenfalls für ein paar Mark mehr, mit zwei integrierten Kindersitzen hinten zum Beispiel oder einem Lamellendach aus Stahl, dessen Bestandteile sich auf Knopfdruck einfach übereinander schieben, bis auch die Rückbank zur Sonnenbank wird. Schon die Ausstattung des Grundmodells Classic umspannt alles Wichtige, von elektrischen Außenspiegeln bis zur Zentralverriegelung, doch wie in der E-Klasse ist die noble Design-Linie Elegance oder die sportliche Version Avantgarde lieferbar. Denn die A-Klasse ist klein aber fein – ganz nach Art des Hauses.

Dans les autres domaines, aussi, la Classe A est effrontée et novatrice, offrant deux sièges enfant intégrés à l'arrière, ou un toit à lamelles en acier dont les éléments se superposent sur simple pression d'un bouton. La dotation du modèle d'appel, Classic, comporte déjà tous les éléments importants, des rétroviseurs extérieurs électriques au verrouillage centralisé, mais, comme pour la Classe E, on peut aussi choisir des niveaux de finition plus relevés, l'Elegance ou la version sportive Avantgarde. En effet, si la Classe A est compacte, elle n'en est pas moins luxueuse, fidèle en cela à la devise de la maison.

What a car! The A-class Mercedes with its footprint of six square meters (64.6 sq ft) combines a revolutionary space and safety concept with cunningly conceived details.

Tausendsassa: Auf sechs Quadratmetern Grundfläche verquickt der Mercedes der A-Klasse ein revolutionäres Raum- und Sicherheitskonzept mit listig ausgedachten Detaillösungen.

Coqueluche : sur six mètres carrés, la Mercedes Classe A allie un concept d'habitabilité et de sécurité révolutionnaire à des solutions de détails astucieuses et sophistiquées.

Thanks to its one-box design and the sandwich
construction method, the drivetrain will be displaced
downwards in the event of a frontal collision, ensuring more
extensive crumple zones. The cockpit is unconventional.
But the way the do-it-all multi-lever and various switches
work conjures up that familiar Mercedes feeling. Note the
unusually steep angle of the steering wheel.

One-Box-Design und Sandwich-Bauweise ermöglichen es:
Bei einer Frontalkollision wird die Antriebseinheit nach
unten weggestoßen und sichert so einen größeren
Deformationsweg. Unkonventionell: das Cockpit. Aber die
Betätigung des alles könnenden Multihebels und diverser
Schalter vermittelt vertrautes Mercedes-Feeling. Auffällig
steil: das Lenkrad.

Design monocorps et construction sandwich sont la clé
de l'énigme : en cas de collision frontale, la chaîne
cinématique glisse sous le plancher de la voiture et crée
ainsi une plus grande zone de déformation programmée.
Le cockpit a jeté par-dessus bord tout ce qui est
conventionnel, mais l'utilisation de la multicommande
à tout faire et des diverses manettes est dans le plus
pur style de Mercedes. Noter la colonne de direction
très verticale.

After seven fat A class years, a successor with just as many engine variations was presented in 2004. The palette of engines on offer for the new generation of 4-cylinders ranges from 95 bhp (A150) to the Turbo with its 194 bhp (A200, from June 2005). The small Mercedes is characterized by greater value, space, and variability despite its compact form.

Nach sieben ergiebigen A-Klassen-Jahren stellt sich 2004 ein Nachfolger mit ebenso vielen Motoren-Varianten vor. Die Triebwerkspalette der neuen Vierzylinder-Generation reicht von 95 PS (A150) bis zum Turbo mit 194 PS (A200, ab Juni 2005). Mehr Wertigkeit, Platz und Variabilität trotz aller Kompaktheit zeichnen den kleinen Mercedes aus.

Après sept années lucratives de Classe A, sa remplaçante se présente en 2004 avec un aussi grand nombre de variantes de moteurs. La palette de motorisations de la nouvelle génération de quatre-cylindres va de 95 ch (A150) à un turbo de 194 ch (A200, à partir de juin 2005). Plus grande qualité perçue, plus de place et variabilité en hausse malgré une compacité indéniable caractérisent la petite Mercedes.

Mercedes-Benz A150 2004

"Everything on the Mercedes M Class is new," said Jürgen Hubbert, a member of the board of management with responsibility for passenger cars, "the vehicle in a new sector, the factory and its workforce in a new location, even its market launch outside Europe." Première for the first ML 320: 21 to 23 July 1997 in Huntsville, Alabama. Production: in Mercedes' newest factory in Tuscaloosa, Alabama. Product: an all-rounder, equally at home on- or off-road, suitable for everyday or more adventurous use. This can be seen in the vehicle's sedan-like exterior in which smooth curves dominate, i.e., this is no solid lump struggling to overcome wind resistance head-on by sheer brute force. Comfort is central to the design of the interior, with air conditioning fitted as standard, as are the adjustable rear seats and the Elcode (for Electronic Code System) driver authority system with remote central locking. Personal requests are accommodated at extra charge, such as for leather upholstery, a third row of seats, or a retractable sectional sunroof.

As in the E 320 or CLK 320, a 3.2-liter v6 engine featuring three valves per cylinder and twin-spark ignition, developing 218 bhp, is the lively powerplant. A further innovation – the 4ETS electronic traction system – replaces three conventional differential locks. A microcomputer increases the braking pressure on the spinning wheel until the difference from the wheels with effective grip is such that its traction is re-established. The driver of the ML 320 has various other electronic aids at his fingertips or, as a precaution, backing up what his feet are doing. The ESP electronic stability program is another extra which also operates to counteract centrifugal motion of the vehicle by intervening in the braking process on individual wheels and by supplementary action on the engine, to maintain straight-line stability.

"Sport utility vehicles" is the term given to this type of car, and the Mercedes is an excellent example, with a particularly rigid chassis, deformable crash boxes at the front ends of the longitudinal members, torsion-resistant cross members, full-size airbags for the driver and front passenger, and sidebags fitted as standard. The safety features are rounded off by a three-fold innovation in the braking system. A special off-road ABS system reduces the braking distance on loose surfaces. The EBV braking force distribution system reduces the load on the front brakes if it detects the need to do so, without impairing roadholding. And the Brake-Assist system which is available in conjunction with the ESP system actuates an automatic emergency stop if required. However, M-class owners can still drive and choose their own suitable route somewhere between the highways and the high passes all for themselves. Naturally the M Class too will not remain a one-model series. To suit a variety of requirements and pockets, potential purchasers will very soon have the additional options of the four-cylinder 150 bhp ML 230 and two V8 versions, the 272 bhp ML 430 and the 374 bhp ML 55 AMG.

An der Mercedes M-Klasse sei alles neu, sagt Jürgen Hubbert, Mitglied des Vorstands für das Geschäftsfeld Personenwagen, das Fahrzeug in einem neuen Segment, das Werk und seine Mitarbeiter an einem neuen Standort, sogar die Markteinführung außerhalb Europas. Premiere des Erstlings ML 320: vom 21. bis zum 23. Juli 1997 in Huntsville, Alabama. Produktion: im jüngsten Mercedes-Werk in Tuscaloosa, Alabama. Das Produkt: ein Allrounder, gleichermaßen versiert Off Road und On Road, in Alltag und Abenteuer. Das beginnt mit der limousinenhaften Verbindlichkeit seines Äußeren, in dem glatte Rundlichkeit dominiert, kein Klotz, der sich wütend gegen den Wind stemmt. Das Interieur ist durch und durch auf Komfort abgestellt, die Klimaanlage ebenso serienmäßig wie die variablen Fondsitze und das Fahrberechtigungssystem Elcode (für *Electronic Code Sytem*) mit ferngesteuerter Zentralverriegelung. Persönliche Wünsche werden gegen Aufpreis befriedigt, etwa der nach Lederpolsterung, einer dritten Sitzreihe oder einem Lamellen-Schiebedach.

Für muntere Fortbewegung sorgt wie im E 320 oder CLK 320 ein v6 mit Dreiventiltechnik, Doppelzündung und 3,2 Litern Hubraum, 218 PS stark. Eine weitere Innovation ersetzt drei herkömmliche Differentialsperren: das elektronische Traktionssystem 4-ETS. Ein Mikrocomputer erhöht solange den Bremsdruck am durchdrehenden Rad, bis die Differenz zu den Rädern mit guter Bodenhaftung ausreicht und somit seine Traktion wieder hergestellt ist. Auch sonst gehen dem Lenker des ML 320 allerlei elektronische Heinzelmännchen zur Hand oder unterstützen fürsorglich seine Beinarbeit. Als Extra wirkt das Electronic Stability Program ESP ebenfalls durch Bremseingriff an einzelnen Rädern sowie durch zusätzliche Einwirkung auf den Motor möglichen Schleuderbewegungen des Wagens entgegen und hält ihn in der Spur.

Sport Utility Vehicles nennt man diese Spezies, und der Mercedes ist ein sicheres Paradigma, mit einem besonders festen Fahrgestellrahmen, deformierbaren Crashboxen an den vorderen Enden der Längsträger, biegesteifen Querträgern, Fullsize Airbags für Fahrer und Beifahrer sowie serienmäßigen Sidebags. Komplettiert wird das Sicherheitssystem durch ein Dreifach-Debüt im Bereich der Bremsanlage. Ein spezielles Gelände-ABS verkürzt den Bremsweg auf losem Untergrund. Die elektronische Bremskraftverteilung EBV entlastet bei erkanntem Bedarf die Vorderradbremsen, ohne die Fahrstabilität zu schmälern. Der in Verbindung mit dem ESP-System lieferbare Brake-Assist leitet in Notfällen eine automatische Vollbremsung ein. Nur: Fahren und ein geeignetes Gelände zwischen Highway und Hohlweg aussuchen darf der M-Eigner noch selbst. Natürlich bleibt es auch im Falle der M-Klasse nicht bei einer Monokultur. Je nach Bedarf und Budget kann der potentielle Kunde sehr bald zusätzlich für den ML 230 mit vier Zylindern und 150 PS oder die beiden v8-Versionen ML 430 mit 272 PS sowie ML 55 AMG mit 374 PS votieren.

Tout est neuf avec la Mercedes Classe M », a décla[ré] Jürgen Hubbert, membre du directoire au titre [du] secteur d'activités Voitures de tourisme : l'autom[o]bile dans un nouveau segment, l'usine et ses collaborateu[rs] sur un nouveau site industriel de même que sa commerci[a]lisation en dehors de l'Europe. La jeune première, la ML 32[0] est dévoilée du 21 au 23 juillet 1997 à Huntsville en Alaba[ma]. Elle est produite dans la plus récente usine de Mercede[s] à Tuscaloosa (Alabama). Le produit, une voiture à tout fai[re] aussi à l'aise en tout-terrain que sur route, pour aller fai[re] ses achats ou se lancer à l'aventure. Cela commence a[vec] une présentation très proche d'une berline, où domine[nt] les galbes et les rondeurs. L'intérieur est conçu pour [le] confort maximal et l'air conditionné est de série au mêm[e] titre que les sièges arrière variables et le système d'auto[ri]sation à la conduite Elcode (pour *Electronic Code Syste[m]*) avec verrouillage centralisé. Les options sont nombreuse[s], par exemple la sellerie cuir, une troisième rangée de sièg[es] ou un toit coulissant.

Elle peut se targuer de performances flatteuses avec s[on] v6 à culasse à trois soupapes, identique à celui qui équi[pe] déjà la E 320 ou la CLK 320, avec double allumage, 3,2 litr[es] de cylindrée et 218 ch. Une autre innovation rempl[ace] simultanément trois blocages de différentiel conventio[n]nels : le système de motricité électronique 4ETS. Un micr[o]ordinateur augmente la puissance de freinage sur tou[te] roue qui risque de s'emballer jusqu'à ce que l'écart [de] régime par rapport aux roues ayant une bonne adhéren[ce] soit résorbé et la motricité, donc, rétablie. Le conducte[ur] de la ML 320 peut faire appel aux magiciens électroniqu[es] qui lui épargnent du travail, notamment avec les pieds. A[u] nombre des options figurent l'*Electronic Stability Progra[m]* (ESP), qui freine une ou plusieurs roues et intervient s[ur] le moteur pour réprimer d'éventuels mouvements inco[n]trôlés de la voiture et la maintenir sur sa trajectoire.

Les Américains ont baptisé ces voitures « Sport Util[ity] Vehicles » et la Mercedes en est un parfait exemple avec [un] cadre de châssis solide, des caissons de collision défo[r]mables aux extrémités avant des longerons longitudinau[x], des poutres transversales résistant à la torsion, des airba[gs] *full size* pour le conducteur et le passager avant ainsi q[ue] des coussins gonflables latéraux de série. Une triple inn[o]vation : un ABS tout-terrain raccourcit la distance de fr[ei]nage sur revêtement peu adhérent ; le dispositif EBV [de] répartition électronique de la puissance de freinage dim[i]nue les sollicitations des roues avant sans porter préjudi[ce] à la stabilité dynamique ; en cas de freinage d'urgence, [le] système d'assistance au freinage Brake Assist proposé av[ec] l'ESP déclenche un freinage d'urgence automatique. [Le] propriétaire de la M n'a plus qu'à conduire et choisir [le] terrain approprié pour ses ébats entre autoroute et chem[in] creux. La monoculture n'est pas de règle pour la Classe [M] non plus. Selon les désirs et le budget, le client potenti[el] peut choisir, à titre supplémentaire, entre la ML 230 [à] moteur à quatre cylindres de 150 ch ou les deux versions [v8] ML 430 de 272 ch ou ML 55 AMG de 374 ch.

Mercedes-Benz ML320 1997

Its aristocratic exterior betrays it: although the ML320 is equipped to handle any mudbath, metaled roads are its preferred domain. The Mercedes family likeness is evident in its radiator grille and headlights.

Sein nobles Äußeres verrät es: Obwohl der ML320 für jede Schlammschlacht gerüstet ist, zählen befestigte Straßen zu seinem bevorzugten Operationsfeld. Die Familienähnlichkeit zu anderen Mercedes zeigt sich in Kühlergrill und Scheinwerfern.

Le luxe de son aspect est sans équivoque. Bien que la ML320 ne craigne pas les chemins boueux, les routes asphaltées sont tout de même son champ d'opération de prédilection. La parenté avec les autres Mercedes s'exprime dans la calandre et les phares.

Functionality in a luxurious setting: the driver of the ML 320 can defy even the most inhospitable weather conditions surrounded by the usual Mercedes comfort.

Arbeiter im Frack: Der Lenker des ML 320 trotzt selbst der unwirtlichsten Natur umgeben vom gewohnten Mercedes-Komfort.

Travailleur en smoking : le chauffeur de la ML 320 défie même la nature la plus impénétrable dans le confort que l'on est en droit d'attendre d'une Mercedes.

This product of "an innovative urban mobility concept" is Smart by name and smart by nature. It's a nippy and street-wise performer, at home in the narrowest of city thoroughfares. It is only 2500 mm (8 ft 2 in) long: half the length of the s-class, and 1350 mm (4 ft 5 in) shorter than the a-class. At 1450 mm (4 ft 9 in) wide, it requires a total of just 3.63 sq m (128 sq ft) of parking space.

This is the lightweight of the Mercedes family, totaling 680 kg (1500 lb), with the power unit taking up 120 kg (265 lb). Production of the engine began on 13 June 1997 at the Berlin Marienfeld Mercedes plant. It is a 600 cc three-cylinder turbo unit with a Suprex charge-cooler producing an impressive 55 bhp. It is a conventional twin-valve engine, with double ignition contributing to its meager fuel consumption of just four liters per 100 km (59 mpg). Later gasoline and diesel models have direct fuel injection. The rear-mounted alloy engine is coupled with a Getrag 6-speed gearbox and a Fichtel & Sachs automatic clutch. A light touch on the relevant shift suffices to change gear up or down, without the left foot having to do anything.

The two-seater is equipped with characteristic Mercedes safety features: two airbags, ABS, a highly stable cage, double telescopic steering column, and built-in seats make this Mercedes Benz co-production with the Swiss Gesellschaft für Mikroelektronik und Uhrenindustrie (Federation for the Microelectronics and Watchmaking Industry) the safest of the micros. It is produced in the Lorraine town of Hambach. The design and internal architecture are innovative, with a storage space increasing from 150 liters to 550 with the removal of the passenger seat. Additionally, new options are always available, even after purchase, the owner can change the interior and the exterior trim at will. Seats, covers, door paneling, and cockpit sections can all be exchanged, as can some of the bodywork fittings.

However, the car was soon in the news. The Smart, which was to have become a common and picturesque sight on the roads, did not sell as quickly as had been hoped. On icy roads it spins like a top at the slightest provocation. In the face of disappointing sales figures even in key markets such as France, Italy and Spain, DaimlerChrysler subsidiary MCC reacted defiantly: a cabriolet followed in March 2000, and by 2004 the youthful vehicle had already penetrated the markets of more than 30 countries.

Er heißt Smart, und smart ist er in der Tat, der Repräsentant eines »innovativen urbanen Mobilitätskonzepts«, ein wahrer Tausendsassa und Hans Dampf in allen Gassen der Stadt, wonnig, wendig und winzig. Lediglich 2500 mm misst der kecke Knirps, ist halb so lang wie die s-Klasse, 1350 mm kürzer als die a-Klasse und beansprucht mit 1450 mm Breite bloß 3,63 Quadratmeter Parkfläche.

Innerhalb der großen Mercedes-Familie fällt ihm zugleich die Rolle des Bruders Leichtfuß zu: 680 kg bringt er komplett auf die Waage, 120 kg entfallen auf die Antriebseinheit. Am 13. Juni 1997 beginnt im Mercedes-Werk Berlin-Marienfelde die Fertigung des Triebwerks, eines Dreizylinder-Turbomotors mit Ladeluftkühlung namens Suprex, der 600 ccm Hubraum stattliche 55 PS entlockt. Ausgelegt ist er durchaus konventionell als Zweiventiler, allerdings mit Doppelzündung. Diese soll seine spartanischen Konsumgewohnheiten fördern: Vier Liter auf 100 Kilometer sind genug. Später werden ein weiterer Benziner und ein Turbodiesel folgen, beide mit Direkteinspritzung. Im Heck installiert, ist die Leichtmetall-Maschine mit einem Sechsgang-Getriebe von Getrag und einer automatischen Kupplung von Fichtel & Sachs zusammengespannt. Ein leichtes Antippen des zuständigen Hebels genügt, und das Getriebe schaltet automatisch vor oder zurück, ohne dass der linke Fuß bemüht würde.

Ganz nach Art des Hauses erweist sich der kurze Zweisitzer bei einem Unfall als treuer Freund: Zwei Airbags, ABS, eine hoch stabile Zelle und eine doppelt teleskopierbare Lenksäule sowie Integralsitze machen den munteren Mini, der im lothringischen Hambach als Koproduktion von Mercedes-Benz und der Schweizerischen Gesellschaft für Mikroelektronik und Uhrenindustrie in Biel auf die stämmigen kleinen Räder gestellt wird, zum sichersten unter den Zwergen. Hinsichtlich Design und Innenarchitektur geht man neue Wege. Das Ladevolumen steigt nach Umlegen des Beifahrersitzes von 150 auf 550 Liter. Öfter mal was Neues: Auch nach dem Kauf kann der Smart-Eigner Innenraum und Äußeres seines Wagens nach Gusto verändern und auffrischen. Sitze, Bezüge, Türverkleidungen und Partien des Cockpits können ebenso ausgetauscht werden wie einige der Kunststoffteile der Karosserie.

Allerdings gerät das Wägelchen bald ins Gerede. Die Smart-Türme, die allenthalben pittoresk in die Landschaft gestellt werden, lassen sich nicht so rasch abbauen wie erhofft. Auf schneeglatten Straßen dreht sich der Winzling auf die geringste Provokation hin wie ein Brummkreisel. Angesichts wenig ermutigender Verkaufszahlen auch in wichtigen Märkten wie Frankreich, Italien und Spanien reagiert die DaimlerChrysler-Tochter MCC mit einem trotzigen Jetzt-erst-recht: Im März 2000 folgt ein Cabrio, und bis 2004 ist das jugendliche Mobil bereits in mehr als 30 Länder vorgedrungen.

Elle s'appelle Smart, mot anglais signifiant dégourd Et, dégourdie, elle l'est en effet, celle qui représen un « concept novateur de mobilité urbaine », ur petite bonne à tout faire qui est chez elle au cœur des ville pratique, élégante et minuscule, irrésistible. Ce petit bou de voiture ne mesure que 2500 mm, à peine la moitié d'un Classe s, soit 1350 mm de moins que la Classe a, et, ave une largeur de 1450 mm, il lui suffit d'un créneau d 3,63 m² pour se garer.

Elle risque fort d'être la coqueluche de la grand famille Mercedes, rôle qu'elle assume avec légèreté : prêt à rouler, elle ne pèse que 680 kg, dont 120 pour la chaîn cinématique. La fabrication du moteur, un trois-cylindre turbo à échangeur d'air baptisé Suprex ne développan pas moins de 55 ch à partir d'une cylindrée de 600 cm³, commence le 13 juin 1997 à l'usine Mercedes de Berlin Marienfelde. Tout à fait conventionnel puisqu'il ne possèd que deux soupapes, il peut toutefois se targuer d'un doubl allumage. Cela afin de lui inculquer une consommatio spartiate : 4 litres aux 100 km devront suffire. Il sera suiv plus tard d'un autre moteur à essence et d'un turbo diesel tous deux à injection directe. Monté à l'arrière, le moteu en alliage léger est accouplé à une boîte Getrag à si vitesses et un embrayage automatique Fichtel & Sachs. suffit d'actionner légèrement le levier correspondant pou monter ou descendre automatiquement les rapports san devoir faire appel au pied gauche.

Tout à fait dans le style de la maison, cette court biplace est un bon compagnon de route en cas d'accident deux airbags, ABS, une cellule passagers ultrarésistante e une colonne de direction télescopique double ainsi que des sièges intégraux font de cette vive mini aux pneu larges construite à Hambach, en Lorraine, en coproductio entre Mercedes-Benz et la Société suisse de microélec tronique et d'horlogerie de Bienne, la plus sûre des microcompactes. En termes de design et de décoratio intérieure, ses pères ont innové. Une fois le siège passage rabattu, la capacité de chargement passe de 150 à 550 litres De plus, ce n'est pas une acquisition pour la vie : mêm après l'avoir achetée, le propriétaire de la Smart peu modifier et rafraîchir à volonté l'habitacle et la carrosseri de sa voiture. Les sièges, les capitonnages, les contre-porte et certaines parties du cockpit sont interchangeables, au même titre que quelques-uns des panneaux de carrosseri en matière plastique.

Mais la voiturette ne tarde pas à susciter des discussions. Les distributeurs automatiques de Smart, qui égaient la nature de leurs couleurs, ne se vident pas aussi rapidement qu'escompté. Sur les routes enneigées, la puce fait la toupie à la moindre provocation. Compte tenu du succès commercial symbolique, même sur des marchés importants comme la France, l'Italie et l'Espagne, MCC, la filiale de DaimlerChrysler, réagit avec un sursaut d'orgueil : en mars 2000 s'y ajoute un cabriolet et, en 2004, cette voiture jeune s'est déjà répandue dans plus de trente pays.

mart 1999

new product needs new terminology. The Smart is in e subcompact class and is the ultimate two-seater city naround. The smiling micro is packed to the brim with e highest of high-tech features.

Mit dem neuen Produkt kommen die neuen Vokabeln: Der Smart gehört zur Subkompakt-Klasse, ist der ultimative City-Zweisitzer. In jedem Fall steckt der schmunzelnde Dreikäselang voller innovativer Lösungen bis hin in die reinen Höhen des High Tech.

À nouveau produit, nouveaux vocables : la Smart appartient au segment des sub-compactes. C'est une citadine à deux places poussée au paroxysme. Cette charmante micro-car regorge en tout cas des solutions novatrices dont certaines sont issues tout droit de la haute technologie.

A giant among dwarves: in some areas the strength of the Smart, its reduction to bare essentials, proved to be a weakness.

Riesenzwerg: Als Schwäche erweist sich auf manchen Gebieten die Stärke des Smart, die radikale Reduktion auf das unbedingt Nötige.

Un nain géant : ce qui est son point faible dans certains registres fait justement la force de la Smart, la réduction radicale à l'essentiel.

When the current s Class was launched at the Paris Motor Show at the end of September opinion was unanimous: it's a beautiful car. And the carping chorus of the critics who had written off its predecessor gave voice one last time, declaring that now one could see what such a car should look like. However, the success of the previous version was vindication enough for its designers: after all, it did sell 407,000.

The new one is not even that much smaller, being just 75 mm shorter and 37 mm narrower. The car contained within this slimmed-down outline, though, is handsome indeed, 41 mm less tall, with graceful, flowing lines yielding an incredibly low drag coefficient of 0.27. Its outward elegance carries over seamlessly to the interior, where the passengers enjoy not only abundant space but also a plethora of beautifully laid out controls and displays. Expectations are high, the s Class being, in automobile terms, the measure of all things. Thus the w 220 represents a distillation of the possibilities offered by the latest in cutting edge automobile technology. Fears that you will not be able to see the wood for the trees are soon dispelled: buttons and switches are grouped together according to function and the operating instructions soon provide enlightenment, so that you soon feel at home in the new top of the range Mercedes.

Traditional extras such as automatic air conditioning or a trip computer come as part of the standard package, but options such as a speech-operated telephone or a multicontour seat that gently massages your back at the press of a button come at a hefty additional price.

The real revolution, though, is underneath the car, where the refined AIRMATIC suspension and an equally perfect adaptive shock absorption system give the occupants a veritable ride on a flying carpet.

At the start of production the w 220 was available as the s 320 v6 plus the s 430 and s 500, both fitted with whispering v8 power units, all of them three-valve engines. Six months later the s 55 AMG was introduced. Its engine was based on the five liter version, but was bored out to 5439 cc, and generated an additional 54 bhp to meet many customer's desire for improved performance. Two petrol versions, the s 280 and the s 600, plus a couple of diesels with six and eight cylinders respectively, round off the model range. All of the engines operate in tandem with a nimble and discrete five-speed automatic gearbox which makes the built-in tiptronic system more or less superfluous.

In line with tried and trusted Mercedes policy, the saloons were followed at the 1999 Geneva Spring Motor Show by two Coupés, the CL 500 and the CL 600. With their four-eyed fronts and conspicuous elegance they rather resemble the CLK. They are fitted with conventional steel suspension controlled by a special hydraulic unit. All this bespeaks a change in model policy: its sporty appearance betrays the fact that Mercedes intends with the CL to encroach on the cosy fiefdom of its rivals Porsche, BMW and Jaguar.

Als die aktuelle s-Klasse auf dem Pariser Salon Ende September 1998 ihre Aufwartung macht, sind sich alle einig: Das Auto ist einfach schön. Und in nörgelndem Nachruf erhebt sich ein letztes Mal der Chor der Kritiker, die den Vorgänger schon immer gescholten hatten: Jetzt sehe man, wie ein solches Fahrzeug auch aussehen könne. Der Erfolg des Alten gab ihm und seinen Vätern gleichwohl recht. Immerhin hat er es auf eine Verbreitung von 407 000 Exemplaren gebracht.

Der Neue ist nicht einmal viel kleiner: nur 75 Millimeter kürzer und 37 Millimeter schmaler. Auf diesem reduzierten Grundriss erhebt sich indessen ein automobiler Beau, 41 Millimeter flacher, geradezu grazil, mit flüssigen Formen, die man in den erstaunlichen c_w-Wert von 0,27 umgemünzt hat. Seine äußere Eleganz setzt sich übergangslos nach innen fort, wo die Passagiere neben Raum in Hülle und Fülle Bedienungselemente und Anzeigen von ungemein attraktiver Gestaltung erwarten. Der Erwartungsdruck ist hoch: Die s-Klasse hat das Maß aller Dinge zu sein. Und so wird der w220 zum Konzentrat des Machbaren auf dem allerletzten Stand der Wissenschaft. Befürchtungen, man könne sich verlieren in einem Zuviel von Lernpensum, sind rasch zerstreut. Knöpfe und Schalter wurden in systembezogenen Einheiten zusammengefasst. Einleuchtend ist die Bedienerführung.

Traditionelle Extras wie Klimaautomatik oder Reiserechner sind ins Basispaket geschnürt, Optionen wie sprachgesteuerte Telefone oder eine Multikonturenlehne, die auf Knopfdruck mild den Rücken massiert, müssen dagegen anständig honoriert werden.

Die eigentliche Revolution findet im Souterrain statt, wo die raffinierte Luftfederung AIRmatic sowie eine gleichermaßen perfekte adaptive Dämpfung die Fahrt zum Reisen auf einem fliegenden Teppich machen. Zum Produktionsstart wird der w220 angeboten als s320 mit einem v6 sowie als s430 und s500, beide mit wispernden v8-Triebwerken. Alle sind Dreiventiler. Ein halbes Jahr später stellt sich der s55AMG ein. Seine Maschine fußt auf dem Fünfliter, wurde aber auf 5439 ccm aufgebohrt und kommt mit 54 Mehr-PS der Lust mancher Kunden auf mehr Leistung entgegen. Zwei Benziner, der s280 und der s600 v12, und zwei Diesel mit sechs und acht Zylindern sollen die Baureihe abrunden. Alle Motoren sind zusammengespannt mit einer Fünfgangautomatik von flinker und diskreter Wirkungsweise, welche die dazugehörige Tiptronic eigentlich überflüssig macht.

Nach bewährtem Mercedes-Brauch folgen den Limousinen auf dem Genfer Frühjahrssalon 1999 die beiden Coupés CL500 und CL600. Sie ähneln mit ihren Vier-Augen-Gesichtern und ihrer auffälligen Zierlichkeit eher dem CLK und sind ausgestattet mit einer konventionellen Stahlfederung, die gleichwohl über eine spezielle Hydraulikeinheit gesteuert wird. Das verrät eine gewandelte Modellpolitik: Auf Grund seiner sportiveren Anmutung soll der CL in die sicher gewähnten Erbhöfe der Rivalen Porsche, BMW und Jaguar einbrechen.

Quand l'actuelle Classe s tire sa révérence, a Salon de Paris à la fin du mois de septembre 1998, tous les spectateurs sont unanimes : la voiture est d'une beauté sculpturale. Et, au moment où es prononcée l'oraison funèbre de l'ancien modèle, s'élève une ultime fois le chœur de ses détracteurs qui n'on jamais cessé de le critiquer : voilà bien la preuve que l'on aurait pu en faire une belle voiture ! Le succès de l'ancien modèle leur aura donné raison, à lui-même et à ses géniteurs. Il aura tout de même été vendu à concurrence de 407 000 exemplaires.

La nouvelle n'est pourtant pas beaucoup plus petite tout juste 75 mm plus courte et 37 mm plus étroite. Mais sur un périmètre de sustentation revu à la baisse, se pavane en rechange une voiture d'anthologie, 41 mm plus basse, littéralement gracile, aux lignes fluides qui se traduisent par un étonnant c_x de 0,27. Son élégance extérieure se poursuit sans rupture à l'intérieur, où les passagers, qui disposent d'un espace pléthorique, ont aussi sous les yeux un tableau de bord et un aménagement intérieur que l'on peut légitimement qualifier de grande réussite. Le cahier des charges était pourtant ambitieux : la Classe s se devait d'être la référence dans sa catégorie. Et c'est ainsi que la w220 est le concentré de tout ce qui est réalisable à condition de représenter le haut de gamme de la science. Ceux qui craignaient de devoir étudier en profondeur le manuel d'utilisation voient leurs réserves s'évanouir rapidement. Les boutons et les commandes ont été regroupés en ensembles logiques. Leur utilisation ne pose aucune énigme. On se sent à l'aise dans la nouvelle grosse Mercedes. Des équipements traditionnels comme la climatisation automatique ou l'ordinateur de bord font partie de la dotation de base, alors que des options comme le téléphone à commande vocale ou le dossier de siège multicontours qui vous masse langoureusement le dos sur simple pression d'un bouton sont en revanche facturées contre espèces sonnantes et trébuchantes.

La révolution proprement dite s'est effectuée dans l'anonymat, en l'occurrence sous la carrosserie, où la raffinée suspension automatique Airmatic ainsi qu'un amortissement adaptatif tout aussi parfait transforment le moindre déplacement en une promenade sur un tapis volant. Pour le lancement de la production, la w220 est proposée dans trois versions : s320 à moteur v6 ainsi que s430 et s500, toutes les deux propulsées par un moteur v8 au murmure irrésistible. Tous ont une culasse à trois soupapes. Six mois plus tard, ce trio est rejoint par la s55 AMG. Son moteur est une évolution du v8 de 5 litres mais réalésé à 5439 cm³ et qui, avec 54 ch supplémentaires va au-devant des clients qui n'en ont jamais assez sous le pied. Deux autres moteurs à essence, le s280 et le s600 v12 et deux diesels, à six et huit cylindres, sont appelés à compléter la gamme. Tous les moteurs sont accolés à une boîte automatique à cinq vitesses au fonctionnement aussi rapide que discret, qui rend à proprement parler superflu la commande Tiptronic intégrée.

MERCEDES-BENZ S320–S55 AMG 1998

Mercedes-Benz S 500 1999

Selon les bonnes vieilles habitudes de Mercedes, les berlines sont suivies, lors du Salon de printemps 1999 à Genève, par les deux coupés CL500 et CL600. Avec leur face avant à quatre yeux et leur gracilité flagrante, ils rappellent immédiatement la CLK et possèdent eux aussi une suspension conventionnelle à ressorts en acier, qui est toutefois commandée par une unité hydraulique spéciale. C'est le signe d'un changement de philosophie pour la politique de gamme : en raison de sa nature plus sportive, la CL est destinée à rouler dans les traces, sinon dans la chasse gardée, de ses rivales : Porsche, BMW et autres Jaguar.

Despite being compressed into the least possible space, the command center with its many features, from preset telephone numbers to controls for the GPS navigation system, is clearly laid out.

Auf knappstem Raum zusammen-gedrängt und dennoch übersichtlich ist die Kommandozentrale mit zahlreichen Funktionen von der Vorwahl fürs Telefon bis hin zum Bedienungszentrum für die GPS-Navigation.

Sur un espace extrêmement restreint, et pourtant clairement lisible, le poste de commande comporte de nombreuses fonctions avec la présélection pour téléphone et même la centrale de commande pour le système de navigation GPS.

While its predecessor's massive and monumental appearance put off some potential customers, the latest S Class appeals at once with its more graceful lines. The five liter engine runs with the quiet discretion of an English butler.

Während der Vorgänger so manchen möglichen Kunden durch wuchtige Monumentalität vergraulte, schmeichelt sich die jüngste S-Klasse durch rundum gefällige Formen sofort ein. Der Fünfliter unter der Haube arbeitet mit der Diskretion eines englischen Filmbutlers.

Alors que son prédécesseur a fait reculer maint client potentiel par son monumentalisme et sa lourdeur, la toute récente Classe S séduit immédiatement par l'élégance de ses lignes. Le moteur de 5 litres sous le capot travaille avec la discrétion d'un majordome britannique.

Mercedes-Benz S320–S55AMG 1998

A liberating act: the lines of the new S Class Coupé are clearly distinguishable from those of the saloon, stressing its manifestly sporty intent.

Emanzipatorischer Akt: Das Coupé zur neuen S-Klasse setzt sich durch ein ganz eigenes Profil vom Basismodell ab. Manifeste Sportlichkeit ist angesagt.

Acte d'émancipation : la version coupé de la nouvelle Classe S se démarque du modèle de base par son profil bien spécifique. La sportivité est manifestement à l'ordre du jour.

Mercedes-Benz S320–S55AMG 1998   529

The new C Class, presented to the public in May 2000, is a delightful vehicle in all ways: mid-range judging by its dimensions, luxurious mid-range in its standard fittings, and in a class of its own with its manifold possibilities for individual variation. And the delighted public greedily snapped it up – as the sales statistics show. Most prospective buyers of a Mercedes range model expect to be offered, without having to stargaze, a wide range of possibilities. The crystal clear answer: no less than 12 engine variations, from the 116 bhp foal to the 231 bhp performance of the v6 power-house from AMG, leave no wish unfulfilled. The variety of tasteful paintwork and upholstery combinations recommended by the producer is amazing. In contrast, the metallic amethyst-violet finish is not to everyone's taste in color. The company's Haute Couture can come up with only one matching color for the seating, irrespective of whether in textile or leather: anthracite.

Indulgence depends on wallet size: either the so-called Classic outfit with its material in "York" design and its high quality – and "Calyptus Linea" wood paneling, or the Elegance furnishing with its "Lauret" wooden applications delightfully spread through the interior. Alloy wheels, much chrome, and a leather steering wheel underline the noble character of this variation. That perhaps a little less pomp can be more enhancing is shown by the Avantgarde matt-black radiator grille blades.

In contrast the knobbly burnished-steel pedals appear to be "in." A firm contact to the pedals is not without a certain justification when dealing with AMG power – especially the C55 with its 5.4-liter v8 (available from 2004 onward) which, with its rich 367 bhp and 510 Newton meter possesses a respectable torque. The front of the vehicle has to be modified to accommodate this engine's large volume. Whoever is willing to pay the costs involved really has to change gear quickly to actually achieve the producer's stated sprint time of 0 to 100 kph (62 mph) in 5.2 seconds.

Let's stay with the modest C220 CDI and its standard fittings, which turn out to be thoroughly luxurious, and contain such important technical components as the electronic stability program (ESP) and the brake assistant (BAS). Some C Class drivers complain that the extremely comfortably designed chassis is too spongy in its steering. Mercedes reacted, in the course of the C Class model refinement in 2004, with stronger stabilizers, a more direct steering, and reworked axle bearings, as well the new standard wheel size 205/55 R16 with which the company had previously shod vehicles of the size of a C240, or larger. The C220 CDI has also been treated to a further 5 bhp for its 4-cylinder diesel engine as part of this live-cell treatment. Since October 2003, the CDI also conforms to the strict EU-4 norm, thanks to a self-regenerating particulate filter.

Small operating changes in the interior have gone hand in hand with the technical interventions. In this way

Mittelklasse, gemessen an den Dimensionen, gehobene Mittelklasse in der serienmäßigen Ausstattung und einsame Klasse in der Vielfalt individueller Variationsmöglichkeiten: Die neue C-Klasse ist rundum ein wonnigliches Gefährt – kein Wunder, wurde es doch im Mai des Jahres 2000 dem Publikum präsentiert. Und das war entzückt und griff – wie die Verkaufszahlen belegen – auch gleich gierig zu. Die breiteste Käufer-schicht für eine Mercedes-Modellreihe erwartet, auch ohne Sterndeutung, ein breit gefächertes Angebot. Stern-klare Antwort: Nicht weniger als 12 Motoren-Varianten, vom 116-PS-Triebling bis zum v6-Kraftquell von AMG mit einer Ausgangs-Leistung von 231 PS, lassen keine Wünsche offen. Ein AMG-v6 mit 354 PS lässt dann auch nicht lange auf sich warten. Verblüffend die vielen geschmackvollen Kombinationen von Lacken und Polstern, die der Herstel-ler empfiehlt. Nicht jedermanns Farbensinn trifft dagegen der Metallic-Sonderlack Amethyst-Violett. Hier fällt der Haute Couture des Hauses freilich nur eine passende Sitz-farbe ein, ganz gleich, ob in Leder oder Stoff: Anthrazit.

Je nach Geldbeutel darf geschwelgt werden: in der so genannten Classic-Ausführung mit dem Stoff-Design »York« – und dazu die Edelholztäfelung »Calyptus Linea«. Oder beim Elegance: hier heißt die Holzapplikation »Lauret«, hübsch im Interieur verteilt. Leichtmetallräder, viel Chrom und ein Lederlenkrad unterstreichen den noblen Charakter dieser Variante. Dass weniger Pomp vielleicht mehr ist, signalisieren schon die mattschwarz lackierten Lamellen des Kühlergrills beim Avantgarde.

»In« scheinen die genoppten Pedale aus gebürstetem Edelstahl zu sein. Der feste Kontakt zur Pedalerie entbehrt im Umgang mit viel AMG-Power nicht einer gewissen Berechtigung – besonders bei dem ab 2004 erhältlichen C55 AMG mit 5,4-Liter-v8, der satte 367 PS abgibt und mit 510 Newtonmetern auch ein ordentliches Drehmoment besitzt. Zur Aufnahme dieses großvolumigen Triebwerks muss der Vorderwagen umgebaut werden. Wer die damit verbundenen Kosten in Kauf nimmt, muss ganz schön schnell shiften, um in 5,2 Sekunden tatsächlich die Werks-angabe für den Sprint von 0 auf 100 realisieren zu können.

Bleiben wir beim bescheidenen C220 CDI und seiner Serienausstattung, die durchaus üppig ausfällt und wichtige technische Komponenten wie das elektronische Stabilitätsprogramm ESP und den Brems-Assistenten BAS beinhaltet. Einige C-Klasse-Lenker monierten, das äußerst komfortabel ausgelegte Fahrwerk sei zu schwammig. Im Rahmen der Modellpflege, 2004 für die C-Klasse, reagiert Mercedes mit stärkeren Stabilisatoren, direkterer Lenkung und überarbeiteten Achslagern sowie der neuen Standard-Reifengröße 205/55 R16, die bislang ab der Größenordnung eines C240 zur Werks-Besohlung zählte. Im Rahmen die-ser Frischzellen-Kur fiel für den C220 CDI auch eine milde Gabe von sieben zusätzlichen PS für den Vierzylinder-Dieselmotor ab. Dank eines Partikelfilters, der sich ohne Zusatzstoffe regeneriert, erfüllt der CDI seit Oktober 2003 die strengen EU-4-Normen.

Segment intermédiaire pour les dimensions, segment supérieur pour la richesse de l'équipement de série, mais un net cran au-dessus pour la diversité des possibilités de personnalisation : la nouvelle Classe C est un véhicule qui met vraiment de bonne humeur – rien d'éton-nant puisqu'elle a été présentée au public en mai 2000, une saison à laquelle les cœurs sont en fête. Ravie, la clientèle ne s'est pas fait prier et – comme les chiffres de vente le prouvent – s'est jetée sur elle. Dans sa grande majorité, la clientèle d'une gamme Mercedes attend, même sans demander la lune, une offre très diversifiée. La réponse est aussi claire qu'un ciel d'été ponctué d'étoiles : pas moins de douze différentes motorisations, du groupe de 116 ch au puissant v6 d'AMG à la puissance nominale de 231 ch comblent tous les désirs. Un v6 AMG de 354 ch ne se fait pas attendre longtemps non plus. Stupéfiant, le nombre de combinaisons réussies pour les vernis et les capitonnages que recommande le constructeur. Une peinture métallisée spéciale, violet améthyste, n'est cependant assurément pas du goût de chacun. Avec elle, le service de haute couture de la maison n'a qu'une nuance à proposer pour les sièges, qu'ils soient en cuir ou en tissu : anthracite.

Le pédalier en acier inoxydable brossé a été parfaite-ment bien conçu, surtout avec ses petites boules en caoutchouc, qui garantissent une bonne adhérence. Faire corps avec sa machine est, de fait, impératif, surtout quand on a autant de chevaux sous le capot qu'avec l'AMG – a fortiori avec la C55 à moteur v8 de 5,4 litres, disponible à partir de 2004. Elle offre en effet la puissance plus que respectable de 367 ch et un couple exceptionnel de 510 newtons-mètres. Pour installer ce moteur de grosse cylindrée, il a fallu revoir toute la partie avant de la voiture. Celui qui n'hésite pas à débourser le supplément de prix occasionné ne doit pas hésiter non plus à changer de vitesse très vite s'il veut réaliser le temps de 5,2 secondes revendiqué par l'usine pour le 0 à 100 km/h.

Mais revenons à la modeste C220 CDI et à son équipe-ment de série, qui est déjà d'une richesse honorable et comporte des équipements techniques aussi importants que le programme de stabilité électronique ESP et l'assis-tance de freinage BAS. Quelques conducteurs de Classe C critiquent le châssis : extrêmement confortable, certes, il serait soit trop mou. À l'occasion de la remise à niveau de la Classe C, en 2004, Mercedes réagit avec des barres anti-roulis de plus grand diamètre, une direction plus directe et des paliers d'essieu revus et corrigés ainsi qu'une nou-velle monte pneumatique standard de 205/55 R16 que le constructeur n'offrait jusqu'à présent qu'à partir de la C240. Dans le cadre de cette « cure de jouvence », la C220 CDI a aussi bénéficié du don miséricordieux de sept chevaux supplémentaires pour son moteur Diesel à quatre cylindres. Grâce à un filtre à particules se régé-nérant sans additifs, la CDI respecte depuis octobre 2003 les sévères normes UE 4.

Les améliorations apportées à la technique vont de pair avec des interventions de cosmétique mineures dans

MERCEDES-BENZ
C 200 CDI – C 55 AMG 2000

Mercedes-Benz C220 CDI 2003

the round, interlocking, instrument fragments have been remodeled into easily readable, really round instruments, and diverse switches arranged more easily at hand. The previously relatively soft side-stability of the seats has adopted orthopedic principles. The seats now provide a sure hold even when cornering sharply.

What would be rejuvenation without a facelift: two powerful ribs replace the fender air intake previously cut in two by a plate, and a modern clear-glass optic has opened the headlights' eyes. The prescription of xenon headlights that adapt to the lie of the road is available at extra cost, and requires a deep dig into the pocket. Speaking of cost: DaimlerChrysler shows quite clearly with the C Class that improvements do not necessarily have to put a strain on the customers' finances. It is an elementary basic that demands a lot of care and attention.

Mit den Eingriffen in die Technik gehen kleinere operative Maßnahmen im Interieur einher. So werden die ineinander greifenden Rundinstrument-Fragmente zu gut ablesbaren, wirklich runden Armaturen ummodelliert und diverse Schalter griffbereiter angeordnet. Der seitlichen Führung der Sitze – bislang relativ weich – nimmt sich die Orthopädie an. Jetzt bieten die Sitze auch bei scharfer Kurvenfahrt sicheren Halt.

Was wären Verjüngungsmaßnahmen ohne Facelifting; Der nur durch einen Steg unterteilte Lufteinlass im Stoßfänger weicht zwei kräftigen Rippen, und moderne Klarglas-Optik öffnet den Scheinwerfern die Augen. Das Verschreiben von Xenon-Strahlern, die sich dem Straßenverlauf anpassen, ist kostenpflichtig und muss mit einem tiefen Griff in die Privatschatulle beglichen werden. Apropos Kosten: Dass Verbesserungen nicht gleich die Finanzlage der Kunden strapazieren müssen, demonstriert DaimlerChrysler bei der C-Klasse recht anschaulich. Sie ist ein tragendes Element, das gehegt und gepflegt sein will.

l'habitacle. Ainsi les cadrans circulaires jusqu'ici partiellement superposés font-ils maintenant place à de vrais cadrans ronds auxquels s'ajoutent, bien positionnées, diverses commandes. Le guidage latéral des sièges – jusqu'ici relativement souples – a été renforcé. Désormais, ceux-ci offrent aussi un bon maintien même dans les virages franchis rapidement.

La prise d'air dans le pare-chocs avant subdivisée avec un seul barreau présente désormais deux énergiques nervures et les projecteurs modernes au verre cristal ouvrent les yeux aux phares. Se faire prescrire des projecteurs xénon qui s'adaptent au déroulement de la route est une médication coûteuse qui implique que l'on puise profondément dans ses deniers personnels. À propos de coûts : ces améliorations ne doivent pas nécessairement mettre en danger l'équilibre financier de la clientèle, comme le prouve DaimlerChrysler, par son succès commercial, avec la Classe C. Elle est un élément porteur et, en tant que tel, mérite d'être cultivée et adulée.

Just about six liters (39 mpg) diesel are consumed by the thrifty C220 CDI engine whose 150 bhp are sufficient to provide the mid-range limousine with a top speed of 208 kph (129 mph).

Knapp sechs Liter Diesel verbraucht das sparsame Triebwerk des C220 CDI, dessen 150 PS aber ausreichen, um der Mittelklassen-Limousine eine Endgeschwindigkeit von 208 km/h zu verleihen.

L'économe moteur de la C220 CDI se contente d'à peine six litres de diesel aux 100 km, mais ses 150 ch suffisent pour propulser, si besoin est, la limousine du segment intermédiaire à une vitesse de pointe de 208 km/h.

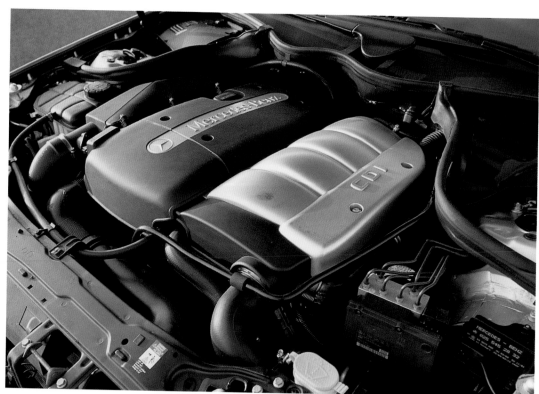

The C class presents itself with an appealing exterior, spacious interior, functional dashboard, and seating with improved side design.

Mit ihrem ansprechenden Äußeren, dem geräumigen Innenleben, funktionellen Armaturen und Sitzen mit verbesserter Seitenführung empfiehlt sich die C-Klasse ebenfalls.

Avec sa présentation séduisante, son habitacle spacieux, son tableau de bord fonctionnel et ses sièges qui offrent un meilleur maintien latéral, on ne peut que recommander la Classe C.

Mercedes-Benz C200 CDI–C55 AMG 2000

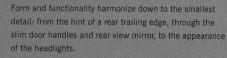

Form and functionality harmonize down to the smallest detail: from the hint of a rear trailing edge, through the slim door handles and rear view mirror, to the appearance of the headlights.

Formen und Funktionalität harmonieren bis ins kleinste Detail: von der angedeuteten Abrisskante des Hecks über die schlanken Türgriffe und Rückspiegel mit integrierten Blinkern bis zur Optik der Scheinwerfer.

Formes et fonctionnalité s'harmonisent jusque dans les moindres détails : du soupçon de becquet sur le couvercle de malle à l'esthétique raffinée des phares en passant par les minces poignées de portières et les rétroviseurs à clignotant intégré.

In reality, only the racing coupé 300 sl, brought into play at the start of the 1950s, is sportingly light, as the abbreviation sl suggests. Even the legendary "gull-wing" weighed 440 kilograms (970 lbs) more, and up until 1988, the sl family had put on a good half a ton. It was only with the fifth generation of this very successful species – with almost a million vehicles sold – that a slight slim-down took place: a whole 35 kilograms (77 lbs). The long engine hood is responsible on its own for 15 kilograms (33 lbs), the aluminum version weighs only half of a comparable steel section. But light alloy in the wings, doors, and trunk lid also has to compensate for the internal overweight.

If you want to acquaint yourself with this muscular beau full of technical finesse, you should once again go back to school. ABC – at DaimlerChrysler these three letters stand for Active Body Control, an active chassis control which prevents chassis swaying at the first signs. As long as the computer is left to its own devices, it is a welcome aid, but one should resist the temptation to confront it with the sport setting on winding stretches. It could react roughly, and certain amount of practice is needed to handle it, otherwise the technically ingenious harmonized symbiosis of ABC, ESP, and the Sensotronic Brake Control (SBC) – wonderfully enabling braking to be administered in exact doses – is of little use.

A small consolation: if the noble sl projectile should ever leave the road and threaten to overturn, the sensor-steered roll bars extend to protect the occupants. As it is succinctly put in the little sl customer manual: "we overturn ourselves to guarantee your wellbeing". Apart from the also manually operational roll bars, safety is ensured by the two-stage airbags for driver and front passenger, head-thorax-sidebags in the doors, well padded integrated seating, and – to a modest degree – the electro-hydraulic operated variable roof. It takes 16 seconds to convert the roadster into a coupé.

This sl bears more masculine features than its predecessors despite all the luxury and comfort. Especially the ventilation ducts in the front wings and on the hood are indicative of a sportsman, whose strength unleashes – a puny 245 bhp for the sl350 – in the case of the sl 500 a cultivated power of 306 bhp. An explosion in performance then begins with the sl 55 AMG and the 12-cylinder biturbo of the sl 600. The latter, with its two ton curb weight more a persiflage of the original sl idea, moves its mass easily – completely without effort. It is also not necessary, for the two turbo-superchargers guarantee 500 bhp. 100 kph (62 mph) can be achieved in 4.7 seconds with this thump on the drive shaft. It is only a pity that the engine management computer electronically blocks higher speeds than 250 kph (155 mph) while the scale on the speedometer lures with its 300 kph (185 mph) marking.

It is interesting that the supercharger model achieves the same acceleration results. A newly developed mechanical supercharger, situated between the cylinder banks,

Sportlich leicht, wie das Kürzel sl suggeriert, ist eigentlich nur das anfangs der 50er Jahre eingesetzte Renncoupé 300 sl. Schon der legendäre Flügeltürer wiegt 440 Kilo mehr, und bis 1988 legte die sl-Familie eine reichliche halbe Tonne zu. Erst in der fünften Generation dieser bis dahin mit fast einer halben Million verkauften Exemplaren recht erfolgreichen Spezies ist es gelungen, ein wenig abzuspecken: ganze 35 Kilo. Davon entfallen allein 15 auf die lange Motorhaube, die in Aluminium nur noch die Hälfte einer entsprechenden Fertigung in Stahl ausmacht. Auch bei Kotflügeln, Türen und Heckklappe muss Leichtmetall übergewichtige Innereien kompensieren.

Um sich mit diesem muskulösen Beau voller technischer Finessen vertraut zu machen, sollte man in die Rolle eines ABC-Schützen schlüpfen. ABC – diese drei Buchstaben stehen bei DaimlerChrysler für Active Body Control, eine aktive Fahrwerksregelung, die Karosserieschwankungen bereits im Ansatz unterbindet. Solange man den Computer gewähren lässt, ist er eine angenehme Stütze, doch sollte man der Versuchung widerstehen, ihn in kurvenreichen Passagen mit der Sporteinstellung zu konfrontieren. Er könnte ruppig reagieren, und es bedarf einer gewissen Übung, mit ihm umzugehen, sonst nützt die Symbiose von ABC, ESP und dem hervorragend dosierbaren Bremssystem Sensotronic Brake Control (SBC) nicht viel.

Kleiner Trost: Falls sich das edle sl-Geschoss jemals in die Botanik verirren sollte und dabei umzukippen droht, fahren sofort die sensorgesteuerten Überrollbügel aus, um die Insassen zu schützen. Wie heißt es in dem sl-Kundenbüchlein doch so treffend: »Für Ihr Wohlbefinden überschlagen wir uns.« Ebenfalls der Sicherheit dienen – neben den auch manuell ausklappbaren Bügeln – zweistufige Airbags für Fahrer und Beifahrer, Head-Thorax-Sidebags in den Türen, gut gepolsterte Integralsitze und – in bescheidenem Maße – auch das elektrohydraulisch betätigte Vario-Dach. 16 Sekunden benötigt es, um den Roadster in ein Coupé zu verwandeln.

Bei allem Luxus und Komfort trägt dieser sl maskulinere Züge als sein Vorgänger. Besonders die Kühlschlitze im vorderen Kotflügel und auf der Motorhaube deuten auf einen Sportler hin, dessen Kraft – beim sl 350 noch mickrige 245 PS – sich bereits beim sl 500 in einer kultivierten Stärke von 306 PS entfaltet. Zur Leistungsexplosion kommt es dann beim Achtzylinder-Kompressor des sl 55 AMG und dem Zwölfzylinder-Biturbo des sl 600. Letzterer, mit zwei Tonnen Leergewicht eher eine Persiflage auf den eigentlichen sl-Begriff, bewegt seine Masse locker – ganz ohne Anstrengung. Die ist auch nicht vonnöten, denn die beiden Abgasturbolader garantieren 500 PS. Mit diesem »Bumms« auf der Antriebswelle sind 100 km/h in 4,7 Sekunden erreicht. Schade nur, dass der Computer für das Motormanagement bei 250 km/h einen elektronischen Riegel vorschiebt, wo doch die Tachoskala mit Tempo 300 lockt.

Interessanterweise kommt die Kompressor-Variante auf den gleichen Beschleunigungswert. Ein neu entwickelter mechanischer Lader zwischen den Zylinderbänken

Sportif et léger, comme le suggère l'abréviation sl, seul le coupé de course 300 sl apparu dans les années 1950 l'est réellement. Le légendaire coupé aux portières en ailes de mouette, déjà, pèse 440 kg de plus et, jusqu'en 1988, la famille sl a pris une surcharge pondérale de 500 kg. Il aura fallu attendre la cinquième génération de cette espèce dont le succès ne s'est jamais démenti jusqu'à ce jour – avec près de 500 000 exemplaires vendus – pour qu'elle réussisse à perdre un peu de poids : en tout et pour tout 35 kg. Dont pas moins de quinze grâce au long capot moteur qui, en aluminium, ne pèse maintenant plus que la moitié de ses homologues en acier. Les ailes, les portières et le couvercle de malle du même métal permettent de compenser la lourdeur des pesantes entrailles.

Avant de se familiariser avec ce coupé aux lignes musclées qui regorge de raffinements techniques, il vaut mieux connaître son alphabet. Dont, parmi une débauche d'abréviations, ABC – chez DaimlerChrysler, ces trois lettres signifient *Active Body Control* –, une régulation active des trains roulants qui étouffe dans l'œuf toute velléité de tangage ou de roulis. Tant que l'on laisse faire l'ordinateur, il s'avère un compagnon de route agréable. Mais il est déconseillé de céder à la tentation d'opter pour les réglages Sport sur les portions de route sinueuses. Il risque de réagir avec brutalité et il faut une certaine accoutumance pour composer avec lui. Sinon, la symbiose d'ABC, d'ESP et de SBC, le *Sensotronic Brake Control*, un système de freinage aux réglages qui frisent la perfection, absolument géniale sur le plan technique, ne sert pas à grand-chose.

Autres facteurs de sécurité – outre les arceaux que l'on peut aussi mettre en place à la main – les airbags à deux seuils de déclenchement pour le conducteur et son passager, les airbags rideau tête-thorax dans les portières, les sièges intégraux remarquablement bien capitonnés et le toit variable à commande électrohydraulique.

En sus de tout ce luxe et de tout ce confort, cette sl a des traits plus masculins que son prédécesseur. Les ouïes d'aération dans les ailes avant et sur le capot moteur sont un indice de sa sportivité. Quant à sa puissance – encore modeste avec 245 ch pour la sl 350 –, plus généreuse avec 306 ch pour la sl 500, elle rend celle-ci plus cultivée. Mais, pour connaître l'explosion de la puissance, il faut opter pour le huit-cylindres à compresseur de la sl 55 AMG ou le douze-cylindres biturbo de la sl 600. Cette dernière, avec un poids à vide de 2 tonnes, arbore plutôt *ad absurdum* la désignation originelle sl. Mais elle ne déplace pas moins cette masse sans le moindre effort. Ce qui est, d'ailleurs, logique quand on sait que les deux turbocompresseurs garantissent une cavalerie de 500 ch. Avec ce coup de pied au derrière, le 0 à 100 km/h en 4,7 secondes seulement n'est qu'une formalité.

Détail intéressant, la variante à compresseur réalise le même chiffre à l'accélération. Un tout nouveau compresseur mécanique entre les deux bancs de cylindres, fonctionnant selon le principe de Lysholm, génère une

Mercedes-Benz SL 350 – SL 55 AMG   2001

Mercedes-Benz SL 500 2003

works according to the Lysholm-supercharger principle that builds up more than 30 percent more boost pressure than comparable systems: with more than 23,000 rpm, 1850 kilograms (4080 lbs) of air per hour are pressed into the eight combustion chambers. Thanks to the electronically steered electromagnetic clutch, the supercharger is driven by a separate v-belt. The direct connection to the crankshaft enables the supercharger to react immediately to the gas pedal.

Even if the sound of the SL is not in the same league as the trumpets of Jericho, it does sublimely intensify itself in the fashion of *The Moldau* by Czech composer Bedrich Smetana.

arbeitet nach dem Prinzip des Lysholm-Kompressors, der bis zu 30 Prozent mehr Ladedruck als vergleichbare Systeme aufbaut: Mit mehr als 23 000 Umdrehungen pro Minute werden stündlich 1850 Kilogramm Luft in die acht Brennräume gedrückt. Dank einer elektromagnetischen Kupplung – elektronisch gesteuert – wird der Kompressor über einen separaten Keilriemen angetrieben. Die direkte Verbindung zur Kurbelwelle bedeutet sofortige Reaktion des Laders auf den Gasfuß.

Auch wenn der Sound des SL die Trompeten von Jericho vermissen lässt, er steigert sich unterschwellig wie *Die Moldau* des tschechischen Komponisten Friedrich Smetana.

pression de suralimentation supérieure jusqu'à concurrence de 30 % à celle des systèmes comparables : à plus de 23 000 tr/min, elle gave les huit chambres de combustion de 1850 kg d'air par heure. Grâce à un embrayage électromagnétique à gestion électronique, le compresseur est entraîné par une courroie crantée séparée. La liaison directe avec le vilebrequin signifie que le compresseur réagit immédiatement à la moindre sollicitation de l'accélérateur.

Même si la sonorité de la SL n'est pas comparable aux trompettes de Jéricho, elle n'en délivre pas moins une mélodie qui pourrait rivaliser avec la célèbre *Moldau* du compositeur tchèque Bedrich Smetana.

The SL 500 transforms itself in only 16 seconds from 2-seater sport coupé into a racy roadster, whose 306 bhp from 8 cylinders display refined power.

In nur 16 Sekunden verwandelt sich der SL 500 von einem zweisitzigem Sportcoupé in einen rassigen Roadster, dessen Achtzylinder mit 306 PS eine kultivierte Stärke entfaltet.

En seulement seize secondes, la SL 500 se métamorphose de coupé sport biplace en un roadster racé dont le huit-cylindres de 306 chevaux brille par sa culture et sa vigueur.

Typical of the SL class: side air outlets, aerodynamically slanted xenon headlights, and a striking almost beefy rear. An orgy of leather and noble woods is to be found in the cockpit with its over-dimensioned light protection screen for speedometer and rev counter. Mercedes also offers a 12-cylinder biturbo with 500 bhp as an alternative to the V8, while the SL 65 AMG manages as much as 612 bhp.

Typisch SL-Klasse: seitlicher Luftauslass, aerodynamisch abgeschrägte Xenon-Scheinwerfer und ein markantes, fast bulliges Heck. Im Cockpit mit über-dimensionalem Blendschutz für Tacho und Drehzahlmesser feiern Leder und Edelhölzer eine Design-Orgie. Alternativ zum V8-Motor bietet Mercedes auch einen 12-Zylinder-Biturbo mit 500 PS an, und der SL 65 AMG leistet gar 612 PS.

Détails typiques de la Classe SL : sorties d'air latérales, phares xénon aérodynamiques en biseau et une poupe caractéristique, presque râblée. Dans le cockpit où une grande casquette abrite le tachymètre et le compte-tours, cuir et bois précieux s'allient pour célébrer le design. Comme alternative au moteur V8, Mercedes propose aussi un douze-cylindres biturbo de 500 ch alors que la SL 65 AMG développe même 612 ch.

In March 2001, this independent c Class model variation from Mercedes-Benz presented itself as concisely as the bmw Compact 3 had done in 1994. This coupé with a youthful emphasis appeared even more dynamic after its 2004 facelift. Although the elegant curved relief of this two-door vehicle coming to an abrupt end behind the c-pillar disturbs the stylistic harmony of the side view a little, it obviously did not disturb the buyers – 190,000 of these sports coupés were sold over a period of three years. The producer happily noted that the majority of these customers had not previously had a star on their bonnet.

The Indianapolis special edition, which received its premiere at the Frankfurt IAA in 2003, was created to push the vehicle once again into the limelight before model refinement. A bi-xenon projection system with clear-glass optic replaced the ribbed headlights of the "Indy-racer"– with its diamond black-metallic or brilliant silver paintwork and fitted with 16-inch, double-spoke alloy wheels.

The sports coupé class of 2004 bears unmistakable characteristics. It appears more powerful from a front view due to the increased track width, from 1465 to 1505 millimeters (4'10" to 5'). This is accentuated by a new fender air intake with its lamellar structure – previously a plain little lattice grill. The radiator grille was also modified by more strongly emphasizing the cross ribs. On request, the fog light housing can incorporate the newly developed turning light. When the low beam is activated, this "around-the-corner headlight" automatically cuts in at low speeds as soon as the blinker is operated or the steering wheel turned.

The newly designed wheel covers and the standard five star alloy wheels for the c230 Kompressor and the c320, enhance the sports coupé as does the "rear lights' diamond optic," as it is called by Mercedes. Whoever finds the vehicle still too sober for their taste, can help themselves from the chrome package as they see fit. The new three spoke steering wheel with its silver colored buttons for telephone system, radio, and central display looks truly attractive. This steering wheel is covered in fine leather and fitted with thumb rests as part of the Evolution package. This proves its worth when the five-gear automatic transmission is to be switched manually using the buttons positioned on the steering wheel.

Regardless of whether it is the instrument panel, the center console, or the seat covers, everything in the Sport coupé that was good before spring 2004, is now even better. The same, but not exactly spacious with its 310-liter (10.9-cu.ft.) capacity: the trunk, whose capacity can be tripled to carry bulky objects by folding down the divided rear seating. The front seats can be tilted forward and upward by folding the backrest, allowing contortion-free passenger access to the rear seats. Actually a simple and not exactly new solution, nonetheless it has been elevated to an Easy-Entry-System by the Mercedes strategists. The explicit information in the Mercedes brochure that the vehicle possesses sport seats, the high sides of which

Kurz und bündig, wie 1994 der 3er Compact von bmw, stellte sich im März 2001 diese eigenständige Modell-Variante der c-Klasse von Mercedes-Benz vor. Ein betont jugendliches Coupé, das nach einem Facelifting 2004 noch dynamischer wirkt. Dass das elegant geschwungene Relief dieses Zweitürers abrupt hinter der c-Säule aufhört, stört ein wenig die Harmonie der Seitenansicht, doch offenbar nicht den Käufer, denn in drei Jahren ließen sich 190 000 dieser Sportcoupés an Mann und Frau bringen. Erfreut registrierte der Hersteller, dass die Mehrzahl der Kunden bislang keinen Stern vor der Nase hatte.

Um diesen Wagen vor der Modellpflege noch einmal in den Blickpunkt zu rücken, kreierte man die Sonder-Edition Indianapolis, die auf der Frankfurter IAA 2003 Premiere feierte. Beim »Indy-Renner« – diamantschwarz-metallic oder brillantsilber lackiert und mit 16-Zoll-Doppelspeichen-Leichtmetallrädern bestückt – lösten Bi-Xenon-Leuchten in Klarglas-Optik die geriffelten Scheinwerfer ab. Serienmäßig eingebaut: eine sensorgesteuerte Klimatisierungs-Automatik, genannt Thermatic.

Der Jahrgang 2004 des Sportcoupés trägt unverwechselbare Merkmale. Frontal wirkt er durch die von 1465 auf 1505 Millimeter verbreiterte Spur kraftvoller. Dazu trägt auch ein neuer Lufteinlass im Stoßfänger mit seiner Lamellenstruktur – bis dato ein braves Rautengitterchen – bei. Der Kühlergrill musste sich durch stärkere Betonung der Querrippen ebenfalls einer Modifikation unterziehen. Auf Wunsch nimmt das Gehäuse der Nebelscheinwerfer das neu entwickelte Abbiegelicht auf. Wenn das Abblendlicht aktiviert ist, schaltet sich dieser »Um-die-Ecke-Scheinwerfer« bei niedrigen Geschwindigkeiten automatisch ein, sobald der Blinker betätigt oder das Lenkrad bewegt wird.

Neu gestaltete Radzierblenden und serienmäßige Fünfstern-Leichtmetallräder für den c230 Kompressor und den c320 werten das Sportcoupé ebenso auf wie die »Brillant-Optik der Rückleuchten«, wie es bei Mercedes heißt. Wem der Wagen immer noch zu nüchtern vorkommt, bediene sich des Chrompakets. Wirklich formschön ist das neue Dreispeichen-Lenkrad mit silberfarbenen Tasten für Telefonanlage, Radio und Zentral-Display. In Verbindung mit einem weiteren Paket, Evolution, ist dieses Lenkrad mit feinem Leder bezogen und Daumenauflagen versehen. Diese bewähren sich, wenn das Fünfgang-Automatik-Getriebe manuell über Tasten am Lenkrad geschaltet werden soll.

Ob Armaturenbrett, Mittelkonsole oder Sitzbezüge, was im Sportcoupé bis zum Frühjahr 2004 gut war, ist jetzt noch besser geworden. Gleich bleibend, aber mit 310 Litern Volumen nicht gerade groß ausgefallen: der Laderaum, der sich durch Umlegen der geteilten Fond-Sitzbank zur Aufnahme sperriger Güter verdreifachen lässt. Um als Passagier ohne Verrenkungen nach hinten zu gelangen, muss man die Vordersitze durch Umlegen der Rückenlehnen nach vorn und oben klappen. Eigentlich eine simple und nicht ganz neue Lösung, die aber von den Mercedes-Strategen zum Easy-Entry-System erhoben wurde. Auch

Court, mais pas à court de sensations, ainsi se présente, en mars 2001, le Coupé Sport, variante à part de la Mercedes-Benz Classe c inspirée de la bmw Série 3 Compact apparue en 1994. Un coupé résolument jeune qui, restylé en 2004, est désormais encore plus dynamique. Si le relief aux galbes élégants de cette deux-portes tronqué brutalement derrière la lunette arrière gène un peu l'harmonie esthétique en vision latérale, cela ne semble pas être le cas des acheteurs. En effet, en trois ans, 190 000 conducteurs et conductrices se sont laissé séduire par ce Coupé Sport. Résultat d'autant plus réjouissant pour le constructeur que la majorité des clients ne se laissait, jusqu'ici, pas encore guider par une étoile.

Le millésime 2004 du Coupé Sport arbore des caractéristiques qui font qu'il est difficile de le confondre : vu de face, il est plus râblé avec ses voies élargies de 1465 à 1505 millimètres. Cela est aussi dû à une nouvelle entrée d'air dans le pare-chocs avant avec une grille de calandre à structure en lamelles – qui remplace l'ancienne brave grille de radiateur grillagé. La calandre a elle également été modifiée avec des barreaux horizontaux de plus grandes dimensions. En option, le boîtier des phares antibrouillard héberge aussi le nouvel éclairage de virage. Lorsque les codes sont actionnés, ces « phares qui regardent dans les coins » se mettent en marche automatiquement, à basse vitesse, dès que l'on actionne les clignotants ou fait tourner le volant.

De nouveaux enjoliveurs de roues ou les jantes en alliage léger à cinq étoiles proposées en série pour la c230 Kompressor et la c320 donnent une touche de noblesse supplémentaire au Coupé Sport, grâce, aussi, au look « diamant ciselé des feux arrière », comme le proclame Mercedes. Vraiment joli, le nouveau volant à trois branches avec touches argentées pour le système de téléphone, l'autoradio et l'écran central. En combinaison avec un autre pack baptisé Evolution, ce volant est gainé d'un cuir fin et comporte des supports pour les pouces. Des supports qui font leurs preuves lorsque l'on désire commander la boîte automatique à cinq vitesses à la main à l'aide des touches intégrées au volant.

Que ce soit le tableau de bord, la console centrale ou les garnissages de sièges, ce qui était déjà bien dans le Coupé Sport jusqu'au millésime 2004 a maintenant encore été amélioré. Quant au coffre, guère généreux avec une capacité de 310 litres, il est resté identique. Mais, en rabattant la banquette arrière fractionnée, on peut faire tripler son volume et transporter des objets encombrants. Pour permettre aux passagers de s'installer à l'arrière sans trop de contorsions, il est possible de rabattre le dossier des sièges avant et de faire basculer ceux-ci vers le tableau de bord. Une solution à vrai dire simple et guère innovante, mais que les commerciaux de Mercedes ont anoblie en la rebaptisant Easy-Entry-System. Quant à la remarque expresse, dans le prospectus Mercedes, que la voiture possède des sièges Sport dont les flancs relevés assurent aussi un excellent maintien latéral dans les virages serrés,

MERCEDES-BENZ
SPORTCOUPÉ C 200 CDI – C 320 2001

Mercedes-Benz Sportcoupé C 230 2003

ensure a safe hold even in tight cornering, is superfluous. What else would you expect of a sports coupé!

As usually is the case in the C class, the sport coupé's engine can be chosen from an extensive list of possibilities: six four-cylinders, three of them with superchargers, a V6, and, the strongest link in this chain, the C 30 CDI from AMG, a five-cylinder engine with 231 bhp. The C 230 Kompressor is to be recommended, for the electronic blocking takes effect at 250 kph (155 mph) anyway. This lively series four-cylinder transports the 1475-kilo (3250-lbs) curb weight of this relatively light vehicle in a racy manner: acceleration from zero to 100 kph (62 mph) in 8.1 seconds and 240 kph (149 mph) top speed. Not exactly racetrack performance, but then that's not what this road sportsman is built for.

der ausdrückliche Hinweis im Mercedes-Prospekt, der Wagen habe Sportsitze, deren hochgezogene Flanken auch in engen Kurven für sicheren Halt sorgen, ist überflüssig. Was sonst erwartet man von einem Sport-Coupé!

Wie in der C-Klasse üblich, steht auch für das Coupé eine reichhaltige Triebwerksauswahl zur Verfügung: Sechs Vierzylinder, davon drei mit Kompressor, ein V6 und als stärkstes Glied in dieser Kette der C 30 CDI von AMG, ein Fünfzylinder mit 231 PS. Da bei 250 Stundenkilometern ohnehin elektronisch abgeriegelt wird, empfiehlt sich der C 230 Kompressor. Dieser muntere Reihen-Vierzylinder bewegt das mit 1475 Kilo Leergewicht einigermaßen leichte Auto recht flott: Beschleunigung von 0 auf 100 km/h in 8,1 Sekunden und 240 Stundenkilometer Endgeschwindigkeit. Keine Werte für die Rennstrecke, aber dafür ist dieser Straßensportler ja auch nicht gebaut worden.

elle est tout à fait superflue : on n'en attend en effet pas moins d'un Coupé Sport !

Comme de coutume avec la Classe C, pour le coupé aussi on n'a que l'embarras du choix quant aux moteurs : six quatre-cylindres, dont trois à compresseur, un V6 et le groupe motopropulseur le plus puissant de la famille, le C 30 CDI d'AMG, un cinq-cylindres de 231 ch. La vitesse étant de toute façon régulée électroniquement à 250 km/h, nous vous recommanderons la version C 230 Kompressor. Ce quatre-cylindres, très volontaire, ne manque pas de tempérament grâce au poids relativement contenu de la voiture, 1475 kg : le 0 à 100 km/h est abattu en 8,1 secondes et elle croise à une vitesse de pointe de 240 km/h. Avec cela, vous n'impressionnerez personne sur les circuits, mais elle a été conçue pour la route et non pour la compétition.

A distinctive rear design and a compact wedge form: the sport coupé, fitted with a 6-gear switching transmission as standard, displays as the C230 a red top above its four-cylinder supercharger engine. Reminiscent of the *testa rossa* from Maranello?

Unverwechselbar im Design der Heckpartie und der kompakten Keilform: Das Sportcoupé, serienmäßig mit einem 6-Gang-Schaltgetriebe ausgerüstet, zeigt als C230 über seinem Vierzylinder-Kompressor-Motor einen roten Deckel. Etwa eine Reminiszenz an die *testa rossa* aus Maranello?

Unique par le design de sa poupe et ses lignes cunéiformes compactes : le Coupé Sport, équipé en série d'une boîte manuelle à six vitesses, est propulsé, en version C230, par un moteur à compresseur et à quatre cylindres avec un couvercle de culasse de couleur rouge. Est-ce un clin d'œil à la *testa rossa* de Maranello ?

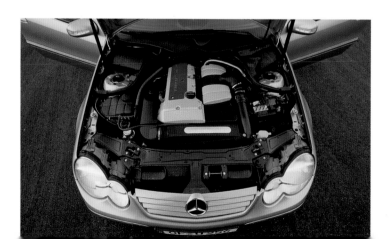

Mercedes-Benz Sportcoupé C200 CDI – C320 2001

As the new E Class was presented in the spring of 2004 after a four-year development phase and a total investment of more than two billion Euros, Dr. Joachim Schmidt, Mercedes-Benz's marketing and sales boss took stock with satisfaction: "with about 1.4 million vehicles produced since 1995, the E Class is the most successful Mercedes model. No other limousine in the top-of-the-range segment is as popular as the E Class. That is proved by the high average worldwide market share of 24 percent". The "heart of the marque", as DaimlerChrysler executive and Mercedes leader Jürgen Hubbert calls this vehicle with its striking four-eyed visage, impresses with its dependability, esthetic, comfort, and high value stability. Apart from the most common model variation, the E320, there are twelve further engines from which to choose, ranging from 123 to 477 bhp. In order to service the world market without exception, the E Class is not only produced in Germany, but also in Egypt, India, Malaysia, Thailand, and the Philippines.

"To do the good even better", that was the task formulation for the bodywork development, according to the principle of "the right material in the right place". Therefore, principally steel and high-strength steel alloys are used, whereas the aluminum contribution is limited to the front wings, hood, trunk lid, as well as the front and rear modules. The side sections, welded together using laser-welding technology, offer even more impact safety than previously.

If the predecessor, the 210-model range from 1995 onward, was considered the most aerodynamic limousine series in the world, with its sensational aerodynamic drag coefficient of 0.27, this E Class undercut its own record by a hundredth. Stylistically it embodies Mercedes design trend to a wedge-shaped, coupé-like side view with arched shoulder and waistline, rear with its subtle trailing edge, and more modern interpretation of the classical radiator grille.

The electro hydraulic braking system developed by Mercedes-Benz, the Sensotronic Brake Control, a "thinking" brake, which belongs to the E Class as a standard, displays a high technical standard. The new four-link front suspension and the principally aluminum multi-link independent rear suspension contribute to better road handling. The pneumatic suspension system of the E 500, which electronically steers both the suspension and shock absorbers at the same time, is a convenience available for all E Class models on payment of a supplement.

Several airbags, the two-step seatbelt pressure inhibitor, in addition to an accident sensor system, ensure passenger safety. Teleaid can be installed, as an option, in connection with an integrated telephone system. An automatic emergency sos signal is sent to the nearest emergency alarm center when the airbags are activated by a crash. There, an attempt is made to contact the unlucky driver by means of the intercom system. If unsuccessful, an ambulance is sent at speed. Of course, the automatic

Als nach vierjähriger Entwicklungszeit und einer Gesamtinvestition von mehr als zwei Milliarden Euro im Frühjahr 2002 die neue E-Klasse präsentiert wurde, zog Dr. Joachim Schmidt, Marketing- und Vertriebschef von Mercedes-Benz, zufrieden Bilanz: »Mit rund 1,4 Millionen Fahrzeugen, die wir seit 1995 produziert haben, ist die E-Klasse eines der erfolgreichsten Mercedes-Modelle. Keine andere Limousine im Segment der Oberklasse ist so beliebt wie die E-Klasse. Das beweist der hohe Marktanteil von weltweit durchschnittlich 24 Prozent.« Das »Herz der Marke«, wie DaimlerChrysler-Vorstand und Mercedes-Dirigent Jürgen Hubbert dieses Auto mit dem markanten Vier-Augen-Gesicht nennt, besticht durch Zuverlässigkeit, Ästhetik, Komfort und hohe Wertbeständigkeit. Neben dem E320, der gängigsten Modell-Variante, stehen zwölf weitere Triebwerke – die Bandbreite reicht von 123 bis 477 PS – zur Auswahl. Um den Weltmarkt lückenlos bedienen zu können, wird die E-Klasse nicht nur in Deutschland, sondern auch in Ägypten, Indien, Malaysia, Thailand und auf den Philippinen produziert.

»Gutes noch besser machen«, so lautete die Aufgabenstellung an die Karosserie-Entwicklung, nach dem Prinzip »der richtige Werkstoff am richtigen Ort«. So werden vornehmlich Stahl und hochfeste Stahllegierungen verbaut, während sich der Aluminium-Anteil auf vordere Kotflügel, Motorhaube, Kofferraumdeckel sowie Front- und Heckmodule beschränkt. Mit Laser-Schweißtechnik zu einem Stück zusammengefügt, bieten die Seitenwände noch mehr Aufprall-Sicherheit als zuvor.

Galt der Vorgänger, Baureihe 210 ab 1995, damals als die strömungsgünstigste Serienlimousine der Welt, mit dem sensationellen Luftwiderstandsbeiwert von 0,27, so unterbietet diese E-Klasse den eigenen Rekord um ein Hundertstel. Stilistisch verkörpert sie den Design-Trend von Mercedes zu keilförmigen, Coupé-ähnlichen Seitenansichten mit bogenförmig gespannter Schulter- und Gürtellinie, Heck mit dezenter Abrisskante und moderner Interpretation des klassischen Kühlergrills.

Höchstes technisches Niveau dokumentiert das von Mercedes-Benz entwickelte elektrohydraulische Bremssystem Sensotronic Brake Control, eine »mitdenkende« Bremse, die bei der E-Klasse zur Serienausstattung gehört. Zum besseren Handling tragen die neue Vierlenker-Vorderachse und die vornehmlich aus Aluminium gefertigte Raumlenker-Hinterachse bei. Das Luftfederungssystem des E500, das gleichzeitig Federung und Dämpfer elektronisch steuert, ist gegen Aufpreis für alle E-Klassen-Vertreter wohlfeil.

Der Insassen-Sicherheit dienen mehrere Airbags, der zweistufige Gurtkraft-Begrenzer sowie eine neue Unfall-Sensorik. Auf Wunsch – in Verbindung mit einer fest installierten Telefonanlage – kann Teleaid eingebaut werden. Mit der Aktivierung der Airbags bei einem Crash geht automatisch ein sos-Signal an die nächste Notrufzentrale. Dort wird versucht, mit dem Unglücksraben über die Gegensprechanlage Kontakt aufzunehmen. Gelingt das nicht, düst

Quand, à l'issue de quatre ans de développeme et au prix de plus de deux milliards d'euro d'investissements, la nouvelle Classe E est pr sentée, au printemps 2002, Joachim Schmidt, responsab du marketing et de la distribution chez Mercedes-Ben dresse un bilan non sans satisfaction : « Avec environ 1. million de véhicules produits depuis 1995, la Classe E rester l'un des modèles de Mercedes qui aura connu le plus d succès. » Le « cœur de la marque » – comme le présiden du directoire de DaimlerChrysler et « grand timonier de Mercedes, Jürgen Hubbert, qualifie cette voiture a marquant visage à quatre yeux – séduit par sa fiabilité son esthétique, son confort et sa faible dépréciation. Outr la E 320, la variante de modèle la plus courante, douze autre moteurs sont proposés au choix – la palette va de 123 477 ch. Afin de pouvoir desservir le marché mondial san aucune lacune, la Classe E n'est pas seulement produite e Allemagne, mais aussi en Égypte, en Inde, en Malaisie, e Thaïlande et aux Philippines.

« Améliorer ce qui était déjà bon », telle est la consign donnée aux ingénieurs chargés de concevoir la carrosser selon le principe « le bon matériau au bon endroit ». Ain ont-ils utilisé essentiellement de l'acier et des alliag d'acier à haute résistance alors que l'aluminium se circons crit aux ailes avant, au capot moteur et au couvercle d coffre ainsi qu'aux modules de la proue et de la poupe Assemblées en un seul bloc grâce à la technique de soudag au laser, les parois latérales offrent une protection cont les collisions latérales encore jamais vue à ce jour.

Tandis que sa devancière, la gamme 210 née en 199 était réputée comme la limousine de série la plus aéro dynamique au monde avec un C_X sensationnel de 0,27 cette Classe E bat son propre record d'un centième. Esthé tiquement, elle incarne la tendance, actuellement en vogu pour le design chez Mercedes, du profil cunéiforme au styl de coupé avec une ligne d'épaules et de ceinture tendue e arc de cercle, une poupe à l'arête de décrochement discrè et une interprétation moderne de la classique calandre.

Avec le système de freinage électrohydraulique Senso tronic Brake Control, un frein « intelligent » qui fait parti de l'équipement de série pour la Classe E, Mercedes-Ben documente sa technicité inégalée à ce jour. Le nouvea train avant à quatre bras et l'essieu arrière multibras essentiellement en aluminium, contribuent à l'amélio ration du comportement. Le système de suspension pneu matique de la E 500, qui gère, simultanément, les ressort et les amortisseurs à l'aide de l'électronique, est propos contre un supplément de prix pour toutes les versions d la Classe E.

Plusieurs airbags, le limiteur à deux niveaux de la forc de tension de la ceinture ainsi que tout un arsenal d nouveaux capteurs de détection d'un éventuel acciden garantissent la sécurité des occupants. Sur demande – e combinaison avec un téléphone embarqué monté à demeure – il est possible d'installer le dispositif Teleaid Le déclenchement d'un ou de plusieurs airbags en ca

Mercedes-Benz E 320 CDI 2003

call for help is only of use when the crashed driver is to be found in a technologically highly developed region with the corresponding communication possibilities.

The fitting of a two-part panorama roof with its view from the front windscreen frame through to the rear roof section is a better prospect. At the press of a button, the front roof section slides slowly to the rear, while a transparent slat is raised at the front as a windbreak. Solar voltaic cells transform sunlight into energy for a cooling fan to prevent the vehicle from overheating unbearably when parked on a hot summer day. "Are you sitting comfortably?" This heretical question is answered by the multi-contoured seats with driving dynamics; the seat flanks pump themselves up – computer-steered – in response to the driving situation of the E Class vehicle, forming a stability pact with the seat occupant.

der Rettungswagen sofort los. Doch nützt der automatische Hilferuf natürlich nur, wenn man sich seinen Unfallpartner in einer technisch hoch entwickelten Zivilisation mit den dazugehörigen Kommunikations-Möglichkeiten sucht.

Bessere Aussichten verheißt die Bestückung mit einem zweiteiligen Panorama-Dach mit Durchblick vom Frontscheiben-Rahmen bis zum hinteren Teil des Daches. Auf Knopfdruck fährt das vordere Dachteil langsam nach hinten, während sich vorn eine durchsichtige Lamelle aufstellt, um als Windabweiser zu fungieren. Damit sich das Fahrzeug beim Parken an heißen Sommertagen nicht unerträglich aufwärmt, wandeln Solarzellen Sonnenlicht in Energie für ein Kühlluftgebläse um. »Sitzt du gut?« Diese ketzerische Frage beantwortet der fahrdynamische Multikontur-Sitz, denn je nach Fahrsituation des E-Klasse-Wagens pumpen sich computergesteuert die Sitzflanken auf und schließen mit dem Sitz-Benutzer einen Stabilitätspakt.

de collision a pour effet l'envoi automatique d'un SOS à la centrale d'appel de détresse la plus proche. De là, les spécialistes s'efforcent de prendre contact par l'Interphone avec le malheureux conducteur. En cas d'échec, une ambulance se rend immédiatement sur place.

Plus agréables sont les perspectives qu'offre le toit panoramique à deux panneaux, qui permet de scruter le ciel du haut du pare-brise jusqu'à la lunette arrière. Il suffit d'appuyer sur un bouton pour faire reculer lentement la partie antérieure du toit tandis qu'à l'avant, une lamelle transparente s'érige et sert de déflecteur. « Es-tu bien assis ? » Cette question insidieuse a sa réponse avec le siège multicontour dynamique, car, selon la situation de conduite de la Classe E, plusieurs coussins du siège – pilotés par ordinateur – se gonflent et se dégonflent à la demande et concluent un pacte de stabilité avec l'occupant du fauteuil.

Mercedes-Benz E 200 CDI – E 55 AMG 2002

The buyer of an E class model has the choice of 48 color combinations for the exterior and diversity of interiors. Twelve further engine variations are available in addition to the V6 of the E320 with its 224 bhp. *A la carte* power up to 500 bhp!

Beim Exterieur und der Vielfalt des Interieurs kann der Käufer eines E-Klasse-Modells zwischen 48 Farbkombinationen wählen. Zum V6 des E320 mit 224 PS, ein Dreiventiler, gesellen sich noch zwölf weitere Triebwerks-Varianten. Kraft nach Wahl bis 500 PS!

Pour l'extérieur et la diversité de l'intérieur, l'acheteur d'un modèle de la Classe E a le choix entre 48 combinaisons de coloris. Au V6 de 224 ch de la E320, un moteur à trois soupapes, s'ajoutent encore douze autres variantes de motorisation. Pour la cavalerie, on n'a que l'embarras du choix : jusqu'à 500 ch !

The 5-gear automatic transmission is a standard fitting for the E 320, while bi-xenon headlights and light metal alloy wheels – here a 5-spoke design – belong to the "Avantgarde" edition.

Serienmäßig beim E 320 ist das 5-Gang-Automatikgetriebe, während Bi-Xenon-Scheinwerfer und Leichtmetallräder – hier im 5-Speichen-Design – zu den Merkmalen der Ausstattungslinie »Avantgarde« gehören.

La E 320 est équipée en série d'une boîte automatique à cinq vitesses tandis que les phares bixénon et les jantes en alliage léger – ici au design à cinq bâtons – figurent parmi les caractéristiques du niveau de finition « Avantgarde ».

This elegant coupé with its silhouette borrowed from the DTM racer, could not have been presented in a more spectacular manner: a joint presentation at the 2002 Geneva Salon of the CLK coupé with its motor sport derivate, the 470 bhp strong model for the German Touring Masters. In the same year, AMG came out with the steam hammer for the road: a CLK with a 5.5-liter engine and 367 bhp that enable an acceleration of 5.2 seconds. The sportiest manner to travel with a CLK captivates with its striking optic: an enormous air intake with spoiler lops in the fender, pronounced side rocker panels, lower back panel, wide-profile tires on alloy wheels all underline the claim to be leader of its class. The speedometer with its calibration up to 320 kph (200 mph) appears somewhat out of place considering that the concentrated power cannot be allowed free rein.

The engine palette for the CLK coupé is identical to that of the cabriolet except for a more economical Common-Rail diesel motor, which despite its 170 bhp swallows an average of only 6.6 liters (36 mpg). This CDI engine is not available for the open-air CLK. Instead, there is a choice of six aggregates: two four-cylinders and two six-cylinders, the CLK 500's 5-liter V8, and the previously mentioned fountain of power which the Mercedes daughter, AMG, lets gush in Affalterbach.

Design boss Peter Pfeiffer – formative of the latest Mercedes products – also drew a line along the waistband of the CLK, emphasized by the hollow beneath which runs out into the front wing. With the new CLS it is even more distinctive, while the new A Class of 2004 displays it with a slight rear cut. The flowing lines are augmented by stylistic precision work such as the interlocking contours of the rocker panel series, the gentle hint of spoiler lips, as well as the analogue accentuation of the lower rear panel area. Well proportioned in this way, all CLKs were adorned with alloy wheels by the producer.

The external impression is strengthened by the ambience of the interior: noble and well thought-out into the smallest detail. The dashboard is dominated by the three round instruments. The central tachometer conceals a multifunctional display, whose eight menus can be activated by four buttons on the heated steering wheel. A "Comand APS" can be built into the center console on payment of a hefty supplement. This term covers a combination of navigation system, radio, CD player, and telephone with e-mail and messaging functions. The addition of a TV tuner is then a mere formality, as is the supplementation of the standard seven-speaker sound system with an "all-surround" sound for each of the four seats. A Linguatronic command is sufficient to mute the acoustic background when necessary. This optional extra, available on payment of a supplement, containing speech-control over radio, CD player, or navigation system, obviously requires a correspondingly modified and clear formulation. Dialects do not go down well at all.

Gemeinsame Präsentation des CLK-Coupés und seines Motorsport-Derivates, der 470 PS starken Ausführung für die Deutsche Tourenwagen Masters, auf dem Genfer Salon 2002: Spektakulärer konnte dieses elegante Coupé, von dem sich der DTM-Renner die Silhouette entliehen hat, nicht eingeführt werden. Noch im gleichen Jahr rückte AMG den Dampfhammer für die Straße heraus: einen CLK mit 5,5-Liter-Triebwerk und 367 PS, die eine Beschleunigung von 5,2 Sekunden ermöglichen. Die sportlichste Form, mit einem CLK unterwegs zu sein, besticht durch ihre auffällige Optik: Ein gewaltiger Lufteinlass im Stoßfänger mit Spoiler-Lippe, ausgeprägte seitliche Schweller, Heckschürze und Breitreifen auf den Leichtmetallrädern unterstreichen den Anspruch, Klassen-Primus zu sein. Da die geballte Kraft nicht ganz ausgetobt werden kann, wirkt der bis 320 Stundenkilometer reichende Tacho etwas deplatziert.

Die Motoren-Palette für CLK Coupé und Cabriolet ist bis auf einen sparsamen Common-Rail-Dieselmotor, der trotz seiner 170 PS lediglich 6,6 Liter im Schnitt schluckt, identisch. Dieses CDI-Triebwerk gibt es nicht für den Open-Air-CLK. Ansonsten stehen sechs Aggregate zur Auswahl: je zwei Vier- und Sechszylinder, der 5-Liter-V8 des CLK 500 und die bereits beschriebene Kraftquelle, die die Mercedes-Tochter AMG in Affalterbach sprudeln lässt.

Design-Chef Peter Pfeiffer spannt – prägnant für die jüngsten Mercedes-Jahrgänge – auch beim CLK einen Bogen über die Gürtellinie und betont diese durch eine darunter liegende Sicke, die im vorderen Kotflügel ausläuft. Beim neuen CLS ist sie sogar noch ausgeprägter, und auch die A-Klasse, Jahrgang 2004, trägt sie mit leichtem Hinterschnitt zur Schau. Stilistische Feinarbeit wie die ineinander greifenden Konturen der Serienschweller, die zarte Andeutung von Spoilerlippen sowie die analoge Betonung im unteren Heckschürzen-Bereich tragen zu der fließenden Form bei. Solchermaßen wohl proportioniert, dürfen sich alle CLK von Haus aus mit Leichtmetallrädern schmücken.

Das Ambiente des Interieurs bekräftigt den äußeren Eindruck: nobel und durchdacht bis ins kleinste Detail. Drei Rundinstrumente beherrschen das Armaturenbrett. Der zentrale Tacho beherbergt ein Multifunktions-Display, dessen acht Menüs durch vier Tasten am beheizbaren Lederlenkrad abgerufen werden können. Gegen saftigen Aufpreis kann in der Mittelkonsole »Comand APS« eingebaut werden. Hinter dieser Bezeichnung verbirgt sich eine Kombination aus Navigationssystem, Radio, CD-Player und Telefon mit E-Mail und SMS-Funktion. Die Addition eines TV-Tuners ist dann nur noch reine Formsache – wie die Ergänzung des serienmäßigen Sound-Systems mit sieben Lautsprechern durch einen Surround-Klang an jedem der vier Sitze. Selbst die Einfach-Ausführung, das Radio Audio 10, kommt nicht ohne 42-seitige Bedienungsanleitung – ohne Register, wohlgemerkt – aus. Um sich bei dieser akustischen Kulisse Gehör zu verschaffen, genügt ein Befehl in die Linguatronic, um sie zum Verstummen zu bringen. Diese gegen Aufpreis erhältliche Sprachbedienung von

Théâtre de la présentation commune du coupé CLK et de sa version course, l'extrapolation de 470 ch destinée au Deutsche Tourenwagen Masters (DTM) : le Salon de Genève 2002 – dévoiler plus spectaculairement cet élégant coupé auquel le bolide du DTM a chipé la silhouette aurait été difficile. La même année encore, AMG dévoile un avion pour la route : une CLK dotée d'un moteur de 5,5 litres développant 367 ch qui la catapulte en 5,2 secondes de 0 à 100 km/h. Le moyen le plus sportif – et le plus exclusif – de se déplacer en CLK séduit par son esthétique qui attire immédiatement le regard : une immense entrée d'air dans le pare-chocs avec lame d'aileron, de volumineux seuils de portière, un imposant tablier arrière et des pneus larges chaussant des jantes en alliage léger soulignent son ambition : être la première de sa classe. Quand on sait qu'il n'est pas possible de laisser libre cours à un tempérament exubérant, le tachymètre gravé jusqu'à 320 km/h semble quelque peu déplacé.

À l'exception d'un économique moteur Diesel à rampe commune qui, malgré ses 170 ch, consomme seulement 6,6 litres aux 100 km en moyenne, la palette de moteurs pour les CLK Coupé et Cabriolet est identique. Ce moteur CDI n'est pas prévu pour la CLK de plein air ; sinon, on a le choix entre six moteurs : respectivement deux quatre-cylindres et six-cylindres, le V8 de 5 litres de la CLK 500 et le groupe motopropulseur source d'émerveillement que fait pétiller AMG, la filiale de Mercedes qui a son siège à Affalterbach.

Pour la CLK aussi, Peter Pfeiffer, le responsable du design, étire un arc de cercle – caractéristique des tout derniers millésimes Mercedes – le long de la ligne de ceinture, que souligne un coup de gouge qui s'efface à l'extrémité de l'aile avant. Avec la nouvelle CLS, il est même encore plus creusé, et la Classe A du millésime 2004, elle aussi, arbore le même coup de griffe. Des détails esthétiques qui témoignent d'une grande finesse tels que les contours des bas de caisse se fondant les uns dans les autres, la discrète ébauche de lame d'aileron ainsi que le léger accent similaire qu'arbore le tablier arrière contribuent à la fluidité des formes.

L'ambiance qui règne dans l'habitacle confirme l'expression extérieure : noblesse de la finition et solutions pensées jusque dans les moindres détails sont au rendezvous. Trois instruments circulaires monopolisent le tableau de bord. Le tachymètre central intègre un écran multifonction dont on peut appeler les huit menus grâce à quatre touches intégrées au volant chauffant gainé de cuir. Ceux qui peuvent se l'offrir trouveront dans la console médiane le système de navigation « Comand APS ». Derrière cette désignation se dissimule une combinaison de systèmes de navigation, d'autoradio, de lecteur de CD et de téléphone avec fonctions e-mail et SMS. Pour se faire entendre dans une telle débauche de raffinements acoustiques, il suffit de donner un ordre avec la commande vocale Linguatronic et le silence règne instantanément. Cette option, disponible contre paiement d'un supplé-

Mercedes-Benz CLK 320 2003

The CLK is not governed solely by high-tech and nobility, but also possesses highly practical lesser features. A wheel change after an irksome tire puncture can be avoided when the repair kit, which includes an electric air pump, is used. Both active and passive safety are written large with the CLK, as is the case with all Mercedes products. Window bags have been installed in addition to the two-part frontal airbags and side bags for driver and passenger. Self-tightening seat belts and seat belt force-limiters are standard. With the cabriolet, roll bars are extended in case of emergency. The chassis, with its front triple-link suspension and its multi-link independent rear suspension, is well balanced, and excuses little mistakes on the part of the driver thanks to ESP. Moreover, if it should come to a crash – for whatever reason – the strengthened side frame and rear-seating crossbeam do their job well.

Radio, CD-Player oder Navigationssystem setzt natürlich eine entsprechend angepasste und deutliche Formulierung voraus. Dialekte kommen ganz schlecht an. Im CLK regieren nicht nur Hightech und Nobilität, sondern er wartet auch mit kleinen, äußerst praktischen Dingen auf. So kann man sich bei einer lästigen Reifenpanne den Radwechsel ersparen, wenn man den Reparatur-Kit, zu dem auch eine elektrische Luftpumpe gehört, benutzt.

Wie bei allen Mercedes wird auch im CLK aktive und passive Sicherheit groß geschrieben. Neben den zweistufigen Frontairbags und Sidebags für Fahrer und Beifahrer sind auch Windowbags installiert. Gurtstraffer mit Gurtkraftbegrenzern für alle vier Sitze gehören zur Standardbestückung. Beim Cabrio fahren im Notfall Überrollbügel aus. Das Fahrwerk mit Dreilenkerachse vorn und Raumlenkerachse hinten ist ausgewogen und verzeiht dank ESP kleinere Fehler des CLK-Lenkers. Und wenn es wirklich – aus welchen Gründen auch immer – einmal krachen sollte, hält die in Seitenwand und Fondsitzquerträger verstärkte Karosserie, was sie verspricht.

ment, comprenant la commande vocale de l'autoradio, du lecteur de CD ou du système de navigation, présuppose naturellement une élocution adaptée et, comme il se doit, bien audible.

Comme dans toutes les Mercedes, dans la CLK aussi la sécurité active et passive est écrite en lettres d'or. Outre les airbags avant à deux seuils de déclenchement et airbags latéraux pour le conducteur et le passager, elle offre aussi des airbags rideaux tête-thorax. Les tendeurs de ceintures avec limiteur de la force de tension à chacune des quatre places font partie de l'équipement de série. Sur le cabriolet, des arceaux de sécurité s'érigent instantanément en cas de danger. Les trains roulants avec essieu à trois bras à l'avant et essieu multibras à l'arrière sont équilibrés et, grâce à l'ESP, pardonnent les petites erreurs d'appréciation du conducteur de la CLK. Et si une collision devait malgré tout se produire, la carrosserie renforcée à hauteur des parois latérales et de la poutre transversale sous la banquette arrière tiendrait sans aucun doute ses promesses.

Distinctive of the younger Mercedes generations: the design arch that spans from the rear lights to the front headlights, and which underlines the flowing roof form without any disturbing B column.

Prägnant für die jüngeren Mercedes-Generationen: der Bogen, den das Design von den Rückleuchten zu den Frontscheinwerfern spannt und den von keiner B-Säule gestörten Dachfluss unterstreicht.

Caractéristiques des récentes générations de Mercedes : le galbe tendu par les designers des optiques arrière aux phares et la ligne de toit qu'aucun pied central ne vient dégrader.

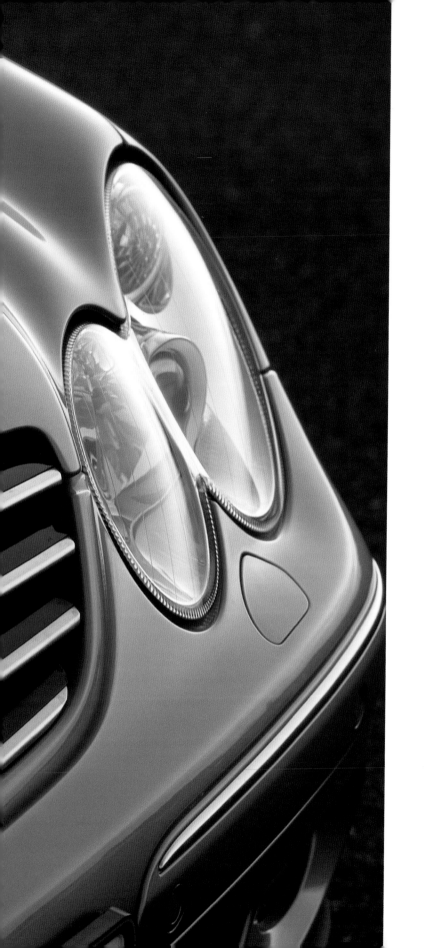

The CLK Coupé, presented at the Geneva
Motor Show of 2002, is an integral part of the
long coupé tradition of Mercedes: fittings,
technology, and road handling – hardly a wish
is left unanswered.

Coupés besitzen bei Mercedes eine lange
Tradition, in die sich das CLK-Coupé, 2002
auf dem Genfer Salon vorgestellt, würdig
einreiht: Ausstattung, Technik, Fahrverhalten –
es bleiben wenig Wünsche übrig.

Chez Mercedes, les coupés ont une longue
tradition dans le droit-fil de laquelle s'inscrit
dignement le Coupé CLK présenté en 2002
au Salon de Genève : équipement, technique,
comportement – difficile de formuler des
critiques.

Engines were his purpose in life, together with Gottlieb Daimler he wrote automobile history, and as he founded his own engine company, Count Zeppelin and other aviators queued up with their engine requirements: Wilhelm Maybach – a legendary personality whose name lives on in the name of luxury limousines from Sindelfingen. The direct competition with Rolls-Royce began as early as 1921, as his son, Karl Maybach, whose ingeniousness complemented that of his father in a most wonderful way, successfully set a Spyker equipped with a Maybach W2 engine on the prestigious Rolls-Royce 30,000 kilometer (18,645 miles) long-distance record. Several British gentlemen were not amused as Maybach presented with the W3 a completely luxurious vehicle at the Berlin Automobile Exhibition of the same year. This Germanic vehicle did not only compete with a comparable degree of comfort and price, it also offered much technically. A novelty: the clutch pedal disappeared, the operation of a separate hill-lever was only needed on steep inclines. The nobility that the bi-colored Maybach Zeppelin DS8 with streamlined body radiated in 1933 is reflected in the present-day Maybach.

"Equipped with the automobile technology of the 21st century, produced in a modern factory and designed with a great love of detail, this vehicle mirrors the competence of the DaimlerChrysler company as the most innovative automobile producer with the richest of traditions", that is how Maybach described its own position in the top-of-the-range class. Here, luxury is a matter of course, and technical tidbits are served on a silver platter.

The chassis consists of high-stability steel alloy in order to create maximum stability with a minimum of material. The front wings, hood, roof, and doors are made from aluminum on the grounds of weight. The trunk lid, under which room is provided for even large items of luggage, consists of glass fiber reinforced plastic. This all means that just 22 percent of the Maybach 62's 2.8-ton total weight can be attributed to the outer hull. The vehicle's name is derived from the vehicle's length of 6.2 meters (20 ft 4 in). The heavy armor-plated version, bulletproof and equipped with splinter protection for the occupants, possesses extra security components on all areas of weakness and tires with emergency running properties. Even the considerable extra weight of this Maybach Guard edition poses no problems for the chassis. The technical blessings of the S Class are fallen back upon: active differential pneumatic suspension with an adaptable shock absorber system that compensate for all burdens as required.

Both the Maybach 62 model and the half a meter (1'8") shorter 57 variation, represent their size in an individual and distinguished manner. The smooth running of the low-noise 12-cylinder Biturbo with its 550 bhp – the renowned tuner Brabus manages to extract up to 640 – and the brilliant 900 Newton meter torque at only 2300 rpm are impressive. Correspondingly rapid is the

Motoren waren sein Leben, zusammen mit Gottlieb Daimler schrieb er Automobilgeschichte, und als er eine eigene Motorengesellschaft gründete, standen Graf Zeppelin und die Luftfahrt mit Triebwerkswünschen Schlange: Wilhelm Maybach – eine legendäre Persönlichkeit, deren Name in Luxuslimousinen aus Sindelfingen weiterlebt. Die direkte Konkurrenz zu Rolls-Royce begann 1921, als sein Filius, Karl Maybach, dessen Ingeniosität die des Vaters wunderbar ergänzte, einen Spyker mit Maybach-W2-Triebwerk auf den prestigeträchtigen Langstreckenrekord über 30 000 Kilometer von Rolls-Royce ansetzte – mit Erfolg! Als Maybach noch im gleichen Jahr auf der Berliner Automobil-Ausstellung mit dem W3 ein komplettes Luxusmobil präsentierte, waren einige Herren auf der Insel *not amused*. Wartete doch dieses germanische Fahrzeug nicht nur mit vergleichbarem Komfort und Preis auf, sondern bot auch technisch viel. Novum: das Kupplungspedal entfiel, nur für starke Steigungen musste ein Berg-Hebel betätigt werden. Die Noblesse, die der zweifarbige Maybach Zeppelin DS8 mit Stromlinien-Karosserie 1933 ausstrahlte, reflektiert der heutige Maybach.

»Ausgestattet mit der Pkw-Technologie des 21. Jahrhunderts, hergestellt in einer modernen Manufaktur und gestaltet mit größter Liebe zum Detail, spiegeln diese Automobile die Kompetenz des Hauses DaimlerChrysler als innovativstem und traditionsreichstem Automobilhersteller wider«, so definiert Maybach die eigene Position in der automobilen Upperclass. Hier ist Luxus selbstverständlich, und technische Leckerbissen werden auf dem Silbertablett dazugereicht.

Um mit einem Minimum an Material ein Maximum an Stabilität zu erreichen, besteht die Karosserie aus hochfesten Stahllegierungen. Gewichtsgründe sprechen für die Fertigung von vorderen Kotflügeln, Motorhaube, Dach und Türen aus Aluminium. Die Kofferraumklappe, unter der auch größeren Gepäckstücken Platz geboten wird, besteht aus Kunststoff. So entfallen beim Maybach 62 – die Typenbezeichnung entspricht der Länge von 6,2 Metern – nur knapp 22 Prozent der 2,8 Tonnen Gesamtgewicht auf die äußere Hülle. Die schwere, armierte Version, schussfest und mit Splitterschutz für die Insassen ausgestattet, besitzt an allen Schwachstellen zusätzliche Sicherheitskomponenten und Reifen mit Notlaufeigenschaften. Selbst das erhebliche Mehrgewicht dieser Guard-Ausführung bereitet dem Fahrwerk keine Probleme. Man greift auf die technischen Segnungen der S-Klasse zurück: Aktiv schaltbare Luftfederung mit einem adaptiven Dämpfersystem, das alle Belastungen bedarfsgerecht ausgleicht.

Ob Maybach 62 oder die einen halben Meter kürzere Variante 57, beide Modelle repräsentieren ihre Größe auf individuelle und vornehme Weise. Der geräuscharme Zwölfzylinder-Biturbo mit 550 PS – der Tuner Brabus entlockt ihm sogar 640 – glänzt durch Laufruhe und das fulminante Drehmoment von 900 Newtonmetern bei nur 2300 Touren. Entsprechend rasant ist die Beschleunigung von 5,4 Sekunden auf 100 km/h beim Maybach 62, und

Les moteurs étaient sa raison de vivre. De concert avec Gottlieb Daimler, il a écrit les tout premiers chapitres de l'histoire de l'automobile et, quand il a fondé sa propre société de fabrication de moteurs, le comte Zeppelin et l'industrie aéronautique naissante ont commencé à faire la queue chez lui pour obtenir ses moteurs : Wilhelm Maybach – une personnalité légendaire dont le nom continue de vivre au travers des somptueuses limousines de prestige de Sindelfingen. La concurrence directe de Rolls-Royce a commencé dès 1921 lorsque son fils, Karl Maybach, dont l'ingéniosité complétait à merveille celle de son père, s'est attaqué, avec une Spyker hollandaise à moteur Maybach W2, au prestigieux record d'endurance de 30 000 km que détenait Rolls-Royce – avec succès ! Quand Maybach, la même année, lors du Salon de l'Automobile de Berlin, présente, avec la W3, une limousine de luxe complète, certains messieurs d'outre-Manche *are not amused* (« ne se montrent guère enjoués »). Non seulement ce véhicule germanique peut se prévaloir d'un confort et d'un prix comparables, mais il peut aussi, qui plus est, proposer de nombreuses innovations techniques. Dont la suppression de la pédale d'embrayage. Face à une côte escarpée, il suffisait de manipuler un levier spécifique pour la montagne. La Maybach d'aujourd'hui reflète la noblesse que diffusait en 1933 la Maybach Zeppelin DS8 à carrosserie aérodynamique deux tons.

Pour offrir un maximum de stabilité avec un minimum de matériau, la carrosserie est réalisée en alliage d'acier à grande résistance. Pour limiter la surcharge pondérale, les ailes avant, le capot moteur, le toit et les portes sont fabriqués en aluminium. Le couvercle de malle, si vaste qu'elle peut héberger les bagages de la plus grande taille, est en matière plastique renforcée de fibre de verre. Ainsi la robe de la Maybach 62 – la désignation correspondant à sa longueur de 6,2 mètres – ne représente-t-elle que 22 % du poids total de 2,8 tonnes. La version blindée, évidemment beaucoup plus lourde, qui résiste aux tirs d'armes à feu et offre une protection des passagers contre les éclats, est habillée, à tous les endroits requis, de renforts de protection supplémentaires et roule sur des pneus anticrevaisons. Même ce supplément de poids considérable laisse imperturbable le châssis de cette exécution Maybach Guard. Celle-ci comporte nombre de raffinements techniques provenant de sa cousine la Classe S : suspension pneumatique à commande active avec un système d'amortisseurs adaptatif qui réagit de manière appropriée face à toutes les sollicitations.

Que l'on opte pour la Maybach 62 ou la variante 57, moins longue de 50 cm, les deux modèles représentent leur grandeur de manière individuelle et sélecte. Le silencieux douze-cylindres biturbo développant 550 ch – le fameux tuner Brabus en extrait même 640 – brille par sa douceur de fonctionnement et son couple phénoménal de 900 newtons-mètres à seulement 2300 tr/min. Logiquement, les accélérations sont fulminantes avec un temps de 5,4 secondes pour le 0 à 100 km/h avec la Maybach 62,

MAYBACH 57–62 GUARD   2002

Maybach 62 2003

acceleration to 100 kph (62 mph) in 5.4 seconds, and even the Guard's 3.2 tons mange the sprint in 5.7 seconds. More than 250 kph (155 mph) cannot be expected of the chauffeur and passengers, although the limousine's aerodynamics with a drag force coefficient of 0.30 would certainly allow more.

Comforts come to the fore when purchasing a Maybach – the 57 starts from 359,600 Euros. Whoever wishes to use this mansion on wheels as an office as well, orders the business package with its laptop, printer, and mobile internet access. Electronic amusements such as radio, DVD player, and TV screen, built into the back of the front seats, are especially enjoyable, accompanied by a glass of champagne, on the rear seats. For a few Euros more, a panorama glass roof arches over a dream landscape of the finest leather and noble woods. The glass contains a liquid crystal layer that loses its clear transparency when electricity is applied. The light falling through the opaque glass now shimmers diffusely.

selbst der Guard mit gut 3,2 Tonnen sprintet noch in 5,7 Sekunden. Mehr als 250 Stundenkilometer werden Chauffeur und Passagieren nicht zugemutet, obwohl die Aerodynamik der Limousine mit einem Luftwiderstandsbeiwert von 0,30 mehr hergäbe.

Beim Kauf eines Maybach – der 57 fängt bei 359 600 Euro an –, stehen die Annehmlichkeiten im Vordergrund. Wer den rollenden Herrensitz auch als Büro nutzen möchte, bestellt das Business-Paket mit Notebook, Drucker und mobilem Internet-Zugriff. Elektronische Kurzweil wie Radio, DVD-Player und TV-Monitor in den Rückenlehnen der Vordersitze lässt sich auf den Fauteuils im Fond bei einem Gläschen Champagner aus der Bordbar besonders genießen. Über der Traumlandschaft aus feinstem Leder und Edelhölzern wölbt sich, für einige Euros mehr, ein Panorama-Glasdach mit einer Flüssigkristallschicht, die unter Wechselspannung die Scheibe undurchsichtig macht. Das einfallende Licht schimmert jetzt in diffusem Glanz.

et même la Guard, malgré ses 3,2 tonnes, accélère encore en 5,7 secondes. Une vitesse maximale de 250 km/h est imposée au chauffeur et à ses passagers bien que l'aérodynamique de la limousine, dont le coefficient de résistance aérodynamique est de 0,30 lui permît d'aller plus vite.

Pour quiconque achète une Maybach – la fourchette de prix de la 57 débute à 359 600 euros –, confort, luxe et raffinement ont la priorité. Celui qui souhaite aussi profiter de ce salon roulant comme d'un bureau commande le pack « Business » avec notebook, imprimante et accès mobile à Internet. Au-dessus du paysage de rêve en cuir le plus fin et en bois précieux s'étend, pour quelques euros de plus, un toit électrique panoramique avec une couche intermédiaire en cristaux liquides qui perd sa translucidité en fonction de la variation de la tension et rend le vitrage opaque. Des rayons ardents du soleil il ne transmet plus qu'une lumière tamisée.

Nomen est omen: the Maybach 62's name is derived from its length of 6.2 meters (20'4"), while the smaller luxury limousine, the 57, correspondingly has a length of only 5.7 meters (18'8"). Good things take their time: in 2003, the annual production was only 702 vehicles.

Nomen est omen: Der Maybach 62 verdankt seine Typenbezeichnung seiner Länge von 6,2 Metern, während es die kleinere Luxus-Limousine, der 57, es analog »nur« auf 5,7 Meter bringt. Gut Ding will Weile haben: Die Jahresproduktion betrug 2003 lediglich 702 Exemplare.

Nomen est omen: la Maybach 62 doit sa désignation à sa longueur de 6,2 mètres à l'instar de la plus petite limousine de luxe, la 57, dont la longueur n'est « que » de 5,7 mètres. Toute bonne chose demande du temps : en 2003, la production annuelle a commencé avec seulement 702 exemplaires.

An electric panorama roof
spans the finest of leather
seating, folding out as a lounger
with a small noble wooden table,
and accompanied by all possible
comforts. Nobility in every detail:
from the entree of stainless steel
to the status symbol on the cover
of the V12 turbo engine with its
550 bhp.

Über feinste Leder-Fauteuils,
ausklappbar als Liegesitze mit
Edelholztischchen, flankiert von
sämtlichen Annehmlichkeiten
im Fond spannt sich ein elektro-
magnetisches Panorama-Dach.
In jedem Detail Noblesse:
vom Entree aus Edelstahl bis
zum Status-Symbol auf dem
Motordeckel des V12-Turbo
mit 550 PS.

Au-dessus des fauteuils
en cuir de très grand luxe
que l'on peut configurer
en siège couchette avec
tablette en bois précieux
et entourés de toutes les
commandes possibles et
imaginables à l'arrière se
tend un toit panoramique
électromagnétique.
Noblesse dans chacun
des détails : du seuil de
portière en acier
inoxydable au symbole
statutaire sur le carénage
du moteur V12 Turbo
développant 550 ch.

Three quarter-liter glasses of a good Württemberg wine would really flood the capacity of this three-cylinder engine to overflowing. However, a super-charger breathes extra power into the small transverse engine in the Smart Roadster's trunk, enabling the mini-capacity of just 698 cc to produce a proud 82 bhp. The economy model has to make do with a modest 61 bhp, too little for a vehicle that wants to be a sports car. As a result, the Mercedes-Benz engine technicians called upon the services of the sports car constructor and tuner Brabus, who combined two of the would-be motors to create a v6 with bi-turbo. This double capacity engine with its proud 170 bhp squeezed itself into the already tight rear of the vehicle, while the enlarged tank spread itself out under the hood. Not enough space remained for even a golf bag.

The per se already very lively vehicle, with its smart appearance, is stimulating for the tuning business. Not only Brabus, but also such companies as cs, Digi-Tec, Lorinser, Michalak, M.L., stc – and all the others – have gone to town, optically, technically, and even more so on the supplementary price tag. For example, Michalak-Design, a family company from Mainz, offers its all-round successful Roadrunner special-edition, limited to 25 vehicles, for an extra 20,000 Euros.

Two roofing variations protect the Roadster's occupants from the elements. Simple but effective is the electrical folding canopy, which disappears in 10 seconds, depriving the luggage compartment of almost half its 86-liter (3-cu.ft.) capacity. As the side roof rails have to be stowed away in the front luggage compartment under the hood, there only remains enough space for a small suitcase. A two-part hardtop has also been available since the summer of 2003. The Roadster weakling was the first to be invigorated by it. Also in possession of a hardtop, the smart rear of the Roadster-Coupé – a somewhat unfortunate choice of terminology – is covered by a glass dome with Spoiler. The placement of Brabus' bi-turbo cooling is similar to that of the Ferrari f40: vents not only on the flanks, but also in the rear glass fairing.

The steel safety cage, around which the synthetic body with its short wheel overhang entwines like a miniskirt, is typical of the Smart. The small turbulences caused by the four cavities for the separated high and low beam headlights, should be of little hindrance in the face of a top speed of 175 kph (109 mph) from the Roadster's 82 bhp and 220 kph (137 mph) from the v6.

The unconventional but clear layout of the cockpit instrumentation is striking. Dominant: two large round instruments in the vehicles colors, on the left the tachometer, on the right the rev counter from the viewpoint of the two-spoke steering wheel, while in the middle of the dashboard two small round instruments provide information about boot pressure and water temperature. The upwardly elongated center console houses sliding vents for heating and ventilation, the onboard music, as well as switches for unlocking the trunk lid and for the

Drei »Viertele« eines guten württembergischen Tropfens hätten das Volumen der drei Zylinder glatt überflutet. Das quer liegende Motörchen im Heck des Smart Roadster produziert trotz des Mini-Hubraums von nur 698 ccm stolze 82 PS, weil ihm ein Turbolader zusätzliche Kraft einhaucht. Die Spar-Version muss sich mit 61 PS bescheiden, zu wenig für ein Vehikel, das Sportwagen sein will. Unter diesem Gesichtspunkt bemühten der Sportwägelchen-Bauer und Tuner Brabus die Motoren-Techniker von Mercedes-Benz. Diese verbandelten zwei Trieblinge zu einem v6 mit Biturbo. Dieser Motor mit doppeltem Hubraum und stolzen 170 PS zwängte sich in das ohnehin recht enge Wagenheck, und der vergrößerte Tank machte sich im Bugraum breit. Da blieb nicht einmal mehr Platz für eine Golftasche.

Das an sich schon recht muntere und pfiffig aussehende Mobil reizt die Tuning-Branche. Da lassen sich neben Brabus Firmen wie cs, Digi-Tec, Lorinser, Michalak, M.L., stc – und wie sie alle heißen – nicht lumpen, weder optisch noch technisch und schon gar nicht beim Aufpreis. Michalak-Design etwa, ein Familienbetrieb aus Mainz, bietet für 25 000 Euro seinen rundum gelungenen Roadrunner an, eine Sonder-Edition, limitiert auf 25 Exemplare.

Zwei Bedachungsvarianten schützen die Roadster-Insassen vor Wetterunbilden. Simpel, aber wirkungsvoll ist das elektrische Faltdach, das in 10 Sekunden verschwindet und das hintere Kofferabteil um fast die Hälfte des Raumangebotes von 86 Litern schrumpfen lässt. Da die seitlichen Dachholme im vorderen Kofferraum direkt unter der Haube verstaut werden müssen, bleibt nur noch für ein Köfferchen Platz übrig. Seit Sommer 2003 ist auch ein zweiteiliges Hardtop erhältlich. Mit diesem wurde zuerst der schwache Roadster aufgepäppelt. Beim Roadster-Coupé – eine etwas unglücklich gewählte Bezeichnung –, ebenfalls mit Hardtop, bedeckt eine Glaskuppel mit Spoiler den smarten Hintern. Bei Brabus wird die Kühlung des Biturbos wie bei einem Ferrari f40 sichergestellt: Schlitze nicht nur in den Flanken, sondern auch in der gläsernen Heckverkleidung.

Typisch Smart ist die Sicherheitszelle aus Stahl, um die sich der Kunststoff mit seinen kurzen Überhängen wie ein Minirock rankt. Dass die vier Löcher, aus denen die Scheinwerfer lugen, getrennt nach Abblend- und Fernlicht, kleine Luftverwirbelungen verursachen, dürfte angesichts der Höchstgeschwindigkeit von 175 km/h beim 82-PS-Roadster und 220 km/h beim v6 kaum hinderlich sein.

Im Cockpit fällt sofort die eigenwillige, aber übersichtliche Anordnung der Instrumente auf. Dominant: zwei große, in Wagenfarbe eingefasste Rundinstrumente, links Tacho, rechts Drehzahlmesser in Blickrichtung auf das zweispeichige Lenkrad. Mittig auf dem Armaturenbrett geben zwei kleinere, ebenfalls runde Instrumente Auskunft über Ladedruck und Wassertemperatur. Die weit nach oben gezogene Mittelkonsole beherbergt Schieber zum Beheizen und Belüften, die Bordmusik sowie Schalter zur Entriegelung der Heckklappe und für das – soweit vor-

Trois *Viertele* – 750 cm³ – d'un bon vin du Wurtemberg feraient largement déborder les trois cylindres de son minuscule moteur. Malgré sa cylindrée modeste de seulement 698 cm³, le petit groupe motopropulseur monté en position transversale à l'arrière de la Smart Roadster n'en développe pas moins 82 ch, grâce au punch que lui insuffle un turbocompresseur. La version économique doit se contenter de 61 ch, trop peu pour un véhicule qui veut jouer les sportives en herbe. C'est ce qui incite à intervenir les constructeurs de la petite voiture de sport, le tuner Brabus et les motoristes de Mercedes-Benz à prendre les choses en main. Ils combinent deux moteurs en un v6 biturbo. Avec une cylindrée multipliée par deux et la puissance enviable de 170 ch, il réussit tout juste à entrer dans la poupe étriquée et bannit le réservoir, à la capacité majorée, sous le capot avant.

L'engin au tempérament flatteur et aux lignes aguichantes de rondeurs a toujours séduit des spécialistes du tuning. Outre Brabus, des préparateurs tels que cs, Digi-Tec, Lorinser, Michalak, M.L., stc – et il y en a bien d'autres encore – n'ont pas hésité à s'attaquer à son esthétique et à sa mécanique, et ni à en revoir le prix à la hausse. Michalak-Design, une entreprise familiale de Mayence, propose pour 20 000 euros son *Roadrunner,* réussi à tout point de vue, une édition spéciale limitée à vingt-cinq exemplaires.

Deux variantes de toit protègent des intempéries les passagers du roadster. Simple mais efficace, le toit pliant électrique qui disparaît en dix secondes divise pratiquement par deux la capacité du coffre arrière, qui est de 86 litres. Comme il faut ranger les montants de toit latéraux dans le coffre avant, directement sous le capot, il ne reste alors plus de place que pour un attaché-case. Depuis l'été 2003, un *hard-top* en deux éléments est également disponible. C'est la solution adoptée en premier lieu pour le roadster à la puissance limitée. Dans le cas du Roadster Coupé – une désignation dont le choix n'est pas très heureux – également à *hard-top,* une coupole en verre avec un aileron coiffe la croupe coquine.

Typiquement Smart, la cellule de sécurité en acier est habillée par une carrosserie qui est tout juste une mini-jupe, en matière plastique avec des porte-à-faux réduits à leur plus simple expression. Compte tenu de la vitesse maximale de 175 km/h pour le roadster de 82 ch et de 220 km/h pour le v6, le fait que les quatre trous du fond desquels les phares – séparés en feux de route et feux de croisement – scrutent la route engendrent des tourbillons ne risque guère d'être un handicap.

Dans le cockpit, on apprécie immédiatement l'agencement particulier mais bien conçu des instruments. Dominants, deux grands instruments circulaires peints dans la couleur de la carrosserie – à gauche le tachymètre, à droite le compte-tours – sont placés dans le champ de vision du conducteur, juste derrière le volant à deux branches. Au centre du tableau de bord, deux autres cadrans circulaires, plus petits, renseignent sur la pression de suralimentation

Smart Roadster 2003

electric folding canopy – where applicable. Thanks to the rather vertical position of the steering wheel, even a lanky beanpole is granted the privilege of unperturbedly piloting the sporty midget, provided that is, he uses the power assisted steering – only available on payment of a surcharge.

The 100-kph mark is reached in just about eleven seconds, if one is successful in jumping over the small turbo lags when sequentially switching up the six-gear automatic transmission. The top speed is not exactly intoxicating, but does not detract from the feeling of sitting in a sports car especially since the appropriate acoustical accompaniment is delivered when in the upper rev region. Driving fun is guaranteed on winding terrain, for the Roadster tends to over-steer when really pushed. Work for ESP!

handen – elektrische Faltverdeck. Dank der ziemlich vertikalen Lenkrad-Position ist es auch einem langen Lulatsch vergönnt, entspannt den sportlichen Winzling zu pilotieren, vorausgesetzt, er dreht an der – nur gegen Aufpreis erhältlichen – Servolenkung.

Ist man beim sequenziellen Hochschalten des automatischen 6-Gang-Getriebes erfolgreich über die kleinen Turbolöcher gesprungen, wird die 100-km/h-Marke in knapp elf Sekunden erreicht. Die Spitzengeschwindigkeit ist nicht gerade berauschend, doch das Gefühl, in einem Sportwagen zu sitzen leidet nicht darunter, zumal er im oberen Drehzahlbereich den entsprechenden akustischen Beitrag liefert. Fahrspaß kommt in kurvenreichen Gefilden auf, denn der Roadster tendiert bei scharfer Gangart zum Übersteuern. Arbeit für ESP!

et de la température d'eau. La console médiane, qui remonte très haut, héberge des commandes coulissantes pour le chauffage et la ventilation, la chaîne audio et le déverrouillage du hayon, ainsi que pour la capote électrique – si cette option a été choisie.

Si l'on parvient à faire oublier le temps de réponse du turbo quand on change à la volée, en mode séquentiel, les rapports de la boîte automatique à six vitesses, on abat le 0 à 100 km/h en tout juste 11 secondes. La vitesse de pointe n'a rien d'époustouflant, mais la sensation de piloter une voiture de sport n'en souffre absolument pas, d'autant plus que l'environnement acoustique à haut régime est en rapport. Le plaisir est garanti sur routes sinueuses, car, dès qu'on lui donne des éperons, le roadster se fait un plaisir de survirer. Du travail pour l'ESP!

The 3-cylinder, 82 bhp engine with turbocharger lies at right angles at the rear. The hardtop roofing segments of the Smart Roadster disappear into a compartment that then only leaves enough room for a mini case.

Quer im Heck liegt der Dreizylinder mit Turbolader, der immerhin 82 PS aktiviert. Die Hardtop-Verdeckteile des Smart Roadster verschwinden in einem Raum, der danach nur noch einen Mini-Koffer akzeptiert.

Le trois-cylindres à turbocompresseur qui développe 82 ch est placé en position transversale arrière.
Le *hard-top* disparaît dans un coffre dans lequel on ne peut plus alors déposer qu'au maximum un attaché-case.

Young and dynamic, sporting and extremely comfortable: already at its introduction, the second SLK generation promised to be an even greater success than the first, and that had topped 308,000 sales. 20,000 advance orders by May 2004 let the salespersons' hearts leap for joy.

The striking nose, reminiscent of the SLR and the Formula 1 vehicles of today, is excellently chiseled into its features. It has been known to motor sport and automobile historians since 1923 – a characteristic of the Benz Tropfenwagen –, and the Mercedes-Benz record-breaking vehicle of 1938 bears a similar facial appearance. The relatively high waistline with its curved beading toward the front contributes to the pleasant optic of this modern compact roadster.

Real enjoyment starts with driving – even with the basic model, the SLK 200 Kompressor, which brings 163 bhp on the road. Closely tiered six-gear transmission, precise steering, and a neutral chassis even with strong lateral acceleration, turn every SLK ride into pure pleasure. At last one can take on the comparable Z4 2.2i, and, after a slight setback at a traffic light start, thumb one's nose at it on maneuvering winding stretches.

That the open-air feeling is very disheveling for the ruff despite a transparent draft stop does not bother the SLK driver in the least. However, he can obtain on payment of a supplement a novelty for a cabriolet: beside the button for the seat heater is another heating activist, which, on demand, fans warm air around the head from slits in the headrest. The fan intensity of this neck hairdryer is regulated by the driving speed.

Whoever feels uneasy about the vehicle's all-weather suitability, can close the hatch by pressing the little button to the right of the hand brake. The closing operation takes 22 seconds. The Vario system opens the trunk lid, pushes the C pillar and roof segment over the roll bar – in doing so the rear window performs a lateral axis turn – and almost silently bolts the roof mechanism.

Exemplary – that is the first impression made by the cockpit. An optimal position to the adjustable steering wheel irrespective of body size is achieved by the anatomically formed sport seats, adjustable in height and with folding magnesium armrests and integrated headrests. The many buttons and dials on the center console have a tidy appearance and are systematically ordered.

Two magnesium tubes, painted silver on the outside, provide an insight into the well legible round instrumentation. In between, displays signal a diversity of data and functions. Any possible movement of the roof is brought to the driver's attention by an exclamation mark, as this is only to take place while standing still. The door handles with integrated window lifts have a futuristic appearance.

The SLK 350 compensates all those who are not satisfied with the humming Kompressor's acceleration performance – from 0 to 100 kph (62 mph) in 7.9 seconds

Jung und dynamisch, sportlich und äußerst komfortabel: Bereits bei ihrer Einführung versprach die zweite Generation des SLK ein noch größerer Wurf zu werden als die erste, und die hatte sich immerhin 308 000-mal verkauft. 20 000 Vorbestellungen bis Mai 2004 erfreuten die Verkäufer-Herzen.

Gar trefflich steht sie ihm ins Antlitz geschnitten, die markante, spitze Nase, die an den SLR und heutige Formel-1-Fahrzeuge erinnert. Motorsport- und Auto-Historikern ist sie allerdings seit 1923 – vom Benz-Tropfenwagen – bekannt, und auch das Mercedes-Benz-Rekordfahrzeug von 1938 trägt ähnliche Gesichtszüge. Zur gefälligen Optik dieses modernen, kompakten Roadsters trägt die relativ hohe Gürtellinie mit einer nach vorn geschwungenen Sicke bei. Ein kleiner stilistischer Kunstgriff, der zur Selbstdarstellung des SLK in der Kunden-Broschüre passt: »Die schönsten Kurven kann man schon im Stand genießen.«

Der richtige Genuss – selbst mit der Basis-Version, dem SLK 200 Kompressor, der 163 PS auf die Straße bringt – kommt erst beim Fahren auf. Eng abgestuftes 6-Gang-Getriebe, präzise Lenkung und ein auch bei höheren Querbeschleunigungen neutrales Fahrwerk machen jeden SLK-Ausritt zum Vergnügen. Kann man sich doch endlich mit dem vergleichbaren Z4 2.2i herumbalgen und ihm nach leichter Unterlegenheit beim Ampel-Start in kurvenreichem Terrain eine ganz lange Nase machen.

Dass die Open-Air-Freiheit trotz transparenten Windschotts ganz schön an der Halskrause rüttelt, stört den SLK-Fahrer herzlich wenig. Darf er doch gegen Aufpreis ein Cabrio-Novum erstehen: Gleich neben dem Druckschalter für die Sitzheizung ist ein weiterer Heizungs-Aktivist, und der fächelt bei Bedarf durch Lamellen in der Kopfstütze warme Luft ums Haupt. Die Gebläse-Intensität dieses Nacken-Föns richtet sich nach der Fahrgeschwindigkeit. Also: Seitenscheiben hoch, alle wärmenden Elemente an und offen in die kalte Jahreszeit, solange der Scheibenwischer-Sensor nicht Regen oder gar Schnee wittert!

Wem die Allwetter-Tauglichkeit mitsamt ihren kleinen Randerscheinungen nicht behagt, möge durch Betätigung eines kleinen Knopfes rechts vor der Handbremse die Luke schließen. Binnen 22 Sekunden öffnet das Vario-System die Heckklappe, schiebt C-Säule und Dachteil über die Überrollbügel hinaus – dabei vollführt die Heckscheibe einen Felgumschwung, also eine Drehung um die Querachse – und verriegelt kaum hörbar den Dachmechanismus.

Vorbildlich – das ist der erste Eindruck vom Cockpit. Die auch in der Höhe verstellbaren, anatomisch geformten Sportsitze mit ausklappbaren Magnesium-Lehnen und Integral-Kopfstützen ermöglichen unabhängig von der Körpergröße eine optimale Position zum ebenfalls justierbaren Lederlenkrad. Zwei auf der Außenseite silbern lackierte Magnesium-Röhren geben Einblick in die gut ablesbaren Rundinstrumente. Dazwischen signalisieren Displays diverse Daten und auch Funktionen.

Wem die Beschleunigung des sirrenden Kompressors – 7,9 Sekunden auf hundert Stundenkilometer – und die

Jeune et dynamique, sportive et extrêmement confortable : dès son introduction, la deuxième génération de la SLK laisse entrevoir une plus grande réussite encore que la première, qui s'était pourtant vendue à 308 000 exemplaires. Avec 20 000 commandes anticipées jusqu'en mai 2004, les vendeurs ont de quoi être optimistes.

Il faut dire qu'elle a tout pour plaire avec son mufle pointu si typique qui rappelle la SLR et les actuelles monoplaces de Formule 1. Les historiens de la compétition et de l'automobile le connaissent bien depuis 1923 – depuis la Benz-Tropfenwagen –, sans oublier la Mercedes-Benz record de 1938 qui arborait un visage similaire. La ligne de ceinture relativement haute, avec une nervure plongeant vers l'avant, n'est pas sans contribuer à l'esthétique séduisante de ce roadster moderne et compact.

Mais le véritable plaisir – même avec la version de base, la SLK 200 Kompressor qui développe 163 ch – ne se manifeste que lors de la conduite. Une boîte de vitesses aux six rapports rapprochés, une direction précise et un châssis stable même en cas d'accélérations latérales violentes font de la moindre excursion en SLK une partie de plaisir sans limite. Ne peut-on pas enfin relever le gant face à la BMW Z4 2.2i, sa rivale directe, et, après avoir cédé un peu de terrain au départ du feu rouge, remettre les pendules à l'heure sur routes sinueuses.

La conduite en plein air s'accompagne parfois, malgré le coupe-vent transparent, de violents tourbillons. Mais le conducteur de SLK n'en sera guère marri. Ne peut-il pas, en effet, mettre à profit une innovation extrêmement originale dans le segment des cabriolets ? Juste à côté de la commande de chauffage des sièges se trouve un autre dispositif générateur de chaleur que l'on ne pourra qu'apprécier. En cas de besoin, à travers les lamelles ménagées au pied de l'appui-tête, celui-ci insuffle des ondes de chaleur qui baignent la nuque du conducteur et de son éventuel passager d'une chaleur bienfaisante. La vigueur de ce sèche-cheveux d'un nouveau genre varie en fonction de la vitesse de la voiture.

Exemplaire – telle est la première impression que l'on a du cockpit. Les sièges sport ergonomiques, réglables en hauteur, avec des accoudoirs en magnésium rabattables et un appui-tête intégré, permettent – quelle que soit la morphologie du conducteur – de trouver une position de conduite idéale par rapport au volant gainé de cuir, également réglable.

Deux cylindres en magnésium dont la paroi extérieure est de couleur argentée offrent une visibilité parfaite sur les instruments circulaires. Entre eux, des écrans affichent diverses données et fonctions.

Ceux pour qui l'accélération de la Kompressor au bruit de sirène – 7,9 secondes pour le 0 à 100 km/h – et la vitesse de pointe de 230 km/h ne suffisent pas peuvent se rabattre sur la SLK 350. Sa vitesse culmine en effet – rapidement – à 250 km/h et il lui faut moins de 5,7 secondes pour franchir la barre des 100 km/h. Mais une conduite aussi soutenue prélève naturellement son tribut. Si, en conduite

MERCEDES-BENZ
SLK 200 KOMPRESSOR– SLK 55 AMG 2004

Mercedes-Benz SLK 200 Kompressor 2004

and a top speed of 230 kph (143 mph). For it accelerates rapidly to 250 kph (155 mph) and leaves the sprint behind it after just 5.7 seconds. Such a full power driving style has its price tag. Whereas a more reasonable style of driving with the Kompressor manages about 770 kilometers (480 miles), the 272 bhp v6 demands a stop at the filling station pump after less than 600 kilometers (370 miles). The SLK 55 AMG guzzles even more – and that from the Super Plus cornucopia. The beefy rear common to all SLKs is a good match for the wide 245 rollers and the powerhouse under the hood: a 5.5-liter v8 with 360 bhp. A hundred kph (62 mph) can be reached in less than five seconds via the rocker switches of the seven-gear automatic transmission. Every game has its limits, for Mercedes-Benz is reluctant to grant permission to let dynamism and sporting spirit develop itself fully at more than 250 kph (155 mph). The exception: the SLR built in England.

Spitze von 230 Sachen nicht ausreichen, dem bietet der SLK 350 Entschädigung. Der akzeleriert nämlich zügig bis 250 km/h und lässt bereits nach 5,7 Sekunden die Sprint-Marke hinter sich. Diese Gangart mit »voller Pulle« fordert ihren Preis. Kommt man bei vernünftiger Fahrweise mit dem Kompressor etwa 770 Kilometer weit, ist mit dem 272 PS starken v6 bei weniger als 600 Kilometern der Stopp an der Super-Zapfsäule fällig. Nach wesentlich kräftigeren Schlucken – und zwar aus dem Super-Plus-Füllhorn – verlangt es den SLK 55 AMG. Zum bulligen Heck aller SLK passen hier die breiten 245er Walzen und dazu wiederum das Aggregat unter der Motorhaube: ein 5,5-Liter-v8 mit 360 PS. Via Schaltwippe der 7-Gang-Automatik sind hundert Stundenkilometer in weniger als fünf Sekunden erreicht. Kein Spiel ohne Grenzen, denn für Dynamik und die volle Entfaltung des Sportsgeistes erteilt Mercedes-Benz jenseits von 250 km/h ungern eine Freigabe – Ausnahme: der in England gebaute SLR.

raisonnable, un plein permet de couvrir environ 770 km avec la version Kompressor, le conducteur de la v6 de 272 ch doit déjà rejoindre la station-service au plus tard au bout de 600 km. Mais leur grande sœur, en l'occurrence la SLK 55 AMG, est encore plus gloutonne, et plus exigeante aussi puisqu'elle ne se contente que de Super Plus. Avec elle, les larges gommes de 245 habillent à la perfection la poupe musclée de toutes les SLK et le moteur, lui aussi, est de la même veine : il s'agit d'un v8 de 5,5 litres et 360 ch. Avec les basculeurs au volant de la boîte automatique à sept rapports, le 0 à 100 km/h est exécuté en moins de 5 secondes. Mais ce n'est pas un jeu sans limites, car, malgré son goût de la dynamique et du libre épanouissement de l'esprit sportif, Mercedes-Benz ne donne pas volontiers l'autorisation de dépasser les 250 km/h. Seule exception : la SLR construite en Angleterre.

The SLK presents itself as an appealing and comfortable vehicle irrespective of whether open or closed, for its electrically lowered roof leaves enough space in the luggage compartment for a trip with baggage.

Offen wie geschlossen präsentiert sich der SLK ansprechend und komfortabel, denn sein elektrisch versenkbares Dach lässt noch genügend Kofferraum für die Reise mit Gepäck übrig.

Ouverte ou fermée, la SLK est tout aussi séduisante et confortable, car son toit à commande électrique laisse suffisamment d'espace pour emmener les bagages nécessaires pour de longs voyages.

Mercedes-Benz SLK 200 Kompressor – SLK 55 AMG 2004

The prominent pointed nose is reminiscent of the SLR, and the rear of the SLK is also powerful. The four-cylinder supercharger engine produces 163 bhp, sufficient for enjoyable driving in the exemplarily fitted out cockpit. More power is to be found in the SLK 55 AMG: a rich 360 bhp.

An den SLR erinnert die markante, spitze Nase, und auch das Heck des SLK ist eine Wucht. Der Vierzylinder-Kompressor-Motor liefert 163 PS, ausreichend für den Fahrspaß in dem vorbildlich eingerichteten Cockpit. Mehr Power steckt im SLK 55 AMG: satte 360 PS.

Le mufle pointu et caractéristique n'est pas sans rappeler la SLR et la poupe de la SLK, elle aussi, en impose. Le moteur à compresseur à quatre cylindres développe 163 ch, suffisamment pour engendrer un agrément de conduite remarquable dans un cockpit à l'aménagement exemplaire. Les amateurs de cavalerie seront comblés avec la SLK 55 AMG et sa puissance affriolante de 360 ch.

Although perhaps not as original as the cute little City-Smart for two, in comparison to its competition in the small car segment it is still a refreshingly cheeky phenomenon that displays all the technology expected of a full-grown automobile. 80,000 sales annually are envisaged for the market section that is home to its Polo, Corsa, Mini, or PSA-youth Citroën C3 and Peugeot 206 competitors. At the same time, the Mitsubishi Colt, which shares half of its structure with the Smart, is also vying for the buyers' favor. The threshold from investment phase to profit zone has been crossed on achieving the envisaged annual production, according to the Smart boss Andreas Renschler. An accompanying drastic drop in material and production costs follows. The link to the spare parts supply system of the Mercedes mother-concern is also a positive factor.

The weakest and at the same time most economical of the Forfour engine trio is a small 1.1-liter transversely mounted front engine with 75 bhp. The 165 kph (103 mph) top speed is nothing spectacular, but perfectly reasonable – that is as long as it is not compared to the 190 kph (118 mph) of the 1.5-liter four-cylinder engine with its 109 bhp. A 1.3-liter aggregate lies between the two, falling into the "neither-nor" category. The joint platform with Mitsubishi is orientated towards global requirements on compelling grounds of cost cutting, although the diehard Smart driver most likely finds it unusual that the motor performs its task at the front, and that there is no automatic transmission to carry out the gear switching.

The optically foreshortened steel cage scaffold bearing the polycarbonate cladding and the doors strengthened with aluminum frames are however, typical of the Smart. Also one hundred percent Smart is the rapid replaceability of those screwed on bodywork sections outside the passenger cage. The repair friendliness is augmented by gratifying consumption figures, to which greater attention deserves to be paid in the face of steadily increasing gasoline prices. The chassis with its sensitive ESP stability program, and the four disk brakes with ABS and brake assistant both deserve extra marks. The Forfour, lowered somewhat and more hardly cushioned, can be navigated around corners at speed with incredible neutrality. One small criticism: the power assisted steering could have been made more direct.

The Forfour's large ventilation outlets are situated where one would expect a Smart to have fixed or swiveling round instrumentation – just like a Ferrari. As a result, three round instruments have wandered to the lower end of the console. The most frequently used instrumentation is also round: the speedometer and rev counter with their red illuminated figures are well legible. For a multi-functional steering wheel and radio, you have dip into your pocket again.

Practical: when completely folded over, the rear seating opens up a large load space, while the front armrest – folded back – offers two drink holders. All

Er ist vielleicht nicht mehr so originell wie der putzige kleine City-Smart für Zwei, aber im Vergleich zu den Konkurrenten im Kleinwagen-Segment eine erfrischend freche Erscheinung, die technisch alles aufweist, was man von einem erwachsenen Auto erwartet. Auf dem Tummelplatz von Polos, Corsas, Minis und der PSA-Jugend Citroën C3 und Peugeot 206 sollen pro Jahr 80 000 Einheiten verkauft werden. Gleichzeitig buhlt der technisch zur Hälfte baugleiche Mitsubishi Colt um die Käufergunst. Mit dem Erreichen der angepeilten Jahresproduktion habe man, so Smart-Chef Andreas Renschler, die Schwelle von der Investitionsphase zur Gewinnzone überschritten. Flankierend erfolgen drastische Senkungen von Material- und Produktionskosten. Positiv ist auch die Anbindung an die Ersatzteilversorgung der Konzern-Mutter Mercedes.

Schwächstes und zugleich sparsamstes Mitglied im Triebwerks-Trio für den Forfour ist ein kleiner, quer gestellter Frontmotor, dessen 1,1 Liter Hubraum 75 PS leistet. 165 Stundenkilometer Spitzengeschwindigkeit sind keine Offenbarung, aber durchaus angemessen – allerdings nicht zu vergleichen mit den 190 km/h des 1,5-Liter-Vierzylinders mit 109 PS. Dazwischen ist ein 1,3-Liter-Aggregat positioniert, dessen Bestimmung in die Rubrik »weder, noch« fällt. Für eingefleischte Smart-Fahrer mag es vielleicht ungewöhnlich sein, dass der Motor vorn seine Arbeit verrichtet und dass keine Automatik die Schaltarbeit übernimmt, doch die gemeinsame Basis mit Mitsubishi richtet sich nach globalen Ansprüchen und zwingenden Ersparnis-Gesichtspunkten.

Typisch Smart dagegen ist die auch optisch abgesetzte Stahlzelle als tragendes Gerüst für die Polycarbonat-Kunststoff-Beplankung, die bei den Türen durch einen Aluminium-Rahmen verstärkt wird. Und ebenfalls ganz smart ist die schnelle Austauschbarkeit der angeschraubten Karosserieteile außerhalb der Fahrgastzelle. Zur Reparaturfreundlichkeit gesellen sich erfreuliche Verbrauchswerte, die angesichts ständig steigender Benzinpreise erhöhte Aufmerksamkeit verdienen. Pluspunkte gebühren auch dem Fahrwerk mit einem sensiblen ESP-Stabilitäts-Programm und den vier Scheibenbremsen mit ABS und Bremsassistent. Etwas tiefer gelegt und härter gedämpft, lässt sich der Forfour unglaublich neutral durch schnelle Kurven dirigieren. Kleiner Kritikpunkt: Die Servolenkung hätte noch direkter ausfallen können.

Wo man bei einem Smart aufgesetzte oder schwenkbare Rundinstrumente erwartet, sitzen beim Forfour große Belüftungsdüsen – wie in einem Ferrari. Dafür wanderten drei Rundinstrumente an das untere Ende der Konsole. Rund geht es auch bei dem am meisten frequentierten Instrumentarium zu: Tacho und Drehzahlmesser mit rot illuminierten Ziffern sind sehr gut lesbar. Für Multifunktions-Lenkrad und Radio muss zusätzlich ins Portemonnaie gegriffen werden.

Praktisch: komplett umgelegt, öffnet die Rückbank einen großen Laderaum, während die vordere Armlehne –

Elle n'est, peut-être, pas aussi originale que l'adorable petite City-Smart pour deux, mais, comparée à ses concurrentes du segment des citadines, elle fait souffler une véritable brise de fraîcheur et possède tout ce que l'on attend, sur le plan mécanique, d'une voiture adulte. Avec comme rivales Polo, Corsa, Mini et les juvéniles Citroën C3 et Peugeot 206 de PSA, il est prévu d'en vendre 80 000 exemplaires par an. Mais une autre rivale, pour moitié identique sur le plan mécanique, la Mitsubishi Colt, brigue elle aussi les faveurs des amateurs. En réalisant l'objectif de ventes annuelles fixé, a déclaré le P.-D.G. de Smart, Andreas Renschler, la marque est passée de la phase des investissements à la zone des bénéfices.

Le plus faible et, aussi, le plus économique membre du trio de moteurs pour la Forfour est un petit groupe en position transversale avant de 1,1 litre de cylindrée qui développe 75 ch. Les 165 km/h de vitesse maximale n'ont rien d'époustouflant, mais suffisent dans la plupart des cas – ils ne sont toutefois pas comparables aux 190 km/h des quatre-cylindres de 1,5 litre et 109 ch. Entre les deux se trouve un groupe de 1,3 litre qui n'est «ni chair ni poisson». Pour les automobilistes familiers de la Smart, il sera sans aucun doute inhabituel que le moteur officie à l'avant et qu'aucune boîte automatique ne leur épargne les changements de vitesses. Mais la base commune partagée avec Mitsubishi doit tenir compte d'exigences mondialistes et de critères d'économie impérieux.

Typiquement Smart, par contre, la cellule passagers en acier, volontairement visible, en tant que structure supportant les panneaux de carrosserie en polycarbonate et matière plastique, qui, pour les portières, sont renforcés par un cadre en aluminium. Également dans la plus pure veine de la Smart, la possibilité de remplacer instantanément, hormis ceux de l'habitacle, les panneaux de carrosserie boulonnés. À la facilité de réparation s'ajoutent des chiffres de consommation réjouissants qui, compte tenu de la spirale montante des prix de l'essence, méritent absolument d'être signalés. Au chapitre des autres atouts, citons le châssis, avec un sensible programme de stabilité dynamique ESP et les quatre freins à disques avec ABS et assistance de freinage. Un peu plus basse et avec un amortissement plus ferme, la Forfour se pilote avec une neutralité incroyable à travers les virages rapides. Une petite critique tout de même: dommage que la direction assistée ne soit pas encore un peu plus directe.

Là où, sur une Smart, on attend de gros instruments circulaires posés sur le tableau de bord ou pivotants, avec la Forfour, on découvre de grandes ouïes de ventilation – comme dans une Ferrari. En revanche, trois instruments circulaires ont été bannis à l'extrémité inférieure de la console médiane. Le cercle est, aussi, de règle pour les instruments les plus fréquemment consultés: le tachymètre et le compte-tours aux chiffres illuminés en rouge sont très lisibles.

Pratique complètement repliée, la banquette arrière donne accès à un vaste espace de chargement tandis que

SMART FORFOUR 1.1–1.5 2004

Smart Forfour 1.5 2004

that is now necessary is to push the front passenger's rest forward, and – due to the firmly upholstered seats – to spread a few cushions, and a rear passenger can already enjoy recliner comfort. All that are missing are the drinks and the reading material that can be illuminated by a light beam from the central roof lighting. For an extra thousand Euros, Smart delivers a transparent roof: a fixed glazed section to the front of the roof cross brace, and as a sliding glass roof to the rear. Spacious storage room can be found in the inner door paneling and cockpit. The electrical window lifts have been placed, on grounds of cost, to the left and to the right of the handbrake, easily accessible for all the occupants, made for four, as it were.

To sum up, the Forfour has succeeded in exuding a large amount of the charisma that has made the new Mini such a success. Things look pretty bleak for such bores as the Polo and the Corsa!

nach hinten geklappt – zwei Getränkehalterungen offeriert. Jetzt nur noch die Lehne des Beifahrersitzes nach vorn gedrückt und – wegen der straff gepolsterten Sitze – ein paar Kissen verteilt, und schon genießt ein Fondpassagier Liegestuhl-Komfort. Fehlen nur noch die Drinks und die Lektüre, auf die man mit der zentralen Deckenleuchte den Lichtstrahl richtet. Für tausend Euro mehr liefert Smart ein durchsichtiges Dach: fest verglast vor der Dachquerstrebe und als Glasschiebedach in der hinteren Hälfte. Geräumige Ablageflächen finden sich in Tür-Innenverkleidungen und im Armaturenbrett. Aus Kostengründen sind die elektrischen Fensterheber links und rechts der Handbremse angeordnet, für alle Passagiere erreichbar, *made for four* sozusagen.

Insgesamt strahlt der Forfour eine gehörige Portion des Charismas aus, das den neuen Mini so erfolgreich gemacht hat. Trübe Aussichten dagegen für Langweiler wie Polo und Corsa!

l'accoudoir avant – rabattu vers l'arrière – dégage deux porte-gobelets. Il suffit maintenant de replier vers l'avant le dossier du siège passager et – les capitonnages des sièges étant plutôt fermes – d'ajouter quelques coussins ici et là pour que le passager arrière ait l'impression de se reposer dans une chaise longue. Il ne manque plus que quelques boissons fraîches et de la lecture sur laquelle l'on peut diriger le faisceau de la liseuse centrale. Pour quelques milliers d'euros de plus, Smart propose un toit vitré: fixe en amont de la poutre de toit transversale et coulissant pour la moitié arrière. On trouvera de vastes vide-poches dans les capitonnages de contre-portes ainsi que dans le tableau de bord. Par souci d'économie, les lève-vitres électriques sont placés à gauche et à droite du frein à main, à portée de tous les passagers, pour ainsi dire *made for four*.

Cheeky and fresh: the Smart Forfour with its transverse 1.5-liter engine, producing 109 bhp, happily delves into the traditional small car market. Designed for four: the interior and the smartly designed cockpit fulfill all the requirements expected of the best of its class.

Frech und frisch: Der Smart Forfour mit querliegendem 1.5-Liter-Motor, der 109 PS leistet, mischt munter im Segment traditioneller Kleinwagen mit. Für Vier konzipiert: Auch der Innenraum und das pfiffig gestaltete Cockpit genügen allen Ansprüchen, die an die Klassenbesten gestellt werden.

Coquine et rafraîchissante : la Smart Forfour à moteur de 1,5 litre en position transversale développant 109 ch fait souffler un vent de jeunesse sur le segment des compactes traditionnelles. Conçue pour quatre : l'habitacle et le cockpit à l'aménagement épris de gaieté satisfont toutes les exigences que l'on pose au meilleure élève de la classe.

Referred to as "Vision CLS," Mercedes-Benz presented a unique synthesis of noble limousine and racy coupé at the Frankfurt International Automobile Exhibition (IAA) in 2003. "With this we are a coupé generation ahead," rejoiced Mercedes boss Prof. Jürgen Hubbert. But first the opinion of the exhibition visitors was to be fathomed, and the decision about the series production of this concept vehicle was to be made dependent on the vote of the public. So, at least, read the official statements; but insiders already knew that the CLS was by now no longer a vision, and would most definitely follow. And how quickly it followed! It celebrated its premiere almost unchanged – just three millimeters longer and the chassis a little lowered – at the Geneva Automobile Show.

From the original concept to the first model phase, the many drawings clearly show how sheer boundless fantasy and creativity can be bundled to form a common design direction, combining the visible polarity of dynamism, power, and functionality with elegance and esthetic. The shoulder curve draws itself and the hollow beneath it in a taught arch, from the dynamically designed curvature of the front wheel well, over the entire body flank, finally ending in the rear light section. The latter picks up the line's flow, and leads it to its end in the rear fender. Even more striking is the course of the roof contour, which flows seamlessly into the sloping rear. Aerodynamically efficient with its gentle emphasis: the small trailing edge on the trunk lid. For the sake of emphasis, the curved surfaces of the side windows are framed with chrome borders, while the wide B pillar of this four-door vehicle – not present in a normal coupé – is forced optically into the background. The leather cladding of the door inner side, and the extensive use of walnut wood on the dashboard, picks up the stylistic elements of the exterior.

The continuously adjustable camshaft of the new lightweight six-cylinder engine with its 272 bhp opens up completely new perspectives. It directs the 24 valves of the aluminum cylinder heads in response to the driving situation in such a way that the energy loss is kept to a minimum. A special module alters the length of the air intake pipe in accordance with the engine speed and regulates the airflow. This enables the V6 engine already to enjoy 87 percent of the torque upper limit of 300 Newton-meter at a modest 1500 rpm. The CLS 500 mobilizes the traditional 5-liter V8 with its 306 bhp well enough to enable a sprint of 0 to 100 kph (62 mph) in 6.1 seconds.

The 7G-Tronic, a revolutionary seven-gear automatic transmission with a direct-drive clutch, is standard with the CLS 500. it adapts optimally to the engine speed, saves fuel and is low in noise. An additional manual switching system operated by buttons on the steering wheel or by tapping the gear selector switch can be ordered. The automatic intervenes immediately if the engine speed suddenly drops, or if the engine is pushed too hard.

Apostrophiert als »Vision CLS« präsentierte Mercedes-Benz auf der Internationalen Automobilausstellung (IAA) 2003 in Frankfurt die einzigartige Synthese aus Nobel-Limousine und rassigem Coupé. »Damit sind wir eine Coupé-Generation voraus«, frohlockte Mercedes-Chef Prof. Jürgen Hubbert. Man wolle aber erst einmal die Meinung der Messe-Besucher ausloten und vom Votum des Publikums die Entscheidung über die Serienfertigung dieses Konzept-Fahrzeuges abhängig machen. So lautete das offizielle Statement, doch Insider wussten längst, dass der CLS zu diesem Zeitpunkt keine Vision mehr war und auf jeden Fall kommen würde. Und wie schnell er kam! Nur ein halbes Jahr später feierte er nahezu unverändert, lediglich drei Millimeter länger und etwas tiefer gelegt, seine Premiere auf dem Genfer Automobil-Salon.

Die vielen Zeichnungen von der Konzept-Idee bis zur ersten Modellphase verdeutlichen, wie sich schier grenzenlose Phantasie und Kreativität zu einer gemeinsamen Design-Linie bündeln, die die scheinbare Polarität von Dynamik, Größe, Kraft und Funktionalität mit Eleganz und Ästhetik verbindet. In spannungsvollen Bögen zieht sich die Schulterlinie mit der darunter laufenden Sicke aus der dynamisch wirkenden Rundung des vorderen Radkastens über die gesamte Karosserie-Flanke und endet in der Rückleuchten-Einheit. Diese greift den Linienfluss auf und lässt ihn sanft in den Stoßfänger einmünden. Noch prägnanter ist der Verlauf der Dach-Kontur, die nahtlos in das abgeschrägte Heck übergeht. Zart betont, aber aerodynamisch effizient: die kleine Abrisskante auf dem Kofferraumdeckel. Zur Betonung der geschwungenen Seitenfenster-Fläche wird diese von einer Chromleiste umrandet und die bei einem normalen Coupé nicht vorhandene breite B-Säule des Viertürers optisch in den Hintergrund gedrückt. Die ledernen Tür-Innenverkleidungen und die großflächige Wurzelnussholz-Beplankung des Armaturenbretts greifen die stilistischen Elemente des Exteriörs auf.

Neue Perspektiven eröffnet die stufenlose, kontinuierliche Nockenwellenverstellung des neuen Leichtbau-Sechszylinders mit 272 PS. Sie dirigiert die 24 Ventile in den Aluminium-Zylinderköpfen je nach Fahrsituation derart, dass Energieverluste auf ein Minimum verringert werden. Ein spezielles Modul verändert die Länge des Saugrohres je nach Drehzahl und reguliert die Luftströmung. Dadurch kommt das V6-Triebwerk bereits bei bescheidenen 1500 Touren in den Genuss von 87 Prozent der Drehmoment-Obergrenze von 300 Newtonmetern. Den CLS 500 mobilisiert der traditionelle 5-Liter-V8 mit 306 PS, gut genug für einen Spurt von 0 auf 100 km/h in 6,1 Sekunden.

Serienmäßig beim CLS 500 ist die 7G-Tronic, ein revolutionäres Siebengang-Automatik-Getriebe mit Wandler-Überbrückungs-Kupplung. Es passt sich optimal der Drehzahl an, spart Sprit und ist geräuscharm. Ergänzend kann ein manuelles Schaltprogramm über Tasten am

Intitulée « Vision CLS » lors de sa présentation par Mercedes au Salon international de l'Automobile de Francfort (IAA), en 2003, elle est une synthèse unique au monde de limousine de prestige et de coupé racé. « Ainsi avons-nous une génération de coupé d'avance », déclare, enchanté, Jürgen Hubbert, le P.-D.G. de Mercedes. Dont l'intention est tout d'abord de sonder les réactions des visiteurs du Salon, la décision de fabriquer en série ce concept-car devant alors dépendre du vote du public. C'est en tout cas ce que proclamait le communiqué de presse officiel. Or les initiés savaient depuis longtemps que la CLS n'était déjà plus, à ce moment-là, une vision et allait bel et bien être produite. D'ailleurs, elle ne se fit pas attendre ! Six mois plus tard à peine, pratiquement inchangée, si ce n'est trois millimètres de plus en longueur et une hauteur légèrement réduite, elle fête sa première au Salon de l'Automobile de Genève.

En un galbe générateur de tension, la ligne de ceinture avec un épaulement marquant au bas des vitres prend naissance dans les rondeurs dynamiques du caisson de roues avant, soulignant sur toute leur longueur les flancs de la carrosserie, pour venir mourir au niveau de la poupe, dans le bloc optique arrière. Celui-ci reprend cette ligne pour la transmettre avec douceur au pare-chocs. Plus caractéristique encore est la courbe des contours du toit, linéaires et tendus, qui lui confèrent une allure très « coupé » en vertu de son arrière oblique. Discret, certes, mais pourtant d'une très grande efficacité : le petit déflecteur sur l'arête du couvercle de malle. Pour souligner la surface galbée des vitres latérales, celles-ci sont cernées d'un jonc chromé tandis que le large pied central de la quatre-portes, qui est inexistant sur un coupé conventionnel, disparaît visuellement.

Le décalage en continu des arbres à cames du nouveau six-cylindres de construction allégée développant 272 ch offre des perspectives inédites. Selon la situation de conduite, il orchestre la cadence des 24 soupapes sous les cache-culasse en aluminium de façon à minimiser le plus possible les pertes d'énergie. Un module spécial modifie la longueur de la tubulure d'aspiration en fonction du régime de rotation et régule l'écoulement de l'air. De ce fait, au régime pourtant modeste de 1500 tours, le moteur V6 permet de bénéficier déjà de 87 % de son couple maximal de 300 newtons-mètres. La CLS 500 est propulsée par le traditionnel V8 de 5 litres et 306 ch, suffisamment de chevaux pour abattre le 0 à 100 km/h en 6,1 secondes.

En série, la CLS 500 est équipée de la boîte 7G-Tronic, une révolutionnaire transmission automatique à sept rapports avec embrayage court-circuitant le convertisseur de couple. Elle s'adapte à la perfection aux régimes de rotation respectifs, économise le carburant et est silencieuse. À titre complémentaire, elle permet de changer de vitesse à la main grâce à des touches intégrées au volant ou en donnant une impulsion au pommeau de vitesse.

L'équipement de série de la CLS 500 comporte aussi la suspension pneumatique Airmatic DC. « DC », qui signifie à

Mercedes-Benz CLS 350 – CLS 500   2004

Mercedes-Benz CLS 320 2004

The pneumatic Airmatic DC suspension also belongs to the standard CLS 500 equipment. "DC," originally the English abbreviation for direct current, stands for "Dual Control" of the system that steers the electric cushioning and vibration absorption. Rubber bellows on telescopic legs, filled with compressed air do the work. The driver determines the chassis setting by means of a level switch on the center console: "0" is for comfort, the system changes relatively late from the softer absorber level to a harder tuning, while in position "1" the characteristics become more sporting. The latter position, signaled by two light-emitting diodes embedded in the switch, activates the sport setting with changed parameters. At the same time, the chassis is lowered by 15 millimeters (0.6 inch). With such a lowered body, this massive vehicle almost becomes a "limousine coupé sports car."

Lenkrad oder Antippen des Wählhebels bestellt werden. Fällt die Drehzahl mal in den Keller oder wird der Motor zu sehr hochgescheucht, greift sofort die Automatik ein.

Zur Serien-Ausstattung des CLS 500 gehört auch die Luftfederung Airmatic DC. »DC«, eigentlich das englische Kürzel für Gleichstrom, steht hier für die Doppelfunktion »Dual Control« der Anlage, die elektrisch Federung und Dämpfung steuert. Gummibälge an den Federbeinen, gefüllt mit komprimierter Luft, übernehmen die Arbeit. Mit einem Niveau-Schalter auf der Mittelkonsole bestimmt der Fahrer seine Fahrwerks-Einstellung: Bei »0« ist Komfort angesagt, das System wechselt relativ spät von der weichsten Dämpferstufe in eine härtere Abstimmung, doch bei Position »1« wird das Kennfeld schon sportlicher. In der zweiten Einstellung, signalisiert von zwei Leuchtdioden im Taster, wird sofort die Sporteinstellung aktiviert, mit veränderten Parametern. Gleichzeitig senkt sich die Karosserie um 15 Millimeter. Solchermaßen tiefer gelegt, wird aus dem wuchtigen Fahrzeug fast ein »Limousinen-Coupé-Sportwagen«.

proprement parler, en anglais, courant continu (direct current), est ici le symbole de la fonction « Dual Control », qui commande électriquement la suspension et l'amortissement. Des soufflets en caoutchouc remplis d'air comprimé à hauteur des jambes élastiques se chargent du travail. Avec, sur la console médiane, un commutateur pour le correcteur d'assiette, le conducteur détermine les réglages de châssis de son choix : « 0 » privilégie le confort, le système passe alors de façon relativement tardive du degré d'amortissement le plus confortable à un réglage plus ferme. Mais, en position « 1 », la transition se fait déjà plus sportive. Et, avec ce second réglage, signalisé par deux diodes lumineuses sur le commutateur, on actionne immédiatement le mode Sport, aux paramètres spécifiques. Simultanément, la carrosserie s'abaisse de 15 millimètres. Dans cette configuration, l'imposant véhicule se métamorphose, presque, en une « limousine-coupé-voiture de sport ».

A leading light (bi-xenon) and a new star in the top of the range firmament: the Mercedes CLS, whose side lines express themselves in an exciting arch, is considered an exceptional success of the new design form. Actually it belongs in a class of its own, the "limousine coupé."

Lichtblick (Bi-Xenon) und neuer Stern am Firmament der Oberklasse: Der Mercedes CLS, dessen Seitenlinien sich in spannungsvollen Bögen ausdrücken, gilt als besonders gelungener Wurf der neuen Design-Linie. Eigentlich müsste man für ihn eine neue Kategorie, das »Limousinen-Coupé«, schaffen.

Regard clair (bi-xénon) et nouvelle étoile au firmament du segment de luxe : la Mercedes CLS, dont les lignes latérales tracent un galbe parfait qui exprime sa puissance, est considérée comme une particulièrement grande réussite esthétique. Il faudrait en réalité créer pour elle une nouvelle catégorie, celle des « limousines-coupés ».

Power and functionality married to elegance and esthetics: the CLS also exudes the skill of the Swabian automobile constructer both under its hood and in its distinguished interior.

Kraft und Funktionalität, gepaart mit Eleganz und Ästhetik: Der CLS strahlt auch unter der Haube und im vornehmen Interieur das Können der schwäbischen Automobilbauer aus.

Quand vigueur et fonctionnel vont de pair avec élégance et esthétique : sous le capot aussi et dans son habitacle distingué, la CLS traduit tout le savoir-faire du constructeur de Stuttgart.

Specifications
Technische Daten
Caractéristiques techniques

		Benz Patent-Motorwagen	Daimler Motorkutsche
Baureihe			
Baujahre		1886–1894	1886
Modell		Modell 1 1886	Daimler Motorkutsche
Motor	Konfiguration	1 Zylinder hinten liegend	1 Zylinder stehend vor der Hinterachse
	Hubraum	984 ccm	462 ccm
	Bohrung x Hub	91,4 x 150 mm	70 x 120 mm
	Kraftstoffversorgung	Oberflächenvergaser	Oberflächenvergaser
	Leistung	0,9 PS bei 400/min	1,1 PS bei 700/min
Getriebe		—	2 Übersetzungen durch verschieden große Riemenscheiben
Chassis	Rahmen	Stahlrohr	Holz, mit Eisen verstärkt
	Aufhängung vorn	Vorderrad in Steuergabel, keine Federung	Starrachse, Vollelliptikfedern
	Aufhängung hinten	Starrachse, Vollelliptikfedern	Starrachse, Vollelliptikfedern
Maße	Radstand	1450 mm	1300 mm
	Länge x Breite x Höhe	2700 x 1400 x 1450 mm	2530 x 1475 x 1695 mm
	Gewicht	265 kg	290 kg
Fahrleistung	Höchstgeschwindigkeit	16 km/h	16 km/h

		Daimler Stahlradwagen	Benz Victoria & Victoria-Familie
Baureihe			
Baujahre		1889	1893–1900
Modell		Daimler Stahlradwagen	Vis-à-Vis 1893
Motor	Konfiguration	V2 stehend vor der Hinterachse	1 Zylinder hinten liegend
	Hubraum	565 ccm	1730 ccm
	Bohrung x Hub	60 x 100 mm	130 x 130 mm
	Kraftstoffversorgung	Oberflächenvergaser	Oberflächenvergaser
	Leistung	1,5 PS bei 920/min	3 PS bei 450/min
Getriebe		4-Gang-Zahnradgetriebe	2-Stufen-Flachriemengetriebe und Vorgelege
Chassis	Rahmen	Stahlrohr	rahmenloser Holzaufbau
	Aufhängung vorn	Fahrradgabel ohne Federung	Starrachse, Vollelliptikfedern
	Aufhängung hinten	Starrachse ohne Federung	Starrachse, Vollelliptikfedern
Maße	Radstand	1400 mm	1650 mm
	Länge x Breite x Höhe		3200 x 1650 x 1750 mm
	Gewicht	300 kg	650 kg
Fahrleistung	Höchstgeschwindigkeit	22 km/h	18 km/h

Baureihe		Benz Velo	Benz Mylord, Break, Dos-à-Dos
Baujahre		1894–1902	1899–1901
Modell		Benz Ideal 1899	Dos-à-Dos 1899
Motor	Konfiguration	1 Zylinder quer über der Hinterachse	2-Zylinder-Boxer liegend hinten
	Hubraum	1140 ccm	1710 ccm
	Bohrung x Hub	115 x 110 mm	100 x 110 mm
	Kraftstoffversorgung	Schwimmervergaser	Schwimmervergaser
	Leistung	4,5 PS bei 960/min	5 PS bei 940/min
Getriebe		3 Vorwärtsgänge, 1 Rückwärtsgang	3 Vorwärtsgänge, 1 Rückwärtsgang
Chassis	Rahmen	Profilstahl, Karosserie aufgesetzt	
	Aufhängung vorn	Starrachse, Vollelliptikfedern	Starrachse, Elliptikfedern
	Aufhängung hinten	Starrachse, Vollelliptikfedern	Starrachse, Elliptikfedern
Maße	Radstand	1560 mm	
	Länge x Breite x Höhe	2400 x 1350 x 1500 mm	
	Gewicht	425 kg	
Fahrleistung	Höchstgeschwindigkeit	35 km/h	25 km/h

Baureihe		Benz Rennwagen	Daimler Phoenix
Baujahre		1899	1899
Modell		Benz Rennwagen	Daimler Phoenix Rennwagen
Motor	Konfiguration	2-Zylinder-Boxer	4-Zylinder in Reihe stehend vorn
	Hubraum	2714 ccm	5503 ccm
	Bohrung x Hub	120 x 120 mm	106 x 156 mm
	Kraftstoffversorgung	Spritzdüsenvergaser	Spritzdüsenvergaser
	Leistung	10 PS bei 1000/min	28 PS bei 950/min
Getriebe		4-Gang-Zahnradgetriebe	4-Gang-Zahnradgetriebe
Chassis	Rahmen	Pressstahl	U-Profil aus Stahlblech
	Aufhängung vorn	Starrachse, Elliptikfedern	starre Faustachse, Blattfedern
	Aufhängung hinten	Starrachse, Elliptikfedern	Starrachse, Blattfedern
Maße	Radstand	1900 mm	1735 mm
	Länge x Breite x Höhe	2960 x 1600 x 1650 mm	(k.A.) x 1630 x 1500 mm
	Gewicht		1400 kg
Fahrleistung	Höchstgeschwindigkeit	50 km/h	81 km/h

Baureihe		Mercedes Simplex	Benz Spider
Baujahre		1902–1910	1902–1907
Modell		26/45 PS 1909	Benz Spider
Motor	Konfiguration	4-Zylinder paarweise	2-Zylinder-Boxer liegend vorn
	Hubraum	6785 ccm	2945 ccm
	Bohrung x Hub	120 x 150 mm	125 x 120 mm
	Kraftstoffversorgung	Kolbenschiebervergaser mit Vorwärmung	Schwimmervergaser
	Leistung	45 PS bei 1100/min	15 PS bei 1100/min
Getriebe		4-Gang-Kulissenschaltung	
Chassis	Rahmen	Pressstahl U-Profil	
	Aufhängung vorn	Starrachse, Halbfedern	
	Aufhängung hinten	Starrachse, Halbfedern	
Maße	Radstand	3540 mm	
	Länge x Breite x Höhe	4800 x 1750 x 1700 mm (offen)	3050 x 1550 x 1650 mm
	Gewicht	1600 kg	870 kg
Fahrleistung	Höchstgeschwindigkeit	85 km/h	60 km/h

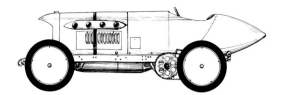

Baureihe		Blitzen-Benz
Baujahre		1909
Modell		Blitzen-Benz
Motor	Konfiguration	4-Zylinder in Reihe
	Hubraum	21 500 ccm
	Bohrung x Hub	185 x 200 mm
	Kraftstoffversorgung	Horizontal-Rundschiebervergaser
	Leistung	200 PS bei 1600/min
Getriebe		4 Vorwärtsgänge, 1 Rückwärtsgang
Chassis	Rahmen	Profilstahl
	Aufhängung vorn	starre Gabelachse, Halbelliptikfedern
	Aufhängung hinten	Starrachse mit Schubstreben, Halbelliptikfedern
Maße	Radstand	2800 mm
	Länge x Breite x Höhe	4820 x 1600 x 1280 mm
	Gewicht	1450 kg
Fahrleistung	Höchstgeschwindigkeit	228,1 km/h

Baureihe		Mercedes-Benz 18/100 Grand Prix
Baujahre		1914
Modell		Mercedes Grand-Prix-Rennwagen 18/100
Motor	Konfiguration	4-Zylinder in Reihe, 4 Ventile und 3 Zündkerzen je Zylinder
	Hubraum	4483 ccm
	Bohrung x Hub	93 x 165 mm
	Kraftstoffversorgung	k.A.
	Leistung	115 PS bei 3200/min
Getriebe		4-Gang
Chassis	Rahmen	Pressstahl
	Aufhängung vorn	Starrachse, Halbelliptikfedern
	Aufhängung hinten	Starrachse, Halbelliptikfedern
Maße	Radstand	2845 mm
	Gewicht	1080 kg
Fahrleistung	Höchstgeschwindigkeit	180 km/h

Baureihe		Mercedes 28/95
Baujahre		1914–1915, 1920–1924
Modell		Sport Phaeton 1922
Motor	Konfiguration	6-Zylinder in Reihe, oben liegende Nockenwelle
	Hubraum	7280 ccm
	Bohrung x Hub	105 x 140 mm
	Kraftstoffversorgung	Mercedes-Vergaser
	Leistung	90 PS bei 1800/min
Getriebe		4-Gang
Chassis	Rahmen	Pressstahl U-Profil
	Aufhängung vorn	Starrachse, Halbelliptikfedern
	Aufhängung hinten	Starrachse, Halbelliptikfedern
Maße	Radstand	3065 mm
	Länge x Breite x Höhe	4650 x 1580 x 1600 mm
	Gewicht	1800 kg
Fahrleistung	Höchstgeschwindigkeit	138 km/h

Baureihe		Mercedes Targa Florio
Baujahre		1924
Modell		Mercedes Targa-Florio-Rennwagen
Motor	Konfiguration	4-Zylinder in Reihe, 2 oben liegende Nockenwellen, Kompressor
	Hubraum	1989 ccm
	Bohrung x Hub	70 x 129 mm
	Kraftstoffversorgung	Druckvergaser
	Leistung	126 PS bei 4300/min
Getriebe		4-Gang
Chassis	Rahmen	Pressstahl U-Profil
	Aufhängung vorn	Starrachse, Halbelliptikfedern, Reibungsstoßdämpfer
	Aufhängung hinten	Starrachse, Halbelliptikfedern, Reibungsstoßdämpfer
Maße	Radstand	2700 mm
	Länge x Breite x Höhe	3800 x 1700 x 1250 mm
	Gewicht	921 kg
Fahrleistung	Höchstgeschwindigkeit	120 km/h

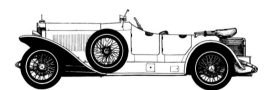

Baureihe		Mercedes 400–630 K
Baujahre		1924–1931
Modell		630K 1926
Motor	Konfiguration	6-Zylinder in Reihe, oben liegende Nockenwelle, Kompressor
	Hubraum	6240 ccm
	Bohrung x Hub	94 x 150 mm
	Kraftstoffversorgung	Drosselvergaser mit Ringschwimmer
	Leistung	160 PS bei 3100/min
Getriebe		4-Gang
Chassis	Rahmen	Pressstahl U-Profil
	Aufhängung vorn	Starrachse, Halbfedern
	Aufhängung hinten	Starrachse, Underslung-Halbfedern
Maße	Radstand	3400 mm
	Länge x Breite x Höhe	4735 x 1760 x 1850 mm
	Gewicht	2000 kg
Fahrleistung	Höchstgeschwindigkeit	145 km/h

Baureihe		Mercedes-Benz S–SSKL
Baujahre		1927–1934
Modell		SSKL 1931
Motor	Konfiguration	6-Zylinder in Reihe, oben liegende Nockenwelle, Kompressor
	Hubraum	7065 ccm
	Bohrung x Hub	100 x 150 mm
	Kraftstoffversorgung	2 Steigstrom-Ringschwimmer-Vergaser
	Leistung	300 PS
Getriebe		4-Gang
Chassis	Rahmen	Pressstahl U-Profil
	Aufhängung vorn	Starrachse, Halbfedern
	Aufhängung hinten	Starrachse, Underslung-Halbfedern
Maße	Radstand	2950 mm
	Länge x Breite x Höhe	4250 x 1700 x 1250 mm
	Gewicht	1500 kg
Fahrleistung	Höchstgeschwindigkeit	235 km/h

Baureihe		Stuttgart	Mannheim
Baujahre		1928–1936	1929–1934
Modell		Stuttgart 260 1930	Mannheim 350 Tourenwagen 1929
Motor	Konfiguration	6-Zylinder in Reihe	6-Zylinder in Reihe
	Hubraum	2581 ccm	3445 ccm
	Bohrung x Hub	74 x 100 mm	80 x 115 mm
	Kraftstoffversorgung	1 Solex 35 MOHLT	Flachstromvergaser Zenith 39 HK Mod. TD
	Leistung	50 PS bei 3400/min	75 PS bei 3200/min
Getriebe		3-Gang + Schnellgang	3-Gang + Schnellgang
Chassis	Rahmen	Pressstahl U-Profil	Pressstahl-Niederrahmen U-Profil
	Aufhängung vorn	Starrachse, Halbfedern	Starrachse, Halbfedern
	Aufhängung hinten	Starrachse, Halbfedern	Starrachse, Underslung-Halbfedern
Maße	Radstand	2810 mm	3200 mm
	Länge x Breite x Höhe	4380 x 1680 x 1800 mm	4900 x 1710 x 1780 mm
	Gewicht	900 kg	1550 kg
Fahrleistung	Höchstgeschwindigkeit	90 km/h	95 km/h

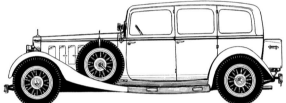

Baureihe		Nürburg	170
Baujahre		1929–1933	1931–1936
Modell		Nürburg 500 Pullman Limousine 1934	170 1931
Motor	Konfiguration	8-Zylinder in Reihe	6-Zylinder in Reihe
	Hubraum	4918 ccm	1692 ccm
	Bohrung x Hub	82,5 x 115 mm	65 x 85 mm
	Kraftstoffversorgung	Doppel-Flachstromvergaser Solex 35 MMOV	Solex 30 FVST
	Leistung	100 PS bei 3100/min	32 PS bei 3200/min
Getriebe		4-Gang + Schnellgang	3-Gang + Schnellgang
Chassis	Rahmen	Pressstahl-Niederrahmen U-Profil	Pressstahl-Niederrahmen U-Profil
	Aufhängung vorn	Starrachse, Halbfedern	2 Querfedern
	Aufhängung hinten	Starrachse, Underslung-Halbfedern	Pendelachse, Doppel-Schraubenfedern
Maße	Radstand	3670 mm	2600 mm
	Länge x Breite x Höhe	5380 x 1820 x 1820 mm	4060 x 1630 x 1650 mm
	Gewicht	2300 kg	1050–1200 kg
Fahrleistung	Höchstgeschwindigkeit	110 km/h	90 km/h

Baureihe		500 K & 540 K	W165
Baujahre		1934–1939	1939
Modell		500 K/540 K Cabriolet A 1936	W165
Motor	Konfiguration	8-Zylinder in Reihe, Kompressor	V8, 2 4-teilige Nockenwellen, Kompressor
	Hubraum	5401 ccm	1495 ccm
	Bohrung x Hub	88 x 111 mm	64 x 58 mm
	Kraftstoffversorgung	Doppel-Steigstromvergaser	3-Stufen-Saugvergaser
	Leistung	180 PS bei 3400/min	254 PS bei 8000/min
Getriebe		4-Gang	5-Gang, Kulisse
Chassis	Rahmen	Pressstahl-Niederrahmen, Kastenprofil	Ovalrohrrahmen mit 5 Quertraversen
	Aufhängung vorn	Doppel-Querlenker, Schraubenfedern	Dreieckslenker, vertikale Schraubenfedern
	Aufhängung hinten	Pendelachse, Doppel-Schraubenfedern, Zusatz-Ausgleichsfeder	Schwingachse, Drehstabfederung
Maße	Radstand	3290 mm	2450 mm
	Länge x Breite x Höhe	5100 x 1880 x 1640 mm	3680 x 1510 x 850 mm
	Gewicht	2300 kg	700 kg
Fahrleistung	Höchstgeschwindigkeit	170 km/h	272 km/h

Glossary of technical terms and abbreviations p. 598 · Glossaire d'abréviations et de termes techniques p. 598

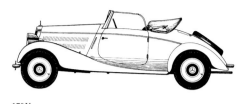

Baureihe		130–170H	170V
Baujahre		1934–1939	1936–1942
Modell		150 Sportroadster 1935	170V Cabriolet A 1937
Motor	Konfiguration	4-Zylinder in Reihe hinten	4-Zylinder in Reihe
	Hubraum	1498 ccm	1697 ccm
	Bohrung x Hub	72 x 92 mm	73,5 x 100 mm
	Kraftstoffversorgung	Doppel-Steigstromvergaser Solex 30 FFVS	Steigstromvergaser Solex 30 BFLVS
	Leistung	55 PS bei 4500/min	38 PS bei 3400/min
Getriebe		3-Gang + Schnellgang	4-Gang
Chassis	Rahmen	Zentralrohrrahmen	X-förmiger Ovalrohrrahmen
	Aufhängung vorn	2 Querfedern	2 Querfedern
	Aufhängung hinten	Pendelachse, Doppel-Schraubenfedern	Pendelachse, Schraubenfedern
Maße	Radstand	2600 mm	2845 mm
	Länge x Breite x Höhe	4200 x 1600 x 1380 mm	4270 x 1570 x 1560 mm
	Gewicht	980 kg	1150 kg
Fahrleistung	Höchstgeschwindigkeit	125 km/h	108 km/h

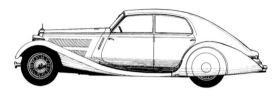

Baureihe		260D	320
Baujahre		1936–1940	1937–1942
Modell		260D Pullman-Limousine 1938	320 Stromlinienlimousine 1937
Motor	Konfiguration	4-Zylinder in Reihe	6-Zylinder in Reihe
	Hubraum	2545 ccm	3208 ccm
	Bohrung x Hub	90 x 100 mm	82,5 x 100 mm
	Kraftstoffversorgung	Einspritzpumpe Bosch	Doppel-Fallstromvergaser Solex 32 JFF
	Leistung	45 PS bei 3000/min	78 PS bei 4000/min
Getriebe		4-Gang	4-Gang
Chassis	Rahmen	Pressstahl-Niederrahmen, Kastenprofil	Pressstahl-Niederrahmen, Kastenprofil
	Aufhängung vorn	2 Querfedern	je 1 Querlenker, 1 Querfeder, Schraubenfedern innen
	Aufhängung hinten	Pendelachse, Doppel-Schraubenfedern	Pendelachse, Doppel-Schraubenfedern, Zusatz-Ausgleichsfedern
Maße	Radstand	3050 mm	3300 mm
	Länge x Breite x Höhe	4790 x 1710 x 1610 mm	4870 x 1730 x 1660 mm
	Gewicht	1550 kg	1850 kg
Fahrleistung	Höchstgeschwindigkeit	94 km/h	130 km/h

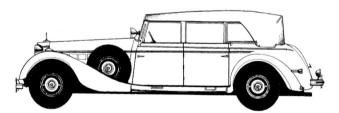

Baureihe		770 »Großer Mercedes«
Baujahre		1938–1943
Modell		770K Offener Tourenwagen, gepanzerte Sonderausführung 1938
Motor	Konfiguration	8-Zylinder in Reihe, 2 Zündkerzen je Zylinder, Kompressor
	Hubraum	7655 ccm
	Bohrung x Hub	95 x 135 mm
	Kraftstoffversorgung	3-Düsen-Doppelvergaser
	Leistung	230 PS bei 3200/min
Getriebe		5-Gang
Chassis	Rahmen	Ovalrohrrahmen
	Aufhängung vorn	Doppel-Querlenker, Schraubenfedern
	Aufhängung hinten	Doppelgelenkachse, Schraubenfedern
Maße	Radstand	3880 mm
	Länge x Breite x Höhe	6000 x 2100 x 1900 mm
	Gewicht	4500 kg
Fahrleistung	Höchstgeschwindigkeit	nur 80 km/h zulässig

Baureihe		230	170 V
Baujahre		1938–1943	1946–1953
Modell		230 Cabriolet D 1939	170 V 1951
Motor	Konfiguration	6-Zylinder in Reihe	4-Zylinder in Reihe
	Hubraum	2289 ccm	1767 ccm
	Bohrung x Hub	73,5 x 90 mm	75 x 100 mm
	Kraftstoffversorgung	Doppel-Fallstromvergaser Solex 30 JFFK	Steigstromvergaser Solex 30 BFLVS
	Leistung	55 PS bei 3500/min	45 PS bei 3600/min
Getriebe		4-Gang	4-Gang
Chassis	Rahmen	X-förmiger Ovalrohrrahmen	X-förmiger Ovalrohrrahmen, Ganzstahlkarosserie
	Aufhängung vorn	2 Querfedern	2 Querfedern
	Aufhängung hinten	Pendelachse, Doppel-Schraubenfedern	Pendelachse, Schraubenfedern
Maße	Radstand	3050 mm	2845 mm
	Länge x Breite x Höhe	4700 x 1720 x 1610 mm	4285 x 1630 x 1610 mm
	Gewicht	1450 kg	1185 kg
Fahrleistung	Höchstgeschwindigkeit	116 km/h	116 km/h

Baureihe		170 S	220
Baujahre		1949–1953	1951–1955
Modell		170 S Cabriolet A 1950	220 1954
Motor	Konfiguration	4-Zylinder in Reihe	6-Zylinder in Reihe, oben liegende Nockenwelle
	Hubraum	1767 ccm	2195 ccm
	Bohrung x Hub	75 x 100 mm	80 x 72,8 mm
	Kraftstoffversorgung	Fallstromvergaser Solex 32 PICB	Doppel-Fallstromvergaser Solex 30 PAAJ
	Leistung	52 PS bei 4000/min	80 PS bei 4850/min
Getriebe		4-Gang	4-Gang
Chassis	Rahmen	X-förmiger Ovalrohrrahmen, Ganzstahlkarosserie	X-förmiger Ovalrohrrahmen, Ganzstahlkarosserie
	Aufhängung vorn	Doppel-Querlenker, Schraubenfedern, Stabilisator	Doppel-Querlenker, Schraubenfedern, Stabilisator
	Aufhängung hinten	Pendelachse, Doppel-Schraubenfedern	Pendelachse, Doppel-Schraubenfedern
Maße	Radstand	2845 mm	2845 mm
	Länge x Breite x Höhe	4510 x 1684 x 1560 mm	4507 x 1685 x 1610 mm
	Gewicht	1270 kg	1350 kg
Fahrleistung	Höchstgeschwindigkeit	122 km/h	140 km/h

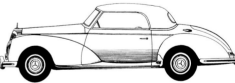

Baureihe		300	300 S
Baujahre		1951–1962	1951–1958
Modell		300 d	300 Sc Coupé 1955
Motor	Konfiguration	6-Zylinder in Reihe, oben liegende Nockenwelle	6-Zylinder in Reihe, oben liegende Nockenwelle
	Hubraum	2996 ccm	2996 ccm
	Bohrung x Hub	85 x 88 mm	85 x 88 mm
	Kraftstoffversorgung	Einspritzpumpe Bosch	Einspritzpumpe Bosch
	Leistung	160 PS bei 5300/min	175 PS bei 5400/min
Getriebe		3-Stufen-Automatik	4-Gang
Chassis	Rahmen	X-förmiger Ovalrohrrahmen, Ganzstahlkarosserie	X-förmiger Ovalrohrrahmen, Ganzstahlkarosserie
	Aufhängung vorn	Doppel-Querlenker, Schraubenfedern, Stabilisator	Doppel-Querlenker, Schraubenfedern, Stabilisator
	Aufhängung hinten	Eingelenk-Pendelachse, Schubstreben, Doppel-Schraubenfedern, elektrisch zuschaltbare Drehstabfederung	Eingelenk-Pendelachse, Doppel-Schraubenfedern
Maße	Radstand	3150 mm	2900 mm
	Länge x Breite x Höhe	5190 x 1860 x 1620 mm	4700 x 1860 x 1510 mm
	Gewicht	1950 kg	1780 kg
Fahrleistung	Höchstgeschwindigkeit	170 km/h	180 km/h

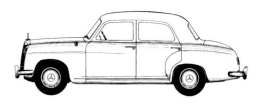

		W194	180
Baureihe		W194	180
Baujahre		1952	1953–1962
Modell		300SL Coupé	180 1954
Motor	Konfiguration	6-Zylinder in Reihe, oben liegende Nockenwelle	4-Zylinder in Reihe
	Hubraum	2996 ccm	1767 ccm
	Bohrung x Hub	85 x 88 mm	75 x 100 mm
	Kraftstoffversorgung	3 Solex-Fallstromvergaser	Fallstromvergaser Solex 32 PICB
	Leistung	175 PS bei 5200/min	52 PS bei 4000/min
Getriebe		4-Gang	4-Gang
Chassis	Rahmen	Gitterrohrrahmen	selbsttragende Ganzstahlkarosserie
	Aufhängung vorn	Parallel-Querlenker, Schraubenfedern	Doppel-Querlenker, Schraubenfedern, Stabilisator
	Aufhängung hinten	Pendelachse	Pendelachse, Schubstreben, Schraubenfedern
Maße	Radstand	2400 mm	2650 mm
	Länge x Breite x Höhe	4220 x 1790 x 1265 mm	4485 x 1740 x 1560 mm
	Gewicht	870 kg	1180 kg
Fahrleistung	Höchstgeschwindigkeit	240 km/h	126 km/h

		W198	W196R
Baureihe		W198	W196R
Baujahre		1954–1963	1954–1955
Modell		300SL Coupé 1955	W196R Monoposto 1954
Motor	Konfiguration	6-Zylinder in Reihe, oben liegende Nockenwelle	8-Zylinder in Reihe, 2 oben liegende Nockenwellen
	Hubraum	2996 ccm	2496 ccm
	Bohrung x Hub	85 x 88 mm	76 x 68,8 mm
	Kraftstoffversorgung	Einspritzpumpe Bosch	Einspritzpumpe Bosch
	Leistung	215 PS bei 5800/min	256 PS bei 8260/min
Getriebe		4-Gang	5-Gang, 4 Gänge synchronisiert, Kulisse
Chassis	Rahmen	Gitterrohrrahmen	Gitterrohrrahmen
	Aufhängung vorn	Doppel-Querlenker, Schraubenfedern, Stabilisator	Querlenker
	Aufhängung hinten	Pendelachse, Schraubenfedern	Pendelachse mit tief gelegtem Drehpunkt
Maße	Radstand	2400 mm	2210 mm
	Länge x Breite x Höhe	4520 x 1790 x 1300 mm	4025 x 1625 x 1040 mm
	Gewicht	1310 kg	835 kg
Fahrleistung	Höchstgeschwindigkeit	228 km/h	≥ 300 km/h

		220a–220SE	190SL
Baureihe		220a–220SE	190SL
Baujahre		1954–1960	1955–1963
Modell		220S Cabriolet A/C 1958	190SL 1961
Motor	Konfiguration	6-Zylinder in Reihe, oben liegende Nockenwelle	4-Zylinder in Reihe, oben liegende Nockenwelle
	Hubraum	2195 ccm	1897 ccm
	Bohrung x Hub	80 x 72,8 mm	85 x 83,6 mm
	Kraftstoffversorgung	Register-Fallstromvergaser Solex 32 PAJTA	2 Register-Fallstromvergaser Solex 44 PHH
	Leistung	106 PS bei 5200/min	105 PS bei 5700/min
Getriebe		4-Gang	4-Gang
Chassis	Rahmen	selbsttragende Ganzstahlkarosserie	selbsttragende Ganzstahlkarosserie
	Aufhängung vorn	Doppel-Querlenker, Schraubenfedern, Stabilisator	Doppel-Querlenker, Schraubenfedern, Stabilisator
	Aufhängung hinten	Eingelenk-Pendelachse, Schubstreben, Schraubenfedern	Eingelenk-Pendelachse, Schubstreben, Schraubenfedern
Maße	Radstand	2700 mm	2400 mm
	Länge x Breite x Höhe	4670 x 1765 x 1530 mm	4220 x 1740 x 1320 mm
	Gewicht	1450 kg	1160 kg
Fahrleistung	Höchstgeschwindigkeit	160 km/h	171 km/h

Baureihe		300SLR	220b–300SE
Baujahre		1955	1959–1965
Modell		300SLR	220Sb 1964
Motor	Konfiguration	8-Zylinder in Reihe, 2 oben liegende Nockenwellen	6-Zylinder in Reihe, oben liegende Nockenwelle
	Hubraum	2982 ccm	2195 ccm
	Bohrung x Hub	78 x 78 mm	80 x 72,8 mm
	Kraftstoffversorgung	Einspritzpumpe Bosch	2 Register-Fallstromvergaser Zenith 35/40 INAT mit Startautomatik
	Leistung	310 PS bei 7400/min	110 PS bei 5000/min
Getriebe		5-Gang, 4 Gänge synchronisiert, Kulisse	4-Gang
Chassis	Rahmen	Gitterrohrrahmen	selbsttragende Ganzstahlkarosserie
	Aufhängung vorn	Parallel-Querlenker	Doppel-Querlenker, Schraubenfedern, Stabilisator
	Aufhängung hinten	Pendelachse mit tief gelegtem Drehpunkt	Eingelenk-Pendelachse, Schubstreben, Schraubenfedern, Ausgleichs-Schraubenfeder
Maße	Radstand	2370 mm	2750 mm
	Länge x Breite x Höhe	4300 x 1740 x 1100 mm	4875 x 1795 x 1500 mm
	Gewicht	901 kg	1845 kg
Fahrleistung	Höchstgeschwindigkeit	≥ 300 km/h	165 km/h

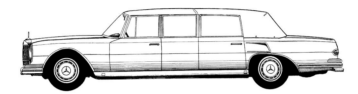

Baureihe		600
Baujahre		1964–1981
Modell		600 Pullman-Landaulet 1971
Motor	Konfiguration	V8, 2 oben liegende Nockenwellen
	Hubraum	6330 ccm
	Bohrung x Hub	103 x 95 mm
	Kraftstoffversorgung	8-Stempel-Pumpe Bosch
	Leistung	250 PS bei 4000/min
Getriebe		4-Stufen-Automatik
Chassis	Rahmen	selbsttragende Ganzstahlkarosserie
	Aufhängung vorn	Doppel-Querlenker, Luftkammer-Federbälge, Gummi-Zusatzfedern, Drehstab-Stabilisator
	Aufhängung hinten	Eingelenk-Pendelachse, Schubstreben, Luftkammer-Federbälge, Gummi-Zusatzfedern, Niveauausgleich, Drehstab-Stabilisator
Maße	Radstand	3900 mm
	Länge x Breite x Höhe	6240 x 1950 x 1510 mm
	Gewicht	2770 kg
Fahrleistung	Höchstgeschwindigkeit	200 km/h

Baureihe		230SL–280SL	250S–280SEL3.5
Baujahre		1963–1971	1965–1972
Modell		250SL 1967	300SEL3.5 1971
Motor	Konfiguration	6-Zylinder in Reihe, oben liegende Nockenwelle	V8, 2 oben liegende Nockenwellen
	Hubraum	2496 ccm	3499 ccm
	Bohrung x Hub	82 x 78,8 mm	92 x 65,8 mm
	Kraftstoffversorgung	6-Stempel-Pumpe Bosch	elektronische Einspritzung Bosch
	Leistung	150 PS bei 5500/min	200 PS bei 5800/min
Getriebe		4-Gang	4-Gang
Chassis	Rahmen	selbsttragende Ganzstahlkarosserie	selbsttragende Ganzstahlkarosserie
	Aufhängung vorn	Doppel-Querlenker, Schraubenfedern, Stabilisator	Doppel-Querlenker, Luftkammer-Federbälge, Gummi-Zusatzfedern, Drehstab-Stabilisator
	Aufhängung hinten	Eingelenk-Pendelachse, Schubstreben, Schraubenfedern, Ausgleichs-Schraubenfeder	Eingelenk-Pendelachse, Schubstreben, Luftkammer-Federbälge, Gummi-Zusatzfedern, Niveauausgleich, Drehstab-Stabilisator
Maße	Radstand	2400 mm	2850 mm
	Länge x Breite x Höhe	4285 x 1760 x 1305 mm	5000 x 1810 x 1440 mm
	Gewicht	1440 kg (mit Coupédach)	1730 kg
Fahrleistung	Höchstgeschwindigkeit	195 km/h	210 km/h

Baureihe		200–240 D 3.0	C 111
Baujahre		1967–1976	1969–1979
Modell		250 CE 1970	C 111 1970
Motor	Konfiguration	6-Zylinder in Reihe, oben liegende Nockenwelle	4-Scheiben-Wankel vor der Hinterachse
	Hubraum	2496 ccm	4 x 600 ccm
	Bohrung x Hub	82 x 78,8 mm	
	Kraftstoffversorgung	elektronische Einspritzung Bosch	
	Leistung	150 PS bei 5500/min	350 PS bei 7000/min
Getriebe		4-/5-Gang	5-Gang
Chassis	Rahmen	selbsttragende Ganzstahlkarosserie	Bodenanlage aus Stahlblech, GFK-Karosserie
	Aufhängung vorn	Doppel-Querlenker, Schraubenfedern, Zusatz-Gummifedern, Drehstab-Stabilisator	Doppel-Querlenker, Drehstab-Stabilisator
	Aufhängung hinten	Diagonal-Pendelachse, Schräglenker, Schraubenfedern, Gummi-Zusatzfedern, Drehstab-Stabilisator	je Rad 3 Querlenker und 2 Längslenker
Maße	Radstand	2750 mm	2620 mm
	Länge x Breite x Höhe	4680 x 1790 x 1395 mm	4440 x 1800 x 1120 mm
	Gewicht	1410 kg	1240 kg
Fahrleistung	Höchstgeschwindigkeit	195 km/h	300 km/h

Baureihe		350 SL–560 SL	280 S–300 SD
Baujahre		1971–1989	1972–1980
Modell		500 SL 1986	350 SEL 1979
Motor	Konfiguration	V8, 2 oben liegende Nockenwellen	V8, 2 oben liegende Nockenwellen
	Hubraum	4973 ccm	3499 ccm
	Bohrung x Hub	96,5 x 85 mm	92 x 65,8 mm
	Kraftstoffversorgung	Bosch KE-Jetronic	Bosch K-Jetronic
	Leistung	245 PS bei 4750/min	205 PS bei 5750/min
Getriebe		4-Stufen-Automatik	4-Gang
Chassis	Rahmen	selbsttragende Ganzstahlkarosserie	selbsttragende Ganzstahlkarosserie
	Aufhängung vorn	Doppel-Querlenker, Schraubenfedern, Gummi-Zusatzfedern, Drehstab-Stabilisator	Doppel-Querlenker, Schraubenfedern, Gummi-Zusatzfedern, Drehstab-Stabilisator
	Aufhängung hinten	Diagonal-Pendelachse, Schräglenker, Schraubenfedern, Gummi-Zusatzfedern, Drehstab-Stabilisator	Diagonal-Pendelachse, Schräglenker, Schraubenfedern, Gummi-Zusatzfedern, Drehstab-Stabilisator
Maße	Radstand	2460 mm	2965 mm
	Länge x Breite x Höhe	4390 x 1790 x 1305 mm	5060 x 1870 x 1430 mm
	Gewicht	1610 kg	1760 kg
Fahrleistung	Höchstgeschwindigkeit	225 km/h	205 km/h

Baureihe		200–300 TD Turbodiesel	280 S–350 SD
Baujahre		1976–1985	1979–1991
Modell		280 E 1983	300 SEL 1986
Motor	Konfiguration	6-Zylinder in Reihe, 2 oben liegende Nockenwellen	6-Zylinder in Reihe, oben liegende Nockenwelle
	Hubraum	2746 ccm	2962 ccm
	Bohrung x Hub	86 x 78,8 mm	88,5 x 80,25 mm
	Kraftstoffversorgung	Bosch K-Jetronic	Bosch KE-Jetronic
	Leistung	185 PS bei 5800/min	188 PS bei 5700/min
Getriebe		4-/5-Gang	5-Gang/4-Stufen-Automatik
Chassis	Rahmen	selbsttragende Ganzstahlkarosserie	selbsttragende Ganzstahlkarosserie
	Aufhängung vorn	Doppel-Querlenker, Schraubenfedern, Drehstab-Stabilisator	Doppel-Querlenker, Schraubenfedern, Gasdruck-Stoßdämpfer, Gummi-Zusatzfedern, Drehstab-Stabilisator
	Aufhängung hinten	Diagonal-Pendelachse, Schräglenker, Schraubenfedern, Drehstab-Stabilisator	Diagonal-Pendelachse, Schräglenker, Schraubenfedern, Gasdruck-Stoßdämpfer, Gummi-Zusatzfedern, Drehstab-Stabilisator
Maße	Radstand	2795 mm	3075 mm
	Länge x Breite x Höhe	4725 x 1786 x 1438 mm	5395 x 1828 x 1407 mm
	Gewicht	1510 kg	1610 kg, mit Automatik 1650 kg
Fahrleistung	Höchstgeschwindigkeit	200 km/h	210 km/h

Baureihe		230 G – G 500 V8	190 – 190 E 1.8
Baujahre		1979→	1982–1993
Modell		G 350 Turbodiesel langer Radstand 1996	190 E 2.5-16 Evolution II
Motor	Konfiguration	6-Zylinder in Reihe, oben liegende Nockenwelle	4-Zylinder in Reihe, 4 Ventile je Zylinder, 2 oben liegende Nockenwellen
	Hubraum	3449 ccm	2463 ccm
	Bohrung x Hub	89 x 92,4 mm	97,3 x 82,8 mm
	Kraftstoffversorgung	6-Stempel-Einspritzpumpe Bosch	Bosch KE-Jetronic
	Leistung	136 PS bei 4600/min	235 PS bei 7200/min
Getriebe		4-Stufen-Automatik	5-Gang
Chassis	Rahmen	gekröpfter Vierkantrohr-Leiterrahmen, Ganzstahlkarosserie	selbsttragende Ganzstahlkarosserie
	Aufhängung vorn	Starrachse, 2 Längslenker, 1 Querlenker (Panhardstab), Schrauben-federn, Gummi-Zusatzfedern, Drehstab-Stabilisator	Doppel-Querlenker mit hydropneumatischen Federbeinen, Schraubenfedern, Drehstab-Stabilisator
	Aufhängung hinten	Starrachse, 2 Längslenker, 1 Querlenker, Schraubenfedern, Gummi-Zusatzfedern	Raumlenkerachse mit hydropneumatischen Federbeinen, Drehstab-Stabilisator
Maße	Radstand	2850 mm	2665 mm
	Länge x Breite x Höhe	4680 x 1760 x 1936 mm	4543 x 1720 x 1342 mm
	Gewicht	2240 kg	1340 kg
Fahrleistung	Höchstgeschwindigkeit	148 km/h	250 km/h

Baureihe		200 – E 420	Sauber-Mercedes C11
Baujahre		1984–1995	1990
Modell		300 E 4matic 1986	Sauber-Mercedes C11
Motor	Konfiguration	6-Zylinder in Reihe, oben liegende Nockenwelle	V8, 2 KKK-Turbolader, 4 Ventile je Zylinder, 4 oben liegende Nockenwellen
	Hubraum	2962 ccm	4973 ccm
	Bohrung x Hub	85,5 x 80,25 mm	96,5 x 85 mm
	Kraftstoffversorgung	Bosch KE-Jetronic	Bosch Motronic MP 1.8
	Leistung	188 PS bei 5700/min	720 PS bei 7000/min
Getriebe		4-Stufen-Automatik, Allradantrieb	5-Gang-Renngetriebe mit Ölkühler
Chassis	Rahmen	selbsttragende Ganzstahlkarosserie	Kohlefaser-Monocoque
	Aufhängung vorn	Dämpferbein-Achse, Dreiecks-Querlenker, Schraubenfedern, Gasdruck-Stoßdämpfer, Drehstab-Stabilisator	Doppel-Querlenker, Schraubenfedern
	Aufhängung hinten	Raumlenkerachse, Schraubenfedern, Gasdruck-Stoßdämpfer, Drehstab-Stabilisator	Doppel-Querlenker, Schraubenfedern
Maße	Radstand	2800 mm	2770 mm
	Länge x Breite x Höhe	4740 x 1740 x 1450 mm	4800 x 2000 x 1030 mm
	Gewicht	1540 kg	905 kg
Fahrleistung	Höchstgeschwindigkeit	215 km/h	≥ 350 km/h

Baureihe		300 SL – SL 600	300 SE – S 300 Turbodiesel
Baujahre		1988–2000	1991–1997
Modell		SL 500 1995	S 320 1996
Motor	Konfiguration	V8, 4 Ventile je Zylinder, 4 oben liegende Nockenwellen	6-Zylinder in Reihe, 4 Ventile je Zylinder, 2 oben liegende Nockenwellen
	Hubraum	4973 ccm	3199 ccm
	Bohrung x Hub	96,5 x 85 mm	89,9 x 84 mm
	Kraftstoffversorgung	Bosch KE 5-Jetronic	elektronische Einspritzung mit Heißfilm-Luftmassenmessung (HFM)
	Leistung	326 PS bei 5500/min	231 PS bei 5600/min
Getriebe		4-Stufen-Automatik	5-Stufen-Automatik
Chassis	Rahmen	selbsttragende Ganzstahlkarosserie	selbsttragende Ganzstahlkarosserie
	Aufhängung vorn	Dämpferbein-Achse, Schraubenfedern auf Dreiecks-Querlenkern, Gasdruck-Stoßdämpfer, Drehstab-Stabilisator, Niveauregulierung	Doppel-Querlenker, Schraubenfedern, Drehstab-Stabilisator
	Aufhängung hinten	Raumlenkerachse, Schraubenfedern, Gasdruck-Stoßdämpfer, Drehstab-Stabilisator, Niveauregulierung	Raumlenkerachse (optional hydropneumatische Niveauregulierung), Schraubenfedern, Drehstab-Stabilisator
Maße	Radstand	2515 mm	3040 mm
	Länge x Breite x Höhe	4465 x 1812 x 1303 mm	5113 x 1886 x 1486 mm
	Gewicht	1880 kg	1890 kg
Fahrleistung	Höchstgeschwindigkeit	250 km/h	230 km/h

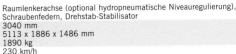

Baureihe		C 200 Diesel – C 43 AMG	Sauber-Mercedes C13
Baujahre		1993–1999	1994
Modell		C 180 T 1996	Sauber-Mercedes C13
Motor	Konfiguration	4-Zylinder in Reihe, 4 Ventile je Zylinder, 2 oben liegende Nockenwellen	V8, 4 Ventile je Zylinder, 4 oben liegende Nockenwellen
	Hubraum	1799 ccm	3499 ccm
	Bohrung x Hub	85,3 x 78,7 mm	93 x 51,5 mm
	Kraftstoffversorgung	elektronische Einspritzung mit Heißfilm-Luftmassenmessung (HFM)	Motor Management Magneti Marelli
	Leistung	122 PS bei 5500/min	765 PS bei 14000/min
Getriebe		5-Gang	6-Gang-Halbautomatik
Chassis	Rahmen	selbsttragende Ganzstahlkarosserie	Kohlefaser-Monocoque
	Aufhängung vorn	Doppel-Querlenker, Schraubenfedern, Drehstab-Stabilisator	Dreiecks-Querlenker, innen liegende Feder-/Dämpfereinheiten, Schubstreben
	Aufhängung hinten	Raumlenkerachse (optional hydropneumatische Niveauregulierung), Schraubenfedern, Drehstab-Stabilisator	Dreiecks-Querlenker, innen liegende Feder-/Dämpfereinheiten, Schubstreben
Maße	Radstand	2690 mm	2930 mm
	Länge x Breite x Höhe	4487 x 1720 x 1460 mm	4330 x – x – mm
	Gewicht	1410 kg	505 kg
Fahrleistung	Höchstgeschwindigkeit	190 km/h	340 km/h

Baureihe		E 200 – E 55 AMG	McLaren-Mercedes MP 4/13
Baujahre		1995–2001	1998
Modell		E 230 1996	McLaren-Mercedes MP 4/13
Motor	Konfiguration	4-Zylinder in Reihe, 4 Ventile je Zylinder, 2 oben liegende Nockenwellen	72° V10, 4 Ventile je Zylinder, 4 oben liegende Nockenwellen
	Hubraum	2295 ccm	2998 ccm
	Bohrung x Hub	90,9 x 88,4 mm	
	Kraftstoffversorgung	elektronische Einspritzung HFM Management Magneti Marelli	TAG 2000 Electronic System
	Leistung	150 PS bei 5400/min	808 PS bei 17600/min
Getriebe		5-Gang	längs eingebaute McLaren-6-Gang-Halbautomatik
Chassis	Rahmen	selbsttragende Ganzstahlkarosserie	Kohlefaser-/Aluminium-Monocoque
	Aufhängung vorn	Doppel-Querlenker, Schraubenfedern, Drehstab-Stabilisator	innen liegende Feder-/Dämpfereinheiten, doppelter Dreiecks-Querlenker, Schubstreben
	Aufhängung hinten	Raumlenkerachse (optional hydropneumatische Niveauregulierung), Schraubenfedern, Drehstab-Stabilisator	innen liegende Feder-/Dämpfereinheiten, doppelter Dreiecks-Querlenker, Schubstreben
Maße	Radstand	2833 mm	3100 mm
	Länge x Breite x Höhe	4795 x 1799 x 1436 mm	4550 x 1800 x – mm
	Gewicht	1450 kg	600 kg (mit Fahrer)
Fahrleistung	Höchstgeschwindigkeit	215 km/h	330 km/h

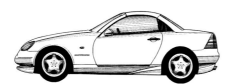

Baureihe		SLK 200 – SLK 230 Kompressor	C-Klasse
Baujahre		1996–2003	1996
Modell		SLK 230 Kompressor 1996	AMG Mercedes C-Klasse (Klasse 1)
Motor	Konfiguration	4-Zylinder in Reihe, 16 Ventile, 2 oben liegende Nockenwellen, Kompressor	V6, 4 Ventile je Zylinder, 4 oben liegende Nockenwellen
	Hubraum	2295 ccm	2499 ccm
	Bohrung x Hub	90,9 x 88,4 mm	
	Kraftstoffversorgung	Bosch Motronic	elektronische Einspritzung
	Leistung	193 PS bei 5300/min	ca. 500 PS bei 11500/min
Getriebe		5-Gang	sequenzielle 6-Gang-Halbautomatik, unsynchronisiert
Chassis	Rahmen	selbsttragende Karosserie mit Hilfsrahmen	selbsttragende verstärkte Stahlblechkarosserie mit verschweißtem Stahl-Überrollkäfig
	Aufhängung vorn	Dreiecks-Querlenker, Schraubenfedern, Stabilisator, Teleskopdämpfer	Doppel-Querlenker mit verstellbaren Dämpfern, verstellbarer GFK-Stabilisator
	Aufhängung hinten	Raumlenkerachse, Schraubenfedern, Stabilisator, Teleskopdämpfer	Raumlenkerachse mit verstellbarem Stabilisator, verstellbare Dämpfer
Maße	Radstand	2400 mm	2690 mm
	Länge x Breite x Höhe	3995 x 1715 x 1265 mm	4666 x 1789 x 1280 mm
	Gewicht	1325 kg	1040 kg
Fahrleistung	Höchstgeschwindigkeit	231 km/h	300 km/h

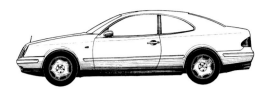

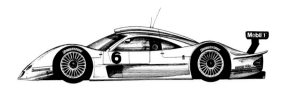

Baureihe		CLK 200 – CLK 430	CLR
Baujahre		1997–2001	1999
Modell		CLK 320 1997	CLR
Motor	Konfiguration	V6, 3 Ventile je Zylinder, 2 oben liegende Nockenwellen	V8, 4 Ventile je Zylinder, 4 oben liegende Nockenwellen, Mittelmotor
	Hubraum	3199 ccm	5721 ccm
	Bohrung x Hub	89,9 x 84 mm	über 600 PS bei 7000/min
	Kraftstoffversorgung	elektronische Einspritzung HFM Bosch	elektronisch gesteuertes Zünd- und Einspritzsystem
	Leistung	224 PS bei 5600/min	Bosch-Motronic
Getriebe		5-Gang-Automatik	Quer eingebautes 6-Gang-Getriebe, unsynchronisiert, sequenzielle Handschaltung
Chassis	Rahmen	selbsttragende Karosserie mit Hilfsrahmen vorn	Monocoque aus Kohlefaser-Verbundwerkstoff mit integrierter Überrollkonstruktion
	Aufhängung vorn	Dreiecks-Querlenker, Schraubenfedern, Stabilisator, Teleskopdämpfer	Doppel-Querlenker mit Pushrod-Anlenkung der Feder/Dämpfereinheiten
	Aufhängung hinten	Raumlenkerachse, Schraubenfedern, Stabilisator, Teleskopdämpfer	Doppel-Querlenker mit Pushrod-Anlenkung der Feder/Dämpfereinheiten
Maße	Radstand	2690 mm	2670 mm
	Länge x Breite x Höhe	4570 x 1720 x 1350 mm	4893 x 1999 x 1012 mm
	Gewicht	1400 kg	900 kg
Fahrleistung	Höchstgeschwindigkeit	240 km/h	370 km/h

Baureihe		A 140 – A 190	ML 320 – ML 55 AMG
Baujahre		1997–2004	1997→
Modell		A 160 1997	ML 320 1997
Motor	Konfiguration	4-Zylinder in Reihe, oben liegende Nockenwelle	V6, 3 Ventile je Zylinder, 2 oben liegende Nockenwellen
	Hubraum	1598 ccm	3199 ccm
	Bohrung x Hub	80 x 79,5 mm	89,9 x 84 mm
	Kraftstoffversorgung	elektronische Einspritzung	elektronische Einspritzung mit Heißfilm-Luftmassenmessung (HFM)
	Leistung	102 PS bei 5250/min	218 PS bei 5600/min
Getriebe		5-Gang	5-Stufen-Automatik
Chassis	Rahmen	selbsttragende Karosserie mit Hilfsrahmen	leiterförmiger Verbund aus Kastenprofilen
	Aufhängung vorn	Dreiecks-Querlenker, Federbeine, Schraubenfedern, Teleskopdämpfer, Stabilisator	Dreiecks-Querlenker, Drehstabfedern, Gasdruck-Stoßdämpfer, Stabilisator
	Aufhängung hinten	Verbundlenkerachse, Schraubenfedern, Teleskopdämpfer, Stabilisator	Dreiecks-Querlenker, Schraubenfedern, Gasdruck-Stoßdämpfer, Stabilisator
Maße	Radstand	2423 mm	2820 mm
	Länge x Breite x Höhe	3575 x 1719 x 1598 mm	4587 x 1833 x 1776 mm
	Gewicht	1020 kg	1930 kg
Fahrleistung	Höchstgeschwindigkeit	182 km/h	180 km/h

Baureihe		Smart	S 320 – S 55 AMG
Baujahre		1998→	1998→
Modell		Smart 1998	S 500 1999
Motor	Konfiguration	3-Zylinder, Turbolader, Doppelzündung, Unterflur hinten	V8, 3 Ventile je Zylinder, 4 oben liegende Nockenwellen
	Hubraum	698 ccm	4966 ccm
	Bohrung x Hub	66,5 x 67 mm	97 x 84 mm
	Kraftstoffversorgung	Bosch Motronic Multipoint	mikroprozessorgesteuerte Einspritzanlage HFM
	Leistung	50 PS	306 PS bei 5600/min
Getriebe		6-Gang-Halbautomatik	5-Gang-Automatik mit Tippschaltung
Chassis	Rahmen	Tridion-Sicherheitszelle	selbsttragende Karosserie mit Hilfsrahmen
	Aufhängung vorn	Einzelradaufhängung	Vierlenker-Vorderachse, volltragendes Luftfedersystem mit Niveauregulierung und adaptivem Dämpfungssystem (ADS), Drehstabilisator
	Aufhängung hinten	De-Dion-Hinterachse mit Stablenkerführung	Raumlenker-Hinterachse, volltragendes Luftfedersystem mit Niveauregulierung und adaptivem Dämpfungssystem (ADS), Drehstabilisator
Maße	Radstand	1812 mm	2965 mm
	Länge x Breite x Höhe	2500 x 1515 x 1549 mm	5038 x 1855 x 1444 mm
	Gewicht	730 kg	1855 kg
Fahrleistung	Höchstgeschwindigkeit	135 km/h	250 km/h

Glossary of technical terms and abbreviations p. 598 · Glossaire d'abréviations et de termes techniques p. 598

		C 200 CDI – C 55 AMG	SL 350 – SL 55 AMG
Baureihe			
Baujahre		2000→	2001→
Modell		C 220 CDI 2003	SL 500 2002
Motor	Konfiguration	4-Zylinder in Reihe, Diesel, 4 Ventile je Zylinder	V8, 3 Ventile je Zylinder, je zwei oben liegende Nockenwellen
	Hubraum	2148 ccm	4966 ccm
	Bohrung x Hub	88,0 x 88,3 mm	97,0 x 84,0 mm
	Kraftstoffversorgung	Common-Rail, Hochdruckeinspritzung	mikroprozessorgesteuerte Einspritzung
	Leistung	143 PS bei 4200/min	306 PS bei 5600/min
Getriebe		6-Gang	5-Gang-Automatik
Chassis	Rahmen	selbsttragende Karosserie	Stahlrahmen mit Aluminium-Karosserie
	Aufhängung vorn	Dreilenkerachse mit Federbein, Drehstab-Stabilisator	Querlenker, Längslenker, Dämpfer, Schraubenfeder, Active Body Control
	Aufhängung hinten	Raumlenkerachse mit Dämpfer, Schraubenfeder, Stabilisator	Raumlenkerachse, Schraubenfeder, Dämpfer, ASP
Maße	Radstand	2775 mm	2560 mm
	Länge x Breite x Höhe	4526 x 1728 x 1427 mm	4535 x 1827 x 1298 mm
	Gewicht	1520 kg	1845 kg
Fahrleistung	Höchstgeschwindigkeit	220 km/h	250 km/h

		Sportcoupé C 200 CDI – C 320	E 200 CDI – E 55 AMG
Baureihe			
Baujahre		2001→	2002→
Modell		C 230 Kompressor 2003	E 320 2003
Motor	Konfiguration	4-Zylinder in Reihe, 4 Ventile je Zylinder, 2 oben liegende Nockenwellen	V6, 3 Ventile je Zylinder, je 2 oben liegende Nockenwellen
	Hubraum	1796 ccm	3199 ccm
	Bohrung x Hub	82,0 x 85,0 mm	89,9 x 84,0 mm
	Kraftstoffversorgung	mikroprozessorgesteuerte Einspritzanlage	mikroprozessorgesteuerte Einspritzung
	Leistung	192 PS bei 5800/min	224 PS bei 5600/min
Getriebe		6-Gang-Schaltgetriebe	5-Gang-Automatik
Chassis	Rahmen		selbsttragende Stahlkarosserie mit Aluminium-Teilen
	Aufhängung vorn	Dreilenkerachse mit Federbein, Stabilisator, Bremsmoment-Unterstützung	Vierlenkerachse, Federbeine, Bremsmomentabstützung, Stabilisator
	Aufhängung hinten	Raumlenkerachse, Schraubenfeder, Gasdruck-Dämpfer, Stabilisator, Anfahr- und Bremskraftunterstützung	Raumlenkerachse, Schraubenfedern, Gasdruckdämpfer, Stabilisator, Anfahr- und Bremsmomentabstützung
Maße	Radstand	2715 mm	2854 mm
	Länge x Breite x Höhe	4343 x 1728 x 1406 mm	4818 x 1822 x 1452 mm
	Gewicht	1475 kg	1645 kg
Fahrleistung	Höchstgeschwindigkeit	240 km/h	245 km/h

		CLK 270 CDI – CLK 55 AMG	Smart Roadster
Baureihe			
Baujahre		2002→	2002→
Modell		CLK 320 Coupé 2003	Smart Roadster-Coupé 2003
Motor	Konfiguration	V6, 3 Ventile je Zylinder, je 2 oben liegende Nockenwellen	3-Zylinder mit Turbolader quer im Heck, oben liegende Nockenwelle
	Hubraum	3199 ccm	698 ccm
	Bohrung x Hub	89,9 x 84,0 mm	66,5 x 67,0 mm
	Kraftstoffversorgung	mikroprozessorgesteuerte Einspritzung	elektronische Einspritzung
	Leistung	218 PS bei 5700/min	82 PS bei 5250/min
Getriebe		5-Gang-Automatik	6-Gang-Automatik, sequenziell geschaltet
Chassis	Rahmen	selbsttragende Stahlkarosserie mit Aluminium-Teilen	Stahlrahmen mit GfK-Karosserie
	Aufhängung vorn	Dreilenkerachse, Federbeine, Stabilisator	Dreiecksquerlenker, Federbeine, Stabilisator
	Aufhängung hinten	Raumlenkerachse, Dämpfer, Schraubenfeder, Stabilisator, Anfahr- und Bremsabstützung	De-Dion-Achsrohr mit Zentrallager, Querlenker, Dämpfer, Schraubenfedern
Maße	Radstand	2715 mm	2360 mm
	Länge x Breite x Höhe	4638 x 1740 x 1413 mm	3427 x 1615 x 1192 mm
	Gewicht	1605 kg	790 kg
Fahrleistung	Höchstgeschwindigkeit	244 km/h	175 km/h

Baureihe		Maybach 57 – Maybach 62 Guard
Baujahre		2002→
Modell		Maybach 62 2003
Motor	Konfiguration	V12, 3 Ventile je Zylinder
	Hubraum	5513 ccm
	Bohrung x Hub	82,0 x 87,0 mm
	Kraftstoffversorgung	mikroprozessorgesteuerte Einspritzung
	Leistung	550 PS bei 5250/min
Getriebe		5-Gang-Automatik
Chassis	Rahmen	selbsttragende Karosserie aus Stahl, Aluminium und GfK
	Aufhängung vorn	Doppelquerlenkerachse, volltragendes Luftfeder-System mit Niveauregulierung, Drehstabstabilisator, Bremsmomentabstützung
	Aufhängung hinten	Raumlenkerachse, volltragendes Luftfeder-System mit Niveauregulierung, Drehstabstabilisator, Anfahr- und Bremsmomentabstützung
Maße	Radstand	3827 mm
	Länge x Breite x Höhe	6165 x 1980 x 1573 mm
	Gewicht	2855 kg
Fahrleistung	Höchstgeschwindigkeit	250 km/h

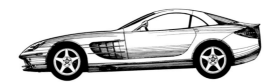

Baureihe		SLR McLaren	SLK 200 Kompressor – SLK 55 AMG
Baujahre		2003→	2004→
Modell		SLR McLaren 2004	SLK 200 Kompressor 2004
Motor	Konfiguration	V8, 3 Ventile je Zylinder, Kompressor, je 2 oben liegende Nockenwellen	4-Zylinder in Reihe, 4 Ventile je Zylinder, Kompressor, 2 oben liegende Nockenwellen
	Hubraum	5439 ccm	1795 ccm
	Bohrung x Hub	97,0 x 92,0 mm	82,0 x 85,0 mm
	Kraftstoffversorgung	elektronische Einspritzung	elektronische Einspritzung
	Leistung	626 PS bei 6500/min	163 PS bei 5500/min
Getriebe		5-Stufen-Automatik	6-Gang
Chassis	Rahmen	Kohlefaser-Monocoque mit Aluminium-Hilfsrahmen für den Motor	selbsttragende Stahlkarosserie mit Aluminium-Teilen
	Aufhängung vorn	Doppelquerlenker, Federbeine, Nickmomentabstützung, Drehstabstabilisator	Dreilenkerachse, Federbeine, Drehstabstabilisator
	Aufhängung hinten	Doppelquerlenker, Dämpfer, Schraubenfedern, Nickmomentabstützung	Raumlenkerachse, Dämpfer, Schraubenfedern, Stabilisator
Maße	Radstand	2700 mm	2430 mm
	Länge x Breite x Höhe	4656 x 1908 x 1261 mm	4082 x 1777 x 1296 mm
	Gewicht	1747 kg	1390 kg
Fahrleistung	Höchstgeschwindigkeit	334 km/h	223 km/h

Baureihe		Smart Forfour 1.1 – 1.5	CLS 350 – CLS 500
Baujahre		2004→	2004→
Modell		Smart Forfour 1.5 2004	CLS 500 2004
Motor	Konfiguration	4-Zylinder in Reihe vorn quer, 2 oben liegende Nockenwellen	V8, 3 Ventile je Zylinder, je 2 oben liegende Nockenwellen
	Hubraum	1499 ccm	4966 ccm
	Bohrung x Hub	75,0 x 84,8 mm	97,0 x 84,0 mm
	Kraftstoffversorgung	elektronische Einspritzung	mikroprozessorgesteuerte Einspritzung
	Leistung	109 PS bei 6000/min	306 PS bei 5600/min
Getriebe		5-Gang	7-Gang-Automatik
Chassis	Rahmen	Stahlrahmen, Aluminium- und GfK-Teile	Leichtbau-Konstruktion aus Stahl und Aluminium
	Aufhängung vorn	Querlenker, Federbeine	Vierlenkerachse, volltragendes Luftfeder-System mit Niveauregulierung, Bremsmomentabstützung
	Aufhängung hinten	Verbundlenker, Stoßdämpfer, Schraubenfedern	Raumlenkerachse, volltragendes Luftfeder-System mit Niveauregulierung, Anfahr- und Bremsmomentabstützung
Maße	Radstand	2500 mm	2854 mm
	Länge x Breite x Höhe	3752 x 1684 x 1450 mm	4913 x 1851 x 1381 mm
	Gewicht	1079 kg	1810 kg
Fahrleistung	Höchstgeschwindigkeit	190 km/h	250 km/h

Glossary · Glossaire

Allgemein	General	Généralités
auf	on	sur
aus	made of	en
außen	external(ly)	extérieur
Doppel-	twin	double
elektrisch	electric	électrique
elektronisch	electronic	électronique
hinten	at rear	arrière
innen	internal(ly)	intérieur
je	per	par
keine	no	aucun(e)
mit	with	avec
verstärkt	reinforced	renforcé
verstellbar	adjustable	réglable
vorn	at front	avant
Zusatz-	supplementary	supplémentaire

Baureihe	Series	Gamme
Baujahre	Production	Millésimes
Modell	Model	Modèle
Motor	Engine	Moteur
Konfiguration	Configuration	Configuration
4-Scheiben-Wankel	4-rotor Wankel	Wankel quadrirotor
4-teilig	4-section	à quatre éléments
Boxer	horizontally-opposed	à plat
Doppelzündung	twin-spark ignition	à double allumage
in Reihe	in-line	en ligne
Kompressor	supercharger	compresseur
liegend	horizontal	horizontal
Mittelmotor	mid-mounted engine	moteur central
oben liegende Nockenwelle	overhead camshaft	à arbre(s) à cames en tête
paarweise	in pairs	en couple
quer	transverse	transversal
stehend	upright	vertical
Turbolader	turbocharger	turbocompresseur
über der Hinterachse	over rear axle	au-dessus de l'essieu arrière
Unterflur	underfloor	sous-plancher
Ventile	valves	soupapes
vor der Hinterachse	ahead of rear axle	devant l'essieu arrière
Zündkerzen	spark plugs	bougies
Zylinder	cylinders	cylindres

Hubraum	Displacement	Cylindrée
ccm	cc	cm³
Bohrung x Hub	Bore x stroke	Alésage x course
Kraftstoffversorgung	Fuel supply	Alimentation en carburant
3-Düsen-	3-nozzle	à 3 gicleurs
3-Stufen-	3-stage	à 3 étages
6-Stempel-	6-stage	à 6 pistons
Drosselvergaser	choke carburetor	carburateur à soupape d'étranglement
Druckvergaser	pressure carburetor	carburateur à pression
Einspritzpumpe	injection pump	pompe d'injection
Einspritzung	injection	injection
Flachstromvergaser	transverse draft carburetor	carburateur horizontal
Heißfilm-Luftmassenmessung (HFM)	hot-film air-mass metering	mesure de la masse d'air à film chaud
Horizontal-Rundschiebervergaser	horizontal variable-jet carburetor	carburateur horizontal à tiroir rond
Kolbenschiebervergaser	piston-slide carburetor	carburateur à robinet à piston
mechanisch	mechanical	mécanique
Oberflächenvergaser	surface carburetor	carburateur à surface
Pumpe	pump	pompe
Ringschwimmer	ring float	flotteur circulaire
Saugvergaser	suction carburetor	carburateur atmosphérique
Schwimmervergaser	float carburetor	carburateur à flotteur
Spritzdüsenvergaser	atomizing carburetor	carburateur à injecteur
Startautomatik	automatic starter	starter automatique
Steigstromvergaser	updraft carburetor	carburateur vertical
Vergaser	carburetor	carburateur
Vorwärmung	preheating	préchauffage

Leistung	Output	Puissance
PS	bhp	ch
bei .../min	at ...rpm	à .../min
Getriebe	Transmission	Boite de vitesses
2-Stufen-	2-stage	à deux rapports
4-Gang	4-speed	à quatre vitesses
Allradantrieb	four-wheel drive	traction intégrale
Automatik	automatic	automatique
Flachriemengetriebe und Vorgelege	flat belt drive and layshaft	boîte de vitesses à courroie plate et renvoi
Halbautomatik	semi-automatic	semi-automatique
Kulisse	gate	grille
Kulissenschaltung	gate shift	commande à grille

Ölkühler	oil cooler	radiateur d'huile
Register-	index	à registre
Renngetriebe	racing gearbox	boîte de vitesses course
Rückwärtsgang	reverse gear	marche arrière
Schnellgang	overdrive	surmultipliée
sequenzielle Halbautomatik	sequential semi-automatic gearbox	semi-automatique séquentielle
sequenzielle Handschaltung	sequential manual gearbox	commande manuelle séquentielle
synchronisiert	synchromeshed	synchronisée
Übersetzungen durch verschieden große Riemenscheiben	transmission by different-sized belt pulleys	démultiplications grâce à des disques de courroie de différentes tailles
unsynchronisiert	non-synchromeshed	non synchronisée
Vorwärtsgänge	forward gears	rapports avant
Zahnradgetriebe	gear transmission	boîte à engrenages

Chassis Rahmen	Chassis Frame	Châssis Cadre
aufgesetzt	mounted	posé
Bodenanlage	floorpan	plate-forme
Eisen	iron	fer
Ganzstahlkarosserie	all-steel body	carrosserie tout acier
gekröpfter Vierkantrohr-Leiterrahmen	box-section longitudinal rails and lateral members	châssis en échelle à tubes de section carrée galbés
GFK	GRP	matière plastique renforcée de fibre de verre
Gitterrohrrahmen	multi-tubular spaceframe	châssis tubulaire
Hilfsrahmen	subframe	berceau auxiliaire
Holz	wood	bois
Karosserie	bodywork	carrosserie
Kastenprofil	box section	profil à caissons
Kohlefaser	carbon fiber	fibre de carbone
Kohlefaser-Verbund	carbon-fiber composite	fibre de carbone-matériaux composites
leiterförmig	with longitudinal and lateral members	en forme d'échelle
Niederrahmen	low-frame	cadre surbaissé
Ovalrohrrahmen	oval-tube frame	cadre à tubes ovales
Pressstahl	pressed steel	acier embouti
Profilstahl	steel sections	acier profilé
Quertraversen	cross members	traverses transversales
rahmenloser Holzaufbau	frameless wooden body	carrosserie en bois sans cadre
selbsttragend	monocoque	autoporteuse
Stahl-Überrollkäfig	steel roll-over cage	arceau de sécurité en acier
Stahlblech	sheet steel	tôle d'acier
Stahlrohr	steel tube	tube d'acier
Teleskopdämpfer	telescopic damper	amortisseur télescopique
tief gelegter Drehpunkt	low pivot point	centre de rotation surbaissé
Tridion-Sicherheitszelle	Tridion safety passenger cell	cellule de sécurité Tridion
U-Profil	U-section	profilé en U
verschweißt	welded	soudé
X-förmig	cruciform	en forme de X
Zentralrohrrahmen	backbone chassis	châssis à poutre centrale

Aufhängung vorn/hinten	Suspension front/rear	Suspension avant/arrière
Ausgleichs-	compensating	de compensation
Blattfedern	leaf springs	ressorts à lames
Dämpfer	damper	amortisseur
Dämpferbein-Achse	axle with MacPherson struts	essieu à jambe d'amortisseur
Drehstabfedern	torsion bar springs	ressorts à barre de torsion
Drehstab-Stabilisator	torsion anti-roll bar	stabilisateur à barre de torsion
Dreieckslenker	wishbone	bras triangulaire
Dreiecks-Querlenker	wishbone	triangle transversal
Eingelenk-Pendelachse	single-pivot swing axle	essieu oscillant à articulation unique
Einzelradaufhängung	independent suspension	suspension à roues indépendantes
Elliptikfedern	elliptical springs	ressorts elliptiques
Fahrradgabel	cycle forks	fourche de bicyclette
Federbeine	struts	jambes élastiques
Feder-/Dämpfereinheit	spring/damper unit	combiné ressort/amortisseur
Federung	springing	suspension
Gasdruck-Stoßdämpfer	gas-compression damper	amortisseur à gaz

Gummi-Zusatzfedern	auxiliary rubber springs	ressorts supplémentaires en caoutchouc	Schwingachse	independent axle	essieu oscillant
			Stabilisator	anti-roll bar	barre antiroulis
			Starrachse	rigid axle	essieu rigide
Halbelliptikfedern	semi-elliptical springs	ressorts semi-elliptiques	starre Faustachse	rigid stub axle	essieu rigide à chapes fermées
Halbfedern	semi-elliptical springs	demi-ressorts			
hydropneumatisch	hydropneumatic	hydropneumatique	starre Gabelachse	rigid forked axle	essieu rigide à fourche
innen liegend	enclosed	in-board	Steuergabel	steering fork	fourche de commande
Längslenker	longitudinal swing arm	levier longitudinal	Underslung-Halbfedern	underslung semi-elliptical springs	demi-ressorts surbaissés
Luftfederung	air suspension	suspension pneumatique			
			Verbundlenkerachse	trailing-arm axle	essieu à bras interconnectés
Luftkammer-Federbälge	air spheres	soufflets de chambre d'air			
			Vollelliptikfedern	fully-elliptical springs	ressorts elliptiques
MacPherson-Federbeine	MacPherson struts	jambes élastiques MacPherson	zuschaltbar	activatable	débrayable
			Maße	**Dimensions**	**Dimensions**
Niveauausgleich	self-leveling	compensation du niveau	Radstand	Wheelbase	Empattement
Niveauregulierung	level control	correction d'assiette	Länge x Breite x Höhe	Length x width x height	Longueur x largeur x hauteur
Panhardstab	Panhard rod	barre Panhard	mm	100 mm = 3.937 in	mm
Pendelachse	swing axle	essieu oscillant	mit Coupédach	with coupé roof	avec toit coupé
Querfedern	transverse springs	ressorts transversaux	offen	open-top	ouvert
Querlenker	transverse arm	bras transversal	**Gewicht**	**Weight**	**Poids**
Rad	wheel	roue	kg	1 kg = 2.205 lb	kg
Reibungsstoßdämpfer	frictional damper	amortisseur à friction	**Fahrleistung**	**Performance**	**Performances**
Raumlenkerachse	multi-link suspension	essieu multibras	Höchstgeschwindigkeit	Maximum speed	Vitesse maximale
Schräglenker	diagonal strut	bras diagonal	km/h	1 km/h (kph)	km/h
Schraubenfedern	coil springs	ressorts hélicoïdaux		= 0.621 mph	
Schubstreben	push rods	poussoirs			

Bibliography · Bibliographie

Daimler-Benz – Das Unternehmen/Die Technik, Kruk/Lingnau/Bartels (Hase & Koehler) Mainz 1986

Der Stern ihrer Sehnsucht: Plakate und Anzeigen von Daimler-Benz. Zeitdokumente der Gebrauchskunst von 1900 bis 1960, Simsa/Sproß/Wendt (Cantz) Ostfildern-Ruit 1995

Magnificent Mercedes – The Complete History of the Marque, Graham Robson (Chevprime Limited) 1988

Mercedes-Benz Grand Prix 1934–1955, George C. Monkhouse (Orell Füssli) Stuttgart 1986

Mercedes-Benz Catalogue Raisonné 1886–1986, Jürgen Lewandowski (Edita)

Mercedes-Benz Personenwagen 1886–1986, Werner Oswald (Motorbuch Verlag) Stuttgart 1994

Deutsche Autos seit 1945, Werner Oswald (Motorbuch Verlag) Stuttgart 1992

Mercedes-Benz Quicksilver Century, Karl E. Ludvigsen (Transport Bookman Publications) Isleworth 1995

Quicksilver, An Investigation into the Development of German Grand Prix Racing Cars 1934–1939, Cameron C. Earl (HMSO) London 1996

Mercedes-Benz: A History, W. Robert Nitske (Motorbooks International) Osceola 1978

Sterne, Stars und Majestäten – Prominenz auf Mercedes-Benz, Simsa/Lewandowski (Stadler) Konstanz 1985

Mercedes-Benz Automobile 1–6, Schrader/Hofner (BLV) München 1985 etc.

Katalog der Automobil Revue 1958–1997 (Hallwag) Bern

Die große Automobilgeschichte Mercedes-Benz, Die multimediale Enzyklopädie aller Typen und Modelle auf CD-ROM (United Soft Media Verlag) München 1996

Photo credits · Fotonachweis · Crédits photographiques

All photographs by Rainer W. Schlegelmilch except:

Alle Fotos von Rainer W. Schlegelmilch außer:

Toutes les photos sont de Rainer W. Schlegelmilch sauf :

DaimlerChrysler-Konzernarchiv: pp 10–99
Jörg Wießmann Sportfotos: p 92

Acknowledgements · Danksagung · Remerciements

I wish to record my very sincere thanks to the following persons, without whose commitment this book could not have got off the ground, for making their cars available and for their active support for this project as as whole:

Für die Bereitstellung ihrer Fahzeuge und die Unterstützung des Gesamtprojekts durch Rat und Tat danke ich ganz herzlich folgenden Personen, ohne deren Engagement dieses Buch nicht hätte entstehen können:

Je remercie très cordialement les personnes mentionnées ci-dessous pour la mise à disposition de leurs véhicules et leur appui en paroles et en actes pour l'ensemble du projet, car ce livre n'aurait pas pu être produit sans leur engagement :

Erhard Aumüller, Helmut Baaden, Marina Bernert, Stefan Bisiani, Waldemar Boroz, Frank Bracke, Stefan Diehl, Andreas Ditzenbach, Dieter Fröbe, Dieter Götz, Thomas Guth, Thomas Hartmann, Heinz Haueisen, Ulrike Hörl, Matthias Jung, Klaus Keck, Peterheinz Kern, Wolfgang Knauth, Hardy Langer, Hermann Layher, Peter Lehmann, Friedhelm Loh, Kay Mertens, Dr. Harry Niemann, Horst Nies, Max von Pein, Steffen Pisoni, Günter Reinhard, Thomas Riedinger, Martin Röder, Stefan Röhrig, Wolfgang Rolli, Berthold E. Rückwarth, Bruno Sacco, Heinz Schacker, Heinrich Schäffler, Horst Schickedanz, Karl-Heinz Schleisick, Heinz Schlosser, Peter Schoene, Uwe Schüler, Oliver Schwarz, Peter Schwarz, Winfried A. Seidel, Klaus Seybold, Alois Singvogel, Markus Stapp, Ditmar Stehr, Norbert Szielasko, Jürgen Tauscher, Willi Vogel, Peter Völker, Ingo Waldschmidt.

I also extend my thanks to the following for their willing cooperation:

Ebenso danke ich für die hilfreiche Kooperation:

Je remercie également pour leur coopération bienveillante :

Mercedes-Benz Museum & Mercedes-Benz Classic, Stuttgart; Flughafen Siegerland; Flugplatz Egelsbach & Flugplatz Michelstadt.

Rainer W. Schlegelmilch

Original title: Mercedes
ISBN 978-3-8331-1056-6

Photography: Rainer W. Schlegelmilch
Text: Hartmut Lehbrink, Jochen von Osterroth (pp. 530–599)
Art direction and design: Peter Feierabend
Layout: Peter Feierabend, Rainer W. Schlegelmilch, Oliver Hessmann
Project manager: Sally Bald, Joachim Schwochert (new edition)
Drawings: Jochen von Osterroth
Typography: Oliver Hessmann
Cover: Oliver Hessmann
Translations into English: Les Telford, Stephen Hunter, Mike Daly, Russell Cennydd
Translation into French: Jean-Luc Lesouëf

Printed in China

ISBN 978-3-8331-3329-9

10 9 8 7 6 5 4 3 2 1
X IX VIII VII VI V IV III II